Lecture Notes in Computer Science 4225

José Francisco Martínez-Trinidad
Jesús Ariel Carrasco Ochoa
Josef Kittler (Eds.)

Progress in Pattern Recognition, Image Analysis and Applications

11th Iberoamerican Congress
in Pattern Recognition, CIARP 2006
Cancun, Mexico, November 14-17, 2006
Proceedings

Springer

Volume Editors

José Francisco Martínez-Trinidad
Jesús Ariel Carrasco Ochoa
National Institute of Astrophysics, Optics and Electronics (INAOE)
Computer Science Department
Luis Enrique Erro No. 1, 72840 Sta. Maria Tonantzintla, Puebla, Mexico
E-mail: {fmartine,ariel}@inaoep.mx

Josef Kittler
University of Surrey
Centre for Vision, Speech and Signal Processing,
School of Electronics and Physical Sciences
Guildford GU2 7XH, UK
E-mail: J.Kittler@surrey.ac.uk

Library of Congress Control Number: 2006933995

CR Subject Classification (1998): I.5, I.4, I.2.10, I.2.7, F.2.2

LNCS Sublibrary: SL 6 – Image Processing, Computer Vision, Pattern Recognition, and Graphics

ISSN 0302-9743
ISBN-10 3-540-46556-1 Springer Berlin Heidelberg New York
ISBN-13 978-3-540-46556-0 Springer Berlin Heidelberg New York

Springer is a part of Springer Science+Business Media

springer.com

Typesetting: Camera-ready by author, data conversion by Scientific Publishing Services, Chennai, India
Printed on acid-free paper SPIN: 11892755 06/3142 5 4 3 2 1 0

Preface

The ongoing success of the Iberoamerican Congress on Pattern Recognition (CIARP) reflects the growing need for developing new theory and applications of pattern recognition, which is being confronted by many reseachers. The 11th Iberoamerican Congress on Pattern Recognition (CIARP 2006) was the 11th event in the premier series of research agenda-defining conferences on pattern recognition in the Iberoamerican community. As in the previous years, CIARP 2006 attracted worldwide participation. The aim of the congress was to promote and disseminate ongoing research and mathematical methods for pattern recognition, image analysis, and applications in such diverse areas as computer vision, robotics and remote sensing, industry, health, space exploration, data mining, document analysis, natural language processing and speech recognition, to name a few.

CIARP 2006, held in Cancun, Mexico, was organized by the Computer Science Department of the National Institute of Astrophysics, Optics and Electronics (INAOE). The event was sponsored by the Advanced Technologies Application Center of Cuba (CENATAV), the Mexican Association for Computer Vision, Neurocomputing and Robotics (MACVNR), the Cuban Association for Pattern Recognition (ACRP), the Portuguese Association for Pattern Recognition (APRP), the Spanish Association for Pattern Recognition and Image Analysis (AERFAI), the Special Interest Group on Pattern Recognition of the Brazilian Computer Society (SIGPR-SBC), and the Chilean Association for Pattern Recognition (ACHRP). CIARP 2006 was endorsed by the International Association for Pattern Recognition (IAPR).

Contributions were received from 36 countries. In total 239 papers were submitted, out of which 99 were accepted for publication in these proceedings and for presentation at the conference. The review process was carried out by the Scientific Committee, composed of internationally recognized scientists, all experts in their respective fields. We are indebted to them for their efforts and the quality of the reviews.

The exciting technical programme formed by the selected contributed papers was complemented by three invited keynote talks, given by:

- Gabriella Sanniti di Baja, Image Analysis Department of the Istitute of Cibernetics "E. Caianiello", CNR, Italy
- Petra Perner, Institute of Computer Vision and Applied Computer Sciences, Germany
- Jim Bezdek, University of West Florida, USA

They enriched the conference with an interesting mix of theoretical and application topics in pattern recognition.

We would like to thank the members of the Organizing Committee for their enormous effort that resulted in these excellent conference proceedings. We trust that the papers in this volume provide not only a record of the recent progress in this rapidly moving field but will also stimulate future research on machine perception for the benefit of industry, commerce, as well as the well-being of society.

November 2006

José Francisco Martínez-Trinidad
Jesús Ariel Carrasco-Ochoa
Josef Kittler

Organization

CIARP 2006 was organized by the Computer Science Department of the National Institute of Astrophysics, Optics and Electronics (INAOE).

General Conference Co-chairs

Josef Kittler	Department of Electrical Engineering of Surrey University, UK
José Francisco Martínez-Trinidad	Computer Science Department, National Institute of Astrophysics, Optics and Electronics (INAOE), Mexico
Jesús Ariel Carrasco-Ochoa	Computer Science Department, National Institute of Astrophysics, Optics and Electronics (INAOE), Mexico

Steering Committee

José Ruiz-Shulcloper	Cuban Association for Pattern Recognition (ACRP)
Alberto Sanfeliu	Spanish Association for Pattern Recognition and Image Analysis (AERFAI)
Aurélio Campilho	Portuguese Association for Pattern Recognition (APRP)
Eduardo Bayro-Corrochano	Mexican Association for Computer Vision, Neurocomputing and Robotics (MACVNR)
Herman Martins Gomes	Special Interest Group on PR of the Brazilian Computer Society (SIGPR-SBC)
Héctor Allende	Chilean Association for Pattern Recognition (ACHRP)

Local Committee

Aurelio López López
Carlos Alberto Reyes García
Eduardo Morales Manzanares
Enrique Sucar Succar
Jesús Antonio González Bernal
Leopoldo Altamirano Robles
Luis Villaseñor Pineda
Manuel Montes y Gómez
Olac Fuentes Chávez

Local Arrangements Committee

Scientific Committee

Gordillo, J. L.	ITESM, Mexico
Graña, M.	University of the Basque Country, Spain
Grau, A.	Universitat Politécnica de Catalunya, Spain
Gibert, K.	Universitat Politécnica de Catalunya, Spain
Gurevich, I.	Russian Academy of Science, Russia
Guzmán-Arenas, A.	CIC-IPN, Mexico
Hancock, E. R.	University of York, UK
Hernando, J.	Universitat Politécnica de Catalunya, Spain
Jain, A. K.	Michigan State University, USA
Kamel, M.	University of Waterloo, Canada
Kasturi, R.	University of Pennsylvania, USA
Kittler, J.	University of Surrey, UK
Koschan, A.	University of Tennessee, USA
Kropatsch, W.	Vienna University of Technology, Australia
Kuncheva, L.	University of Wales, UK
Lazo-Cortés, M.	ICIMAF, Cuba
Levashkine, S.	CIC-IPN, Mexico
Lira-Chávez, J.	UNAM, Mexico
Lopez de Ipiña, K.	University of the Basque Country, Spain
López-López, A.	INAOE, Mexico
Lorenzo-Ginori, J. V.	Universidad Central de Las Villas, Cuba
Marques, J. S.	Instituto Superior Técnico, Portugal
Medioni, G.	University of Southern California, USA
Mejail, M.	Universidad de Buenos Aires, Argentina
Moctezuma, M.	UNAM, Mexico
Morales, E.	INAOE, Mexico
Nascimento, J.	Instituto Superior Técnico, Portugal
Ney, H.	University of Aachen, Germany
Novovicova, J.	UTIA, Czech Republic
Padilha, A. J. M. N.	Universidade de Porto, Portugal
Perales, P.	Universitat de les Illes Balears, Spain
Pereira, F.	Instituto Superior Técnico, Portugal
Pérez de la Blanca-Capilla, N.	Universidad de Granada, Spain
Petrou, M.	Imperial College, UK
Pina, P.	Instituto Superior Técnico, Portugal
Pinho, A. J.	University of Aveiro, Portugal
Pla, F.	Universidad Jaume I, Spain
Randall, G.	Universidad de la República, Uruguay
Reyes, C. A.	INAOE, Mexico
Riazanov, V.	Russian Academy of Science, Russia

Ritter, G.	University of Florida, USA
Rodríguez, R.	ICIMAF, Cuba
Rojas Costa, G. M.	Pontificia Universidad Católica de Chile, Chile
Ross, A.	West Virginia University, USA
Ruiz-Shulcloper, J.	CENATAV, Cuba
Sanfeliu, A.	Universitat Politécnica de Catalunya, Spain
Sanniti di Baja, G.	Istituto di Cibernetica, CNR, Italy
Sansone, C.	Università di Napoli, Italy
Shirai, Y.	Ritsumeikan University, Japan
Sossa Azuela, J. H.	CIC-IPN, Mexico
Sucar, L. E.	INAOE, Mexico
Taboada Crispi, A.	Universidad Central de Las Villas, Cuba
Torres, M. I.	University of the Basque Country, Spain
Torres, S.	Universidad de Concepción, Chile
Verri, A.	University of Genova, Italy
Vidal, E.	Universidad Politécnica de Valencia, Spain
Villanueva, J. J.	Universidad Autónoma de Barcelona, Spain
Zhang, D.	Hong Kong Polytechnic University, Hong Kong
Zhuravlev, Y.	Russian Academy of Science, Russia

Additional Referees

Arias Estrada, M. O.
Cumplido Parra, R. A.
Feregrino Uribe, C.
González Bernal, J. A.
Muñoz Meléndez, A.
Pons Porrata, A.
Sánchez Díaz, G.
Urcid Serrano, G.

Sponsoring Institutions

Advanced Technologies Application Center of Cuba (CENATAV)
International Association for Pattern Recognition (IAPR)
Mexican Association for Computer Vision, Neurocomputing and Robotics (MACVNR)
Cuban Association for Pattern Recognition (ACRP)
Spanish Association for Pattern Recognition and Image Analysis (AERFAI)
Portuguese Association for Pattern Recognition (APRP)
Special Interest Group on PR of the Brazilian Computer Society (SIGPR-SBC)
Chilean Association for Pattern Recognition (ACHRP)

Table of Contents

Skeletonization of Digital Objects

Gabriella Sanniti di Baja

Istituto di Cibernetica "E. Caianiello" – CNR, Pozzuoli (Naples), Italy
g.sannitidibaja@cib.na.cn.it

Abstract. Skeletonization is a way to reduce dimensionality of digital objects and is of interest in a number of tasks for image analysis. In this paper, efficient approaches to skeletonization of 2D and 3D digital objects are illustrated.

1 Introduction

Skeletonization is a process leading to the extraction of a medial representation of a digital object with lower dimension. Algorithms to compute such a medial representation have been called, besides skeletonization, also thinning and medial axis transformation, and the resulting set has received names such as medial line, medial axis transform, skeleton, and labeled skeleton. These medial representations do not necessarily coincide and are characterized by different properties. In this paper, we refer to skeletonization as to a process to compute a subset of the object, the skeleton, topologically homotopic to the object, spatially placed along the medial region of the object and, depending on the problem domain, expected to account for different geometrical and morphological properties of the represented object. In particular, all object parts regarded as significant in the problem domain should be reconstructed starting from the skeleton (i.e., the skeleton enjoys the reversibility feature).

Skeletonization has been initially suggested to compute linear representations of 2D digital objects. During the process, object pixels on the border of the object are changed to background pixels until a subset S of the object is obtained, which is a union of arcs and curves placed symmetrically with respect to the border of the object.

The research on 2D skeletonization has been largely influenced by the work of Blum dealing with a geometry based on the primitive notions of a symmetric point and a growth process [1,2]. A point p of a continuous object at distance d from the boundary of the object is symmetric if at least two points of the boundary exist, having distance d from p. A maximal ball can be associated to every symmetric point p by growth of the symmetric point, where the maximal ball is the largest ball centered on p and contained in the object. The set of symmetric points, labeled with the radii of the associated maximal balls, constitutes the medial axis transform of the object. The union of the maximal balls coincides in shape and size with the object, thus the medial axis transform enjoys the reversibility feature.

The medial axis transform is not necessarily a minimal coding of the object, since a maximal ball can be completely included by the union of other maximal balls. An object can often be reconstructed from proper subsets of its medial axis transform. Moreover, the medial axis does not necessarily reflect the topological properties of the object. For example, if a connected object consists of a number of balls tangent to

J.F. Martínez-Trinidad et al. (Eds.): CIARP 2006, LNCS 4225, pp. 1 – 13, 2006.

each other, its medial axis is the non-connected set consisting of the centers of the balls. Differently from the medial axis transform, the skeleton is a subset of the object, which includes, besides the centers of maximal balls (so that the skeleton enjoys the reversibility feature), also other elements necessary to guarantee that the object and its skeleton are homotopic.

Reducing digital objects to lower dimensions is even more desirable in 3D. The 3D skeleton is either a set of 3D surfaces and curves (called surface skeleton, *SS*) or, if the object does not include cavities, it may consist only of 3D curves (called curve skeleton, *CS*). The basic idea underlying 3D skeletonization does not differ from the 2D case: object voxels are changed to background voxels, provided that topology and geometry are not altered, until the skeleton is obtained.

The literature in the field of skeletonization is very rich and different approaches can be followed to compute the skeleton. A well-known approach is based on the repeated use of topology preserving removal operations. These are applied border after border so as to have a skeleton centered within the object, and hence reflecting its geometrical features. A drawback of this approach, when the algorithm is implemented on conventional sequential computers, is that a number of image scans proportional to the object's thickness is necessary to reach the goal, so that the computation time is quite large. A computationally convenient approach is based on the use of the distance transform of the object. In the distance transform, the layers (i.e., the sets of object elements at the same distance from the background) can be interpreted as the successive borders that characterize the object when this undergoes skeletonization by iterated removal of border elements. In principle, since all layers are available in the distance transform, the skeletal elements can be directly identified and marked in a small and fixed number of inspections of the distance transform.

Both continuous and discrete approaches have been suggested in the literature. We will here focus on discrete approaches to skeletonization. A brief overview of different approaches can be found in [3,4]. This paper is organized as follows. In Section 2, preliminary notions are given. Sections 3 and 4 respectively deal with 2D and 3D skeletonization. Some concluding remarks are given in Section 5.

2 Notions and Definitions

We work with a binary discrete image I in square/cubic grid, where the object O is the set of 1's and the background B is the set of 0's. When working in the discrete space, some problems specific to this space and relevant for skeletonization have to be faced. It is well known that a different connectivity type has to be used for the object and for its complement (the background) to avoid topological paradoxa. The connectivity type depends on which, among the neighbors of a pixel/voxel, are considered as directly connected to the pixel/voxel at hand.

In 2D, a pixel p has four neighbors sharing an edge with p, and four neighbors sharing a vertex with p. The 4-connectivity considers as connected to p the pixels sharing an edge with p, while the 8-connectivity considers both kinds of neighbors.

In 3D, a voxel v has six neighbors sharing a face with v, twelve neighbors sharing an edge and eight neighbors sharing a vertex. Three connectivity types are hence possible: 26-connectivity, when all three kinds of neighbors are considered,

18-connectivity, when neighbors sharing a face or an edge are considered, and 6-connectivity, when only the neighbors sharing a face are considered.

If the same connectivity type is used for both O and B, a closed curve/surface would not divide its complement into disjoint parts, or an open curve/surface would divide its complement into disjoint parts. In the 2D discrete space, the 8-connectivity and the 4-connectivity are generally adopted for the object (and, hence, its skeleton) and for its complement, respectively. In the 3D space, the 26-connectivity and the 6-connectivity are generally used for the object and its complement, respectively.

A second problem, relevant for skeletonization, is related to the nature of the discrete space. In correspondence with regions whose thickness is expressed by an even number of pixels/voxels, the set of centers of maximal balls is 2-pixel/voxel wide. Thus, if a discrete solution to skeletonization is desired, the resulting set (called *nearly-thin skeleton*) can locally be 2-pixel/voxel wide. Alternatively, the nearly-thin skeleton can be reduced to a 1-pixel/voxel thick set by means of a post-processing, generally called *final thinning*, but in this case the complete reversibility is lost, since a number of centers of maximal balls are unavoidably removed from the nearly-thin skeleton. The loss in object recovery starting from the unit-wide S and SS exclusively regards pixels/voxels on the border of the original object and, as such, is generally considered as acceptable. However, if the 3D curve-skeleton CS is computed, reversibility is generally no longer possible, due to the very large number of centers of maximal balls removed from SS to reduce it to CS.

The discrete distance between two elements p and q is the length of a shortest path from p to q. The degree of approximation to the Euclidean distance depends both on the unit moves used to build the path, and on the weights assigned to the unit moves, when these have different Euclidean lengths. A thorough investigation of the distance transforms in 2D and 3D, as well as of weight selection can be found in [5,6]. A good approximation is obtained in 2D by using the weights $w_e=3$ and $w_v=4$, for the edge- and the vertex-neighbors respectively, and in 3D by using the weights $w_f=3$, $w_e=4$ and $w_v=5$, for the face-, the edge- and the vertex-neighbors respectively. For the city-block distance in 2D it is $w_e=1$ and $w_v=\infty$, and for its 3D equivalent distance it is $w_f=1$, $w_e=\infty$ and $w_v=\infty$.

The *distance transform* DT of the object O with respect to the background B is a replica of the image I, where the elements of O are labeled with their distances from B, computed according to the chosen distance function.

A *center of a maximal ball*, CMB, is an object element whose associated ball is not included by any other single ball in the object. To check this condition, a comparison among the label of the element itself and the labels of its neighbors taking into account the relative weights is sufficient [7]. An object element p is center of a maximal ball if for every neighbor q, it is $q < p+w_i$, where $i=\{f, e, v\}$ depending on whether q is a face-, an edge- or a vertex-neighbor of p. Of course, only edge- and vertex-neighbors exist in 2D.

A *hole* in 2D (a *cavity* in 3D) is a maximal 4-connected (6-connected) component of background elements fully surrounded by object elements.

A *tunnel* exists in a 3D object if a path can be found in the object that cannot be deformed to a single voxel [8].

An object element p is *simple* if the object including p is homotopic to the object deprived of p. Simplicity of p means that the numbers of holes and object components in 2D (the numbers of cavities, object components, and tunnels in 3D) are the same, independently of whether p is in the object or in the background.

An object element is a *border element* in the 2D case (in the 3D case) if it has at least an edge-neighbor (a face-neighbor) in the background. Otherwise, an object element is and *inside element*.

An *end point* is an element of S in 2D (of CS in 3D) having only one neighbor in the skeleton.

3 Skeletonization in 2D

The classical approach to skeletonization is based on the repeated use of topology preserving removal operations. Removal of a pixel p should not create holes, which requires that p has at least an edge-neighbor in the background. Disconnections should not occur, which requires that p has exactly one 8-connected component of object neighbors. Simple arithmetic checks, such as the *crossing number* [9] and the *connectivity number* [10], can be used to respectively count the number of 4-connected components of background elements and the number of 8-connected components of object elements in the neighborhood of p. Finally, in order the skeleton reflects the geometrical properties of the object, removal of p should be permitted only provided that p is not necessary to prevent shortening of peripheral branches in the resulting skeleton.

By following the iterated approach, skeletonization requires a number of iterations proportional to the maximal thickness of the object O. If sequential computers are used, each iteration consists of two sub-iterations, respectively dealing with the identification of the current border, and with the sequential deletion of suitable border pixels, i.e., pixels that, when inspected, are not necessary to preserve topology and are not end points. The process is repeated until no border pixel can be removed from the current border. At this stage of the process, all object pixels are expected to be border pixels; some exceptions are discussed later on in this section.

End point detection is a key task to guarantee isotropic object compression and to avoid unwanted shortening of branches in the resulting skeleton. Every significant protrusion of the object should be mapped into a skeleton branch. To achieve a correct mapping, the tip of each protrusion should be identified and an element of the tip should be prevented from removal, so that it will become an end point in the skeleton. Unfortunately, pixel removal often occurs during a *blind* sequential process, that uses the property satisfied by the end points in the resulting skeleton, i.e., the property of having only one neighbor in the skeleton, as a criterion to detect the end points during the process. Thus, in correspondence with identical configurations end points may be originated or not, depending on the order in which the chosen sequence of removal operations is applied to the object's elements.

To solve this problem, the border configurations corresponding to object protrusions should be identified at the beginning of all iterations of the skeletonization process, before applying the removal operations. Effective criteria can be based on the distance of border elements from the inside of the object. Only border subsets including elements at distance from the inside larger than a given threshold correspond to significantly elongated object protrusions and, hence, their pixels should be prevented from being removed [11]. Alternatively, effective criteria can be based on the selection and preservation of all centers of maximal balls in DT. In fact, in correspondence with the tip of an object protrusion, a maximal ball certainly exists, whose border fits the border of the object protrusion for a (large) connected part. The center of such a maximal ball can be selected as the end point of the branch into which the protrusion is mapped. In both cases, the components of skeletal pixels found at a given iteration are likely not to be of unit width. The final identification of the end points is actually postponed to the final thinning, when the nearly-thin skeleton is reduced to unit width.

From an operative point of view, the pixels that should not be removed at the k-th step of the iterated skeletonization process (being necessary for topology preservation, or belonging to border subsets corresponding to significant protrusions) are located where the current border C_k is locally nearly-thin, i.e., where C_k folds on itself. These pixels are called *multiple pixels*, since they prevent C_k from being simple.

In the digital plane a simple 8-connected curve is a set of object pixels dividing the background into two connected subsets, respectively called the outside and the inside of the curve. Pixels of a curve are neighbors of both the inside and the outside of the curve. Since both the inside and the outside of the curve consist of background pixels, the 4-connectness is used for both sets. On the other hand, when the curve is actually the border of an object, the inside consists of object pixels while the outside consists of background pixels, so that 8-connectedness and 4-connectedness are respectively used for the inside and the outside.

In [12], we have proved that the border of an object is simple if and only if both conditions below are satisfied for each of its pixels p:

A1 A pair of opposite edge-neighbors of p exists, such that one of these neighbors belongs to the inside of the object and the other neighbor belongs to the background.

A2 A border pixel v, vertex-neighbor of p, does not exist such that the two edge-neighbors of p that are also edge-neighbors of v both belong to the background.

If the border is not simple, then the border pixels for which any of the above conditions does not hold are multiple pixels. These pixels are the only ones that, at each iteration of skeletonization, cannot be removed. An end point detection criterion is not necessary, when using conditions A1-A2. In fact, the pixel(s) delimiting a peripheral (nearly-thin) part of the border protruding from the object are definitely multiple due to condition A1 (they cannot have an edge-neighbor in the inside). Thus, conditions A1-A2 are more powerful within skeletonization than removal operations based on the notion of simple point. In fact, in the latter case an end point detection criterion should be used to avoid unwanted shortening of peripheral branches, since the end points are simple points.

The process terminates when the current border is completely made up of multiple pixels. Ordinarily, this will occur when the current inside is empty. However, in some pathological cases, a border consisting entirely of multiple pixels can exist, while the inside is not empty. Examples of pathological cases are shown in Fig.1. In both cases, the current border consists exclusively of multiple pixels, but the inside is not empty.

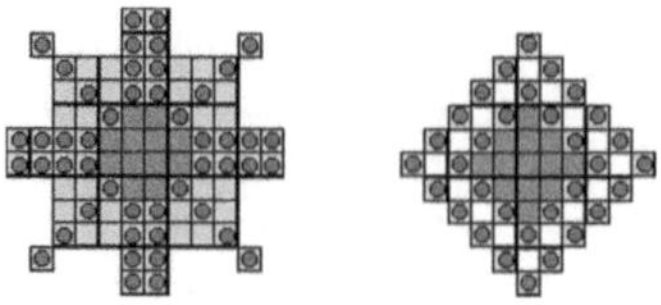

Fig. 1. Object pixels (squares) on a white background. Dots indicate multiple pixels. Light gray and dark gray denote removed object pixels and remaining inside pixels, respectively.

The two conditions A1-A2 can be used more efficiently by employing the city-block distance transform DT of the object during the iterative skeletonization process. In this way, the sub-iteration dealing with current border identification would be no longer necessary, since the DT keeps track of all successive borders. The border of the object at the k-th iteration includes all pixels with distance label k in DT, as well as pixels with distance label smaller than k, if these latter pixels were not removed during previous iterations. Pixels with label greater than k are inside pixels at the k-th iteration. The background is, at all iterations, the set of removed pixels, i.e., the set of 0's. With this interpretation, the skeletonization algorithm can be sketched as follows.

Compute DT. Let m be the maximal distance label in DT
for $k = 1, m$
Remove every pixel p with distance label k, which satisfies conditions A1 and A2, when p is inspected.

It is easy to see that if p is a CMB, condition A1 fails. In fact, no edge-neighbor of p can be labeled more than p, so that p cannot have an edge-neighbor in the inside of the object. Thus, the skeleton includes all the CMBs and complete recovery of the object is possible. The skeleton is nearly-thin, since the set of the CMBs is likely to be 2-pixel thick in some parts.

If the unit-wide S is desired, final thinning is performed by means of topology preserving removal operations. Since inside pixels can exist in the set of skeletal pixels, e.g., for pathological cases or in correspondence of branches crossing each other, only pixels with at least one edge-neighbor in the background are processed, to avoid creation of spurious holes. We suggest a removal operator using the four masks shown in Fig.2. A skeletal pixel p with an edge-neighbor in the background is removed if at least one mask matches the neighborhood configuration of p.

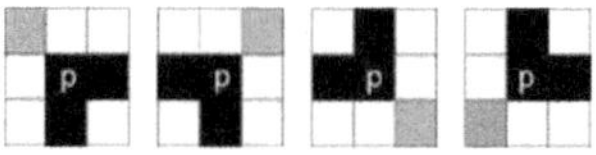

Fig. 2. Masks for final thinning. Black squares and gray squares denote skeletal pixels and background pixels, respectively. White squares are don't care pixels, but among them at least one edge-neighbor of p in each mask must belong to the background.

A post-processing aimed at removal of noisy branches is generally also accomplished (*pruning*). Of course, both final thinning and pruning will remove from the skeleton some CMBs. As a consequence, complete object recovery is not possible, starting from the unit-wide pruned *S*. However, the loss in recovery can be kept under control by using context dependent pruning [13].

The performance of the algorithm can be seen with reference to Fig.3. The skeleton has been reduced to unit thickness and pruning of short branches has been applied. The black pixels in proximity of the border of the object in Fig. 3 are those whose recovery is not possible.

Fig. 3. A mug in three different orientations. The "city-block" skeleton is computed by using conditions A1 and A2.

A different approach to skeletonization can be followed, by exploiting the use of the distance transform. This approach is valid for DTs computed by using any pair of weights w_e and w_v. The DT is interpreted as a landscape, where the label of a pixel indicates its height. Some constraints exist on the heights of neighboring pixels, whose labels can differ only to a limited extent (at most w_e for edge-neighbors, and at most w_v for vertex-neighbors). Thus, the landscape is characterized by gentle slopes converging towards at most two-pixel wide ridges and peaks. The CMBs are located on peaks or ridges and can be detected in one inspection of the DT. Other skeletal pixels detectable in the same inspection of the DT are placed in *saddle configurations*. These pixels have in their neighborhood both (4-connected) components of neighbors with smaller label, and (8-connected) components of pixels with larger label. Indeed, due to the discrete nature of the digital space, in correspondence with parts of the object with even thickness, a special case of saddle configuration occurs, where the pixel *p* at hand is part of a 2×2 block of pixels all with the same label.

The set consisting of the CMBs and the saddle pixels is not necessarily connected, even for a connected object. Thus, to ensure skeleton connectedness, a path growing process is used. Paths originate from already detected skeletal pixels and proceed in the direction of the distance gradient upwards, until another already detected skeletal pixel is found. When determining the gradient, the weights w_i used to measure the unit moves are taken into account. If *p* is an already detected skeletal pixel and *q* is a neighbor of *p* labeled more than *p*, the gradient to *q* from *p* is $grad\ q = (q-p)/w_i$. The neighbor of *p* that maximizes the gradient is the next pixel in the path.

This skeletonization process is computationally very convenient, as it requires only two scans to compute the DT, one scan of the DT plus a path growing process to detect all skeletal pixels, independently of the object's thickness. For more details, see

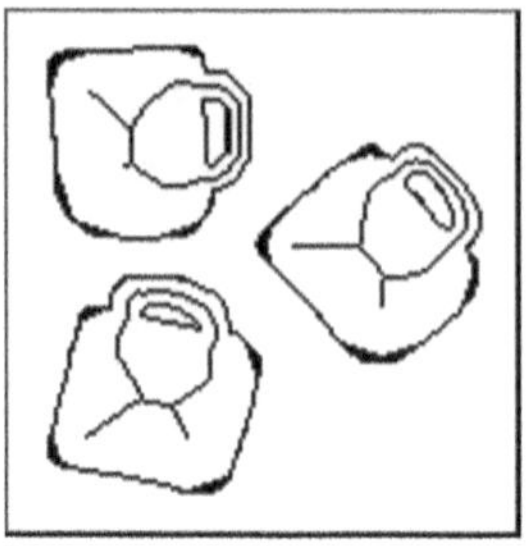

Fig. 4. The skeleton obtained in one inspection of the DT computed with w_e=3 and w_v=4

[13,14]. Also in this case, the skeleton is nearly-thin and the same final thinning already discussed can be employed to obtain the unit-wide skeleton.

An example of the performance of this algorithm by using the DT with weights w_e=3 and w_v=4 is given in Fig.4.

4 Skeletonization in 3D

In 3D, objects can be i) directly reduced to their curve skeletons, e.g., [15,16], or ii) they can be first reduced to their surface skeletons, e.g., [17,18], which are then furthermore compressed to the curve skeletons, e.g., [19,20]. Since object recovery is possible only from the surface skeleton, we prefer algorithms of the latter type.

4.1 Surface Skeletonization

The iterated approach to surface skeletonization requires the identification, iteration after iteration, of the surface bordering the object. Topology preserving removal operations can then be applied. Analogously to the 2D case, where care has to be taken to avoid unwanted shortening of skeleton branches corresponding to significant object protrusions, in 3D removal should not affect peripheral surfaces into which object parts should be mapped. Again, preserving from removal the voxels that are CMBs is a convenient way to achieve this goal.

Also in 3D, topology preserving removal operations can be based on the notion of simple point [21,22], by taking into account that, besides cavities and disconnections, also tunnels have to be considered in the definition of point simplicity. Cavities are not created when removing v from a 26-connected object, if v has at least a face-neighbor in the background. Unfortunately, simple arithmetic checks, analogous to the crossing number or the connectivity numbers available in the 2D case, do not exist to count the number of components in the neighborhood of a voxel v. The number, N_{26}, of 26-connected components of object voxels and the number, N_6, of 6-connected components of background voxels have to be computed by processing the 3×3×3 neighborhood of v. These numbers can be used to determine whether removal of v causes disconnections. Moreover, since removal of v should prevent creation of tunnels, also the number, N_6^{18}, of 6-connected components of background voxels, having v as face-neighbor and computed in the 3×3×3 neighborhood of v deprived of the eight vertex-neighbors, has to be computed. Due to the heavy computation of N_{26}, N_6 and N_6^{18}, alternative removal operations that limit the use of the above numbers are of interest.

The conditions A1-A2 defined in 2D, respectively involve edge- and vertex-neighbors of a pixel p. In 3D, face- and edge-neighbors of a voxel v play the role of the edge- and vertex-neighbors of a pixel p in 2D, respectively. By taking into account that also a third kind of neighbor of a voxel v exists in 3D, the vertex-neighbor, the conditions A1-A2 can be extended to the 3D case, so originating three conditions B1-B3 to detect multiple voxels. A voxel v is not removable if any of the following conditions is satisfied:

B1 No pair of opposite face-neighbors of v exists such that one is an inside object voxel and the other is a background voxel.

B2 There exists a border voxel e, edge-neighbor of v, such that the face-neighbors of both e and v are background voxels.

B3 There exists a border voxel x, vertex-neighbor of v, such that the six common neighbors of both x and v are background voxels.

In Fig.5, the basic configurations involved in conditions B1-B3 are shown. Of course, rotated and mirrored configurations have to be taken into account.

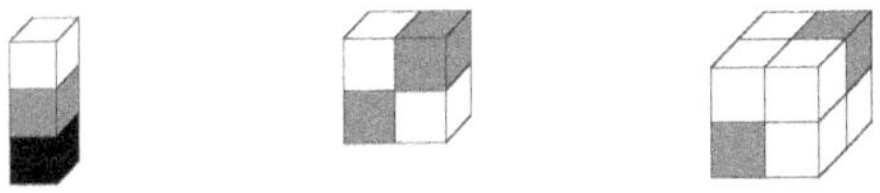

Fig. 5. Voxels involved in Condition B1, left, B2, middle, B3, right. White, gray and black cubes denote background, border and inside voxels, respectively.

If the conditions B1-B3 are sequentially checked for the voxels of the current border, iteration after iteration, a nearly-thin surface skeleton is obtained, as soon as all voxels in the current border are multiple voxels. We point out that the obtained surface skeleton includes the voxels that would be detected as CMBs in the DT computed by using the weights $w_f=1$, $w_e=\infty$ and $w_v=\infty$. These voxels are in fact detected by condition B1 (analogously to the 2D case, where the CMBs in the city-block DT were detected by condition A1).

If a unit wide surface skeleton is desired, final thinning should be accomplished. Since the only voxels that should be removed by this process are those located where the object is 2-voxel thick in face-direction, we should detect the existence of such subsets in the nearly-thin surface skeleton. To this purpose, we use a 4×1 mask consisting of four voxels aligned along one of the three principal directions (top-bottom or bottom-top, left-right or right-left, and front-back or back-front). In each mask, the two external voxels are background voxels and the two internal ones, say v_1 and v_2, are object voxels. The voxels of the surface skeleton are sequentially inspected and if the current voxel plays the role of v_l in the above 4×1 mask, the voxel is removed provided that conditions B2 and B3 do not hold. This is, in fact, sufficient to avoid unwanted reduction of thin peripheral surfaces as well as disconnections.

As an example of the performance of the above algorithm, see Fig.6.

Fig. 6. A 3D object, left, and its surface skeleton, right, obtained by using conditions B1-B3

The distance transform with weights $w_f=1$, $w_e=\infty$ and $w_v=\infty$ can be used, analogously to the 2D case, to reduce the computational effort of the above algorithm. In fact, by computing the DT all the borders that will successively characterize the object are available. As in 2D, at the *k*-th iteration, the border consists of voxels with distance label *k*, as well as of voxels with smaller distance label that have been prevented from being removed at previous iterations. The inside includes all voxels with distance label larger than *k*, and the background the voxels set to 0.

Efficient methods to furthermore exploit the use of the DT with the purpose of computing the surface skeletons in a fixed and small number of scans have been suggested only for the DT computed with weights $w_f=1$, $w_e=\infty$ and $w_v=\infty$ [23].

4.2 Curve Skeletonization

Although curve skeletonization is not reversible since a number of CMBs have unavoidably to be removed from the surface skeleton *SS* to obtain the curve skeleton *CS*, this process is still of interest. In fact, the curve skeleton is a useful representation of the object, provided that it at least maintains some shape information.

To obtain the curve skeleton, an iterated removal process can be applied to the surface skeleton to remove voxels located along the border of the surface skeleton. Thus, a classification of the voxels of the surface skeleton is necessary [20]. Four types of voxels can be identified: internal, edge, curve, and junction voxels. Obviously, internal voxels should not be removed, to avoid creation of spurious tunnels. Curve voxels have to be preserved from removal, since they already constitute parts of the desired curve skeleton. Junction voxels have also to be preserved to avoid disconnections. Thus, the only voxels that should undergo the removal process are the edge voxels. Due to voxel removal during an iteration, some voxels initially classified as internal or junction voxels are likely to become edge voxels at the successive iteration and, as such, should undergo the removal process. However, the basic idea behind curve skeletonization is to postpone as much as possible removal of the voxels classified as junction voxels in the initial surface skeleton, since junctions between different subsets of the surface skeleton retain significant shape information. Thus, curve skeletonization is performed in two phases. During the first phase, removal of voxels classified as junction voxels in the initial surface skeleton is prevented, even if those junction voxels are transformed into edge voxels at some iteration. During the second phase, all current edge voxels are candidate to removal.

Topology preserving removal operations, based on the computation of N_{26}, N_6 and N_6^{18}, are used during both phases. The obtained curve skeleton is at most two-voxel thick, is centered within the surface skeleton, and is homotopic to the surface skeleton (and, hence, is homotopic to the original object). No end point detection criterion is necessary. In fact, end points are automatically preserved, due to their classification as curve voxels whose removal is always prevented.

To reduce the nearly-thin curve skeleton to unit width, final thinning has to be applied. The 4×1 mask introduced in Section 4.1 can be used to identify voxels candidate to removal. These voxels are removed only if this does not alter topology. Actually, two-voxel thickness of the curve skeleton can also be due to pairs of voxels, which are edge-neighbors of each other. Thus, final thinning makes use of different strategies, depending on whether two-voxel thickness is due to pairs of skeletal voxels that are face- or edge-neighbors of each other. Finally, pruning some of the peripheral branches is generally done [24]. Pruning is performed by tracing any peripheral branch and by removing its voxels, provided that the branch includes a small percentage of *significant* voxels, where the notion of significance is still based on the voxel classification accomplished on the surface skeleton.

In Fig.7, a 3D object, its surface skeleton, the nearly-thin curve skeleton, and the unit-wide curve skeleton before and after pruning are shown.

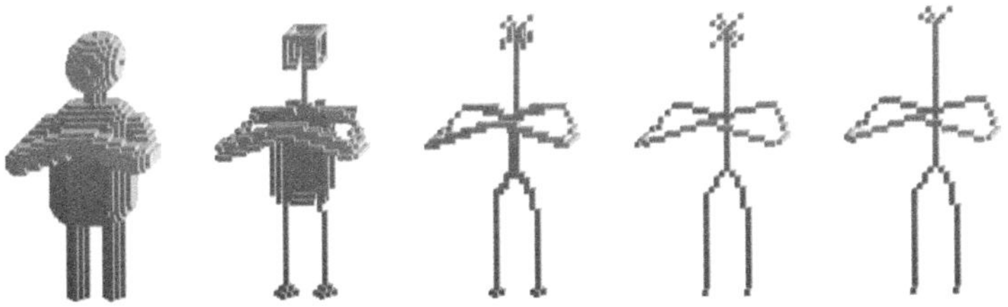

Fig. 7. From left to right: a 3D object, the surface skeleton, the nearly-thin curve skeleton, the unit-wide curve skeleton, and the pruned unit-wide curve skeleton

5 Concluding Remarks

Skeletonization is a convenient process to obtain an object representation with reduced cardinality and suited for image analysis. In the 2D case, the skeleton is union of arcs and curves placed symmetrically within the object. It has been used in many applications, e.g., in optical character recognition. In the 3D case, the skeleton can be either a surface skeleton, or a curve skeleton. The latter can be computed only for objects without cavities. The 3D skeleton is union either of surfaces and curves, or of curves. It has been used in a number of applications, e.g., for the analysis of angiographies starting from magnetic resonance images.

In this paper, approaches to 2D and 3D skeletonization have been presented and algorithms to efficiently compute the skeleton have been briefly illustrated. In particular, it has been shown that the computational load can be significantly reduced when using the distance transform of the object.

References

1. H. Blum, "A transformation for extracting new descriptors of shape", in W. Wathen-Dunn, ed., *Models for the Perception of Speech and Visual Form*, M.I.T. Press, Cambridge, MA, 1967, 362-380.
2. H. Blum, "Biological shape and visual science", *J. Theor. Biol.*, 38, 205-287, 1973.
3. T.Y. Kong and A. Rosenfeld eds., *Topological Algorithms for Digital Image Processing*, Elsevier 1996.
4. C.H. Chen, P.S.P. Wang, Eds., *Handbook of Pattern Recognition and Computer Vision*, World Scientific, Singapore, 2005, chapter 2.3.
5. G. Borgefors, "Distance transformation in digital images", *Comput. Vision Graphics Image Process.*, 34, 344-371, 1986.
6. G. Borgefors, "On digital distance transform in three dimensions", *Computer Vision and Image Understanding*, 64-3, 368-376, 1996.
7. C. Arcelli, G. Sanniti di Baja, "Finding local maxima in a pseudo Euclidean distance transform", *Comput. Vision Graphics Image Process.*, 43, 361-367, 1988.
8. T.Y.Kong, "A digital fundamental group", *Computers and Graphics*, 13, 159-166, 1989.
9. C.J.Hilditch, "Linear skeletons from square cupboards", in B.Meltzer and D.Michie eds., *Machine Intelligence IV*, Edinburgh University Press, UK, 1969, 403-420.
10. S.Yokoi, J.I.Toriwaki, T.Fukumura, "An analysis of topological properties of digitized binary pictures using local features", *Comput. Graphics Image Process.* 4, 63-73, 1975.
11. C.Arcelli, G. Sanniti di Baja, "A thinning algorithm based on prominence detection", *Pattern Recognition*, 13-3, 225 235, 1981.
12. C. Arcelli, G. Sanniti di Baja, "A contour characterization for multiply connected figures", *Pattern Recognition Letters*, 6, 245-249, 1987.
13. G. Sanniti di Baja, E. Thiel, "Skeletonization algorithm running on path-based distance maps", *Image and Vision Computing*, 14, 47-57, 1996.
14. C. Arcelli, G. Sanniti di Baja, "Euclidean skeleton via centre-of-maximal-disc extraction", *Image and Vision Computing*, 11, 163-173, 1993.
15. K. Palagyi, A. Kuba, "A parallel 3D 12-subiteration thinning algorithm", *Graphical Models and Image Processing*, 61, 199-221, 1999.
16. P.K. Saha, B.B. Chaudhuri, D.D. Majumder, "A new shape preserving parallel thinning algorithm for 3D digital images", *Pattern Recognition*, 30-12, 1939–1955, 1997.
17. G. Borgefors, I. Nyström, G. Sanniti di Baja, "Surface skeletonization of volume objects" in P. Perner et al. eds., *Advances in Structural and Syntactical Pattern Recognition*, LNCS 1121, Springer-Verlag, 251-259, 1996.
18. G. Bertrand., "A parallel thinning algorithm for medial surfaces", *Pattern Recognition Letters*, 16, 979–986, 1995.
19. G. Borgefors, I. Nyström, G. Sanniti di Baja, "Computing skeletons in three dimensions", *Pattern Recognition*, 32-7, 1225-1236, 1999.
20. S. Svensson , I. Nyström, G. Sanniti di Baja, "Curve skeletonization of surface-like objects in 3D images guided by voxel classification", *Pattern Recognition Letters*, 23-12, 1419-1426, 2002.

21. P.K.Saha, B.B.Chaudhuri, "Detection of 3D simple points for topology preserving transformations with application to thinning", *IEEE Trans. PAMI*, 16, 1028-1032, 1994.
22. G.Bertrand, G.Malandain, "A new characterization of three-dimensional simple points", *Pattern Recognition Letters*, 15, 169-175, 1994.
23. G.Sanniti di Baja, S.Svensson, "Surface skeletons detected on the D^6 distance transform", in F.J. Ferri et al. eds., *Advances in Pattern Recognition*, LNCS 1121, Springer-Verlag, 387-396, 2000.
24. S. Svensson, G. Sanniti di Baja, "Simplifying curve skeletons in volume images", *Computer Vision and Image Understanding*, 90, 242-257, 2003.

Maximin Initialization for Cluster Analysis

Richard J. Hathaway[1], James C. Bezdek[2], and Jacalyn M. Huband[2]

[1] Department of Mathematical Sciences, Georgia Southern University
Statesboro, GA 30460, USA
r.hathaway@ieee.org
[2] Computer Science Department, University of West Florida
Pensacola, FL 32514, USA
jbezdek@uwf.edu, jhuband@uwf.edu

Abstract. Most iterative clustering algorithms require a *good* initialization to achieve accurate results. A new initialization procedure for all such algorithms is given that is exact when the data contain compact, separated clusters. Our examples use c-means clustering.

1 Introduction

In this note we introduce, analyze and demonstrate a new initialization procedure, called the *maximin initialization* (MMI) algorithm, which is applicable to any clustering method that requires an initial guess for a partition of the data. The core of the proposed initialization strategy appeared as one part of the progressive sampling scheme used in the eNERF (extended non-Euclidean relational fuzzy c-means) algorithm of Bezdek et al. [1] for clustering large relational data sets. MMI is also used in the sVAT (scalable visual assessment of tendency) scheme of Hathaway et al. [2], which produces image displays of large unlabeled data sets. However, neither of these papers discussed the use of MMI in the present context as a standalone tool for initialization of clustering algorithms. In a nutshell, MMI systematically identifies objects that are distributed throughout the data, and uses the identified objects to inexpensively generate an initial partition of the entire data set. We will prove that the MMI partition is exact if the data set consists of compact and separated clusters in the sense of Dunn [3].

Clustering or cluster analysis is the problem of partitioning a set of objects $O = \{o_1,\ldots, o_n\}$ into c self-similar subsets based on available data and some well-defined measure of (cluster) similarity. When each object in O is represented by a (column) vector $\mathbf{x}$ in $\Re^s$, the set $X = \{\mathbf{x}_1,\ldots,\mathbf{x}_n\} \subset \Re^s$ is called an *object data* representation of O. The kth component of the ith feature vector (x_{ki}) is the value of the kth feature (e.g., height, weight, length, etc.) of the ith object. It is in this data space that practitioners sometimes seek geometrical descriptors (often called prototypes) of the clusters. Alternatively, when each *pair* of objects in O is represented by a relationship, then we have *relational data.* The most common case of relational data is when we have (an n×n matrix of) dissimilarity data, say $D = [d_{ij}]$, where d_{ij} is the pair wise dissimilarity (usually a distance) $\mathrm{dis}(o_i,o_j)$ between objects o_i and o_j, for $1 \le i, j \le n$. More

J.F. Martínez-Trinidad et al. (Eds.): CIARP 2006, LNCS 4225, pp. 14–26, 2006.

generally, the relational data can be a matrix of similarities based on a variety of measures (Borg and Lingoes [4]; Kendall and Gibbons [5]).

One of the better-known families of clustering models that must be initialized by a partition of the data is the family of c-means models. There are *hard* (Ball and Hall [6]), *fuzzy* (Bezdek [7]) and *possibilistic* (Krishnapuram and Keller [8]) c-means models and algorithms for object data (HCM, FCM, PCM), and corresponding duals of each of these for relational data (Hathaway et al., [9]). The new initialization procedure can be used with all versions of c-means. We use only HCM and FCM in this note, so clustering is done on object data.

A partitioning of the data (or objects) into c clusters is represented by a c·n partition matrix U. The sets of (nondegenerate) fuzzy and hard c-partitions of n objects are denoted by M_{fcn} and M_{hcn}:

$$M_{hcn} = \left\{ U \in M_{fcn} \mid u_{ik} \in \{0,1\} \right\}; \text{ and} \tag{1}$$

$$M_{hcn} = \left\{ U \in M_{fcn} \mid u_{ik} \in \{0,1\} \right\}. \tag{2}$$

The element u_{ik} of a partition matrix U represents the degree or extent to which object o_k (or datum $\mathbf{x}_k$) belongs to cluster i. The crucial difference between the two sets in (1) is that fuzzy partitions, which were first used by Ruspini [10], allow memberships in [0,1], so that (partial) membership of a datum can be shared between clusters, while hard partitions require membership values to be 0 or 1, so each datum is unequivocally placed into one and only one of the c clusters.

The hard and fuzzy c-means algorithms arise by (approximately) minimizing a member of the family of functionals

$$J_m(U,V) = \sum_{i=1}^{c} \sum_{k=1}^{n} u_{ik}^m d_{ik}^2, \tag{3}$$

where: $d_{ik}^2 = [d(\mathbf{x}_k, \mathbf{v}_i)]^2$ is the distance from $\mathbf{x}_k$ to $\mathbf{v}_i$ in any inner product induced norm, $n = |X|$, $m \in [1, +\infty)$ is a user- defined fuzzification constant, c is the number of clusters assumed, U is in M_{fcn} (m > 1) or M_{hcn} (m = 1), $V = [\mathbf{v}_1,\ldots,\mathbf{v}_c]$ is a matrix whose columns are c prototypes in $\Re^s$, and $d(\mathbf{v}_i, \mathbf{x}_k)$ measures the distance between data point $\mathbf{x}_k$ and prototype $\mathbf{v}_i$ in any inner product induced norm metric. Zeroing the Lagrangian of J_m results in the following first order necessary conditions (m = 1 for HCM, m > 1 for FCM):

$$\text{HCM V Update}: \ \mathbf{v}_i = \left(\sum_{k=1}^{n} u_{ik} \mathbf{x}_k \right) \Big/ \left(\sum_{k=1}^{n} u_{ik} \right) \ \forall i \tag{4}$$

$$\text{HCM U Update}: \ u_{ik} = \begin{cases} 1; & d_{ik} < d_{jk} \ \forall j \neq i \\ 0; & \text{otherwise} \end{cases} \ \forall i,k \tag{5}$$

$$\text{FCM V Update: } \mathbf{v}_i = \left(\sum_{k=1}^{n} u_{ik}^m \mathbf{x}_k\right) \Big/ \left(\sum_{k=1}^{n} u_{ik}^m\right) \quad \forall i \tag{6}$$

$$\text{FCM U Update: } u_{ik} = \left(\sum_{j=1}^{c} \left(d_{ik}/d_{jk} \right)^{\frac{2}{(m-1)}}\right)^{-1} \quad \forall\ i,k \tag{7}$$

The iteration can be initialized using either a partition U or matrix of prototypes V. For example, for either algorithm, a current U is used to update the prior set of prototypes $V = [\mathbf{v}_1,...,\mathbf{v}_c]$, which are in turn used to calculate a new partition U, and then successive estimates (of either set of variables) are compared to a termination threshold. The theory of this *alternating optimization* (AO) procedure is given in Bezdek and Hathaway [11]. Many authors have considered the sensitivity of AO to its initialization. Bezdek et al. [12] contains an extensive discussion of this issue for the c-means algorithms. Our current contribution to this ongoing body of research is a new initialization scheme that has some theoretical substance - viz., the MMI algorithms produces an initial guess for U that is exact when X (or D) contains c compact, separated clusters in the sense of Dunn [3]. In the experiments conducted in Section 3, initialization is always done using an MMI partition $U \in M_{hcn}$.

2 The Maximin Initialization Algorithm

The core of MMI involves selecting c *distinguished objects* $o_{m_1}, o_{m_2},...,o_{m_c}$ that are distributed throughout the set of objects $O = \{o_1,...,o_n\}$, relative to the available measure of dissimilarity between pairs of objects in O. If a relational dissimilarity matrix D is available, then this is used directly to measure dissimilarity of pairs of objects. When using object data set $X = \{\mathbf{x}_1,...,\mathbf{x}_n\} \subset \Re^s$, we pick a metric $d(\cdot\ ,\cdot)$ on $\Re^s \times \Re^s$ and use $d(\mathbf{x}_j, \mathbf{x}_k)$ as a measure of dissimilarity between o_j and o_k. The first distinguished object selected is simply $o_{m_1} = o_1$. The second chosen (o_{m_2}) is the object in O *most dissimilar* to o_{m_1}. All subsequent choices of distinguished objects involve picking the object with the largest minimum dissimilarity to all of the previously selected objects. This selection of distinguished objects is formally described in Step 1 of the statement of the MMI. The second step of the algorithm computes the (hard) partition that corresponds to grouping each object into the same class as its nearest distinguished object. For the case of object data, this amounts to doing (2b) with $\mathbf{v}_i = \mathbf{x}_{m_i}$, for i = 1,...,c. The MMI algorithm follows.

MMI: Maximin Initialization Algorithm

Choose: The number of clusters c, $1 < c < n$; and, $\Re^s \times \Re^s$ if the available data are object data X, an inner product induced metric $d(\cdot\ ,\cdot)$ on.

Input: Object data $X = \{\mathbf{x}_1,...,\mathbf{x}_n\} \subset \Re^s$ or dissimilarity data $D = [d_{ij}] \subset \Re^{n \times n}$.

Step 1 *Select the indices $m_1, \ldots, m_c$ of the c distinguished objects.*
Select $m_1 = 1$ (Remark: this is the "***object seed***";$m_1 = 1$ is arbitrary)
(If the data are X, calculate dissimilarities $\{ d_{1,k} \}$, k = 1 to n.)
Initialize the minimum distance array $\boldsymbol{\delta}^1 = [\delta_1^1,\ldots,\delta_n^1] = [d_{1,1}, \ldots, d_{1,n}]$
For t = 2,..., c:

Update $\boldsymbol{\delta}^t \leftarrow [\min\{ \delta_1^{t-1}, d_{m_{t-1},1} \}, \ldots, \min\{ \delta_n^{t-1}, d_{m_{t-1},n} \}]$

Select $m_t \in \underset{1 \le j \le n}{\arg\max} \{\delta_j^t\}$

(If the data are X, calculate dissimilarities $\{d_{m_t,k}\}$, k = 1 to n.)

Next t

Step 2 *Cluster each object in $\{o_1, \ldots, o_n\}$ with its nearest distinguished object.*
Clear the initialization matrix array $U = [u_{ik}] \subset \Re^{cn} : u_{ik} = 0 \ \forall \ i,k$
For k = 1,..., n:

Select $i \in \underset{1 \le j \le c}{\arg\min} \{d_{m_j,k}\}$ and then set $u_{ik} = 1$

Next k

Output: A crisp c×n initialization partition U in M_{hcn}

If initialization (of the c-means algorithms) by a set of c prototypes rather than by a partition is desired, then it is only necessary to execute Step 1 and terminate with $\mathbf{v}_i = \mathbf{x}_{m_i}$, for i = 1,...,c. The name *maximin initialization* follows by noticing that the loop in Step 1 can be "unrolled" to show that m_t is selected as an index in {1,...,c} that maximizes the minimum of the distances to the previously selected distinguished objects; i.e., m_t is a solution of

$$\underset{1 \le j \le n}{\arg\max} \{\min\{d_{m_1,j}, d_{m_2,j}, \ldots, d_{m_{t-1},j}\}\} \tag{8}$$

Any tie breaking strategy can be used if arg max of Step 1 or arg min of Step 2 does not specify a unique index. The crisp clusters found at Step 2 of MMI are produced by labeling each of the (n-c) remaining objects with the nearest prototype (1-np) rule. Seen in this light, Step 2 of MMI is just a crisp 1-np classifier for the objects in the data that are not selected in Step 1. Finally, notice that MMI requires the user to specify a value for c, the number of clusters that a subsequent clustering algorithm will seek in the data. MMI produces its initialization for any 1 < c < n, and does not offer an uninformed user any means for inferring a "best" choice for this important parameter. This important problem - the *cluster validity* problem - is addressed, for example, by the sVAT algorithm of Hathaway et al. [2]. In this note we simply pick and use (the "correct") value of c for various examples to illustrate how MMI then finds a good initialization for subsequent clustering. In practice, the data should be submitted to an algorithm such as sVAT before using MMI, so that initialization is done at a reasonable value of c.

MMI has about the same computational cost as one iteration of HCM, and is a bit cheaper for relational data D than for object data X. For object data, Step 1 requires calculation of cn distances in $\Re^s$, which is $O(scn)$. Then MMI performs [(c-1)n] min operations involving 2 elements each, and (c-1) max operations involving n elements each. In Step 2, we must do n min operations involving c elements each, which is exactly the cost of performing (2b) one time. Overall then, MMI is $O(scn)$ for object data. For relational data, we don't have to calculate the cn distances in $\Re^s$ because the dissimilarities are already available as elements of the input data set D. Thus, MMI is $O(cn)$ when its input is relational data set D.

The main theoretical result for MMI is that if the clusters are well separated, then the initialization is *exact*. To formalize this, we recall the notion of compact and separated clusters defined by Dunn [3]. For a set of objects $O = \{o_1,...,o_N\}$ with corresponding relational dissimilarity data D, we say that a partitioning $O^{(1)}, O^{(2)}, ..., O^{(c)}$ of O is *compact and separated* (CS) relative to D if each of the possible intra-cluster distances is strictly less than each of the possible inter-cluster ones. When the data has this property, we say simply that "O can be partitioned into c CS clusters". The main result (Theorem 1) is that if the data consists of c CS clusters, and MMI is applied to it with c as the specified number of distinguished objects, then the initial partition produced by MMI will correctly partition O into these c CS clusters. Based on this property - perfect initialization in the compact and separated case - we expect MMI to provide good initializations in most (non-CS) cases. We will investigate this expectation empirically in Section 3.

Theorem 1. Suppose that the set of objects $O = \{o_1,...,o_N\}$, represented by either an object data set X (with metric $d(\cdot\,,\cdot)$ on $\Re^s$) or a relational dissimilarity matrix D, can be partitioned into $c \geq 1$ CS clusters. Then the crisp MMI c-partition of X (or D) partitions O into its c CS clusters.

Proof. We denote the dissimilarity between objects o_j and o_k by $d_{jk} = dis(o_j,o_k)$, understanding that d_{jk} either comes directly from the matrix D if relational data is available or is calculated as $d_{jk} = d(x_k,x_j)$ if object data is available. Also, we denote the c CS clusters of $O = \{o_1,...,o_n\}$ by $O^{(1)}, O^{(2)}, ..., O^{(c)}$, and when convenient, we indicate the cluster of a datum or object by a superscript in parentheses; e.g., $o_7^{(2)}$ indicates that the seventh object is in the second CS cluster. First we prove that Step 1 of MMI selects exactly one distinguished object from each of the c CS clusters. The result is trivially true for c = 1. Now, suppose we can partition $O_n = \{o_1,...,o_n\}$ into $c \geq 2$ CS clusters $O^{(1)}, O^{(2)}, ..., O^{(c)}$. Since the clusters are compact and separated, it is true that for $1 \leq i \neq h \leq c$ and applicable k, p, j, we have

$$d_{kp} = dis(o_k^{(i)}, o_p^{(i)}) < dis(o_k^{(i)}, o_j^{(h)}) = d_{kj} \ . \qquad (9)$$

We first select object o_1, and without loss of generality, assume that it belongs to $O^{(1)}$. Then the initial search array $\boldsymbol{\delta}^1$ is defined (either using elements of D or $d(\cdot\,,\cdot)$ on corresponding object vectors) as $\boldsymbol{\delta}^1 = [dis(o_1,o_1), \ ... \ , dis(o_1,o_n)] = [d_{11},...,d_{1n}]$. Then applying (9) with i = 1, we see that the maximum element in $\boldsymbol{\delta}^1$ (and therefore the choice of the second distinguished feature) must correspond to an object in $O^{(2)}, ...,$

$O^{(c)}$ (but not in $O^{(1)}$). This completes the proof that each CS cluster is represented by exactly one distinguished object for c = 2, and we now continue for the case of $c \geq 3$. Suppose the max occurs in the second entry of $\boldsymbol{\delta}^1$ so that the next object selected is o_2; and further suppose that o_2 belongs to CS cluster $O^{(2)}$. The updated search array $\boldsymbol{\delta}^2$ is:

$$\boldsymbol{\delta}^2 = [\min\{\delta_1^1, d_{21}\}, \ldots, \min\{\delta_n^1, d_{2n}\}].$$

Suppose that a maximum entry is found in the third component of $\boldsymbol{\delta}^2$ and that o_3 is the third object selected ($m_3 = 3$). We will prove that o_3 cannot belong to $O^{(1)}$ or $O^{(2)}$ by contradiction. So, assume that o_3 *does* belong to either $O^{(1)}$ or $O^{(2)}$, say $O^{(1)}$. Selection of o_3 implies that, for all j = 1 to n:

$$\min\{\delta_3^1, d_{23}\} = \min\{dis(o_1, o_3), dis(o_2, o_3)\} \geq \min\{dis(o_1, o_j), dis(o_2, o_j)\} \tag{10}$$

But (10) implies that, for j = 1 to n:

$$dis(o_1, o_3) \geq \min\{dis(o_1, o_j), dis(o_2, o_j)\} \tag{11}$$

Now, let $j \geq 4$ be any index such that o_j is in neither $O^{(1)}$ nor $O^{(2)}$. (At least one such j exists since $c \geq 3$ and for k = 1, 2, 3 we have $o_k \in O^{(1)} \cup O^{(2)}$.) Without loss of generality we suppose that j = 4 satisfies (7) with $o_4 \in O^{(3)}$, and that $dis(o_1,o_4) \leq dis(o_2,o_4)$). Then (11) gives $dis(o_1,o_3) \geq dis(o_1,o_4)$,where $o_1 \in O^{(1)}$, $o_3 \in O^{(1)}$, and $o_4 \in O^{(3)}$; but this contradicts (9) for i = k = 1, p = h = 3, and j = 4. Thus, the third object chosen cannot be in a previously represented cluster. We can now repeat this argument for the 4th, 5th, ..., up to the cth choice. This establishes our claim that each CS cluster is represented by (i.e., contains) exactly one of the distinguished objects $o_{m_1}, o_{m_2}, \ldots, o_{m_c}$. Finally, since Step 1 of MMI has selected one distinguished object from each of the c CS clusters, (5) implies that for i = 1,...,c, each object in cluster $O^{(i)}$ is grouped with object o_{m_i} in Step 2. Thus, our construction produces a crisp c-partition of $O = \{o_1, \ldots, o_n\}$ into its c compact and separated clusters. ■

Theorem 1 guarantees that MMI produces an initial crisp c-partition corresponding to c compact and separated clusters whenever c CS clusters exist in the data. We assert that this provides an excellent initialization for (*any*) partitioning algorithm that initializes at U in M_{hcn}. Indeed, when X (or D) has c CS clusters, the MMI c-partition of it is part of a necessary pair for J_1 at (3, m=1) - i.e., it is part of an HCM solution. The experiments we present in the next section investigate whether MMI also produces useful initializations when the clusters are *not* w¹ell separated.

3 Numerical Examples

In this section we test the MMI algorithm with HCM and FCM. The data sets we choose are samples drawn from mixtures of c = 4 normal distributions in either $\Re^2$ or $\Re^{10}$. Thus, the data sets used for each figure and simulation in this section nominally have c = 4 clusters (or components); and all are of size n = 1000. The parameter we use to control the amount of overlap between the four clusters is the (common) variance σ^2 of the component normals. We call the two types of data sets used **DIAGONAL** data and **SQUARE** data, terms chosen to (roughly) refer to the arrangement of clusters. The DIAGONAL data sets are samples from a mixture distribution of 4 normal distributions with cluster centers arranged along a diagonal line. The specific component parameters in the case of s = 2 (i.e., $X \subset \Re^2$) are:

$$\text{mixing proportions}: \ \alpha_1 = 0.15, \alpha_2 = 0.25, \alpha_3 = 0.25 \text{ and } \alpha_4 = 0.35; \tag{12}$$

$$\text{means}: \ \boldsymbol{\mu}_1 = [0\ 0]^T, \boldsymbol{\mu}_2 = [3\ 3]^T, \boldsymbol{\mu}_3 = [6\ 6]^T \text{ and } \boldsymbol{\mu}_4 = [9\ 9]^T; \text{ and} \tag{13}$$

$$\text{covariance matrices}: \Sigma_1 = \Sigma_2 = \Sigma_3 = \Sigma_4 = \sigma^2\, I_{2\times 2} \tag{14}$$

where $I_{2\times 2}$ is the 2x2 identity matrix and the positive number σ^2 is varied according to the experiment. The SQUARE data distribution is so named because the clusters form the corners of a square configuration, and its component parameters are given by (12), (14), and:

$$\text{means}: \boldsymbol{\mu}_1 = [0\ 0]^T, \boldsymbol{\mu}_2 = [6\ 0]^T, \boldsymbol{\mu}_3 = [0\ 6]^T \text{ and } \boldsymbol{\mu}_4 = [6\ 6]^T. \tag{15}$$

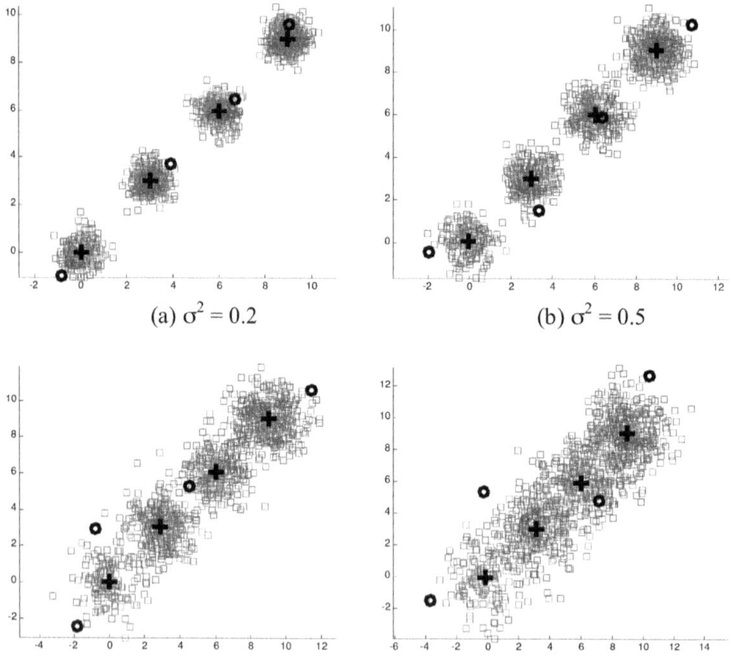

(a) $\sigma^2 = 0.2$ (b) $\sigma^2 = 0.5$

(c) $\sigma^2 = 1.0$ (d) $\sigma^2 = 2.0$

Fig. 1. Typical DIAGONAL data; means (**+**) and MMI selected data (**o**)

Figures 1 and 2 are scatter plots of typical samples from the two dimensional mixtures in $\Re^2$ (n = 1000) for various values of σ^2. The symbol (**o**) represents the c= 4 MMI-selected distinguished objects (i.e., object data in this case).

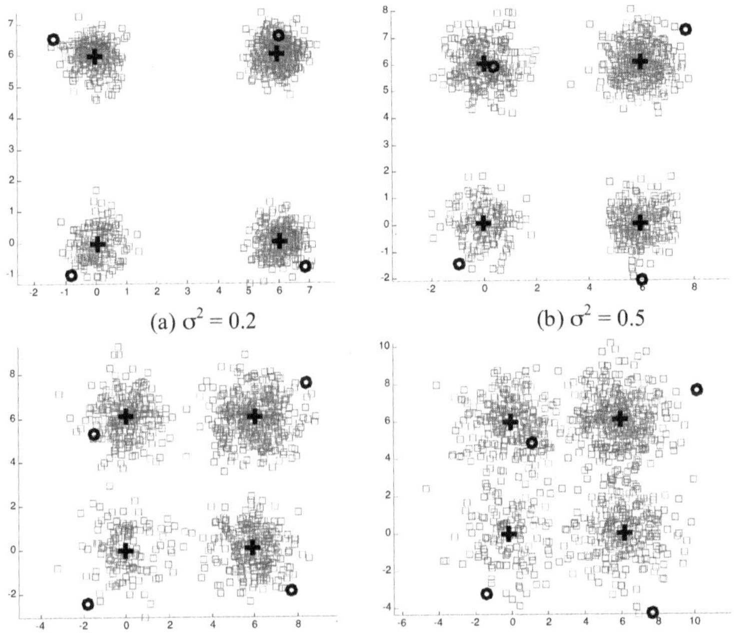

(a) $\sigma^2 = 0.2$ (b) $\sigma^2 = 0.5$ (c) $\sigma^2 = 1.0$ (d) $\sigma^2 = 2.0$

Fig. 2. Typical SQUARE data; means (**+**) and MMI selected data (**o**)

As expected, the distinguished data (**o**) selected by the MMI algorithm are distributed throughout the data sets in the figures and are clearly present in all four clusters in the more separated cases such as those of Figures 1(a) and 2(a). The 2-dimensional simulations that are reported in this section use data sets distributed like those in the figures. Also performed are simulations using 10-dimensional data sets whose first two coordinates are distributed like those in the figures while the 3rd through 10th coordinates are normally distributed with mean 0. Specifically, the mean parameters for the 10-dimensional versions of the DIAGONAL and SQUARE data are:

$$\boldsymbol{\mu}_1 = [0\ 0\ 0\ 0\ 0\ 0\ 0\ 0\ 0\ 0]^T; \boldsymbol{\mu}_2 = [3\ 3\ 0\ 0\ 0\ 0\ 0\ 0\ 0\ 0]^T; \text{ (DIAGONAL)} \quad (16)$$
$$\boldsymbol{\mu}_3 = [6\ 6\ 0\ 0\ 0\ 0\ 0\ 0\ 0\ 0]^T; \boldsymbol{\mu}_4 = [9\ 9\ 0\ 0\ 0\ 0\ 0\ 0\ 0\ 0]^T.$$

$$\boldsymbol{\mu}_1 = [0\ 0\ 0\ 0\ 0\ 0\ 0\ 0\ 0\ 0]^T; \boldsymbol{\mu}_2 = [6\ 0\ 0\ 0\ 0\ 0\ 0\ 0\ 0\ 0]^T; \text{ (SQUARE)} \quad (17)$$
$$\boldsymbol{\mu}_3 = [0\ 6\ 0\ 0\ 0\ 0\ 0\ 0\ 0\ 0]^T; \boldsymbol{\mu}_4 = [6\ 6\ 0\ 0\ 0\ 0\ 0\ 0\ 0\ 0].$$

The component covariance matrices for the 10-dimensional distributions all equal $\sigma^2 I_{10\times10}$, and the mixing proportions in (12) are unchanged. Extension from 2 to 10 dimensions in this way allows us to examine the effect of dimensionality without making the clustering problem substantially easier (or harder) since the separation between components is essentially unchanged and depends only on the first 2 coordinates.

The purpose of our simulations is to investigate the effectiveness of MMI as an initializer of HCM and FCM. We want to compare HCM (and FCM) results obtained using MMI initialization to those obtained using the true class labels as the point of initialization. Toward this end, the true labels are tabulated and represented as a crisp c×n partition (in this case 4×1000) during the generation of each normal mixture data set. We chose this structuring of the tests because we want to know whether or not the MMI works well compared to an "optimal" initialization (i.e., the true labels); not merely whether or not it compares relatively well to some other existing initialization scheme.

The measurement recorded in Tables 1 and 2 is referred to as DIF(✱), which corresponds to the difference between HCM and FCM partitions of the input data obtained from starting the iteration through equations (4)-(5) or (6)-(7) using the MMI and true initializations. We denote the terminal fuzzy partitions obtained using FCM with the two initializations as U^{FCM}_{MMI} and U^{FCM}_{TRUE}; and we similarly denote the HCM results by U^{HCM}_{MMI} and U^{HCM}_{TRUE}. We define DIF(h) and DIF (f) to measure the percentage difference between the crisp (h) or fuzzy (f) clusters obtained using the two initializations. For example, if 45 of n = 1000 data are grouped by HCM into different clusters using the two initializations, then DIF(h) = 4.5%. The percentage can be computed in the crisp case as:

$$\mathrm{DIF(h)} = 50 * \sum_{i=1}^{c}\sum_{j=1}^{n}\left|(u^{HCM}_{TRUE})_{ij} - (u^{HCM}_{MIA})_{ij}\right| \Big/ n . \tag{18}$$

To define the analog of DIF(h) for FCM, we must "harden" the terminal fuzzy partitions obtained by starting FCM at the MMI and True partitions. This amounts to replacing the maximum entry in each column of U by a 1, and replacing all (c – 1) other entries with 0's (this is just Bayes rule when U is a partition of posterior probabilities). We denote the hardening of a partition U by H(U) and define DIF(f) for the FCM results as:

$$\mathrm{DIF(f)} = 50 * \sum_{i=1}^{c}\sum_{j=1}^{n}\left|(H(u^{FCM}_{TRUE}))_{ij} - (H(u^{FCM}_{MIA}))_{ij}\right| \Big/ n \cdot \tag{19}$$

Next, we describe the simulations and the types of entries that appear in Tables 1 and 2. All experiments were done using MATLAB on a PC, with m = 2 in equations (3), (6) and (7) for FCM. The iterations for HCM and FCM were terminated as soon as the maximum change in the (cn) membership values for successive U iterates became less than or equal to 0.00001. Table 1 gives the results for the DIAGONAL data and Table 2 contains the SQUARE data results. Each row of the two tables corresponds to samples from a mixture specified by the component variance σ^2 and dimension s.

The other component parameters are given in the appropriate parts of equations (12-17). For each row, 1000 samples each of size n = 1000 were generated. For each sample, both HCM (results in columns 2-4) and FCM (results in columns 5-7) were initialized using both the true component labels and the MMI initialization. Columns 2 and 5 give the percentage of the 1000 trials for which DIF(✱) = 0; i.e., the percent of trials for which the terminal c-means partitions (hardened in the case of FCM) produced by the MMI initializations are exactly the same as those produced by initialization with the true class labels. Columns 3 and 6 give the average DIF(✱) over the 1000 trials, while columns 4 and 7 give the worst DIF(✱) that occurred for any single trial.

Table 1. 1000 trials for DIAGONAL data : n = 1000

		DIF(h) for HCM			DIF(f) for FCM		
s	σ^2	% Trials where DIF(h) = 0	Ave. DIF(h)	Worst DIF(h)	% Trials where DIF(f) = 0	Ave. DIF(f)	Worst DIF(f)
2	0.2	99.9%	0.0%	0.1%	100%	0%	0%
2	0.5	94.5%	0.3%	35.3%	100%	0%	0%
2	1.0	69.4%	0.1%	39.4%	100%	0%	0%
2	2.0	42.1%	0.8%	45.4%	99.5%	0.0%	0.1%
10	0.2	99.9%	0.0%	33.5%	100%	0%	0%
10	0.5	89.8%	0.7%	34.5%	100%	0%	0%
10	1.0	43.6%	1.8%	42.7%	99.4%	0.0%	0.1%
10	2.0	13.5%	3.1%	49.4%	99.7%	0.0%	0.8%

All clustering algorithms assign numerical labels to their clusters, and these algorithmic labels may or may not correspond to the "true" labels of the input data. Thus, algorithmic cluster 1 might correspond to input cluster 2, and so on. To solve this correspondence problem in the actual computation of DIF(✱), all permutations of the rows of one of the partitions are considered, so that the recorded DIF(✱) is based on the permutation that gives the smallest possible value of (18). This ensures that the calculated disagreement between partitions actually measures a difference in the grouping of the data among clusters, and not simply a difference in the (arbitrary) numerical label assigned to each cluster by HCM or FCM. For c = 4, this amounts to trying 4! = 24 different permutations. This factorial growth in the calculation of DIF is one reason we limited our experiments to the modest value of c = 4. An entry of 0% in either table means *exactly* 0%, while an entry of 0.0% indicates a *rounded* positive number.

A strong implication of the values in Tables 1 and 2 is that MMI works much better for FCM than it does for HCM. This is *not* surprising, since it is well known that initialization sensitivity is more of a problem for the hard c-means algorithm (Bezdek et al., [12]). The performance of MMI with FCM is consistently good throughout the experiments, although the 10-dimensional cases of the SQUARE data with highest overlap (σ^2 = 1.0 and 2.0) resulted in several values of DIF(f) above 20%. The

Table 2. 1000 trials for SQUARE data : n = 1000

		DIF(h) for HCM			DIF(f) for FCM		
s	σ^2	% Trials where DIF(h) = 0	Ave. DIF(h)	Worst DIF(h)	% Trials where DIF(f) = 0	Ave. DIF(f)	Worst DIF(f)
2	0.2	100%	0%	0%	100%	0%	0%
2	0.5	100%	0%	0%	100%	0%	0%
2	1.0	94.2%	0.0%	0.2%	100%	0%	0%
2	2.0	64.0%	0.1%	0.7%	99.7%	0.0%	0.1%
10	0.2	100%	0%	0%	100%	0%	0%
10	0.5	99.8%	0.0%	0.1%	100%	0%	0%
10	1.0	88.9%	0.6%	37.9%	98.8%	0.2%	20.5%
10	2.0	32.8%	1.5%	36.5%	96.4%	0.2%	22.3%

consistently high percentage of cases for which DIF(f) = 0 indicates that with a very high probability, MMI initialization produces the same FCM result as initialization at the true class labels. The average DIF(f) values in both tables show that the average differences between the MMI and true label results are very small: zero for all choices of σ^2 except at σ^2 =1.0 and 2.0 for the 10 dimensional data, and just 0.2% for these two cases.

MMI initialization of HCM worked adequately for very well separated problems (σ^2= 0.2), but even in this case there was a Worst DIF(h) value of 33.5% for s=10 dimensions in Table 1. As σ^2 increases, the cluster separation decreases, and it becomes more and more difficult to obtain the same HCM result using the MMI initialization as that obtained by HCM using the true class labels for initialization. For example, in the worst HCM case, (σ^2 = 2.0 and s = 10 in Table 1), agreement was reached only 135 times in 1000 trials. This is not so much an indictment of MMI initialization as it is an indication that there are a large number of local trap states for minima of J_1 when the data have so much overlap. Even so, the average values of DIF(h) for HCM never got worse than 3.1% for either data set.

The scatter plots of the data in Figures 1 and 2 visually suggest that the SQUARE data clusters are better separated than the DIAGONAL ones, and should therefore be easier for both HCM and FCM. Comparing the tables we see that our intuition is correct for HCM; MMI did significantly better for the SQUARE data than for DIAGONAL. But very surprisingly, the MMI-FCM combination did not have a significantly easier time with the SQUARE data, and in fact, it was this case that produced the only real problems for FCM (Worst DIF(f) values of 20.5% and 22.3%). Finally, we point out that increasing the data space dimensionality from 2 to 10 caused some increase in difficulty, typically more for HCM than FCM.

4 Discussion

The maximin initialization (MMI) algorithm was stated, analyzed and then demonstrated, using samples drawn from a variety of 4 component normal mixtures in two and ten dimensions. The computational cost of executing MMI is essentially equal to a single iteration of HCM or FCM in the case of object data (O(scn)), and even less in the case of relational data (O(cn)). Theorem 1 guarantees that the MMI c-partition corresponds to a compact and separated partitioning of the data whenever such a partitioning exists. MMI identifies c distinguished data (or objects) distributed throughout the data space, and then uses them as "seed" prototypes to build a 1-np partition of the remaining unlabeled data. Our simulations suggest that for a moderate number of clusters, FCM combines particularly well with MMI initialization to produce clustering results comparable to those obtainable when FCM is initialized with the "true" cluster labels.

On the basis of the simulation results, the theoretical implication of Theorem 1, and the inexpensive computational cost, we believe that MMI is a useful tool for generating initializations for FCM, and to a lesser extent, for HCM. Since HCM is notoriously sensitive to initialization, it is probably wise to initialize it from several starting points to make sure a "good" set of clusters is found. MMI can be used to generate multiple, different starting points. How? Just choose an "object seed" other than 1 for m_1 in Step 1 of MMI, and then change $\boldsymbol{\delta}^1$ accordingly. This change to MMI can be used over and over, to produce as many different initializations as desired.

We see several opportunities for future work. The presence of outliers in the data may create some problems for the MMI scheme, although this has yet to be tested. Perhaps a *trimmed maximin* selection, in the spirit of the more robust trimmed mean estimator of centrality, might offer an advantage in the case of data contaminated with outliers. Recently, much effort has been expended to "kernelize" classification and clustering methods. Can kernelized distances be introduced here in a way that causes the selection of better performing distinguished data (or objects)? Two other related clustering approaches that benefit from good initializations are the possibilistic c-means (PCM) algorithm and normal-mixture-based clustering using the expectation-maximization (EM) algorithm (McLachlan and Peel [13]). The EM approach is known to be somewhat sensitive to initialization and PCM produces coincident clusters from some initializations. MMI should stabilize this aspect of both algorithms, but this supposition has yet to be tested.

References

1. Bezdek, J.C., Hathaway, R.J., Huband, J.M., Leckie, C. and Kotagiri, R.: Approximate Clustering in Very Large Relational Data, in press, Inter. J. Intell. Systems (2005)
2. Hathaway, R.J., Bezdek, J.C. and Huband, J.M. 2005: Scalable Visual Assessment of Cluster Tendency for Large Data Sets, in press, Pattern Recognition (2005)
3. Dunn, J.C.:A Fuzzy Relative of the ISODATA Process and its Use in Detecting Compact Well-separated Clusters, J. Cybernetics 3 (1973), 32-57

4. Borg, I. and Lingoes, J.: Multidimensional Similarity Structure Analysis. Springer-Verlag, New York (1987)
5. Kendall, M. and Gibbons, J.D.: Rank Correlation Methods. Oxford University Press, New York (1990)
6. Ball, G. and Hall, D.: A Clustering Technique for Summarizing Multivariate Data, Behavioral Science 12(1967) 153-155.
7. Bezdek, J.C.: Pattern Recognition with Fuzzy Objective Function Algorithms. Plenum, New York (1981)
8. Krishnapuram, R. and Keller, J.M.: A Possibilistic Approach to Clustering, IEEE Trans. On Fuzzy Systems 1 (1993), 98-110
9. Hathaway, R.J., Bezdek, J.C. and Davenport, J.: On Relational Data Versions of c-Means Algorithms, Pattern Recognition Letters 17 (1996), 607-612
10. Ruspini, E.: A New Approach to Clustering, Information and Control 15 (1969), 22-32
11. Bezdek, J. C. and Hathaway, R. J.: Convergence of Alternating Optimization, Neural, arallel and Scientific Computation, 11-4 (2003) 351-368
12. Bezdek, J.C., Keller, J.M., Krishnapuram, R. and Pal, N.R.: Fuzzy Models and Algorithms for Pattern Recognition and Image Processing, Kluwer, Norwell (1999)
13. McLachlan, G. and Peel, D.: Finite Mixture Models. John Wiley & Sons, New York (2000)

Case-Based Object Recognition with Application to Biological Images

Petra Perner

Institute of Computer Vision and applied Computer Sciences IBaI
Körnerstr. 10, 04107 Leipzig
ibaiperner@aol.com
www.ibai-institut.de, www.ibai-research.de

Abstract. There are many biotechnological applications where 3-dimensional objects are represented as 2-d objects in a digital image. The dynamic and variable nature of the microorganism thus creates a formidable challenge to the design of a robust 2-d image inspection system with the ideal characteristics of high analysis accuracy but wide generalization ability. We have developed a novel case-based object recognition method for this kind of problems. The method is able to recognize objects and learn incrementally cases for the recognition process. Such a procedure requires capturing new cases for the further recognition process in order to be able to handle the variability of the natural objects. We describe the theory behind the method and how it works on our problem of fungi spore recognition. The developed case-based object recognition method is flexible and robust enough to be used for different recognition tasks in biotechnology.

Keywords: Object Recognition, Similarity Measure, Image Mining, Case-Based Reasoning.

1 Introduction

There are many biotechnological applications where 3-dimensional objects are represented as 2-d objects in a digital image. The dynamic and variable nature of the microorganism thus creates a formidable challenge to the design of a robust 2-d image inspection system with the ideal characteristics of high analysis accuracy but wide generalization ability.

We have developed a novel case-based object recognition method for this kind of problems. The method is able to recognize objects and learn incrementally cases for the recognition process. Such a procedure requires capturing new cases for the further recognition process in order to be able to handle the variability of the natural objects. Image mining is applied to the newly captured cases in order to keep the case base as small as possible. As a result we obtain groups of similar cases for which we are prototypically calculating cases that are stored into the case base. These learnt cases are applied for case-based object recognition. For the object recognition procedure we have developed a novel similarity measure that can determine similarity between the cases in the case base and the objects in the image. The similarity measure is flexible

J.F. Martínez-Trinidad et al. (Eds.): CIARP 2006, LNCS 4225, pp. 27–37, 2006.

enough in order to get adjusted for different recognition purposes. We describe the theory behind it and how it works on our problem of fungi spore recognition.

The developed case-based object recognition method is flexible and robust enough to be used for different recognition tasks in biotechnology.

2 Material

Some digitized sample images are presented in Table 1 for the different fungal spores. The objects in the images are good representatives for the nature of different kind of biological objects such as yeast, cells, algae, and others.

Table 1. Images of fungal strains

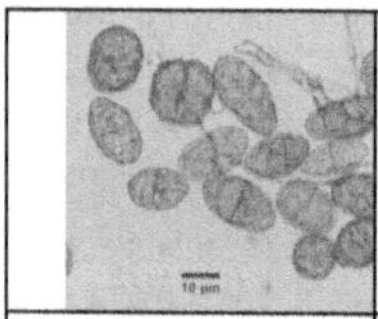	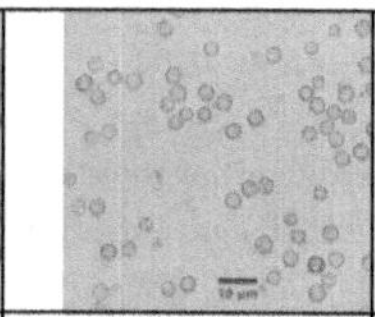	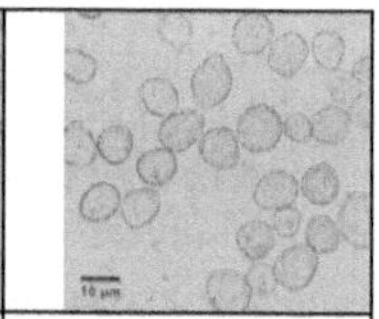
Alternaria Alternata	Aspergillus Niger	Rhizopus Stolonifer
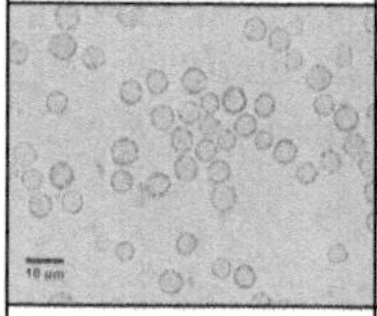	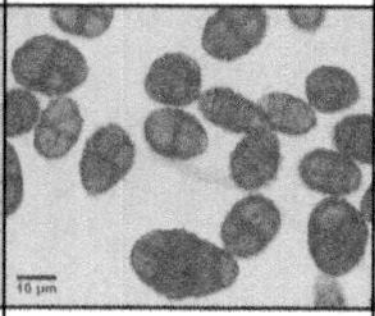	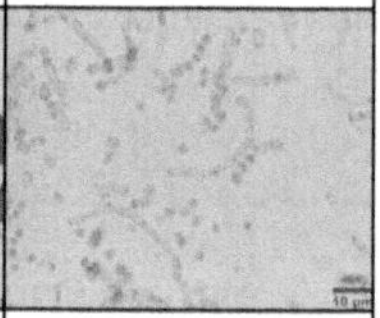
Scopulariopsis Brevicaulis	Ulocladium Botrytis	Wallenia Sebi

3 Case-Base Object Recognition

The objects in the image are highly structured. Our study has shown that these images, represented in Table 1, cannot be segmented by thresholding. The objects in the image can be occluded, touching, or overlapping. It can also happen that only parts of the objects appear in the image. Therefore we decided to use a case-based object recognition procedure for the detection of objects in the image.

A case-based object recognition method uses cases that generalize the original objects and matches these cases against the objects in the image. During the match a score is calculated that describes the goodness of the fit between the object and the case. Well known similarity measures are the normalized cross correlation [1], the Hausdorff distance [2] and the chamfer matching [3]. We did not use the gray values of the objects, but used the object edges instead. For the score of the match between the case and the image we modified the normalized cross correlation in order to measure the average angle between the vectors of the case and the object.

The case can be an object model that describes the inner appearance of the object as well as the contour. In our case the appearance of the whole objects can be very diverse. The shape seems to be the feature that generalizes the objects. Therefore we decided to use the contour of the objects as case representation.

3.1 Similarity Measure

We determine the similarity measure based on the cross correlation by using the direction vectors of an image. This requires the calculation of the dot product between each direction vector of the model $\vec{m}_k = (v_k, w_k)^T$, $k = 1, \ldots, n$, and the corresponding image vector $\vec{i}_k = (d_k, e_k)^T$:

$$s_1 = \frac{1}{n}\sum_{k=1}^{n} \vec{m}_k \cdot \vec{i}_k = \frac{1}{n}\sum_{k=1}^{n} \langle \vec{m}_k, \vec{i}_k \rangle = \frac{1}{n}\sum_{k=1}^{n} (v_k \cdot d_k + w_k \cdot e_k). \tag{1}$$

The similarity measure of Equation (1) is influenced by the length of the vector. That means that *s1* is influenced by the contrast in the image and the model. In order to remove the contrast, the direction vectors are normalized to the length one by dividing them through their gradient:

$$s_2 = \frac{1}{n}\sum_{k=1}^{n} \frac{\vec{m}_k \cdot \vec{i}_k}{\|\vec{m}_k\| \cdot \|\vec{i}_k\|} = \frac{1}{n}\sum_{k=1}^{n} \frac{v_k \cdot d_k + w_k \cdot e_k}{\sqrt{v_k^2 + w_k^2} \cdot \sqrt{d_{k_i}^2 + e_k^2}}. \tag{2}$$

Note that the normalization of *s2* differs from the normalized cross correlation (NCC): The NCC normalizes each pixel value by the expected mean of all values of the considered pixels. Therefore it is sensitive to nonlinear contrast changes whereas our method is not. The similarity measure in Equation (2) takes into account only the angle between the direction vectors, i.e. it is invariant against illumination changes. The value of $arccos\ s_2$ indicates the mean angle between the model vectors and the image vectors.

The values of *s2* can range from *-1* to *1*. In case of *s2* = *1* and *s2* = *-1* the model and the image object are identical. If *s2* is equal to one, then all vectors in the model and the corresponding image vectors have the same direction. If *s2* is equal to *-1* then the vectors have exactly opposite directions, that means only the contrast between the model and the image is changed.

Contrast changes can be ignored if the absolute value of the dot product is calculated:

$$s_3 = \frac{1}{n}\sum_{k=1}^{n} \frac{|\vec{m}_p \cdot \vec{i}_p|}{\|\vec{m}_p\| \cdot \|\vec{i}_p\|}. \tag{3}$$

The aim is to store only one model for objects with similar shapes of different scale and rotation. Therefore a transformed model must be compared to the image at a particular location.

3.2 Case Generation

The acquisition of the templates is done semi-automatically. Prototypical images are displayed to an expert. The screenshot of our developed tool is shown in Fig. 1. The expert manually traces the contour of the object with the help of the cursor of the computer. Afterwards the number of the contour points are reduced for data reduction purposes by interpolating the marked contour by a 1st order polynom. The marked object shapes are then aligned by Procrustes Algorithm [6]. From a set of shapes general groups of shapes are learnt by clustering. Single-linkage technique is used for clustering [4]. The prototype of each cluster is calculated by estimating the median shape [5] of the set of shapes in the cluster and taken as an object model.

3.2.1 Shape Approximation

An approximation of the contour might reduce this set of contour pixels to a sufficiently large set of pixels that will speed up the succeeding computation time of the alignment and clustering process. The numbers of pixels in this set will be influenced by the chosen order of the polygon and the allowed approximation error.

Our approach to the polygonal approximation is based on the area/length ratio according to Wall and Daniellson [6]. We use the first labeled point $s1$ of the object S as the starting point $p1$ for the first approximation. Next, we virtually draw a line segment from the starting point $p1$ to the successor point in B. The area A between this line and the corresponding contour segment of the object S is measured. If the area divided by the length L of the line is smaller than a predefined threshold T, then the same process is repeated for the next successor point in the set B.

This procedure is repeated until the ratio exceeds the threshold T. In that case the current point of set B becomes the end point of the approximated line P and the starting point for the next approximation. The same process is then repeated until the last point in set B is reached. The result of the approximation is a subset C of m points $p1...pm$ where $m < n$ and $pi \in N$.

The ratio A / L controls the maximal error of the approximation, since A is the area and L the side length of a virtual rectangle. If the ratio is low, then the other side of the virtual rectangle is small and wise-versa.

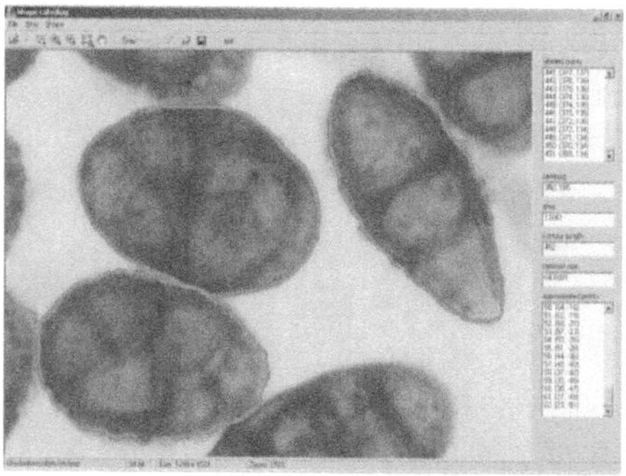

Fig. 1. Labeled and approximated shapes with coordinates

3.2.2 Shape Alignment

The aim of the alignment process is to compare the shapes of two objects in order to define a measure of similarity between them. Consider two shape instances P and O defined by the point-sets $p_i \in R^2$, $i = 1,2,...N_1$ and $o_j \in R^2$, $j = 1,2,...N_2$, respectively. The basic task of aligning two shapes consists of transforming one of them (say P), so that it fits in some optimal way the other one (say O). Generally the shape instance $P = \{p_i(x, y)\}_{i=1...N_1}$ is said to be aligned to the shape instance $O = \{o_j(x, y)\}_{j=1...N_2}$ if a distance $d(P, O)$ between the two shapes can not be decreased by applying a transformation ψ to P. The differences between various alignment approaches is the group of allowed transformations (similarity, rigidity, affinity...) on one side and the chosen distance function on the other side.

In our application we use the Procrustes distance, a least-squares type distance function. The alignment of shapes is limited to a similarity transformation in order to eliminate differences in the translation, the rotation and the scale of the two shapes P and O.

After computing a similarity transformation between P and O, the Procrustes distance is defined by:

$$D(P,O) = \sum_{i=1}^{N} \left\| \frac{(p_i - \mu_P)}{\sigma_P} - R(\theta)\frac{(o_i - \mu_O)}{\sigma_O} \right\|^2 \qquad (4)$$

where θ is the rotation matrix, μ_P and μ_O are the centroids of the objects P and O, respectively and σ_P and σ_O are the sums of squared distances of each point-set from the centroids.

In the basic form, the Procrustes alignment centers and scales each set of points, so that the sum of squared distances of all points in each point-set is unity. Then a similarity transformation based on these centered pre-shapes is computed. Finally the Procrustes average shape and Procrustes residuals can be evaluated. Our algorithm is described in [7].

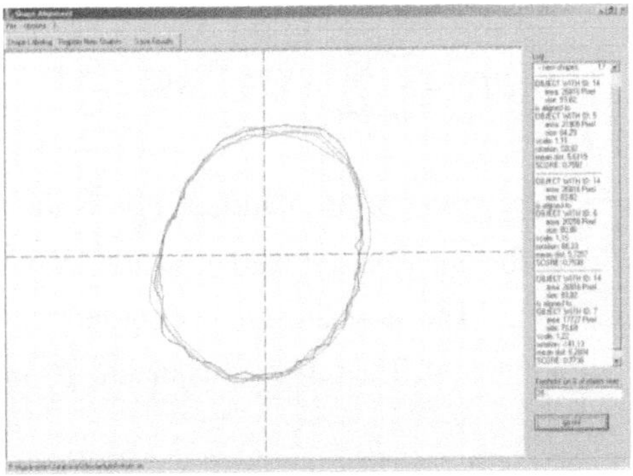

Fig. 2. Aligned shapes of objects Ulocladium Botrytis

4 Our Conceptual Clustering Algorithm

Conceptual clustering [8] is a type of flexible learning the hierarchy by observations. The partitioning of the cases is controlled by a category utility function [4]. Conceptual clustering algorithms can be distinguished by the type of this utility function which can be based on a probabilistic [9], [10] or a similarity concept [11]. Our conceptual clustering algorithm presented here is based on similarities, because we do not consider logical but numerical concepts. The algorithm works directly with structural objects. In our study this is a set of N acquired cases $\{ S_1,\ldots,S_N \}$, each comprised by an ordered array of 2D contour points. In contrast to the agglomerative clustering methods where the distance matrix is used as input it is not necessary to calculate pair-wise distances at first.

In addition to merging cases our algorithm allows incorporating new cases into existing nodes, opening new nodes, and splitting of existing nodes at every position in the hierarchy. Each new case is successively incorporated, so the algorithm dynamically fits the hierarchy to the data. The result will be a sequence of partitions represented a directed graph (concept hierarchy) where the root node contains the complete set of input cases and each terminal node represents an individual case.

Initially the concept hierarchy only consists of an empty root node. The algorithm implements a top-down method. A new case is placed into the actual concept hierarchy level by level beginning with the root node until a terminal node is reached. In each hierarchy level one of these four different kinds of operations is performed:

The new case is incorporated into an existing child node,

A new empty child node is created where the new case is incorporated,

Two existing nodes are merged to form a single node where the new case is incorporated, and

An existing node is splitted into its child nodes.

The new case is tentatively placed into the next hierarchy level by applying all of these operations. Finally that operation is performed which gives the best score of the partition according to the evaluation criteria. A proper evaluation function prefers compact and well separated clusters. These are clusters with small inner-cluster variances and high inter-class variances. Thus we calculate the score of a partition comprised of the clusters $\{X_1, X_2, \ldots X_m\}$ by

$$SCORE = \frac{1}{m} \sum_{i=1}^{m} p_i \left(SB_i - SW_i \right) , \tag{5}$$

where m is the number of clusters in this partition, p_i is the relative frequency of the i-th cluster, SB_i is the inter-cluster variance and SW_i is the inner-cluster variance of the i-th cluster. The normalization according to m is necessary to compare partitions of different size. The relative frequency p_i of the i-th cluster is

$$p_i = \frac{n_i}{n} , \tag{6}$$

where n_i is the number of cases in the i-th cluster and n is the number of cases in the parent node. The output of our algorithm for applying the eight exemplary shape cases of strain Ulocladium Botrytis is shown in Fig. 4. On top level the root node is shown which comprises the set of all input cases. Successively the tree is partitioned into nodes until each input case forms its one cluster.

We also introduced a pruning criterion into the algorithm which can be used optionally. It says that the clusters $\{X_1, X_2, \ldots X_m\}$ in one partition are removed if the sum of their inner-cluster-variances is *zero*. The criterion is fulfilled if the following condition is met

$$\sum_{i=1}^{m} SW_i = 0 \ . \tag{7}$$

Fig. 3 shows the complete, un-pruned concept hierarchy, where a new case called $\{ub\_9\}$ was incorporated supplementary. The darker nodes were those clusters which had to be modified because the new case was incorporated into them. For these nodes the cluster has to be updated. The white nodes in the hierarchy are clusters which were not attached.

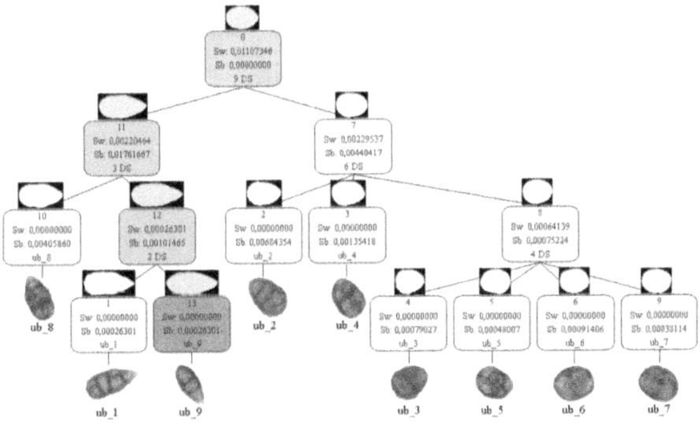

Fig. 3. Complete, not-pruned concept hierarchy after incrementally incorporating a new case

The main advantage of our conceptual clustering algorithm is that it brings along a concept description. Thus, in comparison to agglomerative clustering methods it is easy to understand why a set of cases forms a cluster. The algorithm calculates the inner-cluster-variances direct on the cases within this cluster or rather on their contour points instead of using a given distance matrix. During the clustering process the representative case, and also the variances and maximum distances in relation to this representative case are calculated since they are part of the concept description. It is also possible to incorporate new cases into the existing learnt hierarchy. Thus, the algorithm is of incrementally fashion.

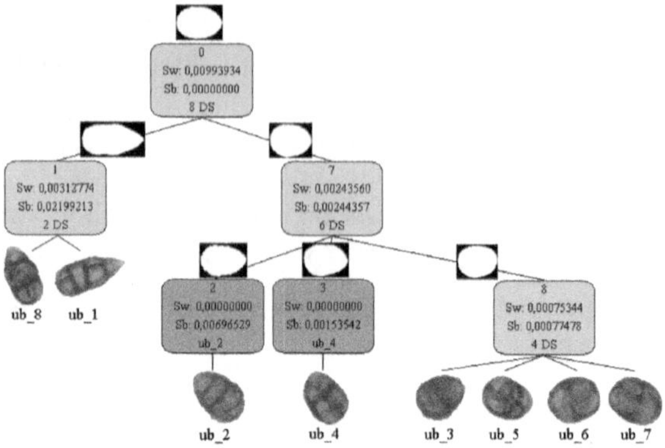

Fig. 4. The pruned version of the concept hierarchy resulting from the eight instances of strain Ulocladium Botrytis is shown

5 Calculation of General Cases

The representative case of a cluster is a more general representation of all cases hosted in this cluster. We select the medoid as a natural representative case for a cluster. The medoid x_{medoid} of a cluster X is the shape case which is positioned closest to the cluster centroid. It is the case which has the minimum distance to all other cases in the cluster

$$\overline{\mu}_X = x_{medoid} = \min_{x \in X} \sum_{i=1}^{n_X} d(x_i, x) \ . \tag{8}$$

In addition to the representative of a cluster we are interested in learning the maximum permissible distance from this generalized case. The maximum permissible distance D_X to the representative case is

$$D_X = \max_{x \in X} d(x, \overline{\mu}_X) \ . \tag{9}$$

When matching objects with a hierarchical casebase of increasing specialized cases it is important to know the degree of generalization for each case. This measure will be used as threshold for the similarity score while matching.

6 Experimental Results

We applied our method to six different airborne fungi spores (see Table 1). We labeled a total of 60 objects for each of the six fungal strains. These objects were taken for the case generation process according to the procedure as described in Section 4. The result was a casebase of 79 cases for the six different fungal strains. Despite the result in [12] where for each separate class the number of models was calculated we get a reduction in the number of models of 27.5%. That is because some of the fungal strain have the same appreance in shape and get clustered into the same cluster with others although the dimension of these objects might be different. Table 3 illustrates this fact.

The 79 cases were inputed in our case base and were applied to a test set of images contaning the same number of images for each class.

The threshold for the score was set to 0.8. We calculated the recognition rate as the number of objects that were recognized correctly in the image to the total number of objects in the images. The results of the matching process are shown in Table 2 and Table 3. Compared to our former results in [12] we got a better recognition rate since with our conceptual clustering method we could better control the grouping of the objects and the level of the hierarchy where the clusters should be taken from. The strategy for finding the cut-off for the grouping by conventional hierarchical clustering methods is a bit more tricky and subjective.

Table 2. Recognized objects in the image

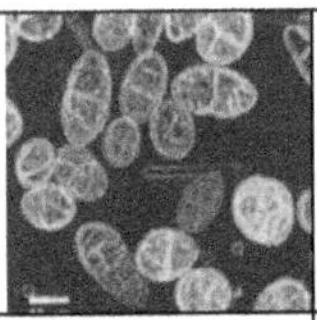	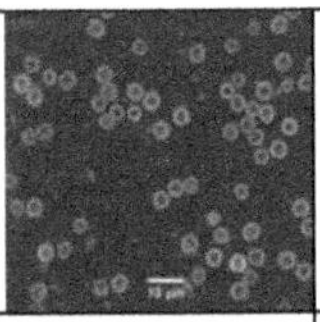	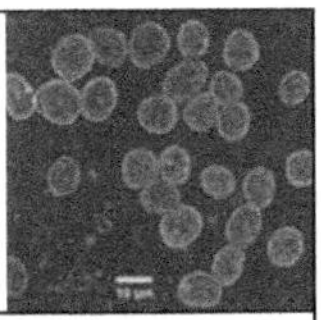
Alternaria Alternata	Aspergillus Niger	Rhizopus Stolonifer
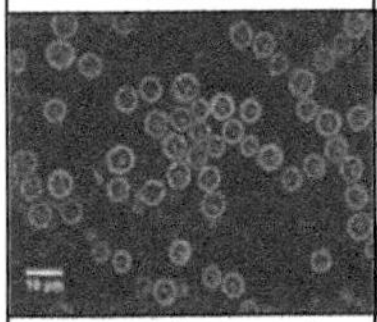	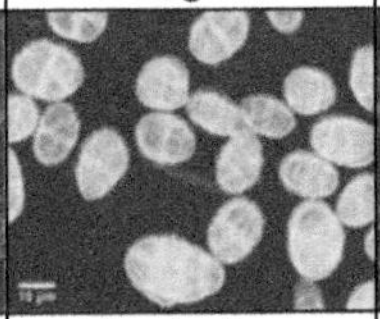	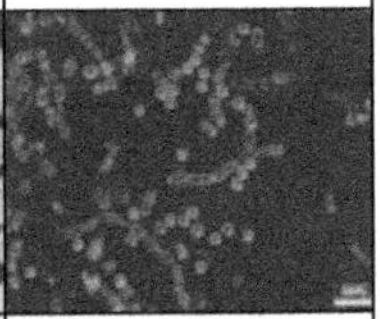
Scopulariopsis Brevicaulis	Ulocladium Botrytis	Wallenia Sebi

Table 3. Cluster number versus class membership

	Cluster Membership of Classes					
Number of Clusters	Alternaria Alterna	Ulocladium Botrytis	Aspergillus Niger	Rhizo. Stol.	Scopul. Brev.	Wallenia Sebi
1		X				
2						X
3	X	X				
...	...	...	...	...	...	...
11	X	X				X
12	X	X				
13		X				
14						X

Table 3. *(continued)*

...	...	...	...	...	...	...
28		X		X		X
29		X				
30				X		
31	X	X		X		
...	...	...	...	...	...	...
63	X	X	X		X	
64	X		X		X	
65	X			X		
66	X		X			
67	X				X	
68			X		X	
69					X	
70					X	
...	...	...	...	...	...	...
77					X	
78					X	
79					X	
Number of Member ship	26	33	9	25	18	26

Table 4. Results of matching

Class	Classification Accuracy in %
Alternaria Alternata	93%
Aspergillus Niger	92%
Rhizopus Stolonifer	94%
Scopulariopsis Brevicaulis	89%
Ulocladium Botrytis	92%
Wallenia Sebi	85%

6 Conclusions

We have described our method for the recognition of biological objects such as e.g. fungi spores in digital microscopic images.

We used a case-based recognition method. The cases are represented by edges and not by the gray-level itself. The similarity measure is based on the scalar product and is invariant against illumination changes and contrast changes. The case generation was done by manually tracing the contour of the object, automatic shape alignment, conceptual shape clustering and prototype calculation. The clustering process is incremental and allows to incorporate a new object into the excisting cluster hierarchy.

Acknowledgement

The project "Development of methods and techniques for the image-acquisition and computer-aided analysis of biologically dangerous substances BIOGEFA" is sponsored by the German Ministry of Economy BMWI under the grant number 16IN0147 and by the European Commission within the project "Multimedia Understanding through Semantics, Computation, and Learning" No. 507752.

References

1. Brown, A Survey of Image Registration Techniques, ACM Computer Surveys 24 (4), 1992, pp. 325-376.
2. C.F. Olson, D.P. Huttenlocher, Automatic Target Recognition by Matching Oriented Edge Pixels, IEEE Transactions on Image Processing 6(1), 1997, p 103-113.
3. G. Borgefors, Hierarchical Chamfer Matching: A Parametric Edge Detection Algorithm, IEEE Transactions on Pattern Analysis and Machine Intelligence 10(6), 1988, p. 848-865.
4. P. Perner, Data Mining on Multimedia Data, Springer Verlag, lnai 2558, 2003.
5. I.L. Dryden and K.V. Mardia, Statistical Shape Analysis, John Wiley&Sons, 1998.
6. K. Wall and P.-E. Daniellson, A fast sequential Method for Polygonal Approximation of digitized Curves, Comput. Graph. Image Process. 28, pp. 220-227, 1984.
7. P. Perner and S. Jänichen, Learning of Form Models from Exemplars, In In: Ana Fred, Terry Caelli, Robert P. W. Duin, Aurelio Campilho, and Dick de Ridder (Eds.), Structural, Syntactic, and Statistical Pattern Recognition, Springer Verlag 2004, lncs 3138, pp. 153-161
8. S. Jänichen and P. Perner, Conceptual Clustering and Case Generalization of 2-dimensional Forms, Journal on Computational Intelligence, to appear 2006
9. D. Fisher and P. Langley, Approaches to conceptual clustering, Proceedings of the Ninth International Joint Conference on Artificial Intelligence, pp. 691-697, Los Angeles, 1985.
10. W. Iba and P. Langley, Unsupervised Learning of Probabilistic Concept Hierarchies, In G. Paliouras, V. Karkaletsis, & C. D. Spyropoulos (Eds)., Machine learning and its applications. Springer Verlag, 2001.
11. P. Perner, Different Learning Strategies in a Case-Based Reasoning System for Image Interpretation, In B. Smith and P. Cunningham (Eds.), Advances in Case-Based Reasoning, pp. 251-261, Springer Verlag, lnai 1488, 1998.
12. P. Perner, H. Perner, and S. Jänichen Recognition of Airborne Fungi Spores in Digital Microscopic Images, Artificial Intelligence in Medicine, Volume 36, Issue 2 , February 2006, p. 137-157 (available on-line 3 October 2005)

A New Method of Illumination Normalization for Robust Face Recognition

Young Kyung Park, Bu Cheon Min, and Joong Kyu Kim

School of Information and Communication Engineering, SungKyunKwan University.
300, Chun-Chun-Dong, Chang-An-Ku, Suwon, Korea 440-746
{multipym, jkkim}@skku.edu

Abstract. In this paper, we propose a novel method of illumination normalization developed on the basis of the retinex theory. In retinex based methods, illumination is generally estimated and normalized by first smoothing the input image and then dividing the estimate into the original input image. The proposed method estimates illumination by iteratively convolving the input image with a 3×3 averaging mask weighted by an efficient measure of the illumination discontinuity at each pixel. In this way, we could achieve a fast illumination normalization in which even face images with strong shadows are normalized efficiently. The proposed method has been evaluated based on the Yale face database B and the CMU PIE database by using PCA. Carrying out various scenarios of test, we have found that our method presented consistent and promising results even when we used images with the worst case of illumination as training sets. We believe that the proposed method has a great potential to be applied to real time face recognition systems, especially under harsh illumination conditions.

1 Introduction

Among many factors affecting the performance of face recognition systems, illumination is known to be the one of the most significant. It has already been shown that illumination causes larger variations in intensity of face images than pose. For example, ambient lighting varies greatly during the course of the day, and from one day to another, as well as between indoor and outdoor environments. Moreover, strong shadows cast from a direct light source can make certain facial features invisible. Therefore, illumination normalization is a major requirement in the face recognition process and also is a central topic in the field of computer vision. In recent years, numerous approaches have been proposed to solve illumination problems in face recognition. Belhumeur et al. [1] extended the eigenface algorithm of Turk and Pentland [2] to fisherfaces by employing a classifier based on Fisher's linear discriminant analysis. They reported that fisherfaces outperform eigenfaces under conditions of varying illumination. Georghiades et al. [3] showed that the illumination cones of human faces can be approximated well by low dimensional linear subspaces. Therefore, the set of face images in fixed pose but under different illumination conditions can be efficiently represented using an illumination cone. However, the above methods either require

J.F. Martínez-Trinidad et al. (Eds.): CIARP 2006, LNCS 4225, pp. 38–47, 2006.

certain assumptions to be made about the light source or need a large number of training sets, and these requirements are not considered practical in real applications. On the other hand, there are alternative methods available which are based on retinex theory. The retinex theory motivated by Land [4] is based on the physical imaging model, in which an image $I(x, y)$ is regarded as the product $I(x, y) = R(x, y)L(x, y)$ where $R(x, y)$ is the reflectance and $L(x, y)$ is the illumination at each pixel (x, y). Here, the nature of $L(x, y)$ is determined by the illumination source, whereas $R(x, y)$ is determined by the characteristics of the imaged objects. Therefore, the illumination normalization for face recognition can be achieved by estimating the illumination L and then dividing the image I by it. However, it is impossible to estimate L from I, unless something else is known about either L or R. Hence, various assumptions and simplifications about L, or R, or both are proposed to solve this problem [5]. A common assumption is that edges in the scene are edges in the reflectance, while illumination spatially changes slowly in the scene. Thus, in most retinex based algorithms, the reflectance R is estimated as the ratio of the image I and its smooth version which serves as the estimate of the illumination L, and many smoothing filters to estimate the illumination have been proposed for robust face recognition. Single Scale Retinex (SSR), the latest version of Land's retinex that was implemented and tested by Jobson et al. [6], employed a simple linear filter with Gaussian kernel. However, halo effects are often visible at large illumination discontinuities in I, and Gross and Brajovie [5] introduced an anisotropic filter to reduce these halo effects to some extent. More recently, self-quotient image (SQI) [7] has been proposed with impressive improvement of performance for illumination problem. SQI employs the weighed Gaussian filter in which the convolution region is divided into two sub-regions with respect to a threshold, and separate values of weights are applied in each sub-region. These retinex based methods have common advantages that they do not require training images and has relatively low computational complexity. However, these methods cannot completely remove large illumination discontinuities, and more fast method is required for real time face recognition system. In this paper, we propose a novel method for illumination normalization based on the retinex theory. The key idea of our method is to estimate illumination by iteratively convolving an input image with a 3×3 averaging mask weighted by an efficient measure of the illumination discontinuity at each pixel. The paper is organized as follows. In section 2, the proposed algorithm is described in detail. In section 3, the experimental results are presented. Finally a conclusion is made in section 4.

2 Illumination Normalization

Since our method is based on the retinex theory, the process of our method for a pixel (x, y) in an image is described as

$$R(x, y) = \frac{I(x, y)}{L(x, y)} \tag{1}$$

As mentioned in section 1, the illumination L is estimated as a smooth version of input image I. Jobson et al. [6] evaluated various functional forms for the smoothing filter and found that the Gaussian form performed better than the inverse square suggested by Land [4]. For face recognition, however, Gaussian filter is known not to satisfy a robustness requirement, which smoothing must be carried out among pixels which having homogeneous illumination. This robustness requirement implies that the estimated illumination must be discontinuous at locations where the input image I has strong discontinuities of intensity [8]. This robust requirement is to more accurately take real world scenes into account, where illumination discontinuities such as shadows frequently occur. On the other hand, the Gaussian kernel, which is currently in wide use for smoothing, has an inherent computational limitation to be applied in real time; that is the computational complexity increases proportionally to the square of the kernel size, causing the overall speed of the smoothing filter very slow. To ensure a fast smoothing satisfying the robustness requirement at the same time, we present a novel method based on iterative convolution.

2.1 Iterative Convolution

Iterative convolution is a fast algorithm, in which an efficient short-length convolution is performed iteratively to build a long convolution [9]. As shown in table 1, iterative convolution is very efficient in terms of the computational complexity. Moreover, it was shown that, by virtue of the central limit theorem, convolving

Table 1. Computational complexity of two convolution methods

	Iterative short-length	Fixed long-length
Complexity	$O(nN^2k^2)$	$O(N^2K^2)$
	N: image size	N: image size
	k: small kernel size(2∼3)	K: kernel size
	n: # of iteration	

a 3×3 averaging kernel n times with an image I approximates the convolution of I with Gaussian kernel of $\sigma = \sqrt{n/3}$ and size of $3(n+1) - n = 2n+3$ [10]. We can formulate the iterative convolution process as follows. Let $I^{(0)}(x, y)$ be the input image at each point (x, y) before smoothing. Then, the smoothed image $I^{(t+1)}(x, y)$ at the $(t+1)th$ iteration is given by: [9]

$$I^{(t+1)}(x,y) = \frac{1}{N^{(t)}} \sum_{i=-1}^{1} \sum_{j=-1}^{1} I^{(t)}(x+i, y+j) w^{(t)}(x+i, y+j) \qquad (2)$$

with

$$N^{(t)} = \sum_{i=-1}^{1} \sum_{j=-1}^{1} w^{(t)}(x+i, y+j) \qquad (3)$$

where

$$w^{(t)}(x,y) = 1, \ \forall(x,y) \text{ and } \forall t. \tag{4}$$

$N^{(t)}$ in (3) represents a normalizing factor, and $w^{(t)}(x,y)$ in (4) indicate the corresponding weights of the convolution mask. This filter smoothes the image everywhere, even across discontinuities because this is just an approximated version of Gaussian filter. Consequently, halo effects might often be visible when we apply the Gaussian filter. Therefore, although iterative convolution is efficient in computational complexity, it doesn't meet the robustness requirement. For robust smoothing, the $w^{(t)}(x,y)$, thus, must be set adaptively based on discontinuities of intensity values. We will present the adaptive weighting method in the next subsection

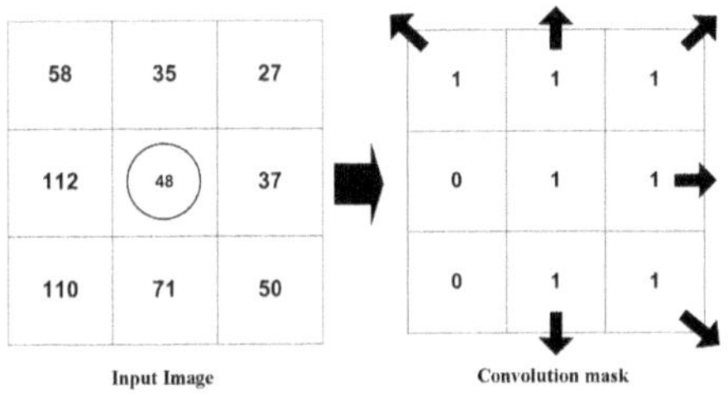

Fig. 1. An example of a convolution mask constructed by applying adaptive weighting ($\alpha = 0.2$) to an input image

2.2 Adaptive Weighting

To set weights of convolution mask $w^{(t)}(x,y)$ adaptively, we must know where illumination discontinuities take place. If we already knew the locations of these discontinuity points, then we could set the corresponding weights of the convolution mask $w^{(t)}(x,y)$ to zero [9]. In the framework of illumination normalization, this means that smoothing must be mainly carried out among pixels with homogeneous illumination. Unfortunately, it is impossible to correctly acquire the locations of illumination discontinuities when only one image is given, and additional information about the scene is not available. To solve this problem, we can set $w^{(t)}(x,y)$ based on the variance between a central pixel and neighboring pixels in convolution mask. Let pixel location (m,n) correspond to a central pixel of a convolution mask with 3×3 size. Then, the variance between the central pixel and neighboring pixels in convolution mask is

$$\tau(m,n) = \sum \sum_{(x,y)\in\Omega} |I(x,y) - I(m,n)| \tag{5}$$

where Ω is a convolution region, and (x,y) indicates the locations of the neighboring pixels. The corresponding weights of the convolution mask $w^{(t)}(x,y)$ are determined according to the variance as follows:

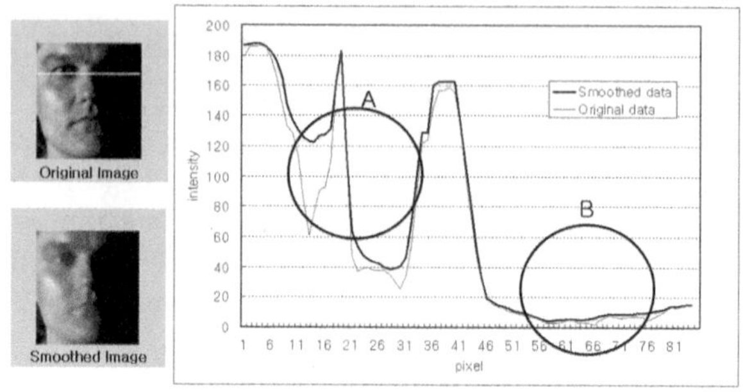

Fig. 2. The intensity profiles of horizontal lines in an original image and a smoothed image after 9 iterations

$$w^{(t)}(x,y) = \begin{cases} 1 & |I(x,y) - I(m,n)| < \alpha\tau(i,j) \\ 0 & \text{else} \end{cases} \tag{6}$$

where α determines the level of strong discontinuity. If α approaches 0, level of strong discontinuity which must be preserved during the process of smoothing decreases. As shown in figure 1, only pixels with relatively little different intensity values from a current pixel are convolved. Once weights of the convolution mask corresponding to each pixel of an input image are determined, iterative convolution is performed. Due to the diffusion characteristic of the iterative convolution, there are two significant operations affecting the image as the iteration proceeds: one is the preservation of strong discontinuities, and the other is the smoothing within regions with small variance. Figure 1 shows these operations well, where diffusion effects of smoothing occur only in the directions of arrow. Now, for more accurate description of real environments, we address an additional constraint that surfaces cannot reflect more light than what is shed on them [8]. Thus, the reflectance R must be always smaller than one. By this constraint, (2) can be modified as follows.

$$\begin{aligned} I^{(t+1)}(x,y) &= \tfrac{1}{N^{(t)}} \textstyle\sum_{i=-1}^{1} \sum_{j=-1}^{1} I^{(t)}(x+i,y+j)w^{(t)}(x+i,y+j) \\ I^{(t+1)}(x,y) &= \max\{I^{(t+1)}(x,y), I^{(t)}(x,y)\} \end{aligned} \tag{7}$$

Figure 2 shows a result of smoothing using the proposed iterative convolution with adaptive weighting with $\alpha = 0.2$. Each region A and B in the graph correspond to two eyes in the face. We can see that regions of facial features are efficiently smoothed while the illumination discontinuities are preserved. Note that the signal variation under light region is much larger than that under shadow region, and the facial features (in this case, the two eyes) have far different scales in these two regions. For a good and stable performance of face recognition, therefore, it is necessary that the small scale signal in the shadow region must be amplified so that both the light and shadow regions have similar signal scales

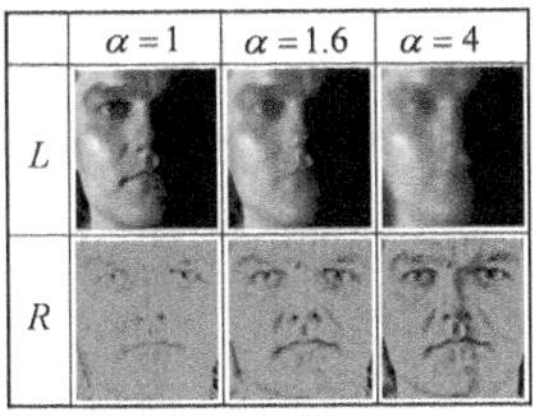

Fig. 3. Effect of different α in adaptive weighting. The first row shows estimated illumination using the proposed smoothing method, and the second row shows final results which are obtained by dividing an input images by estimated illuminations.

after illumination normalization. For this purpose, we apply the retinex theory formulated in (1), and figure 3 shows the results according to some typical values of α. In order to ensure a robust face recognition, the smoothing must be carried out at larger scale than the scale of facial features; that is, we should emphasize the small scale facial features such as mouth, nose, eyes, and eyebrows while removing the illumination. And this mainly depends on the proper choice of α; for example, if α is too small, facial features would not be visible. By some investigations as shown in figure 3, we selected a proper value of $\alpha = 0.2$ for our experiments which will be described in the following section. The number of iterations is also important factor for robust face recognition. If the number of iterations is too large, normalization effects would decrease with the increase of visual effects. For our experiment, we fixed the number of iterations to $n = 9$.

3 Experimental Results and Discussion

In order to evaluate the robustness and effectiveness of the proposed method, we used the images from two publicly available databases: Yale face database B [3] and CMU PIE database [11], and computed the recognition accuracies using Eigenfaces (Principal Component Analysis (PCA)) [2]. The proposed method is also compared with three other existing methods of illumination normalization: SSR [6], SQI [7] and histogram equalization. We present the respective test result for each database.

3.1 Yale Face Database B

The Yale face database B contains 5,760 images taken from 10 subjects under 576 viewing conditions(9 poses $\times$ 64 illumination conditions). Since we are only concerned with the illumination problem in this paper, we selected 640 images for 10 subjects representing 64 illumination conditions under the frontal pose. Images in the database are divided into 5 subsets based on the angle of the light source directions. The 5 subsets are subset 1(0° to 12°), subset 2(13° to 25°), subset 3(26° to 50°), subset 4(51° to 77°), and subset 5(above 78°) [3]. We refer to images in both subset 4 and subset 5 as images with large illumination

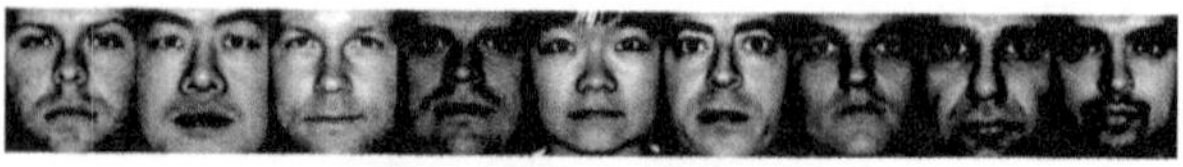

Fig. 4. Representative images of 10 subjects in Yale face database B

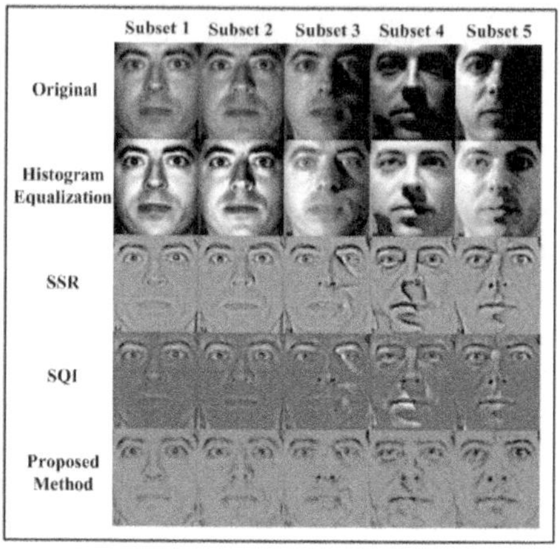

Fig. 5. Illumination normalization effect comparison

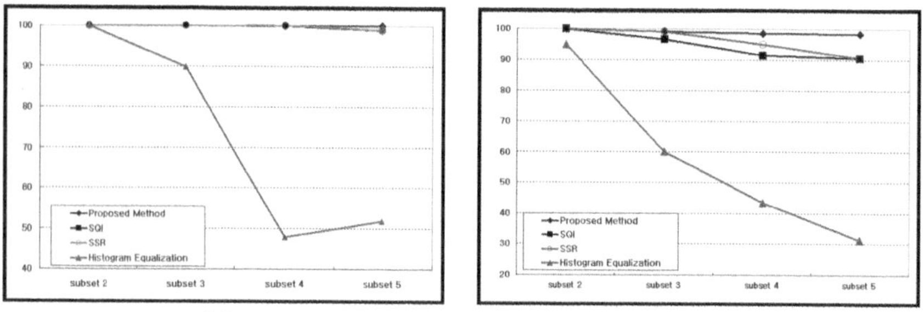

(a) (b)

Fig. 6. Recognition accuracies(%) on the Yale face database B using (a)subset 1, and (b)only the representative images, as the training set

variation. Among the 640 images, we discarded 7 corrupted images and finally constructed total 633 images (70, 118, 118, 138, 189 images in subset 1 to 5). Figure 4 shows the representative images of the 10 subjects, and figure 5 shows illumination normalization results by different methods according to each subset of the one among 10 subjects. To apply our proposed method to a face recognition system, we first used subset 1 as training set and tested other subsets. Figure 6(a) shows the recognition results using each illumination normalization method.

Table 2. Average recognition rate (%) comparison on the Yale face database B using images in all different subsets (from subset 2 to subset 5) as the training set

	Proposed method	SQI	SSR	Histogram equalization
Recognition rate	97.65%	93.11%	94.06%	42.36%

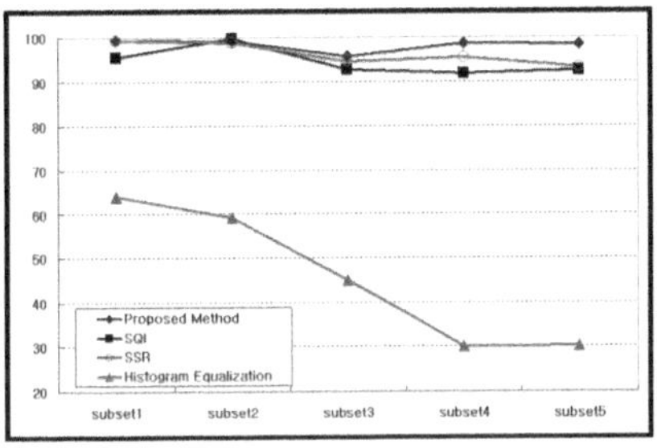

(a)

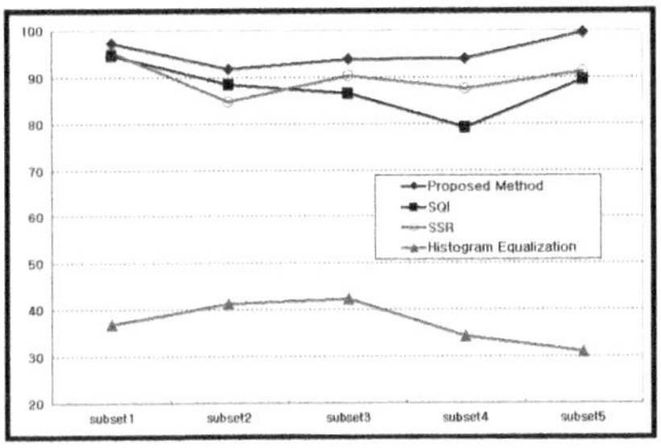

(b)

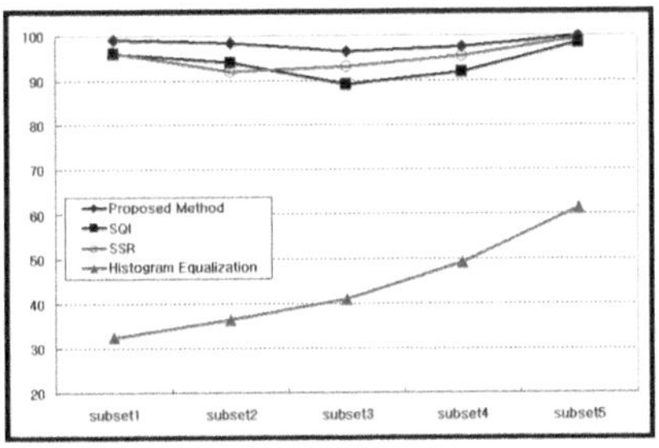

(c)

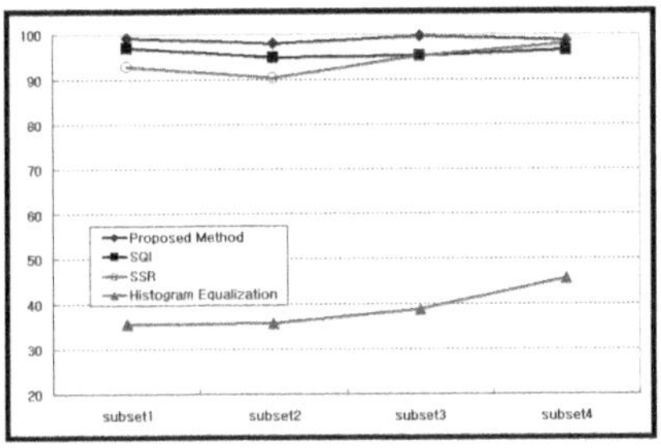

(d)

Fig. 7. Recognition accuracies(%) on the Yale face database B using (a)subset 2 (*test*2), (b)subset 3 (*test*3), (c)subset 4 (*test*4), and (d)subset 5 (*test*5) as the training set

The proposed method achieved recognition rates of 100% in all subsets. As a second test, we only used the 10 images(one for each subject in subset 1) in figure 4 as a training set and tested other subsets. The results are given in figure 6(b), and it is clear that the proposed method outperforms other methods. Finally, we used images in each of the other subsets (2 to 5) as training set and computed the recognition accuracy [12]. Since subset 2 to 5 represent the illumination conditions close to real environments, we can say that this test is more meaningful and practical than the other two previous tests. As shown in figure 7, four tests are carried out. Each $testX$ denotes that the training set is from subset X, where $X = 2, 3, 4, 5$, and the test is done for the remaining subsets. Table 2 compares recognition rates by averaging all results from these four tests. From the figure 7 and the table 2, it is clear that the proposed method has consistent and promising results even when images with large illumination variation (subset 4 and subset 5) are used as the training set.

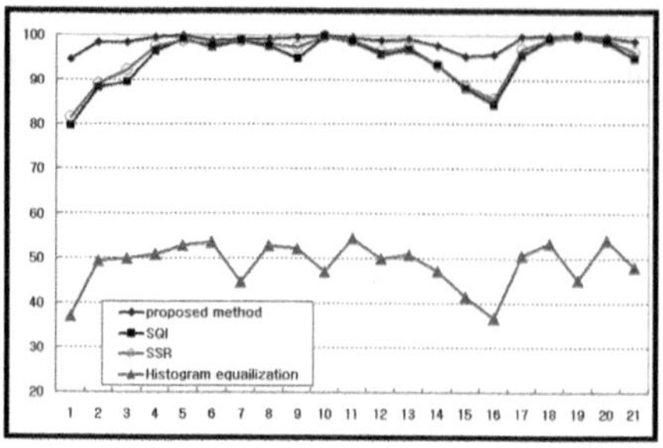

Fig. 8. Recognition accuracies(%) on the CMU PIE database

Table 3. Average recognition rate (%) comparison on the CMU PIE database

	Proposed method	SQI	SSR	Histogram equalization
Recognition rate	98.57%	94.53%	95.32%	48.69%

3.2 CMU PIE Database

The CMU PIE database contains 41,368 images obtained from 68 subjects. We took images of frontal faces with 21 different illumination conditions. Among 68 subjects, we removed one subject because it was not a frontal image. Thus, the total number of images we used for our test is 1,407.

The recognition rates were computed by the k-fold strategy: i.e, k images of each subject (in our test, $k = 1$) are selected for training and the remaining $21 - k$ images of each subject are selected for test. This process was repeated $(21 - k + 1)$ times by changing training images. Figure 8 shows recognition rates according to each trial. The proposed method also outperforms other methods and has consistently high recognition rates over 95%.

4 Conclusion

In this paper, we proposed a new illumination normalization method for robust face recognition. The proposed method, which is based on the retinex theory, estimates the illumination using a novel iterative smoothing methodology, and turned out to be superior to existing smoothing methods in terms of both time complexity and performance. The essence of our proposed method is that the smoothing is carried out by iteratively convolving an input image with a 3×3 averaging mask weighted by a efficient measure of the illumination discontinuity at each pixel. Using the proposed method, we showed that even images with strong shadow are effectively normalized, and consequently the recognition accuracies notably outperformed the existing methods. Especially, our proposed method presented consistent and promising results even when we used images with large illumination variations as training set. We believe that the proposed method has a wide range of applications in real time face recognition systems, especially under harsh illumination conditions.

References

1. Belhumeur,P.N., Hespanha,J., Kriegman,D.J.: Eigenfaces vs. Fisherfaces:Recognition Using Class Specific Linear Projection. IEEE Transactions on Pattern Analysis and Machine Intelligence,20(7), (1997)
2. Turk, M., Pentland, A.: Eigenfaces for Recognition.Journal of Cognitive Neuroscience, 3(1):71-86,(1991)
3. Georghiades, A. S., Belhumeur, P. N., Kriegman, D. J.: From Few to Many: Illumination Cone Models for Face Recognition under Variable Lighting and Pose. IEEE Transactions on Pattern Analysis and Machine Intelligence, 23(6):643-660, (2001)
4. Land, E.: An alternative technique for the computation of the designator in the retinex theory of color vision. Proc. Nat. Acad. Sci., vol. 83, 3078-3080, (1986)
5. Gross, R., Brajovic, V.: An image preprocessing Algorithm for illumination invariant face recognition. In 4th International Conference on Audio and Video Based Biometric Person Authentication, (2003)
6. Jobson, D. J., Rahman, Z., Woodell, G. A.: Properties and performance of a center/surround retinex. IEEE Transactions on Image Processing, vol. 6, 451-462, (1997)
7. Wang, H., Li, S. J., Wang, Y.: Generalized quotient image. IEEE CVPR, (2004)
8. Shaked, D., Keshet, R.: Robust recursive envelope operators for fast retinex. Hewlett-Packard Research Laboratories Technical Report, HPL-2002-74R1, (2002)
9. Saint-Marc, P., Chen, J.-S., Medioni, G.: Adaptive smoothing: a general tool for early vision. IEEE Transactions on Pattern Analysis and Machine Intelligence, 13(6):514-529, (1991)
10. Trucco, E., Verri, A.: Introductory techniques for 3-D computer vision, Prentice Hall, (1998)
11. Sim, T., Baker, S., Bsat, M.: The CMU Pose,Illumination,and Expression Database.IEEE Trans on PAMI, vol. 25, 1615-1618, (2003)
12. Chen, T., Yin, W., Zhou, X. S., Comaniciu, D., Huang, T. S.: Illumination Normalization for Face Recognition and Uneven Background Correction Using Total Variation Based Image Models. IEEE CVPR, (2005)

A Fast Method for Localization of Local Illumination Variations and Photometric Normalization in Face Images

Estela María Álvarez Morales[1], Francisco Silva Mata[1], Eduardo Garea Llano[1], Heydi Mendez Vazquez[1], and Moisés Herrera[2]

[1] Advanced Technology Application Center. 7ma, No. 21812, Siboney, Playa, Cuba, 12200
{egarea, hmendez}@cenatav.co.cu
[2] Empresa de Automatización Integral (CEDAI), Villa Clara, Cuba
moises@cedaivc.co.cu

Abstract. In this paper we present a method for the automatic localization of local light variations and its photometric normalization in face images affected by different angles of illumination causing the appearance of specular light. The proposed approach is faster and more efficient that if the same one was carried out on the whole image through the traditional photometric normalization methods (homomorphic filtering, anisotropic smoothing, etc.). The process consists in using of the Adaboosting algorithms for the fast detection of regions affected by specular reflection combined with a normalization method based on the local normalization that standardizes the local mean and variance into the located region. A set of measures are proposed to evaluate the effectiveness of detectors. Finally, results are compared through two experimental schemes to measure how the similarity is affected by illumination changes and how the proposed approach improves the effect caused by these changes.

1 Introduction

Face recognition algorithms consist in three major parts: Face detection, normalization and face identification [1]. Face recognition starts with the detection of face patterns in sometimes cluttered scenes, continues normalizing the face images to attenuate or eliminate geometrical and illumination problems, then these faces are identified using appropriated classification algorithms, and finally results are post-processed using model-based schemes and logistic feedback [2].

One illumination effect that might cause particular problems in the recognition process is the local reflection of light in the face. Recently many appearance-based algorithms have been proposed to deal with the problem [3-6]. These algorithms work well, but are computationally expensive.

To find a method to efficiently and quickly solve these mentionated problems that obtains face images without the specular illumination effect and maintaining the features necessary for identification is a challenge.

In this paper we present a new approach to perform a fast detection of regions affected by the specular illumination effect by means of a boosted cascade detector

J.F. Martínez-Trinidad et al. (Eds.): CIARP 2006, LNCS 4225, pp. 48 – 57, 2006.

which is based on works of P.Viola and M. Jones [7] and an algorithm proposed by us to attenuate the local specular light through the filtering of the detected regions by mean value of pixels in the four corners of the localized square.

The first contribution of this paper is the fact that we use the Viola and Jones method for region detection instead of object detection. And if in addition we consider that already the integral image has been calculated and that the detection turns into a region previously located by the face detector, the detection process will be extremely fast.

The second contribution of this paper is the fact that this process of photometric normalization is done only in the automatic detected regions and not on the whole image and only in those images where the illumination problem is present; this clearly reports an important saving of time and calculation

The third contribution of this paper is the proposed method for the local normalization that standardizes the local mean and variance of an image region by means of a very fast processing implemented through a lookup table.

The effectiveness of the proposed method was evaluated in several experiments using images from the Yale B database, taken a variety of illumination conditions. Detectors were evaluated using five proposed measures, and obtained results demonstrate that the variations in the image similarity caused by illumination are successfully eliminated or attenuated.

2 Fast Detection of Faces and Their Corresponding Regions Affected by Illumination

Face detection and their corresponding regions affected by illumination is achieved trough the Viola and John's algorithm [7], and are implemented at the OpenCV library [8]. There are several advantages offer by this method: The image representation called integral image, allows a very quickly computation of the features used by the detectors. The learning algorithm based on Adaboost, allows to select a small number of features from the initial set, and to obtain a cascade of simple classifiers to discriminate them [7].

Two cascade detectors were used, the first one was devoted to detect the faces, and the other one devoted to detect the regions affected by specular ligth.

2.1 Training Process

The face training is composed by automatic labeled faces detected by the Stump-based 24x24 Gentle Adaboost frontal face detector, applied on the Yale B Face Database. A region training set was manually prepared by means of selection of the square regions, assigning a positive label (+1) to the samples with local affectations of illumination, and negative labels (-1) to the samples without great affectations of illumination. Then these samples are saved and rescaled to a size of 24 x 24 pixels (Fig. 1). In training phase, the classifier was exhaustively trained using these sets of regions taken from the previously detected faces by the first cascade detector in a wide variety of training images.

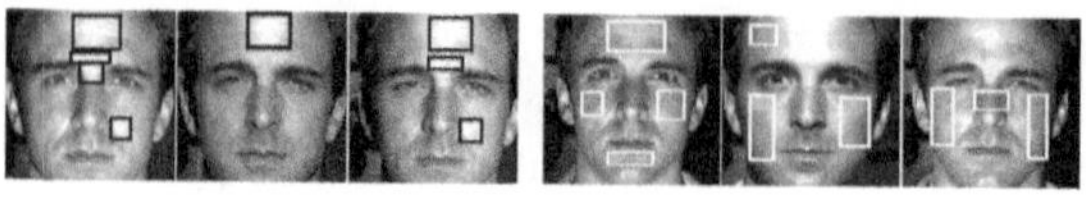

Fig. 1. Region selection for training samples, positive (left) and negatives (right)

2.2 Description of the Detection Process

Detection process begins with the face detection by means of a cascade specialized detector (1). As result, the coordinates of the square which contains the face are obtained. A second cascade detector is triggered to look for the regions affected by specular light but only in the region contained within squares that were detected before (2). The third step is the normalization process, which is made only in the zone detected by the second detector (3). If the face images are going to be used in face recognition the process will continue with the recognition algorithm. If the final objective is to improve the images quality of the processed squares then the normalized regions will be restored to their original position (4). Fig 2 shows the general scheme of the proposed method.

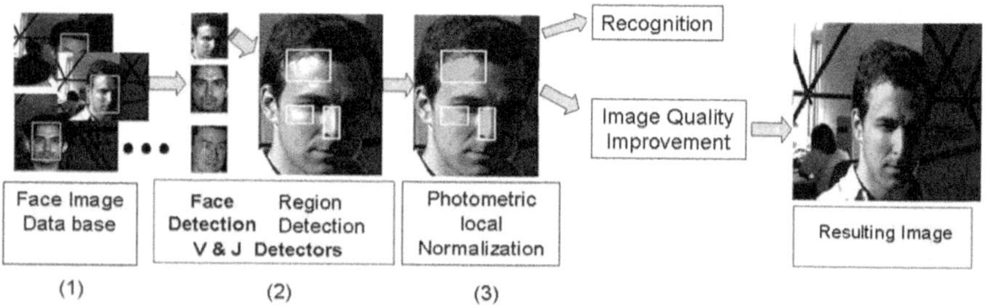

Fig. 2. Basic steps in fast normalization sequence

3 A Fast Local Photometric Normalization Method

The following proposed method is based on the local normalization algorithm that standardizes the local mean and variance of an image [9], [10]. In our approach we make a filtering by the mean value of the pixels of local regions located at the four corners of the automatically localized square window which contains the image parts affected by low frequency illumination effect (specular light) calculated by the expression:

$$I_{(i,j)f} = I_{(i,j)} - \frac{\overline{X}.p}{I_{(i,j)0}} \tag{1}$$

Where, $I_{(i,j)0,}$ is the original value of a pixel located at the position i,j of the square window containing the part of image affected by illumination.

$I_{(i,j)f}$ is the normalized value of a pixel affected by illumination at the position i,j of the rectangular window.

$\overline{X}$. is the mean value of vector formed by four maximum pixel values contained in the windows located at the four corners of the automatic located square that contains the part of the image affected by low frequency illumination effect (specular light). See Fig 3.

p. is the coefficient that depends of the Euclidean distance between the mean value and each value of the image inside the located square window, the values of p are increased on a fixed quantity together with the distance interval, Table 1 shows the distance intervals and their corresponding coefficients used by us.

$$\overline{X} = \frac{[\max(C1) + \max(C2) + \max(C3) + \max(C4)]}{4} \qquad (2)$$

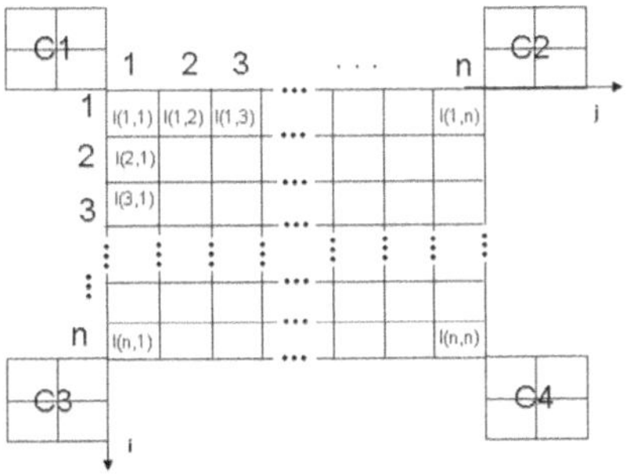

Fig. 3. Distribution of four pixel windows situated in the corners of the automatic localized square window that contains the part of the image affected by low frequency illumination effect (specular light)

Table 1. Distance intervals and its corresponding coefficients p

No. of interval	Distance Interval	Coefficient p
1	1.2 - 1.5	10
2	1.5 - 1.8	40
...	...	...
20	6.9 - 7.2	760

Taking in to account that the automatic localization extracts pixels affected by illumination surrounded by non affected pixels, the normalization algorithm works with the values of these non affected pixels localized in the four corners, the effect is the change of pixel values in the window in function of the mean value calculated, without lost of information (see Fig 4).

3.1 Lookup Table

To increase the speed of normalization process we will set all the possible values that can be obtained with expressions 1 and 2 in a lookup table. A lookup table is a matrix in which the intersection of each column and row represents the value to be returned for one possible combination of pixels in a neighborhood. We produced a multidimensional matrix (256x256x20) containing, one dimension for each distance interval.

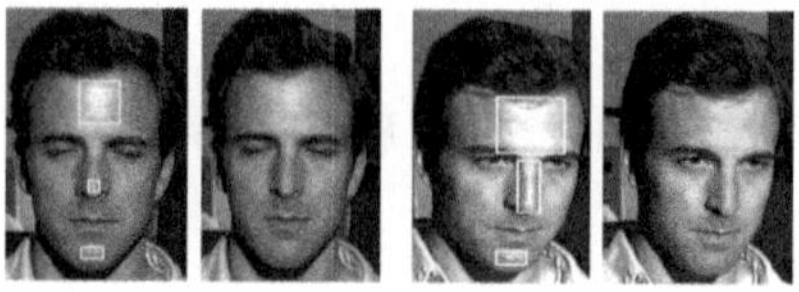

Fig. 4. Example of face image normalization in the Yale B database using the proposed method

4 Experiments

For a complete evaluation of the performance of our proposal we divided the experimental process in two parts, the first one is devoted to measure the effectiveness of the automatic detection process, and the second one is devoted to measure the performance of the photometric normalization method.

4.1 Measurement of the Effectiveness of the Detection Process

We defined a set of measures necessary to accurately know the detector effectiveness behaviour according to the final mission of the process. They are:

$$ESD = \frac{\sum(DA - TA)}{DA.100} \tag{3}$$

ESD (External Square Difference): The difference between the area of automatic detected square (DA) and the area of the optimal square that includes the region to detect (TA), if it was completely detected (Fig.5, A), considering the optimal square like the bounding box of the region affected with specular light, it is given in percentages and calculated by the expression:

ISD (Internal Square Difference): The difference in area between optimal square containing the real region (TA) and the automatically detected one, if the area of the detected square (DA) is situated inside the bounding box (Fig 5, B); it is given in percentages and calculated by the expression:

$$ISD = \frac{\sum(TA - DA)}{\sum TA.100} \tag{4}$$

UED (Unavoidable Error of Detector): Is the difference between the actual area of the region affected by specular light (RA) taken with a certain threshold and the area of the optimal square that is tangential to the region boundaries (TRA) (Fig.5, E).

The value of UED was calculated based on the area of the segmented regions and a threshold calculated according to the process of automatic threshold choosing [13] and the area of the automatically detected square that inscribe the segmented regions, it is given in percentages and calculated by expression:

$$UED = \frac{\sum (RA - TRA)}{\sum RA.100} \quad (5)$$

NDR (Not Detected Region): Is the total area of the region that must be detected but is not detected (Fig 5, C), it is given in percentages and calculated by expression:

$$NDR = \frac{\sum (TA - \sum (DA \cap TA))}{\sum TA.100} \quad (6)$$

EDA (Erroneous Detected Area): Is the total area of the image that was erroneously marked by the detector (Fig 5, D), it is given in percentages and calculated by expression:

$$EDA = \frac{\sum (BDA)}{\sum (AI - TA).100} \quad (7)$$

Where BDA is the bat detected area, and AI is the total area of the image.

We also measured the effectiveness of the automatic detection process by computing the true detected, no detected and falsely detected regions in the test set.

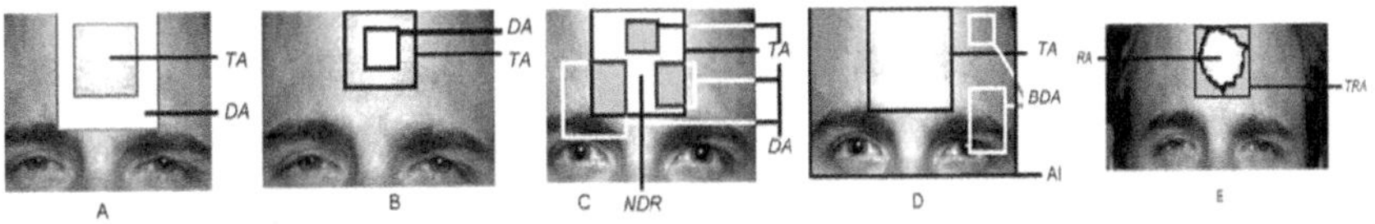

Fig. 5. Proposed measures of the effectiveness of the automatic detection process**,** A-ESD, B-ISD, C-NDR, D-EDA, E-UED

4.2 The Yale B Database

We experimented the proposed approach in images from Yale B database [12].

The Yale B database (Fig. 6) contains 64 different illumination conditions for 10 subjects. The illumination conditions are a single light source, the position of which varies horizontally and vertically. For the evaluation of the effectiveness of the detection process we take a test set composed by 197 images affected by specular reflection.

4.3 Evaluation of the Performance of the Photometric Normalization Method

For evaluation of proposed method we tested it using images from Yale B database. We take 3 images per subject, and from each of these 3 images we created new 5 images introducing high frequency pixel values in some areas of images simulating the low frequency illumination effect (specular light). Fig 6 shows an example of generated images.

With generated images we compared the results in two experimental schemes. The idea was to measure how the similarity is affected by illumination changes and how the proposed approach improves the effect caused by these changes. Normalized correlation has been chosen as it has proved to be a successful similarity measure in face recognition [11]. For identical images it takes the maximum value equal to unity.

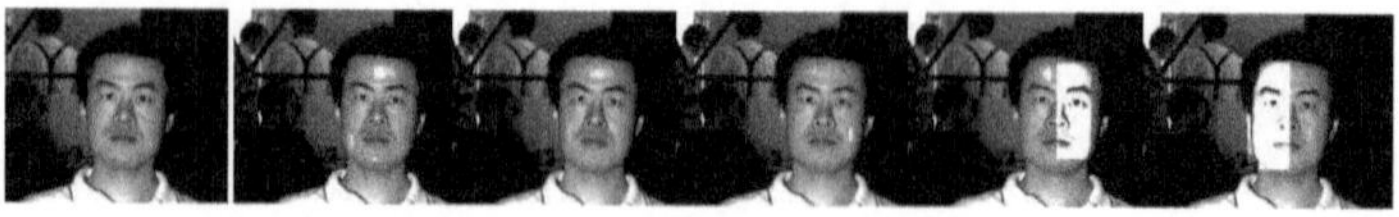

Fig. 6. Example of the new 5 images of one subject created by introducing low frequency pixel values in some areas of images (specular light). The first image in the left is the original image.

To obtain geometrically normalized images we implemented an algorithm [11] that consists of the following steps: Smoothing, rotating, scaling and resampling the input image. The smoothing is performed by convolution with a Gaussian Filter of size5x5, the rotation and scaling outputs an image of size 55 rows x 51 cols. The left-eye is mapped onto the pixel position (19, 38) and the right-eye is mapped onto the pixel position (19, 12).

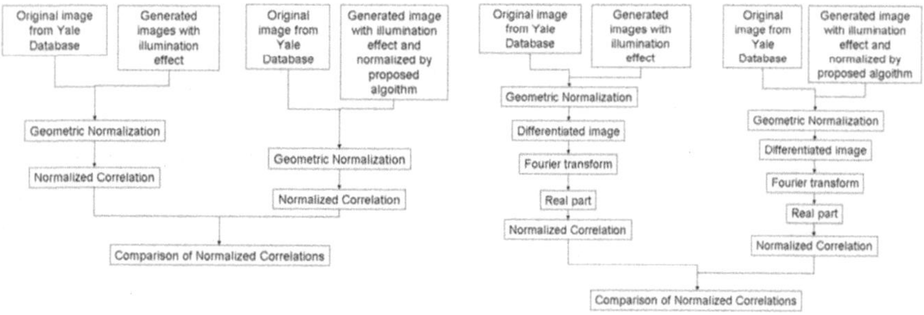

Fig. 7. Experimental schemes. Left, in the image domain; Right, in the frequency domain

The experimental schemes are shown in Fig. 7. Using these schemes we compared results obtained in two different representation spaces, one in the image domain and other in the frequency domain using an illumination insensitive representation [11] based in the complex first derivative image to highlight the high frequency content and transformed it to the frequency domain and extracted the real part as illumination insensitive representation.

For the time consuming evaluation we compared the time taken by our method to normalizing of images affected by illumination taking as the region to be normalized the square that encloses whole image, against the time consumed by four traditional algorithms of photometric normalization [13] (homomorphic filtering, anisotropic smoothing, isotropic smoothing and multiescale retinex) applied to whole image.

5 Experimental Results

5.1 Results of Measurement of the Effectiveness of Detection Process

In Table 2 and 3 we present the results of the evaluation of the detector effectiveness during the detection of regions.

The value of the UED is relatively high. This effect is produced by the fact that the most of affected regions in the Yale B database have shapes near to a rectangle and the detector produces square region

Table 2. Effectiveness of the detection by the proposed measures

UED	ISD	ESD	NDR	EDA
36.1	3.0	31.4	9.0	33.0

Table 3. Performance of the Region Detector

Total of affected regions	True detected	No detected	Falsely Detected
366	334	32	90
100%	91.28%	8.74%	-

Table 4. Difference in the quantity of pixels processed by our method image (region oriented) and processed by traditional methods (whole image oriented)

Total area of 197 images in the database (pixels)	Total area of detected regions in the images (pixels)	Percentage of the processed area vs. total image area (%)
11 824 925	2 963 300	25%

The small value of ISD means that in a little number of cases the detector marks the square smaller than the actual region. The effect of this error is significant in the sense that when we used the proposed normalization method, it will take for the normalization process the mean value from pixels affected by illumination.

The relatively high value of ESD in certain sense increase the computational cost of the normalization process because the number of pixels to be normalized is bigger than the quantity of pixels included in the actual region affected by illumination, but it guarantees that the mean value for photometric normalization will be taken from well illuminated pixels. The effect of normalization on not affected pixels will not considerably change their values since the normalization grade depends of the difference of the pixel value to the mean value.

The low value of the NDR is in correspondence with the low error rate of detector (Table 3)

The value of EDA although is relatively high, principally have implications in the increasing of quantity of pixels to be processed.

Results in Table 3 show that the process of detection reaches high rates; although it leaves a little number of not detected regions. Nevertheless we have achieved a high speed in detection of the 91.28% of affected regions (see Table 4). For the normalization of the not detected regions (9.0%) can be applied one variant of our method that allows the manual selection of the affected region, or can be applied the traditional methods of normalization.

5.2 Results in the Evaluation of the Performance of the Photometric Normalization Method

The distributions of normalized correlations were compared in 4 different combinations. In Table 5 we show the different variants of normalized correlations and results of their comparison. We can see that when we applied the proposed approach and compared the normalized correlations in the image domain, we obtained a significant increase of the correlation coefficients of all normalized images respect to the original image.

Table 5. Normalized correlation and its comparison in Yale B database

Correlations	Description	*Nc*
	In the image domain	
A	165 subjects against the same subjects using 5 different generated images	0.79
B	165 subjects against the same subjects using 5 different generated images (with previous photometric normalization).	0.88
	In the frequency domain	
C	165 subjects against the same subjects using 5 different generated images	0.92
D	165 subjects against the same subjects using 5 different generated images (with previous photometric normalization).	0.98

A similar result is obtained using the representation in the frequency domain, in this case we obtained high correlation coefficients in both correlations, in concordance with results obtained by Garea and Kittler[11] but when applied the proposed approach the correlation coefficients reached nearer values to one.

The time consuming comparison (Table 6) shows that the proposed normalization method is faster than others traditionally used in computer vision even when it is applied to whole image. Taking in to account that the application of the proposed method will be only in those regions affected by illumination the time processing will decrease significantly.

Table 6. Comparison of averages of time consuming in the normalization process in milliseconds

Proposed method	Homomorphic	Multiescale	Anisotropic	Isotropic
0.1	3.4	3.5	10.0	0.8

6 Conclusions

The use of the methods for fast localization of regions with specific features allows the automatic detection of regions affected by illumination specular effects with relatively high accuracy and speed.

The proposed method for photometric normalization offers a set of advantages, the process is carried out only on images affected by illumination and more specifically in those affected regions, and as a result we obtain a good save of time with a low computational cost. The use of a Lookup Table is another factor that influences in the high speed of the proposed method. The total save of computational cost might be measure not only in the quantity of pixels that it avoids to process and also in the fact of having avoided the use of operations with high computational cost like the logarithms and the transformations to the frequency domain.

The proposed experimental scheme for evaluation of the detection effectiveness and the proposed measures allowed proving the high performance of the process.

The proposed method for fast localization and normalization might be used as a previous step in the general face recognition process and also as an independent process for the improvement of the visual effect of face images.

References

1. A. S. Tolba, A.H. El-Baz, and A.A. El-Harby. Face Recognition: A Literature Review. International Journal of Signal Processing Volume 2, N.2-2005.
2. R. Chellappa, C.L. Wilson and C. Sirohey, "Human and machine recognition of faces: A survey," *Proc. IEEE*, vol. 83, no. 5, pp. 705- 740, may 1995.
3. Belhumeur, P., D. Kriegman,: What is the set of images of an object under all possible lighting conditions. Int. J. of Computer Vision 28, 245-260(1998)
4. Georghiades, A., Kriegman, D., Belhumeur, P.: From few to many: Generative models for recognition under variable pose and illumination. IEEE PAMI (2001)
5. Riklin-Raviv, T.,., Shashua, A.: The Quotient image: class-based re-rendering and recognition with varying illumination conditions. In: IEEE PAMI. (2001)
6. Lee, K., Ho, J., Kriegman, D.: 9 Points of Light: Aquiring Subspaces for Face Recognition Under Variable Lighting IEEE Proc. Conf. Computer Vision and Pattern Recognition, (2001).
7. Viola P. and Jones M. Rapid Object Detection Using a Boosted Cascade of Simple Features. Mitsubishi Electric Research Laboratories, Inc., 2004.
8. Lienhart Rainer. Haarcascade_frontalface_default.xml. Intel License Agreement For Open Source Computer Vision Library. 2000.
9. Xiong G, A local normalization algorithm that uniformizes the local mean and variance of an image, URL:http://www.mathworks.com/matlabcentral/fileexchange/loadFile.do? objectId= 8303.
10. Biomedical Imaging Group. Local normalization algorithm, http://bigwww.epfl.ch/demo/ j
11. Garea E., Kittler J.,Messer K., Mendez H., An Illumination Insensitive Representation for Face Verification in the Frequency Domain. Proc.of ICPR 2006, IEEE, in press.
12. The Yale Face Database, URL: http://cvc.yale.edu/projects/yalefaces/yalefaces.html.
13. Gonzales R., Woods, R. and Eddins S., Digital Image Processing using Matlab.pp 404-405 Ed Pearson, 2004.

Gender Classification Using Principal Geodesic Analysis and Gaussian Mixture Models

Jing Wu, William A.P. Smith, and Edwin R. Hancock

Department of Computer Science, The University of York, York, YO10 5DD, UK
{jwu, wsmith, erh}@cs.york.ac.uk

Abstract. The aim in this paper is to show how to discriminate gender using a parameterized representation of fields of facial surface normals (needle-maps) which can be extracted from 2D intensity images using shape-from-shading (SFS). We makes use of principle geodesic analysis (PGA) to parameterize the facial needle-maps. Using feature selection, we determine which of the components of the resulting parameter vector are the most significant in distinguishing gender. Using the EM algorithm we distinguish gender by fitting a two component mixture model to the vectors of selected features. Results on real-world data reveal that the method gives gender discrimination results that are comparable to human observers.

1 Introduction

Humans are remarkably accurate determining the gender of a subject based on the appearance of the face alone. In fact, an accuracy as good as 96% can be achieved with the hair concealed, facial hair removed and no makeup [1]. Experiments by Bruce etc. showed that the gender of the face is conveyed by several cues including: (i) superficial and/or local features, (ii) configural relationships between features, and (iii) the 3-D structure of the face [2]. In [1], Burton etc. attempt to discover a gender discriminator by explicit measurements on the feature points of frontal facial views and profile views. However, their method requires manually labeled 14 landmark points. As a result it is unsuitable for automatic gender classification.

In this paper, we present a statistical framework for gender discrimination that does not require explicit landmark measurements. The method makes use of a representation of facial shape based on a parameterisation of fields of facial surface normals or needle-maps. The needle-map is a 2.5-D shape representation which is mid-way between the 2D intensity image and the 3D surface height function [3]. The representation can be acquired from 2D intensity images using shape-from-shading [4] and is invariant to illumination. To parameterise the facial needle-maps we make use of principle geodesic analysis (PGA) [5], [6]. PGA is a generalization of principle components analysis (PCA) [7]. For data residing on a Riemannian manifold, PGA is better suited to the analysis of directional data than PCA. Our aim is to determine gender using vectors of

J.F. Martínez-Trinidad et al. (Eds.): CIARP 2006, LNCS 4225, pp. 58–67, 2006.

PGA parameters. We aim to distinguish the genders of a sample of subjects by fitting a two-component mixture model to the distribution of vectors of selected features.

The standard method to learn the mixture models is the expectation - maximization (EM) algorithm [8], [9], [10], [11]. However, applying the EM algorithm directly to high dimensional facial needle-maps yields two problems. The first is the analysis of the distribution of needle-maps cannot be effected in a linear way, because a linear combination of unit vectors (normals) is not itself a unit vector. The second problem is that the covariance over the full dimensions of the data is too large to be computationally tractable.

The first of these problems is overcomed if we use PGA parameters (feature vectors) to represent the facial needle-maps since the parameter vectors reside in a vector space. To overcome the problem of dimensionality, we select the most significant feature components for discriminating gender that give the best class separability. Experimental results show that the mixture model learnt by our method has a correct gender classification rate of 87%.

The outline of the paper is as follows. Section 2 reviews the log and exponential maps used in principal geodesic analysis. Section 3 explores how the most significant gender features can be selected. In Section 4, a detailed description of the learning phase and the classification method is given. Experiments are presented in Section 5. Finally, Section 6 concludes the paper and offers directions for future investigation.

2 Principle Geodesic Analysis

The surface normal $n \in R^3$ may be considered as a point lying on a spherical manifold $n \in S^2$, therefore, we turn to the intrinsic mean and PGA proposed by Fletcher et al. [5] to analyze the variations of the surface normals.

2.1 The Log and Exponential Maps

If $u \in T_n S^2$ is a vector on the tangent plane to S^2 at n and $u \neq 0$, the exponential map, denoted Exp_n, of u is the point, denoted $Exp_n(u)$, on S^2 along the geodesic in the direction of u at distance $\| u \|$ from n. This is illustrated in Fig. 1. The log map, denoted Log_n is the inverse of the exponential map. The exponential and log maps reserve the geodesic distance between two points, i.e. $d(n_1, n_2) = d(u_1, u_2)$, where $u_1 = Log_n n_1, u_2 = Log_n n_2$.

2.2 Spherical Medians

It is more natural to treat the surface normal as points on a unit sphere: $n_1, \ldots n_N \in S^2$ rather than points in Euclidian space. Instead of the Euclidian mean, we compute the intrinsic mean: $\mu = \arg\min_{n \in S^2} \sum_{i=1}^{N} d(n, n_i)$, where $d(n, n_i) = \arccos(n \cdot n_i)$ is the arc length. For a spherical manifold,

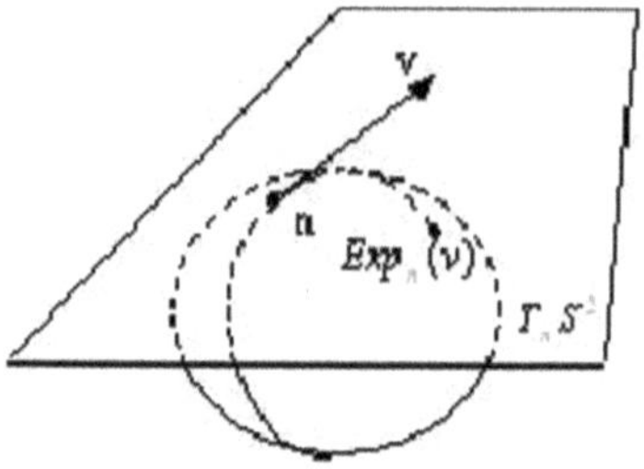

Fig. 1. The exponential map

the intrinsic mean can be found using the gradient descent method of Pennec [6]. Accordingly, the current estimate $\mu^{(t)}$ is updated as follows: $\mu^{(t+1)} = \mathrm{Exp}_{\mu^{(t)}}(\frac{1}{N}\sum_{i=1}^{N}\mathrm{Log}_{\mu^{(t)}}(n_i))$.

2.3 PGA of Needle Maps

PGA is analogous to PCA except that each principal axis in PCA is a straight line, while in PGA each principle axis is a geodesic curve. In the spherical case this corresponds to a great circle. Consider a great circle G on the sphere S^2. To project a point $n_1 \in S^2$ onto a point on G, we use the projection operator $\pi_G : S^2 \longrightarrow G$ given by $\pi_G(n_1) = \mathrm{argmin}_{n \in G}(n_1, n)^2$. For a geodesic G passing through the intrinsic mean μ, π_G may be approximated linearly in the tangent plane $T_\mu S^2$: $\mathrm{Log}_\mu(\pi_G(n_1)) \approx \sum_{i=1}^{K} V^i \cdot \mathrm{Log}_\mu(n_1)$, where $V_1, \ldots V_K$ is an orthonormal basis for $T_\mu S^2$.

Suppose there are K training needle-maps each having N pixel locations, and the surface normal at the pixel location p for the kth training needle-map is n_p^k. We calculate the intrinsic mean μ_p of the distribution of surface normals $n_p^1, \ldots n_p^K$ at each pixel location p. n_p^k is then represented by its log map position $u_p^k = \mathrm{Log}_{\mu_p}(n_p^k)$. $u^k = [u_1^k, \ldots, u_N^k]^T$ is the log mapped long vector of the kth training needle-map. The K long vectors form the data matrix $U = [u^1|\ldots|u^K]$. The covariance matrix of the data matrix is $L = \frac{1}{K}UU^T$.

We use the numerically efficient snap-shot method of Sirovich [12] to compute the eigenvectors of L. Accordingly, we construct the matrix $\hat{L} = \frac{1}{K}U^T U$, and find the eigenvalues and eigenvectors. The ith eigenvector e_i of L can be computed from the ith eigenvector $\hat{e}_i$of $\hat{L}$ using $e_i = U\hat{e}_i$. The ith eigenvalue λ_i of L equals the ith eigenvalue $\hat{\lambda}_i$ of $\hat{L}$ when $i \leq K$. When $i > K$, $\lambda_i = 0$. Providing the effects of noise are small, we only need to retain S eigenmodes to retain p percent of the model variance. S is the smallest integer satisfying:$\sum_{i=1}^{S}\lambda_i \geq \frac{p}{100}\sum_{i=1}^{K}\lambda_i$. In our experiments, we use the 10 leading eigenvectors of L as the columns of the eigenvector matrix (projection matrix) $\Phi = (e_1|e_2|\ldots|e_{10})$.

Given a long vector $u = [u_1, \ldots, u_N]^T$, we can get the corresponding vector of parameters (feature vector) $b = \Phi^T u$. Given a feature vector $b = [b_1, \ldots b_S]^T$, we can generate a needle-map using: $n_p = \mathrm{Exp}_{\mu_p}((Pb)_p)$.

3 Feature Selection

After PGA, we select the most significant S components of the PGA parameter vector (in our experiments, S=10). However, the S dimensional feature vectors still inevitably contain information which is either redundant or irrelevant to the gender classification task. As stated in [13], the classification of patterns as performed by humans is based on a very few of the most important attributes. Therefore, we select the most significant features for gender discrimination.

We examine the distribution for the first 9 components of the PGA parameter vectors for the 200 data samples in our experiments. Here the first 100 are females, and the last 100 are males (see Fig. 2). Table 1 shows the mean values of the first 9 feature components for females and males. By inspection, the 1st, 5th and 6th components have the most significant difference between females and males.

Figure 3 shows the mean face and its variations along the directions of the 1st, 5th and 6th principal geodesic directions. We can see the 3 feature components do convey some gender information. Turning our attention to the 1st component, as λ_1 increases, the face becomes larger and more solid, and, the cheeks thinner. These are all masculine characteristics. In the case of the 5th component, as λ_5 decreases, the face becomes wider and the eyes deepen. Again these are masculine characteristics. In the case of the 6th component, as λ_6 increases, there is a more masculine appearance. Fig. 2 and Fig. 3 therefore indicate the 1st, 5th, 6th features are intuitively the most significant ones for gender discrimination.

To verify our empirical selection, we explore the different feature selection criteria described by Devijver and Kittler [13]. We use the class separability criterion $J(\xi) = \frac{|S_w+S_b|}{|S_w|} = \prod_{k=1}^{d}(1+\lambda_k)$, where S_w and S_b are the between and within class scatter matrices, λ_k, $k = 1 \ldots d$ are the eigenvalues of matrix $S_w^{-1}S_b$. The values of J for the first 9 features are shown in Table 2, from which we can see B(1), B(5), B(6) have the 3 largest values. The result is consistent with our empirical selection. Therefore, the 1st, 5th, and 6th features are the most significant features for gender discrimination. We use them as the selected feature vectors in gender classification using EM algorithm.

Table 1. Mean values of the first 9 feature components

	B(1)	B(2)	B(3)	B(4)	B(5)	B(6)	B(7)	B(8)	B(9)
Female	-8.6776	-3.2660	-0.4854	0.7371	3.0581	-2.4635	0.1951	0.2868	0.8078
Male	8.6776	3.2660	0.4854	-0.7371	-3.0581	2.4635	-0.1951	-0.2868	-0.8078

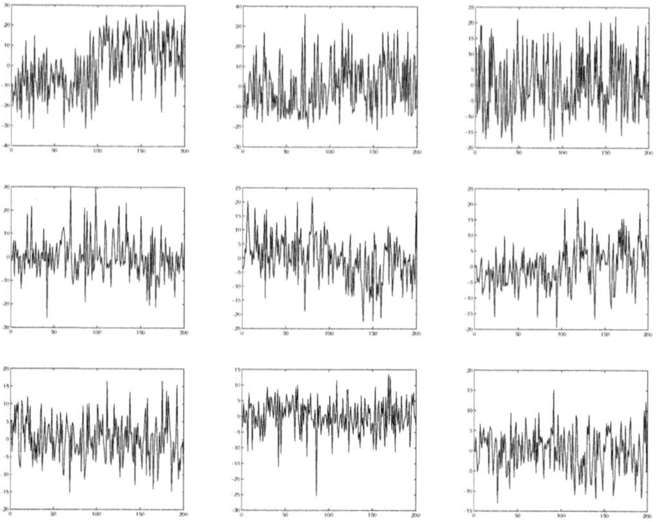

Fig. 2. Plots of the first 9 feature components. From left to right, the first line is B(1), B(2), B(3), the second line is B(4), B(5), B(6), the third line is B(7), B(8), B(9). X axis ranging from 1 to 200 stand for the 200 faces, the first 100 are females, the second 100 are males. Y axis ranging from -25 to 25 is the value of the feature components.

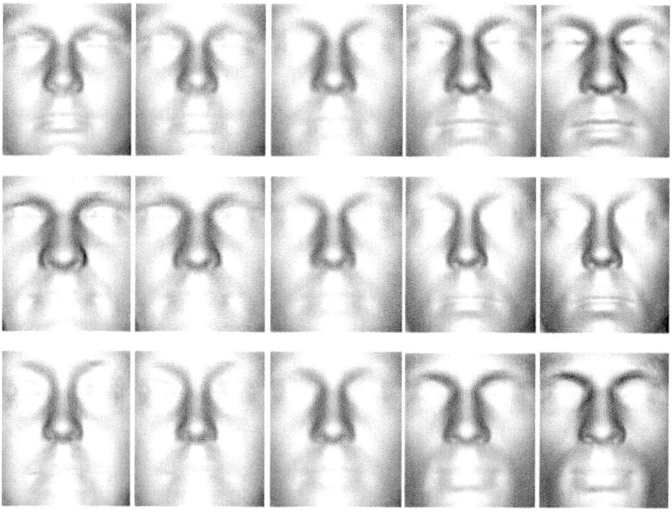

Fig. 3. The mean face and its variances along the 1st, 5th and 6th feature components. The lines are according to the features (from top to bottom): 1st, 5th, 6th features. The columns are according to the variances (from left to right): λ=-30, λ=-20, λ=0 (the mean face), λ=20, and λ=30.

Table 2. J values on the first 9 feature components

	B(1)	B(2)	B(3)	B(4)	B(5)	B(6)	B(7)	B(8)	B(9)
J	1.6231	1.0681	1.0024	1.0073	1.1644	1.1532	1.0010	1.0026	1.0243

4 Learning Gaussian Mixture Models

We use the EM algorithm to fit a two component mixture model to vectors of selected features, and explore whether the a posteriori class probabilities can be used to classify the gender of subjects.

4.1 EM Initialization

In our EM algorithm the a posteriori probability is estimated from the selected feature vectors using the method outlined in [10]. For 2-component Gaussian mixture models, we set $\alpha_1^{(0)} = \alpha_2^{(0)} = \frac{1}{2}$, $\mu_{b1}^{(0)} = \mu_b + \varepsilon_1$, $\mu_{b2}^{(0)} = \mu_b + \varepsilon_2$, and $\Sigma_{b1}^{(0)} = \Sigma_{b2}^{(0)} = det(\Sigma_b)^{1/d} I_d$. Here α_1, α_2 is the a priori probability of each class, μ_b is the overall mean of the selected feature vectors, Σ_b is the overall covariance matrix of the selected feature vectors, ε_1 and ε_2 are two small random vectors.

In our experiments $d = 3$. We can set the class means are $\mu_{b1}^{(0)} = [-\varepsilon_1(1), +\varepsilon_1(2), -\varepsilon_1(3)]$, $\mu_{b2}^{(0)} = [+\varepsilon_2(1), -\varepsilon_2(2), +\varepsilon_1(3)]$. The signs before the ε elements are indicated from Fig. 3. We can see, in our experiments, when the 1st and 6th feature components are negative, the 5th component is positive, the face is more female. Otherwise, the face is more male. Using this information makes the EM initialization more reliable.

4.2 E – Step

In E – Step the a posteriori class membership probability is updated by applying the Bayes law to the class-conditional density. In our application, the class-conditional density is Gaussian:
$p(B_j|\mu_{bc}^{(t)}, \Sigma_{bc}^{(t)}) = \frac{1}{\sqrt{(2\pi)^d |\Sigma_{bc}^{(t)}|}} \exp[-\frac{1}{2}(B_j - \mu_{bc}^{(t)})^T \times (\Sigma_{bc}^{(t)})^{-1} \times (B_j - \mu_{bc}^{(t)})]$. Here, B_j donates the selected feature vector of the jth sample data.

At iteration t+1, the a posteriori probability is updated as follows:

$$W_c^{(j,t)} \equiv P(j \in c|B_j, \mu_{bc}^{(t)}, \Sigma_{bc}^{(t)}) = \frac{\alpha_c^{(t)} p(B_j|\mu_{bc}^{(t)}, \Sigma_{bc}^{(t)})}{\sum_{i=1}^{2} \alpha_i^{(t)} p(B_j|\mu_{bi}^{(t)}, \Sigma_{bi}^{(t)})}. \tag{1}$$

Here, $W_c^{(j,t)}$ means estimate, at iteration t, of the probability that B_j was produced by class c.

4.3 M – Step

In M – Step the parameters for each class are updated to maximize the expected log-likelihood function:
$Q(C^{(t+1)}|C^{(t)}) = \sum_{j=1}^{n} \sum_{c=1}^{2} W_c^{(j,t)} \times \log(\alpha_c^{(t+1)} p(B_j|\mu_{bc}^{(t+1)}, \Sigma_{bc}^{(t+1)}))$.

At iteration t+1, the revised estimate of the a priori probability of class c is $\alpha_c^{(t+1)} = \frac{1}{n}\sum_{j=1}^{n} W_c^{(j,t)}$, the revised estimate of the mean vector is $\mu_{bc}^{(t+1)} = \frac{\sum_{j=1}^{n} W_c^{(j,t)} B_j}{\sum_{j=1}^{n} W_c^{(j,t)}}$, and the revised estimate of the covariance matrix is $\Sigma_{bc}^{(t+1)} = \frac{\sum_{j=1}^{n} W_c^{(j,t)}(B_j-\mu_{bc}^{(t+1)})(B_j-\mu_{bc}^{(t+1)})^T}{\sum_{j=1}^{n} W_c^{(j,t)}}$.

4.4 Classification

After the mixture model of genders has been learnt, we use the a posteriori class probability to classify faces to one of the genders. Given the needle-map n of a test face, first get its selected feature vector b through PGA and feature selection method mentioned in previous sections. Then compute the a posteriori probabilities W_f and W_m through formula (1), using the acquired mean vectors μ_{bf}, μ_{bm} and the covariance matrixes Σ_{bf}, Σ_{bm}. If $W_f > W_m$, then the face is classified as female. Otherwise, the face is classified as male.

5 Experiments

In this section, we evaluate the performance of the method for discriminating gender on the basis of the learnt two-component mixture model for the distribution of shape-features. The data consists of 200 facial needle-maps with known ground truth from the Max Plank dataset. There are 100 females and 100 males.

We first apply PGA and feature selection to the data to extract the shape parameter vectors and perform feature selection. The visualization of the data is shown in the left-hand panel of Fig. 5. Here we show the distribution of the 1st and 5th features as a scatter plot. The data is relatively well clustered according to gender. There is some overlap and this is due to feminine looking males and masculine looking females.

Experiment 1. We use the 200 data for unsupervised learning. Figure 4 shows the initial and final classifications of the data. After convergence of the EM algorithm, the data are reasonably well clustered according to gender. The correct classification rate reaches 89% for females, and 85% for males. Figure 5 visualizes the classification results. From the figure, around 13% of the errors are due to the misclassification of the data in the overlap region. Tests involving human observers give similar error rates.

Experiment 2. We select the 10 needle-maps with the largest and 10 with the smallest female probability W_f from the 100 female faces. The top 10 faces are considered to be typical females, while the bottom 10 are considered to be female faces falling into the overlap region. We repeat this procedure for the male faces. We render the 40 facial needle-maps with facial textures, and present them to 9 subjects (6 males and 3 females). The average classification error rate of the 9 people is shown in Table 3. From the table, the classification performance on

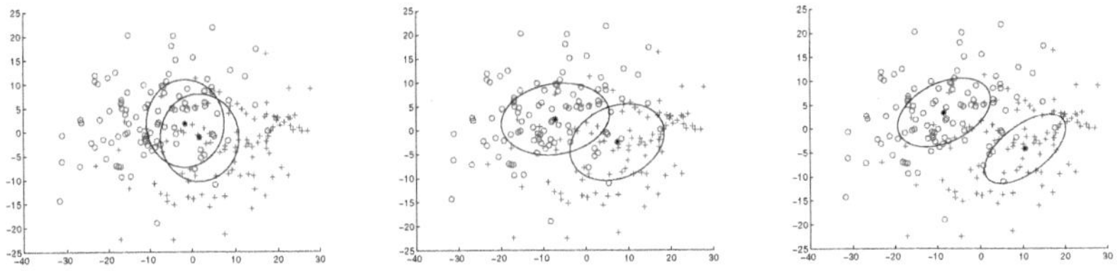

Fig. 4. Learning steps visualized on 1st and 5th features. From left to right, are the results of EM initialization, after 5 iterations and on convergence.

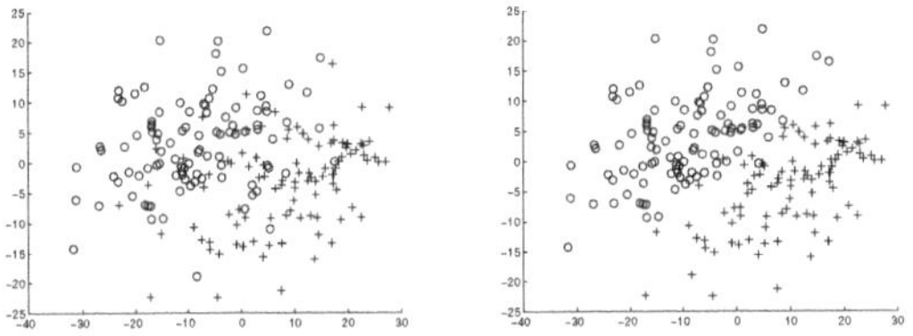

Fig. 5. Classification result on the training data visualized on 1st and 5th features. Left is the original training data, right is the classification result.

the faces in the overlap region is poorer than that of the typical female and male faces. This confirms that the results obtained in experiment 1 are consistent with the performance of human subjects. Interestingly, the classification of the female faces is poorer than that of the males. This may be due to the fact that without hair or makeup the facial appearance is masculine.

Table 3. Error rate of human classification

Total	Overlap	Unoverlap	Females	Males
22.5%	25.6%	19.4%	43.9%	1.1%

Experiment 3. We randomly selected 40 needle-maps from the 200 available for use as test data. The remaining 160 are used as training data. First, we obtain the selected feature vectors of the training and test data using the intrinsic mean and projection matrix using the full sample of 200 data. Then we fit the mixture model to the training data. We visualize the models in the left-hand panel of Fig. 6. The classification rate is evaluated by fitting the mixture models to the test data. The result is shown in the right-hand panel of Fig. 6 and compared with the original test data shown in the middle of Fig. 6. The classification rate for females is 80% and on males 95%. This is a good result and that our method has good generalisation.

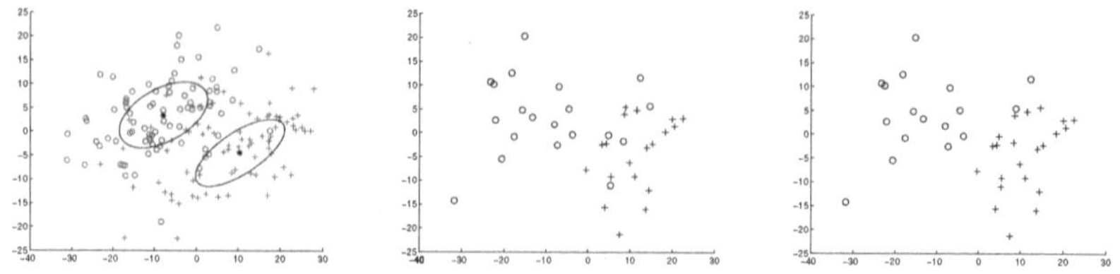

Fig. 6. Training and Testing result visualized on 1st and 5th features. The left is the learnt models on the training data. In the middle is the original testing data. The right is the classification on the testing data.

6 Conclusion

In this paper, we apply feature selection and EM algorithm to PGA shape parameters of the facial needle-maps to perform gender classification. We explore the most significant components of the parameter vectors for gender discrimination, and use the EM algorithm to cluster the selected features. Experimental results show that using the selected feature vectors, facial needle-maps can be well clustered according to gender. Moreover, it demonstrates that it is feasible to construct a 2-component Gaussian mixture models from the facial needle-maps to classify the gender.

However, there are still some problems that require further investigation. First, feature selection is quite empirical and the simplest theoretical verification measure has been used. Our future research will focus on the use of more principled methods for feature selection. Second, in the EM initialization step, we need to analyze the mean face and its variances along each feature component to determine the signs of the initial mean vectors. Thus, although the training data need not to be labeled, the learning phase is not totally unsupervised. Third, our current experiments are based on the ground truth needle-maps extracted from range images. In the future, we will apply our method to needle-maps recovered from facial images using SFS.

References

1. A Mike Burton, Vicki Bruce, Neal Dench: What's the difference between men and women? Evidence from facial measurement. Perception, vol.22, pp.153-176, 1993
2. Vicki Bruce, A Mike Burton, Elias Hanna, Pat Healey and Oli Mason, Anne Coombes, Rick Fright, Alf Linney: Sex discrimination: how do we tell the difference between male and female faces?. Perception, vol.22, pp.131-152, 1993
3. D.Marr: Vision. San Francisco: W.H. Freeman, 1982
4. William Smith , Edwin R. Hancock: Recovering Facial Shape and Albedo using a Statistical Model of Surface Normal Direction. Tenth IEEE International Conference on Computer Vision, vol.1, pp.588-595, 2005
5. P.T. Fletcher,S. Joshi,C. Lu,S.M. Pizer: Principal geodesic analysis for the study of nonlinear statistics of shape. IEEE Transactions on Medical Imaging, vol.23, pp.995-1005, 2004

6. X. Pennec: Probabilities and statistics on riemannian manifolds: A geometric approach. Technical Report RR-5093, INRIA, 2004
7. I.T. Jolliffe: Principle Component Analysis. Springer-Verlag, New York, 1986
8. M.A.T. Figueiredo,A.K. Jain: Unsupervised Learning of Finite Mixture Models. IEEE Transactions on Pattern Analysis and Machine Intelligence, vol.24,No.3,March 2002
9. M.A.T. Figueiredo,J.M.N. Leitao,A.K. Jain: On Fitting Mixture Models. Engergy Minimization Methods in Computer Vision and Pattern Recognition,E. Hancok and M. Pellilo, Eds: Springer-Verlag, pp. 54-69, 1999
10. Naonori Ueda,Ryohei Nakano,Zoubin Ghabramani,Geoffrey E.Hinton: SMEM Algorithm for Mixture Models. Neural Computation, vol.12(9), pp.2109-2128, 2000
11. Christophe Biernacki,Gilles Celeux,Gerard Govaert: Choosing starting values for the EM algorithm for getting the highest likelihood in multivariate Gaussian mixture models. Computational Statistics & Data Analysis, vol.41, Issue 3-4, pp. 561-575, 2003
12. L. Sirovich: Turbulence and the dynamics of coherent structures. Quart. Applied Mathematics, vol.XLV, no. 3,pp.561-590, 1987
13. P. Devijver,J. Kittler: Pattern Recognition: A Statistical Approach. PrenticeHall, 1982

Gender Classification of Faces Using Adaboost*

Rodrigo Verschae[1,2,3], Javier Ruiz-del-Solar[1,2], and Mauricio Correa[1,2]

[1] Department of Electrical Engineering, Universidad de Chile
[2] Center for Web Research, Department of Computer Science, Universidad de Chile
[3] CMLA, ENS Cachan, France

Abstract. In this work it is described a framework for classifying face images using Adaboost and domain-partitioning based classifiers. The most interesting aspect of this framework is the capability of building classification systems with high accuracy in dynamical environments, which achieve, at the same time, high processing and training speed. We apply this framework to the specific problem of gender classification. We built several gender classification systems under the proposed framework using different features (LBP, wavelets, rectangular, etc.). These systems are analyzed and evaluated using standard face databases (FERET and BioID), and a new gender classification database of real-world images.

1 Introduction

The computational analysis of face images plays an important role in many computer vision applications. Among them we can mention visual human-computer interaction, biometry, video conferencing, human-robot interaction, surveillance, video summarizing, image/video indexing and retrieval, and drivers monitoring. So far, face detection systems that perform with high accuracy in real world applications have been developed [13][9][3][11]. However, face classification systems (gender classification, race classification, age classification, etc.) do not achieve similar performance, specifically when analyzing low-resolution faces obtained under uncontrolled conditions (uncontrolled illumination, non-uniform background, etc.).

We aim at reverting this situation by describing a framework for building robust face classification systems using Adaboost [7] and domain-partitioning [8] based classifiers. Within this framework we make use of diverse feature types: (i) rectangular features (similar to Haar wavelets) [12], (ii) LBP-based features [2], (iii) wavelet features [9], and (iv) LBP-based features applied over a wavelet decomposition. Some of these features have not been used before in face classification problems.

We apply this learning framework to the specific problem of gender classification. Gender classification is a relevant problem within many applications: (1) human-robot interaction and visual human-computer interaction: it allows building systems that behaves differently depending on the user's gender, (2) video summarizing, and image/video indexing and retrieval: it allows the use of gender information in the

* This research was funded by Millenium Nucleus Center for Web Research, Grant P04-067-F, Chile.

J.F. Martínez-Trinidad (Eds.): CIARP 2006, LNCS 4225, pp. 68 – 78, 2006.

retrieving/indexing process, and (3) face recognition biometric systems: it allows improving the system performance by having specific models for each gender.

We built several robust gender classification systems using this learning framework and diverse features. Their main strengths are the ability of processing low-resolution faces (up to 24x24 pixels), and being illumination invariant (no preprocessing is needed for photometric normalization). These systems are analyzed and evaluated using standard face databases (FERET, BioID), and a new database of real-world images created with this purpose (UCHGender DB).

The article is structured as follows. In section 2 some related work is outlined. The learning framework is presented in section 3. In section 4 the employed features are described. In section 5 a comparative analysis of different gender classification systems is presented. Finally, in section 6, some conclusions of this work are given.

2 Related Work

Several methods have been proposed for solving the gender classification problem, among them systems based on neural networks (RBF, back propagation, etc.), PCA projections, decision trees, SVM classifiers, and Adaboost classifiers can be mentioned. Best reported results have been obtained using SVM and Adaboost. We will analyze some of these relevant works. In [5] it is proposed a gender classification system based on the use of SVM classifier. The employed features are the pixel elements themselves. The obtained results are very good, 3.38% overall error rate when using a RBF kernel, but the test set consists of only 259 faces. In [1] is proposed a gender classification system based on a SVM classifier and features obtained using PCA (Principal Component Analysis), CCA (Curvilinear Component Analysis) and SOM (Self Organizing Maps). Best results are obtained using 759 PCA components, 7.75% overall error rate, but the size of the faces is restricted to 128x128 pixels and the test set is composed by only 80 faces.

One of the drawbacks of the SVM based system is the fact that they are not real-time. Therefore systems based in Adaboost have been proposed in the last years. In [10] is presented a gender classification system that uses a threshold-weak-classifier based Adaboost algorithm and rectangular features. The system achieves a performance of 79% correct rate in a set of face images obtained from Internet that were manually annotated prior to classification (500 features were employed in this case). This system was favorably compared against the one proposed in [5] using the same dataset; it is 1,000 times faster and it has a higher classification rate (79% against 75.5%). In [14] is described a LUT-based Adaboost system for gender classification that uses rectangular features. Prior to classification faces are aligned. This is done using a face alignment method called SDAM that is a kind AAM (Active Appearance Model). After alignment, grey-level normalization (histogram equalization) is performed. The system achieves a classification rate of 88% in images downloaded form Internet (using 36x36 face windows), and using this database it is favorably compared against a SVM-based system and a threshold-Adaboost system.

Our Adaboost-based gender classification system employs the domain-partitioning approach, and the main improvements over previous works are: (1) the use of more suitable features for addressing this problem (mLBP features behave better than rectangular features; see section 5), (2) the usage of smaller face windows (24x24) which allows analyzing smaller faces, and (3) a faster processing, because, besides the eye alignment, we do not perform any geometric or photometric normalization.

3 A Learning Framework for Building Robust Face Classification Systems

The key concepts used in the considered framework are boosting and domain partitioning classifiers. Adaboost [7] (a Boosting algorithm) is employed for finding highly accurate hypotheses (classification rules) by combining several weak hypotheses (classifiers). We use domain partitioning weak hypotheses [8], each one having a moderate accuracy, and giving self-rated confidence values that estimate the reliability of each prediction. These weak classifiers are linearly combined, obtaining a classifier of the form shown in (1). Each function $h_t(x)$ is a weak classifier, T is the number of weak classifiers, and b is a threshold value that defines the operation point of the classifier. The class assigned to the input corresponds to the sign of $H(x)$.

$$H(x) = \sum_{t=1}^{T} \alpha_t h_t(x) - b \tag{1}$$

The weak classifiers are applied over features computed in every pattern to be processed. Each weak classifier has associated a single feature. Following [8], domain-partitioning weak hypotheses make their predictions based on a partitioning of the domain X into disjoint blocks $X_1,\ldots,X_n$, which cover all X, and for which $h(x)=h(x')$ for all $x, x' \in X_j$. Thus, the weak classifiers prediction depends only on which block X_j a given sample instance falls into. In our case the weak classifiers are applied over features, therefore each feature domain F is partitioned into disjoint blocks $F_1,\ldots,F_n$, and a weak classifier h will have an output for each partition block of its associated feature f:

$$h(f(x)) = c_j \ni f(x) \in F_j \tag{2}$$

For each classifier, the value associated to each partition block (c_j), i.e. its output, is calculated for minimizing a bound of the training error. This value depends on the number of times that the corresponding feature, computed on the training samples (x_i), fall into this partition block (histograms), and on the class of these samples (y_i) and their weight $D(i)$. For minimizing the training error, c_j is set to [8]:

$$c_j = \frac{1}{2}\ln\left(\frac{W_{+1}^{j}+\varepsilon}{W_{-1}^{j}+\varepsilon}\right), \qquad W_l^{j} = \sum_{i:f(x_i)\in F_j \wedge y_i = l} D(i), \text{ where } l = \pm 1 \tag{3}$$

were ε is a regularization parameter. The outputs, c_j, of each the weak classifier, obtained during training, are stored in a LUT for speeding up its evaluation. The pseudo code of the whole algorithm is shown in figure 1.

Given $(x_1, y_1),\ldots,(x_m, y_m)$ were $x_i \in X, y_i \in Y = \{-1,+1\}$

$D_1(i) \leftarrow 1/m, i = 1,\ldots,m$

for t = 1 : T **do**

normalize $D_t()$ to a p.d.f

for each feature $f_p \in F, h_p \in H,\ p = 1,\ldots,P$ **do**

$$h_p(j) = \frac{1}{2}\ln\left(\frac{W_{+1}^j + \varepsilon}{W_{-1}^j + \varepsilon}\right), j = 1,\ldots,J$$

$$Z_p = 2\sum_j \sqrt{W_{+1}^j W_{-1}^j}$$

select h_t for which Z is minimized: $h_t = \arg\min_{h_p \in H} Z_p$

$D_{t+1}(i) \leftarrow D_t(i)\exp(-y_i h_t(x_i)), i = 1,\ldots,m$

$$H(x) = \sum_{t=1}^{T} h_t(x)$$

Fig. 1. Domain-Partitioning Adaboost training algorithm

4 Features

We analyze the use of different kinds of features applied to the problem of face classification: rectangular, mLBP, wavelet, and wavelet+mLBP features. In all cases the feature space is partitioned so it can be used directly with the domain-partitioning Adaboost classifier described in section 3. In all cases LUTs (Look-Up Tables) are used for a fast evaluation of the weak classifiers.

4.1 Rectangular Features

Rectangular features resemble Haar wavelets and can be evaluated very quickly, independently of their size and position, using the integral image [12]. They correspond to the difference between sums of pixels values in rectangular image regions. The output value defines a domain that is partitioned using intervals (or bins) of equal size [13].

4.2 Modified LBP

The LBP (Local Binary Pattern), also known as texture number or census transform, corresponds to an illumination invariant descriptor of the local structure in a given image neighborhood. We use their modified version [2] (mLPB = modified LBP), which overcomes some problems of the original LBP. The mLBP is computed as follows: for a given window of 3x3 pixels, the average of the pixels in the window is calculated. Then, each of the pixel values is compared against the obtained average. From these comparisons, 9 bits are generated, with 0 indicating that a pixel is smaller than the average, and 1 otherwise. After that, the concatenated 9 bits corresponds to the mLBP feature. As it can be noticed, for the mLBP feature the domain partition is already defined, there are 512 bins (actually 511 [2]).

4.3 Wavelet Coefficients

The wavelet transformation allows analyzing images in the spatial-frequency domain. In the context of face detection, wavelets coefficients have been successfully employed as local features. As in [9], the features correspond to groups of 8 neighbor coefficients (in space, orientation or scale) that are used as a partition of the feature space. Each of the coefficients is quantized in 3 levels and then grouped together, defining a partition of 6,561 bins. Given that we use small training sets (see section 5), such a large number of bins may lead to overfitting. Therefore, we partition the wavelet coefficients directly in a small number of bins (16, 32 and 64).

4.4 Modified LBP of the Wavelet Coefficients

The mLBP is applied over the wavelet transform for avoiding the quantization of the wavelet coefficients, and for summarizing information from groups of coefficients. In this way we can reduce the number of partitions to 511 bins.

5 Evaluation

5.1 Evaluated Gender Classification Systems

We use three baseline systems for comparing the performance of our Adaboost based gender classification systems:

- SVM: SVM classifier and face pixels as features. Parameters: RBF kernel, σ=1,125, C=25, 3,082 support vectors.
- SVM+PCA: SVM classifier and PCA projection of the face pixels as features. Parameters: RBF kernel, σ=4,950, C=50, 1,981 support vectors, and 300 PCA components.
- PCA: Face gender is determined using the minimal reconstruction error after projection of the face pixels in a PCA model of men faces and a PCA model of women faces. Parameters: 100 PCA components in each model.

We build different gender classification systems using the described learning framework (domain partitioning Adaboost) and different features:

- Adaboost-Rect: Adaboost & 1,000 rectangular features, 16 bins.
- Adaboost-mLBP: Adaboost & 1,000 mLBP features.
- Adaboost-Wav: Adaboost & 426 wavelet-based features (2-level W), 64 bins.
- Adaboost-Wav-mLBP: Adaboost & 958 wavelet+mLBP features (3 levels WT).

For all systems the selection of the best parameters was done using a validation database (see next section).

5.2 Databases

For the classifiers' training (Adaboost, PCA and SVM based) we built a training database of 4,245 face images, containing images from the CAS-PEAL dataset [4] and UCHGenderTrainDB (our own dataset). We use 2,009 images from CAS-PEAL (1,222 men and 787 women), and 2,165 images from UCHGenderTrainDB (1,150 men and 1,115 women). We use a validation database of 2,745 face images, containing images from CAS-PEAL and UCHGenderValDB (our own dataset). The validation CAS-PEAL dataset contains 1,312 images (768 men and 544 are women), while UCHGenderValDB contains 1,433 images (744 men and 689 women). The validation database is used for model selection during training. In the case of domain-partitioning Adaboost, it is used for selecting the number of weak classifiers and the number of bins in the LUTs. In the case of SVM, it is used for selecting the parameters of the kernel, while in the case of PCA, for selecting the number of components. In both databases, training and validation, for each face a second one was generated, which corresponds to a random variation in the position of cropping. It is important to note that CAS-PEAL includes only Asians, while UCHGenderTrainDB considers other races. With this combination we intend to make our gender classifier race independent to a large degree.

For evaluating the proposed system we use 3 databases: (1) the UCHGender database (real world images, see fig. 2), (2) the Feret database [6], and (3) the BioID database [15]. See table 1 for details on the number of images in each class for these datasets. No image in the evaluation database is also included in the training or in the validation databases.

Faces were cropped using the same procedure during training and evaluation. The cropping was done using the position of the eyes. In the case of the training and validation datasets, the cropping of the faces was done using ground truth data, while in the case of evaluation two cases are considered: cropping using ground truth data and cropping using automatic face and eyes detection (both systems are described in [11]). The obtained results using both alternatives are analyzed (see figs. 3-5).

Table 1. Summary of Databases used for evaluation

Test database	# images	# Faces	# Men	# Women	% Men	% Women
UCHGender	142	343	192	151	55.9	44.1
Feret	2,745	2,745	1,650	1,095	60.1	39.9
BioID	1,521	1,521	975	546	64.1	35.9

The images employed for the training and testing of the SVM and Adaboost based systems were not preprocessed at all. In the case of the PCA based systems (PCA and PCA+SVM) the standard preprocessing required by PCA analysis was employed (subtraction of the mean face image plus variance normalization).

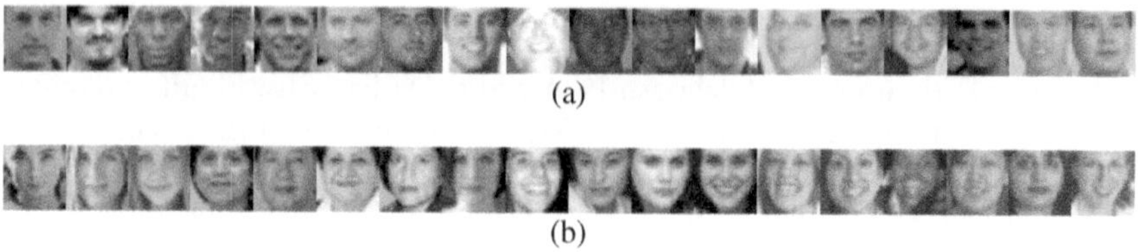

Fig. 2. UCHGender DB (examples) (24x24 pixels): (a) Men, (b) Women faces

5.3 Results

All the here presented results, with the exception of PCA and PCA+SVM, consider faces of 24x24 pixels. PCA based methods use faces of 100x185 pixels. The usage of larger face sizes (48x48) slightly improves the performance of some methods (for example Adaboost-Rect features and Adaboost-Wav), however the training time increases exponentially (from hours to days). Because of this and for not introducing important restrictions in the size of the faces to be analyzed we consider faces of 24x24 pixels.

Figures 3, 4 and 5 show the results of the evaluation of the different methods in the Feret, BioID and UCHGender databases, respectively. Figures 3(a), 4(a) and 5(a) show the results in the case when the eyes were annotated, while figures 3(b), 4(b) and 5(b) show results when the eyes (and faces) were automatically detected. In this last case only correct face detections were considered in the statistics (% of correct face detections: Feret: 99.49%, BioID: 98.22% and UCHGender: 96.79%). Table 2 shows some numerical results for the case of equal error rates in both classes.

Table 2. Correct Classification Rates at Operation points with equal error rates in both classes. Only best performing methods are shown. Faces were cropped using annotated eyes (left), and automatically detected eyes (right). Results are separated by a "/". Best results are shown in bold.

Database	SVM (RBF)	Adab.-Rect	Adab.-mLBP	Adab.-Wav	Adab.-Wav-mLBP
UCHGender	79.2 / 79.82	79.47 / 79.22	**81.23 / 80.12**	79.47 / 75.90	78.01 / 71.99
Feret	83.4 / 84.13	85.24 / 83.95	**85.56 / 85.89**	78.31 / 76.51	78.09 / 83.83
BioID	**81.44** / 79.05	79.66 / 79.52	80.91 / **81.46**	78.54 / 72.96	72.48 / 68.94

It can be noticed that in the Feret database (fig. 3) the best performing method is Adaboost-mLBP followed by Adaboost-Rect, SVM and SVM+PCA. It can also be notice that in this database the results of all methods are relatively independent of the way the eye positions were obtained. Main reason seems to be the fact that due to the characteristics of this database (homogeneous backgrounds and controlled illumination) the face detection rate is very high (99.49%) and the eyes detection very precise.

In the case of the BioID database (fig. 4), the performance of some of the methods increases when the eye detector is used. This happens in particular with the Adaboost-mLBP and Adaboost-Rect. When using annotated eyes (fig. 4(a)), best performing methods are Adaboost-mLBP and SVM depending on the operation point. This is the only case where SVM works better than the other methods, for equal error rates in both classes (see table 2). When using automatic detected eyes (fig. 4(b)), the best performing method is Adaboost-mLBP followed by Adaboost-Rect. This shows that Adaboost-mLBP is more robust (an independent) of the eye detector being used. In the case of the UCHGender database (fig. 5), it can be noticed that again the Adaboost-mLBP outperforms other methodologies. In the case of UCHGender database we do not include results of the PCA and PCA+SVM methods because most faces are smaller than 100x185, and PCA using those images gives poor results.

From figs 3, 4 and 5 it can be noticed that best results are obtained in the Feret database, followed by BioID, and UCHGender. This is probably because the Feret database contains homogeneous backgrounds, controlled illumination, and only completely frontal faces. On the other hand, the UCHGender contains a large variation on backgrounds, races, illumination conditions, and faces are not necessarily frontal -- some of them present yaw (out-of-plane) rotation.

In table 3 it is shown the average time required by the different methods for the gender classification of a given face image. This time does not include the time required for the face detection/cropping, face scaling and eyes detection. It includes just the time required for the face analysis (feature extraction and classification). It can be seen that Adaboost-mLPB is about 10 times faster than SVM, while Adaboost-Rect is 6 times faster than Adaboost-mLPB, and 60 times faster than SVM. This evaluation was done in an Intel Pentium 4 CPU 1.80GHz with 2GB RAM, running Debian GNU/Linux.

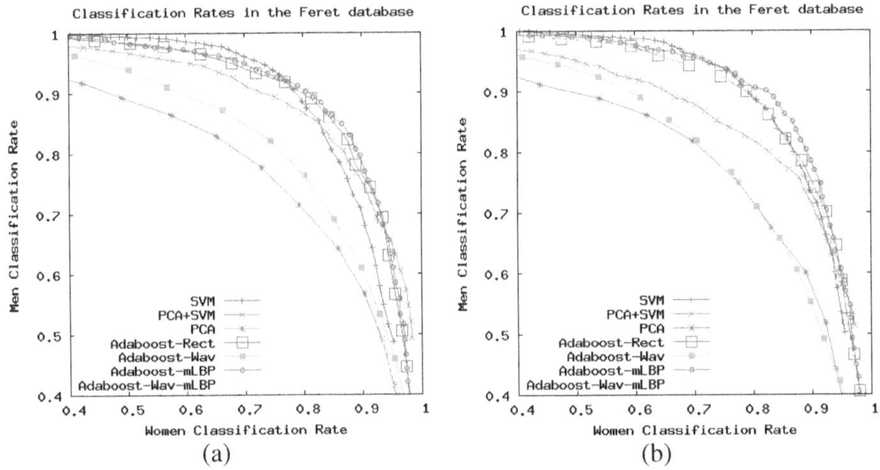

Fig. 3. Classification rates for the FERET dataset. Faces were aligned using: (a) annotated eyes, (b) detected eyes.

Table 3. Processing times of some of the different methods

Method	SVM	PCA	SVM+PCA	Ada-Rect	Ada-mLBP	Ada-Wav	Ada-Wav-mLBP
Time [mseg]	10.48	625	205	0.244	1.465	1.8554	2.7592

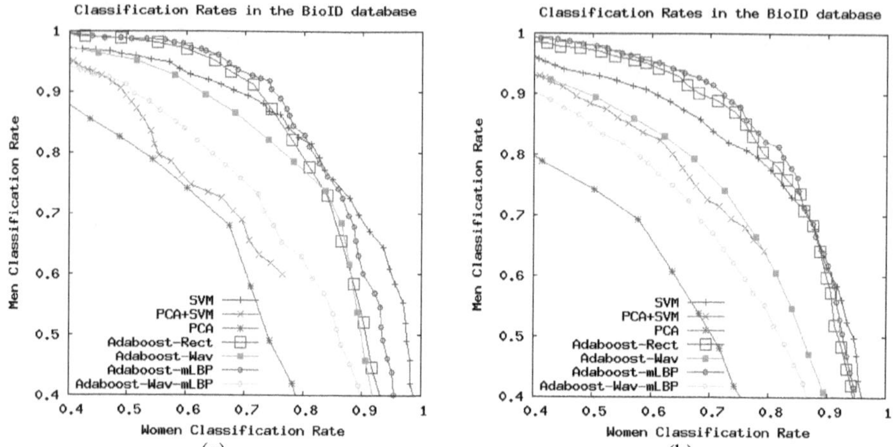

(a) (b)

Fig. 4. Classification rates for the BioID dataset. Faces were aligned using: (a) annotated eyes, (b) detected eyes.

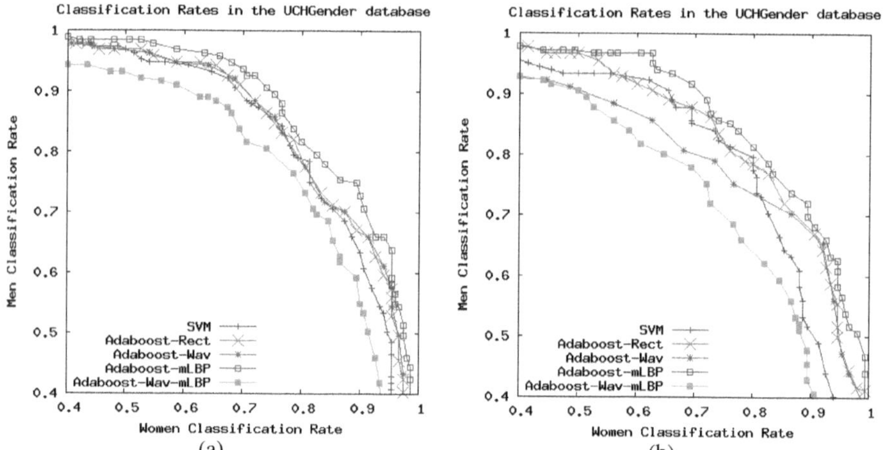

(a) (b)

Fig. 5. Classification rates for the UCHGender dataset. Faces were aligned using: (a) annotated eyes, (b) detected eyes.

6 Conclusions

In this article it was presented a framework for classifying face images using Adaboost and domain-partitioning based classifiers. We built several gender classification systems using the proposed framework and different features (LBP, wavelets, rectangular, etc.). These systems are analyzed and evaluated using three databases (Feret, BioID and UCHGender). The obtained results indicate that Adaboost-mLBP outperforms all other Adaboost-based methods, as well as baseline methods (SVM, PCA and PCA+SVM), in terms for classification rate. The Adaboost-mLBP behavior is robust to changes in the way eyes positions are obtained for performing the face alignment.

The most interesting advantage of the Adaboost-based methods is its high accuracy in dynamical environments, achieved with high processing speed. In terms of processing time, the faster method is Adaboost-Rect, being al least 6 times faster than the other methods (60 times faster than SVM-based methods). It is followed by Adaboost-mLBP, which is 10 times faster than SVM-based methods.

Another interesting characteristic of the developed Adaboost-based methods is their relatively high training speed, about one hour in the case of Adaboost-mLBP and about 48 hours for Adaboost-Rect, for a training database of 4,245 face images and a validation database of 2,745 face images.

Future work can be done in extending this framework to multi-class problems (age and race classification), and finding out a way of using (selecting) different kinds of features at the same time.

Acknowledgements

Portions of the research in this paper use the FERET database of facial images collected under the FERET program, and the CAS-PEAL face database collected under the sponsor of the Chinese National Hi-Tech Program and ISVISION Tech. Co. Ltd.

References

1. S. Buchala, N. Davey, R. J. Frank, T.M. Gale, M. Loomes, W. Kanargard, "Gender Classification of Face Images: The Role of Global and Feature-Based Information", ICONIP 2004, Calcutta, India, *Lecture Notes in Computer Science* 3316, pp. 763-768.
2. B. Fröba and A. Ernst, "Face detection with the modified census transform", *6th Int. Conf. on Face and Gesture Recognition - FG 2004*, pp. 91–96, Seoul, Korea, May 2004.
3. M. Delakis and C. Garcia, "Convolutional face finder: A neural architecture for fast and robust face detection", *IEEE Trans. Pattern Anal. Mach. Intell.*, Vol. 26, No. 11, pp. 1408–1423, 2004.
4. W. Gao, B. Cao, S. Shan, D. Zhou, X. Zhang, D. Zhao, "The CAS-PEAL Large-Scale Chinese Face Database and Evaluation Protocols", *Technical Report No. JDL_TR_04_FR_001*, Joint Research & Development Laboratory, CAS, 2004.
5. B. Moghaddam, M.-H. Yang, "Learning Gender with Support Faces", *IEEE Trans. Pattern Anal. Mach. Intell.*, Vol. 24, No. 5, pp. 707 – 711, 2002.
6. P. J. Phillips, H. Wechsler, J. Huang and P. Rauss, "The FERET database and evaluation procedure for face recognition algorithms", *Image and Vision Computing J.*, Vol. 16, no. 5, pp. 295-306, 1998.
7. R.E. Schapire, "A brief introduction to boosting", *In Proceedings of the Sixteenth International Joint Conference on Artificial Intelligence*, 1999.
8. R.E. Schapire and Y. Singer, "Improved Boosting Algorithms using Confidence-rated Predictions", *Machine Learning*, 37(3):297-336, 1999.

9. H. Schneidermann and T. Kanade, "A statistical model for 3D object detection applied to faces and cars", *IEEE Conf. on Computer Vision and Pattern Recognition*, Vol. 1, pp. 746 – 751, 2000.
10. G. Shakhnarovich, P. Viola, and B. Moghaddam, "A Unified Learning Framework for Real Time Face Detection & Classification", *Int Conf. on Automatic Face & Gesture Recognition – FG 2002*, pp. 16 – 26, May 2002.
11. R. Verschae, J. Ruiz-del-Solar, M. Correa, and P. Vallejos, "A Unified Learning Framework for Face, Eyes and Gender Detection using Nested Cascades of Boosted Classifiers", Technical Report UCH-DIE-VISION-2006-02, Dept. of E. Eng., U. de Chile, 2006.
12. P. Viola and M. Jones, "Fast and robust classification using asymmetric adaboost and a detector cascade", *Advances in Neural Inform. Processing System* 14, MIT Press, 2002.
13. B. Wu, H. Ai, C. Huang, and S. Lao, "Fast rotation invariant multi-view face detection based on real Adaboost", *6th Int. Conf. on Face and Gesture Recognition - FG 2004*, pp. 79–84, Seoul, Korea, May 2004.
14. B. Wu, H. Ai, and C. HUANG. "LUT-based Adaboost for Gender Classification", *4th Int. Conf. on Audio and Video-based Biometric Person Authentication*, June 10-11, 2003, Guildford, United Kingdom.
15. BioID Face Database. Available on april 2006 in: http://www.humanscan.de/support/downloads/facedb.php

General Pose Face Recognition Using Frontal Face Model

Jean-Yves Guillemaut[1], Josef Kittler[1],
Mohammad T. Sadeghi[2], and William J. Christmas[1]

[1] School of Electronics and Physical Sciences, University of Surrey, Guildford, GU2 7XB, U.K.
[2] Department of Electrical Engineering, Yazd University, Yazd, P.O. BOX 89195-741, Iran

Abstract. We present a face recognition system able to identify people from a single non-frontal image in an arbitrary pose. The key component of the system is a novel pose correction technique based on Active Appearance Models (AAMs), which is used to remap probe images into a frontal pose similar to that of gallery images. The method generalises previous pose correction algorithms based on AAMs to multiple axis head rotations. We show that such model can be combined with image warping techniques to increase the textural content of the images synthesised. We also show that bilateral symmetry of faces can be exploited to improve recognition. Experiments on a database of 570 non-frontal test images, which includes 148 different identities, show that the method produces a significant increase in the success rate (up to 77.4%) compared to conventional recognition techniques which do not consider pose correction.

1 Introduction

Face recognition has been a topic of active research in computer vision and pattern recognition for several decades. Applications encompass many aspects of everyday life such as video surveillance, human-machine interface or multimedia applications. Some of the reasons why face recognition has been attracting so much attention is that, unlike other biometrics such as fingerprints or eye iris scan, it does not require cooperation of the subject, it is unobtrusive and it can be done with a relatively cheap equipment. Despite the high recognition rates achieved by current recognition systems in the case of frontal images, performance has been observed to drop significantly if such ideal conditions are not satisfied. In fact, a previous evaluation of face recognition algorithms [1] has identified the face recognition problem from non-frontal images as a major research issue. In this paper, we concentrate on this problem and propose a novel solution.

1.1 Previous Work

Early solutions to the general pose face recognition problem were multi-view generalisations of standard frontal face recognition techniques. In [2], Beymer extends template-based techniques to non-frontal poses by building galleries of views for some pose configurations which sample the viewing sphere. In [3], Pentland et al. apply the eigenspace technique to arbitrary pose images by building a separate eigenspaces for

J.F. Martínez-Trinidad et al. (Eds.): CIARP 2006, LNCS 4225, pp. 79–88, 2006.

each pose configuration. One major limitation of such methods is that a large number of images is required to sample the viewing sphere for each subject.

More recent work focused on eliminating the effects of pose variation by remapping gallery and probe images into similar pose configurations in which case standard recognition techniques are known to perform well. In [4], Vetter and Poggio show that such image transformations can be learnt from a set of prototypical images of objects of the same class that form what they call Linear Object Classes. They synthesised realistic frontal images of faces from non-frontal views, however the decomposition as a sum of basis functions results in a loss of textural information. In [5] Vetter addresses this problem by supplementing the previous method with a generic 3D model which remaps the texture of the original image onto the corrected view. One limitation is that a database of prototype images is needed for each pose that must be corrected or synthesised, which requires the acquisition of a large number of images.

A different line of research concerns the use of parametric surfaces in the recognition feature space. The principle has been formulated in a general object recognition context in [6]. In this work Murase and Nayar consider the set of images of an object undergoing a rotation motion in 3D space and subject to changes of illumination. They observed that the projection of such images into the eigenspace forms a characteristic hypersurface for each object. The recognition problem is then reformulated in terms of finding the hypersurface which lies closest to the projection of the probe image in the eigenspace for a given metric. The principle has been applied in face recognition in the case of single [7] or multiple [8] images. A major limitation of such methods is that the construction of the eigensurface requires a large number of images for each subject.

Another important class of methods consists of model-based methods. The general idea is that a face in an image can be represented by the parameters of a model which can be used for recognition. In [9], Wiskott et al. represent faces by labelled graphs, where each node is labelled with a set of complex Gabor wavelet coefficients, called a jet. In [10], an Active Appearance Model (AAM) [11] is used for face localisation and recognition. The authors used Linear Discriminant Analysis to separate the parameters encoding the identity from the parameters encoding other sources of variation (pose, illumination, expression). In [12], the authors show that the appearance parameters can be used to estimate the pose of a face and synthesise novel views in different poses. They apply the method successfully to tracking images in [12] and face verification [13]. 3D morphable models have also been used to localise faces and identify subjects based on the fitted model parameters [14] or a corrected frontal view [15]. 3D morphable models handle better occlusions than AAM, however they require better initialisation and their convergence may be more difficult.

Finally, in [16] a view synthesis technique based on shape-from-shading is used to correct images with arbitrary poses and illumination into a frontal view under frontal lighting. Unlike other methods, this approach does not require a large number of example images, however light source and pose estimation were done manually.

1.2 Our Approach

Our approach is based on using an AAM to localise the face and synthesise a frontal view which can be then fed into a conventional face recognition system. We require only a gallery of frontal views of each subjects (e.g. mugshots) to train the recognition system, and we use only a single image of a subject in an arbitrary pose (usually non-frontal) for identification. This is a significant advantage compared to techniques requiring multiple example views for training [2,3,7,8]. Another strong point of our system is that it has the potential to localise automatically facial features in the image. This contrasts with a number of approaches which rely more heavily on a good initialisation [14,15,16].

Our approach is different from previous AAM-based face recognition systems [10,12,13] in the sense it does not use the model parameters for recognition. Instead it uses a corrected frontal appearance whose shape is predicted by a statistical model, modelling pose variation, and whose texture is either directly synthesised from the appearance model or obtained by image warping techniques. The latter approach presents the advantage of preserving the textural information (moles, freckles, etc) contained in the original image; such information would be lost in a traditional model parameter representation which models only the principal components of the appearance (low-pass filter equivalent). Another specificity of our pose correction model is that it can accommodate more general head rotations than the original model [12] which was formulated for single axis rotation only.

Our main contributions are the following. Firstly we formulate a novel pose correction method based on AAMs which generalises previous methods [12] as described in the previous paragraph. Secondly we show that AAMs can be used to improve face recognition performance by synthesis of corrected views of the probe images. Finally, we show that the bilateral symmetry of the face can be exploited to attenuate the effect of occlusions and increase the recognition performance.

The paper is structured as follows. We start by giving an overview of the system. We then concentrate on the novel pose estimation and correction algorithm proposed. Experimental results are given on a database of non-frontal images.

2 Methodology

The system is illustrated in Fig. 1. We give a brief description of each module.

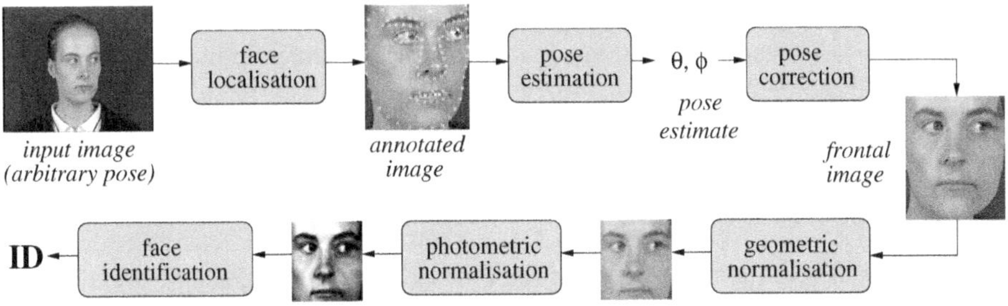

Fig. 1. Illustration of the main modules constituting the system

Face localisation. An AAM [11] is used for localising faces and their characteristic features. Our implementation uses 128 feature points for shape description. For efficiency, a multi-resolution approach with three different resolutions is adopted. The AAM is initialised with the coordinates of the eye centres, which could be obtained for example from an eye detector. In order to improve the convergence properties of algorithm in the case of non-frontal images, we use five different initialisations corresponding to mean appearance for different poses and select the result with lowest residual.

Pose estimation and pose correction. The aim of these modules are firstly to estimate the pose of the face in the probe image and then to synthesise a novel view of the subject in the same pose as the gallery images, i.e. frontal in this case. This is the core of our method. It will be described in detail in the next section.

Geometric and photometric normalisation. Geometric normalisation is done by applying an affine transformation composed of a translation, rotation and scaling in order to align the eye centres with some pre-defined positions; the position of the eye centres in the original image is obtained automatically from the fitted appearance. Photometric normalisation is done by histogram equalisation [17].

Identification. The statistical features used for recognition are obtained by Linear Discriminant Analysis (LDA) [18]. Identification is done by comparing the projection of the probe and gallery images in the LDA subspace and selecting the gallery image which maximises the normalised correlation [19]. Our implementation uses the bilateral symmetry of faces to attenuate the effect of occlusions (see details in result section).

3 Pose Estimation and Correction

Our method is inspired from the work of Cootes et al. described in [12]. In this paper, the authors formulated a pose correction method which handles rotation around a unique axis. Although it was claimed that generalisation to more general rotations was straightforward, no explicit formulation was given. In [13], it was suggested that rotation around two axes could be handled by using sequentially two independent pose correction models trained for pan and tilt motion respectively. Although this may work in practice for small rotations, this is not suitable for correcting rotations which exhibit simultaneously large pan and tilt components because such poses have not been learnt by either pose correction model. We formulate a pose correction method which handles correctly simultaneous pan and tilt head rotations. In addition, we show that image warping techniques can be used to improve the textural content of the corrected images.

3.1 Modelling Pose Variation

Out of plane head rotation is parametrised by two angles: the pan angle θ and the tilt angle ϕ, accounting respectively for rotation around the vertical axis and the horizontal axis attached to the face. This is sufficient to parametrise arbitrary head pose, because in-plane rotation, translation and image scaling are already modelled by the appearance model parameters. In an appropriately defined world reference frame, a feature point attached to the head and with coordinates $(X_0, Y_0, Z_0)^\top$ transforms into the point with coordinates $(X, Y, Z)^\top$ after a rotation parametrised by (θ, ϕ), such that:

$$X = X_0 c_\theta c_\phi - Y_0 s_\theta c_\phi + Z_0 s_\phi, \quad Y = X_0 s_\theta + Y_0 c_\theta, \quad \text{and } Z = -X_0 c_\theta s_\phi + Y_0 s_\theta s_\phi + Z_0 c_\phi, \quad (1)$$

where we use the notations $c_\alpha = \cos\alpha$ and $s_\alpha = \sin\alpha$. Assuming an affine projection model, the 3D point $(X, Y, Z)^\top$ projects into the image point $(x, y)^\top$ such that:

$$x = x_0 + x_1 c_\theta + x_2 s_\theta + x_3 c_\phi + x_4 s_\phi + x_5 c_\theta c_\phi + x_6 c_\theta s_\phi + x_7 s_\theta c_\phi + x_8 s_\theta s_\phi, \quad (2)$$

where $x_0, \ldots, x_8$ are some constant (a similar equation is obtained for y). The shape model being linear, the shape parameters $\mathbf{c}$ follow a similar linear model:

$$\mathbf{c} = \mathbf{c}_0 + \mathbf{c}_1 c_\theta + \mathbf{c}_2 s_\theta + \mathbf{c}_3 c_\phi + \mathbf{c}_4 s_\phi + \mathbf{c}_5 c_\theta c_\phi + \mathbf{c}_6 c_\theta s_\phi + \mathbf{c}_7 s_\theta c_\phi + \mathbf{c}_8 s_\theta s_\phi, \quad (3)$$

where $\mathbf{c}_0, \ldots, \mathbf{c}_8$ are constant vectors which can be learnt from a database of annotated images. Experiments we carried out suggest that this equation can be extended to the appearance parameters. This is consistent with what was observed by Cootes et al. in the case of a single rotation in [12]. Note that if one of the angles is set to a fixed value, (3) simplifies to the equation originally formulated in [12].

3.2 Pose Estimation

We define the matrix $R_\mathbf{c} = [\mathbf{c}_1|\mathbf{c}_2|\mathbf{c}_3|\mathbf{c}_4|\mathbf{c}_5|\mathbf{c}_6|\mathbf{c}_7|\mathbf{c}_8]$. Given a vector $\mathbf{c}$ of shape or appearance parameters, we compute the vector $[a_1, \ldots, a_8]^\top = R_\mathbf{c}^+(\mathbf{c} - \mathbf{c}_0)$, where $R_\mathbf{c}^+$ is the pseudo-inverse of $R_\mathbf{c}$. A closed-form solution for the pan and tilt angles is then given by: $\theta = \tan^{-1}(\frac{a_2}{a_1})$ and $\phi = \tan^{-1}(\frac{a_4}{a_3})$. Such a solution is not optimum because it involves only the values a_1 to a_4. A more accurate solution is obtained by finding the values of θ and ϕ which minimise the following cost function:

$$d_\mathbf{c}(\theta, \phi) = \|\mathbf{c} - (\mathbf{c}_0 + \mathbf{c}_1 c_\theta + \mathbf{c}_2 s_\theta + \mathbf{c}_3 c_\phi + \mathbf{c}_4 s_\phi + \mathbf{c}_5 c_\theta c_\phi + \mathbf{c}_6 c_\theta s_\phi + \mathbf{c}_7 s_\theta c_\phi + \mathbf{c}_8 s_\theta s_\phi)\|. \quad (4)$$

This is a simple two-dimensional non-linear minimisation problem which can be solved e.g. with a steepest descent algorithm initialised with the closed-form solution.

3.3 Synthesising Corrected Views

We assume that the pose in the original image has been estimated as (θ, ϕ) and would like to synthesise a novel view of the same subject in the pose (θ', ϕ'). As in [12], we compute the residual vector $\boldsymbol{r}$ not explained by the pose model in the original image:

$$\boldsymbol{r} = \mathbf{c} - (\mathbf{c}_0 + \mathbf{c}_1 c_\theta + \mathbf{c}_2 s_\theta + \mathbf{c}_3 c_\phi + \mathbf{c}_4 s_\phi + \mathbf{c}_5 c_\theta c_\phi + \mathbf{c}_6 c_\theta s_\phi + \mathbf{c}_7 s_\theta c_\phi + \mathbf{c}_8 s_\theta s_\phi). \quad (5)$$

The shape or appearance parameters $\mathbf{c}'$ of the rotated view in the new pose (θ', ϕ') are then obtained by re-injecting the residual vector $\boldsymbol{r}$ into the new pose equation:

$$\mathbf{c}' = \mathbf{c}_0 + \mathbf{c}_1 c'_\theta + \mathbf{c}_2 s'_\theta + \mathbf{c}_3 c'_\phi + \mathbf{c}_4 s'_\phi + \mathbf{c}_5 c'_\theta c'_\phi + \mathbf{c}_6 c'_\theta s'_\phi + \mathbf{c}_7 s'_\theta c'_\phi + \mathbf{c}_8 s'_\theta s'_\phi + \boldsymbol{r}. \quad (6)$$

If (6) is applied to all appearance parameters, the appearance model can be then used to synthesise a full corrected view of the person (see second row in Fig. 2). We will refer to this method as the *basic pose correction* method.

Fig. 2. Example of non-frontal images (top row) and corrected frontal images (middle rows). For comparison, the bottom row shows example of real frontal images of the same subjects.

3.4 Improving the Textural Content of the Corrected Views

The novel view synthesis method described in the previous section solves elegantly the pose correction problem by predicting the appearance parameters of the novel view and then synthesising a full appearance. There are however two limitations to this approach. Firstly, details such as e.g. moles or freckles are lost in the corrected view, because the appearance parameter representation preserves only the principal components of the image variations. Another limitation is that the basic pose correction method is able to predict the appearance only within the convex hull of the set of feature points, which explains why a black border is present around the face. In practice, this may pose problem during recognition if such border is not present in the gallery images.

We present two methods based on image warping which do not suffer from such limitations. The key idea is to apply (6) only to the shape parameters. This yields an estimate of the position of the feature points in a frontal view. Then the texture of the corrected image is obtained by warping the original image. Two warping techniques have been considered: i) piece-wise affine warping and ii) thin-plate spline warping. Results for all methods are illustrated in Fig. 2 for a few randomly selected subjects. In the first approach, meshes of the original and corrected faces are generated, with vertices placed at the localised or predicted feature points. Triangular meshes are generated automatically by Delaunay triangulation [20]. Then each triangle is warped affinely to its new position (see Fig. 3). The second technique is based on thin-plate splines [21]. It has the advantage of resulting in smoother deformations than the previous method (no artefact at the boundary between triangles), however the behaviour of the method is not always clear in-between feature points, especially in the case of large pose variations.

Experiments carried out on a database of 396 images of unknown subjects (not used for training the pose correction model) with variations of $\pm 22.5°$ for the pan angle and $\pm 30°$ for the tilt angle showed that our pose estimation model is accurate to about $5°$ for the pan angle and $7°$ for the tilt angle. Errors in pose estimation translate into errors in the computation of r in (5), which ultimately result in errors in the corrected frontal view. Typically, errors in estimation of pan and tilt angle result in a compression or expansion of the face in the horizontal or vertical direction respectively. Errors in scale in the horizontal direction are usually less problematic because the distance between the two eyes is normalised for recognition. Unfortunately there exists no such compensation for scaling errors in the vertical direction.

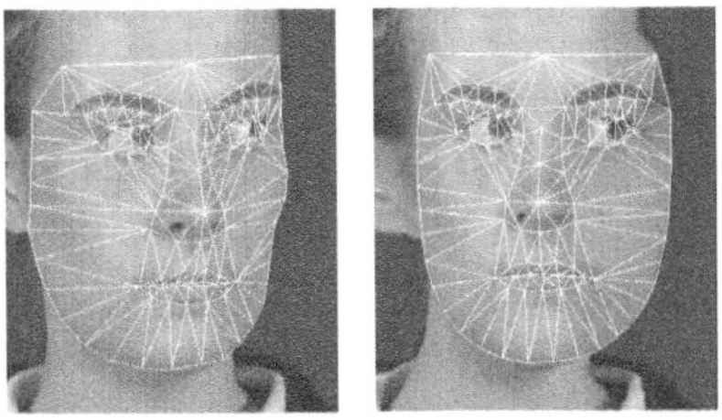

Fig. 3. Illustration of the piece-wise affine warping method. The original image (arbitrary pose) is shown on the left, while the corrected image (frontal pose) is shown on the right. Both images are overlaid with the triangular mesh used for warping.

4 Experimental Results

Experiments were carried out on the XM2VTS database [22]. The database contains eight frontal images and four non-frontal images (corresponding to poses with head turned left, right, up or down) of 295 different subjects. Among all these images, 225 frontal images and 1177 non-frontal images have been manually annotated with facial landmarks. We also use a database of 567 similarly annotated images of 43 subjects for which additional pose information is available. Ground truth pose (pan and tilt angles) was obtained by placing the subjects on a turntable during image acquisition.

For a fair evaluation, the images have been split into two subsets. The first subset contains the images of the first 147 subjects from the XM2VTS database plus the turntable images, and has been used to train the AAM and the pose correction model (when pose ground truth was available). The images of the remaining 148 subjects from the XM2VTS database (570 images in total) are used for recognition experiments; the frontal images were used for training the recognition system (gallery images), while the non-frontal images were used for testing (probe images). None of the subjects used for training the AAM or the pose correction model were used during the recognition experiments.

Two different test sets were considered. *Test set 1* (295 images) contains only the probe images for which the subjects have their eyes open and do not wear glasses. Eyes closed or glasses (which can generate specularities) complicate significantly the problem because the eyes, which contain important information for identification and face localisation, may not be visible. *Test set 2* contains all probe images (570 images). Both test sets are very challenging because of the large pose variations observed (see top row of Fig. 2 for some example of probe images).

Experiments were carried out in two modes: *manual* and *semi-automatic*. In the manual mode, the system is initialised with the manually marked-up feature points; this eliminates potential errors due to AAM fitting and allows us to measure the performance of the system independently from the localisation algorithm. In the semi-automatic mode, faces are localised by the AAM algorithm initialised with the coordinates of the eye centres obtained from manual annotation. In future implementation, the method will be made fully automatic by using an eye detector to initialise the AAM search.

Four different methods are compared. The method with *no pose correction* applies only geometric and photometric normalisation to the test images before projection into the LDA subspace. For geometric normalisation, the images are cropped to a window of dimension 55×51 pixels, where the left and right eyes occupy the points with coordinates $(19, 38)$ and $(19, 12)$. This is a conventional recognition method which is known to perform well in the case of frontal images. The other methods apply additional pose correction based techniques described earlier: *basic pose correction* (see Sect. 3.3), shape correction combined with either *piece-wise affine warping* or *thin-plate spline warping* (see Sect. 3.4).

Given the large changes of pose observed in the images, parts of the face can become largely occluded, which can produce significant artefacts in the corrected images. In order to attenuate such effects, at least in the case of rotations around the vertical axis, the bilateral face symmetry has been used to eliminate the occluded half of the face when needed. In this approach, three different LDA subspaces are build for full image, left half-image and right half-image respectively. Then the pose estimate for the probe images is used to select automatically the most appropriate LDA subspace to use for identification. At the moment, the pose classification is done by thresholding of the pan angle (thresholds of $-15°$ and $+15°$ have been used). All recognition methods are tested with and without this bilateral face symmetry based occlusion removal algorithm; we refer to these methods as *partial face* and *full face* methods respectively.

The success rates (percentage of subjects identified as top matches) obtained for each configuration are shown in Table 1. The best performing method is the one which uses shape correction combined with a piece-wise affine warping, followed very closely by shape correction combined with the thin-plate spline warping. Compared to a conventional face recognition system which does not consider pose correction, the best pose correction method improves the success rate by between 33.7% and 77.4% depending on the difficulty of the test set and the degree of initialisation. The best success rate measured is 69.2%. This is a high recognition score given the number of classes (148 subjects) and the fact that all images are non-frontal (pure chance would be only 0.67%). The basic pose correction method is the least accurate. This suggests that it is important to preserve the textural information contained in original images. The loss of information in the image synthesised from the predicted frontal appearance parameters is accentuated by errors in locating the face in the case of the semi-automatic algorithm. It can be observed that the use of bilateral face symmetry for reducing the effect of occlusions allows to increase the performance by a few percents in the case of the semi-automatic algorithm; it is not as critical in the case of manually localised faces.

Table 1. Success rate for different general pose face recognition methods

		no pose correction		basic pose correction		piece-wise affine warping		thin-plate spline warping	
		full face	part. face	full face	part. face	full face	part. face	full face	part. face
Test set 1	manual	39.0	38.0	33.2	32.2	**69.2**	**69.2**	66.1	66.8
	semi-auto	39.0	38.0	17.3	16.6	60.0	**63.7**	56.9	59.7
Test set 2	manual	40.4	40.0	33.5	33.3	**62.6**	**62.6**	59.3	59.3
	semi-auto	40.4	40.0	13.7	13.7	52.5	**54.0**	50.2	51.9

5 Conclusions and Future Work

We have presented a novel method for face identification which is able to cope with pose variations and requires only a single view of a person in an arbitrary pose for identification. The method relies on the use of a statistical model to estimate and synthesise frontal views of the subjects. When combined with image warping techniques, the method is able to preserve the textural content of the original non-frontal image. The corrected image can be fed directly into a conventional face recognition system. It has been shown that such a correction algorithm is able to improve the performance by up to 77.4% compared to a conventional approach which does not consider correction. We also showed how bilateral face symmetry can be used to alleviate the effects of occlusions by using the pose estimate to classify images into three categories for which separate LDA subspaces have been built.

We have compared several methods for correcting the pose and applied them successfully to the problem of face recognition. We are currently working on comparing these methods with other approaches which carry out the recognition directly in the space of model parameters after having decoupled the parameters encoding the identity from the ones encoding pose, expression and illumination [10]. Although the comparison is still in its early stages, we can already anticipate that such method will probably not be able to achieve as high success rates as the ones given here because of the loss of texture information induced by the model parameter representation.

We think that there is a scope for improving further the technique presented in this paper. One possible avenue for future work is to investigate how pose estimation (and thereby pose correction) can be improved by treating the problem jointly with the face recognition problem; in this approach an optimum pose estimate is found by minimising the metric used for matching in the LDA subspace. Other possible avenues include the use of non-linear techniques such as kernel PCA to improve the performance of our AAM in the case of pose variation, a better handling of occlusions (at the moment we classify faces in only three classes according to pan angle) or the extension of the method to image sequences.

Acknowledgements

This work was initiated under the EU Project VAMPIRE and is now supported by the EU Network of Excellence BIOSECURE, with contributions from EU Project MUSCLE and EPSRC Project 2D+3D=ID.

References

1. Phillips, P., Grother, P., Micheals, R., Blackburn, D., Tabassi, E., Bone, J.: Face recognition vendor test 2002: Evaluation report (2003)
2. Beymer, D.J.: Face recognition under varying pose. In: Proc. IEEE Conference on Computer Vision and Pattern Recognition. (1994) 756–761
3. Pentland, A., Moghaddam, B., Starner, T.: View-based and modular eigenspaces for face recognition. In: Proc. IEEE Conference on Computer Vision and Pattern Recognition. (1994) 84–91
4. Vetter, T., Poggio, T.: Linear object classes and image synthesis from a single example image. IEEE Transactions on Pattern Analysis and Machine Intelligence **19**(7) (1997) 733–742
5. Vetter, T.: Synthesis of novel views from a single face image. International Journal of Computer Vision **28**(2) (1998) 103–116
6. Murase, H., Nayar, S.K.: Visual learning and recognition of 3-d objects from appearance. International Journal of Computer Vision **14**(1) (1995) 5–24
7. Graham, D.B., Allinson, N.M.: Face recognition from unfamiliar views: Subspace methods and pose dependency. In: Proc. IEEE International Conference on Automatic Face and Gesture Recognition. (1998) 348–353
8. Li, Y., Gong, S., Liddell, H.: Constructing facial identity surfaces for recognition. International Journal of Computer Vision **53**(1) (2003) 71–92
9. Wiskott, L., Fellous, J.M., Kruger, N., von der Malsburg, C.: Face recognition by elastic bunch graph matching. IEEE Transactions on Pattern Analysis and Machine Intelligence **19**(7) (1997) 775–779
10. Edwards, G.J., Cootes, T.F., Taylor, C.J.: Face recognition using active appearance models. In: Proc. European Conference on Computer Vision. Volume II. (1998) 581–595
11. Cootes, T.F., Edwards, G.J., Taylor, C.J.: Active appearance models. In: Proceedings of European Conference on Computer Vision. Volume II. (1998) 484–498
12. Cootes, T.F., Wheeler, G.V., Walker, K.N., Taylor, C.J.: View-based active appearance models. Image and Vision Computing **20**(9-10) (2002) 657–664
13. H. Kang, T.F.C., Taylor, C.J.: A comparison of face verification algorithms using appearance models. In: Proc. British Machine Vision Conference. Volume 2. (2002) 477–486
14. Blanz, V., Vetter, T.: Face recognition based on fitting a 3d morphable model. IEEE Transactions on Pattern Analysis and Machine Intelligence **25**(9) (2003) 1063–1074
15. Blanz, V., Grother, P., Phillips, P.J., Vetter, T.: Face recognition based on frontal views generated from non-frontal images. In: Proc. IEEE Conference on Computer Vision and Pattern Recognition. Volume 2. (2005) 454–461
16. Zhao, W., Chellappa, R.: SFS based view synthesis for robust face recognition. In: Proc. IEEE International Conference on Automatic Face and Gesture Recognition. (2000) 285–292
17. Gonzalez, R.C., Woods, R.E.: Digital Image Processing. Second edn. Prentice Hall (2002)
18. Devijver, P.A., Kittler, J.: Pattern Recognition: A Statistical Approach. Prentice-Hall (1982)
19. Li, Y.: Linear Discriminant Analysis and its application to Face Identification. PhD thesis, University of Surrey (2000)
20. de Berg, M., Schwarzkopf, O., van Kreveld, M., Overmars, M.: Computational Geometry: Algorithms and Applications. second edn. Springer-Verlag (2000)
21. Bookstein, F.L.: Principal warps: Thin-plate splines and the decomposition of deformations. IEEE Transactions on Pattern Analysis and Machine Intelligence **11**(6) (1989) 567–585
22. Messer, K., Matas, J., Kittler, J., Luettin, J., Maitre, G.: XM2VTSDB: The extended M2VTS database. In: Proceedings of International Conference on Audio- and VideoBased Biometric Person Authentication (AVBPA). (1999) 72–77

Approximating 3D Facial Shape from Photographs Using Coupled Statistical Models

Mario Castelán*, William A.P. Smith, and Edwin R. Hancock

Department of Computer Science, University of York, York Y01 5DD, UK

Abstract. In this paper we focus on the problem of developing a coupled statistical model that can be used to recover surface height from frontal photographs of faces. The idea is to couple intensity and height by jointly modeling their combined variations. We perform Principal Component Analysis (PCA) on the shape coefficients for both intensity and height training data in order to construct the coupled statistical model. Using the best-fit coefficients of an intensity image, height information can be implicitly recovered through the coupled statistical model. Experiments show that the method can generate good approximations of the facial surface shape from out-of-training photographs of faces.

1 Introduction

One of the simplest approaches to facial shape recovery using shape-from-shading is to extract a field of surface normals and then recover the surface height function by integrating the surface normals [1–3]. Unfortunately, there are a number of obstacles that are encountered when this simple strategy is applied to real-world data. The most important of these is that when integrated, the concave/convex ambiguities in the needle-map can lead to the distortion of the topography of the reconstructed face. One of the most serious instances of this problem is that the nose can become imploded.

In general, shape-from-shading is an under-constrained problem since a surface normal has two degrees of freedom corresponding to the elevation and azimuth angles on the unit sphere which can not be recovered from a single brightness measurement. Domain specific constraints have been used to overcome this problem. Several authors [4–7] have shown that, at the expense of generality, the accuracy of recovered shape information can be greatly enhanced by restricting a shape-from-shading algorithm to a particular class of objects. For instance, both Prados and Faugeras [7] and Castelán and Hancock [6] use the location of singular points to enforce convexity on the recovered surface. Zhao and Chellappa [4] have introduced a geometric constraint which exploited the approximate bilateral symmetry of faces.

On the other hand, Atick et al. [8] proposed a statistical shape-from-shading framework based on a low dimensional parametrization of facial surfaces. Principal components analysis was used to derive a set of 'eigenheads' which compactly captures 3D facial shape. Unfortunately, it is surface orientation and not height which is conveyed by image intensity. Therefore, fitting the model to an image equates to a computationally

* Supported by National Council of Science and Technology (CONACYT), Mexico, under grant No. 141485.

J.F. Martínez-Trinidad et al. (Eds.): CIARP 2006, LNCS 4225, pp. 89–98, 2006.

expensive parameter search which attempts to minimise the error between the rendered surface and the observed intensity. Dovgard and Basri [9] combined the statistical constraint of Atick et al. and the geometric constraint of Zhao and Chellappa into a single shape-from-shading framework. However, asymmetry in real face images results in errors in the recovered surfaces. Blanz and Vetter [10] decoupled surface texture from shape and performed PCA on the two components separately. Their framework could be used regardless of pose and illumination changes, but linear combinations of shape and texture had to be formed separately for the eyes, nose, mouth and the surrounding area. In addition, expensive alignment and parameter fitting procedures had to be carried out. The results delivered by fitting this morphable model proved to be accurate enough to generate photo-realistic views from an input image, though sacrificing efficiency and simplicity.

The aim in this paper is to explore how coupled statistical models can be used to overcome these difficulties. We couple height surface with intensity, developing a coupled statistical model that jointly describes variations in image brightness and height data over the surface of a face. The coupled model is inspired by the active appearance model developed by Cootes, Edwards and Taylor [11], which simultaneously models 2D shape and texture.

2 Principal Component Analysis

In this section we describe how eigenspace models are constructed for Cartesian data. Here we follow the approach adopted by Turk and Pentland who were among the first to explore the use of principal components analysis for face recognition [12]. We make use of the technique described by Sirovich et al. [13] to render the method efficient.

2.1 The Intensity Model

The image data is vectorized by stacking the image columns to form long column vectors $\mathbf{i}$. If the K training images contain M columns and N rows, then the pixel with column index j_c and row index j_r corresponds to the element indexed $j = (N-1)j_c + j_r$ of the long column vector. The training set data-matrix, $\mathbf{I} = [\mathbf{i}_1|\mathbf{i}_2|\cdots|\mathbf{i}_K]$ is then formed by using the long vectors $\mathbf{i}_k$ as columns. The differences from the average face image, $\bar{\mathbf{i}}$ (the sample mean) are used to construct the centered training data matrix

$$\mathbf{I}' = [(\mathbf{i}_1 - \bar{\mathbf{i}})|(\mathbf{i}_2 - \bar{\mathbf{i}})|\cdots|(\mathbf{i}_K - \bar{\mathbf{i}})] = [\mathbf{i}'_1|\mathbf{i}'_2|\cdots|\mathbf{i}'_K]. \quad (1)$$

Principal Component Analysis (PCA) seeks a set of $K-1$ orthogonal vectors which, in a least squares sense, best describe the distribution of the columns of $\mathbf{I}'$. The solution to the least squares problem is found by calculating the eigenvectors of the *explicit* covariance matrix

$$\mathbf{V}^i = \sum_{k=1}^{K} \mathbf{i}'_k \mathbf{i}'^T_k = \mathbf{I}'\mathbf{I}'^T. \quad (2)$$

Unfortunately, due to its size ($MN \times MN$), computing the eigenvalues and eigenvectors of $\mathbf{v}^i$ becomes intractable for large sets of data. However, the numerically efficient method proposed in [13] can be used to overcome these difficulties. According to this method there are only $K-1$ non zero eigenvalues from $\mathbf{V}^i$ and these can be computed from the $K \times K$ *sampled* covariance matrix $\widehat{\mathbf{V}}^i = \mathbf{I}'^T \mathbf{I}'$. The eigen-vector equations for the explicit and sampled covariance matrices, $\mathbf{V}^i$ and $\widehat{\mathbf{V}}^i$, are

$$\mathbf{V}^i \mathbf{u}_k^i = \lambda_k \mathbf{u}_k^i \qquad \text{and} \qquad \widehat{\mathbf{V}}^i \hat{\mathbf{u}}_k^i = \hat{\lambda}_k^i \hat{\mathbf{u}}_k^i, \tag{3}$$

where $\mathbf{u}_k^i$, $\hat{\mathbf{u}}_k^i$ and λ_k^i, $\hat{\lambda}_k^i$ are the eigenvectors and eigenvalues of $\mathbf{V}^i$ and $\widehat{\mathbf{V}}^i$, respectively. To demonstrate the relationship between the two sets of eigenvectors, we note that

$$\widehat{\mathbf{V}}^i \hat{\mathbf{u}}_k^i = \hat{\lambda}_k^i \hat{\mathbf{u}}_k^i, \tag{4}$$

$$\mathbf{I}'^T \mathbf{I}' \hat{\mathbf{u}}_k^i = \hat{\lambda}_k^i \hat{\mathbf{u}}_k^i, \tag{5}$$

$$\mathbf{I}' \mathbf{I}'^T \mathbf{I}' \hat{\mathbf{u}}_k^i = \hat{\lambda}_k^i \mathbf{I}' \hat{\mathbf{u}}_k^i, \tag{6}$$

$$\mathbf{V}^i (\mathbf{I}' \hat{\mathbf{u}}_k^i) = \hat{\lambda}_k^i (\mathbf{I}' \hat{\mathbf{u}}_k^i). \tag{7}$$

As a result $\mathbf{u}_k^i = \mathbf{I}' \hat{\mathbf{u}}_k^i$ and $\lambda_k^i = \hat{\lambda}_k^i$. This means that the eigenvectors of the explicit covariance matrix can be calculated by multiplying the centered training set by the eigenvectors of the sampled covariance matrix. Likewise, the non-zero eigenvalues of the explicit covariance matrix are equal to the eigenvalues of the sampled covariance matrix.

The eigenfaces are then the eigenvectors of $\mathbf{V}^i$ and are constructed by multiplying the centered training-set data-matrix $\mathbf{I}'$ by the eigenvectors of the sampled covariance matrix $\widehat{\mathbf{V}}^i$, i.e.

$$\mathbf{M}^i = \mathbf{I}' \widehat{\mathbf{U}}^i, \tag{8}$$

where $\widehat{\mathbf{U}}^i = [\hat{\mathbf{u}}_1^i | \hat{\mathbf{u}}_2^i | \cdots | \hat{\mathbf{u}}_K^i]$.

An out-of-training-sample face $\dot{\mathbf{i}}$ can be fitted to the eigenfaces $\mathbf{M}^i$ by calculating the parameter vector $\mathbf{b}^i = [b_1^i, b_2^i, \cdots, b_k^i]$ that minimizes the squared error. The solution to this least-squares estimation problem is

$$\mathbf{b}^{\mathbf{i}} = \mathbf{M}^{i^T} (\dot{\mathbf{i}} - \bar{\mathbf{i}}). \tag{9}$$

The vector of parameters $\mathbf{b}^i$ measures the contributions from each eigenface to the recovered approximation of the out-of-training face $\dot{\mathbf{i}}$, and is given by

$$\dot{\mathbf{i}} \approx \bar{\mathbf{i}} + \mathbf{M}^i \mathbf{b}^i. \tag{10}$$

In order to be valid examples of the class represented by the training set, the values of the vector $\mathbf{b}^i$ should be constrained to fall in the interval $b_k \in [-3\sqrt{\lambda_k^i}, +3\sqrt{\lambda_k^i}]$.

2.2 The Surface Height Model

To explain how the surface height model was constructed, let us assume that each of the K surfaces in the training set may be represented by long vectors of height values $\mathbf{h}$. The mean height vector $\bar{\mathbf{h}}$ is given by

$$\bar{\mathbf{h}} = \frac{1}{K}\sum_{k=1}^{K}\mathbf{h}_k. \tag{11}$$

In a similar manner to Equation 1, we form the $MN \times K$ matrix of centered long vectors $\mathbf{H}' = [(\mathbf{h}_1 - \bar{\mathbf{h}})|(\mathbf{h}_2 - \bar{\mathbf{h}})|\cdots|(\mathbf{h}_K - \bar{\mathbf{h}})]$. We calculate the eigenvectors $\hat{\mathbf{u}}_k^h$ of the matrix $\mathbf{H}'^T\mathbf{H}'$ and construct the height statistical model (as in Equation 8)

$$\mathbf{M}^h = \mathbf{H}'\widehat{\mathbf{U}}^h, \tag{12}$$

where $\widehat{\mathbf{U}}^h = [\hat{\mathbf{u}}_1^h|\hat{\mathbf{u}}_2^h|\cdots|\hat{\mathbf{u}}_K^h]$. An out-of-training-sample centered long-vector of height values, $\dot{\mathbf{h}} - \bar{\mathbf{h}}$, can be projected onto the model and represented using the vector of coefficients

$$\mathbf{b}^h = \mathbf{M}^{h^T}(\dot{\mathbf{h}} - \bar{\mathbf{h}}). \tag{13}$$

Note that the intensity model and the height model exhibit different modes of variation. This means that the information encoded by the intensity shape parameters, $\mathbf{b}^i$, is of limited use in directly recovering surface shape from intensity images. This problem has been circumvented by minimizing the distance between rendered views from recovered surfaces and input images, as in the work of Atick [8] and Vetter and Blanz [10]. Unfortunately, the minimization of this distance is badly affected by the presence of local minima. This means that exhaustive search methods must be used, and this sacrifices efficiency. We overcome this problem by using a coupled statistical model to relate 2D intensity variations and variations in surface shape. Once fitted to data, the coupled model allows us to infer the shape-parameters from the best-fit intensity parameters, rather than using the distance between input images and rendered views of the recovered surfaces.

3 The Coupled Model

To construct the coupled model, each training example (i.e. pair of intensity image and corresponding aligned range image) can be summarized by the parameter vectors $\mathbf{b}^i$ and $\mathbf{b}^h$. In both models, we assume that the lower eigenmodes represent small scale noise variation. Hence, if the k_{th} eigenvalue for the intensity model is λ_k^i, we need only S eigenmodes to retain $Perc$ percent of the model variance. We choose S so that $\sum_{k=1}^{S}\lambda_k^i \geq \frac{Perc}{100}\sum_{k=1}^{K}\lambda_k^i$. Similarly, for the 3D models we retain T eigenmodes to capture $Perc$ percent of the variance.

3.1 Eigenmode Concatenation

For the k_{th} training sample we can generate the concatenated parameter vector of length $S+T$:

$$\mathbf{b}_k^c = \begin{pmatrix}\mathbf{W}\mathbf{b}_k^i \\ \mathbf{b}_k^h\end{pmatrix} = \begin{pmatrix}\mathbf{W}\mathbf{M}^{i^T}(\mathbf{t}_k^i - \bar{\mathbf{i}}) \\ \mathbf{M}^{h^T}(\mathbf{t}_k^h - \bar{\mathbf{h}})\end{pmatrix}, \tag{14}$$

where $\mathbf{W}$ is a diagonal matrix of weights for each intensity model parameter, allowing for the different relative weighting of the intensity and surface models. As the elements of $\mathbf{b}^i$ and $\mathbf{b}^h$ represent different classes of data (grayscale and surface shape), they can not be compared directly. We follow Cootes and Taylor [11] and set $\mathbf{W} = r\mathbf{M}^i$, where r^2 is the ratio of the total shape variance to the total intensity variance. The coupled model data matrix is $(\mathbf{b}_1^c|\mathbf{b}_2^c|...|\mathbf{b}_K^c)$.

By applying PCA to the concatenated intensity-shape parameter vectors, we obtain the coupled model:

$$\mathbf{b}^c = \mathbf{C}\mathbf{c} = \begin{pmatrix} \mathbf{C}^i \\ \mathbf{C}^h \end{pmatrix} \mathbf{c}, \tag{15}$$

where $\mathbf{C}$ are the eigenvectors and $\mathbf{c}$ is a vector of coupled parameters controlling the intensity and surface shape models simultaneously. The matrix $\mathbf{C}^i$ has S rows, and represents the first S eigenvectors, corresponding to the intensity subspace of the model. The matrix $\mathbf{C}^h$ has T rows, and represents the final T eigenvectors, corresponding to the surface shape subspace of the model.

We may express the vectors of projected intensity and 3D values directly in terms of the parameter vector $\mathbf{c}$:

$$\mathbf{t}^i = \bar{\mathbf{i}} + \mathbf{M}^i\mathbf{W}^{-1}\mathbf{C}^i\mathbf{c}. \tag{16}$$
$$\mathbf{t}^h = \bar{\mathbf{h}} + \mathbf{M}^h\mathbf{C}^h\mathbf{c}. \tag{17}$$

For compactness we write: $\mathbf{Q}^i = \mathbf{W}^{-1}\mathbf{C}^i$. We retained 95% of the variance for each of the models.

3.2 Fitting the Model to Intensity Data

Fitting the model to intensity data involves estimating the parameter vector $\mathbf{c}$ from input images of faces. To do this we seek the coupled model parameters which minimize the error between the best fit parameters $\mathbf{b}^i$ and the recovered parameters $\mathbf{Q}^i\mathbf{c}$. In doing so, we implicitly recover the surface shape represented by the coupled model parameters.

Suppose that $\mathbf{t}^i$ is a centered vector of length $M \times N$ that represents an intensity image of a face. Its best fit parameter vector, $\mathbf{b}^i$, is calculated using Equation 9. We fit the model to data seeking the vector $\mathbf{c}$ of length $S + T$ that satisfies the condition

$$\mathbf{c} = \arg\min_{\mathbf{c}} \{(\mathbf{b}^i - \mathbf{Q}^i\mathbf{c})^T(\mathbf{b}^i - \mathbf{Q}^i\mathbf{c})\} \tag{18}$$

The corresponding best fit vector of surface shape values is given by

$$\mathbf{t}^h \approx \bar{\mathbf{h}} + \mathbf{M}^h\mathbf{C}^h\mathbf{c} \tag{19}$$

We used a Matlab implementation of the quasi-Newton minimization procedure to solve Equation 18. The fit was constrained such that each coupled parameter lies within ± 3 standard deviations from the mean. One input image took around a couple of seconds to converge to the best solution.

4 Experiments

In this section we report experiments focused on using out-of-training-sample images to evaluate the ability of the coupled model to recover accurate surface information. The face database used for building the models was provided by the Max-Planck Institute for Biological Cybernetics in Tuebingen, Germany [14]. This database was constructed using Laser scans of heads of young adults, and provides head structure data in a cylindrical representation. For constructing the 3D based models, we converted the cylindrical coordinates to Cartesian coordinates and solved for height values. We were also provided with the intensity maps for each 3D face.

We constructed our models using 90 examples. We used 90 out-of-training-sample examples for surface reconstruction tests. We calculated the fractional height difference error $||Ground\_truth - Recovered\_surface||/Ground\_truth$ as an average over the 90 surfaces and over all points on the surfaces. For the purposes of analysis, we ordered the out-of-training-samples examples according to their distance from the mean intensity image $\bar{\mathbf{i}}$. We used the sum of the first ten values of $\mathbf{b}^i$ (to account for at least 50% of the variability), i.e., $\sum_{j=1}^{10} b_j^i$ as a similarity measure. We test how well the coupled model performs using the 90 out-of-training-sample intensity images as input. We compare the recovered surfaces with the ground truth surface height data. In Figure 1 we plot the fractional height difference. The results were ordered according to ascending error for ease of visual comparison. The average surface recovery error was 1.19%. We also calculated the average error from every out-of-training example to the mean height shape, which was 1.71%.

Next, we turn out our attention to real world images. The first set of images used is drawn from the Yale B database [15] and is disjoint from the data used to train the statistical models. In the images, the faces are in frontal pose and were illuminated by

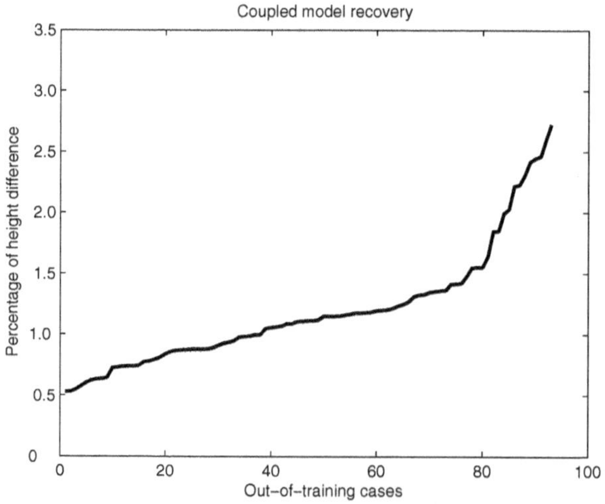

Fig. 1. Plot of the fractional height difference between ground-truth and recovered surface when using the 90 out-of-training intensity images as input

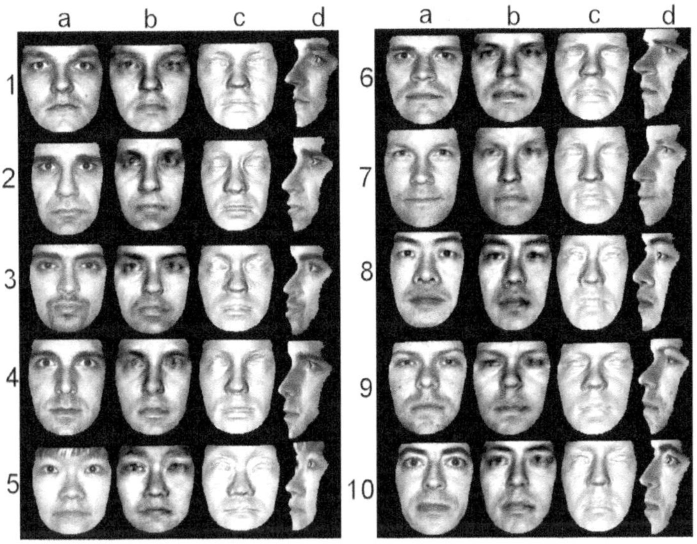

Fig. 2. Experiments with frontal images of 10 individuals of the Yale B database. The figure is divided into two panels, each of which contains five of the ten subjects in the database. In the figure, the rows are labeled with numbers and present the different subjects. The input image, intensity best-fit recovery, frontal illumination of the recovered height and profile view with warped input image are shown column-wise, for each panel.

a point light source situated approximately in the viewer direction. We aligned each image with the mean intensity shape so that the eyes, nose tip and mouth center were in the same position. The surface recovery results using the coupled model are shown in Figure 2. The figure is divided into two panels, with five subjects on the left and five on the right. The result for the different subjects are shown in different rows. From left-to-right in each row we show the input image, the best-fit recovered intensity image, a frontal illumination of the recovered surface height and a profile view of texture mapping the input input image onto the recovered surface. There are a number of features to note from the figure. First, the reconstructed images agree well with the input. Second, the overall shape of the profile view is subjectively convincing.

In Figure 3 we present another set of real world images. In the figure, the columns are labeled with numbers to identify the different subjects. The photographs were taken under uncontrolled lighting conditions. Also, the resolution of the photographs of subjects 3 and 5 was half the size of the one used for training. Note that we did not perform alignment operations to the mean intensity image. The top row of the figure shows the input image, while the bottom row shows the intensity best fit recovery. The intensity best fit recovery results are noisier than those obtained using the Yale database. Only subject 1 achieved a visually convincing reconstruction. The noise can be explained as consequence of not performing alignment operations as well as lower quality resolution.

The artifacts present in the bottom row of Figure 3 occur especially around the mouth and nose regions of the face. This effect may be sufficient to distort the recovered height

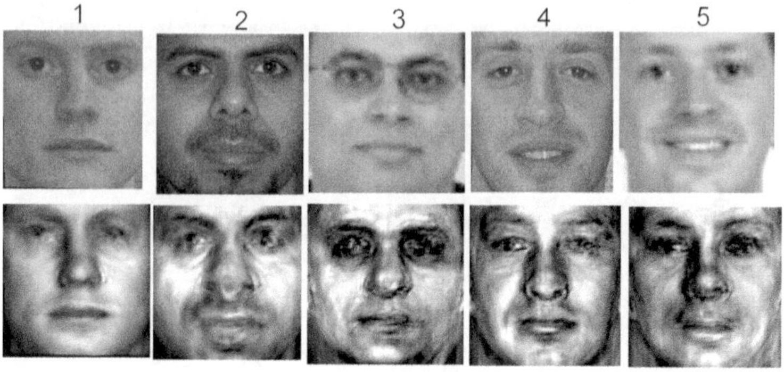

Fig. 3. Experiments with photographs taken under uncontrolled lighting conditions. Top row: input images. Bottom row: best fit recovery from the intensity model.

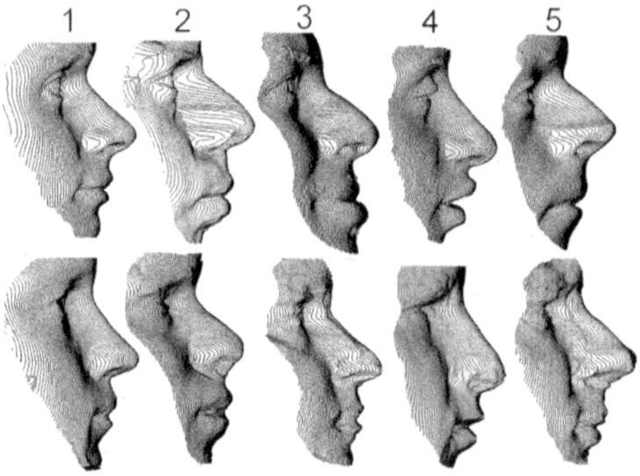

Fig. 4. Surface reconstruction comparison. Top row: ground truth surface. Bottom row: recovered surface using the coupled model.

surface, as we can verify in Figure 4, where we show profile views of the ground truth surfaces (top row) together with profile views of the recovered surfaces using the coupled model (bottom row). The ground truth surfaces of the subjects were acquired with a Cyberware laser scanner. Note that the input photographs are not aligned to the ground truth surfaces, therefore they exhibit slightly different poses and expressions. For this reason we did not perform height difference tests for the experiments on this set of images. A visual examination of both the recovered and the ground truth profiles reveals interesting features. First, the surface recovery of subject 1 presents the best agreement with the ground truth. This is a consequence of the good quality of its best fit intensity recovery. Second, the overall reconstructed facial shape is similar to the ground truth, specially in the nose and mouth shape. The area around the eyes seems to be the most difficult to recover.

Finally, in Figure 5 we present re-illumination experiments on the recovered surfaces for the five subjects. The light source direction makes an angle of -45 and $+45$ degrees to the image normal in the horizontal (x) direction for rows 1 and 2, respectively. In

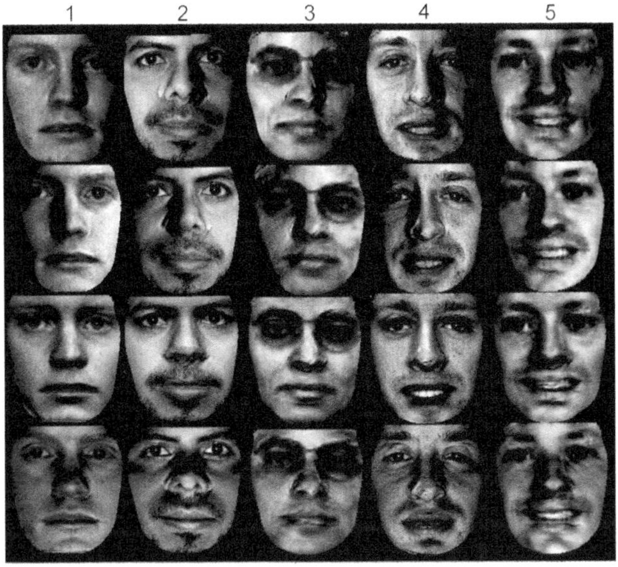

Fig. 5. Experiments on re-illuminating the recovered surfaces The different columns show different subjects. The light source direction makes an angle of -45 and $+45$ degrees in the horizontal (x) direction for rows 1 and 2 respectively. Similarly, the light source is moved in the vertical (y) direction, in rows 3 and 4.

rows 3 and 4, the light source is moved in the same manner in the vertical (y) direction. From the figure we can note that, despite the instabilities around the nose, mouth and eyes, the re-illuminations seem to be in accordance with the overall face structure.

5 Conclusions

We have proposed the use of coupled statistical models of 3D face shape and intensity in order to obtain facial surface approximation from photographs. The coupled model strongly links the best-fit coefficients for intensity and height data into a single statistical model. To recover the parameters of the coupled model, and hence reconstruct height shape, requires an optimization method whose objective function relies on the best-fit intensity parameters. Depending on the quality of the best-fit intensity recovery, the coupled model can be good enough to generate accurate surfaces from intensity imagery in an efficient way.

References

1. H. E. Bors, A.G. and R. Wilson, "Terrain analysis using radar shape-from-shading," *IEEE Trans, on Pattern Analysis and Machine Intelligence*, vol. 25, no. 5, 2003.
2. R. Frankot and R. Chellapa, "A method for enforcing integrability in shape from shading algorithms," *IEEE Transactions on Pattern Analysis and Machine Intelligence*, vol. 10, pp. 438–451, 1988.

3. Z. Wu and L. Li, "A line integration based method for depth recovery from surface normals," *CVGIP*, vol. 43, no. 1, pp. 53–66, 1988.
4. W. Zhao and R. Chellapa, "Illumination-insensitive face recognition using symmetric shape-from-shading," in *Proc. Conference on Computer Vision and Pattern Recognition*, 2000, pp. 286–293.
5. D. Samaras and D. Metaxas, "Incorporating illumination constraints in deformable models for shape and light direction estimation," *IEEE Trans. PAMI*, vol. 25, no. 2, pp. 247–264, 2003.
6. M. Castelán and E. Hancock, "Acquiring height maps of faces from a single image," in *Proc. IEEE 3DPVT*, 2004, pp. 183–190.
7. C. F. Prados, E. and O. Faugeras, "A unifying and rigorous shape from shading method adapted to realistic data and applications," *Journal of Mathematical Imaging and Vision*, 2006.
8. G. P. Atick, J. and N. Redlich, "Statistical approach to shape from shading: Reconstruction of three-dimensional face surfaces from single two-dimensional images," *Neural Computation*, vol. 8, pp. 1321–1340, 1996.
9. R. Dovgard and R. Basri, "Statistical symmetric shape from shading for 3d structure recovery of faces," in *Proc. European Conference on Computer Vision*, May 2004, pp. 99–113.
10. V. Blanz and T. Vetter, "Face recognition based on fitting a 3d morphable model," *IEEE Trans. Pattern Anal. Mach. Intell.*, vol. 25, no. 9, pp. 1063–1074, 2003.
11. E. G. Cootes, T.F. and C. Taylor, "Active appearance models," in *Proc. European Conference in Computer Vision*, 1998, pp. 484–498.
12. M. Turk and A. Pentland, "Face recognition using eigenfaces," in *Proc. IEEE Conference on Computer Vision and Pattern Recognition*, 1991, pp. 586–591.
13. L. Sirovich and R. Everson, "Management and analysis of large scientific datasets," *The International Journal of Supercomputer Applications*, vol. 6, no. 1, pp. 50–68, 1992.
14. V. Blanz and T. Vetter, "A morphable model for the synthesis of 3d faces," in *SIGGRAPH '99: Proceedings of the 26th annual conference on Computer graphics and interactive techniques*. New York, NY, USA: ACM Press/Addison-Wesley Publishing Co., 1999, pp. 187–194.
15. B. D. Georghiades, A. and D. Kriegman, "From few to many: Illumination cone models for face recognition under variable lighting and pose," *IEEE Transactions on Pattern Analysis and Machine Intelligence*, pp. 634–660, 2001.

A Comparative Study of Face Representations in the Frequency Domain

Eduardo Garea Llano[1], Josef Kittler[2], Kieron Messer[2], and Heydi Mendez Vazquez[1]

[1] Advanced Technology Application Center. 7ma, No. 21812, Siboney, Playa, Cuba, 12200
{egarea, hmendez}@cenatav.co.cu
[2] Centre for Vision Speech and Signal Processing, University of Surrey, GU 7HX, UK
{j.kittler, k.messer}@eim.surrey.ac.uk

Abstract. The variation of illumination of an object can produce large changes in the image plane, significantly impairing the performance of face verification algorithms. In this paper we present a comparison of several face representation methods from the point of view of their sensibility to illumination changes. The sensibility is measured in term of the overlap of distribution of normalized correlations for inter class and intra class image comparison. We compared a combination of differentiated image in the frequency domain and the performance of Fourier parameters to obtain an illumination insensitive representation. The result suggests, that better illumination invariance could be achieve in feature spaces developed for a differentiated image rather than using the original input image.

1 Introduction

A number of algorithms [1-4] have been proposed for the face recognition problem, to compensate for illumination changes. In general the variations between images of different faces are smaller than that of the same face taken in a variety of environments. External factors such as pose and illumination can cause different conditions and significant changes in the image plane. It has been shown that illumination causes larger variation in face images than pose [2]. The importance of illumination is further illustrated by examination of the eigenface method [5]. Belhumeur improved the accuracy of a recognition system based on eigenfaces, by removing the first three principal components [4].

In recent years many appearance-based algorithms have been proposed to deal with the problem [7-10]. Belhumeur showed [7], that the set of images of an object in fixed pose but under varying illumination forms a convex cone in the space of images. This method requires a large amount of training data, but Lee showed that the subspace could be generated using only nine images captured under a particular set of illumination conditions [10] Recognition is carried out by finding the distance of the probe image to the illumination cone. These algorithms work well, but are computationally expensive.

Wei and Lai [11] showed that the facial edge feature is an important cue for face recognition and is less sensitive to illumination changes. Barnabas [12] used the Hausdorff distance between the facial edge maps for face recognition. Gao and Leung

J.F. Martínez-Trinidad et al. (Eds.): CIARP 2006, LNCS 4225, pp. 99 – 108, 2006.

[13] furthermore encode the edge map (LEM) by a polygonal line fitting process and computed the similarity of two LEMs with a line segment Hausdorff distance. Savvides [14] showed that modeling the complex phase spectrum in the frequency domain produces a face representation that is tolerant to illumination variations, and also can automatically handle occlusions (i.e. missing features) without any special pre-processing.

In this paper we exploit the fact that although the actual intensity value at each image point is affected by illumination changes, the local differences are much more stable. We propose a novel representation in the frequency domain which is derived from a complex input image with the real and imaginary parts defined by the x and y derivatives of the original image. The sensitivity to illumination is compared with that of the original image and features from the Fourier spectrum.

The contrast XM2VTS database [15] and the Yale B face database [16] are used in the experiments. The images in the XM2VTS database were captured in a controlled environment in which illumination variations are minimized in one set of images but accentuated across another set.

The Yale B database contains images under widely varying illumination conditions and poses of ten subjects. Tests were carried out using the frontal pose set of images with varying illumination

We show that the Real Part of the Fourier transform from differentiated complex image yield the most consistent results across all experimental combinations and can be used as an illumination insensitive representation for face verification.

In the next section, we describe the four representations used in the comparative study. Section 3 details the experimental procedures to obtain and compare the representations. The results of the experiments are presented in Section 4 and we conclude in Section 5.

2 Representations

In this section we describe four face representations that will be compared to identify the most illumination insensitive. They are defined in the frequency domain (magnitude, phase angle, real part and imaginary part) computed from differentiated face images forming a complex input image.

2.1 Fourier Transform

The Fourier transform produces a representation of a signal, in term of a weighted sum of complex exponentials. The defining formulas for the forward Fourier and the inverse Fourier transforms are as follows. Given an image a its forward discrete Fourier transform A is defined as

$$A(\Omega,\Psi) = \sum_{m=-\infty}^{+\infty} \sum_{n=-\infty}^{+\infty} a[m,n] e^{-j(\Omega m+\Psi n)} \tag{1}$$

and vice versa, its inverse as

$$a[m,n] = \frac{1}{4\pi^2} \int_{-\pi}^{+\pi}\int_{-\pi}^{+\pi} A(\Omega,\Psi) e^{+j(\Omega m+\Psi n)} d\Omega d\Psi \quad (2)$$

The Fourier spectrum is the complex function of the real frequency variables and it can be represented by in its real and imaginary parts. Alternatively we can represent it by its magnitude and phase as:

$$A(\Omega,\Psi) = |A(\Omega,\Psi)| e^{j\varphi(\Omega,\Psi)} \quad (3)$$

Where $|A(\Omega,\Psi)|$ is the magnitude and (Ω,Ψ) is the phase corresponding to frequency pair $\varphi(\Omega,\Psi)$.

2.2 Derivatives of Image

Illumination is a low frequency phenomenon the effect of which can be suppressed by differentiation.

In computer vision, image differentiation is traditionally implemented by convolving the signal with some form of linear filter, usually a filter that approximates a first or second derivative operator. An odd symmetric filter will approximate a first derivative.

The gradient of the image is a vector with the derivatives in x and y directions as its components, i.e.

$$\Delta_x(x,y) = \frac{a(x+d_x, y) - a(x,y)}{dx}$$
$$\Delta y(x,y) = \frac{a(x+d_y + y) - a(x,y)}{dy} \quad (4)$$

Rather than in a vector form it is convenient to represent the derivatives in x and y directions as a complex image

$$g(x,y) = \Delta_x(x,y) + j\Delta_y(x,y) \quad (5)$$

3 Experimental Methods

The basic idea of the proposed experimental method is shown in Fig. 1. The principal representation scheme consists in the combination of the elements that we described above. We use the complex first derivative image to highlight frequency content and, then transform it to the frequency domain and determine its characteristics. These characteristics computed for a pair of images will be compared using normalized correlation defined as:

$$Nc = \frac{\sum_i \sum_j (w(i,j) w_1(i,j))}{\sqrt{\sum_i \sum_j w(i,j)^2 \sum_i \sum_j w_1(i,j)^2}} \tag{6}$$

Where the first image is w(i,j), the second image is w_1(i,j). The idea is to measure how their similarity is affected by illumination changes. Normalized correlation has been chosen as it has proved to be a successful similarity measure in face recognition. For identical images it takes the maximum value equal to unity. Examples of generated representations by principal scheme are shown in Fig 2.

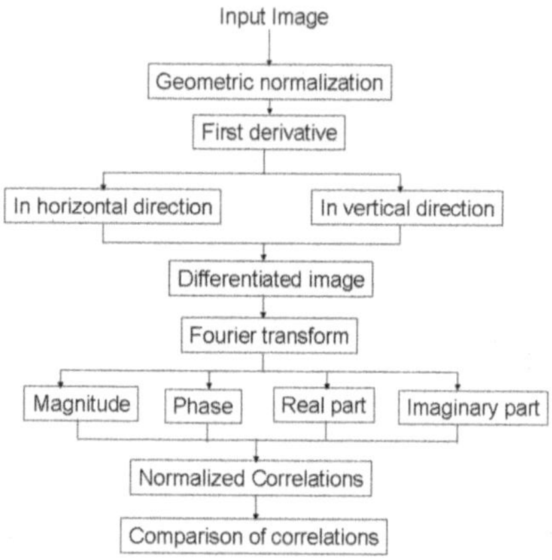

Fig. 1. The flow diagram of the principal proposed experimental method

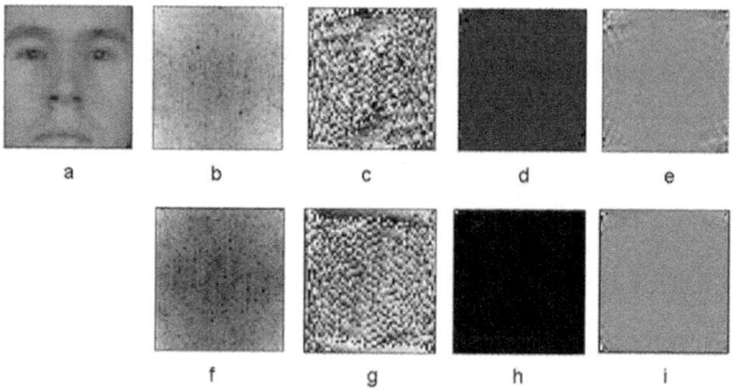

Fig. 2. Image Representations used in the comparative study: a)Geometric normalized input image, b)Magnitude, c)Phase, d)Real part, e) Imaginary part of the frequency spectrum of the differentiated image. f)Magnitude, g)Phase, h)Real part, i) Imaginary part of the frequency spectrum of the input image.

In the second representation scheme the objective is to transform the input image to the frequency domain directly and determine its characteristics.

The third experimental scheme is very simple. It directly involves the original input images geometrically normalized as in the first and second experimental schemes.

3.1 Geometric Normalization Algorithm

The geometric normalization used consists of the following steps: Smoothing, rotating, scaling and resampling the input image. The smoothing is performed by convolution with a Gaussian Filter of size5x5.

The rotation operation is designed to ensure that the line connecting the centres of the two eyes is parallel to the x- axis. The image scaling and resampling scaling outputs an image of size 55 rows x 51 columns. The left-eye is mapped onto the pixel position (19, 38) and the right-eye is mapped onto the pixel position (19, 12), Fig. 3.

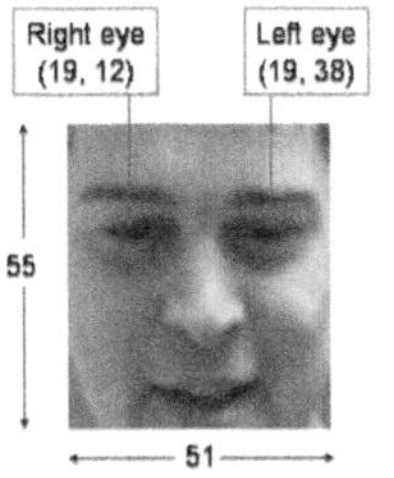

Fig. 3. Geometric normalized image

For a thorough evaluation of the proposed representations, we calculated and compared the normalized correlations using images from the XM2VTS database and Yale B database.

3.2 The XM2VTS Database

For a thorough evaluation of the proposed method, we calculated and compared the normalized correlations using images from the XM2VTS database (Fig. 4).

The XM2VTS database contains images of 295 subjects captured over 4 sessions in a controlled uniformly illuminated environment and with illumination from left and right over 2 sessions. The database uses a standard protocol [15].

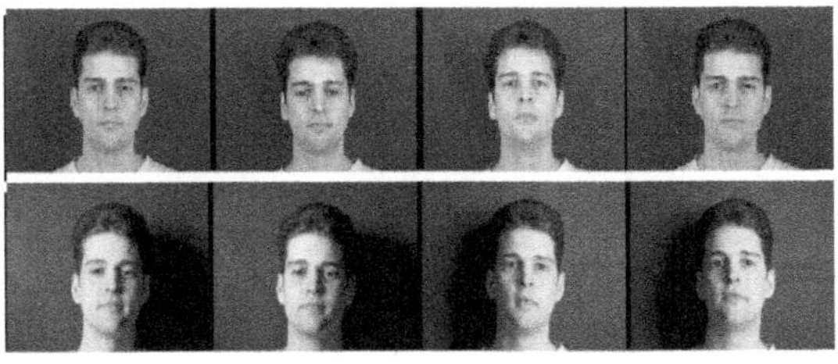

Fig. 4. Examples of the XM2VTS database: Normal illuminated (top), Illuminated from left and right (bottom)

We also used a derivative database obtained by photometric normalization of images of the XM2VTS. The images were normalized using the anisotropic smoothing method [17].

3.3 The Yale B Database

The Yale B database contains 64 different illumination conditions for 10 subjects. The illumination conditions are a single light source, the position of which varies horizontally (from -130°to 130°) and vertically (from –40° to 65°).We take 4 images per each subject with different illumination condition and we also used a derivative database obtained by photometric normalization of one image per person in the Yale B database. The images were normalized using the anisotropic smoothing method [17] (Fig.5).

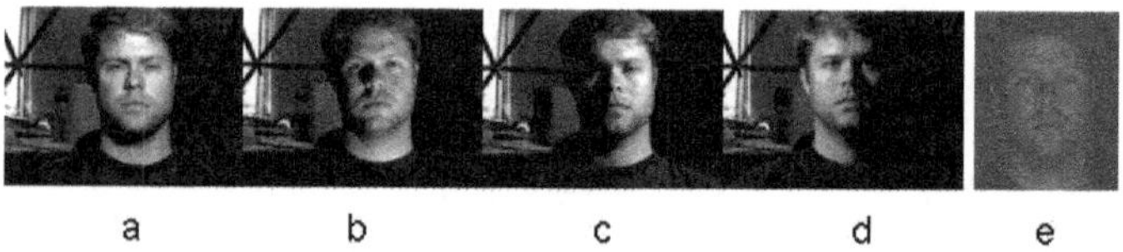

Fig. 5. Examples of the Yale B database: a,b,c,d., illuminated images from above, below, right and left respectively; e, photometrically normalized image

3.4 Comparison of Normalized Correlations

In the XM2VTS database the normalized correlations were compared in two different combinations for each database

- A: 295 subjects of the XM2VTS database against the same subjects using different images for each subject
- B: 295 subjects of the XM2VTS database against 294 different subjects using different images for each subject.

Correlations were carried out among normal illuminated, illuminated from right and left, and photometric normalized images from XM2VTS database to verify in many different conditions the results of comparisons.

In the YaleB database the normalized correlations were compared in two different combinations.

- A: 64 subjects of the Yale B database against the same subjects using different images for each subject
- B: 64 subjects of the Yale B database against 63 different subjects using different images for each subject.

Correlations were carried out among, illuminated from right, left, above and below, and photometric normalized images to verify in different conditions the results of comparisons.

In table 1 we show the different variants of normalized correlations and its comparison.

4 Experimental Results

This section presents a summary of the results of the comparison of the proposed representations by the experimental schemes described.

First, the results of comparisons 1, 2 and 3 from Table 1 are presented in Table 2. We can see that the real part and imaginary part obtained by principal representation scheme are the best spectral properties that reflect the similarity between different images of the same subject and the dissimilarity between images of different subjects taken under controlled illumination conditions of XM2VTS database. The original image in this case best reflects the similarity under controlled normal illumination conditions.

Results on the Yale B database shows that the real part obtained by the principal experimental scheme is consistent representation with high correlation coefficients between images of the same subject taken in different illumination conditions and photometrically normalized.

The second experiment relates to the comparisons 4 and 5 from Table 1. The results are shown in Table 3. The experiment shows that the real part obtained by the principal experimental scheme is consistent representation with high correlation coefficients between images of the same subject taken in normal condition and images taken in different illumination conditions (Fig. 6) and photometrically normalized in both databases.

Table 1. Comparison of normalized correlations

No	Comparison of correlations	Compared images (XM2VTS database)	Compared images (Yale B database)	Compared representations
1	A vs. B	Normally illuminated vs. normal illuminated (8 by 8 images)	Illuminated from right and left vs. Illuminated from right and left (2 by 2 images)	Principal, Second, Third
2	A vs. B	Illuminated from right and left vs. Illuminated from right and left (4 by 4 images)	Illuminated above and bellow vs. illuminated above and bellow (2 by 2 images)	Principal, Second, Third
3	A vs. B	Normally illuminated vs. illuminated from right and left (8 by 4 images)	Illuminated from right and left vs. illuminated above and bellow (2 by 2 images)	Principal, Second, Third
4	A vs. A	Normally illuminated vs. photometrically normalized (2 by 8) images	Illuminated from right and left vs. photometrically normalized (1 by 2 images)	Principal
5	A vs. A	Illuminated from right and left vs. photometrically normalized (4 by 2 images)	Illuminated above and bellow vs. photometrically normalized (1 by 2 images)	Principal

Table 2. Principal results of comparison between normalized correlations (1,2 and 3; Table 1)

Rp	Par	XM2VTS database				Yale B database			
		Av (A)	Av (B)	overlap %	Dist	Av (A)	Av (B)	overlap %	Dist
Comparison		1				1			
Pr.	Mg	0.69	0.63	81.70	0.06	0.78	0.73	93.58	0.05
	Fi	0.12	0.02	12.88	0.09	0.09	0.04	44.44	0.05
	R	**0.83**	**0.67**	**10.17**	**0.16**	**0.92**	**0.56**	**22.88**	**0.36**
	I	**0.57**	**0.25**	**13.83**	**0.32**	0.52	0.51	95.00	0.01
Sec.	Mg	0.73	0.69	63.73	0.03	0.75	0.70	93.33	0.05
	Fi	0.14	0.04	64.41	0.10	0.13	0.02	58.55	0.11
	R	0.99	0.98	22.03	0.01	0.97	0.95	44.06	0.02
	I	0.63	0.35	20.00	0.27	0.58	0.33	18.51	0.25
Th.	**Or**	**0.76**	**0.40**	**4.40**	**0.36**	0.45	0.34	75.55	0.11
Comparison		2				2			
Pr.	Mg	0.72	0.66	50.84	0.09	0.72	0.66	50.84	0.09
	Fi	0.13	0.03	98.64	0.1	0.13	0.03	98.64	0.1
	R	**0.90**	**0.77**	**20.00**	**0.23**	**0.93**	**0.69**	**20.86**	**0.24**
	I	**0.75**	**0.32**	**19.15**	**0.43**	0.69	0.63	91.30	0.06
Sec.	Mg	0.80	0.75	58.64	0.07	0.82	0.73	75.39	0.09
	Fi	0.21	0.07	85.42	0.14	0.17	0.08	54.41	0.09
	R	0.99	0.98	61.69	0.01	0.95	0.93	71.56	0.02
	I	0.96	0.89	67.00	0.07	0.93	0.78	69.00	0.15
Th.	Or	0.89	0.82	64.00	0.07	0.85	0.77	73.14	0.08
Comparison		3				3			
Pr.	Mg	0.68	0.65	86.39	0.04	0.63	0.58	85.50	0.05
	Fi	0.12	0.05	57.82	0.05	0.10	0.03	56.79	0.07
	R	**0.82**	**0.63**	**32.24**	**0.19**	**0.90**	**0.65**	**31.35**	**0.25**
	I	0.57	0.48	58.50	0.09	0.53	0.45	57.45	0.08
Sec.	Mg	0.78	0.67	68.00	0.11	0.81	0.69	67.58	0.12
	Fi	0.25	0.03	12.00	0.22	0.15	0.08	40.00	0.08
	R	0.99	0.99	100.00	0.00	0.97	0.93	75.00	0.04
	I	0.70	0.55	56.32	0.15	0.68	0.62	65.52	0.06
Th.	Or	0.60	0.62	55.00	0.02	0.57	0.53	53.65	0.04

Table 3. Result of comparisons between normalized correlations (4 and 5, Table 1)

Par	XM2VTS database		Yale B database	
	Av(A)	Av(A)	Av(A)	Av(A)
Comparison	4		4	
Mg	0.63	0.67	0.56	0.58
Fi	0.09	0.18	0.11	0.16
R	**0.71**	**0.79**	**0.85**	**0.89**
I	0.46	0.61	0.51	0.63
Comparison	5		5	
Mg	0.56	0.57	0.63	0.67
Fi	0.12	0.13	0.08	0.11
R	**0.81**	**0.83**	**0.92**	**0.96**
I	0.43	0.64	0.45	0.67

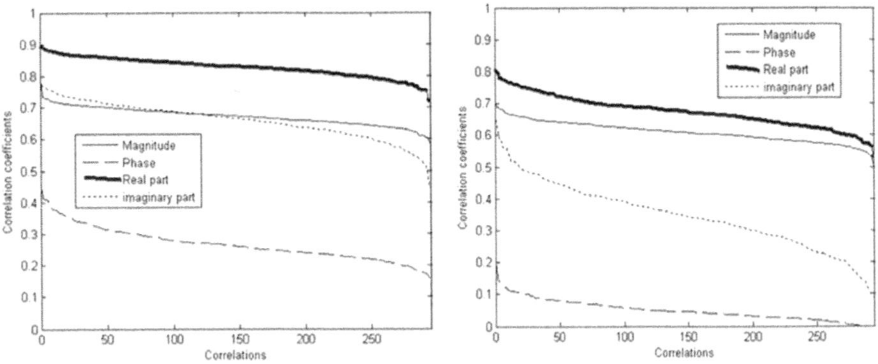

Fig. 6. Results of normalized correlation A (left) and B(right) using normally illuminated and illuminated images from right and left in the XM2VTS database by principal experimental scheme

5 Conclusions

We proposed a novel face image representation in the frequency domain which is derived from a complex input image with the real and imaginary parts defined by the x and y derivatives of the original image. The experimental results show that the real part obtained by the proposed experimental scheme is the most consistent representation with high correlation coefficients between images of the same subject taken in normal condition and images taken in different illumination conditions.

In tables 2 and 3: Mg- Magnitude, Fi- Phase, R-Real part, I- Imaginary part, Or: original image, Pr, Sec. and Th.: Principal, Second and Third representation schemes respectively, Av(A), Av(B): mean of correlation coefficients, overlap%: Percent of overlapping of compared correlations, Distance: Difference between Av(A) and Av(B).

References

1. Acton, S.: Multigrid Anisotropic Diffusion. IEEE Trans. Image Processing, vol. 7, 1998
2. Adini, Y., Moses, Y. and Ullman, S.: Face recognition: the problem of compensating for illumination changes. IEEE Trans. Pattern Anal. Mach. Intelligence, pp721– 732, (1997)
3. Bailly-Bailliere, E.: The BANCA Database and Evaluation Protocol AVBPA, (2003)
4. Belhumeur, P.,. Hespanha, J., Kriegman, D.: Eigenfaces vs. Fisherfaces: Recognition using Class Speci.c Linear Projection. IEEE Trans. Pattern Anal. Mach. Intelligence, vol. 19, pp711-720, (1997).
5. Turk, M., Pentland, A.: Eigenfaces for Recognition. J. Congitive Neuroscience, vol. 3, pp 71-86, (1991)
6. Belhumeur, P., Hespanha, J.P: Eigenfaces vs. Fisherfaces: Recognition using class speci_c linear projection. IEEE PAMI 19, 711-720, (1997)
7. Belhumeur, P., D. Kriegman,: What is the set of images of an object under all possible lighting conditions. Int. J. of Computer Vision 28, 245-260(1998)

8. Georghiades, A., Kriegman, D., Belhumeur, P.: From few to many: Generative models for recognition under variable pose and illumination. IEEE PAMI (2001)
9. Riklin-Raviv, T.,., Shashua, A.: The Quotient image: class-based re-rendering and recognition with varying illumination conditions. In: IEEE PAMI. (2001)
10. Lee, K., Ho, J., Kriegman, D.: 9 Points of Light: Aquiring Subspaces for Face Recognition Under Variable Lighting IEEE Proc. Conf. Computer Vision and Pattern Recognition, (2001).
11. Shou Der Wei and Shang-Hong Lai: Robust Face Recognition under lightinng Variations, Proc. Conf on Pattern Recognition IEE (2004).
12. Barnamas, T.: Comparing face images using the modified Hausdorff distance. Pattern Recognition. Vol. 31, No.12 pp. 1873-1881, (1991).
13. Gao, Y., Leung, K.: Face recognition using line edge map. IEEE Trans. Pattern Analysis Mach. Intel., Vol. 24, No. 6 pp. 764-779, (2002).
14. Savvides, M., Vijaya Kumar, BVK.and Khosla, P.K.: Eigenphases vs. Eigenfaces Proc. Conf on Pattern Recognition, IEEE (2004).
15. Luettin, J. and Maitre, G.: Evaluation Protocol for the XM2FDB Database, (IDIAP, 1998).
16. The Yale Face Database, URL: http://cvc.yale.edu/projects/yalefaces/yalefaces.html.
17. Short, J., Kittler, J. and Messer, K.: A comparison of photometric normalization algorithms for face verification, AVBPA 2005: 617-626, (2004)

Face Recognition with Region Division and Spin Images

Yang Li, William A.P. Smith, and Edwin R. Hancock

Department of Computer Science, University of York, York, YO10 5DD, UK

Abstract. This paper explores how spin images can be constructed using shape-from-shading information and used for the purposes of face recognition. We commence by extracting needle-maps from gray-scale images of faces, using a mean needle-map to enforce the correct pattern of facial convexity and concavity. Spin images [4] are estimated from the needle maps using local spherical geometry to approximate the facial surface. Our representation is based on the spin image histograms for an arrangement of image patches. We demonstrate how this representation can be used to perform face recognition across different subjects and illumination conditions. Experiments show the method to be reliable and accurate, and the recognition precision reaches 98% on CMU PIE sub- database.

1 Introduction

Face recognition is an active research area that has been approached in many ways. Roughly speaking the alternative methods can be divided in two categories. The first of these is the feature-based method, while the second is the model-based method. Recently, it is the model-based method that has attracted the greatest attention [2]. Here one on the most important recent developments is the work of Blanz and Vetter [3]. In this work a 3-D morphable model matched to face data using correspondences delivered by optic flow information. The method gives recognition rates of about 80% when profiles are used to recognise frontal poses. However, the construction of the model requires manually marking feature points, which is labour intensive. Hence, the automatic construction of models remains an imperative in face recognition. There are related feature-based approaches which are based on the assumption that face images are the result of Lambertian reflectance. Under this assumption 3D linear subspaces can be constructed that account for facial appearance under fixed viewpoint but under different illumination [9,1,7].

In this paper we aim to develop a feature based method for face recognition that can be used to recognise faces using surface shape information inferred from image brightness using a Lambertian shape-from-shading scheme. Shape-from-shading is not widely accepted as a technique for face recognition. The reason is that the surface normal is commonly believed to be noisy and is unstable under changes in illumination direction or change of pose. However, recently it has been shown that shape-from-shading can be used to extract useful features from real world face images [8].

One of the problems that hinders the extraction of reliable facial topography using shape-from-shading is the concave/convex inversions that arise due to the bas-relief ambiguity. A recent paper [8] have shown how this problem can be overcome using a statistical model for admissible surface normal variations trained on range data. Here

J.F. Martínez-Trinidad et al. (Eds.): CIARP 2006, LNCS 4225, pp. 109–117, 2006.

we use a simplified version of this algorithm. The surface normals are constrained to fall on the Lambertian reflectance with axis in the light source direction and apex angle given by the inverse cosine of the normalised image brightness. The position of the surface normal on the cone is such that it minimizes the distance to the corresponding mean surface normal direction.

To construct a surface representation from the surface normals, we turn to the spin image first developed by Johnson and Hebert [4]. A spin image is a series of histograms constructed from the polar coordinates of arbitrary reference points on a surface. The representation can capture fine topographic surface detail. Unfortunately, the computational overheads associated with the method are high, since a histogram needs to be generated for each surface location. Moreover, the original spin image representation was developed for range images and hence relies on surface height rather than surface normal information. We demonstrate how these two problems can be overcome by computing local spin images on image patches using surface normal information.

2 Mean Needle Map Alignment

The shape-from-shading algorithm used to extract needle-maps from brightness images is as follows. We follow the work in [10] and place the surface normal on a cone whose axis is the light source direction and whose opening angle is the inverse cosine of the normalised image brightness.

This initial field of surface normals typically contains errors, and in particular locations where the pattern of convexity or concavity is reversed. To overcome this problem we draw on a model that accounts for the distribution of surface normals across ground-truth facial surfaces. To construct this model we use a sample of range images of human faces. From the gradients of the surface height data, we make estimates of surface normal direction. The resulting fields of surface normals are adjusted so that that the faces have the same overall centering, scale and orientation. At each location we compute the mean surface normal direction over the set of training images. Here we use the Max-Planck data-base which has 200 sample images of male and female subjects.

We use the mean facial needle-map to adjust the positions of the surface normals on the reflectance cones. Each initial surface normal is rotated on its cone so that it minimises the angle subtended with the mean surface normal at the corresponding image location.

$$f(x,y) = argmin(tan(\theta_r(x,y) - \theta_{mean}(x,y))) \tag{1}$$

where θ_r and θ_{mean} are the azimuth angles of the aligned surface normal n_r and the mean surface normal n_{mean} on the surface point (x, y).

The simplest way to satisfy 1 is to adjust the azimuth angle of the aligned surface normal n_r so that n_r becomes parallel to n_{mean}.

In Fig. 3 we illustrate the improvements gained using this simple shape-from-shading procedure. In the top row of the figure we show the input images of a single subject with the light source in different directions. In the second row we show the initial estimates of the surface normal directions. Here we have visualised the needle-maps by taking the inner product of the surface normal with the light-source vector perpendicular to the image plane. This is equivalent to re-illuminating the field of surface normals with frontal Lambertian reflectance. From the images in the second row it is clear that there are significant concave/convex inversions in the proximity of the nose and lips when the face is illuminated obliquely. In the third row of the figure we show the field of surface normals that result from the adjustment procedure described above. The re-illuminations reveal that the inversions are removed and the quality of the recovered facial topography is improved (Fig. 4 illustrates the solution of this inversion problem).

3 The Spin Image Approach

The spin image of Johnson and Hebert [4] aims to construct an object-centered representation. The representation consists of a series of 2D histograms and is constructed in the following manner: Commence by selecting an arbitrary point on the surface as the reference point O, and $\vec{n_o}$ is the surface normal at the point O. Then select a second arbitrary point P on the surface, and $\vec{n_p}$ is the surface normal at the point P . Assume the object resides in a 3D coordinate system with the surface normal $\vec{n_o}$ as z axis and the xy plane perpendicular to $\vec{n_o}$. The Euclidean distance $\gamma = \mid \vec{OP} \mid$ can be projected onto the xy plane as α and the z axis as β respectively. After the distances α and β of all the surface points are calculated, we can use them to construct a 2D histogram. The above procedure is performed after each point on the surface has been taken as the point P so that a single 2D histogram is constructed, and then a series of 2D histograms are constructed using the above steps and taking each point on the surface as the reference point O. Figure 1 illustrates the spin image construction. Equation 2 shows the structure of the spin image, in which N is the number of image surface points and n is the number of histogram bins.

$$
\begin{array}{cc}
O_1 & O_2 \\
\begin{bmatrix} a_{11} & a_{12} & \cdots & a_{1n} \\ a_{21} & a_{22} & \cdots & a_{2n} \\ \vdots & & & \vdots \\ a_{n1} & a_{n2} & \cdots & a_{nn} \end{bmatrix} &
\begin{bmatrix} a_{11} & a_{12} & \cdots & a_{1n} \\ a_{21} & a_{22} & \cdots & a_{2n} \\ \vdots & & & \vdots \\ a_{n1} & a_{n2} & \cdots & a_{nn} \end{bmatrix} \\
\cdots & O_N \\
\cdots &
\begin{bmatrix} a_{11} & a_{12} & \cdots & a_{1n} \\ a_{21} & a_{22} & \cdots & a_{2n} \\ \vdots & & & \vdots \\ a_{n1} & a_{n2} & \cdots & a_{nn} \end{bmatrix}
\end{array}
\tag{2}
$$

This object-centered representation is invariant to translation and rotation since the spin image is calculated using only relative distances between object surface points.

The spin image representation is based on the availability of surface height data and can not be applied directly to fields of surface normals or needle maps. Moreover, the spin image histograms need to be constructed at each image location, and this is computationally demanding in both time and storage. In order to obtain this object-centered representation for an object with n surface points/image pixels, the computation cost will be $O(n^2)$.

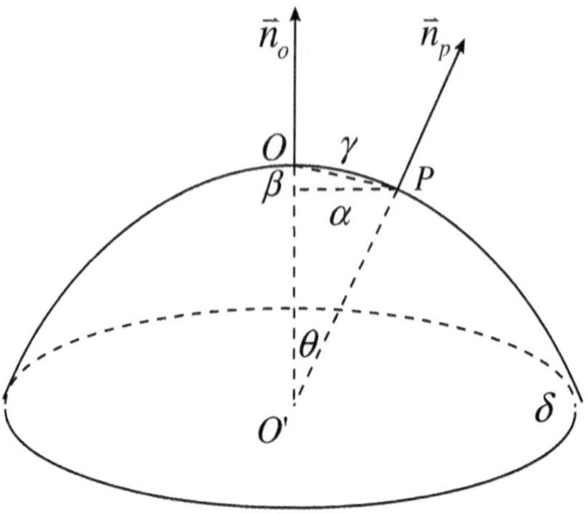

Fig. 1. Illustration of spin image construction

4 Adapting Spin Images to Needle-Maps

We have adapted a patch based approach to spin-image representation. We segment the surface into patches and for each patch we use only the geometric center point O to construct the spin image, rather than use every point of this surface as in the original spin image approach. Our histograms are constructed on a patch-by-patch basis.

From the GGFI [6] we obtain a surface height $\left|\overrightarrow{OP'}\right|$ in the viewing direction $\vec{n_v}$. The surface height $\left|\overrightarrow{OP'}\right|$ and the horizontal distance $\left|\overrightarrow{P'P}\right|$ can not be used to construct the spin image because they are based on the viewing direction. What we need is the surface height and the horizontal distance based on the surface normal $\vec{n_o}$ direction.

To compute these quantities we proceed as follows. From the surface height $\left|\overrightarrow{OP'}\right|$, the distance $\left|\overrightarrow{OP}\right|$ is easy to compute since the distance $\left|\overrightarrow{PP'}\right|$ on the viewing plane can be directly measured from the 2D image. From Fig. 2, we are interested in the distance α, i.e. $\left|\overrightarrow{PP''}\right|$, on the surface normal plane δ and the relative height β, i.e. $\left|\overrightarrow{OP''}\right|$, in the surface normal direction $\vec{n_o}$ between the reference point O and the arbitrary point P. The quantities are related by the following equations:

$$\overrightarrow{OP}=\overrightarrow{OP'}+\overrightarrow{P'P} \tag{3}$$

$$\overrightarrow{P''O}=(\overrightarrow{OP}\cdot\vec{n_o})\times\vec{n_o} \tag{4}$$

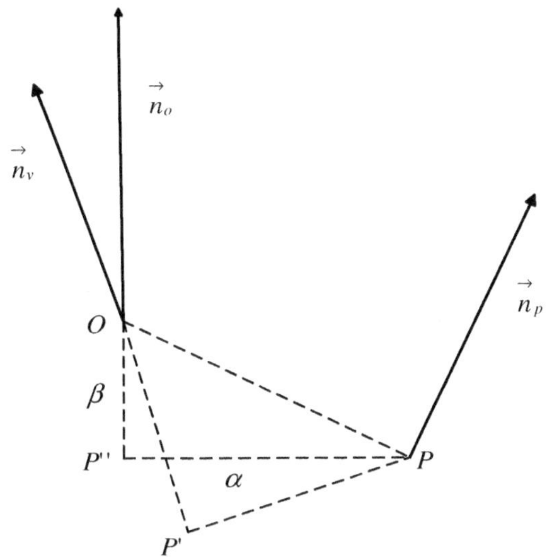

Fig. 2. Illustration of how to obtain the distance α and the relative height β

$$\overrightarrow{P''P} = \overrightarrow{P''O} + \overrightarrow{OP} \tag{5}$$

We now have all the ingredients to construct the 2D histogram of α and β for the surface patch centered at the point O. Equation 6 shows the structure of the patch based spin image, in which M is the number of surface patches and n is the number of histogram bins.

$$\begin{matrix} O_1 & O_2 \\ \begin{bmatrix} a_{11} & a_{12} & \dots & a_{1n} \\ a_{21} & a_{22} & \dots & a_{2n} \\ \vdots & & \vdots & \\ a_{n1} & a_{n2} & \dots & a_{nn} \end{bmatrix} & \begin{bmatrix} a_{11} & a_{12} & \dots & a_{1n} \\ a_{21} & a_{22} & \dots & a_{2n} \\ \vdots & & \vdots & \\ a_{n1} & a_{n2} & \dots & a_{nn} \end{bmatrix} \\ \dots & O_M \\ \dots & \begin{bmatrix} a_{11} & a_{12} & \dots & a_{1n} \\ a_{21} & a_{22} & \dots & a_{2n} \\ \vdots & & \vdots & \\ a_{n1} & a_{n2} & \dots & a_{nn} \end{bmatrix} \end{matrix} \tag{6}$$

In our experiment we construct a 10 by 10 bin 2D histograms of α and β for an image patch of 32 by 32 pixels. The histogram is also normalised so as to be scale invariant.

As an additional step, we have performed PCA on the spin image histograms to reduce the dimensionality of the data. The idea is as follows. We normalise the contents of each spin image histogram to unity. The normalised bin contents of the histograms are concatenated as a long-vector as follows.

$$\begin{bmatrix} \{O_1 : a_{11}\}, \{O_1 : a_{12}\}, \ldots, \{O_1 : a_{1n}\}, \ldots, \\ \{O_1 : a_{n1}\}, \{O_1 : a_{n2}\}, \ldots, \{O_1 : a_{nn}\}, \\ \{O_2 : a_{11}\}, \{O_2 : a_{12}\}, \ldots, \{O_2 : a_{1n}\}, \ldots, \\ \{O_2 : a_{n1}\}, \{O_2 : a_{n2}\}, \ldots, \{O_2 : a_{nn}\}, \\ \ldots, \\ \{O_M : a_{11}\}, \{O_M : a_{12}\}, \ldots, \{O_M : a_{1n}\}, \ldots, \\ \{O_M : a_{n1}\}, \{O_M : a_{n2}\}, \ldots, \{O_M : a_{nn}\} \end{bmatrix} \tag{7}$$

Dimensionality reduction is effected by projecting the long-vector onto the leading eigenvectors of the long-vector covariance matrix.

In the adaptation of spin image on surface normal, the computation cost is reduced to $O(n)$ instead of $O(n^2)$ in the original approach.

5 Recognition

In our preprocessing of the images to extract needle-maps, we perform alignment. This means that we can apply a patch template to the extracted needle-maps to decompose the face into regions. The patch template is constructed from the mean facial needle map, and consists of regions that are either wholly concave or wholly convex. The convexity/concavity test is made using the sign of the changes in surface normal direction. By performing the spin image analysis on these regions, we avoid problems associated with inflexion points when the approximations outlined in Sect. 2 are employed.

As an alternative to constructing the template from the mean needle-map, we have explored constructing it from the needle map extracted from each facial image.

Our measure of facial similarity is based on the normalised correlation of the spin-image histograms for corresponding template patches.

Johnson and Hebert use normalised correlation to evaluate spin image similarity[4]. The method assumes that spin-images from proximal points on the surface for different views of an object will be linearly related. This is because the number of points that fall into corresponding bins will be similar (given that the distribution of points over the surface of the objects is the same). In our case, this assumption still holds. We hence use normalised correlation to compare the patch-based spin images. The correlation is given by

$$r_{xy} = \frac{n \sum x_i y_i - \sum x_i \sum y_i}{\sqrt{(n \sum x_i^2 - (\sum x_i)^2)(n \sum y_i^2 - (\sum y_i)^2)}} \tag{8}$$

where r_{xy} is the correlation of two spin images x and y. n is the bin number of the spin image, x_i and y_i is the bin contents of two spin images respectively.

$$r_{sum} = \sum_{i=1}^{min(M,N)} r_{m_i n_i} \tag{9}$$

6 Experiments

We apply our method to the CMU PIE face database. We use cropped frontal-viewed face images (without background) in this paper. The sub-database contains $67 \times 7 = 469$ (67 subjects (1-67) and 7 lights (3,10,7,8,9,13,16)) images. We apply the two different patch segmentation strategies outlined above.

For the 7 images of the same subject illuminated by different lights, we use 3 for training sets and 4 for testing. To perform recognition for the 67 subjects, we select a probe image from the test set and the closest image in the training set. The results of our experiments are summarised using the precision-recall curves shown in Fig. 5. The star-dotted curve shows the result of patch-based similarity, the circle-dotted curve shows the result of comparing the vectors extracted using PCA and the cross-dotted curve shows the result of using a global histogram of curvature attributes extracted from the needle-maps [5]. The best results are obtained by applying PCA to the spin image histograms.

In Table 1 we compare the recognition results obtained using the spin-image and applying PCA to the spin image long-vectors. Performance is improved using PCA, and this can be ascribed to the fact that PCA effectively discards the histogram bins that are associated with insignificant variance.

Please notice the face component performance is obtained by only comparing the similarity of a single face component (eye, nose, mouth, etc.) instead of the whole face, so the recognition rate will be reasonably low and can only be used to compare the performance of two methods.

Table 1. Recognition performance using the spin image and the dimension-reduced spin image vector

	Spin Image	Spin Image Vector
Face Components	27.81%	29.69%
Whole Face	87.50%	98.75%

In Table 2 we show the effect of applying the different shape-representations to the initial needle maps and the adjusted needle maps obtained using the mean needle map. In each case there is a significant improvement.

Table 2. Recognition performance using the surface normal aligned to mean needle map and and the original surface normal

	Original	MNMA
Global Histogram	47.50%	62.50%
Spin Image	85.00%	87.5%
Spin Image Vector	95.00%	98.75%

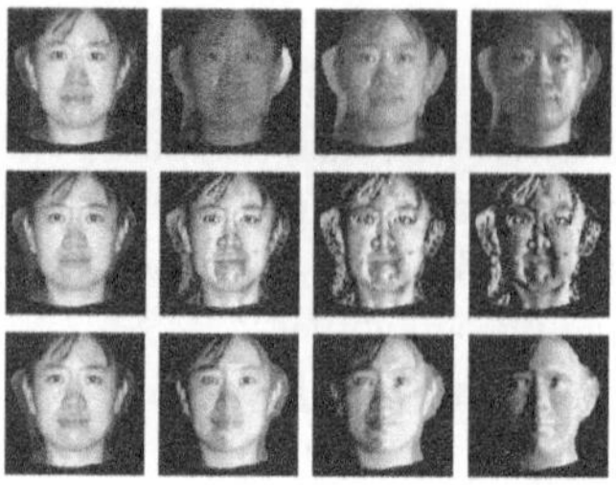

Fig. 3. The images in the first row are real images illuminated by the light sources from different directions. The images in the second row are the original needle maps rendered by the light source different from the real one [10]. The images in the third row are the needle maps after Mean Needle Map Alignment (Sect. 2) rendered by the light source different from the real one. The images in the third row are more photo-realistic and carry less noise than the ones in the second row.

Fig. 4. The first image is the original needle map projected to the x direction of the viewing plane. The second image is the mean needle map that we use as the template. The third image is the needle map projected to the x direction of the viewing plane after the Mean Needle Map Alignment (Sect. 2). The third image compensate the concave/convex problem of the first one.

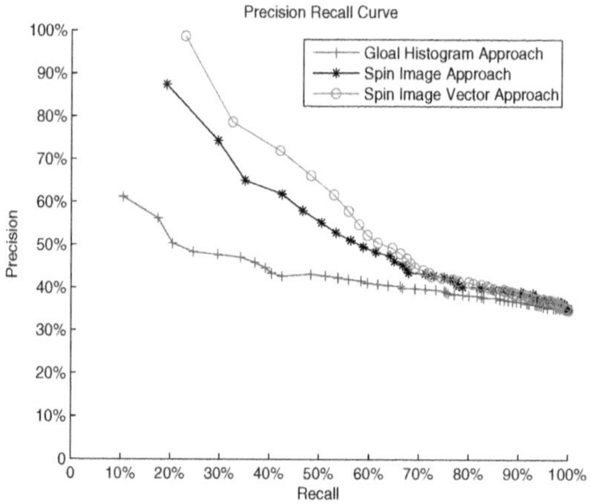

Fig. 5. There are three precision-recall curves of different approaches in this figure: the basic patch-based spin image approach, the spin image vector approach and the previous global histogram approach [5]. All these results are based on the surface normal processed by the Mean Needle Map Alignment because that approach has been proved improving the distinguishing ability in Table 2. Among them the spin image vector approach gives the best performance.

7 Conclusion and Future Work

In this paper we have explored how spin images can can extracted from 2D facial images using shape-from-shading. We make a number of contributions. First, we show how the spin-image histograms can be computed from needle-maps. Second, we show how the complexity of the spin image computation can be reduced using patches, and how the dimensionality of the histograms can be reduced using PCA. Third, we show how the problems of concave/convex inversions in the needle map can be overcome using a mean facial needle-map. The performance of the method is encouraging and can give recognition rates as high as 98.75%.

References

1. P. Belhumeur and D. Kriegman. What is the set of images of an object under all possible illumination conditions? *International Journal of Computer Vision*, 28(3):245–260, 1998.
2. Blanz. Automatic face identification system using flexible appearance models. *IVC*, 13(5):393–401, June 1995.
3. V. Blanz and T. Vetter. Face recognition based on fitting a 3d morphable model. *IEEE Transactions on Pattern Analysis and Machine Intelligence*, 25(9):1063–1074, 2003.
4. A. E. Johnson and M. Hebert. Using spin images for efficient object recognition in cluttered 3d scenes. *IEEE Transactions on Pattern Analysis and Machine Intelligence*, 21(5):433–449, 1999.
5. Y. Li and E. Hancock. Face recognition using shading-based curvature attributes.
6. R.T.Frankot and Z.Chellappa. A method for enforcing integrability in shape from shading algorithms. *IEEE Transactions in Pattern Recognition and Machine Intelligence*, 10:439–451, 1988.
7. T. Sim and T. Kanade. Combining models and exemplars for face recognition: An illuminating example. In *Proceedings of the CVPR 2001 Workshop on Models versus Exemplars in Computer Vision*, December 2001.
8. W. Smith and E. R. Hancock. Recovering facial shape and albedo using a statistical model of surface normal direction. In *Proc. ICCV*, pages 588–595, 2005.
9. M. Turk and A. Pentland. Face recognition using eigenfaces. 1991.
10. P. L. Worthington and E. R. Hancock. New constraints on data-closeness and needle map consistency for shape-from-shaping. *IEEE Transactions on Pattern Analysis and Machine Intelligence*, 21(12):1250–1267, 1999.

Extraction of Blood Vessels in Ophthalmic Color Images of Human Retinas

Edgardo Felipe-Riveron[1] and Noel Garcia-Guimeras[2]

[1] Centre for Computing Research, National Polytechnic Institute,
Juan de Dios Batiz s/n, P.O. 07038, Mexico
[2] Latin American School of Medicine. Havana, Cuba
edgardo@cic.ipn.mx, noelgarciaguimeras@yahoo.com

Abstract. This paper presents a strategy for the extraction of blood vessels from ophthalmoscopic color images of the fundus of human retinas. To extract the vascular network, morphology operators were used, primarily maximum of openings and sum of valleys, and secondly a reconstruction by dilation from two images obtained using threshold by hysteresis. To extract the skeleton of the resulting vascular network, morphological thinning and pruning algorithms were used. Results obtained represent a starting point for future work related to the detection of anomalies in the vascular network and techniques for personal authentication.

Keywords: Blood vessels segmentation, Fundus analysis, Morphology.

1 Introduction

The automatic analysis of human eye fundus images is a task of major importance. The fundamental aim is to help ophthalmologists during the diagnosis of illnesses that present visible affections in the human retina. Some of these illnesses are of concern, because if they are not detected in time, they can lead to blindness. Of particular interest are: glaucoma, diabetic retinopathy, and macular degeneration. Early detection of these conditions is a focus of importance for ophthalmologists.

There are three visible anatomical elements in the fundus of the retina: the macula lutea, the optic disk (or optic papilla), and the vascular network, composed of a thick and dark red vein network, and a thinner arterial network of a clearer reddish tone (Fig. 1).

In order for the ophthalmologist to analyze the retina it is common to induce certain conditions on patients to improve the quality of observation of the eye fundus. To enlarge the observation field the pupils of the patients are dilated; to highlight affections of the retina related with blood, it is common to inject patients with a fluoresceinic substance that makes blood vessels visible with easiness. In this paper we propose a method to detect blood vessels in human retinas from digital ophthalmoscopic color images.

J.F. Martínez-Trinidad et al. (Eds.): CIARP 2006, LNCS 4225, pp. 118 – 126, 2006.

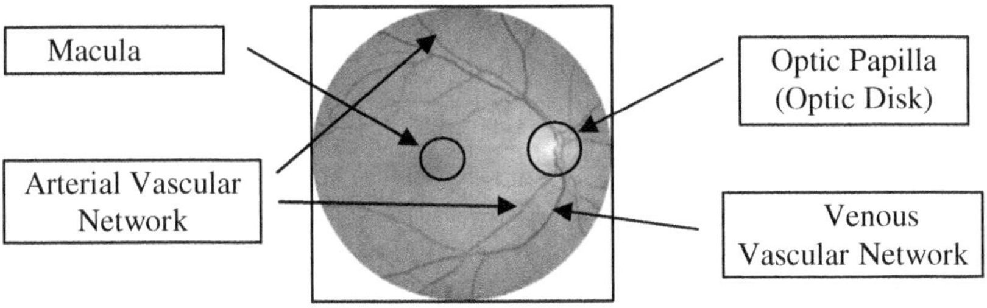

Fig. 1. Anatomic elements of a human eye fundus image

2 The Problem

Our task deals with the extraction of the vascular network from the retina. Due to the normal distribution through the entire retina and the probable non-uniform illumination of the field observed when retina images are captured, this is not a trivial task. Any strategy applied to achieve this purpose should be independent of non-uniform illumination and invariant to translation, rotation, and scale of the images being analyzed.

3 Background

The successful extraction of blood vessels from images of the retina has been treated previously. Filtering by coincidence has being used to separate the blood vessels in eye fundus images [1] [2]. As in their traverse section the blood vessels have the form of an overturned Gauss bell, their segmentation can be carried out by the convolution of images with a Gaussian nucleus. This method used by Chutatape and Zheng [3] is slow because it requires a large Gaussian mask for the convolution, and images need to be rotated several times. Also, the selected mask responds well when it represents the same standard deviation than that of pixels of blood vessels, but it does not respond either for smaller nor bigger blood vessels.

Artificial neural networks have been applied with promising results in the analysis of ophthalmic images [4] [5] [6]. They have demonstrated to be useful, since they can be trained to recognize patterns of blood vessels. In this way it is possible to extract them. A disadvantage of neural networks is that classification is carried out on the basis of statistical methods and logical reasoning.

Algorithms for tracking blood vessels have been used to segment them between two given points [7]. These algorithms work at the level of a single blood vessel and not of the whole vascular network. Usually, while moving through the blood vessel, these algorithms calculate their width, which represents an advantage. Other parameters like the width average and the tortuosity of the blood vessel can also be calculated. The main advantage of this method is that it gives quite exact measures and information about individual blood vessels. Unfortunately, they require a starting point and in most case a terminal point, which works against automation of the process.

Image processing by means of morphological methods is particularly effective when it is required to extract components of the image whose shape is known a priori [8]. The vascular network is linear in small portions, which is ideal for morphological processing. Morphological methods have been applied in segmentation of certain types of vascular networks with the intrinsic advantage of being more efficient and more immune to noise than other methods. In particular, this approach has been applied to gray-level angiographic images captured after patients were injected with a fluoresceinic substance that highlights areas containing blood, as is the case with veins and arterial blood vessels of the vascular network [8] [9].

As mentioned earlier, this paper deals with the extraction of the vascular network from color ophthalmoscopic fundus images. These are images obtained without the necessity of invasive procedures.

4 Our Strategy

The method proposed for the extraction of the vascular network is based on methods proposed by Flynn [10], and by Zana and Klein [9]. The main difference with our strategy is that those methods work well for fluoresceinic gray-level images of retina where blood vessels appear with a higher intensity level and have well-defined contours. In this paper, images were captured from patients that did not require any previous invasive preparation, that is, our solution use color images captured directly and transformed to gray level images.

These images typically are corrupted by significant additive noise that causes the image background to have a non homogeneous gray level. We call background in this paper all parts of the image that do not offer useful information related to our task. On the other hand, the background's gray level is not uniform in all areas through which the vascular network appears. In the region of the optic disk and near to it, the background has a clearer tone of gray, while in regions near the macula the background appears darker. In this aspect, factors related to the illumination of images when they are captured, produce more illuminated areas and also areas where it is not possible to distinguish the location of blood vessels (Fig. 2).

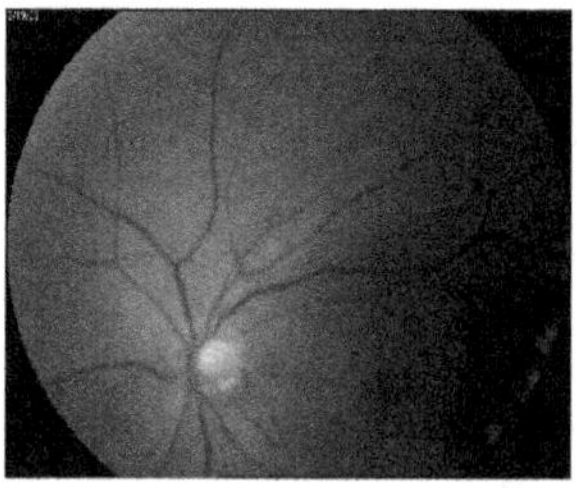

Fig. 2. Human eye fundus image

Generally, blood vessels are darker than the background, although there are areas where the vascular network is not visible because its level is similar to the background. The thickness of blood vessels is variable. In the area near the optic disk, where the two main veins and the two main arteries arise from the choroids through the center of the papilla to the retina, the vascular network is thicker. Other veins and arteries derived from these four are thinner, up to regions where almost they get lost when their thickness is only of one pixel. The last interesting characteristic of the vascular network is its piecewise linear structure. We can say that the vascular network is composed by small linear segments connected to each other [10]. The area near the center of the macula lutea is physiologically avascular.

Before extracting blood vessels images are preprocessed to normalize their size, to reduce additive noise and to enhance the contrast. All images used were obtained from the same source and have a spatial resolution of 300 dpi. Images were normalized to 350 pixels in the longer side.

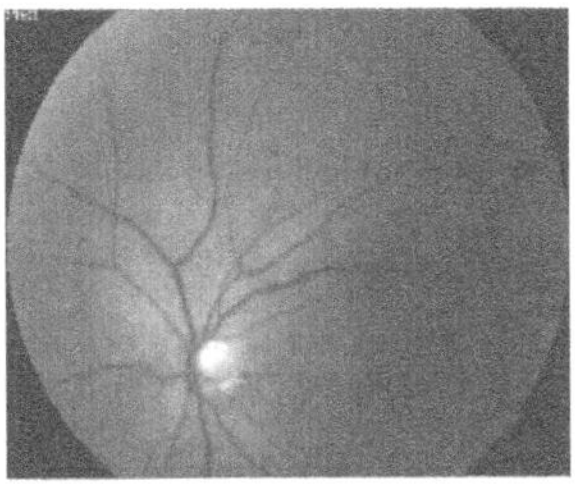

Fig. 3. Gray-level image from the green channel

Experimentally, as the green color is located at the centre of the visible spectrum, it has been observed that from the three-color channels that compose the image in the RGB (Red, Green, and Blue) color model, the green channel offers the higher quantity in information and less additive noise. The red channel still gives some information, and very little the blue channel, in occasions none, but having higher additive noise. Therefore, to avoid the influence of the noise present in these two channels, the conversion of the image to gray levels is based on the information contained in the green channel only (Fig. 3).

Subsequently, a morphological operator proposed by Zana and Klein [8], and Flynn [10] is applied, which diminishes at the same time the additive noise in the background and preserves blood vessels. The operator, called *maximum of openings*, is defined in the following way [12] [13]:

$$I_C = \max_{i=1\ldots16}\{I_0 \circ B_i\}$$

Where I_C is the "cleaned" image, I_0 is the original image, and B_i is a flat structuring element of height h > 0 rotated 16 times. The size of the structuring element (SE) must be chosen in such a way that it preserves the blood vessels and eliminates the additive noise in the image. In our case, we have determined experimentally that 9 pixels length and 5 level unit's height SE gives the best results.

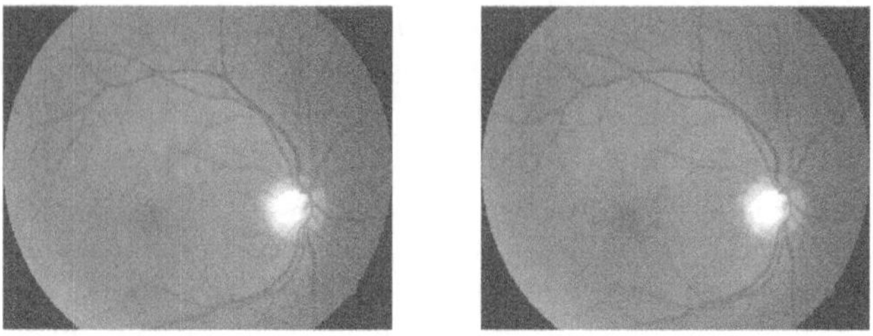

Fig. 4. Effects of the maximum of openings on the background of the image. (a) Original image (green plane). (b) Uniform background, while the structure of the blood vessels is preserved.

Note that after using this filter, the obtained image preserves blood vessels and have a more uniform background (Fig. 4b).

4.1 Primary Detection of the Blood Vessels

Once the image has been preprocessed, a preliminary detection of the blood vessels is carried out. The process is preliminary because in this step some artifacts remain, and have to be eliminated later. The operation is called *sum of valleys* defined as the dual of the operation proposed by Zana and Klein given previously [8]. The resulting image from this operation preserves blood vessels and is sharper, while the background spreads to be black. Figure 5(a) shows an example, in which the intensity has been inverted for clarity.

$$I_{sum} = \sum_{i=1}^{16} BOTHAT(I_C, B_i)$$

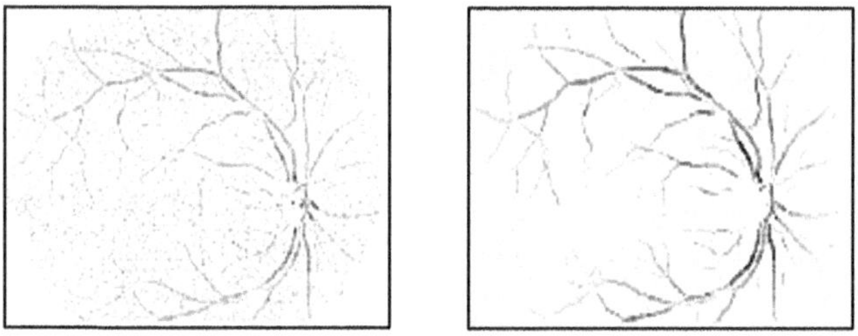

Fig. 5. (a) Image after the operator of sum of valleys is applied. Observe how noise and artifact are conserved in certain regions. (b) Image after suppression of noise and artifacts.

4.2 Extraction of Blood Vessels

The objectives of the next step are to suppress additive noise and artifacts, to preserve the vascular network and to prepare the image for converting it in a binary image.

Again, a maximum of openings is carried out to clean noise and artifacts, and preserve the useful information. The group of structuring elements is formed by a flat linear structure element rotated 16 times. As in previous operations, its longitude depends on the size of the blood vessels in the original image. In our case, two maximum of openings were carried out with structuring elements of different sizes and heights, in order to improve the extraction of the vascular network. Result of one of these maximum of openings is shown in Fig, 5b.

4.3 Thresholding

So far, part of the noise and artifacts still persist in the resulting images. They can be finally eliminated by means of thresholding by hysteresis and a reconstruction by dilation [13]. In this way, when the appropriate thresholds are chosen, the vascular network is isolated. We take advantage of the fact that the additive noise never reaches high gray levels, and that the vascular network is connected. The use of thresholding by hysteresis with an appropriate selection of minimum and maximum thresholds, allows eliminating the noise that still persists in the image, and obtaining a clean image with an isolated vascular network (Fig. 6).

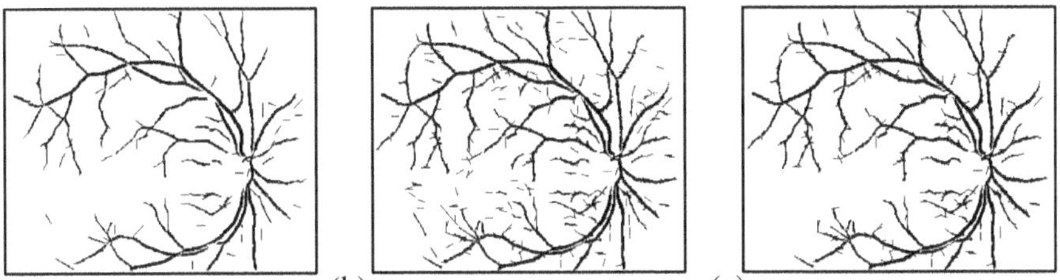

(a) (b) (c)

Fig. 6. (a) Image with threshold in 11. (b) Image with threshold in 6. (c) Image after reconstruction by dilation from previous images.

The image in Fig. 6(a) was obtained with threshold equal to 11. Notice the absence of noise, and that some blood vessels are not connected. This image is the binary mask. Fig. 6(b) shows the image with threshold equal to 6. Here the vascular network is fully connected, although there are also noise and artifacts. This is the binary marker. Figure 6(c) shows the image after being reconstructed by dilation using both the binary mask and the binary marker. Notice how the noise is reduced and the vascular network is now completely connected.

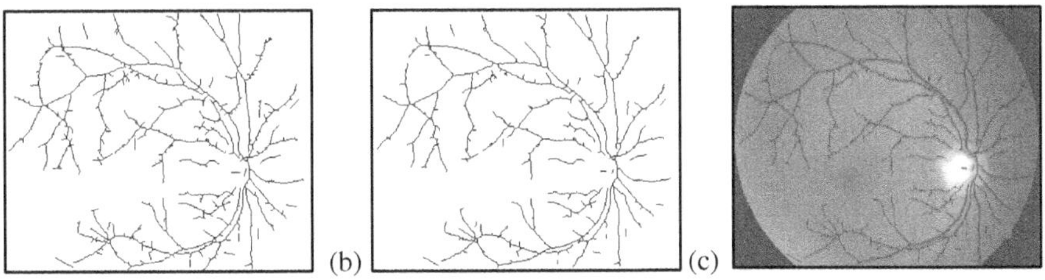

(a) (b) (c)

Fig. 7. (a) Skeleton of final image obtained from the process. (b) After pruning. (c) Segmented vascular network superimposed to the original image.

The skeleton of the vascular network is obtained by means of the morphological operation of thinning. After it, the skeleton is not still smart, because it is common that it presents some non-desirable protuberances, which are eliminated later with several iterations of morphological pruning (Figs. 7a and 7b). In our case, two iterations were enough; finally, Fig. 7c shows the skeleton of the vascular network superimposed to the original image.

5 Discussion of Results

Some problems occurred in the detection of the vascular network due to its relative thickness and length with respect to the characteristics of the SE used. When the vascular network is thicker than the SE, it cannot be detected successfully. It is impossible to achieve a good segmentation if the size of the structuring elements is not adjusted. Generally it is common that all images proceed from the same source, by which once the SE is adjusted it does not present serious problems. In our case, the algorithm was applied to 11 color ophthalmic images with 24 bits/pixel originally, 9 from a Visucam-Lite, Kart Zeiss camera, and 2 from Internet network.

It can happen that once the sizes of structuring elements have been adjusted, there are regions where two blood vessels may be nearly parallel. In this case, they appear like a double cross sized blood vessel, and then a successful segmentation usually is not possible (Figs. 8a and b).

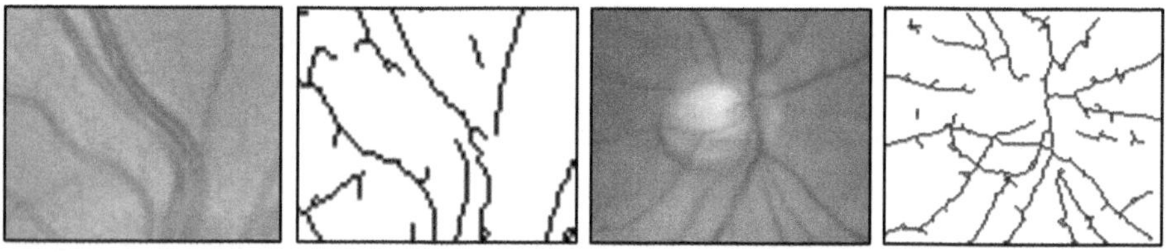

(a) (b) (c) (d)

Fig. 8. (a) Fragment where two blood vessels appear very near. (b) Faulty detection. (c) Image where an area with atrophy is observed in the left inferior border of the optic disk. (d) False detection in this area.

Another problem is the false detection of the border of the optic disk. In a healthy eye this border is presented with a normal transition from clearer to darker shades of gray, and there is no problem. But some atrophy can be present due to glaucoma in the border of the optic disk. In these cases, false detections of the border of the optic disk can occur, as shown in Figs. 8c and 8d. This problem is unavoidable, due to the similar morphology of the blood vessels and the border of the optic disk.

We note that our results presented thus far were obtained without contrast enhancement. That was one of our objectives in order to process images as they were captured.

Osareh, Mirmehdi et al. have obtained good results with preprocessing steps related mainly to color normalization and contrast enhancement of retinal color images, using Fuzzy C-means clustering in the automatic recognition of exudative maculopathies [14].

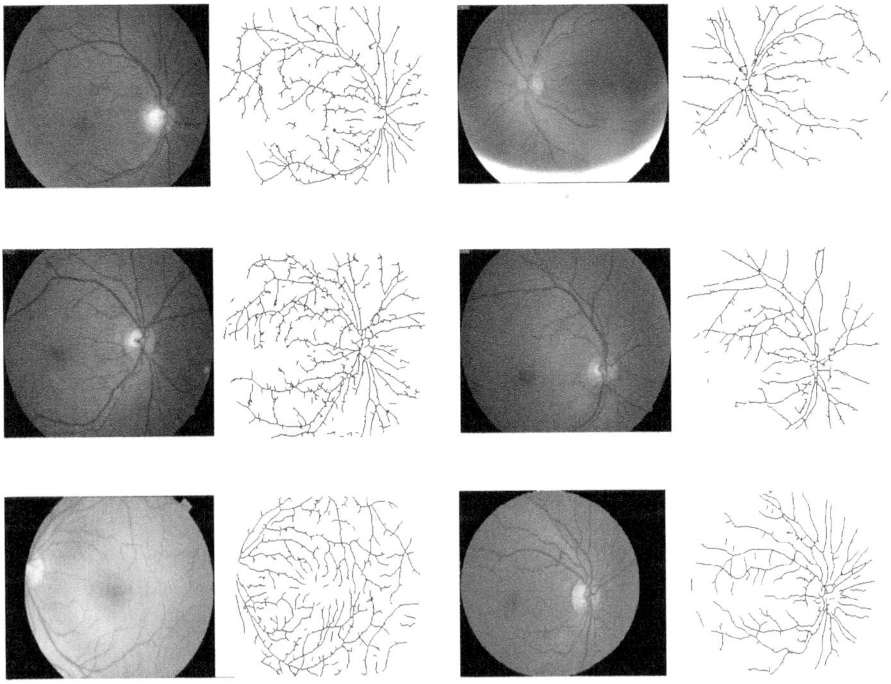

Fig. 9. Original images (left). The skeleton of the vascular network (right). Figures from (a) to (d) are real images. Figures (e) and (f) show images from Internet.

6 Conclusions

In this paper we implemented an algorithm for extracting the blood vessels from real color ophthalmoscopic images of the fundus of the human retina, using morphological methods. Images processed were captured in color without any previous bloody preparation of the patients with fluoresceinic substances to highlight the vascular network. The solution was based on two types of operators: maximum of openings and sum of valleys. The algorithm shows a favorable answer in the detection of blood vessels, although the presence of noise can affect the detection in some degree. The extraction is finally achieved using a reconstruction by dilation of two binary images obtained with two different thresholds. The skeleton was finally obtained by thinning and pruning the extracted vascular network.

Acknowledgements

The authors would like to thank the National Polytechnic Institute (Academic Secretary, COFAA, SIP, and the Centre for Computing Research), for their economical support to develop this work.

References

1. Chaudhury, S., Chatterjee, S., Katz, N., Nelson, M., Goldbaum, M.: Detection of blood vessels in retinal images using two-dimensional matched filters, IEEE Transactions on medical imaging, Vol. 8, No. 3 (1989)
2. Hoover, A., Kouznetsova, V., Goldbaum, M.: Locating blood vessels in retinal images by piecewise threshold probing of matched filter response. IEEE Transactions on Medical Imaging, Vol. 19, No. 3 (2000)
3. Chutatape, O., Zheng, L., Krishnan, S. M.: Retinal blood vessel detection and tracking by matched gaussian and Kalman filters. Proceedings in the 20th Annual International Conference of the IEEE, Engineering in Medicine and Biology Society, Vol. 20, No. 6 (1998)
4. Gardner, G. G., Keating, D., Williamson, T.H., Elliot, A. T.: Automatic detection of diabetic retinopathy using an artificial neural network: a screening tool. British Journal of Ophthalmology (1996)
5. Undrill, P.: Towards the automatic interpretation of retinal images, British Journal of Ophthalmology, 80, 973 (1996)
6. Zana, F., Klein, J. C.: A multimodal algorithm of eye fundus images using vessel detection and Hough transform, IEEE Transactions on Medical Imaging. Vol. 18, No. 5 (1999)
7. Zhoue, I., Rzeszotarski, M., Singerman, L., Cokreff, J.: The detection and quantification of retinopathy using digital angiograms, IEEE Transactions on Medical Imaging, Vol. 13, No. 4 (1994)
8. Zana, F., Klein, J. C.: Robust segmentation of vessels from retinal angiography, Proceedings of the International Conference on Digital Signal Processing, Santorini, Greece (1997)
9. Zana, F., Klein, J. C.: Segmentation of vessel-like patterns using mathematical morphology and curvature evaluation. IEEE Transactions on Image Processing, Vol. 10, No. 7 (2001)
10. Flynn, J.: Automated vessel extraction in digital ophthalmic images.
11. Gang, L., Chutatape, O., Krishnan, S. M.: Detection and measurement of retinal vessels in fundus images using amplitude modified second-order gaussian filter. IEEE Transactions on Biomedical Engineering, Vol. 49, No. 2 (2002)
12. Gonzalez, R., Woods, R. E.: Digital Image Processing, Addison-Wesley, Imington, Delaware, USA (1996)
13. Soille P.: Morphological Image Analysis. Principles and Applications, Springer Verlag, Berlin (1999)
14. Osareh, A., Mirmehdi, M., Thomas, B., Markham, R.: Automatic Recognition of Exudative Maculopathy using Fuzzy C-Means Clustering and Neural Networks. Medical Image Understanding and Analysis (2001) 49-52

A Fast Adaboosting Based Method for Iris and Pupil Contour Detection

Francisco Silva Mata, Eduardo Garea Llano, Estela María Álvarez Morales, and José Luís Gil Rodríguez

Advanced Technology Application Center. 7ma, No. 21812, Siboney, Playa, Cuba 12200
{fjsilva, egarea, ealvarez, jlgil}@cenatav.co.cu

Abstract. The iris localization plays a fundamental role in the recognition process because the speed and performance of the iris recognition system largely depends on the quality of the pupil and iris detection. This process includes the detection of inner (pupil) and outer (iris) boundaries. In this paper we present a new method for iris and pupil boundaries detection based on Adaboosting technique for localization of circular objects and an algorithm based on the elements of analytic geometry, in particular, the determination of the bounded circumference of a tangential square that encloses the pupil and iris. The proposed approach overcomes the limitations that had previous methods regarding the use of images obtained under not controlled conditions like specular light reflected in the pupil or in the iris. We experimented our approach comparing the results in detection with the results obtained by Daugman algorithm using images from two contrasting databases, CASIA and UBIRIS.

1 Introduction

Recognition using the iris texture has been an active investigation field in last years; it has been considered the better phenotypic feature in human face that determines its identity and offers biometric feature acquisition without invasion. Recognition of a person by iris constitutes one of the main applications of the biometrics at present time. The first step in the recognition process is the automatic iris localization. The human eye iris is characterized by a circular or quasi circular form limited by two borders (iris inner border and outer). The iris inner border coincides with the contour of the eye's pupil and the iris outer border establishes the contact iris-sclera (Fig.1). A number of algorithms have been proposed for automatic iris contour detection to obtain both, the iris inner and outer border parameters in order to isolate the iris texture information. [1-7]. The limitations of these algorithms are the fact that they were thought for working using images taken under well controlled illumination conditions [8] where of the specular light reflected in the pupil or in the iris does not represent a problem. The high computational cost is another of their limitations.

In this paper we present a method based on Viola and Johns algorithms [9] that localized the pupil and iris circles. The results of this process are the localization of

J.F. Martínez-Trinidad et al. (Eds.): CIARP 2006, LNCS 4225, pp. 127 – 136, 2006.

the iris inner and outer border enclosed in a tangential to border square. The next step is to draw the circle enclosed in the detected square that describes the iris and pupil borders. We experimented our approach using images from UBIRIS database that incorporates images with several noise factors, thus permitting the evaluation of robustness iris recognition methodologies and compared the results with those obtained using images taken in well controlled environment of CASIA database.

2 Automatic Detection of Tangential Square to Pupil and Iris Borders

Detection of tangential square to pupil and iris borders is achieved through the algorithm of Viola and Johns [9], implemented in the OpenCV library [10]. The advantages that this algorithm offers are several: The image representation called integral image, which allows a very quickly computation of the features used by the detectors. The learning algorithm is based on the Stump-based 24x24 Gentle Adaboost, which lets the selection of a small number of features from the initial set and to obtain efficient classifiers. This method combines classifiers increasingly in a cascade of simple classifiers for discriminate particular features [9].

We trained two cascade detectors, the first devoted to detect the pupil circle (inner contour) with or without specular light reflection, and the second devoted to detect the iris circle detection (outer contour) with or without specular light reflection.

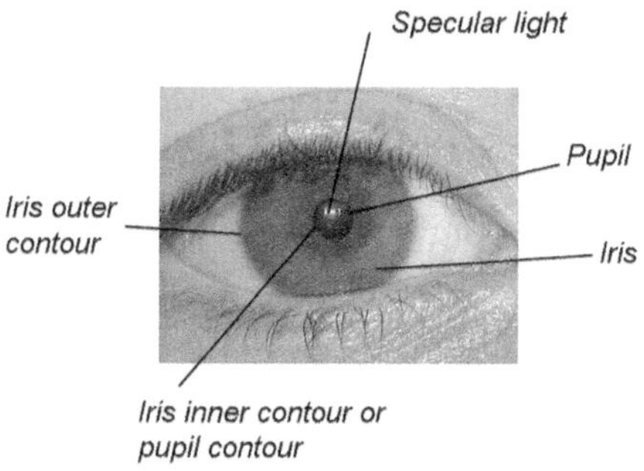

Fig. 1. Circular form of the Iris and pupil

2.1 Training Process

The iris training set consisted of 100 labeled pupil and 100 labeled iris images taken from the UBIRIS and CASIA databases. The region training set was manually prepared by means of the selection of the rectangular regions, and then these samples were saved and rescaled all to a size of 24 x 24 pixels. (Fig. 2). In the training phase, the classifier was exhaustively trained using these sets of regions by the cascade detectors in a wide variety of training images.

2.2 Description of the Automatic Detection Process

The process begins with the pupil border detection by means of the cascade detector specialized in the pupil detection with specular light reflection or without it (1). As a result, the coordinates of the tangential square that contains the pupil are obtained. A second cascade detector is triggered to look for the iris circle, as in the previous step we obtain the coordinates of the tangential square that contains the iris (2).

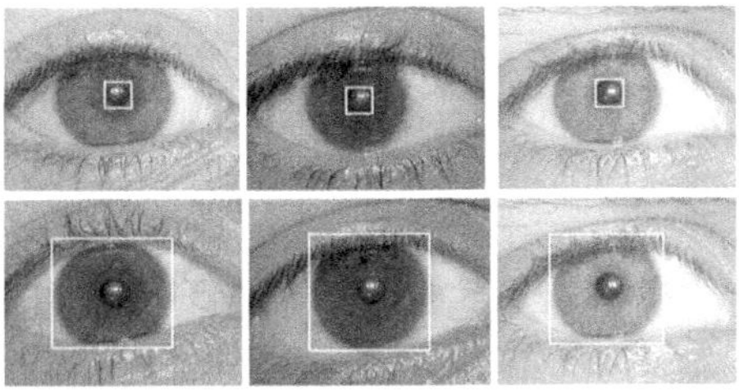

Fig. 2. Region selection for iris training samples in the UBIRIS database

3 Approximation of Pupil and Iris Contour to a Circle Inscribed in a Square

The iris inner contour coincides with the external pupil boundary. Since it is assumed that the pupil and iris possess circular form, the parameters that should be obtained are, the pupil centre coordinates and its radio. To solve this task the algorithm of tangential square circle was designed.

The general idea is very simple, beginning with an automatic localized tangential square; we will calculate the radius of the circumference and the centre of the square that is the centre of the pupil or iris. With the centre and the radius we draw a bounded circumference to the square. The calculated circumference is the pupil or iris contour.

The steps for the proposed approximation are as follows:

***Step1*:** Find the radius of the circumferences

The radius of the circumferences is calculated by expressions:

$$r_{p,i} = \frac{mx_{p,i} - nx_{p,i}}{2} = \frac{my_{p,i} - ny_{p,i}}{2} \tag{1}$$

Where $nx_{p,i}$ and $mx_{p,i}$ are the extreme coordinates of the horizontal or vertical side of the square for the pupil*(p)* and iris*(i)*. (Fig. 3)

***Step 2*:** Find the centres of the tangential squares.

The centres of the squares $C_p(x_p,y_p)$ and $C_i(x_i,y_i)$are calculated by expressions :

$$x_{p,i} = nx_{p,i} + r_{p,i}$$
$$y_{p,i} = ny_{p,i} + r_{p,i} \tag{2}$$

Where $x_{p,i}$ and $y_{p,i}$ are the horizontal and vertical coordinates of the square centres of the pupil *(p)* and iris *(i)* respectively (Fig. 4). The mean centre $[C_m(x_m,y_m)]$ of the eye is calculated by the expression:

$$x_m = \frac{x_p + x_i}{2} \qquad y_m = \frac{y_p + y_i}{2} \tag{3}$$

***Step 3*:** With the circumference parameters we automatically draw the bounded circumference to the square that is the pupil *(p)* or iris *(i)* contour by expression.

$$x_{p,i} = r_{p,i}.\cos\theta,\ y_{p,i} = r_{p,i}.sen\theta \tag{4}$$

Where $x_{p,i}$ and $y_{p,i}$ are the coordinates of the circumferential sector inner and outer borders of the texture codification area.

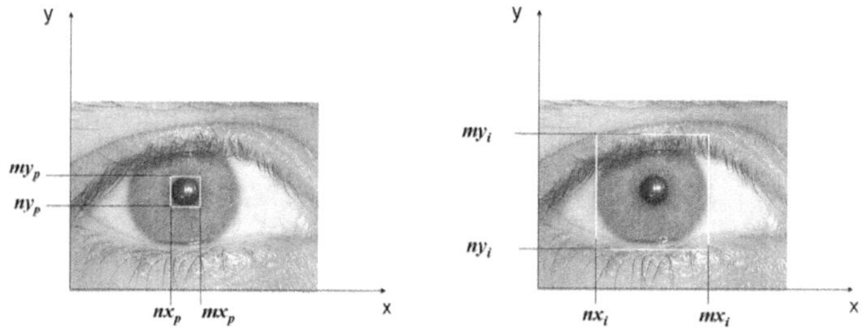

Fig. 3. Coordinates of the squares and centres of the circles

3.1 Lookup Table

To increase the speed of the proposed algorithm we put all the possible values of the circumference coordinates in a lookup table. A lookup table also contents the all possible values of the points x_{im}, y_{im} and x_{pm}, y_{pm} that correspond to all possible values of r_{im} and r_{pm} respectively and for all possible values of the θ angles in the intervals [315°-45°] and [135°-225°].

3.2 The Pupil Pixel Value Change

In a previous work [7] we presented an algorithm that we called "*Three points algorithm*". The proposed algorithm takes advantage of the pupil circular form using elements of analytic geometry, in particular of the determination of the bounded circumference to a triangle. To obtain the parameters that define the external contour the Daugman algorithm [1, 2] was used. This second algorithm receives the output from the first one and after that, searches the abrupt gradient changes of a contour integral to find the iris border. The problem of this proposal was the fact that its effectiveness depends of the quantitative texture feature, as the standard deviation to detect the frontier between the pupil and the iris. When we work on a database with well controlled conditions like the CASIA database [3] composed by images taken with near infrared illumination, without the presence of specular light the performance of the combination of these two algorithms is very high, but when the images are affected by specular light it fails due to the high variability detected in the pupil. To avoid this problem and improve the performance of this combination we implemented an optional step in our new proposal

Step 4: Substitution of the pixel values inside the pupil circumference by zero values, this guarantees that the performance of Daugman algorithm will be effective because the difference between the standard deviation within the pupil and in the iris area increase abruptly.

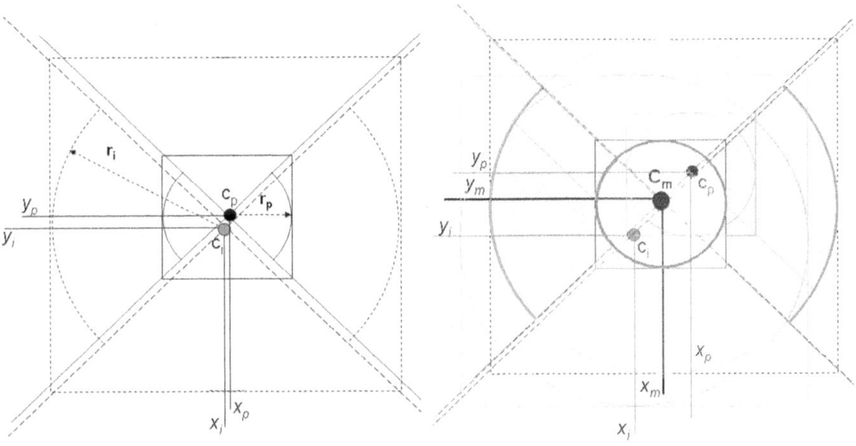

Fig. 4. Determination of the circular sector of the texture codification area for feature extraction

4 Experiments

For a complete evaluation of the performance of our proposal we divided the experimental process in two parts, the first one oriented to the measurement of the effectiveness of the automatic detection of the tangential square enclosing the iris inner and outer contours, and the second one oriented to measure the accuracy of determination of the texture codification area for feature extraction and identification.

4.1 Measurement of the Effectiveness in the Automatic Tangential Square Detection

We defined a set of measures necessary to know accurately the effectiveness behaviour of the detector according to the final mission of the process. They are:

ESD (External Square Difference): The difference in area between optimal square containing the real contour and the one automatically detected if the area of the square detected is bigger (Fig 5, left), it is given in percentage and calculated by the expression:

$$ESD = \frac{\sum (DAS - TAS)}{\sum DAS.100} \tag{5}$$

where *DAS* and *TAS* are the areas of the tangential square automatically detected and the area of the actual tangential square respectively.

ISD (Internal Square Difference): The difference in area between optimal square containing the actual contour and the one automatically detected if the area of the detected square is smaller (Fig 5, right), it is given in percentages and calculated by the expression:

$$ISD = \frac{\sum (TAS - DAS)}{\sum TAS.100} \tag{6}$$

GFT (General effectiveness of automatic detection) is the general percentages of accuracy taking in to account the ISD and ESD, and expresses the precision with which the detector is able to enclose the actual contour. It is calculated by the expression.

$$GFT = 100 - \left[\frac{1}{2} (ESD + ISD) \right] \tag{7}$$

We also measured the effectiveness of the automatic detection process by computing the correctly detected regions, missed regions and falsely detected regions.

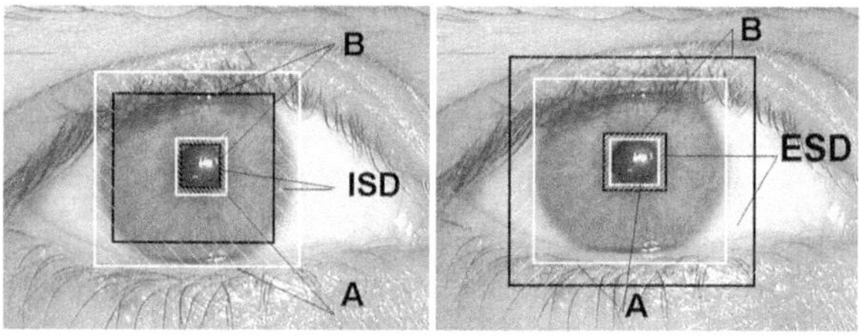

Fig. 5. Measurement of the effectiveness of the automatic iris inner and outer contour detection. A: Optimal square containing the actual contour , B: Automatically detected square.

4.2 The UBIRIS Database

We did the experiments in the UBIRIS database[11]. UBIRIS database is composed of 1877 images collected from 241 persons during September, 2004 in two distinct sessions. Its main characteristic results from the fact that, in opposition to the existing public and free databases (CASIA and UPOL), it incorporates images with several noise factors, thus permitting the evaluation of robustness iris recognition methodologies. For our experiment we took 2 images per person (482 images of 241 persons) and divided the database in two sections, training set, 100 persons (200 images) and test set, 141 persons (282 images), see Fig.7.

4.3 Measurement of the Accuracy in Determination of the Texture Codification Area for Feature Extraction and Identification

The idea was to measure the similarity between images that contain the texture codification area for feature extraction and identification, comparing images generated from the detected automatically contours and the ones detected by Daugman algorithm(Fig 6). As a similarity measure we used normalized correlation. Normalized correlation has been chosen as it has proved to be a successful similarity measure in computer vision. For identical images it takes the maximum value equal to unity, it is defined as:

$$Nc = \frac{\sum_i \sum_j (w(i,j) w_1(i,j))}{\sqrt{\sum_i \sum_j w(i,j)^2 \sum_i \sum_j w_1(i,j)^2}} \tag{8}$$

Where the first image is w(i,j), the second image is $w_1(i,j)$.

For this experiment we used images from CASIA database. We compared 108 images generated from our approach against 108 images of the same individuals generated from Daugman algorithm.

The same procedure we used to compare images from UBIRIS database. For this experiment we compared the *Nc* with the radial difference in pixels between outer contours generated by our approach and the ones generated by Daugman algorithm with previous inner contour detection and normalization of pupil pixel values using our proposed approach (3.2).

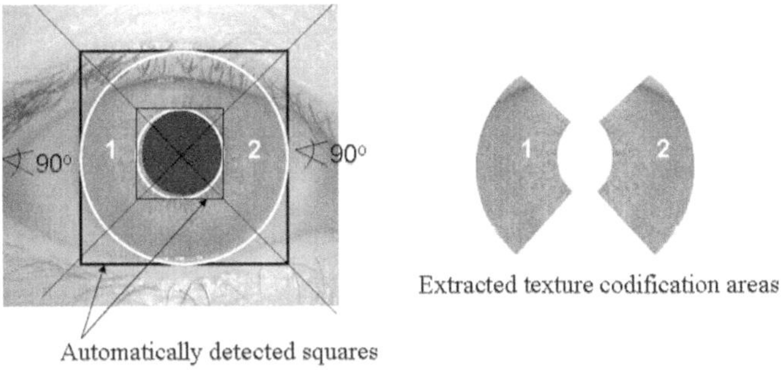

Fig. 6. Extraction of the texture codification area for feature extraction and identification

4.4 The Time Consuming Evaluation

For the evaluation of time consuming in the detection process we compared the time taken for the automatic contour detection using our approach and the time taken using the proposed by Daugman detection algorithm with the same quantity of images and similar hardware configuration. We expressed these measures in milliseconds related to the time consumed for contour detection by Daugman algorithm in 100 images from CASIA database.

4.5 The CASIA Database

The CASIA Iris Image Database [3] includes 108 classes and each class has 7 iris images captured in two sessions with a time interval about a month. So there are totally 756 iris images with a resolution of 320x280 pixels. In our experiment we used 1 image per class (108 images), see Fig 8.

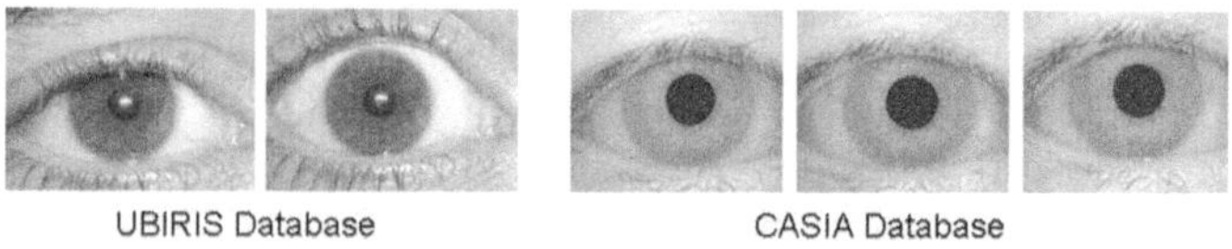

Fig. 7. Samples of the CASIA database used in the experiment

5 Experimental Results

In Table 1 and 2 we present the results obtained by experimental procedure described in 4.1 in the UBIRIS database. We can see that in both cases, ERD and IRD are less than 2.0 % and the GFT is bigger than 98%. The detector only fails in 3 samples detecting the inner contour (0.62%) but in 20 samples detecting the outer contour (4 %).

Table 1. Values of the ERD and IRD in the UBIRIS database

Inner Iris contour		Outer Iris contour	
IRD (%)	ERD (%)	IRD (%)	ERD (%)
0.64	0.33	1.65	0.98
GFT (%)		GFT (%)	
99.51		98.68	

Table 2. Performance of the Detector

Correctly Detected (%)	Missed (%)	Falsely Detected(%)
Pupil Contour (Inner)		
99.3	0.7	0.05
Iris-Contour (Outer)		
95.9	4.1	0

In the Fig. 8 we present the results obtained by experimental procedure described in 4.3. The normalized correlation coefficients (Nc) are in all the cases of the CASIA database (Fig.8A) bigger than 0.9. This result shows that the texture codification areas extracted from images in which the iris contour was automatically detected by our own approach are very similar to the ones obtained from those in which the iris contour was detected by Daugman algorithm. They can be used for the feature extraction and identification. The results in the UBIRIS database (Fig.8B) show that the under not controlled illumination conditions the *Nc* values are in most of cases bigger than 0.7.

From Fig.9, we observe that when our approach is used, the time of processing decreases in approximately 45% of the total of the time used by Daugman algorithm to process the same quantity of images with similar hardware configuration.

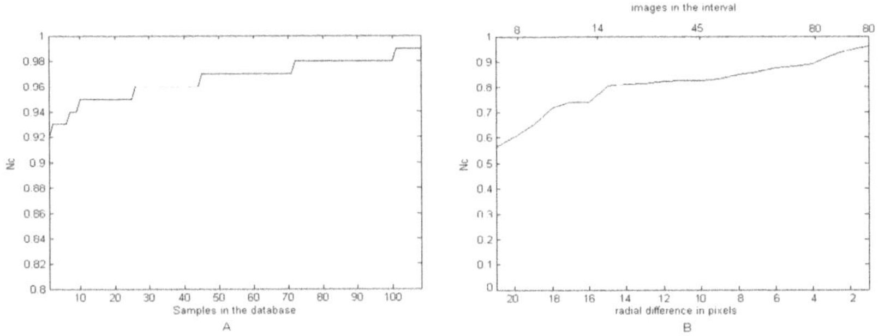

Fig. 8. Comparison of the normalized correlations: A: in the CASIA database, B: in the UBIRIS database

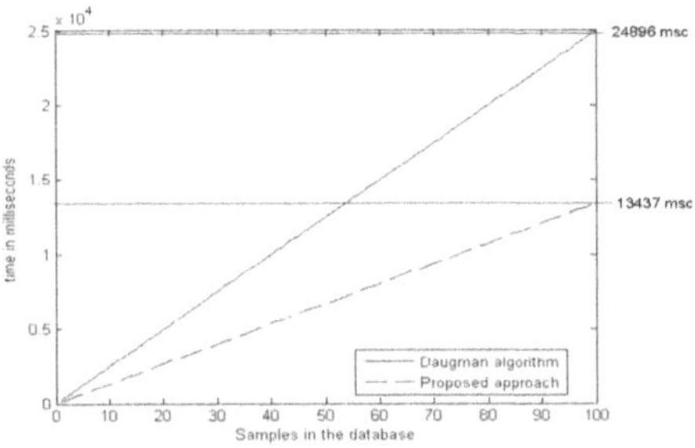

Fig. 9. Comparison of the time consuming (in milliseconds) using Daugman algorithm against proposed approach in the CASIA database

6 Conclusions

In this paper we proposed an approach based on the Adaboosting technique for fast detection of the iris and pupil contour in the images of human eyes. The proposed approach overcomes the problem of the specular light reflected in the pupil or in the iris and allows the detection and localization of the circular sector of the texture codification area for feature extraction. To increase the speed of the proposed algorithm we used the Lookup table containing all the possible values of the circumferential sectors describing the iris contours. The experimental results show that our proposal is equivalent in accuracy in comparison with the well validated Daugman algorithm together with a relevant improvement of the computational time.

Acknowledgements

We want to thank the National Laboratory of Pattern Recognition from Beijing, China and the “Departamento de Informática da Universidade da Beira Interior, Covilhã,

Protugal", for its generosity in allowing us the use of the CASIA and UBIRIS Iris Images Data Bases in our experiments.

References

1. Daugman, J.: High Confidence Visual Recognition of Persons by a Test of Statistical Independence. IEEE Transactions on Pattern Analysis and Machine Intelligence. Vol. 15. No 11. 1148-1160 pp., (1993).
2. Daugman, J.: Demodulation by Complex-Valued Wavelets for Stochastic Pattern Recognition. International Journal of Wavelets, Multiresolution and Information Processing. Vol. 1. No. 1. 1-17 pp., (2003).
3. Center for Biometrics and Security Research (CBSR). CASIA Iris Image Database, http://www.sinobiometrics.com.
4. Cui, J., Y., Wang, T. Tan, L. Ma, Z. Sun: A Fast and Robust Iris Localization Method Based on Texture Segmentation, Center for Biometric Authentication and Testing, National\ Laboratory of Pattern Recognition. Disponible en internet. (2005)
5. Wildes, R.: Iris Recognition: An Emerging Biometric Technology, Proceedings of the IEEE, Vol. 85, pp.1348-1363, (1997).
6. Camus, T. A., R. Wildes: Reliable and Fast Eye Finding in Close-up Images, Proceedings of the IEEE International Conference on Pattern Recognition, (2002).
7. Gil J L , and Díaz Y. A New Method for Iris Pupil Contour Delimitation and its Application in Iris Texture Parameter Estimation,: CIARP 2005, LNCS 3773, pp. 631 – 641, 2005. Springer-Verlag Berlin Heidelberg 2005
8. Center for Biometrics and Security Research (CBSR). CASIA Iris Image Database, http://www.sinobiometrics.com.
9. Viola P. and Jones M. Rapid Object Detection Using a Boosted Cascade of Simple Features. Mitsubishi Electric Research Laboratories, Inc., 2004 201 Broadway, Cambridge, Massachusetts 02139.
10. Lienhart Rainer. Haarcascade_frontalface_default.xml. Intel License Agreement For Open Source Computer Vision Library. 2000.
11. UBIRIS Database. Departamento de Informática da Universidade da Beira Interior, URL: http://iris.di.ubi.pt/.

In-Vivo IVUS Tissue Classification: A Comparison Between RF Signal Analysis and Reconstructed Images

Karla L. Caballero[1], Joel Barajas[1], Oriol Pujol[1,2], Neus Salvatella[3], and Petia Radeva[1]

[1] Computer Vision Center, UAB Bellaterra Barcelona 08193, Spain,
[2] Dept. Matemàtica Aplicada i Anàlisi. University of Barcelona, Barcelona, Spain
[3] Hospital Universitari German Trias i Pujol, Badalona , Spain
klcaballero@cvc.uab.es

Abstract. In this paper we present a novel framework for classification of the different kind of tissues in intravascular ultrasound (IVUS) data. We expose a normalized reconstruction of the IVUS images from radio frequency (RF) signals, and the use of these signals for classification. The reconstructed data is described in terms of texture based features and feeds an ECOC-Adaboost learning process. In the same manner, the RF signals are characterize using Autoregressive models, and classified with a similar learning process. A comparison is performed among these techniques and with DICOM based classification ones obtaining very promising results.

1 Introduction

Plaque rupture is one of the most frequent cause of acute coronary syndromes. Most of them end in myocardial infarction or sudden cardiac death. Many studies, nowadays, report a high correlation between multiple plaque ruptures and acute coronary syndrome. To understand the mechanisms of plaque destabilization and guide a pharmacological treatment, it is of high interest the characterization of the fragile part of the atheromatous plaque and to differentiate between low-risk and high-risk plaques.

Intravascular ultrasound (IVUS) offers a unique view of the morphology of the arterial plaque, it displays the morphology and histological properties of a cross-section of the vessel. It is generally accepted that in these images three are the different kind of plaque tissues distinguishable: calcium formations (characterized by a very high echo-reflectivity and absorbtion); fibrous plaque (medium echo-reflectivity and good transmission coefficient) and lipidic or soft plaque (very low reflectance). The automatic analysis of the IVUS images is of vital importance to the coronary community, since it allows feasible ways to predict vulnerable plaques as well as to quantify the amount of the different tissues, avoiding all the subjectivity due to the physician who performs the study and the amount of hours needed to label the recorded IVUS pullbacks.

J.F. Martínez-Trinidad et al. (Eds.): CIARP 2006, LNCS 4225, pp. 137–146, 2006.

The analysis of IVUS data is approached in two ways in literature: On one hand, several authors propose the analysis of the DICOM images themselves by means of normalization procedures and texture analysis [15,13]. On the other hand, several researchers prefer the use of the original radio-frequency signal when available [5,4]. However, until now there is no evidence of one of the techniques being better than the other.

In this paper we propose two methods that exploit the advantages of both trends of work: we propose a framework to reconstruct normalized IVUS images from the radio frequency signal and to apply the image based characterization process. This data is feeded into an ECOC improved Adaboost framework to perform the final classification. The main advantages of our method are three-fold: firstly, our method offers the advantage of normalizing all cases to a fixed parameter set. Secondly, it allows to use very complex texture-based descriptors. And thirdly, by using a machine learning technique we ensure a proper behavior of the classification approach. In addition, this article presents an approach of tissue classification using RF signals with a similar learning machine technique. Then a comparison between the classification using reconstructed normalized IVUS images with different settings and RF signal analysis is performed.

In section 2, we present an image reconstruction process, in section 3, it is explained an RF signal analysis and characterization. In section 4, it is exposed how to extract the different texture features used in our study. Finally, the results, discussion, and conclusion are presented.

2 Image Reconstruction Process

An IVUS equipment consists of a main computer to reconstruct images, and a catheter which is introduced into the vessel to perform an exploration. This catheter carries an ultrasound emitter which shots a given number of beams, and a transducer that collects their reflections as RF signals. Based on the kind of tissue, these signals vary their frequency and amplitude. There is enough evidence that these signals are suitable to perform a classification process[9,5].

2.1 RF Signal Acquisition

The RF signals are acquired using a 12-bit Acquiris acquisition card with a sampling rate of $200MHz$. The frequency of the catheter transducer is $40Mhz$ for our data, and it is assumed a sound speed in tissue of $1565m/s$. Each IVUS image consists of a total of 256 A-lines (ultrasound beams), and a length of $6.5mm$. Thus, RF data were acquired from patient pullback sequences *in vivo*.

2.2 Image Construction

Having the acquired RF data, an image construction framework is applied to obtain the IVUS images with the same parameters set. Hence as a preprocessing step, the acquired signals are filtered with a band pass filter with 50% of gain located at the transducer frequency. Additionally, a time gain compensation is applied in order to correct the tissue attenuation $\alpha = 1DbMhz/s$.

After the signals are compensated a signal envelope is calculated using the Hilbert transform. This envelope is normalized in a range from 0 to 1, and compressed in a logarithmical form. This is done in order to distribute the gray levels in the histogram and also to enhance the image visualization.

The image is constructed in cartesian form and the missing pixels between each angle are filled using bilinear interpolation. Then, a non linear Digital Development Process (DDP) to regulate the contrast radially is applied. The parameters are fixed in order to normalize all the images with the same contrast. This process allow us to change the contrast of the image easily with low computational cost, which is not an easy task in the DICOM images since the construction parameters are not usually available. Figure 1 shows an example of constructed images with different gains.

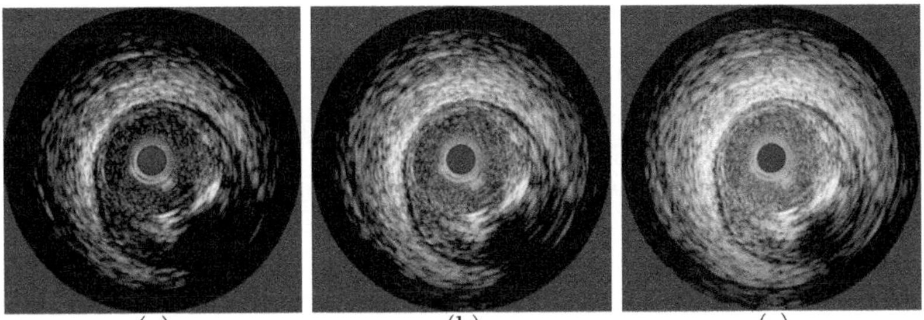

(a) (b) (c)

Fig. 1. Reconstructed IVUS images from RF signals with different DDP gain parameters. (a)DDP gain parameter fixed to 1.04. (b)DDP gain parameter fixed to 2.20. (c)DDP gain parameter fixed to 3.20.

The constructed images are used mainly for: classification with a texture based approach, visualization as a reference for the RF signal correlation, and for manual segmentation used in the training set.

3 RF Signal Analysis

Once the RF signals have been acquired, filtered, and compensated, a characterization process is performed. According to [8,4], one of the most suitable methods to analyze ultrasound signals is the use of Autoregressive (AR) models of their power spectrum. Thus, in this approach the utilization of AR models is explored.

3.1 Autoregressive Models

The autoregressive models can be defined as a linear prediction formula where the output x at a certain point n is equal to a linear combination of its previous outputs p with a given weight a_p[12].

$$x(n) = \sum_{k=1}^{p} a_p(k)x(n-k),$$

The AR models are used to approximate the power spectrum of a RF signal window. In our case it is composed of 64 samples, and 12 of the 256 A-lines. The Burg method is used to estimate the power spectrum, and the optimal model order (21) was obtained using the Akaike's Final Error Prediction [6]. Then, only one side of the spectrum is used because of its symmetry. It is composed of 200 sampled frequencies ranging from 0 to $100MHz$. Thus, each frequency value of the model is used as a signal feature for classification, as it is shown in figure 2.

Here an sliding window of 64 samples and 12 A-lines, and a displacement of 16 samples and 4 A-lines are used for characterization. These is done in order to increase the resolution of the characterization. Note that this window corresponds to a region of 16×12 pixels in the reconstructed polar image.

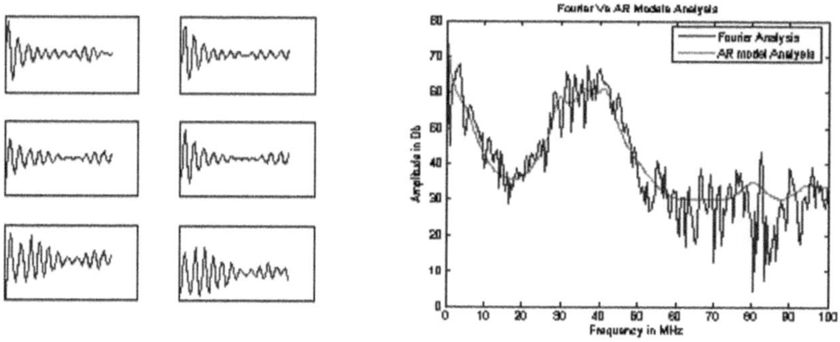

(a) (b)

Fig. 2. The use of a different RF signal sections (a) to create an Autoregressive model(b)

4 Texture Features Extraction

4.1 Co-occurrence Matrix

The co-occurrence matrix can be defined as an estimation of the joint probality density function of gray level pairs in a image [11]. The element values in a matrix are bounded from 0 to 1 and the sum of all element values is:

$$P(i, j, D, \theta) = P(I(l, m) = i \otimes I(l + Dcos(\theta), m + Dsin(\theta)) = j),$$

where $I(l, m)$ is the gray value at the pixel(l, m), D is the distance among pixels and θ is the angle of each of neighbors. The angle orientation θ has been fixed to be $[0^o, 45^o, 90^o, 135^o]$, because, according to [3,11], it is the minimum set of orientations needed to describe a second-order statistic measures of texture. After computing this matrix some characterizing measures are extracted such as energy, entropy, the Inverse Difference Moment, shade, inertia and Promenance, as are defined in [11]. Thus, a 48 feature space is built to perform the classification process for each pixel, since we are estimating 6 different measures at 4 orientations and two distances $D = [5, 8]$.

4.2 Local Binary Patterns

These feature extractor operators are used to detect uniform texture patterns into circular neighborhoods with any quantization of angular space and spatial resolution[10]. It is based on a circular symmetric neighborhood of P members of a circle with radius R. In order to achieve gray level invariance, the central pixel g_c is subtracted to each neighbor g_p, assigning to the result 1 if the difference is positive and 0 if it is negative. Each neighbor is weighted with a 2^p value. Then, the neighbors are added, and the result is assigned to the central pixel.

$$LBP_{R,P} = \sum_{p=0}^{P} s(g_p - g_c) \cdot 2^p$$

The application of this operator generates a 3 dimensional space in texture analysis, by applying a radius of $R = [1, 2, 3]$ and a neighborhood of $P = [8, 16, 24]$.

4.3 Gabor Filters Bank in Texture Analysis

The Gabor Filters is an special case of wavelets [1,2], and is essentially a Gaussian g modulated by a complex sinusoid s. In 2D, a Gabor filter has the following form in the spatial domain:

$$h(x, y) = \frac{1}{2\pi\sigma_{x'}\sigma_{y'}} \exp\{-\tfrac{1}{2}[(\tfrac{x'}{\sigma_{x'}})^2 + (\tfrac{y'}{\sigma_{y'}})^2]\} \cdot s(x, y),$$

where $s(x, y)$ and the Gaussian rotation are defined as:

$$s(x, y) = \exp[-i2\pi(Ux + Vy)]$$
$$x' = x\cos\theta + y\sin\theta,\ y' = -x\sin\theta + y\cos\theta.$$

x' and y' represent the spatial coordinates rotated by an angle θ. $\sigma_{x'}$ and $\sigma_{y'}$ are the standard deviations for the Gaussian envelope. An aspect ratio λ and its orientation are defined as:

$$\lambda = \frac{\sigma_{x'}}{\sigma_{y'}},\ \phi = \arctan V/U$$

where U and V represent the 2D frequencies of the complex sinusoid.

We have fixed $\lambda = 1$ in order to manage with isotropic gaussian envelopes, provoking that both $\sigma_{x'}$ and $\sigma_{y'}$ are equal, leading to discard θ. Then, $\theta = 0$. We have represented the 2D frequency, (U, V), by a polar representation F, ϕ. Thus, we have created a filter bank using the following parameters:

$\sigma_x = \sigma_y = [12.7205, 6.3602, 3.1801, 1.5901]$,
$\phi = [0^o, 45^o, 90^o, 135^o]$,
$F = [0.0442, 0.0884, 0.1768, 0.3536]$,
yielding a 16 dimensional space for each pixel.

4.4 Feature Vector Generation

Now, we have extracted all the features explained above. We have compiled them into a unique feature vector of 67 dimensions for each pixel, which will be used to train the classifier. The main idea is to extract the best of each technique in order to improve the classification performance.

5 Classification

Once we have designed a characterization framework for images using texture and for RF signals using AR models, a classification scheme is developed. We have established 3 classes of tissue: fibrotic plaque, lipid or soft plaque, and calcium. Since we already know how many classes are, and how they behave, we use the Adaptive Boosting (Adaboost) supervised learning technique.

Adaboost is a method that allows us to add "weak" classifiers until some desired training error is obtained [17,16]. In each step of the algorithm a weight is assigned to each feature, which means how accurate this feature can classify the training data. It results into a linear combination of weaker classifiers, and the weight of each one depends on the amount of data it can classify.

Since we have a multiclass problem, we need to establish some combination criteria for the classifier output. Firstly, we used decision tables to combine the outputs but the appearance of draws was common. As a result, we switched to use Error Correction Output Codes (ECOC)[14]. Basically, it consists in assigning a code map table which relates classifiers outputs and classes. Then, the final classification is obtained finding the minimum distance between the resulting code and the classes.

The classification map from the ECOC is the same for both techniques. It is shown in table 1. Here, the number 0's indicate that these classes are not used in the selected classifier. Because there are only two classes left for each classifier, we apply one class versus the other, and not one versus the rest. The 1's indicate that the classifier should output a positive value when this class is found, and negative one (-1) when it is not.

Once we have all the classifiers results, it is found the Euclidean distance between each sample of the test and all the class codes. Thus, the class the minimum distance respect to the sample is assigned.

Table 1. ECOC code map used in the classification

Classes	Classifier 1	Classifier 2	Classifier 3
Calcium	1	1	0
Fibrotic Plaque	-1	0	1
Soft Plaque	0	-1	-1

6 Results

We have the RF signals from *in vivo* sequences, and their IVUS reconstructed images from a set of 10 patients all with the three classes of plaque. Each patient may have 1 or 2 vessel studies or pullbacks. Then, for each one, 10 to 15 different vessel sections are selected to be analyzed.

In order to avoid any kind of bias, the experiment has been repeated ten times by picking one different patient for testing and the rest for training in each iteration. This gives us a roughly idea of how the classification could work with a new unseen patient.

6.1 Tissue Segmentation

We have developed an application to construct IVUS images from the RF signals. It has the advantage of allowing the physicians to move the gain parameter of the DDP to simplify the manual segmentation task. Additionally, it permits the offline manipulation of the images for the physicians. Although the main propose of this step is to segment the training data and label it, the parameters used for the segmentation are stored for future analysis yielding to settings normalization.

The physicians have segmented from the vessel images around of 50 sections of interests per patient. These segmentations were taken as regions of interest (ROI) which were collected into a database categorized by patient. These were mapped in both RF signals and reconstructed images in order to build the data set for this experiment.

6.2 RF Signal Classification

One of the classifications we have done is the one based on the RF signals obtained from the ultrasound transducer. Here, we employ a classifier using the characterization of the signals based on AR models, as it is explained above. Then, we use the ROI selected by the physicians in order to train and test our system. The gentle Boost classifier with 50 stumps is utilized, because in our scheme all the frequencies have the same weight. Hence, the test set is classified, the classification error is calculated based on the number of misclassified samples of each class.

The average accuracy using AR models is 70% for the fibrous plaque, 77.2% for the soft and 75% for the calcium correctly classified. Although the accuracy is lower than some of the rates previously published using RF signals[8,7], it is important to note that this experiment has been performed with a cross validation method. In addition, the test data is taken from different patients of the training data avoiding any kind of bias as in real performance. Notice that the accuracy using the training data is not shown since we think it is useless to measure the real performance of the system.

6.3 Texture Based Classification

In order to test the performance of our texture based classification approach, we have selected 6 different DDP gain parameters to reconstruct the images. Then, there has been created five different data sets, and their extracted texture features have been processed separately using the characterization exposed before. For every DDP gain parameter values a classification error has been computed for each kind of tissue. Thus, the accuracy for different DDP gain parameters is shown in figure 3.

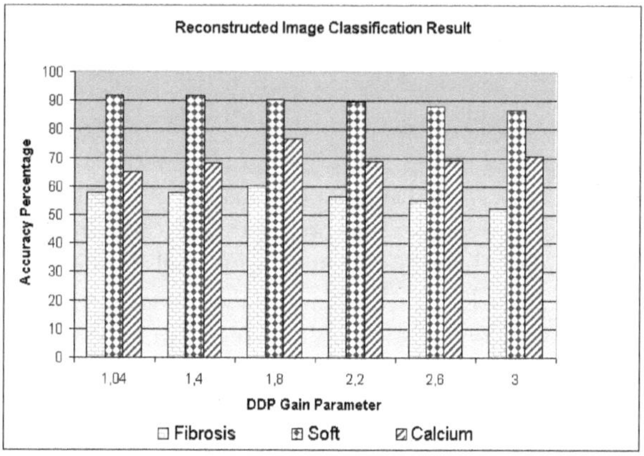

Fig. 3. Classification result among different DDP gain parameters for each type of tissue

It can be seen that the best gain parameter is 1.8 where the classification results are: 70% for fibrotic plaque, 90.5% for lipid, and 77.6% for calcium. Even when it can be chosen a certain gain as the best one for classification, a combination of multiple gain values, one designed for each tissue, could be suitable to improve the performance.

6.4 Classification Comparison

Having tested our classification using the two exposed characterization schemes, we show a comparative table of their performance in table 2. Notice that these results have been obtained with pixel resolution in both schemes, without any kind of postprocessing.

Additionally, a sample image classification result of both techniques is shown in figure 4. Here, a qualitative comparison can be observed. It is worth to mention that RF signal classification presents a border error. It could be caused by the physicians segmentation since it is easy to take little areas out of the real class. Because the RF characterization is based on the power spectrum, it can be easily influenced by the previous and after samples. Thus, this problem affects more in the RF signal based classification performance than in the texture based one.

Table 2. Classification Results from RF Signal Analysis and Texture Based Analysis

Classes	RF signal Analysis	Texture Base Analysis
Fibrosis	70%	70%
Soft	77%	91.2%
Calcium	75%	77.6%

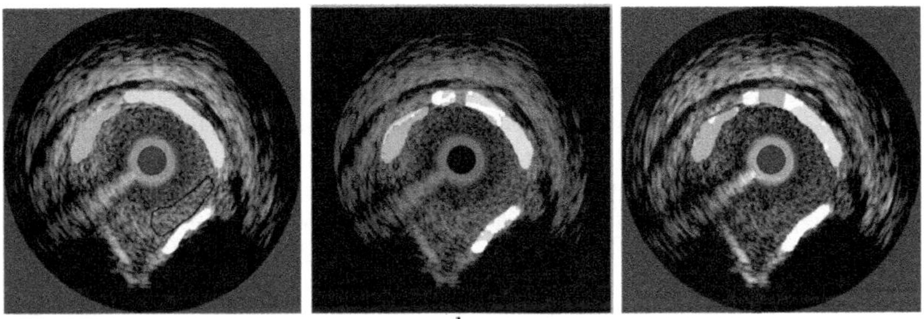

a b c

Fig. 4. Images (a) Segmented by the physician, white is calcium, light gray fibrosis and dark gray soft plaque. (b) Classified with RF signal Analysis. (c)Classified with Texture Based Features.

In any case, the accuracy rates shown here represents an improvement in the tissue characterization problem respect to the DICOM based approaches. Usually, the classifications rates reported in these approaches are around of 76% of the total performance without any kind of postprocessing[13]. The difference is mainly caused by the we use normalized data to test our classification framework.

7 Discussion and Conclusion

Two methods for tissue classification in IVUS from *in vivo* patients have been presented taking into account three types of plaque: fibrotic, soft, and calcium. We have proposed a more accurate technique based on a set of normalized data, which is not possible in conventional approaches based on DICOM images. To do so, an image construction method has been depicted.

The hit rate of the classification is higher in constructed images than in RF signal analysis. However, we suggest a combination of both characterization frameworks, because they provide complementary information. Thus, we are working now in the improvement of RF signal characterization since these represent the raw data and the real plaque response. Additionally, we have shown an application of a multi-class problem using ECOC to combine a set of two-class classifiers based on Gentle AdaBoost.

The classification exposed here has been done for each pixel but without any kind of postprocessing, since we desire to preserve the highest possible resolution. In order to improve the classification, some grouping techniques could be applied to the obtained results.

References

1. J.G. Daugman. Uncertainty Relation for Resolution in Space, Spatial Frequency, and Orientation Optimized by Two-Dimensional Visual Cortical Filters. *Journal of the Optical Society of America*, 2(A):1160–1169, 1985.
2. Hans G. Feichtinger and Thomas Strohmer, editors. *Gabor Analysis and Algorithms: Theory and Applications.* Birkhäuser, 1998.
3. T. Randen J. H. Husoy. Filtering for texture classification: A comparative study. *IEEE Transactions on Pattern Analysis and Machine Intelligence*, 4:291–310, 1999.
4. T. Iwamoto, A. Tanaka, Y. Saijo, and M. Yoshizawa. Coronary plaque classification through intravascular ultrasound radiofrequency data analysis using self-organizing map. In *IEEE Ultrasonics Symposium*, pages 2054–2057, 2005.
5. A. Jeremias, M. Kolz, T. Ikonen, J. Gummert, and A. Oshima. Feasibility of in vivo intravascular ultrasound tissue characterization in the detection of early vascular transplant rejection. *Circulation*, 100:2127–2130, 1999.
6. S. Kay. *Modern Spectral Estimation. Theory and Application.* Prentice Hall, 1988.
7. A. Nair, D. Calvetti, and G. Vince. Regularized autoregressive analysis of intravascular ultrasound backscatter: Improvement in spatial accuracy of tissue maps. *ieee transactions on ultrasonics, ferroelectrics, and frequency control*, 51:420–431, 2004.
8. A. Nair, B. Kuban, E. Murat, P. Schoenhagen, S. Nissen, and D. Vince. Coronary plaque classification with intravascular ultrasound radiofrequency data analysis. *Ciculation*, 106:2200–2206, 2002.
9. A. Nair, B. D. Kuban, N. Obuchowski, and G. Vince. Assesing spectral algorithms to predict atherosclerotic plaque composition with normalized and raw intravascular ultrasound data. *Ultrasound in Medicine & Biology*, 27:1319–1331, 2001.
10. T. Ojala and M. Pietikainen T. Maenpaa. Multiresolution gray-scale and rotation invariant texture classification with local binary patterns. *IEEE Transactions on Pattern Analysis and Machine Intelligence*, 24:971–987, 2002.
11. R. Dubes P. Ohanian. Performance evaluation for four classes of textural features. *Pattern Recognition*, 25:819–833, 1992.
12. J. Proakis, C. Rader, F. Ling, and C. Nikias. *Advanced Digital Signal Processing.* Mc Millan, 1992.
13. O. Pujol. *A semi-supervised Statistical Framework and Generative Snakes for IVUS Analysis.* Graficas Rey, 2004.
14. O. Pujol, P. Radeva, and J. Vitria. Discriminant ecoc: A heuristic method for application dependent design of error correcting output codes. *IEEE Transactions on Pattern Analysis and Machine Intelligence*, 28:1001–1007, 2006.
15. O. Pujol, M. Rosales, and P. Radeva. Intravascular ultrasound images vessel characterization using adaboost. In *Functional Imaging and Modelling of the Heart: Lecture Notes in Computer Science*, pages 242–251, 2003.
16. R. Schapire. The boosting approach to machine learning: An overview, 2001.
17. Paul Viola and Michael Jones. Robust real-time object detection. In *CVPR01*, volume 1, page 511, 2001.

Smoothing Segmented Lung Boundary in Chest CT Images Using Scan Line Search

Yeny Yim[1] and Helen Hong[2,*]

[1] School of Computer Science and Engineering, Seoul National Univ., San 56-1, Shinlim-dong, Kwanakgu, Seoul 151-742, Korea
shine@cglab.snu.ac.kr
[2] Division of Multimedia Engineering, College of Information and Media, Seoul Woman's Univ., 126 Gongreung-dong, Nowon-gu, Seoul 139-774, Korea
hlhong@swu.ac.kr

Abstract. To smooth lung boundary segmented by gray-level processing in chest CT images, we propose a new method using scan line search. Our method consists of three main steps. First, lung boundary is extracted by our automatic segmentation method. Second, segmented lung contour is smoothed in each axial CT slice. Scan line search is proposed to track the points on lung contour and find rapidly changing curvature without conventional contour tracking. 2D closing in axial CT slice is applied to reduce the number of rapidly changing curvature points. Finally, to provide consistent appearance between lung contours in neighboring axial slices, 2D closing in coronal CT slice is applied within pre-defined subvolume. Experimental results show that the smoothness of lung contour considerably increased after applying proposed method.

1 Introduction

Recently, high-resolution X-ray computed tomography (CT) images provide us a detailed abnormal area, and they are increasingly used for applications such as lung nodule detection, lung motion analysis. A critical first step in these applications is the automatic lung segmentation. To separate low density lung regions from the denser surrounding anatomy in chest CT images, most of methods use the difference in gray-level value of pixels [1,2,3]. In gray-level based method, radiodense pulmonary vessels near mediastinum and pleural nodules that contact with the surrounding anatomy, as shown in Fig. 1(a) and (b), are excluded from the segmentation result. This can bring about indentations on segmented lung regions. On the other hand, gray-level based method can include mainstem bronchi into the lung regions because of partial volume effect, as shown in Fig. 1(c). This may not be consistent across slices and therefore causes the lung boundary to have an irregular appearance, especially in coronal and sagittal views [4]. To remove indentations and salience caused by gray-level based method and obtain consistent appearance across slices, smoothing the lung boundary is required after segmentation.

* Corresponding author, Seoul Women's University, Phone: 82-2-970-5756.

J.F. Martínez-Trinidad et al. (Eds.): CIARP 2006, LNCS 4225, pp. 147–156, 2006.

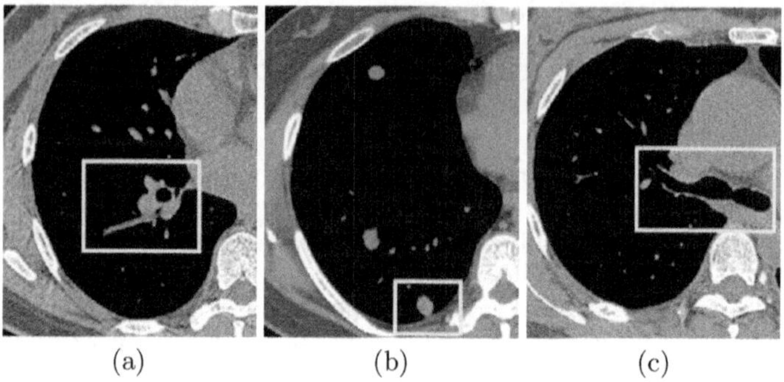

Fig. 1. Original axial CT slices in which gray-level based segmentation method gives rise to indentations and salience of lung regions: (a) axial CT slice with pulmonary vessels, (b) axial CT slice with a pleural nodule, (c) axial CT slice with mainstem bronchi

Several approaches have been suggested for smoothing lung boundary in chest CT images. To compensate the lost pleural nodules, Kanazawa [5] and Ko [6] utilized curvature of points on the initial lung contour. Curvature-based method replaces the contour with rapidly changing curvature using a straight line. To calculate the curvature, however, time-consuming contour tracking is required. Armato [2] rectified indentations that corresponds to pleural nodules by rolling a ball along the lung contour. If the ball overlaps the contour at two contour pixels, linear interpolation is used to identify new contour pixels. However, balls of different radius have to be applied in succession to remove concavities of different dimensions. Shen [7] proposed an algorithm for surface smoothing within a volume of interest (VOI). To segment the pleural lung nodules from the VOI, position and orientation of each point on lung surfaces are transformed into intensity value of 2D image, and then high intensity region which corresponds to nodule is eliminated from this image. This algorithm requires user manipulation for VOI selection and is suitable only for local surface smoothing. For 3D smoothing of the lung surfaces near mediastinum, Ukil [4] performed 3D morphological closing with an ellipsoidal mask using information from the segmented airway tree. Even though this method gives well-smoothed lung surfaces, it requires too excessive time about 5-6 minutes for 3D smoothing of datasets with 300-600 image slices.

To deal with the above limitations, we propose a new method for smoothing segmented lung boundary in chest CT images through scan line search. To track the contour points and find rapidly changing curvature efficiently, we search for intersection points between scan lines and lung contour. To reduce the number of high curvature point, we apply 2D closing in axial slice, as a pre-processing step. For consistent appearance between lung contours in neighboring axial slices, we apply 2D closing in coronal slice. In order not to distort the lung contour away from mediastinum, this operation is performed within predefined subvolume near mediastinum.

2 Methods

The proposed method for smoothing lung boundary is outlined in Fig. 2. Our method consists of three main steps: lung segmentation, smoothing in axial slice and subvolume smoothing in coronal slice.

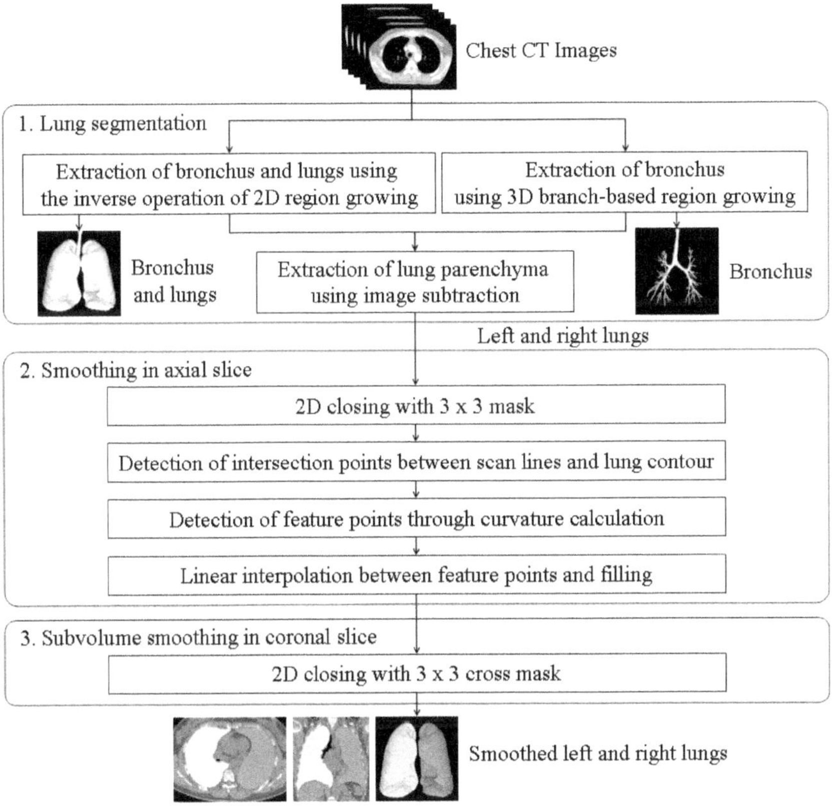

Fig. 2. The pipeline of proposed method for smoothing segmented lung boundary in chest CT images

2.1 Lung Segmentation

The lung boundary is extracted by our automatic segmentation method [3], which is based on density and morphology information in chest CT images. To extract left and right lungs, we use the inverse operation of 2D region growing (2D iRG) that segments the thorax from the background and then the lungs from the thorax. Since the density of bronchus is similar to that of the lungs in CT images, the lungs segmented by 2D iRG still contain the bronchus.

To delineate the bronchus from the lungs, we first extract bronchus and then subtract the result from the segmentation result of bronchus and lungs in voxel-by-voxel manner. To segment bronchus without leakage into lung parenchyma, we use our 3D branch-based region growing [8] that changes the growing condition according to morphology of bronchus. This method differentiates trachea from left and right bronchi based on branch bifurcation and applies different threshold values. For trachea, 3D region growing uses the threshold value determined by optimal thresholding [9]. Fig. 3 shows the process of region growing. Region grows from seed point until bifurcation is found. To detect bifurcation, we perform 3D connected component labeling with 26-connectivity to the grown region in every step and adopt the location where the number of connected component becomes two. For left and right mainstem bronchi, we calculate a new threshold value $\mu - h\sigma$ where μ and σ is respectively mean and standard deviation of gray-level values of voxels that corresponds to trachea and h is a parameter that controls the ease of region growing. To increase robustness of bronchus extraction, we apply additional processing such as median filtering and morphological operations.

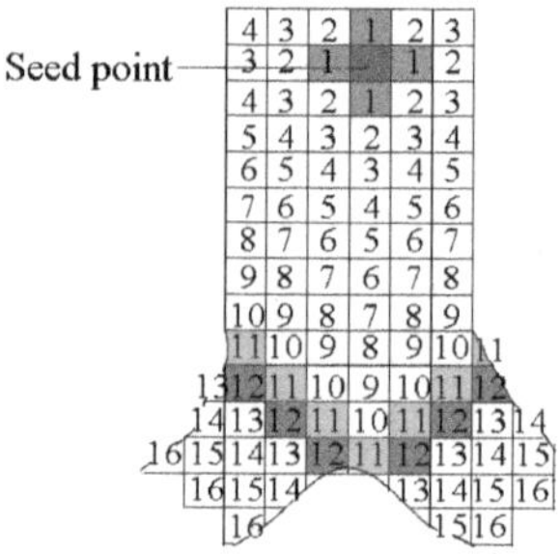

Fig. 3. 3D branch-based region growing. 3D region growing with 6-connectivity is simplified to the 2D region growing with 4-connectivity. The number written in each voxel describes growing step.

2.2 Smoothing in Axial Slice

Since the lung segmentation entirely removes trachea and mainstem bronchi, inconsistent extraction of bronchus across slices can be solved. However, concavities from pleural nodules and pulmonary vessels are still remained. For smoothing the segmented lung contour, curvature-based method is commonly used [5,6]. This method assumes that a rapid change in curvature at points on the lung contour indicates a nodule, large vessel or bronchus, and corrects the lung contour by inserting a border segment. To calculate the curvature of a point, we have to know the previous and next point on lung contour, and therefore contour tracking is required, which takes excessive processing time. To smooth segmented lung contour based on curvature without this time-consuming process, we propose smoothing in axial slice through scan line search.

Smoothing in axial slice tracks the points on lung contour using scan line search, and fills out unwanted cavities by connecting high curvature points. For each lung, we first search for intersection points between scan lines and lung contour by scanning each 2D axial CT slice in horizontal direction at fixed intervals, as shown in Fig. 4(a). For contour tracking, we classify intersection points of ith scan line into three groups: first point $I_i^{first}(x,y)$, last point $I_i^{last}(x,y)$ and middle points $I_i^{middle_j}(x,y)$. By tracking points of identical group on neighboring scan lines, as shown in Fig. 4(b), we can calculate the curvature of point on a scan line. As the scan line interval becomes shorter, we can get more accurate curvature. The scan line interval is experimentally set to 4 pixels.

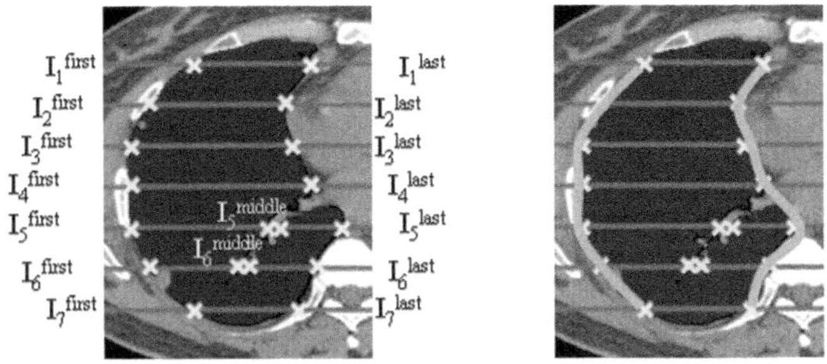

(a) (b)

Fig. 4. Scan line search: (a) detection of intersection points between scan lines and lung contour, (b) tracking of lung contour for curvature calculation

Based on this approximation, we calculate the curvature of the first and last intersection point in each scan line using Eq. (1).

$$\kappa_i = \frac{(x_{i-1} - x_i) \times (y_{i-1} - 2y_i + y_{i+1}) - (y_{i-1} - y_i) \times (x_{i-1} - 2x_i + x_{i+1})}{[(x_{i-1} - x_i)^2 + (y_{i-1} - y_i)^2]^{3/2}} \quad (1)$$

where κ_i is the curvature and (x_i, y_i) is the coordinates of $I_i(x,y)$. To calculate the curvature of the first intersection point of ith scan line, $I_{i-1}^{first}(x,y)$ and $I_{i+1}^{first}(x,y)$ is required as well as $I_i^{first}(x,y)$. After calculating the curvature of intersection points, we adopt high curvature points as feature points. We determine the curvature is high when its absolute value is larger than 0.2. All middle intersection points are also added to feature points to improve accuracy of the above approximation.

The number of feature points detected from left and right lungs is 41 per axial slice, on average. To reduce the number of feature points, we apply 2D closing operation with 3 × 3 mask to each slice, as a pre-processing step. In order to distort lung contour as little as possible, the iteration number is experimentally set to 2. As a result, many concave indentations near mediastinum become gentle and the number of feature points per slice is reduced to 35.

After finding feature points through curvature calculation, we connect all different feature points by linear interpolation when the distance between two points is in the pre-defined range. Experimentally, this range is set from 3 to 40 pixels. The regions that are encompassed by connecting lines are filled by 2D region growing.

2.3 Subvolume Smoothing in Coronal Slice

In smoothing in axial slice, detected feature points and smoothed regions are different across slices. For this reason, smoothed lung contour in one slice can be inconsistent with that of neighboring slice. In coronal or sagittal view, rugged boundary still remains. To solve this problem, we apply 2D closing operation in coronal slice with 3 × 3 cross mask.

Closing consists of dilation followed by erosion. For 2D dilation operation with 3 × 3 cross mask, we perform 2D convolution with 3 × 3 cross mask and maximum filtering. For 2D erosion operation, 2D convolution is followed by minimum filtering. Fig. 5 shows the process of 2D dilation operation with 3 × 3 cross mask. We first convolve the input image with cross mask, and apply gray-level thresholding to convolved image with threshold 30, as shown in Fig. 5(a) and (b). Maximum filtering with 3 × 3 mask sets each pixel in Fig. 5(c) as the maximum value among all the pixel values of thresholded image in the neighborhood of size 3 × 3.

2D closing operation with 3 × 3 cross mask can lead to smooth lung contour in coronal slice while applying the operation with 3 × 3 mask iteratively can cause jagged lung contour. To avoid unwanted distortion of lung contour, closing

0	0	0	0	0	0
0	0	0	0	0	0
0	0	10	10	10	0
0	0	10	10	0	0
0	0	0	0	0	0
0	0	0	0	0	0

⊗

0	1	0
1	1	1
0	1	0

=

0	0	0	0	0	0
0	0	10	10	10	0
0	10	30	40	20	10
0	10	30	30	20	0
0	0	10	10	0	0
0	0	0	0	0	0

(a)

0	0	0	0	0	0
0	0	0	0	0	0
0	0	10	10	0	0
0	0	10	10	0	0
0	0	0	0	0	0
0	0	0	0	0	0

(b)

0	0	0	0	0	0
0	10	10	10	10	0
0	10	10	10	10	0
0	10	10	10	10	0
0	10	10	10	10	0
0	0	0	0	0	0

(c)

Fig. 5. 2D dilation with 3 × 3 cross mask: (a) convolution, (b) the result image after applying gray-level thresholding with threshold value 30, (c) the result image after applying maximum filter operation is applied only within pre-defined subvolume near mediastinum. Fig. 6(a) shows the subvolume, which is in the range of 0.4 × width < x < 0.7 × width, 0.4 × height < y < 0.7 × height, 0.4 × depth < z < 0.8 × depth. Fig. 6(b) and (c) shows the effect of subvolume smoothing in coronal slice. After subvolume smoothing in coronal slice, inconsistency across axial slices is much reduced.

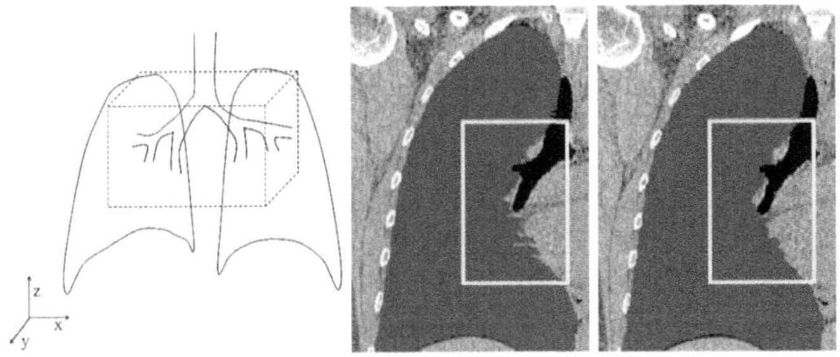

(a) (b) (c)

Fig. 6. Subvolume smoothing in coronal slice: (a) the range of subvolume, (b) the result before subvolume smoothing in coronal slice, (c) the result after subvolume smoothing in coronal slice

3 Experimental Results

All our implementation and test were performed on an Intel Pentium 4 PC containing 2.5 GHz CPU and 2.0 GB of main memory. Our method has been applied to six patients with pulmonary nodule of 16-channel chest CT scans whose properties are described in Table 1. The CT images were obtained with LightSpeed Ultra (GE Healthcare) and Sensation16 (Siemens) multi-detector row CT scanner. Experimental dataset contains 222–446 slices with a slice thickness of 0.75–1.25 mm and a reconstruction size of 512 × 512 pixels.

Fig. 7 shows the lung contours smoothed by proposed method in axial and coronal CT slices. In Fig. 7(b) and (e), lung nodules and pulmonary vessels are excluded from the lung contours. The result in Fig. 7(c) and (f) shows that our smoothing algorithm compensates for these lost parts.

Table 1. Image conditions of experimental datasets

Subject	Slice number	Pixel size (mm)	Slice thickness (mm)
1	222	0.63 × 0.63	1.25
2	291	0.66 × 0.66	1.0
3	279	0.64 × 0.64	1.25
4	258	0.59 × 0.59	1.25
5	446	0.64 × 0.64	0.75
6	305	0.59 × 0.59	2.0

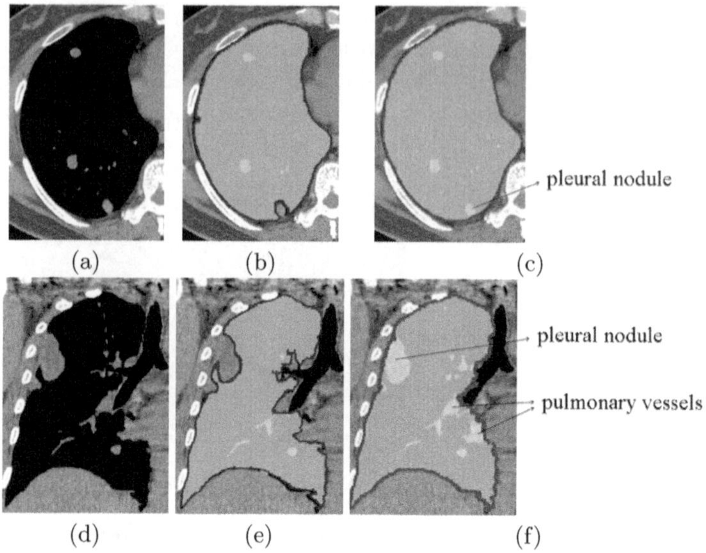

Fig. 7. The result of smoothing: (a) original axial CT slice, (b) automatic segmentation of (a) by [3], (c) smoothing of (b) by proposed method, (d) original coronal CT slice, (e) automatic segmentation of (d) by [3], (f) smoothing of (e) by proposed method

Fig. 8 shows the 3D rendered view of the segmentation result after smoothing. Figures show that the result has smooth lung boundary in all aspects and consistent appearance across slices.

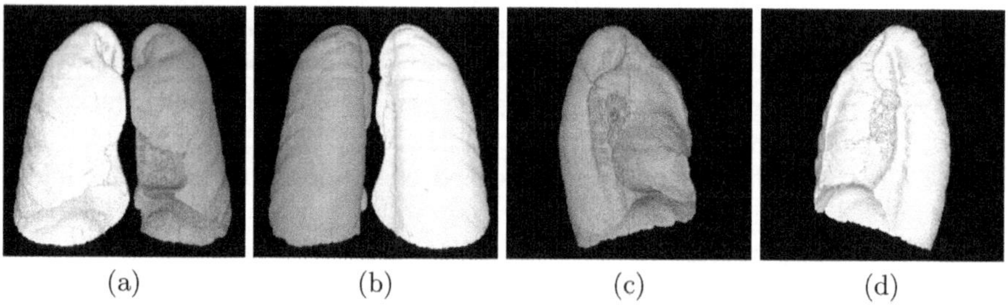

Fig. 8. 3D rendered view of segmentation result after smoothing: (a) anterior view, (b) posterior view, (c) medial view of left lung, (d) medial view of right lung

To evaluate the accuracy of segmented lung contour, we calculated the average of absolute value of curvature over mediastinal axial slices before and after smoothing. For this evaluation, we tracked the contour using chain code [10], which first picks a starting pixel and finds the next pixel on lung contour by searching the eight directions surrounding the current pixel. The value calculated before and after smoothing was 0.0496 and 0.0371, respectively. This result shows that the smoothness of lung contour considerably increased after smoothing.

Processing time for smoothing segmented lung boundary was measured from 6 patient datasets. Total processing time was 5.62 seconds on average, as shown in Fig. 9. For smoothing in axial slice and subvolume smoothing in coronal slice, 3.62 and 2.0 seconds were required, respectively. To prove efficiency of proposed scan line search, we compared the contour tracking time between our method and conventional contour tracking technique. For conventional method, we implemented contour tracking using chain code. From 6 patient datasets, the average contour tracking time of conventional method was 1.281 seconds. On the other hand, the average time needed for scan line search was 0.286 seconds.

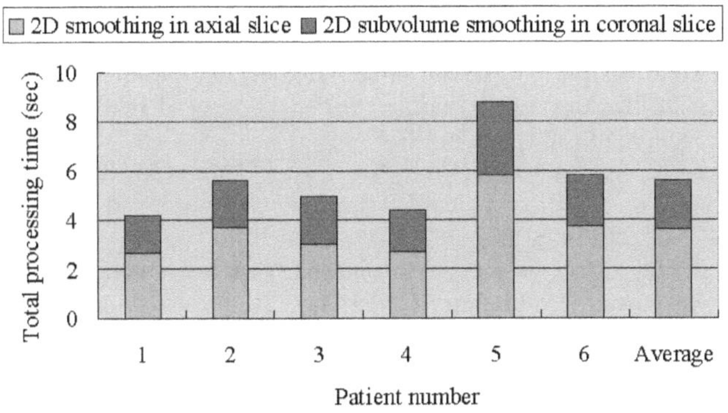

Fig. 9. Total processing time of proposed method for smoothing segmented lung boundary

4 Conclusion

We have developed a new method for smoothing segmented lung boundary in chest CT images. Using scan line search and curvature calculation, we can smooth lung boundary identified by our automatic segmentation method. Scan line search allows us to track the points and find rapidly changing curvature on lung contour efficiently. 2D closing in axial slice can reduce the number of rapidly changing curvature points. Subvolume smoothing in coronal slice provides consistent appearance between lung contours in neighboring axial slices. Six patient datasets with lung nodules have been used for the performance evaluation with the aspects of visual inspection, accuracy and processing time. The results of our method show that the smoothness of lung contour considerably increased by compensating for pulmonary vessels near mediastinum and pleural nodules. Proposed method have been successfully used for lung nodule matching [11,12] and can be used for quantitative evaluation such as measurement of nodule growth rate.

Acknowledgements

This study is supported by research fund from Seoul Womens University, 2006.

References

1. Hu, S., Hoffman, E.A., Reinhardt, J.M.: Accurate Lung Segmentation for Accurate Quantitation of Volumetric X-Ray CT Images. IEEE Transactions on Medical Imaging, Vol. 20, No. 6 (2001) 490–498
2. Armato, S.G., Sensakovic, W.F.: Automated Lung Segmentation for Thoracic CT: Impact on Computer-Aided Diagnosis. Academic Radiology, Vol.11 (2004) 1011–1021
3. Yim, Y., Hong, H.: Automatic Segmentation of Pulmonary Structures in Chest CT Images. Lecture Notes in Computer Science, Vol. 3773 (2005) 654–662
4. Ukil, S., Reinhardt, J.M.: Smoothing Lung Segmentation Surfaces in 3D X-ray CT Images using Anatomic Guidance. Proceeding of SPIE Conference on Medical Imaging, Vol. 5340 (2004) 1066–1075
5. Kanazawa, K., Kawata, Y., Niki, N., et al.: Computer-aided diagnosis for pulmonary nodules based on helical CT images. Computerized Medical Imaging and Graphics, Vol. 22 (1998) 157–167
6. Ko, J.P., Betke, M., Chest CT: Automated Nodule Detection and Assessment of Change over Time - Preliminary Experience. Radiology, Vol. 218 (2001) 267–273
7. Shen, H., Goebel, B., Odry, B.: A New Algorithm for Local Surface Smoothing with Application to Chest Wall Nodule Segmentation in Lung CT Data. SPIE Conference on Medical Imaging, Vol. 5370 (2004) 1519–1526
8. Yim, Y., Hong, H.: Automatic Segmentation of Pulmonary Structures in Chest CT Images. accepted at Computer Assisted Radiology and Surgery 20th International Congress and Exhibition (2006)
9. Gonzalez, R.C., Woods, R.E.: Digital Image Processing. Addison-Wesley Publishing Company (1992)
10. Baxes, G.A.: Digital Image Processing: Principles and Applications. John Wiley & Sons, New York (1994)
11. Hong, H., Lee, J.J., Yim, Y., Shin, Y.G.: Automatic Segmentation and Registration of lung surfaces in temporal chest CT scans. Lecture Notes in Computer Science, Vol. 3523 (2005) 463–470
12. Hong, H., Lee, J.J., Yim, Y., Shin, Y.G.: Automatic lung nodule matching for the follow-up in temporal computed tomography scans. Proc. of RSNA 2005, Chicago, USA (2005)

Automated Ultrasonic Measurement of Fetal Nuchal Translucency Using Dynamic Programming

Yu-Bu Lee[1] and Myoung-Hee Kim[1,2]

[1] Department of Computer Science and Engineering
Ewha Womans University, Seoul, Korea
basilia@ewhain.net
[2] Center for Computer Graphics and Virtual Reality
Ewha Womans University, Seoul, Korea
mhkim@ewha.ac.kr

Abstract. Measurement of nuchal translucency (NT) thickness in the first trimester of pregnancy has recently been proposed as the most useful marker in the early screening for fetal chromosomal abnormalities. Ultrasonic measurement of NT thickness is currently performed by manually tracing the two echogenic lines and locating the electronic calipers on the inner edges of these lines. The drawbacks of this method are inter- and intra-observer variability, and its inefficiency. In particular, accurate caliper placement requires highly skilled operators since the border of the nuchal translucency layer is very thin. We present a computerized method of detecting the border of the NT layer by minimizing a cost function using dynamic programming. Local measurements of intensity, edge strength and continuity are extracted and become weighted terms in a cost function. Our method can obtain accurate and reproducible results, and has been validated by computing the correlation coefficient between manual and automatic measurements.

1 Introduction

Ultrasonography (US) is performed during early pregnancy for dating, determination of the number of fetuses, assessment of early complications, and increasingly for evaluation of the fetus, including measurement of the nuchal translucency (NT) thickness [1]. Measurement of NT thickness in the first trimester of pregnancy has proved to be one of the most discriminating prenatal markers of screening for chromosomal abnormalities such as trisomies 13, 18 and 21 [2]. Furthermore, an increased NT thickness in the presence of a normal karyotype is associated with an increased frequency of structural defects and genetic syndromes [3]. The NT thickness is measured in the sagittal section of the fetus by transabdominal or transvaginal ultrasound examination. Measurement is obtained manually by placing the calipers on the inner edges of the two thin echogenic lines that border the nuchal translucency layer. The crossbar of the caliper should be positioned so that one of its lines is hardly visible as it merges with the white line of the border. This not only requires highly skilled operators but it is also prone to inter- and intra-observer variability. There has been a little research on the computerized automation of

J.F. Martínez-Trinidad et al. (Eds.): CIARP 2006, LNCS 4225, pp. 157 – 167, 2006.

fetal NT measurement. However, Bernardino et al. developed a semiautomated computerized measurement system, which uses the Sobel operator to detect the border of the NT layer [4]. In conventional edge-detection, the location of an edge is entirely determined by local evaluation of a single image feature such as the intensity or the intensity gradient. But a single image feature is not sufficient for reliable border measurement in fetal ultrasound images. These images frequently include weak echoes, echo dropouts, and speckle noise which makes them difficult to analyze using conventional border-detection techniques. Gustavsson et al. [5-7] have suggested a global optimization approach based on dynamic programming (DP) for detecting the boundaries of carotid artery which takes multiple image features into account. This method has obtained accurate and reproducible results for automated ultrasonic measurement by considering multiple image features such as intensity, gradient and border continuity.

In this paper, we will present a procedure based on dynamic programming to measure NT thickness automatically. We start by defining a region of interest in order to reduce the interference from the image boundary and to adapt to different fetal head positions and sizes of the NT layer. We then apply a dynamic programming procedure to determine the location of the border of the NT layer in a way that minimizes a cost function. This cost function is a weighted sum of terms that include local measurements of the echo intensity and the intensity gradient of the image, and a geometrical constraint on the shape of the borders. Our method overcomes the limitations of ultrasound images and accurately detects the border of the NT by combining multiple image features. Moreover, we avoid the variability of manual measurements.

The rest of this paper is organized as follows. In Section 2, we describe the characteristics of nuchal translucency images, definition of the region of interest, the segmentation procedure for detecting the border of the NT layer, and the automated measurement procedure. The results of this method are evaluated in Section 3, and then we draw some conclusions in Section 4.

2 Methods

In this section, we describe the characteristics of nuchal translucency images, the definition of the region of interest and the border detection method, and then we explain the automatic measurement procedure.

2.1 Nuchal Translucency

Nuchal translucency (NT) refers to the normal subcutaneous fluid-filled space between the back of the neck of a fetus and the overlying skin [8]. Fig. 1 shows a representative image of the NT and a schematic illustration of the echo zones (Z1-Z5) and the borders (B1, B2) of the NT layer. The NT thickness is defined as the maximum thickness of the translucent space (Z3) between the skin (Z4) and the soft tissues (Z2) overlying the cervical spine in the sagittal view of the fetus.

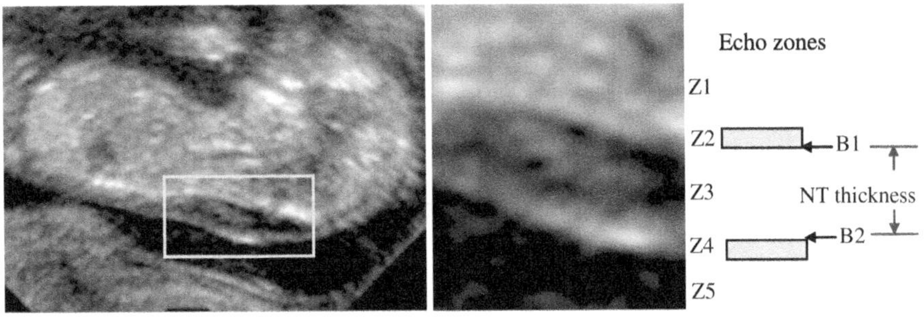

Fig. 1. Echo zones and NT borders

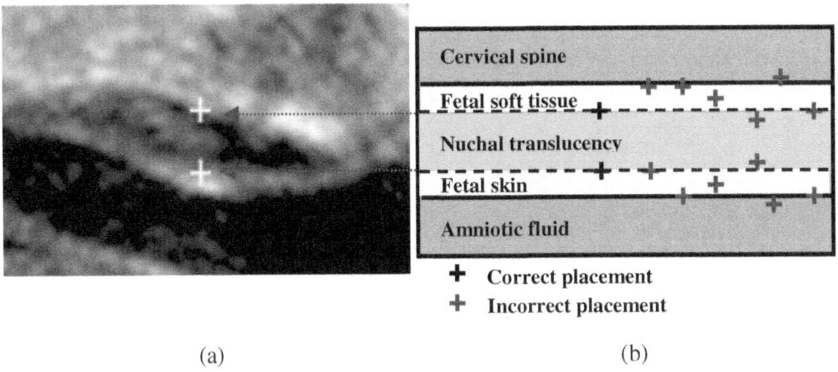

Fig. 2. Caliper method of measuring NT thickness: (a) ultrasonographic sagittal view of fetus with two calipers; (b) calipers placement on anatomical structures of the fetus

To measure the NT thickness, the calipers are located on the inner borders of the NT edges with none of the horizontal crossbars protruding into the NT layer. The + calipers should be only calipers used for NT measurement. The NT thickness should be measured at its maximum thickness with the placement of the calipers perpendicular to the long axis of the fetus [9]. The ultrasonographic sagittal view of a fetus with two calipers is shown in Fig. 2(a) and Fig. 2(b) illustrates the correct and incorrect placement of the calipers on anatomical structures of the fetus [10].

2.2 The Region of Interest

NT images can differ widely because of fetal movement over a scan of several minutes. Fig. 3 shows various NT images corresponding to different fetal positions. In Fig. 3(a) the fetal skin is clearly separate from the amnion, and in Fig. 3(b) there is no clear distinction between fetal skin and the amnion. Fetal images with the head in upside-down or oblique positions are shown in Figs. 3(c) and (d). The ultimate purpose of the identifying the border of the NT layer is to measure the thickness of its widest part. We need to define a region of interest (ROI) which reduces the interference of image boundary and which is adaptable to changes in the fetal head

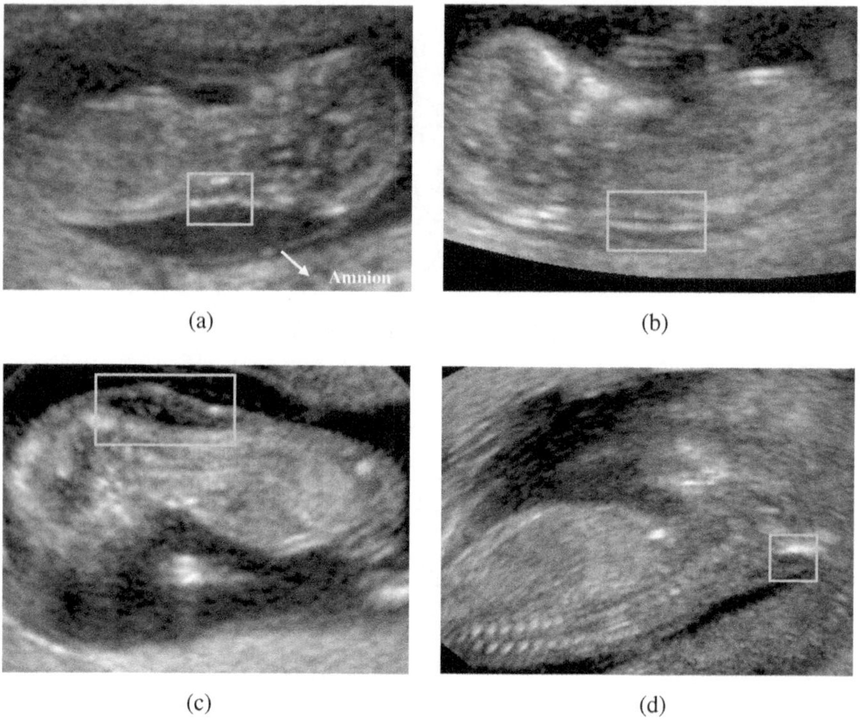

Fig. 3. NT images of different fetal positions (the rectangle indicates the ROI): (a) fetus image with a clear amniotic edge; (b) a fetus image with an indistinct amnion edge; (c) a fetus in an upside-down position; and (d) a fetus in an oblique position

position and the size of the NT layer. An additional requirement of border detection based on dynamic programming is the choice of start and end-point that enclose the interesting region of the NT layer. We create a rectangular region of interest that includes the widest part of the NT layer in the fetal image by user interaction. By creating the ROI in the correct position, we can avoid interference from speckles and from echo zones Z2 and Z4. The coordinates of start and end-point are the top-left and top-right corners of the ROI window.

2.3 Border Detection

The accurate segmentation of a border is a very difficult task since ultrasound images usually have a high level of speckle noise and other imaging artifacts due to random scattering. We apply a global optimization approach based on DP to NT border detection. We will now describe this method in detail.

Cost Function. Cost functions are built for each of the borders of the NT layer, which we will call B1 and B2. If the ROI is an M×N rectangle, then all possible borders B_N can be considered as polylines with N nodes:

$$B_N = \{p_1, p_2, \ldots, p_{N-1}, p_N\}, \tag{1}$$

where p_{N-1} and p_N are horizontal neighbors, and N is the horizontal length of a contour line. The cost function $C(B_N)$ is defined as a sum of local costs along a candidate border B_N:

$$C(B_N) = c_f(p_1) + \sum_{i=2}^{N} (c_f(p_i) + c_g(p_{i-1}, p_i)). \tag{2}$$

At a point p_i, the local cost is made up of two terms $c_f(p_i)$ and $c_g(p_{i-1}, p_i)$, which are defined as follows:

$$c_f(p_i) = \sum_{j=1}^{k} w_j f_j(p_i) \qquad (i = 1, \ldots, N) \tag{3}$$

$$c_g(p_{i-1}, p_i) = w_{k+1} g(p_{i-1}, p_i) \qquad (i = 2, \ldots, N), \tag{4}$$

where $f_j(p_i)$ are image feature terms, k is the number of image features used, $g(p_{i-1}, p_i)$ is a geometrical force term, and w_j (j = 1, 2, 3, 4) is a weighting factor. We use three image features, so k is 3. The cost terms in the cost function associated with a particular type of border must reflect the characteristics of the image features in its neighborhood and the geometrical form of the border. The cost terms are defined such that a stronger image feature at p_i will yield a lower local cost. The desired border corresponds to the B_N which minimizes the cost function $C(B_N)$. The weighting factors are determined empirically for each border using the constraint $w_1 + w_2 + w_3 + w_4 = 1$. Fig. 4 shows a 3D view of the NT layer. Above the NT border B1 (in the y-direction) is a bright and below it is a dark region. The NT border B2 is located above a bright region and below a dark region. From these observations, we can define cost terms that correspond to the characteristics of each border. To be more specific, we will describe the cost terms used in the cost function for B2.

The first term $f_1(p_i)$ measures the average intensity of n (here, n = 3) pixels below a pixel p_i and aims to detect a pixel that belongs to a line above a strong echo zone Z4. The second term $f_2(p_i)$ measures the average intensity of m (here, m = 2) pixels above a pixel p_i, and favors a pixel that belongs to a line immediately below a dark NT space Z3. The third term $f_3(p_i)$ measures the downward intensity gradient which is expected at the upper edge of an echo zone Z4. The intensity gradient is estimated as vertical intensity slope of the pixel p_i using the gradient operator. The final cost term $g(p_{i-1}, p_i)$ is proportional to the square of the difference in vertical distance between the border being estimated and a reference line at node p_i; this term is designed to ensure border continuity. In the case of B2, $g(p_{i-1}, p_i)$ is calculated with a horizontal reference line. In estimating the cost term $g(p_{i-1}, p_i)$ in case of B1, the reference line is the border B2 that has already been detected.

Dynamic Programming. Dynamic programming is typically applied to optimization problems, and can be used as an optimal search method for border detection. The

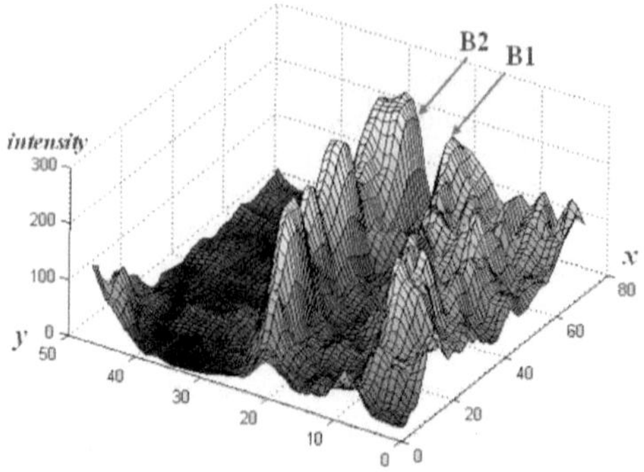

Fig. 4. 3D view of the nuchal translucency layer

optimum border is one that minimizes the given cost function, which is $C(B_N)$ in this case. The search for a solution must be performed globally in the searching region to avoid local minima due to interference patterns such as speckles.

To recast our problem as a DP search, we begin by rewriting Equation (1) in a recursive form as follows:

$$\begin{aligned} &C(B_1) = c_f(B_1), \\ &C(B_n) = C(B_{n-1}) + (c_f(p_n) + c_g(p_{n-1}, p_n)) \qquad (n = 2, \ldots, N). \end{aligned} \tag{5}$$

We denote the candidate minima of the cost function of polyline B_N as $\tilde{C}(B_n)$. Applying Equation (5), the multistage cost accumulation process can now be expressed as

$$\begin{aligned} &\tilde{C}(B_1) = c_f(B_1), \\ &\tilde{C}(B_n) = \min_{p_{n-1}} \{\tilde{C}(B_{n-1}) + (c_f(p_n) + c_g(p_{n-1}, p_n))\} \quad (n = 2, \ldots, N). \end{aligned} \tag{6}$$

To search for the optimum border, costs are accumulated according to Equation (6) and the location of p_{n-1}, which defines $\tilde{C}(B_n)$, is stored in a pointer array at each stage n. The arrows in Fig. 5(a), point to the pixel in the previous column with the minimum accumulated cost, which then allows the points of the optimal border to be derived by back-tracking.

We will now describe the cost accumulation and back-tracking process in detail within an M×N ROI. A vertical scan window of height M is used to scan the border from the start to end-point at N horizontal positions. The locations of the start and end-point are the upper-left and upper-right pixels of the ROI respectively, and correspond to the left and right arrows in Fig. 5(b). At each column n, a candidate minimum of the cost function is found for each point in that column, and its cost is accumulated. After scanning all the columns, the lowest accumulated cost is located. The position of the minimum cost point becomes the end-point of the border. Then

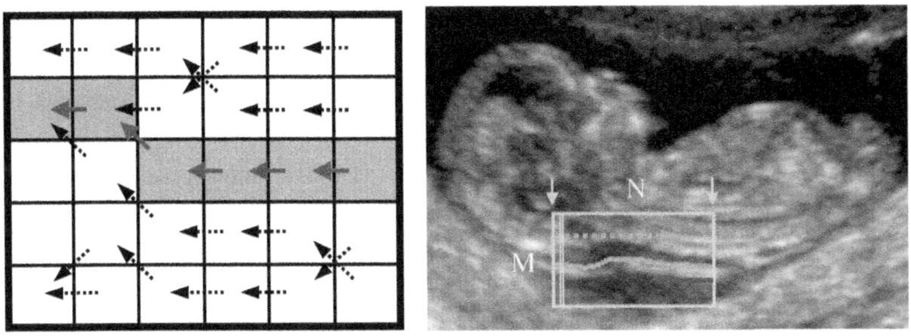

(a) (b)

Fig. 5. Border detection using dynamic programming: (a) the backtracking process, and (b) detecting the border B2 in the NT image

the back-tracking is performed following the pointers until the first column is reached in the ROI. This creates our estimate of the border. B2 can be identified relatively easily since the nearby echogenic zone Z4 is stronger than echogenic zone Z2. Therefore we find B2 first. We then search for B1 using a smoothed line of B2 as a reference line, which forms a lower limit in the search for B1.

2.4 Measurements

We measure the distance between B1 and B2 using linear regression. The process consists of five steps. In the first step, we calculate mid-points between the upper edge and the lower edge at the 2 right and left neighbors centered on a given value of x. The second step is to find the line L1 that bisects the two edges by linear regression. The third step is to find a line L2 that is orthogonal to this bisector L1. The fourth step is to fit lines L3, L4 to B1 and B2 respectively, by linear regression in the range of x that we have previously defined. Finally, we calculate the intersection points between L2 and L3, L4, and then measure the distance between pairs of points. These distances are estimates of the minimum, average and maximum NT thickness.

3 Implementation and Experimental Results

The algorithm that we have described in this paper was implemented in Visual C++ on a Pentium IV. We have applied our method to the sagittal section of 2D and 3D fetus NT images obtained by transabdominal and transvaginal ultrasonography. Fig. 6 compares the conventional edge-detectors and our method. Fig. 7 shows the resulting borders. The strength of the relationship between automated and manual methods is indicated by the correlation $c_{a,\,m}$, which is defined as follows:

$$c_{a,m} = \frac{Cov_{a,m}}{\sigma_a \sigma_m} \tag{7}$$

where $Cov_{a,m}$ is the covariance between the automated and manual and σ_a and σ_m are the standard deviation of automated and manual measurements, respectively. The means (μ_a, μ_m) and standard deviation (σ_a, σ_m) for the differences between the

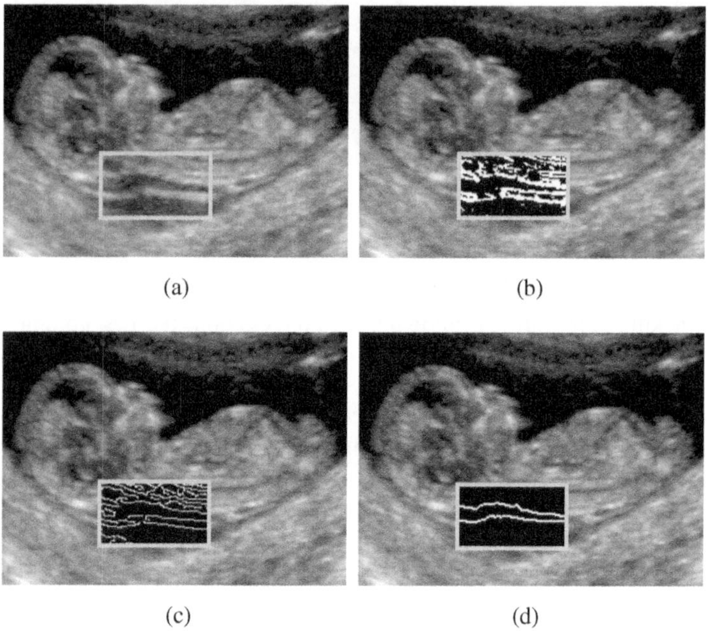

Fig. 6. Comparison of various edge-detectors: (a) original image; (b) Sobel; (c) Canny; (d) edge-detection using dynamic programming

automatic and manual measurements were calculated for the population (n=30). We calculated the correlation which is defined as accuracy between the automatic and manual measurements of the maximum thickness of the NT layer. The resulting values of the parameters μ_a, μ_m, σ_a, σ_m, $c_{a,m}$ are shown in Table 1.

Table 1. Comparison between automatic and manual methods (n = 30)

	Automatic $\mu_a \pm \sigma_a$ (mm)	**Manual** $\mu_m \pm \sigma_m$ (mm)	**Correlation** $c_{a,m}$
NT_{max}	2.68 ±0.18	2.69±0.17	0.98

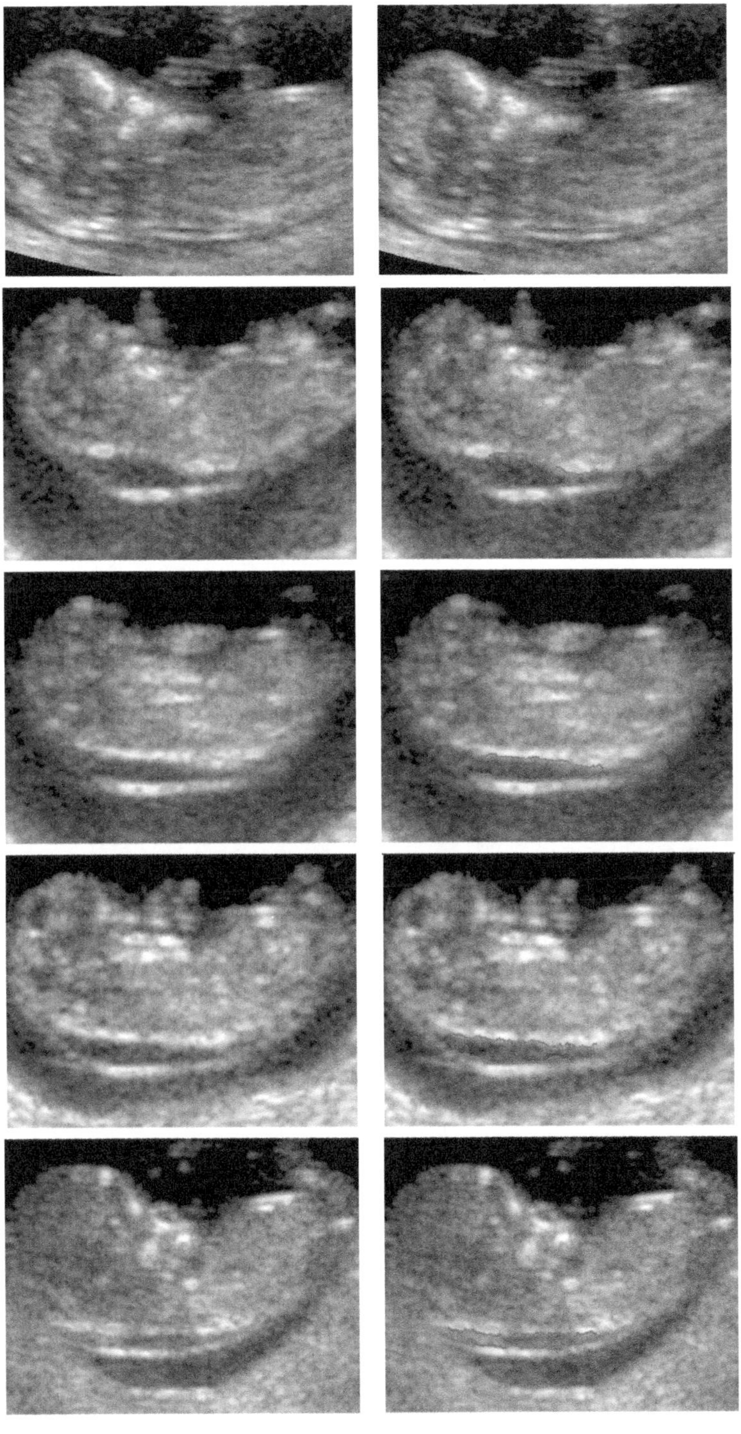

Fig. 7. Experimental results. Left: original image. Right: detecting the border of a fetal NT.

4 Conclusions

We have proposed a method for automated fetal ultrasonic measurements that is based on dynamic programming. Our method detects the borders of the nuchal translucency by constructing a cost function that includes weighted cost terms to represent multiple image features such as intensity, gradient and border continuity. We have obtained superior results to conventional edge-detection procedures that typically consider single image features. In particular, our method has overcome the problem of border continuity which occurs when weak edges are disrupted by the scattering inevitably present in ultrasound images. Our automated measurements were compared with manual measurements, and were found to be equally accurate; and an automated approach reduces the problems of variability and reproducibility that are always present with manual assessments. However, for clinical purposes, some interactive tools may still be needed in order to correct residual detection errors in extremely poor images.

Acknowledgements

This work is financially supported by the Ministry of Education and Human Resources Development (MOE), the Ministry of Commerce, Industry and Energy (MOCIE) and the Ministry of Labor (MOLAB) through the fostering project of the Lab of Excellency, and by the Korea Institute of Science & Technology Evaluation and Planning (KISTEP) under the Real Time Molecular Imaging program. We would like to thank the Medison Co. Ltd. for providing ultrasound image datasets for our experiments.

References

1. W. F. Katherine, A. Toi, S. Salem, K. H. Lisa, D. Chitayat, J. K. Sarah, F. McAuliffe, J. A. Johnson, "Detection of fetal structural abnormalities with US during early pregnancy", *RadioGraphics*, Vol. 24, 157–174, 2004.
2. R.J. Snijders, P. Noble, N. Sebire, A. Souka, K.H. Nicolaides, "UK multicentre project on assessment of risk of trisomy 21 by maternal age and fetal nuchal translucency thickness at 10-14 weeks of gestation", *The Lancet*, Vol. 352, 343–346, 1998.
3. A.P. Souka, E. Krampl, S. Bakalis, V. Heath, K.H. Nicolaides, "Outcome of pregnancy in chromosomally normal fetuses with increased nuchal translucency in the first trimester", *Ultrasound Obstet. Gynecol.* , Vol. 18, 9–17, 2001.
4. F. Bernadino, R. Cardoso, N. Montenegro, J. Bernardes, J. Marques de Sa, "Semiautomated ultrasonographic measurement of fetal nuchal translucency using a computer software tool", *Ultrasound in Med. & Biol.*, Vol. 24, No. 1, 51–54, 1998.
5. T. Gustavsson, Q. Liang, I. Wendelhag, J. Wilkstrand, "A dynamic programming procedure for automated ultrasonic measurement of the carotid artery," *in Proc. IEEE Computers Cardiology*, 297–300, 1994.
6. Q. Liang, I. Wendelhag, J. Wilkstrand, T. Gustavsson, "A multiscale dynamic programming procedure for boundary detection in ultrasonic artery images", *IEEE Trans. Med. Imag.*, Vol. 19, No. 2, 127–142, 2000.

7. I. Wendelhag, Q. Liang, T. Gustavson, J. Wilkstrand, "A new automated computerized analyzing system simplifies readings and reduces the variability in ultrasound measurement of intima-media thickness", *Stroke*, Vol. 28, 2195–2200, 1997.
8. M. Bebbington, R.D. Wilson, M.P. Johnson, "Detection of congenital heart disease in the first trimester of pregnancy", *Progress in Pediatric Cardiology*, Vol. 22, 3–8, 2006.
9. A. Alfred, "Technical Aspects of Nuchal Translucency Measurement", *Seminars in Perinatology*, Vol. 29, Issue 6, 376–379, 2005.
10. K. Nicolaides, N. Sebire, R. Snijders, *"The 11-14 Week Scan: The Diagnosis of Fetal Abnormalities"*, Parthenon Publishing Group, New York, 1999.

A Method for Detection and Modeling of the Human Spine Based on Principal Curvatures

Y. Santiesteban[1], J.M. Sanchiz[2], and J.M. Sotoca[2]

[1] Universidad de Oriente, Santiago de Cuba, Cuba
bonsagitaire@yahoo.fr
[2] Universidad Jaume I, Castellón, Spain
{sanchiz, sotoca}@uji.es

Abstract. The detection and modeling of the human spine from scanned 3D data is an important issue in biomedical shape analysis. It can be useful for avoiding invasive treatments like radiographs, taken for the purpose of monitoring spine deformations and its correction, as is the cases in scoliosis. This is especially important with children.

This work presents a new method for the detection of the human spine from 3D models of human backs formed by triangular meshes, and taken with a range sensor. The method is based on the estimation of the principal curvatures directions, and by joining valley points along these directions. Results are presented with the method applied to scanned 3D models of real patients.

1 Introduction

Serious deformities in the human spine are present in a significant percentage of the population, these includes scoliosis, and abnormal cifosis and lordosis. The idiopathic scoliosis is the most common of these deformities, mainly in children [1], this is an abnormal lateral curvature of the spine of congenital origin, or caused by trauma or disease of the vertebrae or hip bones. This is first noticed as a result of the changes that occur in the shape of the human back during the adolescent growing season. The characteristic feature is the disfiguring hump, caused by the rotation of the vertebrae and ribs, that appears together with a lateral bend of the spine.

In some cases the deterioration of the spine occurs quickly, so an early detection of this disease is very important. The most extended means of assessment has been the use of frequent X-ray examinations. Well known is the noxious effect of radiation over patients, principally in early seasons.

Aiming to find alternatives, several non-invasive methods of surface shape measurements and analysis have been proposed and used, including deformation tests [4], photographic methods [2] [3] [5].

Several works have used the analysis of the principal curvatures from 3D data to detect the human spine on the back surface [6] [7]. In the present paper, we describe a new method for the detection and modeling of the backbone, which

J.F. Martínez-Trinidad et al. (Eds.): CIARP 2006, LNCS 4225, pp. 168–177, 2006.

constitutes a preliminary step for every method that attempts to estimate the deformation of human spines.

For the development and assessment of our method we have used a 3D representation of the human back, as a computerized 3D model, obtained by a non-invasive technique, such as the use of a laser scanner. These 3D models are triangular meshes where the mesh vertices are real scanned points in the back to be represented.

The structure of this paper is as follows: in Section 2 some related works are discussed. Section 3 describes surface curvature and the approach presented in this paper for estimating these geometric features. In Section 5 we explain our approach in detail. Finally, in Section 7 conclusions are drawn and further research directions are discussed.

2 Related Work

The human back presents an almost symmetrical shape, being the spine the symmetry axis. From the lumbar area, in the base of the dorsal thorn, to the cervical region symmetry is preserved. From simple visual inspection of horizontal sections we would be able to locate the whole dorsal thorn estimating their position in each traverse section. The estimation is possible only from the mentioned symmetrical characteristic.

Symmetry of the back is affected by deformations in the spine, mainly due to affections as scoliosis, cifosis or lordosis that produce deviations and torsions. Despite this anomaly it is still possible to find in each horizontal section (profile) the point of best symmetry, that is, the point of minimum asymmetry. This point will, in fact, be a localization of the spine for this horizontal profile. The group of the points in the horizontal profiles will constitute a localization of the dorsal thorn in the all back.

This is the idea followed by Drerup and Hierholzer [6] for the detection of the spine. In their work a fixed coordinate system is attached to the body. The reference points of this reference system were: the prominence of the seventh cervical vertebra, the sacrum point, and the two points dimples of the posterior superior iliac spines. The first two points defined the vertical axis and the others two the horizontal axis. For the localization of reference points the "symmetry line" was detected along the back. Then, by means of anatomical criteria, windows were located where the points of interest were estimated. Inside each region the anatomical points were finally located using digital image processing techniques. These regions were called landmark windows. The authors use as a back surface representation the raster stereographic technique.

Another approach used in order to detect the backbone was presented by Sotoca [8]. In this case the authors use an active shape model [9] based on a statistical scheme trained with a set of samples. This method looked for a curve that represents the shortest path between point matching vertebra *C7* and point matching vertebra *L5*. This curve must fulfill also a criterion of surface smoothness lengthwise. This contribution is based on a raster stereographic technique.

3 Principal Curvatures Estimation

The use of invariant geometric properties is very extended in Computer Vision, like principal curvatures and their directions. Surface curvature is a local shape descriptor invariant to rigid body transformations, this is a concept from Differential Geometry [10] [11]. Several works about 3D object analysis and recognition are based on principal curvatures [12] [13] [14] [15]. Particularly, its use has been adequate in medical imaging applications [16] [17]. The use of polyhedral representations for approximation of real surfaces is also quite common. Actually triangular meshes is the most habitual representation for surfaces because of easiness in latter processing such as estimation of geometric features [18]. However, estimation of surface curvatures on a discrete graphical model is difficult. The main drawback is that curvatures depend on the second derivative of the surface. Some works aim at overcoming this difficulty; they are grouped regarding the techniques used, and can be classified into three main categories [19]. The first one is surface fitting methods, here curvatures are computed from an analytical surface formula that is previously fit to the discrete model points. This approach requires a local surface parameterization [20] [21]. The second class is total curvature methods, in this context curvature is estimated for a surface region and not for singles points [22]. Finally, curve fitting methods fit a family of curves around each surface point in order to estimate the curvatures [23] [24] [25]. When working with large 3D models, as such the ones present in medical applications, it is very important to use a robust estimation method capable of dealing with noise. In this sense, curve fitting based methods are very promising.

The *Normal Vector Voting (NVV)* algorithm introduced by [19] is an extension of the work presented by [26] and [27]. We have used this method, with slight modifications, for estimating principal curvatures and principal directions. This is a two-pass algorithm that can work with large, and probably noisy, triangular meshes. The first step consists of estimating the normal direction for each surface point. In the second step the principal curvatures and their directions are estimated for each surface point.

Basically, the method uses a voting scheme such that all triangles and vertices in a neighborhood of user defined radium, around the current vertex, affect the estimation of curvatures and directions for this vertex. This approach contrasts with other curvature estimation methods that only use a simple one-ring vicinity around the vertex of interest [28]. Interesting in the *NVV* is that the neighborhood of each vertex is defined using geodesic distance and not with traditional Euclidean distance. The search for the geodesic neighborhood of a vertex is related to the *discrete geodesic problem* [29]; this concerns about finding a set of triangles within a specified distance to this vertex. Geodesic distance is computed using a modification of the Kimmel and Sethian method [30], introduced by Sun and Abidi in [31].

Having the vicinity, each triangle in this patch (or geodesic neighborhood) votes for the center vertex. These votes are collected in a covariance matrix, which is decomposed using eigen-analysis. Then eigenvectors and eigenvalues are used respectively for estimating principal directions and principal curvatures for each point.

We have introduced a slight modification of the NVV algorithm that in our case produce better results, we now explain this fact. When collecting votes, in the first pass of the NVV algorithm for estimating the normal vector orientation of each vertex in the mesh, for each triangle in the geodesic neighborhood of vertex v was defined the matrix $V_v = \sum w_i V_i$. In this definition V_i is the covariance matrix $V_i = N_i N_i^t$ where N_i is the normal vector for each triangle in the geodesic neighborhood. w_i is a weighting term defined as $w_i = \frac{A_i}{A_{\max}} \exp\left(-\frac{g_i}{\sigma}\right)$ where A_i is the area of each triangle, g_i is the geodesic distance from the center of the triangle to the vertex v, σ is a constant value defined as function of a maximal geodesic distance defined by the user such that votes from triangle beyond this distance have a negligible influence. The other term in this expression is $A_{\max}$ which is defined as the maximal area in the all mesh. However, the dimension of the triangles in a mesh can vary significantly, and this fact can produce adverse numerical effects in neighborhoods with triangles of small area relative to the maximal area. To overcome this drawback we have used, with better results, the local maximal area in the geodesic neighborhood of the current vertex instead of global maximal area.

4 Method Overview

The proposed approach proceeds by computing the minimum asymmetry point located on each of several horizontal profiles placed on the back surface. Each of these points is an estimation of the position of the spine, so we can model the backbone by means of this set of minimum asymmetry points. But in our approach the model used is a triangular mesh, and the way of defining a horizontal profile is different that what it would be using other model for the back surface, for example if we use raster stereography. When we set a horizontal cutting plane in order to find intersections with the surface and obtain points forming this horizontal profile, in the case of triangular meshes we can not control the amount of points in this intersection. So, when defining horizontal profiles we can not just take vertices of the triangular mesh belonging to the cutting plane (see Figure 1).

On the other hand, we use directions of principal curvatures as local shape descriptor of the back surface. We assume that surface is oriented such the backbone is almost vertical. To obtain horizontal profiles we set several horizontal cutting planes intercepting the surface uniformly along that vertical axis (Figure 1 a). To define a profile we take into account all vertices belonging to the corresponding cutting plane and also all vertices between this cutting plane and the following one. Then we project all these points over the current cutting plane and we use all these projected points as profile definition.

When projecting 3D vertices on a cutting plane several of these point can be very close between them. In general, we are not interested in processing all the projected points placed near the same coordinate in the x axis ((Figure 1) b),

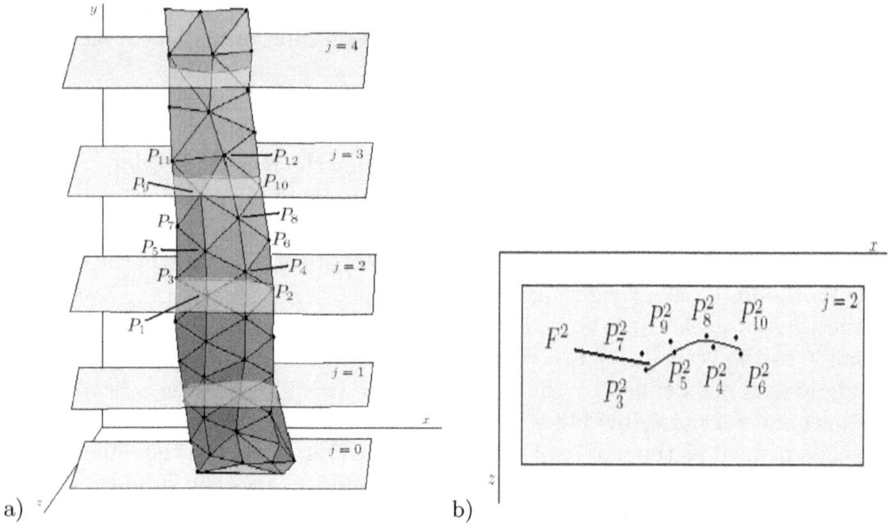

Fig. 1. Horizontal cutting planes defining profiles

regardless coordinate in the z axis. So, we use a clustering method in order to find groups of points close to each other in the cutting plane. Then we use only the central point for each cluster representing all points that have been classified together. This central point is not necessarily a member of the cluster, but the cluster centroid.

So far we have a set of points for each cutting plane, next we need to use a local shape descriptor to analyze the surface behavior in this profile. We select one direction of the principal curvatures for each point as a local shape descriptor. The direction chosen is the most horizontal one. The direction of the curvature for the cluster centroid is obtained from the direction of all points in the cluster.

At this point a profile is formed by a set of points (cluster centroid) and one direction for each of these points. Afterwards we find convex and concave regions taking second derivatives in the profile, then we select one of these regions by a criterion of symmetric position in the profile. The point locating the spine is the middle point of the selected region.

Having a location for the spine on each profile, the entire backbone is modeled by a third degree polynomial. A robust fitting method that can cope with outliers is used to estimate the polynomial parameters.

5 Human Spine Detection Method Based on Principal Directions

At this stage we assume that principal curvatures and directions have been estimated for every vertex in the triangular mesh modeling the back surface. In the following we explain in detail how to obtain the horizontal profiles.

Let $\{v_i^1, v_i^2\}$ be the pair of principal directions for each surface point P_i, $i = 1, 2, \ldots, n$, where n is the number of vertices in the mesh. We associate vector v_i to each point P_i. v_i is defined as

$$v_i = \begin{cases} v_i^1 \text{ if } \left|v_{i_y}^1\right| \leq \left|v_{i_y}^2\right| \\ v_i^2 \text{ other case} \end{cases},$$

where $v_{i_y}^1$ and $v_{i_y}^2$ are the y axis component for the first and second principal directions. In others words, we assign to each point the most horizontal of the two principal curvatures directions.

In the rest of the paper we suppose that the surface orientation and the reference coordinate system is as showed in Figure 2. We also assume that points of minimum coordinate in the y axis lie in the $x - z$ plane. So we can define the height of the surface, L, as the maximum coordinate in the y axis.

We place several cutting planes intercepting horizontally the surface, and then we project all points over some cutting plane. Denoting as $y = j\lambda$ the family of cutting planes, where $j = 0, 1, 2, \ldots, N$, N being the number of cutting planes, we can derive that $N = \left[\frac{L}{\lambda}\right]$, λ being a constant value representing the spacing between any pair of cutting planes and $\left[\div\right]$ representing the integer part operation. We refer to a cutting plane by its factor j, and because there is a single profile for each cutting plane and vice versa, we refer to the profile j which is attached to the cutting plane j.

Next we can define how points are projected onto the cutting planes. A point $P(x_P, y_P, z_P)$ is projected onto cutting plane j if this is the nearest cutting plane, such that $y_P \geq j\lambda$. We denote projection of P on plane j as $P^j(x_P, j\lambda, z_P)$.

In order to simplify the profiles and obtain only useful shape information, we use an incremental clustering technique for grouping close points. Incremental clustering algorithms form clusters dynamically each time a new object is available. These methods are extensively used in document classification, image segmentation and more applications. Given a set of objects to be clustered, clustering algorithms define partitions of this set. For the clustering task a representation space, a similarity measure between objects and a clustering criterion are needed.

In our case, the objects to be grouped are 2D points (3D points projected on a cutting plane). For the clustering algorithm, and as a similarity measure between two point projections $P_1^j\left(x_{i_1}^j, j\lambda, z_{i_1}^j\right)$ and $P_2^j\left(x_{i_2}^j, j\lambda, z_{i_2}^j\right)$ we define the function $s(P_1^j, P_2^j) = |x_{i_1} - x_{i_2}|$. This function take as similar points that are close by the x axis component regardless the z axis component.

It is frequent in the literature to use a *cluster centroid* such that when estimating if new objects will be in a given cluster, comparison is made between the new object and the *cluster centroid* instead of between the new objects and all objects in the cluster. Each time a new objects is inserted into the cluster, the *cluster centroid* is updated. We use this approach and we define the *cluster centroid* for the cluster C^j as the point $P_{C^j}(x_{C^j}, j\lambda, z_{C^j})$ where x_{C^j} and z_{C^j} are the average coordinate in x and z axis respectively for all points in C^j. Here j is the cutting plane.

As a clustering criterion we use the fact that P will be in cluster C^j if and only if $s(P, P_{C^j}) < r$, where r is a user defined threshold.

We have used the *Single-Pass* algorithm by Hill [32] for clustering the set of points projected on each cutting plane. This is a simple method that assigns a point to the first cluster that matches the clustering criterion.

Then, we define the set $M^j = \left\{P^j_{C_1}, P^j_{C_2}, \ldots, P^j_{C_m}\right\}$ as the set of cluster centroid, here m is the number of clusters for cutting plane j. Associated to M^j, we define the set of directions for each *cluster centroid* $V^j = \left\{v^j_1, v^j_2, \ldots, v^j_m\right\}$. Each vector in V^j is obtained by averaging components of the direction vector for each point in the corresponding cluster. We identify the profile for cutting plane j as the set of cluster centroids M^j, and the set of profile directions is V^j.

For each profile j we consider the function $f(v^j_k) = \tan \alpha^j_k$, where α^j_k is the slope angle of v^j_k. All v^j_k are 2D vectors in cutting plane j. Function f has following property: $f(v_k) = (F^j)'$, where F^j is the analytic intersection curve between the cutting plane and the surface. After that, we consider the function $g(v^j_k) = G(f(v^j_k))$, where G is a first derivative Gaussian function. The use of a Gaussian function has the effect of smoothing the profile and obtaining its second derivative, then we have that $g(v^j_k) = (F^j)''$. So far profiles have been defined, the next step is the detection of concave and convex regions for each profile. Aiming at this we use the following statement: $P^j_{C_k}$ is in a concave region if $g(v^j_k) > 0$. On the other hand, if $g(v^j_k) < 0$ then $P^j_{C_k}$ is on a convex region.

In this manner, our method selects points from concave and convex regions for each profile. By means of a symmetry criterion in the profile, using the geodesic distance, we select only one point for each profile. At the end we have selected a set of points that match the spine location on the surface.

Finally the human spine has to be modeled and for that purpose we use a third-degree polynomial. Being $\{P^j(x_{P^j}, j\lambda, z_{P^j})\}$ the set of selected points for each profile, we consider the function $x_{P^j} = h(j\lambda)$ and we use robust linear regression [33] in order to fit x_{P^j} as a function of $j\lambda$. Algorithm used is an iteratively re weighted least squares approach [34]. This method assign lower weight to points that do not fit well, resulting in a fit less sensitive to outliers in the input data. In this manner we have obtained a 2D curve that reflet lateral deviations of backbone. In order to obtain a 3D curve we project the 2D curve over the surface.

6 Results

Several 3D models of patients with spine deformities, consisting of triangular meshes, have been taken using a commercial laser scanner, model FastSCAN by Polhemus. The size of the models is about 26000 vertices and 67000 triangles. The proposed approach to obtain an estimation of the spine was applied to the models. First, the principal curvatures directions were estimated using the modified *NVV* algorithm presented in Section 3. Next, horizontal profiles were

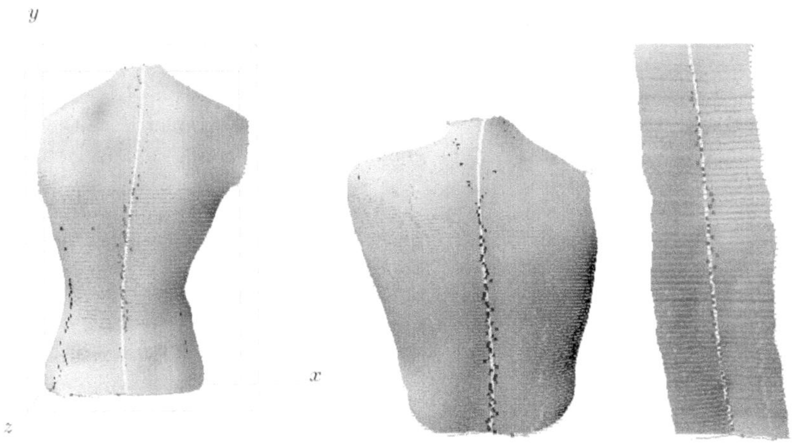

Fig. 2. Horizontal profiles, points of maximum symmetry, and curves modeling the spine in three models of real human backs

defined all along the back using the most horizontal direction of the curvatures. The mesh vertices were projected on the closest profile, and a clustering was done to obtain points all along each profile. Concave and convex regions were bounded in each profile and the best symmetry region was selected according to the concave-convex changes. Then, in each best symmetry region, and for each profile, the best symmetry point was identified. Having one best symmetry point in each profile, a three-degree polynomial curve was fit by robust least squares. Figure 2 shows the curves that model the spines estimated from three example models of real patients.

7 Conclusions and Further Work

We have presented a new method for estimating and modeling the human spine from scanned 3D models of the human back consisting of triangular meshes. The method is based on estimating the principal curvature directions, defining point profiles in horizontal directions, and detecting valley points. The method has been applied to real scanned human backs producing encouraging results. From the spine model important geometric information can be derived, like the Cobb angles. Further work is addressed at estimating and quantifying asymmetries in the spine and in the whole back.

Acknowledgments

This work is partially supported by the Spanish Ministry of Science and Technology under Project TIC2003-06953, and by Fundació Caixa Castelló under project P1-1B2004-08.

References

1. Archer, I.A., Dickson, R.A. Stature and idiopathic scoliosis. A prospective study. Journal of Bone Joint Surg, Vol. 67 (1985) 185-188
2. Frobin, W., Hierholzer, E. Rasterstereography: a photogrametric method for measurement of body surfaces. Photogrammetric Engineering and Remote Sensing, Vol. 47 (1982) 1717–1724
3. Buendía, M., Salvador, R., Cibrian, R., Laguía, M., Sotoca, J.M. Determination of the object surface function by structured light: applications to the study of spinal deformities. Med. Phys. Biol., No. 44, 75–86 (1999)
4. Takasaki, H. Moiré Topography. Applied Optics, Vol. 9 (1970) 1467–1472
5. Turner-Smith, A.R. A Television/Computer three-dimensional surface shape measurement system. Journal of biomechanics, Vol. 21 (1988) 515–529
6. Drerup, B., Hierholzer, E. Automatic localization of anatomical landmarks on the back surface and construction of a body-fixed coordinate system. Journal of Biomechanics, Vol. 20, No. 10 (1987) 961–970
7. Frobin, W., Hierholzer, E. Analysis of human back shape using surface curvatures. Journal of Biomechanics, No. 15 (1982) 379–390
8. Sotoca, J.M., Buendía, M., Iñesta, J.M., Ferri, F.J. Geometric properties of the 3D spine curve. Lecture Notes in Computer Science 2652, F. J. Perales et al (eds.), Springer-Verlag, 1003–1011 (2003)
9. Cootes, T.F., Taylor, C.J., Cooper, D.H., Graham, J. Active shape models: Their Training and application. Computer vision and image understanding, No. 61, 38–59 (1995)
10. do Carmo, M. P. Differential Geometry of Curves and Surfaces. Prentice-Hall, Englewood Cliffs, NJ, (1976)
11. ONeill, B. Elementrary Differential Geometry. 2nd ed., Academic Press, Orlando, FL, (1997)
12. Besl, P.J., Jain, R.C. Invariant surface characteristics for 3d object recognition in range images. Computer Vision, Graphics, and Image Processing, No. 33, (1986) 33-80
13. Brady, M., Ponce, J., Yuille, A., Asada, H. Describing surfaces. Computer Vision, Graphics, and Image Processing, No. 32, 1-28 (1985)
14. Feldmar, J., Ayache, N. Rigid and affine registration of smooth surfaces using differential properties. In Jan-Olof Eklundh, editor, Proceedings, European Conference on Computer Vision, number 801 in Lecture Notes in Computer Science, Springer-Verlag, 397-406 (1994)
15. Medioni, G., Nevatia, R. Description of 3-D surfaces using curvature properties In Proceedings, DARPA Image Understanding Workshop, New Orleans, LA, 291-299 (1984)
16. Guéziec, A., Ayache, N. Smoothing and matching of 3d space curves. International Journal of Computer Vision, No. 12, 79-104 (1994)
17. Monga, O., Benayoun, S., Faugeras, O. From partial derivatives of 3d density images to ridge lines. In Proceedings, IEEE Conference on Computer Vision and Pattern Recognition, 354-359 (1992)
18. Chen, X., Schmitt, F. Intrinsic surface properties from surface triangulation. In Proceedings of the European Conference on Computer Vision, Santa Margherita Ligure, Italy, 739-743 (1992)
19. Page, D. L., Sun, Y., Koschan, A.F., Paik, J., Abidi, A. Normal Vector Voting: Crease detection and curvature estimation on large, noisy meshes. Journal of Graphical Models, Vol. 64 (2003) 1–31

20. Hagen, H., Heinz, S., Thesing, M., Schreiber, T. Simulation based modeling. Int. J. Shape Modeling, No. 4, 143-164 (1998)
21. Rössl, C., Kobbelt, L., Seidel, H. Extraction of feature lines on triangulated surfaces using morphological operators. Smart Graphics (AAAI Symposium 2000), Menlo Park, CA, AAAI Press, New York, 71-75 (2000)
22. C. Lin and M. J. Perry Shape description using surface triangulation. Proceedings of the IEEE Workshop on Computer Vision: Representation and Control, 38–43 (1982)
23. Martin, R.R. Estimation of principal curvatures from range data Int. J. Shape Modeling, No. 4, 99–109 (1998)
24. Tookey, R.M., Ball, A.A. Estimation of curvatures from planar point data. The Mathematics of Surfaces VII, Information Geometers, Winchester, 131-141 (1997)
25. Várady, T., Hermann, T. Best fit surface curvature at vertices of topologically irregular curve networks The Mathematics of Surfaces VI, Oxford University Press, Oxford, 411-427 (1996)
26. Tang, C.K., Medioni, G. Robust estimation of curvature information from noisy 3D data for shape description. Proceedings of the Seventh International Conference on Computer Vision, Kerkyra, Greece, 426–433 (1999)
27. Taubin, G. Estimating the tensor of curvature of a surface from a polyhedral approximation. Proceedings of the Fifth International Conference on Computer Vision, 902-907 (1995)
28. Meyer, M., Desbrun, M., Schroder, P., Barr, A.H. Discrete Differential-Geometry Operators for Triangulated 2-Manifolds. VisMath '02, Berlin, Germany, (2002)
29. Mitchell, J.S.B., Mount, D.M., Papadimitriou, C.H. The discrete geodesic problem. SIAM J. Comput. 16, 647-668 (1987)
30. Kimmel, R., Sethian, J.A. Computing geodesic paths on manifolds. Proc. National Academy of Sciences, 8431–8435 (1998)
31. Sun, Y., Abidi, M.A. Surface matching by 3D points fingerprint. Proceedings of the Eighth International Conference On Computer Vision, Vol. 2 (2001) 263–269
32. Hill, D. R. A vector clustering technique. In Samuelson (ed.), Mechanized Information Storage, Retrieval and Dissemination, North-Holland, Amsterdam (1968)
33. Street, J.O., Carroll, R.J., Ruppert, D. A Note on Computing Robust Regression Estimates via Iteratively Reweighted Least Squares. The American Statistician, No. 42, 152–154 (1988)
34. Holland, P.W., Welsch, R.E. Robust Regression Using Iteratively Reweighted Least-Squares. Communications in Statistics: Theory and Methods, A6, 813–827 (1977)

Linear Radial Patterns Characterization for Automatic Detection of Tonic Intestinal Contractions

Fernando Vilariño[1], Panagiota Spyridonos[1], Jordi Vitrià[1], Carolina Malagelada[2], and Petia Radeva[1]

[1] Computer Vision Center. Universitat Autònoma de Barcelona, Bellaterra 08193, Spain
[2] Hospital Vall d'Hebron, Barcelona 08035, Spain
fernando@cvc.uab.es
http://www.cvc.uab.es/~fernando

Abstract. This work tackles the categorization of general linear radial patterns by means of the valleys and ridges detection and the use of descriptors of directional information, which are provided by steerable filters in different regions of the image. We successfully apply our proposal in the specific case of automatic detection of tonic contractions in video capsule endoscopy, which represent a paradigmatic example of linear radial patterns.

1 Introduction

In this work, we propose a general methodology for the achievement of suitable features for the categorization of linear radial patterns. The interest about categorizing radial patterns is underpinned by the fact that a considerable number of points of interest in computer vision are to be points with an intrinsic radial structure -an interesting and deep review about this issue can be found at [7]-. Recent works presented the characterization of radial patterns to tackle the facial feature extraction, finding blobs in images, processing astronomical images, and starfish tracking, among others. Most of these approaches involve the analysis of the gradient image in a constrained neighborhood, and the application of a symmetry transform which codifies the degree of radial symmetry for each pixel of the image.

Our approach is specifically focused towards the characterization of linear radial patterns by means of the analysis of the overall directional information surrounding the centroid of a given linear pattern. We achieve this by means of the division of the image into several quadrants, and by calculating a set of features which carry the directional information for each quadrant. We also propose an alternative method based on the previous polar transform of the linear pattern. On the one hand, our approach is directly addressed to the specific issue of linear radial patterns ranging the whole image, which lays out of the scope of previous methods, which are focused to the localization of points of interest in a constrained neighborhood by using gradient analysis. On the other

J.F. Martínez-Trinidad et al. (Eds.): CIARP 2006, LNCS 4225, pp. 178–187, 2006.

hand, this orientation appears specially suitable for the specific issue of the automatic detection of tonic intestinal contractions in capsule video endoscopy for intestinal motility assessment [8].

Video capsule endoscopy [4] is a novel clinical technique based on the analysis of the video images provided by a camera attached to a capsule, which is ingested by the patient, in a frame rate of 2 frames per second. Tonic intestinal contractions are rendered in video capsule endoscopy images as a sequence of frames showing a radial pattern of wrinkles, corresponding to the intestinal folds. The manual annotation of these kind of sequences provides a useful source of information for intestinal motility assessment, but this is tedious and time consuming task, which may span for several hours. The use of the linear radial pattern characterization approach which we present in this work appears to deal in a successful way with the automatic detection of this type of events.

The organization of this paper is as follows: Section 2 introduces the visual paradigm of tonic contractions. Section 3 explains the procedure for the obtention of the linear pattern based on the valleys and ridges detection. Section 4 explains the categorization procedure of the linear radial patterns. Section 5 shows the results of our approach for the automatic detection of tonic contractions. We finish our contribution with our conclusions in Section 6.

2 *Tonic Intestinal Contractions*: Visual Paradigms and Video Annotation

Tonic contractions are produced by muscular tone [5], and can be visualized in capsule endoscopy as a continuous closing of the intestinal lumen with a high variability in length. Thus, the visual pattern of tonic contractions corresponds to a sequence of a closed intestinal lumen in a undefined number of frames. This pattern is highly recognizable for the presence of the characteristic wrinkles which the continuous muscular tone produces when the intestinal walls are folded. Figure 1 shows a characteristic example of a tonic contraction -frames are sequentially deployed from left to right and from top to bottom-.

Fig. 1. Sustained contraction (bounded by the green line) spanning 15 frames

The procedure of annotation of tonic contractions in capsule endoscopy consists of the visualization of the whole video by the specialist, and the labelling of the contraction frames. As long as the duration of tonic contractions is not constrained, and varies in a wide range, the specialist labels the first and last frames of the sequence which contains the contraction. The threshold for the consideration of a motility event as a tonic contraction is set by the specialist in at least 10 frames. This procedure becomes a tedious and time consuming task. For a typical study spanning 2 hours of video, and containing about 40 tonic contractions, a trained specialist may last about 3 hours for an accurate annotation.

3 *Intestinal Wrinkles* Detection Through Valleys and Ridges Analysis

Our hypothesis is that the characteristic pattern of radial wrinkles which tonic contractions show is associated with the valleys and ridges analysis of its intensity image. But before the application of a method for the valleys and ridges detection, endoscopy images must be pre-processed in order to smooth them, which we successfully performed by meas of a median filter, with a fixed rectangular window. The size of the median filter window is set to the mean width of wrinkles in sustained contractions, which is set to 6.5 pixels. The application of this filter is justified by the sharpness of the images in areas where a homogeneous view of the intestinal walls is rendered. This is mainly due to the physiological structure of the intestinal walls tissue, and some amount of image noise. Figure 2 (b) renders one example of the results of the median filter smoothing. We tried other sophisticated smoothing methods, such as anisotropic diffusion, which respects the structural information of the image in order to a apply the smoothing by keeping sharpness in edges, obtaining similar results but with a dramatic increase in the computation time.

The valley and ridge detection procedure is performed in the following way: we create a filter mask by calculating the second derivative of an anisotropic gaussian kernel [6]. The implemented anisotropic kernel uses $\sigma_1 = 1$ and $\sigma_2 = 2$ for each direction. We obtain 4 different filter responses $F^i(n)$ for an input image I_n as:

$$F^i(n) = I_n * \ kern_{\alpha_i}, \quad \alpha_i = \frac{i\pi}{4} \tag{1}$$

where, α_i represents 4 different orientations $0^0, 45^0, 90^0$ and 135^0, $kern_{\alpha_i}$ represents the anisotropic kernel rotated α_i radians, and $*$ represents the convolution operator. The valleys and ridges images F^{val} and F^{rid} are calculated as:

$$\begin{aligned} F^{val}(n) &= \quad \max_{(x,y)}\{F^i(n)\} \\ F^{rid}(n) &= \max_{(x,y)}\{(-1) * F^i(n)\} \end{aligned} \tag{2}$$

where $max_{(x,y)}$ represents the maximum value of the F^i functions for the (x, y) pixel. Figure 2 (c) shows the valleys image F^{val} for the example image of Figure 2 (a). In the next step of our procedure, we create a binary image by keeping the 75% percentile of $F^{val}(n)$ and $F^{rid}(n)$. Figure 2 (d) shows the binary image created by this procedure for F^{val}. Finally, we apply a morphological skeletonisation [2] in order to obtain the lines with one pixel connectivity which describe

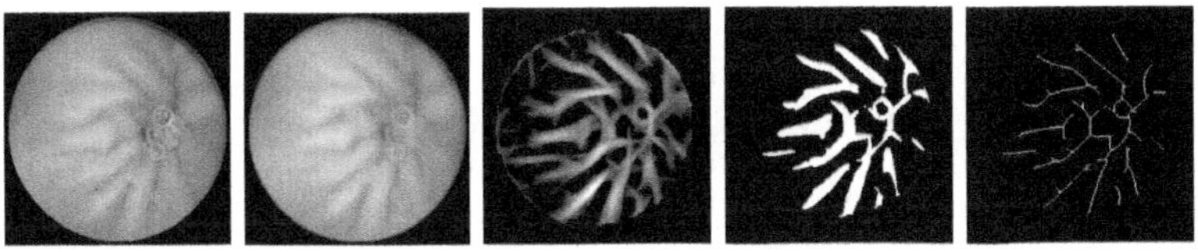

(a) (b) (c) (d) (e)

Fig. 2. (a) Original image. (b) Smoothed image. (c) Valley detection. (d) Binary image. (e) Skeletonisation results.

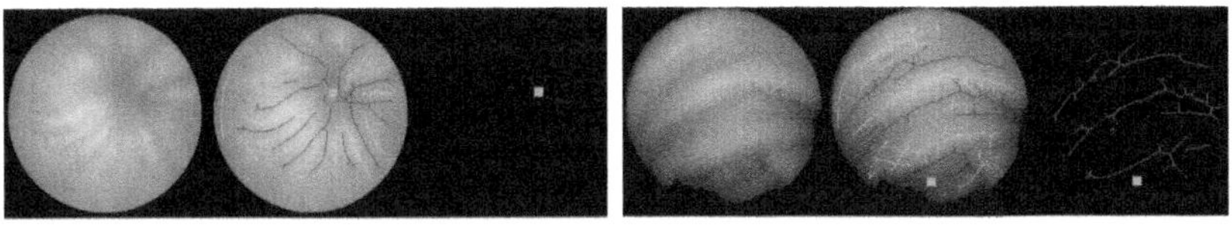

(a) (b)

Fig. 3. Original image, wrinkles detected as valleys (blue) and ridges (cyan), and wrinkles pattern for (a) a frame from a tonic contraction and (b) a randomly selected frame

the valleys and the ridges. Figure 2 (e) shows the skeletons created by this procedure. Figure 3 shows the super-imposition of the valleys and wrinkles for two test frames: (a) a frame from a sustained contraction, and (b) a random frame. The green square corresponds to the center of the intestinal lumen. This point can be straightforward estimated as the centroid of the binary blob obtained by applying a greater-than-zero threshold on the response image of laplacian of gaussian detector with $\sigma = 6$, as [8] demonstrated. Notice that the centroid of the lumen appears in the middle of the radial wrinkle pattern for the contraction frame. On the contrary, for the random frame the position of the centroid of the lumen does not follow a fixed pattern.

4 Descriptors for Linear Radial Patterns

We propose two different strategies for the linear radial patterns characterization. The first approach is based on 4 descriptors which code the multi-directional information of the wrinkles. The second approach simplifies the number of descriptors to 2, by means of a polar transform of the original data. Although the wrinkle pattern is defined both by valleys and ridges, we used only the valleys pattern as a source of wrinkle information because valleys usually show a higher degree of contrast, a more regular radial organization, and keep a more constant orientation for each wrinkle. The inclusion of ridges is shown not to provide a better performance in the specific case of intestinal contractions.

4.1 Multidirectional Approach

For a given wrinkle pattern, we define 4 different quadrants -see Figure 4 (a)-, which we denote by quadrant 1, 2, 3 and 4, using the centroid of the lumen as the

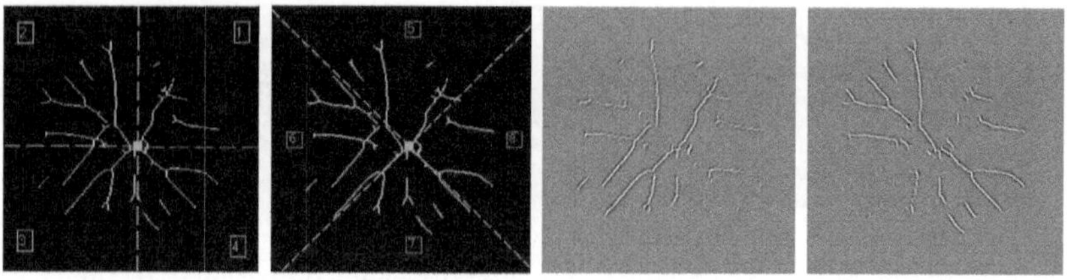

(a) (b) (c) (d)

Fig. 4. Quadrant divisions of a frame -(a) and (b)-, and two filter responses for two different orientations: (c) 45^0, and (d) 135^0

quadrant division middle point. In our preliminary tests, we checked other approaches for the center estimation, such as using as a centroid the center of mass of the wrinkle pattern. However, the results provided by these alternatives were not as satisfactory as those provided by the proposed method. The directional information is obtained by means of 4 second derivative of gaussian steerable filters [1], oriented to 45^0 and 135^0. For both filters, $\sigma = 1$, so they basically operate as line detectors in the direction towards they are oriented. The former output is used to define two descriptors f^1 and f^2 as:

$$\begin{array}{l|l} f^1(n) = G^{45^0}_{1,3}(n) - G^{135^0}_{1,3}(n) & f^3(n) = G^{0^0}_{6,8}(I_n) - G^{90^0}_{6,8}(I_n) \\ f^2(n) = G^{135^0}_{2,4}(n) - G^{45^0}_{2,4}(n) & f^4(n) = G^{90^0}_{5,7}(I_n) - G^{0^0}_{5,7}(I_n) \end{array} \quad (3)$$

where $G^{\theta}_{i,j}(n)$ represents the sum of the response of the filter with orientation θ over all the pixels of the image I_n in the quadrants i and j. Thus, f^1 and f^2 codify the global amount of directional information in the diagonal radial direction for each quadrant. This same analysis was repeated for a 45^0 rotated version of the quadrant distribution as shown Figure 4 (b), defining the new quadrants labelled by 5, 6, 7 and 8. This new quadrant distribution provides two more descriptors f^3 and f^4 defined in equation (3), which codify the global amount of directional information in the vertical and horizontal directions for each quadrant. The paradigmatic response of two filters oriented 45^0 and 135^0 is rendered in Figure 4 (c) and (d). In order to illustrate the behavior of this set of descriptors, we edited a pool of synthetic images and calculated f^1, f^2, f^3 and f^4. Figure 5 shows the feature values for several test images: the four features tend to express high positive values for the linear radial patterns and high negative values for concentric distributions.

4.2 Polar Transform Approach

Polar transform [3] consists of a mapping from the original cartesian image, in which each pixel is referred to by the pair $(row, column)$, into a transformed image in which each pixel is referred to by a pair $(angle, dist)$. In order to perform a polar transform, we need to fix a center. For each pixel with cartesian coordinates $(row, column)$, the $dist$ value is its Euclidean distance to the center, while the angle value is the angle which the vector connecting the center and the pixel

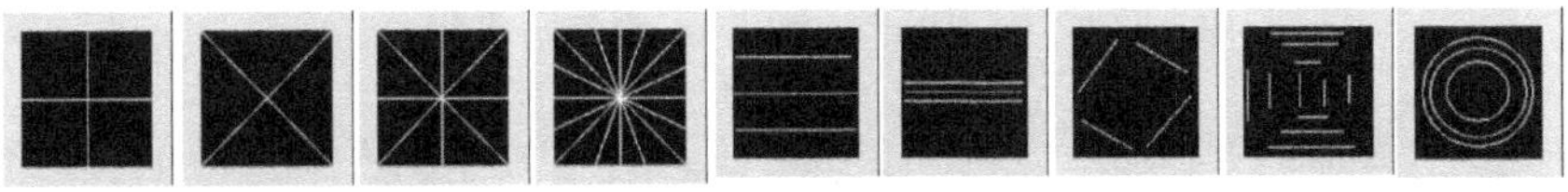

f^1:	00.00	10.00	09.30	26.19	00.00	00.00	-5.40	00.00	-19.65
f^2:	00.00	09.81	09.06	24.86	00.00	00.00	-8.64	00.00	-19.65
f^3:	10.04	-0.25	09.61	17.50	-14.03	-4.39	-0.95	-11.35	-12.29
f^4:	08.85	0.25	08.96	14.91	09.05	24.18	-0.12	-10.46	-10.39

Fig. 5. Directional features for test images

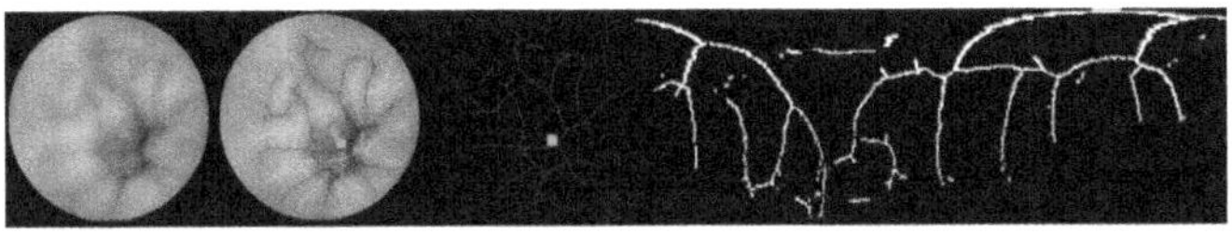

Fig. 6. Wrinkles detected as valleys in polar coordinates

forms with the horizontal axis. In the polar image, the horizontal axis represents the angle parameter, ranging in the interval $[0^0, 360^0]$ from left to right. The vertical axis represents the dist parameter, ranging in the interval $[0, max_{dist}]$ from top to bottom, where max_{dist} corresponds to the maximal distance between two pixels within the camera field of view -which in capsule endoscopy frames corresponds to 240 pixels-.We set the center of the polar transform to be the centroid of the lumen, relating the origin of the transform to the center of the intestinal lumen. Figure 6 shows the result of the polar transform on the wrinkles associated to valleys (blue) for a given frame. Finally, we calculate two descriptors $f^{1'}$ and $f^{2'}$ as follows:

$$\begin{aligned} f^{1'}(n) &= G^{0^0}(I_n^{polar}) \\ f^{2'}(n) &= G^{90^0}(I_n^{polar}) \end{aligned} \tag{4}$$

where $f^{1'}(n)$ and $f^{2'}(n)$ codify the global amount of directional information in the horizontal and vertical direction of the polar image I_n^{polar} of the n frame.

4.3 Definition of the Area of Analysis

As we previously showed, intestinal folds and wrinkles in tonic contractions appear as radial lines in the cartesian image, and as nearly vertical lines in the polar transformed image. However, it must be noticed that this pattern undergoes deformations which are more severe around the the lumen center, and also in distant points from the center -distant parts of the wrinkles usually occur to be curved and no longer respect the radial orientation-. These both regions correspond to the top and bottom areas in the polar plot. To minimize the influence of this phenomenon, we tested the exclusion of the area defined by the lumen detector from the wrinkle analysis. In addition to this, we also excluded all the distant pixels. This exclusion was performed by a simple morphological procedure of dilation and substraction as defined in Figure 7. The region of analysis

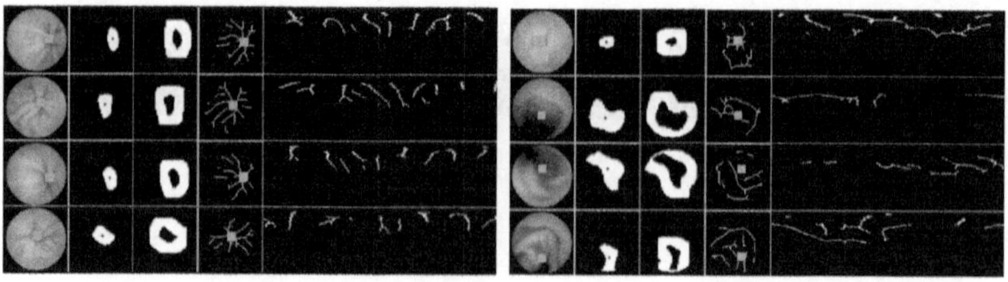

(a) (b)

Fig. 7. (a) Tonic contractions. (b) Randomly selected frames.

is defined by a ring-wise or donut mask, which is to be applied to the valleys wrinkle pattern previously to the feature extraction procedure. Figure 7 shows several examples of (a) frames from tonic contractions and (b) random frames, with their corresponding lumen blobs, masks, wrinkles and polar transform of the valleys wrinkles pattern, restricted to the donut-mask.

5 Results

We tested the features explained in last section, defining 4 different sets: 1) *Quadrant*: features f^1, f^2, f^3 and f^4, 2) *Quadrant-donut*: features f^1, f^2, f^3 and f^4, restricted to the mask defined in Figure 7, 3) *Polar*: features $f^{1'}$ and $f^{2'}$, and 4) *Polar-donut*: the same like quadrant-donut, but using the polar features $f^{1'}$ and $f^{2'}$. For the dilatation step of the donut generation, we used a 40 pixels squared structural element. For each feature set, we run 3 different experimental tests in order to assess the performance of our approach in the detection of frames belonging to tonic contractions, and the final detection rate of tonic contractions: Our first experiment consisted of testing the performance of our system with patterns of frames belonging to sustained contraction without any further restriction. The second experiment tried to quantify the number of *frames* belonging to sustained contractions which were labelled as contraction frames -sensitivity over frames belonging to tonic contractions sequences-. Finally, the third experiment provides the global performance, over one whole video, in terms of sensitivity and precision.

For the performance assessment on general patterns of frames belonging to tonic contractions -from now on, we refer this set to as *wrinkle frames*-, the specialists selected a pool of 2,414 wrinkle frames and 2,414 randomly selected frames which did not belong to any tonic contraction -from now on, we refer this set to as *non-wrinkle frames*-. For all our experiments we trained a SVM classifiers with a radial basis function kernel and $\gamma = 0.05$. We used 80% of the samples for training and 20% for testing, performing 10 runs. Figure 8 show the ROC and PR-curves of the classification experiments for the different features sets. Both *quadrant* and *quadrant-donut* feature sets showed similar behaviors in the ROC curve, although the PR-curve analysis showed that quadrant presented optimal performance in precision in the middle region of recall (sensitivity) of wrinkle frames.

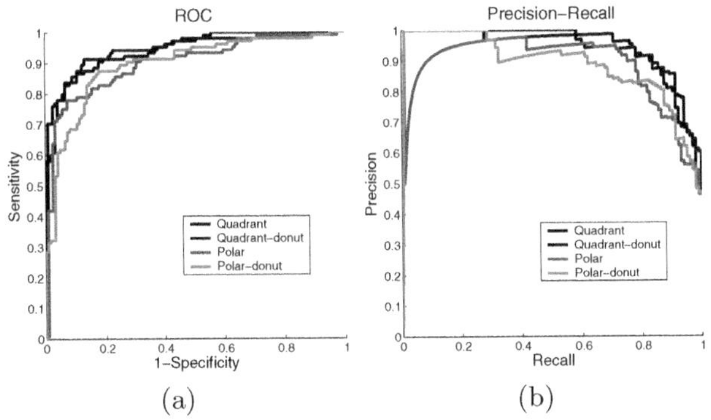

Fig. 8. (a) ROC, and (b) PR curves for the wrinkle frames detection

We used the classifier trained in the last experiment with the *quadrant* feature set in order to label all the frames of the sequences of tonic contractions. The aim of this experiment is to assess the sensitivity of our system for frames of tonic contractions. Table 1 summarizes the results provided by our system. We analyzed 42 sustained contractions with 737 frames. The mean length of the contractions was 14.2(±5.3) frames. Our system detected 454 frames, which represents 61.5% of all the frames belonging to tonic contractions. In average, for each contraction sequence, our system labelled 60.9% of frames as frames showing the radial wrinkle pattern.

Table 1. Detection of frames belonging to tonic contractions

Number of tonic contractions:	42	(737 frames)
Number of annotated frames:	454	(61.5%)
Avg. frame annotation by sequence:	60.9%	(±0.3)

The final step for the validation of our system consists of the automatic labelling of tonic contractions for one video. In order to define the criteria for the detection of a sequence of tonic contraction, we followed the subsequent highlights proposed by the physicians: we consider that we detect a sustained contraction if we detect 5 or more radial wrinkle frames within a window of ±5 frames. Thus, we define a contraction detection by providing at least one frame holding the previous requirement. Our criteria for the calculus of the system performance consisted on the following lines: 1) We automatically annotate all the wrinkle frames in the video. 2) We create all the sequences of sustained contractions following the criterion described above: all the frames belonging to the same sequence have, at least, 5 wrinkle frames within a ±5 frames neighborhood. 3) We consider that a sequence labelled by the experts is detected (a true positive) if there exists a sequence provided by the system which has, at least, one frame in common. 4) We consider that a sequence provided by the system is a false positive if none of its frames belong to a tonic contraction labelled by the experts. Following this criteria we obtain the results showed in Table 2:

Table 2. Detection rate of sequences of sustained contractions

Sustained contractions:	42
System sequences:	106
True positives:	30 (**71.4**% sensitivity)
False positives:	76 (**28.3**% precision)

Our system successfully detected 71.4% of the sustained contractions provided by the experts. In the final output 1 out of 3 suggested sequences are real tonic contractions. In this sense, the visual validation on the false positives sequences shows the difficulty of the labelling of this kind of contractions by the specialists. The visual patterns of the sequences obtained as false positives match, in many cases, with the paradigm of more than 10 frames of sustained contraction, although in some cases it is really difficult to separate the threshold between a phasic and a sustained for such a sort span of time. For the case of the longest contractions, this is not happening, and the specialist and the system provided sequences which intersect for all the cases without exception. Figure 9 (a) shows a set of representative sequences of sustained contractions detected by the system (true positives). The frames detected as wrinkle frames are surrounded by a green square. Figure 9 (b) shows a set of representative false negatives (missed findings). Finally, Figure 9 (c) shows a mosaic of the output of the system for the test video. The sequences detected by the system are surrounded by a green square, the experts' sequences are surrounded by a blue square, and the coincidences are in cyan.

In true positives the wrinkle frames show the sought radial pattern. Regarding the false negatives, the origin of the misclassifications is twofold: some bubbles in the lumen center hinder the detection of the lumen. For other cases the wrinkle

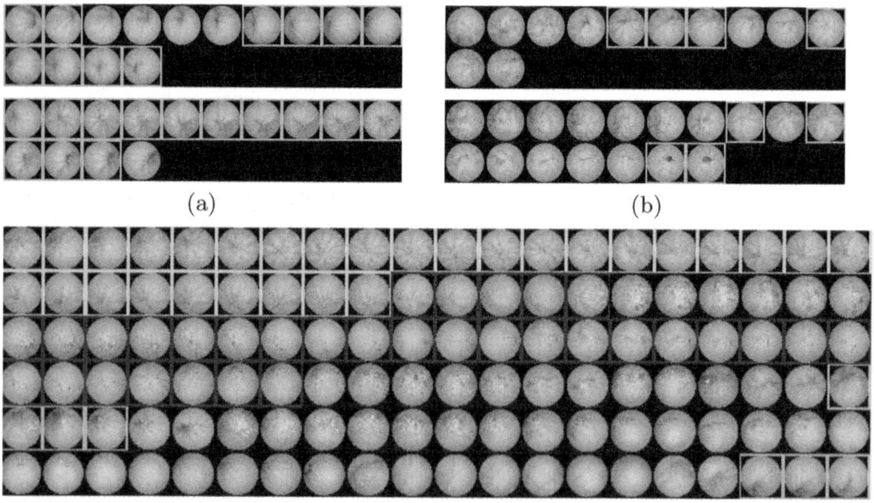

(a) (b)

c)

Fig. 9. (a) True positive, (b) false negative sequences of tonic contractions, and (c) a mosaic: system output (green), experts' findings (blue) and coincidences (cyan) pattern is so weak that no blob was in the binary laplacian image. Finally, it must be noticed that, even with a precision about 30%, the output of our system supposes a valuable tool for the specialists, because they are directly driven to the suggested contractions, and they must not visualize the whole video. For the proposed example of our experiments, assuming the experts to take 10 seconds in the discrimination between a false positive and a true positive of tonic contractions, the total amount of analysis time is reduced to $106 \times 10 = 1060$ seconds, less than 20 minutes. The time consumed by the expert in the labelling of 42 tonic contractions in the analyzed video was reported to be more than 3 hours.

6 Conclusions

In this work, we presented our own general approach for the categorization of linear radial patterns. The obtention of the patterns is performed through a valley and ridge detection algorithm, followed by a morphological processing stage. For the pattern characterization, we propose two different alternatives based on a directional analysis by steerable filters: 1) taking into account the the information of different quadrant divisions of the image, and 2) by means of a polar transform. This general strategy appears to deal well with the specific problem of automatic detection of tonic contractions in capsule endoscopy, providing the experts with a useful tool which achieves a relevant reduction in inspection time.

Acknowledgements

This work was supported in part by a research grant from Given Imaging Ltd., Yoqneam Israel, H. U. Vall d'Hebron, Barcelona, Spain, as well as the projects FIS-G03/1085, FIS-PI031488, TIC2003-00654 and MI-1509/2005. The technology and methods embraced by this disclosure has been filed for patent protection.

References

1. W. T. Freeman and E. H. Adelson. The design and use of steerable filters. *IEEE Trans. Pattern Analysis and Machine Intelligence*, 13(9):891–906, 1991.
2. R.M. Haralick and L.G. Shapiro. *Computer and Robot Vision*, volume I. Addison-Wesley, 1992.
3. A. Hernandez, D. Gil, et al. Anisotropic processing of image structures for adventitia detection in IVUS images. In *Proceedings of Computers in Cardiology*, volume 31, pages 229–232, September 19–22, 2004.
4. G. Iddan, G. Meron, et al. Wireless capsule endoscopy. *Nature*, 405:417, 2000.
5. J.E. Kellow, M. Delvaux, F. Aspriroz, et al. Principles of applied neurogastroenterology: physiology motility-sensation. *Gut*, 45(2):1117–1124, 1999.
6. A. M. Lopez, F. Lumbreras, J. Serrat, and J. J. Villanueva. Evaluation of methods for ridge and valley detection. *IEEE Trans. on PAMI*, 21(4):327–335, 1999.
7. G. Loy and A. Zelinsky. Fast radial symmetry for detecting points of interest. *IEEE Trans. Pattern Anal. Mach. Intell.*, 25(8):959–973, 2003.
8. F. Vilarino, L. Kuncheva, et al. Roc curves and video analysis optimization in intestinal capsule endoscopy. *Pat. Recog. Let.*, 27(8):875–881, 2006.

A Machine Learning Framework Using SOMs: Applications in the Intestinal Motility Assessment

Fernando Vilariño[1], Panagiota Spyridonos[1], Jordi Vitrià[1], Carolina Malagelada[2], and Petia Radeva[1]

[1] Computer Vision Center. Universitat Autònoma de Barcelona, Bellaterra 08193, Spain
[2] Hospital Vall d'Hebron, Barcelona 08035, Spain
fernando@cvc.uab.es
http://www.cvc.uab.es/~fernando

Abstract. Small Bowel Motility Assessment by means of Wireless Capsule Video Endoscopy constitutes a novel clinical methodology in which a capsule with a micro-camera attached to it is swallowed by the patient, emitting a RF signal which is recorded as a video of its trip throughout the gut. In order to overcome the main drawbacks associated with this technique -mainly related to the large amount of visualization time required-, our efforts have been focused on the development of a machine learning system, built up in sequential stages, which provides the specialists with the useful part of the video, rejecting those parts not valid for analysis. We successfully used Self Organized Maps in a general semi-supervised framework with the aim of tackling the different learning stages of our system. The analysis of the diverse types of images and the automatic detection of intestinal contractions is performed under the perspective of intestinal motility assessment in a clinical environment.

1 Introduction

Wireless Capsule Video Endoscopy constitutes a recent technology in which a capsule with an attached camera is swallowed by the patient. The camera travels along the intestinal tract and emits a radio signal, in a ratio of two frames per second, which is recorded as a video in an external device carried by the patient [6]. Once the study is finished, the final record can be easily downloaded into a PC with the appropriate software installed for its posterior analysis by the physicians. Recently, several works have tested the performance of capsule endoscopy in multiple clinical studies. Some of these clinical scenarios include intestinal polyposis and the diagnosis of small bowel tumors, obscure digestive tract bleeding, Crohn's disease and small bowel transplant surveillance [17,11,3,1,8,15,7].

The assessment of intestinal motility using wireless capsule video endoscopy is a novel and challenging fieldwork, which has been the focus of interest in recent publications [20,21]. In this medical image modality, the intestinal contraction sequences constitute the target of the labelling process, which consists

J.F. Martínez-Trinidad et al. (Eds.): CIARP 2006, LNCS 4225, pp. 188–197, 2006.

of video sequences showing the radial contraction of the intestinal lumen. These events have a low prevalence, presenting a typical ratio about 1 frame out of 50 video frames. The clinical procedure associated with this technique implies the visualization of the whole video (1-2 hours per video), which represents a huge amount of time and efforts for the specialist. In addition to this, images from video capsule endoscopy are usually significantly noisy, due to the presence of turbid content from the intestinal juices which hinders the correct visualization of the gut, providing wide range video zones not valid for analysis. All these drawbacks hinder the manual labelling process, and drive a useful clinical routine into a not feasible one. For this reason, we tackle the problem of intestinal motility assessment in a novel approach involving classical machine learning techniques. The main traits of our approach can be listed as follows:

- We state our problem in a cascade-wise strategy, identifying the different features of interest involved in motility assessment, and associating them with different and independent stages.
- We use self organized maps in an exhaustive way in the learning stage of each part of the cascade, adding the possibility of integrating the expert knowledge in a semi-supervised context.
- Finally, we apply a classification step based on a support vector machine in order to accomplish a two-fold objective: the identification of the portion of the video not valid for analysis, and the automatic labelling of intestinal contractions.

By using this strategy we can face several challenges in a simultaneous way: On the one hand, the resulting model is open and flexible, and new features of interest can be easily included adding new stages in the cascade as new necessities appear in the clinical scenario. On the other hand, the intervention of the specialists is reduced to a common framework, implemented with the self organized maps, making the expert-system interactivity bounded to a single common application interface.

In this paper we deploy the former issues according to the following structure: Section 1 is devoted to the explanation of the proposed system as a sequential cascade. Section 2 deploys the main traits exposed in Section 1, focusing on the identification of the portion of the video which is not valid for analysis, the SOM framework for the training stages, and the final classification step for the identification of intestinal contractions. Section 4 presents the results of the system in terms of intestinal motility assessment. We finally conclude this piece of research with the conclusions exposed in Section 5.

2 A General Framework: The Cascade System

Our system is deployed in a sequentially modular way, namely, a cascade, as pictured out in Figure 1. Each part of the cascade receives as an input the output of the previous stage. The main input consists of the video frames, and the main output consists of the frames suggested as contractions. The rejected

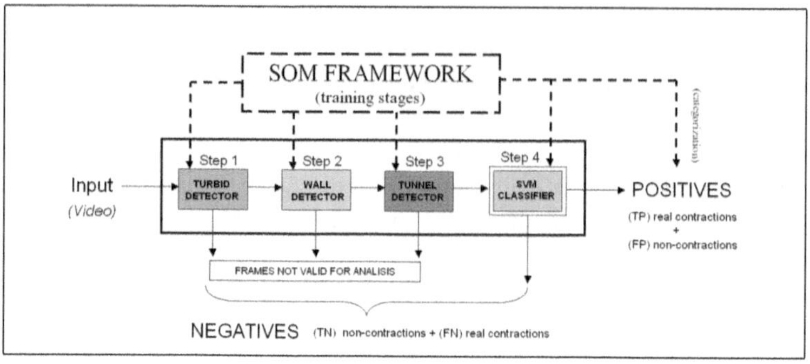

Fig. 1. Sequential Cascade System for Intestinal Motility Assessment

frames are distributed in several classes: turbid frames not valid for analysis, wall frames, and tunnel frames. All the learning stages of each step of the cascade involve a self organized map. The final classification step consists of a support vector machine trained with frames previously labelled by the experts.

In the feature extraction step we used the same set of six features proposed by Vilariño *et al.* [21], [18], based on widely known image descriptors such as, mean intensity, Laplacian response, and statistical descriptors obtained from the concurrence matrices. In addition to this, we included two color descriptors based on the *color opponent* decomposition, using only the two chrominance components *R-G* and *B-Y* [16], [10]. These eight descriptors constitute the feature vector to be associated to each single frame. Since intestinal motility is a dynamic process, not only static information (frame) should be taken into account, but dynamic information also. For this reason, for each frame we construct a feature vector containing the descriptors of the 4 previous and 4 following frames, i.e., containing the descriptors of a whole sequence of 9 frames. The span of 9 frames is based on well known physiological outcomes which bound the minimum time interval between two intestinal contractions in about ten seconds [14].

The choice of the cascade system is underpinned by the fact that each step is designed in order to reject an amount of frames which mainly include images which are not valid for analysis, letting pass through the sequential stages those frames related to intestinal contractions. Finally, the last step of the cascade, consisting of the support vector machine classifier, is to face a classification problem with an imbalance ratio about 1:5 -in contrast with the 1:50 at the input of the system-. This reduction in the imbalanced ratio is shown to be an effective way of tackling the problem of classification in imbalanced data sets. Moreover, the modular shape of the system lets the expert identify new features in order to include them as a new filter stage, adding domain knowledge in a natural way.

Each step of the cascade is trained independently from the others. For each of them, a reduced set of features is utilized, and a self organized map is used to build up the training sets. Self Organizing Maps (SOMs) or Kohonen networks [12] are a specific type of neural networks which provide the possibility of reducing the dimensionality of complex multivariate data sets, allowing their visualization in a 2-dimensional representation. By producing easily comprehensible low-dimensional maps of informative features, SOMs offer a technique for visual understanding and interpretation of hidden structures and correlations in the input dataset. Several works have been published referring medical applications using SOMs in a wide range of fieldworks, including classification of craniofacial growth patterns [13], extraction of information from electromyographic signals [5], magnetic resonance image segmentation [9], cytodiagnosis of breast carcinoma [22], classification of renal diseases [4], and drug design [2], among others. In our case, the use of SOMs is fully justified, since for each step of the cascade, a multidimensional representation of the frames is provided, but the selection of the training sets is strictly related to the visual patterns which the specialist identifies for each case. The SOM shows a clustering of the video sequences based on the information specifically needed for each step, grouping them into cells which correspond to similar descriptors. Each cell is identified by a representative element of the underlying sequences, which gives the specialist a first impression about the visual aspect of the cluster, and all the underlying sequences can be pictured for each cell. Now, the expert can select those cells which best adapt to the sought patterns in order to conform the optimal training sets.

3 System Implementation

3.1 Identification of the Region Not Valid for Analysis

The video frames not valid for analysis are constituted by frames presenting turbid liquid hindering the visualization of the whole image, frames with the camera focusing the intestinal wall, and frames with the camera focusing the intestinal lumen trough a time interval in which no intestinal motion is registered.

The motivation of the first category is straightforward: since the turbid liquid is hindering the visualization of the intestinal tube, no motility information can be inferred, since no intestinal contractions can be visualized. From a visual point of view, these frames are presented as a green-yellowish turbid bath which covers the whole field of view. The second category -frames focusing the intestinal wall-follows a similar reasoning: since the camera is focusing the intestinal wall (due to a lack of contractile activity or a transversal location in the intestinal tube), no intestinal contractions can be visualized. The last category, is related to a lack of motility activity, since the camera is focusing the gut as a tube, appearing as a steady tunnel, with no apparent motion in the intestinal walls.

Figures 2 a) and b) show the SOM resulting from the clustering of all the frames of two different videos, using only the two chrominance features described in Section 1. The number of cells and its shape has been set to a common value for visual comparison purposes. It can be seen how the cell structure is graded in color. After selecting in the SOM the cells corresponding to turbid frames, the feature space is partitioned into two different areas: turbid and not turbid. Figures 2 c) and d) show the two dimensional plots corresponding to the videos in Figures 2 a) and b). The horizontal axis represents the R-G chrominance component, and the vertical axis the B-Y chrominance component. The green points correspond to the frames selected in the SOM as turbid, while blue points are related to the remaining frames, i.e., the frames which are valid for analysis. The red points represent contractions labelled by hand by the specialist for each video. It can be seen that some real contractions fall into the selected not valid for analysis area, resulting as missed contractions (false negatives) of the system.

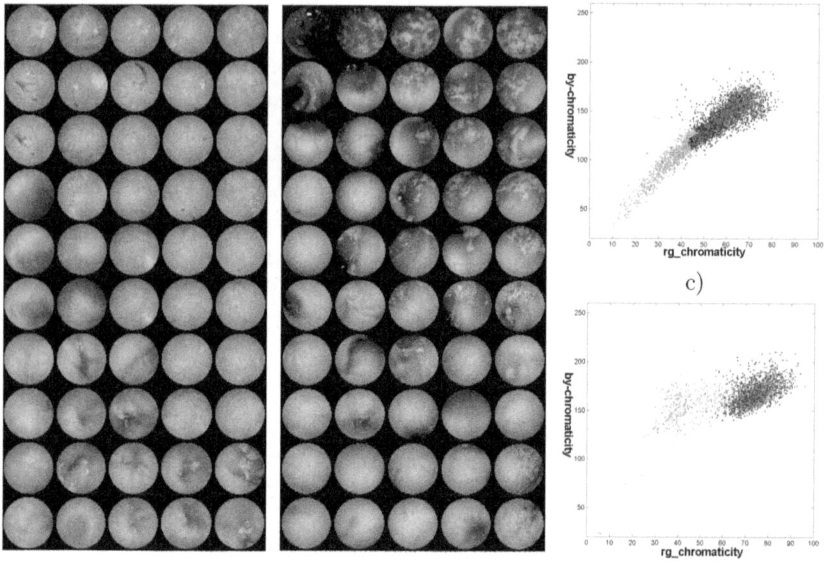

a) b) d)

Fig. 2. a) and b):Two SOMs using color features for two different videos. c) and d): Chrominance plot for both videos.

Figure 3 represents a SOM for the wall detection using as features the number of pixels with positive value of the Laplacian filter, related to the size of the lumen (in order to deal with the size of the hole), and their overall sum, related to the contrast (in order to distinguish between real lumen and shadows). On the left side, we present a SOM where the different cells have been delimited with red lines for visualization purposes. On the right side, an example of a cell content is shown in a), with four video sequences which do not correspond to the wall paradigm, and in b), with seven sequences matching the wall paradigm. For this case, the specialist is to select those sets of cells which best fit the wall paradigm. The same procedure is applied for the case of tunnel sequences.

The classification step for turbid, wall and tunnel is performed with three different support vector machines (SVM) [19] with a radial basis function kernel and $\gamma = 0.1$ for turbid and $\gamma = 0.05$ for wall and tunnel. The choice of the kernel and the γ parameter was obtained in a heuristical way using an exhaustive analysis.

The output of the classification stages is used to construct interactive mosaics. These mosaics deploy the whole video in a sequential way from left to right and

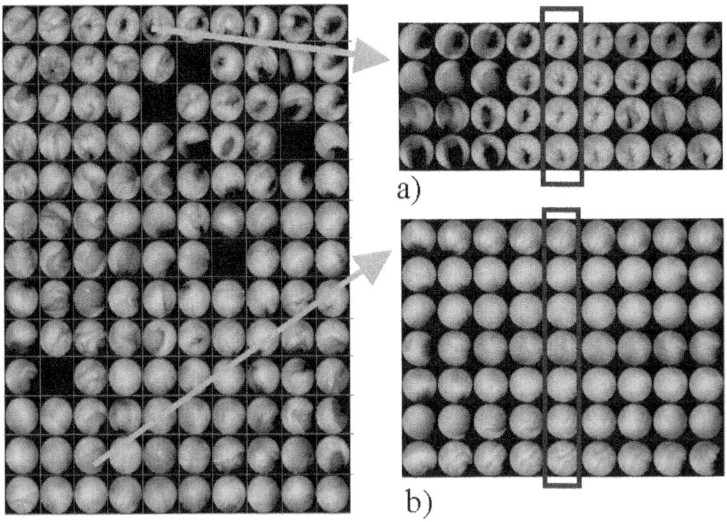

Fig. 3. a) Sequences underlying a cell which does not represent the wall paradigm. b) The wall paradigm is present in this cell. The central frame of each sequence is surrounded by the blue frame.

top to down, associating one pixel to each frame, and showing a different color depending on the the classification performed by the system. Figure 4 shows the interactive mosaics related to the videos in Figure 1. Each frame is assigned with a different color, so the specialist can visualize the valid area (in blue) directly and avoid visualizing the turbid (green), wall (beige) and tunnel frames (brown). For some cases, as it is straightforward to visualize from the mosaic of the video in Figure 4 b) the reduction in visualization time becomes drastic (about 50%).

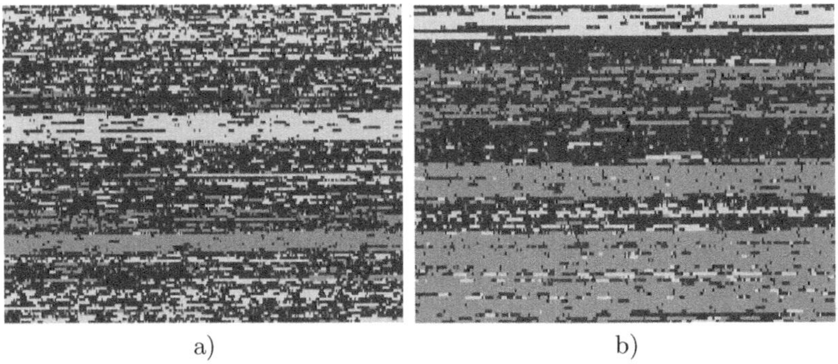

Fig. 4. a) and b): Two color mosaics. Green represents turbid, beige wall, brown tunnel, red labelled contractions and black labelled contract falling into the not valid for analysis area.

3.2 The SVM Classification Step

The aim of the final module of the cascade is to determine in an automatic way whether a frame is to be labelled as a contraction sequence. The input of this stage consists of the frames resulting valid for analysis, and its output consists of the frames which the system suggest as intestinal contractions. This last step is performed by a support vector machine with a kernel of radial basis functions and $\gamma = 0.1$, obtained in a heuristical way using exhaustive search. The feature vectors are constructed using all the existing features except the chrominance values used for turbid detection. The training set consists of a pool of all the previous labelled contractions from the remaining videos for the positives, and a random sample of the same number of non-contractions (under-sampling the negative class).

One of the main difficulties concerning the problem of intestinal motitility assessment lies on the different patterns of intestinal contractions present in each video. From a physiological point of view the different patterns can be gathered into *phasic* and *tonic*. The former are characterized by a sudden closing of the intestinal lumen, followed by a posterior opening, while the latter corresponds to a sequence of a closed lumen in an undefined number of frames. The analysis of the typology of contractions provides the specialist with helpful information for the evaluation of the presence of malfunctions. We used SOMs in order to provide the specialist with a useful tool for the validation of the different typology of intestinal contractions. In this case, the SOM is constructed with the output of the system. The feature set for the SOM is the same used for the final SVM classifier. Figure 5 a) Shows the SOM of the contraction frames corresponding to the video in Figure 2 a). Figure 5 b) Shows the sequences associated to the cell (9,1) (ninth raw, second column) which are to be mainly associated with the pattern of phasic contractions. Figure 5 c) Shows the sequences associated with the cell (4,1), which are to be mainly associated with the pattern of tonic contractions.

4 Results

In order to validate our system, several considerations must be taken into account. On the one hand, the validation of the turbid, wall and tunnel detectors is hard to perform in a direct way, since the large number of frames in video (typically $50,000$) makes the manual labelling of all of them not feasible. On the other hand, we must assume the loss of some frames labelled as contractions both in the intermediate stages of the cascade, and the final SVM classifier (these are the false negatives). In addition to this, we must also assume that the final SVM classifier identifies some frames as contractions in a wrong way (these are the false positives). One usual way of assessment for this kind of problems is tackled by using performance measures such as sensitivity and specificity. Sensitivity is defined as the number of the positives correctly detected over all the existing positives, while specificity is defined as the number of negatives correctly detected over all the existing negatives. Since for imbalanced problems, where

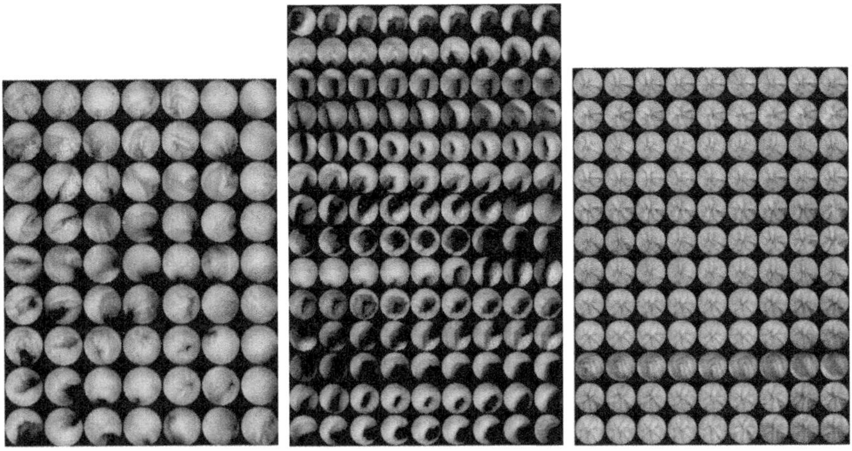

a) b) c)

Fig. 5. a) SOM constructed exclusively with sequences of contractions provided by the system. b) Phasic contraction sequences underlying the cell (9,1). c) Tonic contraction sequences underlying the cell (4,1).

the negative samples outnumber the positives, specificity is not a useful metric, because it is generally close to 1. In our case we define a performance measure as false alarm ratio (FAR) as the number of wrongly classified frames over all the existing frames (false positives / (true positives + false negatives)). Any other performance measure, such as precision (true positives / (true positives + false positives)) could be used as well. For the specialist, the FAR as defined above adds information in the sense that It normalizes the number of wrongly detected frames by the number of existing contractions. In this sense, the FAR measure is not bounded as precision is, and may be greater than one. The pair sensitivity-FAR provides the operation point of our system.

The validation of the system was performed using ten different videos. For each video, the specialists were asked to visualize the whole video and to label all the existing contractions. Then, the specialist was asked to perform the classification stages for the turbid, wall and tunnel. The final SVM was trained for each video with all the contractions of the remaining videos and the same number of a random sample of negatives, in a leave-one-out strategy. The performance results are shown in Table 1.

The resulting overall sensitivity is 74.78 with $\sigma = 7.85$, and the overall FAR is 42.75 with $\sigma = 23.00$. The columns of sensitivity and FAR in Table 1 deserve a separate analysis. On the one hand, the values of sensitivity imply that our system is shown to be able to detect about the 75% of all existing intestinal contractions, with a pick of performance of 85.22% in Video 3. In the specific context of motility assessment, it may not be mandatory to achieve higher levels of accuracy, since the aim of the procedure is to reconstruct the pattern of intestinal contractions along the time. On the other hand, it is important to notice the high value of FAR for Video 10 -a video which has shown to present

Table 1. Performance results for 10 videos

Video	Sensitivity %	FAR%
Video 1	66.01	35.38
Video 2	65.25	25.35
Video 3	**85.22**	69.58
Video 4	73.32	**17.78**
Video 5	70.97	41.47
Video 6	75.35	32.36
Video 7	65.36	43.95
Video 8	82.07	37.56
Video 9	79.77	29.05
Video 10	84.52	**95.01**

a large amount of turbid frames-. If Video 10 is not taken into account, the overall FAR is reduced to 36.94 with $\sigma = 14.67$, while sensitivity does not suffer a significant variation. This means that, as an average, for each three existing contractions in the video, the system is to provide us with a false positive.

5 Conclusions

Intestinal motility assessment in video capsule endoscopy is a tedious task due to the large amount of time needed for the visualization of each studio, the variability of the images present in the video, and the low prevalence of intestinal contractions. We presented a novel approach based on a machine learning system using classical techniques, which overcomes these main drawbacks. The main contribution of our work lies on driving this useful but not feasible technique into a feasible clinical technique. We showed the efficiency of our system designed in a sequential way (cascade), in which each step is trained independently. We introduced a general framework based on self organized maps, which are used in the different training stages of the cascade, providing the specialist with unified way of including expert knowledge. Finally, we presented the classification results obtained by a support vector machine classifier, which represents, as far as we know, the most efficient approach present in the literature for this clinical field. In addition to this conclusions, we expect to continue working in several points for future pieces of research. The seek of optimal descriptors, the development of advanced techniques for dealing with the imbalanced ratio, and the investigation on more efficient classification techniques are some of our current lines of work.

Acknowledgements

This work was supported in part by a research grant from Given Imaging Ltd., Yoqneam Israel, H. U. Vall d'Hebron, Barcelona, Spain, as well as the projects FIS-G03/1085, FIS-PI031488, TIC2003-00654 and MI-1509/2005. The technology and methods embraced by this disclosure has been filed for patent protection.

References

1. A. Ali, J. M. Santisi, and J. Vargo. Video capsule endoscopy: A voyage beyond the end of the scope. *Cleveland Clinic Journal of Medicine*, 71(5):415–424, 2004.
2. S. Anzali and S. Gasteiger. The use of self-organizing neural networks in drug design. Perspectives. *Drug Disc. Des.*, 11:273–299, 1998.
3. TEC Assessments. Wireless capsule endoscopy. Technical Report 17, Blue Cross and Blue Shield Association, 2003.
4. W. Van Biesen and G. Sieben. Application of Kohonen neural networks fort the non-morphological distinction between glomerular and tubular renal disease. *Neph. Dial Transp.*, 13:59–66, 1998.
5. C. I. Christodoulo and C.S. Pattichis. Unsupervised pattern recognition for the classification of EMG signals. *IEEE Trans. on Biom. Eng*, 46(2):169–178, 1999.
6. R. Eliakim. Wireless capsule video endoscopy: three years of experience. *Wd. Journ. Gastro.*, 10:1238–1239, 2004.
7. Z. Fireman and A. Glukhovsky. W. capsule endoscopy. *IMAJ*, 4:717–719, 2002.
8. Z. Fireman and E. Mahanja. Diagnosing small bowel crohns disease with wireless capsule endoscopy. *Gut*, 52:390–392, 2003.
9. J. O. Glass and W.E. Reddick. Hybrid artificial neural network segmentation and classification of dynamic contrast-enhanced MR imaging (DEMRI) of osteosarcoma. *Magn. Res. Im.*, 16(9):1075–1083, 1998.
10. R. C. Gonzalez and R. E. Woods. *Digital Image Processing.* Prentice Hall. 2nd. ed., 2002.
11. C. Gostout and D. G. Adler. State of the art, wireless capsule endoscopy. *Hospital Physician*, 39(5):14–22, 2003.
12. T. Kohonen. *Self-Organized Maps.* Springer, Heidelberg Berlin, 1995.
13. C. L. Lux and A. Atellzig. A neural network approach to the analysis and classification of human craniofacial growth. *Grow. Devel. Asign*, 62(3):95–106, 1998.
14. E. M. Quigley. Gastric and small intestinal motility in health and disease. *Gastroenterology Clinics of North America*, 25:113–145, 1996.
15. J. F Rey. European society of gastroenterology. Guideline for video capsule endoscopy. *Endoscopy*, 36:656–658, 2004.
16. J. C. Russ. *The Image Processing Handbook.* IEEE Press. 2nd. ed., 1994.
17. K. Schulmann and S. Hollerbach. Feasibility and diagnostic utility of video capsule endoscopy for the detection of small bowel polyps in patients with hereditary polyposis syndromes. *Am. Jour. Gastro.*, 100(1):27, 2005.
18. P. Spyridonos, F. Vilariño, et al. Identification of intestinal motility events of capsule endoscopy video analysis. *LNCS.*, 3708:531–537, 2005.
19. V. Vapnik. *The nature of Statistical Learning Theory.* Springer Verlag, 1995.
20. F. Vilariño, L. Kuncheva, et al. ROC curves and video analysis optimization in intestinal capsule endoscopy. *Pat. Recog. Let.*, 27(8):875–881, 2006.
21. F. Vilariño, P. Spyridonos, et al. Experiments with SVM and stratified sampling with an imbalanced problem: Detection of intestinal contractions. *LNCS.*, 3687(2):783–791, 2005.
22. A.J. Walker and S.S. Cross. Visualisation of biomedical datasets by use of growing cell structure networks: A novel diagnostic classification technique. *Lancet*, 354:1518–1521, 1999.

From Lossy to Lossless Wavelet Image Coding in a Tree-Based Encoder with Resolution Scalability

Jose Oliver[1] and Manuel P. Malumbres[2]

[1] Department of Computer Engineering (DISCA), Technical University of Valencia,
Camino de Vera 17, 46017 Valencia, Spain
joliver@disca.upv.es
[2] Departamento de física y ATC, Miguel Hernández University,
Avda. Universidad s/n, 03203 Elche, Spain
mels@umh.es

Abstract. For a lossy encoder, it is important to be able to provide also lossless compression with little or no modification of the usual algorithm, so that an implementation of that algorithm can work in lossy or lossless mode, depending on the specific application, simply by varying the input parameters. In this paper, we evaluate the capability of the Lower Tree Wavelet (LTW) image encoder to work in lossless mode. LTW is a fast and multiresolution wavelet image encoder, which uses trees as a fast mode to group coefficients. In addition, general details on how to implement efficiently (i.e., with only shift and addition/subtraction operations) a reversible integer-to-integer wavelet transform are also given, as a requirement to implement a wavelet-based lossless encoder. Numerical results show that despite being general purpose (i.e., both lossy and lossless) and lacking of complex techniques (such as high-order context and predictive coding), the LTW performs as well as JPEG 2000 in lossless mode, and only 5% below LOCO-I, a specific lossless algorithm.

1 Introduction

Most specific lossless image coders are based on entropy coding with various contexts and predictive techniques. Predictive coding schemes try to predict each sample from the samples that have been previously encoded, which are available to both encoder and decoder. In image compression, prediction is usually performed from nearby pixels. Once a prediction has been calculated, the residual pixel is encoded as the error committed by this prediction. This way, the better a prediction is, the lower it will be the entropy of the residual pixels. The CALIC scheme [1] follows this approach, becoming one of the most efficient lossless image coders in terms of compression performance. A simplification of CALIC was adopted as the JPEG-LS standard, which replaced the lossless mode of the original JPEG standard. This simplified version of CALIC is called LOCO-I [2], and its performance is close to CALIC with lower complexity. Other lossless image encoders are PNG (proposed as a royalty-free alternative to GIF) and JBIG (intended to bi-level image coding and used in fax transmission).

J.F. Martínez-Trinidad et al. (Eds.): CIARP 2006, LNCS 4225, pp. 198 – 207, 2006.

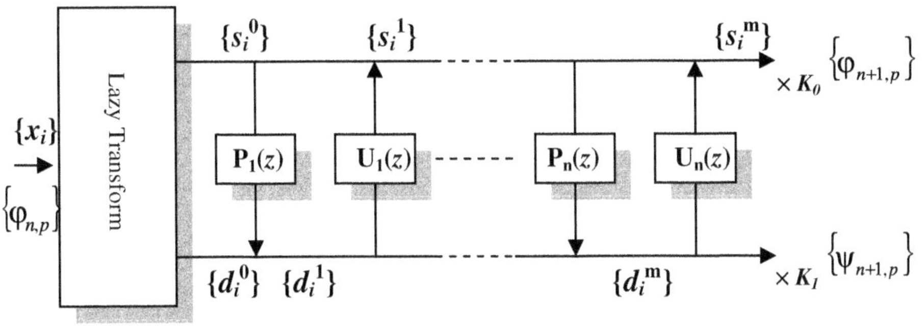

Fig. 1. General diagram for a wavelet decomposition using the lifting scheme

On the other hand, an interesting feature of general lossy image encoders is the ability to losslessly encode an image if no quantization is applied. This way, the emerging JPEG 2000 standard [3] was designed to be able to work in both lossy and lossless mode. SPIHT [4] and EZW [5] are tree-based lossy wavelet image encoders that also can store an image in lossless mode with SNR scalability.

LTW [6] was proposed as a low-complexity multiresolution alternative to the previous encoders. Multiresolution is a very interesting feature in heterogeneous frameworks (such as today's Internet) in which multiple devices with different display capabilities (e.g., image size) are potential clients. For instant, if an image is encoded with spatial scalability, the same bitstream can be employed by a mobile phone (reading only the base layer), a PDA (reading an additional layer to provide a slightly higher resolution) and a desktop computer (maybe needing all the image layers for full resolution).

In this paper, we describe the details to implement the LTW encoder working in a lossless mode, implemented with integer data type. We tackle this problem within the two stages of a wavelet-based image coder, i.e., in the wavelet transform and in the coding stage.

Many applications need to be able to work in lossless mode. Medical imaging is an example of this type of application in which lossless compression is required, since all the image details must be preserved so that medical analysis is not hindered. Another application of lossless coding is image editing. In this type of application, if lossy compression is employed, accumulative errors from successive editions may seriously damage the final image quality.

Lossless compression requires reversibility, which is not guaranteed with regular floating-point operations due to the finite-precision of the operands. In this case, a reversible integer-to-integer implementation is needed. In addition, an integer implementation is not only interesting for lossless image coding to achieve a reversible transform, but also in hardware architectures that only support integer arithmetic, such as some DSPs and many FPGAs. In fact, doing floating-point on FPGAs is difficult due to large amount of hardware required.

The rest of this paper is structured as follows. In Section 2, there is a detailed description of the wavelet transform implemented with the lifting scheme, focusing on a reversible implementation with integer data types. Section 3 describes the LTW algorithm and the required details to work in lossless mode. In Section 4, some experimental results are given, comparing the LTW encoder with JPEG 2000 working in lossless mode, and the specific lossless encoder LOCO-I. Finally, in Section 5 some conclusions are given.

2 Reversible Wavelet Transform

The wavelet transform was earlier defined and implemented using a regular filtering operation following a multiresolution analysis [7], but a more efficient algorithm to compute it was introduced by Sweldens in [8]. This algorithm is called the lifting scheme. The main advantage of this approach is the reduction in the number of operations needed to perform the wavelet transform. An additional advantage is that it allows in-place computation, and hence no extra memory is required to store the resulting coefficients as it happens with any regular filtering method. The third benefit that the lifting scheme introduces is the feasibility of a reversible integer-to-integer wavelet transform with only a slight modification of the usual floating-point implementation. In this section, we will deal with this type of integer wavelet transform.

We have mentioned that the lifting scheme implements an in-place DWT decomposition as an alternative algorithm to the classical filtering algorithm. In the filtering algorithm, in-place processing is not possible because each input sample is required as incoming data for the computation of its neighbor coefficients. Therefore, an extra array is needed to store the resulting coefficients, doubling the memory requirements. In addition, the lifting-scheme reduces the number of operations needed to compute the DWT.

In Figure 1, we present a diagram to illustrate the general lifting process. The whole process consists of a first lazy transform, one or several prediction and update steps, and coefficient normalization. In the lazy transform, the input samples are split into two data sets, one with the even samples and the other one with the odd ones. Thus, if we consider $\{x_i\}$ the input samples, we define both coefficient sets as:

$$\{s_i^0\} = \{x_{2i}\} \qquad \{d_i^0\} = \{x_{2i+1}\}$$

Then, in a prediction step (sometimes called dual lifting), each sample in $\{d_i^0\}$ is replaced by the error committed in the prediction of that sample from the samples in $\{s_i^0\}$:

$$d_i^1 = d_i^0 - P(\{s_i^0\})$$

while in an update step (also known as primal lifting), each sample in the set $\{s_i^0\}$ is updated by $\{d_i^1\}$ as:

$$s_i^1 = s_i^0 + U(\{d_i^1\})$$

After m successive prediction and update steps, the final low frequency coefficients (scaling $\{\varphi_i\}$) and high frequency coefficients (wavelet $\{\psi_i\}$) are achieved normalization:

$$\{\varphi_i\} = K_0 \times \{s_i^m\} \qquad\qquad \{\psi_i\} = K_1 \times \{d_i^m\}$$

A nice feature of the lifting scheme is that it is formed by very simple steps, and each of these steps is easily invertible, which leads to an almost trivial inverse transform. For the inverse transform, we only have to perform the inverse operations in the reverse order. Hence, from the subsets $\{\varphi_i\}$ and $\{\psi_i\}$, we can get $\{s_i^m\}$ and $\{d_i^m\}$ simply by dividing these coefficients by the scaling factors:

$$\{s_i^m\} = \{\varphi_i\}/K_0 \qquad\qquad \{d_i^m\} = \{\psi_i\}/K_1$$

Then, an inverse update operation can be done from these data sets as follows:

$$s_i^{m-1} = s_i^m - U(\{d_i^m\})$$

and at this moment, we can apply the inverse prediction step:

$$d_i^{m-1} = d_i^m + P(\{s_i^{m-1}\})$$

After m successive inverse update and prediction steps, we get the initial sets of even and odd samples, we can interleave these data sets to obtain the original set of samples $\{x_i\}$.

2.1 The Integer-to-Integer Lifting Scheme

With the above scheme, floating-point arithmetic is needed despite having integer input samples (e.g., image pixels), if the weighting factors employed for the prediction/update operations are floating-point and not integer or rational. Actually, even if rational filters are employed, the precision required to perform lossless operation with fixed-point arithmetic grows with each mathematical operation if we do not change the scheme described above.

Fortunately, the lifting scheme can be slightly modified to achieve reversible integer-to-integer wavelet transform [9]. Since the lifting scheme is formed by several simple steps, the whole process can be reversible if we perform each single step in a reversible way.

For the forward transform, we have seen that each prediction step has the form:

$$d_i^m = d_i^{m-1} - P(\{s_i^{m-1}\})$$

In a wavelet transform for integer implementation, the prediction operation $P(\{s_i^{m-1}\})$ involves rational weighting factors (e.g., division by two), and hence the resulting data are not integer. If a rounding operation is added after the prediction operation, an integer variable can be used to store the result of that operation, and hence each d_i^m can be computed from d_i^{m-1} and the $\{s_i^{m-1}\}$ set using integer values as follows:

$$d_i^m = d_i^{m-1} - \lfloor P(\{s_i^{m-1}\}) \rfloor$$

In the inverse transform, the exact value of each d_i^{m-1} can be recovered from d_i^m and the $\{s_i^{m-1}\}$ set as follows:

$$d_i^{m-1} = d_i^m + \lfloor P(\{s_i^{m-1}\}) \rfloor$$

Thereby, perfect reconstruction is guaranteed despite the rounding operation. The same analysis can be performed for an update operation with integer data type.

Although we have used the floor operator for rounding in the above equations, any other rounding operation, such as ceil or rounding to the nearest integer, can be used as long as the same operator is employed in both the forward and inverse transforms.

Finally, a reversible integer-to-integer transform can only be obtained if the normalization factors K_0 and K_1 are integer values.

A drawback of the use of rounding is that the new wavelet transform is no longer linear. Hence, for a 2D wavelet transform, the reverse column-row order of the forward transform has to be used in the inverse transform to achieve perfect reconstruction.

2.2 An Implementation Using the Bi-orthogonal 5/3 Transform

The 5/3 wavelet transform is a typical wavelet for integer-to-integer transform, being part of the JPEG2000 standard for lossless compression. In order to compute it in terms of the lifting scheme, after the lazy transform, the dual lifting is calculated as:

$$d_i^1 = d_i^0 - \left\lfloor \frac{1}{2}\left(s_i^0 + s_{i+1}^0\right) \right\rfloor$$

while the primal lifting is (notice the different rounding):

$$s_i^1 = s_i^0 + \left\lfloor \frac{1}{4}\left(d_i^1 + d_{i-1}^1\right) + \frac{1}{2} \right\rfloor$$

These operations can be easily performed with integer data types and integer arithmetic. For example, in C language, the two above equations can be efficiently computed as:

```
d1[i]=d0[i]-((s0[i]+s0[i+1])>>1);
s1[i]=s0[i]+((d1[i]+d1[i-1]+2)>>2);
```

Where d0, d1, s0 and s1 are arrays of integers, and >> is the right shift operator in C ($a >> b$ is equivalent to the division of a by 2^b with floor rounding).

For a lossless transform, the normalization factors K_0 and K_1 are equal to 1, achieving (1,2) normalization in this case. Thus, the set $\{d_i^1\}$ is directly the final wavelet coefficient set, and the set $\{s_i^1\}$ is the scaling one.

The inverse transform to recover losslessly the original samples is given by:

$$s_i^0 = s_i^1 - \left\lfloor \frac{1}{4}\left(d_i^1 + d_{i-1}^1\right) + \frac{1}{2} \right\rfloor \qquad d_i^0 = d_i^1 - \left\lfloor \frac{1}{2}\left(s_i^0 + s_{i+1}^0\right) \right\rfloor$$

Other reversible integer-to-integer wavelet transforms are given in [10], including an integer version of the popular bi-orthogonal 9/7 transform [11].

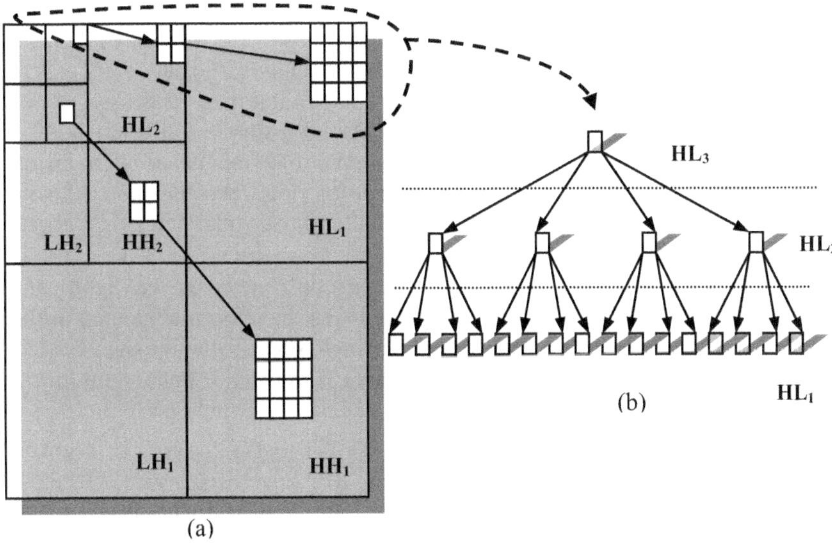

Fig. 2. Definition of wavelet coefficient trees. In (a), it is shown that coefficients of the same type of subband (HL, LH or HH) representing the same image area through different levels can be logically arranged as a quadtree, in which each node is a wavelet coefficient. The parent/children relation between each a pair of nodes in the quadtree is presented in (b).

3 Tree-Based Coding of Wavelet Coefficients with Multiresolution

3.1 Multiresolution in Wavelet Image Coding

One of the features that have turned the wavelet transform so popular is the ability to perform a multiresolution analysis. In order to achieve this type of scalability, the order in which the coefficients are received by the decoder has to follow a decreasing order of the subband level. This way, the first subband that the decoder attains is the LL_N, which is a low-resolution scaled version of the original image. Then, the decoder progressively receives the remaining subbands, from lower frequency subbands to higher ones, which are used as a complement to the low-resolution image to recursively double its size, which is know as Mallat decomposition [7].

In tree-based wavelet image coding, neither EZW [5] nor SPIHT [4] possess multiresolution scalability due to the successive scans that they perform, focusing on a different bit plane in each scan. The Lower Tree Wavelet (LTW) image encoder [6] was one of the first tree-based wavelet encoders to introduce multiresolution, at the expense of losing SNR scalability. In the next subsection, we describe the LTW encoder.

3.2 Lower-Tree Wavelet Coding

In the LTW encoder [6], the quantization process is performed by two strategies: one coarser and another finer. The finer one consists in applying a scalar uniform quantization, Q, to wavelet coefficients. On the other hand, the coarser one is based on removing least significant bit planes. We define *rplanes* as the number of least significant bit planes that have been removed from the wavelet coefficients.

In this encoder, a tree structure (like the one shown in Figure 2) is used, not only to reduce data redundancy among subbands, but also as a simple and fast way of grouping coefficients. As a consequence, the total number of symbols needed to encode the image is reduced, decreasing the overall execution time (because the arithmetic encoder stores less symbols). This structure is called lower tree, and it is a coefficient tree in which all its coefficients are lower than $2^{rplanes}$.

Our algorithm consists of two stages: (a) the construction of the significant map and (b) coefficient coding based on the symbols that have been computed in the first stage. In the first stage, the significance map is built after quantizing the wavelet coefficients (by means of using both Q and *rplanes* parameters). For the arithmetic encoder, the symbol set employed in our proposal is the following one:

(1) A *LOWER* symbol represents a coefficient that is the root of a lower-tree. The rest of coefficients in a lower-tree are labeled as *LOWER_COMPONENT*, but they are never encoded because they are already represented by the root coefficient.

(2) If a coefficient is insignificant (i.e., lower than $2^{rplanes}$), but it does not belong to a lower-tree because it has at least one significant descendant, it is labeled as an *ISOLATED_LOWER* symbol.

(3) For a significant coefficient (i.e., higher or equal to $2^{rplanes}$), we use a symbol indicating the number of bits needed to represent it. Finally, there is a special type of significant coefficient in which all its descendants are insignificant. This type of symbol is able to represent efficiently some special lower-trees, where only the root coefficient is significant, and the descendants are insignificant.

Let us describe now the whole coding algorithm.

In the first stage (symbol computation), all wavelet subbands are scanned in 2×2 blocks of coefficients, from the first decomposition level to the Nth (to be able to build the lower-trees from leaves to root). In the first level subband, if the four coefficients in each 2×2 block are insignificant (i.e., lower than $2^{rplanes}$), they are considered to be part of the same lower-tree, and thereby the are labeled as *LOWER_COMPONENT*. Then, when scanning upper level subbands, if a 2×2 block has four insignificant coefficients, and all their direct descendants are *LOWER_COMPONENT*, the coefficients in that block can be labeled as *LOWER_COMPONENT* as well, increasing the lower-tree size.

However, when at least one coefficient in the block is significant, the lower-tree cannot continue growing. In that case, a symbol for each coefficient is computed one by one. Each insignificant coefficient in the block is assigned a *LOWER* symbol if all its descendants are *LOWER_COMPONENT*, otherwise it is assigned an *ISOLATED_LOWER* symbol. On the other hand, for each significant coefficient, a symbol indicating the number of bits needed to represent that coefficient is employed, but this symbol is marked as a special symbol if its direct descendants are *LOWER_COMPONENT* to be able to identify this type of tree.

Finally, in the second stage, the subbands are encoded from the LL_N subband to the first-level wavelet subbands. Observe that this is the order in which the decoder needs to know the symbols, so that lower-tree roots are decoded before its leaves. In addition, this order provides resolution scalability.

In each subband, for each 2×2 block of coefficients, the symbols that were computed in the first stage are entropy coded by means of an arithmetic encoder with two simple contexts based on the significance of the upper coefficient and the coefficient previously encoded (on the left). Recall that no *LOWER_COMPONENT* is encoded. In addition, for the significant coefficients, the significant bits and its sign are also needed, and therefore they are binary encoded.

3.3 Lossless Mode

As we mentioned in the introduction, it is important for an encoder to be able to provide lossless compression with little or no modification of the usual algorithm, so that an implementation of that algorithm can work in lossy or lossless mode, depending on the specific application, simply by varying the input parameters. The Lower Tree

Table 1. Lossless coding comparison of various image encoders with six greyscale 8 bpp images. Results are given in bits per pixel (bpp) needed to losslessly encode the original image.

codec \ image	LOCO-I	JPEG 2000	LTW
Lena (512×512)	4.24	4.31	4.26
Barbara (512×512)	4.86	4.78	4.83
Goldhill (512×512)	4.71	4.84	4.78
Woman (2560×2048)	4.45	4.51	4.50
Café (2560×2048)	5.09	5.35	5.36
Bike (2560×2048)	4.36	4.53	4.56

Wavelet encoder possesses this feature if no quantization is applied and an integer-to-integer wavelet transform, such as the one presented in the previous section, is used. In order to skip the quantization process, the quantization parameters presented in the description of the algorithm can be set as *rplanes*=0, *Q*=1, although it is faster if we simply omit all the operations related to the scalar quantization. For the wavelet transform, we will use the reversible bi-orthogonal 5/3 filter bank for integer implementation, which is fully described in Section 2.

4 Numerical Results

In Table 1, we compare the results of losslessly encode six images (grayscale 8 bpp) with our encoder, JPEG 2000 and the LOCO-I algorithm (in which the JPEG-LS standard is based). In JPEG 2000, the same bi-orthogonal 5/3 transform is used. In this table, results are expressed as the number of bits per pixel needed for the compressed image, and in general it is reduced from 8 bpp (in the original image) to 4-5 bpp after lossless coding. LTW and JPEG 2000 are general purpose encoders and, if we compare them, they perform almost the same in all the images, with no more than 0.05 bpp difference between them (about 1% in performance). This is a good result for our encoder, if we take into account that lossless coding is mainly based on predictive techniques and context modeling (which are heavily developed in JPEG 2000). LTW, contrary to JPEG 2000, only handles two contexts. As we said in the introduction, LOCO-I [2] is a specific prediction-based lossless technique in which the lossless standard JPEG-LS is based. However, it is not much more efficient than the other two encoders under evaluation, requiring about 0.1-0.2 bpp less than JPEG 2000 and LTW. In particular, LOCO-I's coding efficiency is not higher than 5% compared with JPEG 2000 and LTW.

5 Conclusions

In this paper, we have presented the LTW encoder in a lossless framework, showing that it is also competitive with this type of application. In fact, the coding efficiency is only 5% under the specific lossless algorithm LOCO-I.

In addition, we have presented a detailed description on how to implement the wavelet transform using the lifting scheme. To this end, we have provided the exact instructions in C language to implement this transform with only shift and addition/subtraction operations. This implementation can be used for any wavelet-based encoder, and even to implement the wavelet transform with hardware architectures that only support integer arithmetic.

Acknowledgment

This work was supported by the Spanish Ministry of Education and Science under grant TIC2004-0052.

References

1. X. Wu, N.D. Memon, *CALIC- A Context Based Adaptive Lossless Image Coding Scheme*, IEEE Transactions on Communications, Vol. 45, 437-444, May 1996.
2. M. Weinberger, G. Seroussi, G. Sapiro, *The LOCO-I Lossless Image Compression Algorithm: Principles and Standardization into JPEG-LS*, IEEE Transactions on Image Processing, Vol. 9, 1309-1324, August 2000.
3. ISO/IEC 15444-1: *JPEG2000 image coding system*, 2000.
4. A. Said, A. Pearlman, *A new, fast, and efficient image codec based on set partitioning in hierarchical trees*, IEEE Transactions on circuits and systems for video technology, Vol. 6, no3, June 1996.
5. J.M. Shapiro, *Embedded image coding using zerotrees of wavelet coefficients*, IEEE Transactions on Signal Processing, Vol. 41, n12, December 1993.
6. J. Oliver, M. P. Malumbres, *Fast and Efficient Spatial Scalable Image Compression Using Wavelet Lower Trees*, in Proc. IEEE Data Compression Conference, Snowbird, UT, March 2003
7. S. Mallat, *A Theory for Multiresolution Signal Decomposition*, IEEE Transactions on Pattern Analysis and Machine Intelligence, vol. 11, pp. 674-693, July 1989.
8. W. Sweldens, *The lifting scheme: a custom-design construction of biorthogonal wavelets*, Journal of Applied Computational and Harmonic Analysis, vol. 3, pp. 186-200, 1996.
9. R. C. Calderbank, I. Daubechies, W. Sweldens, B. L. Yeo, Wavelet transforms that map integers to integer, Journal of Applied Computational and Harmonic Analysis, vol. 5, pp. 332-369, 1998.
10. M. Adams, F. Kossentini, *Reversible Integer-to-Integer Wavelet Transforms for Image Compression: Performance Evaluation and Analysis*, IEEE Transactions on Image Processing, vol. 9, pp. 1010-1024, June 2000.
11. M. Antonini, M. Barlaud, P. Mathieu, I. Daubechies, *Imagen Coding Using Wavelet Transform*, IEEE Transactions on Image Processing, vol. 1, no2, April 1992.

3D Mumford-Shah Based Active Mesh

Alexandre Dufour[1,2], Nicole Vincent[2], and Auguste Genovesio[1]

[1] Image Mining group - Institut Pasteur Korea
alexandre.dufour@pasteur.or.kr
[2] Systèmes Intelligents de Perception
Centre de Recherche en Informatique de Paris 5 - Université René Descartes

Abstract. Deformable mesh methods have become an alternative of choice to classical deformable models for 3D image understanding. They allow to render the evolving surface directly during the segmentation process in a fast and efficient way, avoiding both the additional time-cost and approximation errors induced by 3D reconstruction algorithms after segmentation. Current methods utilize edge-based forces to attract the mesh surface toward the image entities. These forces are inadequate in 3D fluorescence microscopy, where edges are not well defined by gradient. In this paper, we propose a fully automated deformable 3D mesh model that deforms using the reduced Mumford-Shah functional to segment and track objects with fuzzy boundaries. Simultaneous rendering of the mesh evolution allows faster tweaking of the model parameters and offers biologists a more precise insight on the scene and hence better understanding of biological phenomena. We present evaluations on both synthetic and real 3D microscopy data.

1 Introduction

3D segmentation and tracking by deformable models is a topic of active research in many domains including medical imaging [1][2][3] and biological imaging [4][5]. Until the early 90's, due to poor machine performances, 3D rendering of the scene used to be done in a post-processing step using surface extraction algorithms, inducing surface approximation errors and an additional time cost for the reconstruction. Advances in 3D computer graphic cards and rendering techniques have thus lead to the development of new techniques where segmentation and 3D rendering are done simultaneously, namely deformable mesh models. The idea, as originally proposed by Miller in [6], is to discretize an initial surface into a closed mesh, i.e. a closed set of polygons, and deform this surface by attracting its vertices toward the features of interest. Most deformable mesh models use edge information to drive the surface. This performs poorly on 3D volumes (depth-stacks of 2D images) obtained in confocal fluorescence microscopy due to several factors: first, a significant blur is introduced by the microscope's Point-Spread Function (PSF), especially along the depth axis. Moreover, like in 2D imaging, the stacks are corrupted by both multiplicative (Poisson) and additive (Gaussian) noise. This has many sources of explanation, including low exposure times, autofluorescence of the medium and shot noise induced by the camera's

J.F. Martínez-Trinidad et al. (Eds.): CIARP 2006, LNCS 4225, pp. 208–217, 2006.

CCD. Finally, in a tracking context, absorption of fluorophore by the entities induces an intensity decrease through time (phenomenon called *photo-bleaching*). To address this problem, a mesh model that uses region-based information instead of edge-based information is proposed. The method is able to detect and track an object with fuzzy boundaries and provides a fast and precise 3D rendering of the evolving surface thanks to the mesh formalism.

In section 2, we review existing work on deformable surfaces and mesh models. Then we detail in section 3 the characteristics of the proposed method. Evaluation on synthetic data and tests on real data are presented in section 4. We conclude the paper in section 5 and discuss possible extensions of the method.

2 Background and Related Work

In this section, an overview of the principles of 3D deformable surfaces is presented, followed by a brief review of existing 3D deformable mesh models.

2.1 3D Deformable Surfaces

To evolve from its initial state to the object boundary, a surface S is driven under the influence of two kinds of forces: data attachment (external) forces, which pull the surface toward specific features of the image, and regularization (internal) forces, which maintain smoothness and regularity of the surface. This evolution can be done by three different ways: a variational, a dynamic and a probabilistic approach.

- The **variational approach** is most popular. The 2D formulation is due to Kass *et. al* [7], and its 3D extension to Cohen and Cohen [8]. The evolving shape is defined as a parametrized surface $S(p) = (x(p), y(p), z(p))^\top$, where $p \in [0, 1]$ is the parametric domain. The surface is then linked to an energy functional, defined to be minimal when the surface fits the desired object correctly. This functional reads

$$F(S) = F_{internal}(S) + F_{external}(S), \tag{1}$$

where

$$F_{internal}(S) = \frac{1}{2}\int_0^1 \alpha \left|\frac{\partial S}{\partial p}\right|^2 + \beta \left|\frac{\partial^2 S}{\partial p^2}\right|^2 dp \tag{2}$$

and

$$F_{external}(S) = -\int_0^1 P(S(p))dp. \tag{3}$$

$F_{internal}$ is the deformation energy, where α is a "tension" parameter that tends to minimize the surface perimeter, and β a "rigidity" parameter that smooths the surface curvature.

The external energy (eq. 3) attracts the surface toward the image features through the scalar potential function P.

Eq. 1 is then minimized using a time-dependent gradient-descent method such as the well-known Euler-Lagrange equations, which give

$$\frac{\partial S}{\partial t} = \alpha \frac{\partial^2 S}{\partial p^2} - \beta \frac{\partial^4 S}{\partial p^4} + \nabla P(S(p,t)). \quad (4)$$

The final surface is obtained after convergence, i.e. when $\partial S/\partial t = 0$.

- In a **dynamic approach**, the shape is defined as a time-varying physical surface $S(p,t) = (x(p,t), y(p,t), z(p,t))^\top$ that evolves until it reaches a steady-state, following the Lagrange equation of motion, which gives

$$\gamma \frac{\partial S}{\partial t} + \mu \frac{\partial^2 S}{\partial t^2} + \alpha \frac{\partial^2 S}{\partial p^2} - \beta \frac{\partial^4 S}{\partial p^4} = \nabla P(S(p,t)) \quad (5)$$

where γ and μ are the surface mass and damping densities, respectively. The final surface is obtained when the system converges to equilibrium, i.e. $\partial S/\partial t = \partial^2 S/\partial t^2 = 0$. This approach allows to quantify both shape and motion evolution through time but complicates the method with two more parameters (γ and μ) to be set by the user.

- Finally, the model can be viewed as a fitting process in a **probabilistic framework** [9][10]. The shape is defined by a set $\mathbf{x}$ of parameters and their probability $p(\mathbf{x})$, being higher for low energy-shapes (this is usually done using a Gibbs distribution). Then, knowing the probability of the image $p(u_0)$ and that of the image knowing the initial shape $p(u_0/\mathbf{x})$, the probability of guessing $\mathbf{x}$ from u_0 is obtained thanks to the Bayes theorem: $p(\mathbf{x}/u_0) = p(u_0/\mathbf{x})p(\mathbf{x})/p(u_0)$. Finally, this probability is maximized to find an estimation of $\hat{\mathbf{x}}$ called the "maximum a posteriori". Probabilistic approaches have the advantage of giving an uncertainty measure of the fitting, but they are computationally much more expensive.

2.2 Deformable Meshes in Computer Vision

3D mesh models find applications in numerous domains including object reconstruction [11], realistic surgery simulation [12] and medical volume segmentation [2][13]. The continuous surface is discretized into a 3D mesh defined as a list of vertices $\mathbf{v}_i = (x_i, y_i, z_i)^\top$ organized in a closed set of oriented polygons representing the boundary of a volumetric object. The surface is then driven by the movement of the mesh vertices. In addition, two reference distances D_{min} and D_{max} are computed from the initial mesh in order to keep a regular mesh sampling during the evolution. The distance between two connected vertices $\mathbf{v}_i$ and $\mathbf{v}_j$ should always satisfy

$$D_{min} \leq dist(\mathbf{v}_i, \mathbf{v}_j) \leq D_{max}.$$

If $dist(\mathbf{v}_i, \mathbf{v}_j) < D_{min}$ or $dist(\mathbf{v}_i, \mathbf{v}_j) > D_{max}$, a local adaptation of the mesh must be applied to respect the above constraint (by splitting or merging problematic faces or edges).

In most models, the external potential P is chosen as an edge map of the image (eventually smoothed to be more robust to noise). This turns out to be efficient for many applications, but fails to detect fuzzy edges in 3D fluorescence microscopy images, where the surface simply shrinks (or inflates, depending on the parameters) and misses the object boundaries. This problem is partially solved in [13], where an additional external term is involved to attract the surface toward a particular iso-value (gray level) of the image. Nevertheless, the detected boundaries are still erroneous, since the object has a much lower intensity at the top and bottom of the volume (along the depth axis) than in the middle plane.

An efficient solution to detect objects with ill-defined boundaries is the Mumford-Shah functional [14], designed for segmentation and denoising in a variational context. The general form of this functional reads

$$F^{MS}(u, S) = \int_{\Omega} |u_0 - u|^2 d\omega + \int_{\Omega/S} |\nabla u|^2 d\omega + \mathcal{H}^{N-1}(S) \tag{6}$$

where Ω is the image domain, u_0 the original image, u the reconstructed image and $\mathcal{H}^{N-1}$ the (N-1) dimensional Hausdorff measure. In case the reconstructed image u should be formed only of regions $R_i \subset \Omega, i \in \{1, n\}$ of constant intensity c_i, then u can be considered piecewise-constant, i.e. $\int_{\Omega \setminus S} |\nabla u|^2 d\omega = 0$, which leads to the reduced Mumford-Shah functional

$$F^{RMS}(c_1, ..., c_n, S) = \sum_{i=1}^{n} \left[\int_{R_i} |u_0 - c_i|^2 d\omega \right] + \mathcal{H}^{N-1}(S). \tag{7}$$

These two functionals have been extensively utilized by region-based deformable models, in 2D (implicit and explicit) methods [15][16],[17][18] and in the 3D implicit case in [5]. To our knowledge, it has not yet been employed in the context of mesh models. We therefore introduce in the next section the new deformable mesh model and its underlying energy term based on the reduced Mumford-Shah functional.

3 Contributed Model

This section describes the proposed method. First, the geometrical aspects of the mesh are presented, then the evolution equation driving the mesh toward the object boundary is described. Finally, we describe the automatic initialization and tracking possibilities of the method.

3.1 Geometrical Mesh Properties

The *simplex mesh* formalism introduced by Delingette in [19] allows the mesh to be formed of different types of geometric primitives (triangles, squares and other polygons). Local mesh adaptation must therefore be done differently for each kind of primitive, which requires to store additional information in the mesh structure. In our approach, we prefer handling a uniform triangle-shaped mesh, which gives satisfactory results in our context. Moreover, a unique scheme is necessary to perform local mesh adaptations, and the mesh structure stores only the vertices and their connectivity.

As presented in section 2.2, the distance between two vertices should be regular over the whole mesh. Therefore we use the initial distance d_0 between two mesh vertices to define a freedom range $[D_{min}, D_{max}]$ such that

$$\begin{cases} D_{min} = d_0/2, \\ D_{max} = 2d_0. \end{cases} \tag{8}$$

The more this interval is chosen narrow, the more the mesh will be regular, and the more it is chosen large, the more freedom is given to the vertices. If the distance between two vertices $\mathbf{v}_i$ and $\mathbf{v}_j$ gets lower than D_{min}, we apply a local mesh adaptation by deleting these two vertices and creating a new one in their center that will share all the neighbors of $\mathbf{v}_i$ and $\mathbf{v}_j$. Inversely, if this distance gets higher than D_{max}, then we isolate the two vertices $\mathbf{v}_k$ and $\mathbf{v}_l$ forming a triangle with $\mathbf{v}_i$ and $\mathbf{v}_j$, separate $\mathbf{v}_i$ and $\mathbf{v}_j$ so that they are no longer neighbors and create a new vertex in their center that is linked to $\mathbf{v}_i$, $\mathbf{v}_j$,$\mathbf{v}_k$ and $\mathbf{v}_l$.

Lachaud proposed in [13] a multi-resolution approach to speed up convergence. The initial mesh is chosen with a low resolution (i.e. the initial distance between two vertices is very high compared to the image resolution), and evolved until convergence. Then the mesh is globally subdivided to obtain a higher-resolution mesh, and evolved again to fit the object boundary more precisely. The evolution-subdivision process is repeated until a suitable mesh resolution is reached (note that subpixel accuracy can be obtained if the distance between two vertices is lower than the image resolution).

The global subdivision strategy should be well chosen, in order to preserve the local mesh curvature as much as possible. We have thus chosen to apply a straightforward subdivision scheme: all faces are splitted into 4 smaller faces by creating a new vertex in the middle of each edge. This turns out to be the first step of the well-known *Loop* subdivision scheme, proposed for mesh refinement and smoothing in computer graphics in 1987 [20]. This scheme outperforms that of Lachaud in [13] which tends to sharpen the mesh corners, increasing its local curvature.

3.2 Evolution Equation

The Mumford-Shah functional is designed to fit into a variational framework, we therefore choose to evolve the surface by an energy-minimization scheme similar to that defined in section 2.1. Our images are typically formed of two phases (the object and the background), thus we may restrict eq. 7 to the two-phase case, which gives

$$F^{RMS}(c_{in}, c_{out}, S) = \int_{in(S)} |u_0 - c_{in}|^2 d\omega + \int_{out(S)} |u_0 - c_{out}|^2 d\omega + \mathcal{H}^{N-1}(S) \tag{9}$$

where c_{in} and c_{out} are variables being respectively the mean intensities of the original image u_0 inside and outside S. We finally construct our energy functional using the same internal energy defined in eq. 2 and the data attachment term of the above equation, and we obtain

$$
\begin{aligned}
F(c_{in}, c_{out}, S) = & \frac{1}{2}\int_0^1 \alpha \left|\frac{\partial S}{\partial p}\right|^2 + \beta \left|\frac{\partial^2 S}{\partial p^2}\right|^2 dp \\
& + \lambda_{in} \int_{in(S)} |u_0 - c_{in}|^2 d\omega \\
& + \lambda_{out} \int_{out(S)} |u_0 - c_{out}|^2 d\omega
\end{aligned} \tag{10}
$$

where λ_{in} and λ_{out} are strictly positive parameters. The Euler-Lagrange equations linked to the minimization of this new energy functional thus give

$$
\frac{\partial S}{\partial t} = \alpha \frac{\partial^2 S}{\partial p^2} - \beta \frac{\partial^4 S}{\partial p^4} - \left[\lambda_{in}(u_0 - c_{in})^2 - \lambda_{out}(u_0 - c_{out})^2\right] \left|\frac{\partial S}{\partial p}\right| \overrightarrow{n} \tag{11}
$$

where $\overrightarrow{n}$ is the surface normal pointing outward. During the evolution, the variables c_{in} and c_{out} have to be recomputed at every iteration.

3.3 Initialization

Deformable models usually rely on user intervention to initialize the model. We prefer employing an automated framework to determine the location and approximate size of the object. First, an automatic thresholding technique is applied (we used the well-known K-means algorithm). The biggest connected component is then extracted from the thresholded image, its mass center $\mathbf{v}_c$ is computed as the average of the objects points coordinates and the mean radius r is defined as the average distance between the mass center and all surface points. Finally, a regular polyhedron of radius r is created and placed in the image domain at the position $\mathbf{v}_c$. Actually, any kind of polyhedron can be used as an initial shape. In our case, a regular 20-face polyhedron was used, also known as the *regular icosahedron*.

3.4 Tracking

As for most deformable models, tracking is done in a straightforward way. Once the object has been segmented on the first frame, we reuse the obtained mesh to initialize the model for the next frame. The new initial mesh being very close from the new object's position, a few number of iterations will be sufficient to track the object movement. This however implies that a significant overlap exist between the object's position at two successive time-points. This overlap should be such that the difference $c_{in} - c_{out}$ is of same sign for both frames. Otherwise, if $c_{in} - c_{out}$ changes sign, the object is interpreted as the background and vice-versa, and the model starts to segment the dual of the object.

There are two possible walk-arounds to such behavior. The first simple way is to reduce the time-lapse between two successive frames during the image acquisition. The second solution is to fix c_{in} and c_{out} after segmentation of the first frame, which are good estimates of the object's and background's mean intensities as long as the global illumination does not vary through time. If photo-bleaching occurs, these estimates must be recalculated regularly, i.e. c_{in} and c_{out} are updated once after convergence on each new frame.

4 Experiments and Results

This section presents several experimentations and evaluations of our method. We shall first discuss results on generated noisy data, and then show results obtained on real microscopy data sets.

4.1 Synthetic Data

We simulated 50 stacks of cell-shaped objects moving in a biological medium, using a method close to that described in [5]. First, binary volumes of size $200 \times 200 \times 200$ voxels are generated, in which a sphere of random radius an center is created (representing the cell body). Then several smaller spheres are generated on the boundary of the bigger sphere to simulate cell protuberances. Then, dark structures are generated randomly within the cell body to simulate inhomogeneous fluorescent marking. Finally, the volumes are convolved by the microscope's PSF and disturbed by multiplicative (Poisson) and additive (Gaussian) noise representing imperfections of the imaging system. To take into account the low depth-resolution of the 3D microscope, we additionally down-scale the volumes depth resolution to $200 \times 200 \times 40$. However, due to major improvements of new microscopy systems, space resolution is now almost isotropic. The left and middle columns of fig. 1 show two slices of an original (left) and noisy (right) stack.

The main calculations were done on a 1.7 GHz mobile cpu, while the rendering was simultaneously performed on a 128 Mb graphic card. The processing time of each stack was approximately 60 seconds including the update of c_{in} and c_{out} after every iteration (an example of segmentation result is shown on the right column of fig. 1). To illustrate the rendering possibilities of the method, we show in fig. 2 three different steps of the mesh evolution at its lower (initial) resolution: the left frame is a snapshot taken before the evolution, where one can see the icosahedron used to initialize the model; the middle frame shows in intermediate stage of the evolution; the right frame shows the converged mesh before it is refined and evolved again to fit the object more precisely.

We evaluated the segmentation by measuring the average distance between the segmentation residue and the original object, as proposed by Ciofolo in [21]. This measure is defined by

$$d_{err}(R, O) = \sum_{v_R \in R} min_{v_O \in O} \frac{dist(v_R, v_O)}{card(R)}$$

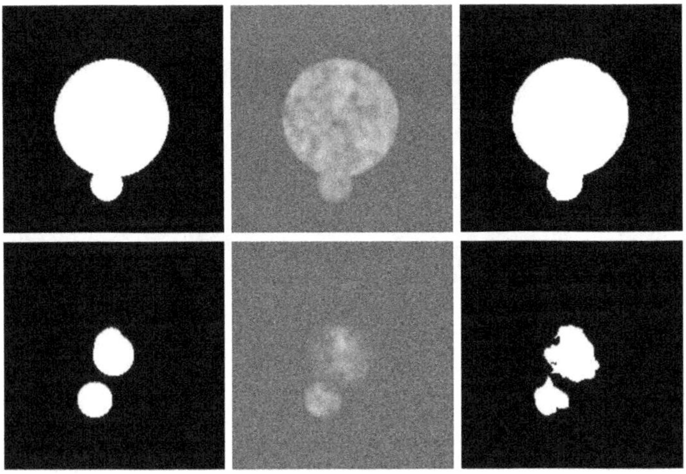

Fig. 1. Two different slices of a synthetic 200 × 200 × 40 stack. left: original image, middle: noisy image, right: result. The top row shows a slice in the middle of the cell, while the bottom row shows a higher slice of the cell. Note the effect of the microscope's PSF on the object boundary.

where v_O and v_R are image voxels forming respectively the original object O the and the segmentation residue R (i.e. the difference between the detected object and O). The average distance d_{err} over the 50 processed stacks is 2 voxels. This measure tends to show that the object boundary has been quite well detected despite the noise, since the errors are mostly located in the vicinity of the object.

4.2 Trial Microscopy Data Sets

Here we present experimental results on a 3D time sequence of a HEK cell changing shape through time while emitting protuberances at its surface. The cell was stained using the Yellow Fluorescent Protein (YFP), and the 3D stacks were acquired on a Zeiss LSM 5 microscope. Fig. 3 shows snapshots of the sequence as well as segmentation and tracking results. The two left-most columns show top and side views of the original stack (left) and segmentation result (right). Note that the model has detected correctly the upper and lower fuzzy boundaries of the cell. The two right-most columns show the same views for the next time-point of the sequence (left), where protuberances appear on the cell surface, and which are correctly detected by the mesh (right).

5 Conclusion and Future Works

A new deformable mesh model based on the reduced Mumford-Shah functional has been proposed, joining the theories of explicit active mesh, region-based information and 3D visualization. The method is able to detect an object with

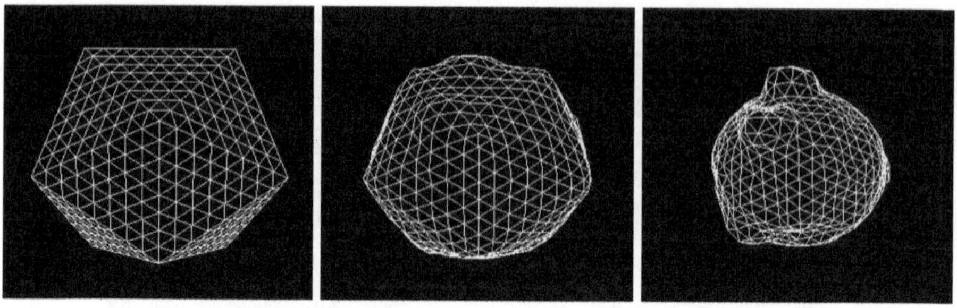

Fig. 2. Rendering of the low resolution mesh at various stages of the evolution: left: before evolution; middle: during evolution; right: after convergence (before refinement)

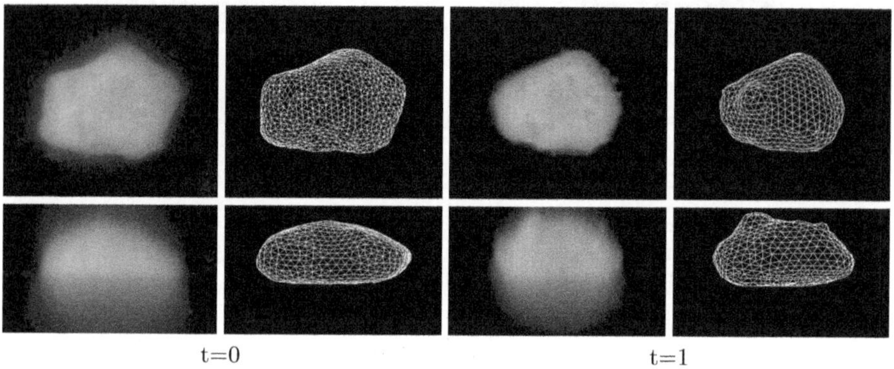

Fig. 3. Tracking results on a HEK cell emitting a protuberance at its top (volume size: 512x512x181): top row: XY plane view from the top of the cell; bottom row: XZ plane view from the side of the cell

fuzzy boundaries and follow its movement and shape changes through time while offering a simultaneous rendering of the evolving scene. Experimental results show that the method is suitable for 3D confocal image analysis, and will be employed in a biological context to study pathogenic diseases involving cellular structures changes through time.

The next step of our work is to detect and track multiple objects simultaneously. To achieve this, multiple meshes will evolve simultaneously within the image domain, and a collision detection strategy will be employed to distinguish correctly two or more objects that might touch each other in time.

References

1. Chakraborty, A., Staib, L., Duncan, J.: Deformable Boundary Finding in Medical Images by Intergrating Gradient and Region Information. IEEE Transactions on Medical Imaging **15**(6) (1996) 859–870

2. Xu, C., Pham, D., Rettman, M., Yu, D., Prince, J.: Reconstruction of the Human Cerebral Cortex from Magnetic Resonance Images. IEEE Transactions on Medical Imaging **18**(6) (1999) 467–480
3. Paragios, N.: A Level Set Approach for Shape-Driven Segmentation and Tracking of the Left Ventricle. IEEE Transactions on Medical Imaging **22** (2003) 773–776
4. Sarti, A., de Solorzano, C.O., Lockett, S., Malladi, R.: A Geometric Model for 3D Confocal Image Analysis. IEEE Transactions on Biomedical Engineering **47**(12) (2000) 1600–1609
5. Dufour, A., Shinin, V., Tajbaksh, S., Guillen, N., Olivo-Marin, J., Zimmer, C.: Segmenting and tracking fluorescent cells in dynamic 3d microscopy with coupled active surfaces. IEEE Transactions on Image Processing **14**(9) (2005) 1396–1410
6. Miller, J.: Geometrically deformed models for the extraction of closed shapes from volume data. Master's thesis, Rensselaer Polytechnic Institute, New York (1990)
7. Kass, M., Witkin, A., Terzopoulos, D.: Snakes : Active contour models. International Journal of Computer Vision **1** (1988) 321–331
8. Cohen, L., Cohen, I.: Finite-element methods for active contour models and balloons for 2-D and 3-D images. IEEE Transactions on Pattern Analysis and Machine Intelligence **15**(11) (1993) 1131–1147
9. Szeliski, R., Terzopoulos, D.: Physically based and probabilistic models for computer vision. In: Geometric Methods in Computer Vision. Volume 1570. (1991) 140–152
10. Staib, L., Duncan, J.: Boundary finding with parametrically deformable models. IEEE Transactions on Pattern Analysis and Machine Intelligence **14**(11) (1992) 1061–1075
11. Delingette, H.: General object reconstruction based on simplex meshes. International Journal on Computer Vision **32** (1999) 111–146
12. Cotin, S., Delingette, H., Ayache, N.: Real-time elastic deformations of soft tissues for surgery simulation. IEEE Transactions on Visualization and Computer Graphics **5** (1999) 62–73
13. Lachaud, J., Montanvert, A.: Deformable meshes with automated topology changes for coarse-to-fine three-dimensional surface extraction. Medical Image Analysis **3**(2) (1999) 187–207
14. Mumford, D., Shah, J.: Optimal approximations by piecewise smooth functions and associated variational problems. Com. Pure App. Math. **42** (1989) 577–684
15. Chan, T., Vese, L.: Active contours without edges. IEEE Transactions on Image Processing **10**(2) (2001) 266–277
16. Tsai, A., Yezzi, A., Willsky, A.: Curve Evolution Implementation of the Mumford-Shah Functional for Image Segmentation, Denoising, Interpolation, and Magnification. IEEE Transactions on Image Processing **10**(8) (2001) 1169–1186
17. Cremers, D., Tischhauser, F., Weickert, J., Schnorr, C.: Diffusion snakes: introducing statistical shape knowledge into the Mumford-Shah functional. International Journal on Computer Vision **50** (2002) 295–313
18. Zimmer, C., Olivo-Marin, J.C.: Coupled Parametric Active Contours. IEEE Transactions on Pattern Analysis and Machine Intelligence **27**(11) (2005) 1838–1842
19. Delingette, H.: Modelisation, Deformation et Reconnaissance d'Objets Tridimensionnels a l'Aide de Maillages Simplexes. PhD thesis, Ecole Centrale de Paris (1994)
20. Loop, C.: Smooth Subdivion Surfaces based on Triangles. PhD thesis, University of Utah (1987)
21. Ciofolo, C.: Segmentation des formes guidee par des modeles en neuro-imagerie. PhD thesis, Universite Rennes I (2005)

Fast 2D-3D Point-Based Registration Using GPU-Based Preprocessing for Image-Guided Surgery

Helen Hong[1,*], Kyehyun Kim[2], and Seongjin Park[2]

[1] Division of Multimedia Engineering, College of Information and Media, Seoul Women's University, 126 Gongreung-dong, Nowon-gu, Seoul 139-774, Korea
hlhong@swu.ac.kr

[2] School of Computer Science and Engineering, Seoul National University, San 56-1 Shinlim-dong, Kwonak-gu, Seoul 151-742, Korea
{iamkgh, sjpark}@cglab.snu.ac.kr

Abstract. We propose a 2D-3D point-based registration method that provides fast and efficient alignment of X-ray fluoroscopy and CT images. Our method is divided into two procedures: pre-operative and intra-operative procedures. For pre-operative procedures, we generate digitally reconstructed radiographs (DRRs) from 3D volume using graphics hardware. In intra-operative procedures, we perform a hierarchical registration that includes in-plane registration using principal axes method and out-plane registration using minimal error searching method in spherical coordinates. This method reduces a degree of freedom from 6-DOF to 2-DOF. Experimental results using 2 cardiac phantoms show that our DRRs generation method is more than 150 times faster than software-based ray casting methods, and our hierarchical registration technique effectively matches DRRs and 2D images.

1 Introduction

Three-dimensional (3D) imaging modalities such as computed tomography (CT) and magnetic resonance (MR) imaging are widely used in clinical diagnosis and treatment planning due to their ability to produce detailed anatomical structures of human organs. However due to the manner in which the images are generated, both techniques have limitations in their use as a modality for guiding interventional procedures. For interventional procedures, images need to be produced in real-time and this is commonly done with ultrasound or X-ray fluoroscopy. The drawbacks of these modalities are that they fail to provide adequate spatial information. Combining the benefits of both types of imaging modalities could produce a system highly suitable for interventional procedures. Therefore, the registration of pre-operative 3D volume to intra-operative 2D images could provide complementary information for tracking the spatial location of medical instruments during image-guided surgery [1-4].

A major obstacle to this proposal is that images obtained with 3D scanning modalities have different dimensions from those obtained using 2D scanning modalities. To estimate geometrical transformation by bringing two modalities into spatial alignment, it

---

* Corresponding author. Seoul Women's University; Phone: 82-2-970-5756.

J.F. Martínez-Trinidad et al. (Eds.): CIARP 2006, LNCS 4225, pp. 218 – 226, 2006.

is essential that two different images are compared in the same space[5]. There are two possible approaches to dealing with this 2D-3D registration.

- Convert the 2D image to a 3D image resulting in a 3D-3D registration
- Convert the 3D image to a 2D image resulting in a 2D-2D registration

From a practical point of view, 3D-3D registration, i.e. reconstructing 3D volume from 2D images requires numerous projection acquisitions and a large computation time[6]. It is consequently more feasible to simulate 2D images from 3D volume[5,7]. To do this, digitally reconstructed radiographs(DDRs) have to be first produced. These images are generated by a ray-casting algorithm that computes the amount of light that a virtual ray from an X-ray light source penetrates the 3D volume as shown in Fig. 1. Since this algorithm visits every voxel of 3D volume and computes while generating the projection image, it needs a large computation time. To reduce the computation time, software-based techniques have been proposed but are limited in their ability to generate simulated projection images in real-time.

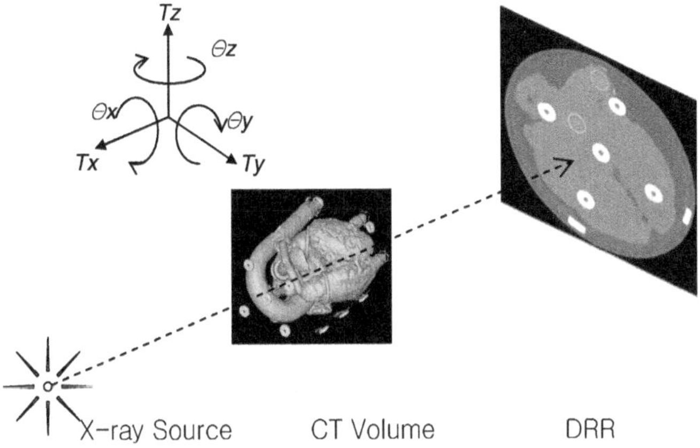

Fig. 1. The principle of DRRs generation from CT volume

In order to overcome this limitation, we propose a fast 2D-3D point-based registration using Graphics Processing Unit (GPU)-based preprocessing. Our main contribution is to accelerate DRRs generation using graphics hardware in pre-operative procedures and to perform hierarchical registration in intra-operative procedure that includes in-plane and out-plane registrations. Our hierarchical registration significantly increases the accuracy by reducing the degrees of freedom from 6 to 2.

The organization of the paper is as follows. In Section 2, we discuss how to generate DRRs using graphics hardware. Then we propose a hierarchical registration to find correspondences between 2D X-ray fluoroscopy images and 3D CT volume. In Section 3, experimental results show how our methods accelerate the procedure for 2D-3D registration. This paper is concluded with brief discussion of the results in Section 4.

2 Fast 2D-3D Point-Based Registration

For the registration of 3D volume and 2D images, we followed the pipeline shown in Fig. 2. The method is divided into two procedures: pre-operative and intra-operative procedures. For the pre-operative stage, DRRs are generated from 3D volumes using graphics hardware. For the intra-operative stage, hierarchical registration is performed by a technique that includes in-plane registration using a principal axes method and out-plane registration using a minimal error searching method in spherical space. In both stages, confirmation markers are automatically detected and segmented.

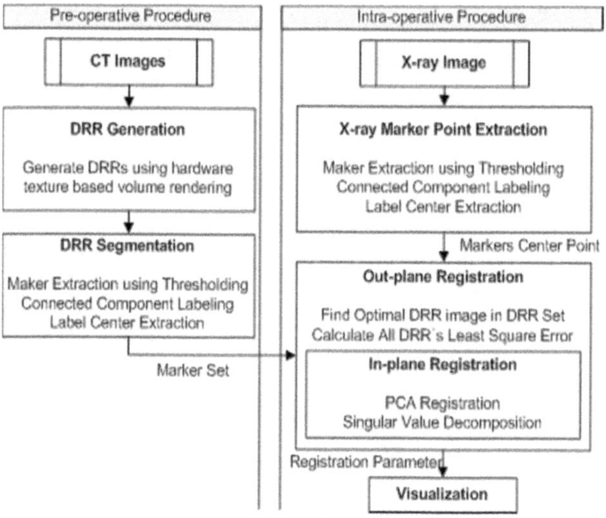

Fig. 2. The pipeline of proposed method using GPU-based preprocessing for Image-Guided Surgery

2.1 The Generation of DRRs Using Graphics Hardware

The DRRs are generated by texture-based volume rendering using hig-level shading language. Generation is composed of three steps. Firstly the 3D volume is changed from 12 bit to 8 bit. Secondly the proxy geometry is generated using perspective projection. Finally the compositing is performed using maximum intensity projection.

The reason for changing the 3D volume from 12 bit to 8 bit is that current graphics hardware has a limitation in loading 3D volume to three-dimensional texture memory in GPU when the resolution of the 3D volume is over 512 x 512 x 512 bits. The main purpose of our method is to align confirmation markers between DRRs projected from 3D volume and 2D images. In addition, the confirmation markers have a high density values. Thus, it is possible to use higher 8 bit from 12 bit in 3D volume. In general, proxy geometry is generated using parallel projection. In order to simulate X-ray images, we have generated proxy geometry using the technique of perspective projection as shown in Fig. 3. We map three-dimensional texture memory in GPU to the proxy geometry. The mapped slices onto the proxy geometry render using compositing modes that include maximum intensity projection, average intensity projection and minimum intensity projection.

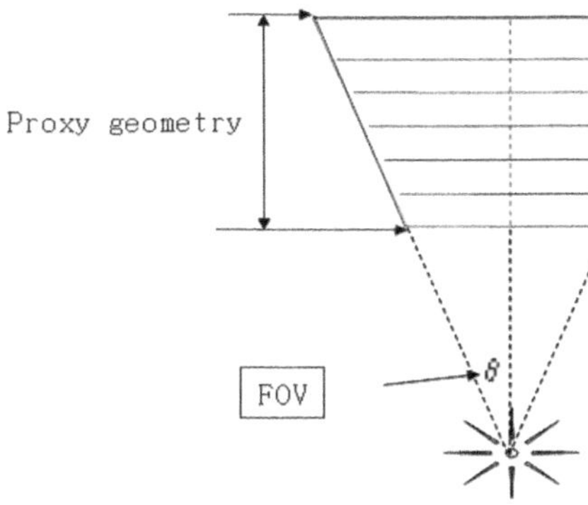

Fig. 3. A generation of proxy geometry using perspective projection

2.2 Automatic Confirmation Marker Segmentation

For point-based registration, confirmation markers are needed to automatically detect and segment. Our method is composed of three steps. Firstly, candidate regions of confirmation markers in each image are segmented by using thresholding [8]. The pixels above 2300 Hounsefield units are considered as the candidate of confirmation markers. Then these candidate regions are saved as binary images as shown in Fig. 4(a). Secondly, noise or other features in the binary images are removed by using connected component labeling. For this, candidate regions of confirmation marker shown in Fig. 4(b) are compared with standard confirmation marker model. If candidate regions of confirmation markers are smaller or larger than the standard confirmation marker model, they are considered as noise or other features and are removed. Finally, centroids of extracted confirmation markers are computed.

2.3 Hierarchical Registration

The purpose of 2D-3D registration is to align the 3D volume obtained from preoperative imaging modalities with 2D images obtained from intra-operative imaging modalities. In order to determine geometrical transformations in three dimensions, translations and rotations in x-, y-, and z-axis are computed with six degree-of-freedom (DOF). However, this approach dramatically increases the number of computations. To address this problem we propose a hierarchical registration that includes in-plane registration and out-plane registration. This method reduces the computation requirement from 6 DOF to 2 DOF.

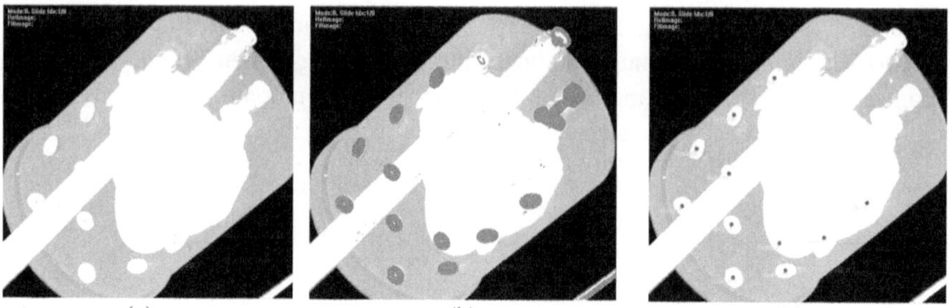

(a) (b) (c)

Fig. 4. A concept of automatic marker detection and segmentation (a) DRR image (b) candidate regions (c) noise removal and centroid extraction

For in-plane registration, we determine optimal translation and rotation vectors of confirmation markers using the principle axes method. Each axis of DRRs and 2D images are computed using Singular Value Decomposition (SVD) and are used to align these two images[9,10]. SVD is defined as Eq. 1. The in-plane rotation vector θ is the differential angle between axes. The in-plane translation vectors, T_X, T_Y for each axes is computed by the weighted mean of the markers' center positions.

$$A = U\Sigma V^T \quad \Leftrightarrow \quad \Sigma = U^T A V \qquad (1)$$
$$\Sigma = diag(\sigma_1, \cdots, \sigma_r)$$

where U and V are unitary, and Σ is real diagonal elements. σ_i is called the singular values.

Out-plane registration is used to compute the position of the source of 2D images in 3D space. To find the source position, we apply two rotation vectors of spherical coordinate systems and search the rotation vectors that optimize the correspondence between 3D volume and 2D images. In order to estimate the similarities, we use the root-mean-squared (RMS) error of the result of in-plane registration like Eq. 2.

$$RMSE = \sqrt{\frac{1}{n}\sum_{j=1}^{n}\left\|P_{ij} - T_j\right\|^2} \qquad (2)$$

where T_i is x-ray marker and P_{ij} is nearest marker of CT with T_i.

3 Experimental Result

All our implementation and tests were performed using a personal computer (PC) equipped with an Intel Pentium 4, 2.4 GHz CPU and 1GB memory. The graphics hardware was ATI Radeon 9600 GPU with 256 MB of memory. Our method was applied to two cardiac phantom datasets to evaluate its accuracy and computation time.

Table 1 shows the datasets derived from the 2 cardiac phantoms used for the study. Three groups of datasets were used:

- Dataset A and B had 3600 DRRs taken at intervals of 0.5 degree
- Dataset C and D had 900 DRRs taken at intervals of 1.0 degree
- Dataset E and F had 225 DRRs taken at 2.0 degree interval

Table 1. Image conditions of experimental datasets

(mm)

Dataset	CT dataset	Image resolution	Slice #	DRR Interval	Slice # (DRR)
A	CT 1	512 x 512	566	0.5	3600
B	CT 2	512 x 512	391	0.5	3600
C	CT 1	512 x 512	566	1.0	900
D	CT 2	512 x 512	391	1.0	900
E	CT 1	512 x 512	566	2.0	225
F	CT 2	512 x 512	391	2.0	225

We have compared our technique with software-based ray casting. This is an image order algorithm used in computer graphics to render three-dimensional scenes to two-dimensional scenes by following rays of light from the eye of the observer to a light source. Table 2 shows a comparison of the DRRs generation time using the 2 different techniques. Our method is over 150 times faster than software-based ray-casting.

Fig. 5 shows the results obtained by generating DRRs using our proposed method based on graphics hardware in comparison with software-based ray casting. It indicates that the image quality of DRRs generated from our method is as good as that of software-based ray-casting.

Fig. 6 shows the result of segmentation of confirmation markers in DRRs. The background image is X-ray fluoroscopy with circles indicating confirmation markers in X-ray fluoroscopy, and crosses indicating confirmation markers in DRRs.

Fig. 7 shows the result of registration of DRRs generated from the 3D cardiac phantoms and X-ray fluoroscopy. In the case of registration of 2-degree interval DRRs, the confirmation markers of the DRRs are not aligned with those of the X-ray fluoroscopy. However, with registration of 1 or 0.5 degree interval DRRs, the confirmation markers are almost perfectly matched.

Table 2. The comparison of DRRs generation time

Dataset	Proposed graphics hardware method (min)	Software-based ray-casting method (min)
A	24.21	5707.85
B	23.48	3664.28
C	6.02	1427.01
D	5.87	916.06
E	1.50	356.67
F	1.47	229.03

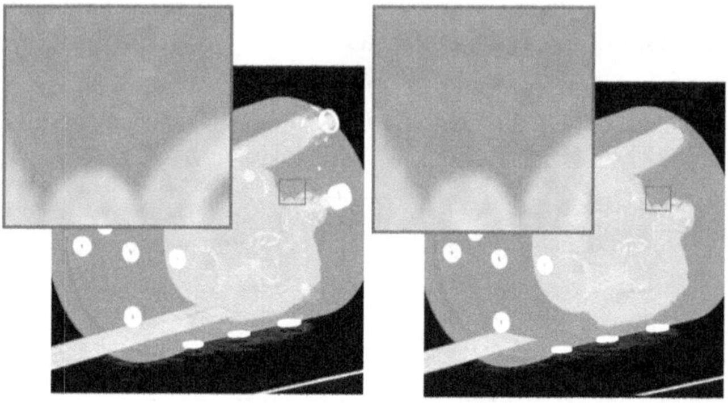

(a) (b)

Fig. 5. The results of DRRs generation (a) proposed graphics hardware-based method (b) software-based ray casting

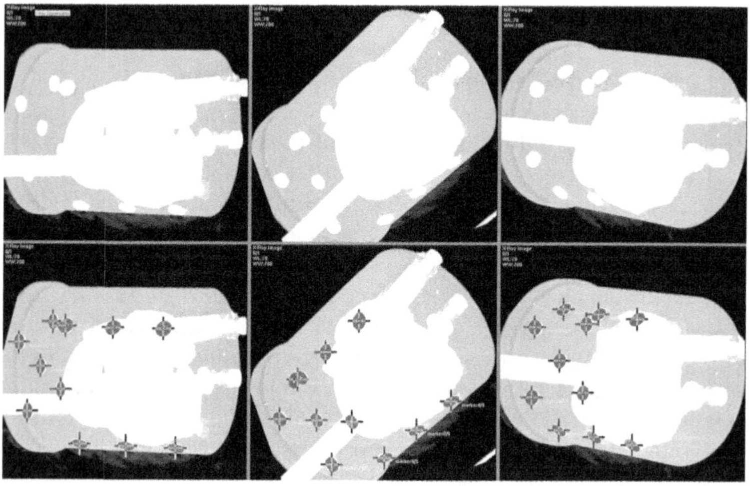

Fig. 6. The results of segmentation of confirmation markers in X-ray fluoroscopy and DRRs

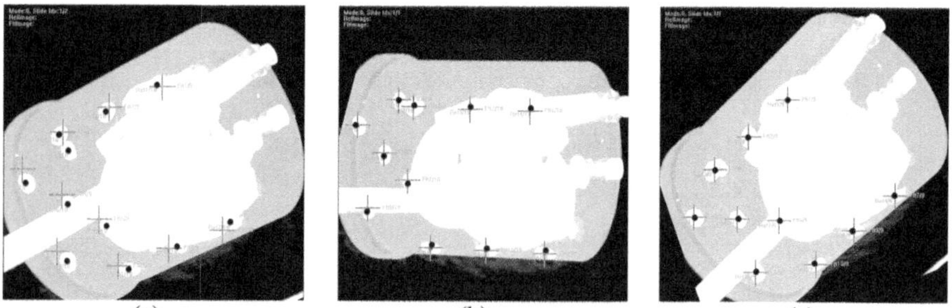

(a) (b) (c)

Fig. 7. The results of 2D-3D point-based registration with (a) registration of 2.0 degree interval DRRs, (b) registration of 1.0 degree interval DRRs, (c) registration of 0.5 degree interval DRRs

To further evaluate the accuracy of the method, we studied the root mean square error between the confirmation markers of DRRs and X-ray fluoroscopy (a distance referred to as the ground truth). If both markers are identically aligned there will be no distance or angulation between them. Our results demonstrated that the distance between the 2 markers varied from 12 to 47mm and the rotation between them varied from 31.6 to 56.5 degrees in all 3 axes (see Table 3). The root mean square error varied between 0.7 and 2.3 mm for distance and 0.5 and 2.8 for angulation.

Table 3. The accuracy evaluation using RMS error

Dataset	Translation Ground-Truth Parameters		Rotation Ground-Truth Parameters			RMSE (mm)
	(T_x, mm)	(T_y, mm)	(θx ,deg)	(θ_y ,deg)	(θ_z ,deg)	
Data A	30.9	30.1	53.5	48.0	56.5	2.7
	31.0	29.0	53.7	47.9	56.3	
Data B	12.3	17.6	35.5	50.5	45.5	1.8
	12.0	18.0	35.7	50.3	45.4	
Data C	29.7	46.4	32.0	50.0	42.0	11.3
	29.0	47.0	31.6	50.5	41.6	
Data D	22.5	30.8	36.0	42.0	42.0	8.6
	24.0	30.0	36.2	41.6	41.9	
Data E	20.6	28.8	54.0	54.0	48.0	19.7
	21.0	27.0	54.9	53.5	49.4	
Data F	15.7	15.8	47.0	36.0	54.0	22.7
	16.0	15.0	46.1	36.9	54.8	

4 Conclusion

We have developed a novel technique of 2D-3D registration of three-dimensional CT dataset and X-ray fluoroscopy. In pre-operative procedure, the DRRs generation method based on graphics hardware was performed rapidly. The automatic confirmation marker segmentation could remove noise and other features in both DRRs and X-ray fluoroscopy. The hierarchical registration including in-plane and out-plane registrations could reduce the search space from 6 DOF to 2 DOF. In our experiments, we use 3D cardiac phantom dataset to evaluate accuracy and computation time. The image quality of DRRs generated from our method is as good as that of software-based ray casting. In addition, the DRRs generation using graphics hardware is over 150 times faster than software-based ray casting. Experimental results showed that our DRRs generation method performs very fast and the hierarchical registration effectively matches the DRRs and 2D images.

Acknowledgement

This study is supported by Bahrom research fund from Seoul Women's University, 2006.

References

1. Gage, B.F., Waterman, A.D., Shannon, W., Boechler, M., Rich, M.W., Radford, M.J., Validation of clinical classification schemes for predicting stroke: results from the National Registry of Atrial Fibrillation, Jama, Vol. 285 (2001) 2864-2870.
2. Cox, J.L., Shuessler, R.B., D'Agostino H.J., Jr., et al., The surgical treatment of atrial fibrillation. III. Development of a definitive surgical procedure, J. Thorac Cardiovasc Surg, Vol. 101 (1991) 569-583.
3. Wyse, D.G., Waldo, A.L., DiMArco, J.P. et al., A comparison of rate control and rhythm control in patients with atrial fibrillation, N Engl J Med, Vol. 347 (2002) 1825-1833.
4. Swartz, J., Perrersels, G., Silvers, J., Patten, L., Cervantez, D., A catheter based curative approach to atrial fibrillation in humans, Circulation (1994).
5. Zollei, E., Grimson, A., Norbash, W. Well., 2D-3D rigid registration of X-ray fluoroscopy and CT images using mutual information and sparsely sampled histogram estimators, IEEE CVPR (2001).
6. Berthold, K.P., Horn, Closed-form solution of absolute orientation using unit quaternions, Journal of the Optical Society of America, Vol. 4, No. 4 (1987) 629-642.
7. J. Weese, R. Gocke, G.P. Penny, P. Desmedt, T.M. Buzug, H. Schumann, Fast voxel-based 2D-3D registration algorithm using a volume rendering method based on shear-warp factorization, Proc. of SPIE Medical Imaging, Vol. 3661 (1999) 802-810.
8. R.G. Gonzalez, R.E. Woods, Digital Image Processing, Addison-Wesley (1993) 443-458.
9. Rusinek, H., Tsui, W., Levy, A.V., Noz, M.E., and de Leon, M.J., Principal axes and surface fitting methods for three-dimensional image registration, J. Nucl. Med., Vol. 34 (1993) 2019-2024.
10. Alpert, N.M., Bradshaw, J.F., Kennedy, D., Correia, J.A., The principal axis transformation – a method for image registration, J. Nucl. Med., Vol. 31 (1990) 1717-1722.

GA–SSD–ARC–NLM for Parametric Image Registration

Felix Calderon, Leonardo Romero, and Juan Flores

Universidad Michoacana de San Nicolás de Hidalgo
División de Estudios de Posgrado. Facultad de Ingeniería Eléctrica
Santiago Tapia 403 Centro. Morelia, Michoacán, México. CP 58000
calderon@umich.mx, lromero@umich.mx, juanf@umich.mx

Abstract. We present the GA–SSD–ARC–NLM, a new robust parametric image registration technique based on the non–parametric image registration SSD–ARC algorithm. This new algorithm minimizes a new cost function quite different to the original non-parametric SSD-ARC, which explicitly models outlier punishments, using a combination of a genetic algorithm and the Newton–Levenberg–Marquardt method. The performance of the new method was compared against two robust registration techniques: the Lorentzian Estimator and the RANSAC method. Experimental tests using gray level images with outliers (noise) were done using the three algorithms. The goal was to find an affine transformation to match two images; the new method improves the other methods when noisy images are used.

1 Introduction

The parametric image registration problem [1] consists of finding a parameter set which allows us to match an origin image with a target image. Many algorithms try to minimize the Sum of Squared Differences (SSD) between the origin and target images. Successful SSD applications, including the classical Least Squared method (LS), are presented in [2,3,4]. Nevertheless the SSD based algorithms have poor performances in cases of noisy images and outliers. In particular, the problem with LS is that outliers have a huge weight in the cost function (and gradient vector) and pull the solution towards them; robust methods try to exclude outliers in some way.

Two well known robust methods in the computer vision literature are the Lorentzian Estimator (LE) and the the Random Sample Consensus method (RANSAC). Some authors, instead of using SSD, use the Lorenzian estimator [5] in cases of noisy images, getting good results. The RANSAC method is a stochastic technique which presents good results with outliers, and its application for image mosaics is presented in [6].

Another robust method is called, Sum of Squared Difference with Adaptive Rest Condition (SSD–ARC), which models outliers rejection inside the SSD cost function. An SSD-ARC application for non-parametric image registration was presented in [7] and another application for non-parametric camera calibration

J.F. Martínez-Trinidad et al. (Eds.): CIARP 2006, LNCS 4225, pp. 227–236, 2006.

is found in [8]. In both articles, the non-parametric SSD–ARC cost function is minimized using a coarse to fine strategy (scale space) and the Richarson Iteration [9].

This paper describes a new robust method named GA–SSD–ARC–NLM that combines the explicit outlier rejection idea from non-parametric SSD–ARC [7] into a new cost function with a searching process in two stages. The first stage is done with a Genetic Algorithm (GA) and the goal is to find an approximate solution inside a bounded parameter space. The second stage refines the solution, reached by GA, using the Newton–Levenberg–Marquardt (NLM) method [9].

An experimental comparison among GA–SSD–ARC–NLM, RANSAC and LE show the robustness pf GA–SSD–ARC–NLM in cases of noisy images.

2 Registration Using an Affine Transformation

The Affine Transformation (AT) [10,11] allows us to compute, at the same time, translation, rotation, scaling, and sharing of images. An AT uses a six-parameter vector Θ, and maps a pixel at position r_i (with integer coordinates $[x_i, y_i]$) to a new position $\widehat{r}_i$ (with real coordinates $[\widehat{x}_i, \widehat{y}_i]$) given by

$$\widehat{r}_i(\Theta) = \begin{bmatrix} \widehat{x}_i \\ \widehat{y}_i \end{bmatrix} = \begin{bmatrix} x_i \; y_i \; 1 \; 0 \;\; 0 \;\; 0 \\ 0 \;\; 0 \;\; 0 \; x_i \; y_i \; 1 \end{bmatrix} \Theta = M(r_i)\Theta \tag{1}$$

where $M(r_i)$ is the matrix of coordinates and $\Theta = [\theta_0 ... \theta_5]$ is the parameter vector.

The image registration problem, try to find the Θ which match an origin or source image I_1 on a target image I_2. However in practical cases both images are corrupted by noise and the problem is to find the best AT to match a transformation of I_1 into I_2. A very well known method to evaluate the match quality is to compute the Sum of Squared Differences (SSD) between the source and target images, pixel by pixel, as in Equation (2).

$$E(\Theta) = \sum_{i=1}^{N} \left[I_1(\widehat{r}_i(\Theta)) - I_2(r_i) \right]^2 = \sum_{i=1}^{N} e_i(\Theta)^2 \tag{2}$$

with a difference vector image e_i given by

$$e_i(\Theta) = I_1(\widehat{r}_i(\Theta)) - I_2(r_i) \tag{3}$$

where $I(r_i)$ is the gray level value of pixel r_i in image I. Using this error measurement, SSD, the registration image task consists of finding Θ^* that makes E reaches a minimum value (Θ^* is the minimizer of Equation (2)). This method is named Least Squared (LS) and some strategies to minimize Equation (2) are presented in [9].

Using the ρ-function, defined by Hampel in [12], the SSD can be defined by Equation (4) with $\rho_{LS}(e_i) = e_i^2$.

$$E_{LS}(\theta) = \sum_{i=1}^{N} \rho_{LS}(e_i(\theta)) \tag{4}$$

The influence function is defined by Hampel in [12], as the derivative of the ρ-function and it helps to see the contribution of the errors to the right solution (see [12]). In the LS case, the influence function is given by (5)

$$\psi_{LS}(e_i) = 2e_i \tag{5}$$

A robust function presented in [5], is the Lorentzian Estimator (LE), which has a ρ-function and influence function given by Equation (6) and (7)

$$\rho_{LE}(e_i) = \log\left(1 + \frac{e_i^2}{2\sigma^2}\right) \tag{6}$$

$$\psi_{LE}(e_i) = \frac{2e_i}{2\sigma^2 + e_i^2} \tag{7}$$

note, the term $\frac{1}{2\sigma^2+e_i^2}$ in (7), reduces the error contribution on the gradient vector and it is not present in Equation (5). This fact explains why LS is notorious sensitive to outliers. Another new function with similar performance is the parametric SSD–ARC function which is described in the following section.

2.1 Parametric SSD-ARC

The Sum of Squared Differences with Adaptive Rest Condition for non–parametric Image Registration was presented, by Calderon in [7], as the minimization of a quadratic energy function $\widehat{E}_{SSD-ARC}$ with a term $l_i h_i$ to reduce huge error contribution given by Equation (8)

$$\widehat{E}_{SSD-ARC}(V, l) = \sum_{i=1}^{N} (e_i(V_i) - l_i h_i)^2 + \mu \sum_{i=1}^{N} l_i^2 + \frac{\tau\mu}{4} \sum_{i=1}^{N} |\nabla V_i|^2 \tag{8}$$

where h_i is an error dependent function, $l_i \in [0, 1]$ is an outlier indicator function under the control of parameter μ, V_i is the displacement vector for each image pixel, and the last term is a homogeneity constrain with regularization parameter τ.

In our case, assuming an AT, $h_i = e_i(\Theta)$, and annulling the homogeneity constraint, a particular parametric SDD-ARC function can be obtained as

$$\widehat{E}_{SSD-ARC}(\Theta, l) = \sum_{i=1}^{N} e_i^2(\Theta)(1 - l_i)^2 + \mu \sum_{i=1}^{N} l_i^2 \tag{9}$$

For this parametric SDD–ARC function, the term $(1 - l_i)^2$ allows us to discard outliers. The second term in Equation (9) restricts the number of outliers by means of μ. The minimizer l_i^* for Equation (9) can be computed by solving $\frac{\partial \widehat{E}_{SSD-ARC}(\Theta,l)}{\partial l_i} = 0$, so the solution for l_i^* is given by Equation (10). We refer to l_i^* as the outlier field.

$$l_i^* = \frac{e_i^2(\Theta)}{\mu + e_i^2(\Theta)} \tag{10}$$

Replacing the value of l_i^* in Equation (9), we have a new parametric SSD–ARC function $E_{SSD-ARC}(\Theta)$ given by Equation (11), which has an unimodal ρ–function and an influence function given by Equations (12) and (13) respectively.

$$E_{SSD-ARC}(\Theta) = \sum_{i=1}^{N} \frac{\mu e_i^2(\Theta)}{\mu + e_i^2(\Theta)} \tag{11}$$

$$\rho_{SSD-ARC}(e_i) = \frac{\mu e_i^2}{\mu + e_i^2} \tag{12}$$

$$\psi_{SSD-ARC}(e_i) = \frac{2\mu^2 e_i}{(\mu + e_i^2)^2} \tag{13}$$

Note, the parametric SSD-ARC influence function exhibits a behavior similar to the Lorentzian Estimator influence function. In both functions, large differences give derivatives values near to zero, as can see in Equations (13) and (7) respectively. The parametric SSD–ARC influence function has a maximum value located at $\widehat{e} = \sqrt{\mu/3}$ and values greater than $2\widehat{e}$ will have a derivative value near to zero. Nevertheless, there is not a gradient-based algorithm capable to reach the minimum, if the initial value gives an error greater than $2\widehat{e}$. For this reason, a minimization method in two steps for the parametric SSD–ARC error function is proposed.

3 Algorithm GA–SSD–ARC–NLM

We propose to begin with a stochastic-based search, as Genetic Algorithm, and then to refine the results using a gradient-based algorithm, the Newton Levenberg–Marquardt (NLM). The following names are used in order to distinguish between the ways to minimize the parametric SSD–ARC Equation. If only the NLM algorithm is used, the minimization process is named SSD–ARC–NLM (see Algorithm 2.); if we use GA, the minimization procedure will be named GA–SSD–ARC (see Algorithm 1.), and when we use a combination, performing first GA and then NLM, the process will be called GA–SSD–ARC–NLM. A similar convention is used with LE.

3.1 GA–SSD–ARC

Haupt and Haupt in [13], describe the steps to minimize a continuous parameter function cost using GA. In our case, the parametric SSD–ARC given by (11) is optimized and the six vector parameter Θ will be the chromosome for each individual and the jth parameter is randomly computed by

$$\theta_j = (\theta_j^{\max} - \theta_j^{\min}) * \alpha + \theta_j^{\min} \tag{14}$$

where $\theta_j^{\max}$ and $\theta_j^{\min}$ are the upper and lower bounds and α is a random number in $[0, 1]$.

Algorithm 1. GA-SSD-ARC

Given μ, $I_1(r_i)$, $I_2(r_i)$ and N_{pop} then

1. Compute a initial population
   - For $k = 1$ to N_{pop}
     Randomly compute $\Theta^{(k)}$ using Equation (14),
     For each $\Theta^{(k)}$ compute $I_1(\widehat{r}_i(\Theta^{(k)}))$ and $e_i(\Theta^{(k)})$, by Equation(3)
     Compute the error $E_{SSD-ARC}(\Theta^{(k)})$ using Equation (11)
   - Select the half population with least $E_{SSD-ARC}(\Theta^{(k)})$; $N_{pop} \leftarrow N_{pop}/2.0$
2. Matting.
   - Randomly select couples over the best population half given more matting probability those elements with least $E_{SSD-ARC}(\Theta^{(k)})$
3. Reproduce
   - Replace the worst population half by the offsprings created by Equation (15)
   - and then, compute the Error $E_{SSD-ARC}(\Theta^{(off)})$ (Equation (11)) for each offspring.
4. Mutation
   - Randomly select the $k-th$ population member and the $j-th$ parameter, and replace it by a new parameter computed by Equation (14)
   - Never mutate the best population member.
5. Repeat steps 2, 3 and 4 until the population do not reach convergence.
6. For the best population member $\Theta^{(0)}$, compute $e_i(\Theta^{(0)})$ using Equation (3), and then, the outliers field l_i by Equation (10)

At each generation, a fitness-based selection process indicates which individuals from the population will mate and reproduce, yielding new offsprings. Once we have selected two individuals $\Theta^{(f)}$, and $\Theta^{(m)}$ for mating, cross-over is accomplished according to the following formulae

$$\begin{aligned} \theta_j^{(k)} &= \theta_j^{(m)} - \beta(\theta_j^{(m)} - \theta_j^{(f)}) \\ \theta_j^{(k+1)} &= \theta_j^{(f)} + \beta(\theta_j^{(m)} - \theta_j^{(f)}) \end{aligned} \tag{15}$$

where β is a random number between zero and one, and $\theta_j^{(k)}$ denotes the $j-th$ parameter of the vector parameter $\Theta^{(k)}$. Newly born offsprings ($\Theta^{(k)}$ and $\Theta^{(k+1)}$) are incorporated to the population replacing the worst elements and their fitness is computed by Equation (11). The final GA-SSD-ARC is presented in the Algorithm 1.

3.2 SSD–ARC–NLM

Equation (16) gives the iterative steps to find the minimum value using the Newton Levenberg–Marquardt NLM [9], and the strategy for computing $\lambda^{(k)}$ is given by Algorithm 2.

$$\Theta^{(k+1)} = \Theta^{(k)} - \left[H\left(\Theta^{(k)}\right) + \lambda^{(k)} I\right]^{-1} \nabla E\left(\Theta^{(k)}\right) \tag{16}$$

Algorithm 2. SSD–ARC–NLM

Given the μ, $I_1(r_i)$, $I_2(r_i)$, $\lambda^{(0)}$ and $\Theta^{(0)}$ then:
1. Set $k = 0$ and compute $E(\Theta^{(0)})$ by Equation (11)
2. Do
   Compute $H(\Theta^{(k)})$ and $\nabla(\Theta^{(k)})$ by Equations (17) and (18)
   Do
      Update $H(\Theta^{(k)}) \leftarrow H(\Theta^{(k)}) + \lambda^{(k)} I$
      Compute $\Theta^{(k+1)}$ by Equation (16) and $E_{SSD-ARC}(\Theta^{(k+1)})$ by Equation (11),
      If $(E_{SSD-ARC}(\Theta^{(k+1)}) > E_{SSD-ARC}(\Theta^{(k)})$ $\lambda^{(k+1)} = 10\lambda^{(k)}$ else $\lambda^{(k+1)} = \lambda^{(k)}$
   While $((E_{SSD-ARC}(\Theta^{(k+1)}) > E_{SSD-ARC}(\Theta^{(k)}))$ and $(\lambda^{(k+1)} < \lambda_{max})$
   If $(\lambda^{(k)} > \lambda_{min})$ then $\lambda^{(k)} \leftarrow \lambda^{(k)}/10$
   If $(E_{SSD-ARC}(\Theta^{(k+1)}) > E_{SSD-ARC}(\Theta^{(k)}))$ then $\Theta^{(k+1)} = \Theta^{(k)}$
   Set $k \leftarrow k + 1$
   While $((E_{SSD-ARC}(\Theta^{(k)}) < E_{SSD-ARC}(\Theta^{(k-1)}))$
3. For the final Θ^*, compute $e_i(\Theta^*)$ using Equation (3), and then l_i by Equation (10)

where $\nabla E(\Theta)$ is the gradient vector and $H(\Theta)$ is the Hessian matriz at each iteration and they are computed by Equations (17) and (18)

$$\nabla E(\Theta) = 2 \sum_{i=0}^{N-1} J(\widehat{r}_i(\Theta)) \frac{\mu e_i^2}{\mu + e_i^2} \tag{17}$$

$$H(\Theta) = 2 \sum_{i=0}^{N-1} J^T(\widehat{r}_i(\Theta)) J(\widehat{r}_i(\Theta)) \frac{2\mu^2(\mu - 3e_i^2)}{(\mu + e_i^2)^3} \tag{18}$$

$$J(\widehat{r}_i(\Theta)) = \left[A^{-T} \nabla I_n(r_i)\right]^T M(r_i)$$

where $J(\widehat{r}_i(\Theta))$ is the Jacobian matrix, $M(r_i)$ is defined by Equation(1), $I_n(r_i) = I_1(\widehat{r}_i(\Theta))$ and $A = \begin{pmatrix} \theta_0 & \theta_1 \\ \theta_3 & \theta_4 \end{pmatrix}$.

4 Experiments

We compare GA–SSD–ARC–NLM, LE and RANSAC methods using pairs of synthetic and real images. For LE, a minimization scheme similar to GA–SSD–ARC–NLM (using GA and NLM) is used in order to give similar minimization conditions (only replacing $E_{SSD-ARC}$ by E_{LE} in Algorithms 1. and 2.). Since in experiments with pairs of synthetic images, we know the right parameter vector $\widehat{\Theta}$, so the Euclidean distance $|\Delta\Theta|$ between the known parameter vector $\widehat{\Theta}$ and the estimated parameter vector Θ, is used as a proximity measure.

4.1 Experiments with Synthetic Images

In synthetic experiments, the NLM uses the vector $\Theta = [1, 0, 0, 0, 1, 0]^T$ as the initial value, and the stop criterion was $1e-5$ or 1000 iterations. For GA, a population of 3000 individuals and 100 generations were used. In order to accelerate the convergence procedure, in some cases the error function was evaluated only on 20% of the image pixels, all these parameters were handpicked in order to have a good performance. The GA search boundaries, for each of the affine transformation parameters, are $\{0.5, 1.5\}$, $\{-0.5, 0.5\}$, $\{-10, 10\}$, $\{-0.5, 0.5\}$, $\{0.5, 1.5\}$, $\{-10, 10\}$. The parameters μ for parametric SSD–ARC and σ for LE were 20 and 25 respectively, in order to give the better performance for both algorithms, and they are the same in all experiments.

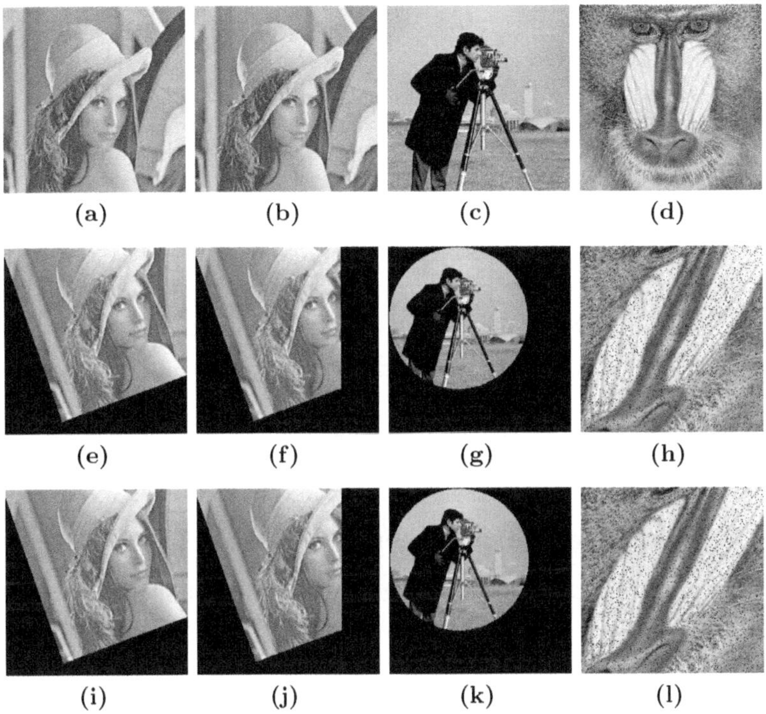

Fig. 1. Experiments with synthetic images. Origin images (a, b, c and d), target images (e, f, g and h), and resulting images using GN–SSD–ARC–NLM (i,j,k and l)

In the first experiment, an affine transformation given by $\widehat{\Theta}$ = [0.9396, -0.3420, 3.0000, 0.3420, 0.9396, 3.0000] is applied to the Lena image (Figure 1(a)) and the target images is shown in Figure 1(e). In the second experiment, in contrast with the previous one, 20% of the image pixels were set to black color (zero value) in order to simulate a regular outlier field. Using the same AT as the experiment one, the target image is shown in Figure 1(f). In the third experiment the complement of a circular-shaped outlier field and an affine transformation, given by $\widehat{\Theta}$ = [1.3, 0, 0, 0, 1.3, 0] are applied to the Cameramen Image (Figure 1(c)), yielding the picture in Figure 1(g). In the fourth experiment we use the

Baboon image (Figure 1(d)), an affine transformation given by $\widehat{\Theta}$ =[0.7, 0.3, 0, 0.3, 0.7, 0] and a random outlier field are applied to the baboon image, the target image is shown in Figure 1(h).

The results for LS, SSD–ARC–NLM, GA-SSD-ARC, GA–SSD–ARC–NLM, LE–NLM, GA–LE, GA–LE–NLM and RANSAC are presented in Table 1. These results show that GA–SSD–ARC–NLM outperforms the other methods, specially in the cameraman and Baboon images. The final images computed by GA–SSD–ARC–NLM in the four experiments are presented in Figures 1(i), 1(j), 1(k) and 1(l). Note the transformed origin images are very close to target images. You can note the bad performance for the same parametric SSD–ARC function when this is minimized using only NLM.

Table 1. Comparative results for parametric SSD-ARC, LE and RANSAC for synthetic experiments

	Lena	**Lena**	**Cameraman**	**Babbon**
Algorithm	$\|\Delta\Theta\|$	$\|\Delta\Theta\|$	$\|\Delta\Theta\|$	$\|\Delta\Theta\|$
LS	0.00010	51.4019	10.0451	1.3056
SSD-ARC-NLM	7.04200	4.2710	8.1507	12.5695
GA-SSD-ARC	0.96880	2.8368	1.3841	1.0910
GA-SSD-ARC-NLM	**0.00010**	**0.0431**	**0.0002**	**0.0000**
LE-NLM	19.60010	262.6573	19.6643	0.0006
GA–LE	0.42630	0.5471	6.7396	0.1371
GA-LE-NLM	0.00014	0.2089	6.3691	0.0006
RANSAC	0.12590	0.5376	0.4082	94.0000

4.2 Experiment with Real Images

This experiment use the origin and target images shown in Figure 2. These images show some differences that can be modelled using an affine transformation. Additionally, the target image has a boy in front of the car (which does not appear in the origin image), in order to introduce more complexity in the outliers, and the camera was rotated. The goal is to obtain the boy image as part of the outlier field and the affine transformation introduced by the camera rotation.

The transformation computed by GA–SSD–ARC–NLM was Θ = [0.9700, -0.2280, 42.7323, 0.2413, 0.9768, -20.6006] and by RANSAC was Θ = [0.9166, -0.2473, 47.1152, 0.2151, 0.9249, -15.3065]. In this case there are differences between the parameter vectors computed by both algorithms but these values do not allow us to conclude which one is the best or produces the nearest image to the target image. Using Equation (10), the outlier field can be computed and its image is presented in Figure 2(c), note in this image the contour of the boy in front of the car. Figure 2(d) shows the resulting image computed by GA–SSD–ARC–NLM. Finally the Figures 2(e) and 2(f) give a clear idea of the accuracy of both AF computed. In both Figures the absolute value of the difference between the target image and the computed image by GA–SSD–ARC–NLM and RANSAC were computed; dark areas correspond to low difference. Note the

(a) *Origin* (b) *Target* (c) *Outlier computed by GA–SSD–ARC–NLM*

(d) *Final Image computing by GA–SSD–ARC–NLM* (e) *Difference between GA–SSD–ARC–NLM and target images* (f) *Difference between RANSAC and target images*

Fig. 2. Car park image registration

quality for the AT computed by GA–SSD–ARC–NLM, shown in Figure 2(e), most static objects like the car or walls are almost perfectly matched; only the boy, and the leaves of trees do not match. In the RANSAC difference image (Figure 2(f)) even the car is not fully matched.

5 Conclusions

In this paper, we presented GA–SSD–ARC–NLM, an algorithm for parametric image registration, based on the non–parametric SSD–ARC algorithm. The Objective function is minimized in two steps, using GA at the beginning and then the NLM to refine the solution found by GA. The final algorithm improved the solution using only GA or using only NLM and it is robust when the images are corrupted by noise. A comparison of GA–SSD–ARC–NLM with other image registration algorithms, such as RANSAC and LE, was presented in order to provide experimental proof of the robustness of GA–SSD–ARC–NLM. We tested GA–SSD–ARC–NLM using different kinds of images and outlier fields. In all these tests, GA–SSD–ARC–NLM improved the results of the RANSAC and LE methods. Our method is similar to GA–LE–NLM but it is less sensitive to the particular parameter σ, and it is easier to find better solutions. Additionally the GA–SSD–ARC–NLM provides an explicit way to compute the outliers and does not need an extra image processing.

With synthetic images, we tested the robustness of GA–SSD–ARC–NLM and presented how the two minimization steps improved the solution using only NLM for the parametric SSD–ARC function. In case of real images, the comparison was done using only the final parameter vector, computed by GA–SSD–ARC–NLM and RANSAC.

Furthermore, GA–SSD–ARC-NLM has the advantage of computing the outliers with accuracy even in case of a random outlier field (as shown in the experiments). In contrast with RANSAC, GA–SSD–ARC–NLM computes the outliers for the whole image using a simple Equation. This outlier Equation is implicit on the parametric SSD–ARC function and the outlier field is computed when the algorithm converges.

References

1. Zitova, B., Flusser, J.: Image registration methods: A survey. Image and vision computing **21** (2003) 977–1000
2. Szeliski, R., Coughlan, J.: Spline-based image registration. Technical Report 94/1, Harvard University, Department of Physics, Cambridge, Ma 02138 (1994)
3. Szeliski, R.: Video mosaics for virtual environments. In: IEEE Computer Graphics and Applications. Volume 16,2., IEEE (1996) 22–30
4. Vemuri, B.C., Shuangying, Huang, Sahni, S., Leonard, C.M., Mohr, C., Gilmore, R., Fitzsimmons, J.: An efficient motion estimator with application to medical image registration. Medical Image Analysis **2** (1998) 79–98
5. Black, M.J., Rangarajan, A.: On the unification of line processes, outlier rejection, and robust statistics with applications in early vision. International Journal of Computer Vision **19** (1996) 57–92
6. Hartley, R., Zisserman, A.: Multiple View Geometry in Computer Vision. Second edn. Cambridge University Press, University of Oxford, UK (2003)
7. Calderon, F., Marroquin, J.L.: Un nuevo algoritmo para el calculo de flujo optico y su aplicacion al registro de imagenes. Computacion y Sistemas **6** (2003) 213–226
8. Calderon, F., Romero, L.: Non-parametric image registration as a way to obtain an accurate camera calibration. In Spriger, ed.: Advances in Artificial Intelligence, Mexico City, MICAI (2004) 584–591
9. Dennis, J.E., Schnabel, R.B.: Numerical Methods for Unconstrained Optimization and Nonlinear Equiations. Society for Industrial and Applied Mathematics. siam, Philadelphia (1996)
10. Hearn, D., Baker, M.P.: Computer Graphics C Version. second edn. Prentice Hall, Inc., Simon and Schuster / A Viacom Upper Saddle River, New Jersey 07458 (1997)
11. Watt, A.: 3D Computer Graphics. 3rd edn. Pearson Education Limited (2000)
12. Hampel, F.R., Ronchetti, E.M., Rousseeuw, P.J., Stahel, W.A.: Robust Statistics: The Approach Based on Influence Functions. John Wiley and Sons, New York, N.Y (1986)
13. Haupt, R.L., Haupt, S.E.: Practical Genetic Algorithms. John Wiley and Sons, New York, N.Y (1998)

Eigenconjugation: An Approach for Computing Image Similarity

V. Ortega-González, A. Angeles-Yreta, J. Medina-Apodaca, V. Landassuri-Moreno, and J. Figueroa-Nazuno

Centro de Investigación en Computación, Instituto Politécnico Nacional
Unidad Profesional "Adolfo López Mateos", 07279, México, D.F.
eortegag631@ipn.mx, malberto@sagitario.cic.ipn.mx, jmmedinaa@ipn.mx, victorm@sagitario.cic.ipn.mx, jfn@cic.ipn.mx

Abstract. We introduce a method for computing similarity between two square matrices based on the information given by their eigenvalues and eigenvectors. The idea is to evaluate the effect of the conjugation of the original matrices and the eigenvectors and eigenvalues of each other. Then, we exemplify its utility for computing similarity between square images from a classified bank of pictures. The performance of the method is evaluated with diverse experiments.

1 Introduction

Comparing matrices is an interesting open problem in computer sciences. Moreover, since matrices are a very useful representation for many kinds of data, it has a lot of applications in many different fields. On the conventional paradigm [1], measuring similarity between entities implies the selection of those properties considered as essential. These subjective elections are commonly erroneous and always incomplete. In many cases, the best techniques are those that use all the information available of the involved entities. For the specific problem of comparing matrices, we should prefer a method that works with all the information contained in each element of the bi-dimensional array.

In Linear Algebra, eigenvalues and eigenvectors are often used to characterize a transformation defined by a square matrix [6]. The determination of those vectors and values is a very well studied problem, and there are a lot of numerical processes which aim to solve it.

Definition 1. *Given a linear transformation M (defined by a square matrix) from Υ into Υ, a nonzero vector v in Υ is an eigenvector of M if*

$$Mv = \lambda v \tag{1}$$

where $v \neq \check{0}$ and $\|v\|_2 = 1$.

The scalar λ is called the eigenvalue of M corresponding to v [3]. Thus, we could say that an eigenvector of a square matrix is a non-null vector whose direction

J.F. Martínez-Trinidad et al. (Eds.): CIARP 2006, LNCS 4225, pp. 237–246, 2006.

is unchanged by the transformation and that the factor by which the magnitude is scaled is called the eigenvalue of that vector.

A square matrix M of $n \times n$ has up to n distinct pairs formed by an eigenvalue and a normalized eigenvector: $Mv^{(1)} = \lambda_1 v^{(1)}$, $Mv^{(2)} = \lambda_2 v^{(2)}$, $\cdots$, $Mv^{(n)} = \lambda_n v^{(n)}$; where $\left\|v^{(i)}\right\|_2 = 0$ for $i = 1, 2, \cdots, n$. It is common to represent the eigenvalues of a square matrix into a diagonal matrix called Λ, and the normalized eigenvectors are often represented as the columns of a square matrix called V, where they occupy their position according to Λ as follows

$$\Lambda = \begin{bmatrix} \lambda_1 & 0 & \cdots & 0 \\ 0 & \lambda_2 & \cdots & 0 \\ \vdots & & \ddots & \vdots \\ 0 & 0 & \cdots & \lambda_n \end{bmatrix} \tag{2}$$

$$V = \left[v^{(1)} \; v^{(2)} \; \ldots \; v^{(n)} \right] \tag{3}$$

It is useful to condense all the information given by the eigenvalues and eigenvectors into a single algebraic expression

$$MV = V\Lambda \tag{4}$$

It is mathematically accepted to say that two $(n \times n)$ matrices A and B are similar if there is an invertible matrix P for which $B = P^{-1}AP$ [3]. This is an equivalence relation on $\Re_{n \times n}$. We also know that if A and B are mathematically similar, they share the same eigenvalues. But this idea is inadequate for real cases where this relation does not describe sufficiently the data. Together, the eigenvectors and eigenvalues describe completely and univocally the intrinsic information of a square matrix. Thus, it is not possible to find two distinct matrices with the same eigenvalues and eigenvectors. We could take advantage of this unique characterization in order to represent a matrix with neither loss of information nor any kind of ambiguity.

2 Eigenconjugation of Two Square Matrices

Definition 2. *Given two square matrices $(n \times n)$ A and B with the matrices of eigenvalues Λ_A, Λ_B and the matrices of eigenvectors V_A, V_B respectively, we know it is true that*

$$V_A = AV_A\Lambda_A^{-1} \tag{5}$$

$$V_B = BV_B\Lambda_B^{-1} \tag{6}$$

where $A, B, \Lambda_A, \Lambda_B, V_A, V_B \in \mathbb{C}_{(n \times n)}$. Then, the matrices V'_A and V'_B know as the eigenconjugation of A and B are defined as

$$V'_A = BV_A\Lambda_A^{-1} \tag{7}$$

$$V'_B = AV_B\Lambda_B^{-1} \tag{8}$$

where $V'_A, V'_B \in \mathbb{C}_{(n \times n)}$.

Since V_A and V_B are matrices composed by column vectors, we considered V'_A and V'_B to have the same structure. Therefore, the column vectors of V'_A express the effect of the conjugation of B with the eigenvalues and eigenvectors of A. And the columns vectors of V'_B express the effect of the conjugation of A with the eigenvalues and eigenvectors of B.

3 Evaluation of the Eigenconjugation as a Similarity Measure for Square Matrices

In this section we introduce a new method which aims to measure an approximated distance between two square matrices based on the algebraic conjugation of the original matrices and the eigenvalues and eigenvectors of each other.

It is possible to represent the distances of each of the column vectors from V_A to V'_A into a sequence of n elements, and the distances from V_B to V'_B into another sequence. An interesting assumption is that if the original matrices A and B are similar, then the behaviours of both sequences are also similar. Now, we define a new matrix operator for determinining the distances between those vectors.

Definition 3. *Given two matrices $(n \times m)$ U and V, both composed by column vectors such as*

$$U = \left[u^{(1)}\ u^{(2)}\ \cdots\ u^{(m)} \right] \tag{9}$$

$$V = \left[v^{(1)}\ v^{(2)}\ \cdots\ v^{(m)} \right] \tag{10}$$

the operator $*$ is defined as

$$U * V = \left[e(u^{(1)}, v^{(1)})\ e(u^{(2)}, v^{(2)})\ \cdots\ e(u^{(m)}, v^{(m)}) \right] \tag{11}$$

where $e(u, v)$ calculates the Euclidean distance between vectors u and v

$$e(u, v) = \left(\sum_{i=1}^{n} (u_i - v_i)^2 \right)^{\frac{1}{2}} . \tag{12}$$

The result is a sequence that contains the distances between the consecutive pairs of columns vectors from both matrices. Now, we define two useful sequences

$$d_1 = V_A * V'_A \tag{13}$$

$$d_2 = V_B * V'_B \tag{14}$$

Therefore d_1 express the Euclidian distances between each of the vectors of V_A and V'_A, and d_2 express the Euclidian distances between each of the vectors of V_B and V'_B. Both sequences characterize the effect of the eigenconjugation of A and B. The characteristic sequences of an Eigenconjugation have always an uptrend.

The hypothesis is that the original matrices A and B are as similar as sequences d_1 and d_2 are:

$$A \approx B \rightarrow d_1 \approx d_2 \tag{15}$$

Since the expression (15) is an one-way logical implication, we must assume that A and B are matrices that belong to the same class.

There are many techniques for comparing sequences as time series. For this work we chose **Dynamic Time Warping** (DTW) for minimize the base distances between these sequences. For more information we suggest to see [4].

Definition 4. *Given two sequences* $Q = \langle q_1, q_2, \cdots, q_n \rangle$ *and* $C = \langle c_1, c_2, \cdots, c_m \rangle$, *the dynamic time warping distance DTW is defined recursively as follows [2]:*

$$DTW(\langle\rangle, \langle\rangle) = 0 \tag{16}$$

$$DTW(Q, \langle\rangle) = DTW(\langle\rangle, C) = \infty \tag{17}$$

$$DTW(Q, C) = d_{base}(f(Q), f(C)) + min \begin{cases} DTW(Q, r(C)) \\ DTW(r(Q), C) \\ DTW(r(Q), r(C)) \end{cases} \tag{18}$$

where

$$d_{base}(q_i, c_j) = |q_i - c_j| \tag{19}$$

and $f(\langle p_1, p_2, \cdots, p_k \rangle) = p_1$, $r(\langle p_1, p_2, \cdots, p_k \rangle) = \langle p_2, p_3, \cdots, p_k \rangle$.

It is assumed that Q and C are the same if $DTW(Q, C) = 0$, they are similar when $DTW(Q, C) \rightarrow 0$, and they are different when $DTW(Q, C) \rightarrow \infty$.

For the experimental results we noticed that the numeric value given by the computation of DTW could be affected by the scale of the magnitudes of the original matrices. So there were many near false positives cases when we compare one image to a bank of hundreds. Therefore we modified (19) in order to employ a kind of normalization similar to the one occupied in **Normalized Root Mean Square Error** (NRMS) measure. Thus, d_{base} is redefined as follows:

$$d_{base}(q_i, c_j) = |\frac{q_i - c_j}{\overline{q} - q_i}| \tag{20}$$

where $\overline{q}$ is the mean value of the fist sequence. Therefore $DTW(Q, C) \neq DTW(C, Q)$ in general. For the implementation we used an optimized version of DTW know as **Fast Dynamic Time Warping** ($FDTW$), which is a non-recursive approximation of computational complexity less than a polynomial of degree 2.

Definition 5. *Given two square matrices A and B of the same class, the similarity measure $sim(A, B)$ is defined as*

$$sim(A, B) = \sqrt{DTW^2(d_1, d_2) + DTW^2(d_2, d_1)} \tag{21}$$

where d_1 and d_2 are the characteristic sequences of the eigenconjugation of A and B.

In the following figures we show four examples of comparisons between pairs of same-class images. In Figure 1 it is possible to appreciate by simple glance, the relation of similarity supposed by (15). In the first case both sequences have a similar behaviour and the original images are also alike. In the second case it is observable the opposite situation.

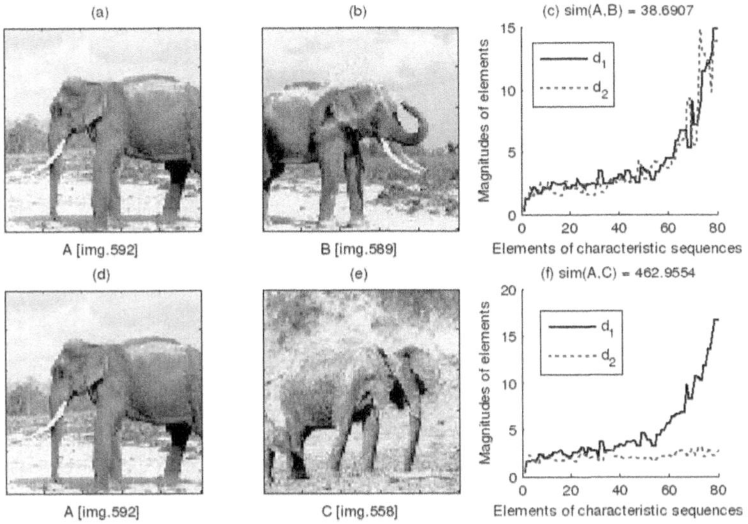

Fig. 1. Image A is compared to B and their characteristic sequences -d_1 & d_2- are showed in (c). Image A is also compared to C, their sequences -d_1 & d_2- are showed in (f). All images are of size 100 × 100 pixels. Only the first 80% of the elements of the sequences are plotted. Codes in brackets are the references of the images.

In Figure 2 two more experiments are showed, where it is important to notice that the numeric values given by *sim* are validated by the similarity relation of the original images.

4 Comparing Square Images Using Eigenconjugation

Although humans are capable of a complex and efficient performance while comparing images, this task is quite difficult for automated systems. Eigenconjugation validates the similarity relation between data matrices using numerical processes that can be easily implemented into a computer.

Although there are many techniques for pre-processing images such as filtering or thresholding, we rather work with the original information without any other stage or process. This is necessary because in this paper we introduce a method for comparing any kind of square matrices, not only for the specific case of square images.

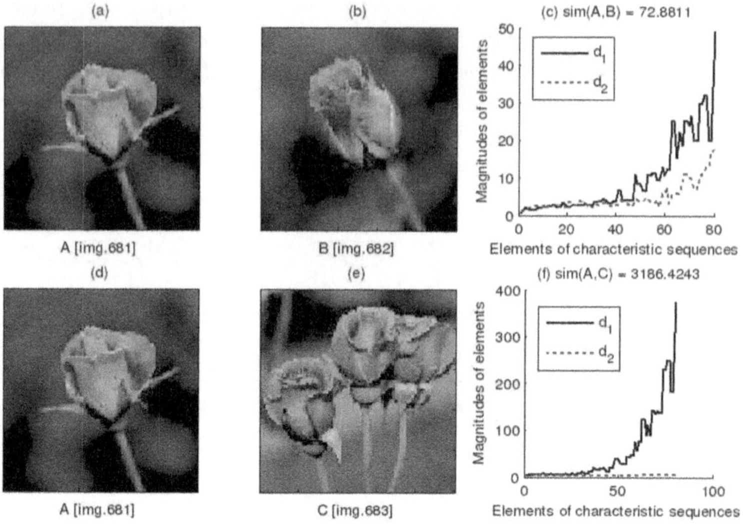

Fig. 2. Image A is compared to B and their characteristic sequences -d_1 & d_2- are showed in (c). Image A is also compared to C, their sequences -d_1 & d_2- are showed in (f). All images are of size 100×100 pixels. Only the first 80% of the elements of the sequences are plotted. Codes in brackets are the references of the images.

Using eigenconjugation, a comparison of two square matrices $(n \times n)$ has a computational complexity of somewhat less than $4n^3 + 12n^2 + 8n$ field operations; where the following stages are considered: algebraic eigenconjugation, construction of the characteristic sequences and the evaluation with $FDTW$.

Given a set of matrix representations of same-class images (Π) the procedure for sorting the elements by its similarity with a query is as follows (it is supposed that all images are square normalized and have the same size):

1. Select the query matrix $A|A \in \Pi$.
2. Calculate the eigenvectors and eigenvalues of A.
3. For each matrix B on the set $(B|B \in \Pi)$:
   (a) Calculate the eigenvectors and eigenvalues of B.
   (b) Obtain the eigenconjugation sequences of A and B: d_1 and d_2.
   (c) Calculate the similarity measure $sim(A, B)$; and save the result into a list.
4. Sort the list and show the results.

At first we worked with simple matrices obtained for the grayscale representation of the images. Obviously the information given by grayscale matrices is not enough for differencing efficiently each image from others. During these first experiments the results were not very satisfactory. It was necessary to include the information given by the colour components. Since the original images were available in RGB format, we decided to make a triple comparison using the matrices of the red, green and blue components. So there were three distances for each comparison. These three values were the components of a vector of distance whose absolute magnitude was defined as the total distance between the coloured matrices. Thus the results were sensibly improved in almost all the cases. But there were still some inconsistencies.

The best results were obtained when we used a unique jointly-coloured matrix representation of each image. This coloured matrix is constructed by an alternative permutation of the bits of the three colour components of each pixel. Thus, one single numeric value is obtained for each pixel. In the former representations the interval for pixel values was small $(0 - 255)$, with the use of coloured matrices the interval or variability is incremented (up to 256^3). Therefore the amount of available information is extended, and the process of similarity measuring is improved.

Every RGB image could be decomposed into three component matrices

$$R = (r_{ij}) \quad G = (g_{ij}) \quad B = (b_{ij}) \tag{22}$$

where each element (r, g and b) of the matrices has a binary representation as

$$r = (r_7 r_6 r_5 r_4 r_3 r_2 r_1 r_0)_2 \tag{23}$$

$$r = \sum_{k=0}^{7} 2^k \cdot r_k \tag{24}$$

where $r_k \in \{0, 1\}$ for $0 \leq k \leq 7$.

Definition 6. *Given a square RGB image $(n \times n)$, its jointly-coloured representation M is defined as follows:*

$$M = C(R, G, B) \tag{25}$$

where $M = (m_{ij})$; and each element m of M has the following binary composition

$$m = (r_7 g_7 b_7 r_6 g_6 b_6 \cdots r_0 g_0 b_0)_2 \tag{26}$$

$$r = \sum_{k=0}^{7} 2^{3k+2} \cdot r_k + 2^{3k+1} \cdot g_k + 2^{3k} \cdot b_k \tag{27}$$

where $r_k, g_k, b_k \in \{0, 1\}$ for $0 \leq k \leq 7$.

This representation prevents us for giving and excessive importance to a specific colour component. Nevertheless there is still an undesirable minimized favouritism. The defined order (r-g-b) in the combination is arbitrary, and it could be changed for optimizing the results in specific cases.

We tried experimentally to use normalization in different steps of the procedure, but the results did not improve except for some specific cases. General applications should not use normalization.

5 Experimental Results

In the following figures we illustrate some experiments where a query image was given, and the five nearest coloured images are showed (among more than 100 elements in each class). In all cases the jointly-coloured matrix representation was used. These results are very interesting and precise although they have to be validated by human inspection. Thus, there is no way to make a rigid objective evaluation of the effectiveness of the method.

In Figure 3, the two more similar images were placed next to the target. The other results could be irrelevant or appear to be erroneous. But the experiment is good because it brought the most similar elements at first.

Fig. 3. Searching over the Elephant class. Image Q "*query*" was compared to all the elements from the class. Images A to E are the nearest found specimens given by the *sim* measure. Codes in brackets are the corresponding references of the images.

Two experiments among the Horse class are showed in Figure 4 and Figure 5. These results are very appropriate for exemplify the correct performance of the method. They are good because the Horse class is correctly classified and the set is homogeneous. Therefore the method could determine with high precision the similarity over an homogeneous set.

Every class of images has a degree of homogeneity which is merely a subjective estimation of resemblance among its elements. In Figure 6 the results are very acceptable; in fact they are almost exactly. It is important to observe that the method is not infallible, that its efficiency depends strongly on the degree of homogeneity between the elements of the class.

6 Conclusions and Future Work

Eigenconjugation is a method for computing similarity between same-class images. And this might be a difficult task because these images are already similar.

Fig. 4. Searching over the Horse class. Images A to E are the nearest specimens of Q given by the *sim* measure. Codes in brackets are the references of the images.

Fig. 5. Searching once again over the Horse class. Images A to E are the nearest specimens of Q given by *sim*. Codes in brackets are the references of the images.

Fig. 6. Searching over the Flower class. Images A to E are the nearest specimens of Q given by the *sim* measure. Codes in brackets are the references of the images.

The proposed method could determine with high precision the similarity over an homogeneous set. Its efficiency depends strongly on the degree of homogeneity between the elements of the class. We have evaluated the method using matrix representations of colour images having better results while working with homogeneous sets. Nevertheless, this method could be applied for every kind of square data matrices. The method evaluates the similarity based on the whole structure of the matrices. In this paper we have discussed about its limitations and characteristics in different cases of use.

Eigenconjugation is a new different approach for computing image similarity. Some other methods [8] need to first process all the elements of the class, but Eigencojugation could evaluate the distance only between two matrices without any information from the other elements. A profound comparison with other techniques is a complicated task which is out of the reach of this paper.

Some future work suggestions are:

1. Using other similarity techniques and measures for time series.
2. Using eigenconjugation for computing similarity with other kinds of data matrices.
3. Complementing eigenconjugation with a classification method for working with non same-class images.
4. Comparing eigenconjugation with other techniques for image similarity.

Acknowledgments. The authors would like to thank the National Polytechnic Institute (IPN) and the National Council for Science and Technology (CONACyT) for supporting young people in academic activities.

References

1. J. Figueroa-Nazuno, A. Angeles-Yreta, J. Medina-Apodaca, V. Ortega-González, K. Ramírez-Amaro, M. Mirón-Bernal and V. Landassuri-Moreno: "Sobre el problema de Semejanza", *Reportes Técnicos*, CIC-IPN, México, 2006.
2. Sang-Wook Kim: "An Index-Based Approach for Similarity Search Supporting Time Warping in Large Sequence Databases", *IBM T.J. WRC*, ICDE 2001.
3. Brinkmann-Klotz: "Linear Algebra and Analytic Geometry", *Addison-Wesley Publishing Company*, 1971.
4. L. Rabiner and B.-H. Juang: "Fundamentals of Speech Recognition", *Prentice Hall*, 1993.
5. E. Keogh: "Exact Indexing of Dynamic Time Warping", in *Proceedings of the 28th VLDB Conference*, pp. 406-417, 2002.
6. J. Medina-Apodaca, J. Figueroa-Nazuno and S. García: "Time Series modeling using Recurrence Plots and Face Recognition techniques", *Congreso Nacional de Física 2002*, México, 2002.
7. A. Angeles-Yreta and J. Figueroa-Nazuno: "Computing Similarity Among 3D Objects Using Dynamic Time Warping", *10th Iberoamerican Congress on Pattern Recognition*, Cuba, 2005.
8. Pentland, T. Starner, N. Etcoff, A. Masoiu, O. Oliyide and M. Turk: "Experiments with Eigenfaces", *International Joint Conference on Artificial Intelligence 1993*, Chamberry, France, 1993.

Image Contrast Enhancement Based on Block-Wise Intensity-Pair Distribution with Two Expansion Forces

Md. Hasanul Kabir, M. Abdullah-Al-Wadud, and Oksam Chae*

Department of Computer Engineering, Kyung Hee University,
1 Seochun-ri, Kiheung-eup, Yongin-si,
Kyunggi-do, Korea, 446-701
hasanul@khu.ac.kr, awsujon@yahoo.com, oschae@khu.ac.kr

Abstract. In this paper, we present a block overlapped intensity-pair distribution based image enhancement algorithm. Instead of using the intensity-pair distribution of the whole image, this proposed algorithm takes the intensity-pair distribution block-wise and maps the intensity of the center pixel according to an expansion function. Analyzing the intensity difference of the intensity-pair, two different expansion force sets are generated for contrast stretch: one for soft edges, another for strong edges. In addition, a set of anti-expansion force is generated for smooth regions to avoid noticeable change. The contrast stretch and over-enhancement are controlled with a linear magnitude mapping function instead of a non-linear one. This linear mapping preserves the relative contrast enhancement ratio between the gray levels. The local information from blocks easily facilitates the contrast enhancement, brings out subtle edge information, and removes noises from the image.

Keywords: Anti-expansion force, expansion force, intensity pair.

1 Introduction

Contrast enhancement is an important issue in image processing for both human and computer vision. It is widely used for medical image processing and as a preprocessing step in speech recognition, texture synthesis, and many other image/video processing applications [4-7]. A very popular technique for contrast enhancement of images is histogram equalization (HE) [9-11]. It is the most commonly used method due to its simplicity. HE performs its operation by remapping the gray levels of the image based on the probability distribution of the input gray levels [8]. The basic idea behind this method is to stretch the dynamic range of the image histogram and resulting in overall contrast improvement. Many researches have already been done on histogram equalization and many methods have already been proposed. Generally, we can classify these methods in two principle categories – global and local histogram equalization [12].

Global Histogram Equalization (GHE) uses the histogram information of the entire input image for its transformation function. Fig. 1(b) shows the result of GHE on the

* Corresponding author.

J.F. Martínez-Trinidad et al. (Eds.): CIARP 2006, LNCS 4225, pp. 247 – 256, 2006.

original image as shown in 1(a). Though this global approach is suitable for overall enhancement, it fails to adapt with the local brightness features of the input image [12] and shifts the brightness to the middle gray level of the image regardless of the input brightness [10]. Local histogram equalization (LHE), also known as Adaptive histogram equalization (AHE) [11], can get rid of such problem. It uses a small window that slides through every pixel of the image sequentially and only the block of pixels that fall in this window are taken into account for HE and then gray level mapping for enhancement is done only for the center pixel of that window. Thus, it takes the advantages of HE, also remarkable use of local statistical information of the input image. But LHE requires high computational cost and sometimes causes over-enhancement in some portion of the image. Another problem of this method is that it also enhances the noises in the input image along with the image features. To get rid of the high computational cost, another approach is to apply non-overlapping block based HE. Nonetheless, most of the time, these methods produce an undesirable checkerboard effects on enhanced images [9].

(a) (b) (c)

Fig. 1. (a) Original image. (b) Enhanced image resulting from GHE. (c) Enhanced image resulting from intensity-pair distribution based method.

Recently, [2] proposes curvelet based method for contrast enhancement. Though in multi-scale edge enhancement, curvelet based approach outperforms wavelet approach [3] in edge representation, but for noiseless or near noiseless images its enhancement is not remarkly better than wavelet based enhancement [2]. On the other hand, [1] proposes an approach for enhancement based on intensity-pair distribution that possesses both the local and global information of the image content. Depending on the intensity difference in the intensity pair, either a set of expansion forces or a set of anti-expansion forces is generated to get an intensity mapping function, which enhances contrast and suppresses the image noise in the output image. This mapping function is more or less like GHE mapping function but incorporating some neighborhood information from intensity pairs. However, still this method cannot sharpen edges with low intensity-pair contribution and remove impulse noises.

In this paper, our proposed algorithm exploits the block-wise intensity-pair distribution for edge enhancement. Generally, digital images contain two-dimensional array of intensity values with locally varying statistics, which results from different combinations of abrupt features, like edges and contrasting homogeneous regions [9]. Since different parts of the image have different statistical characteristics we apply the block based approach to handle local information effectively and leave less chance for the smooth regions from other part of the image to have more influence over the edge pairs and finally lead to better image contrast stretch. To control the contrast stretch of the soft edges and strong edges two different expansion forces are used, where the expansion force for the soft edge pairs are comparatively less than that of strong edge pairs. Unlike [1], where a nonlinear magnitude function was used to avoid over-enhancement and preserve natural look of the processed image, here we present a linear magnitude mapping function to keep the relative contrast enhancement ratio between the gray levels since our search space is small and limited inside the block only. Once we get the final intensity mapping function from the expansion and anti-expansion forces of intensity pairs, only the center pixel of that block is updated and we move to the next pixel to repeat the same procedure. To take care of noises, if the deviation of center pixel's intensity value from its block intensity mean is too high, we replace that intensity value with the mean intensity value of that block, hence suppressing the noise pixels. Here we combined the advantages of conventional intensity-pair distribution method and block based approach for better edge extraction and enhanced image.

This paper is organized as follows. In section 2, we briefly introduce the intensity-pair distribution based image enhancement method [1]. The proposed algorithm is explained in details in section 3. Section 4 lists a few experimental results on different images to illustrate the performance of the proposed approach while section 5 concludes this paper.

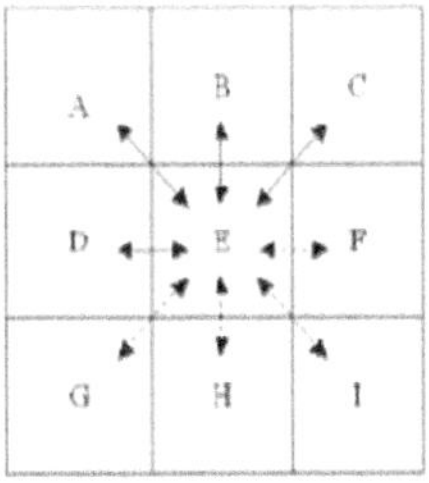

Fig. 2. An illustration of a pixel and its 8-neighbors. The solid arrows show the 4-neighbors from pixel E for intensity-pair generation.

2 Intensity-Pair Distribution Based Method

This section will briefly describe the Intensity-Pair distribution method for image enhancement. The algorithm presented in [1] extracts both the global and local information. It starts with computing the intensity-pair distribution. For a given image, each pixel is checked with its 8-connected neighbors. Due to the commutative property of intensity pair, only 4-neighboring pixels in raster order are scanned. Fig. 2 shows an illustration of 4-neighbors taken into account for the pixel at E from its 8-connection neighbor. Now to find intensity pairs belonging either to the smooth region or the edge region, we take the intensity difference within the pair. If the intensity difference is above a predefined threshold we can treat that pair as an edge pair otherwise that belongs to a flat region. To increase the contrast of the image and make the edges sharp we want to stretch the intensity of the edges pairs. On the contrary we also want to keep the flat regions from being stretched.

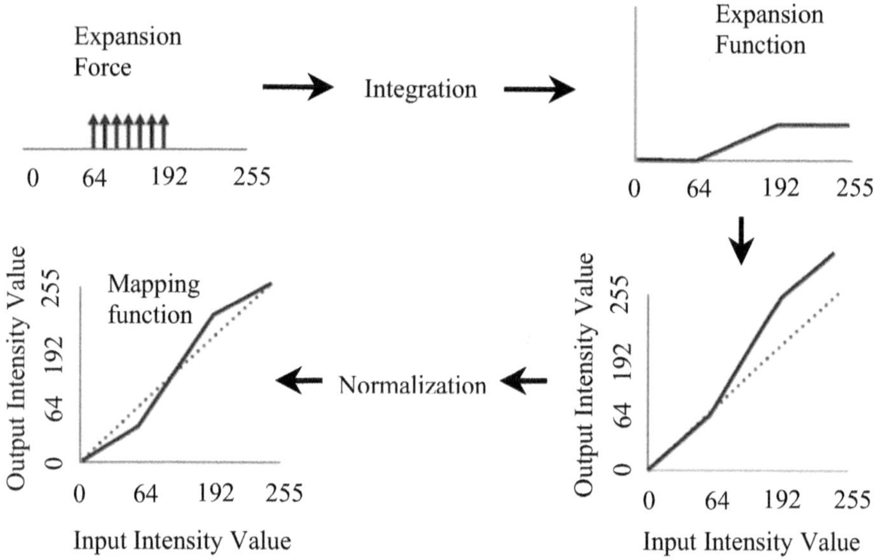

Fig. 3. Intensity mapping function generation procedure

In order to have contrast stretch in the edge pairs, we give a train of expansion forces between the gray level range of the edge pair. In a real 2D image many edge exists. So, we accumulate all the corresponding expansion forces of the edge pairs. Similarly all the anti-expansion forces are generated and accumulated for the intensity pairs of the smooth region. Now the smooth intensity pairs might lie within the gray level range of the edge pair. Due to the contrast stretch of the edge pair, the dynamic range of those smooth regions will also be stretched. To avoid these circumstances, the anti-expansion forces are subtracted from the expansion forces; hence the net-expansion force is obtained. Here, the anti-expansion forces preserve the smoothness for flat regions in the net-expansion force. Still the magnitude of the net-expansion force might be high enough to cause some unnatural and overly enhanced image. To reduce the dynamic range of the net expansion force a magnitude mapping function M(.) is applied which constrains the expansion force to an extent so that the image looks natural. A proposed mapping function is

$$Y = M(X) = X^{1/m} \; . \tag{1}$$

where, X is the net-expansion force, m is the behavior controlling parameter of the mapping function, and Y denoting adjusted net-expansion force. Finally the expansion forces are integrated and normalized to get the expansion function for intensity mapping. Fig. 3 shows the procedure for generation of intensity mapping function and Fig. 1(c) shows the enhanced image resulting from using the just reviewed approach. Notice that the contrast of some of the edges have improved while some others have not improved significantly. This happened because the contrast stretch was done based on the global information irrespective of contrast stretch needed only for a particular region.

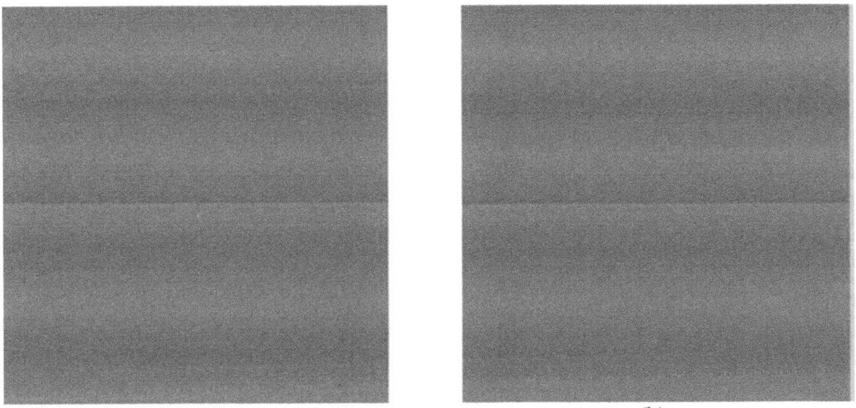

(a) (b)

Fig. 4. (a) Original image. (b) Image resulting from intensity-pair distribution based method, which shows no enhancements made.

3 Proposed Method

In the proposed method, our key objective is to bring out the subtle details of the image by letting the less frequent intensity pairs contribute almost equally to the expansion function. In case of global intensity-pair distribution based method, there are chances that the gray levels of intensity pairs of smooth region might lie and cover the entire gray level range which the edge pairs are expecting to stretch. Since the smooth intensity pairs will generate trains of anti-expansion force, and due to the high occurrences of those pairs the anti-expansion force might nullify the expansion force. As a result, in the net-expansion force there will be no effect from those edge pairs and eventually no contrast stretch. Such an example is shown in Fig. 4. In the original image we have only (0,48) edge pairs because there is sudden intensity jump from 0 to 48 at the middle of the image. Rest of the image contains gray values gradually either increasing from 0 to 48 or decreasing from 48 to 0. So our smooth intensity-pairs are (0,0),(0,1),(1,1),(1,2),…,(47,48),(48,48). Thus the gray level ranges of the smooth regions have covered the entire gray level range of the edge pairs. Now though the edge pairs are generating expansion forces between its gray level ranges, due to high occurrences of smooth pairs the anti-expansion force generated by them will cancel the expansion force. In the end, no enhancement is done. But in case of block-based intensity pair distribution, since we focus only to the intensity pairs falling inside the block, there is no scope for the smooth regions to dominate the edge pair forces. When the block slides over the edges pixels, we have more edge pairs, which then give more expansion force at edge regions. This brings out fine edge information without having any threat from smooth regions. Again, when dealing with edges, we get two types of edges: soft edges and strong edges. Now if the same set of expansion force is applied for both soft edges and strong edges, we might get contrast stretch in intensity but not visually pleasing image. So we give a comparatively low expansion force to the soft edge pairs compared to the strong edge pairs. Low expansion force prevents the soft edges from being too sharp.

Moreover, to avoid unnatural or overly enhanced features due to the large magnitude expansion force, the contrast enhancement approach based on global intensity-pair distribution [1] uses a magnitude mapping function on the net expansion force, which is nonlinear in nature. Due to the nonlinearity, after applying the magnitude mapping function the ratios between the forces at different gray levels do not remain the same as before. So the resultant net expansion forces do not reflect properly the forces of the intensity pairs anymore. Since our proposed method confines attention only inside the block and we have less number of intensity pairs, intuitively there is less scope of having net-expansion force with extremely large magnitude. Here the proposed contrast enhancement algorithm makes use of a linear magnitude mapping function to compress the dynamic range of the net expansion forces and to keep the relative contrast enhancement ratio between the gray levels which otherwise will be lost incase of non-linear mapping function.

In our algorithm, the first step is to define a block and retrieve its intensity pair distribution. This distribution gives us the local information. If an edge falls inside the block then we will have many edge pairs. The expansion force and anti-expansion forces are computed in the same manner as discussed in the previous section with an additional check for soft edge and strong edge. To compress the dynamic range of the net expansion forces, we use a linear magnitude mapping function. An example of such a mapping function M(.) is

$$Y = M(X) = X / \max(f_0, f_1, \ldots, f_i, \ldots, f_{255}) \,. \tag{2}$$

where f_i is the number of times expansion force is added for the *i-th* gray level. The next step is to integrate the net-expansion force to generate the expansion function and normalize it to fit in the range 0 to 255. This function is used as the final intensity mapping function for the center pixel of the block. The presented approach also takes care of impulse noise pixels by computing the mean (μ) and standard deviation (σ) of the block intensity values. For noise pixel removal, if the deviation of the center pixel's intensity value from its block mean is larger than twice the standard

1) Define an $M \times N$ sized output image array for an $M \times N$ input image I.
2) FOR each pixel position (x,y) in the input image
   a. Scan through every pixel within the block centered at pixel position (x,y) to calculate the intensity-pair information, mean μ, and standard deviation σ.
   b. IF $| I(x,y) - \mu | > 2*\sigma$
      THEN
         Put μ as the intensity value at pixel position (x,y) of output image and move to step 2.
   c. FOR each intensity-pair
      IF Intensity difference > Smooth region Threshold AND Intensity difference > Soft edge Threshold
      THEN
         Train of expansion forces for strong edges is generated between the gray level range of intensity-pair.
      ELSE IF Intensity difference > Smooth region Threshold AND Intensity difference <= Soft edge Threshold
      THEN
         Train of expansion forces for soft edges is generated between the gray level range of intensity-pair.
      ELSE
      THEN
         Train of anti-expansion forces is generated between the gray level range of intensity-pair.
   d. Accumulate the expansion and anti-expansion force.
   e. For each gray level k, calculate the net expansion force based on the following equation:

$$NetExpansionForce[k] = ExpansionForce[k] - g \times AntiExpansionForce[k]$$

   here, g is chosen to be 0.1 empirically. If the net expansion force at k is negative, reset that value to zero.
   f. Apply the magnitude mapping function M (.) over the net expansion force.
   g. Integrate the net expansion force to obtain the expansion function T and normalize it to fit within the range 0 to 255.
   h. The intensity value for the output image at pixel position (x,y) is calculated using the following equation:

$$w \times T[I(x,y)] + (1-w) \times I(x,y)$$

   here, w is a combination factor with $0 \le w \le 1$

Fig. 5. Summary of the proposed algorithm

deviation of the block intensity value, the mean value is used instead of using the intensity mapping function-mapped value. Since only the pixels inside the block are taken into account for the generation of the intensity mapping function and computation of center pixel's intensity, we are dealing more with the local information. Next, the block is moved by one pixel and the same procedure is repeated until the end of the image is reached. Here contrast enhancement based on intensity-pair distribution is performed with each block information so it can adapt well to the subtle edge enhancement and partial light condition in the same way the block overlapped histogram equalization works. The proposed algorithm is basically a block overlapped intensity-pair distribution based image enhancement approach with two expansion forces and a linear magnitude mapping function. This idea is summarized more clearly in Fig. 5. In the next section, we will present a detailed experimental result to further display the effectiveness of the proposed algorithm.

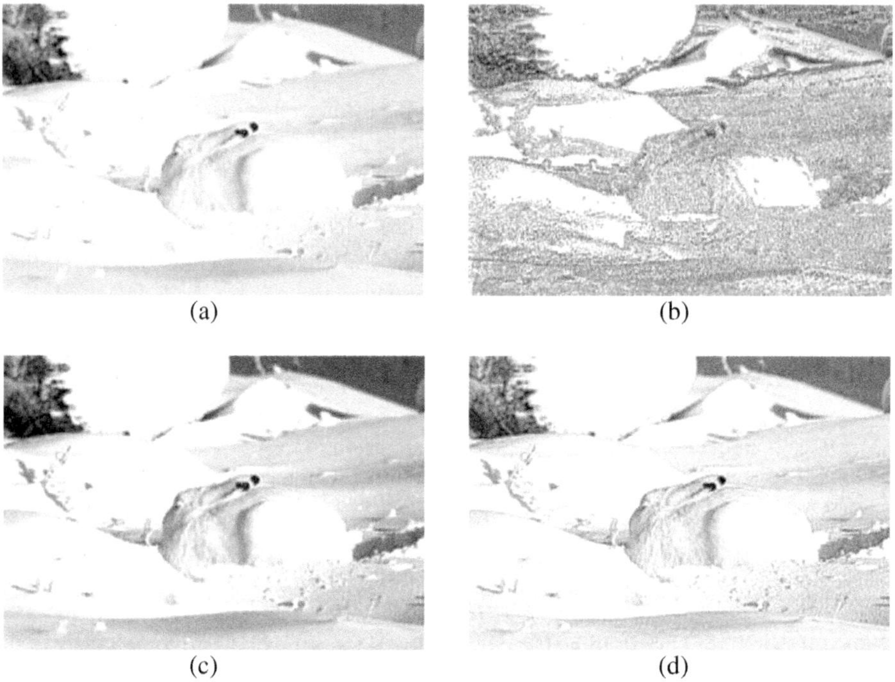

Fig. 6. (a) Original image (b) Enhanced image by LHE (c) Enhanced image by intensity-pair distribution based method with (m, g, k) = (2, 0.1, 0.8) (d) Enhanced image by block based intensity- pair distribution with (g , w) = (0.1, 0.6) and block size 3×3

4 Experimental Results

The results from previous algorithms and the proposed algorithm are simulated on various images, and compared with the enhancement ability of the proposed approach. Fig. 6 shows the original image along with simulation results from LHE, Intensity-Pair Distribution method and the proposed method. Here Block based Intensity-Pair distribution method has given better enhancement of the image, especially with the hare. Moreover, in the original image there are some impulse noises, which still remain for LHE and Intensity-Pair distribution method. Whereas Fig. 6(d) clearly shows our approach has quite efficiently removed those impulse noises.

To further prove the performance of the proposed algorithm, simulation result from applying the proposed method (g = 0.1, w = 0.6 and block size 3×3) on satellite image is shown in Fig. 7(c), compared with Fig. 7(b) resulting from curvelet transform (c = 3, l = p = 0.5 and s = 0). Here the edges and contrast at the upper portion are much more distinct in case of the enhanced image resulting from the proposed algorithm. Moreover, curvelet transform has also increased the overall brightness of the images, which might not be desirable in other images. In edge representation, image brightness and contrast, our proposed approach has done a significant improvement.

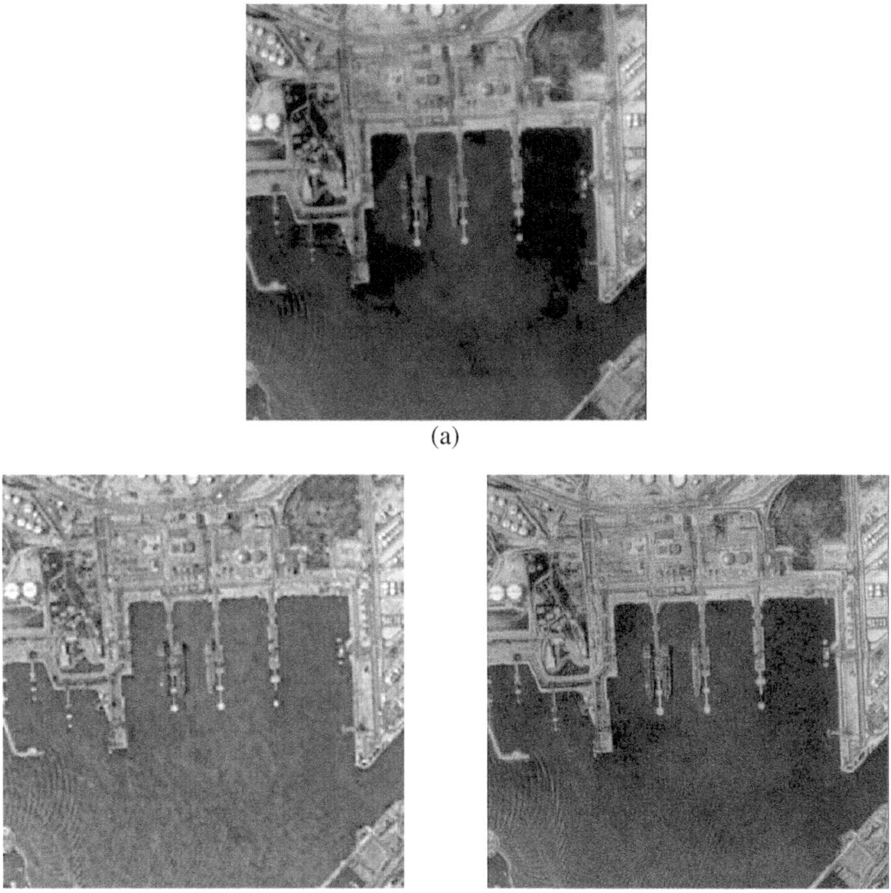

(a)

(b) (c)

Fig. 7. (a) Original satellite image. (b) Image enhanced by curvelet method. (c) Image enhanced by block based intensity-pair distribution method.

5 Conclusion

In this paper, we propose a block based intensity-pair distribution method with two expansion forces and linear magnitude mapping function for image contrast enhancement. Since only the block intensity pairs contribute to the intensity mapping function and smooth regions cannot nullify the expansion force of edge pairs, delicate edges are extracted and image enhanced. An additional noise checking procedure has also suppressed noise effectively from input images. Simulation results have shown that the proposed method has done a better improvement compared with the existing methods.

References

1. Jen, T., Hsieh, B., Wang, S.: Image contrast enhancement based on intensity-pair distribution. In Proc. Int. Conf. Image Processing, Vol. 1, (2005) 913-16
2. Starck, J., Murtagh, F., Candes, E.J., and Donnoho, D.L.: Gray and color image contrast enhancement by the curvelet transform. IEEE Trans. Image Processing, Vol. 12, No. 6, (2003) 706-717
3. Velde, K.V.: Multi-scale color image enhancement. In Proc. Int. Conf. Image Processing, Vol. 3, (1999) 584–587
4. Pei, S.C., Zeng, Y.C., Chang, C.H.: Virtual restoration of ancient Chinese paintings using color contrast enhancement and lacuna texture synthesis. IEEE Trans. Image Processing, Vol. 13, (2004) 416–429
5. Chin, W.A., S.H., Tan, E.C.: Novel approach to automated fingerprint recognition. In Proc. IEE Vision, Image and Signal Processing, Vol. 145, (1998) 160–166
6. Torre, A., Peinado, A.M., Segura, J.C., Perez-Cordoba, J.L., Benitez, M.C., Rubio, A. J.: Histogram equalization of speech representation for robust speech recognition. IEEE Trans. Speech Audio Processing, Vol. 13, (2005) 355–366
7. Pizer, S.M.: The medical image display and analysis group at the university of north carolina: Reminiscences and philosophy. IEEE Trans. Medical Imaging, Vol. 22, (2003) 2–10
8. Chen, S.–D., Ramli, A.R.: Contrast enhancement using recursive mean-separate histogram equalization for scalable brightness preservation. IEEE Trans. Consumer Electronics, Vol. 49, No. 4, (2003) 1301-1309
9. Gonzalez, R.C., Woods, R.E.: Digital Image Processing. 2nd ed. Reading, MA: Addison-Wesley, (1992)
10. Kim, Y.-K.: Contrast enhancement using brightness preserving bi-histogram equalization. IEEE Trans. Consumer Electronics, Vol. 43, No. 1, (1997) 1–8
11. Kim, Y.K., Paik, J.K., Kang, B.S.: Contrast enhancement system using spatially adaptive histogram equalization with temporal filtering. IEEE Trans. on Consumer Electronics, Vol. 44, No. 1, (1998) 82–86
12. Kim, J.-Y., Kim, L.-S, Hwang, S.-H.: An advanced contrast enhancement using partially overlapped sub-block histogram equalization. IEEE Trans. Circuits and Systems for Video Technology, Vol.11, (2001) 475 –484

Guiding a Bottom-Up Visual Attention Mechanism to Locate Specific Image Regions Using a Distributed Genetic Optimization

Eanes T. Pereira and Herman M. Gomes

Universidade Federal de Campina Grande, Departamento de Sistemas e Computação
Av. Aprígio Veloso s/n, 58109-970 Campina Grande PB, Brazil
{eanes, hmg}@dsc.ufcg.edu.br

Abstract. The purpose of this paper is to present an approach to locate specific regions in images. The novelty of the approach is the combination of a weighted bottom-up visual attention mechanism with a genetic algorithm optimization running on a computational grid. The visual attention mechanism is based on the model proposed by Itti and Koch [1]. A saliency map indicates the most interesting points in an image using a number of intermediate low level features, which are detected at different scales and orientations. Using the saliency map weights as parameters, the optimization problem is to minimize the number of most salient points needed to locate a set of reference image regions, previously (and manually) labeled as being interesting. Both an objective and subjective evaluation have demonstrated that the proposed approach is more effective when compared to a fixed weight attention mechanism.

1 Introduction

In any physical computational system, processing capability is limited. A mechanism to deal with this drawback in both biological and machine vision systems is visual attention. Visual attention is the ability that the visual system of superior vertebrates have to select and process only the most relevant regions in a visual scene. In this way, only the major areas in a scene are treated. This selection of relevant information in input stimuli is one of the most important characteristics of visual biological systems that allows fast detection of predators and is very important for perpetuation and evolution of the species [1]. Tsotsos [2] analyzed the computational complexity of visual analyses and confirmed that visual attention is one of the most important contributions to optimize the quantity of computations in visual systems.

For study purposes, visual attention can be divided into bottom-up and top-down. Bottom-up visual attention is related to low level features of the scene, such as: color, orientation and intensity. In this case, attention is not a conscious process. Only subjective interest guides the observer attention. Whereas top-down visual attention is very related with the observer desire or purpose. In top-down mechanisms, attention is guided by a previous interest of the observer.

J.F. Martínez-Trinidad et al. (Eds.): CIARP 2006, LNCS 4225, pp. 257–266, 2006.

Generally, models that require a previous process of learning are used to study top-down visual attention. One of the most used are neural networks. To study bottom-up visual attention, one of the most known models is saliency based model proposed by Koch and Ullman [3].

In a saliency map model, a set of maps is combined to form one single map that represents the most salient regions in the scene [4]. A salient region is the region that attracts most attention. There are several ways to combine feature maps. Itti et al [5] compared four strategies to combine feature maps: simple normalized summation, linear combination with learned weights, global non-linear normalization followed by summation and local non-linear competition between salient locations. Almost all strategies used to combine feature maps are based in learning processes to weight the maps. But none of them use an optimization process like genetic algorithms.

As to each saliency map is associated a weight, top-down knowledge can be used to guide the types of selected regions [6]. For instance, if one is searching for red flowers in a garden picture, the search accuracy can be improved if the weight related with color has a higher value than the other features. So, the system proposed here uses that knowledge to improve the quality of the search and guide the attention to look for previously known objects via an optimization process.

This paper proposes a novel strategy for optimizing the weights of a feature based attention mechanism. This strategy uses genetic algorithms to optimize the arrangement of weights that gives the best results when compared with a weightless map. Optimization is followed by detection and comparison phases. In the detection phase, a saliency map based on three features (color, intensity, and orientation) is constructed. After the detection phase, the resulting salient regions are compared with some previously selected regions and the comparison results are used in the next optimization phase.

The problem of mapping an image region that raises the human visual attention into a function that could be optimized is a complex task. Even when using the linearly weighted saliency model used in this work, there is not a clear way of doing that mapping. Besides that, the quantity of possible feature map combinations is very large and adds more complexity to the problem treated here. Therefore, we chose to use a method that has been used to treat those types of problems: genetic algorithm optimization, which are most appropriate for optimizing complex models in which the location of a global optimum is a difficult task [7].

There are many works that use some kind of evolutionary or genetic approach to treat visual attention [8], [9], but none of them uses a genetic algorithm to weight features maps like the strategy proposed here. Stentiford [8] presents a strategy that maps pixel neighborhoods to individuals in a genetic population. This population is evolved and performs a discrimination between salient and non-salient image features. Treptow et al. [9] present an evolutionary algorithm that uses the Adaboost framework to find new features and to reduce feature search.

The paper starts with a description of the overall optimization architecture proposed, which includes a description of the visual attention mechanism that was employed. This is followed by an objective (numerical) and subjective (based on some test images) evaluations. Finally, some conclusions and proposals of future work are presented. This paper presents and extension of a previous work [10] by giving an improved description of the proposed approach and providing an expanded set of results that uses images publicly available.

2 Proposed Approach

The approach receives as input a reference set of static color images, digitized at 352×240 pixels. The images are grouped in two sets: one containing only objects and other with people. In the set that contains people we consider the faces like the regions that raise more attention. So, in these images, human faces are marked manually by the selection of ears, eyes, mouth and nose of the present faces in the image. After that a file containing the coordinates of these parts is created. In the images without people, all the objects or regions that would intuitively raise the attention of human observers are also manually identified. These images are transfered to remote machines in a grid during the optimization process.

Since the size of the input space for optimization is relatively high (a total of 27 continuously valued weights), a computational grid was employed to cut down the processing time from several weeks on a single computer to just a few days using a grid of dozen computers. The reference input images (100 for people and 80 for objects) are divided into subsets for grid processing. The detection module (which is actually the attention mechanism) will concurrently run on different machines of the grid and process each of the reference image subsets producing as output a list of the most salient points found on those images. A genetic algorithm (which is the optimization module itself) provides the different weight combinations for the attention mechanism. The algorithm uses a cost function that is the percentage of salient points needed to find the previously labeled regions on the reference images. This function is minimized throughout the several iterations of the algorithm. Figure 1 illustrates the whole process.

2.1 Optimization Module

The optimization module is composed by a genetic algorithm that generates sets of weights to be applied in a combination of feature maps. An initial population of weights is randomly generated. After that, this set is sent to remote machines. A group of images and the detection module is sent to remote machines too. In the remote machines, the detection and evaluation processes take place.

When the detection and evaluation processes are finished, the results are sent to the optimization module. Then, the genetic algorithm tries to minimize the number of points needed to find a set of previously selected regions.

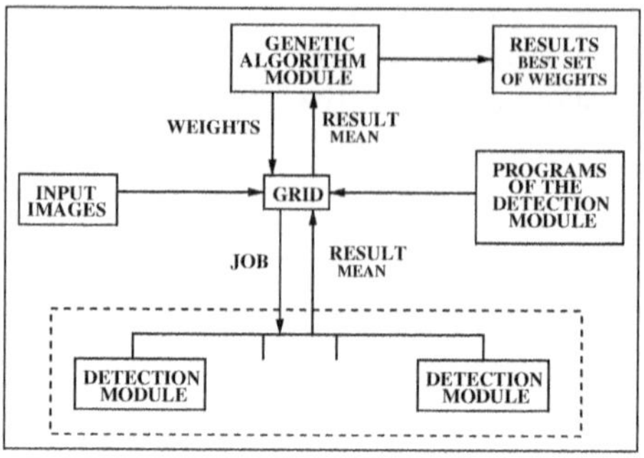

Fig. 1. Optimization architecture of the proposed approach

2.2 Detection Module

The detection module is an adaptation of the model proposed by Itti et al [11]. It uses a saliency-based attention mechanism (bottom-up), which is constructed from a Gaussian Pyramid and locally oriented neighborhood operators. Figure 2 shows a diagram of the detection module.

Initially, three types of primitive visual features are extracted: color, intensity and orientation. After that, four color channels are created (R to red, G to green, B to blue and Y to yellow). Finally, for each channel a Gaussian Pyramid with five levels is created. The Gaussian Pyramid is composed by pass-low filtered versions of the Gaussian convolution applied to the input image. The pyramidal representation is used to get image samples that do not have undesirable details.

To obtain the center-surround differences, it is necessary to create Steerable Pyramids. A Steerable Pyramid is a multi-scale and multi-orientation decomposition of an image. In this type of decomposition, an image is subdivided in a set of sub-bands localized in different scales and orientations. Center-surround operations are implemented as differences among scales. The center is a pixel in the scale $c = \{2, 3, 4\}$ and the surround region is the correspondent pixel in the scale $s = c + \delta$ with $\delta = \{3, 4\}$. Difference between two images is obtained by image interpolation in the scale and point-to-point subtraction. The

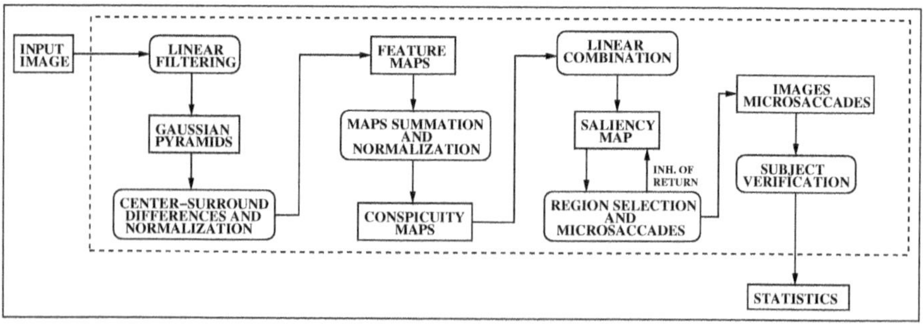

Fig. 2. Detection module

utilization of several scales allows multi-scale feature extraction. After execution of center-surround differences, the feature maps are generated.

Once the feature maps are obtained, they are summed up to produce the Conspicuity Maps: $\overline{\mathcal{I}}$ for intensity, $\overline{\mathcal{C}}$ for color and $\overline{\mathcal{O}}$ for orientation, in the scale $\sigma = 4$. The motivation for create three separated channels $(\overline{\mathcal{I}}, \overline{\mathcal{C}}, \overline{\mathcal{O}})$ is the hypothesis that similar features compete for saliency, while different features independently contribute for Saliency Map [1]. The three Conspicuity Maps contribute to saliency. The purpose of the Saliency Map is to represent salient regions in the image by scalar quantities and guide selection of regions based on spatial distribution of saliency.

Before summing the Conspicuity Maps, the set of weights got from the genetic algorithm are applied. Each combination is applied to all images and the results are written to a file. These weights are applied to the Conspicuity Maps, Feature Maps and Saliency Maps. After the subject detection, the results are compared with the previous manually selected ones. The result of this comparison is returned back to the optimization module.

A pixel sorting scheme (in descending order of saliency) was implemented to select regions of interest. A region around a coordinate of interest (which corresponds to the pixel with greater value) in the Saliency Map is selected. The radius of this region is called by the inhibition radius. In the experiments presented in this work we used inhibition radius of 2 pixels. Besides selecting the region of interest, that region is filled with null intensities. This prevents that the same region of interest be treated another time.

To prevent the same region of interest being selected more than one time, only part of objects are located, a micro-saccadic movement strategy was implemented. For each region of interest displacements are executed, changing the focus of attention to several neighboring points.

A previous work [12] employed an averaging computation in order to obtain the final Saliency Map, and to perform the required visual task using this map (e.g. locating traffic signs, locating faces, etc). In this paper, however, we tune the attention system by changing a set of weights that are used to produce the final attention map, in such a way that the given visual task is performed better. These weights are obtained by an experimental process. In that process, different weights are attributed to each map and results are optimized by the genetic algorithm until it stops.

2.3 Labelling the Regions of Interest

In order to guide the optimization process and to verify if the results of the automatic detection module are satisfactory, one tool was implemented to help manually select objects in images. Satisfactory results are those in which a smaller number of most salient points are required to fall into a set of previously selected image regions.

2.4 Verification Process

After the optimization module achieved a convergence plateau and returned the set of optimized weights, a verification process is performed. That process is performed with images obtained from Internet websites and that were not used in the optimization process.

The verification process is described as follows. Regions of images that raise attention of the observer are manually selected and their coordinates are saved. After that, the visual attention system is applied to those images and the coordinates of all points that raise attention are saved. Then a program is used to verify if the points returned by the attention system are contained in the regions manually selected. This process is done in two ways: using the optimized weights and without using them.

3 Experiments and Results

The purpose of the experiments was to optimize the weights in such a way that the system could find the subject of interest in the images with the least number of points. As mentioned before, the experiments were done using two types of images: with and without people. The goal of using different types of images is to check the generalization capacity of the genetic algorithm.

In this work, grid computing and a genetic algorithm library were used. The computational grid framework *OurGrid (http://ourgrid.org/)* was used to remotely process the detection module. The *GAlib (http://lancet.mit.edu/ga/)* genetic algorithm library was used to make our system. Almost all the code was done in C++ language, the only exception was the manual detection module and the methods related to the grid communication that were done in Java language.

The optimization (or reference) set of images containing people has 100 images and the set of the images without people has 80 images. These images were obtained in an environment that contains great quantity of dispersive elements that can misguide the subject detection process. The image set without people is formed by indoor images and natural environments.

The genetic algorithm uses overlapping populations. Using a previous established percentage, the algorithm creates a new population from a percentage of the best individuals in the early population and from a percentage of the crossovers and mutations of the early population. The algorithm goal is to determine the best mean of points needed to find all previous manually selected regions.

After the optimized weights were found, a verification process was performed. This process was done using 100 images with people and 100 images without people that were not in the optimization set. These images were obtained from Internet websites. In the image set with people, faces regions of people were manually selected. In the other image set, regions that raise attention in accordance with some features (color, intensity, and orientation) were selected. After that, a verification of the most salient points found by the visual attention system that was contained in the faces regions was performed. Fig. 3 shows the results obtained using an inhibition radius of 2 pixels.

The image set with people used in the verification process contains 194 people faces. From the graph of Fig. 3 (left), one can see that using only 1% of the total

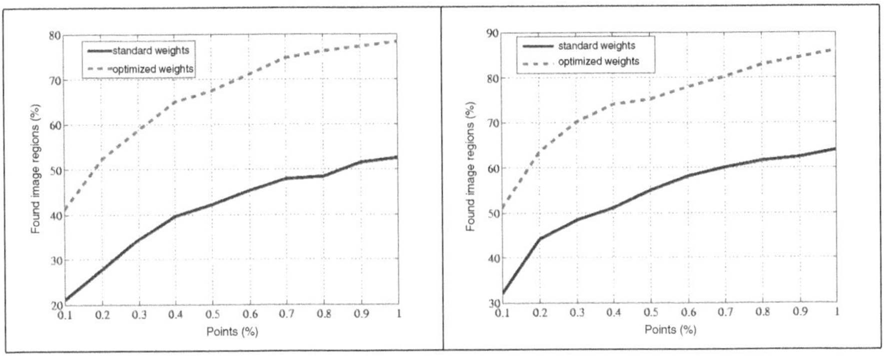

Fig. 3. Region location results for images with (left) and without (right) people, when using the corresponding optimized saliency map weights

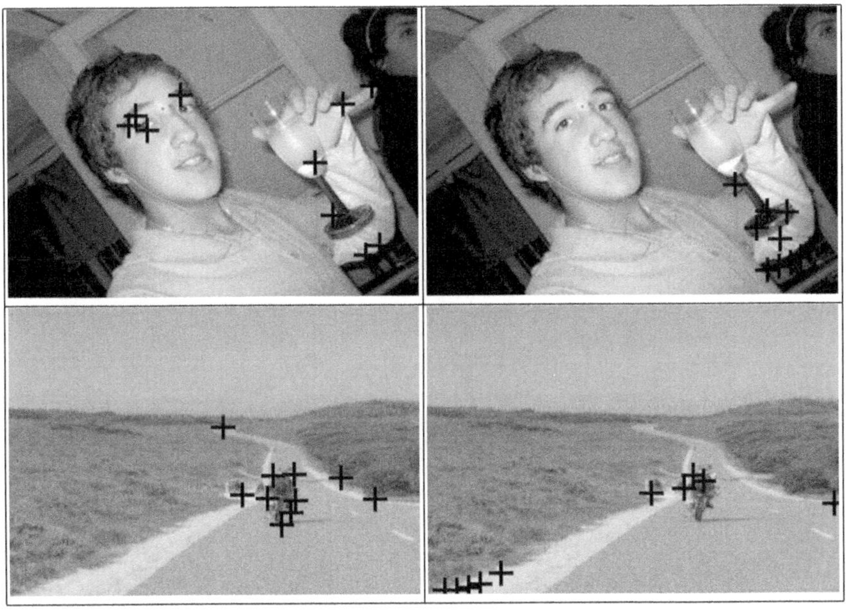

Fig. 4. Results of the attention mechanism with optimized (1st column) and standard (2nd column) weights on arbitrary test images

number of image points the system using optimized weights found points of interest in 152 (78%) people faces previously selected. In the image set without people, 258 objects, or regions that raise attention, were manually selected. The graph from Fig. 3 (right) shows that using 1% of the total number of image points the system using the optimized weights found points of attention in 222 (86%) objects or regions.

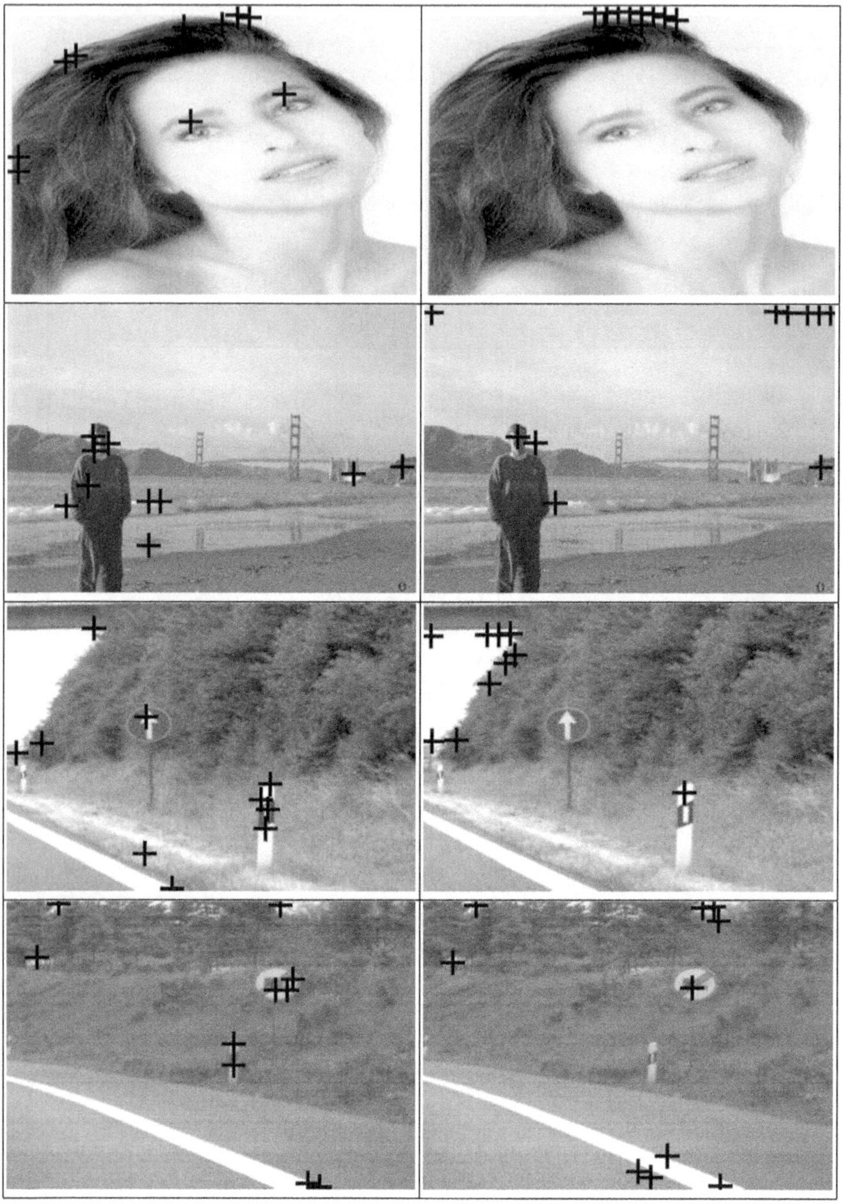

Fig. 5. Results of the attention mechanism with optimized (1st column) and standard (2nd column) weights on test images available at http://ilab.usc.edu/imgdbs/

In Fig. 3, it is clear that the use of optimized weights gives an improvement in the task of finding the subject of images. Besides that, optimized weights guide the subject detection in such a way that the user can previously establish what kind of objects he wants. The graph from Fig. 3 (left) shows an improvement of about 20% to the minor number of points and of about 30% to the greater number of points, and the graph from Fig. 3 (right) shows an improvement of about 19% to the minor number of points and of about 23% to the greater number of points.

For a subjective evaluation, we have applied our optimized attention mechanisms to a number of test images. Figures 4 and 5 contains these results. In Fig. 4, the images were arbitrarily chosen from the Internet. In Fig. 5, we used images from the *Miscellaneous artwork, posters and portraits* (first image) [11], *Miscellaneous outdoors* (second) and *Color images with German traffic signs* (third and fourth images) [13], all available for download at *http://ilab.usc.edu/imgdbs/*. The black crosses in the images indicate the 10 most salient points returned by the visual attention system, using an inhibition radius of 10 pixels. The inhibition radius of 10 was used to help the subjective analysis of the images (reducing the excessive agglomeration of salient points). In these figures, there are two types of images: Images in which the regions of interest are the faces of people, and images in which the regions of interest are general objects. Comparing the results with and without optimized weights one can perceive the improvement brought by the former.

4 Conclusions

This paper presented the application of genetic algorithms in a visual attention system. The genetic algorithm was used to optimize weights that were applied in a saliency map system. These weights were applied to construct the Saliency Map. To obtain results in satisfactory time, the experiments were executed in a computational grid due to the number of free parameters to optimize.

Although the saliency map system used was simple (using only 3 features), the results were very satisfactory. The results using thc optimized weights presented an improvement of about 20% against the results of the system without optimized weights. Another characteristic of the experiments presented is that all images used were obtained in arbitrary (mostly distracting, full of low level details) environments. These environments acted misguiding the system in some cases.

Experiments and results shown here have interesting areas for further improvement: only three features were considered in the saliency map model (more features could be added in the future), and there are many aspects of the evolutionary process that could enhance these results, including, for instance, selection methods, diversity maintenance, multi-objective techniques, and the use of automatically defined functions. Future work will further examine these issues and their application to visual attention systems.

Acknowledgements

We would like to thank HP-Brazil and CNPQ (Brazilian Research Council) for their support.

References

1. Itti, L., Koch. C., Computational Modeling of Visual Attention, *Nature Reviews Neuroscience*, 2(3), 2001, 194-203.
2. Tsotsos, J. Analyzing Vision at the Complexity Level, *The Behavioral and Brain Sciences*, 13(3), 1990, 423–445.
3. Koch, C., Ullman, S. Shifts in selective visual attention: towards the underlying neural circuitry, *Human Neurobiology*, 4, 1985, 219-227.
4. Itti, L., Koch, C. A saliency-based search mechanism for overt and covert shifts of visual attention, *Vision Research*, 40(10-12), 2000, 1489-1506.
5. Itti, L., Koch, C. A comparison of feature combination strategies for saliency-based visual attention systems, *Proc. SPIE human vision and electronic imaging IV*, San Jose, USA, 1999, 473-482.
6. Itti, L. Models of Bottom-Up Attention and Saliency, In: Neurobiology of Attention, (L. Itti, G. Rees, J. K. Tsotsos Ed.), Jan 2005, 576-582, San Diego, CA:Elsevier.
7. Mardle, S., Pascoe, S, An overview of genetic algorithms for the solution of optimisation problems, *Computers in High Education Economics Review*, 3(1), 1999.
8. Stentiford, F. An evolutionary programming approach to the simulation of visual attention, *Proc. Congress on Evolutionary Computation*, Seoul, Korea, 2001, 851–858.
9. Treptow, A., Zell, A. Combining Adaboost learning and evolutionary search to select features for real-time object detection, *Proc. IEEE Congress on Evolutionary Computation*, Portland, USA, 2004, 2107–2113.
10. Pereira, E., Gomes, H., Florentino, V. Bottom-up visual attention guided by genetic algorithm optimization, *Accepted to IASTED International Conference on Signal and Image Processing*, Honolulu, USA, Aug, 2006.
11. Itti, L., Koch, C. Niebur, E. A model of saliency-based visual attention for rapid scene analysis, *IEEE Transactions on Pattern Analysis and Machine Intelligence*, 20, 1998, 1254-1259.
12. Siagian, C., Ititi, L. Biologically-Inspired Face Detection: Non-Brute-Force-Search Approach, *In: First IEEE-CVPR International Workshop on Face Processing in Video*, Jun 2004, 62-69.
13. Itti, L., Koch, C. Feature Combination Strategies for Saliency-Based Visual Attention Systems, *Journal of Electronic Imaging*, 10(1), Jan 2001, 161-169.

ORIENT-CAM, A Camera That Knows Its Orientation and Some Applications

Bertrand Vandeportaele[1,2], Christophe Dehais[1], Michel Cattoen[2], and Philippe Marthon[1]

[1] Institut de Recherche en Informatique de Toulouse, France
bvdp@enseeiht.fr
http://www.enseeiht.fr/~bvdp/
[2] Laboratoire d'Electronique de l'ENSEEIHT, Toulouse, France

Abstract. We introduce a new type of smart cameras. These cameras have an embedded orientation sensor which provides an estimate of the orientation of the camera. In this paper, we describe our prototype orientation sensor and propose some methods for the calibration of the whole camera. We then show two applications. First, the camera is used to create oriented spherical panoramas. Second, it is used for image based localization, in which only the position of the camera has to be retrieved.

1 Introduction

Many researchers are working on methods providing the camera pose (orientation and translation) from the image. These methods use either some knowledge about the observed scene (for example, a 3D model) or more than one image in order to determine the camera pose and a partial model of the scene at the same time. In the first case, the recovered pose is relative to the 3D model. In the second one, the different poses are generally expressed as a function of the first pose and are defined up to a unknown scale.

In this paper, we propose to use an electronic device fastened to a camera in order to determine its orientation. This absolute orientation is defined in a fixed orthonormal world coordinates system in which two axes correspond to the vertical and magnetic north directions.

Some commercial digital cameras contain an embedded orientation sensor. This sensor is not of the same type that the one described here, as it only allows to determine if the captured image is in portrait or landscape orientation. Our sensor, on the other hand, allows to know in which direction each pixel of the camera is pointing.

In [7], a system combining a camera and inertial sensors is proposed to detect the vertical reference. The authors of [8] proposed a more advanced solution, using both inertial sensors an gyroscopes. The magnetic sensors we use do not deviate in time as gyroscopes do, and we can so expect to obtain the correct absolute orientation whereas they can only expect a relative one.

The paper is organized as follows. First, we describe the camera and the orientation sensor. Second, we propose some methods for the calibration of the

J.F. Martínez-Trinidad et al. (Eds.): CIARP 2006, LNCS 4225, pp. 267–276, 2006.

complete sensor. Third, we use the camera to create automatically omnidirectional oriented panoramas. Finally, we show how this camera can be used for image based localization and conclude with some perspectives.

2 Description of the Camera

Our aim was to create an handheld and low cost smart camera. The figure 1 shows the resulting prototype whose dimensions are 100*60*22mm and cost is about 150 USD. Both can be greatly reduced if the sensor is mass produced.

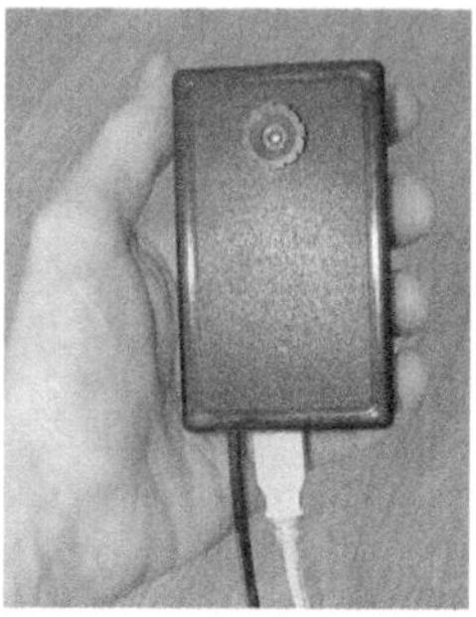

Fig. 1. The complete camera whose thickness is about 2cm

Fig. 2. The orientation sensor and its different axes of sensor. Both a1 and Yb are orthogonal to the main board.

2.1 The Orientation Sensor

The figure 2 shows the orientation sensor prototype we have built and integrated inside the camera. Its dimensions are 45*60*10mm. It is mainly composed of low cost integrated Micro Electro Mechanical Systems (iMEMS), namely accelerometers and magnetometers.

We use the magnetic sensors HONNEYWELL HMC1051Z and HMC1052 in order to have a 3D measurement of the magnetic field (on the axes a1,a2 and a3 shown on the figure 2). We also use two double axis accelerometers MEMSIC MXD3334UL mounted orthogonally to sense the gravity. Each MXD3334UL includes 2 orthogonal accelerometers. A single chip would lead to inaccuracies when one of the two sensor's axis is near the gravity, because each measurement corresponds to the sinus of the angle between the sensor axis and the horizontal plane. When this angle is near 90 degrees, a change of orientation of a few degrees cannot be detected as its sinus changes very few. Using at least 3 sensors allows to always have some sensor axes far away from the gravity axis and hence ensure more accuracy. Finally, the acceleration is sensed on the axes Xa, Ya, Xb and Yb as shown on the figure 2.

A Microchip PIC 18F252 microcontroller gathers the different sensors' measures and send them to the computer using a USB connexion thanks to the

FTDI FT232BM circuit. The complete set of measures is sent at 100Hz allowing a realtime orientation estimation in our computer vision task.

It is noticeable that the sensor provides redundant information as only 3 parameters (the rotations) have to be retrieved from 7 measurements. This allows to compute a more accurate orientation and to detect some incoherences such as parasite accelerations due to movements or magnetic field perturbations. Hence a confidence measure in the retrieved orientation is provided.

2.2 The Camera

The imaging sensor can be either a digital camera or a Webcam. In our prototype, we use the electronic parts of a Logitech QuickCam Pro 4000 at a resolution of 352*288 pixels and at 15 fps. This camera provides the ability to control the shutter speed and gain. Moreover, our model has very low radial distortions, and so can be well approximated by a simple pinhole model.

3 Calibration

3.1 The Orientation Sensor

The data provided by the different sensors have to be corrected in order to determine the orientation. The adequate correction is computed thanks to a calibration procedure that we describe hereafter.

Each magnetometer provide an analogous output. Offsets and gains have to be applied to each channel to ensure that the norm of the magnetic field is approximately constant when the sensor is rotated in any direction. They are estimated by acquiring a sequence of measurements while the sensor is rotating. A cost function whose value is minimal when the variance of the corrected norm is the lowest is then minimized to find the best set of parameters.

Oppositely, the accelerometers needs to be calibrated in static positions to avoid parasite accelerations. The orientation sensor is held in different known orientations and many measurements are done on each channel to compute mean values corresponding to extremal orientations (vertical and horizontal on each axis). The outputs of these circuits are Pulse Width Modulated with a duty cycle between 20 and 70%. The calibration consists in the estimation of a rectification function that provides a duty cycle of 20 or 70% when the sensor is held vertically and of 50% when the sensor is held horizontally.

The next calibration step is optional and only provides better accuracy. It consists in the estimation of the 3D direction of the earth magnetic field at the current location. The field has a different vertical component depending on the latitude on earth. The angle between the magnetic field and the horizontal is estimated by holding the sensor horizontally and deducing the angle directly from the measures given by the sensor.

Once the calibration has been achieved, a first estimate of the orientation is computed using only two accelerometers and a 2D projection of the magnetic field to the estimated horizontal plane. The orientation is then refined by taking into account the data from the 7 sensors. The orientation is parameterized with a quaternion to avoid discontinuity problems and gimbal lock caused by Euler angles parametrization.

Because of the noise in the measurements, we apply a temporal filter to increase the stability and accuracy. Our first idea was to implement a Kalman filter as proposed in [2], but as we have no idea of the movement of the sensor at a given time, we would have modeled it as static. Under this condition, the Kalman filter is equivalent to a standard least squares estimator that we have preferred to implement. Let w defines the size of a temporal window in which the measures of the sensors previously acquired between times $t - w$ and t are used to compute the orientation at instant t. The samples in this windows are weighted differently in order to make the samples which are close in time to the last acquired sample more influent. Increasing (resp. decreasing) w makes the detected orientation more stable (resp. reactive). Values of w between 10 and 20 have provided good results in our applications.

3.2 The Camera and Its Relative Orientation

Once the orientation sensor has been calibrated, it is necessary to calibrate the whole camera, *ie.* estimate its internal parameters and orientation relatively to the orientation sensor.

This is achieved by acquiring pictures I_j of a checkerboard pattern whose one axis is oriented to the magnetic north. We then use the Jean-Yves Bouguet's Complete Camera Calibration Toolbox for Matlab [5] to estimate the pose of the camera for each image (Ri_j, Ti_j) and its intrinsic parameters. Using the orientation given by the orientation sensor for each image Rs_j, we then compute a rotation R_Δ which minimizes $\sum_{j=1}^{n}(R_\Delta Ri_j - Rs_j)^2$ over the n images. This provides the relative orientation of the camera much more accurately than the measure from only one view. Moreover, in order to avoid bias in the estimation of R_Δ, it is better to sample the complete space of possible orientations.

The final detected standard deviation between $R_\Delta Ri_j$ and Rs_j is about 1.5 degree and the max deviation is about 4 degrees.

4 Oriented Panoramas

4.1 Their Inherent Advantages

The most obvious applications for our camera is the automatic stitching of images to create panoramas. It consists in generating a panoramic image from the different images acquired by the camera without needing to detect some common points in the different images, as Brown and Lowe do in [9]. Our approach has mainly four main advantages, thanks to the orientation sensor.

First, the reconstructed panoramas are oriented, so the horizon of the scene is projected on a straight horizontal line and the first column of the panoramic image can point to the magnetic north for example.

Second, as the orientation of the camera is known a priori, homologous points detection is not needed to stitch the images. This allows to deal with panoramas which contains big portions of non textured areas whose images cannot be automatically stitched by standard methods.

Third, the knowledge of the orientation simplifies greatly the creation of complete spherical panoramas. The problem of closings usually appears when one try to stitch images under a full 360 degrees rotation of the camera. Because of the accumulated errors, it is quite hard to stitch the last image and the first one. This problem can be avoided by using bundle adjustment to estimate the whole solution for the stitching instead of stitching iteratively new images to the panorama as proposed in [1] but this method requires a good initial guess for the whole correspondances.

Finally, our camera allows to deal very efficiently with scenes containing moving object which are outliers in the panorama reconstruction. Methods generally used to compute panoramas of such scenes involve a background/foreground segmentation in order to detect the camera orientation relatively to the background. With our sensor, this is done very simply by detecting zones in the images whose movements are incoherent with the orientation provided by the orientation sensor. The pixels of these zones are labeled as foreground and are discarded in the panorama reconstruction.

4.2 How to Create the Panoramas

We recall that a panorama can be created from images if the viewpoint of the camera does not move (or at least, its displacement should be very small compared with the distance to the observed scene), id. that the images are only related by a rotation of the camera. In this paper, we consider that the intrinsic parameters of the camera do not change between the images.

Using the orientation provided by the orientation sensor, it is possible to project each image of the camera to the right location on the panorama. However, due to imprecisions in the orientations of the different images, the different images do not exactly connect together. We first show how to obtain an approximate panorama in real-time and then propose to use the bundle adjustment method to improve its quality.

The resulting panorama we create is spherical, id. each pixel of the resulting image corresponds to a point on the sphere whose spherical coordinates are related to the pixel position. Any surface could be used to sample the image but the sphere allows an omnidirectional field of view.

Let the point P_i be one 3D position on the sphere corresponding to a pixel i. Let the quaternion corresponding to the orientation of the image j be defined by $Q_j = [abcd]^T$. The j indices are omitted in the quaternion parameters for readability purpose. The corresponding rotation matrix R_j is defined in the equation (1).

Let the camera matrix K be defined in the equation (2), α_u (resp. α_v) being the horizontal (resp. vertical) focal length and $[p_u p_v]^T$ being the position of the principal point. The points $P_i = [x_i\ y_i\ z_i]^T$ of the sphere is projected in the image j to the homogeneous point $p_{Hij} = [u_{ij}\ v_{ij}\ w_{ij}]^T$ whose inhomogeneous coordinates are $p_{ij} = [u_{ij}/w_{ij}\ v_{ij}/wij]^T$ obtained by the function $p_{ij} = D(p_{Hij})$. The image p_{ij} of the point P_i in the image j is obtained as shown in the equation (2).

$$R_j = \begin{bmatrix} 1-2\,b^2-2\,c^2 & 2\,ab-2\,cd & 2\,ac+2\,bd \\ 2\,ab+2\,cd & 1-2\,a^2-2\,c^2 & 2\,bc-2\,ad \\ 2\,ac-2\,bd & 2\,bc+2\,ad & 1-2\,a^2-2\,b^2 \end{bmatrix} \quad (1)$$

$$K = \begin{pmatrix} \alpha_u & 0 & p_u \\ 0 & \alpha_v & p_v \\ 0 & 0 & 1 \end{pmatrix} ; p_{ij} = D(KR_jP_i) \quad (2)$$

If p_{ij} lies inside the image boundaries and if the z component of R_jP_i is positive (id. the camera is facing the point), then the point P_i is viewable on the image j and the RGB values of p_{ij} are used in the panorama for the pixel i.

This computation is achieved for the whole sphere at each frame in order to update the panorama. The figure 3 shows an image from the camera and the reconstructed low resolution (1024*512 pixels) oriented panorama obtained in real time from a sequence of approximately 10 seconds. No post processing is applied; the panorama only results from the projections of the different images to the sphere. The left column of the reconstructed panorama points to the north and the horizon of the scene corresponds to an horizontal line in the panorama. Note the narrow field of view of the camera. The scene contains large un-textured areas on the roof, walls and a over exposed area at the window. The images of these parts would be impossible to stitch automatically as they do not contain any discriminant points.

Fig. 3. Left: An image from the camera. Right: The reconstructed oriented panorama.

4.3 Refinement of the Panoramas

The bundle adjustment is used to improve the estimation of the different images orientations. This has already been proposed in [1] but they were not using the a priori knowledge provided by the orientation sensor. The reader can find more information about the bundle adjustment techniques in [6]. This problem can be stated as an iterative minimization of a cost function f defined in equation (3). A detected projection of the point i in the image j is denoted $\widetilde{p_{ij}} = [\,\widetilde{u_{ij}}\ \widetilde{v_{ij}}\,]^T$ and is called an observation. Each observation of a point projection provides 2 residuals (res_u and res_v).

$$f = \sum_{j=1}^{n}(\sum_{i=1}^{m}(||D(KR_jP_i) - [\,\widetilde{u_{ij}}\ \widetilde{v_{ij}}\,]^T||^2)) = \sum_{j=1}^{n}(\sum_{i=1}^{m}(res_u^2 + res_v^2)) \qquad (3)$$

Not all the images (the camera is acquiring images at 15fps) are needed to refine the panorama, so the set of images have to be decimated in order to avoid useless computations. The decimation is very simple and consists in selecting images such that they have at least half their surface in common with the other images. The approximate orientation from the sensor is accurate enough to compute the set of images to keep.

The computations cannot be achieved on every pixels of the retained images and so some of them have to be selected. We use the famous Harris corner detector [3] to detect the projections of corners. Thanks to the knowledge of the approximate orientation of each image, there is no need to use descriptors to detect correspondences between the points in the different images. Instead of this, we simply project the detected Harris points of the different images to the sphere in order to detect the correspondences. A correspondence is established if some projected points from different images are closer than a threshold and if there is no other Harris points in the same images too close in their neighborhood.

Once the correspondences have been detected, the cost function is iteratively minimized. This way, we refine the intrinsic parameters, the quaternions Q_j and the P_i. The convergence is very fast in general and the computation can be achieved very efficiently thanks to the sparse structure of the jacobian. As the accuracy of the orientation sensor is known, we define some limits on the possible values for the quaternion parameters during the iterations. If a quaternion exceed these limits, we take it back to the limit. This ensure that the orientations of the different images cannot deviate too much during the bundle adjustment.

Some images contain no Harris point at all. These images will not have any observation and will not be related in the jacobian matrix. So their orientation will not change. Hopefully, the images which do not contains Harris point are likely to be untextured, so small misalignments due to the orientation sensor inaccuracies are not usually noticeable.

Finally, a post processing is applied in order to smooth the discontinuities at the image boundaries.

The figure (4) shows the results of the bundle adjustment and post processing on a part of the panorama. Only five iterations where necessary to adjust the

(a) (b)

Fig. 4. (a) A part of the panorama from 4 images before the bundle adjustment and post processing. (b) The same part after refinement and post processing.

whole panorama . Only four images are rendered here in order to see the details. Note that the discontinuities are attenuated in the refined image.

We have not deal with radial distortions because our camera does not require it. However it can be included very easily in the model, both in the calibration and bundle adjustment steps.

5 Image Based Localization

Our camera can also be used as an image based substitute for the GPS inside buildings, where the satellite signals cannot be received. In our previous works, we were using catadioptric camera in order to achieve this task. However, these cameras are quite expensive and fragile. Their size do not really allows to use the term "handheld" and special care must be taken in order to avoid scratches and dust that reduce the image quality. Finally, their resolution is lower than the one available from stitched images and the exposure has to be set for the whole scene, resulting in over or under exposed areas. Their main advantage is their ability to acquire more than an hemisphere of the scene in only one shot. Another advantage is that they allow to retrieve the orientation relatively to the horizon using the projection of vertical lines which are numerous inside buildings. However, the orientation to the magnetic north obviously cannot be determined automatically from the image.

In this section, we propose a very simple system to illustrate the ability of our camera. A database B of images I_P of the building in which we want to localize our camera (from its image I_C) is acquired using a catadioptric camera with a parabolic mirror. The acquired area is sampled at a given altitude and every 30cm in an horizontal plane. The paracatadioptric camera is held horizontally and with the columns of the image sensor pointing to the north (using a compass) so the database is at least approximately oriented.

The localization of I_C is achieved after computing a rectified image I_R (which is of the same type than I_P) and finding the closest image I_P in B. Instead of the sphere (as in the section 4), the surface of the paracatadioptric image is sampled. This way I_C is projected to a portion of a paracatadioptric image I_R and can be

(a) (b) (c)

Fig. 5. (a) The image I_C from the camera to be localized. (b) The projection I_R of the image to the surface of the paracatadioptric mirror. (c) The closest panoramic image I_P found in the database.

matched with images from B. Thanks to the orientation knowledge, I_R should superpose to a I_P acquired from the same location.A color rectification is also applied in order to make the images matchable.

In order to avoid costly comparisons of I_R with all the I_P, a first detection is achieved using corners detected by the Harris corner detector. The database is processed offline. Local descriptors are computed to describe every corner points. A famous descriptor widely used in the computer vision community is the Scale Invariant Feature Transform (SIFT) from David Lowe [4]. It provides very good results for matching image points related by affine transformations. However, thanks to the orientation sensor, such a complex descriptor is useless, as the points are observed in similar orientations and from very close positions (less than 20cm). In this experiment, we only use square windows of pixels to describe the points. These descriptors are simpler to compute and are also more discriminant, as they do not give good matching scores to couples which are related by affine transformation.

When an image I_C has to be localized, the Harris points H_C are detected in I_C using a variable size for the gaussian filter in order to deal with the varying resolution of the paracatadioptric camera. I_C and H_C are then projected to the paraboloid and the descriptors corresponding to the projected H_C are computed in I_R.

In order to match the images efficiently, we use a decomposition of the images in annular portions of sectors. The potential Harris points correspondences between I_R and the whole set of I_P are only compared if the points lie in the same or one of the 8 neighbor portions. The computed score is a ZNCC measure between the descriptors, which allows to deal with light variations. Harris points which do not have any correspondence get the worst score. The partial correlation score computed for an image I_P is the sum of the scores of the different points.

A final verification step is applied in order to check the correspondences which have the highest scores, and to decide between different solutions if needed (when many correspondences have nearly the same scores). This step consists in trying to match every pixels of I_R with one pixel in I_P. The ZNCC score is computed for each pixel of the I_R with pixels from I_P in a centered window neighborhood. The lowest score is kept for each pixel, allowing small displacement in the images. The resulting score for each image correspondence is the sum of the pixels' scores.

During our preliminary experiments, we have observed that this simple localization is robust to occlusions up to 30% of the surface of the image. When we integrate many images I_R to create a paracatadioptric panorama from the current location, the robustness of the localization is greatly increased. Obviously, the localization fails if the camera is pointed only to a region which is not discriminant, such as an uniform wall for example.

The figure 5 shows an example of the method. Less than 5 seconds are necessary to retrieve the correct I_P from a database of more than 200 images using a pentium 4 computer. The panoramic images were divided in 10 angular sectors, each one divided in 4 portions.

6 Conclusions and Perspectives

As far as we know, this paper presents the first handheld camera containing a complete absolute orientation sensor. We have shown that this camera is compact, low cost, practical and quite easy to calibrate. This sensor could be improved to obtain more accurate measures but it is sufficient for the proposed applications. We believe that this kind of camera have many other applications and should interest many researchers. Future work will focus on improving the image based localization system in order to avoid the dense sampling of panoramic images while acquiring the database. We are trying to use either a reconstructed 3D model of the scene or a sparse set of panoramic images.

References

1. Philip F.Mc Lauchlanand, Allan Jaenicke: Image Mosaicing using Sequential Bundle Adjustment, BMVC 2000.
2. E.H. Shin: A Quaternion-based unscented Kalman filter for the integration of GPS and MEMS, ION GNSS 2004.
3. C. Harris and M.J. Stephens: A combined corner and edge detector, In Alvey Vision Conference, pages 147-152, 1988.
4. David G. Lowe: Distinctive image features from scale-invariant keypoints, International Journal of Computer Vision, 60, 2 (2004), pp. 91-110.
5. Jean-Yves Bouguet, Complete Camera Calibration Toolbox for Matlab, http://www.vision.caltech.edu/bouguetj/
6. C. Slama: Manual of Photogrammetry, American Society of Photogrammetry, Falls Church, VA, USA, 4th edition, 1980.
7. Jorge Lobo, Jorge Dias:Vision and Inertial Sensor Cooperation Using Gravity as a Vertical Reference, PAMI, December 2003 (Vol. 25, No. 12), pp. 1597-1608.
8. Thomas Schon and Fredrik Gustafsson: Integrated Navigation of Cameras for Augmented Reality, IFAC 2005.
9. M. Brown, D. G. Lowe: Recognising Panoramas, In Proceedings of the 9th International Conference on Computer Vision (ICCV2003).

Irregular Pyramid Segmentations with Stochastic Graph Decimation Strategies*

Yll Haxhimusa, Adrian Ion, and Walter G. Kropatsch

Vienna University of Technology, Faculty of Informatics
Pattern Recognition and Image Processing Group
{yll, ion, krw}@prip.tuwien.ac.at

Abstract. In this paper we use different decimation strategies in irregular pyramid segmentation framework, to produce perceptually important groupings. These graph decimation strategies, based on the maximum independent set concept, used in Borůvka's minimum spanning tree based partitioning method, show similar discrepancy segmentation errors. Global and local consistency error measures do not show big differences between the methods although human visual inspection of the results show advantages for one method. To a certain extent this subjective impression is captured by the new criteria of 'region size variation'.

1 Introduction

It is suggested in [1] to bridge and not to eliminate the representational gap, and to focus efforts on *region segmentation*, *perceptual grouping*, and *image abstraction*. The segmentation process results in 'homogeneous' regions with respect to the low-level cues using some similarity measures. Problems occur since the homogeneity of low levels does not always lead to semantically plausible regions and the difficulty of defining the degree of homogeneity of a region. Thus, using only low-level vision cues cannot produce a complete final 'good' segmentation [2], since there is *an intrinsic ambiguity* in the exact location of region boundaries as well as the problems in defining the context of a digital image. Although the methods that do not use the context of the image cannot produce a 'good' segmentation, they can be valuable tools in image analysis just like efficient edge detectors are. Hence, the low-level coherence of brightness, color, texture or motion attributes should be used to come up sequentially with partitions [4]. A grouping method should have the following properties [3]: capture *perceptually important groupings* (encoding global views of an image); be *highly efficient* (running in time (near) linear), and create *hierarchical partitions* [4]. Computer vision problems could benefit from an efficient computation of segmentation.

Regular image pyramids are an efficient representation for fast grouping and access to image objects in top-down and bottom-up processes. However, it is shown that regular image pyramids are confined to globally defined sampling grids and lack shift invariance [5], and that they have to be rejected as general-purpose segmentation algorithms. To avoid these drawbacks, [6] proposes irregular image pyramids (*adaptive pyramids*), where the hierarchical structure of the

* Supported by the Austrian Science Fund under grants P18716-N13 and S9103-N04.

J.F. Martínez-Trinidad et al. (Eds.): CIARP 2006, LNCS 4225, pp. 277–286, 2006.

pyramid is not *a priori* known but recursively built based on the data. [7] shows that irregular pyramids can be used for segmentation and feature detection.

In the same sense, segmentation can be evaluated purely[1] as segmentation by comparing the segmentation done by humans with those done by a particular method [9]. There is a consistency of segmentation done by humans, even thought humans segment images at different granularity (refinement or coarsening) (Fig. 2, rows 3 – 4). This refinement or coarsening could be thought of as hierarchical structure of the image, i.e. the pyramid. Thus in [9] a segmentation evaluation framework that does not penalize this granularity is used (Sec. 5).

In order to achieve efficiency in image partitioning, Borůvka's algorithm[10] is combined with dual graph contraction (DGC) [11] for building in a hierarchical way a minimum weight spanning tree (of the region)(Sec. 3). We use the idea of building a minimum weight spanning tree (MST) to find region borders quickly and effortlessly in a bottom-up way based only on local differences in a specific feature. Different stochastic strategies (MIS, MIES, D3P, Sec. 2) for contraction kernels are used within the DGC, thus yielding different partitioning methods. We evaluate the normalized cut [4](NCutSeg) and the method based on the Borůvka's MST [12](BorůSeg) (all three flavors depending on the decimation strategy used: MIS, MIES or D3P (BorůSeg (MIS), BorůSeg (MIES) and BorůSeg (D3P)). We compare these methods following the framework of [9], and show that the methods have similar discrepancy error. Although, qualitative inspection of the produced segmentations showed differences between the methods which the pixel-based discrepancy measures did not show (Sec. 5).

2 Irregular Graph Pyramid

In a regular image pyramid, the number of pixels at any level k is λ times higher than the number of pixels at the next (reduced) level $k+1$. The so called reduction factor λ is greater than one and it is the same for all levels k. If s denotes the number of pixels in an image I, the number of new levels on top of I amounts to $\log_\lambda(s)$. This implies that an image pyramid is build in $\mathcal{O}[\log(image\_diameter)]$ time [8], as well as algorithms running on this representation (Fig. 1a).

An irregular pyramid should be used instead of regular ones for segmentation methods [6]. Irregular pyramids can perform all the operations for which their regular counterparts are employed [13]. Each level represents a partition of the pixel set into cells, i.e. *connected subsets of pixels*. The construction of an irregular pyramid is iteratively local [14]. On the base level (level 0) of an irregular pyramid the cells represent single pixels and the neighborhood of the cells is defined by the 4(8)-connectivity of the pixels. A cell on level $k+1$ (parent) is a union of some neighboring cells on level k (children). This union is controlled by so called *contraction kernels* (CK) [11]. Every parent computes its values independently of other cells on the same level. We assume that there is a highest level h. Although adaptive pyramids overcome the drawbacks of their regular ancestors and although they grow to a reasonable height as long as the base is small,

[1] The context of the image is not taken into consideration during segmentation.

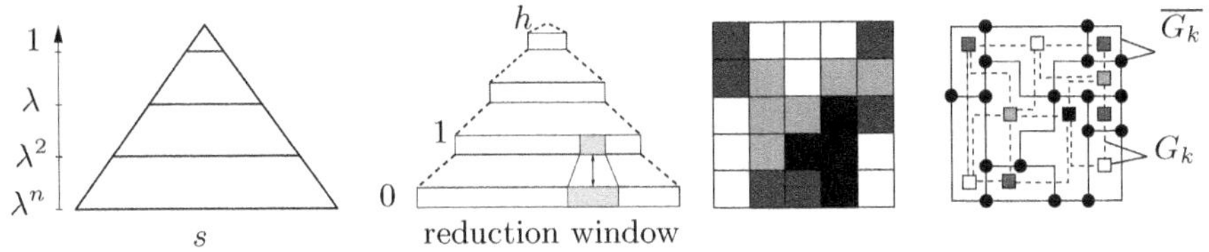

a) Reduction factor b) Discrete levels c) Image to dual graphs $(G_k, \overline{G_k})$

Fig. 1. a,b) Pyramid concept, and c) partition of pixel set into cells and representation of the cells and their neighborhood relations by a dual pair $(G_k, \overline{G_k})$ of plane graphs

they grow higher than the logarithm of base diameter with a larger input size because the progressive deviation from the regular base favors configurations that slow down the contraction process. As a consequence of the greater height the efficiency of pyramids degrades. It is shown in [15] that this problem can be resolved by a new selection mechanism (MIES) which guarantees logarithmic heights. The maximal independent set concept from graph theory is the main principle behind the methods to find the set of CKs: the maximal independent vertex set (MIS)[14]; the maximal independent edge set (MIES) [15] and the data driven decimation process (D3P) [16]. Irregular graph pyramids build by MIS may have a very poor reduction factor and small reduction factors are likely, especially when the images are large [15]. The MIES method guarantees a reduction factor of at least 2.0, proved theoretically, but is applicable only if the edges may be contracted in both directions as in the case of segmentation. The D3P method is proposed to speed up the process of finding the set of CKs.

A level of the graph pyramid consists of a pair $(G_k, \overline{G_k})$ of plane graphs G_k and its geometric dual $\overline{G_k}$ (Fig. 1c). The planarity of graphs restricts us to use only the 4-connectivity of the pixels. The vertices of G_k represent the cells on level k and the edges of G_k represent the neighborhood relations of the cells, depicted with square vertices and dashed edges in Fig. 1c. The edges of $\overline{G_k}$ represent the borders of the cells on level k, solid lines in Fig. 1c, possibly including so called pseudo edges needed to represent neighborhood relations to a cell completely enclosed by another cell. Finally, the vertices of $\overline{G_k}$ (circles in Fig. 1c), represent junctions of boundary segments of $\overline{G_k}$. Moreover the graph is attributed, $G = (V, E, a_v, a_e)$, where $a_v : V \to \mathbb{R}^+$ is a weighted function defined on vertices and $a_e : E \to \mathbb{R}^+$ is a weighted function defined on edges (similar applies for $\overline{G_k}$). The sequence $(G_k, \overline{G_k})$, $0 \leq k \leq h$ is called irregular (dual) graph pyramid and is build using Alg. 1. For simplicity of the presentation the dual $\overline{G}$ is omitted afterward.

3 MST Based Segmentation Algorithm

The segmentation method is supposed to find natural groupings from the pixel set. It is expected that, the measures of dissimilarity capture the expectation that the similarity of pixels within a segment (*internal*) is less than the similarity between pixels in different segments (*external*). The goal is to find the segments

Algorithm 1 – Constructing Dual Graph Pyramid

Input: Graphs $(G_0, \overline{G_0})$

1: **while** further abstraction is possible **do**
2: select contraction kernels by an iterative local method
/* *use MIS, MIES or D3P to determine contraction kernels* */
3: perform dual graph contraction and simplification of dual graph (DGC [11])
4: apply reduction functions to compute content of new reduced level

Output: Graph pyramid – $(G_k, \overline{G_k})$, $0 \leq k \leq h$.

that have strong internal similarities, which optimize the criterion function. The pairwise comparison of neighboring vertices, i.e. partitions, is used to check for similarities [3]. This function measures the difference along the boundary of two components relative to a measure of differences of components' internal differences, i.e. tries to capture the notion of contrast: a contrasted zone is a region containing two connected components whose inner differences (*internal contrast*) are less than differences within it's context (*external contrast*).

Let $G = (V, E, a_v, a_e)$ be a given attributed graph. The goal is to find partitions $P = \{C_1, C_2, ..., C_n\}$ such that these elements are disjoint and satisfy certain properties. Moreover P is a partition of $V \in G$, $\forall i \neq j, C_i \cap C_j = \phi$ and $\bigcup C_i = V$, $\forall i = 1, ..., n$. The graph on level k of the pyramid is denoted by G_k. Every vertex $u \in G_k$ is a representative of a component C_i of the partition P_k. The equivalent contraction kernel of a vertex $u \in G_k$, $N_{0,k}(u)$ is a set of edges forming a tree on the base level $e \in E_0$ that contracts the subgraph $G' \subseteq G = N_{0,k}(u)$ onto the vertex u.

The *internal contrast* of the $C_i \in P_k$ is the *largest dissimilarity* of component C_i i.e. the largest edge weight of the $N_{0,k}(u)$ of vertex $u \in G_k$:

$$I(C_i) = \max\{a_e(e), e \in N_{0,k}(u)\}. \tag{1}$$

Let $u_i, u_j \in V_k$ be the end vertices of an edge $e \in E_k$. The *external contrast* between two components $C_i, C_j \in P_k$ is the *smallest dissimilarity* between component C_i and C_j i.e. the smallest edge weight connecting the trees $N_{0,k}(u_i)$ and $N_{0,k}(u_j)$ of vertices $u_i \in C_i$ and $u_j \in C_j$:

$$E(C_i, C_j) = \min\{a_e(e), e = (v, w) : v \in N_{0,k}(u_i) \wedge w \in N_{0,k}(u_j)\}. \tag{2}$$

The $I(C_i)$ is the *maximum* of edge weights of the tree within C_i, whereas $E(C_i, C_j)$ is the *minimum* of weights of the edges (bridges) connecting component C_i and C_j on the base level G_0. Vertices u_i and u_j are representative of the components C_i and C_j.

The pairwise comparison function $B(\cdot, \cdot)$ is defined as:

$$B(C_i, C_j) = \begin{cases} 1 & \text{if } E(C_i, C_j) > PI(C_i, C_j), \\ 0 & \text{otherwise}, \end{cases} \tag{3}$$

where $PI(\cdot, \cdot)$ is the minimum internal contrast between two components, defined as $PI(C_i, C_j) = \min(I(C_i) + \tau(C_i), I(C_j) + \tau(C_j))$. For the function $B(\cdot, \cdot)$ to be true, i.e. for the border to exist, the external contrast must be greater than

Algorithm 2 – Construct Hierarchy of Partitions (BorůSeg) [12]

Input: attributed graph G_0.
1: $k \leftarrow 0$
2: **repeat**
3: **for all** vertices $u \in G_k$ **do**
4: $E_{min}(u) \leftarrow argmin\{a_e(e) \,|\, e = (u,v) \in E_k$ or $e = (v,u) \in E_k\}$
5: $E_{min} = E_{min} \cup E_{min}(u)$
6: **for all** $e = (u_{k,i}, u_{k,j}) \in E_{min}$ **do**
7: **if** $PI(C_i^k, C_j^k) - E(C_i^k, C_j^k)$ is a strikt local maximum in the edge graph **then**
8: include edge e in contraction edges $N_{k,k+1}$
9: contract graph G_k with contraction kernels, $N_{k,k+1}$: $G_{k+1} \leftarrow C[G_k, N_{k,k+1}]$.
/* MIS, MIES or D3P used as decimation methods */
10: **for all** $e_{k+1} \in G_{k+1}$ **do**
11: set edge attributes $a_e(e_{k+1}) \leftarrow \min\{a_e(e_k) \,|\, e_{k+1} = C[e_k, N_{k,k+1}]\}$
12: $k \leftarrow k + 1$
13: **until** $G_k = G_{k-1}$

Output: a region adjacency graph (RAG) at each level of the pyramid.

the internal contrast. Note that $B(\cdot,\cdot)$ is a boolean comparison function and the resulted segmentation is a so called *crisp* segmentation. Using the comparison function $B(\cdot,\cdot)$ defined previously one can define the algorithm to build the hierarchy of partitions (Alg. 2). Step 10 of this algorithm is the same as steps $2-4$ of Alg. 1. For more details on steps of this algorithm see [12]. A threshold function $\tau(C)$ is used since for small components C, $I(C)$ is not a good estimate of the local characteristics of the data, in extreme case when $|C| = 1$, $I(C) = 0$. Any non-negative function of a single component C can be used for $\tau(C)$ [3]. We define τ to be a function of the size of C: $\tau(C) = \alpha/|C|$, where $|C|$ denotes the size of the component C and α is a constant. A large constant α sets the preference for larger components. The size of $|C|$ gets larger as the algorithms proceeds hence $\tau \to 0$, i.e. the influence of the parameter decreases.

4 Segmentation Results

We start with the trivial partition, where each pixel (vertex) is a homogeneous region. The attributes of edges can be defined as the difference between end point features of end vertices, $a_e(u_i, u_j) = |F(u_i) - F(u_j)|$, where F is some feature. F could be defined as $F(u_i) = I(u_i)$, for gray value intensity images, or $F(u_i) = [v_i, v_i \cdot s_i \cdot \sin(h_i), v_i \cdot s_i \cdot \cos(h_i)]$, for color images in HSV color distance [4]. However the choice of the definition of the weights and the features to be used is in general a hard problem, since the grouping cues could conflict each other. In order to evaluate the methods in our experiments we choose simple gray intensity difference, i.e. $a_e(u_i, u_j) = |I(u_i) - I(u_j)|$. Note that the methods are applicable to any color space as well. The segmentation results of NCutSeg[2], on gray value images are shown in Fig. 2 rows 4-5 of BorůSeg (MIS) in rows

[2] See [4] for NCutSeg default parameters, and for all BorůSeg α is set to 500.

6-7; of BorůSeg (MIES) in rows 8-9 and BorůSeg (D3P) in rows 10-11. These methods use only local contrast based on pixel intensity values. As expected, and shown in Fig. 2, segmentation methods, which are based only on low-level local cues, can not create segmentation results as good as humans. Even thought it looks like, the NCutSeg method produces more regions, actually the overall number of regions in row 4, 6, 8, 10 and 5, 7, 9, 11 are almost the same, but BorůSeg produces more small regions. Anyway all the methods were capable of segmenting the face of a man satisfactory (image #35). BorůSeg did not merge the statue on the top of the mountain with the sky (image #17). Humans do segment this statue as a single region (see Fig. 2). All methods have problems segmenting the see creatures (image #12). Note that the segmentation done by humans on the image of rocks (image #18), contains the symmetry axis, even thought there is no 'big' change in the local contrast, therefore the NCutSeg and BorůSeg methods fail in this respect. None of the methods is 'looking' for this axis of symmetry.

5 Evaluation of Segmentations

For the evaluation, real world images should be used, since it is difficult to extrapolate conclusions based on synthetic images to real images [17], and the human should be the the final evaluator. We use the empirical method for the evaluation, which studies properties of the segmentations by measuring how 'good' a segmentation is close to an 'ideal' one, by measuring this 'goodness' with some function of parameters [18]. The difference between the segmented image and the reference (ideal) one is used to asses the performance of the algorithm [18], and measured by a discrepancy method. The reference image could be a synthetic image or manually segmented by humans. Higher value of the discrepancy means bigger error, signaling poor performance of the segmentation method. In [18], it is concluded that evaluation methods based on "mis-segmented pixels should be more powerful than other methods using other measures". In [9] the error measures used for segmentation evaluation 'count' the mis-segmented pixels.

Segmentations made by humans are used as a reference for benchmarking segmentations produced by different methods. The idea behind this is the observation that, even though different people produce different segmentations for the same image, the obtained segmentations differ, mostly, only in the local refinement of certain regions. This concept has been studied on the human segmentation database (Fig. 2 row $2-3$) in [9] and used as a basis for defining two error measures, which do not penalize a segmentation if it is coarser or more refined than another. They define two error measures based on the pixel error measures (local refinement error), that counts miss-classified pixels between two regions of two segmentations: the *global consistency error* (GCE), which forces all local refinements to be in the same direction; and *local consistency error* (LCE), which allows refinement in different directions in different parts of the image. GCE is a tougher measure than LCE, because GCE tolerates only simple refinements, while LCE tolerates mutual refinement as well. We use the GCE and LCE measures to evaluate the BorůSeg method using the human seg-

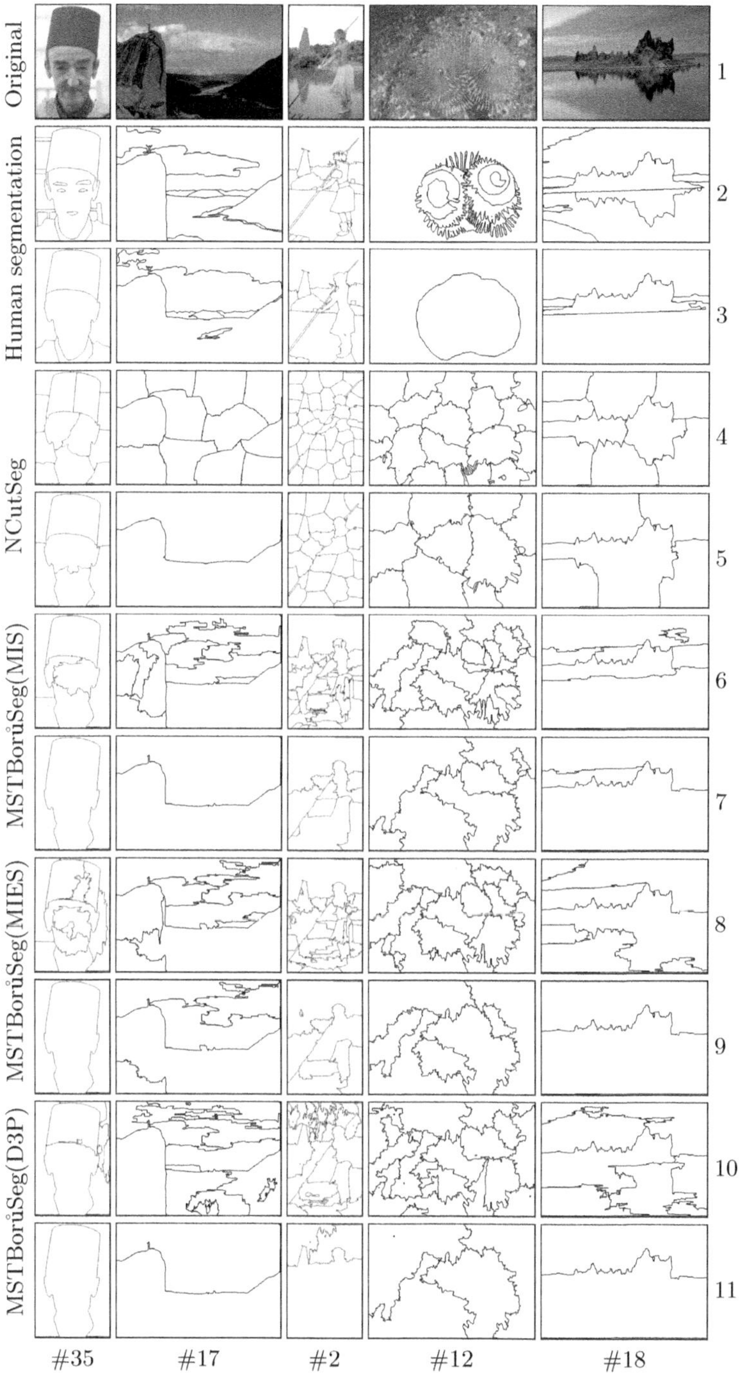

Fig. 2. Segmentation of Humans [9], and NCutSeg and MSTBorůSeg methods

Method		$\widehat{\mu}_{LCE}$	$\widehat{\mu}_{GCE}$
Humans		0.059	0.083
NCutSeg		0.204	0.248
	MIES	0.203	0.278
BorůSeg	MIS	0.200	0.273
	D3P	0.215	0.303

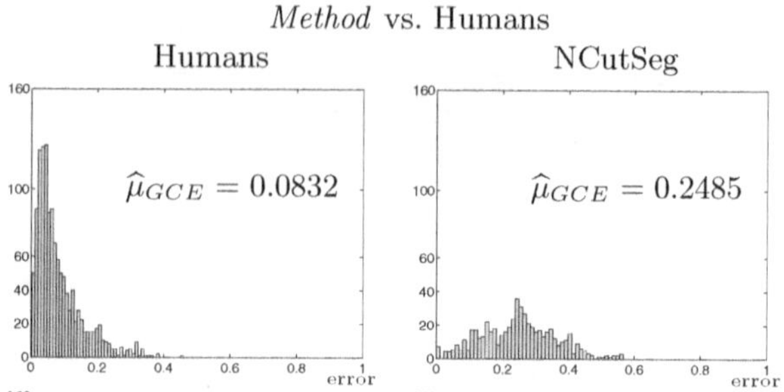

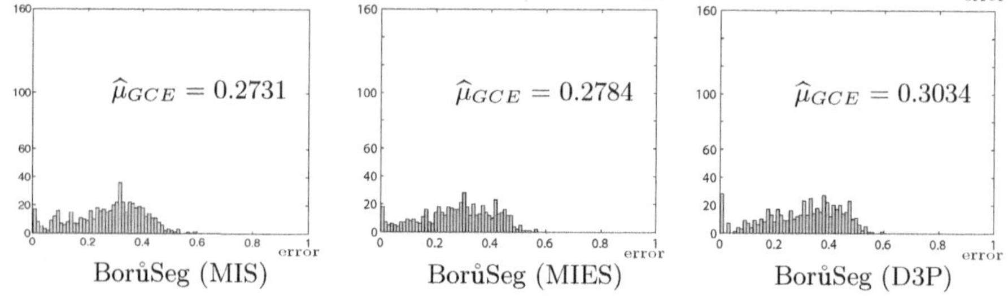

Fig. 3. Histograms of GCE and summary of LCE and GCE discrepancy errors

mented images from the Berkley image database [9]. The results of the NCutSeg method vs Humans and Humans vs Humans are confirmed [9]. A segmentation consisting of a single region and a segmentation where each pixel is a region, is the coarsest and finest possible of any segmentation. In this sense, the LCE and GCE measures should not be used when the number of regions in the two segmentation differs a lot [9]. We take for each image as a region count reference number, the average number of regions from the human segmentations available for that image. We instructed the NCutSeg to produce the same number of regions and for the BorůSeg we have taken the level of the pyramid that has the number of regions closest to the same region count reference number. For the experiments, we use 100 gray level images from the Berkley Image Database[3]. We used the original normalized cuts implementation [4][4], and for the BorůSeg we have our own implementation. For each of the images in the test, we have calculated the GCE and LCE using the results produced by the methods and all the human segmentations available for that image. Fig. 3 shows the histograms of the GCE[5] values obtained ($[0 \ldots 1]$, where zero means no error) for Human vs Human, NCutSeg vs Human, and BorůSeg (MIES, MIS D3P) vs Human. In these images $\widehat{\mu}$ measures the mean the error. Notice that humans are consistent in segmenting the images and the Human vs Human histogram shows a peak very close to 0 (i.e. a small $\widehat{\mu}_{GCE} = 0.0832$). For NCutSeg and BorůSeg there is no significant difference between the values of LCE and GCE (see $\widehat{\mu}$ of the respective histograms). One concludes that the quality of segmentation of these

[3] http://www.cs.berkeley.edu/projects/vision/grouping/segbench/

[4] http://www.cis.upenn.edu/∼jshi/software/

[5] Histograms of LCE are similar and are not shown in this presentation.

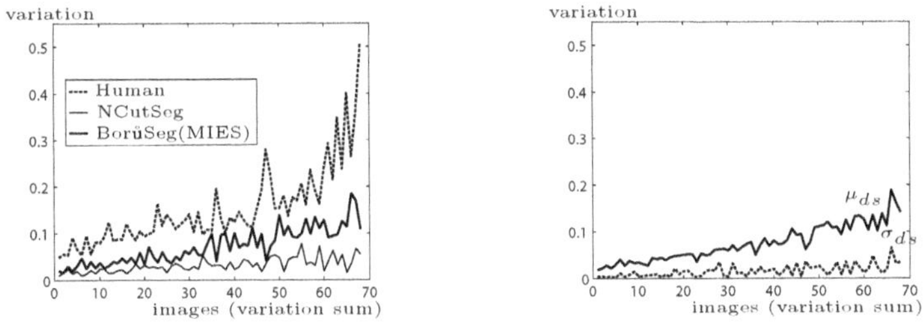

a) σ_s b) μ_{ds}, and σ_{ds} of $\sum$(MIS,MIES, and D3P)

Fig. 4. Variation of region sizes

methods seen over the whole database is not different. The table in Fig. 3 summarizes the histogram mean values of discrepancy errors. Different decimation strategies have similar error, indicating that the segmentation results do not depend on the chosen decimation strategy.

To test how region sizes vary we calculated the standard deviation (σ_s) of the normalized region sizes for each segmentation (normalization is relative to the image size). For humans, the mean of the calculated σ_s for the same image is taken. Fig. 4a) shows the resulting σ_s for 70 images (a majority for which the σ_S order Humans>BorůSeg(MIES)>NCutSeg existed). Results are shown sorted by the sum of the 3 σ_s for each image. The average region size variation for the whole dataset is: Humans 0.1537 , BorůSeg(MIES) 0.0872 and NCutSeg 0.0392. Note, that the size variation is smallest and almost content independent for the NCutSeg and largest for Humans. This shows that, the NCutSeg method is biased toward large regions, since it is defined to avoid the bias of small components of cut criterion in [4]. For the other two decimation strategies, the average region size variation for the whole data set is 0.0893 for BorůSeg (MIS) and 0.1037 for BorůSeg (D3P). One could produce three plots, one for each decimation strategy MIS, MIES, and D3P. In order not to overload the figure with too many plots, we show in Fig. 4b) a solid line representing the mean (μ_{ds}) region size variation of the BorůSeg with three decimation methods MIES, MIS, and D3P; and the doted line the standard deviation (σ_{ds}).

6 Conclusion

In this paper different methods to build an irregular graph hierarchy of image partitions by using different decimation strategies are shown. Although the algorithm makes simple greedy decisions locally, it produces perceptually important partitions in a bottom-up way based only on local differences. We also evaluated segmentation results of three graph-based methods; the well known method based on the normalized cuts (NCutSeg) and the method based on the minimal spanning tree principle (BorůSeg). The NCutSeg method and the BorůSeg are compared with human segmentations. The evaluation is done by using discrepancy measures, that do not penalize segmentations that are coarser or more refined in certain regions. We used gray value images to evaluate the quality of results. For the NCutSeg and BorůSeg segmentation methods, the error measure results are concentrated in the lower half of the output domain and that the mean of the GCE and LCE measure is for both around the value of 0.2. Moreover different decimation strategies (MIS, MIES, D3P) used in BorůSeg have shown similar error results. One can say that for image segmentation choosing any of the decimation strategies will produce satisfiable results. In the experiment with region sizes we show that humans have the biggest variation of the produced region sizes, followed by BorůSeg, and NCutSeg.

References

1. Keselman, Y., Dickinson, S.: Generic model abstraction from examples. IEEE PAMI **27** (2005) 1141–1156
2. Sudhir, B., Sarkar, S.: A framework for performance characterization of intermediate-level grouping modules. IEEE PAMI **19** (1997) 1306–1312
3. Felzenszwalb, P.F., Huttenlocher, D.P.: Efficient graph-based image segmentation. Int'n J. of Computer Vision **59** (2004) 167–181
4. Shi, J., Malik, J.: Normalized cuts and image segmentation. IEEE PAMI **22** (2000) 888–905
5. Bister, M., Cornelis, J., Rosenfeld, A.: A critical view of pyramid segmentation algorithms. Patt. Recog. Lett. **11** (1990) 605–617
6. Montanvert, A., Meer, P., Rosenfeld, A.: Hierarchical image analysis using irregular tesselations. IEEE PAMI **13** (1991) 307–316
7. Cho, K., Meer, P.: Image segmentation from consensus information. Comp. Vis. and Im. Underst. **68** (1997) 72–89
8. Jolion, J.M., Rosenfeld, A.: A Pyramid Framework for Early Vision. Kluwer (1994)
9. Martin, D., Fowlkes, C., Tal, D., Malik, J.: A database of human segmented natural images and its application to evaluating segmentation algorithms and measuring ecological statistics. In Proc. of ICCV, **2** (2001) 416–423
10. Neštřil, J., Miklovà, E., Neštřilova, H.: Otakar Borővka on minimal spanning tree problem translation of both the 1926 papers, comments, history. Discrete Mathematics **233** (2001) 3–36
11. Kropatsch, W.G.: Building irregular pyramids by dual graph contraction. IEE-Proc. Vis., Im. and Signal Process. **142** (1995) 366–374
12. Haxhimusa, Y., Kropatsch, W.G.: Hierarchy of partitions with dual graph contraction. In Milaelis, B., Krell, G., eds.: Proc. of German Patt. Recog. Symp. Vol. 2781 of LNCS, Springer (2003) 338–345
13. Rosenfeld, A.: Pyramid algorithm for efficient vision. Technical Report CAR-TR-299, University of Maryland, Computer Science Center (1987)
14. Meer, P.: Stochastic image pyramids. Computer Vision, Graphics, and Image Processing **45** (1989) 269–294.
15. Kropatsch, W.G., Haxhimusa, Y., Pizlo, Z., Langs, G.: Vision pyramids that do not grow too high. Patt. Recog. Letters **26** (2005) 319–337
16. Jolion, J.M.: Stochastic pyramid revisited. Patt. Rec. Letters **24** (2003) 1035–1042
17. Zhou, Y., Venkateswar, V., Chellappa, R.: Edge detection and linear feature extraction using the directional derivatives of a 2-d random field model. IEEE Trans. on PAMI **11** (1989) 84–95
18. Zhang, Y.: A survey on evaluation methods for image segmentation. Patt. Recog. **29(8)** (1996) 1335–1346

Color Texture Segmentation by Decomposition of Gaussian Mixture Model

Jiří Grim, Petr Somol, Michal Haindl, and Pavel Pudil

Institute of Information Theory and Automation
Academy of Sciences of the Czech Republic
P.O. BOX 18, 18208 PRAGUE 8, Czech Republic
{grim, somol, haindl, pudil}@utia.cas.cz
http://ro.utia.cas.cz/mem.html

Abstract. Recently we have proposed Gaussian mixtures as a local statistical model to synthesize artificial textures. We describe the statistical dependence of pixels of a movable window by multivariate Gaussian mixture of product components. The mixture components correspond to different variants of image patches as they appear in the window. In this sense they can be used to identify different segments of the source color texture image. The segmentation can be obtained by means of Bayes formula provided that a proper decomposition of the estimated Gaussian mixture into sub-mixtures is available. In this paper the mixture model is decomposed by maximizing the mean probability of correct classification of pixels into segments in a way taking into account the assumed consistency of final segmentation.

1 Introduction

The concept of texture segmentation derives from a simple image decomposition suggested e.g. by different colors or by distinct edges. However, it is uneasy to specify the underlying classification problem when the image segments have to be identified by different textural properties. A unique solution of the texture segmentation problem is hardly achievable because a generally accepted definition of texture is also missing. The available texture based image segmentation methods usually consider some local texture properties to identify either boundaries or regions or to combine both approaches [12]. In view of the underlying high-dimensional problems the texture segmentation methods usually apply different feature extraction techniques or subspace approaches [7], [8], [9]. In most applications like image analysis or image database retrieval the segmentation algorithms should be computationally efficient. However, in some areas like medical imaging the computing time is less relevant [13].

In the present paper we propose a novel segmentation procedure based on a local statistical model of the texture properties. We assume that the image to be segmented is composed of different textures which can be characterized by some local statistical properties and simultaneously that the potential texture segments are sufficiently large and homogeneous to enable their identification.

J.F. Martínez-Trinidad et al. (Eds.): CIARP 2006, LNCS 4225, pp. 287–296, 2006.

Recently we have shown in a series of papers [3], [5], [6] that gray-scale textures can be described locally in terms of a joint probability density of gray-levels in a suitably chosen observation window. Unlike other approaches, no feature extraction technique has been applied to pixel variables of the window image patch. Consequently, the dimension of the estimated density may be very high, e.g. of order $10^2 \div 10^3$. By estimating the probability density in the form of Gaussian mixture of product components we succeeded to synthesize artificial textures by sequential prediction. A specific advantage of texture synthesis is the possibility to verify the quality of the estimated mixture model by comparing the original- and synthesized image visually [5], [6]. Motivated by successful experiments we have applied the local mixture model to statistical evaluation of color texture images with the aim to emphasize abnormalities or local defects [4].

The present application of the statistical model to color texture segmentation is based on decomposition of the underlying mixture density into sub-mixtures which correspond to different segments of the source texture image. Considering the framework of statistical classification we suggest a simple criterion in terms of probability of correct classification of pixels into the segments. The criterion is maximized by means of an iterative algorithm which is shown to converge monotonically in a finite number of steps.

In the following we first describe the local statistical texture model in the form of a multivariate Gaussian mixture of product components. In Sec. 3 we propose the basic texture segmentation algorithm and in Sec. 4 its topological modification. In Sec. 5 we illustrate the method by numerical examples from the Prague segmentation benchmark [11]. Finally in the Conclusion we summarize the method and discuss different computational aspects.

2 Gaussian Mixture Model

A digitized color texture image can be described by a matrix of vector variables where each pixel specifies the three RGB spectral values

$$\mathcal{Z} = [\boldsymbol{z}_{ij}]_{i=0}^{I}{}_{j=0}^{J}, \quad \boldsymbol{z}_{ij} = (z_{ij1}, z_{ij2}, z_{ij3}) \in \mathcal{R}^3.$$

Here i, j correspond to row and column indices respectively. We assume that the statistical dependencies between pixels in a suitably chosen observation window do not depend on the window position or, in other words, that the local statistical properties of the texture are shift-invariant. Given a window centered at a position (i, j), we denote

$$\boldsymbol{x}(i, j) = \boldsymbol{x} = (x_1, x_2, \ldots, x_N)$$

the vector of spectral values of window defined context neighborhood in a fixed arrangement, i.e. for each pixel three spectral values. Then in each position the window interior (image patch) $\boldsymbol{x}$ can be viewed as an observation of a random vector and therefore we can describe the statistical properties of the variables x_n

in full generality by a joint probability density. For this purpose we approximate the unknown density function in the form of Gaussian mixture

$$P(\boldsymbol{x}) = \sum_{m \in \mathcal{M}} w_m F(\boldsymbol{x}|\boldsymbol{\mu}_m, \boldsymbol{\sigma}_m), \quad \boldsymbol{x} \in R^N. \tag{1}$$

Assuming conditional independence of variables we define the mixture components as products of univariate Gaussian densities [5], [6]:

$$F(\boldsymbol{x}|\boldsymbol{\mu}_m, \boldsymbol{\sigma}_m) = \prod_{n \in \mathcal{N}} f_n(x_n|\mu_{mn}, \sigma_{mn}), \tag{2}$$

$$f_n(x_n|\mu_{mn}, \sigma_{mn}) = \frac{1}{\sqrt{2\pi}\sigma_{mn}} \exp\left\{-\frac{(x_n - \mu_{mn})^2}{2\sigma_{mn}^2}\right\}. \tag{3}$$

To simplify notation we denote $\mathcal{M} = \{1, 2, \ldots, M\}$ and $\mathcal{N} = \{1, 2, \ldots, N\}$ the index sets of components and variables respectively.

The standard way to estimate mixtures is to use the EM algorithm [10]. By using the "image patch" data set $\mathcal{S}$ obtained by pixel-wise shifting the observation window through the original texture image

$$\mathcal{S} = \{\boldsymbol{x}^{(1)}, \ldots, \boldsymbol{x}^{(K)}\}, \quad \boldsymbol{x}^{(k)} \in \mathcal{R}^N, \quad (K = |\mathcal{S}|), \tag{4}$$

we maximize the corresponding log-likelihood function

$$L = \frac{1}{|\mathcal{S}|} \sum_{x \in \mathcal{S}} \log \left[\sum_{m \in \mathcal{M}} w_m F(\boldsymbol{x}|\boldsymbol{\mu}_m, \boldsymbol{\sigma}_m) \right] \tag{5}$$

by means of the well-known EM iteration equations [1] :

E-step: $(m \in \mathcal{M}, n \in \mathcal{N}, \boldsymbol{x} \in \mathcal{S})$

$$q(m|\boldsymbol{x}) = \frac{w_m F(\boldsymbol{x}|\boldsymbol{\mu}_m, \boldsymbol{\sigma}_m)}{\sum_{j \in \mathcal{M}} w_j F(\boldsymbol{x}|\boldsymbol{\mu}_j, \boldsymbol{\sigma}_j)}, \quad m \in \mathcal{M} \tag{6}$$

M-step:

$$w_m^{'} = \frac{1}{|\mathcal{S}|} \sum_{x \in \mathcal{S}} q(m|\boldsymbol{x}), \quad \mu_{mn}^{'} = \frac{1}{\sum_{x \in \mathcal{S}} q(m|\boldsymbol{x})} \sum_{x \in \mathcal{S}} x_n q(m|\boldsymbol{x}), \tag{7}$$

$$(\sigma_{mn}^{'})^2 = -(\mu_{mn}^{'})^2 + \frac{1}{\sum_{x \in \mathcal{S}} q(m|\boldsymbol{x})} \sum_{x \in \mathcal{S}} x_n^2 q(m|\boldsymbol{x}). \tag{8}$$

Here the apostrophe denotes the new parameter values in each iteration.

The local mixture model $P(\boldsymbol{x})$ provides fully general description of statistical dependencies of pixel variables in the observation window. For any given image patch $\boldsymbol{x} \in \mathcal{S}$ we can compute the corresponding conditional weights $q(m|\boldsymbol{x}), m \in \mathcal{M}$ which can be viewed as highly informative features describing the textural properties of the image patch $\boldsymbol{x}$ in terms of its affinity with the component means $\boldsymbol{\mu}_m$. It is intuitively clear that the context information contained in $q(m|\boldsymbol{x})$ increases with the window size but, simultaneously, the related textural properties become less local. The underlying density estimation problem also becomes more difficult with the increasing dimension N.

3 Segmentation Algorithm

By its nature the EM algorithm produces a set of mixture components which correspond to different local properties of the source texture image, as it can be seen in Fig. 1. The first row shows the color texture examples to be segmented [11] and the second row shows the corresponding mixture models. The component means $\boldsymbol{\mu}_m$ (in the arrangement of the observation window) can be viewed as averaged (smoothed) representants of the typical image patch variants. All the three mixture densities have been estimated in the space of dimension N=1143 without any feature extraction (window size: 21x21 pixels with the corners cut away, i.e. N=381x3=1143). The number of mixture components has been chosen $M_1 = 64,\ M_2 = 59$ and $M_3 = 64$ respectively.

The basic idea of segmentation is to unify similar texture pieces. As the mixture component means $\boldsymbol{\mu}_m$ correspond to different variants of the image patches we assume that different parts of the texture can be characterized by aggregating the related mixture components, i.e. by decomposing the Gaussian mixture $P(\boldsymbol{x})$ into sub-mixtures. In particular, let $\Im$ be a partition of the index set $\mathcal{M}$ into disjunct subsets $\mathcal{M}_k \subset \mathcal{M}$:

$$\Im = \{\mathcal{M}_1, \mathcal{M}_2, \ldots, \mathcal{M}_M\}, \quad \cup_{k \in \mathcal{M}} \mathcal{M}_k = \mathcal{M}, \quad \mathcal{M}_k \cap \mathcal{M}_j = \emptyset, k \neq j. \tag{9}$$

Then we can define the corresponding decomposition of the mixture density (1) into sub-mixtures:

$$P(\boldsymbol{x}) = \sum_{k \in \mathcal{M}} P_k(\boldsymbol{x}) = \sum_{k \in \mathcal{M}} \sum_{m \in \mathcal{M}_k} w_m F(\boldsymbol{x}|\boldsymbol{\mu}_m, \boldsymbol{\sigma}_m), \tag{10}$$

$$P_k(\boldsymbol{x}) = \sum_{m \in \mathcal{M}_k} w_m F(\boldsymbol{x}|\boldsymbol{\mu}_m, \boldsymbol{\sigma}_m). \tag{11}$$

We assume a sub-mixture $P_k(\boldsymbol{x})$ corresponding to $\mathcal{M}_k$ to be zero in case of empty subset $\mathcal{M}_k = \emptyset$. Given the sub-mixtures $P_k(\boldsymbol{x})$ we can classify the image patches $\boldsymbol{x} \in \mathcal{S}$ by means of Bayes formula. Let us recall that each vector $\boldsymbol{x} = \boldsymbol{x}(i,j) \in \mathcal{S}$ uniquely corresponds to the position (i,j) of central pixel of the observation window and also for each $\boldsymbol{x} \in \mathcal{S}$ we can evaluate the probabilities

$$p(k|\boldsymbol{x}) = \frac{P_k(\boldsymbol{x})}{P(\boldsymbol{x})} = \sum_{m \in \mathcal{M}_k} q(m|\boldsymbol{x}), \quad k \in \mathcal{M}. \tag{12}$$

Here $p(k|\boldsymbol{x})$ is the probability that the central pixel of the image patch $\boldsymbol{x}$ belongs to the texture segment $\mathcal{S}_k$ which is characterized by the sub-mixture $P_k(\boldsymbol{x})$. Ignoring some border pixels, we can define a segmentation of the texture image as a partition $\Re$ of the set $\mathcal{S}$ into disjunct subsets $\mathcal{S}_k \subset \mathcal{S}$:

$$\Re = \{\mathcal{S}_1, \mathcal{S}_2, \ldots, \mathcal{S}_M\}, \quad \cup_{k \in \mathcal{M}} \mathcal{S}_k = \mathcal{S}, \quad \mathcal{S}_k \cap \mathcal{S}_j = \emptyset, k \neq j. \tag{13}$$

In view of Eq. (12) the optimal subsets $\mathcal{S}_k$ given $\Im$ can be defined by means of the Bayes decision function [1]

$$d(\boldsymbol{x}|\Im) = \arg\max_{k\in\mathcal{M}}\{p(k|\boldsymbol{x})\} = \arg\max_{k\in\mathcal{M}}\{\sum_{m\in\mathcal{M}_k} q(m|\boldsymbol{x})\} \tag{14}$$

$$\mathcal{S}_k = \{\boldsymbol{x} \in \mathcal{S} : d(\boldsymbol{x}|\Im) = k\},\ k \in \mathcal{M} \tag{15}$$

where $d(\boldsymbol{x}|\Im)$ specifies the sub-mixture with the maximum aposteriori probability $p(k|\boldsymbol{x})$ given $\boldsymbol{x} \in \mathcal{S}$.

In view of the available mixture model a natural way to measure the quality of the texture segmentation $\Re$ is to compute the mean probability of correct pixel classification with respect to the given segments $\mathcal{S}_k \in \Re$:

$$Q(\Im,\Re) = \frac{1}{|\mathcal{S}|}\sum_{k\in\mathcal{M}}\sum_{x\in\mathcal{S}_k} p(k|\boldsymbol{x}) = \frac{1}{|\mathcal{S}|}\sum_{k\in\mathcal{M}}\sum_{x\in\mathcal{S}_k}\sum_{m\in\mathcal{M}_k} q(m|\boldsymbol{x}). \tag{16}$$

In the above criterion $p(k|\boldsymbol{x})$ denotes the probability that the pixel (i,j) has been classified correctly, i.e. that $\boldsymbol{x} = \boldsymbol{x}(i,j) \in \mathcal{S}_k$. Given a segmentation $\Re$ we define the optimal mixture decomposition $\Im$ by Eqs.:

$$\varphi(m|\Re) = \arg\max_{k\in\mathcal{M}}\{\sum_{x\in\mathcal{S}_k} q(m|\boldsymbol{x})\}, \tag{17}$$

$$\mathcal{M}_k = \{m \in \mathcal{M} : \varphi(m|\Re) = k\},\quad k \in \mathcal{M}. \tag{18}$$

Here $\varphi(m|\Re)$ specifies the segment $\mathcal{S}_k$ with the greatest "contribution" of the m-th mixture component. The criterion $Q(\Im,\Re)$ can be maximized by repeating the iterative steps (15), (18). In particular we prove:

Theorem. The iterative use of Eqs. (15) and (18) produces a nondecreasing sequence of values of the criterion $Q(\Im,\Re)$ converging in a finite number of steps to a finite limit.

Proof. Let us note first that any change of the mixture decomposition $\Im$ can be viewed as a result of a sequence of elementary steps. In particular, let $\Im^+$ be defined by an elementary change of $\Im$ (cf. (17)):

$$\mathcal{M}_k^+ = \mathcal{M}_k \cup \{m_0\},\ \mathcal{M}_l^+ = \mathcal{M}_l \setminus \{m_0\},\qquad \mathcal{M}_j^+ = \mathcal{M}_j,\ \ j \in \mathcal{M},\ \ j \neq k,l$$

with m_0 satisfying the condition $\varphi(m_0|\Re) = k$ (cf. (18)). Therefore the following inequality holds (cf. (17))

$$\sum_{x\in\mathcal{S}_k} q(m_0|\boldsymbol{x}) \geq \sum_{x\in\mathcal{S}_j} q(m_0|\boldsymbol{x}),\qquad \forall j \in \mathcal{M} \tag{19}$$

and the corresponding change of the criterion Q (cf. (16)) is non-negative

[1] If the maximum is not unique we choose the smallest index $k \in \mathcal{M}$ with the specified property.

$$Q(\Im^+, \Re) - Q(\Im, \Re) = \frac{1}{|\mathcal{S}|}\left[\sum_{x \in \mathcal{S}_k} q(m_0|\boldsymbol{x}) - \sum_{x \in \mathcal{S}_l} q(m_0|\boldsymbol{x})\right] \geq 0. \quad (20)$$

Consequently, the inequality (20) is also valid for the resulting "cumulative" decomposition as defined by (18).

Analogously, let $\Re^+$ is defined by an elementary change of texture segmentation $\Re$:

$$\mathcal{S}_k^+ = \mathcal{S}_k \cup \{\boldsymbol{x}_0\}, \ \mathcal{S}_l^+ = \mathcal{S}_l \setminus \{\boldsymbol{x}_0\}, \ \mathcal{S}_j^+ = \mathcal{S}_j, \ j \neq k, l$$

with $\boldsymbol{x}_0$ satisfying the condition $d(\boldsymbol{x}_0|\Im) = k$ (cf. (15)). Therefore the following inequality is satisfied (cf. (14)):

$$p(k|\boldsymbol{x}_0) \geq p(j|\boldsymbol{x}_0), \quad \forall j \in \mathcal{M}, \quad (21)$$

and the corresponding change of the criterion (16) is non-negative

$$Q(\Im, \Re^+) - Q(\Im, \Re) = \frac{1}{|\mathcal{S}|}\left[p(k|\boldsymbol{x}_0) - p(l|\boldsymbol{x}_0)\right] \geq 0.$$

It can be seen that the last inequality is also valid for any complex change of the segmentation $\Re$.

Consequently, the iterative segmentation algorithm (15), (18) based on the local mixture model $P(\boldsymbol{x})$ converges to a finite limit in a finite number of steps because the criterion $Q(\Im, \Re)$ is bounded above and the number of possible partitions $\Im$ and $\Re$ is finite.

4 Topologically Modified Segmentation

The "bottom up" segmentation algorithm from Sec. 3 starting with the finest partition $\Im_0 : \mathcal{M}_k = \{k\}, k \in \mathcal{M}$ and maximizing the criterion $Q(\Im, \Re)$ converges in few iterations to a highly over-segmented texture. The tendency to over-segmentation is closely related to the high dimensionality of the estimated density $P(\boldsymbol{x})$. Even in case of a small size the observation window may contain several hundreds of pixels with three spectral values and the resulting dimension N is very high. In multidimensional spaces the mixture components are nearly non-overlapping and therefore there is usually one-to-one correspondence between the mixture components and the initial highly specific texture segments. The examples of the initial over-segmentation are shown in Fig. 1 (third row). Recall that in case of the mixture components from Fig. 1 the underlying densities have dimension $N = 1143$. In high-dimensional spaces the mixture components are well separated and almost non-overlapping and therefore the conditional probabilities $q(m|\boldsymbol{x})$ have nearly binary properties.

In order to increase the senzitivity of the criterion (16) with respect to the topological properties of the texture we include a neighborhood into the underlying decision-making. We define the decision neighborhood $\mathcal{D}(\boldsymbol{x}(i,j))$ of the vector $\boldsymbol{x}(i,j) \in \mathcal{S}$ as a subset of vectors $\boldsymbol{x} \in \mathcal{S}$ which correspond to the pixels near the central point (i,j). In particular, considering a square decision neighborhood with the corners cut away, we can write:

$$\mathcal{D}(\boldsymbol{x}(i,j)) = \{\boldsymbol{x}(k,l) \in \mathcal{S} : |i-k| + |j-l| < (2\rho - r)\}. \tag{22}$$

where $\rho \geq 0$ is a window "radius" and $r = \rho/2$ the corner size (cf. Fig. 1, second row). To simplify notation, the position (i,j) of the observation window will be omitted whenever tolerable.

By using the neighborhood $\mathcal{D}(\boldsymbol{x})$ we can compute the mean probability of correct pixel classification in a more robust way by taking in account the neighbouring pixels:

$$Q(\Im,\Re) \approx \frac{1}{|\mathcal{S}|} \sum_{k\in\mathcal{M}} \sum_{x\in\mathcal{S}_k} p(k|\mathcal{D}(\boldsymbol{x})) \tag{23}$$

Here the probability $p(k|\mathcal{D}(\boldsymbol{x}))$ of correct classification of a pixel $\boldsymbol{x} = \boldsymbol{x}(i,j) \in \mathcal{S}$ can be expressed in the form:

$$p(k|\mathcal{D}(\boldsymbol{x})) = \frac{P_k(\mathcal{D}(\boldsymbol{x}))}{P(\mathcal{D}(\boldsymbol{x}))} = \sum_{y\in\mathcal{D}(\boldsymbol{x})} \frac{P_k(\boldsymbol{y})}{P(\mathcal{D}(\boldsymbol{x}))} = \sum_{y\in\mathcal{D}(x)} \frac{P(\boldsymbol{y})}{P(\mathcal{D}(\boldsymbol{x}))} p(k|\boldsymbol{y}). \tag{24}$$

If we assume the term $P(\boldsymbol{y})/P(\mathcal{D}(\boldsymbol{x}))$ to be approximately constant for all $\boldsymbol{y} \in \mathcal{D}(\boldsymbol{x})$ then it can be replaced by a coefficient $1/|\mathcal{D}(\boldsymbol{x})|$. Denoting $|\mathcal{D}(\boldsymbol{x})| = D_0$ we can write the criterion (23) in the following more suitable form:

$$Q_{\mathcal{D}}(\Im,\Re) = \frac{1}{|\mathcal{S}|} \sum_{k\in\mathcal{M}} \sum_{x\in\mathcal{S}_k} \frac{1}{D_0} \sum_{y\in\mathcal{D}(x)} p(k|\boldsymbol{y}) \tag{25}$$

If we modify definition (15) of the segmentation $\Re$ given the decomposition $\Im$

$$d_{\mathcal{D}}(\boldsymbol{x}|\Im) = \arg\max_{k\in\mathcal{M}} \{ \sum_{m\in\mathcal{M}_k} \sum_{y\in\mathcal{D}(x)} q(m|\boldsymbol{y}) \}. \tag{26}$$

$$\mathcal{S}_k = \{\boldsymbol{x} \in \mathcal{S} : d_{\mathcal{D}}(\boldsymbol{x}|\Im) = k\}, \; k \in \mathcal{M}, \tag{27}$$

and the definition (18) of mixture decomposition $\Im$ given the segmentation $\Re$:

$$\varphi_{\mathcal{D}}(m|\Re) = \arg\max_{k\in\mathcal{M}} \{ \sum_{x\in\mathcal{S}_k} \sum_{y\in\mathcal{D}(x)} q(m|\boldsymbol{y}) \}, \tag{28}$$

$$\mathcal{M}_k = \{m \in \mathcal{M} : \varphi_{\mathcal{D}}(m|\Re) = k\}, \quad k \in \mathcal{M} \tag{29}$$

then the criterion (25) is again maximized by iterating the steps (27) and (29). The proof of this assertion is analogous to that of Sec. 3.

5 Computational Experiments

The practical implementation of the above algorithm starts with the highly oversegmented texture from Sec. 3 which corresponds to the neighborhood radius

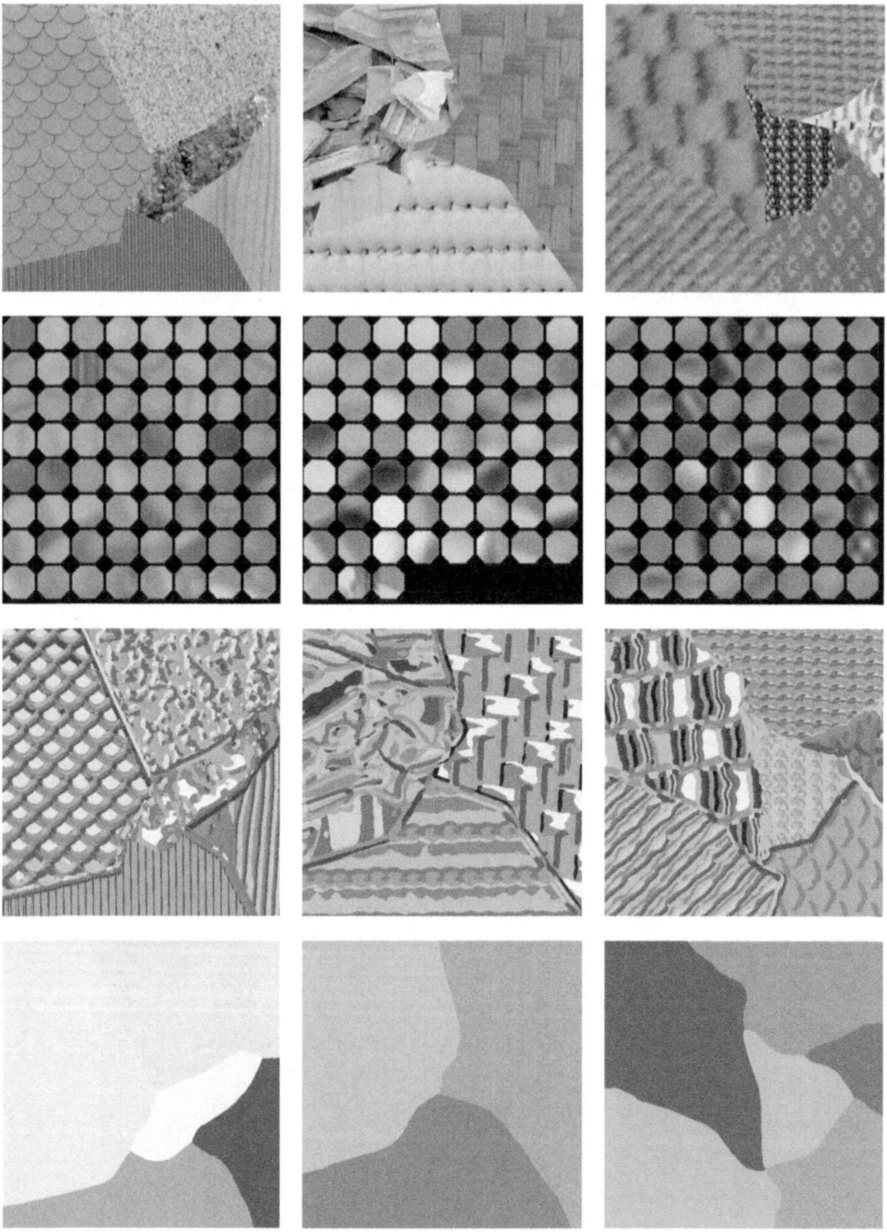

Fig. 1. Texture segmentation experiments. Each column corresponds to one example taken from [11]. The texture image is in the first row, the second row shows the component means $\boldsymbol{\mu}_m$ of the respective Gaussian mixture model and the third and fourth row show the initial and final segmentation respectively. The resulting segmentation is essentially correct despite the strong inhomogeneity of the texture segments. There are only minor "rounding" errors on the segment boundaries.

$\rho = 0$, i.e. to $|D(\boldsymbol{x})| = 1$. Then the topologically modified segmentation algorithm is repeatedly started again with an increased neighborhood $D(\boldsymbol{x})$ and iterated until convergence. The repeated application of the segmentation algorithm represents a hierarchical scheme which can be stopped e.g. when the number of segments does not change for several repetitions or by choosing an ad hoc maximum size of the final decision neighborhood.

In the experiments we have applied the proposed segmentation algorithm to the Prague texture segmentation benchmark which is known to contain very difficult examples. The three test images shown in the first row of Fig. 1 are available at the address [11]. For each texture image we have computed the local statistical model in the form of Gaussian mixture for the window size 21x21 (dimension N=1143, cf. Sec. 3 for details). The second row of Fig. 1 shows the corresponding component means for the three mixtures - as discussed in Sec. 3. The initial "over-segmented" images in the third row illustrate the "discriminative power" of the models and finally the fourth row shows the resulting segmentations. In the considered examples 1-3 the segmentation algorithm has been stopped for the size of decision neighborhood $\rho = 28$, $\rho = 33$ and $\rho = 24$ respectively. The results of segmentation are rather convincing. It can be seen that, despite strong inhomogeneity, all texture segments have been correctly identified, possibly except for some minor "rounding" errors on the segment boundaries.

In the present form the proposed method is rather demanding (several hours) mainly because of the time-consuming mixture estimation. However, the resulting segmentation can be obtained more quickly when the size of the decision neighborhood can be specified in advance.

6 Conclusion

In the present paper we propose a color texture segmentation algorithm based on statistical model of local texture properties. We describe the statistical dependencies between the spectral pixel values in a suitably chosen observation window by a multivariate Gaussian mixture with product components. We estimate the mixture parameters by means of EM algorithm from color image patch data obtained by pixelwise shifting the observation window through the original color texture image. No feature extraction- or dimensionality reduction technique is applied to the spectral pixel variables. As the mixture components correspond to different "averaged" variants of the image patches we identify each texture segment by a corresponding sub-mixture by using Bayes formula. We propose a simple segmentation criterion in terms of probability of correct pixel classification into segments and an iterative algorithm to maximize the proposed criterion. Simultaneously, we prove that the convergence of the algorithm is monotonic in a finite number of steps.

In the present form the proposed texture segmentation method is time-consuming and therefore hardly applicable on-line. On the other hand it may be useful, e.g. for careful off-line evaluation of medical images.

Acknowledgement. This research was supported by the EC project no. FP6-507752 MUSCLE, by the grant No. 1ET400750407 of the Grant Agency of the Academy of Sciences CR and partially by the projects MŠMT 1M0572 DAR and 2C06019 ZIMOLEZ.

References

1. Grim, J., Kittler, J., Pudil, P., Somol, P.,: Multiple classifier fusion in probabilistic neural networks. Pattern Analysis & Applications, 7, **5** (2002) 221-233.
2. Grim, J., Haindl, M.: A discrete mixtures color texture model. In: Texture 2002. The 2nd International Workshop on Texture Analysis and Synthesis, Copenhagen 2002. (Chantler M. ed.). Heriot-Watt Univ., Glasgow, (2002) 59-62
3. Grim, J., Haindl, M.: Texture Modelling by Discrete Distribution Mixtures. Computational Statistics and Data Analysis, 3-4, **41** (2003) 603-615
4. Grim, J., Somol, P., Haindl, M., Pudil, P.: A statistical approach to local evaluation of a single texture image. In: Proceedings of the 16-th Annual Symposium PRASA 2005. (Nicolls F. ed.). University of Cape Town, (2005) 171-176
5. Haindl, M., Grim, J., Somol, P., Pudil, P., Kudo, M.: A Gaussian mixture-based color texture model. In: Proceedings of the 17th IAPR International Conference on Pattern Recognition. IEEE, Los Alamitos, (2004) 177-180
6. Haindl, M., Grim, J., Pudil, P., Kudo, M.: A Hybrid BTF Model Based on Gaussian Mixtures. In: Texture 2005. Proceedings of the 4th International Workshop on Texture Analysis. (Chantler M., Drbohlav O. eds.). IEEE, Los Alamitos, (2005) 95-100
7. Heidemann, G., Ritter, H.: A neural 3-D object recognition architecture using optimized Gabor filters. In: Proceedings of the 13th IAPR International Conference on Pattern Recognition. Vol. IV, 70-74, Los Alamitos CA, IAPR, IEEE Computer Society Press, 1996
8. Ridder, D. de, Kittler, J., Lemmers, O., Duin, R.P.W.: The adaptive sub-space map for texture segmentation. In: Proceedings of the 15th IAPR International Conference on Pattern Recognition, Eds. A. Sanfeliu et al., 216-220, IAPR, IEEE Computer Society Press, 2000
9. Ridder, D. de, Kittler, J., Duin, R.P.W.: Probabilistic PCA and ICA subspace mixture models for image segmentation. In: Proceedings of the British Machine Vision Conference, Eds. M. Mirmehdi et al., (2000) 112-121
10. McLachlan, G.J. and Peel, D.: *Finite Mixture Models*, John Wiley & Sons, New York, (2000)
11. *Prague texture segmentation benchmark (2004):* htpp://mosaic.utia.cas.cz
12. Reed, T.R., du Buf, J.M.H.: A review of recent texture segmentation and feature extraction techniques. CVGIP-Image Understanding, **57** (1993) 359-372
13. Zwiggelaar, R., Planiol, P., Mart, R., Blot, L. Denton, E.R.E., Rubin, C.M.E.: EM Texture Segmentation of Mammographic Images. In: *Proceedings of the 6-th International Workshop on Digital Mammography*, Germany, (2002) 541-543

Texture Features and Segmentation Based on Multifractal Approach

Mohamed Abadi and Enguerran Grandchamp

GRIMAAG UAG, Campus de Fouillole, French West Indies University,
97157 Pointe-à-Pitre Cedex Guadeloupe France
{mabadi, egrandch}@univ-ag.fr

Abstract. In this paper, we use a multifractal approach based on the computation of two spectrums for image analysis and texture segmentation problems. The two spectrums are the Legendre Spectrum, determined by classical methods, and the Large Deviation Spectrum, determined by kernel density estimation. We propose a way for the fusion of these two spectrums to improve textured image segmentation results. An unsupervised k-means is used as clustering approach for the texture classification. The algorithm is applied on mosaic image built using IKONOS images and various natural textures from the Brodatz album. The segmentation obtained with our approach gives better results than the application of each spectrum separately.

Keywords: Multifractal theory, multifractal spectrum, wavelets, texture segmentation, high and very high spatial resolution image.

1 Introduction

This work has been conducted within the CESAR project (Arborescent species classification). The main objective is to reinforce monitoring measurements and to improve durable management of forest resources for ecological considerations. The first step is to obtain a forest identification using very high satellite images such as QUICKBIRD or IKONOS images.

Since we consider that forests could be identified using their texture features our approach is to segment the images into homogeneous textured regions. Indeed, natural images are composed of different and various textures often considered as an infinite combination. With the apparition of very high resolution satellite images, small structures are now textured instead of having a homogeneous mean intensity.

Texture analysis has been studied for a long time using different approaches. A lot of methods are directly based upon the intensity of an image. These include grey-level co-occurrence matrices (GLCM) [1], [2], autocorrelation function analysis [1], moment based texture segmentation [3], two-dimensional filtering in the spatial and frequency domain [4], [5], and the fractal analysis [6].

In order to perform the segmentation we have to characterize each texture. To achieve this goal we have used the multifractal tool based on the Legendre and Large Deviation Spectrum (LS and LDS) [7]. Both spectrums exploit the local and global

J.F. Martínez-Trinidad et al. (Eds.): CIARP 2006, LNCS 4225, pp. 297 – 305, 2006.

regularity of the image using the distribution of singularity exponent [8] (Hölder coefficient or Lipschitz exponent). We justify our choice by the fact that studied images are taken from natural scenes having non-stationary characteristics resulting in complex structures (multifractal) [9]. The analysis of the singular structures of the image [10] enables as to establish a relation between a geometrical description and a statistical description for local and global grey-levels.

These two spectrums are two different ways to compute the same parameter. LS is a statistical approach and LDS a geometrical approach [7].

The article is composed as follow: section 2 explains different approaches used in literature for texture segmentation. Section 3 defines the multifractal approach and the spectrum computation in a two-dimensional case. Section 4 describes the algorithm we use to compute the texture features. Experiments and results are given in Section 5. Section 6 gives some concluding remarks.

2 Texture Segmentation Approach

In the literature there are two important aspects of texture image segmentation procedures, namely feature extraction and classification. There are several methods allowing to extract texture features of images that we can regroup in four large topics: statistical methods (co-occurrence matrices, autocorrelation features [1], [2] moment features [11]), geometrical methods (Voronoi tessellation features [11], structural methods [12]), model based methods (random field models [13], [14], fractals [15], [16]), and signal processing methods (spatial domain filters [17], Fourier domain filtering [18], Gabor and wavelet models [5]). Classification methods are grouped in two categories: supervised and unsupervised classification methods (maximum likelihood classifier [19], Bayesian classification [20], neural networks [21], …).

In the scope of this article we have chosen a multifractal approach and an unsupervised k-means classification.

3 Multifractal Approach

The multifractal formalism is a nice tool for characterizing and describing the statistical and geometrical properties of images from real world scenes [10]. The main idea in this approach is to built a positive measure μ on the image $I(\vec{x})$, where $\vec{x} \in \Re^2$ represents the coordinate vector. Treatments will be made using the measure instead of the image. For each set A, the measure $\mu(A)$ is given by:

$$\mu(A) = \int_A I(\vec{x})\, d\vec{x} \quad (1)$$

hence μ is compactly supported and thus finite.

We quickly present in the following the computation of Legendre and Large Deviation Spectrum.

3.1 Legendre Spectrum (LS)

We define here μ as a Borel probability measure over $[0,1]\times[0,1]$. Let ν_n be an increasing sequence of positive integers, and let us define:

$$I_{i,j,n} = \left[\frac{i}{\nu_n}, \frac{i+1}{\nu_n}\right] \times \left[\frac{j}{\nu_n}, \frac{j+1}{\nu_n}\right] \tag{2}$$

We directly compute some kind of "moments" or generalized dimensions of our measure. To perform this calculation, we will use the Differential Box Counting (DBC) method defined by Chaudhuri and Sarker (1992) [22]. The generalized dimension of order q, $q \in \Re$, is defined by :

$$\mu[I_n(i,j)]^q = \frac{[P_n(i,j)]^q}{\sum_i \sum_j [P_n(i,j)]^q} \tag{3}$$

Where $P_n(i,j)$ is the probability estimation in a ball of radius ν_n.
Then the multifractal spectrum is defined as follows:

$$f(q) = \lim_{n\to\infty} \frac{\sum_i \sum_j \mu[I_n(i,j)]^q * \log\{\mu[I_n(i,j)]^q\}}{\log(\nu_n)} \tag{4}$$

and the singularity exponent as

$$\alpha(q) = \lim_{n\to\infty} \frac{\sum_i \sum_j \mu[I_n(i,j)]^q * \log[P_n(i,j)]}{\log(\nu_n)} \tag{5}$$

3.2 Large Deviation Spectrum (LDS)

Let us consider the projections of the measure μ over an appropriate wavelet ψ around a point $\vec{x}_0$ who allows evaluating μ over balls B centred on $\vec{x}_0$ with different radius $r = \frac{1}{\nu_n}$.

$$T_\psi \mu(\vec{x}_0, r) \equiv \frac{1}{r^2} \int_B \mu(\vec{x}) \psi\left(\frac{\vec{x}_0 - \vec{x}}{r}\right) \tag{6}$$

The wavelet projection provides the same singularity exponents as μ ([9]), that is:

$$T_{\psi}\mu(\vec{x}_0, r) \approx r^{\alpha(\vec{x}_0)} \tag{7}$$

It has been established in [9] that natural images can be modelled by this equation.

Starting from this equation we can estimate the singularity exponents as being the slope of the linear regression in the following way:

$$\alpha(\vec{x}_0) = \lim_{r \to 0} \frac{\log[T_{\psi}\mu(\vec{x}_0, r)]}{\log(r)} \tag{8}$$

After the computation of the singularity exponent at each point by using the above equation, the LDS is estimated [7] by

$$f_g(h) = \lim_{\varepsilon \to 0} \lim_{r \to \infty} \frac{\log[N_r^{\varepsilon}(h)]}{\log(r)} \tag{9}$$

where $N_r^{\varepsilon}(h) = \#\{\alpha / h \in [\alpha - \varepsilon, \alpha + \varepsilon]\} \approx \varepsilon K_{\varepsilon} * p_r(h)$, $*$ is the convolution product, $p_r(h)$ the density of $\alpha(\vec{x})$ and $K_{\varepsilon} = \frac{1}{\varepsilon} K\left(\frac{h}{\varepsilon}\right)$ a rectangular kernel [19]

$$K(t) = \begin{cases} 1 & \text{if} \quad t \in \left[-\frac{1}{2}, \frac{1}{2}\right] \\ 0 & \text{outside} \end{cases}$$

4 Proposed Algorithm

In this section, we expose the method which will allow us to fuse the two previous spectrums (LS and LDS) in order to obtain a single value for each pixel (i, j). This value will be denoted $F(i, j)$ and explained in the following as well as the resulting algorithm.

4.1 EPNSQ Filtering Approach

The Edge Preserving Noise Smoothing Quadrant (EPNSQ) filtering approach was introduced by [23] with the objective of estimating the local statistics and to reduce the misclassification inside texture regions.

This method could be applied on any feature computed from the original image. It has often been applied on fractal dimension estimations and on laws filter, etc. but never on LS and LDS. The EPNSQ can be applied on these two spectrums given the fact that there are two different approaches (geometrical and statistical) to compute the same parameter.

The EPNSQ algorithm performs as follow.

Let us consider q features computed from the image. A sliding window of size $(2w+1) \times (2w+1)$ centered on each coordinate (i, j) will be used for each feature. This window is split into four quadrants. Fig. 1. illustrates this with $w = 2$ and $q = 1$, thus the size of each W_k is $(w+1)\times(w+1) \equiv 3\times 3$.

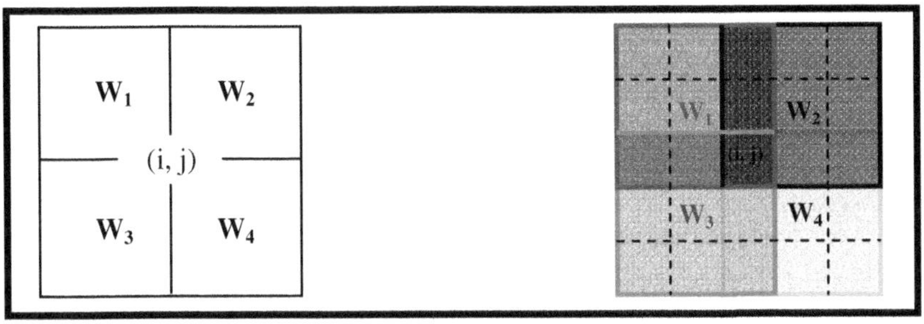

Fig. 1. Four quadrants and an example for a $w = 2$

For each quadrant k and each feature p we compute the local variance $V_{W_k^p}$. We select the quadrant k^* and the feature p^* with the minimal variance

$$V_{W_{k^*}^{p^*}} = \min\left(V_{W_k^p}\right) \qquad k = 1,\cdots,4 \qquad p = 1,\cdots,q \tag{10}$$

The feature value $F(i,j)$ is the average value computed on the $W_{k^*}^{p^*}$ quadrant

$$F(i,j) = \frac{1}{(w+1)^2}\sum_{n=1}^{w+1}\sum_{m=1}^{w+1} W_{k^*}^{p^*}(m,n) \tag{11}$$

This value will be considered as being the most representative spectrum value for each pixel.

4.2 Our Algorithm

The block diagram of our algorithm is described in the following figure and consists in the following steps:

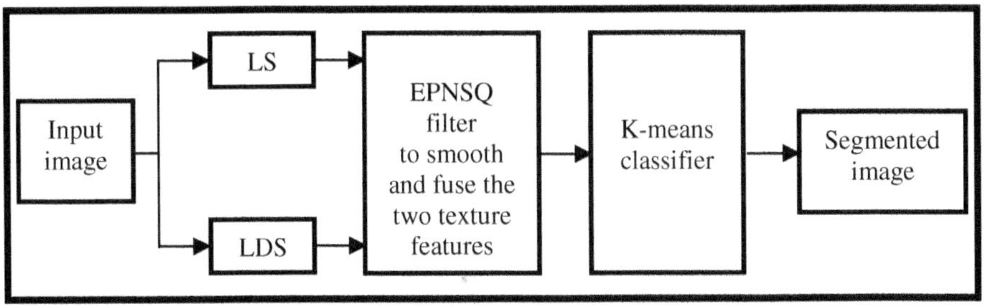

Fig. 2. Block diagram of our algorithm

If the two spectrums (LS and LDS) are computed over the whole image, then each pixel (i, j) is associated with two features and the EPNSQ filtering approach is used to compute $F(i, j)$. We perform the texture segmentation by applying a general k-means clustering algorithm [24] on $F(i, j)$.

5 Experimental Results

This approach, texture features extraction and segmentation, has been tested on different mosaic images built using Brodatz album textures (D9, D57 and D92) (fig. 3) and textures extracted from IKONOS images (fig. 4). Brodatz textures have been chosen because they are close to forest textures extracted from satellite images.

The size of each mosaic image is 256×256 pixels. The texture feature $F(i, j)$ is computed using a sliding window of size 17×17. The number of classes for the k-mean classification algorithm is set to the number of textures (3 in fig. 3 and 4 in fig. 4). For each figure, the k-means classification algorithm was applied on LS (b), LDS (c) and $F(i, j)$ (d).

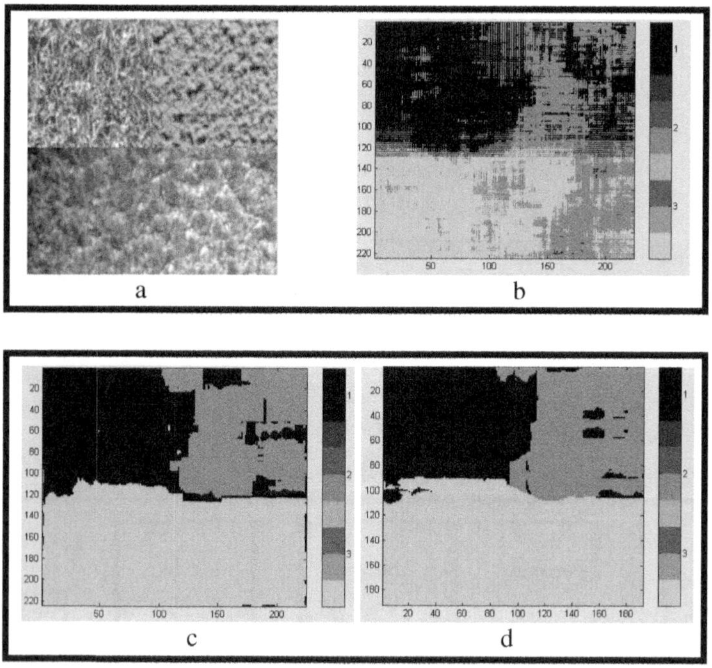

Fig. 3. a: image created from three Brodatz textures (D9, D57, D92). b: segmentation obtained using LS. c: segmentation obtained using LDS. d: segmentation obtained using our algorithm.

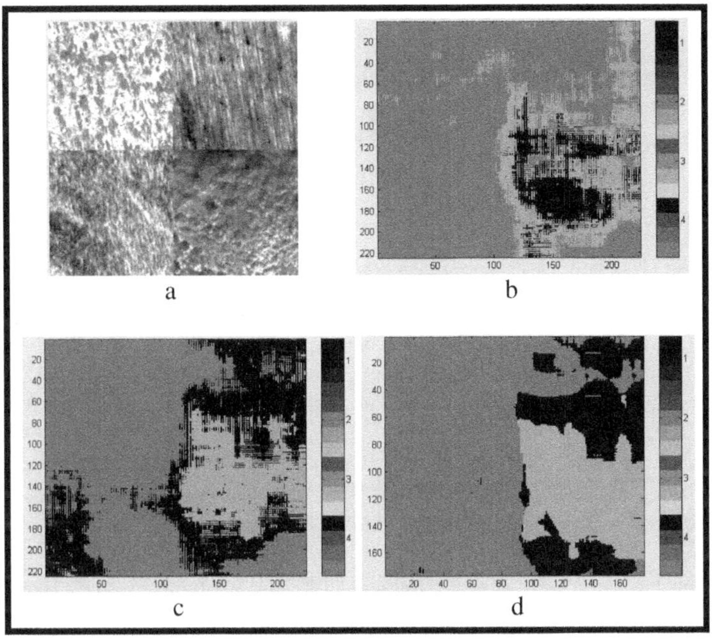

Fig. 4. a: image created from four textures extracted from IKONOS images. b: segmentation obtained using LS. c: segmentation obtained using LDS. d: segmentation obtained using our algorithm.

The results show that the classification algorithm applied on texture features $F(i, j)$ gives a better segmentation on the two kinds of images than the segmentation applied on both spectrums separately. (b) and (c) of fig. 3 and fig. 4 shows that the segmentation based in LDS is better that LS. The main contribution is that spectrum fusion improves the homogeneity of the regions.

6 Conclusion

In this paper we have developed a texture feature segmentation algorithm based on the multifractal spectrums. This approach first computes the Legendre and Large Deviation spectrum within localized regions of the image around each pixel. Then it computes the features $F(i, j)$ for each pixel using the EPNSQ filtering approach. Finally it classifies these features using a k-means clustering algorithm.

We note that the segmentation applied on $F(i, j)$ gives more homogeneous and compact regions. The classification error using $F(i, j)$ is lower than the error using LS or LDS.

In future works we will try to exploit the LDS using different kernel density estimation methods and we will integrate colour information.

Acknowledgements

The authors are thankful to the European institutions for the financing of the CESAR project (Arborescent species classification) and Guadeloupe, Martinique and French Guyana areas within the "INTERREG IIIb Caribbean Space" European program.

References

1. Haralick, R.M.: Statistical and structural approaches to texture. Proceedings of the IEEE (1979) 786–804
2. Haralick, R.M., Shanmugam, K. Dinstein, I.: Textural features for image classification. IEEE Transactions on systems, Man and Cybernetics, (1973) 610–621
3. Tuceryan, M.: Moment based texture segmentation. Pattern Recognition Letters, (1994) 695–668
4. Clark,M., Bovik, A.C.: Texture segmentation using Gabor modulation/demodulation. Pattern Recognition Letters, (1987) 261–267
5. Turner, M.R.: Texture discrimination by Gabor functions. Biological Cybernetics, (1986) 71–82
6. Kaplan, L.M.: Extended Fractal Analysis for Texture Classification and Segmentation. IEEE Transaction on Image Processing, (1999) 1572–1585
7. Levy Vehel, J. : Introduction to the multifractal analysis of images, INRIA
8. Sapiro, G., Tannenbaum, A. : on invariant curve evolution and image analysis. Indiana University Mathematics Journal, (1993) 985–1010
9. Ruderman, D.: The statistics of naturel images. Network 5, (1994) 517–548
10. Grazzini, J.: Analyses multiéchelle et multifractale d'image météorologique Application à la detection de zonnes précipitantes. (2003)
11. Tuceryan, M.: Texture Analysis. In the Handbook of Pattern Recognition and Computer Vision, L.F. Pau and P.S.P. Wang(eds), World Scientific Publishing Co., (1993)
12. Julesz, B.: Textons, the Elements of Texture Perception, and Their Interactions. Nature, (1981) 91–97
13. Chatterjee, S. and Chellappa, R.: Maximum likelihood texture segmentation using Gaussian Markov random field models. P roc. IEEE Coqf Computer Vision, Graph, Pattern Recog., (1985)
14. Derin, H. and Elliot, H.: Modelling and segmentation of noisy and textured images using Gibbs random fields. IEEE Trans on Pattern Anal. and Machine. Intell, (1987) 39–55
15. Keller, J., Crownover, R. and Chen, S. :Texture Description and Segmentation through Fractal Geometry. Computer Vision Graphics and Image Processing, (1989) 150–1 60
16. Chaudhuri, B. B., Sarkar, N. and Kundu, P.: An Improved Fractal Geometry Based Texture Segmentation Technique. Proc. IEE-part E
17. Laws, K. I., Textured Image Segmentation. Ph.D. thesis, University of Southern California, (1980)
18. Campbell, F.W. and Robson, J.G.: Application of Fourier Analysis to the Visibility of Gratings. Journal of Physiology, (1968) 551–566
19. O. Duda, R., E. Hart, P. : Pattern classification and scene analysis. Wiley-Iterscience, New York, (1973).
20. Cheeseman, P., Self, M., Kelly, J., Stutz, J., Taylor, W., Freeman., D. : Bayesian classification. In Seventh National Conference on Artificial Intelligence, (1988) 607–611

21. Grayson, M. : The heat equation shrinks embedded plane curves to round points. J. Differential Geometry, vol. 26, (1987) 285-314
22. Chaudhuri, B.B., Sarker, N.: An Efficient Approach to Estimate Fractal Dimensions of Textural Images, Pattern recognition, (1992) 1035–1041
23. Donnay, J.-P., Barnsley, M.J., Longley, P.A. (eds.) : Remote Sensing and Urban Analysis, GISDATA 9, Taylor & Francis, London, (2000) 3–18
24. Tou, J.T., Gonzalez, R.C.: Pattern Recognition Principles, Addison-Wesley, Reading, MA, (1982)

Object Segmentation Using Growing Neural Gas and Generalized Gradient Vector Flow in the Geometric Algebra Framework

Jorge Rivera-Rovelo[1], Silena Herold[2], and Eduardo Bayro-Corrochano[1]

[1] CINVESTAV Unidad Guadalajara,
Av. Científica 1145, El Bajío, Zapopan, Jalisco, México
{rivera, edb}@gdl.cinvestav.mx
[2] Universidad de Oriente, Santiago de Cuba
silena@csd.uo.edu.cu

Abstract. In this paper we present a method based on self-organizing neural networks to extract the shape of a 2D or 3D object using a set of transformations expressed as versors in the conformal geometric algebra framework. Such transformations, when applied to any geometric entity of this geometric algebra, define the shape of the object. This approach was tested with several images, but here we show its utility first using a 2D magnetic resonance image to segment the ventricle. Then we present some examples of an application for the case of 3D objects.

1 Introduction

The use of neural networks in medical image processing is an area receiving a lot of attention with a variety of applications like segmentation or classification of tissues, etc. The self-organizing neural networks like Kohonen's Map or Self-Organizing Map (SOM), Neural Gas (NG) and Growing Neural Gas (GNG, [3]) have been used broadly when we need to preserve the topology of the data.

In this work we present an approach which uses the *Generalized Gradient Vector Flow (GGVF)* [4] to guide the automatic selection of the input patterns, as well as the learning process of the self-organized neural network GNG to obtain a set of transformations expressed in the conformal geometric algebra framework, which is a coordinate free approach. These transformations help us to define the shape of the object we are interested in. We decided to use such framework because of its coordinate free nature and because it has the advantage that (rigid body) transformations of geometric entities (like points, lines, planes, circles, spheres) are expressed in compact form as operators called *versors*, which are applied in a multiplicatively way to any entity of the conformal geometric algebra. Thus, training the network we do not obtain specific positions for a particular entity (for example, the positions of points when the weights of the network are interpreted in such a way), but we obtain the transformation that can be applied to entities resulting in the definition of the object contour or its shape.

J.F. Martínez-Trinidad et al. (Eds.): CIARP 2006, LNCS 4225, pp. 306–315, 2006.

Note that the authors are proposing a very advanced algorithm using early vision preprocessing and self-organizing neural computing in terms of algebra techniques. We believe that the early vision preprocessing together with self-organizing neurocomputing resembles the geometric visual processing in biological creatures. The experimental results show that approach is very promising.

2 Geometric Algebra

The Geometric Algebra $G_{p,q,r}$ is constructed over the vector space $\mathcal{V}^{p,q,r}$, where p, q, r denote the signature of the algebra; if $p \neq 0$ and $q = r = 0$, the metric is Euclidean; if only $r = 0$, the metric is pseudo euclidean; if $p \neq 0, q \neq 0, r \neq 0$, the metric is degenerate. In this algebra, we have the *geometric product* which is defined as in (1) for two vectors a, b, and have two parts: the inner product $a \cdot b$ is the symmetric part, while the wedge product $a \wedge b$ is the antisymmetric part.

$$ab = a \cdot b + a \wedge b. \tag{1}$$

The dimension of $G_{n=p,q,r}$ is 2^n, and G_n is constructed by the application of the geometric product over the vector basis e_i.

$$e_i e_j = \begin{cases} 1 \; for \; i = j \in 1, \cdots, p \\ -1 \; for \; i = j \in p+1, \cdots, p+q \\ 0 \; for \; i = j \in p+q+1, \cdots, p+q+r \\ e_i \wedge e_j \; for \; i \neq j \end{cases}$$

This leads to a basis for the entire algebra: $\{1\}, \{e_i\}, \{e_i \wedge e_j\}, \{e_i \wedge e_j \wedge e_k\}, \ldots, \{e_1 \wedge e_2 \wedge \ldots \wedge e_n\}$. Any multivector can be expressed in terms of this basis. In the n-D space there are multivectors of grade 0 (scalars), grade 1 (vectors), grade 2 (bivectors), grade 3 (trivectors)... up to grade n.

To work in Conformal Geometric Algebra (CGA) $G_{4,1,0}$ means to embed the Euclidean space in a higher dimensional space with two extra basis vectors which have particular meaning; in this way, we represent particular objects of the Euclidean space with subspaces of the conformal space. The vectors we add are e_+ and e_-, which square to $1, -1$, respectively. With these two vectors, we define the null vectors

$$e_0 = \frac{1}{2}(e_- - e_+); \qquad e_\infty = (e_- + e_+), \tag{2}$$

interpreted as the origin and the point at infinity, respectively. From now and in the rest of the paper, points in the 3D-Euclidean space are represented in lowercase letters, while conformal points in uppercase letters; also the conformal entities will be expressed in the *Inner Product Null Space* (IPNS), and not in the *Outer Product Null Space* unless it is specified explicitly. To map a point $x \in \mathcal{V}^3$ to the conformal space in $G_{4,1}$, we use

$$X = x + \frac{1}{2}x^2 e_\infty + e_0. \tag{3}$$

Let be X_1, X_2 two conformal points. If we subtract X_2 from X_1, we obtain

$$X_1 - X_2 = (x_1 - x_2) + \frac{1}{2}(x_1^2 - x_2^2)e_\infty + e_0 \tag{4}$$

and if we square this result, we obtain

$$(X_1 - X_2)^2 = (x_1 - x_2)^2 \tag{5}$$

So, if we want a measure of the euclidean distance between the two points, we can apply (5). Reader is encouraged to see the CGA representation of other entities consulting [2]. All of such entities and its transformations can be managed easily using the rigid body motion operators described further.

2.1 Rotation, Translation and Dilation

In GA there exist specific operators named *versors* to model rotations, translations and dilations, and are called rotors, translators and dilators respectively. In general, a versor G is a multivector which can be expressed as the geometric product of nonsingular vectors

$$G = \pm a_1 a_2 ... a_k \tag{6}$$

In CGA, such operators are defined by (7) being R the rotor, T the translator, and D_λ the dilator.

$$R = e^{\frac{1}{2}\mathbf{b}\theta}, \qquad T = e^{-\frac{te_\infty}{2}}, \qquad D_\lambda = e^{\frac{-\log(\lambda)\wedge E}{2}}, \tag{7}$$

where $\mathbf{b}$ is the bivector dual to the rotation axis, θ is the rotation angle, $t \in \mathcal{E}^3$ is the translation vector, λ is the factor of dilation and $E = e \wedge e_0$.

Such operators are applied to any entity of any dimension by multiplying the entity by the operator from the left, and by the reverse of the operator from the right. Let be X_i any entity in CGA; then to rotate it, we do $X_1' = RX_1\tilde{R}$, while to translate it we apply $X_2' = TX_2\tilde{T}$, and to dilate we use $X_3' = D_\lambda X_3 \tilde{D}_\lambda$. However, dilations are applied only on the origin, so we must translate the entity X_i to origin, then to dilate it, and finally back translate to its original position.

3 Determining the Shape of an Object

If we want to determine the shape of an object, we can use a topographic mapping which uses selected points of interest along the contour of the object to fit a low dimensional map to the high dimensional manifold of such contour. This mapping is commonly achieved by using self-organized neural networks as Kohonen's Maps (SOM) or Neural Gas (NG); however, if we desire a better topology preservation, we should not specify the number of neurons of the network *a priori* (as specified for neurons in SOM or NG, together with its neighborhood relations), but allow the network to grow using an incremental training algorithm,

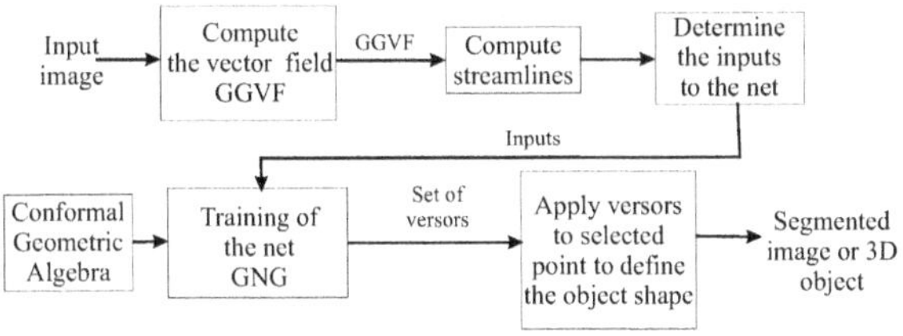

Fig. 1. A block diagram of our approach

as in the case of the Growing Neural Gas (GNG) [3]. In this work we follow the idea of GNG and present an approach to determine the shape of objects by means of applying versors of the CGA, resulting in a model easy to handle in post processing stages, for example modeling the dynamic behavior of the object; a scheme of our approach is shown in Fig. 1. This representation is compact because it uses only one base point and a set of versors in the conformal geometric algebra framework (translators T in 2D, motors M in 3D), which moves such point along the contour of the object we are interested in, to determine its shape. That means that the neural network has versors associated to its neurons, and its learning algorithm determines the parameters of them that best fit the input patterns, allowing us to get every point on the contour by interpolation of such versors.

Additionally, we modify the acquisition of input patterns by adding a preprocessing stage which determines the inputs to the net; this is done by computing the Generalized Gradient Vector Flow (GGVF) and analyzing the *streamlines* followed by particles (points) placed on the vertices of small squares by dividing the 3D space in such squares (a sort of grid for 3D). The streamline or the path followed by a particle that is placed on $\mathbf{x} = (x, y, z)$ coordinates will be denoted as $S(\mathbf{x})$.

3.1 Automatic Samples Selection Using GGVF

Since our goal is to have an approach which needs less as possible the intervention of users, the selection of input patterns must be as automatic and robust as possible; that means that we want to give to the computer only the medical image or the volumetric data in order to find the shape of the object we are interested in. Therefore, we need a method that can provide information to guide the algorithm in this selection. The GGVF [4] is a *dense vector field* derived from the volumetric data by minimizing a certain energy functional in a variational framework. The minimization is achieved by solving linear partial differential equations which diffuses the gradient vectors computed from the volumetric data. To define the GGVF, the edge map is defined at first as

$$f(\mathbf{x}) : \Omega \rightarrow \mathcal{R} \tag{8}$$

(for the 2D image, it is defined as $f(x, y) = -|\nabla G(x, y) * I(x, y)|^2$, where $I(x, y)$ is the gray level of the image on pixel (x, y), $G(x, y)$ is a 2D Gaussian function (for robustness in presence of noise), and ∇ is the gradient operator).

With this edge map, the GGVF is defined as to be the vector field $\mathbf{v}(x, y, z) = [u(x, y, z), v(x, y, z), w(x, y, z)]$ that minimizes the energy functional

$$\mathcal{E} = \int\int g(|\nabla f|)\nabla^2 \mathbf{v} - h(|\nabla f|)(\mathbf{v} - \nabla f) \tag{9}$$

where

$$g(|\nabla f|) = e^{-\frac{|\nabla f|}{\mu}} \quad \text{and} \quad h(|\nabla f|) = 1 - g(|\nabla f|) \tag{10}$$

and μ is a coefficient. An example of such dense vector field obtained in a 2D image is shown in Fig. 2.a, while an example of the vector field for a volumetric data is shown in Fig. 2.b.

a) 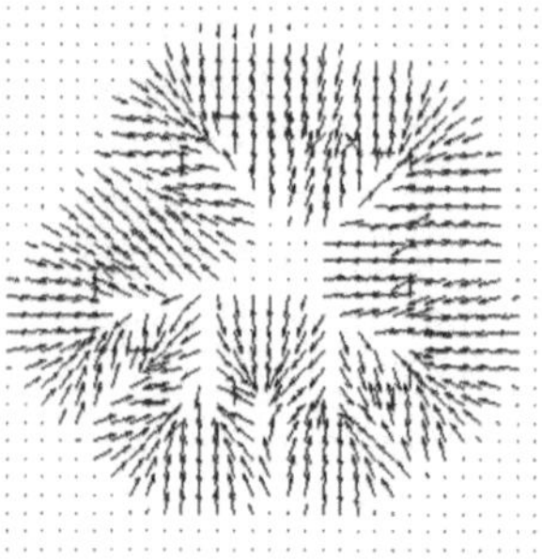 b) 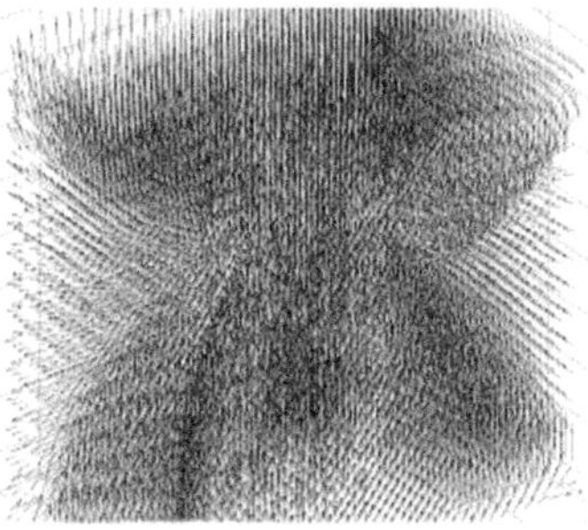

Fig. 2. Example of the dense vector field called GGVF (it is shown not all the vector field, but only representative samples of a grid). a) Samples of the vector field for a 2D image; b) Samples of the vector field for volumetric data.

The automatic selection of input patterns is done by analyzing the *streamlines* of points of a 3D grid topology defined over the volumetric data. It means that the algorithm follow the streamlines of each point of the grid, which will guide the point to the more evident contour of the object; then the algorithm selects the point where the streamline finds a peak in the edge map and gets its conformal representation X (as in equation (3))to make the inputs pattern set. Additionally to the X (conformal position of the point), the inputs have the vector $\mathbf{v}_\zeta = [u,\ v,\ w]$ which is the value of the GGVF in such pixel and it will be used in the training stage as a parameter determining the amount of energy the input has to attract neurons. This information will be used in the training stage together with the position $\mathbf{x}$ for learning the topology of the data. Summarizing, the input set $\mathbf{I}$ will be

$$\mathbf{I} = \{\zeta_k = (X_{\zeta_k}, \mathbf{v}_{\zeta_\mathbf{k}}) | \mathbf{x}_\zeta \in S(\mathbf{x}') \text{ } and \text{ } f(\mathbf{x}_\zeta) = 1\} \tag{11}$$

where X_ζ is the conformal representation of $\mathbf{x}_\zeta$; $\mathbf{x}_\zeta \in S(\mathbf{x}')$ means that $\mathbf{x}_\zeta$ is on the path followed by a particle placed in $(\mathbf{x}')$, and $f(\mathbf{x}_\zeta)$ is the value of the edge map in position $\mathbf{x}_\zeta$ (assuming it is binarized). As some streamlines can carry to the same point or very close points, we can add constraints to avoid very close samples; one very simple restriction is that the candidate to be included in the input set must be at least at a fixed distance d_{thresh} of any other input.

3.2 Learning the Shape Using Versors

Using Growing Neural Gas (GNG) we will define the versors that applied to a point will describe the shape of the object. It is important to note that although we are explaining the algorithm using points, the versors can be applied to any entity in GA that we had selected to model the object (e.g. planes to describe a surface in 3D, spheres, etc). The network starts with a minimum number of versors (neural units) and new units are inserted successively. The network is specified by

- A set of units (neurons) named N, where each $\mathbf{n}_l \in N$ has its associated versor $M_{\mathbf{n}_l}$; each versor is the transformation that must be applied to a point to place it in the contour of the object. The set of transformations will ultimately describe the shape of the object.
- A set of connections between neurons defining the topological structure.

In this approach we will use the information available on GGVF to guide the learning. With this elements, we define the learning algorithm to find the versors that will define the contour as follows:

1. Let P_0 be a fixed initial point over which the transformations will be applied. Such transformations will be expressed as $M = e^{-\frac{t}{2}e_\infty}$ in the conformal geometric algebra. This point corresponds to the conformal representation of p_0, which can be a random point or the centroid defined by the inputs. The vector t will be determined according the distance between X_ζ and P_0 as explained below, but initially it is a random displacement.
2. Start with the minimal number of neurons, which have associated random translators as well as a vector $\mathbf{v_l} = [u_l,\ v_l,\ w_l]$ whose magnitude is interpreted as the capacity of learning for such neuron (initially set to 1).
3. Select one input ζ from the inputs set $\mathbf{I}$ and find the winner neuron; that means to find the neuron n_l having the versor M_l which moves the point P_0 closer to such input:
$$M_{win} = \min_{\forall M} \|X_\zeta - P_0\| \tag{12}$$
4. Modify M_{win} and all others versors of neighboring neurons M_l in such a way that the modified T will represent a transformation moving the point P_0 nearer the input:
$$M_{l_{new}} = e^{-\frac{t_l}{2}e_\infty} e^{-\frac{\Delta t_l}{2}e_\infty} \tag{13}$$
where
$$\Delta t_l = \alpha\ \phi\ \eta\ (\mathbf{v}_\zeta, \mathbf{v_l})(\mathbf{x}_\zeta - p_0) \tag{14}$$
α is a learning parameter, ϕ is a function defining the amount of a neuron can learn according to its distance to the winner one (usually defined as in (15)), and $\eta(\mathbf{v}_\zeta, \mathbf{v_l})$ is defined as in (16).
$$\phi = e^{-(\frac{X_\zeta - TP_0\tilde{T})^2}{2\sigma}} \tag{15}$$

$$\eta(\mathbf{v}_\zeta, \mathbf{v_l}) = \|\mathbf{v}_\zeta - \mathbf{v_l}\|^2 \tag{16}$$

which is a function defining a quantity of learning depending on the strength to teach of the input ζ and the capacity to learn of the neuron, given in $\mathbf{v}_\zeta$ and $\mathbf{v_l}$, respectively. In other words, with $\eta(\mathbf{v}_\zeta, \mathbf{v_l})$ we are taking into account the information of GGVF which guide to the contours. Finally, also update the value $\mathbf{v_l}$:

$$\mathbf{v_l} = [(u_l + \alpha\ \phi\ u_l),\ \ (v_l + \alpha\ \phi\ v_l),\ \ (w_l + \alpha\ \phi\ w_l)]^T \tag{17}$$

5. Insert new neurons as follows:
   - Determine neighboring neurons $\mathbf{n_i}$ and $\mathbf{n_j}$ connected by an edge larger than c_{max}
   - Create a new neuron n_{new} between $\mathbf{n_i}$ and $\mathbf{n_j}$ whose associated M and $\mathbf{v_l}$ will be
   $$M_{n_{new}} = \frac{M_i + M_j}{2}, \qquad \mathbf{v_{l\_new}} = \frac{\mathbf{v_i} + \mathbf{v_j}}{2} \tag{18}$$
   - Delete old edge connecting $\mathbf{n_i}$ and $\mathbf{n_j}$ and create two new edges connecting n_{new} with $\mathbf{n_i}$ and $\mathbf{n_j}$
6. Repeat steps 3 to 5 if the stopping criterion is not achieved. The stopping criterion is when a maximum number of neurons is reached or when the learning capacity of neurons approaches to zero (is less that a threshold c_{min}), the first that happens will stop the learning process.

Training the network we find the set of M defining positions on a trajectory; such positions minimizes the error measured as the average distance between X_ζ and the result of $M_\zeta P_0 \tilde{M}_\zeta$:

$$\chi = \frac{\sum_{\forall\zeta}(\sqrt{(M_\zeta P_0 \tilde{M}_\zeta - X_\zeta)^2}}{N} \tag{19}$$

where M_ζ moves P_0 closer to input X_ζ, and N is the number of inputs.

4 Experiments

To illustrate the algorithm explained in section 3.2 we first present the process for a 2D image. Fig. 3 shows the result when the algorithm is applied to a magnetic resonance image (MRI); the goal is to obtain the shape of the ventricle. Fig. 3.a shows the original brain image and the Region Of Interest (ROI); Fig. 3.b the computed vector field for the ROI; Fig. 3.c the streamlines in the ROI defined for particles placed on the vertices of a 32x32 grid; Fig. 3.d shows the initial shape as defined for the two initial random versors M_a, M_b, which move the point P_0 to $X_a = M_a\ P_0\ \tilde{M}_a$ and $X_b = M_b\ P_0\ \tilde{M}_b$; Fig. 3.e shows the final shape obtained; and finally Fig. 3.f the original image with the segmented object. Many other experiments were carried out, and table 1 shows some quantitative results. Such table shows the errors obtained with the algorithm using and not using the

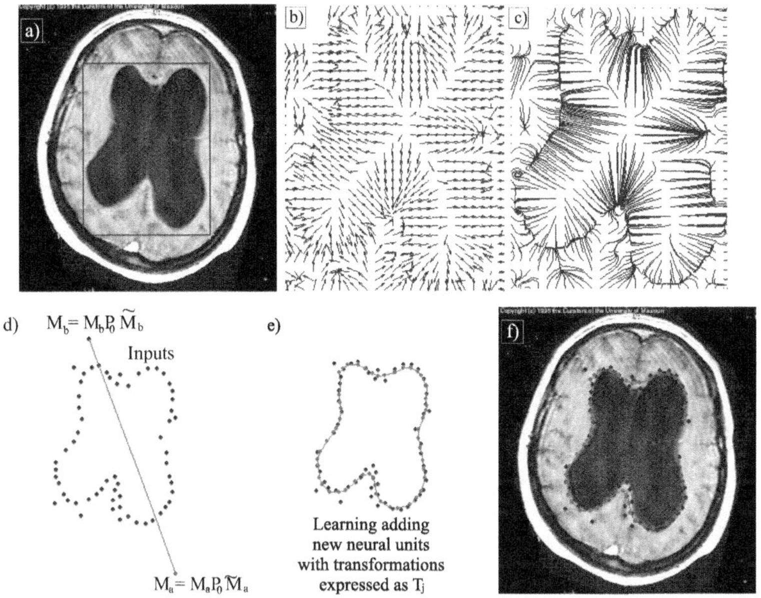

Fig. 3. a) Original image and region of interest (ROI); b) Zoom of the dense vector field of the ROI; c) Zoom of the streamlines in ROI; d) Inputs and initial shape; e) Final shape defined according the 54 estimated translators; f) Image segmented according the results

Table 1. Errors obtained by the algorithm with and without the GGVF information

Example	Error without GGVF	Error with GGVF
Ventricle 1	3.29	2.51
Eye 1	7.63	6.8
Eye 2	3.43	2.98
Column disk 1	4.65	4.1
Tumor 1	3.41	2.85
Tumor 2	2.95	2.41
Free form curve	2.84	1.97
Ventricle 1	3.29	2.51

GGVF information (error measured as in (19)). For the 3D case, Fig. 4.a shows the vectors of the dense GGVF on a 3D grid arrangement of size 32x32x16; Fig. 4.b shows the inputs determined by GGVF and edge map, and also shows the initialization of the net GNG; Fig. 4.c shows Final shape after training has finished with a total of 300 versors M (associated with 300 neural units).

Figure 5 shows the results obtained with other two examples using volumetric data. The first column shows the inputs to the net, selected according the procedure of Sect. 3.1 and the initialization of the net with nine neural units (the topology of the net is defined as a sort of pyramid around the centroid of input

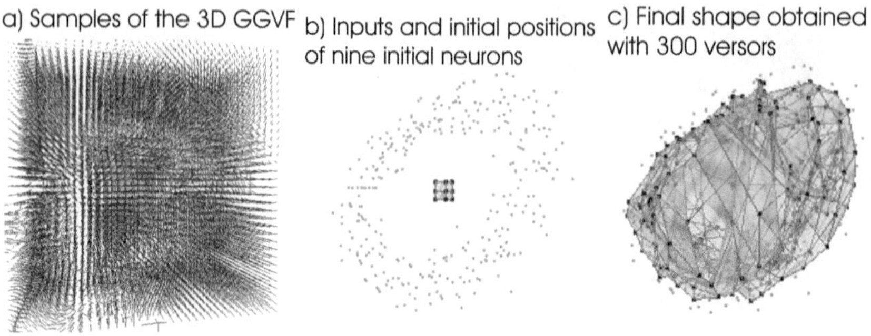

Fig. 4. The algorithm for 3D object's shape determination. a) Vectors of the dense GGVF on a 3D grid arrangement of 32x32x16; b) Inputs determined by GGVF and edge map and the initialization of the net GNG; c) Final shape after training has finished with a total of 300 versors M (associated with 300 neural units).

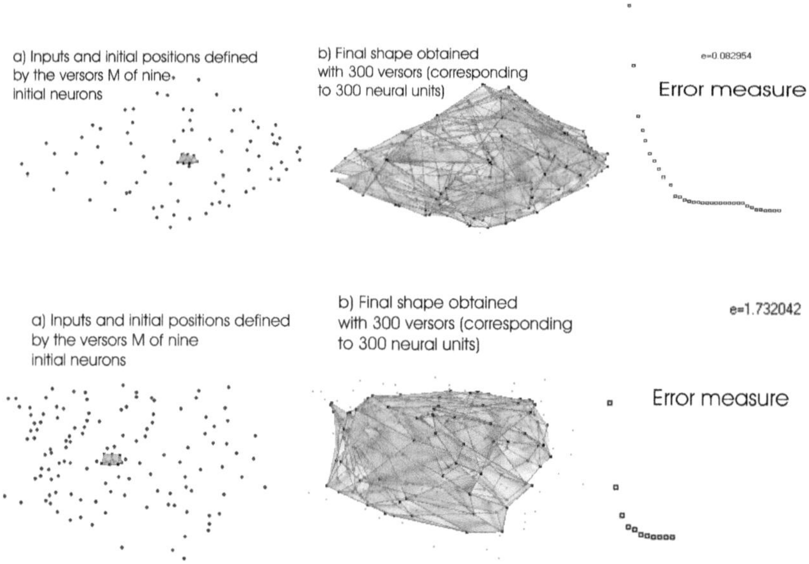

Fig. 5. Two examples of 3D object shape definition. **First column:** inputs to the net selected using GGVF and streamlines, and the initialization of the net with nine neural units; **Second column:** result after the net has been reached the maximum number of neurons (300 neurons); **Third column:** error minimization according to (19).

points); the second column show the result after the net has been reached the maximum number of neurons, which was fixed to 300; the third column shows the minimization of the error according to (19).

It is necessary to mention that the whole process is quick enough; in fact, the computational time required for all the examples showed in this work, took only few seconds. The computation of the GGVF is the most time consuming task in the algorithm, but it only takes about 3 seconds for 64x64 images, 20 seconds for 256x256 images, and 110 seconds for 512x512 images. This is the reason why we decide do not compute it for the whole image, but for selected region of interest. The same criterion was applied to 3D examples.

5 Conclusions

In this work it was shown the use of the dense vector field named Generalized Gradient Vector Flow (GGVF) not only to select the inputs to a neural network, but also as a parameter guiding the learning process of the net. The neural network presented here is the growing Neural Gas, which is used to find a set of transformations expressed in the conformal geometric algebra framework, which move a point by means of a versor along the contour of an object, defining by this way the shape of the object. This is useful because although we have shown examples using points, the versors of the conformal geometric algebra can be used to transform any entity exactly in the same way: multiplying the entity from the left by M and from the right by $\tilde{M}$. There were presented some experiments and results shows that in addition to the set of versors available even if the entity used is other than points, this algorithm is well suited for segmentation tasks.

References

1. E. Bayro-Corrochano, "Robot perception and action using conformal geometry", in *Handbook of Geometric Computing. Applications in Pattern Recognition, Computer Vision, Neurocomputing and Robotics*, E. Bayro-Corrochano (Ed.), Springer Verlag, Heidelberg, 2005, chap. 13, pp. 405-458.
2. B. Rosenhahn, and G. Sommer, "Pose Estimation in Conformal Geometric Algebra", Christian-Albrechts-University of Kiel, Technical Report No. 0206, pp. 13-36, 2002.
3. B. Fritzke, "A growing neural gas network learns topologies", Advances in Neural Information Processing Systems 7, MIT Press, Cambridge, MA, 1995.
4. Ch. Xu, "Deformable models with applications to human cerebral cortex reconstruction from magnetic resonance images", Ph.D. Thesis, Johns Hopkins University, 1999, pp. 14-63.

A Clustering Based Approach for Automatic Image Segmentation: An Application to Biplane Ventriculograms

Antonio Bravo[1], Rubén Medina[2], and J. Arelis Díaz[3]

[1] Grupo de Bioingeniería, Universidad Nacional Experimental del Táchira, Decanato de Investigación, San Cristóbal 5001, Venezuela
abravo@unet.edu.ve
[2] Grupo de Ingeniería Biomédica (GIBULA), Universidad de Los Andes, Facultad de Ingeniería, Mérida 5101, Venezuela
[3] Laboratorio de Investigación en Matemática Pura y Aplicada, Universidad Nacional Experimental del Táchira, Decanato de Investigación, San Cristóbal 5001, Venezuela
jdiaz@unet.edu.ve

Abstract. This paper reports on an automatic method for ventricular cavity segmentation in angiographic images. The first step of the method consists in applying a linear regression model that exploits the functional relationship between the original input image and a smoothed version. This intermediate result is used as input to a clustering algorithm, which is based on a region growing technique. The clustering algorithm is a two stage process. In the first stage an initial segmentation is achieved using as input the result of the linear regression and the smoothed version of the input image. The second stage is intended for refining the initial segmentation based on feature vectors including the area, the gray-level average and the centroid of each candidate region. The segmentation method is conceptually simple and provides an accurate contour detection for the left ventricle cavity.

1 Introduction

Clustering is the division of a dataset into groups of similar objects. Clustering methods have been used for recognition of shapes [1] [2]. Given a set of M data points, the objective is to detect similarities between points of this data set. The clustered data is stored in d-dimension vectors. Each vector represents a particular object which is described by d features that enables comparison to other data vectors. The result of the feature comparison process is used to classify the data into several disjoint subsets. This technique has been used to solve the image segmentation problem. Clustering based segmentation considers features like pixel space positions, topological relations and contour features. Examples of these techniques are the methods for classification [3] and clustering by Region Growing [4].

Region growing methods have been used for performing the segmentation of several medical imaging modalities [5]. The region growing is usually based on

J.F. Martínez-Trinidad et al. (Eds.): CIARP 2006, LNCS 4225, pp. 316–325, 2006.

simple linkage, on multiple connections or centroid based linkage [6]. An alternative classification method is based on clustering by graph theory [7]. According to this method, data is initially represented by adjacent graphs [8] building up several subgraph sets whose union represents a spatially connected region in the image. The fuzzy C–means classification algorithms have also provided good results for image segmentation. These methods require a high computational cost [9][10]. Ventriculograms are obtained from a medical imaging modality based on X–rays, after the injection of a contrast medium in the cavities of the heart aiming to enhance the contrast with respect to other tissues. Such examination enables the assessment of morphology and function of the heart. Ventriculographic image analysis requires a precise description of ventricular shape in order to quantify the parameters associated with the cardiovascular function [11] [12] or alternatively for performing the visualization of this anatomical structure [13]. The accurate description of ventricular shape and their quantitative analysis is important, since cardiovascular disease (CVD) accounts for one third of the deaths in the world [14].

Recently, several robust methods for ventriculographic image segmentation have been proposed. Suzuki *et al.* [15] have developed a ventricular contour detector based on neural networks (NN). The detector was implemented using a multilayer neural network which was trained through a back–propagation algorithm. The training set includes left ventricle images and ventricular contours traced by a cardiologist. Validation was performed by comparison of the area enclosed by the estimated contour with respect to the reference contour traced by the cardiologist. The average contour error obtained at end–diastole was 6.2%. Oost *et al.* [16] have proposed a ventricular cavity automatic segmentation method based on Active Appearance Models (AAMs) and dynamic programming (DP). The active appearance model is used to exploit the existing correlations in shape and texture between end-diastole and end-systole images. A dynamic programming algorithm was used to incorporate cardiac motion features to the method. The method was evaluated by using 140 images. The average border positioning error was smaller than 1.45 mm. These methods provided an accurate representation of ventricular borders, however, they are not yet fully validated and accepted in the clinical work as a gold standard.

The objective of this research is to develop a left ventricle segmentation method based on region growing. This segmentation method consists of two fundamental stages. The first is a preprocessing stage that enhances the image data using statistical tools. The second is a classification stage based on region growing. The method uses a feature vector including the gray-level intensity and the average of pixels included in a neighborhood.

2 Method

2.1 Preprocessing Stage

An average filter is applied to the input image. According to this filter, if a pixel value is greater than the average of its neighbors (the eight closest pixels in a neighborhood of size 3 × 3) plus a certain threshold ε, then the pixel value in the output image is set to the average value, otherwise the output pixel is set equal to the pixel in the input image. The output image is a smoothed version of the input. The threshold value ε was set to the standard deviation of the input image.

A linear regression model is estimated to exploit the functional relation [17] between the data of the input image ($\mathbf{I}_O$) and the data of the smoothed image ($\mathbf{I}_P$). The model is described by:

$$\hat{\mathbf{I}}_P = \beta_0 + \beta_1 \mathbf{I}_O \ , \tag{1}$$

where β_0 and β_1 are the regression coefficients [17], which are estimated by the least squares method according to:

$$\begin{aligned} \beta_0 &= \frac{\sum_{i=0}^{n}(I_{O_i} - \bar{\mathbf{I}}_O)(I_{P_i} - \bar{\mathbf{I}}_P)}{\sum_{i=0}^{n}(I_{O_i} - \bar{\mathbf{I}}_O)^2} \\ \beta_1 &= \bar{\mathbf{I}}_P - \beta_0 \bar{\mathbf{I}}_O \end{aligned} \ . \tag{2}$$

The data obtained by the functional relation between the original image and the smoothed image represents a new image ($\hat{\mathbf{I}}_P$). The pixel values in this image and in the smoothed image are the members of the feature vector used in the clustering method.

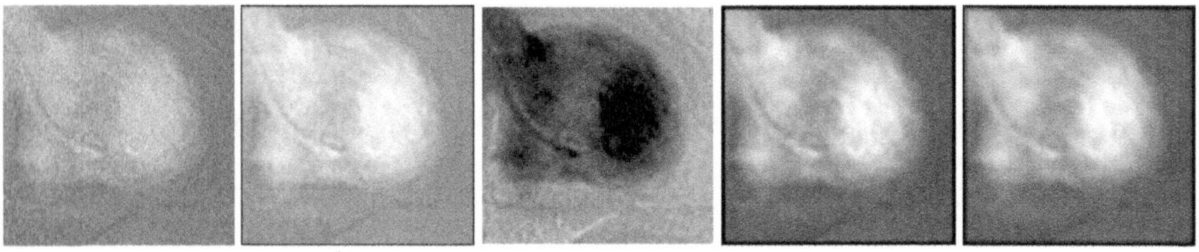

(a) (b) (c) (d) (e)

Fig. 1. Linear regression model. (a) Original image. (b) Smoothed image. (c) Linear regression image. (d) Similarity image. (e) Density function image.

2.2 Clustering Stage

The clustering stage is a four steps process. In the first step a similarity matrix is generated based on a similarity criterion [6] that measures the difference between the gray-level values of pixels in $\hat{\mathbf{I}}_P$ and the smoothed image ($\mathbf{I}_P$). According to this criterion, pixels $p_1(u, v)$ (in $\hat{\mathbf{I}}_P$) and $p_2(u, v)$ (in $\mathbf{I}_P$) have feature vectors denoted as: $\mathbf{pv}_1 = [i_1, a]$ and $\mathbf{pv}_2 = [i_2, b]$, where i_1 and i_2 denote the intensities associated with the corresponding pixel and, a and b are the intensity average in a 5 × 5 neighborhood around each pixel. The neighborhood size was varied between 3 × 3 and 11 × 11. The size 5 × 5 provided the best results and was retained. In general the impact of neighborhood size is not very important;

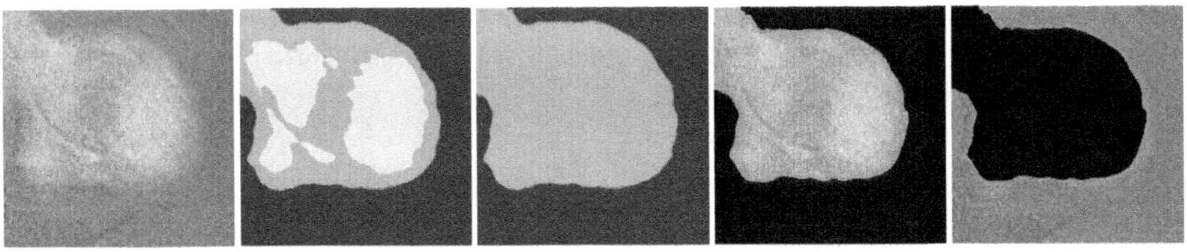

(a) (b) (c) (d) (e)

Fig. 2. (a) Original image (RAO view). (b) Approximate segmentation. (c) Final clustering. (d) Left ventricle cavity. (e) Background region.

however, neighborhood sizes larger than 5×5 increase the computational cost. The similarity matrix ($\mathbf{I}_S$) is an image obtained using the following equation:

$$\mathbf{I}_S = (i_1 - i_2)^2 + (i_1 - b)^2 + (i_2 - a)^2 \ . \tag{3}$$

In the second step a data density function $\mathbf{I}_D$ [18] is obtained by convolving $\mathbf{I}_S$ with a unimodal density mask $\mathbf{K}$ as follows:

$$\mathbf{I}_D = \mathbf{I}_S * \mathbf{K} \ . \tag{4}$$

The density function establishes the degree of dispersion in $\mathbf{I}_S$. A Gaussian distribution with standard deviation σ is used as a density mask [18] as follows:

$$K(i,j) = \left(\frac{1}{2\pi\sigma^2}\right)^{n/2} e^{\frac{-|i+j|^2}{2\sigma^2}}; 0 \leq i,j \leq n \ , \tag{5}$$

where n denotes the mask size. In our case we use $n = 5$ and σ is set as the standard deviation of the smoothed image $\mathbf{I}_P$.

In the third step, an approximate segmentation is performed. All pixels that have an intensity value lower than the standard deviation of image $\mathbf{I}_P$ are considered as seed points for a simple linkage region growing algorithm that is performed on image $\mathbf{I}_D$. A region grows from each of the seed pixels by grouping neighbor pixels that comply with the following uniformity criterion: if the difference between two neighbor pixels is lower than the standard deviation σ_D of image $\mathbf{I}_D$, then both pixels are clustered. This process is applied to the entire image $\mathbf{I}_D$ until all pixels are clustered and tagged. Thus, results achieved provide an approximate segmentation of the input image as more than two regions can be obtained.

The last step of the clustering process improves the segmentation by using a region growing method by multiple linkage [19]. The objective is to obtain only two regions partitioning the ventriculograms: one representing the interior of the left ventricle cavity and the other the background region. Each tagged region obtained in the previous step is a seed region that is represented by a feature vector whose components are the area, the average intensity and the centroid. Neighbor regions are merged when the following uniformity criterion is met: the neighbor regions must provide a minimum for the difference between the average intensity, for the difference between the area and for the Euclidean distance between centroids. This process is applied in an iterative way until only two neighbor regions are left.

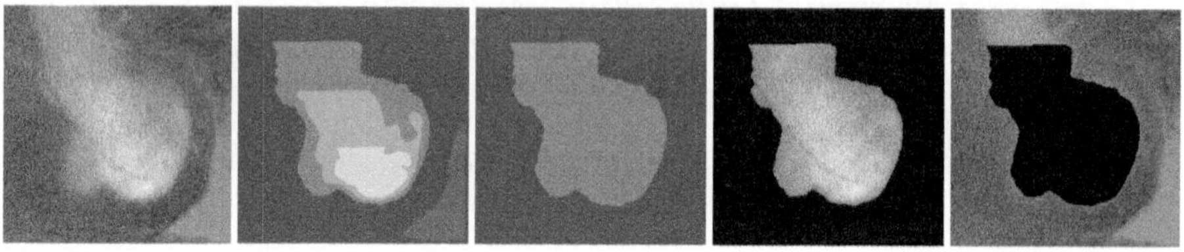

(a) (b) (c) (d) (e)

Fig. 3. (a) End-systole image (LAO view). (b) Approximate segmentation. (c) Clustering results. (d) Left ventricle cavity. (e) Background region.

3 Results

The proposed method has been tested with biplane ventriculograms acquired at several instants of the cardiac cycle. The biplane images were acquired according

Table 1. Components of the feature vector for each of the regions in the end-diastole image

Feature vector	Area (pixels)	Gray-level average	Centroid
Region 0	13305	216	(120,98)
Region 1	16995	152	(105, 106)
Region 2	35236	31	(145, 155)

Table 2. Feature vector for each of the regions in the end-systole image

Feature vector	Area (pixels)	Gray-level average	Centroid
Region 0	35421	52	(62,67)
Region 1	4515	72	(236,220)
Region 2	15172	104	(103,81)
Region 3	7111	156	(135,116)
Region 4	3317	208	(144,174)

Table 3. Feature vector for each of the regions after the first iteration of the multiple linkage clustering in the end-systole image

Feature vector	Area (pixels)	Gray-level average	Centroid
Region 0	39936	52	(62,67)
Region 1	15172	104	(103,81)
Region 2	10428	182	(132,144)

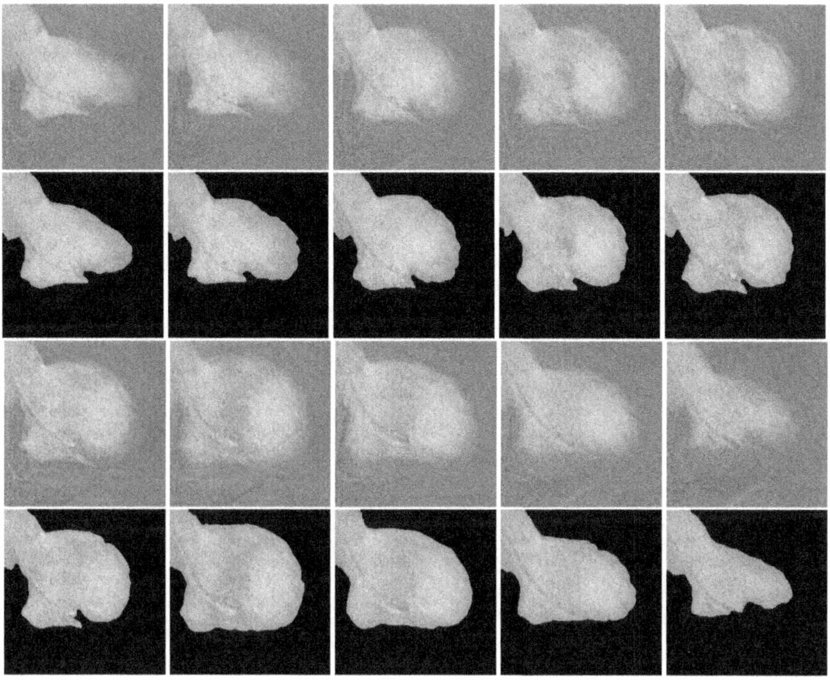

Fig. 4. Segmentation for a RAO view image sequence

to the conventional Left Anterior Oblique (LAO) 60° and Right Anterior Oblique (RAO) 30° views. All images are of size 256×256 pixels. The input images were preprocessed by performing distortion correction and logarithmic subtraction.

Figure 1.a shows the input image that corresponds to the RAO view at the end-diastole instant. Figure 1.b shows the smoothed image using a neighborhood of size 3×3 and figure 1.c shows the image estimated by linear-regression ($\hat{\mathbf{I}}_P$). The similarity image (obtained using equation 3) is shown in figure 1.d. This image is obtained as a quadratic function that combines pixels in the original image with pixels in the smoothed image. As a result the output image has a smoothed appearance. Finally, the density function image is shown in figure 1.e. This image is obtained by convolving a Gaussian function with the similarity image, thus increasing the degree of smoothing. The standard deviation value ($\sigma = 44.63$) is estimated from the smoothed image I_P.

Figure 2.b shows the approximate segmentation where several regions are identified. The standard deviation used for determining the 3 clusters was $\sigma_D = 59.63$. This standard deviation is estimated from the density function image I_D. A feature vector for each of the regions is shown in Table 1. The adjacent regions with a more similar feature vector are regions 0 and 1. The clustering step using multiple linkage provides the final segmentation shown in figure 2.c, where regions 0 and 1 are clustered based on the region growing step. Figure 2.d–2.e shows the two regions obtained from the segmentation process. In figure 3,

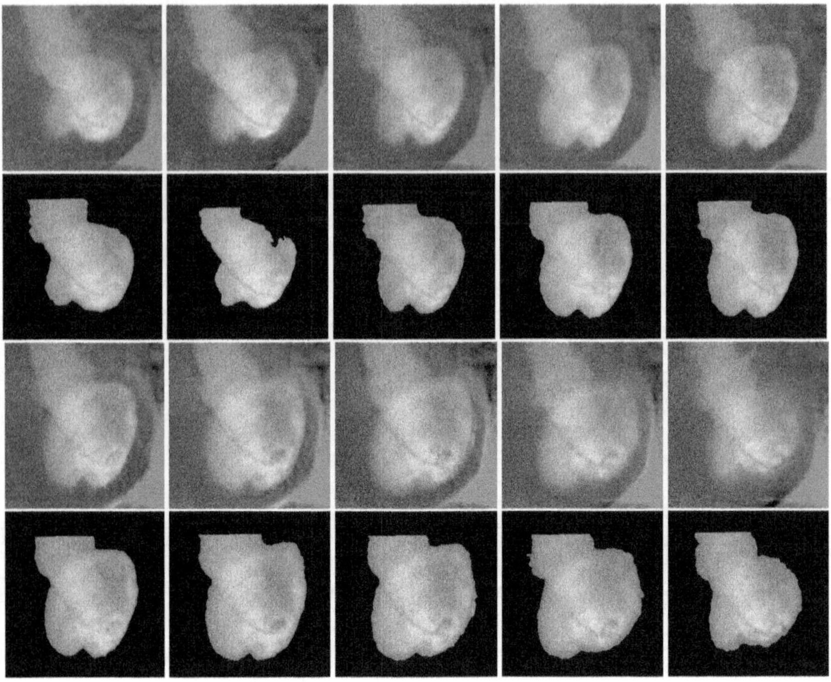

Fig. 5. Segmentation for a LAO view image sequence

results of the segmentation for the end-systole ventriculogram (LAO view) are shown. In this case, five regions have been found at the approximate segmentation step. Table 2 shows the feature vectors for each region. The clustering step is performed using two iterations for attaining the final segmentation. During the first iteration regions 0 and 1 are merged as well as regions 3 and 4. The merged regions have the feature vectors shown in Table 3. During the second iteration regions 1 and 2 are merged providing the final segmentation shown in figure 3.c.

Figure 4 and Figure 5 show the results of the segmentation for a sequence of ventriculograms in the RAO view and LAO view respectively. The first and third rows (from top to bottom) show the original images while the second and fourth rows show the segmentation results.

Validation of the segmentation method is performed by quantifying the difference between the left ventricle shape obtained with respect to the left ventricle shape traced by a cardiologist. The error is expressed as the ratio between the area of the shape difference with respect to area of the union of shapes compared. The error obtained ($mean \pm standard\ deviation$) for a sequence of ventriculograms in the RAO view, including 25 images is 5.47 % ± 1.61 %, with a maximum value of 7.84 % and a minimum value of 2.53 %. When the segmentation is performed for the sequence showing the LAO view (including 25 images) the error is 4.39 % ± 3.41 % with a maximum value of 13.90 % and a minimum value of

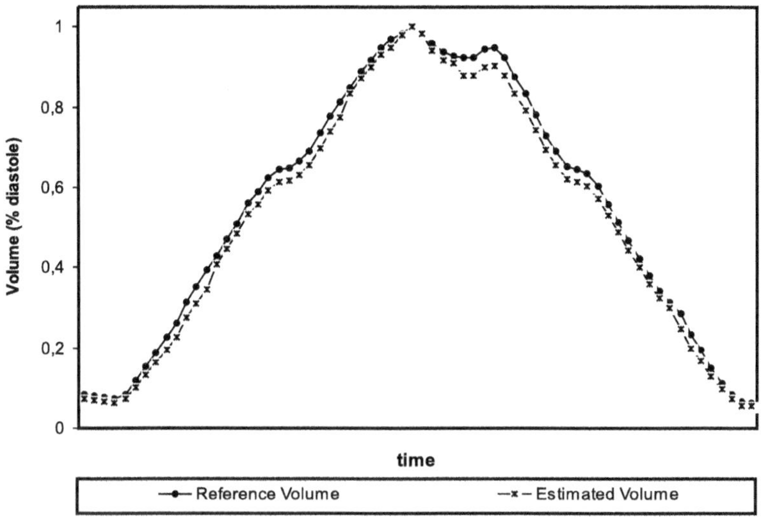

Fig. 6. Left ventricle volume

1.53 %. The error considering the set of 50 images (25 for the RAO view and 25 for the LAO view) is 4.93 % ± 2.69 %. The volume for the left ventricle during the cardiac cycle is estimated using the Area-Length method [20] from the contours obtained using the segmentation method. Fig. 6 shows the left ventricle volume estimated using the contours obtained by the proposed segmentation method (estimated volume) and the volume obtained from contours traced by the cardiologist (reference volume). The volume is normalized with respect to the end-diastole volume. The error obtained by comparing the reference volume with respect to the estimated volume is 4.61 % ± 1.22 %. The ejection fraction [21] for the reference volume is 0.77 and 0.74 for the estimated volume. The percent error is 3.9%.

4 Conclusions

An automatic image segmentation method has been presented. The proposed method is tested using real biplane ventriculograms. The region growing algorithm used as the core of the segmentation process enables the accurate discrimination of the ventricular cavity. The segmentation method does not require any prior knowledge about the ventriculograms and considers the relationship between neighbor pixels.

The segmentation method is conceptually simple and provides an accurate left ventricle contour. The method requires a low computational cost. The proposed approach provides an initial segmentation that is later improved using the multiple linkage region growing algorithm. The initial segmentation could be interpreted as a compression stage that codes the set of groups that represent the image. The initial segmentation could also be considered as the input to other segmentation methods based on clustering or non-supervised learning machines (for instance auto-organized maps or fuzzy logic based techniques). The tests performed on real biplane ventriculograms shows that parameters describing the cardiac function like the volume and the ejection fraction are consistent with the values reported in the literature [22] [23].

As a future research we propose to incorporate other components to the feature vector such as contour curvature and smoothness. In addition, comparison to other methods would be performed. A complete validation is also necessary, including an important number of control subjects as well as cardiac patients. In the validation stage we plan to use other metrics for comparing the segmentation results as for instance the average contour positioning error as in [16]. The validation stage could also include a comparison of estimated parameters describing the cardiac function with respect to results obtained using other imaging modalities like magnetic resonance imaging or multi-slice computerized tomography.

Acknowledgment

The authors would like to thank the Investigation Dean's Office of Universidad Nacional Experimental del Táchira (San Cristóbal, Venezuela) and CDCHT from Universidad de Los Andes (Mérida, Venezuela) for their support to this project.

References

1. R. Duda, P. Hart, and D. Stork. *Pattern Recognition and Scene Analysis (2nd Edition).* John Wiley and Sons, New York, 2000.
2. J. Hubert. Some applications of graph theory to clustering. *Psychometrika*, 39(3):283–309, 1974.
3. R. Horaud and O. Monga. *Vision par ordinateur, outils fondamentaux.* HERMES, Paris, 1993.
4. M. Sonka, V. Hlavac, and R. Boyle. *Image Processing, Analysis and Machine Vision.* PWS Publishing, Pacific Grove, 1999.
5. T. M. Lehmann, D. Beier, C. Thies, and T. Seidl. Segmentation of medical images combining local, regional, global, and hierarchical distances into a bottom-up region merging scheme. In *Proceedings of SPIE*, volume 5747, pages 546–555, 2005.
6. R. Haralick and L. Shapiro. *Computer and Robot Vision*, volume I. Addison-Wesley Publishing Company, USA, 1992.
7. Z. Wu and R. Leahy. An optimal graph theoretic approach to data clustering: Theory and its application to image segmentation. *IEEE Trans. Pattern Recognition Analysis and Machine Inteligence*, 15(11):1101–1113, 1993.
8. R. Urquhart. Graph theoretical clustering based on limited neighborhood sets. *Pattern Recognition*, 13(3):173–187, 1982.
9. R. Medina, M. Garreau, D. Jugo, C. Castillo, and J. Toro. Segmentation of ventricular angiographic images using fuzzy clustering. In *Proceedings of the 17th Annual International Conference of the IEEE EMBS*, pages 405–406, Montreal, 1998.

10. J. Richardt, F. Karl, C. Müller, and R. Klette. The fuzzy local-global duality in detecting pictorial pattern. *Pattern Recognition Letters*, 17(2):187–195, 1996.
11. J. Kennedy, S. Trenholme, I. Kaiser, and S. Wash. Left ventricular volume and mass from single–plane cineangiocardiogram. A comparison of anteroposterior and right anterior oblique methods. *American Heart Journal*, 80(3):343–352, 1970.
12. Osman Ratib. Quantitative analysis of cardiac function. In Isaac Bankman, editor, *Handbook of Medical Imaging: Processing and Analysis*, pages 359–374. Academic Press, San Diego, 2000.
13. R. Medina, M. Garreau, J. Toro, J. L. Coatrieux, and D. Jugo. Three–dimensional reconstruction of left ventricle from two angiographic views: An evidence combination approach. *IEEE Transactions on Systems, Man, and Cybernetics—Part A: Systems and Humans*, 34(3):359–370, 2004.
14. Reducing risk and promoting healthy life. The World Health Report 2002, Geneva, World Health Organization, Julio 2002.
15. K. Suzuki, I. Horiba, N. Sugie, and M. Nanki. Extraction of left ventricular contours from left ventriculograms by means of a neural edge detector. *IEEE Transactions on Medical Imaging*, 23(3):330–339, 2004.
16. E. Oost, G. Koning, M. Sonka, J. Reiber, and B. Lelieveldt. Automated segmentation of X–ray left ventricular angiograms using multi–view active appearance models and dynamic programming. In *Proceedings of the Functional Imaging and Modeling of the Heart: Third International Workshop*, pages 23–31, Barcelona, Spain, 2005.
17. J. Neter, W. Wasserman, and G. Whitmore. *Applied Statistics.* Allyn and Bacon, Boston, 1992.
18. E. Pauwels and G. Frederix. Finding salient regions in images: Non-parametric clustering for images segmentation and grouping. *Computer Vision and Image Understanding*, 75(1,2):73–85, 1999. Special Issue.
19. R. Haralick and L. Shapiro. Survey: Image segmentation techniques. *Computer Vision Graphics and Image Processing*, 29(1):100–132, 1985.
20. H. Dodge, H. Sandler, D. Ballew, and J. Lord. The use of biplane angiocardiography for the measurement of the left ventricular volume in man. *American Heart Journal*, 60:762–776, 1960.
21. S. Yan, B. Lamberto, M. Vladir, and G. Harry. *From Cardiac Catheterization Data to hemodynamic Parameters.* F. A. Davis Company, USA, 1978.
22. J. Kennedy, W. Baxley, M. Figley, H. Dodge, and J. Blackmon. Quantitative angiocardiography. I. The normal left ventricle in man. *Circulation*, 34(2):272–278, 1966.
23. K. Hammermeister, R. Brooks, and J. Warbasse. Rate of change of left ventricular volume in man. I. Validation of peak systolic ejection rate in health and disease. *Circulation*, 49(4):729–738, 1974.

An Image Segmentation Algorithm Using Iteratively the Mean Shift

Roberto Rodríguez and Ana G. Suarez

Institute of Cybernetics, Mathematics and Physics (ICIMAF)
Digital Signal Processing Group
Calle 15 No. 551 e/ C y D CP 10400, La Habana, Cuba
rrm@.icmf.inf.cu

Abstract. Image segmentation plays an important role in many systems of computer vision. The good performance of recognition algorithms depend on the quality of segmented image. According to the opinion of many authors the segmentation concludes when it satisfies the observer's objectives, the more effective methods being the iterative. However, a problem of these algorithms is the stopping criterion. In this work the entropy is used as stopping criterion in the segmentation process by using recursively the mean shift filtering. In such sense a new algorithm is introduced. The good performance of this algorithm is illustrated with extensive experimental results. The obtained results demonstrated that this algorithm is a straightforward extension of the filtering process. In this paper a comparison was carried out between the obtained results with our algorithm and with the *EDISON* System [16].

Keywords: Entropy, image segmentation, mean shift, smoothing filter.

1 Introduction

Segmentation and contour extraction are important steps in many systems of high level. Segmented images are now used routinely in a multitude of different applications, such as, diagnosis, treatment planning, in the robotics, localization of pathology, geology, study of anatomical structure, meteorology, computer-integrated surgery, among others. However, image segmentation remains a difficult task due to both the variability of object shapes and the variation in image quality. In spite of the most complex algorithms developed until the present, segmentation continues being very dependent on the application and it doesn't exist a single method that can solve all the problems that are presented in the universe.

With the aim of obtaining segmentation methods more exact and more effective, several techniques have been proposed in the literature, where a great variety of them has been dedicated to biomedical images [1-7]. Unfortunately, segmentation is a complex problem with no exact solution. Segmentation using traditional low-level image processing techniques, such as thresholding, histogram, region growing and other classical operations requires a considerable amount of interactive guidance in order to attain satisfactory results. Automating these model-free approaches is difficult because of complexity, shadows, and variability within and across individual

J.F. Martínez-Trinidad et al. (Eds.): CIARP 2006, LNCS 4225, pp. 326 – 335, 2006.

objects. Furthermore, noise and other image artifacts can cause incorrect regions or boundary discontinuities in objects recovered from these methods.

At the present time the most robust algorithms in segmentation are the iterative methods, which cover a variety of techniques, from the mathematical morphology, deformable models until the thresholding methods. However, one of the problems of these iterative techniques is the stopping criterion, in which great quantities of methods have been proposed [8-11].

The mean shift is a nonparemetric procedure and it is an extremely versatile tool for feature analysis and can provide reliable solutions for many computer vision tasks. [12]. The mean shift was proposed in 1975 by Fukunaga and Hostetler [13] and largely forgotten until Cheng´s paper [14] rekindled interest in it. The segmentation by using the mean shift as first step carries out a smoothing filter and later on the segmentation process [12].

The term of entropy is not a new concept in the field based on information theory and it has been used in image restoration, edge detection and recently as an objective evaluation method for image segmentation [15].

In this work a new segmentation strategy by using the mean shift is proposed. The new method uses the entropy as stopping criterion, where two steps to obtain the segmented image is not necessary to carry out. The obtained results with our algorithm are compared with the attained results by using *EDISON* System [16]. The results from this preliminary study indicate that the proposed strategy is effective and that at worst these are similar to those reported in [8, 12].

The remainder of the paper is organized as follows: In Section 2, we provide the more significant theoretical aspects of the mean shift. In Section 3, we shortly introduce the entropy concept and we carry out some comments. Then, in Section 4, we describe our segmentation algorithm based on the mean shift and by using the entropy as stopping criterion. The experimental results, comparisons and discussion are presented in Section 5, and Section 6 concludes the paper and discusses future work.

2 The Mean Shift: Analysis

The iterative procedure of the mean shift is introduced as normalized density gradient estimate. By employing a differentiable kernel, an estimate of the density gradient can be defined as the gradient of the kernel density estimate, that is,

$$\hat{\nabla} f(x) \equiv \nabla \hat{f}(x) = \frac{1}{nh^d} \sum_{i=1}^{n} \nabla K\left(\frac{x - x_i}{h}\right) \tag{1}$$

Conditions on the kernel $K(x)$ and the window radio h are derived in [9] to guarantee asymptotic unbiasedness, mean-square consistency, and uniform consistency of the estimate in the expression (1)

For example, for *Epanechikov* kernel

$(K_E(x) = \begin{cases} 1/2\, c_d^{-1}\,(d+2)(1-\|x\|^2) & if\ \|x\|<1 \\ 0 & otherwise \end{cases}$), the density gradient estimate

becomes,

$$\hat{\nabla} f_E(x) = \frac{1}{n(h^d c_d)} \cdot \frac{d+2}{h^2} \sum_{x_i \in S_h(x)} (x_i - x) = \frac{n_x}{n(h^d c_d)} \cdot \frac{d+2}{h^2} \left(\frac{1}{n_x} \sum_{x_i \in S_h(x)} (x_i - x) \right) \quad (2)$$

where the region $S_h(x)$ is a hypersphere of radius h having the volume $h^d c_d$, centered on x, and containing n_x data points, that is, the uniform kernel. The last term in expression (2) is called the *sample mean shift*,

$$M_{h,U}(x) = \frac{1}{n_x} \sum_{x_i \in S_h(x)} (x_i - x) \quad (3)$$

The quantity $\frac{n_x}{n(h^d c_d)}$ is the kernel density estimate $\hat{f}_U(x)$ (the uniform *kernel*) computed with the hypersphere $S_h(x)$, and thus we can write the expression (2) as,

$$\hat{\nabla} f_E(x) = \hat{f}_U(x) \cdot \frac{d+2}{h^2} M_{h,U}(x) \quad (4)$$

which yields,

$$M_{h,U}(x) = \frac{h^2}{d+2} \frac{\hat{\nabla} f_E(x)}{\hat{f}_U(x)} \quad (5)$$

The expression (5) shows that an estimate of the normalized gradient can be obtained by computing the sample mean shift in a uniform kernel centered on x. In addition, the mean shift has the direction of the gradient of the density estimate at x when this estimate is obtained with the *Epanechnikov* kernel. Since the mean shift vector always points towards the direction of the maximum increase in the density, it can define a path leading to a local density maximum that is, to a mode of the density.

A digital image can be represented as a two-dimensional array of p-dimensional vectors (pixels), where $\boldsymbol{p} = 1$ in the gray level case, three for color images, and $\boldsymbol{p} > 3$ in the multispectral case.

As was pointed in [8] when the location and range vectors are concatenated in the joint spatial-range domain of dimension $d = p+2$, their different nature has to be compensated by proper normalization with the h_s and h_r parameters. Thus, the multi-variable kernel is defined as the product of two radially symmetric kernels and the Euclidean metric allows a single bandwidth for each domain, that is,

$$K_{h_s, h_r}(x) = \frac{C}{h_s^2 h_r^p} k\left(\left\| \frac{x^s}{h_s} \right\|^2 \right) k\left(\left\| \frac{x^r}{h_r} \right\|^2 \right)$$

where x^s is the spatial part, x^r is the range part of a feature vector, $k(x)$ the common profile used in both domains, h_s and h_r the employed kernel bandwidths, and C the corresponding normalization constant.

The novelty lies in applying the mean shift procedure for the data points in the joint spatial-range domain.

3 Entropy

From the point of view of digital image processing the entropy is defined according to the following expression,

$$E(x) = -\sum_{x=0}^{2^B-1} p(x) \log_2 p(x) \tag{6}$$

where B is the total quantity of bits of the digitized image and by agreement $log_2 0=0$; $p(x)$ it is the probability of occurrence of a gray-level value. Within a totally uniform region the entropy reaches the minimum value, because one speaking theoretically, the probability of occurrence of the gray-level value is always one. In the practice when one works with real images, the entropy does not reach, in general, the zero value. This is due to the existent noise in the images. Therefore, if we consider the entropy as a measure of the disorder within a system, it could be used as a good stopping criterion into an iterative process by using the mean shift filtering. The entropy within each region diminishes in the measure that the regions become more homogeneous and at the same time in the whole image, until reaching a stable value. When the convergence is reached, a totally segmented image is obtained, because the mean shift filtering is not idempotent as it doesn't happen to some types of filters in the mathematical morphology (for example, with the opening). In addition, as by [8] was pointed out, the mean shift procedure-based image segmentation is a straightforward extension of the discontinuity preserving smoothing algorithm and the segmentation step does not add a significant overhead to the filtering process.

The choice of entropy as a measure of goodness deserves several observations. First, it is known that the addition of two independent random variables (for example, a signal and additive noise) increases the entropy [17]. Entropy reduction reduces the randomness in corrupted probability density function and tries to counteract noise. Then, following this same analysis as the segmented image is a simplified version of the original image, the entropy (segmented image) should be smaller. Recently, it was found empirically that the entropy of the noise diminishes faster than that of the signal [17]. Therefore, an effective criterion would be to stop when the relative rate of change of the entropy, of an iteration to the next one, falls below some threshold.

4 Algorithms

4.1 Filtering Algorithm by Using the Mean Shift

Let X_i and Z_i, $i=1,..,n$, be the input and filtered images in the joint spatial-range domain. For each pixel $p \in X_i$, $p=(x, y, z) \in \Re^3$, where $(x, y) \in \Re^2$ and $z \in [0, 2^\beta - 1]$, β being the quantity of bits/pixel in the image. The filtering algorithm comprises the following steps [8]:

1. Initialize $j=1$ and $y_{i,1} = p_i$
2. Compute through the mean shift (see expression (3), $y_{i,j+1}$), the mode where the pixel converges; that is, the calculation of the mean shift is carried out until convergence, $y = y_{i,c}$.

3. Store at Z_i the component of the gray level of calculated value: $Z_i = (x_i^s , y_{i,c}^r)$, where x_i^s is the spatial component and $y_{i,c}^r$ is the range component.

4.2 Developed Segmentation Algorithm by Using Recursively the Mean Shift Filtering

The proposed algorithm comprise the following steps:

1. Initialize the control values, ***ent1 = 1, errabs = 1, edsEnt***
2. While ***errabs > edsEnt,*** then
3. Do filtrate the image according to the steps of the previous algorithm; store in ***Z*** the filtering image.
4. Do calculate the entropy from the filtered image according to the expression (6); store in ***ent***
5. Do calculate the absolute error with the entropy value obtained in the previous step; ***errabs = abs (ent – ent1)***
6. Do update the value of the parameter; ***ent1 = ent***

It is possible to observe that, in this case, the proposed segmentation algorithm is a straightforward extension of the filtering algorithm, which finishes when the entropy reaches the stability. Note the simplification of this algorithm compared with the one proposed in [8]. A detailed discussion on this issue will be made in the next section.

5 Applications: Discussion

Image segmentation; that is, the decomposition of the gray-level values into homogeneous areas is maybe one of the most important steps in any system of computer vision. Homogeneity, in general, is defined as similarity in pixel values, where a piecewise constant model is enforced over the image [8].

All the segmentation experiments were performed using a uniform kernel. The segmentation of the image lake obtained with the proposed algorithm is shown in Fig. 1b, while in Fig. 1c is presented the obtained results by using *EDISON* System [16].

(a) (b) (c)

Fig. 1. Lake: (a) Original image, (b) Segmented image by our strategy *(hs, hr) = (12, 15)*, (c) Segmented image according to algorithm proposed in en [8], *(hs, hr, M) = (16, 7, 40)*

From the point of view of the visual analysis, it is not observed big differences between the image segmented by our algorithm and the one obtained by the *EDISON* System. However, to say of other observers the sky and the clouds were better segmented with our strategy. Note that all the other details in the segmented image are preserved. Comparing Figs. 1(b) and 1(c), in the part corresponding to the water with our algorithm an additional homogeneous area was obtained. The obtained result in Fig. 1(b) took 9 iterations to reached the convergence; that is, until the stability was reached (no more change). From the point of view of the final result the image segmented with our algorithm has an aspect a little more natural with regard to the original image. In many occasions, given the application, segmentation imposes certain conditions (elimination of regions, prunes or integration of certain maxima, etc). This can originate a biased image with regard to the initial. With our algorithm the resolution is only imposed on the segmentation process; that is, the parameters *hr* and *hs*. For this reason, our algorithm did not make mistakes; that is, a segmented image very different to the original never was obtained.

To better visualize the segmentation process, it is represented in three dimensions in Fig. 2. Observe that the data was reflected over the horizontal axis, while the intensities over *z*. This gives a more informative display. In Fig. 2(a) the segmented image with our algorithm is presented, while in Fig. 2(b) the segmented image with the *EDISON* system. Note that in both representations significant differences are not observed, but in the segmented image with our algorithm one can see other homogeneous areas (do see the central plate of Fig. 2(a) corresponding to the sky and the clouds). It is possible to observe in Fig. 2(a) the integration of large homogeneous regions when the convergence is reached (see the plates). Also, one can see that these plates in both images reached the same level of intensity (see in axis *z*). In spite of with both algorithms very similar results are obtained, the difference underlies in that to obtain the image of Fig. 1(c) it was necessary to carry out a filtering step and other of segmentation. In this last step, one can have certain complexity when adjacency graphs and hierarchical technique are used [8].

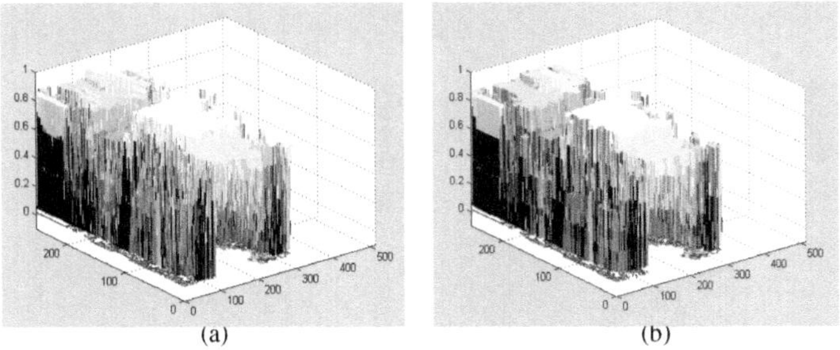

(a) (b)

Fig. 2. Visualization in 3D of the mean shift segmentation. (a) With our algorithm. (b) By using *EDISON* system.

We verified that the segmentation through our algorithm was not very sensitive to the choice of the parameters *hr* and *hs*. This was also tested in [8]. We selected for most of images the same parameters *hr =15* and *hs =12* and ***edsEnt* = *0.005*** as threshold of stopping criterion. This value was empirically found, after carrying out several investigations with different images.

Another segmentation example through our algorithm and using the *EDISON* system is shown in Fig. 3

(a) (b) (c)

Fig. 3. Cameraman: (a) Original image, (b) Segmented image according to our algorithm *hs= 12* and *hr= 15*, (c) Segmented image by using *EDISON* system *hs=8, hr=4*

Note that visually substantial differences are not appreciated between the segmented image with our algorithm and by using *EDISON* system. The convergence with our algorithm in 8 iterations was reached. It is possible to observe that with our strategy the grass is a little more homogeneous as compared with the image of Fig. 3(c). In addition, all the other regions were preserved the same as in the image of Fig. 4(c). Note that the tripod and the buildings were well segmented. However, with our algorithm is not well appreciated the area of the cameraman's hand for an *hr = 15.* In other images segmented with smaller value of *hr* was possible to segment the cameraman's hand. This was not put here for space problem. The range parameter *hr* controls the number of regions in the segmented image [8]. A three-dimensional representation of the segmented images with both methods is shown in Fig. 4.

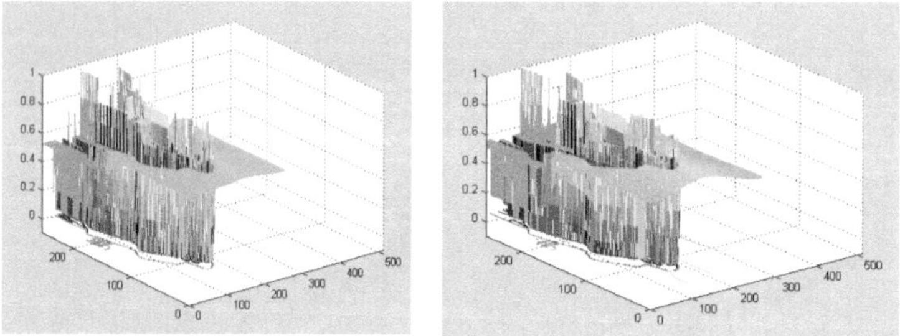

(a) (b)

Fig. 4. Visualization in 3D of the mean shift segmentation. (a) With our algorithm. (b) By using *EDISON* system.

Note in Fig. 4 that in both images is appreciated the plates corresponding to the sky and to the grass, with the slight difference that in the image of Fig. 4(b) the plate of the grass is observed something curved. In the other details, significant differences are not appreciated. The advantage that presents our algorithm compared with the one proposed in [8] is the simplicity of the same one. Our algorithm would be very useful in an automatic segmentation process.

In Fig. 5 another segmentation examples are shown with both methods.

(a) (b) (c)

Fig. 5. (a) Original image, (b) Segmented image according to our algorithm *hs= 12 and hr= 15*, (c) Segmented image using the *EDISON* system; *hs=8, hr=7 y M = 20*

Analyzing, both images visually, one can see that these were segmented well, where it is possible to observe differences in some details, which it are not significant. These differences can be given by the use of different parameters (*hr, hs*). In this case the convergence with our algorithm was reached in 10 iterations. To better visualization of the segmentation process in Fig. 6 are represented in three dimensions.

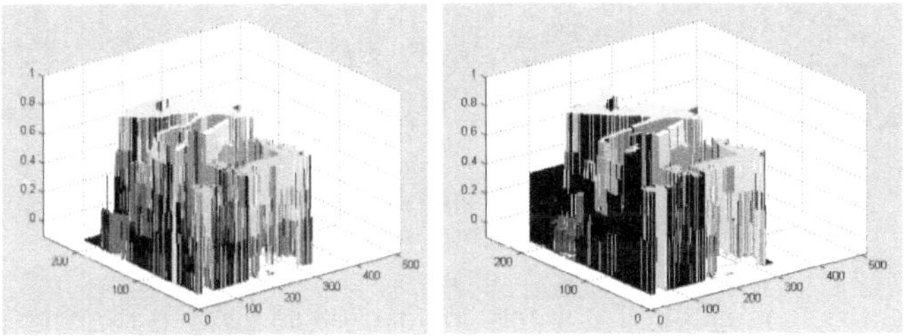

(a) (b)

Fig. 6. 3D visualization of the mean shift segmentation. (a) With our algorithm. (b) By using *EDISON* system.

Note that in both images the plates corresponding to the most homogeneous areas are appreciated with the same levels of intensities (in the axis *z*). It is important to point out that the same as what happened in the segmented images with the *EDISON* system, with those obtained with our algorithm any maximum was not obtained after the convergence was reached.

The abrupt changes that are appreciated in the fall or elevation from a plate to another in the 3D representation are indicative of different regions with different intensities. These correspond to the discontinuities (edges). For example, the window marked in Fig. 5(a) is represented in three dimensions in Fig. 7 (b). It is possible to see in this representation two homogeneous plates corresponding to the sky and the

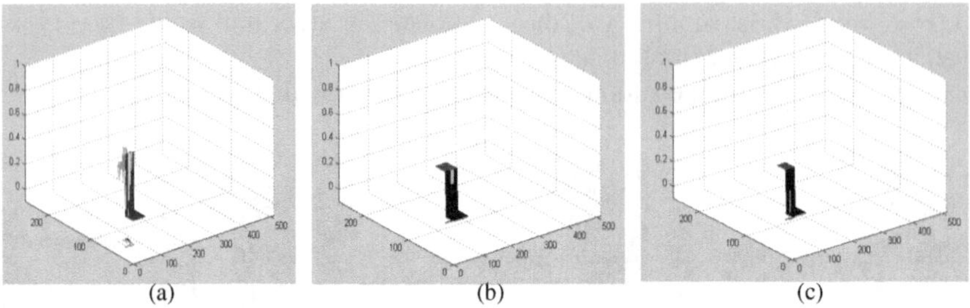

(a) (b) (c)

Fig. 7. Visualization in 3D. (a) Input, (b) Our algorithm, (c) By using *EDISON* system.

roof of the school. Note an abrupt change between a zone and the other one. This means two totally different regions

According to the opinion of some observers with our algorithm the segmented images have a more natural aspect. An example is the result that appears in Fig. 8. Note that the clouds and the sky were better isolated with our algorithm.

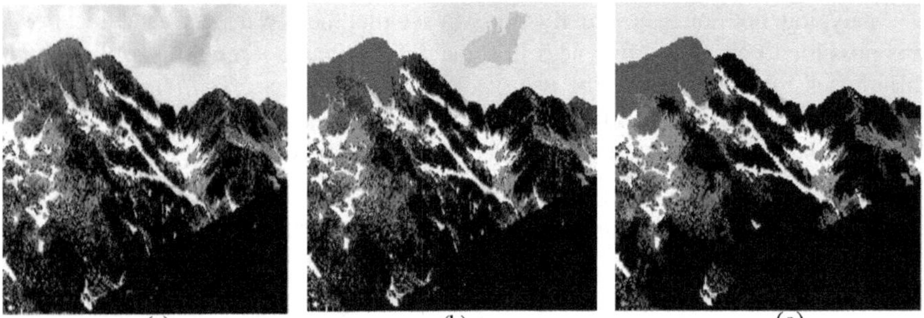

(a) (b) (c)

Fig. 8. (a) Original image, (b) Segmented image according to our algorithm (*hs= 12, hr= 15)*, (c) Segmented image by using *EDISON* system (*hs=8, hr=7 and M = 20*)

It is necessary to point out that in this comparison an analysis from the point of view of the computation time was not carried out, due to that our algorithm was implemented in *MatLab* (ver. 6. 5)), while the *EDISON* system was programmed in *C++*.

6 Conclusions

In this work was proposed a segmentation algorithm using an iterative process of the mean shift filtering. It was tested that the algorithm always converges and through the 3D representation was possible to demonstrate that this convergence always addressed to the homogeneous regions; that is, the different objects. It was verified through the obtained results that our algorithm was effective and that at worst, these (results) were similar to those reported in [8, 12]. From the point of view of the algorithmic complexity this strategy is simpler that the proposal in [8], since adjacency graphs and hierarchical technique is not necessary to use. It was evidenced that this segmentation procedure is a straightforward extension of the filtering algorithm. For this reason, our algorithm did not make mistakes; that is, a segmented image very different to the original never was obtained. This strategy will be extended to the color image segmentation. The results from this preliminary study indicated that the proposed strategy was effective.

References

1. W. Kenong, D. Gauthier and M. D. Levine: "Live Cell Image Segmentation", IEEE Transactions on Biomedical Engineering, vol.42, no. 1, Jun. 1995.
2. J. Sijbers, P. Scheunders, M. Verhoye, A. Van der Linden, D. Van Dyck, E. Raman: "Watershed-based segmentation of 3D MR data for volume quatization", Magnetic Resonance Imaging, vol. 15, no. 6, pp 679-688, 1997.
3. C. Chin-Hsing, J. Lee, J. Wang and C. W. Mao: "Color image segmentation for bladder cancer diagnosis", Mathl. Comput. Modeling, vol. 27, no. 2, pp. 103-120, 1998.
4. Rodríguez, R., Alarcón, T., Wong, R. and Sanchez, L.: "Color segmentation applied to study of the angiogenesis. Part I", Journal of Intelligent and Robotic System, Vol. 34, No.1, May 2002.
5. P. Schmid: "Segmentation of digitized dermatoscopic images by two-dimensional color clustering", IEEE Trans. Med. Imag., vol. 18, no. 2, Feb., 1999.
6. J.E. Koss, F. D. Newman, T. K. Johnson and D. L. Kirch: "Abdominal organ segmentation using texture transforms and a hopfield neural network", IEEE Trans. Med. Imag., vol. 18, no. 7, July, 1999.
7. E. B. Braiek, M. Cheriet and V. Dore: "SKCS-A Separable Kernel Family with Compact Support to improve visual segmentation of handwritten data", Electronic Letters on Computer Vision and Image Anal. 5(1):14-29, 2005
8. Comaniciu, D. and Meer, P.: "Mean Shift: A Robust Approach toward Feature Space Analysis", IEEE Transaction on Pattern Analysis and Machine Intelligence, Vol. 24, No. 5, May 2002.
9. X. Chenyang, P. Dzung and P. Jerry: Image Segmentation Using Deformable Models, SPIE Handbook on Medical Imaging, Medical Image Analysis, Edited by J. M. Fitzpatrick an d M. Sonka, Vol. III, Chapter 3, pp 129- 174, May 2000.
10. Vicent, L ; Soille, P.: "Watersheds in digital spaces: An efficient algorithm based on immersion simulations", IEEE Transact. Pattern Anal. Machine Intell., 13:583-593; 1991.
11. M. Cheriet, J. N. Said and C. Y. Suen: "A Recursive Thresholding Technique for Image Segmentation", IEEE Transactions on Image Processing, Vol. 7, No. 6, June 1998
12. Comaniciu, D. I.: "Nonparametric Robust Method for Computer Vision", Ph.D. thesis, New Brunswick, Rutgers, The State University of New Jersey, January, 2000.
13. Fukunaga, K. and Hostetler, L. D.: "The Estimation of the Gradient of a Density Function", IEEE Trans., Information Theory, Vol. 21, pp. 32-40, 1975.
14. Cheng, Y.: "Mean Shift, Mode Seeking, and Clustering", IEEE Trans., Pattern Analysis and Machine Intelligence, Vol. 17, No. 8, pp. 790-799, Aug. 1995.
15. H. Zhang, J. E. Fritts and S. A. Goldman: "A Entropy-based Objective Evaluation Method for Image Segmentation", Storage and Retrieval Methods and Applications for Multimedia 2004. Edited by Yeung, Minerva M.; Lienhart, Rainer W.; Li, Choung-Sheng, Proceeding of The SPIE Vol. 5307, pp. 38-49 (2003).
16. EDISON: Robust Image Understanding Laboratory, Rutgers University, www.caip.rutgers.edu/riul/
17. Suyash P. Awate and Ross T. Whitaker: "Higher-Order Image Statistics for Unsupervised, Information-Theoretic, Adaptive, Image Filtering", IEEE Trans. Pattern Analysis and Machine Intelligence (PAMI), Pag. 364-376, Vol. 28, No. 3, March 2006.

A Robust Region Based Level Set Framework for Medical Image Segmentation

Yong Yang

School of Information Management, Jiangxi University of Finance and Economics,
Nanchang 330013, P.R. China
greatyyy765@sohu.com

Abstract. In this paper, we present new developments in the formulation of a new class of level set method for medical image segmentation. In this work, a new speed function of level set framework is proposed. The region statistical information, instead of the conventional image gradient information, is fused into the level set fundamental model to improve the robustness of the segmentation for medical images. The new method has some advantages over classical level set methods especially in the situations where edges are weak and fuzzy. A number of experiments on MR, US and CT images were performed to evaluate the new method. Experimental results are given to illustrate the effectiveness and robustness of the method.

1 Introduction

Medical image segmentation is a fundamental problem in medical image processing with numerous applications including but not limited to medical image analysis, 3D visualization, etc. It is the process that automates or facilitates the delineation of anatomical structures and other regions of interest (ROI) based on attributes such as their intensity and spatial location. Many classical segmentation techniques have been developed and detailed surveys can be found in references [1]-[3]. However, medical images are often corrupted by noise and sampling artifacts, which cause considerable difficulties when applying classical segmentation techniques, such as edge detection and thresholding. Therefore, sophisticated automated and semi-automated techniques are required.

To address medical image segmentation problem, active contour model [4]-[5] has recently become one of the most studied techniques for medical image segmentation, where an initial contour is deformed towards the boundary of the object to be detected by minimizing an energy function.

The classical active contour model is a parametric deformable model. Parametric active contour models are very popular and are successfully used in medical image segmentation for extracting image contours such as edges by Kass et al. [4]. However, they have some disadvantages. To make the final result relatively to be insensitive to the initial conditions, Xu and Prince [6] suggested the gradient vector flow (GVF) Snake model. The GVF model is useful when there are boundary concavities. However, the GVF still has topological problems. Chakraborty et al. [7] and Poon et al. [8]

J.F. Martínez-Trinidad et al. (Eds.): CIARP 2006, LNCS 4225, pp. 336 – 344, 2006.

proposed methods to integrate the parametric snake with region segmentation. It requires a priori knowledge of the interest, and can suffer from topological problems. But the parametric deformable models have difficulty in segmentation of topologically complex structures. To overcome this problem, the level set approach was introduced by Osher and Sethian [9] in 1988, and was created to follow the evolution of N-dimensional curves (interfaces) by observing their curvature. Level sets are designed to handle problems in which the evolving interfaces can develop sharp corners and cusps [10]. Most existing shape modeling techniques require that the topology of the object be known before the shape recovery can commence. However, it is not always possible to specify the topology of an object prior to its recovery. One important concern is topological change resulting from tracking the evolution of curve or surface boundaries through time. During their evolution, interfaces may change connectivity and split, thereby undergoing a topological transformation which is often very difficult to follow using traditional approaches. In the level set approach, the convergence to the final result may be relatively independent of the initial shape, and branches, splits and merges can develop without problems as the front moves. Generally, the method may be applied even when no a priori assumptions about the object's topology are made. Most of the challenges in level set approach resulting from the need to construct an adequate model for the speed function.

In this paper, our main contribution is to define a new speed function model, which is based on the image region statistical information. This region statistical information is then incorporated into the level set method instead of the conventional image gradient information. The paper is organized as follows. The level set approach is briefly reviewed in section 2 and our proposed level set framework is described in section 3. The experimental results are discussed in section 4. Some conclusions are drawn in section 5.

2 Level Set Method Model

The level set method was devised by Osher and Sethian [9]. The main idea in the level set method is to describe a closed curve Γ in the image plane as the zero level set of a higher dimensional function $\phi(x,t)$ in $\Re^3$. The value of the ϕ at some point x is defined by

$$\phi(x,t=0)=\pm d \tag{1}$$

where d is the distance from x to $\Gamma(t=0)$, and the sign in Equation (1) is chosen whether the point x lies outside or inside the initial hypersurface $\Gamma(t=0)$. In this manner, Γ is represented by the zero level set $\Gamma(t)=\{x\in R^2 \mid \phi(x,t)=0\}$ of the level set function, and the initial function $\phi(x,t=0)$ with the property that $\Gamma(0)=\{x\in R^2 \mid \phi(x,t=0)=0\}$. The evolution of $\phi(x,t)$ can be modeled as

$$\frac{\partial\phi}{\partial t}+F\|\nabla\phi\|=0 \tag{2}$$

with a given $\phi(x, t = 0)$. At any instant, the position of Γ shall be given as the zero level set of evolving function ϕ. We must have

$$\Gamma(t) = \{x \in R^2 \mid \phi(x,t) = 0\} \tag{3}$$

The speed function F in equation (2) depends on factors like the image gradient. A common choice for F is

$$F = P(I)(1 - \varepsilon k) \tag{4}$$

where $0 < \varepsilon < 1$ is a constant, I is the image intensity and k is the curvature, obtained from divergence of the gradient of the normal vector to the front, curvature k can be defined as

$$k = \frac{\phi_{xx}\phi_y{}^2 - 2\phi_x\phi_y\phi_{xy} + \phi_{yy}\phi_x{}^2}{\left(\phi_x{}^2 + \phi_y{}^2\right)^{\frac{3}{2}}} \tag{5}$$

The term $P(I)$ in equation (4) is an image-dependent halting criteria that can be calculated as

$$P(I) = e^{-|\nabla G_\sigma * I|} \tag{6}$$

where $\nabla G * I$ denotes the image convolved with a Gaussian smoothing filter whose characteristic width is σ. This halting criterion allows model to stop on high image gradient by reducing speed function to zero, thus aligning it to the object boundary. The final level set equation for segmentation is given by

$$\frac{\partial \phi}{\partial t} + P(I)(1 - \varepsilon k)\|\nabla \phi\| = 0 \tag{7}$$

The above motion equation (7) is a partial differential equation in one higher dimension than the original problem. Given the initial value, it can be solved by means of difference operators in a fixed grid via

$$\phi_{ij}{}^{n+1} = \phi_{ij}{}^{n} - \Delta t \cdot h \cdot \begin{pmatrix} \max\left(F_{ij}, 0\right)\nabla^{+} \\ + \min\left(F_{ij}, 0\right)\nabla^{-} \end{pmatrix} \tag{8}$$

where n is the iterative time, h is the grid step, Δt is the time step, F_{ij} is the speed value of pixel (i, j), $\phi_{ij}{}^{n}$ is the level value of pixel (i, j) at time n and where

$$\begin{aligned} \nabla^{+} = [&\max(D_{ij}{}^{-x}\phi, 0)^2 + \min(D_{ij}{}^{+x}\phi, 0)^2 + \\ &\max(D_{ij}{}^{-y}, 0)^2 + \min(D_{ij}{}^{+y}\phi, 0)^2]^{\frac{1}{2}} \end{aligned} \tag{9}$$

$$\nabla^- = [\max(D_{ij}^{+x}\phi,0)^2 + \min(D_{ij}^{-x}\phi,0)^2 + \max(D_{ij}^{+y},0)^2 + \min(D_{ij}^{-y}\phi,0)^2]^{\frac{1}{2}} \tag{10}$$

$$D_{ij}^{-x}\phi = \frac{\phi_{ij}^{n} - \phi_{i-1j}^{n}}{\Delta x} \quad D_{ij}^{+x}\phi = \frac{\phi_{i+1j}^{n} - \phi_{ij}^{n}}{\Delta x} \tag{11}$$

$$D_{ij}^{-y}\phi = \frac{\phi_{ij}^{n} - \phi_{ij-1}^{n}}{\Delta y} \quad D_{ij}^{+y}\phi = \frac{\phi_{ij+1}^{n} - \phi_{ij}^{n}}{\Delta y} \tag{12}$$

This implementation allows the function ϕ to automatically follow topological changes and corners during evolution.

3 Proposed Level Set Method

In this section, a new speed function is proposed which is based on the image region information since the gradient in the conventional level set approach has no meaning for very noisy and low contrast images. This region information is achieved at a global level by a statistical characterization. The core idea is to utilize the probability density function inside and outside of the structure to be segmented. Here, the original speed function proposed by Malladi [11] is employed for it simplicity as:

$$F = h_I(v - \rho k) \tag{13}$$

where v represents an external propagation force, k is the local curvature of the front and acts as a regularization term. The weighting ρ expresses the importance given to regularization and the term h_I is the data consistency and acts as a stopping criterion at the location of the desired boundaries.

Suppose that the image is partitioned into N pixel, labeled by the integers $1,2,\cdots,N$. In most application, the pixel locations or sites will form a regular square lattice. Further suppose that each pixel variable, x_i, $1 \le i \le N$ can take any real value, $x_i \in R$. The values of the pixel variables are called intensities and arbitrary shading will be denoted $x = \{x_1, x_2, \cdots, x_N\}$, hence $x \in R^N$. In general, it is not possible to observe x directly, instead the observed image y is a degraded copy of x .

$$y_i = x_i + \varepsilon_i \ , 1 \le i \le N \tag{14}$$

where $\varepsilon_i \sim N(0,\sigma^2)$,and ε_i and ε_j are independent when $i \ne j$. Let us consider the image $I(x, y)$ could be the Gaussian distribution:

$$P(Y \mid X) = \frac{1}{\sqrt{2\pi}\sigma} \exp\{-\frac{1}{2\sigma^2} \sum_{i=1}^{N} (y_i - x_i)^2\} \tag{15}$$

The goal is to segment the image $I(x, y)$ into two "homogeneous" regions separated by the contour. The region inside the object contour, I_{in}, represents the object region. The region outside the contour, I_{out}, corresponds to the background region. We use the same method as in [12] to incorporate region information into level set method. The sign of v determines the direction of the external propagation force:

$$v = Sign\{a_i p(I_{in}) - (1 - a_i) p(I_{out})\} \tag{16}$$

where $p(I_{in})$ and $p(I_{out})$ denote the likelihood of intensity inside and outside the object, and a_i is the prior of a image to be inside the object. The likelihood $p(I_{in})$ of the curve evolves inside the considered region is given by a Gaussian distribution as follows:

$$p(I_{in}) \propto \frac{1}{\sqrt{2\pi}\sigma_{in}} \exp(-\frac{(I(x) - \mu_{in})^2}{2\sigma^2{}_{in}}) \tag{17}$$

In the same case, where the curve outside the considered region, the likelihood is described by a translated form of the Gaussian as follows:

$$p(I_{out}) \propto \frac{1}{\sqrt{2\pi}\sigma_{out}} \exp(-\frac{(I(x) - \mu_{out})^2}{2\sigma^2{}_{out}}) \tag{18}$$

Set N_{in}, N_{out} to be the number of pixels in the image object and background regions. The corresponding parameters (μ_{in}, σ_{in}) and (μ_{out}, σ_{out}) of the image object and background regions are estimated using maximum likelihood (ML) algorithm.

$$\hat{\mu}_{in} = \frac{1}{N_{in}} \sum_{(x,y) \in I_{in}} I(x, y) \tag{19}$$

$$\hat{\sigma}^2{}_{in} = \frac{1}{N_{in}} \sum_{(x,y) \in I_{in}} I(x, y)^2 - \hat{\mu}_{in}{}^2 \tag{20}$$

$$\hat{\mu}_{out} = \frac{1}{N_{out}} \sum_{(x,y) \in I_{out}} I(x, y) \tag{21}$$

$$\hat{\sigma}^2{}_{out} = \frac{1}{N_{out}} \sum_{(x,y) \in I_{out}} I(x, y)^2 - \hat{\mu}_{out}{}^2 \tag{22}$$

As discussed in [13], the maximum likelihood estimation of the target shape can be obtained by maximizing the likelihood.

$$p(I) = p(I_{in}, I_{out} \mid I) \tag{23}$$

Based on the bayes rule:

$$p(I) = \prod_{(x,y)\in I_{in}} p(I_{in}) \prod_{(x,y)\in I_{out}} p(I_{out}) \tag{24}$$

Since the consistency term h_I is proportion to the probability $p(I)$ of the closest point on the current interface, the final expression of the new consistency term h_I can be defined as:

$$h_I = \exp\{-k \cdot p(I)\} \tag{25}$$

Therefore, according to equation (13) then the new speed function can be defined as:

$$F = h_I(v - \rho k) = (v - \rho k) \cdot \exp\{-k \cdot p(I)\} \tag{26}$$

4 Experimental Results

To demonstrate the results of our new speed function for the level set framework, we carried out a series of experiments on different modalities medical images, such as MR, US and CT images. The performance of the proposed method is compared with that of standard level set method.

We first consider segmenting the cerebrospinal fluid (CSF) from a 2D brain MR corpus callosum image with poor contrast. Fig.1 (a) shows the original image, Fig.1 (b) shows the initial curve. The results of the standard level set method and the proposed method are displayed in Fig.1 (c) and (d) respectively. In order to give clear vision about the results, Fig.1 (e) and (f) give the contours corresponding to the segmented regions in Fig.1 (c) and (d). It is observed from the results that with the standard level set method the CSF is under-segmented especially in the middle extended region as show in Fig.1 (e), while with the proposed method the CSF is accurately segmented as shown in Fig.1 (f).

We then test the two methods using a US image. As we know, the US image quality is very poor and the region boundaries seem to be very fuzzy. Fig.2 shows the results on a US image with both strong and fuzzy region boundaries. Fig.2 (a) shows the original image, Fig.2 (b) shows the initial curve, Fig.2 (c) and (d) give the results of the original level set method and our method, respectively. The segmented contours corresponding to Fig.2 (c) and (d) are illustrated in Fig.2 (e) and (f). Compared to the standard level set method, it is noted that the proposed method can effectively segment the region of interest (ROI) even if the extracting features with fuzzy boundary or with poorly defined edges.

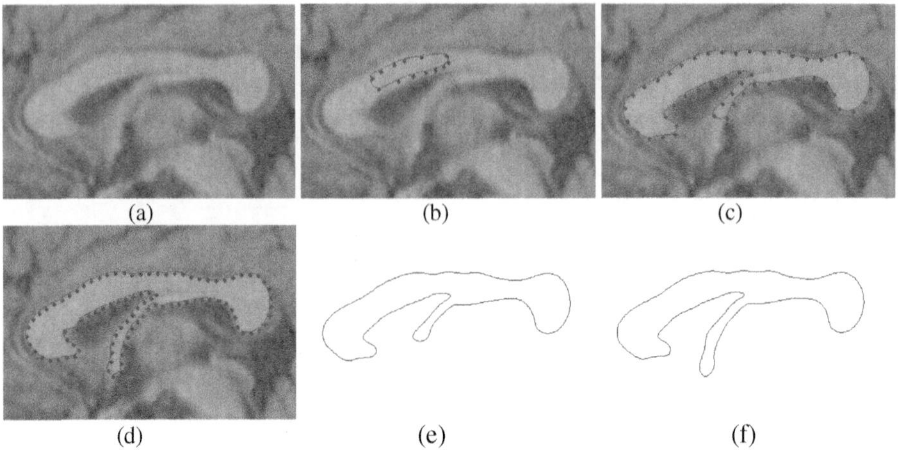

Fig. 1. Brain MR corpus callosum image segmentation results. (a) Original image; (b) Initial curve; (c) Standard level set method result; (d) Our proposed method result; (e) Contour of the segmented region in (c); (f) Contour of the segmented region in (d).

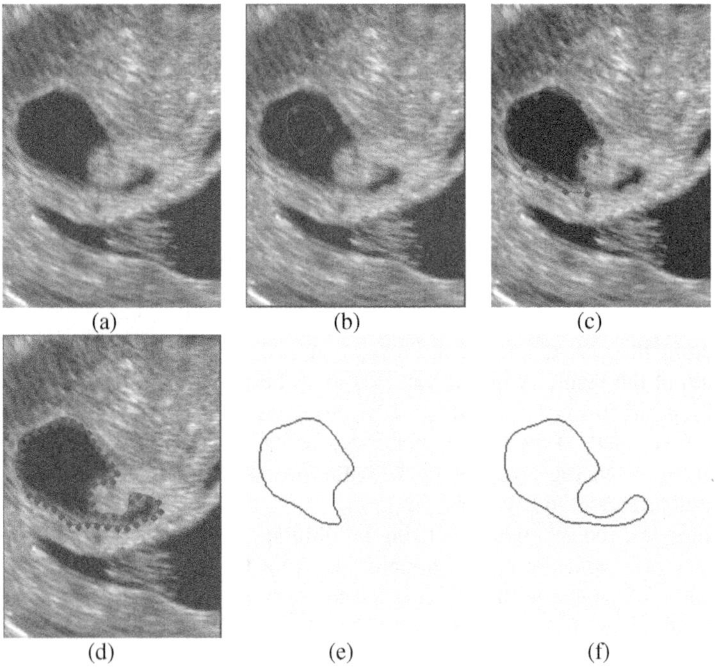

Fig. 2. US image segmentation results. (a) Original image; (b) Initial curve; (c) Standard level set method result; (d) Our proposed method result; (e) Contour of the segmented region in (c); (f) Contour of the segmented region in (d).

We also test the robustness of our algorithm to noise. We add Gussian noise to a CT image of the liver as shown in Fig.3 (a), then segment it. Fig.3 (a) is the original image and Fig.3 (b) is the degraded noisy image. The results for comparison are given in Fig.3 (c)-(g). The results clearly demonstrate the superior segmentation quality of our approach in the noisy situation.

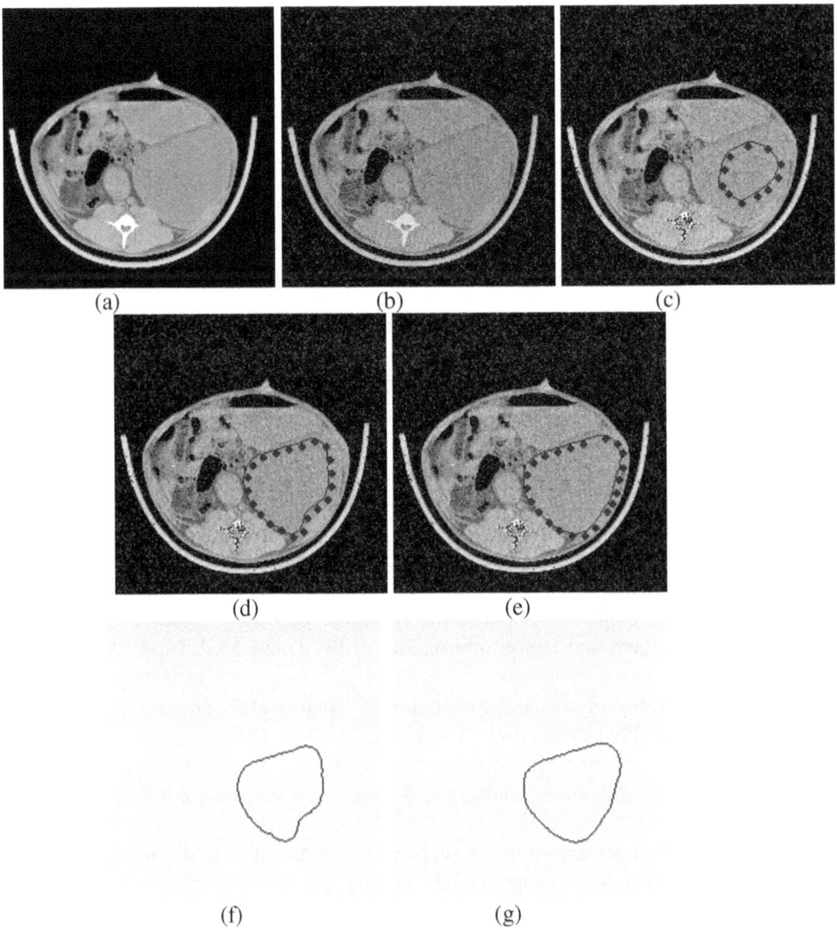

(a) (b) (c) (d) (e) (f) (g)

Fig. 3. CT image segmentation results. (a) Original image; (b) Noisy image; (c) Initial curve; (d) Standard level set method result; (e) Our proposed method result; (f) Contour of the segmented region in (d); (g) Contour of the segmented region in (e).

As mentioned above, we have demonstrated that our method seems ideal for use in a wide variety of medical images. The proposed method can be used to segment images with poor image contrast, fuzzy or diffuse boundary and noise.

5 Conclusions

We have introduced a framework of level set method based on region statistical information. The framework can conveniently incorporate region features into speed function. The method incorporated the region statistical information into the level set fundamental model, instead of the image gradient information. The method has been tested with numerical real modalities medical images, such as MR, US and CT images. We have presented some preliminary experimental results to illustrate the flavor of this technique. The proposed method has been proven to be effective and robust for the segmentation. Future work will focus on the validation of the proposed approach on a variety of medical images.

References

1. S. K. Fu, J. K. Mui: A survey on image segmentation, Pattern Recognition, Vol. 13, (1981) 3-16.
2. R. M. Haralick, L. G. Shapiro: Image segmentation techniques, Comput.Vision Graphics Image Process., Vol. 29, (1985) 100-132.
3. N. Pal, S. Pal: A review on image segmentation techniques, Pattern Recognition, Vol. 26, (1993) 1277-1294.
4. M. Kass, A. Witkin,and D. Terzopoulos: Snakes: Active contour models, International Journal of Computer Vision, Vol. 1, (1987) 321-331.
5. C. Ciofolo, C. Barillot: Brain Segmentation with Competitive Level Sets and Fuzzy Control., Lecture Notes in Computer Science, Vol. 3565, (2005) 333-344.
6. C. Xu and J. Prince: Generalized Gradient Vector Flow External Forces for Active Contours, Signal Processing, Vol. 71, (1998) 131-139.
7. A. Chakraborty, L. Staib, and J. Duncan: Deformable boundary finding in medical image by integrating gradient and region information, IEEE Trans. Med. Imag., Vol.15, (1996) 859-870.
8. C. S. Poon and M. Braun: Image segmentation by a deformable contour model incorporating region analysis, Phys. Med. Biol., Vol.42, (1997) 1833-1841.
9. S. Osher and J. A. Sethian: Propagating with Curvature Dependent Speed: Algorithms Based on Hamilton-Jacobi Formulations, Journal of Computational Physics, Vol. 79, (1998) 12-49.
10. N. Paragios: A level set approach for shape-driven segmentation and tracking of the left ventricle, IEEE Trans. Med. Imag., Vol. 22, (2003) 773–776.
11. R. Malladi, J. Sethian, and B. Vemuri: Shape modeling with front propagation: A level set approach, IEEE Trans. PAMI, Vol.17, (1995) 158-175.
12. C. Baillard and C. Barillot: Robust 3D segmentation of anatomical structures with level sets, Proceedings of MICCAI, (2000) 237-245.
13. F.Reitich and H.M.Soner: Three-Phase Boundary Motions Under Constant Velocities Part One: The Vanishing Surface Tension Limit, Proc. Royal Soc. Edinburgh, Vol. 126, (1996) 837-865.

Color Texture Segmentation Based on Quaternion-Gabor Features

Wang Xiao-Hui, Zhou Yue, Wang Yong-Gang, and Zhu WeiWei

Institute of Image Processing and Pattern Recognition,
ShangHai JiaoTong University, ShangHai, 200240, China
{chocobowang, wygang}@gmail.com,
{zhouyue, zhuww}@sjtu.edu.cn

Abstract. This paper proposed a new framework for color texture segmentation which integrated the color and texture features. Quaternion-Gabor filter was first introduced in this paper for color texture segmentation. The algorithm achieved color texture multichannel Gabor filtering through DRBFT and IDRBFT. And the quaternion-Gabor filter extracted the input color image's color features and texture features at the same time. The proposed method was tested using different mosaic and natural images. Despite the simplicity of the whole algorithm, the segmentation results were rather encouraging.

Keywords: DRBFT, RBs, MCF, k-means.

1 Introduction

Sangwine introduced the first example of a holistic color image filter based on quaternion convolution in 1998 [1]. Although encouraging results have been achieved in color image processing based on quaternions, the multiplication rule of quaternions was not commutative, which restricted the applications of quaternions in signal and image processing. To address this problem, Pei et al. introduced reduced biquaternions (RBs) in digital signal and image processing in 2004 [2]. The multiplication rule of RBs was commutative. One of its advantages was that many existing conventional complex Fourier transform algorithm could be used to implement the discrete reduced biquaternions Fourier transform (DRBFT).

The multichannel filtering (MCF) approaches have appeared to be one of the most successful grey texture segmentation algorithms among all the grey texture segmentation methods. The problem of using MCF algorithm to process color image is how to implement the color image convolution. In this paper color images are represented and processed using RBs. With the DRBFT and corresponding IDRBFT algorithm, we can implement the color image holistic convolution successfully. Therefore, many existing Gabor filtering algorithms which have ever been used to process grey images can be extended to process color images [3][4]. In this paper the Converging Squares Algorithm (CSA) algorithm that has described in [4] is used to design the channels of the MCF. That is to say the number of channels and channel parameters are automatically determined from power spectrum of input color images.

J.F. Martínez-Trinidad et al. (Eds.): CIARP 2006, LNCS 4225, pp. 345 – 353, 2006.

In this paper after the input images are filtered by MCF our method analyzes the color texture using the concept of textons. First we combine each pixel's filtering outputs' amplitudes and phases into a vector. Since the feature vectors are highly correlated, we use the principal components analysis (PCA) [7] to reduce the feature space's dimensionality. Then the k-means [6] method is adopted to cluster the reduced dimension's feature vector and then the region merging algorithm is employed to combine the adjacent clusters that achieved by the k-means method. At last if the texture edge is not very accurate, a special thresholding method will be adopted based on the mean grey value, where each pixel's grey level value is computed with a small neighborhoods (e.g. 7×7) around it.

The rest of this paper is organized as follows: the MCF algorithm and the RBs, DRBFT and IDRBFT are briefly introduced in Section 2 and Section 3 respectively. The principle of the proposed color texture segmentation algorithm is described in Section 4 and some experimental results are given in Section 5 to demonstrate the effectiveness of the proposed color texture analysis algorithm. Finally, we conclude this paper in Section 6 and present future work.

2 Multichannel Filter Model (MCF)

Bovik et al. proposed the multichannel texture filtering technique that relies on 2-D Gabor filters to isolate regions of perceptually homogeneous texture in an image [3]. A special case of the Gabor filter is the daisy petal filter, in which the filter lobes radiate from the origin of the spatial frequency domain [3] [4]. In this paper a bank of daisy petal Gabor filters is used to encode the input color images into multiple complex-modulated sub-images.

The continuous domain impulse response function of the daisy petal Gabor filter can be wrote as the following general form:

$$h(x,y) = g(x',y')\cdot \exp[2\pi jFx'] . \tag{1}$$

where $(x',y') = (x\cos\phi + y\sin\phi, -x\sin\phi + y\cos\phi)$ are notation of coordinates, major oriented at an angle ϕ from the x-axis. F is radial centre frequency, and $j = \sqrt{-1}$.

The Gaussian component is

$$g(x,y) = (\frac{1}{2\pi\lambda\sigma^2})\cdot \exp(-\frac{(x/\lambda)^2 + y^2}{2\sigma^2}). \tag{2}$$

where σ is the Gaussian scale factor and λ is the aspect ratio between the x and y axes. The spatial frequency response of the daisy petal Gabor filter (1) is

$$H(u,v) = exp\{-2\pi^2\sigma^2[(u'-F)^2\lambda^2 + (v')^2]\}. \tag{3}$$

Like the algorithm used in [4], the Converging Squares Algorithm (CSA) proposed by O'Gorman and Sanderson [5] is also used in this paper to detect the spectral peak and determine the channels parameters.

3 Reduced Biquaternions (RBs)

In 2004 Pei et al. adopted RBs to represent and process color image [2]. The representation of RBs is

$$q = q_r + q_i i + q_j j + q_k k = (q_r + q_i i) + (q_j + q_k i) j \equiv q_a + q_b j. \tag{4}$$

where q_a and q_b are two complex numbers, q_r, q_i, q_j and q_k are real numbers, and i, j, k obey the rules as follows:

$$ij = ji = k,\ jk = kj = i,\ ik = ki = -j,\ i^2 = k^2 = -1,\ j^2 = 1. \tag{5}$$

Therefore, from (5) we can find that the multiplication of RBs is commutative. It is a unique advantage over the quaternions.

Similar to the quaternion, an RB can also be uniquely represented by a polar form if $\delta \neq 0$:

$$q = q_r + q_i i + q_j j + q_k k = A e^{i\theta_i} e^{j\theta_j} e^{k\theta_k} \tag{6}$$

where $A = |q| = \sqrt[4]{\delta} \geq 0, \theta_i \in (-\pi, \pi], \theta_j \in R, \theta_k \in (-\pi/2, \pi/2]$,and the definition of δ and the proof of (5) can be found in [2].

In paper [2], the author defined two types' DRBFT. In this paper we use the DRBFT of type 1[2]:

$$F_{(RB1)}(p,s) = \sum_{m=0}^{M-1} \sum_{n=0}^{N-1} f(m,n) e^{-2\pi (i\frac{pm}{M} + j\frac{sn}{N})}. \tag{7}$$

where $f(m,n)$ is a 2-D RBs signal, and $i^2 = j^2 = -1$. The RB Fourier transform can be implemented by decomposing the RBFT into a pair of conventional complex Fourier transform. So first step is to decompose the RB into following form [2]:

$$f(m,n) = f_a(m,n) + f_b(m,n) j \tag{8}$$

Then

$$F_{(\mathrm{RB})}(p,s) = \mathrm{DFT}(f_a(m,n)) + \mathrm{DFT}(f_b(m,n) j). \tag{9}$$

Thus, two conventional complex 2-D DFTs can be used to implement the RBFT.

The definition of RB convolution is

$$g(m,n) = f(m,n) *_{RB} h(m,n) = \sum_{\tau=0}^{M-1} \sum_{\eta=0}^{N-1} f(m-\tau, n-\eta) h(\tau, \eta). \tag{10}$$

where $*_{\mathrm{RB}}$ is RB convolution.

The multiplication rule of RBs is commutative. Here we can get:

$$g(m,n) \equiv \mathrm{IDRBFT}\{F_{(RB)}(p,s) H_{(RB)}(p,s)\} = f(m,n) *_{RB} h(m,n). \tag{11}$$

4 The Proposed Color Texture Segmentation New Algorithm

The principles of the proposed color texture segmentation algorithm can be better explained by referring to the block diagram given in Fig. 1. The whole algorithm is divided into eight successive steps: spectral peak detection, multichannel filtering, channel grouping, dimension reduction, k-means clustering, region merging, thresholding and post-processing.

Spectral peak detection, just as described in the preceding section, using the CSA algorithm determines the number of multichannel filtering channels and frequencies and orientations of each channel.

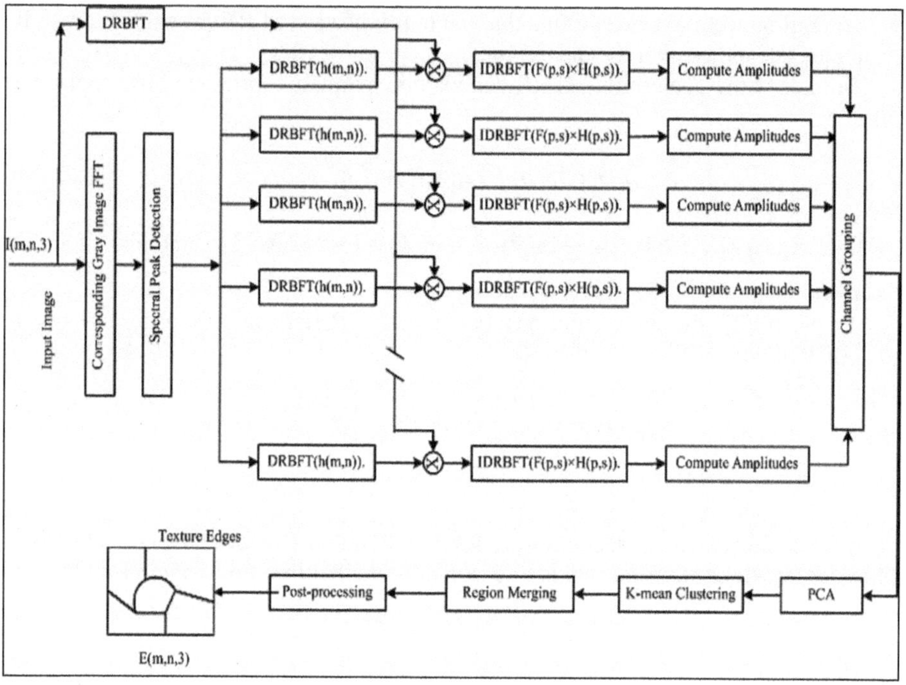

Fig. 1. Block Diagram of the Proposed Algorithm

Then the next step is multichannel filtering. To computer the convolution between the input color image and Gabor filter kernel, the input color image and the Gabor kernel are expressed using RBs firstly. Then we can calculate the RBBDT of the input color image and the Gabor kernel. At last the convolution between the input color image and Gabor filter kernel of each channel can be calculated using (11).

After getting the each channel's filtering result, we compute the amplitudes and phases of each channel's output. And then the amplitudes and phases of each pixel are combined to a feature vector. Just as former explanations, the filtering output of each channel is a RB matrix. So each pixel has the form of formula (4). For each channel we compute three amplitudes of the filtering result. We use (6) to get the first amplitude. And we look on the first two parts of RB: $q_r + q_i i$ and the last two parts of RB: $q_j + q_k i$ as two general complex numbers, so we can use the general definition of a complex number's amplitude compute the other two amplitudes. Through experiments, we find that using three amplitudes can gain much more edge information of the input color image. Therefore, in this paper three amplitudes are used rather than one which can provide better discriminating power. From (6), we can compute three phases from each channel's output. And the three phases can also be used to identify the input color image's edge. Then we combine each pixel's filtering outputs' amplitudes and phases into a vector. Therefore, each pixel (m_i, n_j) is now represented by an n -dimensional feature vector.

Since the extracted feature vectors are highly correlated, we use the principal components analysis (PCA) [7] to reduce the feature space's dimensionality. Then the following stage is to classify each image pixel using the k-means algorithm in terms of the each pixel's feature vector. This segmentation is often referred to the conception of textons. From the output of the k-means clustering, we can get the each pixel's rough classification information.

Then a region merging method is used to combine adjacent clusters which are statistically similar. The initial clustering is based on k-means cluster with k set to be larger than the anticipated number of final regions. As a result, after the initial clustering some regions still need to be merged. The region merging is done in an agglomerative manner where in each iteration the two most similar regions are merged. The similarity of two regions R_i and R_j is given by

$$\zeta_{i,j} = (u_i - u_j)^T [\Sigma_i + \Sigma_j]^{-1} (u_i - u_j) \tag{12}$$

where u_i , u_j are the mean vectors and Σ_i , Σ_j are the covariance matrices computed from the feature vectors of regions R_i and R_j respectively. Here we use the region similarity measure analogous to the one proposed in Nguyen et al.[8].

The last stage is obtaining the segmentation image from the region merging result by a special thresholding method. Each image pixel's thresholding value is determined in terms of average grey level value of $w \times w$ window centered on it. Finally from the thresholding image, the color texture edge can be detected and superimposed on the original color texture image.

5 Segmentation Results

The proposed algorithm has been tested extensively with a variety of synthetic and natural color textures. And the segmentation results using the proposed algorithm are compared with JSEG (J measure based SEGmentation according to [9]) algorithm.

The color textures used in this paper are mainly obtained from the VisTex color texture images database [10] and the Berkeley Segmentation Dataset [11]. The VisTex texture images and Berkeley Segmentation Dataset are both available to the public from their web sites.

Fig. 2 shows the segmentation results of mosaic color images. Owing to only color feature can be used to segment, the JSEG algorithm can not obtain good segmentation result. Fig. 2(a) shows the JSEG algorithm can not identify the color texture because there is only texture feature of different orientation that can be used to segment. Fig. 2(b)(c) show the JSEG algorithm over segment the input images. Fig. 2(d)(e)(f) show the segmentation results of the proposed algorithm. The results are rather good because of the proposed algorithm can adopt the input image's color features and texture features to segment.

The segmentation results of natural color images are shown in Fig. 3. The segmentation results of the JSEG algorithm are showed in Fig. 3(a)(c)(e)(g). Because natural images have enough color features, the segmentation results of the JSEG algorithm are very good. The segmentation results of the proposed algorithm are showed in Fig. 3(b)(d)(f)(h). Not that all the important objects in the images are well identified. The segmentation results are nearly close to or even exceed the segmentation results of JSEG.

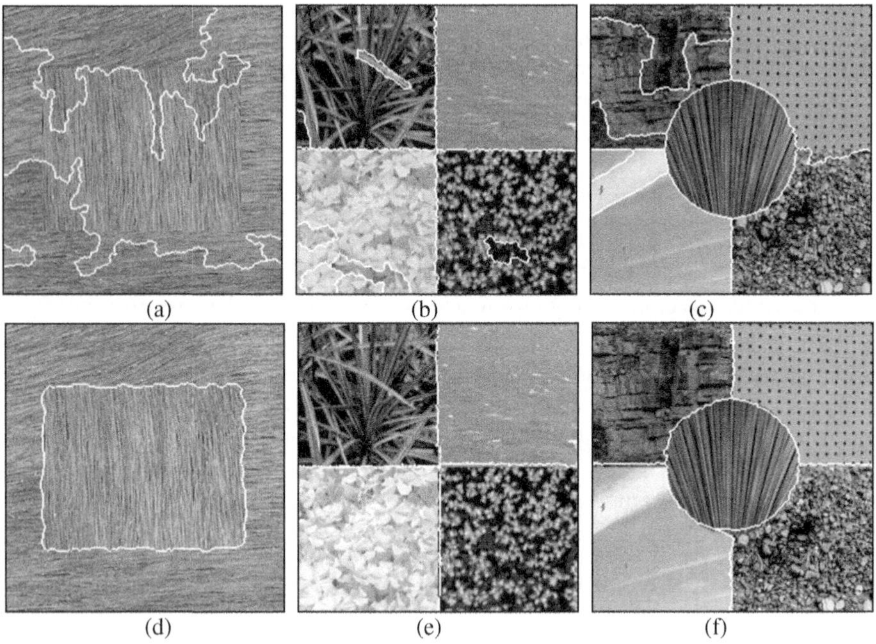

Fig. 2. Segmentation results of mosaic images. (a) (b) (c) Segmentation results using the JSEG algorithm (d) (e) (f) Segmentation results using proposed algorithm.

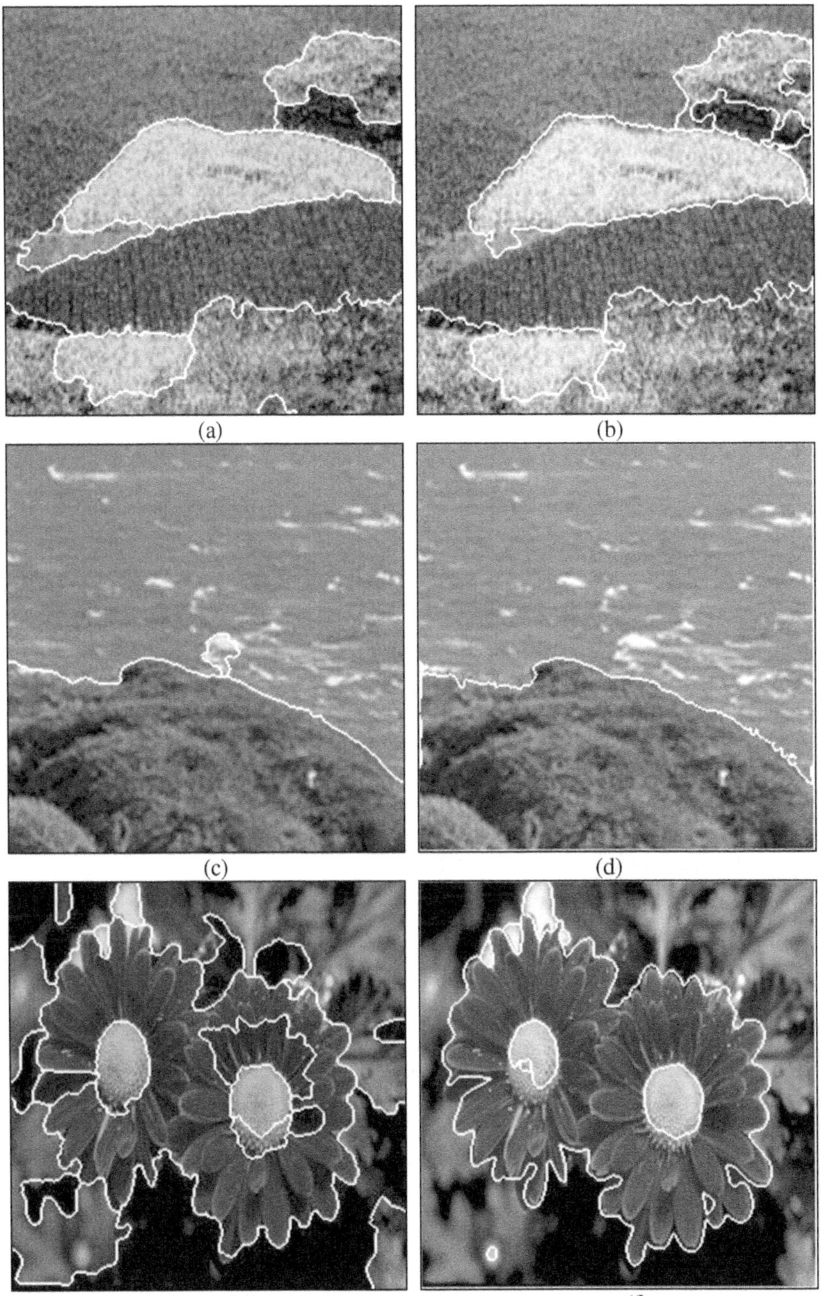

(a) (b) (c) (d) (e) (f)

Fig. 3. Segmentation results of some natural images. (a) (c) (e) (g) Segmentation results using the JSEG algorithm and (b) (d) (f) (h) segmentation results using the proposed algorithm.

(g) (h)

Fig. 3. *(continued)*

6 Conclusions

A new framework was developed for color texture segmentation which integrated the color and the texture features. The contribution of color features and contribution of texture features were both used for color texture discrimination. And the quaternion-Gabor filter extracted the input color image's color features and texture features at one time. The method was applied to various mosaic and natural images. And the segmentation results obtained showed a remarkable segmentation. In conclusion, color texture segmentation and other color image processing techniques based on quaternions will become more and more attractive. In the future work, we plan to find method to fix the k in k-means automatically.

References

1. S. J. Sangwine, "Color image edge detector based on quaternion convolution," Electronics Papers, Vol. 34 No. 10, pp.969-971, May, 1998.
2. Soo-Chang Pei, Ja-Han Chang, and Jian-Jiun Ding, "Commutative reduced biquaternions and their Fourier transform for signal and image processing Applications," IEEE Transactions on Signal Processing, Vol. 51, No. 7, pp.2012-2031, July, 2004.
3. A. C. Bovik, M. Clark and W. S. Geisler, "Multichannel texture analysis using localized spatial filters," IEEE Transactions on Pattern Analysis and Machine Intelligence, No. 12, pp.55-73, 1990.
4. T. N. Tan, "Texture Edge Detection by Modelling Visual Cortical Channels", Pattern Recognition, Vol.28, No.9, pp.1283-1298, 1995.
5. L. O'Gorman and A. C. Sanderson, "The converging squares algorithm: an efficient method for locating peaks in multidimensions," IEEE Transactions on Pattern Analysis and Machine Intelligence, Vol.6, No. 3, pp.280-288, 1984.
6. A. K. Jain and R. C. Dubes, Algorithms for clustering data. Prentice Hall, Advanced Reference Series, New Jersey, 1988.

7. M. Kirby, F. Weissor, G. Dangelmayr, "A model problem in the representation of digital image sequences," Pattern Recognition, Vol. 26, No.1, pp.63-73,1993.
8. H. Nguyen, M. Worring, A. Dev, "Detection of moving objects in video using a robust motion similarity measure," IEEE Transactions on Image Processing, Vol.9, pp.137-141, 2000.
9. Y.Deng, and B.S.Manjunath, "Unsupervised segmentation of color-texture regions in images and video," IEEE Transactions on Pattern Analysis and Machine Intelligence, Vol. 23, No.8, pp.800-810, Aug., 2001.
10. VisTex. http://vismod.media.mit.edu/vismod/imagery/VisionTexture/vistex.html
11. Berkeley Segmentation Dataset. http://www.eecs.berkeley.edu/Research/Projects/CS/vision/grouping/segbench/

Corner Detection by Searching Two Class Pattern Substrings

Hermilo Sánchez-Cruz

Centro de Ciencias Básicas. Universidad Autónoma de Aguascalientes
Av. Universidad 940, Col. Universidad, CP. 20100
Aguascalientes, Aguascalientes. México. Fax: (52 449) 9 10 84 01
hsanchez@correo.uaa.mx

Abstract. A new method for corner detection is proposed. Previous approaches for detecting corners rely on computing angle functions to find changes of curvature. Generally, those methods employ eight different symbols to represent contour shapes. The method of this work is based on using three symbols of a chain code to find pattern substrings, detecting corners in the contour shape. The method relies on searching for the relationship among neighbor points, finding two basic pattern contour chain elements, requiring few computing power to obtain shape corners.

Keywords: Corner; Contour; Chain element; Freeman chain code; Three-symbol chain code; Pattern substrings.

1 Introduction

In literature, usually the aim in obtaining corner points by computing angles of curvature on the contours of shapes is studied. Freeman and Davis [1] proposed to find corners by computing incremental curvature to represent contour shapes by an eight-direction chain code. Since then, many authors have suggested to use this code when representing contour shapes. Part of the algorithm presented by Teh and Chin [2] consists on computing the curvature of contour points and detecting corners by a process of nonmaxima suppression. Liu and Srinath [3] have compared a number of corner detectors due to Medioni and Yasumoto [4], Beus and Tiu [5], Rosenfeld and Johnston [6], Rosenfeld and Weska [7] and Cheng and Hsu [8]. All those authors represented samples of shapes through a sequence of eight direction changes from 0-7, known as the Freeman Chain Code [9]. We propose here to use a method of only three relative direction changes (Fig. 1a). Techniques due to Freeman chain codes in finding corner detection are based on eight different directions (see Fig. 1b).

An advantage in using three symbols is its low storage power, as can be seen by the recent work duo to Sánchez-Cruz & Rodríguez-Dagnino [10]. They found that coding with three symbols is sufficient to represent binary shapes saving storage efficiently. However, recently Yong Kui Liu & Boruk Zalik[11], found efficient storage properties in using the eight directions of Freeman chain code.

J.F. Martínez-Trinidad et al. (Eds.): CIARP 2006, LNCS 4225, pp. 354–362, 2006.

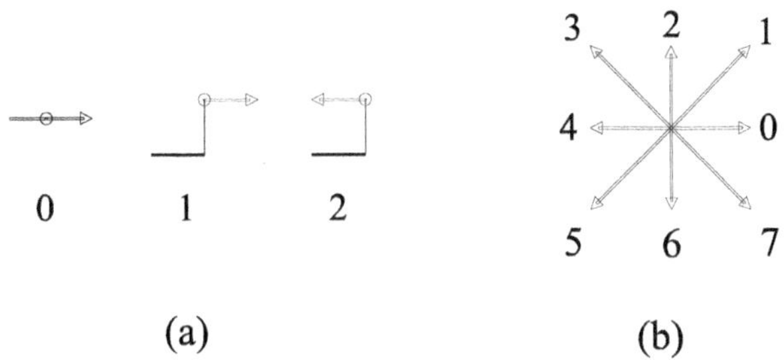

Fig. 1. Two chain codes: (a) Three-symbol, (b) Freeman chain code

However, the number of symbols of Fig. 1a. constitute an advantage in finding a small set of pattern substrings.

For each orthogonal change direction code, chain segments are divided in three parts (given in Fig. 1a.): a *reference segment* (in Fig. 1a. appears as horizontal segment in each code), *a basis segment* (perpendicular to reference segment) and a segment indicating a direction change with regard to reference segment.

The meaning of the three symbols (see Ref[12] for 3D case), given by the set $\mathcal{C} = \{0,1,2\}$, is as follows: the element 0 represents the direction change which means to go straight through the contiguous straight line segments following the direction of the last segment; the 1 indicates a direction change upward with regard to the reference segment; and 2 means to "go back" with regard to the direction of the reference segment. Under certain constrictions, when this particular symbol appears in a contour shape, could easily indicate an existing corner. In Section 2 definitions concerning to this article are presented, seeking the problem as a pattern substring search to obtain corners. In Section 3 some rules to detect corner points are proposed; in Section 4 experimental proving of postulated rules are applied on some binary shapes; and in Section 5 some conclusions are given.

2 Definitions Related to Pattern Chain Substrings

Our proposal method considers to find a specific set of pattern substrings of length l, trying to find all those substrings in a chain code that mach with those patterns. Let us consider, for example $l = 9$ as the length of the substring. Which substrings are all composed of 9 symbols and which of them are considered corner chains? In fact, there are substrings composed of 9 symbols, of course, not all are considered corner chains due to its low curvature or because the region they are associated in the contour shape is not "well behaved", as we explain at once.

Let $\mathcal{P}$ denote the *complete chain code* associated to the shape contour, given by the string of symbols p_i of eq(1).

$$\mathcal{P} = p_1 p_2 \cdots p_n, \tag{1}$$

and P the contour discrete perimeter, given by the number of symbols of the chain code.

Consider a substring template of l symbols: $\mathcal{C} \in \mathcal{P}$, given by eq(2).

$$C = a_1 a_2 \cdots a_l, \quad l \ll P, \tag{2}$$

as a *contour chain element*, or simply: *chain element*, this is, a small piece of contour from the whole shape contour.

Let us consider $m = l/2$ the middle point of a substring of size l, so that a_m, the pivot, be the center of the substring. It is possible to associate a pair of line segments to any chain element. They can be drown up from to the opposite end points, producing an angle φ. We define a *well behaved* chain element when an angle has been subtended by a pair of associated line segments such that the chain does not form loops. In Figure 2 are presented some examples of chain elements. In Figure 2(a), (b) and (d) angles defined by midpoints denoted by a small circle, are well behaved, but that presented by Figure 2(c) is not.

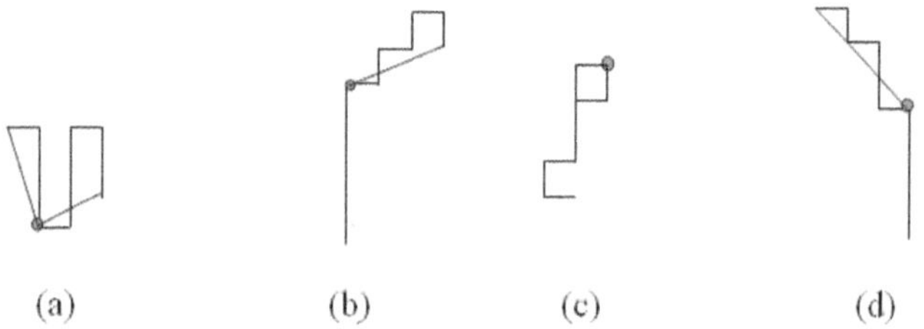

Fig. 2. It is associated a pair of line segments to each of the substring from their middle points

Once well behaved condition is accepted, the angle φ between the two well behaved line segments can be computed, and a threshold is fixed to propose a chain corner.

We define a *neighborhood of radii* r, when considering a piece of the complete string; this region is composed of a small number of symbols in comparing with the whole contour chain code, r symbols on one hand of a particular pivot symbol, and r symbols on the other side of the pivot symbol. An example of neighborhood of radii 5 is: 00000(1+2)10011. This is, a chain element having 00000 in its left first part, 10011 in the right second part, and 1 or 2 (1+2, to abreviate) as a pivot symbol.

To save calculation of corner-angles or curvature changes directly, instead we give a family of substrings and whose angle subtended by well behaved line segments represents a high curvature. Well behaved substrings should not be considered a corner chain when their corner chains associated angles are so much obtuse. Quantitatively, how acute or how obtuse has to be an associated angle to consider a chain element as a corner?

To find pattern substrings, our experimets make us to consider an angle φ associated to a chain corner if $\varphi = [0°, \pm 126°]$ (or $\varphi = [0, \pi \pm \frac{\pi}{3}]$ in radians).

Fig. 3. A well behaved substring and its associated angle

For example, in Fig. 3 a chain element 110110011 is shown, covering the chain from bottom to up, with an associated angle $\varphi = 165.35$, the chain is not considered a corner.

Another definition we need is a *well behaved contour shape*, this is, a contour shape having been smoothed in such a manner that there is no noise or local defects.

3 Rules for Detecting Chain Corners

Part of the study made to find a simple pattern of substrings that represent corners, is to analyse the whole universe of a small vicinity of shape contours, the chain elements. At the begining, to search these patterns, we did our experiments within a vicinity of nine segments in chain elements, giving good results in finding chain corners.

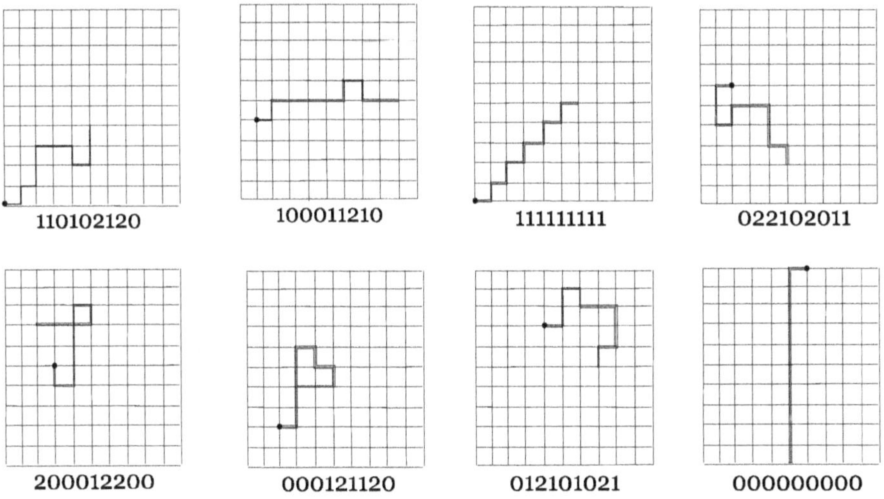

Fig. 4. Eight samples of substrings composed of eleven segments

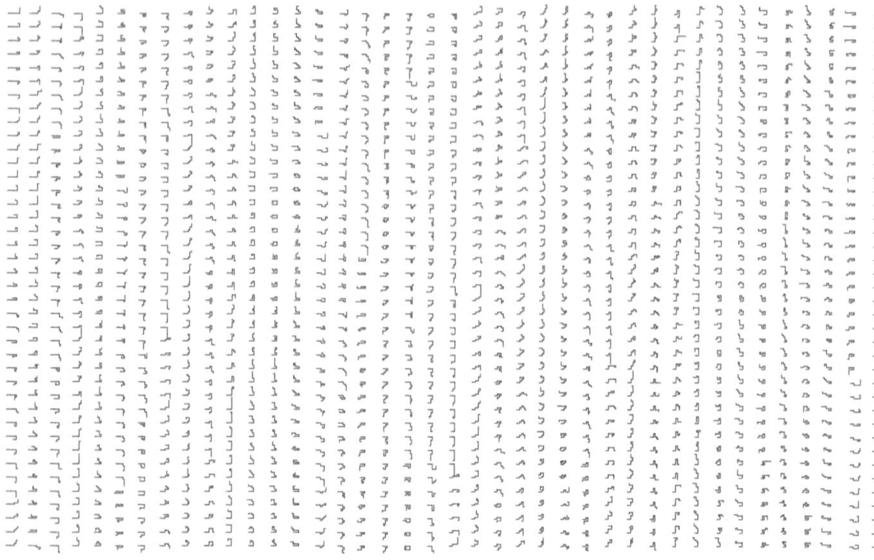

Fig. 5. Part (1 600) of the 6 432 chain elements in the range $[0^o, \pm 126^o]$

We are focused on finding a group of pattern substrings or pattern chain elements considered as chain corners. Eleven chain segments are considered for our study, nine of them are labeled with symbols, representing ortogonal direction changes. The first two are called reference segment and basis segment, respectively. There are a huge number of combinations given by nine symbols (11 segments) in a grid of 10×10. Fig. 4 shows only eight samples.

Even more, fixing the reference segment of the chain, there are 3^9 combinations duo to the other nine chain directions.

There are many possible combinations of chain elements. From this set, we are interested on finding chain elements that have no loops. Looking for these chain elements there are 11 025.

Computing the associated angle to each of these elements, there are 6 432 chain elementes in the range of $[0°, \pm 126°]$. See Fig. 5.

By analizing the different chain sets mentioned, we have observed that pattern substrings representing corners, or even, line elements can be obtained. Parameters we have to take into account are the next:

l: states for the size of substring.

q: represents "many" times a symbol is repeated in a substring. This quantity depends on resolution of binary object. By *many* we define that the number of symbols is greater than the quantity: $l/4$, so $q \in [l/4, l]$.

A way to obtain a complete set of templates considered chains corners, is to search all the substrings arrays composed of l symbols from the set $\mathcal{C} = \{0,1,2\}$, calculate the angle associated to each substring and apply the threshold to see

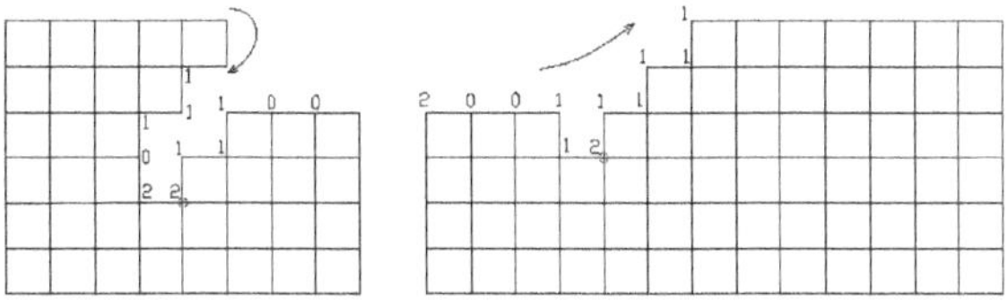

Fig. 6. Examples of chain elements, covering the contour on clockwise sense, of kind S_2. The grid is part of the inner shape.

if it is a chain corner. But we propose a small enough set of template substrings to find the evident chain corners from an arbitrary set of 2D shapes.

As we have computed, from the 6 432 chain elements, there are 4 334 (more than two third parts of the set) chain elements with symbol '2' near the pivot, with associated angles in the range $0° \pm 126°$, whereas only 614 (sligthly more than a third part) from the range $\pm 18°$, that can be considered as a rect lines set (1 547 chain elements). So, to simplify the pattern of chain elements that correspond to chain corners, lets consider only the case where the contour of the image is also a well behaved contour, and consider only those chains that better fit to a pair of associated segments. In this case we are talking about pattern strings of discrete chain corners, postulated by next regular expressions:

$$S_1 = (0 + 1 + 2)^{l/2}(\mathbf{2})(0 + 1 + 2)^{l/2}$$

$$S_2 = (0^q + 1)^{l/2}(\mathbf{1})(0 + 1^q)^{l/2} + (0 + 1^q)^{l/2}(\mathbf{1})(0^q + 1)^{l/2} + (0^q + 1)^{l/2}(\mathbf{1})(0^q + 1)^{l/2} \quad (3)$$

where q represents *many* symbols. For example, pattern S_1 means the pivot is a '2' symbol, independently of the symbols on both sides; whereas S_2 means that substring has many zeros or ones behind the middle symbol and many zeros or ones in the second part of the substring, or many zeros on both sides of a one pivot. Our proposed method relies on looking for these pattern substrings on any contour shape.

We consider shapes represented by resolution cells, each having a value 0 or 1. Contour shape is covered in the clockwise sense. For the implementation of an algorithm to encode this shape we have to visit the ones that represent the contour shape, i.e., the ones of the boundary. Using the three code symbols we follow the contour of the shape counter clockwise, and we give one of the three relative chain codes according to each orthogonal change direction. A manner to fix every orthogonal change is by defining a 3×3 window, then we choose a starting one as the core of the window, and we analyze its neighborhood by finding directed vectors on the boundary of the shape. Hence, we calculate the changes and produce the code. This procedure continues until visiting all ones of the boundary. The object is confined to a minimum rectangle that is visited line by line, from left to right and from top to bottom. The first cell resolution, of the object to be visited, is that which appears at the leftmost and highest part of the occupied region. Fig. 6 shows examples of representing part of contour shape by giving the three symbols of the orthogonal directions given in Figure 1a. When we start to go over the contour the first two discrete segments do not represent a direction change with regard to reference segment. When one ends to go over the contour, it is possible to give chain elements at starting point and contiguous direction change because of last reference segments visited. Given this representation, we can reconstruct the original image by interpreting the code of every symbol in terms of the direction changes that can follow. Finally, the pattern substrings, S_1 and S_2 are parsing the resulting chain string of the complete contour.

4 Proving the Postulated Rules

Consider the set of three shapes $\mathcal{S} = \{Plant,\ Hammer,\ Circles,\ Tigger\}$.

Consider the *Plant* shape object and its corresponding chain code (Fig. 7), 34 chain corners were found in its contour shape. Some of them are so closed, in such a manner that their corresponding pivots are in the neighborhood of each other, in this case we could define only one corner. In Table 1 is listed each of the chain elements and the corresponding class pattern given by eq(3) of the *Plant* shape contour.

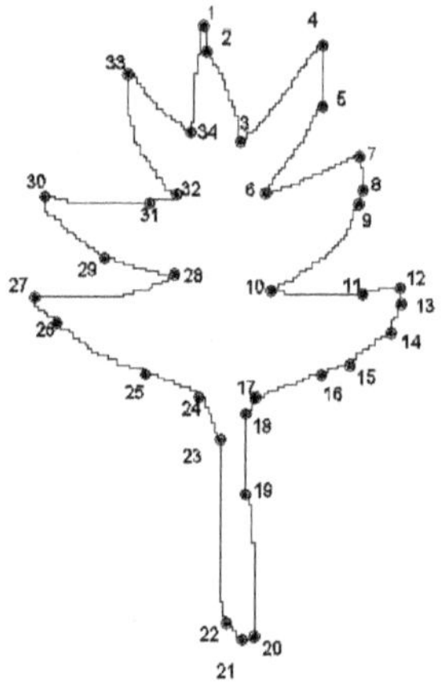

(a)

1211000000110110111101101100110011011001100000000121010101111111111101111111110111111011110111111011111
1010200000000000000000002111011011011011011111110111111011111111011011202100110011001111001100110110110
1101101102000110000000210001101100110011011111111111111110110101011011111110011011012000110000000000000
00000000002100001100000002000021000111100011101101010110110101011111000110011011000110110110001101100111
10010110111100000000000000000000000000021001100000000000001100000000000000000000000000000000211002101011111101
1000011000000000000000000000000000000000000000000000000000110110011001101100101111011001101100110110001
1110001100010100110011011111101101011100101111011110111002000000000000000000000000000001100110000111
0110110120000110001100011001100110011011110111101111111011111010110111000020021000110000000000000000000
0000000210000000001020110101101010111101111110011110000110011000000000000020211011110111111110101111011
1101111112001100000000000000001100000110000000

(b)

Fig. 7. *Plant* shape and its corresponding 3-symbol chain code: (a) the shape; (b) its chain code

Table 1. Chain elements encountered from the Fig. 7 that belong to one of the two classes of chain patterns postulated. Corners 6,30 and 33 are split by two closed chain corners.

Num corner	*Chain element*	*Class pattern*	*Num corner*	*Chain element*	*Class pattern*
1	00001211000	S_1	19	00000210011	S_1
2	00000110110	S_2	20	00000211002	S_1
3	00001210101	S_1	21	21100210101	S_1
4	11010200000	S_1	22	00110110010	S_2
5	00000211101	S_1	23	00110110001	S_2
6a	11011202100	S_1	24	10001111000	S_2
6b	01120210011	S_1	25	11000101001	S_2
7	10110200011	S_1	26	01001100110	S_2
8	00000210001	S_1	27	11100200000	S_1
9	10001101100	S_2	28	01101200001	S_1
10	01101200011	S_1	29	10001100110	S_2
11	00000210000	S_1	30a	10000200210	S_1
12	00000200002	S_1	30b	00200210001	S_1
13	00000200002	S_1	31	00000210000	S_1
14	10001111000	S_2	32	00010201101	S_2
15	00011110001	S_2	33a	00000202110	S_1
16	10001100110	S_2	33b	00020211011	S_1
17	00110110001	S_2	34	11111200110	S_1
18	10001101100	S_2			

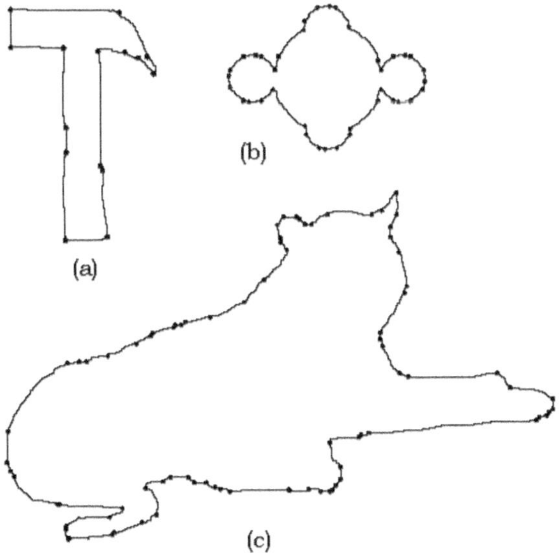

Fig. 8. Sample shapes, (a) *Hammer*, (b) *Circles* and (b) *Tigger* shapes and their corresponding corner points

Figure 8 shows the results of applying the method proposed to search chain corners on the sample objects.

5 Conclusions

With this method we have found shape corners including where shape is apparently circular, like happening with figure constructed by intersecting circles. We used three symbols to represent binary shapes, implying to save time and memory storage to manage this kind of objects. We found patter substrings to obtain most important shape corners in contour shapes preventing to compute angles and curvatures. The method, also, is suitable to find corners on regular shapes, like *Hammer*, or on irregular shapes, like *Tigger*. We have presented a new research topic, in avoiding computing explicitly angles and curvatures. A universal and simplified set of pattern substrings, comparing with other chain codes in literature is suggested to be investigated. As future work most be studied if this method is invariant under scale and rotation transforms.

Acknowledgments

We would like to thank PROMEP program and CONACyT council for their support in finishing this work.

References

1. Freeman, H. and Davis, L. S.: A Corner-Finding Algorithm for Chain-Coded Curves. IEEE Trans. Comput. 26: (1977) 297-303.
2. Teh, C-H. and Chin, R.T.: On the Detection of Dominant Points on Digital Curves. IEEE Trans of Pattern Anal and Mach Int. 11 (8) (1989) 859-872.
3. Liu, H-C; Srinath, M.D.: Corner Detection From Chain-code. Pattern Recognition. 23 (1/2) (1990) 51-68.
4. Medioni, G.; Yasumoto, Y.: Corner detection and curve representation using cubic B-Splines. Comput. Vision Graphics Image Process. 39: (1987) 267-278.
5. Beus, H.L.; Tiu, S.S. H.: An improved corner detection algorithm based on chain-coded plane curves. Pattern Recognition. 20 (1987) 291-296.
6. Rosenfeld, A.; Johnston, E.: Angle detection on digital curves. IEEE Trans Comput. 22: (1973) 875-878.
7. Rosenfeld, A.; Weszka, J.S: An improved method of angle detection on diginal curves. IEEE Trans. Comput. 24: (1975) 940-941.
8. Cheng, F.; Hsu, W.: Parallel algorithm for corner finding on digital curves. Pattern Recognition Lett. 8: (1988) 47-53.
9. Freeman, H.: On the Encoding of Arbitrary Geometric Configurations, IRE Trans. on Electr. Comp. 10 (2) (1961) 260-268.
10. Sánchez-Cruz, H.; Rodríguez-Dagnino, R. M.: Compressing bi-level images by means of a 3-bit chain code. Optical Engineering. SPIE. 44 (9) (2005) pp 1-8. 097004.
11. Liu, Yong K.; Zalik, B.: An efficient chain code with Huffman coding. Pattern Recognition 38 (4) (2005) 553-557.
12. Bribiesca, E.: A chain code for representing 3D curves. Pattern Recognition. 33(5)(2000),755-765.

Model-Based Localization Method by Non-speech Sound Via Wavelet Transform and Dynamic Neural Network

Albert Marzàbal, Antoni Grau, and Yolanda Bolea

Automatic Control Dept, Technical University of Catalonia UPC,
c/ Pau Gargallo 5, 08028 Barcelona, Catalonia, Spain
{albert.marzabal, antoni.grau, yolanda.bolea}@upc.edu

Abstract. Non-speech sound processing is of great interest for indoor mobile robot localization. This paper presents a technique based on feature extraction from continuous wavelet transform (CWT) and a dynamic feed-forward neural network that will approximate the position of the robot in the spatial domain. The link between the function approximation stage (ANN) and the feature extraction stage (CWT) is performed by feature comparative analysis.

1 Introduction

The reverberation effects in a closed room depend mainly on the walls characteristics –such as paralelism, distances and absortion coefficient– and, to a lesser extent, on the objects characteristics located in the room.

Due to reverberations, a sound source located in a specific and known point in the room –a milling machine for instance– characterizes the sound register acquired in different points in the room for the effects of signal bounces feed-forward and cancellation. Since the reverberation effect in the temporal composition of the samples depends on the distance and the signal wavelength, a register composed with different frequencies will also contain information of reverberations in different frequencies. Based on this effect, this work studies the use of non-speech sound information to develop a model-based localization method for mobile robots.

Huang et al. [4] proposed a sound localization method based on a model of human auditory to cope with echoes and reverberations, performing a psychological research over human listener skills, and they propose an acustical preprocess for inhibite input sound when the composition of echoes and reverberations is high. By the other hand, Cowling & Citte [5] presented a comparative study for different techniques that are tipically used in music recognition. They showed that the use of continuous wavelet transform yields good classification rates. In [6], the use of neural networks to sound recognition demostrates to be a useful tool to achieve high rates in patterns identification and recognition.

In a previous work, Bolea et al. [1] have also dealt with non-speech sound localization using wavelet transform and proposed a polynomical transformation

J.F. Martínez-Trinidad et al. (Eds.): CIARP 2006, LNCS 4225, pp. 363–370, 2006.

from the feature domain to the spatial domain. The work presented interesting results but it did not cover the non-linealities that sound reverberation presents. For this reason, in this work we collect a set of sound registers that will be classified with a dynamic *(feed-forward)* neural network in the bidimensional space (Section 4). In [2] the use of continuous wavelet transform has been applied to recognition of industrial sound sources, and [3] also uses wavelet transform to detect defects in laser welding by this industrial sound.

In this work we proposed the use of the continuous wavelet transform (Section 2) for its great capability of characterize the information contained in the sound signal. In Section 3 the feature extraction from the wavelet coefficients is presented, and some interesting experiments with a mobile robot are shown in Section 5.

In Figure 1 the complet procedure is shown. Firstly, the sound is obtained with an ommidirectional microphone in a room (later, in Section 5 there is a description of how the sound is acquired). The signal, digitally sampled and coped, is entered to the wavelet transform block. The output of this stage are the coeffcients of the CWT which are used as input for the feature extraction stage that reduces largely the amount of data and prepares the input for the neural network. There are two steps: the learning step and the recognition step. The network is trained with a huge number of sound samples and it is validated with another subset of samples. In the following sections, the different stages are explained.

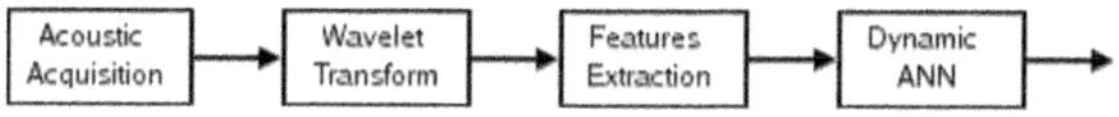

Fig. 1. Localization by non-speech sound features process

2 Continuous Wavelet Transform

Wavelet analysis is similar to Fourier analysis in the sense that it breaks a signal down into its constituent parts for analysis. Whereas the Fourier transform breaks the signal into a series of sine waves of different frequencies, the wavelet transform breaks the signal into its "wavelets", scaled and shifted versions of the "mother wavelet".

When analysing signals of a non-stationary nature, it is often beneficial to be able to acquire a correlation between the time and frequency domains of a signal. The Fourier transform, provides information about the frequency domain, however localised time information is essentially lost in the process. The problem with this is the inability to associate features in the frequency domain with their location in time, as an alteration in the frequency spectrum will result in changes throughout the time domain. In contrast to the Fourier transform, the wavelet transform allows exceptional localisation in both the time domain via translations of the mother wavelet, and in the scale (frequency) domain via dilations. The translation and dilation operations applied to the mother wavelet are performed to calculate the wavelet coefficients, which represent the correlation between the wavelet and a localised section of the signal. The wavelet coefficients are calculated for each wavelet segment, giving a time-scale function relating the wavelets correlation to the signal.

We used the Continuous Wavelet Transform algorithm (figure 2). Here * denotes complex conjugate

$$CWT_{(a,b)} = \frac{1}{\sqrt{|a|}} \int_{-\infty}^{+\infty} \psi^{*}_{\left(\frac{t-b}{a}\right)} \cdot f_{(x)} dx \tag{1}$$

where b represents translation, a represents scale and $\psi_{(t)}$ is the Morlet mother wavelet defined as:

$$\psi_{(t)} = e^{jat} e^{\frac{-t^2}{2s}} \tag{2}$$

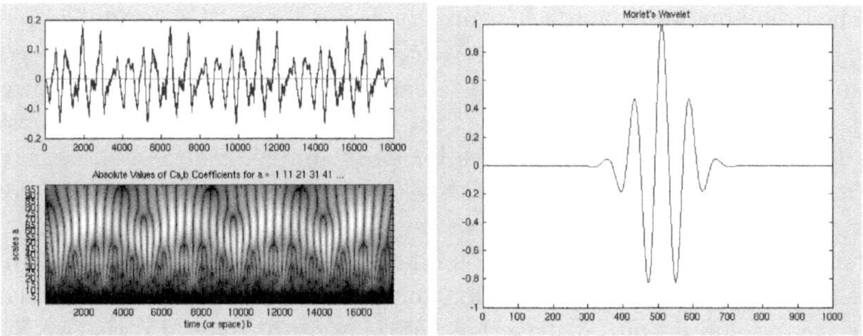

Fig. 2. Wavelet coefficients for a sound register and Morlet's mother wavelet

3 Feature Extraction

Continuous wavelet transform gives frequency and temporal information but, at the same time, it increases the processed data dimensionality. Hence, from a temporal signal in $\Re^2$ (time and intensity) a new signal in $\Re^3$ (time, scale and intensity) is obtained (figure 2). In order to process the information in a reasonable time it is necessary to restrict this processing to a small set of scales that represent the differences among the signals acquired at different locations.

For decades, principal component analysis (PCA) has been widely used to decorrelate spectral bands for reducing dimensionality. It is a useful technique if the spectral class structure of the transformed data is distributed along the first axes. This process is time consuming but it is only needed at the training stage.

First, we analyze the autocorrelation function of the sound register (figure 3) in order to find the lowest repetitive cycle delimitated by two global maxima. Then, the number of samples that feed the ANN will be proportional to this cycle.

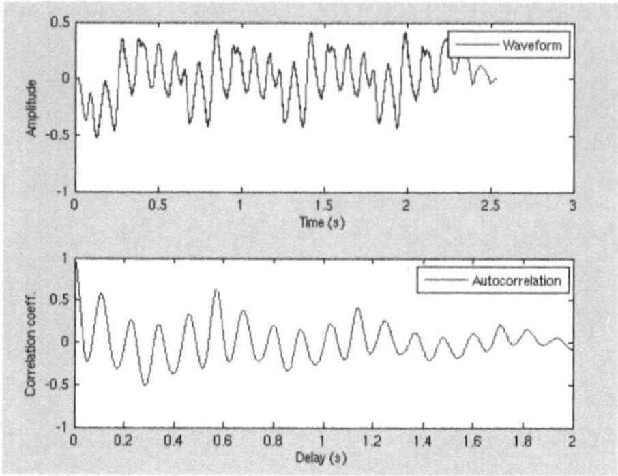

Fig. 3. A register of sound and its autocorrelation function

When the number of samples is already decided, the PCA is applied to determine how many data vectors are necessary for describing the information, that is, the so-called scale vectors. The data to calculate PCA are the vectors formed by all the scales for an specific sample. That implies to have 100-dimension vectors, that is, the CWT returns 100 scales for each sample. Figure 4 shows a Pareto diagram with the percentages of PCA results, and in the table 1 there are their numerical values. From this table we can observe that with 3 components it is explained the 75% of the information and with 5 components the 88%. In order to reduce the amount of information to enter to the ANN, we have chosen 5 components, and despite to have less information in the data, the ANN yields very good results.

Table 1. The five main Principal Components of a sound register

Principal C.	% Information	% Accumuled
First	42.84	42.84
Second	20.11	62.96
Third	12.00	74.97
Fourth	8.29	83.26
Fifth	4.73	87.99

4 Neural Networks

Artificial neural networks are biologically-inspired systems, imitating the physical structure of nervous system with the intention of processing information in a parallel, distributed and adaptive way.

These systems can be considered as universal solvers for their generalization feature based on examples (this is the case of the supervised networks) or based on reinforcement. This behaviour permits to build a system to solve situations without having a deep knolwedge of the problem, and therefore, to consider the neural network systems as black boxes. These features make them specially useful as classifiers and interpolators (ie. *feed-forward* networks).

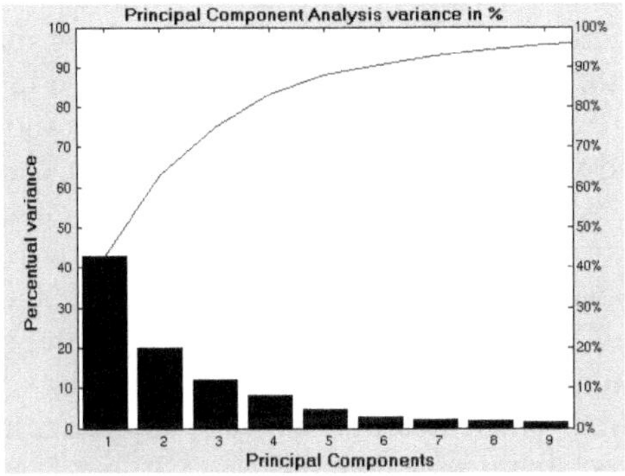

Fig. 4. Pareto diagram of Principal Components

The concept of black box has some drawbacks, such as the fact that it is not possible to extract the system behaviour since the networks is working correctly nor, consequently, the procedure to choose the more suitable network parameters (network structure, number of hidden layers, activation functions, ...).

Dynamic neural networks are divided in only feed-forward connections and feed-back connections (recurrent). Feed-forward dynamic networks (figure 5) have a delayed tapped input and so, the output depends not only on the current input to the network , but also on the current or previous inputs. They are specially good systems for input sequences.

In the first tests, we realized about the importance of the tapped delay length, because the larger the amount of samples the lower the probability of resemblance with another sound registers. The ANN configuration is, specifically, 20 previous samples. Then, the hidden layer is made up with one hundred neurons.

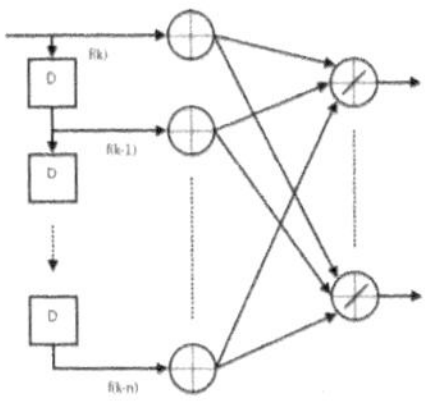

Fig. 5. Dynamic feedforward neuronal network

5 Experimental Results

5.1 Training Data Sets

In order to check the reliability of the method proposed in this paper, we have obtained a set of signals in a room, as it can be seen in figure 7. As sound sources we have used three different industrial machines: milling machine, electric drill and an industrial drill. Each sound source has been placed in three different locations inside the room: at the center, on edge and in one corner of the room. These locations are marked with one crosses in the figure. For each sound source and for each location we have acquired twenty signals in specific locations, where its x-y spatial coordinate is perfectly known. Each signal is approximately recorded for two seconds at 8kHz frequency sampling (more than 20,000 samples/signal). For each signal the CWT is calculated, obtained as many columns of scales as samples. Since the number of scales is approximately 100, the PCA reduces it to five scales. The input of the neural network is a vector with these five components (with its x-y coordinates for training, and without them for classification). Furthermore, the number of input vectors for each signal is equal to the number of samples. This huge amount of data generates the same number of outputs, with are depicted in figure 6. In this figure, it can be seen some clouds of points around a central points which is the training example, numbered in rows and columns as shown in figure 7, together with the sample number. For each set of twenty sound register, we use 18 registers for training and 2 registers for validation (crossed validation). In summary, we have obtained 180 signals that will be used to train three separated neural networks, with the consequent amount of information explained above.

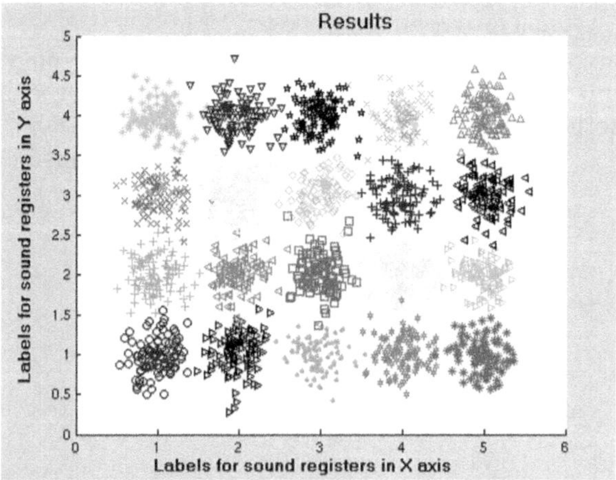

Fig. 6. Network output: x-y localization for the sound registers. The axes indicate the label shown in figure 7.

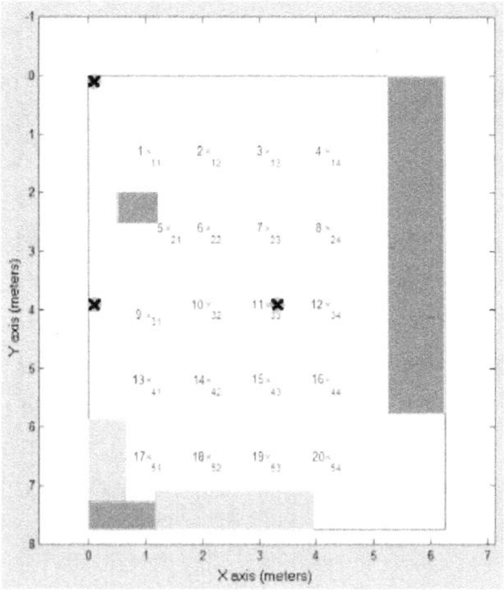

Fig. 7. Localization map of sounds registers and sound sources (big crosses)

Table 2. Classification ratio for training and validation with the milling machine in a corner of the room

validation sound registers		training %	validation %
1/1	1/4	77.2	62.1
1/2	3/4	76.2	65.1
1/3	5/4	81.1	64.2
2/1	4/3	72.5	69.4
2/2	4/3	76.1	71.5
2/2	4/1	83.7	68.8
2/3	5/3	79.8	78.0
2/3	4/1	81.3	72.1
3/1	2/4	74.1	73.6
3/2	3/3	86.2	45.1
3/2	3/4	80.5	63.0
3/3	4/1	83.1	69.5
3/4	4/2	76.0	61.2
4/2	2/2	84.5	79.5
4/2	5/4	84.9	66.7
4/3	5/1	73.7	71.6
4/4	4/1	87.1	66.5
5/2	3/4	82.6	71.3
5/3	3/3	79.9	61.2
5/4	3/4	86.0	81.3

5.2 Results

The results are slightly different depending on the localization and the source of sound. Table 2 shows some of these results, concretely obtained with a milling machine located in a corner of the room. The neural network have been trained for giving two coordinates (x,y) of a spatial 2D position. Since the output layer transfer function is linear, the x-y output from the network will be considered classified within the area of the closest sample in the training stage. Table 2 shows the classification results. Each row in the table corresponds to the classification rate for a pair of samples used as crossed validation. The column "validation" means the average success in the classification of a specific sound register when it is used as a validation sample, whereas the column "training" means the average success in the classification of the eighteen remaining samples in the training stage.

6 Conclusions

In this work, a non-speech-based localization method is presented. This method uses the continuous wavelet transform (CWT) to capture frequency-time information of sound which, after a dimensionality data reduction process, feeds a dynamic neural network. The system is trained with samples with known x-y position which have been acquired from 3 sound sources in three different sites in a room. The training process is relatively slow as well as the PCA analysis but this is an off-line process. The results demonstrate that the ANN localizes the new sound registers with a relative small error.

References

1. Bolea, Y., Grau, A., Sanfeliu, A.: Non-speech sound feature extraction based on model identification for robot navigation. CIARP 2003, LNCS 2905, pp. 221-228, 2003.
2. Bolea, Y., Grau, A., Pelissier, A., Sanfeliu, A.: Structural Pattern Recognition for Industrial Machine Sounds based on Frequency Spectrum Analysis. CIARP 2004, LNCS 3287, pp. 287-295, 2004.
3. Luo, H., Zeng, H., Hu, L., Hu, X., Zhou, Z.: Application of Artificial Neural Network in Laser Welding Defect Diagnosis. Journal of Materials Processing Technology vol. 170, pp. 403-411, 2005.
4. Huang, J., Supaongprpa, T., Terakura, I., Wang, F., Ohnishi, N., Sugie, N.: A model-based sound localization system and its application to robot navigation Robotics and Autonomous Systems vol. 27, pp. 199-209, 1999.
5. Cowling, M., Sitte, R.: Comparison of techniques for enviromental sound recognition. Pattern Recognition Letters vol. 24, pp. 2895-2907, 2003.
6. Orozco-García, J., Reyes García, Carlos A.: A study on the Recognition of Patterns of Infant Cry for the Identification of Deafness in Just Born Babies with neural Networks. CIARP 2003, LNCS 2905, pp. 348-349, 2003.

An Application of Neural Networks for Image Reconstruction in Electrical Capacitance Tomography Applied to Oil Industry

Norberto Flores[1], Ángel Kuri-Morales[2], and Carlos Gamio[3]

[1] Instituto Mexicano del Petróleo, Eje Central Lázaro Cárdenas 152, San Bartolo Atepehuacan 07730, Distrito Federal, México
nfloresg@imp.mx
http://www.imp.mx

[2] Instituto Tecnológico Autónomo de México, Río Hondo 1, Progreso Tizapán 01080, Distrito Federal, México
akuri@itam.mx
http://www.itam.mx

[3] Glasgow Caledonian University, 70 Cowcaddens Road, Glasgow G4 0BA United Kingdom
carlos.gamio@gcal.ac.uk
http://www.gcal.ac.uk

Abstract. The article presents a possible solution to a typical tomographic images generation problem from data of an industrial process located in a pipeline or vessel. These data are capacitance measurements obtained non-invasively according to the well known ECT technique (Electrical Capacitance Tomography). Every 313 pixels image frame is derived from 66 capacitance measurements sampled from the real time process. The neural nets have been trained using the backpropagation algorithm where training samples have been created synthetically from a computational model of the real ECT sensor. To create the image 313 neuronal nets, each with 66 inputs and one output, are used in parallel. The resulting image is finally filtered and displayed. The different ECT system stages along with the different tests performed with synthetic and real data are reported. We show that the image resulting from our method is a faster and more precise practical alternative to previously reported ones.

1 Introduction

Process tomography consists of obtaining images from the inside of pipelines, reactors or other type of containers that are part of industrial processes [1] [4]. Such visualization is performed non-invasively. There are several techniques for obtaining images, depending on the type of measurement used (acoustic, magnetic resonance, electrical, etc.). One way is to obtain capacitance measurements according to the ECT technique [1] [3].

Image reconstruction techniques from Artificial Neural Nets (ANN) trained by means of a supervised learning algorithm, require large number of samples (capacitance measurements for several known permittivity distributions) to be trained.

J.F. Martínez-Trinidad et al. (Eds.): CIARP 2006, LNCS 4225, pp. 371 – 380, 2006.

Because of the difficulty in obtaining such examples experimentally, we need to develop a methodology which allows us to generate synthetic examples from a real-sensor model.

From the set of generated samples the ANN is trained assuming the capacitance information as the input and the permittivity distribution information as the output. The ANN thusly trained has the capability to respond to new sensor data, giving adequate permittivity distribution which allows us to reconstruct a tomographic image.

1.1 Electrical Capacitance Tomography

ECT is an innovating technique (late 80s) [1] [10] for industrial multiphase process visualization, suitable for electrically insulating materials. Its potential applications in the petroleum industry [4] range from multiphase flow measurement and monitoring in producing wells to separator and fluidized bed optimization [2].

The ECT technique consists in placing an electrode array around a pipeline or vessel made of an insulating material that contains the process to be visualized. By using the adequate tools, the capacitances between all possible electrode pairs needs to be measured [6]. The obtained readings depend on the dielectric constant value (electrical permittivity) of the different phases or components of the mixture and the way they are distributed inside the pipeline or vessel. The next step is to obtain an image of such distribution from the measured capacitance data by means of an adequate image reconstruction algorithm. Figure 1 shows a schematic diagram of an ECT system with its main components. Besides the capacitance sensor, a basic ECT system is made up with a data acquisition system and a computer for image reconstruction [10].

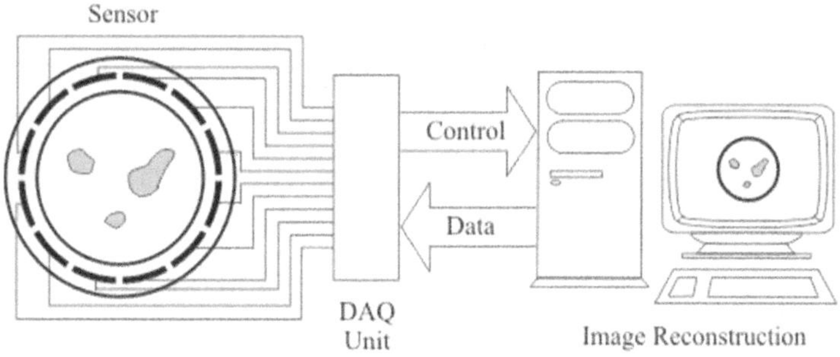

Fig. 1. ECT system components

2 ECT Sensor Used

The number and the size of electrodes depend on the specific application. Most of the applications developed until now make use of sensors with 8, 12, or 16 electrodes [1] [3] [6], they must be inside a grounded screen to cut down noise and the influence of external fields (see Fig 2). Besides, the sensor used has two grounded cylindrical end guards to eliminate the changes on the electric field borders.

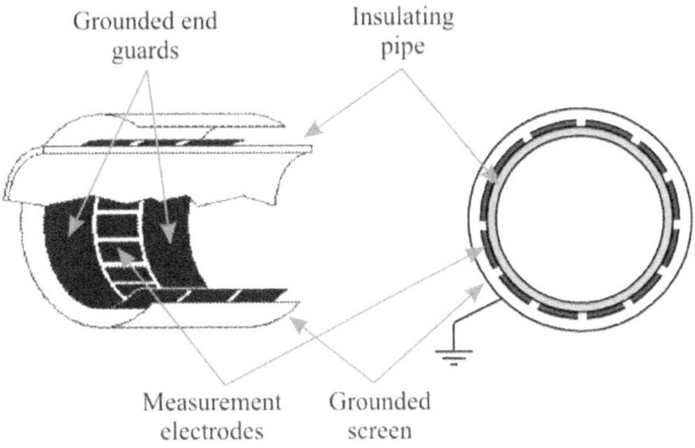

Fig. 2. ECT Sensor Schematic Diagram

The sensor from the Mexican Petroleum Institute used in this research has 12 electrodes (see Fig. 3a), so it is possible to measure 66 capacitance values between them (see Figure 3b). These capacitances are extremely small and, due to this, very sensitive measurement circuits are needed. Such values are in the 0.1 to 500 femtofarads range (1 femtofarad = 10 e-15 farads).

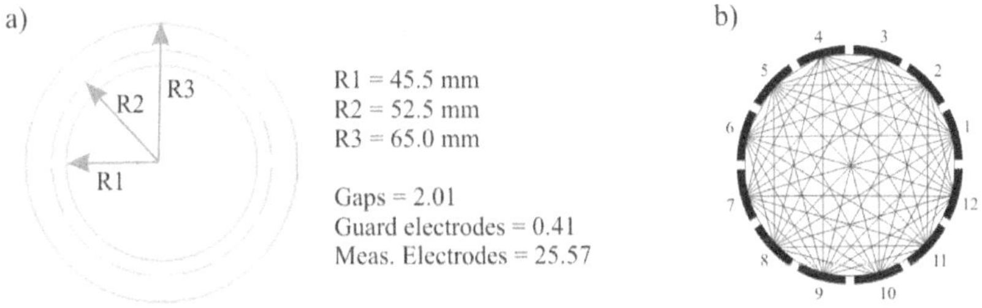

Fig. 3. Mexican Institute of Petroleum ECT Sensor. a) Dimensions, b) 66 electrode-pair combinations

2.1 Numeric ECT Sensor Model

Although the sensor is a three-dimensional device, it is possible to use a two dimension model due to the fact that it is representative of a central transversal section. The natural deformation of the electric field at the edges of the pipe formed by the measurement electrodes is controlled by means of the grounded electrodes placed in both edges (see Figure 2). Apart from the insulating pipe, measurement electrodes, guard electrodes and shielded screen dimensions, the model geometry includes the spatial discretization of the inner part of the sensor (R1 in Figure 3). It has been discretizated into 313 uniform size zones, as shown in Figure 4.

The model allows us to have a method from which numerical calculation can be carried out for the electric potential ϕ in the space of the sensor. This is necessary as an intermediate step towards the capacitance calculation. An ECT sensor can be considered as an electrostatic field problem. The electric potential ϕ within the sensor [3] is calculated by solving the following second order partial differential equation

$$\nabla \cdot [\varepsilon(x,y) \nabla \phi(x,y)] = 0 \tag{1}$$

where $\phi\,(x,y)$ is the potential distribution in two dimensions, and $\varepsilon\,(x,y)$ is the relative permittivity distribution in two dimensions.

To complete the model, the boundary conditions (Dirichlet boundary conditions) related to the measurement technique are shown in (2). When electrode i is the excitation electrode, such conditions are:

$$\psi_i = \begin{cases} V_{exc} & (x,y) \subseteq \Gamma_i \\ 0 & (x,y) \subseteq \Gamma_j \quad (j = 1, \ldots, n;\ j \neq i) \quad and \quad (x,y) \subseteq (\Gamma_s + \Gamma_g) \end{cases} \tag{2}$$

where Γ_i is the spatial location of the measurement (excitation) electrode; Γ_j is the spatial location of the 11 detecting electrodes; Γ_s the one of the sensor screen; and Γ_g the one of the 12 grounded guard electrodes placed between the 12 measurement electrodes.

The sensor model will be used to simulate a real sensor. This means that it will be able to solve the ECT forward problem calculating capacitances between all possible electrode pairs. To achieve this, equation (1) has to be solved first such that the potential distribution $\phi\,(x,y)$ is obtained within the sensor.

One way to calculate $\phi\,(x,y)$ is through the finite element method (FEM) [7]. Using this method, an approximation to the potential ϕ will be obtained in the sensor at a finite set of points corresponding to the nodes of the triangular mesh that is normally used in the finite element method.

Once the potential distribution is found within the sensor, the electric charge Q_j on each detector electrode is calculated by using Gauss law

$$Q_j = \oint_{j} (\varepsilon(x,y) \nabla \phi(x,y) \cdot \mathbf{n}) \mathrm{d}s \tag{3}$$

where Γ_j is a closed curve surrounding the detector electrode and $\mathbf{n}$ is the normal vector along the Γ_j.

Finally the capacitance can be computed by an energy method, the energy required to charge a capacitor is given by the expression

$$W_e = \frac{Q^2}{2C} \tag{4}$$

which is equal to the energy of the electrostatic field. So the capacitance is easily obtained from (5).

$$C = \frac{Q^2}{2W_e} \tag{5}$$

3 ANN Solution's Description

The tomography problem is, mathematically speaking, an inverse problem, since from the observed effects (the change in magnitude of capacitances) our aim is to obtain the causes which originate them (material distribution in the inner part of the sensor). The solution of an inverse problem, for our ECT case, consists on obtaining the discretized permittivity distribution **ε** (**ε** = $\{\varepsilon_1, \varepsilon_2, .., \varepsilon_{313}\}$) starting from the set of capacitance measurements, represented by the **c** vector (**c** = $\{c_1, c_2, .., c_{66}\}$).

$$\begin{aligned} \varepsilon_1 &= f_1(c_1, c_2, c_3, \ldots, c_{66}) \\ \varepsilon_2 &= f_2(c_1, c_2, c_3, \ldots, c_{66}) \\ &\vdots \\ \varepsilon_{313} &= f_{313}(c_1, c_2, c_3, \ldots, c_{66}) \end{aligned} \tag{6}$$

As mentioned before, an ECT process consists of two stages: 1) capacitances obtained in a specific moment; 2) image construction (see Fig. 4). This last stage has been implemented by using an ANN.

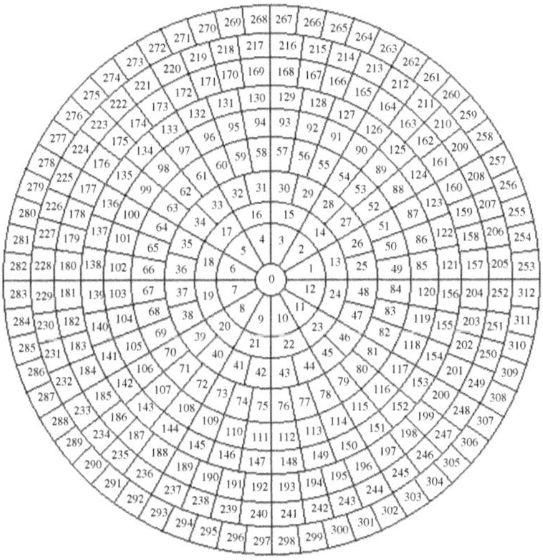

Fig. 4. Pixels distribution that forms the tomographic image

Multilayer Perceptron is the ANN selected type as they are universal function aproximators for a nonlinear input-output mapping [5]. An MLP is used to solve each of the 313 f_p functions (with p= 1, … , 313) obtaining **ε**.

In the image creation stage, **c** is input by several ANNs (see Fig. 5) calculating individually the ε_p pixel values. As a result each pixel is assigned a 1-3 permittivity value corresponding to a substances mixture (For instance, petroleum will have a permittivity close to 3; gas will have a value close to 1; while in the case of a mixture, an intermediate value will be observed). Afterwards, the pixel value will be mapped to the range [0-255] that corresponds to its final gray level (represented with 8 bits).

3.1 Use of Neural Networks in the Image Reconstruction Stage

The ANNs are now grouped in a module: Its full architecture consists of 313 ANNs in parallel (see Fig. 5). Vector **c** is fed and the module outputs the corresponding **ε** vector. Therefore, **ε** represents permittivity distribution in the sensor transversal section. The image is made up according to the pixel numbers as shown in Figure 4.

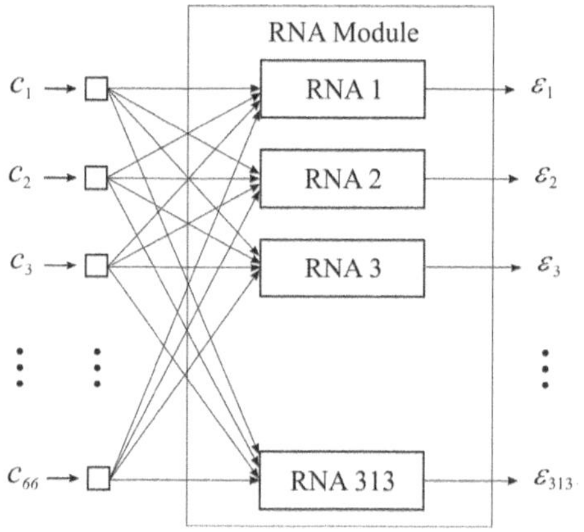

Fig. 5. RNA module for solving the TCE problem

For each ε_p pixel calculation identical ANNs are used: one per pixel. Its architecture is 66-4-7-1 (see Fig. 6), meaning 66 inputs; a first hidden 4 neuron layer, a second 7 neuron one, and a unique neuron in the output layer supplying the permittivity value for ε_p.

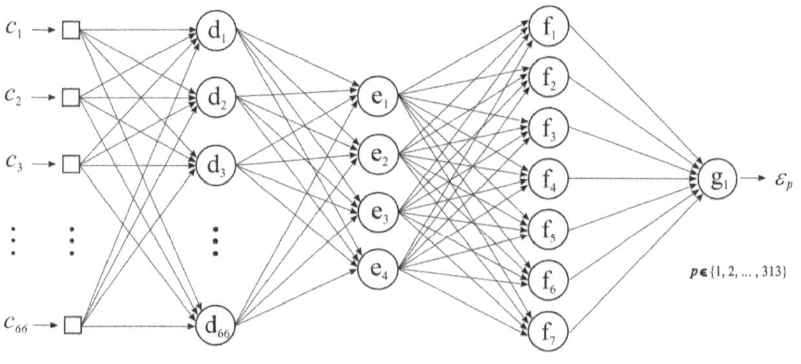

Fig. 6. ANN Architecture

These ANNs have been trained by using the traditional backpropagation algorithm. 1000 training and 150 test examples have been created to achieve such training. Examples are created in the following manner: a p pixel discretized permittivity distribution is chosen. Such distribution makes up vector $\boldsymbol{\varepsilon}$ which is then fed to the computational sensor model to get n capacitances making up $\mathbf{c}$ vector. Later on, both are merged resulting into a training or test example as shown in Figure 7. These items of the sample have 379 elements for p=313 and n=66.

$\mathbf{c}$						$\boldsymbol{\varepsilon}$					
c_1	c_2	c_3	c_4	...	c_n	ε_1	ε_2	ε_3	ε_4	...	ε_p

Fig. 7. Examples structure for training and test

A large majority of these examples were randomly generated. 100 training examples were created by using known distribution patterns of materials in the flow, such as: stratified, annular and with bubbles. Training was performed for 1500 epochs, reaching a 0.19 training error, and a 0.24 testing error. A 0.1 learning rate has been used for the three computational layers. Also, a 0.1 momentum constant has been used in them.

4 ANN Recall and Digital Image Processing Module

The general method's performance is now described. As mentioned before capacitance values are in order of femtofarads. Vector $\mathbf{c}$ is normalized in the [0, 1] interval, and input the trained ANN module. A normalized permittivity value is obtained in [0, 1] at the module output. Such a value is now denormalized and a grey level value (from 0 to 255) is displayed as the output value in the corresponding pixel.

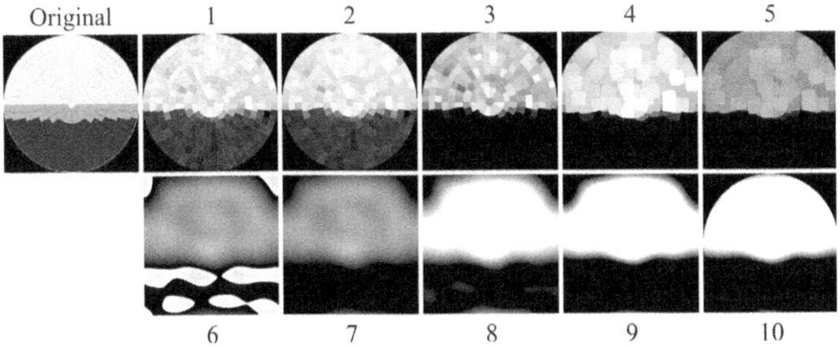

Fig. 8. Digital Image Processing steps

Finally the image made up with the 313 pixel aggregate is passed through a Digital Image Processing (DIP) module mainly to get dissemination among the pixels to present a tomographic aspect image. The DIP module is made up by applying a ten step sequence (see Figure 8) as follows: 1) Circular mask to eliminate the four black corners, outside the circle, from the treatment; 2) Median filter to add blur (slight fading at the edges between the pixels); 3) A lookup table (LUT) 1/x type, with x= 0.4, for a better brightness, turning the darker zones into even darker ones; 4) Dilation of the light zones; 5) Decreasing brightness; 6) Low pass FFT Filter (Consisting of three steps: a) Finding the FFT, b) Filtering low frequencies from the resulting images and, c) Going back to the image dominium by means of the inverse FFT); 7) Noise elimination from the saturation zones in the former step (The noise is inverted and then subtracted from itself); 8) The image is added to itself to double the gray level from the light parts to recover the brightness withdrawn in 3 and 5 steps; 9) Brightness and contrast are adjusted; 10) A circular mask (as in step one) is applied again.

5 Test Using Synthetic Data for Validation

The process for 4 synthetic images is described in what follows. Both the ANN and the DIP module results are shown. First the desired image (original image) is defined and put in $\boldsymbol{\varepsilon}$ form. Later the ECT sensor model is used to get the corresponding $\mathbf{c}$ vector. Then $\mathbf{c}$ and $\boldsymbol{\varepsilon}$ are merged and RNA module is used to simulate ECT system performance. Finally, the resulting images are passed by the DIP module. The results can be easily validated. Figure 9 displays the ANN module's output and results after applying DIP.

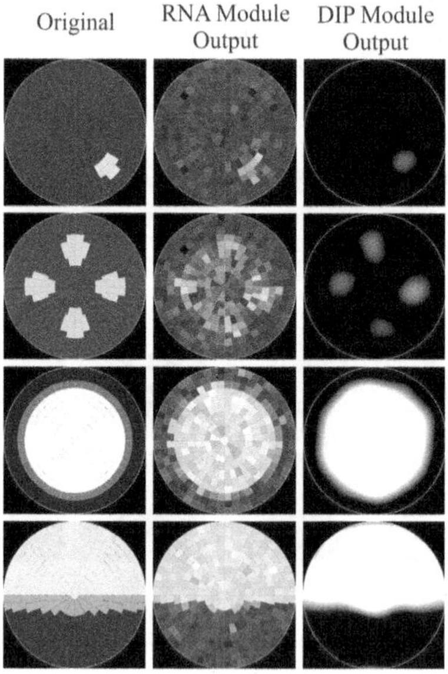

Fig. 9. Original Synthetic Images versus generated ones by using the ECT system

These results show that the ANN method effectively yields satisfactory results for tomographic images reconstruction from capacitance measurements. The light zones represent gas zones (permittivity close to 1), while the dark zones represent oil (permittivity close to 3). All the examples were integrated with different permittivity values; examples 3 and 4 have three different levels, representing oil, foam and gas. The first two examples represent a pipeline filled with oil with 1 and 4 gas bubbles respectively.

6 Experiments Using Real Data

Results from tests performed with real data from a petroleum reservoir simulator are now shown. Real gas and oil at different pressures and amounts were passed through the sensor.

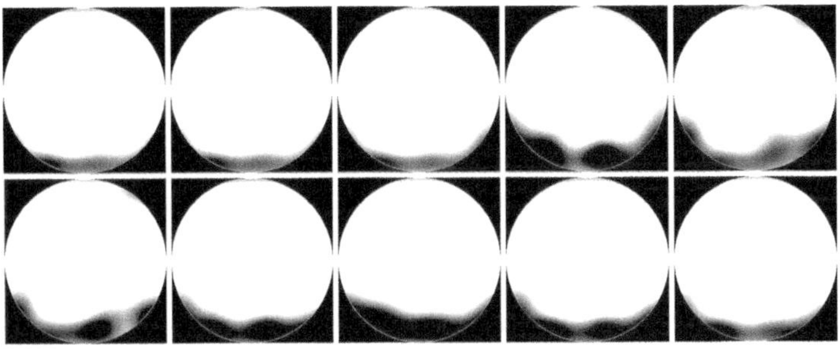

Fig. 10. Experiment using gas and oil. Frames were acquired at 10 ms intervals

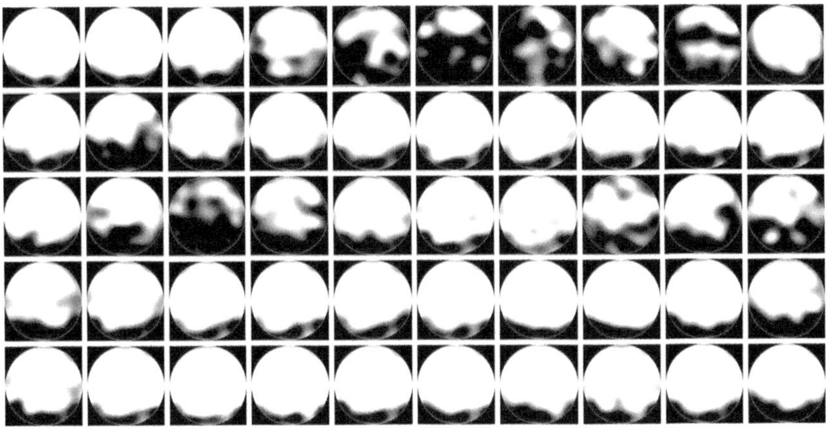

Fig. 11. Experiment using gas and oil. Frames were acquired at 10 ms intervals

Figures 10 and 11 show tomographic images obtained from two experiments. Figure 10 shows an experiment with 0.246 million scfd (standard cubic feet per day) for gas and 182.37 bpd (barrels per day) for oil, having a mixture pressure of 5.5 barbg (barg gauge). Experiment in Figure 11 was carried out with 0.248 million scfd and 2,263.33 bpd, making a 5.7 barbg pressure.

7 Conclusions

The ANN is a proven functional method for ECT image reconstruction. Several worldwide researchers have already reported promissory results by using this technique [8] [9] [11]. Experiments displayed in this paper have reached 0.24 maximum error image results. This can be measured only when testing known synthetic patterns. Error measurements from real data cannot be supplied because the transversal distribution reference from different flow phases going through a pipe is unknown. And it is precisely here where our method is most useful. The proven effectiveness of the ANN model capabilities allows us to extrapolate the observed and known results to unknown areas of operation, thus fulfilling the original aim of accurately modeling the phenomenon under study.

References

1. Beck, M., Byars, M., Dyakowski, T., Waterfall, R., He, R., Wang, S. J., Yang, W. Q.: Principles and industrial applications of electrical capacitance tomography. Measurement + Control, Vol. 30 (1997) 197–200.
2. Dyakowski T., Jeanmeure, L. F., Jaworski, A. J.: Applications of electrical tomography for gas-solids and liquid-solids flows – A review. Powder technol, Vol. 112 (2000) 174–192.
3. Gamio, J. C., Ortiz-Alemán, C.: An interpretation of the Linear Back-Projection Algorithm Used in Capacitance Tomography. 3rd World Congress on Industrial Process Tomography. Bannf (2003) 427-432.
4. Hammer, E. A., Johansen, G.: A Process tomography in the oil industry – State of the art and future possibilities. Measurement + Control. Vol. 3 (1997) 11-14.
5. Hecht-Nielsen, R.: Kolmogorov's mapping neural network existence theorem. First IEEE International Conference on Neural Networks. Vol. 30 (1987) 212-216.
6. Huang, S. M., Xie, C. G, Thorn, R., Snowen, D., Beck, M. S.: Design of sensor electronics for electrical capacitance tomography. IEE Proc. G. Vol. 139 (1992) 83-88.
7. Khan, S. H. y Abdullah, F.: Finite element modeling of multielectrode capacitive systems for flow imaging. IEE Proceedings-G. Vol. 140(3) (1993) 216-222.
8. Nooralahiyan, A. Y., Hoyle, B., Bailey, N.: Neural network for pattern association in electrical capacitance tomography. IEE Proc.-Circuits Devices Syst. Vol. 141(6) (1994) 517-521.
9. Sun, T. D., Mudde, R., Schouten, J.C., Scarlett, B., van den Bleek, C.M.: Image reconstruction of an electrical capacitance tomography system using an artificial neural network. 3rd World Congress on Industrial Process Tomography. Buxton 1999) 174-180.
10. Yang, W. Q., Peng, L.: Image reconstruction algorithms for electrical capacitance tomography – Review Article. Measurement Science and Technology. Vol. 14 (2003) R1 – R13.
11. Warsito, W., Fan, L-S.: Neural network based multi-criterion optimization image reconstruction technique for imaging two- and three-phase flow systems using electrical capacitance tomography. Measurement Science and Technology. Vol. 12 (2001) 2198 – 2210.

Combining Neural Networks for Gait Classification

Nigar Sen Koktas[1], Nese Yalabik[2], and Gunes Yavuzer[3]

[1] Informatics Institute, METU, Ankara, Turkey
nigar@ii.metu.edu.tr
[2] Computer Engineering Department, METU, Ankara, Turkey
yalabik@ceng.metu.edu.tr
[3] Department of Physical Medicine and Rehabilitation, Ankara University Medical School, Ankara, Turkey
gyavuzer@ankara.medicine.edu.tr

Abstract. Gait analysis can be defined as the numerical and graphical representation of the mechanical measurements of human walking patterns and is used for two main purposes: human identification, where it is usually applied to security issues, and clinical applications, where it is used for the non-automated and automated diagnosis of various abnormalities and diseases. Automated or semi-automated systems are important in assisting physicians for diagnosis of various diseases. In this study, a semi-automated gait classification system is designed and implemented by using joint angle and time-distance data as features. Multilayer Perceptrons (MLPs) Combination classifiers are used to categorize gait data into two categories; healthy and patient with knee osteoarthritis. Two popular approaches of combining neural networks are experimented and the results are compared according to different output combining rules. In the first one, same set is used to train all networks and afterwards the features are decomposed into five different sets. These two experiments show that using entire data set produces more accurate results than using decomposed data sets, but complexity becomes an important drawback. However, when a proper combining rule is applied to decomposed sets, results are more accurate than entire set. In this experiment sum rule produces better results than majority vote and max rules as an output combining rule.

1 Introduction

Gait analysis is the process of collecting and analyzing quantitative information about walking patterns of people and it is important for developing treatment plans or tracking the improvement of persons having gait problems (i.e. Parkinson, cerebral palsy, arthritis). This process is facilitated by the use of computer-interfaced video cameras to measure patient motion, by the use of electrodes placed on the surface of the skin to appreciate muscle activity, and by the use of force platforms imbedded in a walkway to monitor the forces and torques produced between the patient and the ground. After collecting data the essential part of the process is the interpretation of these by experts and related software. Gait analysis, when considered as an automated system, is used for two main purposes: human identification and clinical applications.

J.F. Martínez-Trinidad et al. (Eds.): CIARP 2006, LNCS 4225, pp. 381 – 388, 2006.

Human identification is an important security issue. In most cases it is not so easy to determine the identity of the person but many applications work well for some special cases, such as gender classification [1], age classification [2] etc. In most of these studies data sources are image sequences, but it is inappropriate to measure joint and segment gait kinematics directly from the videotape or monitor. They do not give an indication of the cause of the gait abnormality and so have limited value in clinical decision-making.

The application of automatic gait analysis in medicine is also a well-studied subject. There are studies that have shown that the number of surgical procedures is reduced after a three-dimensional (3-D) gait analysis [3]. In medical applications measurements are obtained more sensitively. Kinetic and kinematical temporal changes are obtained from the subject. In addition to temporal changes of joint angles and force data, time-distance parameters of the gait such as velocity, cadence, stride length, step length are recorded.

The outcome of musculoskeletal diseases can be followed in two ways, as shown in Figure 1. The first one is the traditional method, and the second one is the gait analysis method. Traditional diagnosis starts with the examination of patients according to their complaints. Two mostly used and expensive traditional methods are based on determining cartilage damages. The first one is MR technique which determines the degree of damage. The second one is the determination of cartilage damage by blood and urine analysis. Since these traditional methods are expensive and harmful to subjects to some degree, they are not suitable for frequent long term follow-up of the patients.

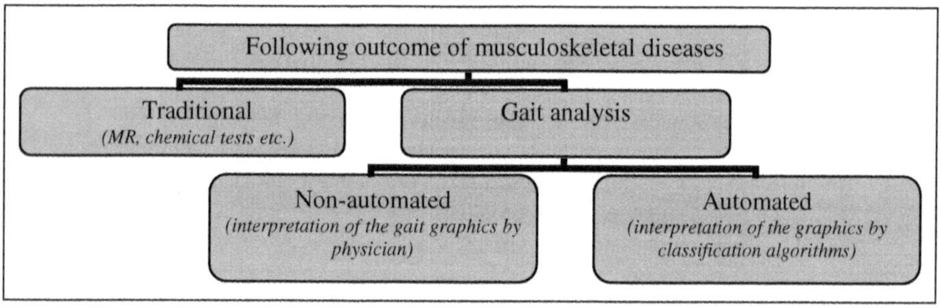

Fig. 1. The role of gait analysis in clinical context

Gait analysis helps the physician in both the diagnosis and follow-up non-automatically or automatically. If the physician him/herself interprets the obtained gait data, then this is a non-automated diagnosis. But if this data is interpreted by software, then it is called automated diagnosis. Since non automated diagnosis requires high level of expertise, only specifically trained orthopedists or physiatrist can use gait data. Automated system is expected to decrease this requirement which may help to increase the number of physicians and patients, making use of the laboratory. In addition, automated systems save experts' time and decrease the possibility of human made errors.

Here the word *automated* does not mean that gait systems are tools to replace physicians. Rather, it is an assisting tool to search the diseases that physicians suspected, to determine the level of the already diagnosed diseases, or to examine invisible changes of patients.

For the design of automated diagnoses systems some well known pattern recognition algorithms are used. These are neural networks (NNs) [2, 4, 5, 6, 11], support vector machines (SVMs) [2, 8], and radial basis functions (RBFs) [7]. The use of NNs for experimental gait classification is not new. There are studies in which NNs are trained by force platform data to distinguish 'healthy' from 'pathological' gait [4, 5, 7, 9]. In addition to these, there are studies to recognize walking people among a few subjects (less than 10) by using joint angles as features [6, 10, 12]. These studies produce reasonable results (about %51-%83 on testing set and about %76-%98 on training set) for NNs use in gait classification. Since these studies differ from each other in description of gait variables (such as subject type, measurement tools, type of variables, anatomical levels), and in construction of classifiers, comparing the performances of them with the current one may not be reasonable.

As the dimension of the features and the size of the data increase same accuracies may not be guaranteed. In similar pattern recognition studies this problem is tried to be solved by combining classifiers. Combination of NNs are widely used today especially in speech recognition [14] and character recognition [13] studies and they have showed an increase in the performance of the classifiers. In [16] Sharkey made a comprehensive experiment to compare two different NNs combining methods; modular and ensemble ones. She concluded that using an entire set for training produces more accurate results than decomposing it. In this study comparison of these two approaches are done in the context of gait classification. There are also different approaches on combining outputs of classifiers. Kittler et. al. [17] has comparative studies on efficiency of output combination rules such as majority voting, sum, product, max., and min. rules. In [17], they concluded that sum rule is superior to others in most of the cases.

The objective of this study is to design a software system for physicians for supplying accurate and practical ways to diagnose and further classify a musculoskeletal disease using only gait data. The accuracy of the proposed system will be safeguarded by using all features used for diagnoses. To be able to combine all features in one classification system, combination methods are expected to be most suitable. As our previous studies [11] and similar studies proved MLP usage for gait classification produces reasonable results. A group of MLPs are used to classify the subjects as healthy or sick, using temporal changes of knee joint angle and time-distance parameters as features. Current study is one of the first studies in which classifier combination techniques have been applied to gait data. Two different NNs combination methods are tried. In the first experiment data set is decomposed into five different sets and five MLPs are trained and tested by these sets. Then test set results are combined by sum, majority vote and max rules to produce final class label. In the second experiment, entire data set is used to train three different architectural MLPs and again outputs are combined by three different rules and accuracy rates on test set are compared.

The remainder of the report is organized as follows. Section 2 introduces data collection process and the characteristics of data. This is followed by details of our experiments and results. Finally, in last section conclusions are presented.

2 Characteristics of Data

There are many data collection methods in gait analysis literature. However, some have disadvantages over others because of harmful effects to the subjects. The stereo metric method is the most popular one currently used. It employs visible markers attached to the skin on rigid segments of the body structure and tracks their motion using imaging equipment. This technique is implemented using charge coupled device (CCD) cameras and frame-grabber electronics to allow digital images to be captured as the subject moves within the field of view. Digital image analysis allows the physical location of each marker to be computed, using triangulation of the views from an array of camera systems. This technique has minimal impact on the natural motion of the subject and allows data capture without the need to tether the subject to the data acquisition hardware. But, it is not feasible to measure gait patterns or variability with only one traversal of the instrument walkway. Thus, multiple walking trials need to be collected, which may fatigue the subject.

While data collection techniques for gait analysis have continually evolved over the past 40 years, the method of data presentation has not changed much. The data is still reported in 2-D charts with the abscissa usually defined as the percentage of the gate cycle and the ordinate displaying the gait parameter. Figure 2 shows the graphical representation of the gait data used in this study for both a healthy and with knee osteoarthritis person.

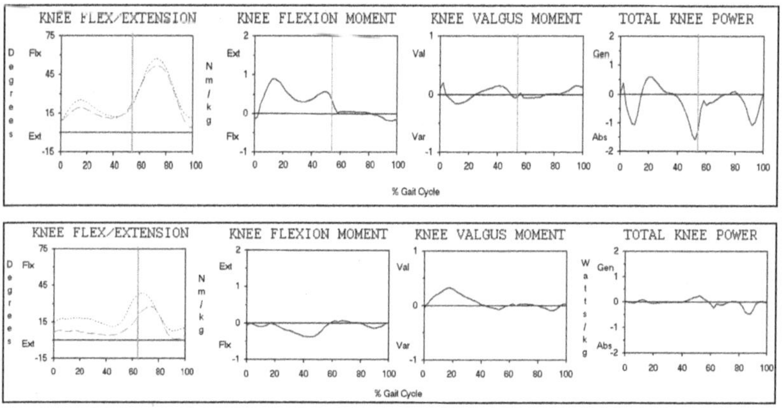

Fig. 2. Graphs of the gait data (*healthy (a) and knee osteoarthritis (b)*)

In this study, data are collected in Ankara University Faculty of Medicine Department of Physical Medicine and Rehabilitation Gait Laboratory by the gait analysis experts. In this laboratory, there are standard gait laboratory equipments which are supported by "VICON" a commercial system for gait analysis. Subject is walked on the platform and in one cycle of gait, temporal changes of joint angles, joint moments, joint powers, force ratios and time-distance parameters are gathered and recorded to database. Decision of which features to use is done according to inspected illness. In this study, Osteoarthritis, a disease that affects knee joints is selected as an example;

therefore, by the advice of the medical expert, knee flexion, knee flexion moment, knee valgus moment and total knee power are selected as the features of the knee joint angle. In addition, walking velocity, single support and step length are selected as the time-distance parameters of the gait.

Each of joint angle related features are represented by a graph that contains 51 samples taken in equally spaced intervals in the time for gait cycle, which is the time spent for one step. These points composed feature vectors which are used as inputs of the related MLP. On the other hand, time-distance parameters are static numerical values which are also used to train a MLP.

Before passing to classification phase data is cleaned by eliminating rows having missing values. Finally, 91 healthy and 110 sick subjects' data is prepared for classification purpose and shared for training and testing purposes as shown in Table 1 (H: healthy, S: Sick, SMP: Samples).

Table 1. Dataset characteristics

<table>
<tr><th rowspan="2">FEATURE VECTOR (FV)</th><th rowspan="2">DATASET</th><th rowspan="2">#SMP.</th><th colspan="2">#TRAIN</th><th colspan="2">#TEST</th></tr>
<tr><th>H</th><th>S</th><th>H</th><th>S</th></tr>
<tr><td>FV1</td><td>KFlex: Knee flexion/extension</td><td>51</td><td rowspan="6">61</td><td rowspan="6">77</td><td rowspan="6">30</td><td rowspan="6">33</td></tr>
<tr><td>FV2</td><td>KMFlex: Knee flexion/ extension moment</td><td>51</td></tr>
<tr><td>FV3</td><td>KMVal: Knee Valgus Moment</td><td>51</td></tr>
<tr><td>FV4</td><td>KPTot: Total Knee Power</td><td>51</td></tr>
<tr><td>FV5</td><td>Time-dist: Velocity, single support, step length</td><td>3</td></tr>
<tr><td>FV6</td><td>Entire set (all of above)</td><td>207</td></tr>
</table>

3 Experiments and Results

The basic classifier structure, used in this study is MLPs combination. Weaknesses of each classifier are diminished by combining classifiers, and more accurate results are expected.

In [15], two methods are described for combining multiple networks. The first one is the modular approach, in which the task is first decomposed into several subtasks and a specialist network is then trained using the inputs pertaining to the corresponding subtask. The second approach is the ensemble one, in which each network is trained using the same inputs and provides a different solution to the same task. Outputs from these networks are combined to reach an integrated result. Complexity is an important issue to be considered in this case. Differentiation among classifiers may be done by using initial random weights, different topologies, and varying the input data.

As stated previously the final data that is used here has five feature vectors; four for temporal changes of knee joint angle (KFlex, KMFlex, KMVal, KPTot) and one for time-distance parameters. Before training all data sets are scaled to interval [-1, 1]. Totally eight MLPs are trained using Matlab neural network toolbox. These MLPs are combined in different schemas for experiment 1 and experiment 2 as shown in

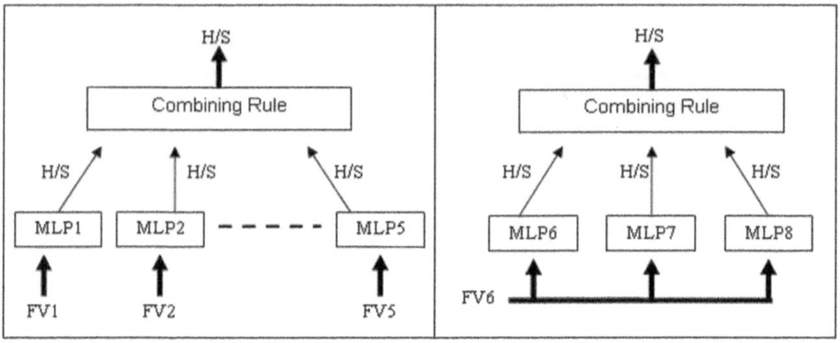

Fig. 3. MLP combination schemas for experiment 1 (a), and experiment 2 (b) H/S: Healthy or sick, FV: Feature vector

Figure3. Table 2 and Table 3 show the topology of each network and their individual success rates on test data. For the first five networks number of hidden nodes and hidden layers are determined experimentally.

Experiment 1: Input data is decomposed in five sets composed of different feature vectors. Five MLPs are trained by these input sets and then outputs of test set are combined by three different combining rules to reach a final result. So, accuracy of different combining rules is compared.

Table 2. Properties of MLPs used in experiment 1

NETWORK	#NODE			#MIS-CLASSIFIED	SUCCESS RATE (%)
	input	*hidden1*	*hidden2*		
MLP1	51	35	10	10	84
MLP2	51	35	10	8	87
MLP3	51	35	10	15	76
MLP4	51	35	10	18	71
MLP5	3	2	-	13	79

Experiment 2: Three different MLPs are trained by using the same composite input set without any decomposition. Here, differentiation of each network is done by different number of hidden layers and hidden nodes.

In both experiments different combination approaches are used, but in both cases combining outputs of classifiers became and important issue. In this study three of these rules, sum, majority vote and max rules, are experimented and results are compared by success rates on test data set.

After training each network with corresponding input set, test data are presented and the outputs are normalized to use them as posterior probabilities. Since *tansig* function is used as the activation function in all layers of networks, outputs are in interval [-1, 1]. To normalize an output, its absolute value is taken as posterior

Table 3. Properties of MLPs used in experiment 2

NETWORK	#NODE			#MIS-CLASSIFIED	SUCCESS RATE (%)
	input	*hidden1*	*hidden2*		
MLP6	207	50	-	6	90
MLP7	207	150	40	6	90
MLP8	207	207	50	7	89

probability, and its sign is taken as class label (i.e minus sign is for normal and plus sign is for sick subject). Then, its 1-complement is recorded as posterior probability of the other class. Thus, sum and max rules for combining outputs can be applied.

For sum rule, created posterior probabilities are added up for two classes and higher value determined the class label. In max rule, the network, producing the maximum of posterior probabilities determined the class label and the others are ignored. To find the majority vote, each networks' output is converted to class labels by applying a threshold and three agreeing classifiers determine the class label of the test datum. Table 4 shows the obtained success rates on test set by applying these combining rules.

Table 4. Success rates (number and percentage) for combining rules

Combining rule	Combined networks			
	MLP1-MLP5		MLP6-MLP8	
	#misclassified	*success rate (%)*	*#misclassified*	*success rate (%)*
Sum	4	94	6	90
majority vote	5	92	6	90
Max	5	92	6	90

4 Conclusion

According to these results, it can be concluded that the best individual performance is produced by MLP6 and MLP7 in which entire data set is used for training and testing purpose. However, as the dimension of the data and relatively network size increase, complexity becomes an important drawback. Since it is difficult to process a large set of data training time increases. However, smaller MLPs which use only one feature vector produce less accurate results and combining their outputs increase the accuracy reasonably.

In addition, combining outputs do not increase the accuracy in experiment 2 as much as in the first one. Increasing the number of networks does not cause any improvement after an optimum number, which is "three" in our experiment.

The combining rules show equal performance in experiment 2, but in experiment 1 sum rule is superior to others. Then, as complexities are considered combining many small networks may be preferred when dealing with large dimensional data.

In further stages of the study, to improve classification accuracy, some feature reduction and/or selection techniques can be tried to reduce the dimension of data and so more features can be included in classification process.

References

1. Lee L., Grimson W.: Gait analysis for recognition and classification, Proceedings of the IEEE Conference on Face and Gesture Recognition, (2002)
2. Beggy R., Kamruzzaman J.: A Comparison of Neural Networks and Support Vector Machines for Recognizing Young-Old Gait Patterns, Proceeding of IEEE TENCON Conference, (2003)
3. Davis R. B., DeLuca P. A., Romness M. J.: Clinical Gait Analysis and Its Role in Treatment Decision-Making", Medscape General Medicine 1-1, (1999)
4. Kohle M., Merkl D., Kastner J.: Clinical gait analysis by neural networks: issues and experiences, Proceedings of the 10th IEEE Symposium on Computer-Based Medical Systems, pp.138, (1997)
5. Wu W., Su F., Cheng Y., Chou Y.: Potential of the Genetic Algorithm Neural Network in the Assessment of Gait Patterns in Ankle Arthrodesis, Annals of Biomedical Engineering, 29, pp. 83–91, (2001)
6. Barton J. G., Lees A.: An application of neural networks for distinguishing gait patterns on the basis of hip-knee joint angle diagrams, Gait & Posture, 5, pp. 28-33, (1997)
7. Kohle M., Merkl D.: Analyzing human gait patterns for malfunction detection, Proceedings of the 2000 ACM symposium on Applied computing, 1, (2000)
8. Begg R. K., Palaniswami M., Owen B.: Support Vector Machines for Automated Gait Classification, IEEE Transactions On Biomedical Engineering, 52-5, (2005)
9. Bertani B., Cappello A., Benedetti M.G., Simoncini L., Catani F.: Flat foot functional evaluation using pattern recognition of ground reaction data, Clinical Biomechanics 14, pp. 484-493, (1999)
10. Lakany H., Hayes G.: An algorithm for recognizing walkers, Proceedings of the International Conference on AVBPA, pp. 112-118, (1997)
11. Anonymous
12. Tanawongsuwan R., Bobick A.: Gait Recognition from Time-Normalized Joint-Angle Trajectories in the Walking Plane, CVPR, 02-2, pp. 726, (2001)
13. Mao J., A case study on bagging, boosting and basic ensembles of neural networks for OCR, Proceeding of IJCNN-98, 3, pp.1828-1833, (1998)
14. Kim J., Ahn J., Cho S.: Ensemble competitive learning neural networks with reduced input dimension, Int J Neural Syst., pp 133-42, (1995)
15. Sharkey A. J. C: On combining artificial neural networks, Connection Science, 8, pp 299-314, (1996)
16. Sharkey A. J. C: Types of multinet system, Lecture Notes in Computer Science, Vol. 2364. Springer-Verlag, Berlin Heidelberg, (2002)
17. Kittler J., Hatef M., Duin R. P.W., Matas J.: On Combining Classifiers, IEEE Transactions on Pattern Analysis and Machine Intelligence, 20-3, (1998)
18. R. O. Duda, P. E. Hart, and D. G. Stork, *Pattern Classification*, 2nd. ed., Wiley, New York (2001)

Training of Multilayer Perceptron Neural Networks by Using Cellular Genetic Algorithms

M. Orozco-Monteagudo, A. Taboada-Crispí, and A. Del Toro-Almenares

Center for Studies on Electronics and Information Technologies, Universidad Central de Las Villas, Carretera a Camajuaní, km 5 ½ , Santa Clara, VC, CP 58430, Cuba
morozco@uclv.edu.cu, ataboada@uclv.edu.cu, anestodt@uclv.edu.cu

Abstract. This paper deals with a method for training neural networks by using cellular genetic algorithms (CGA). This method was implemented as software, CGANN-Trainer, which was used to generate binary classifiers for recognition of patterns associated with breast cancer images in a multi-objective optimization problem. The results reached by the CGA with the Wisconsin Breast Cancer Database, and the Wisconsin Diagnostic Breast Cancer Database, were compared with some other methods previously reported using the same databases, proving to be an interesting alternative.

Keywords: Neural networks, genetic algorithms, cellular automata, multi-objective classification.

1 Introduction

The trend of using Multilayer Perceptron Neural Networks (MLP) [1] for the solution of classification problems in pattern recognition applications is understandable due to their capacity to imitate the nature of the human brain (learning capacity), and the fact that their structure can be formulated mathematically. The functionality of the topology of the MLP is determined by a learning algorithm able to modify the parameters of the net. The algorithm of Backpropagation (BP), based on the method of steepest descent [1] in the process of upgrading the connection weights, is the most commonly used by the scientific community. The main limitations and problems that present the BP algorithm in training the MLP are exposed in [2]. Recently, numerous works have been reported trying to overcome their main limitations. However, the topology selection issue [3] for MLP still leaves margin for improvements. At the same time, it is not clear what algorithm, or combination of algorithms, is the most appropriate to achieve the objective of reducing complexity of the classifiers and, simultaneously, increasing their benefits in terms of classification effectiveness, for a particular application, and much less for one with a more general character.

On the other hand, Evolutionary Algorithms (EA) have demonstrated great effectiveness to solve problems of Multiobjective Optimization (MO) [4]. In addition, the use of Hierarchical Codification [5] (Fig. 1), combined with the EA, provides advantages in the determination of solutions for problems where the determination of a good structure (ignored *a priori*), is of vital importance. The enormous capacity of computation of the Cellular Automata (CA) [6] gives, in conjunction with EA, a very

J.F. Martínez-Trinidad et al. (Eds.): CIARP 2006, LNCS 4225, pp. 389 – 398, 2006.

desirable characteristic: the population, when having a certain space distribution, will be more representative of the search space and, therefore, the method will be less vulnerable to the phenomenon of premature convergence.

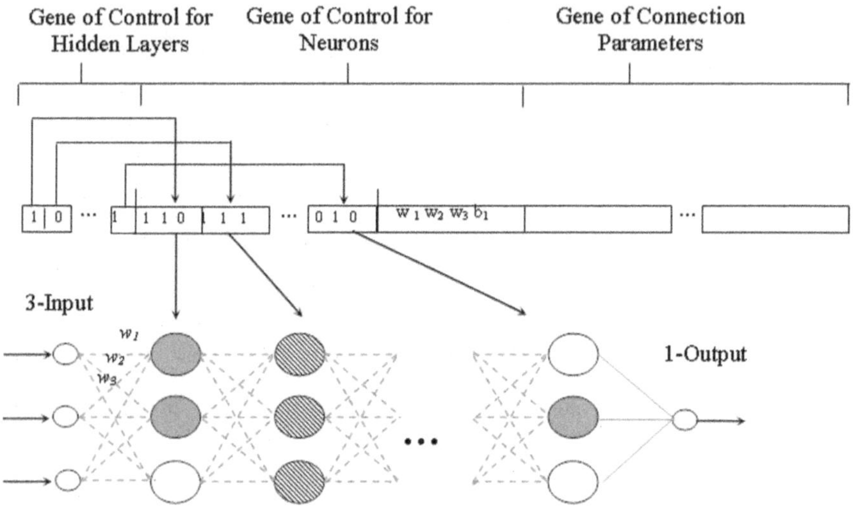

Fig. 1. MLP Hierarchical Codification

2 Materials and Methods

This work is conceived to build general purpose classifiers for pattern recognition, so its use is feasible for any classification problem where it is necessary to discern between two or more classes. This kind of problem is very common, therefore, the field of application of the developed method is very wide, and the definition of materials to be used depends on the problem to be solved.

2.1 CGA for the Construction of Binary Classifiers Based on MLP

A cellular genetic algorithm (CGA) [7] is represented by a probabilistic cellular automaton where the state of each cell is represented by a chromosome.

Each cell should reproduce with some other of its neighborhood, being the descending chromosomes those that substitute the previous generation, according to the replacement technique that is used. The differences between CGA and conventional genetic algorithms reside in three fundamental aspects:

1. There is a space distribution that determines the reproduction processes.
2. The selection process is for every element of the population (better or worse adapted) and the candidates to mate will be only those that are in the neighborhood inside the cellular automata.

3. The replacement will be for the population's individuals and it will be in:
   - Generational Genetic Algorithm, where the offspring always replaces the progenitor.
   - Elitist replacement, where the replacement occurs only if the offspring has more adaptation than its father.

These characteristics guarantee a better representation of the population for the search space, for being the reproduction mechanism less elitist and the population's individual compete only with its neighborhood.

2.2 Punctuation by Means of Successive Refinement of the Pareto Optimal Set

From the multiobjective formulation of the problem of construction of binary classifiers, and the description of the cellular genetic algorithms, the combination of both is presented to create the CGA that solves the outlined problem.

Fig. 2 shows the complete process that governs the developed CGA. The relationships among the main stages that compose this process are illustrated here. Next, every stage is described, as well as the interactions among them.

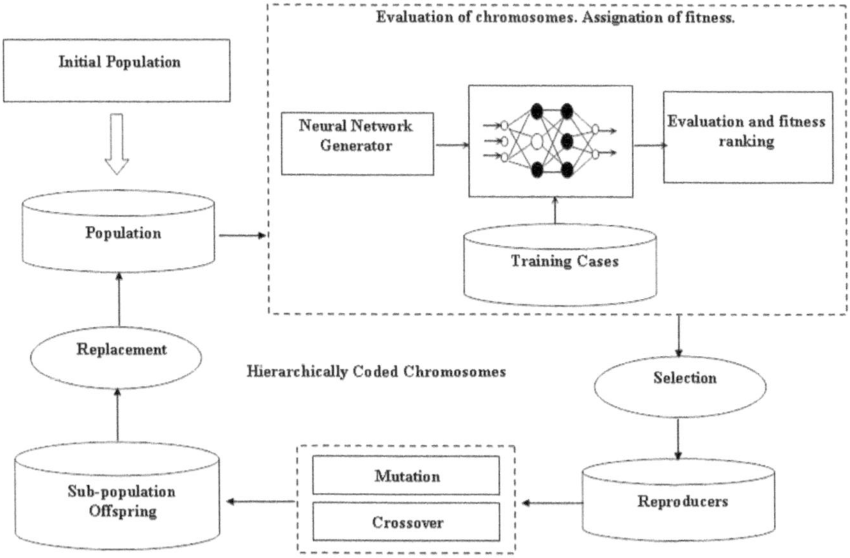

Fig. 2. Scheme for construction of classifiers based on MLP by using CGA

Initial population: A population of chromosomes where each chromosome codes a MLP (topology and connection weight randomly assigned) that constitutes a potential solution of the problem of MO to solve.

Evaluation and punctuation of chromosomes: The assignment of fitness is carried out by using the punctuation outline developed in [8]. The ranking of an individual is calculated as the weighting sum of the dominances of an individual in each one of the corresponding schemes, obtained by suppressing objective functions corresponding to the problem. This method of fitness assignment reduces the effect introduced by not dominated solutions in a local way, the specialization phenomenon, and it is capable, also, of sampling uniformly regions of the space of solutions.

Selection: A stochastic scheme of selection is used to allow that the individuals with more fitness have bigger probability of being selected and, as a result, they can give place to a bigger number of descending.

Mutation operators and crossover: The characteristics of the structure used in the Hierarchical Code of the chromosomes, presuppose the employment of specific genetic operations, developed for levels, by using any variant of the traditional methods: one-point crossover, multipoint crossover, or uniform crossover [2].

Subpopulation of offspring: This stage comprises those descendants that will participate in the replacement process. This offspring subpopulation will be the initial population's image and each individual has an offspring that occupies, in the subpopulation, the same place that the father in the initial population.

Replacement: A strategy of generational or elitist replacement is used. The process of optimization finishes when a specific number of iterations has been reached.

2.3 Evaluation of the Method to Train Multilayer Perceptron by Using CGA

In this work, specifically, the model developed for the problem of diagnostic of breast cancer will be used. Two standard databases, the Wisconsin Breast Cancer Database (WBC) and the Wisconsin Diagnostic Breast Cancer Database (WDBC) are used for evaluation. Next, these databases are briefly described, along with the works where they are used for evaluation of algorithms of classification.

Wisconsin Breast Cancer Database (WBC). The Wisconsin Breast Cancer Database (WBC) was obtained in the Hospitals of the University of Wisconsin, USA. This contains 699 examples belonging to two different classes: malign and benign. Sixteen of these cases present incomplete information, so only 683 were used, 444 (65%) of the Benign Class and 239 (35%) of Malign class. Each case is described by nine attributes, corresponding to subjective evaluations (Clump Thickness, Uniformity of Cell Size, Uniformity of Cell Shape, Marginal Adhesion, Single Epithelial Cell Size, Bare Nuclei, Bland Chromatin, Normal Nucleoli, and Mitoses), with values between 1 and 10, corresponding to descriptions of the cells obtained by means of microscopic examination. An additional attribute indicates the class associated to this description.

The methods reported with the WBC and used to compare with the results of the cellular genetic algorithms (CGA) here implemented are:

- M1: Uses the multi-surface method [9], [10], [11].
- M2: Uses instance-based learning [12].
- M3: Uses linear programming to train neural networks [13].
- M4: Uses evolutionary algorithms to build classifiers based on MLP, by means of elimination of connections among the hidden neurons [3].
- M5: Uses neural networks after a previous process of selection of features [14], [15].
- M6: Uses a group of extracted rules of an MLP [16].
- M7: Uses a fuzzy system built by means of evolutionary algorithms [17].

- M8: Uses evolutionary algorithms with hierarchical code to build classifiers based on MLP [2].
- M9: Uses classification rules by means of a scheme of weighting of the nearest neighborhood method [18].

Wisconsin Diagnostic Breast Cancer Database (WDBC). The Wisconsin Diagnostic Breast Cancer (WDBC), similarly, was obtained in the Hospitals of the University of Wisconsin. This database contains a total of 569 cases, 357 Benign (63%) and 212 Malign (37%). Observations are described by 30 attributes corresponding to three statistical values that are calculated from ten geometric measurements of the cells (Radius, Texture, Perimeter, Area, Softness, Compactness, Concavity, Number of Points of Concavity, Symmetry, and Fractal Dimension), plus one corresponding to its classification: benign or malign. The observations are based on descriptions of the cells, obtained by means of the microscopic observation.

The methods reported with the WDBC and used to compare with the results of the cellular genetic algorithms (CGA) here implemented are:

- D1: Uses Machine Learning with linear programming [19].
- D2: Uses classification rules by means of an outline of weighting of the nearest neighborhood method [18].

During the processing stage, in this work (CGA), the attributes of the WDBC database were normalized between 0 and 1 by using a linear transformation.

Software CGANN-Trainer. To validate the proposed method, the software CGANN-Trainer was implemented. This software allows changing the input parameters of the algorithm such as: MLP topology (the widest), transfer functions, objective functions to optimize with their respective grade of importance, dimensionality, and type of neighborhood of the CA, crossover and mutation probabilities of the genes of every layer in which the chromosome is divided. The process of training can be supervised by monitoring the evaluations of every objective function. When finishing, the nets with the best benefits can be saved in a text file, which can be used by other applications later.

Formulation of optimal binary classifiers, based on MLP, as a problem of multiobjective optimization. The formulation of the problem for the construction of classifiers based on MLP as a problem of MO tries to find a binary classifier, based on a MLP that minimizes some of the objective functions (f_1, f_2, f_3, f_4, f_5, f_6) related with the acting of the classifier and, simultaneously, with the complexity of the associated topology.

Five of these objective functions (f_1, f_2, f_3, f_4, f_5) are calculated by using well-known indexes: Sensibility (*Se*), Specificity (*Sp*), Positive Predictivity (*PP*), Negative Predictivity (*NP*) and Rate of Classification (*RC*). In turn, these approaches are calculated by using four basic measures recommended by the AAMI (American for the Advancement of Medical Instrumentation): True Positive (TP), False Positive (FP), True Negative (TN) and False Negative (FN).

Sensibility (*Se*): Is the fraction of elements of the main class (in this case, Malign) correctly classified and it is calculated as,

$$Se = \frac{TP}{TP + FN} = 1 - \frac{FN}{TP + FN}. \tag{1}$$

Specificity (*Sp*): Is the fraction of elements of the complementary class (in this case, Benign) correctly classified and it is calculated as,

$$Sp = \frac{TN}{TN + FP} = 1 - \frac{FP}{TN + FP}. \tag{2}$$

Positive Predictivity (*PP*): Is the fraction of elements of the main class (in this case, Malign) correctly classified with regard to the positive classifications and it is calculated as,

$$PP = \frac{TP}{TP + FP} = 1 - \frac{FP}{TP + FP}. \tag{3}$$

Negative Predictivity (*NP*): Is the fraction of elements of the complementary class (in this case, Benign) correctly classified with regard to the negative classifications and it is calculated as,

$$NP = \frac{TN}{TN + FN} = 1 - \frac{FN}{TN + FN}. \tag{4}$$

Rate of Classification (*RC*): Is the total fraction of correct classifications and it is calculated as,

$$RC = \frac{TP + TN}{TP + TN + FP + FN} = 1 - \frac{FP + FN}{TP + TN + FP + FN}. \tag{5}$$

In this context, *TP* is the number of elements of the main class (Malign) correctly classified; *FP* and *TN* correspond to the number of elements of the complementary class (Benign) incorrectly and correctly classified, respectively, and *FN* is the number of elements of the main class incorrectly classified.

From these indexes, some of the following objective functions were considered to minimize, during the process of optimization:

$$f_1 = 1 - Se = \frac{FN}{TP + FN}, \tag{6}$$

$$f_2 = 1 - Sp = \frac{FP}{TN + FP}, \tag{7}$$

$$f_3 = 1 - PP = \frac{FP}{TP + FP}, \tag{8}$$

$$f_4 = 1 - NP = \frac{FN}{TN + FN}, \text{ and} \tag{9}$$

$$f_5 = 1 - RC = \frac{FP + FN}{TP + TN + FP + FN}. \tag{10}$$

In general, it is desirable that these objective functions, simultaneously, reach values near to zero. However, solutions of compromise are usually selected. Among the used indexes, sensibility is generally considered the most critical one. This is given by the importance that has to classify correctly an element of the main class (Malign), in comparison with the false alarms that can be emitted.

The sixth objective function (f_6) is related to the complexity of the topology associated to the classifier and it is calculated as the number of active neurons (N_A) of the MLP divided by the maximum number of neurons that admits the topology (N_{Ad}):

$$f_6 = \frac{N_A}{N_{Ad}}. \tag{11}$$

The specification of the grade of importance, that is, the associated weight, of every objective function is determined by the specific characteristics of the problem to solve and corresponds to the specialist its assignment.

By means of the optimization of these four objective functions simultaneously, it is guaranteed that the classifiers have a drop error rate, as well as a topology of reduced complexity, increasing the benefits during their exploitation.

During the process of optimization were used the functions f_1, f_5 and f_6. f_1 depends directly on the FN, which is the most sensitive variable of a problem of classification of cancerous cells. The function f_5 involves all the other ones. f_6 guarantees to find the simplest classifier.

Experiment 1: WBC database classification

Training Cases: 333 cases from WBC (49 %), randomly selected. The rest (51 %) was used as the test set.

Topology of the MLP:

9 input neurons; 2 hidden layers; 6 neurons per layer; and one output neuron.

Hidden layer transfer function: $$lsigm(n) = \frac{1}{1+e^{-n}} \tag{12}$$

Output layer transfer function: $$hardl(n) = \begin{cases} 1, & n \geq 0 \\ 0, & n < 0 \end{cases} \tag{13}$$

Population Size: 121

Population Topology: Square with Moore (8-element) neighborhood.

Objective functions (to minimize): f_1, f_5, f_6

Weights associated: 0.45, 0.45, 0.10, for f_1, f_5, f_6, respectively.

Replacement: Elitist.

Experiment 2: WDBC database classification

Training Cases: 350 cases from WDBC (61 %), randomly selected. The rest (39 %) was used as the test set.

Topology of the MLP:

30 input neurons; 2 hidden layers; 8 neurons per layers; and one output neuron.

Hidden layer transfer function: $$\tanh(n) = \frac{e^{n} - e^{-n}}{e^{n} + e^{-n}} \tag{14}$$

Output layer transfer function: $$hardl(n) = \begin{cases} 1, & n \geq 0 \\ 0, & n < 0 \end{cases}$$

Population Size: 121
Population Topology: Square with Moore (8-element) neighborhood.
Objective functions (to minimize): f_1, f_5, f_6
Weights associated: 0.45, 0.45, 0.10, for f_1, f_5, f_6, respectively.
Replacement: Elitist.

3 Results and Discussion

Fig. 3 and Fig. 4 show how the sensibility and the rate of classification (actually f_1 and f_5) behaved during the first 200 iterations of the training process in the experiments 1 and 2, respectively.

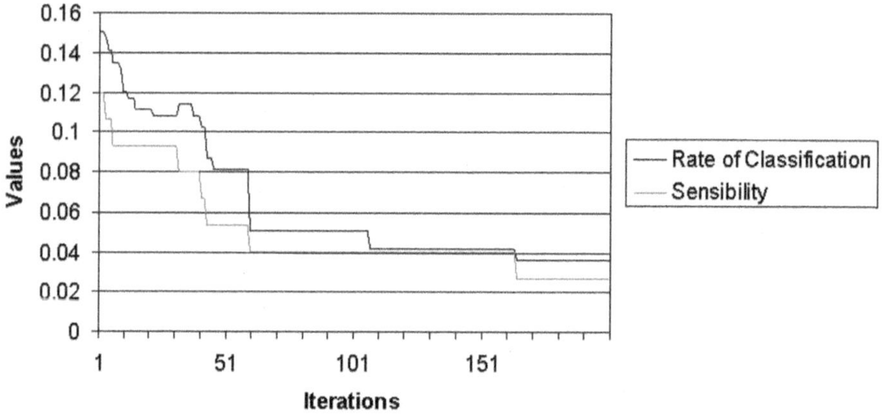

Fig. 3. Behavior of sensibility and rate of classification (f_1 and f_5) during the first 200 iterations of the training process in experiment 1

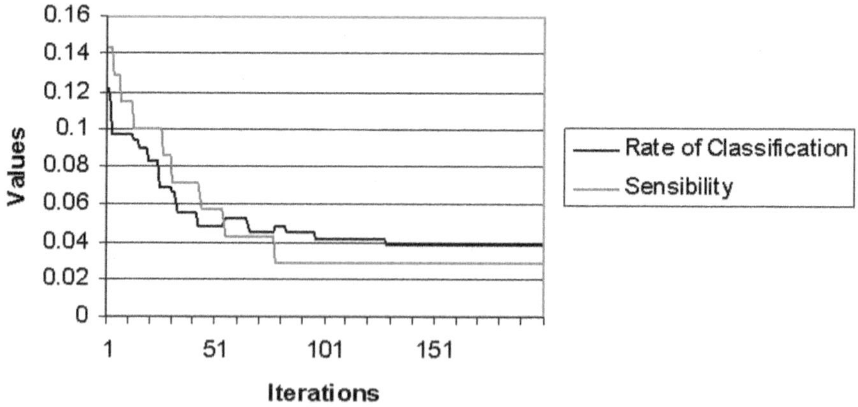

Fig. 4. Behavior of sensibility and rate of classification (f1 and f5) during the first 200 iterations of the training process in experiment 2

Table 1 presents the results reached by the two classifiers, based on MLP, built by means of the experiments 1 and 2, respectively. Its selection was motivated from its behavior in all indexes under optimization, with regard to the rest of the solutions corresponding to the set of best individuals of each experiment. Every index was calculated for the training cases (TC1), the test cases (TC2) and for the complete database (TC1+TC2), in each experiment. The information on the topology of the MLP, corresponding to the opposing classifiers is also shown in Table 1.

Table 1. Indexes obtained with the CGA for experiments 1 and 2

	Experiment 1			*Experiment 2*		
Criteria	*TC1*	*TC2*	*TC1+TC2*	*TC1*	*TC2*	*TC1+TC2*
Se (%)	98.67	96.95	97.49	98.57	95.77	96.70
Sp (%)	98.06	95.70	97.07	100	99.27	99.72
PP (%)	93.67	95.21	94.71	100	99.27	99.51
NP (%)	99.60	97.27	98.63	99.54	95.80	98.07
RC (%)	98.19	96.28	97.22	99.65	97.50	98.59
Topol.	1 hidden layer, 3 neurons			1 hidden layer, 4 neurons		

The results obtained for both experiments were compared with those reported by different methods in the specialized literature, for the same databases.

This comparison is shown in the Table 2, for the experiments 1 and 2. The CGA proved to be an interesting alternative for pattern recognition applications, obtaining results comparable and sometimes better than those previously reported. The software CGANN-Trainer was very useful to generate the neural network and to evaluate its performance.

Table 2. RC (%) reported for different algorithms used to classify cases from the WBC and WDBC databases

WBC									
M1	**M2**	**M3**	**M4**	**M 5**	**M6**	**M7**	**M8**	**M9**	**CGA**
95.9	93.7	97.4	97.5	97.2	97.9	97.8	95.5	97.0	**97.2**

WDBC		
D1	**D2**	**CGA**
97.1	98.1	**98.6**

Acknowledgement

This work was partially supported by the Canadian International Development Agency Project Tier II-394-TT02-00 and by the Flemish VLIR-UOS Programme for Institutional University Co-operation (IUC).

References

1. H. Demuh, Neural Network Design, PWS Publishing Company, 1996.
2. K.F. Man, K.S. Tang, S. Kwong, Genetic Algorithms: Concepts and Designs, Springer, 1999. Chapter 7, Hierarchical Genetic Algorithm in Computational Intelligence, 155-174.
3. G. Bebis, K. Takis, Coupling Weight Elimination and Genetic Algorithms, Proc. of Int. Conf. on Neural Networks, Washington D.C., USA, 2 (1996) 1115-1121.
4. F. Menczer, R. Belew, Local Selection, Evolutionary Programming, VII, LNCS 1447, Berlin, Springer, (1999).
5. K.F. Man, K.S. Tang, S. Kwong, Genetic Algorithms: Concepts and Designs, Springer, 1999. Chapter 4, Hierarchical Genetic Algorithm, 65-74.
6. O. Lafe, "Cellular Automata Transforms" KLUWER ACADEMIC PUBLISHERS, 2000.
7. D. Whitley, "An overview of Evolutionary Algorithms: Practical Issues and Common Pitfalls" Information and Software Technology, 43(14):817-831, 2001.
8. A. del Toro, M. Orozco, C. A. Ferrer, M. Mendoza, A. Taboada, "A Novel Pareto-Based Fitness Assignment Method and its Evaluation in Genetic Programming", I Congreso Nacional de Reconocimiento de Patrones, Havana, 2003, ISBN 959-7056-19-4.
9. O.L. Mangasarian, R. Setiono, W.H. Wolberg, Pattern Recognition for Linear Programming, Theory and Applications in Medical Diagnosis, (1990) 22-30.
10. O.L. Mangasarian, W.H. Wolberg, Cancer Diagnosis Via Linear Programming, SIAM News, 23 (5) (1990) 1-18.
11. W.H. Wolberg, O.L. Mangasarian, Multi-Surface Method of Pattern Separation for Medical Diagnosis Applied to Breast Cytology, Proc. of the National Academy of Sciences, U.S.A., 87 (1990) 9193-9196.
12. J. Zhang, Selecting Typical Instances in Instance-Based Learning, In Proc. of the Ninth International Machine Learning Conference, Aberdeen, Scotland: Morgan Kaufmann, (1992) 470-479.
13. K.P. Bennett, O.L. Mangasarian, Neural Network Training via Linear Programming, Advances in Optimization and Parallel Computing, (1992) 56-67.
14. R. Setiono, Extracting Rules from Pruned Neural Networks for Breast Cancer Diagnosis, Artificial Intelligence in Medicine, (1996) 37-51.
15. R. Setiono, R.H. Liu, Symbolic Representation of Neural Networks, Computer, (1996) 71-77.
16. L. Taha, J. Ghosh, Evaluation and Ordering of Rules Extracted from Feed-Forward Networks, Proc. IEEE International Conference on Neural Networks, (1997) 221-226.
17. C.A. Peña-Reyes, M. Sipper, A Fuzzy-Genetic Approach to Breast Cancer Diagnosis, Artificial Intelligence in Medicine, (1999) 131-155.
18. S.C. Bagui, S. Bagui, K. Pal, N.R. Pal, Breast Cancer Detection using Rank Nearest Neighbor Classification Rules, Pattern Recognition, 36 (2003) 25-34.
19. N. Street, Cancer Diagnosis and Prognosis via Linear-Programming-Based Machine Learning, Ph.D. Dissertation, University of Wisconsin-Madison, Available as UW Mathematical Programming Technical Report 94-14, (1994).

Combining Neural Networks and Clustering Techniques for Object Recognition in Indoor Video Sequences

Francesc Serratosa[1], Nicolás Amézquita Gómez[1], and René Alquézar[2]

[1] Departament d'Enginyeria Informàtica i Matemàtiques, Universitat Rovira i Virgili, Campus Sescelades, Av. dels Països Catalans 26, 43007, Tarragona, Spain
[2] Dept. Llenguatges i Sistemes Informàtics, Universitat Politècnica de Catalunya, Campus Nord, Edifici Omega, 08034 Barcelona, Spain
{francesc.serratosa, amezquita}@urv.cat, alquezar@lsi.upc.edu

Abstract. This paper presents the results obtained in a real experiment for object recognition in a sequence of images captured by a mobile robot in an indoor environment. Objects are simply represented as an unstructured set of spots (image regions) for each frame, which are obtained from the result of an image segmentation algorithm applied on the whole sequence. In a previous work, neural networks were used to classify the spots independently as belonging to one of the objects of interest or the background from different spot features (color, size and invariant moments). In this work, clustering techniques are applied afterwards taking into account both the neural net outputs (class probabilities) and geometrical data (spot mass centers). In this way, context information is exploited to improve the classification performance. The experimental results of this combined approach are quite promising and better than the ones obtained using only the neural nets.

Keywords: Clustering, Spot, Class probabilities, Neural Nets.

1 Introduction

One of the most general and challenging problems a mobile robot has to confront is to identify and locate objects that are common in its environment. To this end, a teacher may show what the object is from images taken in different views and a robot may apply some learning abilities to obtain a certain model of the object and an associated recognition procedure.

A very important issue is to determine the type of object model to learn. In our point of view, a useful model should be relatively simple and easy to acquire from the result of image processing steps. For instance, the result of a color image segmentation process, consisting of a set of regions (spots, from now on) characterized by different features (related to color, size and shape), may be a good starting point to learn the model. Although structured models like adjacency attributed graphs or random graphs can be synthesized for each object from several segmented images [1], we have decided to investigate first a much simpler approach in which the object is just represented as an unstructured set of spots. One of the main drawbacks

J.F. Martínez-Trinidad et al. (Eds.): CIARP 2006, LNCS 4225, pp. 399–405, 2006.

of the structural methods is that the segmented images from one frame to the other can be quite different, and so, it is difficult to match the actual spots (usually represented by nodes of the graphs) with the previous ones. The main aim of our approach is to accept these differences between segmented images and use a more coarse approach in which the basic element is not the spot or region of the segmented image but its pixels.

In a previous recent work [2], feed-forward neural networks were used to classify the spots independently as belonging to one of a finite set of objects or the background (defined as everything else). In this work, clustering techniques are applied afterwards taking into account both the neural net outputs (class probabilities) and geometrical data (spot mass centers). In this way, context information can be exploited to improve the classification performance.

The classification of segmented image regions for object recognition has been addressed in several works. Neural networks are used in [3] not only to classify known objects but to detect new image objects as well in video sequences. In [4], objects of interest are first localized, then features are extracted from the regions of interest and finally a neural network is applied to classify the objects. Support vector machines are used in [5] to classify a segmented image region in two categories, either a single object region or a mixture of background and foreground (multiple object region), in order to derive a top-down segmentation method.

2 Image Acquisition, Pre-processing, Segmentation and Feature Extraction

The input of our system is a digital video sequence. The images in the sequence were preprocessed by applying a median filter on the RGB planes and segmented by the Felzenszwalb – Huttenlocher algorithm [6]. The output of the segmentation and feature extraction process for each image consists of a list of spots (that represent regions) with their features.

Two types of information were extracted from the spots: color and geometry. With regards to color, average and variance values for each one of the three RGB bands were calculated for each spot on the basis of the corresponding intensity values of the spot pixels in the original image. This is, the result of the segmentation algorithm served to identify the pixels of every spot, but their color features were computed from the original RGB image.

Regarding the geometrical information, we were mainly interested in shape descriptors that were invariant to translation and scale, and to this end, we decided to use the seven invariant geometric moments defined by Hu [7] (whose equations are also reproduced in [2]). In addition and since the range of variation of the objects' size was rather limited in the video sequence, we also calculated and used the size of each spot, i.e. its area measured in number of pixels. Hence, 14 features (6 for color and 8 for geometry) were computed for each spot. Moreover, the mass center was also calculated.

3 Spot Classification Methodology

A neural net is first trained to classify each spot within certain regions of the images in the sequence. The inputs of the neural net are the features of each spot and the target is the class that we impose to each spot. To impose the class of each spot, we manually marked on the images a rectangular box for each object of interest. Thus, the spots whose mass centers are inside each box are forced to belong to the class that the box represents. Figure 1 shows one of the images and its segmentation together with the boxes used to impose the classification.

Fig. 1. One of the original images (left) and the corresponding segmented image (right), with four boxes marked on them. Spot mass centers are also displayed in the right image.

In the recognition stage, each image from the video sequence is segmented, then for each spot of the segmented image, a first classification was made using the neural net.

A second step for spot classification involves the detection and reclassification of possibly misclassified spots based on the context information provided by the mass centers of the spots classified as the same class (or object) in the same frame.

For each one of the classes (or objects) o and for each frame f, a weighted mass center wmc(o,f) was computed as

$$wmc(o,f) = \frac{\sum_{s=1}^{ns(o,f)} p(o/s)a(s)mc(s)}{\sum_{s=1}^{ns(o,f)} p(o/s)a(s)} \tag{1}$$

where ns(o,f) is the number of spots classified as object o in frame f, p(o|s) is the a-posteriori class probability of object o for spot s given by the net, and a(s) and mc(s) are respectively the area and mass center of s.

Then, for every spot in the segmented image classified by the net as an object, the distance between its mass center and the weighted mass center of the assigned object was computed. If this distance exceeded a given threshold, the spot was marked as possibly misclassified and it was optionally reclassified to the object with the nearest mass center. Note that this step is a kind of spot clustering process that is inspired in both the dynamic and k-means clustering algorithms, but starting from the clusters (class assignments) given by the neural network.

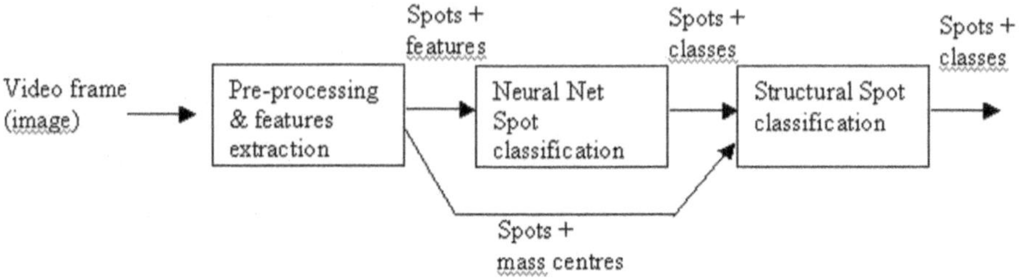

Fig. 2. Classification process based on three main steps. First, the extraction of the spots and features. Second, spot classification based on a Neural Net and third, reclassification of the spots based on its position respect the other spots within the same class.

Figure 3 displays an example of the beneficial effects of performing the reclassification based on structural information. In the left hand image, there are two spots that were misclassified by the net, one in the chair was classified as wastebasket and one in the wastebasket was classified as chair. These spots could be correctly reclassified after this step, as shown in dark green and dark blue in the right hand image.

Fig. 3. Spots classified as belonging to the three objects by the net (left) and the result of the reclassification after the clustering (right)

4 Experimental Results

A digital video sequence of 88 images was captured by an RGB camera installed on the MARCO mobile robot at the Institute of Robotics and Industrial Informatics (IRI,

UPC-CSIC) in Barcelona. The sequence shows an indoor scene with some slight perspective and scale changes caused by the movement of the robot while navigating through a room. The objects of interest in the scene were a box, a chair and a pair of identical wastebaskets put together side by side (see Figure 1), and the objective was to discriminate them from the rest of the scene (background) and locate them in the images.

For the training stage, four rectangular boxes were manually marked on the images with a graphics device to encompass the three objects of interest and a large region on the floor (figure 1). In order to assign a class label to each spot, to be used as target for the spot pattern in the neural network training and test processes, a simple decision was made: each one of the four rectangular boxes constituted a class and all the spots that had its mass center inside the window and a size large than 100 pixels were assigned the same class label.

We used a neural net with a feed-forward 2-layer perceptron architecture using standard backpropagation as training algorithm. From previous experiments reported in [2], we set the number of hidden units to 180, although it was shown in [2] that the results were not very sensitive to this choice. Hyperbolic tangent and sine functions were used as activation functions in the hidden layer and the output layer, respectively. For backpropagation, we set a learning rate of 0.003, a momentum parameter of zero and a maximum number of 500 training epochs for each run.

A dataset containing 3,411 labeled patterns (spots) was available after the segmentation of all the 88 images. For each subset of features, a double cross-validation procedure was carried out that generated 90 different partitions of this dataset, each including 80% of the patterns for the training set, 10% for the validation set and 10% for the test set. The validation sets were used for early stopping the training phase. Actually, the network chosen at the end of the training phase was the one that yielded the best classification result on the validation set among the networks obtained after each training epoch.

The results of the double cross-validation procedure obtained for different subsets of features are displayed in Table 1, ordered decreasingly by test classification performance. For each one of the three sets (training, validation and test set), the classification performance is measured as the average percentage of correctly classified patterns in the 90 cross-validation partitions, evaluated in the networks selected after training (the ones that maximize the performance on the validation set). It can be noted that similar results are obtained if the average RGB color features are taken into account, but the performance falls down dramatically when they are not used. The best result was 92.93% test classification performance for a subset comprising color features (both RGB averages and variances) and spot size (and without the shape invariant moments).

These results are in agreement with those reported in [2] with regards to the relative usefulness of the different spot features (i.e., invariant moments are shown to be practically useless and RGB color averages are shown to provide almost all the relevant information), but the absolute classification rates are notably better here, due to a more accurate definition of the rectangular boxes that eliminated from the dataset most of the spots that were incorrectly labeled in [2].

Table 1. It presents the classification results for several groups of selected variables to assess the relative importance of the different types of features (size, color averages, color variances and shape invariant moments)

Classification performance (with feature subsets)			
Feature Subsets	Training	Validation	Test
spot size, average and variance RGB	94.20	93.38	92.93
spot size and average RGB	93.29	93.26	92.75
all 14 features	94.58	93.19	92.72
spot size, average RGB and three first moments	93.47	92.92	92.22
Average RGB and three first invariant moments	92.11	92.37	91.93
Average RGB and the seven invariant moments	92.04	92.35	91.60
spot size and variance RGB	62.12	63.54	63.06
spot size, variance RGB and three first moments	62.46	63.52	62.79
seven invariant moments and variance RGB	55.98	57.48	57.33
seven invariant moments	32.29	32.49	32.38

Using spot size and RGB averages and variances as features, the network (and associated dataset partition) that gave the best result in the training set (97.25%) was selected for computing the weighted mass centers and to assess the effect of the clustering process on the spot classification performance. Table 2 compares the results obtained without clustering with those obtained after clustering and reclassification to the nearest object. A 78.8% of the spots misclassified by the network were correctly reclassified by the clustering and only a 0.1% of the correctly classified spots were incorrectly reclassified.

Table 2. Spot classification results before and after clustering using the net that maximized the result in the training set

Classification performance (with the best feature subsets)			
Classifier	Training	Validation	Test
Only the neural network	97.25	95.01	96.18
Combining the neural net and the clustering	99.34	98.53	99.71

5 Conclusions and Future Work

A simple approach to object recognition in video sequences has been successfully tested combining neural networks and clustering techniques to classify image segmentation regions (spots) as belonging to one of the objects of interest or to the background. Objects are implicitly represented as an unstructured set of spots; no adjacency graph or description of the structure of the object is used. The method is robust to changes between successive frames in the number and shape of the spots associated with each object, as given by the image segmentation algorithm.

In this work, spatial context information has been obtained through the distances between the mass centers of the spots, which allow the formation of semi-supervised clusters, since both the classification labels and probabilities given by the neural net are taken into account as well for the clustering. Other ways of aggregating spatial context can be studied in future work, e.g. relaxation labeling may be used for updating the class probabilities of neighboring spots.

The obtained classification results are quite good, but it must be noted that only the spots in some regions of interest were processed and just three objects (plus background) were considered as classes. A more realistic experiment would involve the spots of whole images in the test phase and eventually more objects to recognize. Moreover, the dynamic nature of the visual data should be exploited by somehow integrating the tasks of object detection, recognition and tracking in consecutive video frames.

In the long-term, our purpose is to design a robust dynamic approach to object recognition and tracking in video sequences based on unstructured sets of spots, which can deal with the variations in the object views resulting from the movement of a mobile robot in an indoor environment.

References

1. Sanfeliu A., Serratosa F., Alquézar R., "Second-order random graphs for modeling sets of attributed graphs and their application to object learning and recognition", Int. Journal of Pattern Recognition and Artificial Intelligence, Vol. 18 (3), 375-396, (2004).
2. Amezquita Gómez N. and Alquézar R. "Object recognition in indoor video sequences by classifying image segmentation regions using neural networks", Proc. 10th Iberoamerican Congress on Pattern Recognition, CIARP 2005, Havana, Cuba, M. Lazo and A. Sanfeliu (eds.), Springer-Verlag, LNCS 3773, Berlin, pp.93-102, (2005).
3. Singh S., Markou M., Haddon J., "Detection of new image objects in video sequences using neural networks", Proc. SPIE Vol. 3962, pp.204-213, Applications of Artificial Neural Networks in Image Processing V, Nasser M. Nasrabadi; Aggelos K. Katsaggelos; Eds., (2000).
4. Fay R., Kaufmann U., Schwenker F., Palm G., "Learning object recognition in a neurobotic system". In: H-M. Groß, K. Debes, H-J. Böhme (Eds.) 3rd Workshop on SelfOrganization of AdaptiVE Behavior (SOAVE 2004). Fortschritt -Berichte VDI, Reihe 10 Informatik / Kommunikation, Nr. 743, pp. 198-209, VDI Verlag, Düsseldorf, (2004).
5. Wang W., Zhang A. and Song Y., "Identification of objects from image regions", IEEE Int. Conf. on Multimedia and Expo (ICME 2003), Baltimore, July 6-9,(2003).
6. Felzenszwalb P. and Huttenlocher D., "Efficiently computing a good segmentation". In IEEE Conference on Computer Vision and Pattern Recognition, 98-104, (1998).
7. Hu M-K., "Visual pattern recognition by moment invariants", IRE Trans. on Information Theory, Vol. 8 (2), pp. 179-187, (1962).
8. Bishop C.M., Neural Networks for Pattern Recognition, Oxford University Press,(1995).

Evaluation of Time and Frequency Domain-Based Methods for the Estimation of Harmonics-to-Noise-Ratios in Voice Signals

Carlos A. Ferrer, Eduardo González, and María E. Hernández-Díaz

Center for Studies on Electronics and Information Technologies, Central University of Las Villas, Zip code: 54830, Santa Clara, Cuba
{cferrer, moreira, mariae}@uclv.edu.cu

Abstract. In this paper several approaches of time and frequency domain-based algorithms to estimate harmonics-to-noise ratios (HNR) in voice signals are compared. The approaches covered incorporate a recent time-domain correction to a classic method, as well as a frequency-domain adjustment introduced here. The experimental comparisons include the number of pitch periods needed to obtain the best HNR estimates, as well as the sensitivity of the methods to different perturbations of the periodicity pattern, like shimmer, jitter, noise and combinations of them. Time domain methods show better performance than frequency-based approaches, and moreover, the correction to the ensemble-average time domain technique reduces the required number of pulses by an order of magnitude.

1 Introduction

It has been widely reported that estimates of additive noise levels in voice signals are of diagnostic value to several speech pathologies ([20], [8], [4], [18]). The determination of Harmonics-to-Noise Ratios (HNR) in voiced speech signals is intended to yield a measure of additive noise in the acoustic waveform. For this purpose, several methods have been proposed [11], both in time and frequency (or transformed) domain, and there is no definitive satisfactory solution. A most troubling issue is the interaction of other perturbations of the periodicity pattern, like pulse duration variability (jitter) and pulse amplitude variability (shimmer), in the measured HNR [5]. According to the derivations described analytically in [17], it is not possible to perform separate measurements of each type of perturbation by using spectral-based methods. On the other hand, time domain methods have been criticized ([6][15]) for depending on the correct determination of the individual pulse (pitch epoch) boundaries, among many other method-specific factors.

A much referenced time-domain method was proposed by Yumoto *et al.* [20], who introduced the finding of a pitch epoch "template" by averaging the ensemble of individual pitch pulses. The averaged waveform is known to present a noise variance reduced by a factor of N, the number of averaged pulses. Yumoto proposed to measure HNR as the ratio of the variance of the template to the variance of the differences of the individual pulses with the template (see equation 5). It has been

J.F. Martínez-Trinidad et al. (Eds.): CIARP 2006, LNCS 4225, pp. 406–415, 2006.

criticized [7] for the need of a relatively large number of pulses (30-50) to effectively remove the noise from the template, and influences of jitter and shimmer in the resulting measures of HNR [5].

In spite of this, Yumoto's method remains "the most commonly used time-domain technique" [11] and several authors have worked on its improvement. In [1], a single-pass method was proposed which accounted, under certain considerations, for jitter, shimmer and offset effects. Later, Dynamic Time Warping [13] and Zero Phase Transforms [14] of individual pulses prior to the averaging were used to reduce waveform variability influences in the template. For the same purpose, the ensemble averaging technique was applied [11] to the spectral representations of individual glottal source pulses. Dealing again with waveform variability, Functional Data Analysis was used [9] to perform an optimal time-alignment of pulses prior to averaging. Recently, a theoretical formula (see equation 6) was derived to correct the ensemble averages estimates of HNR for any number of pulses [3], suppressing the need of using a large *N*.

The objective of this paper is to address two issues that remain unclear. First, the ability of the Ensemble-Averages correcting formula in [3] to actually determine the HNR for any number of pulses is tested using simulated signals. Second, the practical extent to which the frequency-domain HNR estimation methods are affected by jitter and shimmer perturbations. The validity of the results in [3] is tested for different pulse lengths, in samples, allowing a more realistic understanding of its practical usefulness. The method in [3] is also compared to the original time-domain version [20] and a correction (developed in this paper) to a frequency domain method [8][2].

2 Description of Signals, Methods and Experiments

2.1 Signals

Simulated vowels were generated according to the method used in [10] and [12], where the speech signal $s(t)$ is obtained as the convolution of two signals, the vocal tract impulse response $h(t)$ and an excitation impulse train $i(t)$:

$$i(t) = \sum_n k(t_n)\delta(t - t_n)$$
$$h(t) = \sum_{m=1}^{M} a_m e^{-b_m t} \cos(2\pi f_m t) \qquad (t \geq 0) \tag{1}$$

This convolution results in:

$$s(t) = \sum_n k(t_n) h(t - t_n) \tag{2}$$

where t_n is the time instant of the *n-th* excitation and k is its amplitude. The terms a_m, b_m and f_m represent the amplitude, bandwidth and central frequency, respectively, of the M resonators (formants) used to model the vocal tract. The values of a_m, b_m and f_m used for these resonators are the same as in [10] and [12], corresponding to a vowel /a/ and M=5.

The use of equations (1) and (2) to synthesize the vowel yields an easy way to vary the amount of jitter by controlling t_n, while k can be used to vary shimmer, and the HNR can be controlled by adding noise to $s(t)$.

The sampling frequency F_S was set to 22.05 kHz, and the mean value of fundamental period T0 is t_m=1/150 seconds ('mean' fundamental frequency F0=150 Hz, t_m=147 samples). These values for Fs and F0 are the same than in [12]. For simplicity reasons, only the closest two precedent impulses to the current "t" were considered in the synthesis of (2), since $h(t)$ decays to negligible values for $3{*}t_m$. In any case, a certain amount of interference between two consecutive pulses is introduced. The length of the generated speech signals was set to two seconds, which gives, together with the value of t_m used, an average of 300 pitch pulses on each signal. Four types of signals were generated, according to the presence of jitter, shimmer, additive noise, or a combination of the three periodicity perturbations.

Jittered Signals: The amplitude factor of equations (1) and (2) is left constant ($k=1$) and no noise is added to the signal $s(t)$. The impulse excitation instants are obtained as $t_n = t_{n-1} + t_m + u(n)$, where $u(n)$ is a random real value uniformly distributed in the interval $\pm u_m$. The time difference between two adjacent excitation instants will have then a uniform probability distribution in the range $t_m \pm u_m$. The average pitch duration in samples is t_m= 147. Different values for u_m were used, varying from 0 to 35, in steps of 5 samples, corresponding to values from 0 to 23.8% of t_m in steps of 3.4%. According to [10] jitter almost never exceeds the 25% of t_m.

Shimmered Signals: The amplitude $k(n)$ of the impulses used to generate $s(t)$ are obtained as: $k(n)=1+v(n)$, where $v(n)$ is a random real value, uniformly distributed in the interval $\pm v_m$. The values of v_m used were twice the values of u_m in the previous experiment, measured in percent of the unaltered amplitude k=1, going from 0 to 47.6% in steps of 6.8. This relationship was chosen to keep the ratio of usually accepted limits of jitter (25%) [10] and shimmer (50%) [19]. The temporal separation between the pulses was kept constant, equal to t_m. No noise was added to $s(t)$.

Additive Noise Only: A clean signal $s(n)$, obtained for constant values of $k=1$ and $t_{n+1}=t_n+t_m$, was contaminated with additive white gaussian noise $e(n)$, such that the ratio of the variances of $s(n)$ and $e(n)$ met an intended value of HNR in dB. The values of HNR used (in dB) were ∞, 22, 18, 15, 12, 8, 5, and 2.

Combined Perturbations: All the parameters (u_m, v_m and HNR) were varied simultaneously, in ascending order of perturbation, in the same amounts as in the three previous experiments. In this way, eight different cases are obtained, ranging from the perfectly periodic $s(t)$ to the most distorted waveform with u_m=23.8%, v_m=47.6% and HNR=2 dB.

2.2 HNR Estimation Methods

The HNR estimation methods compared in this paper are the original ensemble averaging technique [20] and its correction to any number of pulses [3] in the time domain. In the frequency domain, the approach proposed in [8] and generalized in [2] was chosen. A brief description of the methods follows.

Time-Domain Method

The ensemble averaging technique departs from assuming each pulse representation $x_i(t)$ prior to averaging as a repetitive signal $s(t)$ plus a noise term $e_i(t)$:

$$x_i(t) = s(t) + e_i(t) \tag{3}$$

A "template" of the periodic component is obtained as the average of the N individual pulses:

$$\bar{x}(t) = \frac{\sum_{i=1}^{N} x_i(t)}{N} = s(t) + \frac{\sum_{i=1}^{N} e_i(t)}{N} \tag{4}$$

and an expression to estimate the HNR is proposed as:

$$HNR_{Yum} = \frac{N \times E\left[\bar{x}^2(t)\right]}{\sum_{i=1}^{N} E\left[(x_i(t) - \bar{x}(t))^2\right]} \tag{5}$$

with E[] denoting the expected value operation. In 3 it is shown that, if noise and signal are uncorrelated, the actual HNR can be expressed in terms of (5) as:

$$HNR = \frac{N-1}{N} HNR_{Yum} - \frac{1}{N} \tag{6}$$

Frequency-Domain Method

The frequency-domain approaches are mostly based in the calculation of a Discrete Fourier Transform to a segment of the signal containing several pulses. Amongst the many transformed-domain approaches ([2][4][6][7][8][11][15][16]) the one proposed by Kojima [8] was chosen, since it shares many of their limitations, but at least suppresses the windowing effects in the HNR estimation. The basic difference of [8] compared to the others is that the segment of analysis is chosen so that it contains an **exactly integer** number of pulses (*N*), regardless of its length in samples (*T*). This method has not been favored by researchers, preferring values of *T* multiples of 2 to use FFT algorithms.

Since the signal is assumed quasi-periodic, the harmonic energy should be concentrated every *N* spectral component, corresponding to the numerator (*Num*) in (8), while the noise energy can be assumed as the difference of the total energy and the harmonic one, as written in the denominator (*Den*) of (8). *T* is the length in samples of the sum of the *N* pulses.

$$HNR_{Koj} = \frac{Num}{Den} = \frac{\sum_{i=1}^{T/N} X(i*N)^2}{\sum_{i=1}^{T} X(i)^2 - \sum_{i=1}^{T/N} X(i*N)^2} \tag{7}$$

The original approach in [8] used N=3 and established spectral bands where the calculated HNR correlated best to the perceived hoarseness. In [2] the method was generalized to use any N and frequency bands.

A Correction to Kojima's Method

Revisiting the idea behind Kojima's method two corrections are apparent: the numerator overrates the harmonic energy, due to the contribution of the noise present at $X(i*N)$, which has been neglected, and the denominator underrates the noise energy, because of the removal of the noise at the same frequencies.

Assuming that the noise has a flat power spectral density and limiting the analysis in the spectral domain to a number of bins B equal to the closest multiple of N smaller than L, it can be shown that the total noise energy E_N in the interval of B bins is:

$$E_N = Den\frac{N}{N-1} \tag{8}$$

Similarly, the total harmonic energy E_H in the B bins can be expressed as:

$$E_H = Num - (N_M * H) = Num - \frac{E_N}{B}\frac{B}{N} = Num - \frac{E_N}{N} = Num - \frac{Den}{N-1} \tag{9}$$

where $N_M=E_N/B$ is the mean noise energy, and $H=B/N$ is the number of harmonics in the B bins. The actual HNR=E_H/E_N is then given by:

$$HNR = \frac{E_H}{E_N} = \frac{Num - \frac{Den}{N-1}}{Den\frac{N}{N-1}} = \frac{Num}{Den}\frac{N-1}{N} - \frac{1}{N} = HNR_{Koj}\frac{N-1}{N} - \frac{1}{N} \tag{10}$$

The resemblance of (10) and (6) is remarkable, and it suggests both methods to be equivalent. The equivalence of time and spectral domain HNR estimations has also been assumed in [15], although the results favored the time-domain approach. It is evident that the correction in (10) is largely relevant for Kojima's method, where small values of N were used (N=3).

2.3 Experiments

The experiments performed were all programmed in ***MatLab 6.5***, and can be separated in two sets:

Time-Domain HNR Sensibility to the Number of Pulses and Pulse Lengths

In this set of experiments the actual ability of the theoretical derivation in [3] (given by (6)) to correct the results of Yumoto's approach (5) is tested. Theoretically, (6) can correct (5) for any number of pulses (N) given that the noise and the repetitive components, as well as each realization of noise, are uncorrelated. A result of zero correlation in stochastic processes is more probable as the number of samples considered approaches infinity. In practice, pitch pulse duration and sampling frequencies impose limits to the pulse lengths (L). For instance, with a typical telephone-quality sampling frequency (8 kHz) a child or an adult woman with moderately high F0 = 400 Hz would generate only 20 samples per period. No study of HNR is likely to be conducted under such circumstances, but this example is illustrative in terms of practical low limits of L. In this work the original [20] and corrected [3] ensemble averages approaches were tested for values of N between 2 and 50, and L between 30 and 10000.

The experiment consisted in evaluating (5) and (6) for a set of N pulses generated randomly by adding N random vectors $\boldsymbol{x}_i$ of length L to a common random vector $\boldsymbol{s}$ of the same length. The variances of $\boldsymbol{s}$ and $\boldsymbol{x}_i$ were chosen to be 4 and 1, respectively, such that calculated HNR should be 4, equivalent to 6 dB. This value is in the range of HNRs tested in the "Additive Noise Only" signals described in section 2.1, allowing the results of this experiment to be extended to those signals.

Sensitivity of HNR Estimation Methods to Different Periodicity Perturbations
This set of experiments consists in the evaluation of the different methods (both time and frequency-domain based) abilities to estimate HNR in the presence of the perturbations shown by the signals described in section 2.1. The objective in this paper is to explore each method's ability to correctly estimate the HNR, and thus, no band limits were imposed on the frequency domain estimation of HNR. More specific configuration settings are described in section 3. A preliminary experiment is conducted comparing the original and corrected Kojima's frequency-domain method (given by (7) and (10)) in the case of "Additive Noise Only", to illustrate the importance of the correction.

3 Results and Discussion

The results of the experiments are divided in the same two sets that were described in section 2.3.

Ensemble-Averages HNR sensibility to Number of Pulses and Pulse Lengths
The results of the comparison of (5) and (6) for different N and L are shown in Fig. 1. The figure plots the mean absolute differences between actual and obtained HNRs for 1000 realizations of the random variables involved in the experiment. The results are normalized with respect to the actual HNR (HNR=4).

The original HNR estimation method shows the criticized need of large N to reach values closer to the minimum "steady state" errors, which occurs for N in the range from 30 to 50 in correspondence with what is stated in [7]. The plot of corrected HNR can be used to realize the limits of the theoretical "complete" suppression of the effect of N in HNR estimation. It can be seen that the mean "steady state" error is reached for different values of N, depending on the number of samples comprised in a pulse length. For a relatively low number of samples (i.e. 30 or 100) a steady error (22% and 12%, respectively) is obtained for 8 or 7 averaged pulses. A "medium" sized pulse (300 samples) reaches a steady error from 4 to 7 pulses (from 8% to 7% mean errors). No more than 4-5 pulses are needed to reach the steady mean error value when the pulse L is above 300 samples.

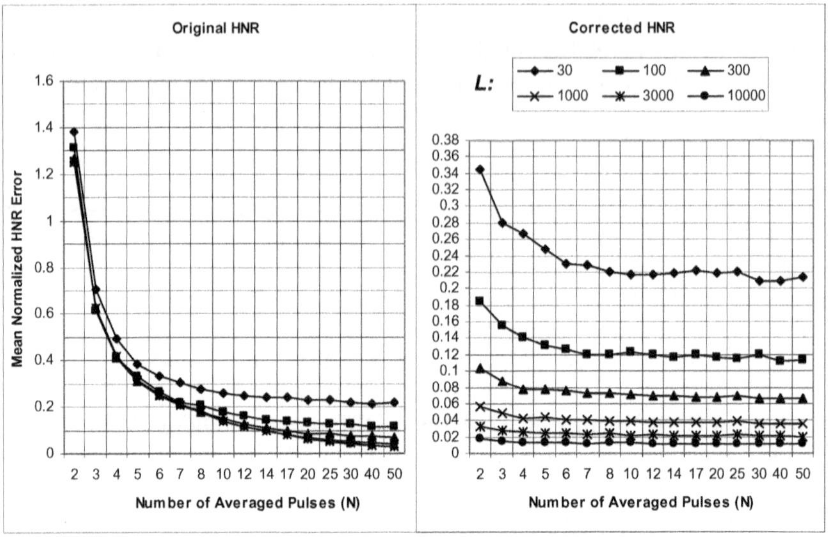

Fig. 1. Original (left) and corrected (right) values of HNR obtained for different cases of averaged pulses (*N*) and pulse lengths (*L*)

Sensibility of HNR estimation methods to Periodicity Perturbations
The illustration of the importance of the correction in (10) of the frequency-domain approach in [8] given in (7) is depicted in Fig. 2. Segment sizes were fixed at 3 (original option in [8]) and 7 pulses, to test the influence of the number of pulses. The latter limit was set to avoid the already criticized use of a large *N*.

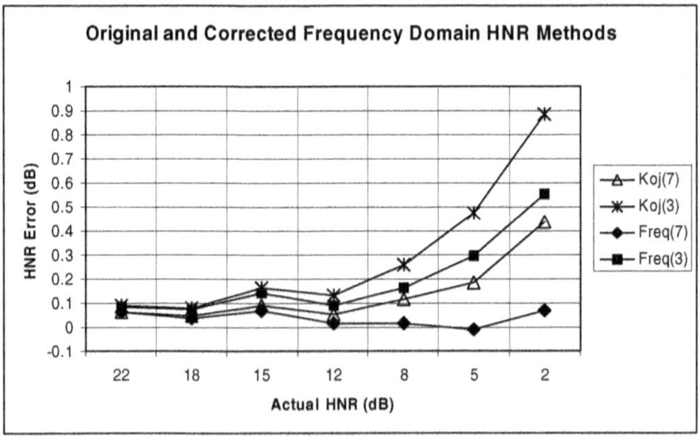

Fig. 2. Comparison of original (Koj) and corrected (Freq) values of HNR in the presence of "Additive Noise Only", calculated for 3 and 7 pulse segments

These results demonstrate that in the absence of other perturbations of the periodicity pattern, the correction works better for larger *N*. It is also relevant that the effect of changing *N* from 3 to 7, moving from "Koj(3)" to "Koj(7)", causes a larger error reduction than the one introduced by correcting "Koj(3)" to "Freq(3)". The frequency-domain alternatives compared to the time domain approaches in the other perturbation types are only "Freq(3)" y "Freq(7)".

The signals generated according to the procedure described in section 2.1 were used to evaluate the ability of the different HNR estimation methods to cope with the perturbations present in the signals. Two different *N* (7 and 50) were considered in the original "Orig" and corrected "Corr" time-domain approaches. The lower limit was set considering the results of the experiment in Fig. 1 and the pulse length (*L*) of the signals used (147 samples). The results are shown in Fig. 3.

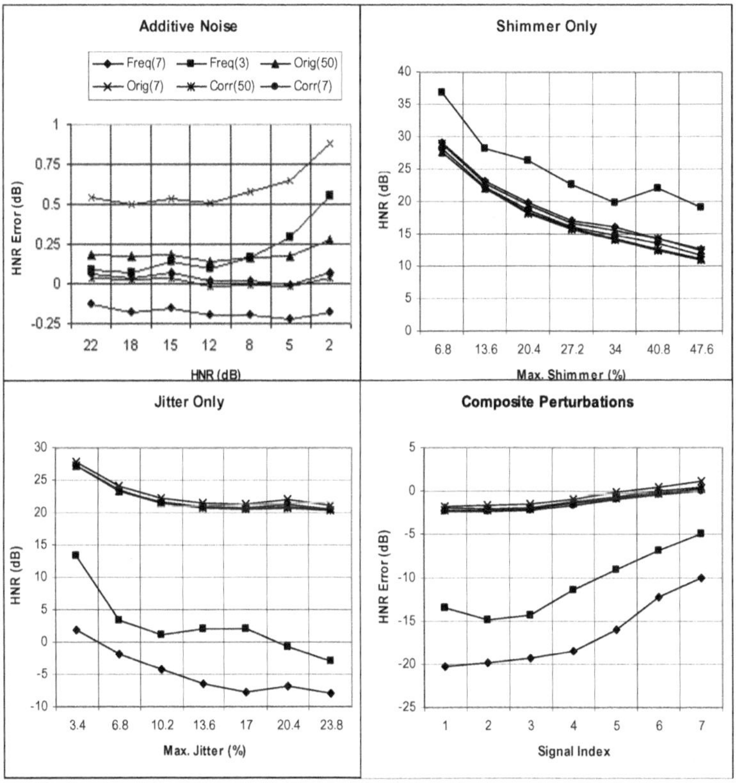

Fig. 3. Results obtained in the experiment on HNR sensibility to periodicity perturbations

The results of the methods facing additive-noise perturbations (upper-left graph in Fig. 3) are demonstrative of their intrinsic ability to measure HNR. An important issue in the time-domain is the similar results of "Corr(7)" and "Orig(50)", showing the importance of using equation (6). The most accurate of the time-domain alternatives is, as expected, "Corr(50)", but "Freq(7)" performs with similar exactitude with an N almost an order of magnitude smaller. This indicates that in the absence of jitter and shimmer, the frequency-domain approach performs better.

In the presence of shimmer (upper-right graph in Fig. 3) all the methods show similar deteriorations in the estimated HNR (theoretically infinite), with the exception of "Freq(3)", which is visibly superior. We don't have at this moment an elaborate explanation for this phenomenon. The only guess we can make is that in so few pulses (N=3) the random AM modulation is not so variable to significantly affect the spectrum, but a strict mathematical derivation is not readily available. The coincidence of the time-domain based methods with "Freq(7)" strengthens the idea that all of them are similarly shimmer-sensitive, and the effect in "Freq(3)" should be caused by a calculation bias related to the small value of N.

The "Jitter Only" experiment (bottom-left graph in Fig. 3) confirms the predicted [17] sensitivity to jitter of frequency-domain approaches, with estimated HNR (theoretically infinite) more than 15 dB below the time-domain methods. After the third level of perturbation (maximum jitter of 10.2%) the deterioration due to jitter in time-domain HNR calculation stabilizes at 21-22 dB, being less representative than shimmer-caused deterioration. The reason for this stabilization is that the HNR within the pulse is not constant. The smallest size of the N pulses is used as pulse length in the averages (4). Since the synthetic signals consist of exponentially-damped sinusoids, the suppressed portions of the pulses, the endings, are the ones with lower signal energy, resulting in an overestimation of HNR. As the jitter grows the portions removed enlarge, increasing this effect that counters the expected reduction in measured HNR.

When mixed-perturbation signals are used (bottom-right graph in Fig. 3), frequency-domain approaches fail due to their jitter sensitivity, with time-domain methods showing a similar, more acceptable, performance. The effect of pulse length reduction produced by jitter causes the gradual increment of the measured HNR with the level of perturbation.

4 Conclusions and Future Work

The correction of the ensemble-average time-domain approach demonstrates to produce satisfactory results using considerably less pulses (4-7) than the original approach (30-50). However, a practical limitation of the correction in (6) has been shown in this work, related to the actual lengths, in samples, of the pulses considered. In general, time domain approaches produced better results than frequency-domain approaches, even with the correction introduced in (10), due to the frequency-domain sensitivity to jitter. This is in correspondence with the predictions in [17].

The results obtained in this paper can serve as a reference regarding error limits in the calculation of Harmonics-to-Noise-Ratios in the presence of different perturbations of the periodicity pattern. However, more extensive experiments can still be performed, including the use of colored and non-uncorrelated noise. Also, other more sophisticated methods could be included in the comparisons, along with a richer set of perturbations levels and combinations.

Acknowledgments. This work was supported partially by the Canadian International Development Agency Project Tier II-394-TT02-00 and by the Flemish VLIR-UOS Programme for Institutional University Co-operation (IUC).

References

1. Cox, N. B., Ito, M. R., and Morrison, M. D. Data labeling and sampling effects in harmonics-to-noise ratios. J. Acoust. Soc. Am. 85, 2165-2178. (1989).
2. Cox, N. B., Ito, M. R., and Morrison, M. D. Technical considerations in computation of spectral harmonics-to-noise-ratios for sustained vowels. 32, 203-218. (1989).
3. Ferrer, C. A., González, E. and Hernández-Díaz, M. E. Correcting the use of ensemble averages in the calculation of harmonics to noise ratios in voice signals. J. Acoust. Soc. Am. 118, 605-607. (2005).
4. Fukazawa, T.; El-Assuooty, A. & Honjo, I. A new index for evaluation of the turbulent noise in pathological voice. Journal of the Acoustical Society of America. Vol. 83, No 3. pp 1189-1193. March. (1988).
5. Hillenbrand, J. A methodological study of perturbation and additive noise in synthetically generated voice signals. J. Speech Hea. Res. 30, 448-461. (1987).
6. Hillenbrand, J., Cleveland, R. A. and Erickson, R. L. Acoustic correlates of breathy vocal quality. J. Speech Hea. Res. 37, 769-778. (1994).
7. Kasuya, H., Ogawa, S., Kazuhiko, M. and Ebihara, S. Normalized noise energy as an acoustic measure to evaluate pathologic voice. J. Acoust. Soc. Am. 80, 1329-1334. (1986).
8. Kojima, H., Gould, W. J., Lambiase, A., and Isshiki, N. Computer analysis of hoarseness. Acta Otolaringol. 89, 547-554. (1980).
9. Lucero, J. C. and Koenig, L. L. Time normalization of voice signals using functional data analysis. J. Acoust. Soc. Am. 108, 1408-1420. (2000).
10. Medan, Y., Yain, E., and Chazan, D. Super resolution pitch determination of the speech signals. IEEE Transactions on Signal Processing. 39, 40-48. (1991).
11. Murphy, P. J. Perturbation-free measurement of harmonics-to-noise ratio in voice signals using pitch-synchronous harmonic analysis. J. Acoust. Soc. Am. 105, 2866-2881. (1999).
12. Parsa, V. and Jamieson, D.G. A comparison of high precision Fo extraction algorithms for sustained vowels. Journal of Speech, Language & Hearing Research. 42. 112-126. (1999).
13. Qi, Y. Time-normalization in voice analysis. J. Acoust. Soc. Am. 92, 2569-2576. (1992).
14. Qi, Y., Weinberg, B., Bi, N. and Hess, W. J. Minimizing the effect of period determination on the computation of amplitude perturbation in voice. J. Acoust. Soc. Am. 97, 2525-2532. (1995).
15. Qi, Y. and Hillman, R. E. Temporal and spectral estimations of harmonics-to-noise ratio in human voice signals. J. Acoust. Soc. Am. 102, 537-543. (1997).
16. Schoentgen, J., Bensaid, M. and Bucella, F. Multivariate statistical analysis of flat vowel spectra with a view to characterizing dysphonic voices. J. Speech, Lang. Hear. Res. 43, 1493-1508. (2000)
17. Schoentgen, J. Spectral models of additive and modulation noise in speech and phonatory excitation signals. J. Acoust. Soc. Am. 113, 553-562. (2003).
18. Shrivastav, R., and Sapienza, C. M. Objective measures of breathy vocal quality using an auditory model. J. Acoust Soc. Am. 114, 2217-2224. (2003).
19. Titze, I. R. Summary Statement. *Workshop-on acoustic voice analysis*. National Center of Voice and Speech. Iowa. (1994).
20. Yumoto, E., Gould, W. J., and Baer, T. The harmonics-to-noise ratio as an index of the degree of hoarseness. J. Acoust Soc. Am. 71, 1544-1550. (1982).

A Combined Classifier of Cry Units with New Acoustic Attributes

Sergio Cano[1], Israel Suaste[2], Daniel Escobedo[1],
Carlos A. Reyes-García[2], and Taco Ekkel[3]

[1] CENPIS, University of Oriente, Ave Las Américas 90900 Stgo de Cuba, Cuba
[2] INAOE, Carretera de Cholula s-n, Puebla, Mexico,
[3] Faculty of Informatics, University of Twente, The Netherlands
{scano, daniele}@fie.uo.edu.cu,
{kargaxxi, isuaste}@inaoep.mx, taco @utwente.nl

Abstract. The present work proposes a combined classifier of infant cry units that links in a single structure two focuses: a threshold-based classification and ANN-based classification. The threshold-based classifier considers 4 new acoustic features: *stridor, melody, voicedness, shifts,* that show properly their robustness in front of alterations of the acoustics of infant cry concerned with the presence of some diseases. In order to satisfy the automatic estimation their practical implementations are also considered. The ANN-based classifier consists in a feed-forward network using the method of Scale Gradient Conjugate (MSGC) as learning algorithm and the MFCCs as input vectors to the net. Each focus or classification stage gives in the exit one indicator (FN1 and FN2) that generates to the output a decision on two classes with gradation (*normal, moderately-pathologic and pathologic*). The results demonstrate the potentiality of these types of combined classifiers when the advantages of each focus in particular are properly emphasized

Keywords: Cry classification, pattern recognition, neural network.

1 Introduction

The problem of cry classification has been recently on the centre of many research efforts because of the avalanche of new focuses in the soft-computing area like *the artificial neural networks (ANN´s), genetic algorithms, evolutionary computing and fuzzy logic* [1-3]. The works of Petroni and Schonweiller using supervised and not supervised ANN´s respectively demonstrated the robustness of these models in the detection of abnormalities like deafness in newborns and their ability to classify different cry types. The Group of Speech Processing (GPV) in the University of Oriente developed several experiences with different ANN architectures (MLP, SOM, RBF networks) obtaining good results for the classification of 4 control groups of CNS pathologies (linked with hypoxia: *hypoxia, hypoxia with aggravating factors, hyperbilirubinaemia and delay on intra-uterine growth*). In the 2000 the Mexican group of Cry Analysis of the INAOE began interesting experiences using

J.F. Martínez-Trinidad et al. (Eds.): CIARP 2006, LNCS 4225, pp. 416–425, 2006.

neural networks with *fuzzy logic* and *genetic algorithms*. Nevertheless until now no cry-based clinical routines have been achieved for diagnostic purpose, at least in the reported scientific literature. Probably the above-mentioned could be concerned with: the lack of a wide corpus of data to train the learning structures, the inconsistency of the soft-computing algorithms in order to generalize all the patterns learned in the training tests, and the necessity to measure diverse parameters in the acoustics of the cry connected to the infant's neurophysiologic status. Because of which research efforts looking for new approaches in the cry classification continue still being developed.

A current trend is looking for combinations or hybrids of classifiers that could empower the advantages of each one (e.g. genetic-fuzzy approach) [2, 4]. The paper presents a new proposal that combines a traditional focus as the threshold-based classification and the focus using ANN-based classification, resulting in a combined system which displays an abnormality index (with gradation) as output. Moreover the combination of 4 acoustic features of the cry signal is also implemented. Those features have been reported in the bibliography as moderate indicators of certain disorders [5-8] but in this paper, in a combined environment they've shown relevant performances in front of the presence of abnormal cry.

2 Methods and Materials

Despite of the four parameters above mentioned are well known and reported in the literature, they have received insufficient attention according to their potentialities to characterize the neurophysiologic status of the child, raising the attention on other more robust ones as fundamental frequency, formants, latency, etc. Maybe the lack of models or formulas for their automatic calculation has influenced on it.

First, It becomes indispensable to manage some concepts related to these four acoustic parameters:

Fundamental Frequency (F0)[1]: it is the lowest frequency component of a complex tone and is the determinant of the pitch that one hears. In infant cries, the fundamental frequency mostly resides in the range of 400 to 600 Hz [8].

Voicedness is defined as being the ratio of the amount of periodic sound versus the amount of noise. The higher the voicedness, the weaker the noise component in comparison to the periodic sound. Hence, the higher the voicedness, the more clearly one could audibly determine the pitch of the sound. Synonyms for a low voicedness are *turbulence*, *disphonation*, *unpitched sound* or simply *noise*.

[1] It is known that in a voiced segment when it is passed through a frequency filter of narrow band in the spectrogram the harmonics appear. The first of these harmonics is the Fundamental Frequency, being the rest of harmonics multiples of the first harmonic. This Fundamental Harmonic has the frequency of the Glottal Pulse (The Glottal Pulse is the impulse of air of the glottal stream produced by movements of opening or closing of the vocal cords. The Fundamental Frequency is proportional in inverse mode to these periods and the unity of measurement is the Hertz, Hz). The Fundamental Harmonic tends to determine the intonation and the melodic curve of any voiced utterance.

Melody is defined as the description of the behavior of the fundamental frequency over time, *within one cry unit.* Normally, cry research identifies six types: rising-falling, falling, flat, falling-rising, rising and glottal plosive.

Shift: it's a sudden large change in pitch (fundamental frequency) caused by the vocal cords crashing into 'overdrive' thereby instantly increasing the fundamental frequency to a much higher value. Those sudden changes are a change of melody or intonation seen on a very relative short time that shows the relation between the fundamental frequency with the stability on the larynx control. [5, 8].

Stridor: another form vocal cord hyperfunction. In this case, a rapid increase in air pressure causes the vocal cords to enter a turbulent state resulting in the sudden loss of pitch. This creates a short noisy (voiceless) segment in the sound, often of about the same energy as the voiced regions surrounding it.

2.1 Acoustical Indicators of Disorder

Various studies have been undertaken to discover possible acoustical features in the infant crying sound that can be correlated to a certain state of the central nervous system. Since the goal is to discriminate between normal and abnormal cases, we need to find these features to perform this classification, in which we could view upon the features as 'decision variables'.

Our four parameters considered in this paper have been connected with certain abnormalities according with the international scientific reports [5,8]: (1) *instant changes in the fundamental frequency of four or more octaves occur significantly more often in abnormal cases; (2) the melody type in test cases is, more often than in normal cases, of the rising type, (3) the number of turbulent noises (stridors) is increased in abnormal cases, (4) in general, the number of shifts and stridors tends to be higher in abnormal cases.* Finally, cries of non-healthy infants are, in general, more often considered to be either hyperfunctional (higher, louder and shriller) or hypofunctional (lower, weaker and thinner) [8].

The research goal is to be able to classify a cry sound as originating from either a healthy (normal) infant or an infant suffering from a CNS disorder (based on hypoxia). In order to perform this classification, the sound needs to be expressed in absolute (as opposed to subjective) terms, and therefore variables that describe the sound are needed. Then, based on the values of these variables, a decision can be made. Considering all of the above, the acoustic parameters to be extracted from the crying sound in order to measure all of the aforementioned indicators are:

- *fundamental frequency over time (just to estimate the melody pattern)*
- *voicedness over time*
- *number of occurrences of shift*
- *number of occurrences of stridor*
- *melody type*

2.2 Procedures to Estimate the Acoustic Features

Voicedness

To extract a measure of 'voicedness' from the sound data, information from the spectral domain can be used. When the data consists primarily of noise, there are few peaks in the spectral domain of a signal at that time point. However, when the sound consists mostly of periodic sound, clear peaks can be distinguished. To get a measure of this difference, the spectral information is first smoothed over a few frames. This has the effect of a low-pass filter on the frequency data, cancelling out most variability due to white noise. After this, a vector is created containing the differences from one frequency component to the next, effectively creating a numerical derivative. Since peaks in the voiced data create larger differences than the relatively 'flat' data from the noise, the sum of absolute numerical derivatives results in a relatively large value for a voiced region and a small one for a noisy region. The voicedness v is now calculated from an array of amplitudes a (where the indices correspond to frequencies) with length N:

$$v = \sum_{i=1}^{N-1} \left| a_{i+1} - a_i \right| \quad (1)$$

Melody

When we visually inspect one cry unit in the spectrogram, coupled with aural inspection the sound, we can determine which melody type is applicable to the unit. For automatic extraction however, things are a bit more complicated. First, there is the fact that the pitch detection is not flawless. If we were to take, for example, only the first frequency value as *start frequency*, a measurement error in this one value could seriously compromise correct detection. To cope with this, a scheme is devised in which all frequency values of one cry unit are pre-processed by multiplying the data within a segment with smoothing windows, as shown in Fig. 1. In doing so, the influence of a single measurement error is greatly reduced while preserving locally relevant information. For smoothing, the frequency values Fi are convolved with a Hanning window to produce a local average, yielding the following equation for calculating the averaged midpoint frequency Fm, where M is the total number of frequency values in the cry unit:

$$F_m = \frac{\sum_{i=1}^{M} \frac{1}{2} F_i \left[1 - \cos\left(\frac{2\pi}{M} i \right) \right]}{\int_{i=1}^{M} \frac{1}{2} \left(1 - \cos(\frac{2\pi}{M} i) \right)} \quad (2)$$

It results in three values: an average frequency representing the beginning of the cry (start), one representing the center of the cry (midpoint), and one representing the end of the cry (end). Secondly, the decision boundaries for the melody type have to be defined in order to answer the question under what numerical situation a certain set of values can be assigned to a certain category. Only the occurrence of a rising melody type will be used in classification. This is considered a valid strategy since, in earlier work, it was concluded that occurrence of the rising melody type was allegedly greater in disorder cases, but no similar significance was found for other melody types [10].

Stridor

Since both voicedness and the energy are calculated over time, stridor can be detected by using the following rule: *when the voicedness suddenly drops within an area of high energy, one occurrence of stridor is marked.* Tangibly, the following thresholds were selected: when the voicedness drops to less than 30% of its maximum

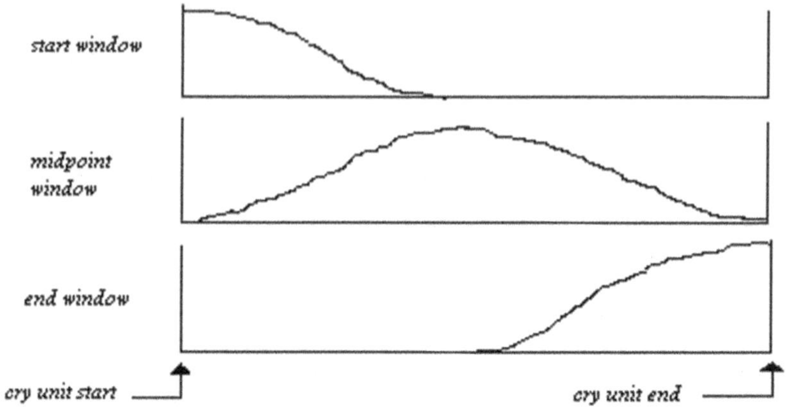

Fig. 1. Windowing procedures used for melody detection

while the energy level remains above -35dB, one occurrence of stridor is marked [5]. An exception is made at the end of a cry unit, because the voicedness of the cry usually drops sharply a little bit before the cry stops. This is a normal consequence of stopping the air stream and it should therefore not be considered a vocal cord hyperfunction. Using this algorithm on the real life data, the number of stridor occurrences per cry unit is usually zero, and sometimes one or two.

Shift

In detecting shift, the definition as used by the GPV in earlier work is followed [9]: when the fundamental frequency instantly (i.e., from one frame to the next) rises four octaves or more, the presence of a shift is marked. One octave represents a doubling of the fundamental frequency, so a stridor is marked when, from one frame to the next,

$$\frac{F_{o_{current}}}{F_{o_{previous}}} > 4$$

2.3 Estimation of Mel Frequency Cepstral Coefficients (MFCC)

The well-known Mel cepstral coefficients were selected to build up the input vectors for the ANN architecture. They have been used with high efficiency in recent works concerned with cry classification. [1,11] The Mel scale filter bank is a series of L triangular band pass filtering believed to occur in the auditory system (corresponding to series of band pass filters with constant bandwidth and spacing on a Mel frequency scale as you see in Fig. 2.

As it is also represented in Fig. 2 the MFCC´s can be computed by: (1) generating small segments from the signal, (2) calculating the DFT for each segment, (3) the spectrum is then converted into a logarithmic scale, (4) the scale is transformed into a soft Mel spectrum, (5) the discrete cosine transform DCT is calculated.

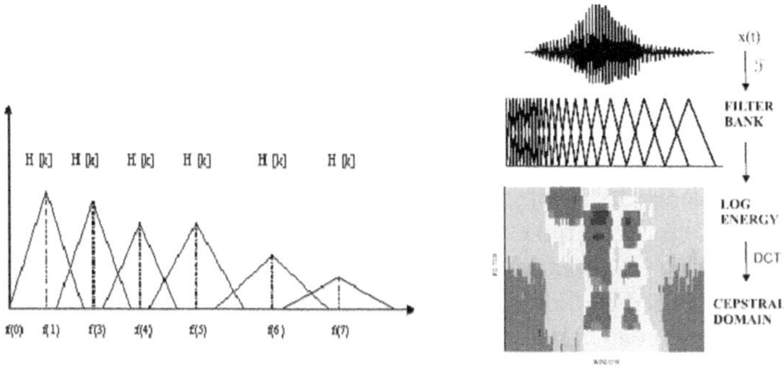

Fig. 2. The Triangle-filters use for MFCC computation and the steps required for computing the cepstrum of a cry signal

2.4 The Use of an Artificial Neural Network

The use of ANN´s has been a great impact in the development of several research areas like computer vision, autonomous vehicle, pattern recognition, connected-speech synthesis and more recently into the classification of cry units [3-4, 11-12]. The ANN used in this work is shown in Fig. 3. It is a Feed-Forward network in which *x1, x2, ..., xn* represent the acoustic features of signals and *y1, y2, ..., yn* the n classes to be identified. This kind of supervised ANN has been also used in cry classification with succeed [11-12].

For an efficient learning of the classification patterns one important aspect to be considered is the training method of the ANN. An optimal learning supposes the minimization of the error function which depends on the weights. For this purposes some algorithms are based on the gradient descendent. Cry data are not static, and any cry sample at any instance in time is dependent on crying patterns before and after

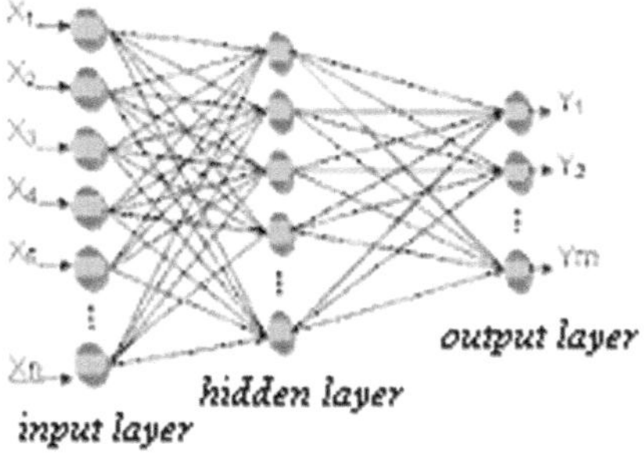

Fig. 3. A Feed-Forward Artificial Neural network

that instance in time. A common flaw in the traditional Back-Propagation algorithm is that it does not take this into account. In the paper we choose the *Method of Scaled Conjugate Gradient* (MSCG) [13].

The MSCG finds out a direction to a new point and then decide what so far to go in that direction (*step size*) using 2nd order information

$$E_{qw}(y) = W(w) + E^{l}(w)^{T} y + \frac{1}{2} y^{T} E^{ll}(w) y \tag{3}$$

where y is a point in the weight vector. The 2nd order technique uses second derivatives of the objective function and, generally it finds a local minimum but with a high computational cost. The algorithm MSGC shows a linear convergence accentuated in most of the problems [13]. Using a mechanism to decide what so far to go in a specified direction MSGC avoids a time of consumption in the linear learning iteration, which makes the algorithm faster than other second order algorithms.

The soft tools used in this experience were: BDLlanto database with 12 seconds-cry recordings of Cuban children, BPVOZ soft-package, PCVOX and *praat* software for the acoustic signal processing. The ANN implementation (including the MSGC algorithm) was done with *Neural Network Toolbox of Matlab* v. 6.0. [14-15]. The Principal Component Analysis (PCA) was implemented using *Matlab* v 6.0.

3 Results and Discussion

Starting from the primary information in BDLlanto database (32 cases: 16 healthy children and 16 pathological children) a segmentation process was developed to generate the cry units being obtained 73 healthy (normal) cry units and 68 pathological cry units (relative to hypoxia). 58 cry units were chosen (for each class) for training and 10 for classification. The segmentation stage was semi-automatic combining a *begin/end detection* (based on function energy and zero-crossing rate) and a manual correction to reduce the negative effect of considering inappropriate sections within the cry unit. From the cry units obtained from database a parameter estimation for every cry unit is done, following two possible ways:

(a) *estimation of 4-acoustic features for the threshold-based classifier:*
The estimated feature is then compared with the normal threshold values associated to each one of the 4 selected parameters, generating to the exit an index FN1 with the following gradation:

FN1: 0.25 for 1 parameter altered [2]
0.5 for 2 parameters altered
0.75 for 3 parameters altered
1.0 for 4 parameters altered
0 for no one parameter altered (normality index)

(b) *estimation of MFCC´s for the ANN-based classifier.*
500 MFCC´s were computed for each generated cry unit (16 Mel-cepstral coefficients were estimated for each 50 milliseconds frame). The original input vectors were reduced to 50 components by means of Principal Component Analysis

[2] One parameter altered means that it is out of the threshold boundary for *normality*.

(PCA). Then the input vector to the feed-forward ANN was presented, with the following structure: 50 nodes in the input layer, 15 nodes for the hidden layer and finally 2 nodes for the output layer.

To detect the cry type in the newborn the output values of the net are analyzed. The output values of the net are coded between 0 and 1. If the value of the output node 1 is bigger than the value of the output node 2 the sample is assigned to the class *"normal"* (N) generating a FN2 index equal to 0, otherwise it is assigned to the class *"pathologic"* (P) generating a FN2 index equal to 1.

Finally both FN1 and FN2 indexes are processed in a decision block ($D = \frac{FN1 + FN2}{2}$) resulting in two classes-based decisions with 3 qualitative levels:

Normal	*D <=0.5*
Moderately- pathologic	*D = 0.75*
Pathologic	*D = 1.0*

Tables 1, 2, 3 and 4 display the results from the threshold-based classifier, ANN-based classifier and the Combined Classifier respectively. From these results some comments can be done:

- The present performance is higher than other similar works [1-2]
- In Table 4 the gradation of the D index let physicians to use properly the output of the cry classifier in order to compare and to evaluate its *"possible meaning"* in front of the results from the neurophysiologic evaluation of the newborn (how much abnormal the infant cry is from the acoustical point of view and its "weight" for diagnostic purpose.
- The need to include more acoustic features in cry classifier for better classification rates proposed and argued by Schonweiller in 1996 [2], is well demonstrated here. As you see the FN1 index displayed a strong correlation between the altered status of acoustic feature and the pathologic status of cry unit.
- Of particular interest was the fact that the only two cry units misclassified as normal obtained a FN1 equal to 0.75 (abnormal for the threshold-based classifier), so both outputs from the classifiers also offer valuable information to be considered by the specialists (see table 2).
- The higher frequency of altered parameters for pathological cry units seems to be representative of the robustness of the four acoustic features used as detectors of abnormality. (see table 3)

Table 1. Results from the Threshold-based classifier

		FN1 Index				
		0	**0.25**	**0.5**	**0.75**	**1.0**
Normal	10	9	1	-	-	-
Pathologic	10	-	2	5	2	1

Table 2. Frequency of altered parameters for both classes (p/n)

	Altered Parameter			
	Stridor	**Voicedness**	**Melody**	**Shift**
Normal (10)	-	-	-	1
Pathologic (10)	6	5	5	6

Table 3. Results from the ANN-based classifier

		Confusion Matrix		**%**
	Cry Units	**Normal**	**Pathologic**	**Classification**
Normal	10	7	3	70%
Patolog.	10	2	8	80%
Total	20			**75%**

Table 4. Results from the Combined Classifier

		Confusion Matrix		**D index**			**%**
		N	**P**	**X<= 0.5**	**0.5<x<=0.75**	**0.75<x**	
Normal	10	10	0	10	0	0	100
Pathologic	10	2	8	2	7	1	80
Total	20			12	7	1	90

4 Conclusions

In the presented work we have developed a new combined-cry classifier which uses two focuses for cry classification (a threshold-based classifier and an ANN-based classifier) with satisfactory results. Moreover four acoustic features as *shift, voicedness, melody* and *stridors* were estimated and efficiently combined, showing their potentialities to detect abnormal behaviour related to the neurophysiologic status of the newborn. Both output indexes FN1 and FN2 offer also valuable information for specialists when they analyze them together or in separate environment.

Another interesting aspect was concerned with the successful use of *cry unit* as the basic processing unit for cry classification validating the assessment done by Ekkel in 2000 [16]. The asseveration made by Schonweiller in [2] about to include other parameters in the domain frequency it is also supported here.

Further tests should focus on using different acoustic features and different soft-computing paradigms. Also the use of hybrid structures for cry classifiers seems to be a promise alternative.

Acknowledgments

This work is in part supported by National Council for Science and Technology CONACYT-Mexico under project (C01-46753).

References

1. Petroni, M., Malowany, A., Johnston, C., Stevens, B. "*Identification of Pain from Infant Cry Vocalizations Using Artificial Neural Networks* (ANN´s)". The International Infant Cry Research Group. Applications and Science of Artificial Neural Networks. The International Society for Optical Engineering. Volumen 2492. 1995. pp.729-738.
2. Schonweiler,R. et el. "Neuronal networks and self-organizing maps: new computer techniques in the acoustic evaluation of the infant cry". Int. Journal of Pediatric Otorhinolaryngology,. Elsevier Science, 38, 1996, pp. 1-11
3. Suaste, I, Reyes-Galaviz, O., Dias, A., Reyes, C. A Fuzzy Relational Neural Network for Pattern C.assification. A.Sanfeliu et al (Eds.): CIARP 2004, LNCS 3287, pp. 358-365, 2004.
4. Alonso, L. et al. *Reconocimiento de Patrones con Redes Neuronales*. Ed. L.Alonso, Editorial Imprenta Catedral, 2001, pp 37-56
5. Wasz-Höckert, O., Lind, J., Vuorenkoski, V., Partanen, T., Valanne, E. "*The Infant Cry: A Spectrographic and Auditory Analysis* ". Spastics International Medical Publication, Lavenham, U.K., 1968.
6. Hurlock, E.B. "*Child Development*". Nueva York. McGraw-Hill. 1950.
7. Zeskind P.S., Lester B. "Acoustic features and auditory perceptions of the Cries of Newborns with Prenatal Complications". Child development, pp. 580-589. 1978.
8. Michelsson, K. "Sound Spectrographic cry analysyis of normal and abnormal newborns". Folia Phoniatria, 28, 1982, pp. 161-173
9. Escobedo,D., Cano,S., Coello,E., Regueiferos,L., Capdevila,L.: Rising Shift of Pitch Frequency in the Infant Cry pf Some Pathologic Cases. 2nd >Int. Conf. MAVEBA 2001, Firenze, Italy, 2001-
10. Cano,S. et al. "The Spectral Analysis of Infant Cry: An Initial Approximation". Proceedings of EUROSPEECH'95 (sponsored by ESCA & IEEE), Madrid, Sept 18-21,1995
11. Orozco, J., Reyes, C. "Extracción y Análisis de Características Acústicas del Llanto de Bebés para su Reconocimiento Automático Basado en Redes Neuronales". Tesis de Maestría, INAOE, Puebla, Mex., 2002.
12. Cano, D., et al. "Análisis preliminar de los resultados de una clasificación de unidades de llanto según tres arquitecturas de redes neuronales". Memorias de TELEC'2002 (en CD'Rom). Centro de Convenciones HEREDIA, Julio 2002.
13. Moller. "*A Scaled Conjugate Gradient Algorithm for Fast Supervised Learning*". Neural Networks 6 (4). 1993. pp. 525-533.
14. Boersma, P., Weenink, D., *Praat v. 4.0.27. "Sistema para hacer fonética por computadora"*. University of Amsterdam. The Netherlands. 1992-2002.
15. The MathWoks, Inc., MATLAB®. "*Neural Network Toolbox*". Version 6.0.0.88. 1984 - 2000.
16. Ekkel, T. "Neural Network-Based Classification of Cries from Infants Suffering from Hypoxia-Related CNS Damage". Tesis de Maestría. University of Twente. The Netherlands, 2002.

Practical Considerations for Real-Time Implementation of Speech-Based Gender Detection

Erik Scheme[1], Eduardo Castillo-Guerra[2], Kevin Englehart[1,2], and Arvind Kizhanatham[3]

[1] Institute of Bimedical Engineering, University of New Brunswick, P.O. Box 4400, Fredericton, NB, Canada, E3B 5A3
[2] Dept. of Electrical and Computer Engineering, University of New Brunswick, P.O. Box 4400, Fredericton, NB, Canada, E3B 5A3
[3] Diaphonics Inc., 1310 Hollis Street, Halifax, Nova Scotia, Canada B3J 3P3
{escheme, eduardo.castillo, kengleha}@unb.ca

Abstract. This paper describes a detailed analysis and implementation of a robust gender detector for audio stream applications. The implementation, based on melcepstral features and a Gaussian mixture model classifier, is designed to maximize gender classification performance in continuous speech. The described detector outperforms other reported systems based on statistically significant numbers of gender verifications (2136 unique speakers) obtained from the FISHER speech corpus. The system yields high accuracies for long and short utterances while a confidence figure of merit score for the decision ensures reliability in continuous audio streams.

Keywords: Gender detection, GMM classification, audio streaming.

1 Introduction

The importance of accurate speech-based gender detection is rapidly increasing with the emergence of technologies which exploit gender information to enhance performance. Currently, gender identification is used in security-related applications such as gender mining large volumes of audio recordings, automatic speech monitoring, automatic data labeling and multimedia indexing. Other applications use gender information to train more effective models for speech recognition or speaker identification and verification. Some commercially oriented applications use gender detection for closed captioning and gender-oriented advertisement in audio driven applications. The emergence of these new applications imposes demanding requirements on gender detection system, which may include one or all of the following: Real-time audio stream processing; high confidence for the decision and analysis of a limited amount of useful speech.

Previous investigations in gender identification have proposed a variety of features and classification techniques. Feature extraction is often performed using gender related characteristics of speech such as pitch [1],[3], formant and harmonic structure

J.F. Martínez-Trinidad et al. (Eds.): CIARP 2006, LNCS 4225, pp. 426 – 436, 2006.

[3],[4]. Other approaches rely on spectral features such as Mel-Frequency Cepstral or Spectral Coefficients (MFCC or MFSC) [2],[5], Linear Prediction Coefficients [6], Reflection Coefficients [6] and Log area Ratio Coefficients [5]. Classification techniques use Hidden Markov Models (HMM) [1],[4], Gaussian Mixture Models (GMM)[5],[7],[8] or Neural Networks [2]. Multi-expert approaches have also been developed combining classification techniques [2],[5] .

Despite the abundance of research literature on gender detection, little is focused on its implementation for audio streaming applications and few papers provide practical considerations for performance optimization in real world scenarios.

Harb & Chen [2] have described a general audio classifier for content-based multimedia indexing in continuous speech. They used the mean and variance of 20 MFSCs taken from one second windows to train a collection of eight neural network classifiers based on speech coded with different techniques. They obtained a good dimensionality reduction of features assuming a linear relationship between MFSCs across frames in each one-second segment with results. They performed continuous gender identification with no preprocessing of the incoming signal, so, gender decisions can be made in segments composed solely of silence segments. The gender decisions are also made based upon average MFSCs across one second segments allowing the estimation to possibly include speech from both genders.

This paper describes a detailed analysis of a robust gender detector that addresses some of the limitations observed in previous reports, keeping the classification technique simple to facilitate the implementation. The detector herein is based on a pattern recognition approach where the speech is processed to obtain a representation of the most relevant information for gender identification. The system uses a GMM classifier approach with preprocessed speech, normalized features and provides a decision with a confidence figure of merit (CFM) for each analyzed segment. The performance of two features extraction techniques (MFCC and MFSC [2]) is studied. Different aspects of the GMM are also optimized and practical issues are considered for the real-time implementation of the resulting identification system.

2 Gender Detector

Signal Preprocessing: Audio streaming applications require that a decision be made within a constrained schedule, regulated by specific performance goals. This is typically achieved by analyzing short segments. However, the composition of each processed segment can vary drastically, as well as the amount of noise that is present. Therefore in order to obtain data-independent performance, silent frames are removed using speech activity detection.

The algorithm used herein is based on a combination of zero-crossing (ZC), autocorrelation and energy analysis (EN) of the speech. The ZC analysis discards those frames that the number of crossings is outside a typical range observed in male and female speech (corresponding to a pitch range from 60-400Hz). The computed ZC is normalized by the number of samples corresponding to the pre-selected analysis window (32ms and 8ms increment) according to the sampling frequency of the utterance. The segments that meet the ZC criteria are submitted to autocorrelation analysis where further periodicity of the processed speech is analyzed. A threshold of 0.15 is applied to the normalized correlation values. The segments meeting both previous analyses are then processed with the EN, while the others are used to estimate an adaptive energy threshold. The EN is then performed using two thresholds: an adaptive and absolute threshold. The adaptive threshold is used to discard those frames with energy below the threshold estimated based on the estimated noise segments which should provide an estimation of the utterance noise. The absolute threshold is a fix maximum and minimum hard thresholds were obtained from average telephone speech levels. These thresholds were applied to avoid incorrect estimation of the adaptive threshold due to overly noisy data or other extraneous data conditions. The incoming data stream is continuously preprocessed until a buffer of predefined size is filled with clean data.

Feature Extraction: The feature extraction was tailored to specifically maximize performance for gender detection and not for speech recognition or speaker identification[1]. Consequently, channel compensation and speech normalization techniques were specifically chosen to avoid distortion of gender information. In the speech domain, the mean was subtracted and variance normalization was implemented. The MFCCs were extracted using Hamming windows of 32ms and 8ms increments. In the feature domain, Cepstral mean subtraction[2] and low-pass filtering were implemented. The filtering was used to remove low-amplitude high-frequency content of the spectrum which is highly susceptible to noise and typically consists of unvoiced fricatives containing little information about gender. Variance normalization was not used because it was found to warp the spectral magnitude which decreases observable differences between genders in the extracted features. RASTA [7] technique was found to also decrease the gender discrimination power of the extracted features.

Two variants of Mel frequency coefficients, MFSC and MFCC, were studied. MFSC places emphasis on spectral differences in the mid and high frequencies while MFCC emphasizes differences in the lower spectral content [9]. In each case, 26 Mel filters were used with 19 coefficients and deltas. This effectively results in a low-pass filtering of the framed data in the feature domain at 3 KHz.

Classifier: Classification was performed by selecting the maximum of the log likelihood produced by two gender-dependent GMMs (λ_{Male} and λ_{Female}). The expectation maximization algorithm was used to fit the Gaussians to gender-dependent data obtained from the Fisher database [10]. Data from 312 unique speakers of each gender were used to train gender specific models. The amount of training speech per speaker was varied in order to study its effect on classification performance. The optimal number of Gaussian components was also studied in terms of performance and identification speed.

---

[1] The tailoring of the feature extraction was achieved by empirical optimization of classification performance using the Fisher speech corpus.

[2] Consist on subtracting the mean of each MFCC coefficient for the collection of frames.

Confidence Figure of Merit (CFM) and Decision: A CFM was added to provide feedback about lower quality segments and segments that contain varying levels of speech from both genders. The CFM was estimated by mapping the boundaries of the difference between the mean-log likelihood for each gender model ($\Delta\lambda = \lambda_{Male} - \lambda_{Female}$) into the interval [0,1] when varying the composition of testing segments between male and female. In this case, the threshold between genders is mapped into the center of the interval. The effect was observed for 10,000 verifications using 100 unique speakers from each gender. All combinations of the test segments were used to obtain the performance of the system when presented with segments containing both genders (expressed in percentage of speech that is female in Fig 1).

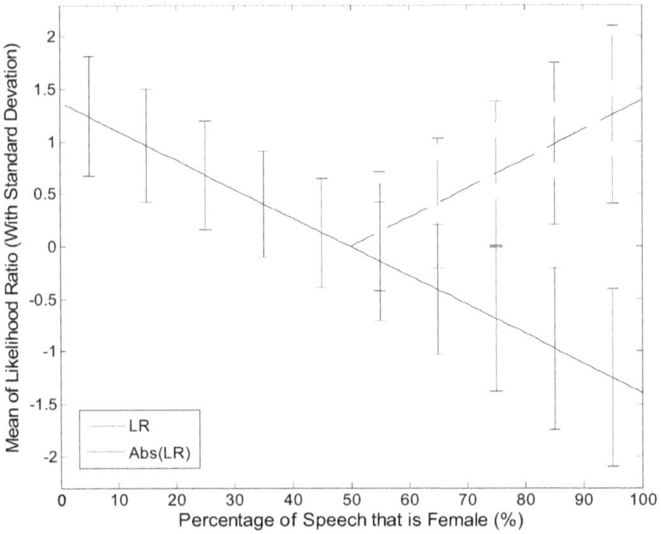

Fig. 1. Likelihood ratio when the composition of the testing segment varies from 0-100% female speech. Dashed lines indicate absolute value.

A positive differential of the log likelihood ratios is shown when the composition consists of more male than female speech indicating that the male model is predominant. However when the speech becomes predominantly female, the differential log likelihood ratio turns negative. A definite trend away from zero exists as a more biased gender composition (greater than 50% male or female) is introduced. This reveals that the system's response is linearly proportional to the constitution of the testing segment and the contribution provided by each gender feature is equally balanced. Mixed gender utterances result in a lower CFM for the decision because their log likelihood ratios tend to be closer to 0. The application controller can therefore monitor for segments with low CFM, and perform further analysis. The gender models used in this section were trained with 30s of speech from 312 unique speakers of each gender and tested with 15s segments extracted from varying combinations of 100 pairs of male-female speakers.

3 Experiments

Three main experiments were conducted throughout this investigation. The first compares the use of MFCC and MFSC features for capturing gender information. Their impact on the performance of models created with variable amounts of speech per speaker (SPS) and variable length of the testing segments (VLTS) was also considered. Pairs of gender models were trained with 60s, 30s, 15s, 10s, 5s and 3s of speech obtained from unique speakers. The models were validated using testing utterances of seven different lengths in order to observe the effect of varying training and testing data length on overall performance.

The second experiment considered the effect of a varying number of GMM components on the performance of gender models created with 30s of SPS and VLTS. Models were trained with 64, 128, 256, 512 and 1024 Gaussians and tested using test utterances of several different lengths.

The last experiment tests the performance of the best performing models from previous sections (MFCC features, 30s SPS, 512 Gaussians) with a continuous stream of speech. The audio stream was composed of alternating male/female speech segments of random-size (between 20 and 30s) from 200 unique speakers taken from the National Institute of Standard Technology (NIST) evaluation data, 2005. Time labels of gender transitions were maintained and used to determine the performance of the system. Trials were completed using 1, 3 and 5 second segments.

In all tests, the models were trained with speech from 312 unique gender-specific speakers obtained from the Fisher database [10]. All utterances were manually verified prior to use to avoid mislabeled and cross-gender cross-talk content. The testing speech for experiments 1 and 2 was taken from 2136 unique speakers of NIST evaluation data, 2005.

4 Results

MFCC-MFSC Performance: The performance of the gender detection system, when extracting MFCC and MFSC features, is shown in Tables 1 and 2. The accuracy obtained when using each feature set is shown for varying lengths of training and testing data for each gender and overall.

A comparison between both tables show that MFCCs outperform MFSCs, with the difference approached 3%. These results contradict those reported in [2], however, the classification approach used herein also differs from that used by Harb & Chen. It can be observed from Table 1 that the overall performance decreases with diminishing amounts of training data. However, the performance for individual gender does not show the same trend for both genders. This could be originated because providing less training speech the model captures more non-stationary characteristics of the waveform disguising the boundaries between genders. It is appreciated that female models perform more consistently across changes in training set length than males. This can be caused due to female gender information is more readily captured by the MFCC features and requires less data amounts to perform compared to male gender.

Table 1. System Performance with MFCC Coefficients

			Speech Per Speaker Used to Train Gender (Seconds)					
		Gender	**60**	**30**	**15**	**10**	**5**	3
Length of the Testing Segments (Seconds)	**60**	M	**96.01**	**96.01**	**95.58**	**95.69**	**95.36**	95.03
		F	**98.51**	**98.59**	**98.68**	**98.51**	**98.18**	97.93
		Both	97.43	97.47	97.33	97.28	96.95	**96.67**
	30	M	**95.79**	**96.12**	**95.90**	**95.90**	**95.79**	95.47
		F	**98.68**	**98.43**	**98.43**	**98.10**	**97.44**	97.44
		Both	97.43	97.42	97.33	97.14	96.72	**96.58**
	15	M	**95.36**	**95.68**	**94.50**	**95.47**	**94.50**	94.28
		F	**98.35**	**98.18**	**98.59**	**97.51**	**97.68**	97.60
		Both	97.05	97.09	96.82	96.63	96.30	**96.16**
	5	M	**93.96**	**93.42**	**93.42**	**91.91**	**92.56**	91.15
		F	**96.94**	**97.44**	**96.86**	**97.44**	**95.62**	96.44
		Both	95.65	95.69	95.37	95.04	94.29	**94.15**
	3	M	**93.96**	**90.83**	**90.94**	**90.72**	**89.32**	89.21
		F	**94.79**	**97.02**	**96.69**	**96.61**	**96.53**	95.12
		Both	94.43	94.33	94.19	94.05	93.40	**92.56**
	1	M	**87.91**	**90.06**	**88.66**	**86.93**	**88.76**	86.61
		F	**95.21**	**92.98**	**94.30**	**94.63**	**91.32**	92.40
		Both	**92.04**	**91.71**	**91.85**	**91.29**	**90.22**	**89.89**

The spectral differences between each gender, including pitch, formants and high frequency energy distribution also accentuate this difference, impacting differently the MFCC estimation.

The testing utterance also has a direct impact on the performance of the system, with larger testing segments providing best performances. This is because larger testing segments contain more information. However, it is noticeable that the effect of the length of training data is more profound. This is beneficial for streaming applications because while training can be performed offline with large amounts of data, high performance is desired with shorter test utterances.

Upon further analysis of Table 1, it is appreciated that the performance gap between both genders increases while the length of the testing segments decrease. This is created by a combination between the differences in the descriptive power of the MFCC features for the female gender and the decrement of information provided. This creates a fussier delimitation between both genders, causing overlap among them. Table 1 shows that no substantial gain when more than 15s of speaker data is used for training the models. Therefore, this is a good tradeoff between performance and speech length requirements to build the gender models. Table 2 shows deeper differences in data trends for each gender since MFSC capture different information. However, the overall trend keeps decreasing when the length of the training and testing sets decrease.

Table 2. System Performance with MFSC Coefficients

Length of the Testing Segments (Seconds)		Speech Per Speaker Used to Train Gender (Seconds)					
	Gender	**60**	**30**	**15**	**10**	**5**	3
60	**M**	**95.79**	**96.12**	**96.87**	**97.09**	**98.17**	98.38
	F	**96.20**	**95.53**	**93.88**	**92.72**	**88.01**	86.52
	Both	95.99	95.83	95.38	94.90	93.09	**92.45**
30	**M**	**94.82**	**95.79**	**96.44**	**97.20**	**98.06**	98.38
	F	**96.20**	**95.53**	**93.80**	**92.14**	**87.01**	84.78
	Both	95.51	95.66	95.12	94.67	92.54	**91.58**
15	**M**	**94.82**	**95.47**	**96.53**	**96.98**	**98.17**	98.27
	F	**96.77**	**95.12**	**93.22**	**91.89**	**86.10**	84.53
	Both	95.80	95.30	94.88	94.44	92.14	**91.40**
5	**M**	**92.56**	**93.20**	**93.96**	**95.04**	**96.44**	96.66
	F	**94.87**	**94.46**	**92.14**	**90.07**	**84.45**	82.55
	Both	93.72	93.83	93.05	92.56	90.45	**89.60**
3	**M**	**90.40**	**90.51**	**91.91**	**92.23**	**94.28**	94.82
	F	**94.79**	**93.80**	**91.81**	**90.41**	**83.95**	81.64
	Both	92.59	92.15	91.86	91.32	89.19	**88.23**
1	**M**	**86.50**	**87.58**	**89.01**	**90.36**	**93.20**	93.30
	F	**91.65**	**91.16**	**89.04**	**87.60**	**82.56**	79.92
	Both	**89.07**	**89.36**	**89.02**	**88.98**	**87.88**	**86.61**

Effect of Number of Gaussians on Performance: The performance of models with different number of Gaussians is shown in Table 3. It can be seen that accuracy of decisions increases as the number of Gaussians increases, but the computational load increases likewise. For this reason, the optimal selection of performance (a tradeoff of speed and accuracy) may be system specific. Applications requiring extremely fast processing may forfeit minimal accuracy to achieve speed gains. Offline applications desiring peak accuracies may choose a larger number of Gaussians. Herein, 256 Gaussians were chosen as the most efficient compromise between speed and accuracy. Lower number of Gaussians than 64 followed the same trend as the values shown in the table with the respective decrement in performance.

Audio Stream Evaluation: Fig. 2 shows the performance of the system applied to a pseudo-random streaming audio input. The continuous curve represents the gender composition of each tested segment (where 1 signifies 100% male and -1 signifies 100% female). The stem plot denotes the difference of likelihood ratios (clipped to ±1 for visibility) obtained for the previous segment. It can be seen that the decision made in the segments containing speech from both genders (shown as a change in sign of the continuous curve) produce lower likelihood values. These lower scores will correspond to a decision with low CFM. It may therefore be desirable for an application to further scrutinize, or reject, low CFM for the decisions which tend to indicate cross-gender segments. Given this possibility, it is interesting to note the performance of the system under specific CFM restrictions.

Table 3. System Performance with Variable Number of Gaussians

Length of the Testing Segments (in Seconds)		Gender	Number of Gaussians*				
			1024	**512**	**256**	**128**	64
	60	M	**97.19**	**97.74**	**95.79**	**94.82**	94.61
		F	**97.35**	**96.03**	**95.20**	**94.79**	94.38
		Both	97.27	96.88	95.50	94.81	**94.49**
	30	M	**96.65**	**97.09**	**94.82**	**94.39**	94.18
		F	**97.02**	**96.28**	**94.96**	**94.46**	94.54
		Both	96.83	96.68	94.89	94.43	**94.36**
	15	M	**96.11**	**96.66**	**94.93**	**94.39**	94.07
		F	**96.94**	**96.11**	**94.87**	**94.79**	94.13
		Both	96.53	96.38	94.90	94.59	**94.10**
	5	M	**94.60**	**95.47**	**92.13**	**91.91**	91.48
		F	**96.36**	**94.79**	**93.38**	**93.55**	92.39
		Both	95.48	95.13	92.75	92.73	**91.93**
	3	M	**93.74**	**93.74**	**89.97**	**89.64**	88.89
		F	**96.20**	**94.29**	**93.30**	**92.97**	92.06
		Both	94.97	94.02	91.63	91.31	**90.47**
	1	M	**90.28**	**91.36**	**86.61**	**86.27**	86.01
		F	**91.40**	**90.58**	**90.89**	**90.33**	89.73
		Both	**90.84**	**90.97**	**88.75**	**88.30**	**87.87**

* Gender models were trained with 30s of speech from 312 speakers per gender.

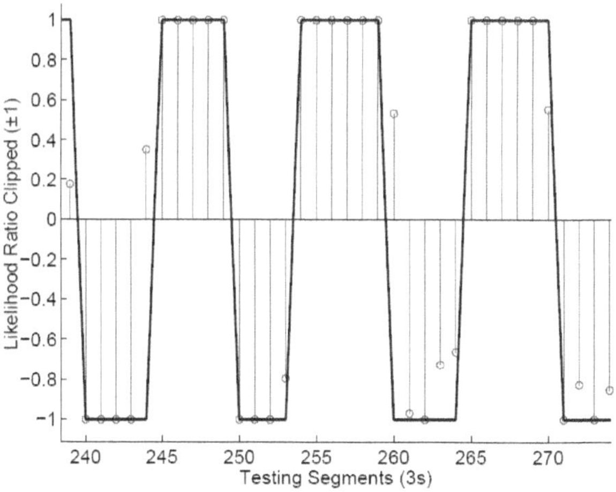

Fig. 2. System performance when applied to an audio stream. Continuous line: composition of the testing segment. Stems: $\Delta\lambda$ of segment.

Specifically, Fig. 3 (top) shows the overall performance of the system when a minimum CFM threshold is applied. Fig. 3 (bottom) shows the percentage of total frames that fall into the accepted CFM. Operation of the system without CFM restrictions yields accuracies of 91%, 92.3% and 92.1% on all segments for 1, 3 and 5 second testing segments, respectively. By applying a CFM threshold of 70% -only those segments with CFM over 70% are considered- the system would yield an accuracy of 96.18%, 97.02% and 96.73% (for 1, 3 and 5 second segments), using approximately 80% of the segments.

Computational Complexity: The computational complexity required for the implementation of the gender detector is proportional to the number of Gaussians components used as well as the processing time. The implementation of the algorithms reported was accomplished code generated with Visual Studio 2005 on a 3.2GHz Xeon processor based workstation. The system required 147ms to provide a decision with the most computational demanding setting using 60s of testing speech and 1024 Gaussians. For the setting using 64 Gaussians and 1s of testing speech provided the system required 11ms to provide a decision. In all cases the system performed several times real-time.

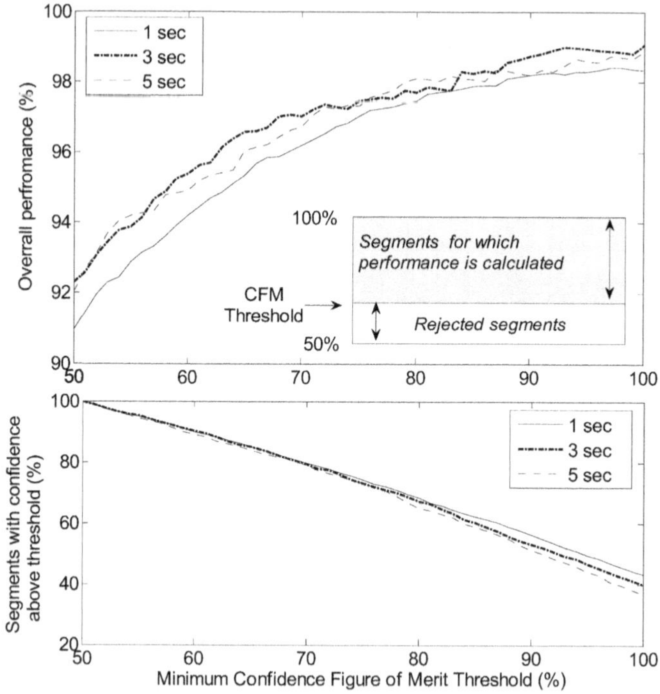

Fig. 3. System performance for testing segments with CFM above threshold (top). Segments meeting minimum CFM threshold (bottom).

5 Conclusion

The experiments performed herein address issues dealing with the implementation of a gender identification system tailored to operate efficiently for audio stream applications. It was observed that the MFCC features that emphasize gender differences observed in the lower part of the spectrum provide more discriminative ability than MFSC features which accentuate the upper spectral band. It was shown that a simple GMM classification approach can be used effectively to provide high classification performance with short-length testing segments performing better or similar to other more complex techniques reported.

The results obtained with the classifier revealed that the amount of speech per speaker used to train the gender models highly influences the performance of the system. Fifteen seconds of speech per speaker was found to be sufficient for training gender models, since longer sequences did not significantly improve performance.

The performance of the system was observed to improve with a greater number of Gaussians, with diminishing returns beyond 512 Gaussians. For streaming audio applications, the optimal number of Gaussians should be chosen to balance accuracy and real-time viability. This research indicated that the system described herein, can reliably perform gender classification at several times real-time in audio streams.

The CFM described enables a measure of quality in the gender decision and improve significantly the performance of the system when a threshold greater than 50% is selected, as showed in experiment 4.3. This metric is very desirable to aid in the detection of cross-gender segments, and to permit higher precision of audio stream applications.

References

1. Parris, E. S., Carey, M. J.: Language Dependent Gender Identification. Acoustics, Speech, and Signal Processing. ICASSP-96 Conference Proceedings, vol. 2. (1996) 685 - 688.
2. Hurb, H., Chen, L.: Gender Identification Using a General Audio Classifier. ICME '03 Proceedings, vol. 2. July (2003) 733-736.
3. Kamran, M., Bruce, I. C.: Robust Formant Tracking for Continuous Speech with Speaker Variability. IEEE Trans. Speech and Audio Proc. Accepted for publication, Jan. 19, (2005).
4. Vergin, R., Farhat A., O'Shaughnessy D.: Robust Gender-dependent Acoustic-phonetic Modelling in Continuous Speech Recognition Based on a New Automatic Male/female Classification. ICSLP-96 Conference Proceedings, vol. 2. October (1996) 1081-1084.
5. Slomka, S., Sridharan, S.: Automatic Gender Identification Optimised for Language Independence. TENCON '97 IEEE Region 10 Annual Conference. Speech and Image Technologies for Computing and Telecommunications Conference Proceedings, vol. 1. December (1997) 685 - 688.
6. Childers, D. G., Ke, W., Bae, K. S., Hicks, D.M.: Automatic Recognition of Gender by Voice. Acoustics, Speech, and Signal Processing. ICASSP-88 Conference Proceedings, vol. 1. (1988) 603-606.

7. Torres-Carrasquillo, P. A., Singer, E., Kohler, M. A., Greene, R. J., Reynolds, D. A., Deller, J. R.: Approaches to Language Identification Using Gaussian Mixture Models and Shifted Delta Cepstral Features, International Conference in Spoken Language. Denver. (2002).
8. Chen, T., Huang, C., Chang, E., Wang, J.: Automatic Accent Identification Using Gaussian Mixture Models. Workshop in Automatic Speech Recognition and Understanding ASRU '01. (2001) 343 – 346.
9. Andrianaki, I., White, P. R.: Modeling of Mel Frequency Features for Non Stationary Noise. Institute of Sound and Vibration Research. University of Southampton. Available: http://dea.brunel.ac.uk/cmsp/ Projnoise2003/Presentation25052004Ioannis.ppt.
10. Fisher English Training Speech Part 1, Linguistic Data Consortium, LDC2004S13, 2004.

On the Processing of Fuzzy Patterns for Text Independent Phonetic Speech Segmentation

Luis D. Huerta-Hernández[1,2] and Carlos A. Reyes-García[1]

[1] Instituto Nacional de Astrofísica Óptica y Electrónica (INAOE)
Luis Enrique Erro No. 1, Sta. Ma. Tonanzintla, Puebla, 72840, México
{luisdh2, kargaxxi}inaoep.mx
[2] Instituto Tecnológico Superior de Acatlán de Osorio,
Unidad Tecnológica, Acatlán de Osorio, Puebla, 73440, México

Abstract. In this work we propose an algorithm for continuous speech segmentation with text independency. In our approach we do not use feature vectors in order to detect phoneme boundaries, instead we only make use of the intensity measure. Obtaining with this a remarkable reduction in the amount of information needed and simplified rules on the processing. In the process only a pre-emphasis filter, and one strategy based on a distance measure with normalized fuzzy memberships over the signal patterns are used. In the preliminary results the method reaches up to 77.54% of correct segmentation with a 20 msec. accuracy and an over segmentation rate near to 0%. The algorithm implementation, the experiments, as well as some results are shown.

1 Introduction

From the arrival of computers, we have the need to communicate with them, and the recent tendency is to try to do it by natural means, like through the use of speech. We need to implement methods to communicate with machines, by developing friendly interfaces. In order to understand human oral expressions by mean of machines, they have to perform speech recognition. One way to do it is by first performing speech segmentation and later recognizing the found segments. The continuous speech recognition process is highly dependent of the segmentation process, being a crucial factor for automatic speech recognition (ASR) systems. We need to develop methods with features aimed to increase the performance and speed, such as the use of reduced speech units to be treated; reduced amount of information extracted from the speech, and simplified processing. Currently, many speech recognition systems are using phoneme like units because they bring the following advantages: phonemes are linguistically well defined units and can be looked up easily on a dictionary; pronunciation variability due to linguistic context, accent or dialogues can be easily represented by applying rules to basic forms; the number of units is small; and the phonemes require significantly less data to train than would be needed for whole word modeling [1]. There have been reported phoneme segmentation methods; with acceptable results, but with some of the following restrictions imposed: restricted vocabulary [1], speaker dependency [2], isolated words [3], and text dependency [4]. There are some

J.F. Martínez-Trinidad et al. (Eds.): CIARP 2006, LNCS 4225, pp. 437–445, 2006.

reported works, with complex processing based on rules derived from acoustic phonetic knowledge for phoneme segmentation [5, 6, 7, 8]. Recently, new methods have been proposed for phoneme segmentation, without the restrictions mentioned above but having to deal with over-segmentation and text-independency. They have minimized the complexity of the processing; however, they use speech feature vectors or set of features per sequence of time [2, 9, 10,11] and a post processing in order to reduce the insertion rate, but increasing the response time. The feature of speech commonly used with success in recognition and segmentation are LPC, and bank filter of models like MFCC, PCBF (Perceptual Critical Band Features) to mention some. Nonetheless, the encoded representation given on vectors is extracted from basic features presented on time domain.

The main goal of this work is to develop a phoneme speech segmentation algorithm with text independency and low computational cost, that can obtain high phoneme boundary detection rates without over segmenting, using a simplified approach on the feature extraction, segmentation process, fuzzy pattern and distance measure.

We tested the utility of basic features, like intensity, to get phoneme segmentation, and we found similar performance to the one reported on the state of art without presenting over-segmentation. It is important to remark that the intensity is one basic feature easily obtained from speech with light processing. Two remarkable issues of the proposed method are; the reduced information and the simple rules used, obtaining with them an almost real time phoneme segmentation. The testing was done over the same corpus and under similar conditions to the used in [9, 10].

2 The Auditory System Model

The human ear is able to perceive a range of frequency between 20 and 20000 Hz approximately. Since the speech wave is composed by many frequencies, these are not perceived with the same sensitivity. The high and low frequencies are perceived with less intensity. In general, following the Bark scale, the variations of sensitivity below 1000 Hz follow a constant variation with 100 Hz. bands, and when the frequency increases above the 1000 Hz, the sensitivity of frequencies follows a logarithmic scale. These obtained scales, show that low frequencies are increased significantly between 100 and 1000 Hz, and are based on the hearing functioning.

Methods to obtain cepstral vectors using filter banks have been developed, like the previously mentioned, which model the hearing functioning. In recent phoneme segmentation algorithms, the features of speech have been extracted by following some model of the auditory system, having an encoded speech in form of time sequence vectors, which has been taken in [10] as a constraint. Depending of the codification scheme used, the feature extraction might involve a time consuming process, and might obtain too much information to be treated. Doubtlessly some of these schemes like MFCC have reported success on speech recognition, because they give a detailed representation on the speech wave. For segmentation these details are not totally necessary, to show this we have used only scalar values of intensity per sequence of time.

3 The Basic Features of Speech

The Sound is composed of waves of pressure variations that oscillate from positive to negative relative to the surrounding medium, usually the air. The number of air pressure oscillations per second, determines the pitch of the sound, whose physical correlate is frequency. The amplitude is defined like the pressure applied by the vibration, on the elastic mean. If we have a sine wave, the y-value for any given x-value is the amplitude of the sine wave at that point in time. The amplitude is given in Pascal (Pa) units. On the other hand, the intensity is the size of the pressure vibrations determining the loudness of the sound. Acoustic scientists measure the intensity in a base 10 logarithmic scale called decibels (dB) [13]. The term intensity is used to refer to the overall power of a sound.

The phonemes used in words, have different intensity, for example, most aperture of the mouth is required for relative long time in order to pronounce vowels, releasing most energy and resulting in high intensity, in contrast with the intensity of the majority of consonants, and although plosives have high intensity their duration is very short.

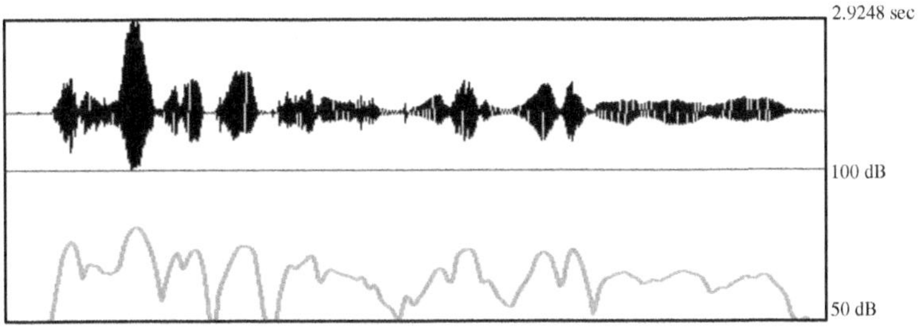

Fig. 1. Speech waveform and its respective intensity

Basic features as zero crossing rate, energy and pitch have been used in previous works in order to obtain sentence segmentation without speech recognition; details of one of those works are presented in [15]. The authors remark its accuracy comparable to methods using speech recognition but to a lower computational cost. Our work is oriented in a similar way, it is, to obtain phoneme segmentation based only on intensity changes without phoneme recognition.

4 The Fuzzy Algorithm

Some kind of speech codification scheme like the previously mentioned was avoided; instead, minimal information like the obtained from the intensity was used. In order to carry out the phoneme segmentation, we implemented a fuzzy distance measure between contiguous frames, and a set of simples rules aimed to detect significant distances, which could be tried like phoneme transition changes on continuous speech. We took advantage of fuzzy memberships of the intensity in order to obtain details on cases where the differences between frames are vague. Different from other approaches [2], this fuzzy algorithm does not require any training and has a reduced computational load due to its simplicity. The details are next described.

4.1 Preprocessing

First, the pre-emphasis filter on the speech signal was applied. The pre-emphasis filter gives a resultant sound with a high spectral slope. A frequency *F*, above which the spectral slope will be increased by 6 dB/octave, is given. The pre-emphasis factor α is computed as:

$$\alpha = \exp\left(-2\pi F \Delta t\right) \quad (1)$$

Where Δt is the sampling period of the sound. The resultant sound y_i is obtained with (2).

$$y_i = x_i - \alpha x_{i-1} \quad (2)$$

Where every sample x_i of the sound is changed, going down from the last sample [14]. According to the acoustical theory, in order to approximate the unequal sensitivity of human hearing at different frequencies [12], pre-emphasis process is used. In contrast, with the smoothing preprocessing techniques, we can enhance certain frequency intervals from another ones containing less relevant information. In our case, the pre-emphasis filter setting 50 Hz to the *F* argument in (1) was applied.

4.2 Phoneme Segmentation

The pre-emphasized signal is used in order to obtain the intensity with a minimal pitch of 93 Hz, and 3 msec. frames without overlapping were used. We also tested 4 and 5 msec. frame size, the results are shown in the experiments section.

For each signal, the maximum and minimum intensity were obtained, in order to establish the fuzzy space. The average between the maximum and minimum intensity, in order to obtain the medium point of the fuzzy space, was calculated. Three triangular fuzzy functions, representing low, median and high intensity, were applied. Membership values from the fuzzy sets are obtained for each intensity measure, and then they are normalized as follows: $\lambda=max(M)$, where *M* represents the fuzzy membership obtained from the compared frames. The maximum fuzzy membership denoted as λ is obtained. Then $\mu_i = \mu_i / \lambda \ \forall \mu_i \in M$ is applied. Since our strategy is based on the difference between contiguous frames, in order to detect phoneme boundaries, the normalized memberships are used in (3), and we denote the values obtained as *V*.

$$D(f_t, f_{t-2}) = \sqrt{(\mu_{high}(f_t) - \mu_{high}(f_{t-2}))^2 + (\mu_{mid}(f_t) - \mu_{mid}(f_{t-2}))^2 + (\mu_{low}(f_t) - \mu_{low}(f_{t-2}))^2} \quad (3)$$

Our approach is simple, because we focus on detecting the local maxima on the V values, which indicate the significant differences between the compared frames, and, therefore, the presence of a phoneme boundary. The rules used to detect the local maxima are the following:

1) $V_t > V_{t-1}$ & $V_t > V_{t+1}$
2) $V_t > 46.8\ dB$
3) $V_t > \Phi$

In condition 1) a V value at time t is treated as local maximum if it is greater than the previous and following V value on the sequence of time. Condition 2) is used to discriminate potential boundary values, because low intensity V_t values generally are not representative of phoneme boundaries. Condition 3) selects local maxima representing significant changes, when they are over the threshold Φ. The last two conditions are used in order to avoid unwanted insertions; although some valid phoneme boundaries are incorrectly discarded by them. On the other hand, erroneous points detected by the algorithm are rejected, resulting in a competitive performance. A limitation of this algorithm is that segments shorter than 0.021 msec are not allowed, this condition reduces the over segmentation problem and, at the same time, some of the valid phoneme boundaries are sacrificed too.

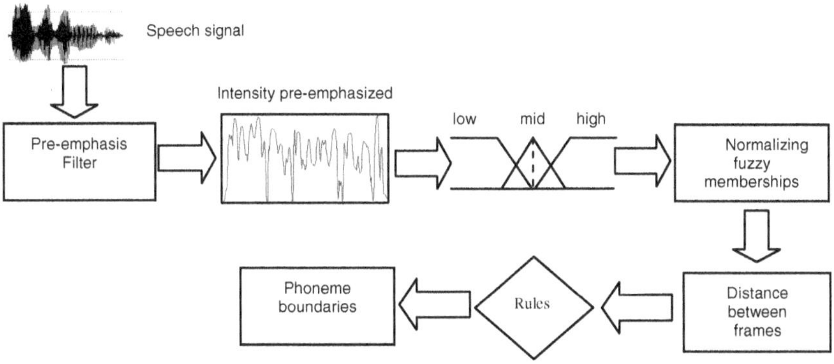

Fig. 2. Algorithm diagram

5 Implementation and Experiments

The feature extraction and segmentation processing was implemented using the freeware PRAAT v.4.4.04 [14].

For the experiments we used continuous speech expressed naturally, and with text and speaker independency. The algorithm was tested with 544 speech signals sampled at 16 kHz of the American English DARPA-TIMIT database, corresponding to 68 speakers (34 males and 34 females) of all dialect regions. The phoneme segmentation performance of the algorithm was compared with the true phoneme boundaries obtained from the transcription associated to the speech signals, which was made manually by phonetician experts. The subset of sentences has a total of 20647 phonetic boundaries.

5.1 Measurement Performance

The performance of the algorithm was evaluated with commonly used measures, like the one used in [9, 10, 11].

$$D = 100 \cdot \left(\frac{S_d}{S_t} - 1 \right) \tag{4}$$

Where D is the measure of over-segmentation, S_d is the number of segmentation points detected by the algorithm, and S_t is the number of the true segmentation points.

$$P_c = 100 \cdot \left(\frac{S_c}{S_t} \right) \tag{5}$$

Where P_c is the percentage of correct detection, and S_c is the number of correct segmentation points. The segmentation points detected by the algorithm are defined as correct if its distance from the true segmentation point is within the range of ± 20 msec.

5.2 Experiments and Results

Many changes aimed to improve, were implemented on the algorithm. Results of different algorithm versions are shown, in order to remark the effects of the experimented modifications. The first version of our algorithm, was using a frame size of 5msec, without normalized fuzzy memberships, and using the measure computed by (6), which obtains the distance between adjacent frames. The results are shown in table 1.

When the frame size was 5 msec without normalized fuzzy memberships, a poor performance was observed, and while the frame size was reduced the performance was slightly improved. The best observed performance was obtained when a frame size of 3 msec was used. That is why, in the remaining experiments, a 3 msec frame size was used.

$$D(f_t, f_{t-1}) = \sqrt{(\mu_{high}(f_t) - \mu_{high}(f_{t-1}))^2 + (\mu_{mid}(f_t) - \mu_{mid}(f_{t-1}))^2 + (\mu_{low}(f_t) - \mu_{low}(f_{t-1}))^2} \tag{6}$$

Table 1. Algorithm performance, with different frame size and its respective parameters

Size	Φ	Sd	Sc	% Correct Detection	% Over Segmentation
5 msec	0.040	20946	15046	72.87	1.44
4 msec	0.036	21039	15353	74.35	1.89
3 msec	0.032	20910	15485	74.99	1.27

Another remarkable improvement was when the fuzzy memberships were normalized, which increased the correct detection rate and reduced over segmentation to near to 0%. The results are shown in table 2.

Table 2. Algorithm performance, using normalized fuzzy memberships

Φ	Sd	Sc	% Correct Detection	% Over Segmentation
0.050	20642	15567	75.39	-0.02

When the distance between adjacent frames is being used, many phoneme changes are not detected, because their significant difference does not appear in adjacent frames. So a frame distance between compared frames was used in order to detect those slowly reflected changes, applying (3). The frame distance between compared frames is referred in this work as inter-frame. Finally, we used a minimum intensity of 25 dB instead the relative minimum intensity of each signal, in order to obtain the fuzzy space, increasing the performance. The results are shown in table 3.

Table 3. Algorithm performance, using inter frame

Φ	Sd	Sc	% Correct Detection	% Over Segmentation
0.0855	20668	16010	77.54	0.09

This modification to the distance measure and the minimum intensity of the fuzzy space, results on a correct detection increased above of 2 %, maintaining a percentage of over segmentation of near to 0%. Starting, in the preliminary experiments, with a correct detection performance of near to 73% and an over segmentation rate above of 1%, with simple modifications like the frame size, normalization of fuzzy membership functions, using an inter frame between compared frames and a minimum intensity of 25 dB in the fuzzy space, we improved the correct detection rate to near to 5%, and the over segmentation rate was reduced in more than 1%.

5.3 Comparison with Similar Works

The results are compared to algorithms alike [9,10,11], dealing with text and speaker independency, with over segmentation and some other previously mentioned conditions. Relevant aspects like amount of phoneme boundaries treated, information extracted from the speech, number of speakers and percentage of correct detection are used for the comparison, they are shown in table 4.

Table 4. Algorithm comparatives on different issues

Used features	Extracted values per 20 msec	Treated Speaker	Treated Phoneme Boundaries	% Correct detection
Intensity	6.66	68	20647	77.54
PCBF [9]	15	48	17930	73.56
Mel spectrum [10]	8	48	17930	76.53
PCBF [11]	15	20	6200	75.80

In the first row, significant aspects of our algorithm are presented, the remaining rows contain the reported aspects of the mentioned algorithms in the listed order as presented in [9, 10, 11]. The compared algorithms use feature vectors on frames of 20 msec, with 10 msec overlapping; and the "jump" term is used to denote significant changes (peaks) between compared frames; algorithms [10,11] are modifications of the algorithm presented in [9].

These algorithms have a fundamental process to combine, in a unique indication of phoneme boundary, the "jump" events detected around the same frame. The process is called "fitting" and was introduced to place the segmentation boundary in the middle of a cluster of quasi-simultaneous "jumps". The fitting process is used after the "jump" detection.

On the other hand, our approach use scalar values per time sequence, and no fitting process is used. Although the difference in number of features used among the algorithms is insignificant, we are not using overlapping frames, and our process to extract the features is remarkably simple and effective. Generally, the compared and the proposed algorithm present difficulties to detect vowel-vowel phoneme boundaries, and, specifically the proposed algorithm rejects those consecutive correct boundaries separated by only 0.021 msec.

7 Conclusions

The proposed phoneme segmentation algorithm has shown some advantages over others due to its lower computational cost in the extraction of features and boundaries detection. Our approach achieves competitive performance with fast execution due to the reduced information used and its simplified processing. In the preprocessing phase, only a pre-emphasis filter to enhance spectral changes was used. The strategy of using a fuzzy distance measure between frames shows to be simple and effective. The use of fuzzy normalized membership in an Euclidean distance, in order to obtain details of vague phoneme boundaries difficult to detect, lead to an increase in the overall algorithm performance. The use of inter frames was useful to detect phoneme boundaries, which present slow changes. The algorithm detected 77.54% of the boundaries without over segmentation. As future works we will try to improve the performance by enhancing the algorithm with more efficient strategies and rules.

References

1. Hu Z., Schalwyk J., Bernard E., Cole R., "Speech recognition using syllabe-like units", ICSLP '96, 2: 1117—1120, 1996.
2. Suh Y. and Lee Y., "Phoneme Segmentation of Continuous speech using multi-layer perceptron", IEEE Trans. Speech and Audio Proc., 7(6):697-708, 1999.
3. Ratsameewichai S., Theera N., Vilasdechanon J., Uatrongjit S., and Likit-Anurucks K., "Thai phoneme segmentation using dual-band energy contour", ITC- CSCC-2002.
4. Pellom B., Hansen J., "Automatic segmentation of speech recorded in unknown noisy channel characteristics", Speech Communication, 1998, 25, 97-116.
5. Schwartz R. And Makhoul J., "Where the Phonemes Are: Dealing with Ambiguity in Acoustic Phonetic Recognition", IEEE Trans. ASSP, Vol. 23, pp 50-53, Feb. 1975.
6. Zue V., "The Use of Speech Knowledge in Automatic Speech Recognition", Proceeding of the IEEE, Vol. 73, pp. 1602-1615, Nov. 1985.
7. Weinstein C., McCandless S., Mondstein L., and Zue V., "A system for Acoustic-Phonetic Analysis of Continuous Speech", IEEE Trans. ASSP, Vol. 23, pp. 54-67, Feb. 1975.
8. Grayden D. and Scordilis M., "Phonemic Segmentation of Fluent Speech, "Proc. ICASSP-94, pp. 73-76, 1994.
9. Aversano G. and Esposito A., "A new text-independent method for phoneme segmentation". in Proc. the 44th IEEE Midwest Symposium on Circuits and Systems, vol. 2, pp. 516--519, 2001.

10. Aversano G. and Esposito A., "Automátic Parameter Estimation for a Context-Independent Speech Segmentation Algorithm", TSD 2002, LNAI 2448, pp. 293-300, 2002 Springer Verlag Berlin Heidelberg 2002
11. Saraswhati S., Geetha T.V, and Saravanan K., "Integrating Language Independent Segmentation and Language Dependent Phoneme Based Modeling for Tamil Speech Recognition System", Asian Journal of Information Technology 5 (1) : 38-43, 2006.
12. Gold B., Morgan N., "Speech and audio signal processing", John Wiley & Sons Inc., 2000
13. Rodman R., "Computer Speech Technology", Artech House Inc., 1999.
14. Boersma, P. "Praat, a system for doing phonetics by computer". Glot International 5:9/10, 341-345.
15. Wang D., Le L., Zhang H., "Speech segmentation without speech recognition". Proc. of IEEE International Conference on Acoustics, Speech and Signal Processing (ICASSP03), Vol. I, pp. 468-471, Hong Kong, 2003.
16. Petek B., Andersen O., Dalsgaard P., "On the robust automatic segmentation of spontaneous speech", in proceedings of ICSLP'96, 1996, pp. 913-916.

A RLS Filter for Nonuniformity and Ghosting Correction of Infrared Image Sequences*

Flavio Torres[1], César San Martin[1,2], and Sergio N. Torres[2]

[1] Department of Electrical Engineering, University of La Frontera, Casilla 54-D, Temuco, Chile
ftorres@ufro.cl

[2] Department of Electrical Engineering, University of Concepción, Casilla 160-C, Concepción, Chile
sertorre@udec.cl
http://nuc.die.udec.cl

Abstract. In this paper, a technique to improve the convergence and to reduce the ghosting artifacts of a previously developed adaptive scene-based nonuniformity correction method is presented. The nonuniformity correction method estimates detector parameters based on the recursive least square filter approach. We propose, three parameters to reduce ghosting artifacts and to speed up the convergence of such method by using only the read-out data. The parameters proposed are based in identify global motion between consecutive frames as well as evaluate the main assumption used in the previous method in the uncertainty on the input infrared irradiance. The ability of the method to compensate for nonuniformity and reducing ghosting artifacts is demonstrated by employing several infrared video sequences obtained using two infrared cameras.

Keywords: Image Sequence Processing, Infrared Imaging, RLS.

1 Introduction

Infrared imaging systems are employed in several applications such as defense, astronomy and medical science. In general, those systems are based on the infrared focal-plane array IR FPA technology. An IR-FPA is a die composed of a group of photodetectors placed in a focal plane forming a matrix of $X \times Y$ pixels, which gives the sensor the ability to collect the IR information.

It is well known that nonuniformity noise in IR imaging sensors, which is due to pixel-to-pixel variation in the detectors' responses, can considerably degrade the quality of IR images since it results in a fixed-pattern-noise (FPN) that is superimposed on the true image. Even more, what makes matter worse is that the

* This work was supported by Universidad de La Frontera, Proyecto DIUFRO EP N° 06-0253 . The authors wish to thank Ernest E. Armstrong (OptiMetrics Inc., USA) and Pierre Potet (CEDIP Infrared Systems, France) for collecting the data.

J.F. Martínez-Trinidad et al. (Eds.): CIARP 2006, LNCS 4225, pp. 446–454, 2006.

nonuniformity slowly varies over time, and depending on the technology used, this drift can take from minutes to hours. In order to solve this problem, several scene-based nonuniformity correction (NUC) techniques have been developed [1,2,3,4,5,6]. Scene-based techniques perform the NUC using only the video sequences that are being imaged, not requiring any kind of laboratory calibration technique.

Our group has been given special attention to NUC methods based on estimation theory. Seeking for more effectiveness in the reduction of NUC, we propose to improve our previously published adaptive scene-based NUC method [7], based in a RLS (recursive least square) filter [8]. The NUC method based in a RLS algorithm exhibits the advantages of fast convergence rate and unbiased stationary error [9,10]. However, the method has shown the following weakness: the supposition that the input scene is constantly moving, in general, is not valid and ghosting artifacts are generated; the assumption that the best target for the unknown input infrared irradiance is an average over its neighboring pixels is scene dependent generating a poor correction in pixels, which are part of objects boundaries. Then, for improving the performance of the NUC RLS algorithm, we propose three parameters to mitigate the ghosting artifacts and speed up the convergence in pixels that are part of the edges of objets being imaged. The effect of the parameters are tested with simulated and real IR data.

This paper is organized as follows. In Section 2 the IR-FPA model and the RLS- NUC method with the proposed enhancement are presented. In Section 3 the RLS- NUC technique is tested with video sequences of real raw IR data captured using two infrared cameras. In Section 4 the conclusions of the paper are summarized.

2 The RLS NUC Method for Infrared Video Sequences

In this section, the previously published scene-based NUC method [7] is presented for completeness. We begin reviewing the most common model used for the nonuniformity presented IR-FPA technology, and we finish developing three parameters with the ability of being used to reduce ghosting artifacts and to speed up convergence of such method.

2.1 RLS Filter Method

In this paper, we adopt the commonly used linear model for the infrared detector. For the $(ij)^{\text{th}}$ detector in IR-FPA, the measured read-out signal Y_{ij} at a given time n can be expressed as:

$$Y_{ij}(n) = g_{ij}(n) \cdot X_{ij}(n) + o_{ij}(n) + v_{ij}(n) \tag{1}$$

where $g_{ij}(n)$ and $o_{ij}(n)$ are the gain and the offset of the ij^{th} detector, $X_{ij}(n)$ is the real incident IR photon flux collected by the respective detector, and $v_{ij}(n)$ is the additive electronic noise. Re-writing equation (1) in a vectorial form we obtain:

$$Y_{ij}(n) = \Psi_{ij}^T(n)\Theta_{ij}(n) + v_{ij}(n) \tag{2}$$

where, $\Psi_{ij}(n) = [X_{ij}(n), 1]^T$ is the IR data vector and $\Theta_{ij}(n) = [g_{ij}(n), o_{ij}(n)]^T$, is the detector parameter vector. Then, an estimator for Θ_{ij} can be formulated like:

$$\hat{Y}_{ij}(n) = \Psi_{ij}^T(n)\hat{\Theta}_{ij}(n) \tag{3}$$

and the estimation error is given by:

$$e_{ij}(n) = Y_{ij}(n) - \Psi_{ij}^T(n)\hat{\Theta}_{ij}(n) \tag{4}$$

From (3) is possible to obtain a solution only if the unknown real incident IR is known. The key assumption of the method is that X_{ij} can be initially estimated from the read-out data Y_{ij}. Then, we initially estimate the real IR X_{ij} with the spatial mean value of the corrupted image at ij sensor [4], that is:

$$X_{ij}(n) = \bar{Y}_{ij}(n) = \frac{1}{(2v+1)^2} \sum_{k=i-v}^{i+v} \sum_{l=j-v}^{j+v} Y_{kl}(n) \tag{5}$$

where $\bar{Y}$ is a smoothing version of Y and v fixes the averaging window size. This assumption is valid when the scene is constantly moving with respect to the detector. Because $\bar{Y}$ is more uniform than Y, a spatial nonuniformity correction is performed. Then, equation (3) will be used to estimate the detector parameters with $\Psi_{ij}(n) = \left[\bar{Y}_{ij}(n), 1\right]^T$, i.e., we suppose that the gain parameters have a spatial normal distribution with unit mean, and the offset have a spatial normal distribution with zero mean.

Then, we minimize the functional

$$\epsilon_{ij}(n) = \sum_{k=1}^{n} \lambda_{ij}^{n-k} e_{ij}^2(n) \tag{6}$$

where λ is the forgetting factor which varies to in $0 < \lambda < 1$, and weighs the influence of past error values. Deriving $\epsilon_{ij}(n)$ with respect to the parameter vector $\Theta_{ij}(n)$, equalling to zero and solving for the parameter vector, we obtain

$$\hat{\Theta}_{ij}(n) = \left[\sum_{k=1}^{n} \lambda^{n-k} \Psi_{ij}(k) \Psi_{ij}^T(k)\right]^{-1} \sum_{k=1}^{n} \lambda^{n-k} \Psi_{ij}(k) y_{ij}(k) = P_{ij}(n) \psi_{ij}(n) \tag{7}$$

For a recursive update of the parameters, the RLS algorithm is used, hence all necessary equations to form the algorithm are:

$$\hat{\Theta}_{ij}(n+1) = \hat{\Theta}_{ij}(n) + \mathrm{K}_{ij}(n+1)\left[Y_{ij}(n+1) - \Psi_{ij}^T(n+1)\hat{\Theta}_{ij}(n)\right]$$

$$\mathrm{K}_{ij}(n+1) = \mathrm{P}_{ij}(n)\Psi_{ij}(n+1)\left[\lambda - \Psi_{ij}^T(n+1)\mathrm{P}_{ij}(n)\Psi_{ij}(n+1)\right]^{-1}$$

$$\mathrm{P}_{ij}(n+1) = \left[I - \mathrm{K}_{ij}(n+1)\Psi_{ij}^T(n+1)\right]\mathrm{P}_{ij}(n) \cdot \frac{1}{\lambda} \tag{8}$$

where, $\hat{\Theta}_{ij}(n) = [\hat{g}_{ij}(n), \hat{o}_{ij}(n)]^T$, is the estimated parameter vector, $\mathrm{K}_{ij}(n)$ is the gain vector and $\mathrm{P}_{ij}(n)$ is the covariance matrix.

Finally, to remove the nonuniformity noise of the corrupted image sequence, we use the parameters estimated by the RLS algorithm like the following:

$$\hat{X}_{ij}(n) = Y_{ij}(n)/\hat{g}_{ij}(n) - \hat{o}_{ij}(n)/\hat{g}_{ij}(n) \tag{9}$$

where $\hat{X}_{ij}(n)$ is the corrected image.

2.2 Performance of the RLS NUC Method

The main problems detected on the performance of the RLS NUC method are originated by three basic constraints used in the development of the method. The first is related to the supposition that the scene is constantly moving with respect to the detector. Then, the problem is that when the scene is not moving for a few frames, this equality is not valid, and the ghosting effect appears. This consists in a ghost present in the next frames.

The second is related to the supposition that the readout data has imaged object with low spatial diversity in the integrate IR radiation, which in the general case, is also not valid. The spatial uniformity in the image is used to obtain an accurate parameter estimation of the RLS NUC method because the spatial variance of the read-out data and the true IR data are near to zero, and only variance of the offset and the electronic noise are presented.

The third constraint is that the RLS NUC method does not satisfies the orthogonality principle. This means that the variance of the error is not minimal. This generates an estimation with a considerable variability in the error.

In the next section, we propose parameters to be included in the algorithm to reduce the effects generated by the foregoing constraints.

2.3 Nonuniformity and Ghosting Correction Algorithm

The algorithm is improved considering three parameters,which are based on the following: motion detection, nonuniformity degree estimation and error variance. We propose an indicator for the motion detection between consecutive frames, i.e., between frames at n and $n-1$ as follows:

$$z_1(n) = \sum_{k,l} |Y_n(k,l) - Y_{n-1}(k,l)|$$

where $z_1(n)$ is used to reduce ghosting. If $z_1(n)$ is close to zero, ghosting is presented on the corrected image. And, we propose an indicator for spatial variance of the IR radiation by considering the local spatial variance of $Y_{ij}(n)$, $\sigma^2_{Y_{ij}(n)}$ calculated by

$$\sigma^2_{Y_{ij}(n)} = \frac{1}{(2v+1)^2} \sum_{k=i-v}^{i+v} \sum_{l=j-v}^{j+v} (Y_{kl}(n) - \bar{Y}_{ij}(n))^2$$

The frame by frame calculus allows us to estimate a new temporal variable $z_2(n) = \sigma^2_{Y_{ij}(n)}$ that is used as an indicator in the algorithm. Note that, small values of $z_2(n)$ means that the input data meets the required assumption, on the IR radiance, by the proposed method.

The last indicator is obtained using the error defined in equation (4) as $z_3(n) = e^2_{ij}(n)$, i.e., the error variance. In this case, a good performance of the method takes place when $z_3(n)$ is minimal.

Then, the NUC algorithm is enhanced by the use of these parameters as described in the following steps:

- For each frame, we obtain $z_1(n)$, $z_2(n)$ and $z_3(n)$,
- After L frames, $\sigma^2_{z_2}$ is calculated
- Then, we calculate the H value, defined as

$$H = \frac{\sigma^2_{z_2} z_3}{1 + z_1}$$

- If at the current iteration, the calculated value of H is lower in magnitude than any previously calculated value, the estimated gain and offset are updated on this iteration. Otherwise, the gain and offset calculated at the previous iteration are not updated.

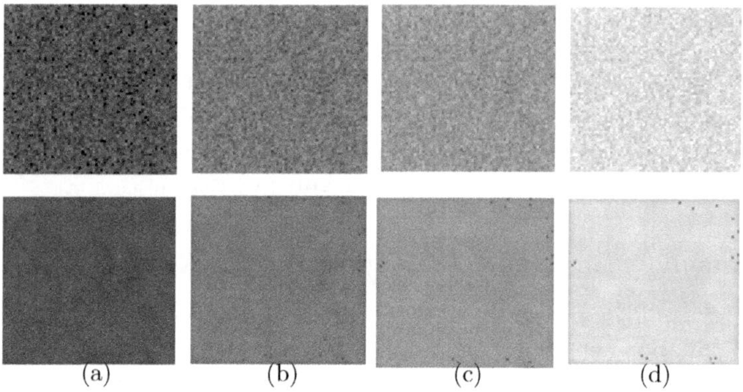

Fig. 1. Four frames of a simulated black bodies sequence (first row) and the correction with the enhanced NUC RLS method (second row). a) The 335 - th frame. b) The 500 - th frame. c) The 665 - th frame. d) The 845 - th frame.

3 Evaluation of the Proposed Methods Upgrades

The main goal of this section is to test the ability of the proposed method to reduce nonuniformity on simulated and real infrared video data. In the first place, we use simulated black body images. In the second place, the algorithm is tested with two real infrared image sequences taken by two different IR cameras.

As a quantitative measure of performance, we use the Root Mean Square Error (RMSE), which measures the difference between the true infrared image with the corrected image using the proposed method. The RMSE is calculated by:

$$RMSE(n) = \{\frac{1}{pm}\sum_{i=1}^{p}\sum_{j=1}^{m}(\hat{x}_{ij}(n) - x_{ij}(n))^2\}^{1/2} \tag{10}$$

(a) (b) (c)

Fig. 2. Results on Real IR data with emphasis in ghost artifacts reducction. The first row shows the 770- th frame and the second row shows the 1600-th frame of the first set of IR data, a) The raw corrupted frames, b) The corresponding frames corrected by the previous RLS method [7] and c) The corresponding frames corrected by the enhanced method.

where $p \times m$ is the number of detectors in the FPA. A low value of RMSE means a better correction of the frame data. The evaluation procedure for each set of data is detailed in the following sections.

3.1 Results with Simulated Black Bodies

The simulated black bodies has been generated using flat images, where the intensity or gray level indicates the black bodies temperature. FPN is added to each image generating the corrupted sequence. An example is presented in the first row of Fig. 1. Those images present only nonuniform noise, hence the black bodies constitute a good test for the NUC algorithm. In the second row of Fig. 1, it is clear, using the naked eye, that the proposed method reduced the FPN and performed an accurate nonuniformity correction.

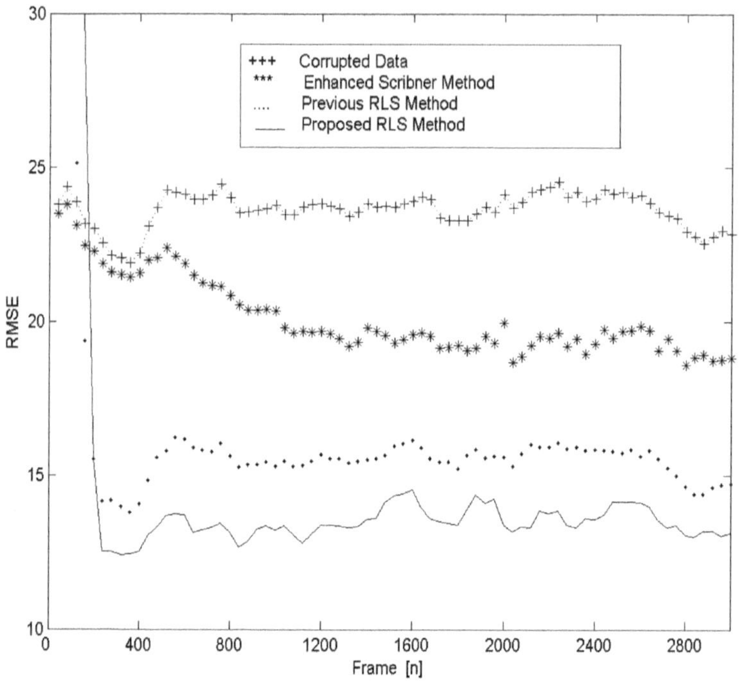

Fig. 3. The evolution of the RMSE between the reference (set 1 calibrated with black bodies) and the corrected frames of IR data set 1. Line with a plus represents the corrupted data; line with a star represents the RMSE computed for the enhanced Scribners NUC method [4]; line with a dot represents the previous NUC RLS method [7]; and solid line represents the RMSE computed for the proposed enhanced NUC-RLS method.

3.2 Results with Two Real Infrared Image Sequences

The first sequence has been collected using a 128×128 InSb FPA cooled camera (Amber Model AE-4128) operating in the $3 - 5\mu m$ range. As an example, Fig. 2a shows a corrupted readout data frame. In Fig. 2b and 2c the corresponding corrected frame by the NUC RLS method and the enhance RLS method are presented, respectively. In Fig. 2b and Fig. 2c we have shown a zooming of the corrected image, specifically of the zones indicated by boxes. In them, using only the naked eye is clear that the non-uniformity is notably better in the proposed NUC RLS method (Fig. 2c) than in the previous published method (Fig. 2b).

The NUC performance, in this case, is evaluated by employing the index RMSE computed between a reference (the real IR sequence calibrated with black bodies) and the corrected IR video sequence. Figure 3 shows the calculated RMSE for the corrupted data, for each frame corrected using enhanced Scribner's NUC method [4], the RLS, and the enhanced RLS method. Further, the average RMSEs computed for the whole infrared sequence are equal to 20.15, 16.62 and 14.23 for the Scribner NUC method, the NUC-RLS algorithm and the enhanced NUC RLS algorithm, respectively. It can be seen in Fig. 3 that the RMSE value obtained for the enhanced NUC RLS method has a greater convergence speed, because, for the same number of frame, it reaches a lower RMSE value than any other method.

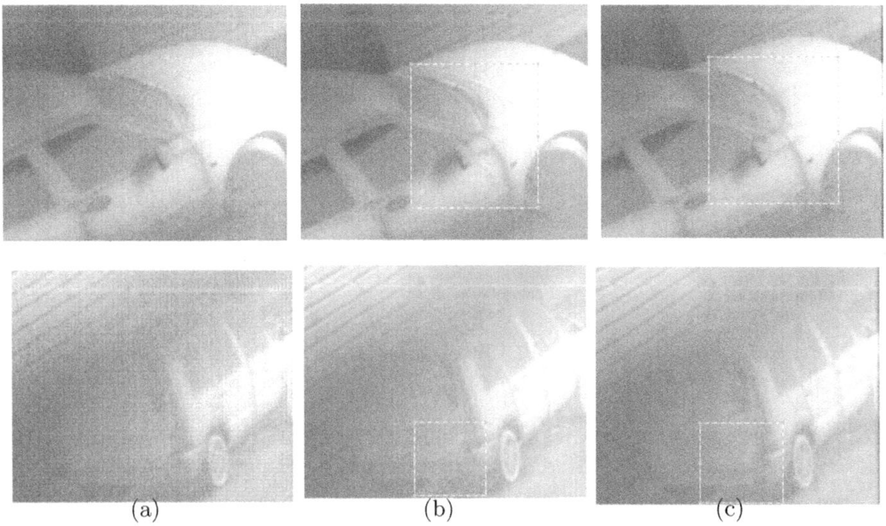

Fig. 4. Performance of the enhanced NUC-RLS method under real IR data. The first row shows the 297- th frame and the second row shows the 467-th frame of the second set of IR data, a) The raw corrupted frames, b) The corresponding frames corrected first by the RLS method and c) The corresponding frames corrected by the proposed enhance method.

The second sequence of infrared data has been recorded using a 320×240 HgCdTe FPA cooled camera (CEDIP Jade Model) operating in the $8 - 12\mu m$ range. As an example, Fig. 4a shows the corrupted readout data for two frames. In Fig. 4b, and Fig. 4c the corresponding corrected frames by the previous published method and the NUC method proposed in this paper are shown, respectively. The non-uniformity, visually presented in the raw frame, has been notably reduced by the proposed method; in Fig. 4b and Fig. 4c this is specially noticed in the marked region. In Fig. 4b it is possible to appreciate the ghosting present on both frames. This ghost effect disappears when we used the RLS method with nonuniformity and ghosting correction algorithm, as it is shown in Fig. 4c. Thus, we have shown experimentally with real IR data that the proposed scene-based NUC RLS method with ghost correction has the ability of notably reduce both the non-uniformity noise presented in IR-FPA sensors and the ghosting generated by lack of motion in the recorded IR data.

4 Conclusions

In this paper an enhanced version of our previously published NUC method, based in a RLS filter is presented. The new method has the ability to improve the nonuniformity correction and to eliminate ghosting artifacts more efficiently than the previous method. This is obtained by means of three parameters based in identifying global motion between consecutive frames as well as, evaluate the main assumption used in the previous method in the uncertainty on the input infrared irradiance. Furthermore, the evaluation with simulated and real data has demonstrated that the proposed method reduces ghosting artifacts and improves the RMSE parameter when compared with the previous published method. Using read-out data taken from cameras of two different technologies we were able to observe that the method is capable to reduce nonuniformity, minimizing ghosting, with fast convergence and low RMSE.

References

1. Torres, S., Hayat, M.: Kalman Filtering for Adaptive Nonuniformity Correction in Infrared Focal Plane Arrays. The JOSA-A Opt. Soc. of America. **20**. (2003) 470–480.
2. Torres, S., Pezoa, J., Hayat, M.: Scene-based Nonuniformity Correction for Focal Plane Arrays Using the Method of the Inverse Covariance Form. OSA App. Opt. Inf. Proc. **42**. (2003) 5872–5881.
3. Scribner, D., Sarkady, K., Kruer, M.: Adaptive Nonuniformity Correction for Infrared Focal Plane Arrays using Neural Networks. Proceeding of SPIE. **1541**. (1991) 100–109.
4. Scribner, D., Sarkady, K., Kruer, M.: Adaptive Retina-like Preprocessing for Imaging Detector Arrays. Proceeding of the IEEE International Conference on Neural Networks. **3**. (1993) 1955–1960.
5. Torres, S., Vera, E., Reeves, R., Sobarzo, S.: Adaptive Scene-Based Nonuniformity Correction Method for Infrared Focal Plane Arrays. Proceeding of SPIE. **5076**. (2003) 130–139.
6. Vera, E., Torres, S.: Fast Adaptive Nonuniformity Correction for Infrared Focal Plane Arrays. EURASIP Journal on Applied Signal Processing. (2005).
7. Torres, F., Torres, S., San Martin, C.: A Recursive Least Square Adaptive Filter for Nonuniformity Correction of Infrared Image Sequences. LNCS, **3773**. (2005) 540–546.
8. L. Ljung and T. Sderstrm: Theory and practice of recursive identification, MIT Press, Cambridge, 1983.
9. E. Eleftheriou, D.D. Falconer, Tracking properties and steady-state performance of RLS adaptive filter algorithms, IEEE Trans. Acoust. Speech Signal Process. ASSP **34** (1986) 1097-1110.
10. E. Ewada, Comparasion of RLS, LMS and sign algorithms for tracking randomly time-varying channels, IEEE Trans. Signal Process. **42** (1994) 2937-2944.

Correlation Filters for Detection and Localization of Objects in Degraded Images

Erika M. Ramos-Michel and Vitaly Kober

Department of Computer Sciences, Division of Applied Physics, CICESE
Km 107 Carretera Tijuana-Ensenada, Ensenada, B.C. 22860, México
rmichel@cicese.mx, vkober@cicese.mx

Abstract. Several correlation filters are derived to improve pattern recognition of a noisy target embedded into nonoverlapping background, when the input image is degraded with a linear system. With the help of computer simulation we analyze and compare the performance of various correlation based methods for reliable detection and localization of objects in blurred and noisy images.

Keywords: Object recognition, correlation filters, degraded image.

1 Introduction

In pattern recognition detection and localization of objects in pictures are tasks of extreme importance. Since the pioneering paper by Vanderlugt [1] various correlation filters have been suggested. When a correlator is used the pattern recognition can be done in two steps. First, the detection is carried out by searching the highest correlation peaks at the filter output, and then the coordinates of the peaks are taken as position estimations of targets in the scene image [2-13].

Several criteria were proposed to characterize the filter performance in terms of signal-to-noise ratio, peak sharpness, light efficiency, discrimination capability, etc. [3]. Correlation filters can be designed by maximizing one of these criteria. Many solutions were proposed when the input scene contains a reference object corrupted by additive noise (overlapping model). For instance, the matched spatial filter (MSF) [1] is derived by maximizing the signal-to-noise ratio (SNR). Horner and Gianino [2] suggested the phase-only filter (POF) that maximizes light efficiency. The optimal filter (OF) [13] was proposed to minimize the probability of anomalous errors (false alarms) [6, 9]. When the input scene contains a reference object embedded into a disjoint background (nonoverlapping model) and additive noise the following correlation filters were obtained: the generalized optimum filter, which is designed to maximize the ratio of the expected value of the squared correlation peak to the average expected value of the output signal energy (POE) [4,5,7,10]; the generalized matched filter that maximizes the ratio of the expected value of the squared correlation peak to the average output variance (S$\tilde{N}$R) [4,7,10].

The mentioned filters were derived for the overlapping and nonoverlapping models. However, these two models do not take into account possible blurring of input scenes. These kinds of degradation frequently appear during image formation

J.F. Martínez-Trinidad et al. (Eds.): CIARP 2006, LNCS 4225, pp. 455–463, 2006.

and recording [14-16]. For this reason, these degradations should be considered in the design process of filters.

The purpose of this paper is to investigate the performance of correlation filters in terms of accuracy of localization and discrimination capability for a modified nonoverlapping model, which takes into account blurring of the input scene. Two schemes of degradation of the input scene are considered; that is, 1) degradation (blurring) is caused by a linear system with a given point spread function (PSF); 2) degradation consists of blurring by a linear system and further corruption with additive white Gaussian noise. For the proposed signal model new correlation filters optimized with respect to pattern recognition measures are derived. With the help of computer simulation we analyze the performance of the obtained and known filters in terms of discrimination capability (DC) and localization distance errors. We assume that the information of degradation is known. In other words, the parameters of blurring and noise can be estimated taking into account the nature of the degradations. Note that although the degradation information is known, no restoration techniques are utilized because the objective is a reliable recognition and localization of a reference object. The presentation is organized as follows. In Section 2, new correlation filters for the modified nonoverlapping model are presented. Computer simulation results are presented and discussed in Section 3. Finally, Section 4 summarizes our conclusions.

2 Correlation Filters for Pattern Recognition in Blurred and Noisy Images

Several causes produce blurred images during the process of image formation: optical diffraction, atmospheric turbulence, out of focus, relative motion between the recording medium and the scene, object moving through a fixed background, etc. In our experiments we consider the blurring degradation due to a relative motion of a camera, while an input scene is still. In this case the captured image is completely blurred. Assume that the input image is always corrupted by additive noise (for instance, sensor's noise).

Let us consider that an input scene $s(x)$ contains a target $t(x-x_0)$ having unknown coordinate x_0 and a nonoverlapping background $b(x,x_0)$. Because of the image formation process, this image is degraded by a uniform PSF and additive noise as follows:

$$s(x,x_0)=\left[t(x-x_0)+b(x,x_0)\right]*h_d(x)+n(x) , \tag{1}$$

where we use the following notations and assumptions.

1. The nonoverlapping background signal $b(x,x_0)$ is regarded as a product of a realization $b(x)$ from a wide-stationary random process and an inverse support function of the target $w(x)$ defined as zero within the target area and unity elsewhere; that is,

$$b(x,x_0)=b(x)w(x-x_0) . \tag{2}$$

2. The coordinate x_0 is considered as a random variable with a uniform probability density function.
3. It is assumed that the wide-sense stationary noise and the target location x_0 are statistically independent of each other.
4. μ_b is the expected value of $b(x)$.
5. $B_0(\omega)$ is the power spectral density of $(b(x) - \mu_b)$, and it is calculated as

$$B_0(\omega) = \left| F\left\{ \left[b(x, x_0) - \mu_b \right] V(x) \right\} \right|^2 , \tag{3}$$

where F{.} denotes the Fourier transform. This can be done because $b(x)$ is considered as an ergodic process [17]. $V(x)$ is a sinusoidal window that is utilized for smoothing the image in order to obtain a better estimation of the power spectral density. Actually, other windows can be used as well for the estimation [18]. However, the used sinusoidal window is separable, that leads to an easy implementation of the estimation.
6. The input scene is completely degraded by blurring. $h_d(x)$ is the real impulse response, which is represented with a uniform PSF as

$$PSF_d = \frac{1}{d^2} \begin{bmatrix} 1 & \cdots & 1 \\ \vdots & \ddots & \vdots \\ 1 & \cdots & 1 \end{bmatrix}_{d \times d} , \tag{4}$$

and $H_d(\omega)$ is its transfer function.
7. $n(x)$ is additive white Gaussian noise with the zero mean and the power spectral density $N(\omega)$.
8. $T(\omega)$ y $W(\omega)$ are the Fourier transforms of $t(x)$ and $w(x)$, respectively.

Next, for the modified nonoverlapping model we derive new optimal correlation filters. Actually, these filters are modified versions of the correlation filters: generalized matched filter (GMF), generalized phase-only filter (GPOF), and generalized optimal filter GOF [4, 9, 10, 11], which are optimal with respect to various recognition measures for the nonoverlapping signal model. The proposed filters are denoted as follows: GMF+, GPOF+, and GOF+. For simplicity, through this paper we use the one-dimensional notation.

The GOF+ filter can be obtained by maximizing the POE criterion defined as

$$POE = \frac{\left| E\left[y(x, x_0) \right] \right|^2}{\overline{E\left\{ \left[y(x, x_0) \right]^2 \right\}}} = \frac{\left| E\left[y(x, x_0) \right] \right|^2}{\overline{Var\left\{ y(x, x_0) \right\}} + \overline{\left| E\left\{ y(x, x_0) \right\} \right|^2}} . \tag{5}$$

First, $\left| E\left[y(x, x_0) \right] \right|^2$, $\overline{Var\left\{ y(x, x_0) \right\}}$, and $\overline{\left| E\left\{ y(x, x_0) \right\} \right|^2}$ are calculated taking into account (1), and then they are substituted in (5) as follows:

$$POE = \frac{\frac{1}{4\pi^2} \left| \int \left[T(\omega) + \mu_b W(\omega) \right] H_d(\omega) H(\omega) d\omega \right|^2}{\frac{1}{2\pi L} \int \left\{ \left[\alpha B_0(\omega) \circ \left| W(\omega) \right|^2 + \left| T(\omega) + \mu_b W(\omega) \right|^2 \right] \left| H_d(\omega) \right|^2 + N(\omega) \right\} \left| H(\omega) \right|^2 d\omega} . \tag{6}$$

Finally, applying the Schwarz inequality [19], we have the filter that maximizes the POE criterion:

$$H_{GOF+}(\omega) = \frac{\left[T^*(\omega) + \mu_b W^*(\omega)\right] H_d^*(\omega)}{\left[\left|T(\omega) + \mu_b W(\omega)\right|^2 + \alpha B_0(\omega) \circ \left|W(\omega)\right|^2\right] \left|H_d(\omega)\right|^2 + N(\omega)} . \tag{7}$$

The asterisk denotes the complex conjugate and the symbol "∘" indicates the convolution operation. α is a normalizing constant [10].

In a similar manner, the modified filters GMF+ and GOF+ are derived and given, respectively, by

$$H_{GMF+}(\omega) = \frac{\left[T^*(\omega) + \mu_b W^*(\omega)\right] H_d^*(\omega)}{\left[\alpha B_0(\omega) \circ \left|W(\omega)\right|^2\right] \left|H_d(\omega)\right|^2 + N(\omega)} , \tag{8}$$

$$H_{GPOF+}(\omega) = \frac{\left[T^*(\omega) + \mu_b W^*(\omega)\right]}{\left|T(\omega) + \mu_b W(\omega)\right|} e^{-j\theta_{H_d}} . \tag{9}$$

If the observed image has no blurring, the classical generalized filters and obtained modified filters are equal. Note that the filters GPOF and GPOF+ do not take into account the additive noise influence. If the PSF is symmetric, its Fourier transform has zero phase.

3 Discussion and Computer Simulations

In this section computer simulation results are presented and discussed. In our experiments the target image *t(x)* and the background image *b(x)* possess characteristics given in Table 1. All the correlation filters are implemented with the use of the Discrete Fourier Transform [15].

Table 1. Parameters of the used images

Statistical Description	Background Image	Target Image
Mean	133.0900	143.9833
Standard Deviation	22.5315	70.23
Size (pixels)	256 × 256	41 × 69

The signal range is [0-255]. The target is shown in Fig. 1(a). The nonoverlapping background scene is shown in Fig. 1(b). The observed image is degraded with 1) only a linear system possessing the PSF of different sizes (d); 2) a linear system and additive white Gaussian noise (AWGN) with zero mean and the standard deviations (σ_n): 5, 10, 15, 20, 25, 30, 35, 40 and 43. Figure 2 shows an example of the observed image, which is degraded by the PSF with d=5, and the noise with σ_n=20.

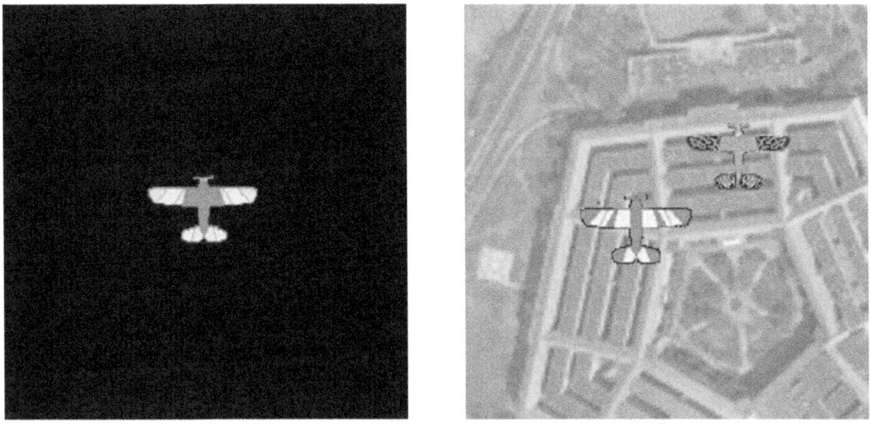

(a) (b)

Fig. 1. (a) Image target, (b) background image

Fig. 2. Observed image with a uniform PSF (size d=5) and AWGN with μ_n=0 and σ_n=20

The discrimination capability is formally defined as ability of a filter to distinguish a target among other different objects. If a target is embedded into a background that contains false objects, then the DC can be expressed as follows:

$$DC = 1 - \frac{\left|C^B(0,0)\right|^2}{\left|C^T(0,0)\right|^2}, \tag{10}$$

where C^B is the maximum in the correlation plane over the background area to be rejected, and C^T is the maximum in the correlation plane over the area of target position. The area of target position is determined in the close vicinity of the actual target location. The background area is complementary to the area of target position. The DC gives a detection ability of a filter. The location errors can be characterized by deviation between actual and obtained target positions. Formally, the distance error of localization is calculated as the distance between the known exact position of the target (x_T, y_T) and the position corresponding to the coordinates of the maximum value in the correlation plane over the area of object to be recognized was found $(\tilde{x}_T, \tilde{y}_T)$.

$$\mathrm{DE} = \sqrt{(x_T - \tilde{x}_T)^2 + (y_T - \tilde{y}_T)^2} . \tag{11}$$

3.1 Results of Scenario 1

In this scenario, the observed image is non-degraded. Table 2 shows the performance of the correlation filters in terms of the DC. To obtain these results the 30 statistical trials were carried out. In each trial the target position randomly was changed. We see that all the filters are able to detect and to localize the target. Note that the GOF and the OF filters yield the best results.

Table 2. Mean and Standard Deviation (*SD*) of *DC* of Scenario 1

Statistics	MSF	POF	OF	GMF	GPOF	GOF
Mean	0.1333	0.8698	0.9284	0.3954	0.8734	0.9395
SD	0.0078	0.0087	0.0092	0.0080	0.0131	0.0084

3.2 Results of Scenario 2

In this scenario, the observed image is degraded only by a linear system with the uniform PSFs, whose the sizes are 3, 5, 7, 11, and 15. Table 3 shows the performance of the correlation filters in terms of the DC. For each blurring degradation 30 statistical trails were conducted.

Table 3. Mean and Standard Deviation (*SD*) of *DC* of Scenario 2

Size of PSF	**3**		**5**		**7**		**11**		**15**	
Filters	**Mean**	**SD**	**Mean**	**SD**	**Mean**	**SD**	**Mean**	**SD**	**Mean**	**SD**
POF	0.7889	0.0192	0.6359	0.0246	0.4505	0.0311	0.3095	0.0297	0.1710	0.0302
OF	0.9271	0.0076	0.9189	0.0081	0.9172	0.0090	0.8960	0.0173	0.9108	0.0079
GMF	0.2945	0.0081	0.2102	0.0085	0.1484	0.0089	-	-	-	-
GPOF, GPOF+	0.7611	0.0191	0.6973	0.0120	0.5363	0.0185	0.3796	0.0236	0.2484	0.0260
GOF	0.8794	0.0152	0.8460	0.0207	0.7682	0.0334	0.7405	0.0346	0.6486	0.0690
GMF+	0.3954	0.0080	0.3954	0.0080	0.3954	0.0080	0.3954	0.0080	0.3954	0.0080
GOF+	0.9395	0.0084	0.9395	0.0084	0.9395	0.0084	0.9395	0.0084	0.9395	0.0084

We see that in this case the proposed filters taking into account the blurring parameters yield essentially better performance than those of the classical filters. The modified GOF+ is the best. The MSF filter always fails to recognize the object. The GMF begins to fail when the size of the PSF is greater than 9. Note that if a filter is able to detect the object then this filter localizes exactly the position of the target.

Because the number of observations is sufficient, it is possible to employ a normal distribution and to calculate a 95% confidence interval as follows:

$$P\left(\mu - 1.96\frac{\sigma}{\sqrt{N}} \le DC \le \mu + 1.96\frac{\sigma}{\sqrt{N}}\right) = 0.95 \ . \tag{12}$$

With 95% confidence the DC interval of each of the filters can be calculated. For instance, for the *GOF+* the confidence intervals for different PSFs are (0.9366, 0.9424).

3.2 Results of Scenario 3

In this scenario, the observed image is degraded both by a linear system with the uniform PSFs, whose sizes are 3, 5, 7, 9, 11, 15, and due to additive noise with standard deviations of 5, 10, 15, 20, 25, 30, 35, 40, and 43.

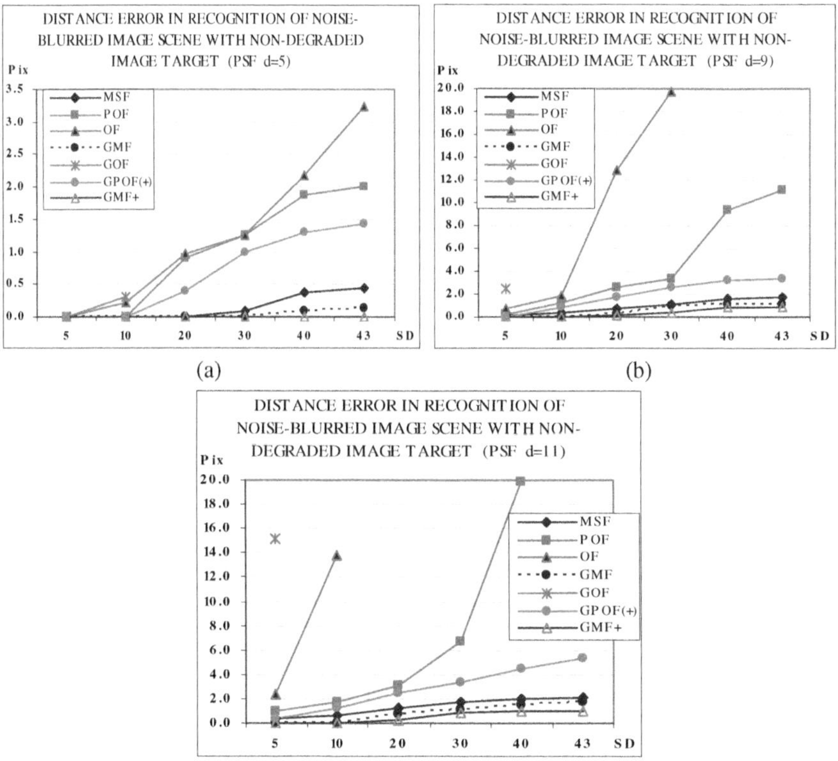

(c)

Fig. 3. Distance errors of localization with the PSF's sizes: (a) d=5, (b) d=9, (c) d=11

In this case the performance of the correlation filters in terms of the DC is similar to that of Scenario 2. However, the distance errors of localization increase, while the standard deviation of the noise increases. Figure 3 shows the performance of the filters with respect to the distance errors of localization. It can be seen that the *GMF+* yields the best performance in terms of this criterion.

4 Conclusions

In this paper three correlation filters were proposed in order to improve detection and localization of a noisy target embedded into nonoverlapping background degraded with a linear system. With the help of computer simulation we showed that the proposed filters taking into account information about degradation yield better results in terms of detection and localization than those of the known correlation filters.

It is necessary to investigate the performance of pattern recognition systems consisting of the two separate steps; that is, the first step is image restoration, and then is object recognition with a correlation filter.

References

1. VanderLugt A. B., Signal Detection by Complex Filtering. IEEE Trans. Inf. Theory, Vol. 10, (1964) 139-135.
2. Horner J. L. and Gianino P. D., Phase-Only Matched Filtering. Applied Optics, Vol. 23, No. 6, (1984) 812-816.
3. Vijaya-Kumar B. V. K. and Hassebrook L., Performance Measures for Correlation Filters. Applied Optics, Vol. 29, No. 20, (1990) 2997-3006.
4. Javidi B. and Wang J., Design of Filters to Detect a Noisy Target in Nonoverlapping Background Noise. Journal OSA (A), Vol. 11, No. 10, (1994) 2604-2612.
5. Vijaya-Kumar B. V. K., Correlation Filters Minimizing Peak Location Errors. Journal OSA (A), Vol. 9, No. 5, (1992) 678-682.
6. Yaroslavsky L. P., The theory of optimal methods for localization of objects in pictures. In: Progress in Optics XXXII, E. Wolf, Ed., Elsevier, (1993) 145-201.
7. Javidi B. and Horner Joseph L., Real-Time Optical Information Processing. Academic Press, San Diego, California (1994).
8. Ahouzi E., Campos J. and Yzuel, M. J., Phase-Only Filter with Improved Discrimination. Journal OSA (A), Vol. 19, No. 17, (1994) 1340-1342.
9. Javidi B., Parchekani F. and Zhang G., Minimum-Mean-Square-Error Filters for Detecting a Noisy Target in Background Noise. Applied Optics, Vol. 35, (1996) 6964-6975.
10. Kober V. and Campos J., Accuracy of Location Measurement of a Noisy Target in a Nonoverlapping Background. Journal OSA (A), Vol. 13, No. 8, (1996) 1653-1666.
11. Towghi N. and Javidi B., Generalized Optimum Receiver for Pattern Recognition with Multiplicative, Additive, and Nonoverlapping Background Noise. Journal OSA (A), Vol. 15, No. 6, (1998) 1557-1565.
12. Yaroslavsky L. P., Is the Phase-Only Filter and Its Modifications Optimal in Terms of the Discrimination Capability in Pattern Recognition?. Applied Optics, Vol. 31, No. 11, (1998) 1677-1679.
13. Kober, V. I. and Ovseyevich A., Phase-Only Filter with Improved Filter Efficiency and Correlation Discrimination. Pattern Recognition and Image Analysis, Vol. 10, No 4, (2000) 514-519.
14. Jain Anil K., Fundamental of Digital Image Processing. First Edition. Prentice Hall, NJ, (1988).

15. Biemond J., Lagendijk R. L. and Mersereau R. M., Iterative Methods for Image Deblurring. Proceedings of the IEEE. Vol 78, No. 5, (1990) 856-883.
16. Bertero M. and Boccacci P. Introduction to Inverse Problems in Imaging. Institute of Physics Publising, Bristol and Philadelphia, (1998).
17. Pratt, W. K. Digital Image Processing. Wiley-Interscience Publication. New York, (1981).
18. Jähne, B. Digital Image Processing. Springer. Germany, (2002).
19. Papoulis, A. Probability, Random Variables, and Stochastic Processes. McGraw-Hill, New York, (1984).

Statistical Recursive Filtering Estimation of Detector Offset Nonuniformity in Infrared Imaging Systems*

César San Martin[1,2] and Sergio N. Torres[1]

[1] Department of Electrical Engineering, University of Concepción. Casilla 160-C, Concepción, Chile
cesanmartin@udec.cl, sertorre@udec.cl
[2] Department of Electrical Engineering, University of La Frontera. Casilla 54-D, Temuco, Chile
csmarti@ufro.cl

Abstract. In this paper, a recursive filter to estimate the offset nonuniformity for infrared focal plane array imaging systems, using only the scene data, is presented. The proposed algorithm operates frame by frame in a pixel-by-pixel basis and there is not inter-related operations among the detectors. The method assumes that the input irradiance at each detector is a random and uniformly distributed variable in a range that is common to all detectors in the infrared focal plane array. The method is designed to operate in infrared imaging system, which exhibit important offset nonuniformities with slow temporal drift. The ability of the method to compensate for offset nonuniformity is demonstrated by employing several infrared video sequences obtained using an infrared camera.

Keywords: Image Sequence Processing, Infrared Focal Plane Arrays, Recursive Filtering.

1 Introduction

Infrared (IR) cameras use an IR sensor to digitize the information, and due to its high performance, the most employed integrated technology in IR sensors is the Focal Plane Array (FPA). An IR-FPA is a die composed of a group of photodetectors placed in a focal plane forming a matrix of $X \times Y$ pixels, which gives the sensor the ability to collect the IR radiation.

Nonuniformity noise in IR imaging sensors, which is due to pixel-to-pixel variation in the detectors' responses, can considerably degrade the quality of IR images since it results in a fixed-pattern-noise (FPN) that is superimposed on

* This work was partially supported by Grants Milenio ICM P02-049 and by FONDECYT 1060894. The authors wish to thank Ernest E. Armstrong (OptiMetrics Inc., USA) and Pierre Potet (CEDIP Infrared Systems, France) for collecting the data, and the United States Air Force Research Laboratory, Ohio, USA.

J.F. Martínez-Trinidad et al. (Eds.): CIARP 2006, LNCS 4225, pp. 464–473, 2006.

the true image. Further, what makes matter worse is that the nonuniformity slowly varies over time, and depending on the FPA technology, this drift can take from minutes to hours. In order to solve this problem, several scene-based nonuniformity correction (NUC) techniques have been developed [1,2,3,4]. Scene-based techniques perform the NUC using only the video sequences that are being imaged, not requiring any kind of laboratory calibration technique. Our group has been active in the development of novel scene-based algorithms for NUC based on statistical estimation theory. In [5,6] we have developed a Gauss-Markov model to capture the slow variation in the FPN and have utilized the model to adaptively estimate the nonuniformity in blocks of infrared video sequences using a Kalman Filter.

In this paper, a recursive filter [7] to estimate the offset of each detector on the FPA from scene data is developed. The method is developed using two key assumptions: i) the input irradiance at each detector is a random and uniformly distributed variable in a range that is common to all detectors in FPA; ii) The FPA technology exhibits important offset nonuniformity with slow temporal drift. The proposed algorithm is developed to operate on one block, short enough to assume that the offset is constant within the block, of infrared images. In this block, the offset of each detector is optimally and recursively estimated.

This paper is organized as follows. In Sections 2 and 3 the IR-FPA model and the scene based method for NUC by means of a recursive filtering are presented respectively. In Section 4 the main parameters that the algorithm needs for a computer implementation are discussed. In Section 5 the recursive filtering technique is tested with video sequences of real raw IR data captured using an infrared camera. In Section 6 the conclusions of the paper are summarized.

2 Model

In this paper, we model the pixel-to-pixel variation in the detectors' responses (nonuniformity) using the commonly used linear model for each pixel on the IR FPA. For the $(ij)^{\text{th}}$ detector, the measured readout signal y_{ij} at a given time n can be expressed as:

$$y_{ij}(n) = A_{ij}(n)x_{ij}(n) + B_{ij}(n) + v_{ij}(n),$$

where $A_{ij}(n)$ and $B_{ij}(n)$ are the gain and the offset of the ij^{th} detector respectively and $x_{ij}(n)$ is the real incident infrared photon flux collected by the detector. It is assume that $x_{ij}(n)$ is a uniform distribute random variable in range common to all detectors in the IR FPA. The term $v_{ij}(n)$ is additive electronic noise represented by a zero mean Gaussian random variable that is statistically independent of noise in other detectors.

In this work, we are focused in IR FPA in which the nonuniformity is mainly generated by spatial and temporal variations in the detectors offset. Then, we suppose that A_{ij} is a known constant given by the IR camera manufacturer or it can be initially calculated by using known information of the particular IR camera. Using the foregoing, we re-write the model of each detector as

$$y(n) = Ax(n) + B(n) + v(n), \tag{1}$$

the subscript ij is omitted with the understanding that all operations are performed on a pixel by pixel basis. In the next section, we present the deduction of the proposed method: a recursive filtering for estimate the offset $B(n)$ in a block of frames of read-out IR data.

3 Recursive Estimation of the Offset

The goal of this paper is to develop a scene-based nonuniformity correction method for estimating the offset of each detector on the IR FPA using a block of frames short enough to assume that the offset is a constant in noise within the block. To do so, we first propose to estimate the offset frame by frame recursively in the form

$$\hat{B}(n) = C_n \hat{B}(n-1) + K_n y(n), \tag{2}$$

where $\hat{B}(n)$ and $\hat{B}(n-1)$ are the estimate of $B(n)$ and $B(n-1)$ respectively, C_n and K_n are the coefficients of the recursive filter. To find the C_n and K_n coefficients, we apply the orthogonality principle

$$E[(B(n) - \hat{B}(n))y(n-l)] = E[(\varepsilon(n)y(n-l)] = 0, \tag{3}$$

where $\varepsilon(n)$ is the estimation error and $l = 0, 1, ..., n$. In order to find an expression for the error variance, $\sigma^2_{\varepsilon(n)}$, we use

$$E[\varepsilon(n)B(n)] = \sigma^2_{\varepsilon(n)}, \tag{4}$$

where $E[\cdot]$ denotes the expectation operation.

Now, the main assumptions used in the develop of the filter are that the IR radiance $x(n)$ is random and uniformly distributed [5] within a known range $[X_{min}, X_{max}]$. We also consider that $x(n)$ is independent of $B(n)$ and $v(n)$, and that $B(n)$ is a zero mean random variable independent of $v(n)$. Before solving the equation (2), we introduce the necessary expressions for the development of the method.

The IR radiance $x(n)$ has a mean value given by $E[x(n)] = \mu_x = \frac{(X_{max}+X_{min})}{2}$ and variance $\sigma^2_x = \frac{(X_{max}-X_{min})^2}{12}$, and the correlation function is denoted by $E[x^2(n)] = R_x(0) = \sigma^2_x + \mu^2_x$. How $x(n)$ is independent of $B(n)$ and $v(n)$ then $E[x(n)B(n)] = E[x(n)]E[B(n)]$ and $E[x(n)v(n)] = E[x(n)]E[v(n)]$, are both equal to zero.

Now, based on the latter deduction, we want to obtain an expression for $E[y(n)y(n-l)]$ for $l = 0, 1, ..., n$ using equation (1), that is

$$E[y(n)y(n-l)] = AE[x(n)y(n-l)] + E[B(n)y(n-l)] + E[v(n)y(n-l)]. \tag{5}$$

It can be easily shown that this expectation is reduced to

$$E[y(n)y(n-l)] = A^2 R_x(l) + R_B(l) + \sigma^2_v \delta(l), \tag{6}$$

where $R_x(l)$ is the correlation function of the IR radiance $x(n)$, $R_B(l)$ is the correlation function of the offset $B(n)$ and $\sigma^2_v \delta(l)$ is the correlation function of the electronic noise.

3.1 Solution for K_n: Case Where $l = 0$

In this case, substituting $y(n)$ by (1) in (3), and using (4) yields

$$E[\varepsilon(n)y(n)] = E[\varepsilon(n)Ax(n)] + \sigma^2_{\varepsilon(n)} + E[\varepsilon(n)v(n)] = 0, \tag{7}$$

the first and third terms are calculated individually. In the first term, equations (1), (2) and (6) are used, since the irradiance $x(n)$ is independent of the offset, we get

$$E[\varepsilon(n)x(n)] = E[B(n)x(n)] - E[C_n\hat{B}(n-1)x(n)] - E[K_n y(n)x(n)] = -AK_n R_x(0), \tag{8}$$

and in the third term, (1), (2) and (6) are used, and that since the noise is white and orthogonal to the signal, we can write

$$E[\varepsilon(n)v(n)] = E[B(n)v(n)] - E[C_n\hat{B}(n-1)v(n)] - E[K_n y(n)v(n)] = -K_n\sigma^2_v. \tag{9}$$

Now, substituting these results in (7) yields

$$K_n = \frac{\sigma^2_{\varepsilon(n)}}{\sigma^2_v + A^2 R_x(0)}. \tag{10}$$

3.2 Solution for C_n: Case Where $l > 0$

In this case,

$$E[\varepsilon(n)y(n-l)] = E[(B(n)y(n-l)] - C_n E[\hat{B}(n-1)y(n-l)] - K_n E[y(n)y(n-l)] = 0, \tag{11}$$

and using (1), (5) and (6) we obtain

$$E[\varepsilon(n)y(n-l)] = (1-K_n)R_B(l) - A^2 R_x(l)K_n - C_n E[\hat{B}(n-1)y(n-l)] = 0, \tag{12}$$

and for the term $E[\hat{B}(n-1)y(n-l)]$ we use $\varepsilon(n-1) = B(n-1) - \hat{B}(n-1)$ and (4), getting

$$E[\hat{B}(n-1)y(n-l)] = E[B(n-1)y(n-l)] - E[\varepsilon(n-1)y(n-l)] = R_B(l-1), \tag{13}$$

now, rewriting (12) for C_n we obtain

$$C_n = \frac{R_B(l) - K_n(R_B(l) + A^2 R_x(l))}{R_B(l-1)}. \tag{14}$$

Assuming that $R_B(l) = \alpha^l R_B(0)$, i.e., $B(n)$ is a signal that has an exponential correlation function, we obtain

$$C_n = \alpha\{1 - K_n(1 + A^2\frac{R_x(l)}{\alpha^l R_B(0)})\}. \tag{15}$$

Using an auxiliary variable $\beta = 1 + A^2\frac{R_x(l)}{\alpha^l R_B(0)}$ we finally get

$$\hat{B}(n) = \alpha\hat{B}(n-1) + K_n(y(n) - \alpha\beta\hat{B}(n-1)). \tag{16}$$

3.3 Solution for $\sigma^2_{\varepsilon(n)}$

We start using (2) and the previous results. Then, we can write

$$\sigma^2_{\varepsilon(n)} = E[(B(n) - \hat{B}(n))B(n)] = (1 - K_n)R_B(0) - \alpha(1 - \beta K_n)E[B(n)\hat{B}(n-1)]. \quad (17)$$

Using the fact that $B(n)$ is a signal with an exponential correlation function, i.e., $B(n) = \alpha B(n-1) + \omega(n)$, where $\omega(n)$ is a zero mean gaussian process independent of $B(n)$, we obtain that

$$E[B(n)\hat{B}(n-1)] = \alpha E[B(n-1)\hat{B}(n-1)]. \quad (18)$$

Note that $\sigma^2_{\varepsilon(n-1)} = E[\varepsilon(n-1)B(n-1)] = R_B(0) - E[B(n-1)\hat{B}(n-1)]$. Then, solving for $E[B(n-1)\hat{B}(n-1)]$ result in

$$\sigma^2_{\varepsilon(n)} = (1 - K_n)R_B(0) - \alpha^2(1 - \beta K_n)(R_B(0) - \sigma^2_{\varepsilon(n-1)}), \quad (19)$$

and finally replacing K_n and solving for $\sigma^2_{\varepsilon(n)}$ allow us to obtain

$$\sigma^2_{\varepsilon(n)} = \frac{\alpha^2\sigma^2_{\varepsilon(n-1)} + (1-\alpha^2)R_B(0)}{1 + \frac{\alpha^2\beta(\sigma^2_{\varepsilon(n-1)} - R_B(0)) + R_B(0)}{\sigma^2_v + A^2R_x(0)}}. \quad (20)$$

In the next section, we modified the foregoing filter to estimate the offset as a constant in noise.

4 Estimation of the Offset as a Constant in Noise

In this section the theoretical development of the main goal of this paper is finished. The idea is to develop an algorithm able to estimate the offset $B(n)$ as a constant in noise. As an example, we know this assumption is practically valid in block of frames taken within two to three minutes in several IR FPA technologies.

Then, the foregoing filter will have to be modified using $B(n) = B(n-1) = B$ a constant, i.e., $\alpha = 1$ and $\omega(n) = 0$. Then (16) is simplified to

$$\hat{B}(n) = \hat{B}(n-1) + K_n(y(n) - \beta\hat{B}(n-1)), \quad (21)$$

and equation (20) is simplified to

$$\sigma^2_{\varepsilon(n)} = \frac{\sigma^2_{\varepsilon(n-1)}}{1 + \frac{(1-\beta)R_B(0) + \beta\sigma^2_{\varepsilon(n-1)}}{\sigma^2_v + A^2R_x(0)}}. \quad (22)$$

Note that if $\beta = 1$, i.e., the IR irradiance at a current frame is uncorrelated with previous frames, and equation (22) can be reduced to

$$\sigma^2_{\varepsilon(n)} = \frac{\sigma^2_{\varepsilon(n-1)}}{1 + \frac{\sigma^2_{\varepsilon(n-1)}}{\sigma^2_v + A^2R_x(0)}}. \quad (23)$$

Now, each step of the recursive filter for nonuniformity correction is listed.
Algorithm:

1. Establish the range $[X_{min}, X_{max}]$ and calculate all the initial conditions.
2. Choose the length of the block of frames n_b.
3. Update $K_n = \frac{\sigma^2_{\varepsilon(n)}}{\sigma_v^2 + A^2 R_x(0)}$ and $\sigma^2_{\varepsilon(n)} = \frac{\sigma^2_{\varepsilon(n-1)}}{1+\frac{\sigma^2_{\varepsilon(n-1)}}{\sigma_v^2+A^2R_x(0)}}$ from the value $n = 1$.
4. Obtain the signal estimation $\hat{B}(n) = \hat{B}(n-1) + K_n(y(n) - \hat{B}(n-1))$.
5. Generate the corrected frame using $\hat{x}(n) = (y(n) - \hat{B}(n))/A$.
6. If $n \leq n_b$ then, go to step 3 and increase n.
7. If $n > n_b$ maintains the correction with $\hat{x}(n) = (y(n) - \hat{B}(n_b))/A$.

4.1 Initial Parameters

In order to initialize the algorithm the parameters $[X_{min}, X_{max}]$, A, $\sigma^2_{\varepsilon(0)}$, $R_B(0)$ and σ_v^2 have to be calculate for each particular IR camera. First of all, anyone with experience with his IR camera can easily propose a range $[X_{min}, X_{max}]$ for a particular block of frames. Then, $R_x(0) = \frac{(X_{max}-X_{min})^2}{12} + \frac{(X_{max}+X_{min})^2}{4}$. Also, knowing $[Y_{min}, Y_{max}]$ from the read-out IR data and employing (1) we can obtain

$$A = \frac{Y_{max} - Y_{min}}{X_{max} - X_{min}}.$$

To compute $\sigma^2_{\varepsilon(0)}$, we use (23) and.

$$\sigma^2_{\varepsilon(n-1)} = R_B(0) - E[B(n-1)\hat{B}(n-1)],$$

assuming that no prior observations are available, i.e., $\hat{B}(-1) = 0$, then $\sigma^2_{\varepsilon(-1)} = R_B(0)$, now replacing in (23)

$$\sigma^2_{\varepsilon(0)} = \frac{R_B(0)}{1 + \frac{R_B(0)}{\sigma_v^2 + A^2 R_x(0)}}. \quad (24)$$

Finally, to get a good estimation of $R_B(0)$, detectors offsets of a particular camera obtained previously with another nonuniformity correction method are used [4]. Also, the variance of electronic noise σ_v^2 can easily be calculated from previous IR raw data.

4.2 Convergence Analysis

An important aspect for any nonuniformity correction algorithm is its convergence analysis. For this case, the convergence is determinate by $\sigma^2_{\varepsilon(n)}$, i.e., the estimation error variance. Let us define $a = \frac{R_B(0)}{\sigma_v^2+A^2R_x(0)}$ and replacing it in equation (24)

$$\sigma^2_{\varepsilon(0)} = \frac{R_B(0)}{1+a}, \quad (25)$$

then, (23) and (10) can be expressed by

$$\sigma^2_{\varepsilon(n)} = \frac{R_B(0)}{1 + a(n+1)} \tag{26}$$

$$K_n = \frac{a}{1 + a(n+1)}, \tag{27}$$

i.e., $\sigma^2_{\varepsilon(n)}$ and K_n correspond to a decreasing succession, where a parameter is responsible of the convergence. For the case $a > 1$, the convergence is faster than when $a < 1$. In other words, for the case in which $R_B(0) > \sigma_v^2 + A^2 R_x(0)$ the convergence of the method occurs within a few frames, whereas when $R_B(0) < \sigma_v^2 + A^2 R_x(0)$ a greater number of frames is required. In infrared system, a practical consideration is that $R_B(0)$ is approximately equal to 10% of the dynamic range of the readout infrared data. Further, supposing that it is possible to consider $A^2 R_x(0) >> \sigma_v^2$ and that $R_B(0)$ is approximately equal to 10% of $A^2 R_x(0)$, which implies that $a \approx 0.1$. Then, to obtain a reduction of until the 2% of the initial estimation error we need $n = 490$ frames. Note that for the case $a = 1$ the initial error estimation is reduced to 2% when $n = 48$ frames.

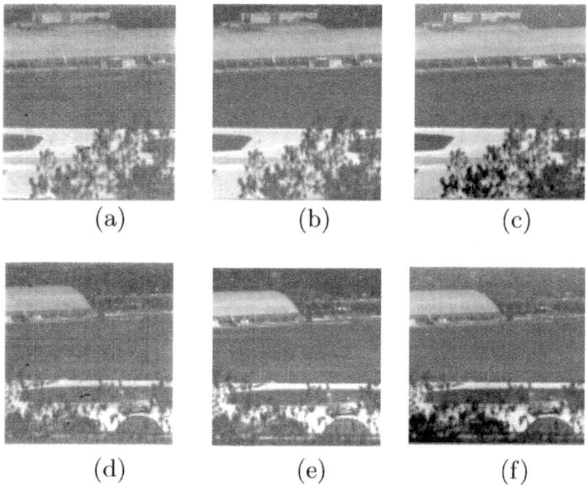

Fig. 1. Performance of the proposed method on real IR data. The first row shows the $570-th$ frame, and the second row shows the $1570-th$ frame of the set of IR data. (a) (d) Real corrupted frames, (b) (e) Real frames corrected by using black bodies (c) (f) Real frames corrected by the proposed method.

5 Applications to Real Infrared Image Sequences

The main goal of this section is to test the ability of the proposed method for reduce nonuniformity on real infrared video data. The sequence has been collected using a 128×128 InSb FPA cooled camera (Amber Model AE-4128) operating in the $3-5\mu m$ range. In the set data, 3000 frames were collected at a rate of 30 frames per second, with 16 bits of resolution. For purposes of comparison black bodies radiator are used under laboratory conditions to generate flat-field images in the linear range of the detectors. These data is used to estimate the gain and the offset associated with each detector. With these parameters, the best correction of nonuniformity is performed, obtaining a sequence that is used like a reference.

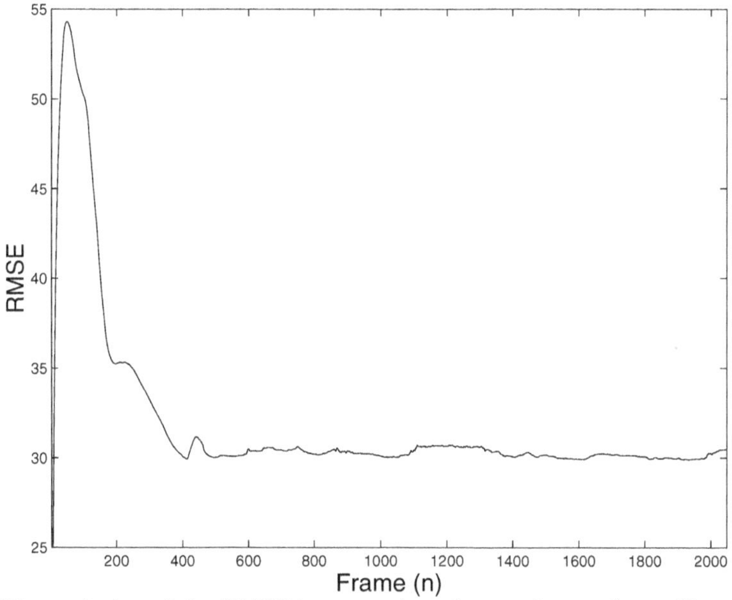

Fig. 2. The evolution of the RMSE between the reference frames (set calibrated with black bodies) and the corrected frames by the proposed NUC method

As a quantitative measure of performance, we use the Root Mean Square Error (RMSE), which measures the difference between the reference infrared image with the corrected image using the proposed method. The RMSE is calculated by:

$$RMSE(n) = \{\frac{1}{pm}\sum_{i=1}^{p}\sum_{j=1}^{m}(\hat{x}_{ij}(n) - x_{ij}(n))^2\}^{1/2}, \tag{28}$$

where $p \times m$ is the number of detectors in the FPA. $\hat{x}_{ij}(n)$ is the infrared irradiance calculated with the offset estimated by the recursive filter. $x_{ij}(n)$ is the infrared irradiance calculated with the offset estimated by using the black-body radiator data (Laboratory calibration offset). A lower value of RMSE means a good correction of the frame data.

Before using the algorithm, the initial conditions are calculated. Firstly, we have assumed that the range of the input irradiance is between [0, 255], this is that all the pixels were exposed to minimum and maximum possible in the gray scale. We use a block of frames with a length of $n_b = 500$, this is approximate 17 seconds of data. With this and the raw infrared data, $R_x(0) = 21.68 \times 10^3$, $A = 257$, $R_B(0) = 1.43 \times 10^8$ and $\sigma_v^2 = 3.10 \times 10^5$. In addition, $a = 9.99 \times 10^{-2}$ and $(\%)\sigma^2_{\varepsilon(500)}/\sigma^2_{\varepsilon(0)} = 2.35\%$.

Figure 1 (a)(b)(c) (d) (e) (f) shows from left to right a frame of real noisy readout data, the corresponding corrected frame by using black bodies, and the corresponding corrected frame by the NUC method proposed in this paper. It can be clearly seen by using the naked eye that our method mitigate the nonuniformity noisy as well as the calibration method. The NUC performance, in this case, is evaluated employing the index root mean square error (RMSE) computed between a reference (the real IR sequence calibrated with black bodies) and our corrected IR video sequence. Figure 2 shows the calculated RMSE for each frame corrected using the proposed method. Figure 3 presents the convergence for the recursive filter. It's clear that the gain and the error variance converge to minimal value after the $500 - th$ frames.

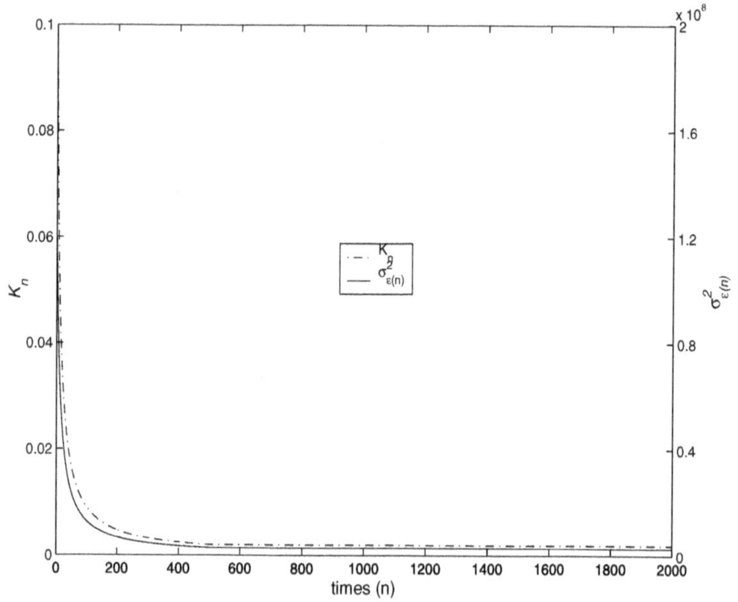

Fig. 3. Convergence parameters of the proposed method. The dashed line correspond to the gain K_n and the solid line represents the error variance $\sigma^2_{\epsilon(n)}$.

6 Conclusions

In this paper a recursive filter for NUC on IR imaging system is proposed. It was shown experimentally using real IR data that the method is able to notably reduce the non-uniformity. Indeed, the method has shown good reduction of nonuniformity after processing only around 300 frames. The main advantage of the method is based in its simplicity using only fundamental estimation theory. Further, the method during the estimation process generates two convergence parameters, which can be used for determining the method ON-OFF time in real infrared camera operations. The keys assumptions of the proposed method are that the input irradiance at each detector is a random and uniformly distributed variable in a range that is common to all detectors in the infrared focal plane array and that input infrared sequences of frames exhibits important offset nonuniformities with slow temporal drift.

References

1. Scribner, D., Sarkady, K., Kruer, M.: Adaptive Nonuniformity Correction for Infrared Focal Plane Arrays using Neural Networks. Proceeding of SPIE. **1541**. (1991) 100–109.
2. Scribner, D., Sarkady, K., Kruer, M.: Adaptive Retina-like Preprocessing for Imaging Detector Arrays. Proceeding of the IEEE International Conference on Neural Networks. **3**. (1993) 1955–1960.
3. Torres, S., Vera, E., Reeves, R., Sobarzo, S.: Adaptive Scene-Based Nonuniformity Correction Method for Infrared Focal Plane Arrays. Proceeding of SPIE. **5076**. (2003) 130–139.
4. Vera, E., Torres, S.: Fast Adaptive Nonuniformity Correction for Infrared Focal Plane Arrays. To be published in EURASIP Journal on Applied Signal Processing. (2005).
5. Torres, S., Hayat, M.: Kalman Filtering for Adaptive Nonuniformity Correction in Infrared Focal Plane Arrays. The JOSA-A Opt. Soc. of America. **20**. (2003) 470–480.
6. Torres, S., Pezoa, J., Hayat, M.: Scene-based Nonuniformity Correction for Focal Plane Arrays Using the Method of the Inverse Covariance Form. OSA App. Opt. Inf. Proc. **42**. (2003) 5872–5881.
7. Therrien, Charles W.: Discrete Random Signal and Statistical Signal Processing, Prentice Hall Press, USA, 1992.

3D Vector Directional Filters to Process Video Sequences

Volodymyr Ponomaryov[1], Francisco Gallegos-Funes[2], Alberto Rosales-Silva[1], and Igor Loboda[1]

[1] National Polytechnic Institute of Mexico,
Mechanical and Electrical Engineering Higher School
ESIME-Culhuacan; Av. Santa Ana 1000, Col. San Francisco Culhuacan,
04430, Mexico D.F., Mexico
vponomar@ipn.mx
[2] ESIME-Zacatenco; Av. IPN s/n, U.P.A.L.M. Col. Lindavista,
07738, Mexico D.F., Mexico
fgallegosf@ipn.mx

Abstract. We present novel algorithms to suppress impulsive noise in video color sequences. They use order statistics, directional and adaptive processing techniques. Extensive simulation results in known reference video color sequences have demonstrated that the proposed filters consistently outperform other filters by balancing the tradeoff between noise suppression, detail preservation, and chromaticity characteristics. The criteria used to compare the performance or various filters were the PSNR, MAE, and NCD.

Keywords: Adaptive and directional processing, Order statistics, 3D Video color sequences.

1 Introduction

Several filters have demonstrated good ability to remove impulsive noise, preserve fine details, and provide chromatic properties in multichannel processing applications [1-3]. One of the useful and promising approaches being proposed was the multichannel signal processing based on vector processing [1-3]. In this case the correlation in chromacity that exists between the channels is employed. The value of each a 2D pixel is represented by a 3D (three dimensional) vector, so, the color image is translated into a set of vectors with the directions and lengths that are related to the chromatic properties of the pixels. Nonlinear filtering techniques apply the robust order statistics theory that is the basis for design of the different novel approaches in digital multichannel processing [4-8].

In this paper we introduce novel methods to process 3D multichannel images that are based on order statistics and vectorial processing techniques [1, 2]. We propose the Video Adaptive Vector Directional (VAVDF) filter. This filter can use in its filtering scheme the median or α-trimmed mean filters to obtain the Video Adaptive Vector Directional Median (VAVDMF) filter and the Video Adaptive Vector Directional α-trimmed mean (VAVDATMF) filter, respectively. We also proposed the Video Vector Directional K-Nearest Neighbour (VVDKNNF) filter with the

J.F. Martínez-Trinidad et al. (Eds.): CIARP 2006, LNCS 4225, pp. 474–480, 2006.

estimation of vector median filter in its filtering scheme to obtain the VVDKNNVMF filter.

Finally, we present some adapted versions of 2D filters that can process 3D video colour sequences. The filters used during the implementations were: the median filter to obtain the Video Median filter, the Vector α-trimmed mean (VATM) filter to realize the Video Alpha Trimmed Mean filter, the K-Nearest Neighbour filter that is adapted to implement the Video KNNF, and the Vector Median Filter to present the Video Vector Median (VVMF) Filter.

2 Proposed Methods

We denote an image pixel as $I(x, y, t)$, where (x, y) and t indicate the spatial and temporal location in the video sequence or, maybe third spatial coordinate in the case of 3D image, respectively. The 3D window (cube) contains the pixels (x', y', t') where $|x-x'|<3$, $|y-y'|<3$ and $|t-t'|<3$ [7]. The window is used to compute the filtered value $I'(x, y, t)$.

2.1 Video Generalized Vector Directional (VGVDF) Filter

Vector directional processing is one of the most important techniques implemented recently [4, 7, 8]. The vector processing separates the signal vector processing in directional processing and magnitude processing. The pixels are denoted as vectors in m-dimensional spaces, in the case of color images, $m = 3$. The vectors have to be ordered in certain way, in the majority of cases they are ordered as follows:

$$\sum_{i=1}^{n} A(x_{BD}, x_i) \leq \sum_{i=1}^{n} A(x_j, x_i), \quad \forall j = 1, 2, \ldots, n, \tag{1}$$

where $A(x_j, x_i)$ is the angle among vectors x_i and x_j, and x_{BD} satisfies to minimum deviation value among vectors. So, x_{BD} gives the output of known filter, the Basic Vector Directional Filter (BVDF). The Generalized Vector Directional Filter (GVDF) is selected from a set of vectors, which present the minimum deviation with respect to other vectors:

$$x^{(1)} = BVDF[x_1, x_2, \ldots, x_n] \tag{2}$$

$$\{x^{(1)}, x^{(2)}, \ldots, x^{(k)}\} = GVDF[x_1, x_2, \ldots, x_n], \quad 1 \leq k \leq n \tag{3}$$

$$x_0 = \Im\{x^{(1)}, x^{(2)}, \ldots, x^{(k)}\} = \Im\{GVDF[x_1, x_2, \ldots, x_n]\} \tag{4}$$

According to (2)-(4) the GVDF produces set of vectors with typical directions and this set should be passed after through a magnitude processing filter $\Im$ to produce an only vector for each a pixel. The GVDF involves the k parameter that needs to be specified for each particular implementation. This parameter can be selected in an adaptive and non adaptive way described in [1].

There are realized two operations using different windows to preserve image details and suppress noise effectively. We apply the following operations:

$$x_O = \Im\left\{x^{(1)}, x^{(2)}, \ldots, x^{(K)}\right\} = \Im\left\{VGVDF\left[x_1, x_2, \ldots, x_n\right]\right\}, \tag{5}$$

where VGVDF is the Video Generalized Vector Directional Filter using to find the vectors with the minimum angle deviation from the vectors that are under processing $x_{2j} \in W_2 - W_1$ and α'_2, which corresponds to x_{2j} and is defined as:

$$\alpha'_{2j} = \sum_{i=1}^{n} A\left(x_{2j}, x_{1i}\right). \tag{6}$$

During the next stage the vector x_{2j} is added to set $\left\{x_1^{(1)}, x_1^{(2)}, \ldots, x_1^{(k)}\right\}$ if the condition $\alpha'_{2j} \le \alpha_1^{(k)}$ is satisfied. In this way, the external window contributes with vectors x_{2j} that diverges less than the last vector considered $x_1^{(k)}$ from x_1.

2.2 Video α-Trimmed Mean Filter

The α-trimmed mean filter is applicable to process color images [7]. In here, we adapt this filter to process 3D video color sequences.

All pixel values from the 3D window are ordered in one dimensional array according to order chosen:

$$x_L = \left(x_1, x_2, \ldots, x_N\right)^t, \tag{7}$$

where $N = 27$ denotes the number of the pixels in the 3D sliding window.

Then, the pixels values in x_L are ordered in ascending order to get a new 1D array,

$$x_\alpha = \left(x_{(1)}, x_{(2)}, \ldots, x_{(N)}\right)^t, \tag{8}$$

where $x_{(1)} > x_{(2)} > \ldots > x_{(N)}$.

Finally, the filter output is calculated as follows:

$$y = \frac{1}{\theta} \sum_{i=[\alpha^* N]+1}^{N-[\alpha^* N]} x_{(i)}, \tag{9}$$

where $\theta = N - 2*\lceil \alpha * N \rceil$ and $\lceil \cdot \rceil$ is the ceiling function, which rounds up to the nearest integer.

2.3 Video Vector Directional K-Nearest Neighbour Vector Median (VVDKNNVMF) Filter

The proposed Video KNN filter is based in the approach of ref. [7]. We sort the pixel values in x_L according to their difference with $I(x, y, t)$ to get a new 1D array,

$$x_l = \left(x_{(1)}, x_{(2)}, \ldots, x_{(N)} \right)^t, \tag{10}$$

where $x_{(1)} = I(x, y, t)$ is the central pixel en the sliding 3D window, $x_{(i)}, i = 2,3,\ldots,N$ are the pixels that satisfy the condition $A\left(x_{(1)}, x_{(i)}\right) \leq A\left(x_{(1)}, x_{(j)}\right)$, $j = i \ldots N$, and $A(\cdot)$ is the angle between the central pixel and the other N-1 pixels. So, the novel 1D array can be written as:

$$x_l = \left(x_{(2)}, \ldots, x_{(N)} \right)^t. \tag{11}$$

The set of the K-Nearest Neighbour vectors with respect to central pixel is obtained as,

$$\left\{x^{(1)}, x^{(2)}, \ldots, x^{(K)}\right\}^t = VDKNNF\left[x_{(2)}, \ldots, x_{(N)}\right]^t, 1 \leq K \leq (N-1). \tag{12}$$

The first K terms of the ordered sequence $\left\{x^{(i)}\right\}^t$ constitute the output of VDKNN (Vector Directional K-Nearest Neighbour) filter. At the final stage the magnitude processing filter should be applied to obtain an only output vector for each a pixel. It is done using the Vector Median (VMF) Filter that defines the VVDKNNVMF to process 3D video sequences:

$$VMF\left\{x^{(1)}, x^{(2)}, \ldots, x^{(K)}\right\}^t = x_{VMF}. \tag{13}$$

3 Experimental Results

During the simulations the 176x144 video sequences "Miss America" and "Flowers" were corrupted with noise of different intensity. The noise was independently added in each a plane of the frame. The criteria applied to evaluate the performance of various filters were: the Pick Signal-to-Noise Relation (PSNR) used to characterize noise suppression level, the Mean Absolute Error (MAE), which characterizes a quality of edge and detail preservation, and the Normalized Color Difference (NCD) to qualify and quantify chromaticity preservation given by color perceptual error.

The proposed Video Generalized Vector Directional (VGVDF) Filter with the α-trimmed mean and median filters as a magnitude ones, the Video Adaptive Vector Directional α-trimmed mean (VAVDATM), the Video Adaptive Vector Directional median (VAVDMF) filters, the Video Vector Directional K-Nearest Neighbour (VVDKNNF) filter, and the VVDKNNVMF filter that have been introduced in this paper were compared with other filters proposed here.

We utilize the following filters as a comparative ones to evaluate the properties of noise suppression, detail preservation, and chromaticity preservation of the proposed filters: the median filter that was been adapted to 3D processing to obtain the Video MF, the Vector Median Filter that gives the Video Vector Median (VVMF) Filter, the Vector ATM filter improving the Video ATM, and the KNNF [1] in two variants in the 3x3x3 window named as filter KNNF_1, and in the CrossXCrossXCross window named as KNNF_2, These filters were adapted to realize 3D processing and to obtain the Video KNN Filter.

Table 1 presents the comparative filtering results in a frame of video sequences "Flowers" and "Miss America" obtained by different filters. From the performance results one can see that the proposed filters demonstrate the best results in the terms of criteria used.

Table 1. Comparative results in a frame of video sequences "Flowers" and "Miss America"

Algorithm	Flowers (15%)			Miss America (20%)		
	PSNR	MAE	NCD	PSNR	MAE	NCD
VATM	27,002	6,305	0,01260	34,585	2,534	0,00906
KNNF_1	26,144	7,386	0,01398	28,113	5,477	0,02021
KNNF_2	26,903	6,140	0,01150	27,644	5,144	0,01929
VAVMF	25,384	6,996	0,01300	32,099	2,876	0,00989
Video-MF	26,973	6,150	0,01241	34,571	2,454	0,00917
VVMF	26,919	6,108	0,01235	34,446	2,413	0,00876
VAVDMF_1	26,722	5,871	0,01209	33,256	2,196	0,00836
VAVDMF_2	27,285	5,240	0,01059	35,237	1,719	0,00674
VAVDATM	27,331	5,328	0,01068	35,25	1,765	0,00664
VVDKNNVMF	26,176	6,932	0,01399	32,292	3,208	0,0113

Figure 1 displays the filtered frames and error images in the case of 15% of impulsive noise contamination for video color sequence "Flowers". This figure clearly shows that the Video Adaptive Vector Directional Alpha-trimmed Mean (VAVDATM) filter can suppress noise corruption and provide detail preservation better than other filters.

Figure 2 presents the processed images in the case of 30% impulsive noise in a frame of video sequence "Miss America". The restored image found applying the proposed filters appears to have a very good subjective quality.

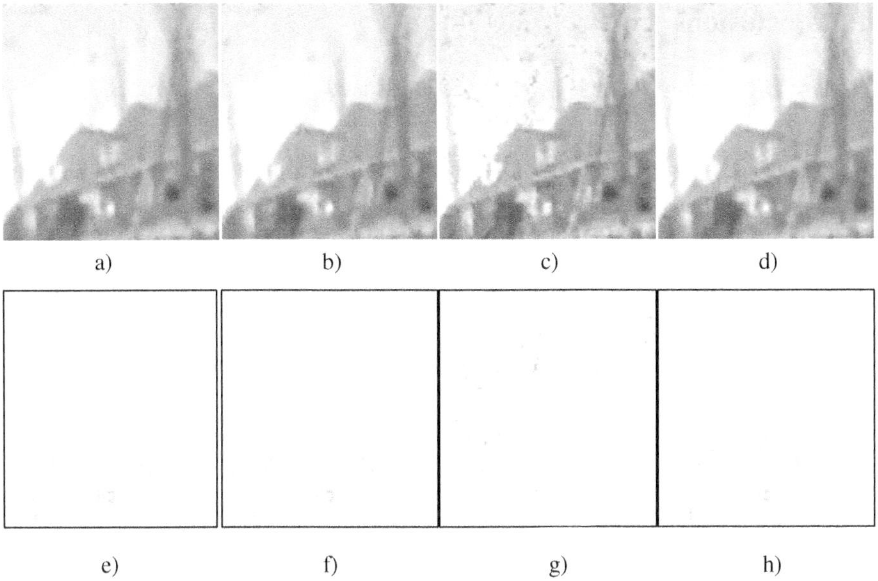

Fig. 1. Visual results in a frame of video sequence "Flowers", a) Restored frame applying VATM filter, b) Restored frame applying VVMF Filter, c) Restored frame applying KNNF_1 filter, d) Restored frame applying VAVDATM filter, e) Error image applying VATM filter, f) Error image applying VVMF Filter, g) Error image applying KNNF_1 filter, h) Error image applying VAVDATM filter

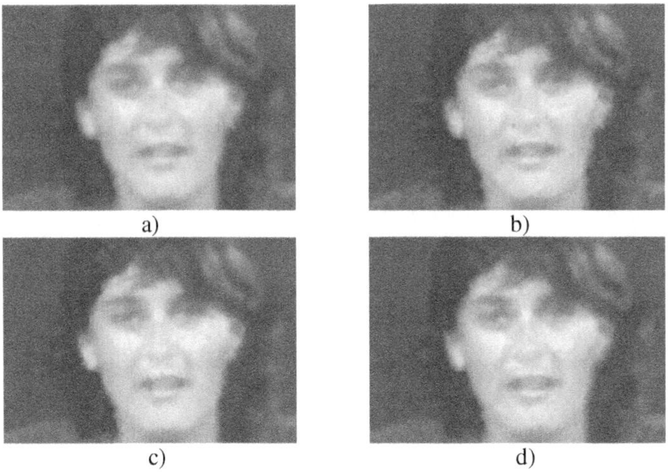

Fig. 2. Filtered Images with 30% of impulsive noise in a frame of video sequence "Miss America": a) Restored frame applying VATM filter, b) Restored frame applying VVMF filter, c) Restored frame applying VMMKNN filter [6], and d) Restored image applying VAVDATM filter

4 Conclusions

Proposed filtering methods have demonstrated their effectiveness in noise suppression, detail preservation and chromaticity characteristics. The novel VAVDATM and VAVDMF filters appear to demonstrate the best results in terms criteria used and visually in noise suppression and detail and color preservation. Several filters that work in 2D processing have been adapted in here to process 3D video information demonstrating good properties in terms of criteria PSNR, MAE, and NCD.

Acknowledgments. This work is supported by National Polytechnic Institute of Mexico and CONACyT (project 42790).

References

1. Trahanias P. E., Karakos D., Venetsanopoulos A. N.: Direccional Processing of Color Images: Theory and Experimental Results. IEEE Trans. on Image Process. Vol. 5 No. 6. (1996) 868-880.
2. Plataniotis K. N., Androutsos D., Vinayagamoorthy S., Venetsanopoulos A. N.: Color Image Processing Using Adaptive Multichannel Filters. IEEE Trans. on Image Process. Vol. 6 No. 7. (1997) 933-949.
3. Shkvarko YV.: Unifying regularization and Bayesian Estimation methods for enhanced imaging with remotely sensed data. IEEE Trans. On GSRS, Vol. 42 No. 5. (2004) 923-931.
4. Lukac R.: Adaptive Vector Median Filtering. Pattern Recognition Lett. Vol. 24. (2003) 1889-1899.
5. Gallegos-Funes F., Ponomaryov V., De-La-Rosa J.: ABST M-type K-nearest neighbor (ABSTM-KNN) for image denoising. IEICE Trans. on Funds. of Electronics Comms. and Computer. Science. Vol.E88A, No.3, (2005) 798-799.
6. Ponomaryov V. I., Gallegos-Funes F. J., Rosales-Silva A.: Real-Time Color Imaging Based on RM-Filters for Impulsive Noise Reduction. J. Imaging Science and Technology, Vol. 49, No. 3. (2005) 205-219.
7. Zlokolica V., Philips D., Van De Ville D.: A New Non-Linear Filter for Video Processing. IEEE Benelux Signal Processing Symposium, March 2002, Belgium
8. Koschan T., Abidi M.: A comparison of Median Filter Techniques for Noise Removal in Color Images. Proc. 7th German Workshop on Color Image Processing, Vol. 34, No. 15, (2001) 69-79.

Object Recognition and Tracking in Video Sequences: A New Integrated Methodology

Nicolás Amézquita Gómez[1], René Alquézar[2], and Francesc Serratosa[1]

[1] Departament d'Enginyeria Informàtica i Matemàtiques, Universitat Rovira i Virgili, Campus Sescelades, Av. dels Països Catalans 26, 43007, Tarragona, Spain
[2] Dept. Llenguatges i Sistemes Informàtics, Universitat Politècnica de Catalunya, Campus Nord, Edifici Omega, 08034 Barcelona, Spain
{francesc.serratosa, nicolas.amezquita}@urv.cat,
{amezquita, alquezar}@lsi.upc.edu

Abstract. This paper describes a methodology that integrates recognition and segmentation, simultaneously with image tracking in a cooperative manner, for recognition of objects (or parts of them) in image sequences. A probabilistic general approach at pixel level is depicted together with a practical heuristic simplification in which pixels' class probabilities are approximated by a finite small set of class possibility values. These possibility values are updated iteratively along the image sequence for each class and each pixel taking into account both the prior tracking information and the spot-based object recognition results provided by a trained neural network. A further segmentation of the class possibility images allows the tracking of each object of interest in the sequence. The good experimental results obtained so far show the viability of the approach under certain conditions.

Keywords: Object recognition, object tracking, image segmentation, neural networks, probabilistic approach, video sequences.

1 Introduction

This work presents a methodology that integrates segmentation, recognition and tracking, for recognition of objects in image sequences. To the best of our knowledge there are few existing works that combine segmentation, recognition and tracking in an integrated framework [1]. These tasks often are treated separately and/or sequentially on intermediate representations obtained by the segmentation and grouping algorithms [2, 3, 4]. In [5], object recognition techniques are applied to a scene where the objects of interest do not move most of the time and makes tracking a discrete process of watching for object disappearances and reappearances.

The procedure that we used is based on the iterative and adaptive processing of consecutive frames. A similar methodology is presented in [6]. Another related work is [7], where a probabilistic approach that combines segmentation, object recognition, 3D localization and tracking in an integrated and unified framework is described. In our case, the original images are firstly segmented in homogeneous regions (spots) and color and geometric features are extracted from these regions. As reported in [8], neural networks can be trained to classify spots into different objects using the spot

J.F. Martínez-Trinidad et al. (Eds.): CIARP 2006, LNCS 4225, pp. 481 – 490, 2006.

features as input, provided that an enough large set of labeled spots is given from the supervised segmentation of representative views of these objects. In [8], the trained networks were shown to classify quite correctly test spots located in the same regions of interest that the training spots (ROI that were defined around each object). However, the spot classification performance impairs significantly outside these regions or in different images than those used for training.

In the current work, we address this problem (object recognition in full new images) through the use of a dynamic iterative approach in which a probabilistic model at pixel level (or an approximation of it) is updated taking into account both the neural net outputs and prior object tracking information from the previous image.

A scheme of the whole process integrating object recognition and tracking is displayed in Fig.1.

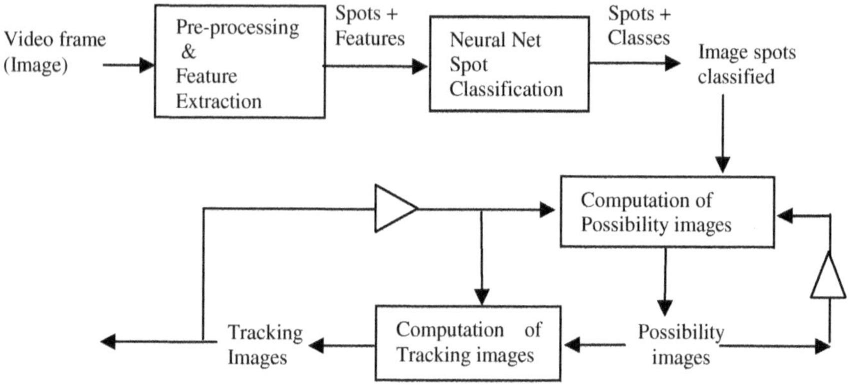

Fig. 1. Block diagram of the iterative object recognition and tracking process

The rest of the paper is organized as follows. A more formal definition of the addressed problem is given in Section 2, together with the entire notation used throughout the paper. In Section 3, the proposed methodology is described in more detail. Experimental results are included in Section 4 and, finally, conclusions and future work are discussed in Section 5.

2 Problem Statement and Notation

Let us assume that we have a sequence of 2D color images $I^t(x,y)$ for $t=1,\dots,L$, and a corresponding sequence $S^t(x,y)$ of segmented images resulting from the application of an image segmentation algorithm to the former. Also, let us consider that there are (or can be) N objects of interest in the sequence of different types (associated with classes $c=1,\dots,N$), and that a special class $c=N+1$ is reserved for the background. Furthermore, let us assume that the initial position of each object is known and represented by N binary images, $p_c^0(x,y)$, for $c=1,\dots,N$, where $p_c^0(x,y)=1$ means that the pixel (x,y) belongs to a region covered by an object of class c in the first image.

We would like to obtain N sequences of binary images $T_c^t(x,y)$, for $c=1,\dots,N$, that mark the pixels belonging to each object in each image; these images are the desired output of the whole process and can also be regarded as the output of a tracking process for each object. Note that we can initialize these tracking images (for t=0) from the given initial positions of each object, this is:

$$T_c^0(x,y) = p_c^0(x,y) \tag{1}$$

For notational purposes, let MC_c^t, for $c=1,\dots,N$, refer to the mass centers of each object in the corresponding tracking image $T_c^t(x,y)$.

Suppose that a neural network has been trained to classify regions (spots) of the same objects using a different but similar sequence of labeled segmented images. Hence, the trained network is able to produce a sequence of class probability images $Q_c^t(x,y)$ for $t=1,\dots,L$ and $c=1,\dots,N+1$, where the value $Q_c^t(x,y)$ represents the a-posteriori probability given by the net output that the pixel (x,y) of the segmented image $S^t(x,y)$ belongs to the class c. From these probabilities, a class can be assigned to each pixel simply by choosing the class with maximum probability:

$$C^t(x,y) = \arg\max_c \left(Q_c^t(x,y)\right) \tag{2}$$

In order to obtain the tracking images, a probabilistic approach could be followed in which we would need to store and update $N+1$ probability images $p_c^t(x,y)$, for $c=1,\dots,N+1$, where the value $p_c^t(x,y)$ represents the probability that the pixel (x,y) in time t belongs to an object of class c (for $c=1,\dots,N$) or to the background (for $c=N+1$). In general, these probabilities should be computed as a certain function f of the same probabilities in the previous step, the class probabilities given by the neural net for the current step and the tracking images resulting from the previous step:

$$p_c^t(x,y) = f\left(p^{t-1}(x,y), Q^t(x,y), T^{t-1}(x,y)\right) \tag{3}$$

Now, the tracking images could be computed dynamically using these probabilities according to some decision function d:

$$T_c^t(x,y) = d\left(p^t(x,y), T_c^{t-1}(x,y)\right) \tag{4}$$

In the present work, as a first simple approach to test, we have relaxed the normalization constraint required for probabilities and have approximated the probability values with a small set of "possibility" values (e.g. 0, ½, 1) computed heuristically. Hence, instead of using the probability images $p_c^t(x,y)$ we have used the so-called "possibility" images $H_c^t(x,y)$, that contain the possibility values that a pixel (x,y) belongs to a class c in time t. Note that these images can be initialized as well from the given initial positions of each object:

$$H_c^0(x,y) = p_c^0(x,y) \tag{5}$$

Consequently, the update function f and the decision function d have been defined in this work using the possibility images $H_c^t(x,y)$ instead of the probability images $p_c^t(x,y)$, in the way described in next section. In particular, the class assignments given by the net $C^t(x,y)$ have been used instead of the probabilities $Q_c^t(x,y)$ in the update function *f*.

3 Methodology

The methodology proposed can be split in two phases: the object learning phase and the object recognition and tracking phase. Next subsections describe both phases.

3.1 Object Learning

For object learning, a sequence of segmented images showing the objects of interest is required. Furthermore, a subset of the spots (segmentation regions) obtained must be selected and labeled manually (or semi-automatically as described in [8]) with the target classes. These target classes include the different object types and a special class for the background. In addition, for each selected spot, a number of features have to be computed that may include both color and geometric properties.

The spot features and target classes are collected in a pattern file. Then, a neural network is trained to classify the selected spots using most of the patterns as training set and the rest as validation set. Once trained, when a new pattern (spot feature vector) is introduced, the network is able to estimate the a-posteriori class probabilities for this pattern, according to the statistical model it has learnt previously from the given examples. From these probabilities, a class can be assigned to each spot simply by choosing the class with maximum probability. Note that if we represent the probabilities and classes at pixel level rather than at spot level, all pixels of a given spot will have the same probabilities and class that the entire spot.

A more detailed description of the learning phase that includes the specific features used for the spots is available in [8].

3.2 Object Recognition and Tracking

For object recognition and tracking, another sequence of segmented images showing the same objects of interest is required. Furthermore, for each object of interest, its approximate location in the first image of the sequence is needed. This information is supposed to come as a binary image for each object, where the white pixels represent the object and the black pixels represent the background or other objects. These binary images are used to set the initial values of both the tracking images and the possibility images, as defined in Section 2, equations (1) and (5). For the following time steps $t=1, 2, ...L$, the binary images that represent the approximate positions of the objects of interest (tracking images) will be computed as explained later.

The neural network obtained in the learning phase is applied to all the spots of all the images in the recognition sequence. This means that all the spot features must be computed previously. From the network outputs, all spots (and their constituent pixels) can be classified according to equation (2).

In order to update the tracking images, first a possibility image is computed for each class and time step. The update function *f* for the possibility image $H_c^t(x, y)$ is defined heuristically taking into account the classification of pixel (x, y) given by the neural network, $C^t(x,y)$, and the previous values of the pixel in the tracking image $T_c^{t-1}(x, y)$ and the possibility image $H_c^{t-1}(x, y)$. Specifically, we used as function f the mapping shown in Table 1.

Table 1. Update function for the possibility image $H_c^t(x, y)$. The two shadowed entries correspond to impossible cases, since $T_c^{t-1}(x,y)=1 \Rightarrow H_c^{t-1} \geq ½$.

T_c^{t-1}	H_c^{t-1}	$C_c^t=c$	H_c^t
0	0	No	0
0	½	No	0
0	1	No	0
0	0	Yes	½
0	½	Yes	½
0	1	Yes	½
1	0	No	0
1	½	No	0
1	1	No	½
1	0	Yes	½
1	½	Yes	1
1	1	Yes	1

Then, this possibility image $H_c^t(x,y)$ is segmented inside a *region-of-interest* ROI_c^t, which is estimated from the bounding box BB_c^{t-1} of the previous tracking image T_c^{t-1}. In order to compute the bounding box of a binary image, such as T_c^{t-1}, we use the method described in [9]. In fact, ROI_c^t and BB_c^{t-1} share the same center and shape, but the size of region ROI_c^t is determined to be greater than that of BB_c^{t-1} according to a given fixed scale ratio r (e.g. r=1.25) to take into account a possible displacement of

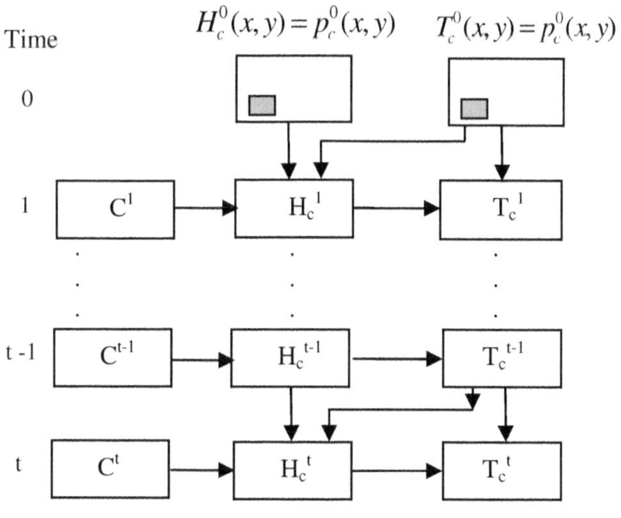

Fig. 2. Dynamic calculation of $H_c^t(x, y)$ and $T_c^t(x, y)$

the object between consecutive frames. The region of interest ROI_c^t is then passed to a seed-based segmentation algorithm [10] that yields the next tracking image T_c^t by finding a single connected region of the image $H_c^t(x,y)$, within the limits of ROI_c^t, such that all their pixels have a possibility value ≥ than a threshold z (e.g. z=½) , where the seed pixel is defined as MC_c^{t-1} , the mass center of T_c^{t-1}.

Summarizing, for the each time step t the next processes are carried out sequentially:

1. Calculate the class assignment $C^t(x, y)$ from the outputs given by the neural network when the features of the spot that includes the pixel (x,y) are entered to the net.
2. Compute $H_c^t(x, y)$ from $H_c^{t-1}(x, y)$, $T_c^{t-1}(x, y)$ and C^t, for each class $c=1,...,N$, using the heuristic mapping defined in Table 1.
3. Calculate $T_c^t(x, y)$ from $H_c^t(x, y)$ and $T_c^{t-1}(x, y)$, for each class $c=1,...,N$, by finding the region of interest ROI_c^t and applying within it the seed segmentation algorithm to $H_c^t(x, y)$.

These steps are shown graphically in figure 2 for a sequence of time steps.

4 Experimental Results

We illustrate our methodology and approach using two sequences of images that correspond to the left and right image sequences of a stereo vision system installed on a mobile robot. These sequences display an indoor scene where we chose three objects of interest (N=3): a box, a chair and a pair of adjacent wastebaskets. The slow relative motion of the objects in the sequences is due to the slow motion of the mobile robot during its navigation in an indoor environment, and this small displacement of the objects is an expected characteristic of the video sequences we are dealing with. In our initial work described in [8], only the left sequence was used and only the spots inside some predefined ROIs were selected for neural network training and test; a cross-validation procedure was followed using 25% of the spots for testing with a correct classification performance of around 76%. In a more recent work [11], this performance was raised to a 96% by adjusting more accurately the ROIs and to a 99% by combining the neural net with a reclassification process based on clustering. The performance of the selected neural net on the right sequence was a 90% of correctly classified patterns in the same ROIs.

However, for the test phase, it is somewhat tricky to restrict the object recognition to predefined ROIs, since we cannot rely on having the ROIs marked on every frame in a realistic experimental scenario. Hence, in the new experiments reported here, the same neural network trained from selected ROIs in the left sequence was used, but the whole right sequence including all spots was taken for testing both object recognition and tracking. A ROI for each object was only defined in the first image to initialize the tracking images. To the contrary of the results in [8] and [11], in this work we were not so interested in achieving a high spot classification ratio but a sequence of tracking images of good quality for each object of interest, as a first validation of the methodology proposed in Section 3.

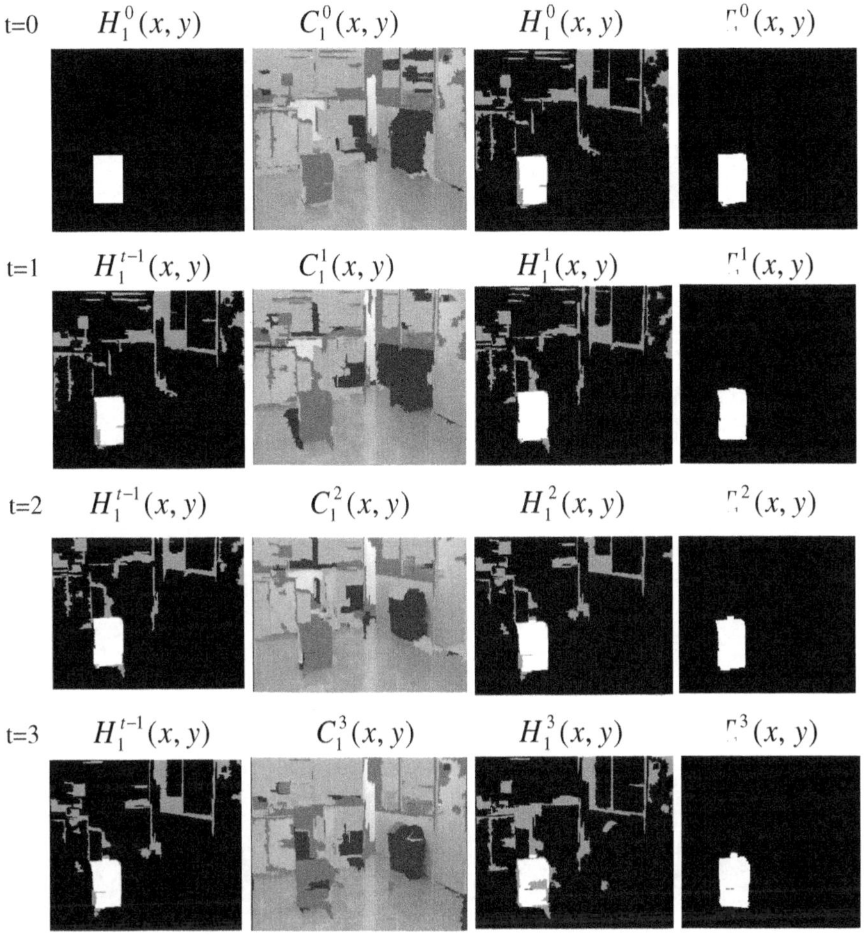

Fig. 3. Recognition and tracking results for class 1 (the box) in the first 4 frames of the test sequence

Figures 3 and 4 illustrate the process depicted in Figure 2 for two of the objects of interest (the box and the wastebaskets, respectively) in some consecutive images of the test sequence. Using the obtained tracking binary images as a visualization mask, the results of tracking both objects on the original images are displayed in Figures 5 and 6. It can be observed that the proposed approach obtained rather satisfactory results on these images. Similar good results were obtained for these two objects in the rest of the sequence, but those for the other object (the chair) were not so stable. Concerning the computation time of our current non-optimized implementation, the process of recognition and tracking takes about 20 seconds in average for each object and frame in a Pentium IV processor at 3.4 GHz with 512 MB RAM.

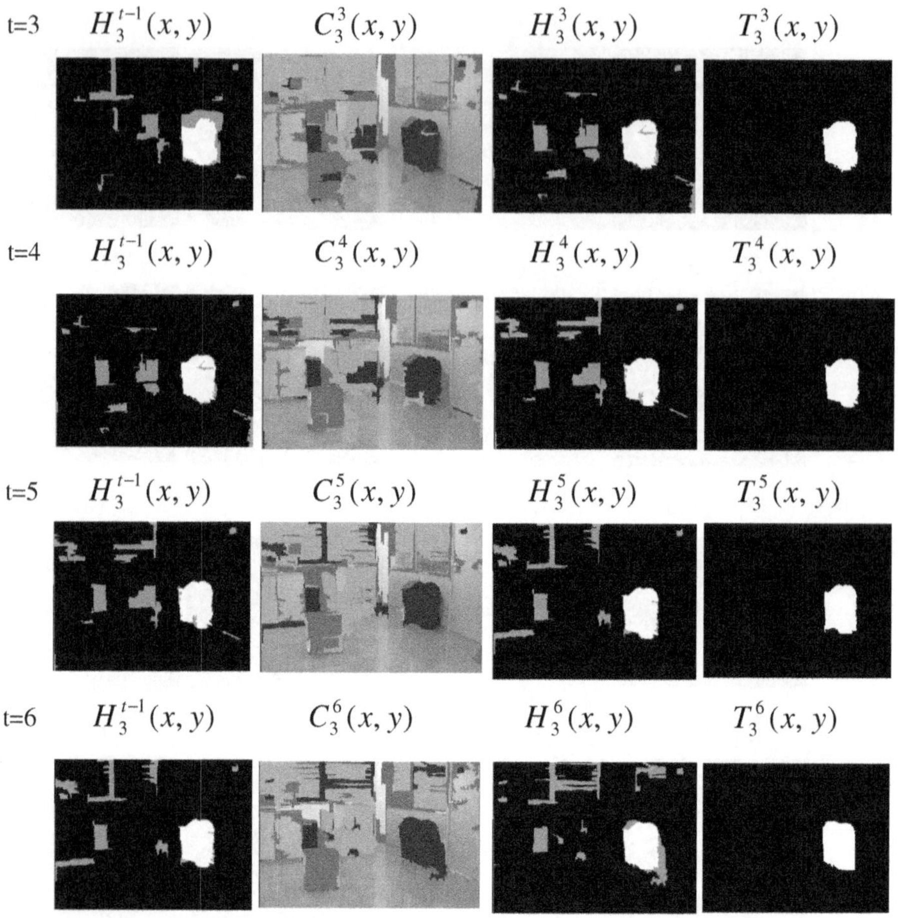

Fig. 4. Recognition and tracking results for class 3 (the wastebaskets) in four frames of the test sequence

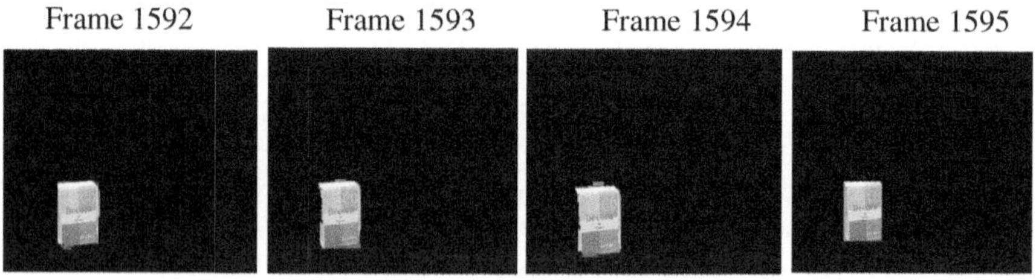

Fig. 5. Tracking of the box on part of the original image sequence

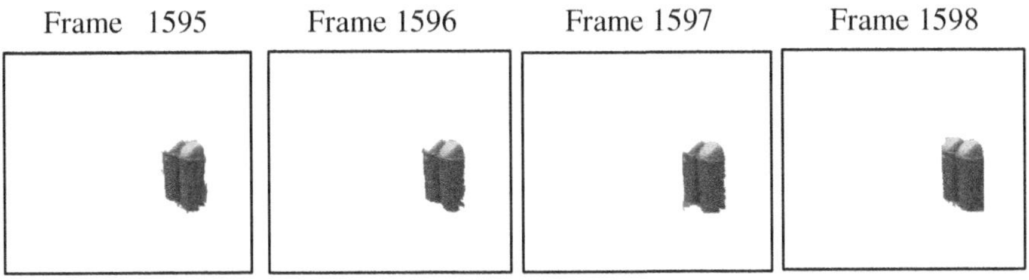

Fig. 6. Tracking of the wastebaskets on part of the original image sequence

5 Conclusions and Future Work

A dynamic iterative approach for object recognition and tracking in video sequences has been presented in which a probabilistic model at pixel level (or an approximation of it) is updated taking into account both the spot classification given by a trained neural net and prior object tracking information from the previous image. In this work, possibility images for each object of interest have been updated using a heuristic rule instead of applying a fully probabilistic model.

The use of the dynamic possibility images combined with the tracking information allows the gradual discrimination of the pixels classified as belonging to an object by the neural network but which do not really belong to it. It also helps to recover object pixels that have been classified as belonging to the background by the network but that really belong to an object. This can be made because the values in the possibility images save information of *how* the pixels have been classified in previous steps. Thus, this helps to decide at each iteration if a pixel belongs to an object or not. The experiments carried out have indicated that the proposed approach is viable and can provide satisfactory results.

In a future work, we would like to substitute the possibility images by actual probability images and to define the update and decision functions in a more principled way. We would also like to reduce the recognition and tracking computation time in order to approach the run-time processing. Our final objective is to design a robust dynamic approach to object recognition and tracking in video sequences based on unstructured sets of spots, which can deal with the variations in the object views resulting from the (relatively slow) motion of a mobile robot in an indoor environment.

References

1. Tu Z. Chen X., Yuille A.L., Zhu S.C., "Image Parsing: Unifying Segmentation, Detection, and Recognition", *Proceedings in Ninth IEEE International Conference on Computer Vision*, pp 18- 25 ISBN: 0-7695-1950-4 (2003).
2. Malik J., Belongie S., Leung T. and Shi J., "Contour and Texture Analysis for Image Segmentation", *IJCV*, vol.43, no.1, (2001).
3. Tu Z. and Zhu S.C., "Image segmentation by Data Driven Markov chain Monte Carlo", *IEEE Trans. PAMI*, vol. 24, no. 5, (2002).

4. Zhu S.C. and Yuille A., "Region competition: unifying snakes, region growing, and Bayes/MDL for multiband image segmentation", *IEEE Trans. on Pattern Analysis and Machine Intelligence*, Vol: 18, Issue 9, pp:884 – 900 Sept. (1996).
5. Nelson, R.C.; Green I.A. "Tracking objects using recognition", *Proceedings 16th International Conference on Pattern Recognition*, ISSN: 1051-4651, ISBN: 0-7695-1695-X Vol: 2, pp:1025-1030 (2002).
6. Yuya Iwasa, Ryuichi Oka "Spotting recognition and tracking of a deformable object in a time-varying image using two-dimensional continuous dynamic programming", *CIT '04. The Fourth International Conference on Computer and Information Technology*, ISBN: 0-7695-2216-5, pp:33 – 38. (2004).
7. Von Wichert G., "A probabilistic approach to simultaneous segmentation, object recognition, 3d localization, and tracking using stereo", in *Lecture Notes in Computer Science* 2191, pp 100, (2001).
8. Amézquita Gómez N. and Alquézar R. ,"Object Recognition in Indoor Video Sequences by Classifying Image Segmentation Regions Using Neural Networks ", *Proceedings 10th Iberoamerican Congress on Pattern Recognition, CIARP 2005*, LNCS Springer Berlin / Heidelberg ISSN: 0302-9743, Vol. 3773, Chapter: pp. 93 - 102 (2005).
9. Gerke, M, Heipke, C, Straub, B.-M. "Building extraction from aerial imagery using a generic scene model and invariant geometric moments", in *Remote Sensing and Data Fusion over Urban Areas, IEEE/ISPRS Joint Workshop*, ISBN: 0-7803-7059-7 8,pp: 85-89, (2001).
10. Ballard D.H. and Brown C.M., *Computer Vision*, Prentice Hall, New Jersey (1982).
11. Serratosa F., Amézquita Gómez N. and Alquézar R. ,"Combining neural networks and clustering techniques for object recognition in indoor video sequences", *Proceedings 11th Iberoamerican Congress on Pattern Recognition, CIARP 2006*, Cancun, Mexico (2006).

Conceptual K-Means Algorithm Based on Complex Features

I.O. Ayaquica-Martínez, J.Fco. Martínez-Trinidad, and J. Ariel Carrasco-Ochoa

National Institute of Astrophysics, Optics and Electronics
Computer Science Department
Luis Enrique Erro # 1, Santa María Tonantzintla, Puebla, Mexico, C.P. 72840
{ayaquica, fmartine, ariel}@inaoep.mx

Abstract. The k-means algorithm is the most studied and used tool for solving the clustering problem when the number of clusters is known a priori. Nowadays, there is only one conceptual version of this algorithm, the conceptual k-means algorithm. One characteristic of this algorithm is the use of generalization lattices, which define relationships among the feature values. However, for many applications, it is difficult to determine the best generalization lattices; moreover there are not automatic methods to build the lattices, thus this task must be done by the specialist of the area in which we want to solve the problem. In addition, this algorithm does not work with missing data. For these reasons, in this paper, a new conceptual k-means algorithm that does not use generalization lattices to build the concepts and allows working with missing data is proposed. We use complex features for generating the concepts. The complex features are subsets of features with associated values that characterize objects of a cluster and at the same time not characterize objects from other clusters. Some experimental results obtained by our algorithm are shown and they are compared against the results obtained by the conceptual k-means algorithm.

1 Introduction

The conceptual clustering problem was first addressed in the 80's by Michalski [1]. It consists on finding, from a data set, not only the clusters but also a conceptual interpretation of them. Starting from the Michalski's works several algorithms have been developed to solve the conceptual clustering problem. Some of them can be found in [2-8].

The k-means algorithm is the most studied and used tool for solving the clustering problem when the number of clusters is known a priori. The conceptual k-means algorithm proposed by Ralambondrainy [8] is the unique conceptual version of this algorithm. Then, we are going to focus in this algorithm.

The conceptual k-means algorithm [8] was developed to solve problems where the number of clusters is known a priori. This algorithm consists of two phases: an aggregation phase, in which the clusters are built and a characterization phase, in which the concepts are generated. In the aggregation phase, the k-means algorithm was extended to work with mixed data. In order to solve the mixed data problem, a

J.F. Martínez-Trinidad et al. (Eds.): CIARP 2006, LNCS 4225, pp. 491 – 501, 2006.

distance function given as the weighted sum of the Euclidean distance, for quantitative features; and the Chi-square distance, for qualitative features was used. For applying the Chi-square distance, a transformation of each qualitative feature into a set of Boolean features, must be done. The new features are handled as numeric features, which is inadequate. Additionally, this distance function does not work with missing data. On the other hand, this algorithm uses the same distance function for comparing objects in any problem.

In the characterization phase, a generalization lattice for each feature is required. For the qualitative features, it is difficult to determine the best generalization lattice for each feature; moreover there are not automatic methods to build the lattices, therefore this task must be done by the specialist; while for the quantitative features a codification into qualitative features to allow building a generalization lattice is done. In addition, the missing data is not taken into account when the generalization lattice is built.

In this paper, we propose a new conceptual k-means algorithm, which allows working with mixed and missing data; our algorithm does not require any transformation of features neither generalization lattices for the construction of the concepts.

This paper is organized as follows: in Section 2, some basic concepts are given. In Section 3, we introduce a new conceptual clustering algorithm. In Section 4, a measure to evaluate the quality of the concepts is proposed. The tests made with the proposed algorithm are shown in Section 5. In Section 6, a comparison between the conceptual k-means algorithm and the proposed algorithm is presented. Finally, in Section 7, conclusions and future work are presented.

2 Basic Concepts

The goal of this paper is to propose a new conceptual clustering algorithm, such that similar objects belong to the same cluster while dissimilar objects belong to different clusters. Besides, the concept associated to each cluster should characterize objects of the cluster and at the same time not characterize objects from other clusters. The complex features [9] are combinations of values for a subset of features such that these values appear sufficiently in the objects into a cluster and at the same time not appear in the objects outside the cluster. For this reason, they could be used to generate concepts.

The formal outline of the problem is the following:

Let $U=\{O_1,\dots,O_m\}$ be a set of m objects. Each object is described by a set of n features $R=\{x_1,\dots,x_n\}$. Each feature x_i takes values in a set of admissible values, D_i, i=1,... ,n. The features can be of any nature (qualitative: Boolean, multi-valued, etc. or quantitative: integer, real).

Also, it is assumed that in D_i exists a symbol "?" that denotes missing data, so incomplete descriptions of objects can be considered.

For each feature x_i, a comparison function $FC_i : D_i \times D_i \rightarrow L_i$, i=1,...,n is defined, where L_i is a completely ordered set. The FC_i function is an evaluation of the similarity degree between two values of the feature x_i. In addition, let

$\Gamma: (D_1 \times ... \times D_n)^2 \rightarrow [0,1]$ be a similarity function, which allows evaluating the similarity degree between two object descriptions.

The conceptual clustering problem consists on structuring the objects in k clusters and also generating the concept associated to each cluster.

As we mention above, the complex features could be used for generating concepts because, they are subsets of features with associated values that characterize objects of a cluster and at the same time not characterize objects from other clusters.

In order to obtain the complex features, some subsets of features, Ω, denominated *support sets* are needed. The support sets indicate the parts of the objects where the complex features will be searched. These support sets can be obtained in different ways. In this paper, the Γ-discriminating, the Γ-characterizing and support sets that are Γ-discriminating and Γ-characterizing at the same time are used.

In the following definitions, ΩO is a subdescription of the object O taking into account only the features of Ω.

1) Γ-discriminating support sets are subsets of features that do not increase the similarity among the objects from different clusters and they are defined as follows:

   Def. 1: $\Omega \subseteq R$ is a Γ-*discriminating support set* of features if all pairs of objects (O_i,O_j) of different clusters satisfy $\Gamma(\Omega O_i, \Omega O_j) \leq \Gamma(O_i, O_j)$, i.e., Ω is a Γ-discriminating support set of features, if objects in different clusters do not have a greater similarity in Ω than in R.
2) Γ-characterizing support sets are subsets of features that do not reduce the similarity among the objects in the same cluster and they are defined as follows:

   Def. 2: $\Omega \subseteq R$ is a Γ-*characterizing support set* of features if all pairs of objects (O_i,O_j) in the same cluster satisfy $\Gamma(O_i, O_j) \leq \Gamma(\Omega O_i, \Omega O_j)$, i.e., Ω is a Γ-characterizing support set of features, if objects of the same cluster do not have a lesser similarity in Ω than in R.
3) Support sets that are Γ-discriminating and Γ-characterizing at the same time.

For calculating the support sets, the degree in which each subset Ω satisfies the Γ-discriminating, Γ-characterizing or both properties, respectively is evaluated. It is to say:

1) For Γ-discriminating support sets, the degree in which the subset Ω satisfies the definition of Γ-discriminating support set is evaluated measuring the number of pairs of objects in different clusters, such that their similarity in Ω is lesser or equal than their similarity in R, as well as how much their similarity values differ in Ω and R.
2) For Γ-characterizing support sets, the degree in which the subset Ω satisfies the definition of Γ-characterizing support set is evaluated measuring the number of pairs of objects in the same cluster, such that their similarity in Ω is greater or equal than their similarity in R, as well as how much their similarity values differ in R and Ω.
3) For support sets that are Γ-discriminating and Γ-characterizing at the same time, the degree in which the subset Ω satisfies both definitions is evaluated. This degree

is evaluated as the sum of the degree in which the subset Ω satisfies the definition of Γ-discriminating support set and the degree in which the subset Ω satisfies the definition of Γ-characterizing support set.

Additionally to the support sets it is also necessary a set of values associated to these features, such that these values appear sufficiently in the objects into the cluster and at the same time do not appear in the objects outside the cluster. For this reason we use the complex features.

Def. 3: Let $\Omega = \{x_{i_1},...,x_{i_p}\}$ be a support set and $(a_1,...,a_p)$ values associated to the features $x_{i_1},...,x_{i_p}$ from an object of the sample, then $\{x_{i_1},...,x_{i_p}\}$ and $(a_1,...,a_p)$ form a complex feature of the cluster A_i, if and only if:

1) $\sum_{O \in A_i} \Gamma(\Omega O,(a_1,...,a_p)) \geq \beta_i$

2) $\sum_{O \notin A_i} \Gamma(\Omega O,(a_1,...,a_p)) < \lambda_i$

where β_i is the minimum similarity that the objects of the cluster A_i should have with the subdescription $(a_1,...,a_p)$ and λ_i is the maximum similarity that the objects outside of the cluster should have with $(a_1,...,a_p)$. For this work, we used $\lambda_i = 1$, because we are interested in obtaining concepts, with the smallest number of complex features, that do not recognize objects of other clusters. We tried $\lambda_i = 0$ but there were some clusters without any complex feature. Also, we tried $\lambda_i = 2$ and in this case we obtained too much complex features. The value of β_i is calculated automatically. The procedure to calculate β_i is the following: Initially, β_i is the number of objects in the cluster; then β_i is decremented taking as value the maximum similarity obtained by the subdescriptions that do not satisfy the complex feature definition. Then the complex features are computed with the new value of β_i; this process is repeated while $\beta_i > 0$.

3 Conceptual K-Means Algorithm Based on Complex Features

We will follow the same idea of Ralambondrainy proposing a conceptual k-means algorithm in two phases: a clustering phase, in which the k-means with similarity functions algorithm (KMSF) [10] is used to obtain the clusters; and a characterization phase, in which the complex features are used to generate the concepts.

3.1 Clustering Phase

In this phase, the k-means with similarity functions algorithm is used to build the clusters. This algorithm allows working with mixed, qualitative and quantitative, features defining a similarity function. In this way, the similarity function does not require transformations of features as the distance of the conceptual k-means algorithm does. Also, the similarity function is usually defined in terms of comparison functions, which express how the values of the features are compared. This algorithm contrary to the conceptual k-means algorithm (CKM) allows using different functions to compare the values of features depending on the problem to solve.

For example, in this work we use the following similarity function:

$$\Gamma(O_i,O_j)=\frac{\sum_{x_s\in R} FC_s\left(x_s(O_i),x_s(O_j)\right)}{|R|}$$

where $FC_s\left(x_s(O_i),x_s(O_j)\right)$ is the comparison function used for comparing two values of the feature x_s.

The comparison functions used for the tests were the following:

i) For quantitative features:

$$FC_s\left(x_s(O_i),x_s(O_j)\right)=\begin{cases}0 & \text{if } x_s(O_i)=?\vee x_s(O_j)=?\vee\left|x_s(O_i)-x_s(O_j)\right|\geq\sigma\\ 1 & \text{in other case}\end{cases}$$

where σ is the standard deviation for the feature x_s.

ii) For qualitative features:

$$FC_s\left(x_s(O_i),x_s(O_j)\right)=\begin{cases}0 & \text{if } x_s(O_i)=?\vee x_s(O_j)=?\vee x_s(O_i)\neq x_s(O_j)\\ 1 & \text{in other case}\end{cases}$$

Notice that, when a value for the feature is missing then the value is different from any other value even from other missing value.

On the other hand, the KMSF algorithm, selects objects of the sample as centroids of the clusters (see details in [10]) instead of the mean, as occur in the modified k-means algorithm proposed by Ralambondrainy [8].

3.2 Characterization Phase

In this phase, the complex features are used to generate the concepts. In order to use the complex features, some support sets are needed. In this work, the Γ-discriminating (Γd), Γ-characterizing (Γc) and Γ-discriminating and Γ-characterizing (Γd and Γc) support sets are used.

For calculating the support sets, a genetic algorithm was used. In this genetic algorithm, each individual represents a support set and it is formed by n genes, where each gene represents a feature. A gene takes value 1 if the feature is included and 0 if it is not included. This algorithm uses the 1-point crossover operator, it is to say, a cross point is selected and starting from it, the information of the chromosomes is exchanged. As mutation operator, the uniform mutation is used, it is to say, a gene of a chromosome is randomly selected and its value is changed (0 by 1 or 1 by 0). As aptitude function, the degree in which a subset Ω satisfies the definition of Γ-discriminating, Γ-characterizing or both respectively is used. From these sets, those that satisfy with the highest degree the Γ-discriminating property, Γ-characterizing property or both, respectively, are selected.

Example: For the sample of Table 1, suppose that after applying the clustering phase, the following clusters were obtained: $A_1=\{O_1,O_2\}$ and $A_2=\{O_3,O_4\}$.

For these clusters, the genetic algorithm obtained the support sets shown in Table 2.

Table 1. Sample with four objects described by three features

Objects	Features		
	Color (C)	**Weight (W)**	**Shape (Sh)**
O_1	Red	20	Round
O_2	Red	25	Round
O_3	Yellow	30	Triangle
O_4	Yellow	35	Triangle

Table 2. Support sets obtained by the genetic algorithm for the sample of the Table 1 with $A_1=\{O_1,O_2\}$ and $A_2=\{O_3,O_4\}$

Support sets		
Γd	**Γc**	**Γd y Γc**
{C}	{C,Sh}	{C,W,Sh}
{C,W}		{C,W}
{W}		{W}

Once obtained the support sets, the complex features are obtained applying the definition 3.

In this phase, the similarity function used to calculate the complex features is the same one used in the clustering phase. An advantage of using the same similarity function in both phases of the algorithm is that the way in which the concepts are generated maintains a relationship with the cluster construction. This does not happen in the conceptual k-means algorithm, where the comparison used to generate the concepts is different from the one used to build the clusters.

The complex features obtained with the support sets of Table 2 and the dataset of Table 1 are shown in Table 3.

Table 3. Complex features for the example

	Complex Features for each support set		
Cluster	**Γd**	**Γc**	**Γd y Γc**
1	{C}- (Red) {C,W} – (Red,20) {C,W} – (Red,25) {W} – (20)	{C,Sh}- (Red,Round)	{C,W,Sh}- (Red,20,Round) {C,W,Sh} – (Red,25,Round) {C,W} – (Red,20) {C,W} – (Red,25) {W} – (20)
2	{C}- (Yellow) {C,W} – (Yellow,30) {C,W} – (Yellow,35) {W} – (35)	{C,Sh}- (Yellow,Triangle)	{C,W,Sh}- (Yellow,30,Triangle) {C,W,Sh} – (Yellow,35,Triangle) {C,W} – (Yellow,30) {C,W} – (Yellow,35) {W} – (35)

Afterwards, in order to generate the concepts, a predicate is associated to each complex feature. This predicate is built in the following way: to each feature $x_i \in R$ that appears in the complex feature, the associated value a_i is assigned to this feature; and for the features $x_i \in R$ that do not appear in the complex feature * is assigned. The symbol * means "any value is possible".

For the example, the predicates formed for the complex features of Γ-discriminating (Γd) sets of the cluster 1, in Table 3 are:

P1: C=Red ∧ W=* ∧ Sh=*
P2: C=Red ∧ W=20 ∧ Sh=*
P3: C=Red ∧ W=25 ∧ Sh=*
P4: C=* ∧ W=20 ∧ Sh=*

The set of predicates obtained from the complex features can contain two or more predicates that recognize the same objects. Therefore, this set of predicates can be reduced by eliminating predicates that recognize the same objects than another predicate. This reduction is made using the strategy proposed by Ralambondrainy [8] that works as follows: first, the predicates are sorted, in a descending way, according to the amount of objects that each one recognizes. The first predicate will be part of the concept. For the remaining predicates, if a predicate recognizes some objects not recognized by the stored predicates, then it is added to the concept; otherwise it is eliminated. The concept is formed by the disjunction of the stored predicates.

For the example, the concepts obtained after the reduction process are shown in Table 4.

Table 4. Concepts obtained for the example

Kind of support set	Cluster	Concept
Γd	1 2	C = Red C = Yellow
Γc	1 2	C = Red ∧ Sh = Round C = Yellow ∧ Sh = Triangle
Γd y Γc	1 2	C = Red ∧ W = 20 ∧ Sh = Round C = Yellow ∧ W = 30 ∧ Sh = Triangle

4 Quality Measure

In 1995, Ralambondrainy proposed to take as a quality measure, the percentage of objects in the cluster that are recognized by the concept. However, we consider that it is also necessary to take into account the objects outside of the cluster that are recognized by the concept. Therefore, we propose the following quality measure:

$$quality(C_1,\ldots,C_k)=\frac{1}{k}\sum_{i=1}^{k}\frac{examples(C_i)}{total(C_i)+counterexamples(C_i)}$$

where:

k is the number of clusters.

C_i is the concept associated to the i-th cluster, $i = 1,\ldots,k$.

$examples(C_i)$ is the number of objects into the i-th cluster, which are recognized by the concept C_i.

$counterexamples(C_i)$ is the number of objects outside of the i-th cluster, which are recognized by the concept C_i.

$Total(C_i)$ is the number of objects in the i-th cluster.

This function obtains higher values if the number of examples recognized by the concept increases and the number of counterexamples recognized by the concept decreases. The function obtains 1.0 when the concept recognizes all the objects in the cluster and it does not recognize any object outside the cluster, which is the ideal case.

For the example, the quality of the concepts obtained with each kind of support sets (see Table 4) is:

1) for the Γ-discriminating sets = 1.0
2) for the Γ-characterizing sets = 1.0
3) for the Γ-discriminating and Γ-characterizing sets = 1.0

5 Experimentation

The CKMCF algorithm was applied on different supervised databases taken from the UCI repository [12].

For selecting the support sets, we did tests using different number of iterations: 10, 20 and 30, and different number of individuals: 5, 10, 20, 50, 100 and 500. We obtained the best results with 10 iterations and 500 individuals. In Table 5, we show only the results obtained with the genetic algorithm with 10 iterations and 500 individuals, using the three kinds of support sets.

Table 5. Results obtained with the CKMCF algorithm using three kinds of support sets

Conceptual K-means algorithm based on Complex Features							
		Γd		Γc		Γd and Γc	
Databases	No. clusters	No. predicates	Quality	No. predicates	Quality	No. predicates	Quality
Autos_mpg	3	29	0.69	29	0.69	29	0.69
Credit	2	86	0.99	79	1.00	184	0.99
Diabetes	2	63	0.72	62	0.72	64	0.72
Electro	3	31	0.95	32	0.97	35	0.95
Glass	6	23	0.99	23	0.95	23	0.98
Hayes	3	32	1.00	31	1.00	32	1.00
Hepatitis	2	69	0.75	58	0.95	59	0.87
Import85	6	97	0.65	60	0.87	104	0.94
Iris	3	5	0.93	5	0.93	5	0.92
Lenses	3	5	1.00	5	1.00	5	1.00
Tae	3	24	0.98	24	0.98	24	0.98
Zoo	7	28	1.00	19	1.00	27	1.00
Average		45.9	0.89	41.1	0.88	52.5	0.92

In Table 5, we can observe that the results obtained with the different kinds of support sets, in most of the cases, are very similar. Therefore, we can use any of these support sets for obtaining good quality concepts. For the Hepatitis and the Import85 databases, we obtained lowest quality concepts using Γ-discriminating sets (see Figure 1).

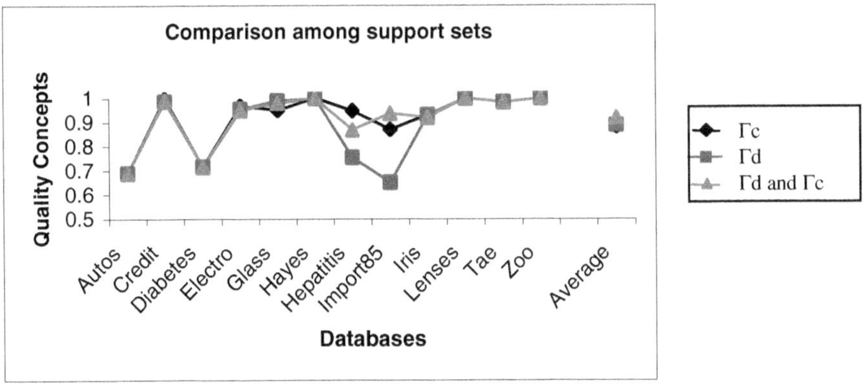

Fig. 1. Comparison among the three kinds of support sets for the CKMCF algorithm

6 Comparison Between the CKM and the CKMCF Algorithms

In this section, a comparison between the conceptual k-means (CKM) [8] and the conceptual k-means based on complex features (CKMCF) algorithms is presented. In Table 6, the results obtained by both algorithms are shown.

Table 6. Results obtained with the CKMCF and the CKM algorithms

Databases	No. Clusters	CKMCF						CKM	
		Γd		Γc		Γd and Γc			
		No. Pred	Quality	No. Pred	Quality	No. Pred	Quality	No. Pred	Quality
Diabetes	2	63	0.72	62	0.72	64	0.72	307	0.90
Glass	6	23	0.99	23	0.95	23	0.98	39	0.84
Hayes	3	32	1.00	31	1.00	32	1.00	26	0.97
Iris	3	5	0.93	5	0.93	5	0.92	17	0.90
Lenses	3	5	1.00	5	1.00	5	1.00	13	1.00
Tae	3	24	0.98	24	0.98	24	0.98	13	0.96
Zoo	7	28	1.00	19	1.00	27	1.00	13	0.99
Average		25.7	0.88	24.1	0.95	25.7	0.94	62.13	0.94

Comparing the results obtained with the CKMCF and CKM algorithms, we can observe that, with the Diabetes database the CKM algorithm was better than the CKMCF algorithm. However, for the rest of databases the CKMCF algorithm obtains concepts with better quality than the concepts obtained by the CKM algorithm (Figure 2). In Table 6, we can see that, in average, the set of predicates obtained by the CKMCF algorithm is smaller than those obtained by the CKM algorithm, then the concepts obtained by the CKMCF algorithm are shorter and easier for handling than those obtained by the CKM algorithm.

We compared the CKMCF and the CKM algorithms using only six databases from those used in the previous section (see Table 5) since for the Autos_mpg, Credit, Electro, Hepatitis and Import85 databases was not possible to apply the CKM algorithm because these databases contain missing data, which cannot be processed by the CKM algorithm.

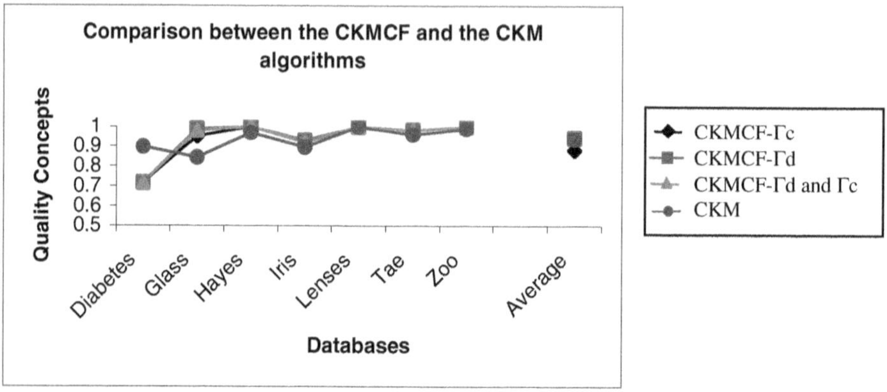

Fig. 2. Comparison between the CKMCF and the CKM algorithms

7 Conclusions and Future Work

In this paper, the conceptual k-means algorithm based on complex features (CKMCF) for solving conceptual clustering problems when the number of clusters is known a priori was proposed.

We consider that the CKMCF algorithm is a good alternative for the solution of conceptual clustering problems, because this algorithm allows working with mixed and missing data without any transformation of features; the centroids of the clusters are objects of the sample instead of elements that cannot be represented in the same space of the sample. Also, this algorithm does not depend on generalization lattices.

Based on the experimental results, we can observe that the CKMCF algorithm obtains very similar results with the three kinds of support sets. Then we can use any of these support sets for obtaining good quality concepts.

From the comparison between the CKMCF and the CKM algorithms we could observe that, in most of the cases, the CKMCF algorithm obtains better quality concepts with smaller set of predicates than those obtained by the CKM algorithm. Even though the number of predicates was decreased, the concepts of the clusters are formed by many predicates then as future work we will propose some modifications in order to generate smaller concepts.

References

1. Michalski R.S. (1986), *A theory and methodology of inductive learning*. In R.S. Michalski, J. G. Carbonell and T. M. Mitchell, editors, Machine Learning: An artificial intelligence approach, volume 2, pp. 83-129. Morgan Kaufmann, Los Altos, CA.
2. Briscoe G. and Caelli T. (1996), *A compendium of Machine Learning, Volume 1: Symbolic Machine Learning*, Ed. Ablex.

3. Stumme G. et. al. (2001), *Conceptual Clustering with Iceberg Concept Lattices*, In: R. Klinkenberg, S. Ruping, A. Fick, N. Henze, C. Herzog, R. Molitor, O. Schroder (Eds.): Proc. GI-Fachgruppentre#en Maschinelles Lernen '01,Universitat Dortmund 763.
4. Jonyer I., Holder L.B. and Cook D.J. (2001), *Graph-based hierarchical conceptual clustering*. International Journal on Artificial Intelligence Tools, 10 (1-2), pp. 107-135.
5. Pons-Porrata A., Ruiz-Shulcloper J. and Martínez-Trinidad J.F. (2002), *RGC: a new conceptual clustering algorithm for mixed incomplete data sets*. In Mathematical and Computer Modeling 36, pp. 1375-1385.
6. Osinski S. and Weiss D. (2004), *Conceptual clustering using lingo algorithm: Evaluation on open directory project data*. Advanced in Soft Computing, Intelligent Information Processing and Web Mining, Proceedings of the International IIS: IIPWM'04 Conference, Zakopane, Poland, pp. 369-378.
7. Jänichen S. and Perner P. (2005), *Acquisition of Concept Descriptions by Conceptual Clustering*, In P. Perner and A. Imiya (Eds.): MLDM 2005, LNAI 3587, pp. 153-162.
8. Ralambondrainy H. (1995), *A conceptual version of the K-means algorithm*, Pattern Recognition Letters 16, pp. 1147-1157.
9. De la Vega Doria, L.A, Carrasco Ochoa J.A. and Ruiz Shulcloper J. (1998), *Fuzzy Kora-Ω Algorithm*, 6th European Congress on Intelligent Techniques and Soft Computing EUFIT 98, Aachen Germany, vol. 2 pp. 1190-1194.
10. García Serrano J.R. and Martínez-Trinidad J.F. (1999), *Extension to c-means algorithm for the use of similarity functions*. 3rdEuropean Conference on Principles of Data Mining and Knowledge Discovery Proceedings. Prague, Czech. Republic, pp 354-359.
11. http://www.ics.uci.edu/pub/machine-learning-databases/

Spatial Data Description by Means of Knowledge-Based System

Víctor Montes de Oca, Miguel Torres, Serguei Levachkine, and Marco Moreno

Geoprocessing Laboratory - Centre for Computing Research - National Polytechnic Institute, Mexico City, Mexico
vicmoca@sagitario.cic.ipn.mx,
{mtorres, sergei, marcomoreno}@cic.ipn.mx

Abstract. In this paper, we propose the use of a knowledge based system, which has been implemented in SWI-Prolog to approach the automatic description of spatial data by means of some logic rules. The process to establish the predicates is based on the topological and geometrical analysis of spatial data. These predicates are handled by a set of rules, which are used to find the relations between geospatial objects. Moreover, the rules aid the searching of several features that compose the partition of topographic maps. For instance, in the case that any road *intersects* with other, we appreciate that a *connection relation* exists between different destinies, which can be accessed by these roads. Furthermore, the rules help us to know each possible access for this case. Therefore, this description assists in the tasks of geospatial data interpretation *(map description)* in order to provide quality information for spatial decision support systems.

1 Introduction

The technique of knowledge-based systems consists of manipulating the information to support human decision-making, learning and action. Such systems are capable of cooperating with human users and so the quality of support given, as well as the knowledge representation *(the information quality)* are important issues to consider when developing such systems.

Through pattern recognition, the process of acquisition of spatial data is automated, which is generally stored in raster or vector format, being this last one the most useful to make topological and geometrical analysis from which spatial knowledge is acquired. It is necessary to count with a correct representation of this knowledge to assist to understand, manage and share information of a spatial domain region.

Expert systems are attempting to introduce human knowledge about problem solving into computer software. The general objective is to emulate the problem-solving capabilities of the human expert [1]. Traditionally, expert systems were employed to aid on specific domain tasks, and its solution set was delimited by the knowledge base that constitute them, which could not be extended to other related domain tasks without reengineering the database. Knowledge based systems (KBS) extend this principle by allowing new knowledge to be inferred from the existing one adding it to the database.

J.F. Martínez-Trinidad et al. (Eds.): CIARP 2006, LNCS 4225, pp. 502 – 510, 2006.

In this paper, we propose the use of a KBS, which has been implemented in SWI-Prolog to approach the automatic description of spatial data by means of some logic rules. The process to establish the predicates is based on a topological and geometrical analysis of the spatial data to find some basic properties. These predicates are handled by a set of rules, which are used to find the relations between geospatial objects. Moreover, the rules aid the searching of several features that compose topographic maps. The focus is on development and execution of knowledge-based "micro systems", specialized for a specific region (case study) by means of logic predicates, built in a pattern recognition process. These predicates compose the knowledge base and are used by "universal" rules that infer new knowledge for the domain of topographic maps.

For instance, in the case that any road *intersects* with other, we appreciate that a *connection relation* exists between different destinies, which can be accessed by these roads. Furthermore, the rules help us to know each possible access for this case and this knowledge is valuable for the tasks of geospatial data interpretation *(map description),* in order to provide quality information for spatial decision support systems.

Because we manage "basic data" obtained by means of a pattern recognition process and rely on that data to generate knowledge, we are convinced of its importance on the automation of task and data manipulation.

The rest of the paper is organized as follows. In section 2 we present an overview related to knowledge-based systems (KBS), their importance on AI's research and how we address the issues of knowledge representation, acquisition and processing. Also we show a brief example on how spatial knowledge can be derived through PROLOG's inference capabilities and what kind of information composes of the knowledge base. Section 3 contains the algorithm and logic that we use as the workforce toward generating the map description, and also a brief example of a description generated so far with the KBS developed. Our conclusions are outlined in section 4.

2 Why Knowledge-Based Systems Are Important?

Knowledge is of paramount importance, and AI research has shifted its focus from an inference-based paradigm to a knowledge-based paradigm. Knowledge is viewed as consisting of facts and heuristics. The *facts* constitute a body of information that is widely shared, publicly available, and generally agreed-upon by experts in a field. The *heuristics* are most private, little-discussed rules of good judgment (rules of plausible reasoning, rules of good guessing) that characterize expert-level decision making in a field [9]. "...however, this does not restrict the knowledge base to a traditional ES (Expert System) approach but it could include more indirect forms of knowledge representation" [1]. Heuristics are also embedded into the process of pattern recognition and in the results obtained by such algorithms.

Three major research issues of AI's knowledge-based paradigm are grouped as issues of knowledge representation, knowledge utilization, and knowledge acquisition [9]. In this paper, we specify how we approach these issues to obtain the automatic spatial data description by means of a knowledge-based system (KBS).

2.1 Knowledge Representation

Since we use SWI-Prolog as the platform to develop our KBS, it is necessary to build the knowledge in the form of predicates or *facts* about the spatial data. We propose to use these facts to generate a description of the spatial data.

2.2 Knowledge Utilization

The knowledge is used as first order logic statements that help us to discover, by means of inference procedures, more advanced (or complex) relations that topologic and geometric analysis are not aware of because they are out of their scope at runtime.

With that, we would like to state that even when we still use inference to acquire *new knowledge* about spatial relations among the objects that compose a map (the spatial data). There is an interesting twist on the way the *basic knowledge* base is constructed; instead of a human expert being the one who inputs the knowledge, this is acquired by the automatic process of topologic and geometric analysis (a kind of pattern recognition), which is done to a map, whose in turn, uses heuristic methods to obtain this information.

How logic rules can help to describe spatial data? Logic rules are formed by two elements: facts and a consequence. The consequence is considered true if all the facts that the rule needs to prove turn out to be true (see Fig. 1).

a)		b)

'fact' -- > 'consequence'
IF *{fact is true}*
THEN *{consequence}*
	⟺	`new_fact :-  /* rule or consequence */`
		`fact_1,  /* Facts to be proved */`
		`...,`
		`fact_n.`

Fig. 1. Methods to express rules. a) From the traditional way. b) To the PROLOG way.

In Fig. 1 1a) we note that the traditional way is a series of *facts* (or just a single fact) that triggers a *consequence*. In PROLOG 1b) we search for all those *facts* (they must be in the knowledge base, so they can prove to be true) so if and only if every fact proves true then the *rule* is said to be true [12]. This reveals a *new fact,* we did not know, but always existed *implicitly* in the knowledge base, we could add this new knowledge *explicitly* to the knowledge base to aid on more advanced inferences. That is the very essence of a KBS.

In Fig. 2, we used first order logic predicates together with the topological relations of the 9-intersection model [6][7], because in this model two spatial objects 'A' and 'B' share a topological relation, we can group and compare them (even as a single entity) with other objects that have the same relation (and different ones) and make more complex analysis.

If **A** *contains* **B** then **B** *is inside* **A**
also
if **C** *contains* **B**
then we conclude that
C *contains* **A** or that **A** *is inside* **C**

Fig. 2. Example of a inference process, in which a topological relation between *A* and *C* is discovered, by means of a common *relation* they both share with *B*

2.3 Knowledge Acquisition

Straight from topologic and geometric analysis [10][11][13], we can automatically construct a knowledge base containing the following *basic facts* about the spatial objects that compose a map:

- Topologic relations: *disjoint, meet, overlap, coveredBy, covers, contains, inside, equal.*
- Relative directions: *north, south, east* and *west* [8].
- Geometric measures: *area, perimeter, distance, large…*
- Type attribute: *area, line, point.*

If the map is already classified into a spatial database, we can *import* the following elements:

- Theme attribute: *road, population, hydrological, land type …*
- Descriptive attribute: *name …*

Although there are many possible advanced 'functions' or 'rules', we would like to have in the inference engine of the KBS, we concentrate on a few and we think that they are the most useful to describe a map such as Fig. 3, which is very important to consider in the following sections.

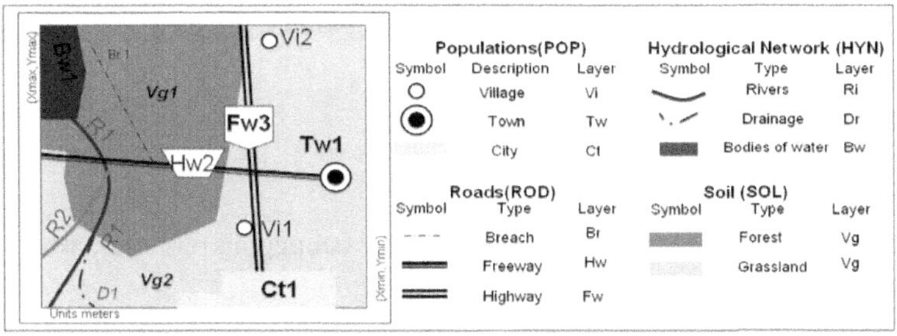

Fig. 3. Case study map for testing a KBS spatial data description. This map[1] is composed of 13 objects: 4 areal, 6 linear and 3 punctual. They are organized on 4 themes: *Population, Hydrology, Roads and Soil.*

[1] The legend of the map shows the geospatial objects types of each thematic, in this case they are 11 representations. However the map is composed of 13 objects, because it has 2 rivers (R1, R2) and 2 villages (Vi1, Vi2).

Interconnects() – Returns those spatial objects that constitute urban places or 'destinies' like villages, towns and cities, that are related *(or can be reached)* to an object that suggests some kind of communication as roads, highways and freeways.

We shall note that the logic of this relation can be extended to search for interconnections of objects of the same theme, such as body of water objects are connected by rivers, or even connections among the nodes of river networks. For example, the following PROLOG query:

```
          interconnects(fw3, Ans).
should return:
          Ans = vi1
          Ans = vi2
          Ans = ct1
```

It turns out that with this information added to the knowledge base, we could generate the following rule:

Destinations() – Returns all those 'destinies' that can be reached from one place by any number of 'roads' that *intersects* between them, which turns out to be the 'cross product' of all the destinies that *interconnects* each of those 'roads'. Since the highway **Hw2** interconnects with town **Tw1** and intersects the freeway **Fw3** the query is the following:

```
          destinations(ct1, Ans).
should return:
          Ans = vi1
          Ans = tw1
          Ans = vi2
```

A more general rule, mainly used for debugging the knowledge base construction is:

What_Relation() – This rule returns *true* for all the relations that the knowledge base states between two specified objects. For this purpose, it is necessary to prove each rule seen so far, from the basic to the derived ones, so special care should be taken to include in the code every new rule generated or derived. For example the query:

```
          what_relation(r1, bw1).
should return:
          connects = yes.
          south = yes.
```

Even though the last rule was conceived for debugging purposes, we can use the information provided to construct a rule called:

Explain() – It mentions everything that we know *(that is in the knowledge base)* about a spatial object. For instance, how it is related to other objects *(topology)*, its name, classification attributes as *type (line, point, area)*, also its *theme: {[Roads(freeway, highway,...)]; [population(city, village, town,...)]; [hydrological(body of water, river, drainage,...)]; [land(grassland, forest, breach,...)]}* and its metrics, if we have such information. The query is:

```
          explain(bw1).
should return:
          type = area
          theme = hydrological
          is_a = body of water
          inside = vg1
          covered_by = vg1
          meet = vg1 ; meet = r1
          north_of = hw2 ; north_of = r2 ;
          north_of = d1 ; north_of = ct1
          west_of = br1 ; west_of = vi2 ;
          west_of = tw1 ; west_of = vi1 ;
          west_of = ct1
```

It should be obvious that, while all the basic predicates or facts in the knowledge base are generated through topological and geometrical analysis and some more advanced facts are inferred through rules, is this last rule along with the algorithm explained in the following section, the workforce of the map description generation.

3 Map Description Process

Verbal descriptions of spatial situations are frequently ambiguous and may easily lead to misinterpretations, because geographic concepts are often vague, imprecise, little understood, or not standardized [2].

Experiments in psychology and cartography showed that topology is among the most critical information people refer to when they assess spatial relationships in geographic space, while metrical changes are frequently considered to be of lesser importance. This is based on the premise *topology matters, metrical refines.* In [2] referring to [4, 5].

For this reason, we only consider topology characteristics for the "first levels" of spatial descriptions, which involve the metrics only for those spatial objects that arc selected to be of relevance, as in the rule *(early in detail)*:

```
explain(object).
```

3.1 The Description Generator Algorithm

The KBS constructs sentences about the spatial state of the map and the relations between spatial objects that constitute it, in such a way that this knowledge generated as sentences can be looked out on a search by exact word match.

The description is generated considering the following algorithm:

1. Start from the 'leftmost' spatial object at the top and work to the right toward the bottom of the map.
2. For each spatial object:
3. Describe its type, theme and name.
4. Describe its topological relations in order of similitude *(more on this later...)*
5. IF the description level > 1 AND we have metric data, describe it.
6. Search the object to the east with which it has the following topological relation, in order of importance:

- Overlap.
- Meet.
- Disjoint.

7. Set it as the new work object and repeat from the step 3.
8. If there is no object to the east, look for objects to the south considering conditions in the step 6
9. Repeat from the step 2
10. If there are no more objects to the east and south, end.

In the step 4, we use the "Conceptual neighborhood graph of the eight region-region relations" [3] shown in Fig. 4 to determine the order in which the elements of description should appear, basing on the importance and similarity of topological relations.

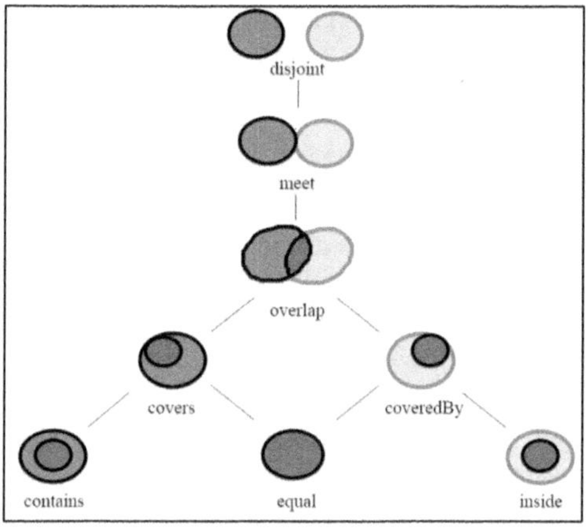

Fig. 4. Conceptual neighborhood graph of the eight region-region relations. It states the similitude between the binary topological relations.

This procedure produces the following map description:

[a body of water](bw1) *inside* [a forest](vg1) *connects* [a river](r1) {to the east} *disjoint* [a breach](br1).

[a forest](vg1) *inside* [a grassland](vg2) *contains* [a body of water](bw1) *contains* [a breach](br1) *contains* [a river](r1) *contains* [a river](r2) *covered by* [a grassland](vg2) *meets* [a freeway](fw3) *intersects* [a highway](hw2)

[a grassland](vg2) *contains* [a river](r1) *contains* [a river](r2) *contains* [a forest](vg1) *contains* [a village](vi2) *contains* [a freeway](fw3) *contains* [a highway](hw2) *contains* [a town](tw1) *contains* [a village](vi1) *contains* [a drainage](d1) *contains* [a city](ct1)

. . .

4 Conclusions

In this paper, we propose a set of logic predicates that state some basic characteristics of spatial objects, which can be generated after some pattern recognition analysis such as topology, relative direction, and geometric measures.

In addition, we propose automatic methods based on the measures above mentioned, to construct the knowledge base. These predicates or facts can be managed by rules to infer new knowledge that reveals more sophisticated relations that typical analysis are not aware of, or are out of their scope. With this information, it is possible to automatically generate richer descriptions that make sense of the map as it 'explains' more attributes about each spatial object. The rules presented are "universal" in the sense that they can be used for any given map to generate its description as long as its predicates are formed in the same way suggested in this work.

The advantages of this approach is that the analysis and inference processes are executed only once for each map, since the new knowledge is stored on the knowledge base, which is the foundation to make more complex analysis and generate richer descriptions. Also, this approach is used to *share* new data and provide them for spatial decision support systems.

Future works are related to allow us changes on the map at runtime in order to update the knowledge base, which should reflect the new state of the relations between the spatial objects of the map.

References

1. Openshaw, S. and Openshaw, C.: *Artificial Intelligence in Geography.* John Wiley & Sons (1997).
2. Egenhofer, M.: Query Processing in Spatial-Query-by-Sketch, *Journal of Visual Languages and Computing,* 8(4), (1997) 403-424.
3. Bruns, T. and Egenhofer, M.: "Similarity of Spatial Scenes", *Seventh International Symposium on Spatial Data Handling,* M.-J. Kraak and M. Molenaar, eds., Delft, The Netherlands, (1996) 31-42.
4. Mark, D.: "Counter-Intuitive Geographic "Facts:" Clues for Spatial Reasoning at Geographic Scales" *Theories and Methods of Spatio-Temporal Reasoning in Geographic Space, Pisa, Italy,* A. Frank, I. Campari, and U. Formentini, eds., *Lecture Notes in Computer Science,* 639, Springer-Verlag, Berlin, (1992) 305-317.
5. Stevens, A. and Coupe, P.: "Distortions in Judged Spatial Relations" *Cognitive Psychology,* vol. 10, (1978) 422-437.
6. Egenhofer, M. and Franzosa, R.: "Point-Set Topological Spatial Relations", *International Journal of Geographical Information Systems,* 5(2), (1991) 161-174.
7. Egenhofer, M. and Herring, J.: Categorizing Binary Topological Relationships Between Regions, Lines, and Points in Geographic Databases, *Technical Report of the Department of Surveying Engineering*, University of Maine, Orono, ME, (1991).
8. Frank, A.: "Qualitative Spatial Reasoning about Cardinal Directions", *Autocarto 10,* D. Mark and D. White, eds., Baltimore, MD, (1991) 148-167.
9. Randall, D. and Lenat, D.: *Knowledge-Based Systems in Artificial Intelligence.* Advanced Computer Science Series, Mc Graw Hill, (1982).

10. Verastegui, K.: Conceptualization of Geometrical Aspects of Geospatial Data, *Proceedings of the First International Conference on Geospatial Semantics*, Poster Session GeoS 2005. ISBN: 970-36-0304-2 (2005).
11. Rosales, M.: Semantic Topological Descriptor for Topographic Maps, *Proceedings of the First International Conference on Geospatial Semantics*, Poster Session GeoS 2005. ISBN: 970-36-0304-2 (2005).
12. Townsend, C.: *Mastering Expert Systems with Turbo Prolog*. Howard W. Sams & Company, First Edition, (1987).
13. Torres, M., Moreno, M., Quintero, R. and Fonseca, F.: Ontology-driven description of spatial data for their semantic processing. *Proceedings of the First International Conference on Geospatial Semantics*, Springer-Verlag, 3799, Mexico City, Mexico (2005) 242-249.

Search Method of Time Sensitive Frequent Itemsets in Data Streams

Tae-Su Park[1], Ju-Hong Lee[2], Sang-Ho Park[1], Bumghi Choi[2] , and Deok-Hwan Kim[3]

[1,2] Dept. of Computer Science & Information Engineering, Inha University, Incheon, Korea
{taesu, parksangho}@datamining.inha.ac.kr,
{juhong, neural}@inha.ac.kr
[3] Dept. of Electronics Engineering, Inha University
deokhwan@inha.ac.kr

Abstract. Recently, due to technical improvements of storage devices and networks, the amount of data increases rapidly. In addition, it is required to find the knowledge embedded in a data stream as fast as possible. Data stream is influenced by time. Therefore, the itemsets which were not the frequent itemsets can become frequent itemsets. The volume of data stream is so large that it can hardly be stored in finite memory space. Current researches do not offer appropriate method to find frequent itemsets in which flow of time is reflected but provide only frequent items using total aggregation values. In this paper we propose a novel algorithm for finding the relative frequent itemsets according to the time in a data stream. We also propose a method to save frequent items and sub-frequent items in order to take limited memory into account and a method to update time variant frequent items. By applying the proposed technique, we can improve the accuracy of searching for a change in the frequent itemsets according to the time in a data stream. Moreover, it will be able to use the limited memory space efficiently and store all frequent itemsets.

Keywords: Data Stream, Frequent Itemsets, Data Mining.

1 Introduction

Recently, due to technical improvements of storage devices and network developments, data continues to increase in a very short time. Huge amount of data, for example, have been generated in many fields of applications, such as network invasion detection, sensor network and e-commerce. Many efforts have been made to extract valuable information from such application environments. One of the key realms of research is to extract information from data streams through a data mining method.

A data stream is data that continues to be inputted at high speed. In data streams, data continues to increase at high speed. So, there are two requirements for dealing with data streams by a data mining method.

First, since it is impossible to store large increments of data in a limited space, a new method is required to efficiently store data without losing information by using memory space flexibly.

Second, it is imperative to generate mining results at request because data streams generate large amounts of data in a short time period and the result of mining must be

J.F. Martínez-Trinidad et al. (Eds.): CIARP 2006, LNCS 4225, pp. 511 – 518, 2006.

output immediately. This implies that the mining result must be generated by one reading of each transaction of data streams.[3]

One of the most fundamental challenges of data streams is to find frequent itemsets [4]. The conventional data mining method takes a lot of time and memory because it initially reads off from static transactions to compose candidates for frequent itemsets, and then searches for items that have values higher than the defined threshold.

In data streams, items that weren't regarded as frequent itemsets can be converted over time. Thus, it is necessary to update actively and store the frequency of each item. In addition, all unit items cannot be stored because of continuous inputs of too much data in data streams, which makes it improper to apply the conventional data mining method. Many researchers come up with new algorithms that can search for frequent itemsets in data streams [2, 3, 4, 5, 6, 7, 8, 9, 10, 11].

Frequent itemset searching methods in data streams, however, can't guarantee the reliability of the search because they merely aggregate and search for frequent itemsets or find them within a time, or a range, after randomly setting a certain size of sliding window. In addition, they again aggregate the total frequent itemsets as time goes by, which results in failure to demonstrate efficiently current changes in frequent itemsets and overlooks frequent itemsets converted over time.

To solve these problems, this paper proposes a new mining method which searches for frequent itemsets more efficiently, taking into account time in data streams.

This paper has 5 sections including the introduction. Section 2 describes related works and section 3 proposes a method to search for frequent itemsets. Performance of the proposed method is evaluated in section 4 through various experiments. Section 5 gives the conclusion and suggestions for improvement.

2 Relate Works

Conventional data mining methods search frequent itemsets by searching max itemsets with a support higher than the predefined minimum support, which were derived by simple searching transactions of the database. Most of algorithms on frequent itemsets are based on the principle of Apriori [1]. This principle states that all subset of frequent itemsets must also be frequent itemsets. When a frequent itemset has a full rank of n, the Apriori algorithm searches up to $n+1$ to generate candidate sets and then begins to search a frequent itemset. Therefore, the Apriori algorithm requires a big memory and a lot of time due to repetitive database searches.

On the other hand, the FP-growth using a divide-and-conquer method does not generate candidate sets [8].

FP-growth is very efficient in mining either long or short frequent itemsets and has a feature of expandability. It also proves to be much faster than the Apriori algorithm. But, both methods must search data sets more than once and must re-search the whole database every time whenever a new transaction takes place. Moreover, when a data set continues to increase at a fast pace, performance drops due to a limited memory.

Data is being generated very quickly due to advanced storage devices and network development. These data are called data stream. Many researchers are studying frequent itemset searching methods in data streams [2, 3, 4, 5, 6, 7, 8, 9, 10, 11].

The Count Sketch algorithm focuses on frequency of unit items in data streams [4], and the Lossy Counting algorithm searches for frequent itemsets in data streams only when a minimum support and a maximum allowable error are given [9]. These algorithms only focus on finding the frequent itemsets without taking account of time.

The Moment algorithm, which can search for not only frequent itemsets in a sliding window using limited available memory, but also items close to frequent itemsets. This algorithm uses a tree structure similar to a prefix tree known as CET (Closed Enumeration Tree) [6]. CET stores maximally frequent itemsets, frequent itemsets and approximate frequent itemsets. Thus, it can recognize the changes in frequent itemsets over time and search for frequent itemsets managing the memory efficiently.

The FP-stream algorithm is a revision of the FP-growth algorithm to better fit for data streams [7]. This algorithm classifies data sets into a frequent itemset, a sub frequent itemset and a non-frequent itemset by using a minimum support and maximum allowable errors. It uses a Pattern tree and a tilted time window. Also, it accumulates frequent itemsets up to the current point by storing them in a pattern tree and utilizing a fixed window, a tilted time window and recognizes the latest changes in frequent itemsets efficiently. However, unfixed frequent itemsets are difficult to search for since it uses only fixed time slots.

3 Frequent Itemset Search in Data Streams

3.1 Searching for Relatively Frequent Itemsets

In data streams, data continues to accumulate at a fast rate. This is why the data cannot be stored in a conventional way. Also, a data stream is affected by time, changing the frequent itemset over time. Therefore Non-frequent itemsets can't be discarded or overlooked. To resolve such problems effectively, we classifies data into 3 groups, *frequent itemsets*, *sub frequent itemsets*, and *non-frequent itemsets*, by using a predetermined minimum support and maximum support error, as in the FP-stream[7] algorithm. The FP-stream algorithm uses fixed time window, but our method uses unfixed time window due to find relative frequent itemset. If the frequency is greater than the minimum support value, it is considered *a frequent itemset*. When the frequency is below the minimum support value but has a greater error than the predetermined maximum error, it is classified as *a sub frequent itemset*. Data is disregarded when it has less value than the maximum support error.

The conventional methods search frequent itemsets only by comparing the aggregate values between frequent itemsets and sub frequent itemsets. Hence, time-sensitive and relatively frequent itemsets cannot be accounted for. This implies a necessity of a method to take account of items with a relative frequency of appearance higher than the currently frequent itemsets, even though a value aggregated up to now is smaller than the currently frequent itemsets. Therefore, we define the relatively frequent itemsets as follows:

A relatively frequent itemset is defined as a set of items having a frequency smaller than total frequency of the currently frequent itemsets but greater than current frequency (not total frequency) of the currently frequent itemset, f refers to the currently frequent itemset.

Table 1. Elements of relative frequent itemset

Symbol	Mean
N	Total number of transactions
m	Number of consecutive transactions
f	A frequent itemset
h_t	Time that occurs t'th transactions
T_t	t'th transaction
R_t	Relative Frequent itemset at time of t'th transactions
$A_i(x)$	Appearance function of x in i'th transactions
$F(x)$	Frequency of item x
$C_{m,t}(x)$	Interval of appearance of item x with fixed m and time t'th transactions
$E_{m,t}(x)$	Relative frequency of item x with fixed m and time t'th transacions

$$R_t = \{x \mid F(f) > F(x),\ E_{m,t}(x) > E_{m,t}(f)\} \tag{1}$$

A relative frequency can be regarded as the number of consecutive transactions (m) divided by the sum of differences among intervals of appearances. This is the starting point of finding the relatively frequent itemsets.

$$E_{m,t}(x) = \frac{m}{C_{m,t}(x)}\ ,\quad C_{m,t}(x) = h_t - h_{t-m+1} \tag{2}$$

Also, a frequency is an aggregate value of appearance of a specific item in continuous transactions.

$$F(x) = \sum_{i=1}^{N} A_i(x)\ ,\quad A_i(x) = \begin{cases} 1 & x \in T_i \\ 0 & otherwise \end{cases} \tag{3}$$

Also, the difference of each interval of appearance is meaningful in such that it can determine the time when relatively frequent itemsets exist. It represents a time difference between its current appearance time and the previous appearance time. The y_t implies the point of time when a transaction T_t containing item x happens.

We examine relative frequent itemsets based upon the abovementioned materials. Figure 1 depicts the concept of relatively frequent itemsets. Where each x, y, z is a frequent itemset with a value greater than the minimum support or a sub frequent itemset with a value smaller than the minimum support but greater than the maximal support error, and each dot on the arrow is the frequency. T_t stands for transactions up to now. Here, window size is user-defined because window size effects the result, also, the window not overlapped previous that. In the first row x, we see that the frequency is 28, the highest among the three, implying a frequent itemset. The second and third rows are sub frequent itemsets. By examining Figure 1, we see that the first item shows high frequency in the early period but is dispersed gradually as time goes by. The second row shows a sharp increase in frequency in the middle of the row. Seemingly, it makes more sense to designate the second item as the frequent itemset in this specific time period since it appears more frequently than the past, and even more than the first item which is the currently frequent itemset. Thus, the second item becomes the relatively frequent itemset compared to the first item in the middle part of the time period.

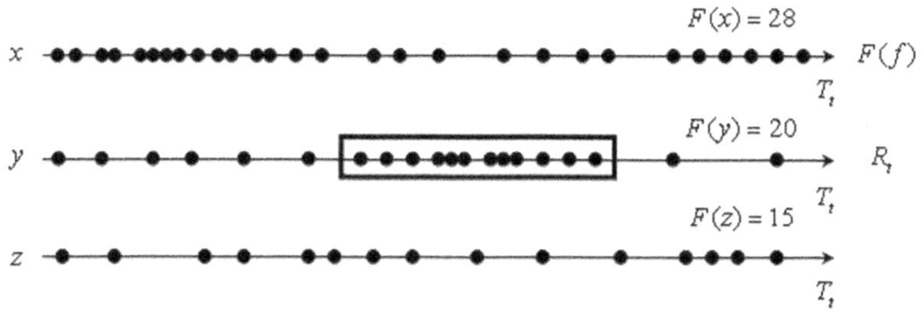

Fig. 1. Concept of relative frequent itemset

The important point here is to find the time when it begins to become a relatively frequent itemset. Therefore, this study suggests a standard for relatively frequent itemsets as follows:

1. A relative frequency must be greater than the relative frequency of frequent itemsets.

$$E_{m,t}(f) < E_{m,t}(x) \tag{4}$$

2. The appearance time of a relatively frequent itemset is the interval from the time(a) to the time(b). a is the latest time at which the currently relative frequency is larger than the just previous relative frequency. b is the latest time at which the currently relative frequency is less than zero.

$$E_{m,a-1}(x) \le E_{m,a}(x)\,,\ E_{m,b-1}(x) > E_{m,b}(x),\ a > b \tag{5}$$

That is, it is the time period when a relatively frequency of frequent itemsets becomes higher and the interval between each appearance has becomes very short, compared to the frequent itemset. This study takes the relative frequencies only to tenths for generalizing the numbers and easing the calculation process.

3.2 Storing Method Using the FP-Tree Algorithm

In this section, we suggest an efficient storing method using the FP-Tree algorithm of a prefix tree structure that can maintain and manage all frequent itemsets and relatively frequent itemsets within a limited memory.

As stated earlier, a data stream is assumed to be an infinite set of data. It follows that all data cannot be stored. Hence, the FP-Tree stores only three kinds of key relevant information, items, frequency and TID, to maintain and manage frequent itemsets and relative frequent itemsets efficiently. Here, items mean either frequent itemsets or relatively frequent items, and frequency refers to the total number of appearance of such items. TID refers to the current transaction id, which is used to measure the starting point of a relatively frequent itemset.

The FP-Tree algorithm has four main steps, each of which is reiterated when a new transaction is added.

The first step is a phase where data stream transactions are searched to update the frequency of each item. The total dataset $|S_N|$ is incremented by 1 when a new transaction occurs. The frequency and TID values are updated when items appearing in such a new transaction happen to exist in a node of FP-Tree.

The second step is a phase where a sub frequent itemset is added. When there is no node in the FP-Tree corresponding to the items that appear in the new transaction, items with a value smaller than the minimum support but greater than the maximum support error are added to the FP-Tree node as sub frequent itemsets. Those with errors smaller than the maximum allowable error are discarded in that it has little chance to become frequent itemsets. It results in less performing time because it uses less memory and reduces a process to insert new nodes to the FP-Tree.

The third step is searching for the currently frequent itemset. Upon users' request, this step outputs those items' information, items, frequency and TID, with the greatest total frequency up to now and a support more than the minimum support value.

The fourth step is searching for the relatively frequent itemset. When the relative frequency of a frequent itemset becomes bigger, that is, when the intervals become much shorter, searching items that appear relatively more frequently than the current frequent itemset starts at this step.

This method guarantees reliability and accuracy by searching not only the currently frequent itemset but also the relatively frequent itemset which can be easily overlooked, moreover, it can efficiently utilize the limited memory because it holds only three kinds of information, items, frequency and TID.

4 Test and Evaluation

Our algorithm was written in C and compiled using gcc. The stream data was generated by the IBM test data generator [1]. Generated datasets are T10.I4.D1000K and T15.I6.1000K, where the numbers denotes the average transaction size (T), the average large itemset size (I) and the number of transactions respectively.

The experiment evaluated the accuracy and memory space of the proposed method in comparison with Lossy Counting algorithm [9]. Jeffrey Xu Yu's method is using less memory than Lossy Counting algorithm[10]. James Cheng's method runs faster than Lossy Counting algorithm[5]. Figure 2 shows the results of this experiment.

The Lossy counting algorithm using a minimum support finds frequent itemsets through the aggregation. Therefore if the number of transactions is small, then the accuracy of the Lossy counting algorithm is low. On the other hand, the proposed method finds frequent itemsets with relative frequent itemsets as time goes by.

Although the number of transactions is small, the proposed method achieves better accuracy than the Lossy counting algorithm. As the number of transactions increases, the accuracy of both methods is getting higher because transactions include more frequent itemsets.

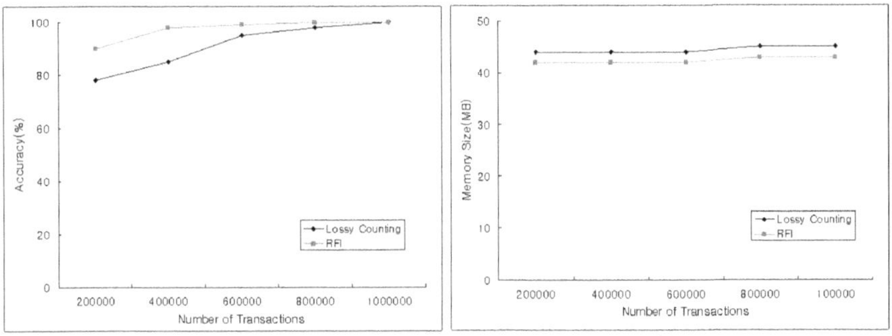

(a) (b)

Fig. 2. The result of experiment according to the accuracy and memory space; a) Accuracy according to the number of transactions, b) Memory size according to the number of transactions

Fig. 2 (b) shows the memory size according to the number of transactions. Above all, we must find the optimal minimum support value. Because too low minimum support value leads to a wide range of permission for frequent itemsets and too high minimum support value leads to a narrow range of permission for those. Here, minimum support value sets 0.3 according to our experiments. In the proposed method, the FP-Tree stores only three kinds of key relevant information, items, frequency and TID, to maintain and manage frequent itemsets and relative frequent itemsets efficiently. Therefore, it is clear that the proposed method uses less memory space than the Lossy counting algorithm.

As shown above, we can see that the proposed method find the frequent itemsets more accurately and our method is able to compute all frequent itemsets using less memory than the Lossy Counting algorithm.

5 Conclusion

One of the most fundamental problems in data streams is how to search frequent itemsets generated from the stream. The frequent itemsets change because the stream itself is affected by time. Therefore Non-frequent itemsets can not be discarded. Data streams may be defined as infinite sets of data, making it impossible to store every item in the stream. To solve these problems, we introduced relatively frequent items and the FP-Tree algorithm in this paper.

We classify data into 3 groups, frequent itemsets, sub frequent itemsets, and non-frequent itemsets, by using a predetermined minimum support and maximum support error. The suggested algorithm computes the total number of frequencies and relative frequencies derived from intervals between frequencies using unfixed time window. It searches the frequent itemset and, by comparing relative frequencies of sub frequent itemsets, the relatively frequent itemset that can be easily overlooked. The FP-Tree tries to efficiently manage frequent itemsets and sub frequent itemsets by storing only 3 kinds of information, items, frequency and TID. The FP-Tree has four main steps, updating the frequency of each item, adding a sub frequent itemset, searching for the currently frequent itemset, searching for the relative frequent itemset. All these enable us to search time-sensitive frequent itemsets, to increase reliability of the searches and to utilize limited memory efficiently.

Acknowledgement. This work was supported by INHA university Research Grant.

References

1. R. Agrawal and R. Srikant.: Fast algorithms for mining association rules. In Proc. of the 20th Intl. Conf. on Very Large Databases (1994)
2. B. Babcock, S. Babu, M. Datar, R. Motwani, and J. Widom.: Models and issues in data stream systems. In Proc. of SIGMOD/PODS, Madison, Wisconsin, USA (2002) 1–16
3. J. Chang. and W. Lee.: Finding recent frequent itemsets adaptively over online data Streams. In Proc. of the 9th ACM SIGKDD Intl. Conf. on Knowledge Discovery & Data Mining, Washington, DC (2003) 226–235
4. M. Charikar, K. Chen, and M. Farach-Colton.: Finding frequent items in data streams. In Procedings of the International Colloquium on Automata, Languages and Programming (2002) 693–703
5. James Cheng, Yiping Ke, and Wilfred Ng, "Maintaining Frequent Itemsets over High-Speed Data Streams", PAKDD 2006
6. Y. Chi, H. Wang, P. Yu, and R. Muntz.: MOMENT: Maintaining closed frequent itemsets over a stream sliding window. In Proc. of 4th IEEE Intl. Conf. on Data Mining, Brighton, UK (2004) 59–66
7. C. Giannella, J. Han, J. Pei, X. Yan, and P.S. Yu.: Mining Frequent Patterns in Data Streams at Multiple Time Granularities. in H. Kargupta, A. Joshi, K. Sivakumar, and Y. Yesha (eds.), Next Generation Data Mining, AAAI/MIT (2003)
8. J. Han, J. Pei, and Y. Yin.: Mining frequent patterns without candidate generation. In Proceedings of the SIGMOD Conference, Dallas, Texas, USA: ACM Press (2000) 1–12
9. G. Manku and R. Motwani.: Approximate frequency counts over data streams. In Proceedings of 28th International Conference on Very Large Data Bases (2002) 346–357
10. Jeffrey Xu Yu, Zhihong Chong, Hongjun Lu, Aoying Zhou, "False Positive or False Negative : Mining Frequent Itemsets from High Speed Transactional Data Streams", VLDB 2004, 204-215
11. D. Zhang, D. Gunopulos, V. J. Tsotras and B. Seeger.: Temporal Aggregation over Data Streams using Multiple Granlarities. Proc. of 8th International Conference on Extending Database Technology (EDBT), Prague, Czech Republic (2002)

Image Compression Algorithm Based on Morphological Associative Memories

Enrique Guzmán[1], Oleksiy Pogrebnyak[2], Cornelio Yáñez[2], and José A. Moreno[1]

[1] Universidad Tecnológica de la Mixteca
{eguzman, jamoreno}@mixteco.utm.mx
[2] Centro de Investigación en Computación del Instituto Politécnico Nacional
{olek, cyanez}@pollux.cic.ipn.mx

Abstract. A new method for image compression based on Morphological Associative Memories (MAM) is proposed. We used MAM at the transformation stage of image coding, thereby replacing the traditional methods such as Discrete Cosine Transform or Wavelet Transform. After applying the MAM, the informative image data are concentrated in a minimum of values. The next stages of image coding can be obtained by taking advantage of this new representation of the image. The main advantage offered by the MAM with respect to the traditional methods is the speed of processing, whereas the compression rate and the obtained signal to noise ratios compete with the traditional methods.

Keywords: Image compression, Morphological Associative Memories, Morphological Hetroassociative Memories *min*.

1 Introduction

Traditional methods in image compression often use the Discrete Cosine Transform (DCT) or the Wavelet Transform at the data transformation stage. Actually, DCT is used in many image compression standards like JPEG, MPEG at image transformation stage [6], [7].

1992 was a vitally important period for the area of image compression. Ronald A. DeVore and his collaborators developed a mathematical theory that enables us to use the Wavelet Transform in image compression in [8]. Daubechies and his collaborators proposed a scheme for image compression by the use of the Wavelet Transform. This decomposition provides sub-images corresponding to different levels of resolution and orientation [9]. Lewis and Knowles propose a scheme for image compression based on the 2-D Wavelet Transform [10]. In this scheme, the image is separated into its spatial elements and spectral coefficients using the 2-D Wavelet Transform.

Various methods for coding of image wavelet coefficients are proposed. The first wavelet image coding algorithm "Embedded Zerotree Wavelet Algorithm" (EZW) was proposed by Shapiro in 1993 [11]. Next, Said and Pearlman in [12] proposed a new and better implementation of the EZW, the SPIHT algorithm (Seth Partitioning in Hierarchical Trees), based on the use of data sets organized in hierarchical trees. A new algorithm for image compression known as EBCOT (Embedded Block Coding

J.F. Martínez-Trinidad et al. (Eds.): CIARP 2006, LNCS 4225, pp. 519 – 528, 2006.

with Optimized Truncation) was proposed by Taubman in 2000 [13]. The Standard JPEG2000 is based fundamentally on the Discrete Wavelet Transform and Embedded Block Coding with Optimal Truncation (EBCOT) [14].

In this paper, a new method for image compression based on Morphological Associative Memories (MAM) created by Ritter, Sussner and Diaz de León in 1998 [15] is proposed. The operations in MAM are based on the morphological operations, dilation and erosion; in other words, they make use of maximums or minimums of sums [15]. This feature distinguishes them from the Hopfield memories [16], which use sums of products. The MAM have turned out to be an excellent tool for recognizing and recovering patterns, even if these display dilative, erosive or random noise [15], [17], [18].

We used MAM (to be more exactly, morphological heteroassociative memories) at the transformation stage of an image compression system. The main advantage offered by the MAM technique with respect to traditional methods used in this stage is the processing speed meanwhile the compression rate and the signal to noise ratio obtained compete with the traditional methods.

2 Morphological Associative Memories

The "**Mg**" generic associative memory scheme is shown in Figure 1, the input patterns and output patters are represented by **x** and **y** respectively.

Fig. 1. Associative memory scheme [23]

$$\mathbf{x}^T = (x_1, x_2, \ldots, x_n);\ \mathbf{y}^T = (y_1, y_2, \ldots, y_n) \tag{1}$$

n and m are integer positive numbers and represent the dimensions of the input and output patters respectively. Henceforth, let $\{(\mathbf{x}^1,\mathbf{y}^1),(\mathbf{x}^2,\mathbf{y}^2),\ldots,(\mathbf{x}^k,\mathbf{y}^k)\}$ be k vector pairs defined as the *fundamental set of associations* [18] that is represented by

$$\{(\mathbf{x}^\mu,\mathbf{y}^\mu) \mid \mu = 1, 2, \ldots, k\}\ . \tag{2}$$

The **Mg** associative memory is represented by a matrix and it is generated from the fundamental set of associations. Once the fundamental set is delineated, we define the necessary operations for the learning process and recovery process of a MAM; these operations make use of the maximum $\bigvee$ and minimum $\bigwedge$ operators [18], [19].

Let D be a column vector of dimension m, and F a row vector of dimension n, the *maximum product* is given by

$$D \,\nabla\, F = C = \left[c_{ij}\right]_{mxn}\ . \tag{3}$$

where $c_{ij} = (d_i + f_j)$. Ggeneralizing for a fundamental set of associations:

$$c_{ij} = \bigvee_{l=1}^{k} \left(d_{il} + f_{lj} \right) \tag{4}$$

The *minimum product* is given by

$$D \, \Delta \, F = C = \left[c_{ij} \right]_{mxn} \tag{5}$$

for a fundamental set of associations c_{ij} is defined by

$$c_{ij} = \bigwedge_{l=1}^{k} \left(d_{il} + f_{lj} \right) \tag{6}$$

On the other hand, let $D = \left[d_{ij} \right]_{mxn}$ be a matrix and $F = \left[f_i \right]_n$ a column vector, the calculation of the maximum product $D \nabla F$ gives as result a column vector $C = \left[c_i \right]_m$, where c_i is defined by

$$c_i = \bigvee_{j=1}^{n} \left(d_{ij} + f_j \right) \tag{7}$$

For the *minimum product* $C = D \, \Delta \, F$

$$c_i = \bigwedge_{j=1}^{n} \left(d_{ij} + f_j \right) \tag{8}$$

According to the mode of operation, the associative memories are classified in two groups:

- morphological auto-associative memories (MAAM).
- morphological hetero-associative memories (MHM).

2.1 Morphological Heteroassociative Memories *min*

A MAM is Hetero-associative if $\exists \mu \in \{1, 2, \ldots, k\}$ such that $\mathbf{x}^{\mu} \neq \mathbf{y}^{\mu}$. There are two types of MHM: *max*, symbolized by **M**, and *min*, symbolized by **W**. The MHM *min* (**W**) are those that use the maximum product and the minimum operator in their learning phase and the maximum product in their recovery phase.

Learning Phase:

1. The matrices, $\mathbf{y}^{\mu} \nabla \left(-\mathbf{x}^{\mu} \right)^t$, are calculated for each one of the *k* elements of the fundamental set of associations $\left(\mathbf{x}^{\mu}, \mathbf{y}^{\mu} \right)$.

2. The **W** memory is obtained having applied the minimum operator $\wedge$ to the resulting matrices of step 1. **W** is given by

$$\mathbf{W} = \bigwedge_{\mu=1}^{k} \left[\mathbf{y}^{\mu} \nabla \left(-\mathbf{x}^{\mu} \right)^t \right] = \left[w_{ij} \right]_{mxn}, \; w_{ij} = \bigwedge_{\mu=1}^{k} \left(y_i^{\mu} - x_j^{\mu} \right) \tag{9}$$

Recovery Phase:

1. The maximum product $\mathbf{W} \nabla \mathbf{x}^{\omega}$ is calculated, where $\omega \in \{1, 2, \ldots, k\}$, obtaining a column vector $\mathbf{y} = \left[y_i \right]_m$, which represent the output patterns associated with $\mathbf{x}^{\omega}$ input patterns,

$$\mathbf{y} = \mathbf{W} \nabla \mathbf{x}^{\omega}, \quad y_i = \bigvee_{j=1}^{n} \left(w_{ij} + x_j^{\omega} \right) \tag{10}$$

Theorem 2 and Corollary 2.1 of [20] govern the conditions that must be satisfied by MHM *min* to obtain a perfect recall to output patterns.

Theorem 2: $\mathbf{W} \nabla \mathbf{x}^{\omega} = \mathbf{y}^{\omega} \ \forall \omega = 1,\ldots,k$ if and only if for each ω and each row index $i = 1,\ldots,m$ there are column indexes $j_i^{\omega} \in \{1,\ldots,n\}$ such that $m_{ij_i^{\omega}} = y_i^{\omega} - x_{j_i^{\omega}}^{\omega}$ $\forall \omega = 1,\ldots,k$. **Corollary 2.1:** $\mathbf{W} \nabla \mathbf{x}^{\omega} = \mathbf{y}^{\omega} \ \forall \omega = 1,\ldots,k$ if and only if for each row index $i = 1,\ldots,m$ and each $\gamma \in \{1,\ldots,k\}$ there is a column index $j_i^{\gamma} \in \{1,\ldots,n\}$ such that

$$\mathbf{x}_{j_i^{\gamma}}^{\gamma} = \bigvee_{\varepsilon=1}^{k} \left(x_{j_i^{\gamma}}^{\varepsilon} - y_i^{\varepsilon} \right) + y_i^{\gamma} \tag{11}$$

On the other hand, Theorem 6 of [20] indicates the amount of noise that is permissible in the input patterns to obtain a perfect recall to output patterns.

Theorem 6: For $\gamma = 1,\ldots,k$, let $\tilde{\mathbf{x}}^{\gamma}$ be a corrupted input pattern of $\mathbf{x}^{\gamma}$. Then $\mathbf{W} \nabla \tilde{\mathbf{x}}^{\gamma} = \mathbf{y}^{\gamma}$ if and only if it satisfies that

$$\tilde{x}_j^{\gamma} \le x_j^{\gamma} \vee \bigwedge_{i=1}^{m} \left(\bigvee_{\varepsilon \neq \gamma} \left[y_i^{\gamma} - y_i^{\varepsilon} + x_i^{\varepsilon} \right] \right) \forall j = 1,\ldots,n \tag{12}$$

and for each row index $i \in \{1,\ldots,m\}$ there is a column index $j_i \in \{1,\ldots,n\}$ such that:

$$\tilde{x}_{ji}^{\gamma} = x_{ji}^{\gamma} \vee \left(\bigvee_{\varepsilon \neq \gamma} \left[y_i^{\gamma} - y_i^{\varepsilon} + x_{ji}^{\varepsilon} \right] \right) \tag{13}$$

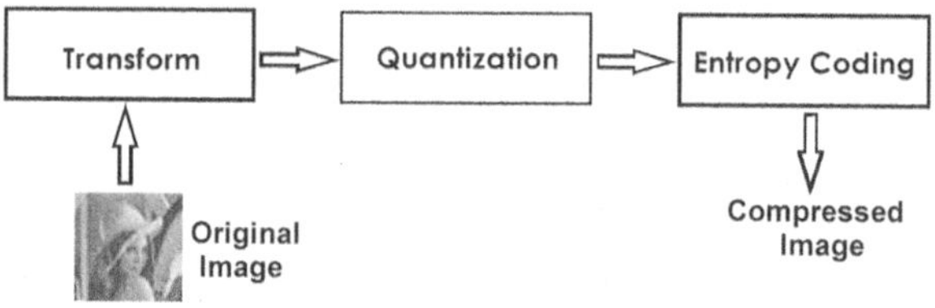

Fig. 2. Scheme of image compression system

3 Image Transformation Using MHM *min*

An image compression system can be composed of three principal stages shown in Figure 2. The transformation stage is the main focus of this study; traditional methods of image compression use the DCT or the Wavelet transform in this stage. We propose the use of the MAM in the transformation stage. MAM satisfies the features of a transformation method: the transformed MAM information is concentrated into a minimum of values; the transformed MAM is reversible; the MAM has low memory requirements, uses limited arithmetical precision, and few arithmetical operations.

Let image **A** is divided into **N** $m' \times n'$ sub-matrix or image blocks, obtaining $\mathbf{N} = (m/m') \cdot (n/n')$ blocks, each of these blocks is divided into m' vectors of dimension n'; these vectors represent the output patterns, $\mathbf{y}^{m'} = [y_i]_{n'}$, of the MHM *min*. On the other hand, the input patterns must be known for both image coding and image decoding; besides, the generation of these input patterns is governed by Theorem 2 and the Corollary 2.1 of [20]. m' input patterns of dimension n' are created

$$\begin{aligned} \mathbf{x}^1 &= [x_1^1, x_2^1, x_3^1, \ldots, x_{n'}^1] \\ \mathbf{x}^2 &= [x_1^2, x_2^2, x_3^2, \ldots, x_{n'}^2] \\ \mathbf{x}^3 &= [x_1^3, x_2^3, x_3^3, \ldots, x_{n'}^3] \\ &\vdots \\ \mathbf{x}^{m'} &= [x_1^{m'}, x_2^{m'}, x_3^{m'}, \ldots, x_{n'}^{m'}] \end{aligned} \tag{14}$$

To satisfy Theorem 2 and the Corollary 2.1, choose the elements of the input patterns with the following conditions:

$$x_{n'}^{m'} \begin{cases} = 0 & si \;\; m' \neq n' \\ > a & si \;\; m' = n'; \forall a \in \mathbf{A} \end{cases} \tag{15}$$

Where a is the maximum value that can take an element of the **A** matrix. Once the input and output patterns are defined, **W** is obtained by applying (9) to every sub-matrix of the image with the set of chosen input patterns shown in Figure 3.

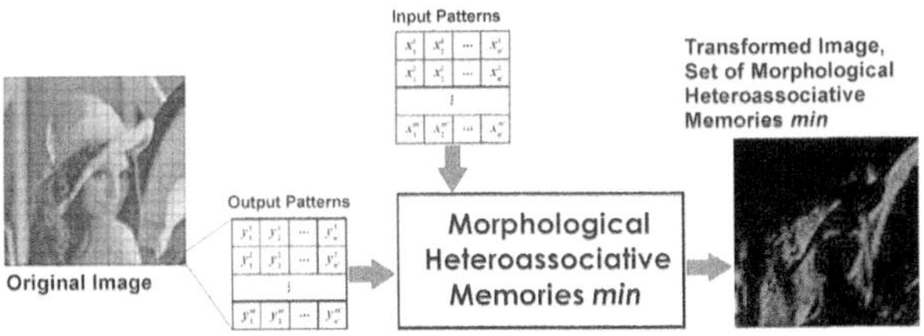

Fig. 3. Scheme of the MHM *min* applied to an image

As a result of applying a MHM *min* to an image, **N** $m' \times n'$ associative memories **W** are obtained. The image information remains concentrated in a minimum of values. It is possible to take advantage of this new representation of the image in the following stages of image coding.

The next stage of image coding is a uniform scalar quantization. This stage modifies each of the associative memories **W.** Lets remember that the perfect recall to output patterns is based on the fact that noise appears in the input patterns and not in the associative memories; how, then, does it affect this noise in the associative memory for the recovery of the original output patterns (blocks of the original image)?

To answer this question, let $\tilde{\mathbf{W}}$ be a corrupted version of the associative memory $\mathbf{W}$:

$$\begin{aligned}\tilde{\mathbf{W}} &= \mathbf{W} \pm r \\ \tilde{w}_{ij} &= w_{ij} \pm r\end{aligned} \tag{16}$$

where r represents the noise associated with $\mathbf{W}$.

Considering Theorem 2, its respective Corollary 2.1 and Theorem 3 of [15], we have $\mathbf{y}^{\gamma} = \mathbf{W}\,\nabla\,\mathbf{x}^{\gamma}$, bearing in mind the corrupted version of the associative memory, then $\mathbf{y}^{\gamma} = \tilde{\mathbf{W}}\,\nabla\,\mathbf{x}^{\gamma}$.

The equation (17) shows that the noise r associated with the associative memory directly affects the output patterns and the perfect recovery of the image.

$$\begin{aligned}\left(\mathbf{W}\nabla\mathbf{x}^{\gamma}\right)_i &= \bigvee_{j=1}^{n}\left(\tilde{w}_{ij} + x_j^{\gamma}\right) \geq \tilde{w}_{ij_i} + x_j^{\gamma} = \tilde{w}_{ij_i} + \left(\bigvee_{\varepsilon=1}^{k}\left(x_{j_i}^{\varepsilon} - y_i^{\varepsilon}\right) + y_i^{\gamma}\right) \\ &= \tilde{w}_{ij_i} + y_i^{\gamma} - \bigwedge_{\varepsilon=1}^{k}\left(y_i^{\varepsilon} - x_{j_i}^{\varepsilon}\right) = \tilde{w}_{ij_i} + y_i^{\gamma} - w_{ij_i} = w_{ij_i} \pm r + y_i^{\gamma} - w_{ij_i} = y_i^{\gamma} \pm r\end{aligned} \tag{17}$$

The noise r is associated with the set of associative memories and depends directly on the quantization factor Q used. As a uniform scalar quantization is used, then each of the associative memories is modified as $\tilde{\mathbf{W}} = \mathbf{W}/Q$.

This process is realized using R numbers to facilitate the coding process, $\tilde{\mathbf{W}}$ is truncated to Z numbers by

$$\tilde{\mathbf{W}} = \begin{cases}\tilde{\mathbf{W}} - 1 & \text{if} \quad \tilde{\mathbf{W}}^{\mathbf{R}} - \tilde{\mathbf{W}}^{\mathbf{Z}} \leq -0.5 \\ \tilde{\mathbf{W}} & \text{if} \quad \tilde{\mathbf{W}}^{\mathbf{R}} - \tilde{\mathbf{W}}^{\mathbf{Z}} > -0.5\end{cases},$$

where $\tilde{\mathbf{W}}^{\mathbf{R}} \in$ R, $\tilde{\mathbf{W}}^{\mathbf{Z}} \in$ Z is the integer part of $\tilde{\mathbf{W}}^{\mathbf{R}}$. The $\tilde{\mathbf{W}}$ range is $[-249,-13]$, if the recovery value of $\mathbf{W}$ is given for $\tilde{\mathbf{W}} \times Q$, then noise added to associative memory $\mathbf{W}$ is from 0 % to 23 %, and this will directly affect the output patterns or sub-blocks of the image.

The range of $\tilde{\mathbf{W}}$ was obtained from three image fields that Y, Cb and Cr. The range of noise was obtained from all the levels of quantification, therefore, the highest percentage of noise corresponds to $Q = 10$. Due to characteristics of the quantization, the percentage of noise does not affect the entire image, only a very low percentage of elements of the same.

3.2 Decoding Process

After the stages of entropy decoding and inverse quantification, the recovery process is applied using the set of associative memories.

Once the image is transformed into a set of associative memories and knowing the input patterns, the image transformation using MHM *min* is reversible (see Fig. 4).

When dealing with MMH *min,* the inverse transformation process makes use of the maximum product $\mathbf{W}\,\nabla\,\mathbf{x}^{\omega}$, where $\omega \in \{1, 2, \ldots, k\}$, the input patterns $\mathbf{x}$ are defined in

(14) and **W** is an associative memory belonging to the set that forms the transformed image. As a result a set of vectors $\mathbf{y}^{m'} = [y_i]_{n'}$ are obtained that represent a block of the original recovery image. Since the associative memory **W** is affected by noise, then $\tilde{\mathbf{W}} \nabla \mathbf{x}^{\gamma} = \tilde{\mathbf{y}}^{\gamma}$.

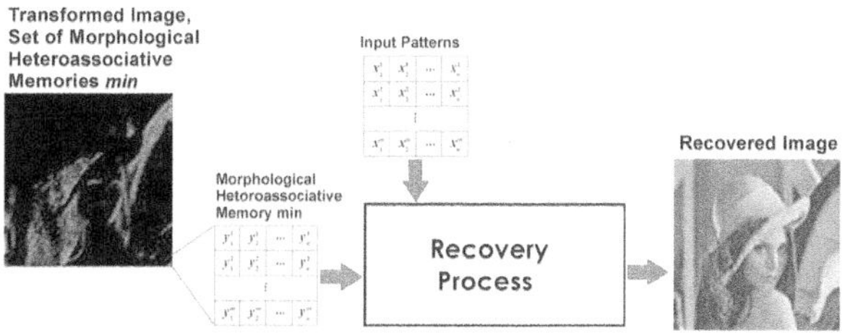

Fig. 4. Recovery algorithm scheme

4 Results

The test images are: Lena 512x512, Foreman 352x288 and Akiyo 176x144. The result of applying the MHM *min* to these images can be seen in Figure 5.

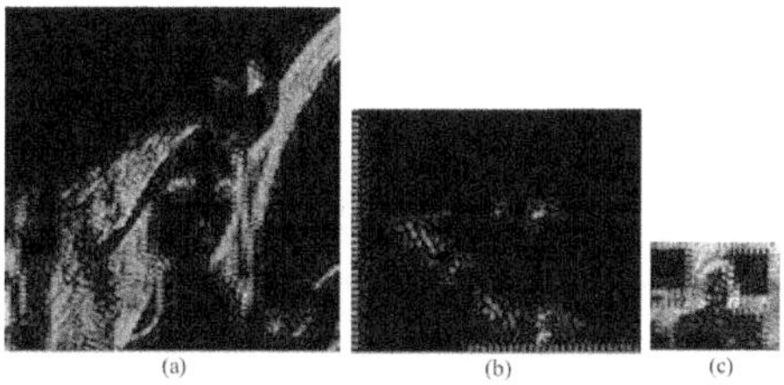

Fig. 5. Results of applying the MMH *min* on Y of: (a) Lena 512x512, (b) Foreman 352x288, (c) Akiyo 176x144.

The image transformed by MHM *min* is quantified using an uniform scalar quantization. Then, standard methods of codification were applied. Such methods include statistical coding, such as arithmetical, Huffman, range and PPM, and dictionary coding, LZ77 and LZP. The results of compression using MHM *min* on Lena, at different levels of quantification and using diverse codifiers of entropy, is available in Table 1.

From these results one can conclude that the coder which offers best results of compression and signal to noise ratio obtained on the image transformed by a MMH *min* is the PPM coding; it is an adaptive statistical method and its operation is based on partial equalization of chains, that is, PPM coding predicts the value of an element based on a sequence of previous elements.

The efficiency of the image coder based on an MAM was compared with results of other image compression methods, JPEG [21], [22], DCT *Based Embedded* [21], EZW [11], [22], SPIHT [12], [22], EBCOT [13], proving to be competitive with them in the characteristics of compression and signal to noise ratio, Table 2 and Fig. 5.

Table 1. Comparative results of applying MHM *min* and several coders on Lena

Coder	Morphological Heteroassociative Memories *min* (8x8 block) Lena (512x512=786486 bytes, 24 bpp)					
	Q=1 PSNR=44.19	Q=2 PSNR=42.14	Q=4 PSNR=38.12	Q=6 PSNR=35.08	Q=8 PSNR=32.84	Q=10 PSNR=31.02
Range	108238 bytes	95971 bytes	84246 bytes	77937 bytes	74124 bytes	69919 bytes
Comp. ratio	7.27:1	8.19:1	9.33:1	10.09:1	10.61:1	11.25:1
Bit rate	3.3 bpp	2.93 bpp	2.57 bpp	2.38 bpp	2.26 bpp	2.13 bpp
LZ77	76903 bytes	56420 bytes	37893 bytes	30201 bytes	25041 bytes	20386 bytes
Comp. ratio	10.23:1	13.94:1	20.75:1	26.04:1	31.41:1	38.58:1
Bit rate	2.35 bpp	1.72 bpp	1.16 bpp	0.92 bpp	0.76 bpp	0.62 bpp
LZP	74727 bytes	58393 bytes	40478 bytes	31505 bytes	27059 bytes	20801 bytes
Comp. ratio	10.52:1	13.47:1	19.43:1	24.96:1	29.06:1	37.81:1
Bit rate	2.28 bpp	1.78 bpp	1.24 bpp	0.96 Bpp	0.83 bpp	0.63 bpp
PPM	46504 bytes	32858 bytes	21682 bytes	16793 bytes	14205 bytes	11426 bytes
Comp. ratio	16.91:1	23.93:1	36.27:1	46.83:1	55.36:1	68.83:1
Bit rate	1.42 bpp	1 bpp	0.66 bpp	0.51 bpp	0.43 bpp	0.35 bpp

Table 2. Comparison between MMH *min* and traditional methods on Lena 512x512

Lena 512x512	Bit Rate	PSNR
Bseline JPEG [21], [22]	0.25	31.6
	0.50	34.9
DCT-Based Embedded [21]	0.25	32.25
	0.50	36.0
EZW [11], [22]	0.25	33.17
	0.50	36.28
SPIHT [12], [22]	0.25	34.1
	0.50	37.2
EBCOT [13]	0.25	34.40
	0.50	37.49
MHM *min*	0.43	32.84
	0.51	35.08

Table 3. Processing speed comparison between MHM *min*, DCT and DWT on Lena 512x512

	Number of operations
Discrete Cosine Transform	7,340,032 sums, 1, 310,720 multiplications
Wavelet Transform (three-stage)	1,032,192 sums, 344,064 shifts
MHM *min*	262,144 sums, 262,144 comparisons

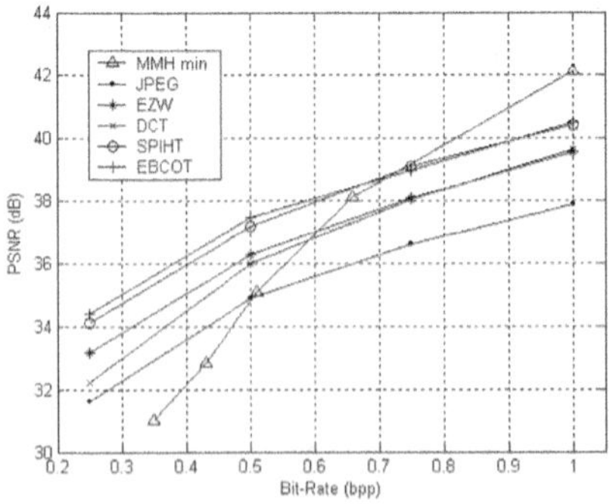

Fig. 6. MMH *min* in comparison to traditional methods on Lena 512x512

Morphological associative memories were shown to be a more efficient transformation process in the processing speed with regard to the traditional methods of transformation. Table 3 shows the number of operations the MHM *min*, the DCT and the WT needed to transform the image Lena 512x512.

5 Conclusions

The use of Morphological Associative Memories in the transformation stage of an image compressor has demonstrated a high competitiveness in its efficiency compared to traditional methods based on DCT or wavelet transform. Furthermore, a MAM has low computational complexity since its calculation is based on operations of comparisons and sums. A better response in the signal to noise ratio can be achieved using associative morphologic bidirectional memories (AMBM) that are robust to random noise.

The quantization process used in this coder is the simplest and thereby offers limited efficiency in compression. Vector quantization is an alternative method that can be used to obtain better results of compression ratio and signal to noise ratio. By basing its functioning on an algorithm of search of equalization, vector quantization makes it a slow process and of considerable computational complexity..

Acknowledgements. This study was supported by the Centro de Investigación en Computación of the Instituto Politécnico Nacional as part of research project CGPI No. 2004285.

References

1. N. Ahmed, T. Natrajan and K. R. Rao. "Discrete Cosine Transform". *IEEE Transactions on Computer*, Vol. 23, 1974, pp. 90-93.
2. W. H. Chen, C. H. Smith and S.C Fralick. "A Fast Computational Algorithm for the Discrete Cosine Transform". *IEEE Transactions on Communications*, Vol. COM-25, 1977, pp. 1004-1009.
3. Y. Arai, T. Agui y M. Nakajima. "A Fast DCT-SQ Scheme for Image" *Transactions of the IEICE*, Vol. E 71, No 11, 1988, pp. 1095-1097.
4. B. D. Tseng and W. C. Miller. "On Computing the Discrete Cosine Transform". *IEEE Transactions on Computer*, C-27, 10, 1978, pp. 966-968.
5. S. Winograd. "On Computing the Discrete Fourier Transform". *Proceedings of the National Academy of Sciences of the United States of America*, Vol. 73, No. 4, 1976, pp. 1005-1006.
6. G. K. Wallace. "The JPEG Still Picture Compression Standard". *Communications of the ACM*, Vol. 34, No. 4, 1991, pp. 30-44.
7. ISO, *Digital compression and coding of continuous-tone still images: Requirements and guidelines*, ISO/IEC IS 10918-1, 1994.
8. R. A. DeVore, B. Jawerth and B. J. Lucier. "Image Compression Through Wavelet Transform Coding". *IEEE Transactions on Information Theory*, Vol 38, No. 2, 1992, pp 719-746.

9. M. Antonini, M. Barlaud, P. Mathieu and I. Daubechies. "Image Coding Using Wavelet Transform". *IEEE Transactions on Image Processing*, Vol. 1, No. 2, 1992, pp. 205-220.
10. A. S. Lewis and G. Knowles. "Image Compression Using the 2-D Wavelet Transform". *IEEE Transactions on Image Processing*, Vol. 1, No. 2, 1992, pp. 244-250.
11. J. M. Shapiro. "Embedded Image Coding Using Zerotrees of Wavelet Coefficients". *IEEE Transactions on Signal Processing*, Vol. 41, No. 12, 1993, pp. 3445-3462.
12. A. Said and W. A. Pearlman. "A New, Fast, and Efficient Image Codec Based on Set Partitioning in Hierarchical Trees". *IEEE Transactions on Circuits and Systems for Video Technology*, Vol. 6, No. 3, 1996, pp. 243-250.
13. D. Taubman. "High Performance Scalable Image Compression with EBCOT". *IEEE Transactions on Image Processing*, Vol. 9, No. 7, 2000, pp. 1158-1170.
14. Joint Photographic Experts Group. *JPEG 2000 Part I* Final Committee Draft Version 1.0 ISO/IEC JTC 1/SC 29/WG 1, N1646R, (ITU-T SG8), 2000.
15. G. X. Ritter, P. Sussner and J. L. Díaz de León. "Morphological Associative Memories". *IEEE Transactions on Neural Networks*, Vol. 9, No. 2, 1998, pp. 281-293.
16. J. J. Hopfield. "Neural Networks and Physical Systems with Emergent Collective Computational Abilities". *Proceedings of the National Academy of Sciences of the USA*, Vol. 79, 1982, pp. 2554-2558.
17. C. Castellanos, J. L. Díaz De León y A. Sánchez. "Análisis Experimental con las Memorias Asociativas Morfológicas". *XXI Congreso Internacional de Ingeniería Electrónica, Electro 99*, Instituto Tecnológico de Chihuahua, Chih., México, 1999, pp. 11-16.
18. C. Yáñes y J. L. Díaz de León. *Memorias Morfológicas Heteroasociativas*. Centro de Investigación en Computación, IPN, México, IT 57, Serie Verde, ISBN 970-18-6697-5, 2001.
19. C. Yáñes y J. L. Díaz de León. *Memorias Morfológicas Autoasociativas*. Centro de Investigación en Computación, IPN, México, IT 58, Serie Verde, ISBN 970-18-6698-3, 2001.
20. G. X. Ritter, J. L. Díaz de León and P. Sussner. "Morphological Bidirectional Associative Memories". *Neural Networks*, Vol. 12, No. 6, 1999, pp. 851-867.
21. Z. Xiong, O. G. Guleryuz and M. T. Orchard. "A DCT-Based Embedded Image Coder". *IEEE Signal processing Letters*, Vol. 3, No. 11, 1996, pp. 289-290.
22. Z. Xiong, K. Ramchandran, M. T. Orchard and Y. Zhang. "A Comparative Study of DCT- and Wavelet-Based Image Coding". *IEEE Transactions on Circuits and Systems for Video Technology*, Vol 9, No 5, 1999, pp. 692-695.

A Novel Approach to Automatic Color Matching

Cornelio Yáñez, Edgardo Felipe-Riveron, I. López-Yáñez, and R. Flores-Carapia

Center for Computing Research, National Polytechnic Institute, Mexico,
Juan de Dios Batiz s/n, Col. Nueva Industrial Vallejo, C.P. 07738

Abstract. In this paper the design and operation of an Automatic Color Matching system is presented. This novel system takes advantage of the improvements introduced by Alpha-Beta associative memories, an efficient, unconventional model of associative memory of recent creation. The results are demonstrated through experiments on a relatively small database with 1001 samples prepared by the authors. However, the approach is considered valid according to the tendency of the results obtained, in part, thanks to the performance exhibited by Alpha-Beta associative memories.

Keywords: Color matching, Autoassociative memory, Alpha-Beta associative memories.

1 Introduction

Color mapping or color matching is a process by mean of which, a color is transformed to its visually closest color in a given destination color space. The final goal of the system herein presented consisted of industrial application, which is related to the problems faced by companies that manufacture paints. It is well known that usually, the factories that produce paints match colors through a color swatchbook prepared from the paints and mixes of colors particularly produced by them. The cost in equipments of color matching in real time is relatively high, and it is done only *in situ*, never at distance over the Internet, which is a potential future extension of our system, currently in development [1]. Many industrial, e.g. plastics, paint, and textile applications exploit color matching and mixing devices and techniques, but industries solve the problem of color matching always in a pragmatic way. Due to industrial secret there is not any information in the open literature in order to know the method the industry uses for matching colors.

On the other hand, associative memories have been an active area for research in computer sciences by roughly half a century. In this respect, computer scientists are interested in developing mathematical models that are able to learn and recall patterns (the two phases of an associative memory model) representing objects, organisms, or concepts [2-4]. The ultimate goal of an associative memory is to correctly recall complete patterns from input patterns. These patterns might be altered with noise. The classical era in associative memories is represented by Hopfield's memory [5], while in recent years the morphological associative memories [6] gave place to the rise of the Alpha-Beta ($\alpha\beta$) associative memories [7]. This new model is based on two new

J.F. Martínez-Trinidad et al. (Eds.): CIARP 2006, LNCS 4225, pp. 529–538, 2006.

operators (alpha and beta), and has become the most efficient and robust model of an associative memory.

In this paper we present the design and operation of an Automatic Color Matching system. This novel system takes advantage of the improvements introduced by $\alpha\beta$ associative memories. The results are demonstrated in a relatively small database with 1001 samples prepared by the authors. However, we consider valid the approach according to the tendency of the results obtained, in part, thanks to the performance exhibited by $\alpha\beta$ associative memories. The task of color matching is not a trivial one, because it depends on the preparation of color samples and their maintenance. Color matching is a process by means of which an unknown mix of color is located in a particular position in a given known color space. The system was created when it was necessary to find a procedure to achieve a fast, robust, and error-free procedure for color matching. A different possible solution to carry out the color matching task could be the Self-Organizing Maps or Kohonen Maps. However, they present some drawback which must be solved first. One major problem with SOMs is getting the right data. Another problem is that every SOM is different and finds different similarities among the sample vectors. The final major problem with SOMs is that they are very computationally expensive which is a major drawback since as the dimensions of the data increases, dimension reduction visualization techniques become more important, but unfortunately the time to compute them also increases [8].

Our solution is another alternative that gives valid results in a short time, it is not computational extensive, and does not need any previous selection or ordering of data in the data base.

The remaining of the paper is organized as follows. In Section 2 some concepts about color are provided. Section 3 is focused on explaining the $\alpha\beta$ associative memory model. Section 4 contains the core proposal and section 5 the experimental results. Section 6 is finally devoted to conclusions and directions for future research in this topic.

2 Color

Color is a sensation, such as warmth or a touch in our skin: it is caused by a physical reality. Color is not a property of the things that cause the sensation: grass is not green and the sky is not blue. Rather, they have physical properties that make us perceive them as green and blue, but even that is true only in some circumstances. Also, colors are not qualified in the same way by everybody that sees them. It is our trained visual system that decides on a color.

Color mixes can be obtained by means of an additive method or of a subtractive method. Primary colors in the additive method are red, green and blue. Every mix of two of them produces cyan, magenta or yellow colors. These colors are called secondary colors for this method. The mix of all of them produces white that contains all colors. Primary colors in the subtractive method are cyan, magenta and yellow. Every mix of two of them produces red, green or blue colors. These colors are called secondary colors for this method. The mix of all of them produces black that is absence of color. In both types of mix, complementary colors are those that combining together gives us the color resulting from the mix of three primaries of the respective method, that is, white in the additive method and black in the subtractive method. Then, complementary colors are those that when one of them is pure it means the other one is not present, so one color in pure state excludes the other. Green and magenta, red and cyan, and yellow and blue are complementary colors. In a given color space, each color has its particular unique position.

3 $\alpha\beta$ Associative Memories

Basic concepts, results and notation about associative memories were taken from the Yáñez-Márquez's PhD Thesis [8]. An associative memory M is a system that relates input patterns, and outputs patterns, as follows: $x \to \mathrm{M} \to y$ with x and y the input and output pattern vectors, respectively. Each input vector forms an association with a corresponding output vector. For k integer and positive, the corresponding association will be denoted as (x^k, y^k). Associative memory M is represented by a matrix whose ij-th component is m_{ij}. Memory M is generated from an *a priori* finite set of known associations, known as the fundamental set of associations. If μ is an index, the fundamental set is represented as: $\{(x^\mu, y^\mu) \mid \mu = 1,2,\ldots,p\}$ with p the cardinality of the set. If it holds that $x^\mu = y^\mu, \forall \mu \in \{1,2,\ldots,p\}$, M is autoassociative, otherwise it is heteroassociative. In this case it holds that $\exists \mu \in \{1,2,\ldots,p\}$ for which $x^\mu \neq y^\mu$.

The $\alpha\beta$ associative memories are of two kinds and are able to operate in two different modes. Operator α is useful at the learning phase, and operator β is the basis for the pattern recall phase.

The core of the mathematical tools used in the αβ model, are two binary operators designed specifically for these memories. These operators are defined in [9] as follows: First, we define the sets A = {0,1} and B = {00,01,10}, then the operators α and β are defined in tabular form, as shown in Table 1.

Table 1. Definition of the Alpha and Beta operators

$\alpha : A \times A \to B$

x	y	$\alpha(x,y)$
0	0	01
0	1	00
1	0	10
1	1	01

$\beta : B \times A \to A$

x	y	$\beta(x,y)$
00	0	0
00	1	0
01	0	0
01	1	1
10	0	1
10	1	1

The sets A and B, the α and β operators, along with the usual $\wedge$ (minimum) y $\vee$ (maximum) operators, form the algebraic system $(A, B, \alpha, \beta, \wedge, \vee)$ which is the mathematical basis for the $\alpha\beta$ associative memories. The ij-th entry of the matrix $y \oplus x^t$ is: $[y \oplus x^t]_{ij} = \alpha(y_i, x_j)$. If we consider the fundamental set of patterns:

$\{(x^\mu, y^\mu) | \mu = 1,2,\ldots,p\}$ where $x^\mu \in A^n$ and $y^\mu \in A^m$ then: $\left[y^\mu \oplus (x^\mu)^t\right]_{ij} = \alpha(y_i^\mu, x_j^\mu)$.

Because there are two kinds of $\alpha\beta$ associative memories $\vee$ and $\wedge$, and considering that each of these kinds is able to operate in two different modes, heteroassociative and autoassociative, we have four different available choices. In this issue, we only talk about the $\alpha\beta$ autoassociative memories of kind $\vee$. Therefore, the fundamental set takes the form: $\{(x^\mu, x^\mu) | \mu = 1,2,\ldots,p\}$. Besides, the input and output patterns have the same dimension *n*, and the memory is a square matrix: $\mathrm{V} = [v_{ij}]_{n \times n}$.

Learning Phase (two steps)
STEP 1:

For each $\mu = 1,2,\ldots,p$, and from (x^μ, x^μ) build the matrix: $\left[x^\mu \oplus (x^\mu)^t\right]_{n \times n}$.

STEP 2:

Apply the binary $\vee$ operator to the matrices obtained in step 1 to get **V** as follows: $\mathbf{V} = \bigvee_{\mu=1}^{p}\left[x^\mu \oplus (x^\mu)^t\right]$. The *ij*-th entry is given as: $v_{ij} = \bigvee_{\mu=1}^{p} \alpha(x_i^\mu, x_j^\mu)$. It is obvious that, $v_{ij} \in B, \forall i \in \{1,2,\ldots,n\}, \forall j \in \{1,2,\ldots,n\}$.

Recalling Phase

A pattern x^ϖ , with $\omega \in \{1,2,\ldots,p\}$ is presented to the $\alpha\beta$ autoassociative memory of kind **V** and the following operation is done: $\mathrm{V} \bigcap_\beta x^\varpi$. The result is a column vector of dimension *n*, where: $\left(\mathbf{V} \bigcap_\beta x^\varpi\right)_i = \bigwedge_{j=1}^{n} \beta\left\{\left[\bigvee_{j=1}^{n} \alpha(x_i^\mu, x_j^\mu)\right], x_j^\varpi\right\}$.

The greatest limitation of $\alpha\beta$ associative memories is perhaps that they only work with binary data, being unable to manipulate integer or real numbers. However, there have been numerous efforts to extend the original model [10-11]. With these advances, $\alpha\beta$ memories can be applied to binary and integer pattern recognition.

4 Our Proposal

In this section the proposal of the intelligent system for Automatic Color Matching is presented. First, it will be explained how the color samples database was prepared, and the methodology used to take measurements. Based on these and the concepts given on sections 2 and 3, the design and operation of the proposed intelligent system is discussed.

4.1 Preparation of Color Samples

If color samples to be measured are not rigorously prepared, the color recognition is prone to errors, making this preparation of utmost importance. The color samples produced by mixing three primary colors cyan, magenta and yellow, together with black and distilled water in previously defined proportions will constitute the patterns to be recognized. On the other hand, colors parameters can be measured by colorimeters, spectrophotometers, and other equipments. In our case a spectrophotometer was used. The color measurement by means of a spectrophotometer could be by transmittance or by reflectance. Thus, several considerations were imposed to the color samples to be used to carry out our experiments.

First, the type of the color source must be selected; that is, the material having the required primary colors to prepare the mixes to be recognized. It could be liquid, powder, pastes, and others. If transmittance is used to measure the colors, like in the case of liquids, the use of expensive quartz vessels is obligatory, since the transparence of the vessel must be considerably high in order to guarantee that its contribution in color be practically null. Therefore it was decided to measure colors by reflectance. For all these reasons, it was decided to use as the color source to prepare the color samples the Hewlett Packard cyan, magenta, yellow and black printer inks. It was used also distilled water in order to simulate the presence of the white color when the mixes were prepared over a white substrate [12].

As a second step, the choice of the substrate where the printer inks will be applied became of great importance. The main characteristic to be fulfilled by the substrate was that its contribution in color when the inks are applied over it, be a minimum and non-dependent on the mix prepared, according to our convenience. A second requirement was that the application of a liquid or a paste onto it does not moisten the substrate in such a form that makes it useless. Also its white color and its reflectivity must be uniform in the whole range of visible wavelengths. With all this in mind, three types of substrate were considered: photographic paper, white *couche* paper and common white kromekote paper. The reflectance vs wavelength curves obtained from the spectrophotometer for these three types of papers showed that the kromekote paper gives a better behavior than the other two.

The number of drops of ink to be deposited over the substrate was crucial also. The first condition to be fulfilled was that the reflectance of the paper does not affect the reflectance of the color sample. The second condition is that an excessive number of drops do not moisten the paper, in a measure that the color reflectances vary with the characteristics of the paper. In this sense some tests were done. Table 2 show the luminance level L^* of the three primary colors cyan, magenta and yellow, respectively, when measured for 1 to 10 ink drops, with respect to the standard cyan, magenta and yellow colors reflectance given by the calibrated spectrophotometer.

It may be noted that except for yellow, for every color the luminance with six drops of ink on the substrate is similar to the standard one (first row in the tables), which means that the "pure" primary color covers completely the substrate; that is, the influence of the higher luminance of the white color of the substrate is minimum or nearly null. It can be noted also that yellow gives higher luminance values than the other two primary colors, shows a more uniform characteristic and its luminance value is nearest to that of the substrate (94.29). The fact that only five drops of yellow cover the substrate (lesser luminance value), it means that it is the color that better covers the substrate. The variable values of luminance obtained in all cases when more than six drops of ink were used, is a sign that the substrate has been already moistened and due to this, the color properties changed. Then, as a conclusion, using only six drops of mixed inks carried out the covering of the substrate with all color samples.

Table 2. Luminance values for cyan, magenta and yellow ink

Color of Ink	Cyan ink		Magenta ink		Yellow ink	
Number of drops	Luminance Level	Difference	Luminance Level	Difference	Luminance Level	Difference
Standard	59.05	-35.90	49.59	-44.28	87.39	-6.65
1	69.08	10.02	60.94	11.35	87.69	0.30
2	66.83	7.78	57.01	7.42	87.44	0.05
3	67.80	8.75	55.07	5.48	87.42	0.03
4	66.86	7.81	53.81	4.22	87.37	-0.01
5	60.59	1.53	52.96	3.36	87.12	-0.27
6	58.39	0.66	50.01	-0.42	87.65	-0.26
7	62.34	3.29	53.43	3.84	85.18	-2-21
8	60.17	1.12	50.49	0.90	85.53	-1.86
9	60.69	1.64	52.98	3.38	84.92	-2.47
10	61.37	2.32	48.35	-1.25	87.78	0.39

To achieve different shadows and tints of pure primary colors and their mixes, it was necessary to mix pure primary color inks with black ink and distilled water in the corresponding proportions, respectively. The white color of the substrate contributed to give tint when distilled water was used in the mixes. Afterward, other particular mixes were prepared using the corresponding shadowed and tinted primaries. The total number of drops used in the preparation of every color mix was limited always to one hundred drops. Each color mix prepared was kept in a small previously sterilized dropper glass, sealed with a cap and protected from light in order to guarantee that its quality does not deteriorate.

To calculate the exact number of possible color patterns that must be prepared according to the conditions stated, generating function models were used [13]. Suppose a_r is the number of ways to select r objects in a certain procedure. Then $g(x)$ is a generating function for a_r if $g(x)$ has the polynomial expansion:

$$g(x) = a_0 + a_1 x + a_2 x^2 + \cdots + a_r x^r + \cdots + a_n x^n .$$

For example as: $(1+x)^n = 1 + \binom{n}{1} x + \binom{n}{2} x^2 + \cdots + \binom{n}{r} x^r + \cdots + \binom{n}{n} x^n$. Then $g(x) = (1+x)^n$ is the generating function for $a_r = C(n,r)$, the number of ways to select an r-subset from an n-set. The problem of determining the coefficient of x^r when we multiply several such polynomial factors together can be restated in terms of exponents. As an example, consider the expansion of $(1+x+x^2)^4$. The number of formal products $x^{e_1}x^{e_2}x^{e_3}x^{e_4}$, $0 \le e_i \le 2$ equaling x^r in the expansion, will be the number of integer solutions to: $e_1+e_2+e_3+e_4=r$, $0 \le e_i \le 2$. In our case, the total number of drops of the five possible components to create each color mix was limited to 100 drops for convenience. Additionally, the concentration of samples created for each one out of five components was established in steps of ten drops, that is, r = *100/10* = *10* steps. This means that: $e_1+e_2+\cdots+e_5=10$, *where* $0 \le e_i \le 10$. This is equivalent to solving the polynomial: $P(x)=(x^0+x^1+\cdots+x^9+x^{10})^5$. In the expansion of this polynomial $P(x)$ in its formal products, the coefficient a_{10} of x^{10} gives the total number of combinations under our conditions. That coefficient is 1001. Then, the number of combinations (to be) prepared was 1001 combinations.

4.2 Measurements

In taking measurements, the spectrophotometer was calibrated to measure the samples under a known specific set of conditions. These conditions involve the illuminant (light source) type, the observer's viewing angle, and the spectral exclusion (not taking gloss into consideration). The spectrophotometer used was a Milton Roy COLOR MATE™ HDS Color Analyzer. Before its use and after warmed, it was always meticulously calibrated with a white tile accompanying the equipment. The parameters established in the equipment by us to measure the color samples were: Observation Angle: 10º; Sight Window (Area of View): small; Color Space: CIE $L^*a^*b^*$; Illuminants: D65 and D50; and Average number of lectures: 5.

Five lectures were done facing onto it different zones of the covered substrate. The equipment then averaged the results of the five lectures and finally gave us thirty one values of the reflectance of the sample for each one of the thirty one wavelengths ranging from 400 to 700 nanometers of the visible spectrum, in steps of ten, of the standard and the color sample, as well as the difference between both values. The standard color could be selected by the user, between the standard white, standard black, one of the primary color selected from cyan, magenta and yellow, or another one of our convenience. From the two illuminants selected, that is D50 and D65, the spectrophotometer gave us the values of the components L^*, a^*, b^* of the color model CIELAB selected and the values of the three primary three-stimulus values X, Y and Z, for both the standard and the sample, together with the respective difference. In order to carry out the color matching, the value of L^* related to the illuminant D65 was used as reference for daylight. Then, after reading the 1001 color samples, prepared with colors cyan, magenta, yellow, black and distilled water in steps of ten drops, and taking into account that the total number of drops be 100 drops for each mix prepared and used 6 drops to cover the substrate, a database was created with patterns of thirty one values of the reflectance, which vary from 6.24 to 102.58.

4.3 System Description

The system consists of three modules: the input module, the processing module and the output module; and operates in two phases: the learning phase and the pattern recall phase. The first module has as main purpose to convert each input pattern made up of 31 real values into its corresponding binary pattern, requirement imposed for the design and operation of the $\alpha\beta$ associative memories. The third module does the reverse procedure: converts the binary patterns which result from operating the system into their corresponding 31 real components patterns, which make up the pattern for a specific color. Module 2 is the core of the system, and is conformed by two complementing redundant sub-modules: the first sub-module is an autoassociative $\alpha\beta$ memory of type max, and the second sub-module is an autoassociative $\alpha\beta$ memory of type min. In this intelligent system, the fundamental patterns of each $\alpha\beta$ associative memory are precisely the patterns of 31 real valued reflectance components representing the different colors. Since the memories are autoassociative, it holds that $x^{\mu} = y^{\mu}, \forall \mu \in \{1,2,\ldots,p\}$, where p is the fundamental set cardinality; that is, $p = 1001$.

Learning phase.-

- Every pattern in the fundamental set is presented to the system and module 1 converts into binary patterns the 31 real component patterns.
- Both $\alpha\beta$ associative memories, max and min, do their respective learning phases.

Matching Phase.-

- An unknown 31 real valued pattern is presented to the system and module 1 converts it to a binary pattern.
- Each $\alpha\beta$ associative memory, max and min, executes its pattern recall phase, producing two binary patterns.
- Module 3 converts each of these two binary patterns into a 31 real valued pattern.

Given the redundancy of both submodules of module 2, it is expected that both obtained patterns be equal. However, they were different. The worst case occurs when both patterns are a valid version of a color resulting from the matching. It is left to the user to select by visual inspection the *best* of them.

5 Experimental Results

The experimental design is quite simple. In each individual experiment, the following was done: (a) At random one out of 1001 samples was selected from the database. Then, the database had only 1000 elements (color combination) in this case; (b) the learning phase of the system was undertaken with the resulting 1000 patterns database; (c) the color that was retired in step 1 was used as sample. Then the results given by the system was analyzed by several human observers, who dictated whether the color resulting from the matching was close enough to the testing color, or not.

In Table 3 are shown the values of the number of drops of 24 samples to match selected at random from the database, the number of drops of the matching calculated by the matching module and the majority opinion of the observers group.

In this table we can notice that all results are positive, except when pure colors were presented to the system, that is, colors which have presence of only one primary color. Since these colors are known in advance, the system failure with them is irrelevant.

Table 3. Experimental results

Number of drops of the color sample to match					Number of drops of the matching with the color sample					Yes/ No
Cyan	Mag.	Yellow	Water	Black	Cyan	Mag.	Yellow	Water	Black	
0	60	20	0	20	0	40	20	20	20	yes
80	0	0	0	20	0	0	0	0	100	no
40	0	30	10	20	50	0	30	0	20	yes
50	30	10	0	10	40	30	10	10	10	yes
40	30	20	0	10	40	30	10	10	10	yes
20	0	50	30	0	20	0	60	20	0	yes
30	10	0	10	50	20	10	20	20	30	yes
0	10	0	10	80	0	10	0	0	90	yes
0	40	0	0	60	20	10	10	0	60	no
0	50	40	10	0	0	60	30	10	0	yes
30	50	0	0	20	30	40	0	10	20	yes
0	20	60	20	0	0	40	60	0	0	yes
20	10	10	50	10	30	10	10	30	20	yes
0	0	70	30	0	0	0	40	60	0	no
0	0	10	80	10	0	0	10	70	20	yes
0	50	10	30	10	0	50	0	30	20	yes
0	40	0	0	60	20	10	10	0	60	no
30	0	0	60	10	40	0	0	40	20	no
40	0	50	0	10	40	0	30	20	10	yes
20	0	10	50	20	30	0	10	20	40	yes
0	60	30	10	0	0	70	30	0	0	yes
0	10	20	0	70	0	10	10	20	60	yes
0	20	20	50	10	0	30	20	30	20	yes
10	60	30	0	0	10	50	30	10	0	yes

6 Conclusions

This work has been oriented toward the use of $\alpha\beta$ associative memories for colors matching. The universe of samples is a relatively small database with 1001 carefully prepared samples. The experiments consisted in excluding a randomly selected sample from the full database, then building both $\alpha\beta$ memories with the remaining 1000 samples, in order to operate the system with the excluded pattern. After the system delivered the recalled patterns, a group of observers decided whether the results were satisfactory or not. The results manifest the validity of its use in a relatively easy way, in this relatively particular application, except when presented with pure colors; that is, colors which have presence of only one primary color. Since these colors are known in advance, the system failure with them is irrelevant. Therefore, the approach can be considered valid according to the tendency of the results obtained.

Acknowledgements

The authors would like to thank the Instituto Politécnico Nacional (Secretaría Académica, COFAA, SIP, and CIC), the CONACyT, and SNI for their economical support to develop this work.

References

1. Aquino, D., Cervantes, F., Linares, B., Felipe, E., De la Cruz, C.: Telecolorimetría basada en el reconocimiento de patrones de color, Thesis. Interdisciplinary Professional School in Engineering and Advanced Technologies, National Polytechnic Institute, Mexico (2004)
2. T. Kohonen.: Correlation Matrix Memories. IEEE Transactions on Computers. 21(4). (1972) 353-359
3. Kohonen, T.: Self-Organization and Associative Memory. Springer-Verlag, Berlin Heidelberg New York (1989)
4. Hassoun, M. H.: Associative Neural Memories. Oxford University Press, New York (1993)
5. Hopfield, J. J.: Neural networks and physical systems with emergent collective computational abilities, Proceedings of the National Academy of Sciences, 79 (1982), 2554–2558
6. Ritter, G. X., Sussner, P., Diaz-de-Leon, J. L.: Morphological Associative Memories. IEEE Transactions on Neural Networks. 9 (1998) 281-293
7. Yáñez-Márquez, C., Díaz de León-Santiago, J. L.: Memorias Asociativas Basadas en Relaciones de Orden y Operaciones Binarias. Computación y Sistemas. México, 6(4). (2003) 300-311
8. Honkela, T.: Self-Organizing Maps in Natural language Processing, PhD Thesis (1997)
9. Yáñez-Márquez, C.: Associative Memories Based on Order Relations and Binary Operators (In Spanish). PhD Thesis. Center for Computing Research, México (2002)
10. Yáñez-Márquez, C., Díaz de León-Santiago, J. L., Salgado, J. C.: New V-Alpha-Beta Associative Memories able to Learn and Recall Patterns with Integer Components. Technical Report 210, Blue Series. National Polytechnic Institute. Center for Computing Research, México (2005)
11. Sossa, H., Barrón, R., Cuevas, F., Aguilar, C.: Associative Gray Level Pattern Processing Using Binary Decomposition and α β Memories. Neural Processing Letters, Vol. 22 (1) (2005) 85
12. Zhang, H., Dong Bi, J., Back, B.: The Design and Implementation of Color Matching System Based on Back Propagation, Lecture Notes in Computer Science, Vol. 2358, Springer-Verlag, Berlin (2002) 557-566
13. Tucker A.: Applied Combinatorics, John Wiley & Sons, 4th Edition, Chapter 6 (2002)

The Associative Recall of Spatial Correlated Patterns

Jana Štanclová

Department of Software Engineering,
Faculty of Mathematics and Physics, Charles University
Malostranské nám. 25, 118 00, Praha 1, Czech Republic
jana.stanclova@mff.cuni.cz

Abstract. The strategies for an associative recall can be based on associative memory models. However, the performance of standard associative memories is very sensitive to the number of stored patterns and their mutual correlations. With respect to huge amounts of spatial patterns (mostly correlated) to be processed, we have focused on an arbitrary number of associative memories grouped into several layers (Hierarchical Associative Memories - HAM). In the newly presented HAM2-model, the patterns are hierarchically grouped according to the "previous-layer" patterns. The HAM2-model uses the information recalled by the "previous-layer" to find an appropriate subset of "next-level" associative memories. To evaluate the performance of the HAM2-model, extensive simulations are carried out. The experimental results show the recall ability of the model in the area of associative pattern recall.

1 Introduction

Let us consider a situation when a traveler moves along a familiar scenery. In such a situation, he can usually see only his close surroundings. Based on is previous knowledge about the whole area, he might be able to recall also some part of the environment that he can not see yet, but will see soon as he moves. The newly recalled scenery in his mind can trigger other associations, he is also able to recall another part of the environment further ahead of him. Thus, he can recall in his mind the scenery of a wide environment by a chain of such recall processes. This process of an associative recall could be used e.g. when building an autonomous robot "warehouse keeper" or an automatic hoover. It would help with robot localization and thus its better overall control.

For an associative recall of patterns, we use the approach introduced by Fukushima et al. [5]. The actual "seen" scenery is represented in the form of a spatial pattern with an egocentric coordinate system. During the movement, the actual area becomes shifted relatively to the previous position of the move (in order to keep the body always in the center of the pattern to be recalled). As the scenery image shifts following the movement, a vacant region appears in the "not yet seen" part of the image. The pattern with a vacant "not yet seen" region (the so-called incomplete pattern) is presented to an associative memory and the empty part of the pattern is expected to be filled (see Figure 1).

J.F. Martínez-Trinidad et al. (Eds.): CIARP 2006, LNCS 4225, pp. 539–548, 2006.

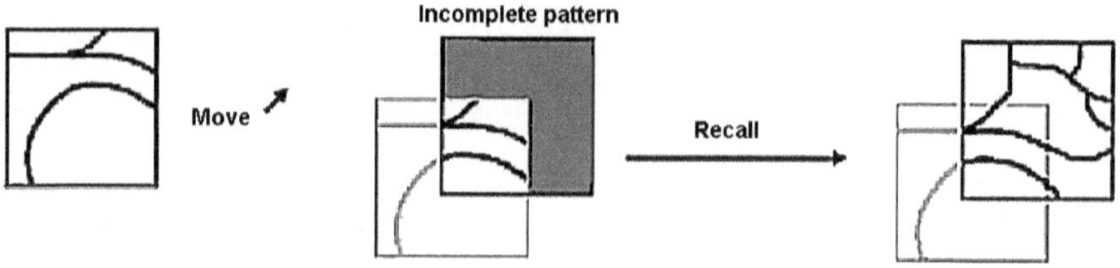

Fig. 1. The associative pattern recall inspired by Fukushima et al. [5]

Anyway, the associative memory by itself does not reliably recall shifted patterns, and each presented pattern has to be placed accurately at the location of one of the memorized patterns. Different approaches to an associative recall (e.g. in spatial maps) can be based on the so-called cognitive maps. Different approaches have been developed to build hierarchical cognitive maps (e.g. [2], [4], [12]).

For an associative recall, standard associative memories can be used. However, this model is not suitable for the associative recall mentioned above, as it cannot cope with the need for a high number of stored patterns and the fact that the patterns are not orthogonal. Therefore, we decided to focus our research on the models of Hierarchical Associative Memories (HAM) developed with an emphasis on the necessity to process large amounts of (correlated) data. They consist of an arbitrary number of associative memories grouped into several layers. In our original model HAM1 (described e.g. in [11]), the patterns are stored in "any suitable" associative memory. The HAM1-model does not use the "previous-layer" information to find an appropriate associative memory at the "next" layer. In this paper, we present the HAM2-model. The associative memories of the HAM2-model form a tree structure. A disjoint subset of associative memories is assigned to every "previous-layer" associative memory. We expect that the HAM2-model improves the HAM1-model and allows a reliable storage and "sufficiently reliable" recall of correlated patterns with respect to an associative pattern recall.

The organization of the paper is as follows: a basic concept of associative memories is reviewed in section 2. In section 3, the models HAM1 and HAM2 are described. In section 4, we present experimental results evaluating the performance of the models HAM1 and HAM2. The paper concludes with Section 5, which outlines the directions of our future work.

2 Models of Associative Memories

The standard associative memory is a neural network, for which all its neurons are input and output neurons simultaneously and there are oriented interconnections among all neurons. All their weights are symmetric and each neuron is connected to all other neurons except itself. Other basic notions and characteristics of this memory can be found e.g. in [7]. If the number of stored patterns does not exceed the limit ($0.15n$ where n is the dimension of stored patterns [7]), the models have robust recall ability. Although the robust recall ability is very attractive, patterns to be stored in the standard associative memory must be almost orthogonal one to each other. Storing correlated patterns can cause serious problems and previously stored training patterns can even become lost because the cross-talk does not average to zero [1].

To overcome this problem, many researchers have extended the standard associative memory to process correlated patterns (e.g. [3], [6], [8], [9], [10]). Morita [10] proposed a model that enhances the ability of associative memories with non-monotonic dynamics. Gutfreund [3] proposed a model consisting of two associative memories - one for each level of the two-level hierarchy. The first associative memory (AM1) and the second one (AM2) store the first-level patterns (called ancestors) and their second-level patterns (called descendants), respectively. However, Gutfreund's model has a parameter on which the storage capacity strongly depends [3]. Hirahara et al. [6] proposed a model of Cascade Associative Memory (CASM) similar in the structure to Gutfreund's model. The CASM-model is characterized by the AM2 storing not the descendants but the so-called difference patterns. The difference patterns become sparser with increasing correlation, which allows the CASM-model to have a larger storage capacity. Unfortunately, the upper limit of the storage and the recall abilities of the CASM-model are bounded by that of the AM1 ($\sim 0.15n$) [6].

3 The Hierarchical Associative Memory (HAM)

The performance of standard associative memories is limited by the number of patterns which can be stored in it and the fact that the patterns have to be orthogonal. To avoid (at least to a certain extent) these limitations, we have designed the Hierarchical Associative Memory models. These models are based on the concept of the CASM-model [6]. Our goal is to use the CASM-model more generally by allowing an arbitrary number of layers with more memories grouped in each layer.

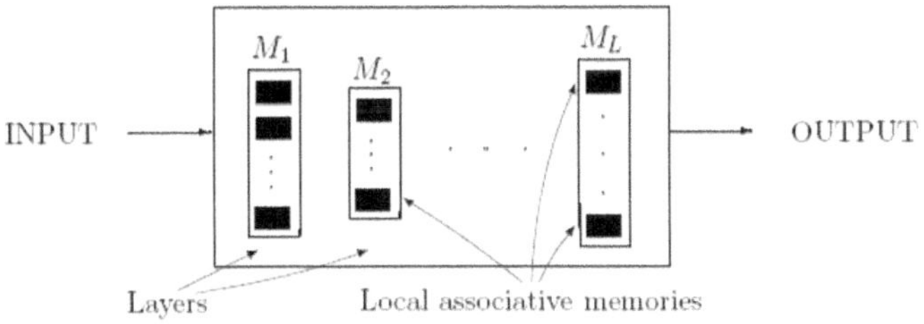

Fig. 2. The structure of the Hierarchical Associative Memory with L layers $M_1,\ldots, M_L$

A Hierarchical associative memory H with L $(L>0)$ layers is an ordered tuple $H=(M_1,\ldots,M_L)$ where $M_1,\ldots,M_L$ are finite non-empty sets of associative memories (the so-called local associative memories). A set M_k $(k=1,\ldots,L)$ is called the layer of the memory H. $|M_k|$ denotes the number of local associative memories in the layer M_k $(k=1,\ldots,L)$. Every local associative memory of the same layer has the same number of neurons n $(n>0)$. A training tuple T of H is an ordered tuple $T=(T_1,\ldots, T_L)$ where T_k $(k=1,\ldots,L)$ is a finite non-empty set of training patterns for the layer M_k. The structure of the HAM2-model, as well as the HAM1-model, is shown in Figure 2. The difference between the HAM1-model and the HAM2-model is in the network dynamics.

3.1 The HAM1-Model

To train the HAM1-model, we have designed the so-called dynamical layer training algorithm (DLT-algorithm) [11]. Each of the layers M_k $(k=1,...,L)$ is trained separately. The training patterns from the set T_k are stored in local associative memories of the corresponding layer M_k.. During the training of the layer M_k, training patterns from the set T_k are presented to the layer M_k sequentially. Each training pattern $\boldsymbol{x}$ is stored in such a local associative memory of the layer M_k where the pattern $\boldsymbol{x}$ (or its "noisy" version[1]) is recalled correctly. If there is no "suitable" local associative memory, a new local associative memory is created, added to the layer M_k and the pattern $\boldsymbol{x}$ is stored in the newly created associative memory.

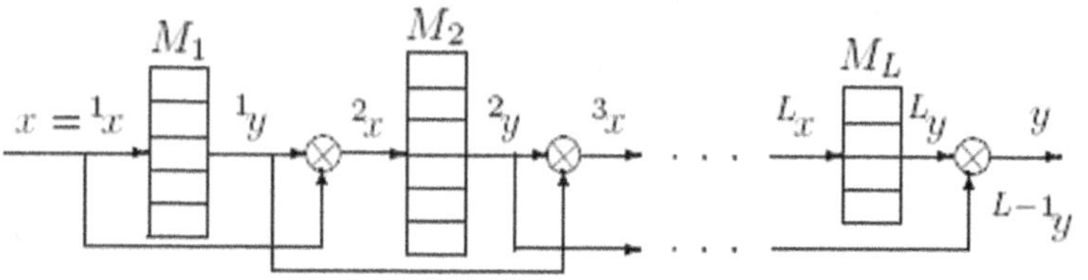

Fig. 3. The recall process in the HAM1-model with the layers M_1, ..., M_L

The recall process of the HAM1-model is depicted in Figure 3. During the recall, a pattern $\boldsymbol{x}$ is an input to the HAM1-model. The input pattern $\boldsymbol{x}$ represents an input for the first layer M_1 (i.e. $\boldsymbol{x}={}^1\boldsymbol{x}$). Within every time step k $(1 \leq k \leq L)$, the layer M_k produces the corresponding output ${}^k\boldsymbol{y}$. The output ${}^k\boldsymbol{y}$ combined with the output ${}^{k-1}\boldsymbol{y}$ of the "previous" layer M_{k-1} is used as the input ${}^{k+1}\boldsymbol{x}$ to the "next" layer M_{k+1}. The function of the circle "⊗" in Figure 3 is to produce the "next" input (in our implementation, the difference pattern calculation is used). The output ${}^L\boldsymbol{y}$ of the "last" layer M_L combined with the output of the layer M_{L-1} represents the output $\boldsymbol{y}$ of the HAM1-model.

At the layer M_k, the input pattern ${}^k\boldsymbol{x}$ is propagated to all local associative memories of the layer M_k and each of them recalls the corresponding outputs ${}^k\boldsymbol{y}^i$ $(i=1,..., /M_k/)$. The output ${}^k\boldsymbol{y}$ of the layer M_k is an output ${}^k\boldsymbol{y}^i$ which is "the most similar" to the input pattern ${}^k\boldsymbol{x}$ (we use Hamming distance, but other metrics may be considered too).

3.2 The HAM2-Model

A basic concept of the HAM2-model is similar to the HAM1-model. The main difference is that the local associative memories of the HAM2-model form a tree structure. A disjoint subset of local associative memories is assigned to every "previous-layer" local associative memory. The HAM2-model groups the associative memories according to their "previous-layer" information. The subsets of local associative memories are organized in a tree structure (Figure 4).

[1] A pattern in which certain number of randomly selected elements change their value.

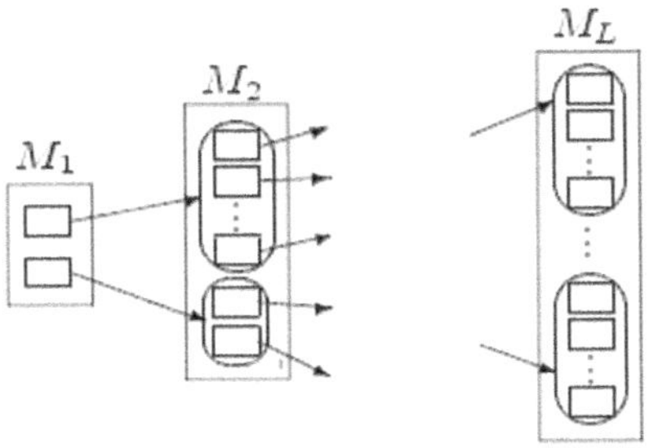

Fig. 4. The tree structure of the HAM2-model with the layers M_1, ..., M_L

All layers M_k $(k=1,...,L)$ in the HAM2-model are trained sequentially. The training patterns from the training set T_k are presented to the corresponding layer M_k sequentially. The training of every pattern $\boldsymbol{x}$ consists of two steps. First, the pattern $\boldsymbol{x}$ from T_k is presented to already trained layers $M_1,\ldots,M_{k-1}$ to be recalled. The output of the layer M_{k-1} provides the information into which subset of the currently trained layer M_k the pattern $\boldsymbol{x}$ belongs (S denotes the corresponding subset of the layer M_k for the pattern $\boldsymbol{x}$). As the corresponding subset S is detected, the "suitable" local associative memory in the subset S of the layer M_k is found and the pattern $\boldsymbol{x}$ is stored in it. If there is no "suitable" local associative memory in the subset S of the layer M_k, a new local associative memory is created and added to the subset S of the layer M_k. In this case, the training pattern $\boldsymbol{x}$ is stored in the newly created associative memory.

The recall process is similar to the recall process of the HAM1-model, but it utilizes the tree structure of the HAM2-model. The recall process takes place sequentially in the layers of the HAM2-model. During the recall, a pattern $\boldsymbol{x}$ is an input to the HAM2-model (i.e. $\boldsymbol{x} = {}^{1}\boldsymbol{x}$). At every time step k $(1 \leq k \leq L)$, the layer M_k receives the input ${}^{k}\boldsymbol{x}$ and the recall process at this layer proceeds. First, the output ${}^{k-1}\boldsymbol{y}$ of the "previous" layer M_{k-1} $(k>1)$ gives the information into which subset S of the layer M_k the input pattern ${}^{k}\boldsymbol{x}$ belongs. Then, the pattern ${}^{k}\boldsymbol{x}$ is sent only to such local associative memories that belong to the subset S of the layer M_k. Each of these local associative memories recalls the outputs ${}^{k}\boldsymbol{y}^{i}$ $(i=1,...,|S|)$. The output ${}^{k}\boldsymbol{y}$ of the layer M_k is an output ${}^{k}\boldsymbol{y}^{i}$ which is "the most similar" to the input pattern ${}^{k}\boldsymbol{x}$ (we use Hamming distance, but other metrics may be considered too). The output ${}^{k}\boldsymbol{y}$ combined with the output ${}^{k-1}\boldsymbol{y}$ of the "previous" layer M_{k-1} is used as the input ${}^{k+1}\boldsymbol{x}$ to the "next" layer M_{k+1}. The output of the "last" layer M_L represents the output of the HAM2-model.

3.3 Characteristics of the HAM2-Model

In the HAM2-model, there is no need to state the number of the local associative memories before the training process starts because the local memories are automatically added to corresponding layers during training. The training process can start with one local associative memory in every layer. The initial structure of the HAM2-model forms a path (i.e. a degenerated tree). Other local associative memories are added to the HAM2-model during the training process according to the incoming patterns. The number of local associative memories in the HAM2-model varies with the structure of incoming data. The number of subsets in every layer depends on the structure of incoming patterns, too.

In the training algorithm, we use a simple heuristics how to choose the "suitable" local associative memory for storing a pattern. The above-sketched heuristics is quick, simple and easy to implement, but it is not optimal. A pattern remains stored in such a local associative memory (of the corresponding subset) where the pattern or its "noisy version" is recalled correctly. However, using this training algorithm we cannot predict anything about recalling previously stored patterns. After storing another pattern, some of the previously stored patterns can be recalled incorrectly or even become lost.

4 Experimental Results

One of the key points in neural network performance is the recall ability. Applying the HAM2-model to obtain an associative recall (e.g. in an autonomous robot), a robust recall of presented patterns (images) is required, often unknown in some parts of their surface. The experimental simulations are focused on the analyses of the HAM2-model recall abilities (in comparison with the HAM1-model and the standard associative memory model).

4.1 The Implementation of the HAM2-Model

Our experimental simulations are restricted to a two-layer hierarchy of the HAM2-model (and the HAM1-model as well). The two-layer hierarchy is chosen for an easy geometrical interpretation of data. We can believe that the patterns in an input space are grouped into clusters. In the centers of the clusters are representative patterns (called ancestors) that form the first-layer patterns. Other patterns similar (correlated) to any ancestor are distributed in a cluster around it. They represent the second-level patterns, called descendants. The generalization of the data structure to an arbitrary number of layers is straightforward but the geometrical interpretation does not have to be so simple (in the future, we plan to extend the experiments to a high number of layers).

With respect to the robust recall ability requirement, the second layer of the implemented HAM2-model deals with difference patterns instead of descendants. The difference patterns contain only the information on the differences between the descendants and the corresponding ancestor. During the training, the ancestors are stored in the first layer of the HAM2-model. Afterwards, the corresponding ancestor is found for every descendant (e.g. by recalling in the first - already trained - layer of the HAM2-model). The difference pattern (descendant – recalled ancestor) is calculated and stored in the second layer according to the training algorithm. The second layer of the HAM2-model is in the form of a pile of associative memory subsets. Each subset is responsible for recalling only the difference patterns belonging to the ancestor stored in the corresponding local associative memory of the first layer.

During recalling, an input pattern is presented to the first layer of the HAM2-model to recall the corresponding ancestor. Once the ancestor is recalled, the corresponding difference pattern is calculated by combining the recalled ancestor with the input pattern. The difference pattern is propagated to the second layer of the HAM-model to be recalled. The output of the HAM2-model is produced by combining the recalled difference pattern with its recalled ancestor (by the operation inversed to the difference pattern calculation).

4.2 The Generation of Patterns

For experiments, we generate 100 sets of 100 randomly generated bipolar patterns; each of size 15×15 elements. In a bipolar pattern, every element takes the value +1 or -1. Every experiment is run on its set of patterns independently on other sets. Experiments are repeated for every data set. In our experiments, we process "relatively small" patterns, as it is necessary to perform huge number of experiments to analyze the HAM2-model recall ability. We have performed also experiments with "bigger" data (75×75elements) and the results have been very similar (or even a little better). After pattern generation, the patterns of every data set with the smallest cumulative correlation between the respective patterns are chosen to be the ancestors and the remaining patterns are used to form the descendants. We define the pattern rate r as a ratio between the number of ancestors and descendants in a set of patterns.

4.3 The Associative Recall of Stored Patterns

First, we analyze the HAM2-model ability to recall the stored patterns and compare the HAM2-model abilities with the HAM1-model and standard associative memory abilities. We measure the percentage of patterns (from a set of patterns) that are recalled correctly. A pattern is recalled correctly if it coincides with its original. We define the capacity coefficient c that reduces the maximum number of patterns stored in a local associative memory. The maximum storage capacity α of a local associative memory is given by formula $\alpha=0.15 \cdot n \cdot c$. The capacity coefficient c takes the value of 1 for a standard associative memory. For decreasing c, the maximum storage capacity is reduced and the HAM2-model recall ability rises. The results are shown in Figure 5.

In Figure 5, the surface represents the average number of patterns recalled correctly. If $c \leq 0.5$, the results are very similar in both models (for every pattern rate r). In this case, more than 97% of stored patterns are recalled correctly. As the capacity coefficient c (and the pattern rate r) increases, the differences between the HAM1- and the HAM2-model become significant. The increasing pattern rate r corresponds to the increasing number of ancestors (and the increasing number of local associative memories in the first layer). The recall abilities are enhanced in the HAM2-model (especially for $r>1/2$) due to the influence of the tree structure.

The same experiments are performed with the standard associative memory. As the number of patterns to be stored exceeds the theoretical storage capacity [7], the standard associative memory is not able to recall correctly any of the stored patterns. The experiments show that the HAM2-model has a robust recall ability to recall correctly the stored patterns. The performance of the model depends on the capacity coefficient c and the pattern rate r. Several patterns are recalled with an error, but the error does not exceed 2.5%.

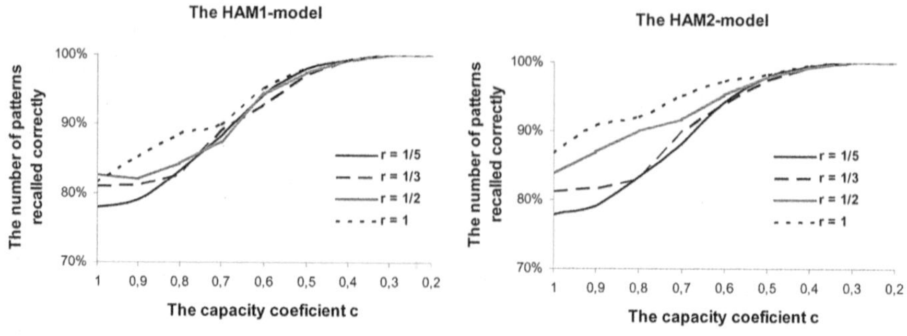

Fig. 5. The number of patterns recalled correctly in the HAM1-model (left) and the HAM2-model (right) with respect to the capacity coefficient c and the pattern rate r

4.4 The Associative Recall of Incomplete Patterns

Now, we focus on the HAM2-model ability to recall incomplete patterns (e.g. images). According to the above-mentioned results (Figure 5), we concentrate on the HAM2-model with the capacity coefficient $c=0.7$ and the pattern rate $r=1$. We create three groups of incomplete patterns containing 13%, 25% and 36% of unknown elements, respectively. Each of the groups corresponds to a diagonal shift of the pattern (image) by 1, 2, or 3 points, respectively. We process four types of diagonal directions: ⇖ (northwest), ⇗ (northeast), ⇙ (southwest) and ⇘ (southeast). In practice, other directions are also possible. The experiments are processed for every diagonal direction separately and the results are averaged for the corresponding size of the shift.

We analyze the model ability to recall the incomplete patterns with respect to the diferent size of the shift. With the increasing number of the „unknown“ elements, the recall ability decreases. In practice, it is not necessary to recall the incomplete patterns correctly (i.e. a small error is acceptable). The results of incomplete pattern recall with the shift by 1 and 2 points are shown in Figure 6.

The horizontal axis in Figure 6 corresponds to the acceptable error (the number of elements in a pattern that can be recalled incorrectly). The vertical axis shows the number of patterns in which the recall error is bellow the corresponding acceptable error level. Figure 6 shows the recall abilities of the HAM2-model are higher than the HAM1-model but the differences are just minor. We also perform the same experiments with the standard associative memory. Because of the incapability to recall any of the stored patterns, the standard associative memory is not able to recall the incomplete patterns correctly either. The detailed results of the HAM2-model for two selected acceptable errors are summarized in the Table 1.

With increasing error acceptance the number of patterns increases. When the "unknown" area is small and the error acceptance is about 6%, the HAM2-model has a relatively robust recall ability with respect to the incomplete pattern recall (82%). Moreover, theory says that for every pattern associative memories store an inverse pattern as well. It is possible that the inverse pattern is recalled instead of the original one. In this situation, the pattern is considered to be recalled incorrectly. If we could detect the situation, the recall ability of the HAM2-model would be improved.

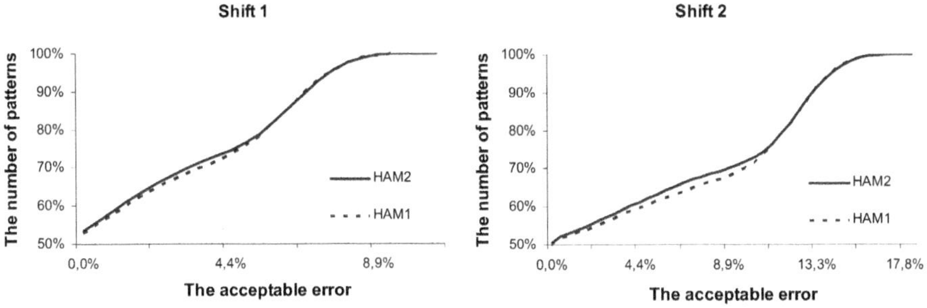

Fig. 6. The number of incomplete patterns recalled by the HAM2-model (the solid line) and the HAM1-model (the dotted line) with the error bellow the acceptable error. The "unknown" elements correspond to the diagonal shift by 1 point (left) and 2 points (right)

Table 1. The number of incomplete patterns recalled by the HAM2-model where the recall error is bellow 1% and 6%

Acceptable error	Shift by 1	Shift by 2	Shift by 3
$\leq 1\%$	59%	53%	51%
$\leq 6\%$	82%	64%	57%

Experiments for the HAM2-model with different pattern rates r are also performed. The results show that the HAM2-model ability to recall incomplete patterns are increased with the increasing pattern rate r.

5 Conclusions

Our current research in the area of associative memories is focused on an associative pattern recall with necessity to handle large number of correlated patterns. Here, we have presented the HAM2-model that improves the storage/recall ability of standard associative memories and our previous HAM1-model as well. The HAM2-model has a tree structure and the patterns are hierarchically grouped according to the "previous-layer" information. The recall ability of the HAM2-model can be further improved by restricting the storage capacity of local memories. The experiments carried out have confirmed the legitimacy of the proposed HAM2-model and shown promising results for the associative pattern recall. However, for real applications it is necessary to further improve the robustness of recall process with respect to incomplete patterns.

The right choice of a local associative memory for storing a pattern represents an important point of a successful overall performance of the model. We have used a basic straightforward method, which we try to improve. We hope it will further increase the robustness of the HAM2-model. In the future, we plan to compare the HAM2-model with the CASM-model of Hirahara [6] and carry out the experiments with the HAM2-model consisting of more than two layers.

Acknowledgments. This work was partially supported by the Ministry of Education of the Czech Republic (grant MSM0021620838).

References

1. Amit, D. J., Gutfreund, H., Sompolinsky, H.: Information storage in neural networks with low levels of activity, in: Physical Review A, 35, 2293-2303, 1987
2. Donnart, J. Y., Meyer, J. A.: Hierarchical-map building and selfpositioning with Mona-Lysa, Adaptive Behavior, 5(1), 29–74, 1996
3. Gutfreund, H.: Neural networks with hierarchically correlated patterns. Physical Review A, 37, 570–577, 1988
4. Kuipers, B.: The spatial semantic hierarchy, Artificial Intelligence, 119, 191–233, 2000
5. Fukushima, K., Yamaguchi, Y., Okada, M.: Neural Network Model of Spatial Memory: Associative Recall of Maps, Neural Network, Vol. 10, No. 6, 971-979, 1997.
6. Hirahara, M., Oka, N., Kindo, T.: A cascade associative memory model with a hierarchical memory structure, Neural Networks, Vol. 13, No. 1, 41-50, 2000.
7. Hopfield, J. J.: Neural Networks and physical system with emergent collective computational abilities, Proc. Natl. Acad. Sci. USA, 79, 2554-2558, 1982.
8. Kimoto, T., Okada, M.: Coexistence of memory patterns and mixed states in a sparsely encoded associative memory model storing ultrametric patterns, Biological Cybernetics, 90, 229–238, 2004
9. Matsumoto, N., Ide, D., Watanabe, M., Okada, M.: Synaptic Depression Enlarges Basin of Attraction, Neurocomputing, 65-66, 571-577, 2005
10. Morita, M.: Associative memory with nonmonotone dynamics. Neural Networks, 6, 115–126, 1993
11. Štanclová, J., Zavoral, F.: Hierarchical Associative Memories: The Neural Network for Path Prediction in Spatial Maps, Proc. ICIAP 2005, Springer-Verlag LNCS3617, 786-793, 2005
12. Voicu, H. : Hierarchical cognitive maps, Neural Networks, Vol. 16, pp. 569-576, 2003

Associative Memories Applied to Image Categorization

Roberto A. Vázquez and Humberto Sossa

Centro de Investigación en Computación – IPN
Av. Juan de Dios Batíz, esquina con Miguel Othón de Mendizábal
Ciudad de México, 07738, México.
ravem@ipn.mx, hsossa@cic.ipn.mx

Abstract. In this paper we describe how associative memories can be applied to categorize images. If we present to an associative memory (AM) an image we would expect that the AM would respond with something that describes the content of the image; for example, if the image contains a tiger we would expect that the AM would respond with the word "tiger". In order to achieve this goal, we first chose a set of images. Each image is next associated to the word that better describes the content of the image. With this information an AM is trained as in [10]. We then use the AM to categorize instances of images with the same content even if these images are distorted by some kind of noise. The accuracy of the proposal is tested using a set of images containing different species of flowers and animals.

1 Introduction

Research on associative memories (AMS) has been carried out during the last 40 years. AMS can be seen as a particular kind of neural networks. AMS are a mathematical device specially designed to recall output patterns in terms of input patterns which can be contaminated by some kind of noise, see for example [1-9]. Some of these AMS have several constraints that limit their applicability in the solution real life problems. Most common applications of AMS are as filters [5-7]; in this case the AM is fed with a signal (an image, for example), possibly altered by noise; at the output the original image (without noise) should be obtained. However, in order to achieve the best performance the input patterns have to satisfy some restrictions; for example in [5-6] the input pattern can only be distorted by additive or subtractive noise, but not both. These conditions limit their applicability in real life problems. In [7] the patterns can be contaminated with both types of noise. Another application of AMS is as classification tools [8-9], however they were only tested in the classification of simple objects. Recently in [10] it was introduced a new associative model which has demonstrated to be useful for both applications (as a filter and as a classification tool); due to its robustness, the model has been recently applied to retrieve images from a database [11]. In this paper, we adopt the same model to solve the problem of image categorization.

Most of the information on the web is disposed as images; however this information is not well organized. In order to organize those millions of images it is necessary categorize them in some manner. In [12], for example, the authors use objective

J.F. Martínez-Trinidad et al. (Eds.): CIARP 2006, LNCS 4225 , pp. 549–558, 2006.

semantic cues for the semantic indexing and quering of images. In this paper we describe how images can be categorized using the AM model recently introduced in [10]. If we feed an AM with a picture we expect that it would respond with something indicating the content of the picture. If, for example the picture contains a tiger, we would expect that the AM would respond with the word "tiger". With this goal in mind, we first select a set of images; we then manually associate these images with a description of the images. With these associations we finally train the corresponding AM. To test the proposal we use a set of images containing different species of flowers and animals; we expect to categorize instances of these images even if they appear distorted by noise.

The remaining of the paper is organized as follows. In section 2, we describe the adopted AM model. In section 3, we describe how the proposal is implemented, while in section 4, we present the obtained experimental results. In section 5, we finally conclude and give some directions for further research.

2 Associative Model

An association between input pattern $\mathbf{x}$ and output pattern $\mathbf{y}$ is denoted as $(\mathbf{x}^k, \mathbf{y}^k)$, where k is the corresponding association. The associative memory $\mathbf{M}$ is represented by a matrix whose component m_{ij} can be seen as the synapses neuron i and neuron j. $\mathbf{M}$ is generated from a finite a priori set of know associations, known as the fundamental set of association and is represented as: $\{(\mathbf{x}^k, \mathbf{y}^k) \mid k = 1,2,\ldots,p\}$ where p is the number of associations. If $\mathbf{x}^k = \mathbf{y}^k \ \forall k \in \{1,2,\ldots p\}$ then $\mathbf{M}$ is auto-associative, otherwise it is hetero-associative. A distorted version of a pattern $\mathbf{x}$ to be restored will be denoted as $\tilde{\mathbf{x}}$. If an associative memory $\mathbf{M}$ is fed with a distorted version of $\mathbf{x}^k$ and the output obtained is exactly $\mathbf{y}^k$, we say that recalling is perfect.

2.1 Building and Testing the Associative Memory

Two main phases are used to build and test the AM model.

Training Phase:

1. For each couple $\{(\mathbf{x}^k, \mathbf{y}^k) \mid k = 1,2,\ldots,p\}$ build matrix $\mathbf{y} \Diamond_{\mathrm{A}} \mathbf{x}^t$ as:

$$\mathbf{y} \Diamond_{\mathrm{A}} \mathbf{x}^t = \begin{pmatrix} \mathrm{A}(y_1, x_1) & \mathrm{A}(y_1, x_2) & \cdots & \mathrm{A}(y_1, x_n) \\ \mathrm{A}(y_2, x_1) & \mathrm{A}(y_2, x_2) & \cdots & \mathrm{A}(y_2, x_n) \\ \vdots & \vdots & \ddots & \vdots \\ \mathrm{A}(y_m, x_1) & \mathrm{A}(y_m, x_2) & \cdots & \mathrm{A}(y_m, x_n) \end{pmatrix}_{m \times n}$$

with $\mathrm{A}(x, y) = x - y$.

2. Apply the median operator to the matrix obtained in step1 to get matrix $\mathbf{M}$.

$$m_{ij} = \underset{k=1}{\overset{p}{\mathbf{med}}} \mathrm{A}\left(y_i^k, x_j^k\right) \tag{1}$$

Recalling Phase:

A pattern $\mathbf{x}^k$ is presented to the memory $\mathbf{M}$ and the following operation is done to recall $\mathbf{y}^k$:

$$\left(\mathbf{M} \Diamond_{\mathrm{B}} \tilde{\mathbf{x}}^k\right)_i = \underset{j=1}{\overset{n}{\mathbf{mid}}} \mathrm{B}\left(m_{ij}, \tilde{x}_j^k\right) \tag{2}$$

In this case $\mathrm{B}(x, y) = x + y$ and operator **mid** is defined as $\mathbf{mid}\ \mathbf{x} = x_{(n+1)/2}$.

2.2 A Dynamic Associate Memory

Humans, in general, do not have problems to recall patterns even in the presence of noise. Before an input pattern is learned or processed by the brain, it is hypothesized that it is transformed and codified by the brain. This process can be simulated using the algorithm described in [8]:

Procedure 1. Transform the fundamental set of associations into codified patterns and de-codifier patterns:

```
Input: FS Fundamental set of associations:
{
  1. Make d = const and make (x̄¹,ȳ¹) = (x¹,y¹)
  2. For the remaining couples do {
       For k = 2 to p {
         For i = 1 to n {
              x̄ᵢᵏ = x̄ᵢᵏ⁻¹ + d ;  x̂ᵢᵏ = x̄ᵢᵏ − xᵢᵏ
              ȳᵢᵏ = ȳᵢᵏ⁻¹ + d ;  ŷᵢᵏ = ȳᵢᵏ − yᵢᵏ }
       }
}
Output: Set of codified and de-codifier patterns.
```

This procedure allows computing codified patterns from input and output patterns denoted by $\overline{\mathbf{x}}$ and $\overline{\mathbf{y}}$, respectively. On the other hand $\hat{\mathbf{x}}$ and $\hat{\mathbf{y}}$ are the de-codifier patterns. In addition a simplified version of $\mathbf{x}^k$ denoted by s_k is obtained using:

$$s_k = s\left(\mathbf{x}^k\right) = \mathbf{mid}\ \mathbf{x}^k \tag{3}$$

When the brain is stimulated by an input pattern, some regions of the brain are stimulated by its information, also are the synapses belonging to that region. We call these regions *active regions* and are computed as follow:

$$ar = r(\mathbf{x}) = \arg\left(\bigwedge_{i=1}^{p} \left| s(\mathbf{x}) - s_i \right| \right) \tag{4}$$

Principal synapses (kernel of the AM) are located in the middle column of matrix $\mathbf{M}$ and is denoted by $\mathbf{K}_\mathbf{M} = \mathbf{mid}_{i=1}^{m} w_i$. The synapses that belong to $\mathbf{K}_\mathbf{M}$ are modified as a response to the input pattern. This pattern stimulates some regions, interacts with these active regions and then, according to those interactions modifies the synapses. Adjusting factor is denoted by Δw and is given as:

$$\Delta w = \Delta(\mathbf{x}) = s(\overline{\mathbf{x}}^r) - s(\mathbf{x}) \tag{5}$$

where r is the index of the active region.

Finally synapses belonging to $\mathbf{K}_\mathbf{M}$ are updated as:

$$\mathbf{K}_\mathbf{M} = \mathbf{K}_\mathbf{M} \oplus (\Delta w_{new} - \Delta w_{old}) \tag{6}$$

where operator $\oplus$ is defined as $\mathbf{x} \oplus d = x_i + d \ \forall i = 1, \ldots, m$.

Using this dynamic approach an AM can be built using the following procedure:

1. Transform the fundamental set of association into codified and de-codifier patterns using procedure 1.
2. Compute simplified versions of input patterns using equation 3.
3. Build matrix $\mathbf{M}$ in terms of codified patters: apply step 1 and 2 of the training procedure described at the beginning of section 2.

Given a pattern $\mathbf{x}^k$ or a distorted version of it $\tilde{\mathbf{x}}^k$, pattern $\mathbf{y}^k$ can be recovered as follows:

1. Obtain index of active region ar by means of equation 4.
2. Transform $\mathbf{x}^k$ using de-codifier pattern $\hat{\mathbf{x}}^{ar}$ as: $\widehat{\mathbf{x}}^k = \mathbf{x}^k + \hat{\mathbf{x}}^{ar}$.
3. Compute adjusting factor $\Delta w = \Delta(\widehat{\mathbf{x}})$ by using equation 5.
4. Modify synapses of associative memory $\mathbf{M}$ that belong to $\mathbf{K}_\mathbf{M}$ by means of equation 6.

5. Apply step 1 of the recalling phase described in section 2.
6. Obtain $\mathbf{y}^k$ by transforming $\widehat{\mathbf{y}}^k$ by using de-codifier pattern $\hat{\mathbf{y}}^{ar}$ as: $\mathbf{y}^k = \widehat{\mathbf{y}}^k - \hat{\mathbf{y}}^{ar}$.

3 Categorizing Images

Image categorization is not trivial when pictures are taken from real life situations. This implies that categorization must be invariant to several image transformations such as translations, rotations, scale changes, illumination changes, orientation changes, noise, and so on.

A first step to solve this problem, we provide a solution when the concerned images are distorted only by mixed noise. For this we use the associative model described in section 2. Firstly, we select a set of images. We then associate these images with describing words. The images and the describing words are our set of associations, with $\mathbf{x}^k$ is the k-image and $\mathbf{y}^k$ the k-describing word. With this set of associations we next proceed to build the corresponding associative memory as explained in section 2.1.

Either for learning or recall, each color image $f_k(i,j)$ is converted to a vector by means of standard scanning method. If image $f_k(i,j)$ is of size $M \times N$ pixels, then its corresponding vector is $\mathbf{x}^k = \begin{bmatrix} x_1^k & x_2^k & \dots & x_{M\times N}^k \end{bmatrix}^T$.

The elements $y_r^k, r = 1,\dots,R$ of vector $\mathbf{y}^k$ correspond to the ASCII codes of the letters of each describing word. R is the number of letters of a given word.

Something important with this proposal is that we can control the degree of detail of categorization going from something general to something particular. Let us suppose, for example, that the set of selected images contain just animals, and that then we can categorize these animals into oviparous or viviparous. If we want more detail, we can categorize oviparous animal in reptiles and birds, and so on.

4 Experimental Results

In this section, we test the accuracy of the proposal with a set of 40 images containing flowers and animals as shown Figure 1.

Three experiments where performed in order to determine the accuracy of the proposal. We use different description levels. In the first experiment we categorized the set images into classes: flowers or animals. In second experiment we went more in detail and split flowers and animals into different families of species, eleven families for flowers and six families for animals; seventeen classes in total. In the last experiment, we categorized each flower and animal into its particular name; here we categorized the images into forty classes.

Fig. 1. Set of images of flowers and animals used in the experiments

In the first experiment we associated whole flowers with the description word **"flowers"** and complete animals with the description word **"animals".** These associations allow us to categorize the images into two classes; this is a description of level 1, see Figure 2.

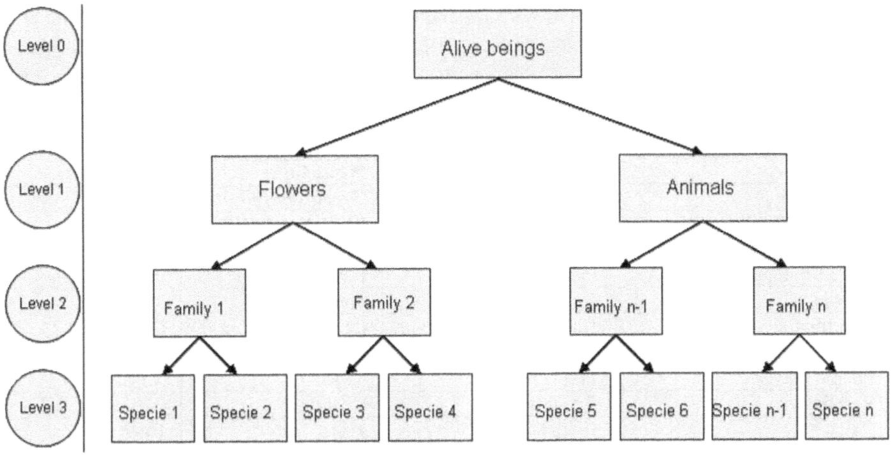

Fig. 2. Description levels used to train the associative memory in the three different experiments

For the second experiment we decided to categorize the images into different families, see Table 1. In this case we associated the flower and the animals belonging to a specific family with the name of the family.

Table 1. Different species of flowers and animals associated to a specific family. This implies that if the associative memory is fed with an image of a lion, leopard or tiger, the associative memory will respond with the word "felines" and so on.

Family (description word)	Species
Agapanthus	Agapanthus
Calla lily	White calla lily, yellow call lily
Bougainvillea	Yellow bougainvillea, purple bougainvillea
Cactaceae	Cactus, nopals
Dianthus	Dianthus
Dahlia	Dahlia
Other flowers	Purple flower, red flower, white flower, green-red flower, black flower
Geranium	White geranium, pink geranium, cranesbills
Daisy	Daisy
Gazania	Gazania
SunFlower	Sunflower
Birds	Ostrich, peacock, flamingo, goose, macaw
Primates	Chimpanzee, spider monkey
Felines	Lion, leopard, tiger
Dogs	Wild dog, domestic dogs
Big animals	Bison, elephant, hippopotamus, rhinoceros, bear
Small animas	Impala, turtle, zebra

For the last experiment we associated each image with the name of the specie appearing on the image, see Table 2.

Table 2. Each species is associated with the name of the specie. This implies that if the associative memory is fed with the image of the tiger, the associative memory will respond with the word "tiger" and so on.

Description word	Specie	Description word	Specie
Agapanthus	Agapanthus	**White flower**	White flower
White calla lily	White calla lily	**Green-red flower**	Green-red flower
Yellow calla lily	Yellow calla lily	**Black flower**	Black flower
Yellow bougainvillea	Yellow bougainvillea	**White geranium**	White geranium
Purple bougainvilie	Purple bougainvilie	**Pink geranium**	Pink geranium
Cactus	Cactus	**Sunflower**	Sunflower
Dianthus	Dianthus	**Cranesbills**	Cranesbills
Dahlia	Dahlia	**Daisy**	Daisy
Purple flower	Purple flower	**Nopal**	Nopal
Red flower	Red flower	**Gazania**	Gazania
Ostrich	Ostrich	**Tiger**	Tiger
Bison	Bison	**Turtle**	Turtle
Chimpanzee	Chimpanzee	**Zebra**	Zebra
Elephant	Elephant	**Domestic dog**	Domestic dog
Impala	Impala	**Flamingo**	Flamingo
Lion	Lion	**Goose**	Goose
Leopard	Leopard	**Hippopotamus**	Hippopotamus
Peacock	Peacock	**Spider monkey**	Spider monkey
Wild dog	Wild dog	**Bear**	Bear
Rhinoceros	Rhinoceros	**Macaw**	Macaw

Once the associative memory in each experiment was trained we manually contaminated the images with noise and then we fed the associative memories with the contaminated image in order to obtain its categorization.

As you can appreciate in Figure 3, whole images were perfectly categorized in the three experiments. These results support the accuracy of the proposal.

5 Conclusion and Ongoing Research

In this paper we have described how an associative memory can be used for categorizing images containing complex objects as flowers and animals. Although only the proposal was tested with images manually modified, the results were highly acceptable.

It is important to mention that this is the first time that an associative memory is used to categorize images, and the most important, complex images with flowers and animals.

In addition, we have categorized images in three different description levels. We performed three experiments going from a general description to a particular description. These descriptions can also be arranged into a hierarchical tree of descriptions. On the other hand we have demonstrated the robustness of the associative model categorizing images in more than twenty classes.

The associative model used is robust under some affine transformations but only when the images contain plastic objects; however with complex images the associative model could provide a low accuracy.

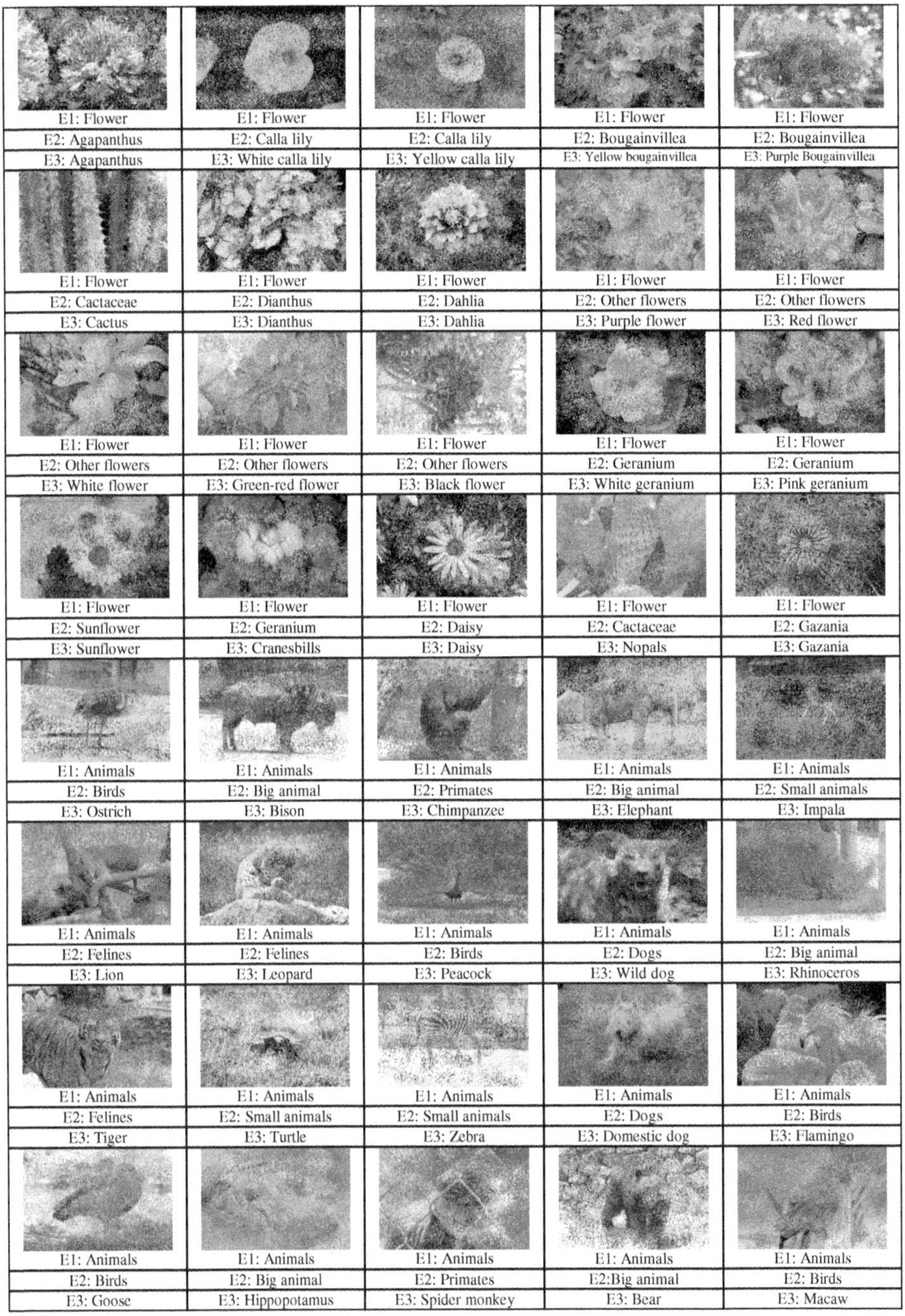

Fig. 3. Results obtained in the experiments using altered images. E1:xx represents the description word obtained by feeding the memory with the image in experiment 1. The same occurs for E2 and E3.

Nowadays we are facing more complex problems, for example when the images present illumination changes and some image transformations, such as translations, rotations, scale changes, and so on. By solving all of these problems and by combining the solution with a hierarchical arrangement of associative memories it might be possible to develop a powerful image retrieval system.

Acknowledgements. This research was economically supported by SIP-IPN under grants 20050156 and 20060517 and SEP-CONACYT by means of grant SEP-2004-C01-46806/1215.

References

1. K. Steinbuch (1961). Die Lernmatrix. Kybernetik, 1(1):26-45.
2. J. A. Anderson (1972). A simple neural network generating an interactive memory. Mathematical Biosciences, 14:197-220.
3. T. Kohonen (1972). Correlation matrix memories. IEEE Trans. on Computers, 21(4): 353-359.
4. J. J. Hopfield (1982). Neural networks and physical systems with emergent collective computational abilities. Proceedings of the National Academy of Sciences, 79: 2554-2558, 1982.
5. P. Sussner (2003). Generalizing operations of binary auto-associative morphological memories using fuzzy set theory. Journal of mathematical Imaging and Vision, 19(2): 81-93.
6. G. X. Ritter, G. Urcid, L. Iancu (2003). Reconstruction of patterns from noisy inputs using morphological associative memories. Journal of mathematical Imaging and Vision, 19(2):95-111.
7. H. Sossa and R. Barron (2003). New associative model for pattern recall in the presence of mixed noise. In Proceedings of the fithh IASTED International Conference on Signal and Image Processing, SIP2003. Acta Press 399:485-490.
8. H. Sossa, R. Barrón, R. A. Vázquez (2004). Transforming Fundamental set of Patterns to a Canonical Form to Improve Pattern Recall. LNAI 3315:687-696. Springer Verlag.
9. H. Sossa, R. Barrón, R. A. Vázquez (2004). New associative memories for recall real-valued patterns. LNCS 3287:195-202. Sprinegr Verlag.
10. R. A. Vázquez, H. Sossa and R. Barrón (2006). Enhanced associative memory model for pattern restoration. To be submitted.
11. R. A. Vázquez and H. Sossa (2006). Associative memories applied to image retrieval. Submitted to MICAI 2006.
12. A, Mojsilović, J. Gomes and B. Rogowitz (2004). Semantic-Friendly Indexing and Quering of Images Based on the Extraction of the Objective Semantic Cues. International Journal of Computer Vision, Special Issue on Content-Based Image Retrieval, 56(1-2):79-107.

Robustness Analysis of the Neural Gas Learning Algorithm*

Carolina Saavedra[1], Sebastián Moreno[1], Rodrigo Salas[1,2], and Héctor Allende[1,3]

[1] Universidad Técnica Federico Santa María;
Dept. de Informática; Casilla 110-V; Valparaíso-Chile
{smoreno, saavedra, hallende}@inf.utfsm.cl
[2] Universidad de Valparaíso; Departamento de Computación
rodrigo.salas@uv.cl
[3] Universidad Adolfo Ibañez; Facultad de Ciencia y Tecnología

Abstract. The Neural Gas (NG) is a Vector Quantization technique where a set of prototypes self organize to represent the topology structure of the data. The learning algorithm of the Neural Gas consists in the estimation of the prototypes location in the feature space based in the stochastic gradient descent of an Energy function. In this paper we show that when deviations from idealized distribution function assumptions occur, the behavior of the Neural Gas model can be drastically affected and will not preserve the topology of the feature space as desired. In particular, we show that the learning algorithm of the NG is sensitive to the presence of outliers due to their influence over the adaptation step.

We incorporate a robust strategy to the learning algorithm based on M-estimators where the influence of outlying observations are bounded. Finally we make a comparative study of several estimators where we show the superior performance of our proposed method over the original NG, in static data clustering tasks on both synthetic and real data sets.

Keywords: Neural Gas, Robust Learning Algorithm, M-estimators.

1 Introduction

The Neural Gas (NG), introduced by Martinetz et. al. [6], is a vector quantization technique that has been successfully applied in several areas as pattern recognition and data mining (see [9]). The NG is a variant of the Kohonen Self-Organizing Map [5] where the neighborhood relation is adaptively defined by the ranking order of the distance between the prototypes and the sample data. The NG has the advantage of being flexible and capable of both quantizing topologically heterogeneously structured manifolds and learning the similarity relationships among the input signals without the necessity of specifying a network topology.

The learning algorithm for the parameter estimation of neural networks models rely on the data. In real engineering and scientific applications, data are noisy with the presence of outlying observations. Assumptions of the underlying data generation process

* This work was supported in part by Research Grant Fondecyt 1061201, 1040365 and 7060040; and in part by DGIP-UTFSM.

J.F. Martínez-Trinidad et al. (Eds.): CIARP 2006, LNCS 4225, pp. 559–568, 2006.

no longer holds and the model estimates are badly affected obtaining a poor performance (see for example [1] and [8]).

In [2] and [7] the authors empirically show that the Neural Gas lacks of robustness and they incorporated several robust strategies such as outlier resistant scheme. In this paper we show that when deviations from idealized distribution function assumptions occurs, the behavior of the Neural Gas model can be drastically affected and will not preserve the topology of the feature space as desired. In particular, we show that the learning algorithm of the NG is sensitive to the presence of outliers due to their influence in the adaptation step. We incorporate a robust strategy to the learning algorithm based on M-estimators where the influence of outlying observations is bounded.

The remainder of this paper is organized as follows. In the next section we briefly introduce the Neural Gas model. In section 3 we review some concepts of Robust M-estimator applied to the learning process. In section 4 we investigate the robustness properties of the NG by casting the learning algorithm as a statistical estimation problem, furthermore, we introduce the M-estimators as a robust scheme for the parameter estimation process. In section 5 we provide a comparative study of several estimators where we show the superior performance of the robust methods over the original NG, in static data clustering tasks on both synthetic and real data sets. Conclusions and further work are given in section 6.

2 Neural Gas

The "Neural-Gas" (NG) model consists of an ordered set $\mathbf{m} = \{\mathbf{m}_1, ..., \mathbf{m}_M\}$ of M prototypes, neurons or "codebooks" vectors $\mathbf{m}_j \in \mathcal{M} \subseteq \mathbb{R}^d$, $j = 1, .., M$ arranged according to a neighborhood ranking relation between the units.

When the data vector $\mathbf{x} \in \mathcal{X} \subseteq \mathbb{R}^d$ is presented to the NG model, it is projected to a neuron position by searching the best matching unit (bmu), i.e., the prototype that is closest to the input, and it is obtained as $c(\mathbf{x}) = \arg\min_{j=1..M} \{\|\mathbf{x} - \mathbf{m}_j\|\}$, where $\|\cdot\|$ is the classical Euclidean norm. This procedure divides the manifold $\mathcal{X}$ into a number of subregions $V_j = \{\mathbf{x} \in \mathcal{X} | \ \|\mathbf{x} - \mathbf{m}_j\| \leq \|\mathbf{x} - \mathbf{m}_i\| \forall i\}$, called Voronoi polygons or Voronoi polyhedra, where each data vector $\mathbf{x}$ is described by its corresponding reference vector $\mathbf{m}_j$.

The neighborhood relation of the prototypes in the NG model is defined by the ranking order of the distance of the codebook vectors to the given sample. When a data vector $\mathbf{x}$ is presented, the "neighborhood-ranking" $(\mathbf{m}_{i_0}, \mathbf{m}_{i_1}, ..., \mathbf{m}_{i_{M-1}})$ is determined, with $\mathbf{m}_{i_0}$ being the closest to $\mathbf{x}$, $\mathbf{m}_{i_1}$ being second closest to $\mathbf{x}$, and $\mathbf{m}_{i_k}, k = 0, .., M-1$, being the reference vector for which there are k vectors $\mathbf{m}_j$ with $\|\mathbf{x} - \mathbf{m}_j\| < \|\mathbf{x} - \mathbf{m}_{i_k}\|$. If $k_j(\mathbf{x}, \mathbf{m})$ denotes the number k associated with each vector $\mathbf{m}_j$, which depends on $\mathbf{x}$ and the whole set $\mathbf{m}$ of reference vectors, then the adaptation step for adjusting the $\mathbf{m}_j$'s is given by:

$$\mathbf{m}_j(t+1) = \mathbf{m}_j(t) + \alpha h_\lambda(k_j(\mathbf{x}, \mathbf{m}))(\mathbf{x} - \mathbf{m}_j) \qquad j = 1, .., M \tag{1}$$

with both the learning parameter function $\alpha = \alpha(t) \in [0, 1]$ and the characteristic decay function $\lambda = \lambda(t)$ are monotonically decreasing functions with respect to time. For example for α the function could be linear $\alpha(t) = \alpha_0 + (\alpha_f - \alpha_0)t/t_\alpha$ or exponential

$\alpha(t) = \alpha_0(\alpha_f/\alpha_0)^{t/t_\alpha}$, where α_0 is the initial learning rate (< 1.0), α_f is the final rate (≈ 0.01) and t_α is the maximum number of iteration steps to arrive α_f. Analogously for λ (See [10] for further details).

The neighborhood kernel $h_\lambda(k_j(\mathbf{x}, \mathbf{m}))$ is unity for $k_j = 0$ and decays to zero for increasing k_j. In this paper we use $h_\lambda(k_i(\mathbf{x}, \mathbf{m})) = \exp^{k_i(\mathbf{x},\mathbf{m})/\lambda}$. Note that if $\lambda \to 0$ then (1) is the K-means adaptations rule, whereas for $\lambda \neq 0$ not only the "winner" (bmu) $\mathbf{m}_{i_0}$ but the second closest reference vector $\mathbf{m}_{i_1}$, third closest vector $\mathbf{m}_{i_2}$, etc., are also updated.

Martinetz et. al. [6] showed that the dynamics of the $\mathbf{m}_j$'s obeys a stochastic gradient descent on the cost function:

$$E_{ng}(\mathbf{m}, \lambda) = \frac{1}{2C(\lambda)} \sum_{i=1}^{M} \int h_\lambda(k_i(\mathbf{x}, \mathbf{m}))(\mathbf{x} - \mathbf{m}_i)^2 dF(\mathbf{x}) \tag{2}$$

where $C(\lambda) = \sum_{i=1}^{M} h_\lambda(k_i) = \sum_{k=0}^{M-1} h_\lambda(k)$ is a normalization factor that only depends on λ. $F(\mathbf{x})$ is the probability distribution measure of the data generating process.

3 Robust M-Estimators for the Learning Process

The learning process of the NG can be seen as a parameter estimation process, and their inference relies on the data [2]. When observations substantially different from the bulk of data exist, they can influence badly the model structure bringing degradation in the estimates. In this work we seek for a robust estimator of the NG parameters based on M-estimators (see [4]).

Let the data set $\{\mathbf{x}_1, ..., \mathbf{x}_n\}$ consists of an independent and identically distributed (i.i.d.) sample of size n obtained from the input space $\mathcal{X} \subseteq \mathbb{R}^d$ of dimension d, i.e., $\mathbf{x}_i \in \mathcal{X}$. An M-estimator $\hat{\theta}_n^M$ is defined as

$$\hat{\theta}_n^M = \arg\min\{RL_n(\theta) : \theta \in \Theta\} \quad \text{with} \quad RL_n(\theta) = \frac{1}{n}\sum_{i=1}^{n} \rho(\mathbf{x}_i, \theta)$$

where $\Theta \subseteq \mathbb{R}^D$ is the parametric space, $RL_n(\theta)$ is a functional cost and $\rho : \mathcal{X} \times \Theta \to \mathbb{R}$ is the function that we will name it robust when it introduces a bound to the influence of outliers data during the training process. By assuming that the function ρ is differentiable with respect the parameter $\theta = (\theta_1, ..., \theta_D)$, we obtain the score function $\psi(\mathbf{x}, \theta) = (\psi_1, ..., \psi_D)'$ whose components are the partial derivatives $\psi_j(\mathbf{x}, \theta) = \frac{\partial \rho(\mathbf{x}_i, \theta)}{\partial \theta_j}$, $j = 1..D$. Then the M-estimator can be defined implicitly as the solution of the vector equations $\frac{1}{n}\sum_{i=1}^{n} \psi_j(\mathbf{x}_i, \theta) = \mathbf{0}$, $j = 1..D$. Table 1 shows the Least Square (LS), Huber (H) and Tukey's biweight (B) methods as examples of M-estimators. Please refer to [4] for further examples of robust functions.

We consider estimators T which are functionals of the distribution functions, i.e., $T = T(F)$, and estimators that are Fisher consistent $T(F) = \theta$. The *influence function* (IF) of the functional T at the distribution function $F = F(\mathbf{x})$ is defined as

$$IF(\mathbf{x}; T, F) = \lim_{t \to 0} \frac{T((1-t)F + t\Delta_{\mathbf{x}}) - T(F)}{t}$$

where $(1-t)F + t\Delta_{\mathbf{x}}$ is the t-contaminated model of the distribution $F(\mathbf{x})$, where $\Delta_{\mathbf{x}}$ is the probability measure which puts mass 1 at the point $\mathbf{x}$. The influence function is a local measure introduced by Hampel [4] that describes the effect of an infinitesimal contamination at the point $\mathbf{x}$ on the estimate.

Table 1. Examples of M-estimators

Name	$\rho(x)$	$\psi(x)$
Least square	$x^2/2$	x
Huber	$\begin{cases} x^2/2 & \lvert x\rvert \le \kappa \\ \kappa\,\lvert x\rvert - \kappa^2/2 & \lvert x\rvert > \kappa \end{cases}$	$\begin{cases} x & \lvert x\rvert \le \kappa \\ \kappa\ sign(x) & \lvert x\rvert > \kappa \end{cases}$
Tukey's biweight	$\begin{cases} \kappa^2(1-[1-x^2/\kappa^2]^3)/ & \lvert x\rvert \le \kappa \\ \kappa^2/6 & \lvert x\rvert > \kappa \end{cases}$	$\begin{cases} x[1-x^2/\kappa^2]^2 & \lvert x\rvert \le \kappa \\ 0 & \lvert x\rvert > \kappa \end{cases}$

An important summary value based on the IF is the gross error sensitivity that measure the worst (approximate) influence which a small amount of contamination of fixed sized can have on the value of estimator. The *gross error sensitivity* of the estimator T at the distribution F is defined as $\gamma(T, F) := \sup_{\mathbf{x}}\{\|IF(\mathbf{x}, T, F)\|\}$. It is a desirable feature that $\gamma(T, F)$ be finite and in such case we say that T is B-Robust at F.

4 Robustness Analysis of the Learning Algorithm

Let the data set $\{\mathbf{x}_1, ..., \mathbf{x}_n\}$, $\mathbf{x}_i \in \mathcal{X} \subseteq \mathbb{R}^d$, consists of an independent and identically distributed (i.i.d) sample of size n with common probability distribution $F(\mathbf{x})$. The cost function of equation (2) is generalized to the following form:

$$\begin{aligned} E_{ng}(\mathbf{m}, \lambda) &= \frac{1}{C(\lambda)} \sum_{i=1}^{M} \int_{\mathcal{X}} h_\lambda(k_i(\mathbf{x}, \mathbf{m}))\rho(\mathbf{x} - m_i) dF(\mathbf{x}) \\ &= \frac{1}{C(\lambda)} \int_{\mathcal{X}} \sum_{i=1}^{M} h_\lambda(k_i(\mathbf{x}, \mathbf{m}))\rho(\mathbf{x} - m_i) dF(\mathbf{x}) \\ &= \frac{1}{C(\lambda)} \int_{\mathcal{X}} \eta(\mathbf{x}, \mathbf{m}) dF(\mathbf{x}) \end{aligned} \tag{3}$$

where the second equation is obtained by interchanging the integral with the summand. Let the function $\eta : \mathcal{X} \times \mathcal{M} \longrightarrow \mathbb{R}$ be defined as $\eta(\mathbf{x}, \mathbf{m}) = \sum_{i=1}^{M} h_\lambda(k_i(\mathbf{x}, \mathbf{m}))\rho(\mathbf{x} - m_i)$ and $\rho : \mathcal{X} \times \mathcal{M} \longrightarrow \mathbb{R}$ is the function of the M-estimator functional cost (see table 1 for examples).

An M-estimator is defined as the value $\hat{\mathbf{m}} = \{\hat{\mathbf{m}}_1, ..., \hat{\mathbf{m}}_M\}$ such that

$$\hat{\mathbf{m}} = arg\ \min_{\mathbf{m}} \{E_{ng}(\mathbf{m}, \lambda)\}$$

Assuming that ρ is differentiable whose derivative is given by $\psi(r) = \frac{\partial \rho(r)}{\partial r}$ then

$$\varphi_j(\mathbf{x}, \mathbf{m}) = \frac{\partial \eta(\mathbf{x}, \mathbf{m})}{\partial \mathbf{m}_j} = -h_\lambda(k_j(\mathbf{x}, \mathbf{m}))\psi(\mathbf{x} - \mathbf{m}_j) + R_j \qquad j = 1, ..., M$$

with $R_j = \sum_{i=1}^{M} h'_\lambda(k_j(\mathbf{x}, \mathbf{m}))\rho(\mathbf{x} - \mathbf{m}_j)\frac{\partial k_i(\mathbf{x},\mathbf{m})}{\partial \mathbf{m}_j}$. Martinez et al. [6] demonstrated that $\int R_j dF(x) = 0$ for each $j = 1, .., M$. An M-estimator $\hat{\mathbf{m}}$ can be defined implicitly by the solution of the vector equation $\varphi_j(\mathbf{x}, \mathbf{m}) = 0, \forall j = 1, ..., M$.

The influence function $IF_j(\mathbf{x}, \mathbf{m}, F)$ associated to the M-estimator $\hat{\mathbf{m}}_j$ is given by the following equation:

$$IF_j(\mathbf{x}, \mathbf{m}, F) = h_\lambda(k_j(\mathbf{x}, \mathbf{m}))\psi(\mathbf{x} - \mathbf{m}_j)H^{-1} \qquad \forall j = 1, ..., M$$

where $H = -\int \frac{\partial}{\partial \mathbf{m}} \left[\varphi_j(\mathbf{x}, \mathbf{m})\right]_{\hat{\mathbf{m}}} dF(\mathbf{x})$. Note that if the classical Least Square estimator is used, then the gross error sensitivity is $\gamma(\hat{\mathbf{m}}^{LS}, F) = \infty$, this reflect the fact that, for any samples size, even a single outlier can carry the estimates over all bounds (if it is far enough).

4.1 Robust Learning Algorithm

The updating rule (1) employed in the original NG algorithm lacks of robustness as was shown in the previous section. The gross error sensitivity is infinity implying that the learning step is biased toward the location of the outlying observations. To overcome this problem the following updating rule that obeys a stochastic gradient descent on the cost function (3) is used instead:

$$\mathbf{m}_j(t+1) = \mathbf{m}_j(t) + \alpha h_\lambda(k_j(\mathbf{x}, \mathbf{m}))\psi(\mathbf{x} - \mathbf{m}_j) \qquad j = 1, ..., M \tag{4}$$

where the $\psi(\cdot)$ function diminish the influence of the outliers (see table 1 for examples). Unfortunately, the learning rule of equation (4) is not invariant with respect to scale, which is often a nuisance parameter. To overcome this problem we can standardized each data sample $\mathbf{x}_i = (x_1, ..., x_d)'$ as $\hat{S}_j^{-1/2}(\mathbf{x} - \mathbf{m}_j)$, where $\hat{S}_j$ is the robust estimation of the covariance matrix of the difference $\mathbf{x} - \mathbf{m}_j$ of all the data that belong to the Voronoi polygon V_j, and $\hat{S}_j^{-1/2} = \sqrt{\hat{S}_j^{-1}}$ is the square root of the inverse of the covariance matrix. Now we can redefine the robust learning rule as follows

$$\mathbf{m}_j(t+1) = \mathbf{m}_j(t) + \alpha h_\lambda(k_j(\mathbf{x}, \mathbf{m}))\psi\left(\hat{S}_j^{-1/2}(\mathbf{x} - \mathbf{m}_j)\right) \qquad j = 1, .., M \tag{5}$$

One could compute $\mathbf{m}$ and $\hat{S}$ simultaneously as M-estimators of location and scale respectively. However, simulations have shown the superiority of M-estimators with scale estimated iteratively during the learning process by the scaled version of the *median of the absolute deviations from the median* (sMAD):

$$sMAD(x_1, ..x_n) = \frac{1}{\Phi^{-1}(\frac{3}{4})} \underset{l=1..n}{median} \left\{ \left| x_l - \underset{k=1..n}{median}(x_k)) \right| \right\}$$

where $\Phi^{-1}(p)$ is the inverse of the standard Gaussian cumulative distribution function at the probability p. The constant $\frac{1}{\Phi^{-1}(\frac{3}{4})} \approx 1.483$ is needed to make the $sMAD$ scale estimator Fisher consistent when the data behave as Gaussian distribution. We apply the sMAD function for each dimension component of the sample $\{(\mathbf{x_i} - \mathbf{m}_j)\}_{i=1}^{n}$ and for each prototype $j = 1..M$.

The robust M-estimators of the learning update rule have initialization problems. To overcome this situation the constant κ of the $\psi(\cdot)$ function is considered as a function of time and the standard deviation, i.e., $\kappa = \kappa(t)\sigma$, where $\kappa(t)$ monotonically decreases with time. In this paper we use a linear decreasing function $\kappa(t) = \kappa_0 + (\kappa_f - \kappa_0)t/t_f$, where κ_0 is the initial value (bigger than 6); and κ_f is the final value (between 3 and 6) and t_f is the maximum number of iteration steps to arrive κ_f.

5 Simulation Results

In this section we provide a comparative study of the Least Square (LS), Huber (H) and Biweight (B) M-estimators applied to the learning process of the NG, in static data clustering tasks on both synthetic and real data sets, the latter were obtain from the UCI benchmark [3].

In the experiments, all the dimensions of the training data set were scaled to interval $[-1, 1]$, and the test data set were scaled using the same scale applied to the training data set. The test data set will not necessarily fall in the same interval. The number of epochs utilized for all experiments is $t_f = 500$ and the α and λ decay in exponential form with values: $\alpha_0 = 0.9$, $\alpha_f = 0.05$, $\lambda_0 = M/3$, $\lambda_f = 0.01$, $\kappa_0^H = 30$, $\kappa_0^B = 40$ and $\kappa_f = 3$.

5.1 Performance Evaluation of the NG

In the experiments we use the following metrics to evaluate the performance of the NG model. The *Classification Accuracy* (CA) is the right classification percentage

$$CA = \frac{1}{n}\sum_{i=1}^{n} \mathcal{I}(\mathbf{x}_i, \mathbf{m}_{c(\mathbf{x}_i)}) \cdot 100\% \tag{6}$$

where we label the neuron $\mathbf{m}_j$ with the class that has the majority in its Voronoi polygon V_j. $\mathcal{I}(\mathbf{x}_i, \mathbf{m}_{c(\mathbf{x}_i)})$ takes the value of one if the label of the data $\mathbf{x}_i$ is equal to the label of its best matching unit $\mathbf{m}_{c(\mathbf{x}_i)}$, and takes the value of zero in the other case.

The *Mean Square Quantization Error* is given by

$$MSQE = \frac{1}{n}\sum_{i=1}^{n} \left\|\mathbf{x}_i, \mathbf{m}_{c(\mathbf{x}_i)}\right\|^2 \tag{7}$$

The *Mean Distance from the Neurons to the closest cluster Center* measures the average Euclidean distance between the neurons $\mathbf{m}_j$ and its closest cluster center $\mu(\mathbf{m}_j)$:

$$MDNC = \frac{1}{M}\sum_{j=1}^{M} \|\mathbf{m}_j - \mu(\mathbf{m}_j)\|^2 \tag{8}$$

Finally, the *Numbers of clusters Center in the Voronoi polygon* is given by

$$NC = \sum_{\mathbf{m}_j \in \mathcal{M}} |\tau_j - 1| \tag{9}$$

where τ_j correspond to the number of clusters center that are inside the Voronoi polygon V_j. A desirable feature is that each neuron model no more and no less than one cluster center.

5.2 Experiment #1: Computer Generated Data

The synthetic experiments were constructed by generating a square grid of twenty five cluster drawn from two-dimensional Gaussian distributions $\mathbf{X}_l \sim \mathcal{N}(\mu_l, \Sigma_l)$, $l = 1, ..., L = 25$, where μ_l is the mean vector of the cluster l and $\Sigma_l = \Sigma$ is its covariance matrix. A total of 2500 samples for the training and the same quantity for the test were generated, where each cluster has an expected size of 100 samples.

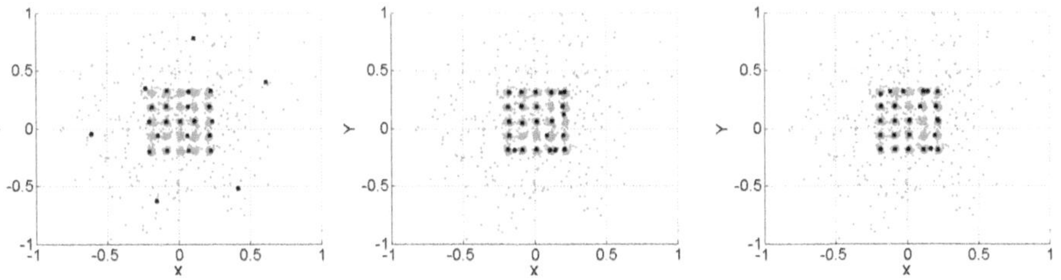

Fig. 1. Topology adaptation of the NG. Comparative results of the NG model to the synthetic data with 15% of outliers for the Least Square (left), Huber (middle) and Biweight (right) estimators.

The observational process is obtained by adding additive outliers: $\mathbf{Z}_l = \mathbf{X}_l + V_l\, U_l$, where V_l is zero-one process with $P(V_l \neq 0) = \varepsilon$, $0 < \varepsilon \ll 1$ and U_l has distribution $\mathcal{N}(\mathbf{0}, \Sigma_U)$ with $|\Sigma_U| \gg |\Sigma|$. The generating process was affected with $\varepsilon = 5\%, 10\%, 15\%$ and 20% of outliers with $\Sigma_U = 27\Sigma$.

Figure 1 shows the adaptation of the NG to the data with 15% of outliers for the three estimators: Least Square (left), Huber (middle) and Biweight (right). The LS estimator was badly affected by locating five prototypes far from the square grid. Nevertheless, the robust estimators (Huber and Biweight) were much less affected and their respective neurons were located inside the grid of 25 clusters, with each neuron close to the some of the clusters center. The robust estimators diminished the influence of the outlying observations and they had a better topology preservation than the LS-estimator.

Table 2 shows the summary results of the performance evaluation of the NG with the three estimators.The LS estimator obtained the lowest $MSQE$ evaluated in the data with outlier for all the experiments (columns $E1$ and $E2$), this result was expected because the LS-estimator minimizes the cost function (3) while the robust estimators minimize the cost function (3). However, if we compute the MSQE in the data without outliers (columns $E3$ and $E4$), the robust estimators outperforms the LS-estimator.

The $CA1$ and $CA2$ show the classification accuracy of the training and test set respectively, as was expected, the robust estimators obtained better performance than the LS-estimator when the percentage of outliers are increased. The column NC computed with equation (9) show how the robust estimators remains stable with an increasing percentage of outliers, while the LS-estimator got worse. Finally, the last column show that the robust estimators outperforms the LS-estimator, meaning that the former locate the prototypes closer to the clusters center. Note that the last two columns measures the quality of the topology preservation of the square grid.

Table 2. Summary results of the performance evaluation of the NG model with 25 prototypes with the LS, H and B estimators used in the training process. The second column is the percentage of outliers in the data. From the columns $E1$ to $E4$ are the value of Mean Square Quantization Error (7), column $E1$ and $E2$ correspond to the error evaluation of training and test set respectively by considering the outliers, while columns $E3$ and $E4$ are the error evaluation of training and test data sets without considering the outliers. The columns $AC1$ and $AC2$ are the value of the Classification Accuracy (6) of the training and test sets respectively by considering the outliers. Finally the column NC and $MDNC$ are the values obtained with equations (9) and (8) respectively.

Estimators	% Outliers	$E1$	$E2$	$E3$	$E4$	$CA1(\%)$	$CA2(\%)$	NC	$MDNC$
LS	5	**0.0039**	**0.0045**	**0.0009**	**0.0009**	**88.7**	**88.0**	**3.8**	0.0171
H	5	0.0063	0.0066	0.0012	0.0013	86.9	85.5	4.8	**0.0004**
B	5	0.0064	0.0067	0.0016	0.0016	82.5	81.6	6.8	0.0005
LS	10	**0.0054**	**0.0065**	0.0013	0.0013	78.4	77.1	7.6	0.0263
H	10	0.0102	0.0112	**0.0011**	**0.0012**	**82.4**	**81.0**	**5.2**	**0.0004**
B	10	0.0103	0.0113	0.0015	0.0016	80.4	79.1	6.0	0.0005
LS	15	**0.0056**	**0.0069**	0.0016	0.0017	69.2	66.4	11.4	0.0388
H	15	0.0134	0.0141	**0.0010**	**0.0011**	76.4	75.9	6.0	**0.0003**
B	15	0.0134	0.0141	0.0013	0.0013	**76.7**	**76.0**	**5.2**	0.0004
LS	20	**0.0065**	**0.0072**	0.0019	0.0019	62.5	59.6	13.6	0.0432
H	20	0.0171	0.0170	**0.0010**	**0.0010**	**74.7**	**73.9**	**5.0**	0.0003
B	20	0.0175	0.0174	0.0013	0.0014	72.5	71.9	6.2	**0.0002**

5.3 Experiment #2: Real Data Sets

In the second experiment we test the algorithm with four real datasets obtained from the UCI Machine Learning repository [3]. The *Wine recognition*, *Glass Identification*, *Cancer* and *Pima Indians Diabetes* data sets were selected.

Figure 2 displays the Mean Square Quantization Error of the M-estimators computed for all the data sets. Similarly to the previous section, the LS-estimator obtained better performance in this metric with respect to the robust estimators. Nevertheless, we can not assure the topology preservation of the LS-estimator as the robust estimators, if the real data are contaminated.

Figure 3 shows the Classification Accuracy of the NG modelling all the real data sets. In the Cancer data set (upper-left) the best performance were obtained with a low number of neurons, while in the other experiments better performance were obtained with increasing number of prototypes. When the number of the prototypes are less than

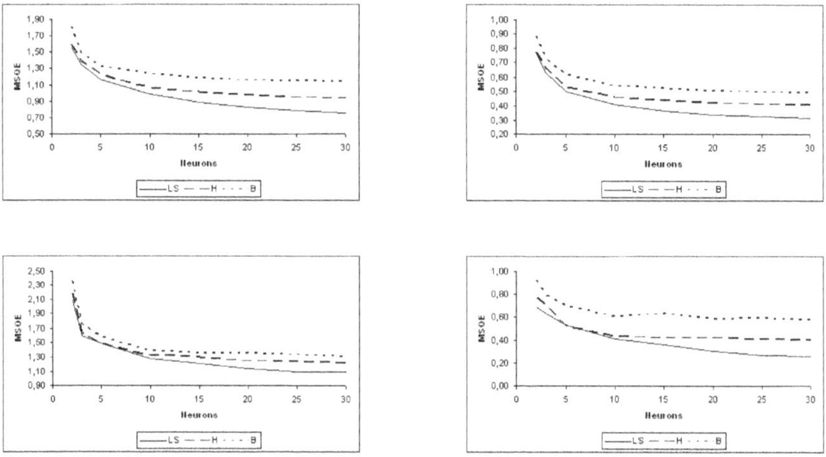

Fig. 2. MSQE performance evaluation for the Real data sets. Neural Gas modelling the Cancer (Upper-Left), Pima Indians Diabetes (Upper-Right), Glass Identification (Bottom-Right) and the Wine Recognition (Bottom-Left) data sets respectively.

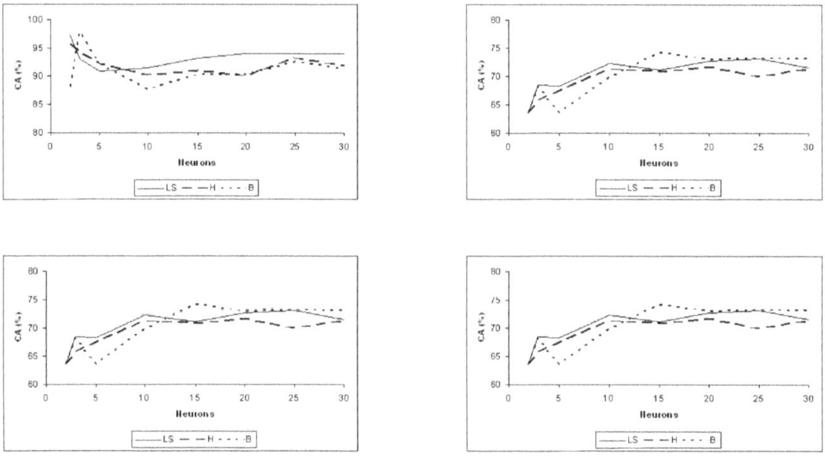

Fig. 3. Classification Accuray for the Real data sets. Neural Gas modelling the Cancer (Upper-Left), Pima Indians Diabetes (Upper-Right), Glass Identification (Bottom-Right) and the Wine Recognition (Bottom-Left) data sets respectively.

the number of classes the performance of the NG model for all the estimator was very poor (the Cancer, the Pima Indians Diabetes, the Glass Identification and the Wine Recognition data sets were composed of 2, 2, 8, 3 classes respectively). Only in the Wine Recognition data set one of the estimators (biweight) outperforms the others, while in the other cases we can not see the superiority of any of the estimators.

6 Concluding Remarks

In this paper we analyzed the robustness properties of the learning process of the Neural Gas model based on the M-estimator robust theory. We have demonstrated that the classical Neural Gas learning algorithm lacks of robustness and with small amount of contamination the codebooks are biased towards the outliers. We have introduced robust M-estimator to diminish the influence of outlying observations and making the learning process more stable.

In the synthetic experiment the robust estimators outperforms the LS-estimator in the topology preservation. However, we empirically showed that the $MSQE$ was not a good performance metric of the adaptation quality under contaminated data.

In the real data experiments, all the estimators showed similar performance in the classification accuracy. But we were not able to assure the topology preservation for the LS-estimator as in the robust estimator case. It is of great importance find algorithms to determine the learning parameters and the ordering properties. Finally, due to the similar behavior in real data sets of all algorithms is better to use a robust function learning to explore the data because it works with or without presence of outliers.

Further studies are needed to extend the results to other class of estimators (L, M and R estimators) as well as other self organizing models. Furthermore, index that measures the quality of topology preservation are needed instead of the MSQE.

References

1. H. Allende, S. Moreno, C. Rogel, and R. Salas, *Robust self organizing maps*, CIARP. LNCS **3287** (2004), 179–186.
2. H. Allende, C. Rogel, S. Moreno, and R. Salas, *Robust neural gas for the analysis of data with outliers*, IEEE-CS Press. SCCC 2004 (2004), 149–155.
3. C.L. Blake and C.J. Merz, *UCI repository of machine learning databases*, 1998.
4. F.R. Hampel, E.M. Ronchetti, P.J. Rousseeuw, and W.A. Stahel, *Robust statistics*, Wiley Series in Probability and Mathematical Statistics, 1986.
5. T. Kohonen, *Self-Organizing Maps*, Springer Series in Information Sciences, vol. 30, Springer Verlag, Berlin, Heidelberg, 2001, Third Extended Edition 2001.
6. T. Martinetz, S. Berkovich, and K. Schulten, *Neural-gas network for vector quantization and its application to time-series prediction*, IEEE Trans. on Neural Networks **4** (1993), no. 4, 558–568.
7. A. Qin and P. Suganthan, *Robust growing neural gas algorithm with application in cluster analysis*, Neural Networks **17** (2004), 1135–1148.
8. R. Salas, S. Moreno, and H. Allende C. Moraga, *A robust and flexible model of hierarchical self organizing maps for nonstationary environments*, To appear in Neurocomputing (2006).
9. U. Seiffert and L. Jain (eds.), *Self-organizing neural networks: Recent advances and applications*, Studies in Fuzziness and Soft Computing, vol. 78, Springer Verlag, 2002.
10. M. Su and H. Chang, *Fast self-organizing feature map algorithm*, IEEE Trans. on Neural Networks **11** (2000), no. 3, 721–733.

Feature Selection Based on Mutual Correlation

Michal Haindl[1], Petr Somol[1],
Dimitrios Ververidis[2], and Constantine Kotropoulos[2]

[1] Institute of Information Theory and Automation,
Academy of Sciences CR,
Prague, CZ182 08, Czech Republic
{haindl, somol}@utia.cas.cz
http://ro.utia.cz

[2] Dept. of Informatics, Aristotle Univ. of Thessaloniki
Box 451, Thessaloniki 541 24, Greece
{jimver, costas}@aiia.csd.auth.gr
http://poseidon.csd.auth.gr

Abstract. Feature selection is a critical procedure in many pattern recognition applications. There are two distinct mechanisms for feature selection namely the wrapper methods and the filter methods. The filter methods are generally considered inferior to wrapper methods, however wrapper methods are computationally more demanding than filter methods. A novel filter feature selection method based on mutual correlation is proposed. We assess the classification performance of the proposed filter method by using the selected features to the Bayes classifier. Alternative filter feature selection methods that optimize either the Bhattacharrrya distance or the divergence are also tested. Furthermore, wrapper feature selection techniques employing several search strategies such as the sequential forward search, the oscillating search, and the sequential floating forward search are also included in the comparative study. A trade off between the classification accuracy and the feature set dimensionality is demonstrated on both two benchmark datasets from UCI repository and two emotional speech data collections.

1 Introduction

Feature selection is defined as the process of selecting D most discriminatory features out of $d \geq D$ available ones [1]. Feature subset selection aims to identify and remove as much irrelevant and redundant information as possible. Feature transformation is defined as the process of projecting the d measurements to a lower dimensional space through a linear or non-linear mapping. Principal component analysis and linear discriminant analysis are probably the most common feature transformations [2]. Both feature extraction and feature transformation reduce data dimensionality and allow learning algorithms to operate faster and more effectively on large datasets and even to improve classification accuracy in some cases. Depending on the available knowledge of class membership, the feature selection can be either supervised or unsupervised.

The feature selection problem is NP-hard. So, the optimal solution is not guaranteed to be found unless except exhaustive search in the feature space is

J.F. Martínez-Trinidad et al. (Eds.): CIARP 2006, LNCS 4225, pp. 569–577, 2006.

performed [1]. Two approaches to feature selection are commonly used namely the wrapper methods and the filter methods. The former use the actual classifier to select the optimal feature subset, while the latter select features independently of the classifier. The filter methods use probability based distances independent of the classification such as the Bhattacharya distance, the Chernoff distance, the Patrick Fisher distance, and the divergence. Both filter and wrapper methods may employ efficient search strategies such as branch and bound, best individual N method, sequential forward selection (SFS), sequential backward selection (SBS), and sequential floating forward search (SFFS).

A novel filter feature selection method based on mutual correlation is proposed. Both filter and wrapper techniques have their advantages as well as drawbacks. The major problem with wrapper methods and filter methods employing search strategies is their high-computational complexity, when applied to large data sets. For feature sets of large dimensionality, any feature selection method that would approximate an exhaustive search in these large data spaces is infeasible due to the many possible combinations

$$\frac{d!}{(d-D)!\,D!} .$$

On the other hand, any non-exhaustive search method is not guaranteed to find the optimal feature set. We can only hope to reach a reasonable local optimum. While the literature has shown no clear superiority of any particular feature selection method, some feature selection methods are more suitable for large-dimension applications than others.

2 Correlation-Based Method

Correlation is a well-known similarity measure between two random variables. If two random variables are linearly dependent, then their correlation coefficient is ± 1. If the variables are uncorrelated, the correlation coefficient is 0. The correlation coefficient is invariant to scaling and translation. Hence two features with different variances may have the same value of this measure. Let us have n d-dimensional feature vectors

$$X_i = [{}^i x_1, \ldots, {}^i x_d] \qquad i = 1, \ldots, n$$

from K possible classes. The mutual correlation for a feature pair x_i and x_j is defined as

$$r_{x_i,x_j} = \frac{\sum_k {}^k x_i \, {}^k x_j - n\bar{x}_i\bar{x}_j}{\sqrt{(\sum_k {}^k x_i^2 - n\bar{x}_i^2)(\sum_k {}^k x_j^2 - n\bar{x}_j^2)}} \tag{1}$$

If two features x_i and x_j are independent then they are also uncorrelated, i.e. $r_{x_i,x_j} = 0$. Let us evaluate all mutual correlations for all feature pairs and compute the average absolute mutual correlation of a feature over δ features

$$r_{j,\delta} = \frac{1}{\delta} \sum_{i=1, i \neq j}^{\delta} |r_{x_i,x_j}| . \tag{2}$$

The feature which has the largest average mutual correlation

$$\alpha = \arg\max_j \; r_{j,\delta} \tag{3}$$

will be removed at each iteration step of the feature selection algorithm. When feature x_α is removed from the feature set, it is also discarded from the remaining average correlations, i.e.

$$r_{j,\delta-1} = \frac{\delta\, r_{j,\delta} - |r_{x_\alpha,x_j}|}{\delta - 1} \; . \tag{4}$$

2.1 Proposed Feature Selection Algorithm

The proposed correlation based feature selection algorithm can be summarized as follows.

1. Initialize $\delta = d - 1$.
2. Discard feature x_α for α determined by (3).
3. Decrement $\delta = \delta - 1$, if $\delta < D$ return the resulting D dimensional feature set and stop. Otherwise,
4. Recalculate the average correlations by using (4).
5. Go to step 2.

The algorithm produces the optimal D-dimensional subset from the original measurements with respect to the correlation criterion

$$X = [x_1, \ldots, x_D] \; .$$

The algorithm is very simple and so it has low computational complexity.

3 Evaluation Criteria

The presented method was compared with three wrapper based alternatives: SFS [3], SFFS [3], and oscillating search (OS) [4] used to directly optimize the Bayes error when each class probability density function is modelled by a single Gaussian. We also compared it with the Bayes error committed by two filter methods that select optimal feature subsets either with respect to the Bhattacharyya distance

$$B = \frac{1}{8}(\mu_i - \mu_j)^T \left(\frac{\Sigma_i + \Sigma_j}{2}\right)^{-1} (\mu_i - \mu_j) + \frac{1}{2} \ln \frac{|\frac{\Sigma_i + \Sigma_j}{2}|}{\sqrt{|\Sigma_i||\Sigma_j|}}, \tag{5}$$

or the divergence (assuming normality)

$$DIV = (P_i - P_j) \ln \frac{P_i |\Sigma_j|^{\frac{1}{2}}}{P_j |\Sigma_i|^{\frac{1}{2}}} + \frac{1}{2} tr\{[P_i \Sigma_i + P_j \Sigma_j][\Sigma_j^{-1} - \Sigma_i^{-1}]\} + \frac{1}{2}(\mu_i - \mu_j)^T \left(P_i \Sigma_j^{-1} + P_j \Sigma_i^{-1}\right)(\mu_i - \mu_j) \; , \tag{6}$$

where Σ_i and μ_i are the class covariance matrices and mean vectors, respectively and P_i are prior class probabilities. The criterion functions (5) and (6) are extended for multi-class problems by summing the criterion values for all combinations of 2 out of K classes.

4 Experimental Results

4.1 UCI Datasets

In this section, we demonstrate results computed on 2-class datasets from the UCI repository [5] namely the SPEECH data originating from British Telecom (15 features, 682 utterances of the word "yes" and another 736 utterances of the word "no") and the mammogram Wisconsin Diagnostic Breast Center (WDBC) data (30 features, 357 benign and 212 malignant samples). The parameters of the two datasets are summarized in Table 1.

Table 1. UCI repository set parameters

Parameter	SPEECH	WDBC
K	2	2
D	15	30
n_1	682	357
n_2	736	212
n	1418	569

The progress of the algorithm at the several iterations of the proposed algorithm is illustrated in Table 2.

Although the proposed method selects less optimal feature subsets on average for specific numbers of retained features, as can be seen from Tables 3 and 4, the corresponding Bayes error increases up to 7%. The latter deterioration in accuracy is compensated by the speed of the method.

4.2 Emotional Speech Data Collections

In this section, the Bayes error committed by the subset of features determined with respect to the mutual correlation is compared to that of filter methods employing B or DIV and wrapper methods employing SFS, and SFFS on 2 emotional speech data collections. The first data collection is Danish Emotion Speech (DES) containing recordings of speech utterances expressed by 4 actors in 5 emotional states [6]. The second data collection uses a subset of Speech Under Simulated and Actual Stress (SUSAS) data collection which includes words uttered under low and high stress conditions as well as speech in various talking styles expressed by 9 native American English speakers [7,8]. Several statistics of *pitch, formants,* and *energy* contours were extracted as features [9]. In Table 5, the parameters of DES and SUSAS are summarized. For DES, $n_k = 72$, $k = 1, 2, \ldots, 5$, while for SUSAS $n_k = 630$, $k = 1, 2, ldots, 8$.

Table 2. Recalculated average correlation at the several iterations of the proposed algorithm for the SPEECH dataset

step	class 1	class 2
1	$r_{6,15} = 0.59$	$r_{7,15} = 0.54$
2	$r_{7,14} = 0.57$	$r_{10,14} = 0.51$
3	$r_{4,13} = 0.54$	$r_{11,13} = 0.48$
4	$r_{9,12} = 0.51$	$r_{4,12} = 0.47$
5	$r_{3,11} = 0.50$	$r_{3,11} = 0.44$
6	$r_{11,10} = 0.49$	$r_{8,10} = 0.43$
7	$r_{5,9} = 0.46$	$r_{12,9} = 0.41$
8	$r_{10,8} = 0.44$	$r_{14,8} = 0.39$
9	$r_{15,7} = 0.44$	$r_{1,7} = 0.38$
10	$r_{1,6} = 0.39$	$r_{6,6} = 0.37$
11	$r_{8,5} = 0.37$	$r_{15,5} = 0.34$
12	$r_{13,4} = 0.32$	$r_{5,4} = 0.31$
13	$r_{2,3} = 0.30$	$r_{9,3} = 0.24$
13	$r_{12,2} = 0.25$	$r_{2,2} = 0.21$
14	$r_{14,1} = 0.16$	$r_{13,1} = 0.13$

Table 3. Bayes error for different feature selection algorithms on SPEECH dataset

Number of retained features	Correlation	SFS	OS	*B*	*DIV*
14	0.077	0.074	0.074	0.081	0.081
13	0.082	0.068	0.066	0.076	0.073
12	0.092	0.069	0.062	0.076	0.076
11	0.089	0.066	0.060	0.072	0.077
10	0.084	0.060	0.056	0.079	0.089
9	0.115	0.061	0.058	0.074	0.087
8	0.113	0.055	0.050	0.074	0.098
7	0.108	0.052	0.052	0.087	0.102
6	0.092	0.053	0.053	0.086	0.118
5	0.113	0.053	0.052	0.076	0.108
4	0.118	0.068	0.061	0.079	0.098
3	0.108	0.081	0.081	0.111	0.111
2	0.119	0.119	0.119	0.187	0.226
1	0.345	0.139	0.139	0.221	0.221
average	0.118	0.073	0.070	0.099	0.112

The feature selection methods are evaluated according to their execution time and the classification error achieved by the Bayes classifier that classifies the speech segments into emotional states. The crossvalidation method was used to obtain an unbiased error estimate [10]. For wrapper techniques based on SFS and SFFS, the crossvalidation method has been speeded up by two mechanisms

Table 4. Bayes error for different feature selection algorithms on WDBC dataset

Number of retained features	Correlation	SFS	OS	*B*	*DIV*
30	0.053	0.059	0.084	0.079	0.089
29	0.053	0.052	0.053	0.056	0.053
28	0.053	0.049	0.042	0.053	0.049
27	0.056	0.049	0.032	0.046	0.042
26	0.056	0.053	0.028	0.049	0.049
25	0.053	0.053	0.025	0.046	0.063
24	0.060	0.053	0.021	0.046	0.049
23	0.056	0.046	0.018	0.056	0.060
22	0.067	0.039	0.018	0.053	0.067
21	0.063	0.032	0.014	0.046	0.063
20	0.056	0.028	0.018	0.042	0.067
19	0.056	0.021	0.018	0.039	0.056
18	0.053	0.018	0.011	0.039	0.056
17	0.074	0.014	0.014	0.035	0.053
16	0.056	0.014	0.014	0.042	0.046
15	0.077	0.011	0.011	0.053	0.046
14	0.088	0.014	0.011	0.035	0.056
13	0.074	0.011	0.011	0.039	0.053
12	0.077	0.011	0.014	0.053	0.046
11	0.070	0.011	0.007	0.046	0.053
10	0.074	0.018	0.007	0.053	0.046
9	0.063	0.018	0.004	0.053	0.060
8	0.102	0.018	0.007	0.053	0.062
7	0.105	0.018	0.007	0.053	0.042
6	0.109	0.025	0.011	0.063	0.063
5	0.250	0.028	0.021	0.056	0.053
4	0.253	0.042	0.032	0.077	0.077
3	0.274	0.046	0.042	0.067	0.067
2	0.372	0.049	0.056	0.077	0.077
1	0.345	0.084	0.084	0.109	0.105
average	0.098	0.032	0.025	0.054	0.059

that reduce its computational burden and improve its accuracy [9]. In the experiments, feature set A is declared to be better than feature set B, if the error achieved by using A is smaller than that obtained using B by at least 0.015. The error difference 0.015 was chosen according to observations made in [9] and the available computational power.

A comparison of the execution time needed by each feature selection method is made in Table 6 for each data collection. Filter methods such as those employing correlation, B, and DIV are 50 times faster than wrapper ones based on SFS and SFFS. The execution time for correlation and DIV is comparable, whereas the filter method based on B is twice slower.

Table 5. Parameters of emotional speech data collections

Parameter	DES	SUSAS
K	5	8
D	90	90
n_k	72	630
n	360	5040

Table 6. Execution time (in sec)

Method	Databases	
	DES	SUSAS
SFFS	18107	53494
SFS	9446	21092
correlation	276	458
B	351	633
DIV	292	454

To evaluate the efficiency of the proposed filter method based on correlation, we compare the classification errors measured on DES and SUSAS. The classification errors on DES are plotted in Figure 1 for the number of retained features (SFS,SFFS) and the number of discarded features (correlation, B, DIV). It is seen that SFS and SFFS achieve about 48% classification error, whereas the error for filter methods is about 10% higher. The lowest error rates achieved by wrappers are for 10-15 retained features. Similarly, the lowest error rates obtained by filter methods are accomplished when 60-70 features are removed from the entire feature set. From the error rates of the Bayes classifier plotted in Figure 1, we infer that correlation method is equivalent to the other filter methods but it is clearly inferior to wrapper methods.

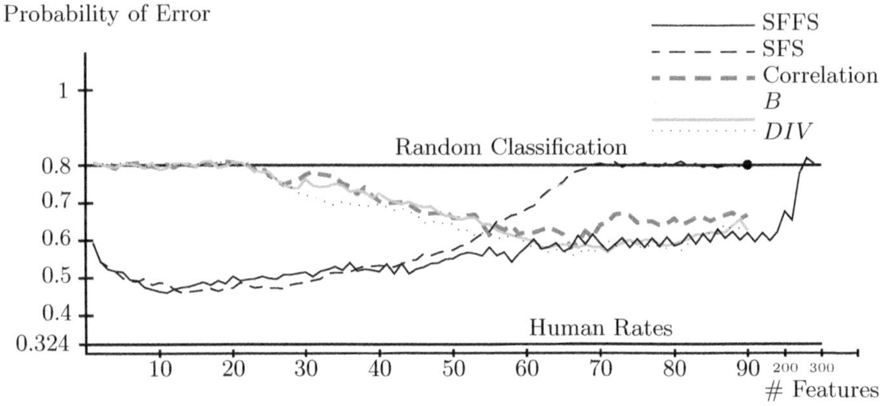

Fig. 1. Probability of classification error versus the number of features retained/discarded by feature selection method on DES

From the experimental results on data collection SUSAS plotted in Figure 2, it is inferred that the lowest error rates are achieved when almost all the features are selected, either in the first steps of filters or the last steps of wrappers. So, feature selection here is not used to reduce error rates but to remove redundant features. The optimal feature set for wrappers as well for filters is achieved after

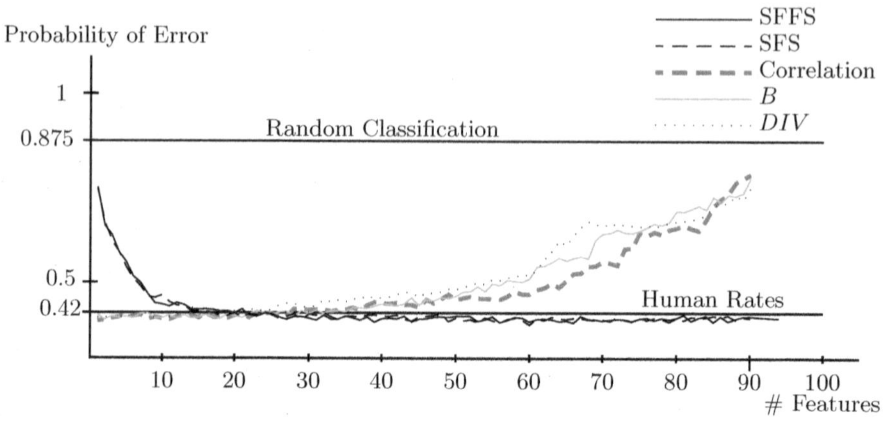

Fig. 2. Probability of classification error versus the number of features retained/discarded by feature selection method on SUSAS

20-30 iterations. Wrappers select 20-30 features, whereas filters remove 20-30 features out of the 90 initial ones. Therefore, wrappers yield a smaller feature set than filters. Regarding the time requirements, wrappers select the optimal feature subset of 20 features within 2000 sec., whereas filters based on correlation and divergence can yield a subset of 50 features yielding comparable error rates to wrappers within 150 sec. There is a great difference between the results obtained for DES and SUSAS. By using all features in DES for classification, the error is at random level, whereas the error rates in SUSAS are minimized when the entire feature set is employed. This abnormal behavior of classification error regarding the size of feature set could be a topic of further research.

5 Conclusions

A filter method for feature selection based on mutual correlation has been proposed. Being a filter method, it yields features independent of the classifier to be used. Hence, in principle, the proposed method can only approach the feature selection quality of methods based on direct estimation of the Bayes classifier error rate (i.e. wrapper methods with SFS or OS, filter methods using B or DIV). At the same time, the proposed filter method can easily cope with classification tasks in feature spaces of large dimensionality. The method is extremely fast in comparison with the other compared methods (except DIV). The presented method can also be used when alternative filter methods based on B or DIV cannot be applied due to limited measurements which prevent the robust estimation of necessary covariance matrices. The method can be used either in supervised or unsupervised mode.

Acknowledgements

This research was supported by the EC project no. FP6-507752 MUSCLE, grants No.A2075302, 1ET400750407 of the Grant Agency of the Academy of Sciences CR and partially by the MŠMT grant 1M0572 DAR.

References

1. Devijver, P.A., Kittler, J.: Pattern Recognition: A Statistical Approach. Prentice-Hall (1982)
2. Fukunaga, K.: Introduction to Statistical Pattern Recognition: 2nd edition. Academic Press, Inc. (1990)
3. Somol, P., Pudil, P.: Feature selection toolbox. Pattern Recognition **35** (2002) 2749–2759
4. Somol, P., Pudil, P.: Oscillating search algorithms for feature selection. In: 15th Int. Conf. on Pattern Recognition, Barcelona, Spain (2000) 406–409
5. Murphy, P., Aha, D.: Uci repository of machine learning databases [ftp.ics.uci.edu] (1994)
6. Engberg, I., Hansen, A.: Documentation of the danish emotional speech database DES. Technical report, Center for Person Kommunikation, Aalborg Univ., Aalborg (1996)
7. Womack, B., Hansen, J.: N-channel hidden markov models for combined stressed speech classification and recognition. IEEE Trans. Speech and Audio Processing **6** (1999) 668–667
8. Bolia, R., Slyh, R.: Perception of stress and speaking style for selected elements of the (susas) database. Speech Communication **40** (2003) 493–501
9. Ververidis, D., Kotropoulos, C.: Sequential forward feature selection with low computational cost. In: Proc 13th European Signal Processing Conf., Antalya, Turkey (2005)
10. Efron, B., Tibshirani, R.: An Introduction to the Bootstrap. Chapman & Hall/CRC (1993)
11. Duda, R., Hart, P., Stork, D.: Pattern Classification. J. Wiley, New York (2001)
12. F.J.Ferri, P.Pudil, M.Hatef, J.Kittler: Comparative Study of Techniques for Large-Scale Feature Selection with Nonmonotonic Criterion Functions. In: Pattern Recognition in Practice IV. Elsevier (1994) 403–414
13. Jain, A.K., Zongker, D.: Feature selection: Evaluation, application and small sample performance. IEEE Transactions on Pattern Analysis and Machine Intelligence **19** (1997) 153 – 158
14. Kohavi, R., John, G.: Wrappers for feature subset selection. Artificial Intelligence **97** (1997) 273–324
15. Kudo, M., Sklansky, J.: Comparison of algorithms that select features for pattern classifiers. Pattern Recognition **33** (2000) 25–41
16. Theodoridis, S., Koutroumbas, K.: Pattern Recognition. Elsevier (2003)
17. Webb, A.: Statistical Pattern Recognition. John Wiley & Sons (2002)

Oscillating Feature Subset Search Algorithm for Text Categorization

Jana Novovičová[1,2], Petr Somol[1,2], and Pavel Pudil[1,2]

[1] Dept. of Pattern Recognition, Institute of Information Theory and Automation, Academy of Sciences of the Czech Republic
{novovic, somol}@utia.cas.cz
http://ro.utia.cz/

[2] Faculty of Management, Prague University of Economics, Czech Republic
pudil@fm.vse.cz
http://www.fm.vse.cz

Abstract. A major characteristic of text document categorization problems is the extremely high dimensionality of text data. In this paper we explore the usability of the Oscillating Search algorithm for feature/word selection in text categorization. We propose to use the multiclass Bhattacharyya distance for multinomial model as the global feature subset selection criterion for reducing the dimensionality of the bag of words vector document representation. This criterion takes into consideration inter-feature relationships. We experimentally compare three subset selection procedures: the commonly used best individual feature selection based on information gain, the same based on individual Bhattacharyya distance, and the Oscillating Search to maximize Bhattacharyya distance on groups of features. The obtained feature subsets are then tested on the standard Reuters data with two classifiers: the multinomial Bayes and the linear SVM. The presented experimental results illustrate that using a non-trivial feature selection algorithm is not only computationally feasible, but it also brings substantial improvement in classification accuracy over traditional, individual feature evaluation based methods.

1 Introduction

The application of machine learning (ML) and pattern recognition (PR) in the real-world domain data often encounters problems caused by the high dimensionality of the input space. More and more often, data sets in numerous research fields contain a very large number (from hundreds to tens of thousands) of features. The situation becomes worse if the ratio of relevant features to the irrelevant ones is low, as for example in text document categorization problem. By removing these insignificant features, the learning process becomes more effective, and the performance of the classifier improves.

Text categorization (also known as text classification) is the task of automatically sorting a set of documents into predefined classes based on its contents. This task is of great practical importance. Document classification may appear in many applications including e-mail filtering, mail routing, spam filtering, news monitoring, selective dissemination of information to information consumers, automated indexing of scientific articles, and so on.

J.F. Martínez-Trinidad et al. (Eds.): CIARP 2006, LNCS 4225, pp. 578–587, 2006.

An increasing number of statistical classification methods and ML algorithms have been explored to build automatically a classifier by learning from previously labelled documents, e.g., *naive Bayes* ([1], [2]), *k-nearest neighbor* ([3]), *neural networks* ([4]), *decision trees* ([1]), *symbolic rule induction* ([5], [6]), *regression* ([7]), *support vector machines* ([8]), *boosting* ([9]). The overview of Sebastiani [10] discusses the main approaches to text categorization (TC).

In TC, usually a document representation using a *bag of words* approach is employed (each position in the feature vector representation corresponds to a given word). This scheme leads to very high-dimensional feature space, too high for conventional classification methods. Dimensionality reduction (DR) is a very important step in TC because irrelevant and redundant features often degrade the performance of classifiers both in speed and classification accuracy. Two approaches for DR exist, either selecting a subset of the original features (feature selection), or transforming the features into new ones (feature extraction).

In TC problem the dominant approach is feature selection (FS) using various criteria. Traditional methods for feature subset selection in TC use an evaluation function that is applied to single words. All words are independently evaluated and sorted according to the assigned criterion. Then, a predefined number of the best features is taken to form the best feature subset. Scoring of individual words can be performed using some measure like, e.g., *document frequency* (Yang and Pedersen [11]), *mutual information* [11], *information gain* (also known as average mutual information) or χ^2 *statistic* (Caropreso et al. [17], Yang and Pedersen [11], Yang and Liu [18]) and *odds-ratio* (Mladenić [12]). Yang and Pedersen [11] and Mladenić and Grobelnik [13] give experimental comparison of the above mentioned measures in TC. The information gain (IG) and several very simple frequency measures were reported to work well on text data. Forman [14] presents an extensive comparative study of twelve FS criteria for the high-dimensional domain of text categorization.

In Section 2 and 3 the standard methodology of feature selection for text categorization is discussed. Section 4 introduces our novel approach. Section 5 shows experimental results. Conclusions are given in Section 6.

2 Text Categorization Task

The *text categorization* task is the task of assigning free documents expressed in natural language into one or more thematic *classes* (*categories*) belonging to the predefined set $\mathcal{C} = \{c_1, \ldots, c_{|\mathcal{C}|}\}$ of $|\mathcal{C}|$ classes. The construction of a *text classifier* relies on an *initial collection* of documents pre-classified under $\mathcal{C}$. Let $\mathcal{D} = \{d_1, \ldots, d_{|\mathcal{D}|}\}$ be the finite training document set and $\mathcal{V} = \{w_1, \ldots, w_{|\mathcal{V}|}\}$ be the vocabulary set containing $|\mathcal{V}|$ distinct words occurring in training documents. Given a set of document vectors $\{d_1, \ldots, d_{|\mathcal{D}|}\}$ and their associated class labels, the problem is to estimate the true class label of a free document. The construction of a text classifier consists of essentially three phases: *document indexing* and *dimensionality reduction*, *classifier learning*, and *classifier evaluation*.

In TC a document d_i is usually transformed into a vector in the *term space*. The indexing process is characterized by a definition of what a term is. In TC applications of the thematic kind, the set of terms for a document is usually made to coincide with the set of words occurring in the document. The number of features can be dramatically reduced by the domain dependent methods, which include the elimination of stop words, stripping of special characters as well as stemming algorithms or morphological analysis. For further DR the domain independent methods can be used.

A wide variety of supervised learning approaches have been explored to construct automatically a classifier by learning from previously labelled documents. All of the classification methods mentioned in Section 1 still retain their popularity, but in recent years Support Vector Machines (SVM) and boosting have become the two dominant learning techniques in TC. The reasons for this are twofold. First, these are the two methods that have unquestionably shown the best performance in comparative TC experiments performed so far. Second, these are the newest methods in the classifier learning area, and the ones with the strongest justifications from computational learning theory. A further factor that has determined their success is the free availability, at least for research purposes, of respective software packages, such as SVMlight and BoosTexter.

3 Feature Subset Selection

Because of computational complexity the filter approach is preferable over the wrapper approach to feature subset selection in TC. Given a predefined integer $|\mathcal{V}'|$, the methods for word selection attempt to select from the original set $\mathcal{V}$, the set $\mathcal{V}'$ of words with $|\mathcal{V}'| \ll |\mathcal{V}|$ that, when used for document representation, yields the highest effectiveness. Different methods for feature subset selection have been developed in ML and PR using different evaluation functions and search procedures. In the following we consider the global (a feature subset is chosen for the classification under all classes) filter FS approach.

3.1 Traditional Feature Selection Evaluation Functions

A simple and effective global word selection function is the *document frequency* of a word w, that is, only the terms that occur in the highest number of documents are retained.

Information-theoretic functions for FS have been used in the literature, among them *mutual information*, *information gain*, χ^2 *statistic* and *odds-ratio*. The mathematical definitions of the main functions used for DR in text classification task are summarized in the paper of Sebastiani [10]. All functions are specified locally to a specific class $c_j \in \mathcal{C}$. In order to assess the value of word w in a *global* class-independent sense, either the sum or the weighted sum, or the maximum of their class-specific values are usually computed.

Information gain, used in our experiments for comparison as a ranking measure for selection of the best individual features, is defined as

$$IG(w_v) = \sum_{j=1}^{|\mathcal{C}|} P(c_j, w_v) \log \frac{P(c_j, w_v)}{P(c_j)P(w_v)} . \qquad (1)$$

Here $P(w_v)$ is the probability, that the word w_v occurred in document, $P(c_j)$ is the probability of the class c_j. $P(c_j, w_v)$ is the joint probability of the class c_j and the occurrence of the word w_v.

3.2 Traditional Feature Selection Search Methods

Most methods for feature subset selection that are used for text processing tasks are very simple in comparison to the other methods known in ML and PR.

Best individual features (BIF) method (see e.g. [15]) evaluates all the $|\mathcal{V}|$ words individually according to a given criterion, sorts them and selects the best $|\mathcal{V}'|$ words. Since the vocabulary usually consists of several thousands or tens of thousands of words, the BIF methods are popular in TC because they are rather fast, efficient and simple. However, they evaluate each word separately and completely ignore the existence of other words and the manner how the words work together.

Forward selection algorithms start with an empty set of features and add one feature at a time until the final feature set is reached. *Backward elimination* algorithms start with a feature set containing all features and remove features one at a time. As opposed to the BIF methods these feature selection procedures reflect to a certain extent the dependencies between words (see e.g. [15]). However, despite their relative simplicity even these basic sequential methods can show to be too slow to yield results in reasonable time.

4 Proposed Feature Selection Algorithm

For the exceedingly high-dimensional problem of text categorization we have found the Oscillating Search (OS) algorithm [16] to be a rare case of a more advanced algorithm being capable of yielding promising results in reasonable time. In the following we show the simplified (thus the fastest) modification of the algorithm to consistently improve the selected subsets of terms and, consequently, improve the classification performance. This is made possible by using the following form of Bhattacharyya distance as the term subset evaluation criterion.

4.1 Bhattacharyya Distance for Multinomial Model

We proposed to use the *multiclass Bhattacharyya distance* developed for multinomial model for class conditional densities in Novovicova [20] as the FS criterion in text categorization.

In the *multinomial* model, the document d_i is represented by a feature vector, each feature variable N_{iv} is the number of times certain word w_v occurs in that document. In this model each document d_i is drawn from a multinomial distribution over the set of all words in the vocabulary $\mathcal{V}$ with as many independent trials as the length $|d_i|$ (the number of words from $\mathcal{V}$ occurring in the document). The order of the words is lost, however the number of occurrences is captured. The *multiclass Bhattacharyya distance* of document d_i is given as

$$B(d_i) = \sum_{j=1}^{|\mathcal{C}|-1} \sum_{k=j+1}^{|\mathcal{C}|} P(c_j)P(c_k)B_{jk}(d_i), \tag{2}$$

where $P(c_j)$ and $P(c_k)$ are the prior probabilities of the class c_j and c_k, respectively. $B_{jk}(d_i)$ is the *pairwise Bhattacharyya distance* of d_i defined as

$$B_{jk}(d_i) = -|d_i| \, \log \sum_{v=1}^{|\mathcal{V}|} \sqrt{P(w_v|c_j)P(w_v|c_k)}. \tag{3}$$

Here $P(w_v|c_j)$ and $P(w_v|c_k)$ are the probabilities of w_v in c_j and c_k, respectively. The Bhattacharyya distance for one feature corresponding to the word w_v between classes c_j and c_k, to be denoted *individual Bhattacharyya distance* is then

$$B_{jk}(w_v) = -|d_i| \log \left(\sqrt{P(w_v|c_j)P(w_v|c_k)} + \sqrt{(1 - P(w_v|c_j))(1 - P(w_v|c_k))} \right). \tag{4}$$

4.2 Oscillating Search

As opposed to other sequential subset selection methods the *Oscillating Search* (OS) [16] is not dependent on pre-specified direction of search (forward or backward). It is based on repeated modification of the current subset $\mathcal{V}_r$ of r features. This is achieved by alternating the so-called *down-* and *up-swings*. The *down-swing* removes successively o worst features from the current set $\mathcal{V}_r$ to obtain a new set $\mathcal{V}_{r-o}$ at first, then adds o best ones to $\mathcal{V}_{r-o}$ to obtain a new current set $\mathcal{V}_r$. The *up-swing* adds o "good" features to the current set $\mathcal{V}_r$ to obtain a new set $\mathcal{V}_{r+o}$ at first, then removes o "bad" ones from $\mathcal{V}_{r+o}$ to obtain a new current set $\mathcal{V}_r$ again. The up- and down-swings are repeated as long as the set $\mathcal{V}_r$ gets improved. The value of o shall be set to 1 initially and may be later increased to allow more thorough search at a cost of more computational time. The algorithm then terminates when o exceeds a user-specified *limit* Δ.

The OS algorithm starts the search from some initial set $\mathcal{V}_r$ of r features and brings improvement after each pair of swings (terminates otherwise). This is very advantageous for the high-dimensional problem we deal with here, as no time is lost in evaluating term subsets of sizes far from the desired one. Note that while the sequential forward search (see Section 3.2) needs 400 complex steps to find a subset of 400 features, the OS may achieve the same or better result in a couple of steps, provided it is initialized properly. The perfect way of initializing OS for TC is taking use of some of the standard fast BIF methods.

Let us describe the essential form of the algorithm formally:

Step 1: (*Initialization*) Find the initial set $\mathcal{V}_r$. (For TC do it by means of BIF). Let $c = 0$. Let $o = 1$.

Step 2: (*Down-swing*) Remove such o-tuple from $\mathcal{V}_r$, so that the new set $\mathcal{V}_{r-o}$ retains the highest criterion value. Add such o-tuple from $\mathcal{V} \setminus \mathcal{V}_{r-o}$ to $\mathcal{V}_{r-o}$, so that the new subset $\mathcal{V}_r^{new}$ yields the highest criterion value. If $\mathcal{V}_r^{new}$ is better than $\mathcal{V}_r$, let $\mathcal{V}_r = \mathcal{V}_r^{new}$, $c = 0$, $o = 1$ and go to Step 4.

Step 3: (*Last swing did not find better solution*) Let $c = c + 1$. If $c = 2$, then none of previous two swings has found better solution; extend the search by letting $o = o + 1$. If $o > \Delta$, stop the algorithm, otherwise let $c = 0$.

Step 4: (*Up-swing*) Add such o-tuple from $\mathcal{V} \setminus \mathcal{V}_r$ to $\mathcal{V}_r$, so that the new set $\mathcal{V}_{r+o}$ has the highest criterion value. Remove such o-tuple from $\mathcal{V}_{r+o}$, so that the new set $\mathcal{V}_r^{new}$ yields the highest criterion value. If $\mathcal{V}_r^{new}$ is better than $\mathcal{V}_r$, let $\mathcal{V}_r = \mathcal{V}_r^{new}$, $c = 0$, $o = 1$ and go to Step 2.

Step 5: (*Last swing did not find better solution*) Let $c = c + 1$. If $c = 2$, then none of previous two swings has found better solution; extend the search by letting $o = o + 1$. If $o > \Delta$, stop the algorithm, otherwise let $c = 0$ and go to Step 2.

The OS algorithm can be considered a "higher level" procedure, as it may take use of other feature selection methods as sub-procedures in place of up- and down-swings. One notable property of the OS algorithm is the fact that the fastest improvement of the target subset may be expected in initial phases of the search. This behavior is advantageous, because it gives the option of stopping the search prematurely without too serious result-degrading consequences.

In the context of TC it is desirable to keep the procedure as simple and fast as possible, thus we consider only the set-up with $\Delta = 1$ and the simplest form of up- and down-swings as described here. For more details see [16].

5 Experimental Study

Our experiments are conducted to illustrate that using a non-trivial Oscillating Search feature selection algorithm is not only computationally feasible, but it also brings substantial improvement in classification accuracy.

We adopted the bag of words approach. After text preprocessing the global filter feature selection is performed. For evaluating the classification performance assuming single-label TC we use the standard classification accuracy.

5.1 Data Set

In our experiments we examined the commonly used Reuters-21578 data set.[1] Our text preprocessing included removing all non-alphabetic characters, ignoring

[1] http://www.daviddlewis.com/resources/testcollections/reuters21578

all the words that contained digits or non alpha-numeric characters, removing words from a stop-word list. We replaced each word by its morphological root, removed all the words which had less than three occurrences. After pre-processing the data set contained 33 classes of document-representing vectors of dimensionality 10105. The largest class contained 3924, the smallest only 19 non-zero documents. All tests have been done by means of 10-fold cross-validation over the whole data set.

5.2 Examined Criteria and Search Methods

In our experiments we used the Bhattacharyya distance (4) and information gain (1) as ranking measures for the selection of the best individual features. The proposed oscillating algorithm then uses the Bhattacharyya distance (2) to evaluate groups instead of individual features only.

For selecting r salient words from the complete vocabulary set $\mathcal{V}$ we used not only the proposed oscillating procedure (Section 4), but for comparison also the best individual features method (BIF) based on individual Bhattacharyya distance (BIF IB) and information gain (BIF IG) presented in Section 3.1. We initialize the OS algorithm by feature subsets found by means of BIF IB. In our experiments, we set $r = \{6, 12, 25, 50, 100, 200, 400, 600, 1000, 1500, 2000, 3000, 4500, 6000\}$, respectively.

5.3 Classifiers

All feature selection methods were examined on two classifiers: the Bayes classifier for multinomial probabilistic model and the linear SVM.

Bayes classifier. We use the multinomial model as described by McCallum and Nigam in [2]. The predicted class for document d_i is the one that maximizes the posterior probability of each class given the test document $P(c_j|d_i)$,

$$P(c_j|d_i) \propto P(c_j) \prod_{v}^{|\mathcal{V}|} P(w_v|c_j)^{N_{iv}}.$$

Here $P(c_j)$ is the prior probability of the class c_j, $P(w_v|c_j)$ is the probability that a word chosen randomly in a document from class c_j equals w_v, and N_{iv} is the number of occurrences of word w_v in a document d_i. We smoothed the word and class probabilities using Bayesian estimate with word priors and a Laplace estimate, respectively.

Linear Support Vector Machine. The SVM method has been found recently one of the best performing tools in TC. Especially its excellent generalization ability in high-dimensional sparse spaces is very suitable for text related problems. Linear kernel has been found sufficient in this context. For our experiments we used the LibSVM implementation [21]. We used the standard C-SVC form of the classifier with default value of $C = 1$. No data scaling has been done.

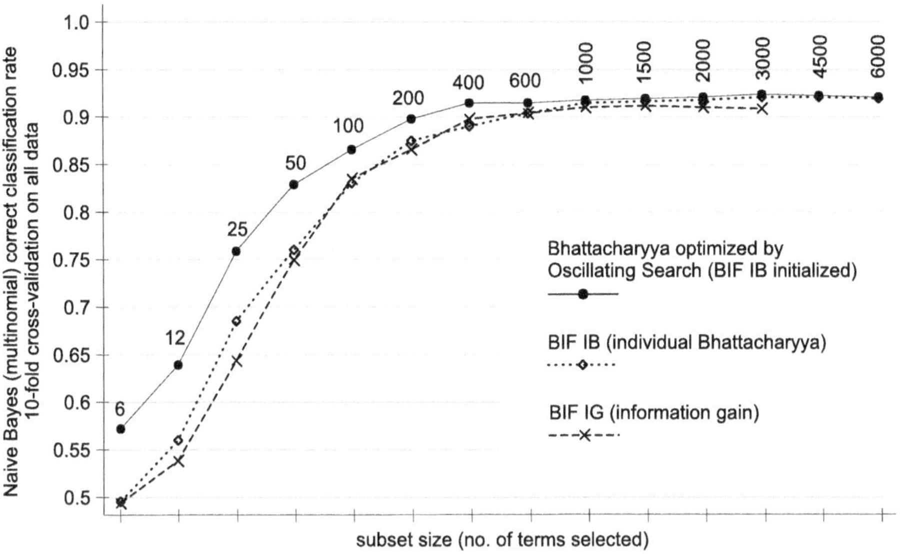

Fig. 1. Multinomial Bayes classifier 10-fold cross-validated classification rate.

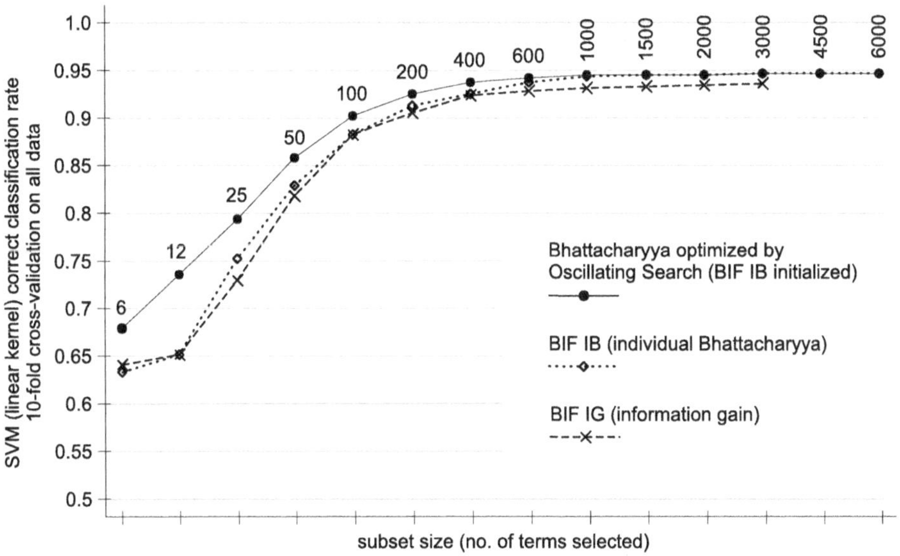

Fig. 2. SVM classifier 10-fold cross-validated classification rate

5.4 Results

It can be clearly seen in Figs. 1 and 2 that feature selection based on Oscillating Search that optimizes Bhattacharyya distance on groups of terms is constantly

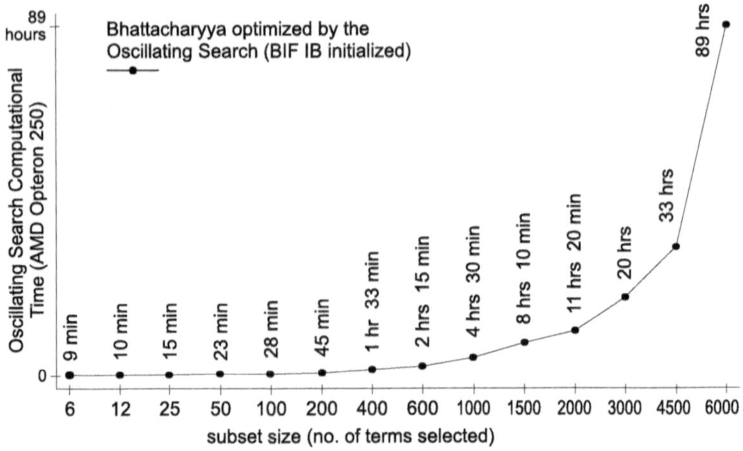

Fig. 3. Oscillating Search computational time

superior to BIF approaches for subset sizes roughly ≤ 1000. For larger subsets the improvement is hardly observable or not present at all; the search time then becomes inadequate as well (see Fig. 3). Note, that the improvement is equally notable for both of the tested classifiers. This also adds to the discussion about the impact of feature selection on SVM performance.

A second notable observation is the slight superiority of individual Bhattacharyya over information gain in BIF based search.

6 Conclusions and Future Work

We have shown that in text categorization tasks it is possible to achieve considerable classification accuracy improvement by employing a feature search procedure, that, unlike traditional approaches, evaluates feature groups instead of individuals. The most notable improvement is to be expected with subsets of lower sizes, where the time requirements of the discussed Oscillating Search procedure stay in reasonable limits. We have also shown that the multinomial Bhattacharyya distance is a good measure for both group-wise and individual feature selection, capable of identifying features that are good for fundamentally different classifiers.

In the future we intend to investigate in more detail the applicability of alternative Oscillating Search versions and other even more complex search procedures to text categorization problems. Another option for further research is including SVM parameter optimization in the feature selection process.

Acknowledgement. The work has been supported by EC MUSCLE project FP6-507752, the Grant Agency of the Academy of Sciences of the Czech Republic (CR) project A2075302, CR MŠMT grant 2C06019 and 1M0572 DAR.

References

1. Lewis, D.D., Ringuette, M.: A comparison of two learning algorithms for text categorization. In: Proceedings of SDAIR-94, 3rd Annual Symposium on Document Analysis and Information Retrieval, Las Vegas, US (1994) 81–93
2. McCallum, A., Nigam, K.: A comparison of event models for naive Bayes text classification. In: Proc. Workshop Learning for Text Categorization AAAI (1998)
3. Yang, Y., Liu, X.: A re-examination of text categorization methods. In: Proc. 22nd ACM SIGIR-99 Int. Conf. on R. & D. in Information Retrieval (1999) 42–49
4. Ng, H.T., Goh, W.B., Low, K.L.: Feature selection, perceptron learning, and a usability case study for text categorization. In: Proc. 20th ACM Int. Conf. on R. & D. in Information Retrieval SIGIR-97 (1997) 67–73
5. Apté, C., Damerau, F.J., Weiss, S.M.: Automated learning of decision rules for text categorization. ACM Transactions on Information Systems **12**(3) (1994) 233–251
6. Cohen, W.W., Singer, Y.: Context-sensitive learning methods for text categorization. ACM Transactions on Information Systems **17**(2) (1999) 141–173
7. Yang, Y., Chute, C.G.: An example-based mapping method for text categorization and retrieval. ACM Transactions on Information Systems **12**(3) (1994) 252–277
8. Joachims, T.: Transductive inference for text classification using support vector machines. In: Proc. 16th Int. Conf. on Machine Learning ICML-99 (1999) 200–209
9. Schapire, R.E., Singer, Y.: BoosTexter: a boosting-based system for text categorization. Machine Learning **39**(2/3) (2000) 135–168
10. Sebastiani, F.: Machine learning in automated text categorization. ACM Computing Surveys **34**(1) (2002) 1–47
11. Yang, Y., Pedersen, J.O.: A comparative study on feature selection in text categorization. In: Proc. 14th Int. Conf. on Machine Learning ICML-97. (1997) 412–420
12. Mladenić, D.: Feature subset selection using in text learning. In: 10th European Conference on Machine Learning. (1998) 95–100
13. Mladenić, D., Grobelnik, M.: Feature selection for unbalanced class distribution and naive Bayes. In: Proceedings of the Sixteenth International Conference on Machine Learning. (1999) 258–267
14. Forman, G.: An experimental study of feature selection metrics for text categorization. Journal of Machine Learning Research **3** (2003) 1289–1305
15. Mladenić, D.: Machine Learning on non-homogeneous, distributed text data. PhD thesis, J. Stefan Institute, University of Ljubljana, Ljubljana, SL (1998)
16. Somol, P., Pudil, P.: Oscillating search algorithms for featute selection. In: Proc. of the 15th IAPR Int. Conference on Pattern Recognition. (2000) 406–409
17. Caropreso, M., Matwin, S., Sebastiani, F.: A learner-independent evaluation of the usefulness of statistical phrases for automated text categorization. In: Text Databases and Document Management: Theory and Practice. Idea Group Publishing, Hershey, PA (2001) 78–102
18. Yang, Y., Liu, X.: A re-examination of text categorization methods. In: Proc. 22nd Int. ACM SIGIR Conf. on R. & D. in Information Retrieval. (1999) 42–49
19. Jain, A.K., Duin, R.P.W., Mao, J.: Statistical pattern recognition: A review. IEEE Transactions on Pattern Analysis and Machine Intelligence **22** (2000) 4–37
20. Novovičová, J., Malík, A.: Text document classification using finite mixtures. Research Report 2063, ÚTIA AVČR, Prague, Czech Republic (2002)
21. Chang, C.C., Lin, C.J.: LIBSVM: a library for support vector machines. (2001) Software available at `http://www.csie.ntu.edu.tw/~cjlin/libsvm`.

Two Step Ant Colony System to Solve the Feature Selection Problem

Rafael Bello[1], Amilkar Puris[1], Ann Nowe[2],
Yailen Martínez[1], and María M. García[1]

[1] Department of Computer Science, Universidad Central de Las Villas, Cuba.
[2] Comp Lab, Department of Computer Science, Vrije Universiteit Brussel, Belgium.
{rbellop, ayudier, yailenm, mmgarcia}@uclv.edu.cu,
ann.nowe@vub.ac.be

Abstract. In this paper we propose a new model of ACO called Two-Step Ant Colony System. The basic idea is to split the heuristic search performed by ants into two stages. We have studied the performance of this new algorithm for the Feature Selection Problem. Experimental results obtained show the Two-Step approach significantly improves the Ant Colony System in term of computation time needed.

1 Introduction

Ant Colony Optimization (ACO) is a metaheuristic used to guide other heuristics in order to obtain better solutions than those that are generated by local optimization methods. In ACO a colony of artificial ants cooperates to look for good solutions to discrete problems. Artificial ants are simple agents that incrementally build a solution by adding components to a partial solution under construction. This computational model was introduced by M. Dorigo. Information about this metaheuristic can be found in [6], [8] and [10].

Ant System (AS) is the first ACO algorithm; it was introduced using the Travelling Salesman Problem (TSP) [7] and [9]. In TSP, we have a set of N fully connected cities $\{c_1, \ldots, c_n\}$ by arcs (i,j); each arc is assigned a weight d_{ij} which represents the distance between cities i and j, the goal is to find the shortest possible trip visiting each city once before returning to initial city. When ACO is used to solve this problems, pheromone trails (τ_{ij}) are associated to arcs which denote the desirability of visiting city j directly from city i. Also, the function $\eta_{ij} = 1/d_{ij}$ indicates the heuristic desirability of going from i to j, where d_{ij} is the distance between cities i and j. Initially, ants are randomly associated to cities. In the successive steps ant k applies a random proportional rule to decide which city to visit next according to expression (1):

$$p_{ij}^k = \frac{(\tau_{ij})^\alpha * (\eta_{ij})^\beta}{\sum_{l \in N_i^k} (\tau_{il})^\alpha * (\eta_{il})^\beta} \quad if \quad j \in N_i^k \quad (neighborhood \quad of \quad ant\, k) \tag{1}$$

J.F. Martínez-Trinidad et al. (Eds.): CIARP 2006, LNCS 4225, pp. 588 – 596, 2006.

where α and β are two parameters to point out the relative importance of the pheromone trail and the heuristic information respectively. After all ants have built their tours the values τ_{ij} are updated in two stages. First, τ_{ij} values are decreased by evaporation, $\tau_{ij}=(1-\rho)*\tau_{ij}$, using the parameter ρ, where $0<\rho<1$. This to avoid unlimited accumulation of pheromone. Second, all ants increase de value of τ_{ij} on the arcs they have crossed in their tours, $\tau_{ij}=\tau_{ij}+Inc_{ij}$, where Inc_{ij} is the amount of pheromone deposited by all ants which included the arc (i,j) in their tour. Usually, the amount of pheromone deposited by ant k is equal to $1/C_k$, where C_k is the length of the tour of ant k.

Some direct successor algorithms of Ant Systems are: Elitist AS, Rank-based AS and MAX-MIN AS. A more different ACO algorithm is Ant Colony System (ACS). ACS uses the following pseudorandom proportional rule to select the next city j from city i.

$$j = \begin{cases} \arg\max_{l \in N_i^k} \left\{ \tau_{ij} * (\eta_{il})^{\beta} \right\} & if \quad q \leq q_0 \\ random\ selection\ according\ to\ (1) & otherwise \end{cases} \quad (2)$$

where q is a random variable uniformly distributed in [0,1], q_0 which is a constant taken in the interval [0,1], controls the amount of exploration. In ACS, ants have a local pheromone trail update ($\tau_{ij}=(1-\xi)*\tau_{ij}+\xi*\tau_{ij}(0)$) applied after crossing an arc(i,j), where $\tau_{ij}(0)$ represents the initial value for the pheromone, and a global pheromone trail update ($\tau_{ij}=(1-\rho)*\tau_{ij}+\rho*Inc_{ij}$) executed only by the best-so-far ant.

In this paper, we propose a new approach to ACO in which the search process developed by ants is splitted into two stages. We have studied the performance of this proposal using the ACS algorithm. In the following, we first introduce the new algorithm. After that, the performance of it is studied in the case of the Feature Selection Problem (FSP). Finally we conclude our findings.

2 Two-Step ACS Algorithm

The Two-Step Ant Colony System algorithm proposed in this investigation is based on the following idea: to divide the search process made by the ants in two stages, so that in the first stage preliminary results are reached (partial solutions) that serve as an initial state for the search made by the ants in the second stage. In the case of FSP, this means that subsets containing a subset of features are generated in the first stage; in the second stage, these subsets will serve like an initial state for the ants.

The determination of the initial state in which the search process starts has been an interesting problem in heuristic search. It is well known that the initial state has an important effect in the search process. The aim is to be able to approach the initial state to the goal state. Of course, it is necessary to consider an adequate balance between the computational cost of obtaining that initial state and the total cost; in other words, the sum of the cost of approaching the initial state to the goal state plus the cost of finding the solution from that "improved" initial state should not be greater than the cost of looking for the solution from a random initial state.

More formally, the purpose is the following. Let E_i be an initial state randomly generated, or obtained by any other method without a significant computational cost, E_i* is an initial state generated by some method M that approaches it to the goal state, $C_M(E_i, E_i*)$ denotes the cost of obtaining E_i* from state E_i using the method M, and $CC_{HSA}(x)$ is the computational cost of finding a solution from state x using a Heuristic Search Algorithm (HSA). Then, the objective is that $C_M(E_i,E_i*) + CC_{HSA}(E_i*) < CC_{HSA}(E_i)$.

In the TS-ACS approach proposed here, the procedure to generate Ei* and the HSA are both the ACS algorithm, so the objective is $C_{ACS}(E_i, E_i*) + CC_{ACS}(E_i*) < CC_{ACS}(E_i)$. As ACS is used in both stages, the difference between the 2 stages is obtained by giving different values to some parameters of the model in each step. A ratio (r) is introduced in order to establish the relative setting of the values of the parameters of the algorithm in both stages; the ratio indicates which proportion of the complete search is given to the first stage. For example, if r=0.3, means that the first step will cover 30% of the search process and the second step the remaining 70%.

The setting of the ratio r has a high influence on the overall performance of the algorithm. A high value of r, that is, about value 1, causes the state E_i* to be closer to the goal state, then the value of $C_{ACS}(E_i, E_i*)$ may increase and the value of $CC_{ACS}(E_i*)$ will decrease. But, in addition to this balance between the costs of $C_{ACS}(E_i,E_i*)$ and $CC_{ACS}(E_i*)$, we have the problematic about how much the space search is explored; while more greater is the rate r, the search in the second stage decreases for several reasons: (I) there are less ants working, (II) the amount of cycles decreases, and (III) although the quantity of possible initial states for the second stage must grow when r grows, that amount is already limited by the result of the previous stage.

Therefore, a key point is to study what value of rate r is the best in order to obtain the best balance between the searches in both stages. This value must allow:

- To diminish the value of $C_{ACS}(E_i,E_i*) + CC_{ACS}(E_i*)$.
- To allow an exploration of the search space that guarantees to find good solutions.

3 Two-Step ACS in the Feature Selection Problem

In this section we dicuss some results we obtained when applying the two stage approach to the feature selection problem. Feature selection is useful in different computational tasks, for instance, in machine learning processes. An appropriate representation space for learning by selecting relevant attributes to the problem domain is a crucial issue for learning systems [11], [16] and [17]. Usually, not all features describing the examples are relevant to the classification process and some of them are irrelevant or redundant. Too many irrelevant features increase the complexity of learning process and decrease the accuracy of induced knowledge. Feature selection is useful to reduce the dimensionality problem; it results not only in improving the speed of data manipulation [14], but even in improving the classification rate by reducing the influence of noise [5] and [15].

The FSP can be viewed as a particular case of a more general subset selection problem in which the goal is to find a subset maximizing some adopted criterion. Feature selection methods search through the subsets of features and try to find the best subset among the competing 2^N-1 candidate subsets according to some evaluation measure, where N denotes the total number of features.

Each state represents a subset of features in the search space. All feature selection methods contain two important components: an Evaluation function used to evaluate a candidate feature subset and a Search algorithm to search through the feature space. Search strategies are important because the feature selection process may be time consuming and an exhaustive search for the "optimal" subset is impractical for even moderate sized problems [18]. Examples of search strategies are heuristic search, probabilistic methods and hybrid algorithms.

ACO has been used as a search algorithm for the FSP. Methods which combine ACO and Rough Set Theory (RST) to find reducts with promising results were proposed in [1], [2], [3] and [12]. They are based on the reduct concept.

A Decision System is a pair DS=(U, $A\cup\{d\}$), where U is a non-empty finite set of objects called the Universe, A is a non-empty finite set of features, and $d\notin A$ is the decision feature. The basic concepts of RST are the lower and upper approximations of a subset $X\subseteq U$ [13]. These were originally introduced with reference to an indiscernibility relation IND(B), where objects x and y belong to IND(B) if and only if x and y are indiscernible from each other by features in B.

Let $B\subseteq A$ and $X\subseteq U$. It can be proved that B defines an equivalence relation. The set X can be approximated using only the information contained in B by constructing the B-lower and B-upper approximations of X, denoted by B_*X and B^*X respectively, where $B_*X=\{x : [x]_B \subseteq X\}$ and $B^*X=\{x : [x]_B \cap X\neq\phi\}$, and $[x]_B$ denotes the class of x according to B-indiscernible relation. The objects in B_*X are sure members of X, while the objects in B^*X are possible members of X. If $B^*X- B_*X$ is not empty, then X is a rough set.

RST offers several measures about a Decision System. Among them is the quality of the approximation of classification (expression 3). It expresses the percentage of objects which can be correctly classified into the given classes Y= $\{Y_1,..., Y_n\}$ employing only the set of features in B.

$$\gamma_B(Y) = \frac{\sum_{i=1}^{n} |B_* Y_i|}{|U|} \tag{3}$$

An important issue in the RST is feature reduction based on the reduct concept. A reduct is a minimal set of features that preserves the partitioning of universe and hence the ability to perform classifications. The subset B is a reduct if IND(A)=IND(B); that is, $\gamma_A(Y)=\gamma_B(Y)$. The concept of reduct is one of the most important concepts in the Rough Set Theory.

However, this beneficial alternative is limited because of the computational complexity of calculating reducts. The problem of finding a globally minimal reduct for a given information system is NP-hard. For that reason, methods for calculating reducts have been developed using heuristic search, such as is studied in [12].

When ACO is used to solve the feature selection problem the graph representation is lightly different to the TSP case. This problem can be modeled in the following way. Let $A=\{a_1, a_2, a_{na}\}$ be a set of features. You can view this set as a network in which nodes represent features, and all nodes are connected by bi-directional links. Pheromone values τ_i are associated to nodes a_i, τ_i represents the absolute contribution of the feature a_i to a reduct. In the first step, each ant k is assigned to one node, it can move to all nodes in the network ($b_k \leftarrow \{a_i\}$, where b_k is the subset ant k has to build). Ants perform a forward selection in which each ant k expands its subset b_k step-by-step by adding new features; for performing it, each ant k looks for all features in the set $A\text{-}b_k$ and selects the next feature among them to include in b_k according to the ACO rule. This rule is the pseudorandom proportional rule (expression 2) in the case of ACS. The quality of the approximation of classification measure of RST (expression (3)) is used like a heuristic function (η) in the ACO model ($\eta(B)=\gamma_B(Y)$).

The ACS algorithm showed the best performance when a comparative study about several ACO algorithms was developed to solve the feature selection problem, see [2] and [3]. For this reason, we use the Ant Colony System algorithm to study the two stage approach.

The Two-step ACS algorithm in the FSP is based in the following key idea: to split the process of finding reducts in two stages. In the first stage, the algorithm builds candidate subsets, which are used in the second stage as initial subsets for each ant. In order to apply the two stage approach we need to decide how to set some parameters. The number of ants and the number of cycles per stage is calculated according to the ratio r; that is, let m the quantity of ants to use and NCmax the number of cycles to perform, these values are divided for each stage in the following form: First stage $\{m_1=m*r$ and $NCmax_1=NCmax*r\}$, and Second stage $\{m_2=m*(1-r)$ and $NCmax_2=NCmax*(1-r)\}$. Also, we must define what a partial solution is in the first stage. In this case, the reference value is the quality of the approximation of classification measure $\gamma_A(Y)$, and ants have to build subset of features with a quality of the approximation of approximation equal to $r*\gamma_A(Y)$. In the second stage we are looking for a solution to the original problem, so the subset has to obtain the value $\gamma_A(Y)$.

In other words, in the first stage m_1 ants during $NCmax_1$ cycles will be looking for subset of features with a quality of the approximation of classification equal to $r*\gamma_A(Y)$. In the second stage, m_2 ants will perform $NCmax_2$ cycles using the subsets resulting from the first stage as initial states in order to generate reducts.

The TS-ACS-RST-FS algorithm has the following structure:

Given parameters alpha, beta, NCmax (total number of cycles), na, ratio, ro and epsilon

```
P0: Calculate the quantity of ants (m) according to the
     number of features (na).
    Calculate the quality of the classification using
     all features (γB(Y) for B=A).
P1: Stage 1
     Calculate value for parameters in the first stage:
            NCmax1=ratio*NCmax
            m1= ratio*m  ; γB1(Y)=ratio* γA(Y)
     Apply ACS-RST-FS algorithm.
     Candidate subsets ← subSetselected by the ACS-RST-
     FS algorithm.
```

```
P2: Stage 2
     Calculate value for parameters in the second stage:
          NCmax2=NCmax-NCmax1
          m2= m-m1      ;   γB2(Y)= γA(Y)
     Apply ACS-RST-FS algorithm, in each cycle assign a
     random subset from Candidate subsets as initial
     subset for each ant.
```

The value of the ratio is an important parameter. Values near to 1 produce subsets near to the definition of reducts in the first stage.

For the experiments, we have used the following values for parameter ratio {0.2, 0.3, 0.36, 0.5, 0.6, and 0.8}. We have studied the effect of the ratio in three aspects, the quantity of reducts, the length of reducts and the computation time. Each algorithm was executed 10 times and the results were averaged over these 10 runs.

In Table 1, we present the results obtained using a decision system that contains 20 objects which are described by 16 discrete features (na=16) and belongs to two classes. The first class contains 9 objects and the second one contains 11 objects, the quality of the approximation of classification is equal to 1 ($\gamma_A(Y)=1$); so, this is a consistent decision system (each pair of indiscernible objects belongs to the same class). The quantity of cycles was 21 (NCmax=21). In columns number 6 and 7 the information is presented in the following form: averaged number of reducts/averaged length of reducts/time.

Table 1. A comparison between algorithms ACS-RST-FS and TS-ACS-RST-FS

Algorithm	NC max_1	NC max_2	m_1	m_2	beta=5 q_0=0.9	beta=1 q_0=0.3
ACS			--	--	46.7/3.95/228s	123/4.19/274s
TS-ACS rate=0.2	4	17	3	13	32.7/4.2/82s	76.3/4.2/89.9s
TS-ACS rate=0.3	6	15	5	11	43.3/4.1/53s	71/4.2/64s
TS-ACS rate=0.36	8	13	6	10	38.7/3.9/39s	67.3/4.1/47s
TS-ACS rate=0.5	10	11	8	8	29.7/3.8/32s	43.3/4.1/44s
TS-ACS rate=0.6	13	8	10	6	20.33/3.8/41s	37/4.2/49s
TS-ACS rate=0.8	17	4	13	3	9/3.8/82s	10.67/4.2/97s

You can see the ratio about to 0.3 yields the best results. This setting obtains a quantity of reduct near to ACS-RST-FS algorithm [3] but only in the 23% of the time. Similar results were obtained using other databases. This is an expected result, because the value ratio=0.3 offers a good balance between both stages; a higher numbers of ants and cycles in the second stages allows the algorithms to perform a larger exploration of the search space from of initial subsets having certain quality.

In Table 2, we present a similar study using Breast Cancer database from UCI Repository [4], in this database na=9 and we used 9 ants (m=9). In columns number 4 and 5 the information is presented in the following form. In the first row, the results obtained by the ACS algorithm (average number of reducts/time) are presented; in the rest of the rows we present the results yielded for the TS-ACS-RST-FS algorithm (percent of average number of reducts/percent of time) respects to the results showed in the first row. For instance, the TS-ACS-FSP algorithm with r=0.3, β=5 and q_0=0.9 obtained an average of 50.9 reducts (109% respects to 46.7 reducts) in only 71 seconds (31% respects to 228s). These results are very interesting because the Two-Step ACS approach enable us to obtain equal or greater quantity of reducts in lower time than ACS-RST-FS algorithm.

From tables 1 and 2, it is possible to see the time cost in the case of TS- ACS-RST-FS algorithm is very low. From this advantage, we propose a second idea: to increase the quantity of ants in order to yield a greater exploration of the search space. We developed experiments in which the number of ants was increased by the factors {1.33, 1.5, 1.8, 2.1}. In the last row of Table 2 the results with value 2.1 are showed. The relation is established respect the quantity of reducts and the time. For instance, when the number of ants is increased to 2.1*m (m=2.1*9=19), the algorithm TS-ACS-RST-FS obtains 124% number of reducts respect to the quantity of reducts obtained by ACS-RST-FS algorithm in only 67% of the time used by this last algorithm (for beta=5 and q_0=0.9). We used the rate=0.3 because this value shows the best results in experimental results.

Table 2. A comparison between ACS-RST-FSP algorithm and several alternatives to TS-ACS-RST-FS algorithm ($NCmax_1$=6, $NCmax_2$=15)

Algorithm	m_1	m_2	beta=5 q_0=0.9	beta=1 q_0=0.3
ACS m=9	--	--	46.7/228s	123/274s
TS-ACS rate=0.2	2	7	60%/34%	70/49%
TS-ACS rate=0.3	3	6	109%/31%	73%/37%
TS-ACS rate=0.36	3	6	105%/25%	77%/31%
TS-ACS rate=0.5	4	5	100%/22%	73%/26%
TS-ACS rate=0.6	5	4	65%/13%	50%/20%
TS-ACS rate=0.8	7	2	33%/27%	31%/26%
TS-ACS rate=0.3 m=2.1*m=19	6	13	124%/67%	103%/83%

4 Conclusion

We have presented an improvement of the Ant Colony Optimization which consists on splitting the search process developed by ants into two stages. The study was developed using the Ant Colony System algorithm. In this approach some parameters (number of ants, quantity of cycles, etc.) receive different values in each stage according to a ratio parameter which indicates what proportion of the complete search corresponds to each stage.

We studied the performance using different ratio values in the Feature selection problem. The experimental results showed the performance of ACO was increased strongly; the best results were obtained when the value of ratio is about 0.3.

This new approach to ACO which produces an important reduction of the computation time cost, yet preserving the solution quality.

Acknowledgments

The authors would like to thanks VLIR (Vlaamse InterUniversitaire Raad, Flemish Interuniversity Council, Belgium) for supporting this work under the IUC Program VLIR-UCLV.

References

1. Bello, P.R., Nowe, A., et al. Using ACO and Rough Set Theory to Feature Selection. WSEAS Transactions on Information Science and Applications, Issue 5, Vol. 2, May 2005, pp. 512-517.
2. Bello, P.R., Nowe, A., et al. A Model based on Ant Colony System and Rough Set Theory to Feature Selection. Proceedings of Genetic and Evolutionary Computation Conference (GECCO05), June 25-29, Washington DC, USA, 2005, pp. 275-276. ACM Press, ISBN 1-59593-038-8.
3. Bello, P.R., Nowe, A., et al. Using Ant Colony System meta-heuristic and Rough Set Theory to Feature Selection. Proceedings of The 6th Metaheuristics International Conference (MIC2005), August 22-26, Vienna, Austria. 2005. Printed by University of Vienna.
4. Blake, C.L. and Merz, C.J.. UCI repository of machine learning databases, 1998. http://www.ics.uci.edu/~mlearn/MLRepository.html.
5. Dong, M. and Kothari, R.. Feature subset selection using a new definition of classifiability. Patter Recognition Letter, vol. 24, issues 9-10, pp. 1215-1225. 2003.
6. Dorigo, M. et al. The Ant System: Optimization by a colony of cooperating agents. IEEE Transactions on Systems, Man and Cybernetics-Part B, vol. 26, no. 1, pp. 1-13. 1996.
7. Dorigo, M. and Gambardela, L.M.. Ant colonies for the traveling salesman problem. BioSystems no. 43, pp. 73-81, 1997.
8. Dorigo, M. et al. Ant algorithms for Discrete optimization. Artificial Life 5(2), pp. 137-172. 1999.
9. Dorigo, M. and Stützle, T.. ACO Algorithms for the Traveling Salesman Problem, 1999, Evolutionary Algorithms in Engineering and Computer Science: Recent Advances in Genetic Algorithms, Evolution Strategies, Evolutionary Programming, Genetic Programming and Industrial Applications, John Wiley & Sons., EEUU.

10. Dorigo, M. and Stutzle, T.. Ant Colony Optimization. MIT Press. 2004.
11. Inza, I.et al.. Feature subset selection by bayesian networks based optimization. Artificial intelligence, vol. 123, No. 1-2, pp. 157-184. 2000.
12. Jensen, R. and Shen. Q.. Finding rough set reducts with ant colony optimization. Proceedings of UK Workshop on Computational Intelligence, pp. 15-22. 2003.
13. Komorowski, J. Pawlak, Z. et al.. Rough Sets: A tutorial. In Pal, S.K. and Skowron, A. (Eds) Rough Fuzzy Hybridization: A new trend in decision-making. Springer, pp. 3-98. 1999.
14. Kudo, M. and Sklansky, J.. Comparison of algorithms that select features for pattern classifiers. Pattern Recognition 33, pp. 25-41. 2000.
15. Somol, P. and Pudil, P.. Feature selection toolbox. Pattern Recognition 35, pp. 2749-2759. 2002.
16. Stefanowski, J.. An experimental evaluation of improving rule based classifiers with two approaches that change representations of learning examples. Engineering Applications of Artificial Intelligence 17, pp. 439-445. 2004.
17. Xing, H. and Xu, L.. Feature space theory –a mathematical foundation for data mining. Knowledge-based systems 14, pp. 253-257. 2001.
18. Zhang, H. and Sun, G.. Feature selection using tabu search method. Pattern Recognition 35, pp. 710-711. 2002.

Simultaneous Features and Objects Selection for Mixed and Incomplete Data

Yenny Villuendas-Rey[1], Milton García-Borroto[2], Miguel A. Medina-Pérez[1], and José Ruiz-Shulcloper[3]

[1] University of Ciego de Ávila, Cuba
{migue, yennyv}@bioplantas.cu
http://www.unica.cu
[2] Bioplants Center, UNICA, C. de Ávila, Cuba,
mil@bioplantas.cu
http://www.bioplantas.cu
[3] Advanced Technologies Applications Center, MINBAS, Cuba.
jshulcloper@cenatav.co.cu
http://www.cenatav.co.cu/

Abstract. In this paper a new simultaneous editing and feature selection method for the Most Similar Neighbor classifier is proposed. It is designed for databases with objects described by features no exclusively numeric or categorical. It is based on Testor Theory and the Compact Set Editing method, mixing edited projections until a good accuracy is achieved. Experimental results with several databases show a good performance compared to previous methods and the classifier using the original sample.

1 Introduction

The Nearest Neighbor classifier [1] is widely used on supervised classification. This classifier stores a training set (T) and each new object is assigned to the class of its closest object on T. According to this rule, a distance function is necessary for comparing objects.

In many applications we usually deal with Mixed and Incomplete Data (MID), because objects are described by features not purely numeric or categorical. Also, missing values could be present. In these cases, we usually have a similarity measure that is not an opposite of a distance function: it is not positive defined or does not assure the triangle inequality or is not symmetric. So, the Nearest Neighbor rule should be extended to the Most Similar Neighbor rule (MSN), allowing any similarity function. Though, it has the main disadvantages of the Nearest Neighbor rule: significant computational costs (similarities with all the objects in the training sample T must be assessed) and high storage requirements (all T must be stored).

Researches to reduce these drawbacks have been focused mainly on two separated approaches: reducing the number of objects and selecting a feature subset. Nevertheless, few studies have been addressed to solve the two problems jointly [2-5].

In this paper we introduce a new method for solving both problems with MID over non-metric spaces. In section 2 we summarize some jointly approaches reported in the literature. We also underline some of the main drawbacks of these methods. In

J.F. Martínez-Trinidad et al. (Eds.): CIARP 2006, LNCS 4225, pp. 597–605, 2006.

section 3 our method is described, and section 4 contains the experimental results. Finally, conclusions and future works are presented.

2 Related Works

Just a few authors (Skalak [5], Kuncheva [4], Ishibushi [3] and Dasarathy [2]) have faced the problems of simultaneously (or combined) feature and object selection for the NN classifiers.

Skalak [5] uses a Random Mutation Hill Climbing algorithm. It consists on the random generation of a binary string, which represents the inclusion/exclusion of an object or feature in the current solution. At each step, an element of the string is mutated, generating a new one. Accuracy with 1-NN is computed, and the best solution (in a fixed number of iterations) is selected.

Kuncheva [4] uses a Genetic Algorithm. In this case, the chromosome is a binary string of length $|F|+|T|$ (where F is the feature set and T is the training sample) which represents the selected features and objects. A value 1 in a bit of the string means the inclusion of this feature/object in the selected sample, 0 otherwise.

The fitness function used by the Genetic Algorithm is:

$$fitness = A_{1-NN}(V) - \alpha\left(\frac{sf + so}{|F| + |T|}\right) \tag{1}$$

where A_{1-NN} is the 1-NN accuracy in a validation sample V, sf is the number of the selected features, so is the number of the selected objects and α a constant parameter (user defined).

Analogously, Ishibushi [3] employs a Genetic Algorithm, but with a different fitness function:

$$fitness = w_{1-NN} * nwc(T) - w_f * sf - w_o * so \tag{2}$$

where nwc is the number of well classified objects in a training sample T, sf is the number of the selected features, so is the number of the selected objects and w_{1-NN}, w_f and w_o are the user defined weights associated with the accuracy, feature count and object count respectively.

The chromosome encoding of the algorithm is similar to the strategy used by Kuncheva.

These approaches have an important random component, so two different application of the algorithm with the same data could have dramatically different results. Besides, the results reached by these methods lack of a comprehensive meaning in the problem domain. Also, as pointed out by Kuncheva [4], Genetic Algorithms spent a long time to get to a good solution.

Dasarathy [2] proposes the application of a Sequential Backward Search (SBS), introduced by Kittler [6]. The SBS uses as Optimization Function a combined measure of the reduction ratio and the accuracy of the classifier with respect to (wrt) the edited sample. This sample is obtained applying the Relative Neighborhood Graph based Editing (RNG-Edit) [7] and the Minimal Consistent Subset (MCS) [8].

This method have a big computational cost because their components (SBS, RNG-Edit and MCS), are all time consuming.

3 The Proposed Method

Specially designed to feature subsets selection with MID is the typical testors computation [9]. Typical testors are feature subsets that have two main properties: they do not confuse objects of different classes and are irreducible. So, a typical testor is a highly discriminative feature subset, with a clear meaning for specialists such as physicians, geologist, etc.

Typical testors have two main drawbacks: the computational cost and, in some databases, the amount of typical testors.

An object selection method designed to deal with MID is the Compact Set Editing (CSE) [10]. This algorithm has the desired property that is subclass consistent. So, the inner subclass structure of the training sample is preserved. CSE calculates the maximum similarity graph and make an ascending sort of the vertexes according to their indegree and outdegree. The nodes are iteratively discarded, starting from the firs, taking some actions to guarantee the subclass consistency.

The proposed algorithm is designed to deal with mixed and incomplete data, finding a new sample by reducing the numbers of features and objects in a simultaneous way. Besides, it tries to keep the 1-MSN classifier accuracy wrt a validation set as high as possible, using the selected sample.

The Simultaneous Object and Feature Selection Algorithm (SOFSA) proceeds as follows: firstly, we calculate the typical testors (TT) using the LEX algorithm [11],

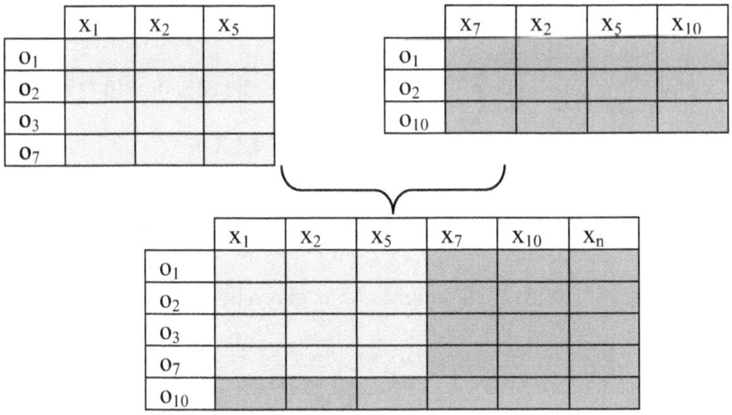

Fig. 1. Joint subsamples procedure used by SOFSA. All the features and objects of the parents are in the new subsample.

which has a good computational behavior for this task. Then, the TT are sorted according to their informational weights. Objects in the training sample are projected by the features presented in the first TT and CSE is applied to this projection. If accuracy wrt the validation sample is greater than the initial accuracy, calculated using all features and objects, a solution is returned, else the next TT is considered. In each previous step, we obtain a subsample. These subsamples generate a new subsample formed by the union of objects and features of each of them. See Fig 1.

Note that the process could be repeated for finding more accurate solutions than the initial one, but with more features and / or objects; until all projections are explored. In the cases that no solution improves the initial accuracy, we can choose an optimization function [2-4] that depends on accuracy result, object reduction ratio and feature reduction ratio. For example, we could use:

$$fitness = w_{1-NN} * A_{1-NN}(V) - w_f * \frac{sf}{|F|} - w_o * \frac{so}{|T|} \quad (3)$$

where A_{1-NN} is the classifier accuracy wrt the validation set, sf is the number of the selected features, so is the number of the selected objects and w_{1-NN}, w_f and w_o are the user defined weights associated with the accuracy, object reduction ratio and feature reduction ratio respectively.

Algorithm Parameters:

T	Training Sample
V	Validation Sample
CSE	Compact Set based Editing method
$\varepsilon_M^{Clasif}(V)$	Accuracy function wrt *V*, using *Clasif* as classifier and *M* as training sample
ΩM	Partial objects descriptions of sample *M* using only the features in Ω

To compute the relevance of a feature *x*, we use the equation in [12]:

$$\rho(x) = \alpha * P(x) + \beta * L(X) \quad (4)$$

where $P(x)$ and $L(x)$ are the frequency informational weight and the length informational weight of feature *x*, respectively.

The frequency informational weight of *x* is given by:

$$P(x) = \frac{\tau_x}{\tau} \quad (5)$$

where τ_x is the amount of typical testors in which *x* appears and τ is the total typical testors amount.

The length informational weight of feature *x* is given by:

$$L(x) = \frac{\sum\limits_{t \in TT_x} \frac{1}{|t|}}{|TT_x|} \tag{6}$$

where TT_x is the family of all typical testors in which x appears.

In our experiments, we use $\alpha = \beta = 0.5$ following [12]

SOFSA Algorithm:

1.	$TT \leftarrow LEX(T)$	Typical testors of T are computed using the LEX algorithm.
2.	*forEach tt in TT* $Weight_{tt} \leftarrow \sum_{X \in tt} \rho(x)$	The informational weight of each typical testor is calculated as the sum of the relevance of the features in the testor.
3.	$TT \leftarrow Sort(TT)$	The typical testors are sorted according to their weights.
4.	$InitialAcc \leftarrow \varepsilon_T^{1-MSN}(V)$	The accuracy of 1-MSN classifier is computed.
5.	$Solution \leftarrow []$	
6.	$found \leftarrow false$	
7.	*while not found* $\Omega \leftarrow next(\Omega) \in TT$	While no solution is found, the algorithm proceeds to project the objects of the training sample by the features of the typical testor $\Omega \in TT$.
	$Edited \leftarrow CSE(\Omega T)$	Then, the CSE method is applied to obtain an edited sample.
	$Solution \leftarrow Join(Solution, Edited)$	The edited sample is joined with the last solution, that is, all objects in the edited sample and all features in the typical testor are added to the solution.
	If $\varepsilon_{Solution}^{1-MSN}(V) > InitialAcc$ then	If the accuracy of the 1-MSN using the new solution is greater than initial accuracy,
	return Solution $InitialAcc \leftarrow \varepsilon_{Solution}^{1-MSN}(V)$ $found \leftarrow true$	a new solution is found and returned.
8.	End	

4 Experimental Results

Traditional methods for selecting features and objects simultaneously assume metric spaces. In this paper they were extended to deal with MID in non-metric spaces, for making numerical comparisons. For brevity, we name the extensions as: eDasarathy, eKuncheva, eIchibushi and eRMHC-FP respectively.

The experimental results were made using 4 databases from UCI, with Mixed and Incomplete Data. The description of these databases is shown in Table 1. In the experiments the databases were divided in Training (10% of the total of objects), Validation (20%) and Testing (70%).

Table 1. Description of the used databases

UCI name	Objects	Numerical Features	Categorical Features	Missing Values
Credit-screening	690	6	9	67
Hepatitis	155	6	14	167
Heart	270	6	7	0
Import-85 (symboling)	205	16	10	59

The similarity function used in our experiments was:

$$\Gamma(o,p)=\frac{\left|\{r\in F \mid C_r(o_r,p_r)=1\}\right|}{|F|} \tag{7}$$

where F is the set of all features, C_r the comparison criterion for the feature r; o_r and p_r are the values of the feature r of the objects o y p, respectively.

The Boolean similarity comparison criteria for numeric features were:

$$C_r(o_r,p_r)=\begin{cases}0 & \text{if } (o_r=?)\vee(\mathrm{p}_r=?)\vee(|o_r-p_r|\geq\sigma)\\ 1 & \text{otherwise}\end{cases} \tag{8}$$

where "?" denote a missing value, and σ is the standard deviation of the values of the feature.

For categorical data we use the criterion:

$$C_r(o_r,p_r)=\begin{cases}0 & \text{if } (\mathrm{o}_r=?)\vee(\mathrm{p}_r=?)\vee(o_r\neq p_r)\\ 1 & \text{otherwise}\end{cases} \tag{9}$$

The results for each used database are shown in tables 2-5. The accuracy function used was the ratio of well classified objects and the total amount of objects. The difference between accuracy without editing and accuracy after editing is shown in the Delta (Δ) column. As the databases are split randomly, we repeated the process 3 times to reduce the influence of randomness in partition, showing the mean in tables.

Table 2. Experimental results for database credit-screening. Accuracy without editing: 0.7428.

Method	Object Reduction (%)	Feature Reduction (%)	Edited Accuracy	Delta (Δ)
SOFSA	33.40	29.17	0.7590	0.0125
eDasarathy	83.61	6.67	0.7514	0.0086
eRMHC-FP	42.62	68.89	0.6707	-0.0722
eKuncheva	73.22	77.78	0.6071	-0.1357
eIshibushi	62.30	66.67	0.7377	-0.0052

In database credit-screening, the best method according to classifier accuracy is SOFSA, followed by eDasarathy. Both outperform the original accuracy of the 1-MSN classifier using only a reduced number of features and objects. According to reduction in both features and objects, eKuncheva shows the best performance; although the classifier accuracy is degrade in about 10%. Finally, eIshibushi shows a good reduction with a slightly drop in accuracy.

Table 3. Experimental results for database hepatitis. Accuracy without editing: 0.7161.

Method	Object Reduction (%)	Feature Reduction (%)	Edited Accuracy	Delta (Δ)
SOFSA	27.50	36.84	0.6938	-0.0223
eDasarathy	85.42	5.26	0.6615	-0.0547
eRMHC-FP	47.92	43.86	0.6797	-0.0365
eKuncheva	58.33	71.93	0.6094	-0.1068
eIshibushi	56.25	54.39	0.5000	-0.2161

In database hepatitis, no method outperforms classifier accuracy. SOFSA and eRMHC-FP give the best results according to accuracy. Both methods slightly degrade classifier accuracy, using a reduced number of features and objects. According to reduction, eKuncheva and eIshibuchi show the best performance, but the classifier accuracy is dropped in approximately 10% and 20% respectively.

Table 4. Experimental results for database heart. Accuracy without editing: 0.7619.

Method	Object Reduction (%)	Feature Reduction (%)	Edited Accuracy	Delta (Δ)
SOFSA	26.09	30.77	0.7619	0
eDasarathy	88.41	5.13	0.7904	0.0285
eRMHC-FP	44.93	51.28	0.6761	-0.0857
eKuncheva	52.17	79.49	0.6000	-0.1619
eIshibushi	52.17	61.54	0.6571	-0.1047

On database Heart, the best method according to accuracy results is eDasarathy. This method outperforms the unselected 1-MSN. SOFSA maintains original accuracy, reducing the 30% approximately of features and objects. All the other methods show a significant drop in accuracy. According to reduction, eKuncheva and eIshibushi both reduce about 50% to 70% of features and objects, with a drop of 10% in accuracy.

Table 5. Experimental results for database import-85. Accuracy without edititng: 0.4603.

Method	Object Reduction (%)	Feature Reduction (%)	Edited Accuracy	Delta (Δ)
SOFSA	8.33	37.00	0.4583	-0.0060
eDasarathy	84.03	4.00	0.4048	-0.0556
eRMHC-FP	45.14	42.67	0.4087	-0.0516
eKuncheva	27.08	36.00	0.2778	-0.1825
eIshibushi	27.08	36.00	0.3452	-0.1151

Finally, on database import-85, no method improves the classifier accuracy. SOFSA shows a little degradation, followed by eRMHC-FP. This last method shows the best results according to reduction in features and objects. The eRMHC-FP method obtains about a 45% of reduction in both features and objects.

The experimental results show that our method has a good performance over most of the databases. It reduces approximately 25 percent the number of features and objects with none or little degradations in classifier accuracy. In the numerical experiments it outperforms the other methods, except for database Heart, although in the database import-85 no significant reduction could be done.

eDasarathy had a stable behavior over all databases, but with insignificant reductions in the number of features. Random Mutation Hill Climbing and Genetic Algorithms show a good performance in some cases and in others the classifier performance is dramatically degraded. In these last three methods the reduction percent is always around half of features and objects.

5 Conclusions

Simultaneously (or combined) feature and object selection for improving the classifiers accuracy is a very important task in supervised classification problems. It was faced by several authors, but assuming metric spaces for 1-NN classifier. No procedure has been developed for MID in non-metric spaces for MSN classifiers. In this paper the methods introduced for metric spaces were extended for dealing with MID in non-metric spaces. Besides, a new algorithm is proposed to select jointly features and objects for the 1-MSN classifier. This is the first simultaneous features and objects selection algorithm specially designed to deal with databases containing objects described by features no exclusively numeric or categorical.

In most databases a good performance is showed by the proposed method, with respect to our extensions of earlier reported methods. Improvements or little degradations in the 1-MSN accuracy with a reduced number of features and objects are obtained by the method in all databases.

Several solutions could be returned by the method, which could be selected based on certain optimization criterion. These solutions have better accuracy, but the reduction in the number of objects and/or features is lesser.

All solutions returned by the method are formed by a highly discriminative feature subset, with a clear meaning for specialists. Also, the selected objects preserve the inner structure of the domain classes. Furthermore, this is a deterministic procedure, so we get unique solutions in two different application of the algorithm with the same data.

References

1. Duda, R.O., Hart, P.E.: Pattern Classification and Scene Analysis. John Wiley & Sons, N.Y. (1973)
2. Dasarathy, B.V.: Concurrent Feature and Prototype Selection in the Nearest Neighbor Decision Process. 4th World Multiconference on Systemics, Cybernetics and Informatics, Vol. VII, Orlando, USA (2000) 628/633
3. Ishibushi, H., Nakashima, T.: Evolution of reference sets in nearest neighbor classification. LNCS **1585** (1999) 82-89
4. Kuncheva, L.I., Jain, L.C.: Nearest neighbor classifier: Simultaneous editing and feature selection. Pattern Recognition Letters (1999)
5. Skalak, D.B.: Prototype and Feature Selection by Sampling and Random Mutation Hill Climbing Algorithms. Eleventh International Conference on Machine Learning (1994)
6. Kittler, J.: Feature set search algorithms. In: Chen, C.H. (ed.): Pattern recognition and signal proccessing. Sijthoff and Noordhoff, The Netherlands (1978)
7. Toussaint, G.T.: Proximity Graphs for Nearest Neighbor Decision Rules: Recent Progress. 34 Symposium on Computing and Statistics INTERFACE-2002, Montreal, Canada (2002)
8. Dasarathy, B.D.: Minimal consistent set (MCS) identification for optimal nearest neighbor decision systems design. IEEE Transactions on systems, man and cybernetics. **24** (1994) 511-517
9. Ruiz-Shulcloper, J., Abidi, M.A.: Logical combinatorial pattern recognition: A Review. In: Pandalai, S.G. (ed.): Recent Research Developments in Pattern Recognition. Transword Research Networks, USA (2002) 133-176
10. García-Borroto, M., Ruiz-Shulcloper, J.: Selecting Prototypes in Mixed Incomplete Data. Lecture Notes in Computer Science **3773** (2005) 450-459
11. Santiesteban, Y., Pons, A.: Un nuevo algoritmo para el cálculo de los testores típicos. Revista de Ciencias Matemáticas **21** (2003) 85-95
12. Lazo-Cortés, M., Ruiz-Shulcloper, J.: Determining the feature informational weight for non-classical described objects and new algorithm to calculate fuzzy testors. Pattern Recognition Letters **16** (1995) 1259-1265

Selecting Objects for ALVOT

Miguel Angel Medina-Pérez[1], Milton García-Borroto[2], Yenny Villuendas-Rey[1], and José Ruiz-Shulcloper[3]

[1] University of Ciego de Ávila, Cuba
(migue, yennyv)@bioplantas.cu
http://www.unica.cu
[2] Bioplants Center, UNICA, C. de Ávila, Cuba
mil@bioplantas.cu
http://www.bioplantas.cu
[3] Advanced Technologies Applications Center, MINBAS, Cuba
jshulcloper@cenatav.co.cu
http://www.cenatav.co.cu/

Abstract. ALVOT is a model of supervised classification based on partial precedences. In this paper a new object selection method based on a voting procedure for ALVOT is proposed. The method was developed for dealing with databases having objects described by features that are not exclusively numeric or categorical. A comparative numerical experiment was performed with different algorithms of object selection. The experimental results show a good performance of the proposed method with respect to the other algorithms.

1 Introduction

To achieve high-quality results, supervised classifiers need a good training matrix. It is usually accomplished by removing "noisy" as well as redundant objects. Several techniques have been developed to deal with these two problems, increasing the quality of classification: editing and condensing methods respectively [1].

On the other hand, in real world problems, sometimes the objects are described simultaneously in terms of qualitative and quantitative features. Some of the object descriptions could also be incomplete (missing values). In these cases, the tools of the Logical Combinatorial Pattern Recognition (LCPR) [2] should be used.

ALVOT [3, 4], introduced by Zhuravlev, is a model of supervised classification in the LCPR. The original algorithm has been applied to different real world situations, with the introduction of new similarity functions. Also, the fuzzy set theory concepts have been used in order to adequately model some problems in geosciences, medicine, and others [5, 6].

ALVOT is based on partial precedence. Partial precedence is the principle of calculating the similarity between objects using comparisons between their partial descriptions. A partial description is a combination of features with a clear meaning in the problem domain. This is the way that physicians, and other natural scientists, establish comparisons among objects in real world problems [4].

For a new object to be classified, many partial comparisons with all the objects in the training matrix have to be calculated. This can be very time consuming, while the

J.F. Martínez-Trinidad et al. (Eds.): CIARP 2006, LNCS 4225, pp. 606 – 613, 2006.

cardinality of the matrix increases. That is why we propose an object selection method, which improves the quality of classification with ALVOT.

2 Previous Works

The first editing method for ALVOT was introduced in [7, 8]. This method uses a set of genetic algorithms to select the support sets system, the features weights, and the objects in the training matrix. Nevertheless, there are several problems where this optimization procedure can not be applied, because the parameters have a meaning in the problem definition domain. For example, the specialist might determine the support sets system and assign the feature weights according to his background knowledge. He can also use some procedures, with a comprehensive meaning in his model. Based on these facts, we compared our algorithm only with the object selection procedure.

The chromosomes used by the genetic algorithm were binary strings consisting of m bits, one for each object, representing the subsets of those which are selected. The ith bit has value 1 when the respective element is included, and 0 otherwise.

In general, the algorithm works as follows:

1 The initial population is generated randomly. The population size and iteration number are input parameters of the algorithm.
2 The population's individuals are sorted according to their fitness. The first and last individuals are crossed, the second is crossed with the penultimate and this process is repeated until finishing the population. They are crossed using a 1-point crossover operator in the middle of the individual. The fitness function is the ratio of well classified objects.
3 For each individual in the population the mutation operator is applied. It takes randomly an individual's gene and changes its value. The fitness is evaluated for this new population.
4 The original individuals together with those obtained by crossing and mutation are sorted in descending order according to their fitness and those with highest fitness are chosen (taking into account the population size). The new population is used in the next iteration of the algorithm.

This method has an important random component, so two different executions of the algorithm with the same data could have dramatically different results. Besides, the results reached by this procedure lack of a comprehensive meaning in the problem domain. As pointed out by Kuncheva and Bezdek [9] selecting prototypes by Random Searches and Genetic Algorithms could be computationally demanding and, for large data sets, may be infeasible.

3 A First Approach to a New Object Selection Method for ALVOT

For selecting objects for ALVOT we can apply a classical editing methods based on NN rule. An analogue solution were reported by Decaestecker [10] and Konig et. al [11], in which the training matrix is edited for a Radial Based Function network, using a procedure originally designed for k-NN. A deep study about editing methods is outside of the scope of this paper, but a revision can be found in [1].

Considering that we are working with MID, in this paper we use the Compact Set Editing method(CSE) [12], an extension of Wilson's [13] Edited Nearest Neighbor rule (ENN) for MID, and a modification of the ENN using ALVOT as classifier (EALVOT).

Despite these procedures can be applied, as we can see below, a better solution could be achieved considering the way ALVOT works.

4 Voting Based Object Selection (VOS)

Any algorithm of ALVOT A works in six stages:

Stage 1.- Determine the support sets system Ω_A, which is a set of subsets of features.

Stage 2.- Find out the feature comparison criteria and similarity function between sub-descriptions of objects $\beta(\Omega O, \Omega O_i)$, $\Omega \in \Omega_A$. ΩO is a sub-description of object O using only features in Ω; and β is a similarity function.

Stage 3.- Rule for evaluating the partial similarity between a fixed sub-description of a new object and the corresponding sub-descriptions of previously classified objects $\Gamma_\Omega(O_p, O)$ (partial evaluation by rows).

Stage 4.- Rule for summarizing the partial evaluation by rows of a fixed sub-description of a new object for each class $\Gamma_\Omega^j(O)$ (partial evaluation by classes).

Stage 5.- Rule for summarizing all partial evaluations by class with respect to the whole support sets system of a new object $\Gamma^j(O)$ (total evaluation by classes).

Stage 6.- Decision-making rule based on the total evaluation by classes Γ_A.

In this paper we introduce a new method to select objects for ALVOT, named Voting based Object Selection (VOS). Objects are selected according to their *voting power* in the training data, which is calculated with the following expression:

$$\iota(O) = \frac{V_{K_j}(O)}{\alpha_{K_j}(O) + \left(1 - V_{K_j}(O)\right)} - \max_{i \neq j}\left\{\frac{V'_{K_i}(O)}{\alpha'_{K_j}(O) + \left(1 - V'_{K_i}(O)\right)}\right\} \quad (1)$$

where:

- $V_{K_j}(O) = \frac{1}{|K_j| - 1} \sum_{\substack{O_i \in K_j \\ O_i \neq O}} I_{K_j}(O, O_i)$; summarizes the votes that O gives to the objects of its own class (K_j).
- $I_{K_j}(O, O_i) = \frac{1}{|\Omega_A|} \sum_{\Omega \in \Omega_A} \frac{1}{|K_j| - 1} \cdot \rho(O) \cdot \rho(\Omega) \cdot \beta(\Omega O, \Omega O_i)$; a voting function obtained from ALVOT stages 3 to 5. This function express the vote that the object

O gives to O_i, being $\rho(O_p)$ the weight of the object O_p, $\rho(\Omega) = \sum_{\chi_i \in \Omega} \rho(\chi_i)$, and $\rho(\chi_i)$ the weight of the feature χ_i.

- $\alpha_{K_j}(O) = \frac{1}{|K_j| - 1} \sum_{\substack{O_i \in K_j \\ O \neq O_i}} \left| V_{K_j}(O) - I_{K_j}(O, O_i) \right|$ the variance between the mean $V_{K_j}(O)$ and the vote that the object O gives to the other objects in K_j; so when the variance decreases, the values of $\iota(O)$ increases.
- $V'_{K_i}(O) = \frac{1}{|K_i|} \sum_{O_h \in K_i} I'_{K_i}(O, O_h)$; analogous to $V_{K_j}(O)$, but $O \notin K_i$.
- $I'_{K_i}(O, O_h) = \frac{1}{|\Omega_A|} \sum_{\Omega \in \Omega_A} \frac{1}{|K_j|} \cdot \rho(O) \cdot \rho(\Omega) \cdot \beta(\Omega O, \Omega O_h)$, analogous to $I_{K_j}(O, O_i)$, but $O \notin K_i$.
- $\alpha'_{K_i}(O) = \frac{1}{|K_i|} \sum_{O_h \in K_i} \left| V'_{K_i}(O) - I'_{K_i}(O, O_h) \right|$; analogous to $\alpha_{K_j}(O)$, but $O \notin K_i$.

Let be $Q_A(S,V) = W_a \cdot Acc - W_o \cdot \frac{|S|}{|T|}$ a quality function; where W_a is the weight associated to the accuracy obtained from classifying the objects in V using S as training matrix; T the original training matrix; and W_o, the weight associated to the reduction ratio.

The algorithm VOS works as follows:

Step 0: Calculate $Q_A(T,V) = q_0$, the quality of A classifying the validation matrix V using the training matrix T.

Step 1: Calculate the voting power of each object using (1).

Step 2: Sort descendent the objects per class according to $\iota(O)$.

Step 3: Calculate $c_0 = \min_{i \in 1 \ldots r} \left\{ \left| \{ O \in K_i : \iota(O) > 0 \} \right| \right\}$, where r is the total amount of classes. This value is the minimal number of objects in any class with a positive $\iota(O)$. Select an initial solution S_0 taking the first c_0 objects from each class.

Step 4: Calculate q_1, the quality of A classifying V using S_0 as the training matrix.

Step 5: If $q_1 \geq q_0$, keep removing from S_0 the object with less $\iota(O)$ per class, while the quality is above q_0 and no empty class is obtained.

Step 6: If $q_1 < q_0$, keep adding from $T \setminus S_0$ to S_0 the object with greater $\iota(O)$ per class, until the quality reaches at least q_0.

Step 7: Return S_0.

5 Experimental Results

The experiments were made using 7 databases from UCI [14] Repository of Machine Learning, with mixed and incomplete data. A description of these databases can be found in Table 1.

Table 1. Databases used in the experiments

Database	Objects	Features	Missing Values	Classes
Breast-cancer	286	9	9	2
Breast-cancer-breast	286	9	9	2
Credit-screening	690	15	37	2
Credit-screening-A9	690	15	37	2
Credit-screening-A12	690	15	37	2
Hepatitis	155	19	75	2
Import-85	205	25	46	7

Breast-cancer-breast is the same database as Breast-cancer, but with the feature breast used as class feature. Credit-screening-A9 (Credit-screening-A12) is the same database as Credit-screening, but with the feature A9 (A12) used as class feature.

Each database was split taking 70% for training and 30% for testing. We repeated the process 5 times and average the results.

In our experiments we used a voting algorithm A with the following parameters:

- The support sets system was the set of all typical testors of the training matrix.
- $\beta(\Omega O_i, \Omega O_j) = \dfrac{\sum_{\chi_p \in \Omega} C_p(\chi_p(O_i), \chi_p(O_j))}{|\Omega|}$; partial similarity function, where Ω is a subset of features, C_p the comparison criterion for the feature χ_p, and $\chi_p(O_i)$ is the value of the feature χ_p in the object O_i.
- $C_p(\chi_p(O_1), \chi_p(O_2)) = \begin{cases} 1 & \text{if } |\chi_p(O_1) - \chi_p(O_2)| < \sigma_p \\ 0 & \text{otherwise} \end{cases}$; similarity comparison criteria for numeric features, where σ_p is the standard deviation of the values of the feature χ_p in the training matrix.
- $C_p(\chi_p(O_1), \chi_p(O_2)) = \begin{cases} 1 & \text{if } \chi_p(O_1) = \chi_p(O_2) \\ 0 & \text{otherwise} \end{cases}$; similarity comparison criteria for non-numeric features.
- $\Gamma_\Omega(O_p, O) = \rho(O_p) \cdot \rho(\Omega) \cdot \beta(\Omega O_p, \Omega O)$; partial evaluation by rows for a fixed support set, where $\rho(\Omega) = \sum_{\chi_i \in \Omega} \rho(\chi_i)$. In the experiments $\rho(O_p) = 1$ was used.

- The weight of the feature χ_i is calculated, following [15], with the equation: $\rho(\chi_i)=\alpha\cdot P(\chi_i)+\beta\cdot L(\chi_i)$ with $\alpha,\beta>0$ and $\alpha+\beta=1$, being α and β two parameters, which weight the influence of $P(\chi_i)$ and $L(\chi_i)$ respectively in $\rho(\chi_i)$. We used $\alpha=\beta=0.5$. $P(\chi_i)$ is computed: $P(\chi_i)=\frac{\tau(i)}{\tau}$, where $\tau(i)$ is the number of typical testors, which contain the feature χ_i and τ the amount of all typical testors. $L(\chi_i)$ is computed: $L(\chi_i)=\frac{\sum_{t\in\Psi^*(\chi_i)}\frac{1}{|t|}}{|\Psi^*(\chi_i)|}$, where $\Psi^*(\chi_i)$ is the family of all typical testors, which contain the feature χ_i.
- $\Gamma_\Omega^j(O)=\frac{1}{|K_j|}\sum_{O_t\in K_j}\Gamma_\Omega(O_t,O)$; partial evaluation by classes for a fixed support set.
- $\Gamma^j(O)=\frac{1}{|\Omega_A|}\sum_{\Omega\in\Omega_A}\Gamma_\Omega^j(O)$; total evaluation by classes.
- $\Gamma_A(\Gamma^1(O),\ldots,\Gamma^r(O))=(\alpha_1^A(O),\ldots,\alpha_r^A(O))$; decision – making rule, where $\alpha_1^A(O)=\begin{cases}1 & if\ \Gamma^i(O)\geq\Gamma^j(O)\ for\ i\neq j\\ 0 & otherwise\end{cases}$.
- The quality function used, $Q_A(S_0,V)$, was the well classification ratio; hence, $W_a=1$ and $W_o=0$.
- The training matrix was used as validation matrix; $V=T$.

To make numerical comparisons, we denoted as GA the algorithm introduced in section 2.

The accuracy of A with the original matrix, CSE, ENN, GA, EALVOT and VOS are shown in Table 2 and 3. These results show that no method was clearly superior in all databases.

The compression ratios achieved by the algorithms are shown in Table 4.

It is clear that the proposed method reach higher compression ratios affecting lesser the classifier accuracy than any other methods.

Table 2. Accuracy of A without editing compared with methods that do not use ALVOT

Database	A	CSE	ENN
Breast-cancer	0.754	0.767	0.774
Breast-cancer-breast	0.58	0.624	0.547
Credit-screening	0.801	0.790	0.785
Credit-screening-A9	0.739	0.744	0.734
Credit-screening-A12	0.620	0.606	0.598
Hepatitis	0.738	0.691	0.740
Import-85	0.495	0.498	0.451

Table 3. Accuracy of A without editing compared with methods that use ALVOT

Database	A	GA	EALVOT	VOS
Breast-cancer	0.754	0.714	0.785	0.749
Breast-cancer-breast	0.58	0.522	0.560	0.578
Credit-screening	0.801	0.788	0.773	0.782
Credit-screening-A9	0.739	0.738	0.717	0.705
Credit-screening-A12	0.620	0.616	0.614	0.616
Hepatitis	0.738	0.738	0.740	0.743
Import-85	0.495	0.422	0.460	0.489

Table 4. Compression ratio

Database	CSE	ENN	GA	EALVOT	VOS
Breast-cancer	0.29	0.21	0.51	0.27	0.60
Breast-cancer-breast	0.22	0.21	0.53	0.32	0.55
Credit-screening	0.50	0.10	0.50	0.13	0.60
Credit-screening-A9	0.44	0.11	0.50	0.14	0.52
Credit-screening-A12	0.21	0.24	0.49	0.42	0.48
Hepatitis	0.54	0.12	0.51	0.19	0.69
Import-85	0.44	0.13	0.50	0.61	0.87

6 Conclusions

ALVOT is a model for supervised classification based on partial precedences. It is mainly used in problems where the objects are described in terms of qualitative and quantitative features simultaneously, and some features have missing values.

Classifying with ALVOT turns expensive while the training matrix increases. In this paper a new object selection method (VOS) for ALVOT is introduced. It is based on the voting power of the objects, a magnitude calculated according the way ALVOT works. Several experiments were carried out and the comparisons with other methods showed that the proposed method reaches higher compression ratios affecting lesser the classifier accuracy than any other method.

References

1. Bezdek, J.C., Kuncheva, L.I.: Nearest Prototype classifiers designs: an experimental study. International Journal of Intelligent Systems 16 (2001) 1445 - 1473
2. Martínez Trinidad, J.F., Guzmán-Arenas, A.: The logical combinatorial approach to Pattern Recognition, an overview through selected works. Pattern Recognition 34 (2001) 741-751
3. Zhuravlev, Y.I., Nikiforov, V.V.: Recognition algorithms based on voting calculation. Journal Kibernetika 3 (1971) 1-11

4. Ruiz-Shulcloper, J., Abidi, M.A.: Logical Combinatorial Pattern Recognition: A Review. In: Pandalai, S.G. (ed.): Recent Research Developments in Pattern Recognition. Transword Research Networks, USA (2002) 133-176
5. Gómez-Herrera, J., Rodríguez-Morán, O., Valladares-Amaro, S., Ruiz-Shulcloper, J., Pico-Peña, R.: Prognostic of Gas-oil deposits in the Cuban ophiological association, applying mathematical modeling. Geofísica Internacional 33 (1995) 447-467
6. Ortiz-Posadas, M.R.: Prognosis and evaluation of cleft palate patients' rehabilitation using pattern recognition techniques. World Congress on Medical Physics and Biomedical Engineering 35 (1997) 500
7. Carrasco-Ochoa, J.A., Martínez-Trinidad, J.F.: Editing and Training for ALVOT, an Evolutionary Approach. Lecture Notes in Computer Science 2690 (2003) 452-456
8. Carrasco-Ochoa, J.A., Martínez-Trinidad, J.F.: Combining Evolutionary Techniques to Improve ALVOT Efficiency. WSEAS Transactions on Systems 2 (2003) 1073-1078
9. Kuncheva, L.I., Bezdek, J.C.: Nearest prototype classification: clustering, genetic algorithms or random search. IEEE Transactions on Systems, Man and Cybernetics. Part C 28 (1998) 160-164
10. Decaestecker, C.: NNP: A neural net classifier using prototype. International Conference on Neural Networks, San Francisco, California (1993) 822-824
11. König, A., Rashhofer, R.J., Glesner, M.: A novel method for the design of radial-basis-function networks and its implication for knowledge extraction. International Conference on Neural Networks, Orlando, Florida (1994) 1804-1809
12. García-Borroto, M., Ruiz-Shulcloper, J.: Selecting Prototypes in Mixed Incomplete Data. Lecture Notes in Computer Science 3773 (2005) 450-459
13. Wilson, D.L.: Asymptotic properties of nearest neighbor rules using edited data. IEEE Transactions on Systems, Man and Cybernetics 2 (1972) 408-421
14. Merz, C.J., Murphy, P.M.: UCI Repository of Machine Learning Databases. University of California at Irvine, Department of Information and Computer Science, Irvine (1998)
15. Lazo-Cortés, M., Ruiz-Shulcloper, J.: Determining the feature informational weight for non-classical described objects and new algorithm to calculate fuzzy testors. Pattern Recognition Letters 16 (1995) 1259-1265

Feature Extraction Using Clustering of Protein

Isis Bonet[1], Yvan Saeys[3], Ricardo Grau Ábalo[1], María M. García[1], Robersy Sanchez[2], and Yves Van de Peer[3]

[1] Center of Studies on Informatics, Central University of Las Villas, Santa Clara, Villa Clara, Cuba
[2] Research Institute of Tropical Roots, Tuber Crops and Banana (INIVIT), Biotechnology Group, Santo Domingo, Villa Clara, Cuba
[3] Department of Plant Systems Biology, Flanders Interuniversity Institute for Biotechnology (VIB), Ghent University, Belgium
isisb@uclv.edu.cu, yvsae@psb.ugent.be,
{rgrau, mmgarcia, robersy}@uclv.edu.cu,
yves.vandepeer@psb.ugent.be

Abstract. In this paper we investigate the usage of a clustering algorithm as a feature extraction technique to find new features to represent the protein sequence. In particular, our work focuses on the prediction of HIV protease resistance to drugs. We use a biologically motivated similarity function based on the contact energy of the amino acid and the position in the sequence. The performance measure was computed taking into account the clustering reliability and the classification validity. An SVM using 10-fold crossvalidation and the *k-means* algorithm were used for classification and clustering respectively. The best results were obtained by reducing an initial set of 99 features to a lower dimensional feature set of 36-66 features.

Keywords: HIV resistance, SVM, clustering, k-means, similarity function.

1 Introduction

Nowadays, Bioinformatics is an area of research that is rapidly gaining in importance worldwide. It comprises several scientific fields, and is becoming a multidisciplinary science where input from e.g. machine learning research plays an important role.

Most of the problems in bioinformatics concern the analysis of DNA or protein sequences. In order to analyze these sequences, a common approach is to use the representation based on the sequence. However, in the case of protein sequences, more information could be conveyed by the three-dimensional structure. Studies on 3D structure are just another investigation problem in bioinformatics, yet unfortunately predicting the structure from the sequence is not evident. For this reason, we focus in this paper on a classification problem, starting from the primary sequence. The classification problem we consider here is the prediction of HIV drug resistance.

Given the protein sequence of protease, which is an important viral protein, the goal is to predict its resistance to drugs. The protease protein mutates constantly, and therefore resistance emerges easily after the application of a drug.

J.F. Martínez-Trinidad et al. (Eds.): CIARP 2006, LNCS 4225, pp. 614–623, 2006.

To solve the resistance prediction problem, several machine learning techniques have been applied previously, such as decision trees, k-nearest neighbor technique (KNN) classifiers, and support vector machines (SVM) [1], [4], [10].

Usually, in problems on sequence analysis, the primary sequence is described using a feature for each amino acid. This representation consists of too much features. Given a problem where the length of the sequences is n and taking into account that there exist 20 amino acids, this results in 20^n possible features, the value of which correspond to the possible mutations of the sequence. The large number of possible mutations results in the fact that existing databases only represent a few of them, mostly having no known instances for each possible type of mutation. However, it can be considered that positions in the protein sequence that never mutate, will not influence the solution found by a machine learning algorithm.

On other hand, sequences are frequently very large, resulting in many possible features. These two observations motivate our work on reducing the dimensionality of the features that represent the protein sequence. Thinking in a first step, we start from a clustering process that looks for associations between amino acids in the sequence. Subsequently, an SVM is used as classification algorithm, where the idea is to find a small number of features that are sufficient to obtain good performance (i.e. values better or at less equivalent to the results obtained using all features).

2 Methods

2.1 Datasets

We used the information in the Stanford HIV Resistance Database Protease to develop our work because it is the one mostly used in the literature and it contains information about the genotype and phenotype for seven of the most widely used protease inhibitors. These inhibitors are: amprenavir (APV), atazanavir (ATV), nelfinavir (NFV), ritonavir (RTV), saquinavir (SQV), lopinavir (LPV) and indinavir (IDV). The genotype is described by the mutated positions with the corresponding change in amino acid. The phenotype is described by the resistance-fold based on the concentration for the drug to inhibit the viral protease as the resistance value. This database is available at http://hivdb.stanford.edu/cgibin/PIResiNote.cgi.

To eliminate missing values, the instances in the dataset with unknown changes in amino acid were discarded. Finally, seven databases were constructed, one for each drug. We took as reference sequence (wild type) the HXB2 protease and built the mutated sequences by changing the amino acid in the corresponding reported mutated positions. For the resistance-fold we used the 3.5 cut-off value, as previously reported in the literature for these drugs [2], [10]. If the drug resistance is greater than this cut-off value, the mutant is classified as resistant and otherwise as susceptible. In this way we obtain a binary (i.e. two-class) classification problem: {resistant, susceptible}.

2.2 Pattern Representation

As in any classification problem, one of the first steps is looking for appropriate features to represent the input information. In problems of sequences analysis like this, it is common to use each amino acid as the information for the features. In this way, we will have the same number of features as the sequence has amino acids.

In some approaches, the simple representation of each sequence position being a binary vector of 20 elements (i.e. the amino acids) has been used. In that case, a value of 1 is given to the analyzed amino acid position and a 0 to all the others. Mutual information profiles have also been used to represent each sequence of the Protease enzyme [1].

Some methods using information of protein structure have also been reported in the literature [4]. The idea to use the information related to the 3D structure would be ideal, because this structure would allow us to know whether the drug has perfect contact with the protein to inhibit its functionality or not. However, the amount of available 3D data on HIV mutants is not enough in order to build a good training database. Since the amount of primary structure data is significantly higher than the number of 3D structures available, we used data based on primary structures. However, we use a representation of the sequence that allows to some extent to take into account some features related to the 3D-structure. In particular, we chose the amino acid contact energy as an adequate representation because it determines the (un)folding of the protein. Miyazawa and Jernigan (1994) showed that the contact energy changes the protein structure, and the substitution of a simple amino acid suffices to observe this [13], [14]. For this reason, the energy associated with each amino acid is used to represent the Protease sequence and will be referred to from now on as Energy (equation 1).

$$\text{Energy: } A \rightarrow R \tag{1}$$

where A is the set of 20 amino acids and R is the set of real numbers.

In particular, we have 7 databases, one for each drug. The problem was transformed into seven similar binary classification problems. The target function of each problem is the same (equation 2).

$$F: A \rightarrow O \tag{2}$$

where O = {resistant, susceptible} and $A \subseteq R99$, because the database consists of sequences of the same length, namely 99 amino acids. Each element of A is a protease sequence identified by an amino acid vector. All amino acids are represented by their Energy, which is a real value.

As was explained in the introduction, the databases have some features that never change, which have the same value in all cases. One of the possible solutions to this problem is to find association between positions in the sequence and to do a transformation in the space building new features. Feature extraction can be a technique to compute new features taking into account the information of other features.

2.3 Feature Extraction

In mathematical terms, dimensionality reduction is based on the following: given a p-dimensional variable that defines the features $x = (x_1;\ldots; x_p)^T$; look for a lower dimensional representation of it $(s_1;\ldots;s_k)^T$ with $k<p$, that captures the content in the original data, according to some criterion.

Dimensionality reduction can be focused on feature selection or feature extraction. The first idea is based on finding a subset s of features from the original data x. The second objective is focused on finding a transformation that can be applied to the space in all features.

Any of these techniques can be chosen. Features selection can help to select the positions with more influence in the resistance. However, in our case we did not want to lose the information of each position, as it could be biologically relevant in having an influence on the classification of the resistance. Therefore, we focus in this work on feature extraction.

Feature extraction consists of finding a matrix $C_{k\times p}$, with $k<p$, from the matrix $X_{n\times p}$ where n is the number of data in the database and p the number of features. The idea is to transform the matrix X from the matrix C to obtain the matrix U representing the new features (equation 3).

$$U^T = C \times X^T \tag{3}$$

There are many feature extraction techniques commonly used in the literature for different problems [6]. Due to the characteristics of the problem, the transformation was focused on finding associations between the positions with biological meaning. In this way we can find groups of positions that relate to each other for reasons of resistance modeling. To compute the associations, there exist many statistical and artificial intelligence techniques. We select a clustering method to find the groups of positions in the sequence, as a fast way to do feature extraction. This technique has been used by other authors in other problems of pattern recognition [5], [15], [16].

Clustering is a technique that groups patterns into classes (termed clusters) based on similarity.

Any clustering task can be characterized by the following three principles [9]:

1. Pattern representation
2. Definition of a pattern similarity measure
3. Clustering algorithm

The first step was described in the section 2.2. Step 2 will be explained further in the paper. The last step includes the selection of the clustering algorithm In the literature there are several clustering techniques., reviewed by Jain, A. K. et al. (1999) [9]. One of them, *k-means,* is a classical algorithm and was chosen to be used in this work.

2.4.1 K-Means

k-means is a popular clustering algorithm which has been used in several applications. Given a set of n data points in R^p and an integer k, the *k-means* algorithm finds a set of k points R^p, called "centroids", and associates each point in the data to the nearest centroid. It is very important to select an appropriated similarity function [11].

This method has the disadvantage that it needs the number of clusters as input information (prior information). However, for our application this is not problematic, as we want to test all possible clusters number.

For the implementation of the clustering, we used Weka, which is a free software package that has implemented this algorithm. Furthermore, it has the advantage that it is easy to add a new similarity function. Weka is available at the following URL: http://www.cs.waikato.ac.nz/ml/weka.

2.4.2 Similarity Function

Selecting a similarity function is a key step for a good clustering process. There are already several functions defined in the literature, depending on the problem. Between the most popular are: Euclidean distance, Minkowski metric, squared Mahalanobis distance [3], [7].

In this paper, we defined our own similarity function, which has a biological meaning related to the clustering of sequence positions for drug resistance modeling With this type of function we can keep the interpretability of the data that precisely is a disadvantage of most feature extraction techniques.

As already discussed above, the data of our problem are defined by equations 1 and 2. Each element represents the Energy associated to the corresponding amino acid. However, we need to group the positions of the sequences taking into account the repercussions of the mutations in these positions. Using only the Energy information is not enough to build these groups. One can observe that the positions with the same amino acid will be member of the same group and this result is not valid. In order to keep the idea to find information relative to the 3D structure, we take the position as an additional type of information into account. We combined both *Energy* and *position* of each element in the sequence to obtain the following similarity function:

$$d(k,l) = \sum_{i=1}^{n}\left(Z\left(k*e_{a_k}(i)\right)-Z\left(l*e_{a_l}(i)\right)\right)^2 \quad (4)$$

where Z(x) represents the Z-score normalization of the variable x, defined in the equation 5:

$$z(X) = \frac{X - \overline{X}}{S_x} \quad (5)$$

Here, $\overline{X}$ is the mean of X and S_x is the standard deviation. In our case:

You can define $k*e_{ak}=X_1$ and $l*e_{al}=X_2$, and one can consider equation 4 as the square of the Euclidean distance (see equation 6).

$$d(k,l) = \sum_{i=1}^{n} \left(z\left(x_1(i)\right) - z\left(x_2(i)\right)\right)^2 \quad (6)$$

2.5 Classification Method

2.5.1 SVM

Support Vector Machines (SVM) are a technique developed by Vapnik in 1996 from statistical learning theory [17]. SVM have become an important machine learning technique for many pattern recognition problems, especially in computational biology. For SVM training and testing we also used the Weka software.

2.5.2 Performance Measure

The performance measures used in this work were divided in two parts: one to evaluate the clustering, and the other to evaluate the classification.

To evaluate the classification results we use the Receiver Operating Characteristic curve (ROC curve) to evaluate the results of an SVM [12].

ROC curves have the advantage that they encapsulate all information contained in the confusion matrix. It is a plot of the true positive rate (TPr) against the false positive rate (FPr). To measure the classification performance, we used the area under the curve (AUC) [8].

3 Results and Discussion

The objective of this paper is focused on searching the best features to predict HIV drug resistance starting from feature extraction. We used *k-means* as clustering algorithm to find associations between the amino acids that describe the protein sequence. In a next step, we used an SVM as a classification method, and compared the results obtained using all features to those using the new features derived from the clustering.

First, we train the SVM using all features and afterwards, we applied *k-means* for all possible values of *k*, *k*=1,,.., *p*-1 (p denotes the sequence length). With small values of k we obtained good results, as is shown in Table 1. The first row in this table represents the results for all features (i.e. 99 amino acids). The rows 2 and 3 describe the results of 25 and 28 clusters respectively for each drug. As can be observed, the results for 25 clusters are better or at least as good as those using all features, for 6 of the 7 drugs. Using 28 clusters we already obtain good results for all drugs.

Table 1. Prediction performance (AUC) of SVM for the seven drugs using 99, 25 and 28 features

Number of features	APV	ATV	IDV	NFV	RTV	SQV	LPV
99	83.5	75.2	89.3	85.7	89.9	85.2	65
25	**83.6**	**81**	**89.8**	83.8	**92.9**	**87.6**	**77.2**
28	84	80.2	90.3	**85.9**	92.7	86.8	78.1

With these results, however, we only check the validity of the SVM prediction. In this case we use a non-supervised technique (*k-means*) and a supervised technique (SVM). To do the validation of the results we need to check the validity of the classification, but we also need to check the reliability of the clustering.

In short, our process is based on the following steps:

1. Run *k-means* with the matrix X^T for k=1,2,..,p-1. Where k is the number of clusters and p is the number of features.
2. Check clustering reliability. Compute the subset SK of reliable clusters number.
3. Build new features and new data matrix.
4. Run SVM for each $sk_i \in$ SK.
5. Check validity of results.

In the first step, we use the algorithm *k-means* implemented in Weka, with a variation of the similarity function, as was shown in equation 4. This algorithm is run with all possible values of k.

However, the way to check the performance of a clustering process depends on the distribution of the elements in the clusters. In other words, if an element is very far from the centroid of a cluster, this could means that we do not have chosen enough clusters to group our data, i.e. this element could define another cluster.

To check the reliability, we defined another measure that from now on will be called "maxim centroid distance" (MCD) defined as follow:

$$MCD = \max(CD(f_i)) \tag{7}$$

where F is the feature set for clustering. For each $f_i \in$ F, $CD(f_i)$ represent the distance of the feature f_i to the centroid of the corresponding cluster.

A value of MCD being too large is not desirable, because it would mean that at least one of the clusters contains some points that are located too far from the centroid. In order to answer the question of finding an appropriate value for MCD, we first need to analyze the similarity function (defined in equation 4) into more detail. The normalization of a variable using equation 5 guarantees that the mean and the standard deviation will be 0 and 1 respectively. The difference of two variables, normalized in this way, has mean 0 and constant variance 2. Based on a basic probability theory the square sum of variables with normal distribution, mean zero and constant variance has a chi-square (χ^2) distribution. For this reason, equation 4 is χ^2 distributed.

Due to the χ^2 distribution of the similarity function, we can do a reliability analysis based on a χ^2 test. We can define the MCD value as $\chi^2_{observed}$. We compute χ^2_{critic} depending on the number "*n*" of proteins and the level of significance α. We work with α=0.05 i.e., in such a way that the probability or χ^2 was greater than χ^2_{critic} is lesser than 0.05. This constant χ^2_{critic} will be compared with $\chi^2_{observed}$ (for each k of clustering). That is, the idea is the following: if the maximum square Euclidean distance between the instances and the centroid ($\chi^2_{observed}$) is greater than the value of

χ^2_{critic} we have too few clusters. The objective is then to take a low number of clusters, without elements being too far from the corresponding centroids.

The second step is then to check the reliability of the clustering technique, in other words, to look for the minimum number of clusters needed to describe the variability of the data, and select the subset SK of value of k, which $\chi^2_{observed} < \chi^2_{critic}$.

The next step is based on the computation of the matrix U (defined in equation 3), after finding the matrix C in the previous step with the clustering. For a given k, a clustering with k clusters is obtained. In general, the elements c_{ij} of the matrix C represent the membership of *feature j* (f_i) to the *cluster i* (K_i) as shown the following equation:

$$c_{ij} = \begin{cases} 1 & \text{if } f_j \in K_i \\ 0 & \text{in other cases} \end{cases} \quad (8)$$

SK is the subset of all clusters chosen in the previous step. For each $sk_i \in$ SK we build a new database. The database i has sk_i features computed from the matrix U defined in equation 3.

For each sk_i, a matrix $C_{p\times ki}$ is represented in order to compute the matrix U^T, where U represents the new database with the new features. This database will have as features the clusters present in C. Each feature represents a cluster and it is computed as the sum of all features grouped in the cluster.

In short, in this step for each $sk_i \in$ K, we compute the matrix U, which represents a new database. An SVM is then trained for this new database using Weka.

In the last step we check the classification performance of the SVM using AUC criterion, using 10-fold crossvalidation.

Table 2. Classification measure (AUC ROC) of the better cluster for each database take into account the classification validity and clustering reliability

Clusters	APV	ATV	IDV	NFV	RTV	SQV	LPV
36					94		
39							82.3
41						89.4	
54		84.3					
62	85						
65			92.2				
66				89.7			

Table 2 shows the results obtained in the process described above for the seven databases. It can be observed that the best results for each drug are obtained using a different number of clusters. These results could be expected, because the associations of positions are related in a different way with regard to each drug. In all cases we obtained results that were better than those obtained using all features. This demonstrates that the clustering process effectively reduces the dimensionality.

Table 3. Comparison of the best cluster for each drug with previuos results. Prediction performance is measured in terms of accuracy. (1) Results by James (2004) (2) Results by Beerenwinkel et al. (2002). (3) Results using SVM with all features. (4) Results using SVM with the features computed from the best clustering.

Drug	KNN (1)	Dtree (1)	New DTree (1)	Dtree (2)	SVM (3)	SVM (4)
APV	80.9	75.8	75.8	87.4	83.5	87.3
ATV					75.2	**84.3**
IDV	80.6	85	85.5	89.1	89.3	**92**
NFV	73.6	91.8	93.7	88.5	85.7	93.1
RTV	82	89	89.5	89.8	89.9	**94.1**
SQV	81.7	80	85.7	87.5	85.2	**89.4**
LPV	81.1	-	89.5	-	65	**91.4**

Table 3 shows the comparison between the results obtained previously by James (2004) and Beerenwinkel (2002) [1],[10]. The column 5 represents the results using SMV with the 99 features and these are similar or better than the previous results obtained by James or Beerenwinkel. All results in this table are described using the accuracy as classification measure. Last column represent the results based on the best clustering described in the Table 2 for each drug. Only in APV and NFV the results are similar to the best results obtained previously, in the rest of the cases, our new method performs best.

4 Conclusions

In this paper, we focused on the problem of predicting Human Immunodeficiency Virus (HIV) Drug Resistance. We applied a clustering technique as a feature extraction method to sequence features in protein sequences. In applying this technique, a new similarity function with a biological meaning was defined, in order to look for associations between positions in the protein sequence of HIV protease.

We define a process to find the appropriate number of cluster based on the reliability of the results obtained with the *k-means* algorithm as a clustering method.

SVMs were then used to classify, and averaging using a 10-fold cross-validation we can conclude that the clustering process is a good way to do feature extraction, as well as reduce the dimensionality of the problem. We compared the results to those using all features, and to existing techniques for resistance prediction, concluding that our approach yields better results.

Acknowledgments. This work was developed in the framework of a collaboration program supported by VLIR (Vlaamse InterUniversitaire Raad, Flemish Interuniversity Council, Belgium).

References

1. Beerenwinkel, N., Schmidt, B., Walter, H., Kaiser, R., Lengauer, T., Hoffmann, D., Korn, K., Selbig, J.: Diversity and complexity of HIV-1 drug resistance: A bioinformatics approach to predicting phenotype from genotype. PNAS 99 (2002) 8271-8276
2. Beerenwinkel, N., Daumer, M., Oette, M., Korn, K., Hoffmann, D., Kaiser, R., Lengauer, T., Selbig, J., Walter, H.: Geno2pheno: estimating phenotypic drug resistance from HIV-1 genotypes. Nucl. Acids Res. 31 (2003) 3850-3855
3. Bergo, A.: Text Categorization and Prototypes. www.illc.uva.nl/Publications/ResearchReports/MoL-2001-08.text.pdf. (2001)
4. Cao, Z.W., Han, L.Y., Zheng, C.J., Ji, Z.L., Chen, X., Lin, H.H., Chen, Y.Z.: Computer prediction of drug resistance mutations in proteins. Drug Discovery Today 10 (2005) 521-529
5. Duda, R.O., Hart, P.E., Stork, D.G.: Pattern Classification. Wiley-Interscience (1997)
6. Fodor, I.K.: A survey of dimension reduction techniques. LLNL technical report. UCRL-ID-148494. (2002)
7. Gabrielsson, S.: MOVSOM-II- analysis and visualization of movieplot clusters. http://www.pcpinball.com/movsom. (2004)
8. Hanley, J.A., McNeil, B.J.: The meaning and use of the area under a receiver operating characteristic (ROC) curve. Radiology 143 (1982) 29-36
9. Jain, A.K., Murty, M.N., Flynn, P.J.: Data Clustering: A review. ACM Computing Surveys 31 (1999)
10. James, R.: Predicting Human Immunodeficiency Virus Type 1 Drug Resistance from Genotype Using Machine Learning. University of Edinburgh (2004)
11. McQueen, J.: Some methods for classification and analysis of multivariate observations. Fifth Berkeley Symposium on Mathematical Statistics and Probability (1967) 182-297
12. Metz, C.E.: Basic principles of ROC analysis. Seminars in Nuclear Medicine 8 (1978) 283-298
13. Miyazawa, S., Jernigan, R.L.: Protein stability for single substitution mutants and the extent of local compactness in the denatured state. Protein Eng. 7 (1994) 1209-1220
14. Miyazawa, S., Jernigan, R.L.: Residue Potentials with a Favorable Contact Pair Term and an Unfavorable High Packing Density Term, for Simulation and Threading. J. Mol. Biol. 256 (1996) 623-644
15. Slonim, N., Tishby, N.: The power of word clusters for text classification. 23rd European Colloquium on Information Retrieval Research (2001)
16. Steinbach, M., Karypis, G., Kumar, V.: A comparison of document clustering techniques. KDD Workshop on Text Mining (2000)
17. Vapnik, V.: The Nature of Statistical Learning Theory. Springer-Verlag, New York (1995)

A Theoretical Comparison of Two Linear Dimensionality Reduction Techniques

Luis Rueda[1] and Myriam Herrera[2]

[1] Department of Computer Science and Center for Biotechnology
University of Concepción
Edmundo Larenas 215, Concepción, Chile
lrueda@inf.udec.cl
[2] Department and Institute of Informatics
National University of San Juan
Cereceto y Meglioli, San Juan, 5400, Argentina
mherrera@iinfo.unsj.edu.ar

Abstract. A theoretical analysis for comparing two linear dimensionality reduction (LDR) techniques, namely Fisher's discriminant (FD) and Loog-Duin (LD) dimensionality reduciton, is presented. The necessary and sufficient conditions for which FD and LD provide the same linear transformation are discussed and proved. To derive these conditions, it is first shown that the two criteria preserve the same maximum value after a diagonalization process is applied, and then the necessary and sufficient conditions for various cases, including coincident covariance matrices, coincident prior probabilities, and for when one of the covariances is the identity matrix. A measure for comparing the two criteria is derived from the necessary and sufficient conditions, and used to empirically show that the conditions are statistically related to the classification error for a post-processing quadratic classifier and the Chernoff distance in the transformed space.

1 Introduction

Linear classifiers have been widely used in pattern recognition due to their simplicity and processing speed. Various schemes that lead to linear classification have been proposed, including the well known *Fisher's discriminant* (FD) approach [5,20], the *perceptron algorithm* (the basis of the back propagation *neural network* learning algorithms) [7,11,14,15], *piecewise recognition models* [12], *random search optimization* [13], *removal classification structures* [1], *adaptive linear dimensionality reduction* [10] (which outperforms Fisher's classifier for some data sets), *linear constrained distance-based classifier analysis* [4] (an improvement to Fisher's approach designed for hyperspectral image classification), and *recursive Fisher's discriminant* [3]. Rueda et al. [18,19] have shown that the optimal classifier between two normally distributed classes can be linear even when the covariance matrices *are not equal*. In [16], a new approach to selecting the *best hyperplane classifier* (BHC), which is obtained from the optimal pairwise linear classifier, has been introduced.

A generalization of linear classification can be seen as the process of linear dimensionality reduction (LDR), which aims to reduce high-dimensional data to a lower dimension in such a way that the classification of the new data is more tractable, and

J.F. Martínez-Trinidad et al. (Eds.): CIARP 2006, LNCS 4225, pp. 624–633, 2006.

can still be done efficiently. In this paper, we consider the traditional two-class case, and assume that we are dealing with two classes, ω_1 and ω_2, which are represented by two normally distributed n-dimensional random vectors, $\mathbf{x}_1 \sim N(\mathbf{m}_1, \mathbf{S}_1)$ and $\mathbf{x}_2 \sim N(\mathbf{m}_2, \mathbf{S}_2)$, and whose *a priori* probabilities are p_1 and p_2 respectively. The aim is to linearly transform $\mathbf{x}_1$ and $\mathbf{x}_2$ into new normally distributed random vectors $\mathbf{y}_1$ and $\mathbf{y}_2$ of dimension d, $d < n$, using a matrix $\mathbf{A}$ of order $d \times n$, in such a way that the classification error in the transformed space is as small as possible.

A typical approach to reduce the dimension of the data is principal component analysis (PCA) [5,20,21], but it better applies to unsupervised learning problems, since it takes the whole data as a "single" class, losing the discriminability power of labeled data. We consider two well-known LDR techniques, Fisher's discriminant (FD), and Loog-Duin (LD) dimensionality reduction, and theoretically analyze their common aspects. Let $\mathbf{S}_W = p_1\mathbf{S}_1 + p_2\mathbf{S}_2$ and $\mathbf{S}_E = (\mathbf{m}_1 - \mathbf{m}_2)(\mathbf{m}_1 - \mathbf{m}_2)^t$ be the within-class and between-class scatter matrices respectively. The FD criterion consists of maximizing the distance between the transformed distributions by finding $\mathbf{A}$ that maximizes the following function [5]:

$$J_{FD}(\mathbf{A}) = tr\left\{(\mathbf{A}\mathbf{S}_W\mathbf{A}^t)^{-1}(\mathbf{A}\mathbf{S}_E\mathbf{A}^t)\right\} . \quad (1)$$

The matrix $\mathbf{A}$ that maximizes (1) is obtained by finding the eigenvalue decomposition of:

$$\mathbf{S}_{FD} = \mathbf{S}_W^{-1}\mathbf{S}_E , \quad (2)$$

and taking the d eigenvectors whose eigenvalues are the largest ones. Since the eigenvalue decomposition of the matrix (2) leads to only one non-zero eigenvalue, $(\mathbf{m}_1 - \mathbf{m}_2)^t(\mathbf{m}_1 - \mathbf{m}_2)$, whose eigenvector is given by $(\mathbf{m}_1 - \mathbf{m}_2)$, we can only reduce to dimension $d = 1$.

Loog and Duin have recently proposed a new LDR technique for normally distributed classes [8], namely LD, which takes the Chernoff distance in the original space into consideration to minimize the error rate in the transformed space. They consider the concept of *directed distance matrices*, and a linear transformation in the original space, to finally generalize Fisher's criterion in the transformed space by substituting the within-class scatter matrix for the corresponding directed distance matrix. The LD criterion consists of obtaining the matrix $\mathbf{A}$ that maximizes the function [9]:

$$\begin{aligned} J_{LD}(\mathbf{A}) &= tr\left\{(\mathbf{A}\mathbf{S}_W\mathbf{A}^t)^{-1}\right. \\ &\left.\left[\mathbf{A}\mathbf{S}_E\mathbf{A}^t - \mathbf{A}\mathbf{S}_W^{\frac{1}{2}}\frac{p_1\log(\mathbf{S}_W^{-\frac{1}{2}}\mathbf{S}_1\mathbf{S}_W^{-\frac{1}{2}}) + p_2\log(\mathbf{S}_W^{-\frac{1}{2}}\mathbf{S}_2\mathbf{S}_W^{-\frac{1}{2}})}{p_1p_2}\mathbf{S}_W^{\frac{1}{2}}\mathbf{A}^t\right]\right\} \end{aligned} \quad (3)$$

The solution to this criterion is given by the matrix $\mathbf{A}$ that is composed of the d eigenvectors (whose eigenvalues are maximum) of the following matrix:

$$\mathbf{S}_{LD} = \mathbf{S}_W^{-1}\left[\mathbf{S}_E - \mathbf{S}_W^{\frac{1}{2}}\frac{p_1\log(\mathbf{S}_W^{-\frac{1}{2}}\mathbf{S}_1\mathbf{S}_W^{-\frac{1}{2}}) + p_2\log(\mathbf{S}_W^{-\frac{1}{2}}\mathbf{S}_2\mathbf{S}_W^{-\frac{1}{2}})}{p_1p_2}\mathbf{S}_W^{\frac{1}{2}}\right] . \quad (4)$$

In [2], it has been empirically shown that LD outperforms FD in many cases when coupling the LDR technique with a quadratic (Bayesian) classifier in the one dimensional space, namely when the optimal classifier under the assumption of normally distributed classes. As opposed to this, for the linear classifier, FD performs better than LD. In this paper, we derive the necessary and sufficient conditions for which both criteria FD and LD yield the same linear transformation. We also show empirically that the theoretical analysis is related to the probability of error obtained by coupling the LDR technique with quadratic and linear classifiers in the one-dimensional space.

2 Theoretical Comparison

Prior to deriving the necessary and sufficient conditions for which FD and LD produce the same linear dimensionality reduction transformation, we show that the maximum for both criteria can be preserved after a simultaneous diagonalization process is applied. We see afterwards that diagonalization allows to simplify the derivations and understanding the conditions. The following lemma shows that if simultaneous diagonalization is applied, the maximum for the FD criterion is preserved.

Lemma 1. *Let* $\mathbf{x}_1 \sim N(\mathbf{m}_1, \mathbf{S}_1)$ *and* $\mathbf{x}_2 \sim N(\mathbf{m}_2, \mathbf{S}_2)$ *be two normally distributed* n*-dimensional random vectors whose* a priori *probabilities are* p_1 *and* p_2 *respectively, where* $\mathbf{S_1}$ *and* $\mathbf{S_2}$ *are two arbitrary positive definite and symmetric matrices. Then, there exist two diagonal positive definite matrices* $\mathbf{D}_1 = \mathbf{I}$ *and* $\mathbf{D}_2$*, and an* n*-dimensional vector* $\boldsymbol{\nu}$*, such that* $max_{\{\mathbf{A}\}} J_F(\mathbf{A}) = max_{\{\mathbf{A}\}} J'_F(\mathbf{A})$*, where* $J_F(\mathbf{A})$ *is given by (1) and*

$$J'_F(\mathbf{A}) = tr\left\{(\mathbf{A}\mathbf{D}_W\mathbf{A}^t)^{-1}(\mathbf{A}\mathbf{M}_E\mathbf{A}^t)\right\} , \qquad (5)$$

with $\mathbf{D}_W = p_1\mathbf{D}_1 + p_2\mathbf{D}_2$ *and* $\mathbf{M}_E = \boldsymbol{\nu}\boldsymbol{\nu}^t$. □

The proof of this lemma is accomplished by considering the the following linear transformation: $T(\mathbf{x}) = \boldsymbol{\Phi}_2^t\mathbf{S}_1^{-\frac{1}{2}}(\mathbf{x} - \mathbf{m}_1)$. Then, the transformed random vectors have the following parameters: $N(\mathbf{0}; \mathbf{I})$ y $N(\boldsymbol{\nu}; \mathbf{D}_2)$, where $\boldsymbol{\nu} = \mathbf{m}_1 - \mathbf{m}_2$. Defining $\mathbf{D}_W = p_1\mathbf{I}+p_2\mathbf{D}_2$ and $\mathbf{M}_E = \boldsymbol{\nu}\boldsymbol{\nu}^t$, it follows that $\mathbf{D}_W = (\boldsymbol{\Phi}_2^t\mathbf{S}_1^{-\frac{1}{2}})\mathbf{S}_W(\boldsymbol{\Phi}_2^t S_1^{-\frac{1}{2}})^t$ and $\mathbf{M}_E = (\boldsymbol{\Phi}_2^t\mathbf{S}_1^{-\frac{1}{2}})\mathbf{S}_E(\boldsymbol{\Phi}_2^t\mathbf{S}_1^{-\frac{1}{2}})^t$, which are used to prove that $J'_F(\mathbf{A}) = J_F(\mathbf{A}(\boldsymbol{\Phi}_2^t\mathbf{S}_1^{-\frac{1}{2}}))$, and so the maximum values are the same. The complete proof can be found in the unabridged version of this paper [17].

In the following two axioms we prove that the maximum for the LD criterion is the same for any parameters of the normal distribution, and for the corresponding parameters after diagonalization. Although the maximum for both cases coincide, we do not provide the linear transformation that relates the transformation matrix in both cases, before and after diagonalization. This is quite intricate and remains an open problem that we are currently investigating.

Lemma 2. *Let* $\mathbf{x}_1 \sim N(\mathbf{m}_1, \mathbf{S}_1)$ *and* $\mathbf{x}_2 \sim N(\mathbf{m}_2, \mathbf{S}_2)$ *be two normally distributed* n*-dimensional random vectors whose* a priori *probabilities are* p_1 *and* p_2 *respectively, where* $\mathbf{S_1}$ *and* $\mathbf{S_2}$ *are two arbitrary positive definite and symmetric matrices. Then, there* *exist two diagonal positive definite matrices* $\mathbf{D}_1 = \mathbf{I}$ *and* $\mathbf{D}_2$*, and an* n*-dimensional vector* $\boldsymbol{\nu}$*, such that* $tr\{\mathbf{S}_{LD}\} = tr\{\mathbf{D}_{LD}\}$*, where*

$$\mathbf{D}_{LD} = \mathbf{D}_W^{-1}\left[\mathbf{M}_E - \mathbf{D}_W^{\frac{1}{2}}\frac{p_1\log(\mathbf{D}_W^{-\frac{1}{2}}\mathbf{D}_1\mathbf{D}_W^{-\frac{1}{2}}) + p_2\log(\mathbf{D}_W^{-\frac{1}{2}}\mathbf{D}_2\mathbf{D}_W^{-\frac{1}{2}})}{p_1p_2}\mathbf{D}_W^{\frac{1}{2}}\right] \tag{6}$$

with $\mathbf{D}_W = p_1\mathbf{D}_1 + p_2\mathbf{D}_2$ *y* $\mathbf{M}_E = \boldsymbol{\nu}\boldsymbol{\nu}^t$. □

The proof of this lemma follows by observing that the eigenvalues of a matrix of the form $\mathbf{B}^{-\frac{1}{2}}\mathbf{C}\mathbf{B}^{-\frac{1}{2}}$, where $\mathbf{B}$ is a non-singular matrix, are the roots of the polynomial $|\mathbf{C} - \lambda\mathbf{B}|$. In this way, it follows that the eigenvalues of $\mathbf{D}_w^{-\frac{1}{2}}\mathbf{D}_1\mathbf{D}_w^{-\frac{1}{2}}$ coincide with those of $\mathbf{S}_w^{-\frac{1}{2}}\mathbf{S}_1\mathbf{S}_w^{-\frac{1}{2}}$. Also, it is easy to see that the eigenvalues of $\mathbf{D}_W^{-\frac{1}{2}}\mathbf{D}_2\mathbf{D}_W^{-\frac{1}{2}}$ and $\mathbf{S}_W^{-\frac{1}{2}}\mathbf{S}_2\mathbf{S}_W^{-\frac{1}{2}}$ coincide. The proof is accomplished by proving that $tr\{\mathbf{S}_{LD}\} = tr\{\mathbf{D}_{LD}\}$, after showing that $tr\{\mathbf{S}\} = tr\{\mathbf{D}\}$, where:

$$\mathbf{D} = \frac{p_1\log(\mathbf{D}_W^{-\frac{1}{2}}\mathbf{D}_1\mathbf{D}_W^{-\frac{1}{2}}) + p_2\log(\mathbf{D}_W^{-\frac{1}{2}}\mathbf{D}_2\mathbf{D}_W^{-\frac{1}{2}})}{p_1p_2}, \tag{7}$$

and

$$\mathbf{S} = \frac{p_1\log(\mathbf{S}_W^{-\frac{1}{2}}\mathbf{S}_1\mathbf{S}_W^{-\frac{1}{2}}) + p_2\log(\mathbf{S}_W^{-\frac{1}{2}}\mathbf{S}_2\mathbf{S}_W^{-\frac{1}{2}})}{p_1p_2}. \tag{8}$$

The complete proof can be found in [17].

Conjecture 1. *Let* $\mathbf{x}_1 \sim N(\mathbf{m}_1, \mathbf{S}_1)$ *and* $\mathbf{x}_2 \sim N(\mathbf{m}_2, \mathbf{S}_2)$ *be two normally distributed* n*-dimensional random vectors whose* a priori *probabilities are* p_1 *and* p_2 *respectively, where* $\mathbf{S}_1$ *and* $\mathbf{S}_2$ *are two arbitrary positive definite and symmetric matrices. Then, there exist two diagonal positive definite matrices* $\mathbf{D}_1 = \mathbf{I}$ *and* $\mathbf{D}_2$*, and an* n*-dimensional vector* $\boldsymbol{\nu}$*, such that* $max_{\{\mathbf{A}\}}J_{LD}(\mathbf{A}) = max_{\{\mathbf{A}\}}J'_{LD}(\mathbf{A})$*, where* $J_{LD}(\mathbf{A})$ *is given by (3) and*

$$J'_{LD}(\mathbf{A}) = tr\left\{(\mathbf{A}\mathbf{D}_W\mathbf{A}^t)^{-1}\left[\mathbf{A}\mathbf{M}_E\mathbf{A}^t - \mathbf{A}\mathbf{D}_W^{\frac{1}{2}}\frac{p_1\log(\mathbf{D}_W^{-\frac{1}{2}}\mathbf{D}_1\mathbf{D}_W^{-\frac{1}{2}}) + p_2\log(\mathbf{D}_W^{-\frac{1}{2}}\mathbf{D}_2\mathbf{D}_W^{-\frac{1}{2}})}{p_1p_2}\mathbf{D}_W^{\frac{1}{2}}\mathbf{A}^t\right]\right\} \tag{9}$$

with $\mathbf{D}_W = p_1\mathbf{D}_1 + p_2\mathbf{D}_2$ *y* $\mathbf{M}_E = \boldsymbol{\nu}\boldsymbol{\nu}^t$. □

Proving this result for $d = n$, follows by using Lemma 2, which states that $tr\{\mathbf{S}_{LD}\} = tr\{\mathbf{D}_{LD}\}$. It can be shown that $tr\left\{(\mathbf{A}\mathbf{D}_W\mathbf{A}^t)^{-1}\mathbf{A}\left[\mathbf{M}_E - \cdots\right)\mathbf{A}^t]\right\} = tr\{\mathbf{D}_{LD}\}$, and hence using the same reasoning, this can be shown for $tr\{\mathbf{S}_{LD}\}$. For $d < n$, although $tr\{\mathbf{S}_{LD}\} = tr\{\mathbf{D}_{LD}\}$, it does not easily follow that the d ($d < n$) eigenvalues of $\mathbf{S}_{LD}$ and $\mathbf{D}_{LD}$ are the same. This has been verified numerically[1], but formally proving it remains an open problem. The complete sketch of proof can be found in [17].

[1] Proving this formally is not trivial, since one needs to find a *linear* transformation of the matrix $\mathbf{A}$ from the original to the diagonalized space. However the underlying expressions contain *non-linear* functions such as, log and powers of $\frac{1}{2}$.

Note that even if we would have shown that the eigenvalues of $\mathbf{D}_W$ and $\mathbf{S}_W$ are the same, this does not imply that the eigenvectors are coincident too. This can be easily seen as follows. Let $\mathbf{D}$ be any diagonal, non-singular matrix of order $n \times n$, and $\mathbf{S} = \mathbf{F}^{-1}\mathbf{D}\mathbf{F}$ any non-singular matrix of order $n \times n$, where $\mathbf{F} \neq \mathbf{I}$ is an arbitrary non-singular matrix of order $n \times n$. Clearly, the eigenvalues of $\mathbf{S}$ can be obtained by means of the decomposition $\mathbf{F}\mathbf{S}\mathbf{F}^{-1}$, resulting in $\mathbf{D}$. Then, the eigenvalues of $\mathbf{S}$ and $\mathbf{D}$ are the same; however, the corresponding eigenvectors are given by $\mathbf{F}$ and $\mathbf{I}$. For this reason, showing that the eigenvectors of $\mathbf{S}_{LD}$ and $\mathbf{D}_{LD}$ (whose eigenvalues are the largest) are given by $\mathbf{A}$ and $\mathbf{AC}$ respectively, where $\mathbf{C}$ is an arbitrary transformation matrix, is an interesting problem in the sense that it would allow to find the solution in the "diagonalized" space, allowing to transform the matrix $\mathbf{A}$ back to the "original" space. This is a problem that we are currently investigating.

We now formalize the necessary and sufficient conditions for which the two LDR methods we study, FD and LD, produce the same linear transformation.

Theorem 1. *Let* $\mathbf{x}_1 \sim N(\mathbf{m}_1, \mathbf{S}_1)$ *and* $\mathbf{x}_2 \sim N(\mathbf{m}_2, \mathbf{S}_2)$ *be two normally distributed* n*-dimensional random vectors whose* a priori *probabilities are* p_1 *and* p_2 *respectively, where* $\mathbf{S}_1$ *and* $\mathbf{S}_2$ *are two diagonal positive definite and symmetric matrices. Then,* $J_F(A) = J_{LD}(A)$ *if and only if:*

$$\mathbf{S}_1^{p_1}\mathbf{S}_2^{p_2} = p_1\mathbf{S}_1 + p_2\mathbf{S}_2 \,. \tag{10}$$

□

The proof of this theorem is accomplished by finding the conditions for which $J_F(\mathbf{A}) = J_{LD}(\mathbf{A})$ holds if and only if:

$$\mathbf{S}_W^{\frac{1}{2}} \frac{p_1 \log(\mathbf{S}_W^{-\frac{1}{2}}\mathbf{S}_1\mathbf{S}_W^{-\frac{1}{2}}) + p_2 \log(\mathbf{S}_W^{-\frac{1}{2}}\mathbf{S}_2\mathbf{S}_W^{-\frac{1}{2}})}{p_1 p_2} \mathbf{S}_W^{\frac{1}{2}} = \mathbf{0} \,, \tag{11}$$

where $\mathbf{0}$ is a zero matrix of order $n \times n$. Using Lemma 1 and Conjecture 1, it is always possible to obtain the same result for both criteria). We ensure, in this way, that $\mathbf{S}_1 = diag(\lambda_{1_i})$ and $\mathbf{S}_2 = diag(\lambda_{2_i})$. For the two LDR criteria to coincide the following must hold:

$$\forall i : \lambda_{1_i}^{p_1}\lambda_{2_i}^{p_2} = p_1\lambda_{1_i} + p_2\lambda_{2_i} \,, \tag{12}$$

which can be written in a matrix-form-like manner as in (10). The complete proof of this theorem can be found in [17]. The following results show the necessary and sufficient conditions for various cases, including coincident covariance matrices, coincident prior probabilities, and for when one of the covariances is the identity matrix. The complete proofs of the corollaries can be found in [17].

Corollary 1. *Under the conditions of Theorem 1, if* $\mathbf{S}_1 = \mathbf{S}_2$*, then* $J_F = J_{LD}$ *for any values of* p_1 *and* p_2*.* □

Corollary 2. *Under the conditions of Theorem 1, if* $\mathbf{S}_1 \neq \mathbf{S}_2$*, and (10) holds, then* $p_1 \neq p_2$*.* □

Corollary 3. *Under the conditions of Theorem 1, if* $\mathbf{S}_1 = \mathbf{I}$ *and* $\mathbf{S}_2 = diag(\lambda_i)$*,* $J_F(\mathbf{A}) = J_{LD}(\mathbf{A})$ *if and only if:*

$$\lambda_i^{p_2} - p_2\lambda_i - p_1 = 0 \,. \tag{13}$$

□

Note that the formulas we found, although are the necessary and sufficient conditions for the *coincidence* of both criteria, can also be used to evaluate the "similarity" between the classifiers used after the transformation. Also, this kind of analysis can be done using the parameters of the distributions without transforming the data onto the new "diagonalized" space, as it is required by Lemma 1 and Conjecture 1. As a measure for this similarity, and assuming that the underlying covariance matrices are given by $\mathbf{I}$ and $\boldsymbol{\Lambda} = diag(\lambda_1, \ldots, \lambda_n)$ respectively, we can use the condition given in (13), and average over all the n dimensions as follows:

$$\delta = \frac{1}{n}\sum_{i=1}^{n} |\lambda_i^{p_2} - p_2\lambda_i - p_1| \tag{14}$$

$$= \left| \frac{1}{n}\left[tr\left\{\boldsymbol{\Lambda}^{p_2}\right\} - p_2 tr\left\{\boldsymbol{\Lambda}\right\}\right] - p_1 \right| \,. \tag{15}$$

In the following section, we utilize this measure to empirically compare the result of the two LDR techniques when coupled with either of two classifiers, linear or quadratic.

3 Empirical Results

The tests involve ten different datasets of dimensions $n = 10, 20, \ldots, 100$ each with two randomly generated normally distributed classes. The underlying parameters of the distributions were generated as follows. Each element of the means, $\mathbf{m}_1$ and $\mathbf{m}_2$, was generated by following distributions $\mathrm{U}[0, b/n]$ and $\mathrm{U}[b/n, 2b/n]$, where b was set to 10. Dividing by n makes sure that the classification task is not easier when increasing the dimension. The eigenvalues of the covariances, $\mathbf{S}_1$ and $\mathbf{S}_2$, were randomly generated as $\mathrm{U}[0, b]$, and the corresponding eigenvectors from a random matrix in $\mathrm{U}(0, b/n)$ followed by a QR decomposition, taking the orthogonal matrix $\mathbf{Q}$. This ensures that the covariances are positive and definite. A linear transformation using $\mathbf{S}_1^{-\frac{1}{2}}$ was applied, obtaining covariances $\mathbf{I}$ and $\mathbf{S}_1^{-\frac{1}{2}}\mathbf{S}_2\mathbf{S}_1^{-\frac{1}{2}}$ respectively, followed by a subsequent linear transformation using $\boldsymbol{\Phi}_2$, which contains the eigenvectors of $\mathbf{S}_1^{-\frac{1}{2}}\mathbf{S}_2\mathbf{S}_1^{-\frac{1}{2}}$. After all the transformations, the underlying covariance matrices resulted in $\mathbf{I}$ and $\boldsymbol{\Lambda}_2$. We also randomly generated p_1 as a $\mathrm{U}[0.3, 0.7]$ and assigned $p_2 = 1 - p_1$. We trained two LDR techniques, FD and LD, using these parameters, and for each dataset we generated 10,000 samples for testing purposes. After a linear transformation to dimension $d = 1$ is performed we have tested two classifiers: the linear (L) classifier, which is obtained by averaging the covariances matrices in the transformed space, and the quadratic (Q) classifier which is the one that minimizes the error rate assuming that the parameters in the transformed data are given by $\mathbf{Am}_i$ and $\mathbf{AS}_i\mathbf{A}^t$.

The classification error for FD and LD and the corresponding values of δ are shown in Table 1. The second and third columns contain the classification error for FD and LD coupled with a quadratic (Q) classifier, and the fourth column the difference (in absolute value) between the two errors. The fifth, sixth and seventh columns represent the same but for the linear (L) classifier, and the last column contains the value of δ, which is computed as in (15). For the quadratic classifier, the smallest value of δ coincides with the smallest difference, and the third difference corresponds to the fourth value of δ. Note that the four largest values of δ correspond to values which are among the five largest difference of errors. For the linear classifier, we note that the four largest values of δ correspond to the differences which are among the fifth largest ones; however not all small values of δ correspond to the smallest error differences. To numerically assess this correspondence, we computed the Spearman rank correlation coefficient for two pairs of lists [6], the differences for the quadratic classifier and δ, and the differences for the linear classifier and δ, respectively. The coefficients obtained are 0.62 for the quadratic classifier, and 0.32 for the linear classifier. This denotes that in both cases, the values of δ and the differences are positively correlated. The high value for the quadratic classifier indicates that the latter is quite related with the differences between the eigenvalues of the underlying covariance matrices for the optimal classifier in the transformed space. This is not the case for the linear classifier.

Table 1. Error rates and differences for two LDR techniques, FD and LD, coupled with quadratic and linear classifiers

d	FD(Q)	LD(Q)	Diff.	FD(L)	LD(L)	Diff.	δ
10	0.2629	0.2460	0.0169	0.2639	0.3404	0.0765	0.1280
20	0.2004	0.1132	0.0872	0.2012	0.2083	0.0071	0.4572
30	0.2865	0.1803	0.1062	0.2870	0.4296	0.1426	0.4801
40	0.2747	0.2179	0.0568	0.3053	0.3524	0.0471	0.4690
50	0.2646	0.1262	0.1384	0.2659	0.2858	0.0199	0.2712
60	0.2190	0.0778	0.1412	0.2216	0.3646	0.1430	0.6132
70	0.2026	0.0407	0.1619	0.2281	0.3809	0.1528	0.6919
80	0.3313	0.0989	0.2324	0.3318	0.3500	0.0182	0.6702
90	0.3859	0.0835	0.3024	0.3920	0.2968	0.0952	0.9946
100	0.3191	0.1433	0.1758	0.3195	0.3417	0.0222	0.2308

To analyze the relation between δ and the quadratic classifier, we computed the Chernoff distance between both distributions in the transformed space as follows

$$k(\beta, \mathbf{A}) = \frac{\beta(1-\beta)}{2}(\mathbf{A}\mathbf{m_1} - \mathbf{A}\mathbf{m_2})^t[\beta\mathbf{A}\mathbf{S}_1\mathbf{A} + (1-\beta)\mathbf{A}\mathbf{S}_2\mathbf{A}]^{-1}(\mathbf{A}\mathbf{m_1} - \mathbf{A}\mathbf{m_2}) + \frac{1}{2}\log\frac{|\beta\mathbf{A}\mathbf{S}_1\mathbf{A} + (1-\beta)\mathbf{A}\mathbf{S}_2\mathbf{A}|}{|\mathbf{A}\mathbf{S}_1\mathbf{A}|^{\beta}|\mathbf{A}\mathbf{S}_2\mathbf{A}|^{1-\beta}} . \quad (16)$$

where $\beta = p_1$ and $\mathbf{A}$ is the linear transformation matrix obtained by either FD or LD, and compared it with the corresponding values of δ. The results are tabulated in

Table 2. The Chernoff distances in the transformed space for FD and LD are given in the second and third columns, while their difference in absolute value is given in the fourth column. We observe that, as in the error for the quadratic classifier, the four largest values of δ correspond to those differences which are among the five largest ones. A similar situation occurs with the smallest values of δ. Again, to numerically assess the relation between the difference ("Diff." in the table) and δ, we computed the Spearman rank correlation coefficient, resulting in 0.65, which is a significantly large value, and indicates a high positive correlation between the two lists.

Table 2. Chernoff distance in the transformed space after the two LDR transformations, FD and LD, are applied

d	FD	LD	Diff.	δ
10	1.5286	2.2260	4.2803	0.1280
20	0.7924	4.5833	0.6974	0.4572
30	1.1314	3.5879	3.7908	0.4801
40	1.1156	2.5607	2.4565	0.4690
50	0.4929	5.1266	1.4452	0.2712
60	2.1272	8.5170	4.6337	0.6132
70	2.6234	12.2768	6.3899	0.6919
80	0.3178	6.8664	9.6534	0.6702
90	0.3454	7.3926	6.5486	0.9946
100	0.2593	4.5395	7.0472	0.2308

4 Conclusion

We have formalized the necessary and sufficient conditions for which two well-known LDR techniques, FD and LD, provide the same linear transformation. To derive these conditions, we have first shown that the two criteria preserve the same maximum value after a diagonalization process is applied. For FD, we have found the linear transformation that allows to obtain the LDR in the original space. For the LD criterion, however, we have only shown that the maximum values coincide in both original and diagonalized space, and conjectured that this holds for lower dimensional spaces.

We have derived the necessary and sufficient conditions for various cases, including coincident covariance matrices, coincident prior probabilities, and for when one of the covariances is the identity matrix. We have empirically shown that the conditions are statistically related to the classification error for a post-processing quadratic classifier and the Chernoff distance in the transformed space.

One of the problems that constitute a future extension of this work is to analyze the correspondence between the two LDR methods for more than two classes. Another problem involves deriving the expressions for obtaining the LD dimensionality reduction in the original space, when the diagonalized distributions are given. This is, though quite intricate, an interesting problem as it would allow to speed up the LDR derivation significantly.

Acknowledgments. This research has been supported by the Chilean National Council for Technological and Scientific Research, FONDECYT grant No. 1060904, and the Institute of Informatics, National University of San Juan.

References

1. M. Aladjem. Linear Discriminant Analysis for Two Classes Via Removal of Classification Structure. *IEEE Trans. on Pattern Analysis and Machine Intelligence*, 19(2):187–192, 1997.
2. M. Ali, L. Rueda, and M. Herrera. On the Performance of Chernoff-distance-Based Linear Dimensionality Reduction Techniques. In *Proc. of the 18th Canadian Conference on Artificial Intelligence*, volume LNAI 4013, pages 469–480. Springer, 2006.
3. T. Cooke. Two Variations on Fisher's Linear Discriminant for Pattern Recognition. *IEEE Transations on Pattern Analysis and Machine Intelligence*, 24(2):268–273, 2002.
4. Q. Du and C. Chang. A Linear Constrained Distance-based Discriminant Analysis for Hyperspectral Image Classification. *Pattern Recognition*, 34(2):361–373, 2001.
5. R. Duda, P. Hart, and D. Stork. *Pattern Classification*. John Wiley and Sons, Inc., New York, NY, 2nd edition, 2000.
6. E. Lehmann and H. D'Abrera. *Nonparametrics: Statistical Methods Based on Ranks*. Prentice-Hall, 1998.
7. R. Lippman. An Introduction to Computing with Neural Nets. In *Neural Networks: Theoretical Foundations and Analsyis*, pages 5–24. IEEE Press, 1992.
8. M. Loog and P.W. Duin. Linear Dimensionality Reduction via a Heteroscedastic Extension of LDA: The Chernoff Criterion. *IEEE Transactions on Pattern Analysis and Machine Intelligence*, 26(6):732–739, 2004.
9. M. Loog and R. Duin. Non-iterative Heteroscedastic Linear Dimension Reduction for Two-Class Data. In *Proceedings of the Joint IAPR International Workshops SSPR 2002 and SPR 2002*, volume LNCS 2396, pages 508–517. Springer, 2002.
10. R. Lotlikar and R. Kothari. Adaptive Linear Dimensionality Reduction for Classification. *Pattern Recognition*, 33(2):185–194, 2000.
11. O. Murphy. Nearest Neighbor Pattern Classification Perceptrons. In *Neural Networks: Theoretical Foundations and Analysis*, pages 263–266. IEEE Press, 1992.
12. A. Rao, D. Miller, K. Rose, , and A. Gersho. A Deterministic Annealing Approach for Parsimonious Design of Piecewise Regression Models. *IEEE Transactions on Pattern Analysis and Machine Intelligence*, 21(2):159–173, 1999.
13. S. Raudys. On Dimensionality, Sample Size, and Classification Error of Nonparametric Linear Classification. *IEEE Transactions on Pattern Analysis and Machine Intelligence*, 19(6):667–671, 1997.
14. S. Raudys. Evolution and Generalization of a Single Neurone: I. Single-layer Perception as Seven Statistical Classifiers. *Neural Networks*, 11(2):283–296, 1998.
15. S. Raudys. Evolution and Generalization of a Single Neurone: II. Complexity of Statistical Classifiers and Sample Size Considerations. *Neural Networks*, 11(2):297–313, 1998.
16. L. Rueda. Selecting the Best Hyperplane in the Framework of Optimal Pairwise Linear Classifiers. *Pattern Recognition Letters*, 25(2):49–62, 2004.
17. L. Rueda and M. Herrera. Necessary and Sufficient Conditions for the Equivalence of two Linear Dimensionality Reduction Techniques. *Submitted for Publication*, 2006. Electronically available at http://www.inf.udec.cl/~lrueda/papers/FisherLoogDuinJnl.pdf.

18. L. Rueda and B. J. Oommen. On Optimal Pairwise Linear Classifiers for Normal Distributions: The Two-Dimensional Case. *IEEE Transations on Pattern Analysis and Machine Intelligence*, 24(2):274–280, 2002.
19. L. Rueda and B. J. Oommen. On Optimal Pairwise Linear Classifiers for Normal Distributions: The *d*-Dimensional Case. *Pattern Recognition*, 36(1):13–23, January 2003.
20. S. Theodoridis and K. Koutroumbas. *Pattern Recognition*. Elsevier Academic Press, third edition, 2006.
21. A. Webb. *Statistical Pattern Recognition*. John Wiley & Sons, N.York, second edition, 2002.

A New Approach to Multi-class Linear Dimensionality Reduction

Luis Rueda[1] and Myriam Herrera[2]

[1] Department of Computer Science and Center for Biotecnology
University of Concepción
Edmundo Larenas 215, Concepción, Chile
lrueda@inf.udec.cl
[2] Department and Institute of Informatics
National University of San Juan
Cereceto y Meglioli, San Juan, 5400, Argentina
mherrera@iinfo.unsj.edu.ar

Abstract. Linear dimensionality reduction (LDR) is quite important in pattern recognition due to its efficiency and low computational complexity. In this paper, we extend the two-class Chernoff-based LDR method to deal with multiple classes. We introduce the criterion, as well as the algorithm that maximizes such a criterion. The proof of convergence of the algorithm and a formal procedure to initialize the parameters of the algorithm are also given. We present empirical simulations on standard well-known multi-class datasets drawn from the UCI machine learning repository. The results show that the proposed LDR coupled with a quadratic classifier outperforms the traditional LDR schemes.

1 Introduction

The linear dimensionality reduction (LDR) problem is well-known in pattern recognition due to its linear time complexity and its simplicity to be implemented and understood. Various schemes that yield LDR to dimension one have been proposed, including the well known *Fisher's discriminant analysis* approach [5], *direct Fisher's discriminant analysis* [6], the *perceptron algorithm* (the basis of the back propagation *neural network* learning algorithms) [12], *piecewise recognition models* [11], *removal classification structures* [1], *adaptive linear dimensionality reduction* [9] (which outperforms Fisher's classifier for some data sets), *linear constrained distance-based classifier analysis* [4] (an improvement to Fisher's approach designed for hyperspectral image classification), *recursive Fisher's discriminant* [2], *pairwise linear classifiers* [16,17], and the *best hyperplane classifier* [13].

The problem we deal with consists of k classes, $\omega_1, \ldots, \omega_k$, whose *a priori* probabilities are given by $p_1, \ldots, p_k$, and which are represented by k n-dimensional normally distributed random vectors, $\mathbf{x}_1 \sim N(\mathbf{m}_1; \mathbf{S}_1), \ldots, \mathbf{x}_k \sim N(\mathbf{m}_k; \mathbf{S}_k)$. The aim is to linearly transform $\mathbf{x}_1, \ldots, \mathbf{x}_k$ into new normally distributed random vectors $\mathbf{y}_1, \ldots, \mathbf{y}_k$ of dimension d, $d < n$, using a matrix $\mathbf{A}$ of order $d \times n$, in such a way that the classification error in the transformed space is as small as possible.

J.F. Martínez-Trinidad et al. (Eds.): CIARP 2006, LNCS 4225, pp. 634–643, 2006.

A typical approach to reduce the dimension of the data is principal component analysis (PCA) [5,18,21], but it better applies to unsupervised learning problems, since it takes the whole data as a "single" class, losing the discriminability power of labeled data. As opposed to this, linear discriminant analysis (LDA) aims to consider the class-conditional distributions to maximize the separability of the data in the transformed space. One of such approaches is Fisher's discriminant (FD). Let $\mathbf{S}_E = \sum_{i=1}^{k} p_i(\mathbf{m}_i - \mathbf{m})(\mathbf{m}_i - \mathbf{m})^t$, where $\mathbf{m} = \sum_{i=1}^{k} p_i \mathbf{m}_i$, be the *between-class* scatter matrix, and $\mathbf{S}_W = \sum_{i=1}^{k} p_i \mathbf{S}_i$ be the *within-class* scatter matrix. The FD approach aims to find a matrix $\mathbf{A}$ that maximizes the following criterion function [5]:

$$J_{FD}(\mathbf{A}) = tr\left\{(\mathbf{A}\mathbf{S}_W\mathbf{A}^t)^{-1}(\mathbf{A}\mathbf{S}_E\mathbf{A}^t)\right\}\ , \tag{1}$$

and which is obtained by finding the d eigenvectors (whose eigenvalues are the largest ones) of $\mathbf{S}_W^{-1}\mathbf{S}_E$.

The Loog-Duin LD criterion for the multi-class problem aims to find the transformation $d \times n$ matrix $\mathbf{A}$ that maximizes the following function [8]:

$$\begin{aligned} J_{LD}(\mathbf{A}) = \sum_{i=1}^{k-1}\sum_{j=i+1}^{k} p_i p_j tr\Big\{(\mathbf{A}\mathbf{S}_W\mathbf{A}^t)^{-1}\mathbf{A}\mathbf{S}_W^{\frac{1}{2}} \\ \Big[(\mathbf{S}_W^{-\frac{1}{2}}\mathbf{S}_{ij}\mathbf{S}_W^{-\frac{1}{2}})^{-\frac{1}{2}}\mathbf{S}_W^{-\frac{1}{2}}\mathbf{S}_{E_{ij}}\mathbf{S}_W^{-\frac{1}{2}}(\mathbf{S}_W^{-\frac{1}{2}}\mathbf{S}_{ij}\mathbf{S}_W^{-\frac{1}{2}})^{-\frac{1}{2}} + \frac{1}{\pi_i\pi_j}\Big(\log(\mathbf{S}_W^{-\frac{1}{2}}\mathbf{S}_{ij}\mathbf{S}_W^{-\frac{1}{2}}) \\ -\pi_i\log(\mathbf{S}_W^{-\frac{1}{2}}\mathbf{S}_i\mathbf{S}_W^{-\frac{1}{2}}) - \pi_j\log(\mathbf{S}_W^{-\frac{1}{2}}\mathbf{S}_j\mathbf{S}_W^{-\frac{1}{2}})\Big)\Big]\mathbf{S}_W^{\frac{1}{2}}\mathbf{A}^t\Big\}\ , \end{aligned} \tag{2}$$

where $\mathbf{S}_{E_{ij}} = (\mathbf{m}_i - \mathbf{m}_j)(\mathbf{m}_i - \mathbf{m}_j)^t$, $\pi_i = \frac{p_i}{p_i+p_j}$, $\pi_j = \frac{p_j}{p_i+p_j}$, and $\mathbf{S}_{ij} = \pi_i\mathbf{S}_i + \pi_j\mathbf{S}_j$. The LD criterion is maximized as it is done for the two-class case, by finding the matrix $\mathbf{A}$ composed of the d eigenvectors (whose eigenvalues are the largest ones) of the following matrix:

$$\begin{aligned} \mathbf{S}_{LD} = \sum_{i=1}^{k-1}\sum_{j=i+1}^{k} p_i p_j \mathbf{S}_W^{-1}\mathbf{S}_W^{\frac{1}{2}}\Big[(\mathbf{S}_W^{-\frac{1}{2}}\mathbf{S}_{ij}\mathbf{S}_W^{-\frac{1}{2}})^{-\frac{1}{2}}\mathbf{S}_W^{-\frac{1}{2}}\mathbf{S}_{E_{ij}}\mathbf{S}_W^{-\frac{1}{2}}(\mathbf{S}_W^{-\frac{1}{2}}\mathbf{S}_{ij}\mathbf{S}_W^{-\frac{1}{2}})^{-\frac{1}{2}} \\ +\frac{1}{\pi_i\pi_j}\Big(\log(\mathbf{S}_W^{-\frac{1}{2}}\mathbf{S}_{ij}\mathbf{S}_W^{-\frac{1}{2}}) - \pi_i\log(\mathbf{S}_W^{-\frac{1}{2}}\mathbf{S}_i\mathbf{S}_W^{-\frac{1}{2}}) - \pi_j\log(\mathbf{S}_W^{-\frac{1}{2}}\mathbf{S}_j\mathbf{S}_W^{-\frac{1}{2}})\Big)\Big]\mathbf{S}_W^{\frac{1}{2}}\ , \end{aligned} \tag{3}$$

The traditional classification problem has usually been solved by maximizing the separability between the underlying distributions using different criteria. FD aims to minimize the error by maximizing the Mahalanobis distance between distributions, resulting in an optimal criterion when the covariance matrices are equal. In case the covariances are different, the optimal classifier is quadratic; the linear classification results in maximizing the separability between the distributions by generalizing the Mahalanobis distance [7]. On the other hand, the LD criterion utilizes, as pointed out above, a directed distance matrix, which is incorporated in Fisher's criterion assuming the within-class scatter matrix is the identity.

In this paper, we extend the two-class LDR criterion as proposed in [14], and which takes advantage of the properties of the Chernoff distance to maximize the separability of the distributions in the transformed space. Since we are assuming the original distributions are normal, the distributions in the transformed space are also normal. Thus, the Bayes classifier in the transformed space is quadratic and deriving a closed-form expression for the classification error is not possible. However, the probability of classification error in the transformed space can be bounded in terms of the Chernoff distnace between two distributions given by:

$$k(\beta, \mathbf{A}) = \frac{\beta(1-\beta)}{2}(\mathbf{Am_1} - \mathbf{Am_2})^t[\beta\mathbf{AS}_1\mathbf{A} + (1-\beta)\mathbf{AS}_2\mathbf{A}]^{-1}(\mathbf{Am_1} - \mathbf{Am_2}) + \frac{1}{2}\log\frac{|\beta\mathbf{AS}_1\mathbf{A} + (1-\beta)\mathbf{AS}_2\mathbf{A}|}{|\mathbf{AS}_1\mathbf{A}|^{\beta}|\mathbf{AS}_2\mathbf{A}|^{1-\beta}}. \quad (4)$$

The larger the value of $k(\beta, \mathbf{A})$ is, the smaller the bound for the classification error is, and hence, in this paper, we propose to maximize (4). To clarify this, we note that the FD criterion also aims to maximize the separability between distributions in the transformed space, but coincides with the optimal classifier only when the latter is linear, i.e. when the covariance matrices are coincident, a rare case. As observed above, the LD criterion utilizes the Chernoff distance in its directed distance matrix but in the original space. This criterion, however, does not optimize such a distance in the *transformed* space, as it can be observed in the following example.

Consider two normally distributed random vectors, $\mathbf{x}_1 \sim N(\mathbf{m}_1, \mathbf{S}_1)$ and $\mathbf{x}_2 \sim N(\mathbf{m}_2, \mathbf{S}_2)$, whose parameters are: $\mathbf{m}_1 = [0.5001, 0.4947]^t$, $\mathbf{m}_2 = [2.1069, 1.4324]^t$, $\mathbf{S}_1 = [0.8205, 0.4177; 0.4177, 2.8910]$, $\mathbf{S}_2 = [5.1150, -4.3990; -4.3990, 5.7119]$, $p_1 = p_2 = 0.5$. Consider also a linear transformation $\mathbf{y} = \mathbf{Ax}$ to the one-dimensional space, i.e. $\mathbf{A}$ is of order 1×2, namely a two-dimensional vector. As shown later in the paper, we can just "rotate" $\mathbf{A}$ and produce different values for the Chernoff distance in the transformed space, and *only one* value for each angle. Thus, in Fig. 1, we plot three different criteria for all possible values of the angle θ between $\mathbf{A}$ and $[0, 1]^t$, including $J_F(\mathbf{A})$ computed as in (1), $J_{LD}(\mathbf{A})$ computed as in (2), and the Chernoff distance in the transformed one-dimensional space computed as in (4), where $\beta = 1/2$. As we will also see later, we note that maximizing the criterion $J_F(\mathbf{A})$ or $J_{LD}(\mathbf{A})$ does not necessarily imply maximizing the Chernoff distance in the transformed space (as our criterion aims to), and hence minimizing the classification error. Also, we observe that the $k(\beta, \mathbf{A})$ function has more than one peak and so, as shown later, this makes it difficult to find a closed-form expression for the optimal solution.

2 The Proposed LDR Criterion

In this section, we formalize the proposed LDR criterion for the multi-class case, which aims to maximize the Chernoff distance in the transformed space. We suppose that we are dealing with k classes, $\{\omega_i\}$, whose *a priori* probabilities are given by $\{p_i\}$, with $i = 1, 2, \ldots, k$. By following the notation used above, we define $\mathbf{S}_{E_{ij}} = (\mathbf{m}_i - \mathbf{m}_j)(\mathbf{m}_i - \mathbf{m}_j)^t$ and $\mathbf{S}_{W_{ij}} = \pi_i\mathbf{S}_i + \pi_j\mathbf{S}_j$ as the between-class and within-class scatter

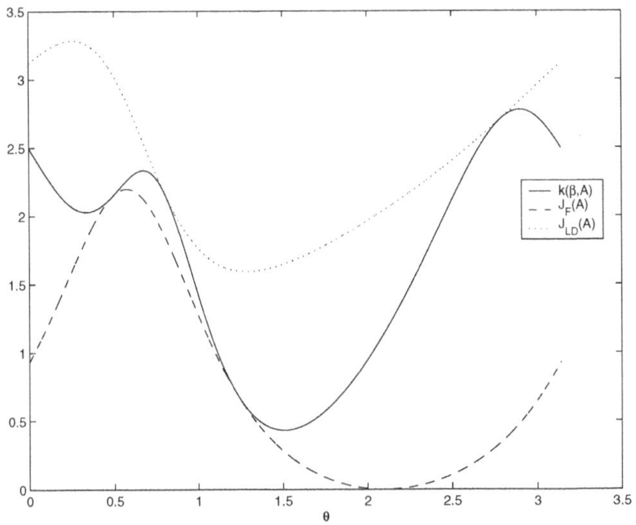

Fig. 1. Plot of three different dimensionality reduction functions, namely Fisher's, Loog-Duin's, and the Chernoff distance in the transformed space, for a two-dimensional to one-dimensional reduction example. The x-axis represents the different angles of the transformation vector $\mathbf{A}$.

matrices respectively, where $\mathbf{m}_i$ and $\mathbf{S}_i$ are the mean and covariance matrices for ω_i respectively, $\pi_i = p_i/(p_i + p_j)$ and $\pi_j = p_j/(p_i + p_j)$.

The extension of the two-class classification is not straightforward, as there is no general formula for the Chernoff distance between more than two distributions. This is also the case of other classifiers, such as the well-known support vector machines or kernel-based classifiers, for which majority votes of $k(k-1)/2$ decisions are among the most efficient schemes [19], as opposed to other schemes like one-against-all or all-at-once, which suffer the problem of yielding unclassifiable regions [5,20]. In our case, however, it is natural to maximize the *weighted* sum of pairwise Chernoff distances between classes ω_i and ω_j, for all $i = 1, \ldots, k-1, j = i, \ldots, k$. The "weights" used for the pairwise class criterion are given by the normalized joint prior probabilities between classes ω_i and ω_j, $\pi_i\pi_j$. Thus, the criterion that we propose for multiple classes consists of finding the transformation $\mathbf{Ax}$, where $\mathbf{A}$ is a matrix of order $d \times n$ that maximizes the function, where we have adopted a natural way to set the value of β, as $\beta = \pi_1$ and $1 - \beta = \pi_2$.:

$$J_c^*(\mathbf{A}) = \sum_{i=1}^{k-1} \sum_{j=i+1}^{k} J_{c_{ij}}^*(\mathbf{A}), \tag{5}$$

with:

$$J_{c_{ij}}^*(\mathbf{A}) = tr\left\{\pi_i\pi_j(\mathbf{A}\mathbf{S}_{W_{ij}}\mathbf{A}^t)^{-1}\mathbf{A}\mathbf{S}_{E_{ij}}\mathbf{A}^t + \log(\mathbf{A}\mathbf{S}_{W_{ij}}\mathbf{A}^t) - \pi_i \log(\mathbf{A}\mathbf{S}_i\mathbf{A}^t) - \pi_j \log(\mathbf{A}\mathbf{S}_j\mathbf{A}^t)\right\} \tag{6}$$

Taking the Chernoff distance between $\mathbf{x}_i$ and $\mathbf{x}_j$ as in (4), and doing some algebraic manipulations, it can be written in terms of $tr\{\ldots\}$ as in (6) (cf. [15]). We show there always exists an orthogonal matrix $\mathbf{Q}$ for which the Chernoff distance in the new space is the same as that of using the matrix $\mathbf{A}$. The proof of the lemma can be found in [15].

Lemma 1. *Let $\mathbf{A}$ be any real $d \times n$ matrix, $d \leq n$, whose rows are linearly independent, and $J_c^*(\mathbf{A})$ be defined as in (5). Then:*

$$max_{\{\mathbf{A}\}} J_c^*(\mathbf{A}) = max_{\{\mathbf{A}:\mathbf{A}\mathbf{A}^t=\mathbf{I}_d\}} J_c^*(\mathbf{A}) . \qquad (7)$$

Proof (Sketch). Let $\mathbf{A}$ be any matrix of order $d \leq n$ whose rows are linearly independent. Then, by applying the QR decomposition [3], $\mathbf{A}$ can be decomposed as follows $\mathbf{A} = \mathbf{RQ}$, and it follows that $J_c^*(\mathbf{A}) = J_c^*(\mathbf{Q})$. In this way, we ensure that $max_{\{\mathbf{A}\}} J_c^*(\mathbf{A}) = max_{\{\mathbf{A}:\mathbf{A}\mathbf{A}^t=\mathbf{I}_d\}} J_c^*(\mathbf{A})$. □

To obtain $\mathbf{A}$, we first find the gradient matrix given by the first-order necessary condition. That is, we differentiate (5) with respect to $\mathbf{A}$, resulting in:

$$\nabla J_c^*(\mathbf{A}) = \frac{\partial J_c^*(\mathbf{A})}{\partial \mathbf{A}} = \frac{\partial}{\partial \mathbf{A}} \sum_{i=1}^{k-1} \sum_{j=i+1}^{k} J_{c_{ij}}^*(\mathbf{A}) = \sum_{i=1}^{k-1} \sum_{j=i+1}^{k} \nabla J_{c_{ij}}^*(\mathbf{A}) , \qquad (8)$$

where

$$\begin{aligned}\nabla J_{c_{ij}}^*(\mathbf{A}) = 2\pi_i\pi_j \big[&\mathbf{S}_{E_{ij}}\mathbf{A}^t(\mathbf{A}\mathbf{S}_{W_{ij}}\mathbf{A}^t)^{-1} \\ &-\mathbf{S}_{W_{ij}}\mathbf{A}^t(\mathbf{A}\mathbf{S}_{W_{ij}}\mathbf{A}^t)^{-1}(\mathbf{A}\mathbf{S}_{E_{ij}}\mathbf{A}^t)(\mathbf{A}\mathbf{S}_{W_{ij}}\mathbf{A}^t)^{-1}\big]^t \\ +2\big[\mathbf{S}_{W_{ij}}\mathbf{A}^t(\mathbf{A}\mathbf{S}_{W_{ij}}\mathbf{A}^t)^{-1} &- \pi_i\mathbf{S}_i\mathbf{A}^t(\mathbf{A}\mathbf{S}_i\mathbf{A}^t)^{-1} - \pi_j\mathbf{S}_j\mathbf{A}^t(\mathbf{A}\mathbf{S}_j\mathbf{A}^t)^{-1}\big]^t \qquad (9)\end{aligned}$$

To maximize $J_c^*(\mathbf{A})$ we propose Algorithm **Chernoff_LDA_Multi** given below.

Algorithm **Chernoff_LDA_Multi**
Input: Threshold τ
begin
$\mathbf{A}^{(0)} \leftarrow \max_{\mathbf{A}}\{J_{c_{12}}^*(\mathbf{A}_{FD}), J_{c_{12}}^*(\mathbf{A}_{LD})\}$ // Maximum of FD or LD
$k \leftarrow 0$
repeat
$\eta_k \leftarrow max_{\eta>0}\phi_k(\eta)$
$\mathbf{B} \leftarrow \mathbf{A}^{(k)} + \eta_k \sum_{i=1}^{k-1}\sum_{j=i+1}^{k} \nabla J_{c_{ij}}^*(\mathbf{A}^{(k)})$
Decompose $\mathbf{B}$ into $\mathbf{R}$ and $\mathbf{Q}$
$\mathbf{A}^{(k+1)} \leftarrow \mathbf{Q}$
$k \leftarrow k+1$
until $|J_{c_{ij}}^*(\mathbf{A}^{(k-1)}) - J_{c_{ij}}^*(\mathbf{A}^{(k)})| < \tau$
return $\mathbf{A}^{(k)}, \sum_{i=1}^{k-1}\sum_{j=i+1}^{k} J_{c_{ij}}^*(\mathbf{A}^{(k)})$
end

At each step, the value of η_k is obtained as the one that maximizes the following function:

$$\phi_k(\eta) = J_c^*(\mathbf{A}^{(k)} + \eta \nabla J_c^*(\mathbf{A}^{(k)})) . \tag{10}$$

The algorithm initializes the matrix $\mathbf{A}$ by using the result of either FD or LD, depending on the one that gives the maximum value of the Chernoff distance in the transformed space. At each step, the matrix $\mathbf{A}$ is decomposed using the RQ decomposition, as shown in Lemma 1. Let us now see how the algorithm converges, using the convergence properties of the two-class case [15].

Theorem 1. *Let $\{\mathbf{A}^{(k)}\}_{k=1}^{\infty}$ be the sequence of matrices generated by Algorithm* **Chernoff_LDA_Multi**. *If $\nabla J_c^*(\mathbf{A}^{(k)}) \neq 0$, then $J_c^*(\mathbf{A}^{(k)}) < J_c^*(\mathbf{A}^{(k+1)})$. Otherwise, the algorithm terminates.*

Proof (Sketch). From (5), we have that $J_c^*(\mathbf{A}^{k)}) = \sum_{i=1}^{k-1} \sum_{j=i+1}^{k} J_{c_{ij}}^*(\mathbf{A}^{(k)})$. By using the result of the two-class case [15], it is true that $J_{c_{ij}}^*(\mathbf{A}^{(k)}) < J_{c_{ij}}^*(\mathbf{A}^{(k+1)})$ if $\nabla J_{c_{ij}}^*(\mathbf{A}^{(k)}) \neq 0$. Also, since for all $i, j = 1, \ldots, k$, $J_{c_{ij}}^*(\mathbf{A}^{(k+1)}) \geq 0$, we have that $J_c^*(\mathbf{A}^{(k)}) = \sum_{i=1}^{k-1} \sum_{j=i+1}^{k} J_{c_{ij}}^*(\mathbf{A}^{(k)}) < \sum_{i=1}^{k-1} \sum_{j=i+1}^{k} J_{c_{ij}}^*(\mathbf{A}^{(k+1)}) = J_c^*(\mathbf{A}^{(k+1)})$.

On the other hand, if $\nabla J_c^*(\mathbf{A}^{(k)}) = 0$, we have that $\mathbf{A}^{(k)} = \mathbf{A}^{(k+1)}$. Since we also know that $\tau > 0$, then we have that $|J_c^*(\mathbf{A}^{(k+1)}) - J_c^*(\mathbf{A}^{(k)})| < \tau$, and hence the algorithm terminates. The complete proof can be found in [15]. □

We note that it is quite important to compute, at each step, a value of η_k that maximizes the function ϕ_k given in (10). Computing the first derivative of this function results in:

$$\frac{d\phi_k}{d\eta}(\eta) = [\nabla J_c^*(\mathbf{A}^{(k)} + \eta \nabla J_c^*(\mathbf{A}^{(k)}))] \cdot \nabla J_c^*(\mathbf{A}^{(k)}) . \tag{11}$$

Using this expression, we compute $\eta^{(j+1)}$ as follows:

$$\eta^{(j+1)} = \eta^{(j)} - \frac{\eta^{(j)} - \eta^{(j-1)}}{\frac{d\phi_{k12}}{d\eta}(\eta^{(j)}) - \frac{d\phi_{k12}}{d\eta}(\eta^{(j-1)})} \frac{d\phi_{k12}}{d\eta}(\eta^{(j)}) , \tag{12}$$

where the values of $\eta^{(0)}$ and $\eta^{(1)}$ are obtained using the following theorem.

Theorem 2. *Let $\phi_k : \mathbb{R}^{d \times n} \to \mathbb{R}$ be the continuously differentiable function defined in (10), where $J_c^*(\cdot)$ is defined in (5), and whose first derivative is given by (8).*

Then, the initial values of the secant method are given by $\eta_0 = 0$ and

$$\eta_1 = \frac{d^2\epsilon - d}{tr\{\mathbf{A}^{(k)}[\nabla J_c^*(\mathbf{A}^{(k)})]^t\}} , \tag{13}$$

where $\epsilon = \cos\theta$, with θ being the angle between $\mathbf{A}^{(k)}$ and $[\mathbf{A}^{(k)} + \eta_k \nabla J_c^*(\mathbf{A}^{(k)})]$.

Proof (Sketch). From Lemma 1, we have that[1] $[\mathbf{A}^{(k)}][\mathbf{A}^{(k)}]^t = [\mathbf{A}^{(k+1)}][\mathbf{A}^{(k+1)}]^t = \mathbf{I}_d$, and hence both matrices are located in the boundary of the environment of zero (null

[1] Note that we are considering that $\mathbf{A}^{(k)}$ is the matrix $\mathbf{Q}$, which is orthogonal and obtained by means of the RQ decomposition.

matrices) of radius d in the matrix space. The angle difference between the matrices at steps 'k' and '$k+1$' are given by:

$$\cos\theta = \frac{1}{d} + \frac{\eta_k tr\{[\mathbf{A}^{(k)}][\nabla J_c^*(\mathbf{A}^{(k)})]^t\}}{d^2} \quad (14)$$

The result follows by setting $\cos\hat{\theta} = \epsilon$, and observing that the secant leads to a maximum. The complete proof can be found in [15]. □

To conclude this section, we emphasize that the geometric interpretation of $\mathbf{A}^{(k)}$ that we did for the two-class case is also valid for the multi-class case [14]. Again, the rows of the matrix $\mathbf{A}^{(k)}$ are "rotated" independently using the same scalar, n_k. In the same way, we could also imagine a more general mechanism for updating $\mathbf{A}^{(k)}$ using a vector, $\boldsymbol{\eta}$, instead of a scalar. This problem is a possible future avenue for extending this work.

3 Empirical Results

In order to evaluate the classification performance of the proposed criterion, we present an empirical analysis of the classification accuracy and Chernoff distance in the transformed space on real-life data drawn from the UCI machine learning repository [10]. Three LDR techniques are compared, namely FD and LD as discussed in Section 1, and the proposed method, as presented in Section 2, namely RH. In order to analyze the classification power of the LDR techniques, two classifiers are used in the transformed space, the linear (L) and quadratic (Q) classifiers. The datasets involved in the experiments are Iris plants, Letter recognition, Pendigits, Thyrod gland, Wine, Glass identification, Landsat satellite, and Vowel context. In order to avoid ill-conditioned covariance matrices, we have applied principal component analysis (PCA) to Glass and reduced the data from dimension nine to eight, and removed class '6' to apply the 10-fold cross validation method. As in the two-class case, we trained the three LDR techniques, namely FD, LD and RH, followed by a quadratic or linear classifier, in a 10-fold cross-validation experiment. The average classification errors are given in Table 1, in which d^* indicates the dimension that yields the lowest error rate. For each classifier, quadratic and linear, the LDR method(s) that produce(s) the lowest error rate is(are) marked with a '*'. For the quadratic classifier, we note that the RH method yields to lower error rate in four times, while FD and LD reach the best error rate in three times. For the linear classifier, both FD and LD are superior to RH. This is as expected, since the RH aims to maximize the Chernoff distance in the transformed space, which is related to the Bayesian quadratic classifier, but not necessarily to the linear classifier. Also, the error rates obtained using RH and the quadratic classifier are in all cases (except in Iris and Glass) much smaller than the corresponding rate for the linear classifier, independently of the LDR technique coupled with the latter.

Fig. 2 (a) shows the plots for the error rates obtained after coupling the LDR techniques with the quadratic classifier on the Pendigits dataset. The plot shows the error rates for dimensions $d = 1, \ldots, 15$. After dimension $d = 3$, the error rates corresponding to LD and RH become relatively lower than that of FD, and in general, the error rate of RH is lower than that of LD, showing the superiority of the former over the latter on

Table 1. Average error rates obtained from the three LDR techniques coupled with quadratic and linear classifiers on the multi-class datasets drawn from the UCI machine learning repository

Dataset	FD+Q	d^*	LD+Q	d^*	RH+Q	d^*	FD+L	d^*	LD+L	d^*	RH+L	d^*
Iris	0.0266	1	0.0200*	1	0.0200*	1	0.0200*	1	0.0200*	1	0.0200*	1
Letter	0.1186	15	0.1169*	15	0.1200	15	0.2973*	15	0.2997	14	0.3048	14
Pendigit	0.0493	9	0.0232	15	0.0223*	14	0.1240*	9	0.1291	15	0.1301	15
Thyroid	0.0329*	1	0.0422	1	0.0374	4	0.0935*	1	0.0935*	4	0.0935*	1
Wine	0.0111	2	0.0055*	2	0.0055*	2	0.0222	2	0.0111*	5	0.0164	2
Glass	0.4333*	2	0.4468	4	0.4496	4	0.3387*	4	0.3968	6	0.4106	6
Landsat	0.1518*	5	0.1597	18	0.1543	5	0.1722	5	0.1705*	10	0.1857	5
Vowel	0.3788	9	0.3222	6	0.3040*	6	0.4656	6	0.4444*	2	0.4444*	2

the quadratic classifier. For the linear classifier, the error rates for different dimensions are shown in Fig. 2 (b). After dimension $d = 4$, the error rate for FD is relatively lower than that of LD and RH, while the error rate for the latter is higher than that of LD. In all cases, the error rate tends to decrease as the reduced dimension becomes larger. Fig. 3 (a) shows the error rates for the quadratic classifier on the Vowel dataset. The error rate of FD is quite larger than that of the other two methods, while the error rate for RH starts decreasing to reach its minimum at $d = 6$, to increase a little bit on greater dimensions. Although LD exhibits a similar behavior, it does not reach the minimum as RH, which demonstrates that the former does not capture all the information for the Chernoff distance in the transformed space. For the linear classifier on the Vowel dataset, Fig. 3 (b), LD and RH lead to a minimum error rate for most of the values of d, but they show the minimum is reached early at dimension $d = 2$. Also, the peak shown by RH at $d = 3$ shows how maximizing the Chernoff distance in the transformed space does not necessarily imply minimizing the error rate for the linear classifier. Note, however, that the converse is not always true for the quadratic classifier, but the behavior exhibited in the figures shows how the RH criterion is more appropriate for a quadratic classifier in

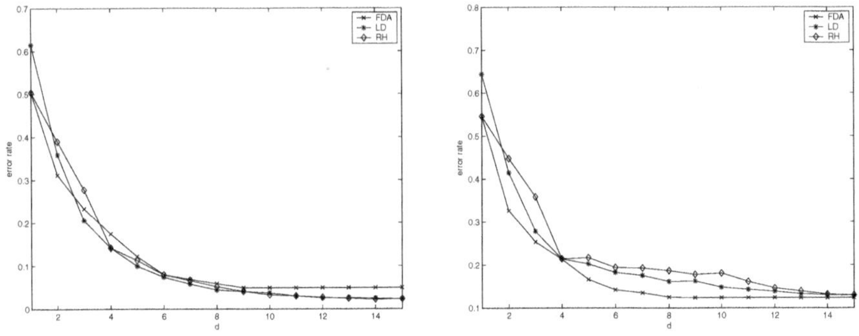

(a) Quadratic classifier. (b) Linear classifier.

Fig. 2. Error rates for all reduced dimensions on Pendigits

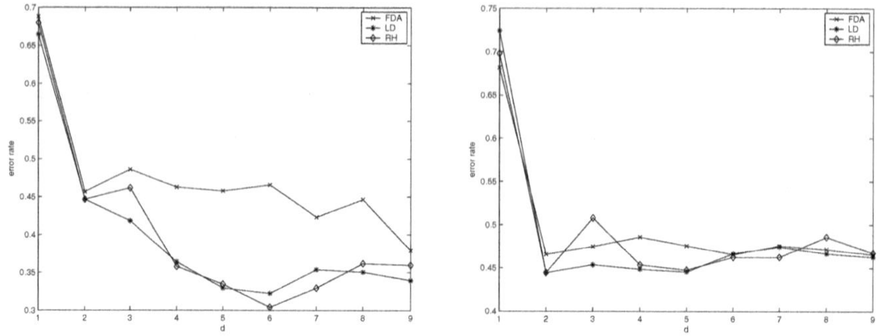

(a) Quadratic classifier. (b) Linear classifier.

Fig. 3. Error rates for all reduced dimensions on the Vowel dataset

the transformed space, because it captures more information on the Chernoff distance which provides a good approximation of the error rate for that classifier.

4 Conclusion

We have introduced a new criterion for linear dimensionality reduction (LDR), which, unlike previous approaches such as Fisher's and Loog-Duin's, aims to maximize the Chernoff distance in the transformed space. We have extended the corresponding criterion for the multi-class case, and provided proofs for the convergence of the optimizing gradient-based algorithms. The empirical results on real-life datasets show the superiority of RH over the existing FD and LD criteria, mainly when the techniques are coupled with the *quadratic* classifier, demonstrating the importance of maximizing the Chernoff distance in the transformed space for such a classifier. One of the possible extensions for this work is to use a vector η to update the matrix $\mathbf{A}^{(k)}$, instead of a scalar. This is a problem that we are currently investigating.

Acknowledgments. This research has been supported by the Chilean National Council for Technological and Scientific Research, FONDECYT grant No. 1060904, and the Institute of Informatics, National University of San Juan.

References

1. M. Aladjem. Linear Discriminant Analysis for Two Classes Via Removal of Classification Structure. *IEEE Trans. on Pattern Analysis and Machine Intelligence*, 19(2):187–192, 1997.
2. T. Cooke. Two Variations on Fisher's Linear Discriminant for Pattern Recognition. *IEEE Transations on Pattern Analysis and Machine Intelligence*, 24(2):268–273, 2002.
3. D. Harville. *Matriz Algebra from a Statisticians Perspective*. Springer-Verlag, New York, 1997.
4. Q. Du and C. Chang. A Linear Constrained Distance-based Discriminant Analysis for Hyperspectral Image Classification. *Pattern Recognition*, 34(2):361–373, 2001.

5. R. Duda, P. Hart, and D. Stork. *Pattern Classification*. John Wiley and Sons, Inc., New York, NY, 2nd edition, 2000.
6. H. Gao and J. Davis. Why Direct LDA is not Equivalent to LDA. *Pattern Recognition*, 39:1002–1006, 2006.
7. M. Herrera and R. Leiva. Generalización de la Distancia de Mahalanobis para el Análisis Discriminante Lineal en Poblaciones con Matrices de Covarianza Desiguales. *Revista de la Sociedad Argentina de Estadística*, 3(1-2):64–86, 1999.
8. M. Loog and P.W. Duin. Linear Dimensionality Reduction via a Heteroscedastic Extension of LDA: The Chernoff Criterion. *IEEE Transactions on Pattern Analysis and Machine Intelligence*, 26(6):732–739, 2004.
9. R. Lotlikar and R. Kothari. Adaptive Linear Dimensionality Reduction for Classification. *Pattern Recognition*, 33(2):185–194, 2000.
10. D. Newman, S. Hettich, C. Blake, and C. Merz. UCI repository of machine learning databases, 1998. University of California, Irvine, Dept. of Computer Science.
11. A. Rao, D. Miller, K. Rose, , and A. Gersho. A Deterministic Annealing Approach for Parsimonious Design of Piecewise Regression Models. *IEEE Transactions on Pattern Analysis and Machine Intelligence*, 21(2):159–173, 1999.
12. S. Raudys. Evolution and Generalization of a Single Neurone: I. Single-layer Perception as Seven Statistical Classifiers. *Neural Networks*, 11(2):283–296, 1998.
13. L. Rueda. Selecting the Best Hyperplane in the Framework of Optimal Pairwise Linear Classifiers. *Pattern Recognition Letters*, 25(2):49–62, 2004.
14. L. Rueda and M. Herrera. A New Linear Dimensionality Reduction Technique based on Chernoff Distance. In *Proceedings of the 10th Iberoamerican Conference on Artificial Intelligence*, Ribeirao Prieto, Brazil, October 2006, pp. 299–308.
15. L. Rueda and M. Herrera. Linear Discriminant Analysis by Maximizing the Chernoff Distance in the Transformed Space. *Submitted for Publication*, 2006. Electronically available at http://www.inf.udec.cl/~lrueda/papers/ChernoffLDAJnl.pdf.
16. L. Rueda and B. J. Oommen. On Optimal Pairwise Linear Classifiers for Normal Distributions: The Two-Dimensional Case. *IEEE Transations on Pattern Analysis and Machine Intelligence*, 24(2):274–280, 2002.
17. L. Rueda and B. J. Oommen. On Optimal Pairwise Linear Classifiers for Normal Distributions: The d-Dimensional Case. *Pattern Recognition*, 36(1):13–23, January 2003.
18. S. Theodoridis and K. Koutroumbas. *Pattern Recognition*. Elsevier Academic Press, third edition, 2006.
19. D. Tsujinishi and S. Abe. Fuzzy Least Squares Support Vector Machines for Multi-class Problems. *Neural Networks*, 16:785–792, 2003.
20. V. Vapnik. *Statistical Learning Theory*. Wiley, New York, 1998.
21. A. Webb. *Statistical Pattern Recognition*. John Wiley & Sons, N.York, second edition, 2002.

Automatic Band Selection in Multispectral Images Using Mutual Information-Based Clustering

Adolfo Martínez-Usó, Filiberto Pla, Pedro García-Sevilla, and J.M. Sotoca

LSI Department, Jaume I University. Castellón, Spain
{auso, pla, pgarcia}@uji.es
http://www.vision.uji.es

Abstract. Feature selection and dimensionality reduction are crucial research fields in pattern recognition. This work presents the application of a novel technique on dimensionality reduction to deal with multispectral images. A distance based on mutual information is used to construct a hierarchical clustering structure with the multispectral bands. Moreover, a criterion function is used to choose automatically the number of final clusters. Experimental results show that the method provides a very suitable subset of multispectral bands for pixel classification purposes.

1 Introduction

Works in multispectral imaging are producing many emerging applications in several disciplines. Multi or hyperspectral sensors acquire information from a range of wavelengths in the spectrum and, unquestionably, they have produced an important improvement of the results obtained from just one or three bands in some demanding application fields, like remote sensing, medical imaging, product quality inspection, fine arts, etc. The work we present here is not focused on a specific field and could be applied to any kind of multispectral images. However, due to the lines of work that we follow, we are strongly interested in SAR images as well as in fruit quality inspection tasks.

Obviously, from the point of view of pixel classification tasks, a very desirable step when we have a large amount of input spectral information is a process to reduce this initial information without losing classification accuracy in a significant way. This reduction could be done in two different ways: feature extraction [9,7] or feature selection [2]. In feature extraction we would obtain a new and reduced data set representing the transformed initial information, whereas in feature selection we would have a subset of relevant data from the original information. In this work we will focus on feature selection rather than feature extraction due to the fact that in feature extraction the total amount of information is needed to obtain the new set of input bands. On the other hand, selecting the relevant range of wavelengths in the spectrum, where the process obtains better results, allows the acquisition step to deal with a reduced set and makes the analysis simpler.

In multispectral applications, the question is how to select the correct bands from the multispectral range to characterise the problem. In this case, regarding to feature selection for pixel classification, this question could be addressed using information theory and, more concretely, by measures based on the mutual information concept [11].

In recent years, clustering techniques are becoming more popular, being hierarchical clustering one of the most used approaches. Important advances have been made

J.F. Martínez-Trinidad et al. (Eds.): CIARP 2006, LNCS 4225, pp. 644–654, 2006.

in different fields as segmentation [1] [10], text classification [3] or even in semantically meaningful grouping [12]. A comprehensive analysis of these methods can be also found in [4]. In our work, we take advantage of this representation because it is a very intuitive way to group the input data in order to progressively reduce the amount of information.

The methodology of the algorithm presented in this work can be summarised as follows. A similarity space is defined among image bands, where a dissimilarity measure is defined based on the mutual information between a pair of bands. From the initial set of bands that form a multispectral image, the process starts with a hierarchical clustering in the defined dissimilarity space. In order to progressively construct a hierarchical family of derived clusters the method uses a linkage strategy with an inter-cluster distance as the objective function to optimise. The number of final clusters is calculated automatically by means of a functional. The maximum values in this function indicate which number of clusters is suitable in order to form an accurate partition. Finally, for each of the final clusters, a band representing the cluster is chosen, providing the final bands selected, which are considered the most relevant.

2 Band Selection Algorithm

In this section the dimensionality reduction algorithm is introduced. To this end, the method proposed tries to identify the subset of bands that are as much independent as possible among them. It is known that independence between bands [9] is one of the key issues to obtain relevant subsets of bands for classification purposes. As we will show in the experimental results, the resulting bands obtained by means of our method produce very satisfactory classification rates with respect to other feature selection approaches.

To find the subset of K bands that are as much independent as possible among them, our approach defines a dissimilarity space based on mutual information between bands. In this dissimilarity space, a clustering process is performed. As a result of the clustering, bands are grouped according to the amount of information they share. Therefore, all the bands in the same cluster are highly dependent among them. In a final stage, a band representing each cluster is chosen, in such a way that the band selected will be the band that share as much information with respect to the other bands in the cluster. Eventually, the K selected bands from the final K clusters will have a significant degree of independence, and therefore, will provide an adequate reduced representation that will provide satisfactory classification results.

2.1 Mutual Information-Based Distance

Let us calculate mutual information from entropy measures according to the well-known expression $I(X,Y) = H(X) + H(Y) - H(X,Y)$, where $H(X)$, $H(Y)$ are the entropies of random vectors X, Y respectively and $H(X,Y)$ is the joint entropy. I is an absolute measure of common information between two sources, however, as we can infer from the previous equation, I by itself would not be a suitable distance measure. The reason is that it can be low because the X, Y variables present a weak relation (such as it should be desirable) or because the entropies are small (in such case, the variables contribute with few information). Thus, it is convenient to obtain a proper measure so that it works independently from the marginal entropies and also measures the statistical dependence as a distance.

Let us consider a set of n bands $X_1, ..., X_n$ from a multispectral image and let us suppose that each band represents a random variable. From this input data, we shall employ a measure of similarity between any two random images, $NI(X_i, X_j) = \frac{2 \cdot I(X_i, X_j)}{H(X_i)+H(X_j)}$, which is a normalised measure of I. This measure is used to calculate distance $D_{NI} = \left(1 - \sqrt{NI(X_i, X_j)}\right)^2$. Both D_{NI} and NI had been proposed in [5].

2.2 Hierarchical Clustering

The hierarchical structures are commonly represented by a tree diagram or *dendrogram* with a nested set of partitions. In this representation, called hierarchical clustering, the sequence of disjoint partitions is obtained using only the information contained in a distance matrix. This matrix of dissimilarities calculates the distance D_{NI} for each pair of groups and is used to decide how to link nested clusters in consecutive levels of the hierarchy.

There are several linkage strategies that we can use as the rule to decide how the distance matrix has to be updated [6]. Different linkage strategies create different tree structures. The algorithm here proposed uses an agglomerative strategy, that is, it starts with n initial clusters and, at each step, merges the two most similar groups to form a new cluster. Thus, the number of groups is reduced 1 by 1 until there is just one cluster. Our hierarchical clustering algorithm is based on a Ward's linkage method [13]. Ward's linkage method has the property of producing minimum variance partitions. Thus, this method is also called minimum variance method because it pursues to form each possible group in a manner that would minimise the loss associated with each grouping (internal cohesion). To this end, the hierarchical grouping merges the pair of clusters that minimise the increment in the square error of the whole partition. The error used to this calculation is the intra-cluster dispersion. In addition to several studies that conclude that this method outperforms other hierarchical clustering methods [6], the process helps us to form groups with not much variance in their level of independence, that is, clusters with similar D_{NI} distances will be joined together.

2.3 Fully Automated K-Assessment

Most of the applications that imply a band selection process suffer from a lack of an $automatic - K - selection$, that is, the final number K of selected bands is not chosen automatically. This drawback is usually solved by a manual introduction of the K value or by determining a threshold value in order to control the progression of certain functional [4]. Therefore, a method with an $automatic - K - selection$ would be desirable in order to finish correctly the hierarchical process and make the method completely unsupervised.

In this paper, we introduce a functional that automatically calculates how many clusters would be desirable as a final subset, that is, the K number. In our work, we have compared this result with the classification rates for each number of final clusters in order to check the validity of the K taken. Thus, a valid K number would be a value from which the classification accuracy does not improve or even become worse.

The developed functional will begin in the stage where each band, from the N starting bands, is a single cluster and will finish in the stage with only two clusters. Let us suppose certain stage where the bands are grouped in n clusters (where $n \leq N$) forming a partition $C = \{c_0, c_1, ..., c_n\}$, that is, a set of clusters. Let us also suppose that we have a cluster of bands c_i and $\bar{C}_i = \{c_0, c_1, ..., c_n\}$ is the complementary subset of clusters where $c_i \notin \bar{C}_i$, $C \equiv \{c_i\} \cup \bar{C}_i$.

Let us define $I(c_i)$ as the average of the *internal* distances[1] among the bands b_i belonging to c_i. We shall also define $E(c_i)$ as the average of the *external* distances between the bands belonging to c_i and the bands in $\bar{C}_i$. Thus,

$$I(c_i) = \frac{1}{\|c_i\|^2} \sum_{b_i \in c_i} \sum_{b_j \in c_i} D_{NI}(b_i, b_j) \qquad E(c_i) = \frac{1}{\|C_i\| \cdot \|\bar{C}_i\|} \sum_{b_i \in c_i} \sum_{b_j \in \bar{C}_i} D_{NI}(b_i, b_j)$$

Note that $I(c_i)$ calculates an intra-cluster average difference whereas $E(c_i)$ calculates the inter-cluster average difference. Both of them use mutual information among bands (as described in 2.1) and are related to a particular cluster c_i. Hence, we will define $P_I(C)$ and $P_E(C)$ as the global average measures among all the clusters in a particular partition C as follows:

$$P_I(C) = \frac{1}{\|C\|} \sum_{c_i \in C} I(c_i) \qquad P_E(C) = \frac{1}{\|C\|} \sum_{c_i \in C} E(c_i)$$

In an ideal partition, we would hope the inter-cluster value $P_E(C)$ to be very large, and the intra-cluster value $P_I(C)$ to be very small. Thus, left side of figure 1 plots the function $P_E(C) - P_I(C)$ against the number of clusters in C. As we can see, the maximum difference between $P_E(C)$ and $P_I(C)$ is obtained when each band is considered as an independent cluster. Since our aim is a band reduction, this measure is not enough by itself. Hence, we plot the linear function that ranges from 0 to $P_E(C_0) - P_I(C_0)$ where C_0 is the initial partition when each band is considered as a single cluster. This linear behaviour would be the graph we will expect if all steps in the clustering process would provide the same variation in the values of $P_E(C)$ and $P_I(C)$.

Taking into account the two described functions, we shall consider the resulting functional from the difference between the first one, which could be considered as the *real* behaviour, and the second one, which could be considered as the expected *linear* behaviour. The maximum value in this $K\_functional$ is considered the better K value for the final number of clusters. For some application, other local peaks around the maximum of the $K\_functional$ could also be taken into account. Plotting the functional values for each number of clusters (Fig. 1 on the right) we can see that the graph draws an increasing function from right (where each band is an independent cluster) to left (where several bands are grouped in a few clusters) until a maximum value which is the selected K number. In short, the functional equation has the following form:

$$K\_func(C) = (P_E(C) - P_I(C)) - \|C\| \frac{P_E(C_0) - P_I(C_0)}{\|C_0\|}$$

[1] It is important to point out that when we talk about distance we are referring to D_{NI}.

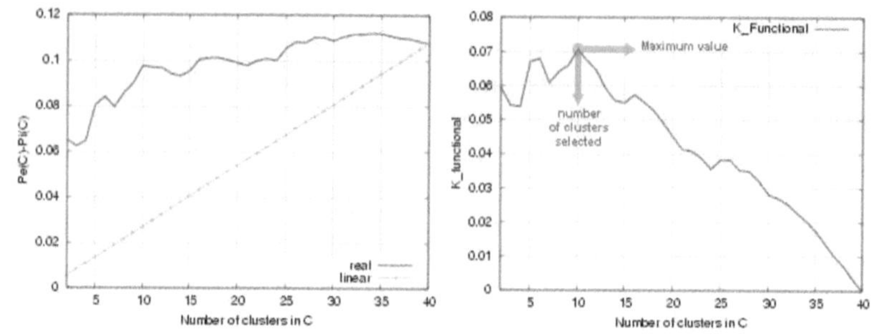

Fig. 1. Left picture shows *real* and expected *linear* graphs for NIR database. Resulting $K\_functional$ is plotted on the right.

2.4 Choosing the Cluster Representatives

After the distance matrix is initialised, the algorithm looks for the two most similar clusters that will have the minimum distance value in the matrix. These two clusters are merged into one and the matrix is updated using Ward's linkage method. Of course, the rows/columns corresponding to the merged clusters are deleted and a row/column for the new cluster is added.

The described process is repeated until the stage with just one band. After that, by means of the previous described functional, the algorithm selects the K number of final clusters. The resulting mutually exclusive groups represent groups of highly correlated bands, and bands from two different clusters will have low correlation. Thus, let us consider now the resulting cluster c_i with n bands. The weight of each band $i \in c_i$ is calculated as $W_i = \frac{1}{n} \sum_{j \in c_i, j \neq i} \frac{1}{\epsilon + D(i,j)^2}$ where ϵ is a very small value to avoid singular values, and function $D(i,j)$ returns the distance value between bands i,j. The representative band from each group is selected as the band with the highest W of the cluster. A low value of W_i means that the band i has an average large distance with respect to the other bands in the cluster, that is, in this case, the band i will have an average low correlation with respect to the other bands in the cluster. In a reverse way, a high value of W_i means that band i has, in average, a high correlation with respect to the other bands in the cluster. Thus, choosing the band in the cluster with the highest average correlation (mutual information) with respect to the other bands in the cluster, what we are doing is choosing the band that better predicts the information content of the other bands, since the more mutual information two random variables have, the more can predict one of the variable about the other one.

As a result of the algorithm, K bands will be selected that represent K clusters. These K bands will be significantly separated in the dissimilarity space defined, thus, having a low correlation and, therefore, having a high degree of independence among them.

3 Results

To test the proposed approach, several multispectral images from different databases are used in the experimental results:

1. Multispectral images of oranges obtained by an imaging spectrograph (RetigaEx, Opto-knowledge Systems Inc., Canada). This database has two groups, VIS collection (400-720 nm in the visible) and NIR collection (650-1050 nm in the near infrared). In both cases, the camera has a spectral resolution of 10 nm. The database includes several kinds of orange defects. It has eight classes, obtaining 1463346 labelled pixels from VIS and 1491888 labelled pixels from NIR.
2. The $92AV3C$ source of data corresponds to a spectral image (145 X 145 pixels, 220 bands, 17 classes) acquired with the AVIRIS data set and collected in June 1992 over the Indian Pine Test site in Northwestern Indiana[2].
3. $DAISEX'99$ project provides useful aerial images about the study of the variability in the reflectance of different natural surfaces. This source of data corresponds to a spectral image (700 X 670 pixels, 6 classes) acquired with the 128-bands HyMap spectrometer during the DAISEX-99 campaign (http:/io.uv.es/projects/daisex/).

In addition to the previous description, images in Fig. 2 show some instances of the database collections used. These images are presented as RGB compositions.

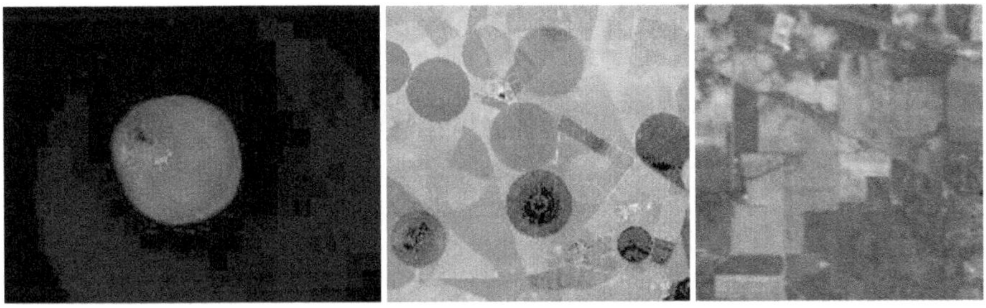

Fig. 2. Examples of RGB composition. First for an orange image in the Visible spectrum, second for HyMap spectrometer and third for AVIRIS (92AV3C)

On $92AV3C$ and $DAISEX'99$ databases, because of the labelled "background", which corresponds to pixels with an undetermined class, we can divide each database into two groups, one with background and another without background.

Since we perform the Ward's linkage method using a distance based on Mutual Infor-mation, we shall name hereafter $WaLuMI$ to our proposed algorithm. It has been tested with these six databases described, that is, the VIS and NIR collections from the database of oranges, $92AV3C$ database with and without background and $DAISEX'99$ database with and without background.

In order to assess the performance of the method, a Nearest Neighbour (NN) classifier was used to classify pixels into the different classes. The performance of the NN classifier was considered as the validation criterion to compare the significance of the subsets of selected image bands obtained by the proposed approach.

To analyse the accuracy of the ranking of bands obtained by the proposed approach, two supervised filter feature selection methods were also tested. Thus, the band selection process was considered as a supervised feature selection approach, in this case

[2] http:/dynamo.ecn.purdue.edu /~biehl/MultiSpec

using the labelled data set for the feature selection process. The main motivation about comparing the proposed method with supervised approaches is that the labelled data contains information about the distribution of classes existing in the hyperspectral data, and they allow the search for relevant feature subsets. By comparing the performance with those approaches, we can measure the capability to obtain subsets of relevant features (image bands) by the introduced algorithm without a prior knowledge of the class distributions in the multispectral image, allowing the labelling of data.

The first method is the well-known *ReliefF* algorithm [8] based on pattern distances. This algorithm initialises every feature weight to zero and then iterates m times looking for a set of feature weights that optimises a criterion function.

The second technique is related to divergence measures between classes. One of the best-known distance measures used for feature selection in multi-class problems is the average Jeffries-Matusita (JM) distance [2].

In terms of class separability, the higher is the JM distance between two classes, the more separability between them. To obtain suboptimal subsets of features, we have applied a search strategy based on a Sequential Forward Selection applying this distance ($(SFS)JMdistance$). This technique starts from an empty feature subset and adding one feature at a time, reaching a feature subset with the desired cardinality.

3.1 Performance Evaluation Including Background Pixels

During the image labelling process, there are always pixels in an image that are not assigned to any class of interest, mainly because they are pixels that either do not clearly belong to some of the predefined classes or they are assigned to a complementary class. The pixels that have not been assigned to any class are labelled as "background" class. In this subsection, we include the background information in the databases for its evaluation.

In order to increase the statistical significance of the results, the experimental results shown in this section about the classification rates correspond to the average classification accuracy obtained by the NN classifier over five random partitions. The samples in each partition were randomly assigned to the training and test set with equal sizes as follows: VIS = 43902 pixels, NIR = 44758 pixels, HyMap = 37520 pixels, 92AV3C = 2102 pixels.

On the other hand, given the huge size of the data sets and the trouble in computational cost to apply the supervised approaches, particularly in the case of VIS, NIR and HyMap, the following independent partitions with respect to the data sets were randomly extracted maintaining the prior probability of the classes: VIS = 87805 pixels, NIR = 89516 pixels, HyMap = 93804 pixels and 92AV3C = 10512 pixels. Using these databases, the supervised approaches and the proposed method were applied in order to obtain a ranking of relevance of the features, that is, of bands.

Figures 3, 4 (left) and 5 (left) represent in their top row the classification rates with respect to the subset of N bands selected by each method for each database. In all cases, we show the performance of the *NN* classifier with respect to the number of features obtained by $WaLuMI$, $(SFS)JMdistance$ and $ReliefF$. Note that the proposed method obtained better performance with respect to the rest of methods in all databases. It is worthwhile mentioning that the $WaLuMI$ approach has a good behaviour in all cases when choosing the smaller sets of bands (one to ten), where the decision is more critical.

$ReliefF$ performs poorer with respect to the other approaches except with HyMap image, where the performance of $(SFS)JMdistance$ is worse.

Therefore, regarding to the band selection problem, where there exists high correlation among different features (image bands), the principle of looking for non-correlated bands from the different regions of the spectrum, by reducing the mutual information in the ensemble of image bands, has proven to be an effective approach to obtain subsets of selected image bands that also provide satisfactory results from the classification accuracy point of view.

3.2 Performance Evaluation Without Background Pixels

The hyperspectral data assigned to the "background class" are usually very scattered and overlapped with other classes, and this fact damages the classification accuracy. Moreover, the elimination of this information supposes a supervised knowledge to detect those regions of the image.

These regions are very difficult to detect with precision from unsupervised information. Therefore, the goal of this experiment is analysing the advantages that suppose the knowledge of the class distribution without the noise that the *background* class can introduce. In this case, we will focus on HyMap and 92AV3C hyperspectral data, where the background information is much more undefined.

In the case of HyMap, we added the *background* class to the training set and validation set: training = 26190 pixels and validation = 65479 pixels. The test set contains all classes except the *background* class. The total number of test samples is 327336 pixels. Thus, the experiment classifies the test using the ranking of relevance of the features obtained by the validation set with the proposed method and the supervised methods used in the comparison.

The image 92AV3C only contains 10366 instances without the *background* class. Therefore, we apply a holdout partition, where the training and the validation set have the same size with 5181 pixels and the rest of pixels represent the test set = 5185 pixels.

Figures 4 and 5 represent, in their right side of the top row, similar classification results than the previous subsection, but without "background class". The best performance is obtained by $WaLuMI$, even better in the first bands where the decision is more critical.

3.3 Selection of the K Final Clusters

For the experiments shown in previous subsections, we also present the values of the $K\_functional$ described in section 2.3. Figures 3, 4 and 5 show the results[3] of this $automatic - K - selection$ process in their bottom rows. We can realise how the maxima of the functional approximately fit with K values which provide satisfactory classification rates. Of course, we could make this comparison each time we carry out a

[3] Note that, in order to achieve a clearly graph, figures only show the 30 last partitions in VIS and NIR databases and the 50 last partitions in $HyMap$ and $92AV3C$ databases.

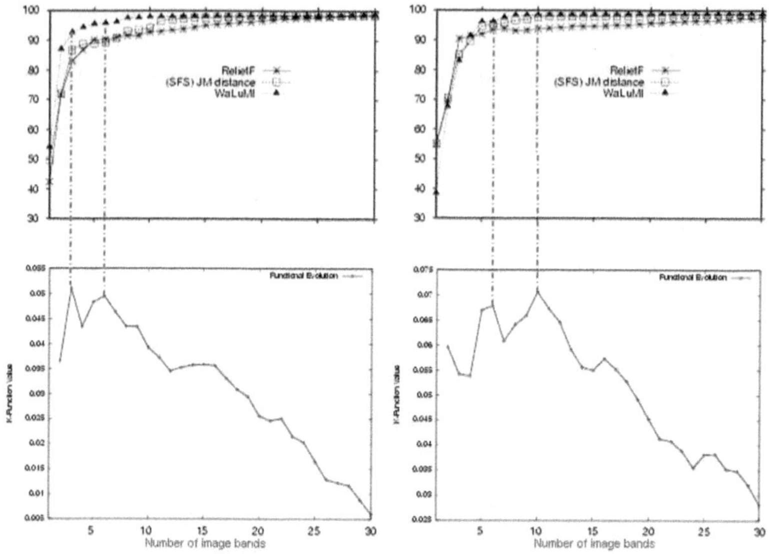

Fig. 3. $Automatic - K - selection$ (x-axe) in VIS/NIR databases. Top row shows the classification rates. Bottom row shows the corresponding K_functional. Left column shows the results for VIS multispectral image. Right column shows the results for NIR multispectral image.

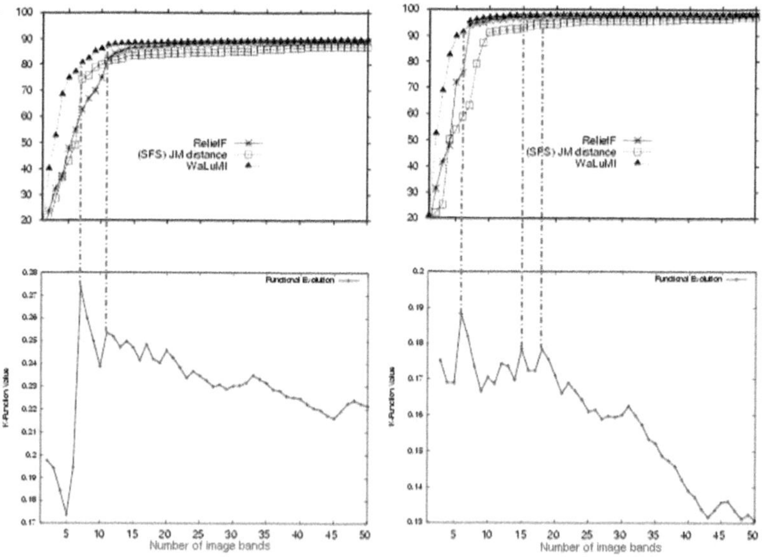

Fig. 4. $Automatic - K - selection$ (x-axe) in HyMap database. Top row shows the classification rates. Bottom row shows the corresponding K_functional. Left column shows the results for HyMap multispectral image. Right column shows the same results, but this time the image is considered without "background class".

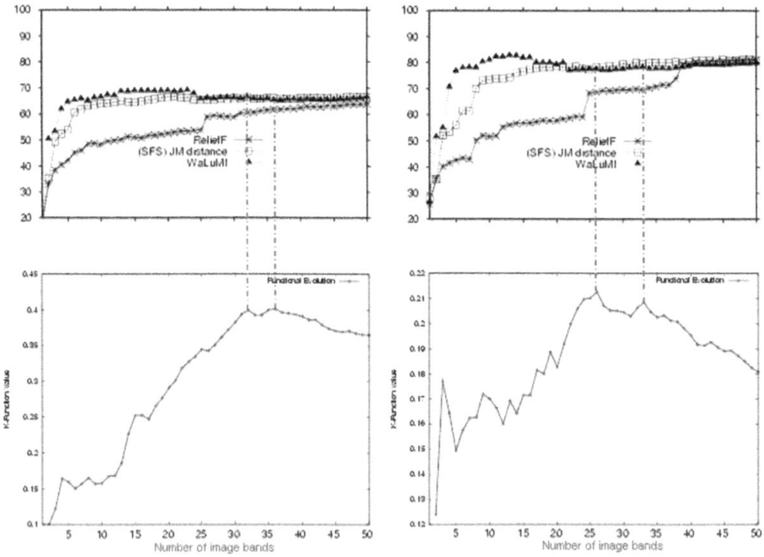

Fig. 5. $Automatic - K - selection$ (x-axe) in 92AV3C database. Top row shows the classification rates. Bottom row shows the corresponding K_functional. Left column shows the results for 92AV3C multispectral image. Right column shows the same results, but this time the image is considered without "background class".

band reduction, that is, testing the classification rates for each possible number of final clusters. The problem is the high computational/temporal cost it involves. So, in order to avoid this expensive process, we provide an automated method that selects as good partitions as we would choose manually according to classification rates but without having to run the classification experiments.

Figures 3 and 4 show in their bottom row the $K\_functional$ values for the oranges and HyMap databases respectively. In both databases a good number of clusters has been selected according to the classification accuracy graph. On the other hand, figure 5 does not achieve as good results as would be desirable because the selected K is a little bit away from the values that we manually would have chosen. However, taking into account that this image starts from 220 clusters (image bands), the K selected is a reasonable band reduction.

4 Conclusions

An unsupervised approach to select image bands in multispectral images based on mutual information measures has been introduced. The method uses a clustering process to group bands correlated among them, and selecting a subset of bands with a high degree of independence in a completely unsupervised way.

The results obtained from the point of view of pixel classification in multispectral images provide experimental evidence about the importance that independence among bands plays in the problem of classification. The method here presented is computationally affordable, avoiding the problem of labelling, and providing very satisfactory classification results with respect to other well known supervised feature selection criteria. In addition, an $automatic - K - selection$ process contributes to achieve a fully unsupervised algorithm that improves our previous work.

References

1. Jean-Marie Beaulieu and Morris Goldberg. Hierarchy in picture segmentation: A stepwise optimization approach. *IEEE Transactions on PAMI*, 11:150–163, 1989.
2. L. Bruzzonne, F. Roli, and Serpico S.B. An extension to multiclass cases of the jeffreys-matusita distance. *IEEE Trans on GRS*, 33:1318–1321, 1995.
3. I. Dhillon, S. Mallela, and R. Kumar. A divisive information-theoretic feature clustering algorithm for text classification. *JMLR*, 3:1265–1287, 2003.
4. Chris Ding and Xiaofeng He. Cluster merging and splitting in hierarchical clustering algorithms. *ICDM'02*, 1:139–146, 2002.
5. Raquel Dosil, Xosé R. Fdez-Vidal, and Xosé M. Pardo. Dissimilarity measures for visual pattern partitioning. *LNCS*, (3523):287–294, 2005.
6. A.K. Jain and R.C. Dubes. *Algorithms for Clustering Data.* Prentice-Hall, 1988.
7. L. Jimenez and D. Landgrebe. Supervised classification in high dimensional space: Geometrical, statistical, and asymptotical properties of multivariate data. *IEEE Transactions on System, Man, and Cybernetics*, 28, Part C(1):39–54, 1998.
8. I. Kononenko. Estimating attributes: analysis and extensions of relief. *In Proceedings of 7th European Conference on Machine Learning, Catania, Italy*, pages 171–182, 1994.
9. S. Kumar, J. Ghosh, and M.M. Crawford. Best basis feature extraction algorithms for classification of hyperspectral data. *IEEE Trans on GRS*, 39(7):1368–1379, 2001.
10. E. Sharon, A. Brandt, and R. Basri. Fast multiscale image segmentation. *CVPR*, 1:70–77, 2000.
11. G.D. Tourssari, E.D. Frederick, M.K. Markey, and C.E.Jr. Floyd. Applications of mutual information criterion for feature selection in computer-aided diagnosis. *Machine Learning Research*, 3:2394–2402, 2001.
12. A. Vailaya, M. Figueiredo, A.K. Jain, and H.J. Zhang. Image classification for content-based indexing. *IEEE Transactions on Image Processing*, 10:117–130, 2001.
13. John H. Ward. Hierarchical grouping to optimize an objective function. *American Statistical Association*, 58(301):236–244, 1963.

Orientation Invariant Features for Multiclass Object Recognition*

Michael Villamizar[1], Alberto Sanfeliu[1], and Juan Andrade-Cetto[2]

[1] Institut de Robòtica i Informàtica Industrial, UPC-CSIC
Llorens Artigas 4-6, 08028 Barcelona, Spain
{mvillami, sanfeliu}@iri.upc.edu
[2] Computer Vision Center, Universitat Autònoma de Barcelona
Edifici O, Campus UAB, 08193 Bellaterra, Spain
cetto@cvc.uab.es

Abstract. We present a framework for object recognition based on simple scale and orientation invariant local features that when combined with a hierarchical multiclass boosting mechanism produce robust classifiers for a limited number of object classes in cluttered backgrounds. The system extracts the most relevant features from a set of training samples and builds a hierarchical structure of them. By focusing on those features common to all trained objects, and also searching for those features particular to a reduced number of classes, and eventually, to each object class. To allow for efficient rotation invariance, we propose the use of non-Gaussian steerable filters, together with an Orientation Integral Image for a speedy computation of local orientation.

1 Introduction

Object detection is a fundamental issue in most computer vision tasks; particularly, in applications that require object recognition. Early approaches to object recognition are based on the search for matches between user-generated geometrical object models and image features. To overcome the need of such models, appearance-based object recognition gained popularity in the past two decades using dimensionality reduction techniques such as PCAs for whole-image matching. Unfortunately, appearance based matching as such, is prone to fail in situations with modest occlusions or under varying backgrounds. Lately, a new paradigm for object recognition has appeared based on the matching of geometrical as well as appearance local features. The most popular of these, perhaps, the SIFT descriptor [1].

* Financial support to M. Villamizar and A. Sanfeliu comes from the EURON Network Robot Systems Research Atelier NoE-507728, and the Spanish Ministry of Education and Science project NAVROB DPI 2004-05414. J. Andrade-Cetto is a Juan de la Cierva Postdoctoral Fellow of the Spanish Ministry of Education and Science under project TIC2003-09291, and is also funded in part by the EU PACO-PLUS project FP6-2004-IST-4-27657. The authors belong to the Artificial Vision and Intelligent Systems Group funded in part by the Catalan Research Commission.

J.F. Martínez-Trinidad et al. (Eds.): CIARP 2006, LNCS 4225, pp. 655–664, 2006.

Instead of using general saliency rules for feature selection as in the case of the SIFT descriptor, the use of boosting techniques for feature selection has proven beneficial in choosing the most discriminant geometric and appearance features from training sets. Despite their power in achieving accurate recognition from trained data, early boosting mechanisms such as [2], were tailored to single class object recognition, and are not suitable for multiclass object recognition given the large amount of features that need to be trained independently for each object class. Lately however, there have been some extensions to the general idea of classfication with boosting that allow the combined training of multiple classes [3,4]. In the computer vision doamin, Torralba *et al.* [5] proposed an extension to one such boosting algorithm (gentleboost), with the purpose of sharing features across multiples object classes so as to reduce the total number of classifiers. They called it JointBoost, and in this approach, all object classes are trained jointly, and for each possible subset of classes ($2^n - 1$ excluding the empty set), the most useful feature is selected to distinguish that subset from the background class. The process is repeated until the overall classification error reaches a minimum, or until a limit on the number of classifiers is achieved.

The type of weak classifier features used in [5] are very simple template matching masks, that would presumibly fail if sample objects are to be found at different orientations than as trained. In this work we investigate on the use of similar multiclass feature selection, but with keen interest in fast computation of orientation invariant weak classifiers [6] for multiclass rotation invariant object recognition.

In [2], Viola introduced the integral image for very fast feature evaluation. Once computed, an integral image allows the computation of Haar-like features [7] at any location or scale in real time. Unfortunately, such system is not invariant to object rotation or occlusions. Other recognition systems that might work well in cluttered scenes are based on the computation of multi-scale local features such as the previously mentioned SIFT descriptor [1]. One key idea behind the SIFT descriptor is that it incorporates canonical orientation values for each keypoint. Thus, allowing scale and rotation invariance during recognition. Even when a large number of SIFT features can be computed in real time for one single image, their correct pairing between sample and test images is performed via nearest neighbor search and generalized Hough transform voting, followed by the solution of the affine relation between views; which might end up to be a time consuming process.

Yokono and Poggio [8,9] settle for Harris corners at various levels of resolution as interest points, and from these, they select as object features those that are most robust to Gaussian derivative filters under rotation and scaling. As Gaussian derivatives are not rotation invariant, they use steerable filters [10] to steer all the features responses according to the local gradient orientation around the interest point. In the recognition phase, the system still requires local feature matching, and iterates over all matching pairs, in groups of 6, searching for the best matching homography, using RANSAC for outlier removal. Unfortunately, the time complexity or performance of their approach was not reported.

In [6] we realized that filter response to Haar masks can be not only be computed efficiently with an integral image scheme; but also, that such masks can be approximately rotated with some simplifications of the Gaussian steerable filter. Thus, allowing for fast computation of rotation invariant filter responses as week classifiers.

In this paper, we incorporate these two ideas, multiclass boosting, and rotation invariance, for the selection of joint and specific local features to construct a hierarchical structure that allow recognizing multiples objects independently of position, scale and orientation with a reduced set of features. In our system, key-points are chosen as those regions in the image that have the most discriminant response under convolution with a set of wavelet basis functions at several scales and orientations. Section 2 explains how the most relevant features are selected and combined to classify multiples objects. The selection is based on JointBoost, in which a hierarchical structure is composed by sets of joint and specific classifiers. A linear combination of these weak classifiers produces a strong classifier for each object class, which is used for detection. Rotation invariance is achieved by filtering with oriented basis functions. Filter rotation is efficiently computed with the aid of a steerable filter, that is, as the linear combination of basis filters, as indicated in Section 3.

During the recognition phase, sample image regions must be rotated to a trained canonical orientation, prior to feature matching. Such orientation is dictated by the peak on a histogram of gradient orientations, depicted in Section 4. Section 5 explains our proposed Orientation Integral Image for the speed of kernel orientation computation, and Section 6 presents some experiments.

2 Feature Selection

The set of local features that best discriminates an object is obtained by convolving positive sample images with a simplified set of wavelet basis function operators [7] at different scales and orientations. These filters have spatial orientation selectivity as well as frequency selectivity, and produce features that capture the contrast between regions representing points, edges, and strips, and have high response along for example, contours. The set of operators used is shown in Figure 1. Filter response is equivalent to the difference in intensity in the original image between the dark and light regions dictated by the operator. Figure 1 d) exemplifies how an object can be represented by a small set of the most useful local features.

Convolving these operators at any desired orientation is performed by steering the filter (Section 3), and fast convolution over any region of the entire image is efficiently obtained using an integral image (Section 5).

Feature selection is performed as in JointBoost [5], choosing one at a time, from the $2n-1$ subsets of the classes $c = 1...n$ (empty set excluded), the weak classifier $h(I, s)$ that best discriminates any subset s from the background class

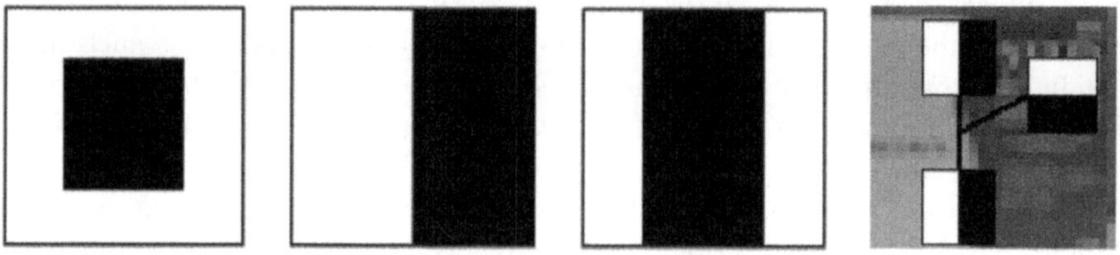

Fig. 1. Simplified wavelet basis function set. a) center-surround b) edge, and c) line; and d) object local features.

(lowest classification error). The weak classifier is defined by the parameters filter type, size, location, orientation and threshold, taking the binary decission value

$$h(I, s) = \begin{cases} 1 & : \quad I * f > t \\ 0 & : \quad \text{otherwise} \end{cases} \tag{1}$$

where I is a training sample image of class c in the subset s, f is the filter being tested, with all its parameters, $*$ indicates the convolution operation, and t is the filter response threshold.

At each iteration during the training phase, the algorithm must find for all of the $2n - 1$ subsets, the weak classifier that best discriminates that subset from the background class by minimizing the squared error over weighted samples of all classes in that subset

$$J_{wse} = \sum_{c=1}^{n} \sum_{s=1}^{m} w_i^c (z_i^c - h(I, s))^2 \tag{2}$$

where z_i^c and w_i^c are the membership label and weight of the sample i for class c respectively, and m the total number of training samples. The algorithm also updates sets of weights over the training samples. The number of sets corresponds with the number of classes to learn. Initially, all weights are set equally, but on each round, the weights of missclassified samples are increased so that the algorithm is forced to focus on such hard samples in the training set the previously chosen classifiers missed. Finally, choosing the weak classifier for the subset that had the minimum squared error J, and iteratively adding it to the Strong Classifier for every class c in s, $H(I, c)$,

$$H(I, c) := H(I, c) + h(I, s) \tag{3}$$

Scale invariance is obtained by iterating also over scaled filters within the classifier H. Scaling of the filters can be performed in constant time for a previously computed integral image.

3 Steerable Filters

In order to achieve orientation invariance, the local filters must be rotated previous to convolution. A good alternative is to compute these rotations with steerable filters [10], or with its complex version [11]. A steerable filter is a rotated filter comprised of a linear combination of a set of oriented basis filters

$$I * f(\theta) = \sum^{n} k_i(\theta) I * f(\theta_i) , \tag{4}$$

where $f(\theta_i)$ are the oriented basis filters, and k_i are the coefficients of the bases.

Consider for example, the Gaussian function $G(u, v) = e^{-(u^2+v^2)}$, and its first and second order derivative filters $G'_u = -2ue^{-(u^2+v^2)}$ and $G''_u = (4u^2 - 2)e^{-(u^2+v^2)}$. These filters can be re-oriented as a linear combination of filter bases. The size of the basis is one more than the derivative order.

Consequently. the first order derivative of our Gaussian function at any direction θ is

$$G'_\theta = \cos\theta G'_u + \sin\theta G'_v , \tag{5}$$

and, the steered 2nd order Gaussian filter can be obtained with

$$G''_\theta = \sum_{i=1}^{3} k_i(\theta) G''_{\theta_i} \tag{6}$$

with $k_i(\theta) = \frac{1}{3}(1 + 2\cos(\theta - \theta_i))$; and G''_{θ_i} precomputed second order derivative kernels at $\theta_1 = 0$, $\theta_2 = \frac{\pi}{3}$, and $\theta_3 = \frac{2\pi}{3}$. See Figure 2.

Convolving with Gaussian kernels is a time consuming process. Instead, we propose in [6] to approximate such filter response by convolving with the Haar basis with the objective of using the integral image. Thus, we approximate the oriented first derivative response with

$$I * f_1(\theta) = \cos\theta I * f_1(0) + \sin\theta I * f_1(\tfrac{\pi}{2}) . \tag{7}$$

and in the same sense, the filtering with our line detector at any orientation θ is obtained with

$$I * f_2(\theta) = \sum_{i=1}^{3} k_i(\theta) I * f_2(\theta_i) . \tag{8}$$

The similarity of the response between the Gaussian and the Haar filters allows us to use the later basis instead as weak classifiers for the detection of points, edges, and lines; just as the Gaussian filters do. The main benefit of the approach is in speed of computation. While convolution with a Gaussian kernel takes time O(n) the size of the kernel, convolution with the oriented Haar basis can be computed in constant time using an integral image representation. Figure 3 shows some results.

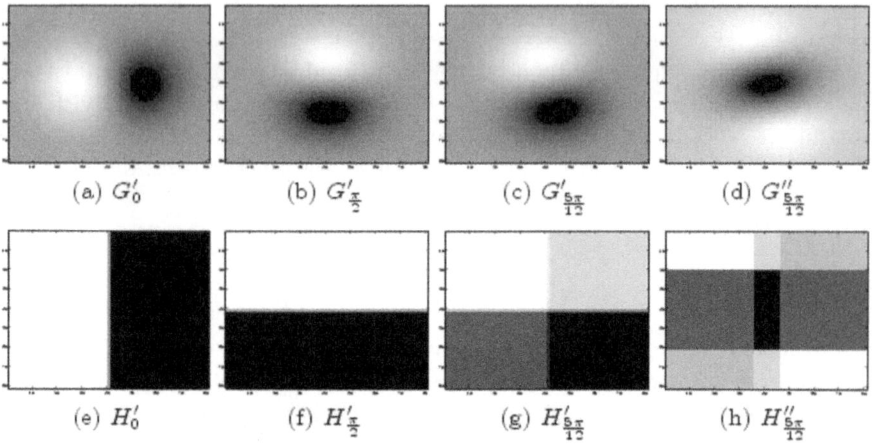

Fig. 2. First and second order steerable filters. (a-b) Gaussian basis, (c-d) Gaussian oriented filters, (e-f) Haar basis, (g-h) Haar oriented filters.

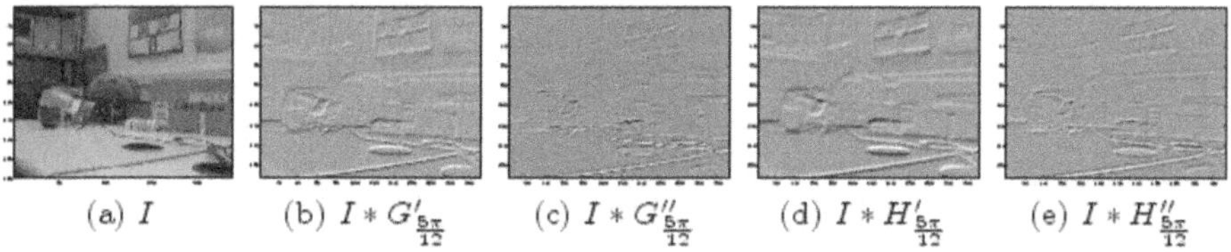

Fig. 3. Filter responses. (a) original image, (b-e) filter responses.

4 Local Orientation

Consider a training session has produced a constellation H of local features h as the one shown in Figure 4. Now, the objective is to test for multiple positions and scales in each new image, whether such constellation passes the test H or not. Instead of trying every possible orientation of our constellation, we chose to store the canonical orientation θ_0 of H from a reference training image block, and to compare it with the orientation θ of each image block being tested. The difference between the two indicates the amount we must re-orient the entire feature set before the test H is performed.

On way to compute block image orientation is with ratio of first derivative Gaussians G'_u and G'_v [9], $\tan\theta = \frac{I*G'_v}{I*G'_u}$. Another technique, more robust to partial occlusions, is to use the mode of the local gradient orientation histogram (see Figure 4 c-d), for which it is necessary to compute gradient orientations pixel by pixel, instead of a region convolution as in the previous case.

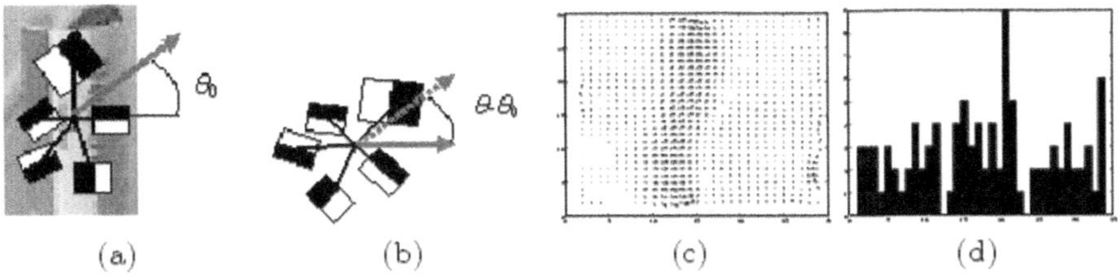

Fig. 4. Local orientation a) canonical orientation, b) rotated constellation, c) image gradients, b) gradient orientation histogram

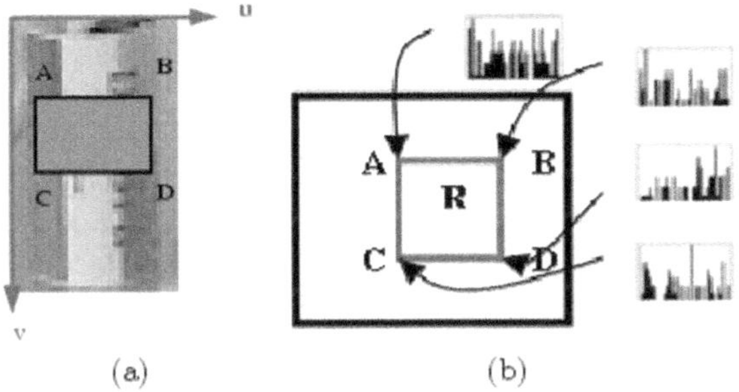

Fig. 5. Integral Images, a) Integral Image b) Orientation Integral Image

5 The Local Orientation Integral Image

An integral image is a representation of the image that allows a fast computation of features because it does not work directly with the original image intensities. Instead, it works over an incrementally built image that adds feature values along rows and columns. Once computed this image representation, any one of the local features (weak classifiers) can be computed at any location and scale in constant time.

In its most simple form, the value of the integral image M at coordinates u, v contains the sum of pixels values above and to the left of u, v, inclusive.

$$M(u,v) = \sum_{i \leq u, j \leq v} I(i,j) \tag{9}$$

Then, it is possible to compute for example, the sum of intensity values in a rectangular region simply by adding and subtracting the cumulative intensities at its four corners in the integral image (Figure 5a). Then, the response from the Haar-filters can be calculated in a fast way independently of size or location.

$$\text{Area} = A + D - B - C \tag{10}$$

Extending the idea of having cumulative data at each pixel in the Integral Image, we decide to store in it orientation histogram data instead of intensity sums. Once constructed this orientation integral image, it is possible to compute a local orientation histogram for any given rectangular area within an image in constant time. see Figure 5b.

$$\begin{aligned}\text{Histogram}(\text{Area}) = \ & \text{Histogram}(A) + \text{Histogram}(D) \\ & - \text{Histogram}(B) - \text{Histogram}(C)\end{aligned} \tag{11}$$

6 Experiments

In this communication we report on initial recognition results for a limited number of objects in gray scale images. The training set had 100 images for each class, and 500 negatives or background images. These negatives images were extracted from exterior and interior scenes. The positive class images used for training presented some small translation, orientation, and scale, as shown in Figure 6.

Figure 7 a) and b) show examples of extracted feature constellation for each object class. Each one is composed by 8 weak classifiers (Haar-like features), with 4 of them common to both classes, and the remaining 4 specific to each class.

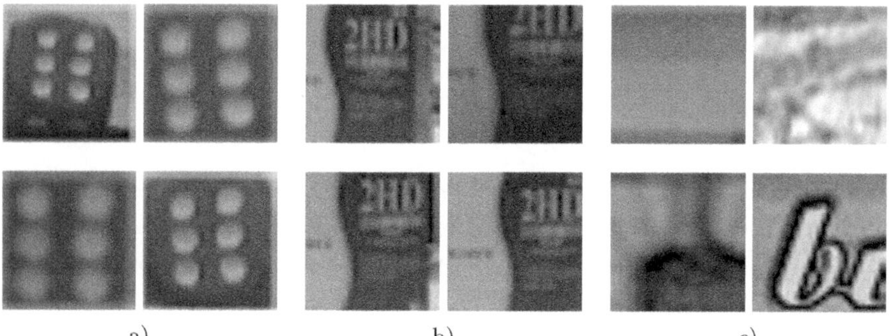

Fig. 6. Training object classes. a) dice images, b) CD box images, and c) background images.

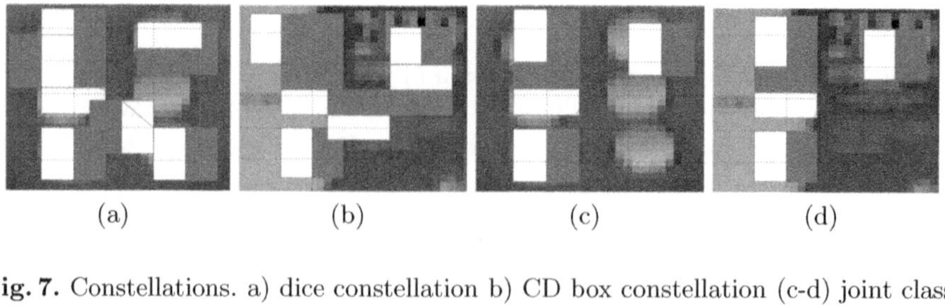

Fig. 7. Constellations. a) dice constellation b) CD box constellation (c-d) joint classifiers.

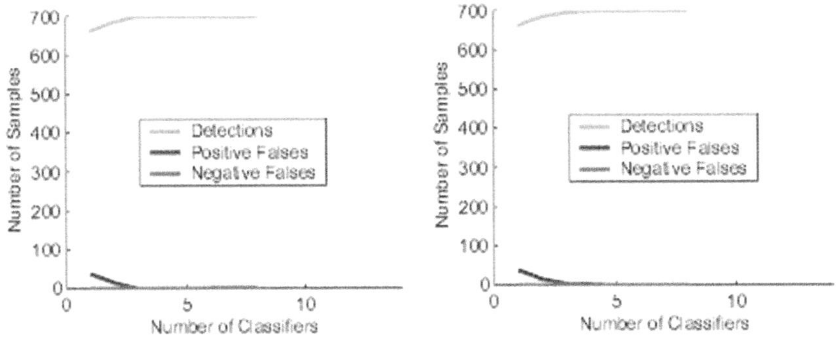

(a) (b)

Fig. 8. Training performance. a) dice b) CD box.

Fig. 9. Examples of correct detection of classifiers trained jointly (dice and Cd box). The last image shows also under what circumstances a false detection might occur.

Thus, producing a hierarchical structure of weak classifiers. Frames c) and d) show only those four classifiers that are common to both classes. They capture simmilar local information in both classes, separating them from the background set, without the need to be class specific.

The Strong Classifiers can be expressed as the combination of joint and specific weak classifiers. Consider the dice to be class 1, the CD box to be class 2, and c_{12} the set of training samples containing either one or both objects. Then

$$H(I, c_1) = \sum h(I, c_{12}) + \sum h(I, c_1) \tag{12}$$

$$H(I, c_2) = \sum h(I, c_{12}) + \sum h(I, c_2) \tag{13}$$

The training curves are shown in Figure 8.They illustrate how the correct classification of the training set is achieved. Some results in detection process over a image sequence are visualized in Figure 9.

7 Conclusions

In this paper we have introduced a hierarchical feature selection structure that reduce the total number of weak classifiers needed to detect multiples object classes. With this method the system finds common features among objects and generalizes the detection problem.

Our approach is based on boosting over a set of simple local features. In contrast to previous approaches, and to efficiently cope with orientation changes, we propose the use of Haar basis functions and a new orientation integral image for a speedy computation of local orientation.

References

1. Lowe, D.: Distinctive image features from scale-invariant keypoints. Int. J. Comput. Vision **60** (2004) 91–110
2. Viola, P., Jones, M.: Rapid object detection using a boosted cascade of simple features. In: Proc. 15th IEEE Conf. Comput. Vision Pattern Recog., Kauai (2001) 511–518
3. Li, L.: Multiclass boosting with repartitioning. In: Proc. 23rd Int. Conf. Machine Learning, Pittsburgh (2006) To appear.
4. Eibl, G., Pfeiffer, K.P.: Multiclass boosting for weak classifiers. J. Mach. Learn. Res. **6** (2005) 189–210
5. Torralba, A., Murphy, K., Freeman, W.: Sharing features: efficient boosting procedures for multiclass object detection. In: Proc. 18th IEEE Conf. Comput. Vision Pattern Recog., Washington (2004) 762–769
6. Villamizar, M., Sanfeliu, A., Andrade-Cetto, J.: Computation of rotation local invariant features using the integral image for real time object detection. In: Proc. 18th IAPR Int. Conf. Pattern Recog., Hong Kong, IEEE Comp. Soc. (2006) To appear.
7. Papageorgiou, C.P., Oren, M., Poggio, T.: A general framework for object detection. In: Proc. IEEE Int. Conf. Comput. Vision, Bombay (1998) 555
8. Yokono, J., Poggio, T.: Oriented filters for object recognition: An empirical study. In: Proc. 6th IEEE Int. Conf. Automatic Face Gesture Recog., Seoul (2004) 755–760
9. Yokono, J., Poggio, T.: Rotation invariant object recognition from one training example. Technical Report 2004-010, MIT AI Lab. (2004)
10. Freeman, W.T., Adelson, E.H.: The design and use of steerable filters. IEEE Trans. Pattern Anal. Machine Intell. **13** (1991) 891–906
11. Schaffalitzky, F., Zisserman, A.: Multi-view matching for unordered image sets, or "How do I organize my holiday snaps?". In: Proc. 7th European Conf. Comput. Vision, Copenhagen, Springer-Verlag (2002) 414–431

On the Design and Implementation of a High Performance Configurable Architecture for Testor Identification

René Cumplido, J. Ariel Carrasco-Ochoa, and Claudia Feregrino

Computer Science Department, INAOE, Apdo. Postal 51 & 216
Tonantzintla, Puebla, México
rcumplido@inaoep.mx, ariel@inaoep.mx, cferegrino@inaoep.mx

Abstract. Typical testors are a useful tool to do feature selection in supervised classification problems with mixed incomplete data. However, the complexity of computing all typical testors of a training matrix has an exponential growth with respect to the number of columns in the matrix. For this reason different approaches like heuristic algorithms, parallel and distributed processing, have been developed. In this paper, we present a configurable custom architecture for the efficient identification of testors from a given input matrix. The architectural design is based on a brute force approach that is suitable for high populated input matrixes. The architecture has been designed to deal with parallel processing and can be configured for any size of matrix. The architecture is able to evaluate if a vector is a testor of the matrix in a single clock cycle. The architecture has been implemented on a Field Programmable Gate Array (FPGA) device. Results show that it provides runtime improvements over software implementations running on state-of-the-art processors. FPGA implementation results are presented and implications to the field of pattern recognition discussed.

1 Introduction

Feature selection is an important task in supervised classification. It consists in identifying those features that provide relevant information for the classification process. Into the framework of the Logical Combinatorial Pattern Recognition [1], feature selection is solved using Testors Theory [2].

Yu. I. Zhuravlev introduced the testor concept to Pattern Recognition problems [3]. Zhuravlev defined a testor as a subset of features that allows differentiating objects from different classes.

This concept has a special application in the problem of feature selection for supervised classification; working in situations where there are qualitative and quantitative features and may be incomplete object descriptions, this is, mixed incomplete data. Since, computing all typical testors is very expensive, all the algorithms developed until now have exponential complexity, different approaches have been developed like heuristic algorithms, parallel and distributed computing, etc.

J.F. Martínez-Trinidad et al. (Eds.): CIARP 2006, LNCS 4225, pp. 665 – 673, 2006.

Although the theoretical aspect of testor identification algorithms is advanced, there is not practical hardware implementations reported previously. The intensive computational requirements due to the exponential complexity of the algorithms can only be met by a combination of technology improvements and efficient hardware architectures based on parallel computational models. Specific parallel architectures can be designed to exploit the parallelism found in the algorithms to speed up the processing. Further optimizations such as incremental processing and the use of multiple processing elements are also possible.

The rest of the paper is organized as follows. Section 2 provides the theoretical foundation of testor identification. Section 3 presents a data parallelism analysis of the algorithms and details of the proposed hardware architecture. In section 4 the FPGA implementation and experimental result are presented. In section 5, a brief discussion on the performance improvements is presented and the obtained results are compared against software implementation. Finally, section 6 presents the concluding remarks and directions for further research.

2 Algorithms for Testor Identification

Let *TM* be a training matrix with *K* objects described through *N* features of any type $(x_1,\ldots,x_N)$ and grouped in *r* classes. Let *DM* be a dissimilarity Boolean matrix (0=similar,1=dissimilar), obtained from feature by feature comparisons of every pair of objects from *T* belonging to different classes. *DM* has *N* columns and *M* rows, where $M>>K$.

Testors and Typical Testors are defined as follows:

Definition 1. A subset of features *T* is a testor if and only if when all features are eliminated, except those from *T*, there is not any row of *DM* with only 0´s.

Definition 2. A subset of features *T* is a typical testor if and only if *T* is a testor and there is not any other testor *T*' such that $T'\subset T$.

We can find two main strategies to compute all typical testors. One of them is to analyze the matrix and find conditions, which guarantee that a feature subset is a typical testor. The algorithms that use this strategy are called *internal scale algorithms*. The other one is to look over the whole power set of features. The algorithms that use this strategy are called *external scale algorithms*. In this paper we are interested in the last strategy. An example of this kind of algorithms is BT. In order to review all the search space, BT codifies the feature subsets as binary *N*-tuples where 0 indicates that the associated feature is not included and 1 indicates that the associated feature is included. BT supposes the order induced by the increasing order of binary natural numbers. The BT algorithm is as follows:

Step 1.- Generate first no null *N*-tuple $\alpha=(0,\ldots,0,1)$.
Step 2.- Determinate if the generated *N*-tuple is a testor of *DM*.
Step 3.- If α is a testor of *DM*, store it and and take $\alpha'=\alpha+2^{n-k}-1$ where let *k* be the index of the last 1 in α.

Step 4.- If α is not a testor of *DM*, determine a row v of *DM* with only 0´s in the columns where α has 1´s and generate α' as:

$$\alpha'_j = \begin{cases} \alpha_j & if \quad j < k \\ 1 & if \quad j = k \\ 0 & if \quad j > k \end{cases},$$

where let k be the index of the last 1 in v.
Step 5.- Take $\alpha=\alpha'$
Step 6.- If α is not after (1,1,...,1,1) then, go to step 3
Step 7.- Eliminate from the stored testor those, which are not typical testors.

For the proposed architecture, we used the next modified algorithm, which follows the reverse order:

Step 1.- Generate first *N*-tuple $\alpha=(1,...,1,1)$.
Step 2.- If α is a testor of *DM*, store it and take $\alpha'=\alpha-1$
Step 3.- If α is not a testor of *DM*, take $\alpha'=\alpha-2^{k-1}$, where k is the index of the first 0 in α, (index starts from the right or least significant bit LSB).
Step 4.- Take $\alpha=\alpha'$
Step 5.- If α is not (0,0,...,0) then, go to step 2
Step 6.- Eliminate from the stored testor those, which are not typical testors.

3 Parallel Hardware Implementation

3.1 Analysis of Algorithms

In most of the algorithms for computing typical testors, deciding if a candidate is a testor is a task that must be done many times. This decision involves comparing the candidate against each one of the *DM*'s rows, but for matrices with many rows, these decisions could take a lot of time. For this reason, we addressed the problem of deciding if a candidate is a testor as fast as possible, taking advantage of the concurrency that can be implemented through a specific hardware architecture based on a parallel computational model.

3.2 Configurable Architecture

The main hardware components of the architecture are a register file, a counter and a control unit. (See Fig. 1). The counter produces an *N*-tuple that is evaluated by the register file to find out if it is a testor of *DM*. If the *N*-tuple is a testor, the output port *Is_testor* will be TRUE and the value present at the output port *Testor* is stored. If the *N*-tuple is not a testor, the counter will decrease its value as indicated by the Step 3 of the modified algorithm shown in Section 2.

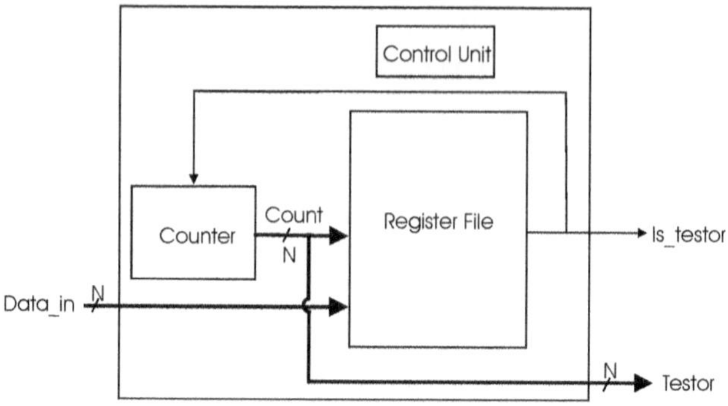

Fig. 1. Top-level architecture

The core of the architecture consists of the register file module shown in Fig 2. The module takes data from the input port during the initialization process. The data are read in a linear-stream based scheme and sent to the register file where propagates through the registers until the full *DM* has been loaded. Once the register file has been completely filled, the control unit starts the testor identification process. It is important to mention that only one clock cycle is needed to test if an *N*-tuple is a testor of *DM*. This is possible because the input data are fed simultaneously to the *M* Store-and-Compare (*SC*) modules to be processed in parallel.

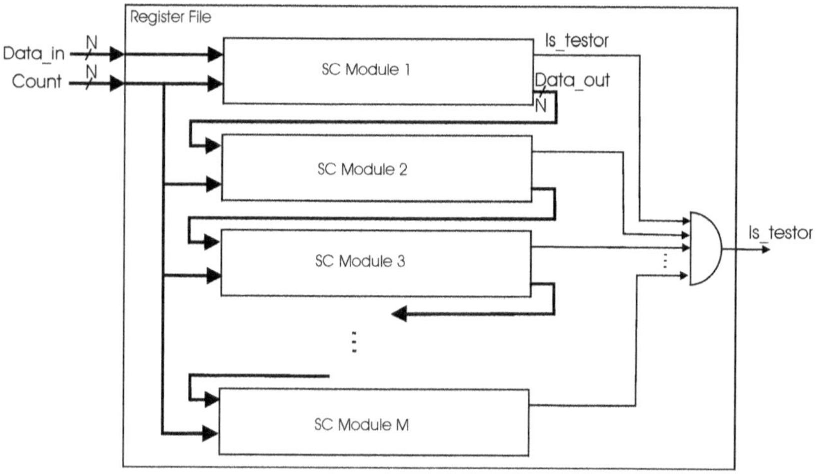

Fig. 2. Register file

The basic element of the architecture is shown in figure 3. The *SC* module is composed of an *N*-bit wide register plus a number of gates. The register in each *SC* module stores a row of the *DM*. A bitwise AND operation is performed between the value stored in the register and the input port Count. If at least one bit of the result is

TRUE, then the output port *Is_testor* will be TRUE. Finally, if the output port *Is_testor* of all *SC* modules is TRUE, then the *N*-tuple *Count* is a testor of *DM*.

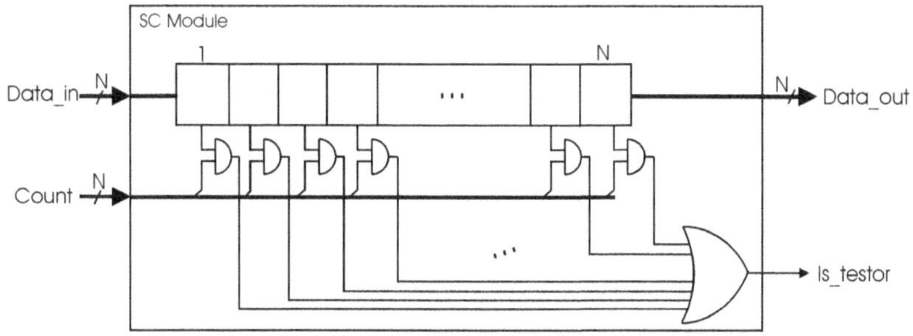

Fig. 3. Store-and-Compare (*SC*) Module

The register file is the configurable element in the architecture as it can be adapted for any size of the *DM*. In the following section, the hardware implementation of the proposed architecture, targeted to an FPGA device, is presented.

4 FPGA Implementation and Results

The proposed architecture was modeled using the VHDL Hardware Description Language under a structural approach. The VHDL model of the proposed architecture for the register file and counter unit is fully parameterizable in terms of the matrix dimensions (*N*,*M*). The VHDL model was simulated and validated both functional and post-synthesis with ModelSim v6.0. The VHDL model was synthesized with Xilinx ISE Software targeted for a XC3S200 Spartan-III device from Xilinx [4]. The use of the FPGA technology was chosen because it provides a rapid prototyping platform and is specially suited for implementing algorithms based on bit level operations. Some important advantages of FPGAs over general-purpose processors are:

i) FPGAs provide massive parallel structures and high density logic arithmetic with short design cycles compared to ASICs.
ii) In FPGA devices, tasks are implemented by spatially composing primitive operators rather than temporally.
iii) In FPGAs, it is possible to control operations at bit level to build specialized data-paths.
iv) FPGA technology can offer potentially several orders of magnitude more raw computational power per unit of area than conventional processors.
v) FPGA technology is well suited for implementing parallel architectures such as pipelined and systolic processors.

Table 1 summarizes the FPGA hardware resource utilization and timing performance for a case study with N=38 and M=45. According to the FPGA synthesis results, the proposed architecture provides good trade-off between performance and hardware resource utilization and it is suitable to be used as a high performance processing module in a hardware-in-the-loop approach [5]. Most FPGA resources are employed as storage elements to implement a *SC* module within the register file.

Table 1. FPGA resource utilization for N=38 and M=45

Synthesis summary for the architecture targeted for a XC3S200 Spartan-III device	
Number of slices	1210 (63%)
Number of 4-input LUTs	1276 (33%)
Number of flip-flops	1711 (44%)
Maximum clock frequency	87 MHz

The hardware resource utilization is directly proportional to the size of the matrix. Due to the regular structure of the register file, the size of the matrix does not affect the speed at which the architecture can operate. This makes possible to accurately estimate the processing time for a specific input matrix, based on the value of N and the operating frequency according to the following equation:

$$t = \frac{2^N}{f}$$

where t is the processing time and f is the clock frequency of the architecture.

The design was implemented on a Spartan-III based board. To program the device, the System Generator tool from Xilinx that runs in the Matlab/Simulink environment was used. This tool allows performing hardware-in-the-loop type of simulation using a JTAG interface. The system set-up is illustrated in Fig. 4.

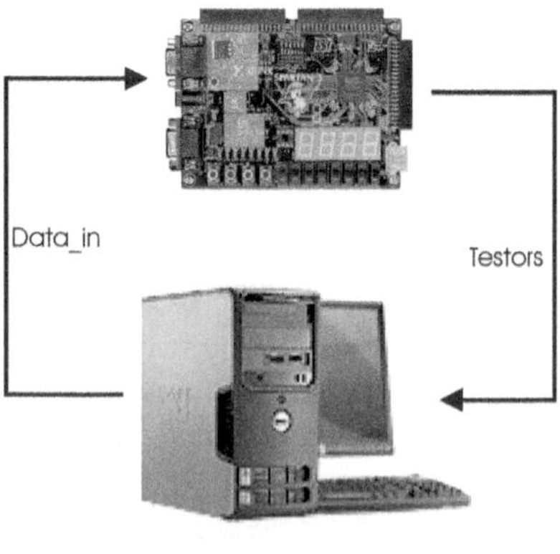

Fig. 4. System set-up

Although the synthesis results show that the architecture can operate up to 87MHz, the clock oscillator on the board is limited to an operating frequency of 50MHz. Thus the reported results were calculated considering the latter frequency.

4.1 Results

In order to show the performance of the proposed architecture it was compared against software implementations of the original BT algorithm, which is an *external scale* algorithm, and the CT algorithm, an *internal scale* algorithm that is one of the most successful algorithms for calculating all typical testors. For the experiments, square matrices from 18 to 30 columns were randomly generated. Figure 5 shows the processing time for the proposed architecture and software implementations of BT and CT for these matrices. For BT and CT we used optimized programs, which implements modifications for performance improvement, such as sorting the matrix [8]. These experiments show that the proposed architecture allows computing all typical testors about 20 times faster that BT and about 3 times faster than CT. The experiments were done on a PC with an Intel Pentium 4 processor running at 2.8GHz with 512MB of RAM memory. In the figure 5, the runtimes of the proposed architecture were estimated for the worst case, where the step 3 of the modified algorithm never happens.

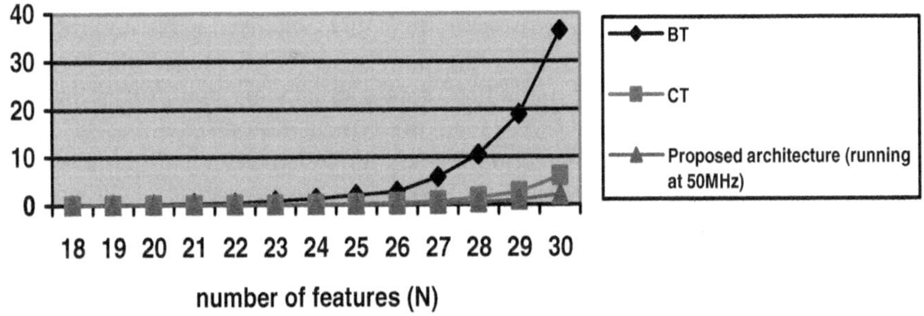

Fig. 5. Processing times in seconds, for several values of *N*

5 Discussion

The proposed architecture provides high performance processing capabilities with low hardware resource utilization. The architecture performs the number of operations needed to know if a value is a testor of the matrix in a single clock cycle. The architecture efficiently stores data in a flexible register like structure. The initial latency period is just *M* clock cycles. The latency arises at the start of processing since the register file must be full before processing can begin.

According to the reported maximum clock frequency from the synthesis process for the case of study, the architecture can operate up to 87MHz. The performance comparison of the architecture is difficult since there are not similar architectures reported in the literature.

The experiments show that the proposed architecture allows computing all typical testors much faster than BT and slightly faster than CT. However, the proposed architecture needs the same time to process any matrix of *N* columns, independently of the number of rows, whereas BT and CT performance will decrease when the number of rows grows.

It is important to highlight that the proposed architecture compute testors and the decision about which of them are typical has to be make after each testor is found (as in BT).

Even though the proposed architecture is a first approach to computing testors and typical testors in a reconfigurable intensive computing special architecture, it allows computing testors and typical testors much faster than following a similar strategy by a computer program, and for problems with not too many features, it is faster than the most sophisticated algorithms for computing typical testors.

6 Conclusions

In this work, an efficient hardware implementation of a testor identification algorithm was presented. The high performance of the proposed architecture was feasible due to the high level of parallelism implicit in the BT algorithm that can be efficiently implemented on the FPGA.

As future work, a number of optimizations are being considered for to further improve the performance. Such optimizations include modifying the control unit for implementing steps 2-4 of the BT algorithm in order to reduce the number of candidates to be verified, and including a post-processing unit for reducing the number of testors, which would speed up the typical testor selection. In addition, because the architecture resource requirements are relatively small, a new scheme where the processing core can be replicated is also explored; this will effectively reduce the processing times proportionally to the number of processing cores that can be accommodated on the FPGA device. Early results show that a state-of-the-art Virtex-4 XCE4LX200 FPGA [7] could accommodate 100+ processing cores and run up to 190MHz, potentially resulting on 380x processing time improvement over CT runtimes. Another research direction is exploring the construction of architectures for implementing more sophisticated *external scale* algorithms like LEX [9], which follows a different search order.

References

1. Martínez-Trinidad J. F. and Guzmán-Arenas A. "The logical combinatorial approach to pattern recognition an overview through selected works", Pattern Recognition, Vol 34, No. 4, pp. 741-751, 2001.
2. Lazo-Cortes M., Ruiz-Shulcloper J. and Alba-Cabrera E. "An overview of the evolution of the concept of testor", Pattern Recognition, Vol. 34, No. 4, pp. 753-762, 2001.
3. Dmitriev A.N., Zhuravlev Y.I., Krendeliev F.P. "About mathematical principles of objects and phenomena classification", Diskretni Analiz Vol 7, pp. 3-15, 1966. (In Russian).
4. Spartan-3 Data sheet. Available at www.xilinx.com.

5. Martin Gomez, "Hardware-in-the-Loop Simulation", Embedded Systems Programming, Vol. 14, No. 13, December 2001.
6. Spartan-3 Starter Board Data Sheet. Available at www.digilentinc.com.
7. Virtex-4 Data sheet. Available at www.xilinx.com.
8. Sánchez Díaz G. and Lazo Cortés M., "Modifying BT Algorithm for improving its runtimes", Revista Ciencias Matemáticas. Vol. 20, No. 2, pp. 129-136. ISSN: 0256-5374, 2002. (In Spanish)
9. Santiesteban-Alganza Y. and Pons-Porrata A., "LEX: a new algorithm for computing typical testors" Revista Ciencias Matemáticas. Vol. 21, No. 1, pp. 85-95. ISSN: 0256-5374, 2003. (In Spanish)

Proposal for a Unified Methodology for Evaluating Supervised and Non-supervised Classification Algorithms

Salvador Godoy-Calderón [1], J. Fco. Martínez-Trinidad [2], and Manuel Lazo Cortés [3]

[1] Center for Computing Research, IPN, Mexico
sgodoyc@prodigy.net.mx
[2] Computer Science Department, INAOE, Puebla, Mexico
fmartine@inaoep.mx
[3] Pattern Recognition Group, ICIMAF, Havana, Cuba
mlazo@icmf.inf.cu

Abstract. There is presently no unified methodology that allows the evaluation of supervised and non-supervised classification algorithms. Supervised problems are evaluated through *Quality Functions* that require a previously known solution for the problem, while non-supervised problems are evaluated through several *Structural Indexes* that do not evaluate the classification algorithm by using the same pattern similarity criteria embedded in the classification algorithm. In both cases, a lot of useful information remains hidden or is not considered by the evaluation method, such as the quality of the supervision sample or the structural change generated by the classification algorithm on the sample. This paper proposes a unified methodology to evaluate classification problems of both kinds, that offers the possibility of making comparative evaluations and yields a larger amount of information to the evaluator about the quality of the initial sample, when it exists, and regarding the change produced by the classification algorithm.

1 Introduction

When one works in pattern recognition, whether in field applications or in research, it is a common need to evaluate the result of a classification algorithm [1-4]. On many occasions the objective of such evaluation is, either to study the behavior of the classification algorithm used, or to establish the appropriateness of applying such algorithm to the type of problem being evaluated. Classification problems may be shown in three different ways [5] known as s*upervised* problems, p*artially-supervised* problems and *non-supervised* problems. Unfortunately, nowadays there is no methodology that allows us to evaluate, under the same criteria, the action of an algorithm in any of the forms of a problem.

A classification problem is informally called supervised when there is previous knowledge (called supervision sample or learning information) on the classes or categories into which it is possible to classify the objects or patterns being studied.

A classification problem is considered non-supervised when such previous knowledge does not exist. In that case, the problem starts with a universe of patterns without structure that must be classified. Finally, the other form that a classification problem

J.F. Martínez-Trinidad et al. (Eds.): CIARP 2006, LNCS 4225, pp. 674 – 685, 2006.

can adopt is an intermediate state between supervised and non-supervised problems. A classification problem is considered partially-supervised when the previous knowledge regarding the nature of its solution is partial.

2 Traditional Evaluation Methods

In order to evaluate supervised problems, the classification algorithm is applied to a test sample and its result is compared with a previously known solution considered as valid [3,4]. This comparison is made by means of a *Quality Function* that generates a score, which is typically a real number, that synthesizes the evaluation of the problem and thus measures the performance of the classification algorithm.

In many cases, simple quality functions, such as the following, are applied: Let A be a supervised classification algorithm and let $\Phi(A)$ be the quality function that evaluates it and which expression is $\Phi_1(A) = x/(x+y+z)$, where x is the number of patterns correctly classified by the algorithm, y is the number of patterns incorrectly classified, z is the number of abstentions. Other times, much more detailed quality functions are applied, such as $\Phi_2(A) = \frac{1}{n}\left(\sum_{i=1}^{k}\sum_{i=}^{k}\alpha_{ij}E_{ij} + \sum_{s=1}^{k}\beta_s A_s\right)$, where: n is the total number of patterns in the control sample, k is the number of classes in the problem, α_{ij} is the amount of objects that belong to class i, mistakenly classified in class j, E_{ij} is the specific weighting of the mistake counted in α_{ij}, β_s is the amount of objects that belong to class i in which the algorithms refrained from classifying, and A_s is the specific weight of the error counted in β_s.

Of course, the decision regarding the quality function to be used in the evaluation of a specific problem depends largely on the conditions and semantics of the problem, so there is an infinite amount of possible quality functions. Regardless of how complex the selected quality function may be, the result of the evaluation is always expressed with only one number, which hides the details and the specific reasons for the assigned classification.

In the case of non-supervised problems, there is no explicit formula to evaluate the quality of the classification algorithm. However, opposite to what happens in the supervised case, the idea of measuring the quality of the resulting covering in terms of its structural conditions [6] is quite common. The structural aspects evaluated in a covering are several, but commonly aspects considered include the compacting of clusters, the separation between clusters, the max and min degree of membership of each cluster, etc. (See [7,8]).

Several indexes have been proposed to evaluate partitions and coverings. Three of the more widely used are the *Partition Coefficient* and the *Entropy index* proposed by Bezdek [9], and the *Xie-Beni index*[6]. Let us examine each one of them.

For a non-supervised classification problem, with n patterns and with k being the pre-determined number of classes to be formed, Bezdek defines the partition coefficient (*PC*) in [9] as $PC = \sum_{i=1}^{n}\sum_{j=1}^{k}(\mu_{ij})/n$, with μ_{ij} being the membership of pattern i to class j. Under the same assumptions, Bezdek also defines the partition entropy (*PE*) as $PE = \sum_{i=1}^{n} \sum_{j=1}^{k} \left(\mu_{ij} \log\left(\mu_{ij} \right) \right) / n$. The main disadvantage of these indexes, as Bezdek himself states in [9] is that they evaluate each class by considering exclusively the degrees of membership assigned to the patterns and not their (geometric) structure or the structure of the whole covering. X. L. Xie and G. Beni proposed an index that evaluated two structural aspects: the *Compactation* and the *Separation* of the classes [6]. For them, an optimum partition is that which has a strong compacting and a noticeable separation between clusters. Therefore, they proposed the compacting measure as $\Psi = \sum_{i=1}^{k} \sum_{j=1}^{n} \mu_{ij} \left\| x_j - v_i \right\|^2$ with v_i being the centroid of each class. The second factor then represents the Euclidean norm of the difference between each object and the corresponding centroid in each class. The separation between classes, is calculated as $\Xi = n \left(\underbrace{\min}_{i \neq k} \left\| v_i - v_k \right\|^2 \right)$. Lastly, the Xie-Beni (*XB*) index is formed as the quotient of these two quantities, i.e., $XB = \Psi / \Xi$.

Like in the case of supervised problems, all of these structural indexes limit their evaluation to only one number which, in this case, represents the quality of the structuring in the solution covering generated by the classification algorithm.

Most authors do not even consider partially-supervised problems as a different category of problems [10]. These problems are treated as supervised in what regards the evaluation of the classification algorithms. Therefore, in the rest of this paper, no explicit reference will be made to partially-supervised problems and the same conditions of supervised problems will be assumed for them.

3 Advantages and Disadvantages of Traditional Evaluation Methods

The most evident advantage of evaluating supervised problems through quality functions is the flexibility of the latter. The researcher can build a quality function as thorough as the problem requires, and one that can encompass situations of very different kind, such as abstentions of the classifying algorithm or a different weighing for each type of error made in assigning memberships. In return for this, the way of evaluating supervised problems has some evident disadvantages. The first and most noticeable one is the need for having a previously known solution for the problem being evaluated, and its consideration as "the correct solution to the problem". This requirement makes it impossible to evaluate problems for which such a solution is not available, and even more: the consideration of such solution as the correct one may cause important biases in the evaluation of the algorithm. There are two main reasons for these biases in the evaluation: first, the quality of the supervision sample used for the evaluated classification algorithm. Second: the quality of the structure induced on the solution covering by the evaluated algorithm is not measured.

Not evaluating the quality of the supervision sample used for a supervised problem seriously limits the ability to judge the action of the classifying algorithm. It is not hard to imagine that a very well built sample (with the more representative patterns of each class) may induce the generation of the same solution even by less precise algorithms, while a poorly built sample (with patterns not very representative of each class) may induce errors or abstentions in the algorithms based on the similarity of patterns. The criteria through which a solution can be selected and considered as correct, are not clear. Should the methodology include any type of measurement of the structure of the solution covering generated by the classification algorithm, the evaluation would not depend so much on the quality of the supervision sample. Nonetheless, the quality function is limited to comparing the membership to each of the classes assigned by the classifying algorithm to each pattern. Lastly, notice that most of the classification algorithms (both for supervised and for non-supervised problems) are based on measuring the similarity between two patterns. The criterion or set of criteria through which the similarity is measured is called *Pattern Analogy Function* and it is evident that in spite of the fact that this function is the most important element for the algorithm, it is in no way considered by the evaluation methodology for supervised problems. In summary, the following disadvantages may be noticed:

1. The quality of the supervision sample is not measured.
2. The structural quality of the solution covering is not measured.
3. The pattern analogy function is not involved in the evaluation.

The way to evaluate non-supervised problems has very different characteristics. The evaluation is made based on the quality of the structure of the solution instead of comparing with a previously known solution is by far the most evident advantage of this method. Unlike what happens with supervised problems, no elements, such as the magnitude of the membership assigned to each pattern or the number of abstentions in which the algorithm incurs are considered (although non-supervised classification algorithms almost never have the possibility of abstaining from classifying any pattern). In general, the elements considered to make the evaluation are precisely those which are not considered in supervised problems. These evaluation methods are radically different in both cases, but the diverse conditions of each type of problem do not allow the indiscriminate use of the respective methods. Nevertheless, in both cases the evaluation of the algorithm is reduced in its expression to only one number which generally hides more information than the one it gives, because it does not allow an analysis of the specific situation of a pattern or category. Therefore, the list of deficiencies of classical methods may be completed as follows:

4. The evaluation is synthesized in only one number which does not allow alternative interpretation.
5. The evaluation methods are not unified for all types of problems.

This leads us to ask the following question: Is it possible to devise an evaluation methodology that can overcome the deficiencies found in the present methods and produces unified criteria to evaluate classification algorithms applied to any type of problem?

4 The Main Definitions and Proposed Methodology

Before presenting the methodology proposed by the authors for the solution of the question mentioned above, we now introduce the three most important theoretical concepts on which the design and methodology are based. These concepts are: the *Covering*, the *Classification Problem* and the *Classification Algorithm*. For a more detailed description see [10].

Let Ω be a known universe of objects under study and let $O \subseteq \Omega$.

Definition 1. A Covering of O is a tuple $(O, \Re, \delta, Q, \pi, C_c, f)$ where O, $\Re$ and Q (called structural sets) are respectively sets of objects, descriptive features for the objects and classes. Components δ and π (called structural relations) are, respectively, description and membership functional relations. The first one describes the objects of O in terms of the features in $\Re$ and the second one assigns to each o_i object a membership to each of the C_j classes. Last, C_c and f are respectively a set of comparison criteria and the pattern analogy function (see [10]).

According to the definition given above, the special types of coverings shown in the following table may be characterized.

Table 1. Types of Coverings.

Covering	Conditions
Total	Every object belongs to a class
Partial	There is an object that does not belong to any class
Blind	No object belongs to any class
Strict	All classes are not empty
Flexible	There is an empty class

Definition 2. A classification problem is a tuple of the form (Z_0, Θ) where Z_0 is an initial cover.

Following definition 2 a problem is supervised if and only if its initial covering is strict; partially supervised if and only if its initial covering is flexible and non-supervised if and only if its initial covering is blind.

Definition 3. A classification algorithm is an algorithm of the form $A(P) = Z_1$ such that, as a parameter, it receives a classification problem (in any of its forms) and delivers a total final covering which is the solution to this problem.

When the design of this evaluation methodology was made, two general objectives were established: 1) to generate a unified methodology for all types of classification problems, and 2) to keep the advantages of each classical method, but to overcome their disadvantages. According to the definitions of the previous section, the methodology designed to evaluate classification algorithms is based on the structural comparison between the initial covering of a problem and the final covering generated as a solution by the classifying algorithm. Such a comparison can always be made, even in cases in which one of the two compared coverings is a blind covering (as in the case of an initial covering in non-supervised problems). The comparison of all types of properties in the covering that involve the membership of patterns to classes and the similarity between them, in accordance with the analogy function between patterns is considered as a structural comparison.

The proposed evaluation methodology obviously starts with the application of the classifying algorithm to the problem being solved. From that moment on, the evaluation process is developed in the following three stages:

Stage 1 (Structural Analysis of the coverings) During this stage the initial and final coverings of the problem are analyzed separately, calculating for each of them the same set of structural properties. These properties are discussed in detail in a later section. The analysis takes place at three levels for each covering:

Level of the Objects: The structural properties are calculated for each object, making reference to each class in the covering.

Level of the Classes: The values corresponding to each of the structural properties in the patterns that form the support of each class are accumulated and averaged.

Level of the Covering: The indexes for the structural properties for the covering under study are calculated.

Stage 2 (Comparison between Coverings) The difference in the value of each one of the structural properties calculated for each covering during the previous stage is calculated. The calculated set of differences is called *Difference Tuple* and it is the score assigned to the classifying algorithm. This tuple expresses the structural change generated by the classifying algorithm in the initial covering of the problem.

Stage 3 (Interpretation of the Score) Once we have the partial results of each of the previous stages, particularly those corresponding to the three levels of structural analysis of the coverings, the researcher interprets the obtained score.

Unlike classical methods, the one proposed here refrains from reducing the evaluation process to only one final score that hides the details involved in the evaluation process. The partial results obtained in each stage are valuable sources of information for the researcher, where he can study particular situations regarding the problem being solved. Another distinctive characteristic of this methodology is the fact that it is useful independently of the quantity and selection of the structural properties calculated during the first stage. Sometimes the researcher may be interested in using a specific set of structural properties, according to the characteristics of the problem under study. For this reason, the methodology described above was introduced without any reference to the specific properties used in the analysis of coverings. In this sense, the set of structural properties that have been used and are described in the next section are shown for the sole purpose of clarifying all of the elements involved in the methodology. Nonetheless, the researcher is free to use the set of properties that he deems to be more adequate for his particular study.

5 Application Details

For the structural analysis stage, only four properties, considered as determining factors in the structure of a covering, are calculated:

The *Tipicity* (T) of an o_i object, with regard to a C_j class, understood as the degree to which the object is representative of such class and it is calculated as follows:

$$T(o_i, C_j) = \sum f(o_i, o_s)\pi(o_s, C_j) / |Sop(C_j)|$$

where $f(o_i,o_s)$ is the similarity between the objects (calculated by the pattern analogy function), $\pi(o_s, C_j)$ is the membership of the o_i object to the C_j class, $|Sop(C_j)|$ is the cardinality of support of the C_j class.

The *Contrast* (*C*) of an o_i object with regard to a C_j class, understood as the degree to which the object is representative of all of the other classes in the covering is defined as:

$$C(o_i, C_j) = \sum_{Cs \neq Cj} T(o_i, C_s) / k - 1$$

where $T(o_i,C_s)$ is the tipicity of the o_i object, in the C_j class, and k is the total number of classes in the covering.

The *Discrimination Error* (ε) of an o_i object with regard to a C_j class, understood as the degree of confusion of the object in the covering is defined as:

$$\varepsilon(o_i, C_j) = \sum_{Cs \neq Cj} \pi(o_i, C_{js})$$

where $\pi(o_i, C_{js})$ is the degree of membership of o_i to the intersection of the C_j and C_s classes.

The *Characterization Error* (γ) of an o_i object with regard to a C_j class, understood as the difference between the belonging of the object to the class and its Tipicity in this same class is defined as:

$$\gamma(o_i, C_j) = |\pi(o_i, C_j) - T(o_i, C_j)|$$

During the analysis at the level of the classes, each of these structural properties is averaged in the analyzed class. During the analysis at the level of the covering, the structural indexes corresponding to each property are calculated. In every case, the index is calculated as one minus the corresponding property averaged in the whole covering.

Striving to give this methodology the same flexibility shown by the quality functions in supervised problems, a special technique for the structural analysis of the coverings during the first stage was developed. This technique consists of adding to each covering an additional class which represents the complementing set for the rest of the classes in the covering and then calculating all the structural properties, also regarding this class. In the initial covering of a problem all of the patterns that are not classified will be considered to have maximum membership to the complementing class. This technique allows the proposed analysis to account for the abstentions incurred by the classification algorithm although, evidently, without achieving the same degree of flexibility achieved by the quality functions.

6 Experimental Results

In order to test the designed methodology, we used the famous *IrisData* set consisting of 150 Iris flowers, described by 4 features (length and width of petals and sepals, all measures in centimeters) and grouped in 3 classes called *Iris Setosa*, *Iris Versicolor* and *Iris Virginica* (See [11]). This data set was used to evaluate two different algorithms: a (supervised) simple voting algorithm and the (non-supervised) Fuzzy C-Means algorithm. Two experiments were performed with the supervised algorithm, one of them with a very well built training sample and the other one with a badly built one. In the non-supervised case the algorithm was simply applied to the whole Iris-Data set to study the solution covering generated. In every experiment, the action of the classification algorithm was evaluated with the traditional methods as well as with the proposed methodology, and both evaluations were compared.

Table 2. Training samples for the supervised experiments

Well-built sample:

Iris Setosa					Iris Versicolor					Iris Virginica				
object No.	length & width Petals		length & width Sepals		object No.	length & width Petals		length & width Sepals		object No.	length & width Petals		length & width Sepals	
27	5	3.4	1.6	0.4	84	6.0	2.7	5.1	1.6	117	6.5	3.0	5.5	1.8
8	5	3.4	1.5	0.2	56	5.7	2.8	4.5	1.3	148	6.5	3.0	5.2	2.0
24	5.1	3.3	1.7	0.5	64	6.1	2.9	4.7	1.4	104	6.3	2.9	5.6	1.8
29	5.2	3.4	1.4	0.2	74	6.1	2.8	4.7	1.2	138	6.4	3.1	5.5	1.8
40	5.1	3.4	1.5	0.2	79	6.0	2.9	4.5	1.5	105	6.5	3.0	5.8	1.8

Badly-built sample:

Iris Setosa					Iris Versicolor					Iris Virginica				
object No.	length & width Petals		length & width Sepals		object No.	length & width Petals		length & width Sepals		object No.	length & width Petals		length & width Sepals	
16	5.7	4.4	1.5	0.4	94	5	2.3	3.3	1	107	4.9	2.5	4.5	1.7
42	4.5	2.3	1.3	0.3	58	4.9	2.4	3.3	1	110	7.2	3.6	6.1	2.5
15	5.8	4	1.2	0.2	51	7	3.2	4.7	1.4	114	5.7	2.5	5	2
82	5.5	2.4	3.7	1	22	5.1	3.7	1.5	0.4	25	4.8	3.4	1.9	0.2
121	6.9	3.2	5.7	2.3	113	6.8	3	5.5	2.1	80	5.7	2.6	3.5	1

In the supervised experiments, both training samples consisted of five objects representing each class. For the well-built case the five objects with more intra-class similarity were selected and for the badly-built case, each class was represented by the three less intra-similar objects and two more objects randomly selected from the other two classes. Both samples are shown in table 2.

Table 3. Traditional evaluation for the two supervised experiments

	$\Phi_1(A)$	$\Phi_2(A)$
Case 1 well-formed sample	0.793	0.854
Case 2 badly-formed sample	0.760	0.837

The two quality functions $\Phi_1(A)$ and $\Phi_2(A)$ introduced in section 2 were used for the traditional evaluation of these supervised experiments. When the rest of the objects not contained in the training sample were submitted for classification, the supervised algorithm produced, for each experiment, the results shown in table 3.

Notoriously, in both cases, the traditional evaluation showed very similar results for the well-built and the badly-built samples. This can only be explained due to the restrictive nature of evaluation methodology using quality functions. This traditional evaluation method measures only the degree of matching between the results obtained by the algorithm and the results contained in the previously known solution. All other aspects of the evaluation are not taken into account, including the quality of the test sample.

In contrast, the unified methodology proposed herein measures the structural quality of both the initial and final coverings on the problem. As stated in section 4, this unified methodology unfolds over three stages. During stage #1 both coverings (initial and final) are analyzed separately and the four structural properties introduced in section 5 are calculated for each one (tipicity, contrast, discrimination and characterization). Since the analysis of each covering takes place at three levels (objects, classes and covering), this stage produces very large tables of intermediate results. These tables are not included in this paper for space reasons. During stage #2, the analysis of both coverings is compared and the Difference Tuples depicted in table 4 are produced.

Table 4. Unified methodology results for the supervised experiments

Case 1 (well-built sample):

T	C	ε	γ
-0.213	-0.016	-0.299	-0.114

Case 2 (badly-built sample):

T	C	ε	γ
-0.038	-0.196	-0.411	+0.342

Finally, during stage #3 the difference tuples are interpreted. The interpretation of these results indicates that by establishing the quality of the initial sample given to the algorithm, the unified methodology manages to evaluate both cases in a notoriously different way. The above results show the structural change produced by the algorithm between the initial and final coverings of each experiment. Interpreting each index of the above table the following observations may be stated:

1. The Tipicity index (T) was reduced reduced much more in the well-built case than in the badly-built one. This means that in the first case the quality of the training sample was so high that the algorithm did not manage to group the rest of the objects with the same representativity in each class. By contrast, in the second case the quality of the sample was low enough that the algorithm kept almost the same covering quality while classifying the rest of the objects.
2. The Contrast index (C) had the expected opposite behavior of the tipicity index, meaning that classified objects kept to be equally representative to all classes in the first case but not in the second one.
3. The Discrimination index (ε) reduction in the second case nearly doubled that of the first case. This means that, after applying the classification algorithm in the second case, the resulting covering has more overlapping in its memberships than the first case. This is an expected result if one considers the quality of the respective samples and the behavior of the tipicity and contrast indexes.

4. The Characterization index (γ) shows the most dramatic change by reducing its value in the first case and growing considerably in the second case. This is also the most unexpected and significant result of this evaluation. In the first case the slight reduction is explained because of the high quality of the training sample. In the second case, the classification algorithm behaves very consistently with the low inter-class similarity of the objects contained in the sample, so by classifying the rest of the objects it reduces the average difference between the membership and the tipicity of all objects.

These arguments lead to the following conclusion: the supervised algorithm used in this experiments is highly sensitive to the quality of the initial sample, especially to the inter-class similarity of the objects. The proposed evaluation methodology allows the researcher to consider different structural aspects that the traditional evaluation methods hide when synthesizing to only one number. This evaluation takes into account both, the structure of the initial and final coverings in the problem, and the change induced by the classification algorithm separately.

In order to traditionally evaluate the non-supervised experiment, the *PE* and *XB* indexes were used yielding the results shown in table 5.

Table 5. Traditional evaluation for the non-supervised experiment

	PE	*XB*
non-supervised experiment	0.157	0.395

The low partition entropy is a good score for the classification algorithm and it means that the final covering has a very clear structure. Nevertheless the middle-range magnitude of the *XB* index indicates an unbalanced ratio between compactation and separation among classes. So these indexes are not very consistent with each other.

For this experiment, the proposed methodology overcomes the inconsistency of the structural indexes and their inability to evaluate by using the same pattern analogy function used by the classification algorithm. Again, the unified methodology unfolds over its three stages and once more the tables containing intermediate results for stage #1 are not shown. Stage #2 (comparison between coverings) yields the difference tuple shown in table 6.

Table 6. Unified methodology results for the non-supervised experiment

T	C	ε	γ
+0.421	+0.421	+0.883	+0.815

During stage #3 the interpretation of each index in the same way as it was done in the supervised experiments, leads to the following observations:

1. In contrast with the supervised experiments, the change in all indexes has a positive magnitude. This is to be expected since the initial covering was blind and so it had no structure.

2. The growth in tipicity and contrast is exactly the same. Also the growth in discrimination and characterization is very similar and notoriously high.
3. Tipicity and contrast are consistent with each other, and they mean that the classification algorithm produces an increase in the tipicity of all classes almost in 42%.
4. Discrimination and characterization are also consistent with each other and they indicate that the algorithm produces 80% more distinguishable objects with 80% more consistency between their tipicity and their membership in each class.
5. The pattern analogy function used by the algorithm is also used in the calculation of each of the four indexes.

In summary, this experiment shows that the consistency of interpretation among the four structural indexes is far superior to that of other structural indexes used in traditional evaluation methods, and that each calculation uses the same pattern analogy function employed by the classification algorithm. So, the methodology proposed herein showed that it fulfills its design objectives and at the same time, it gives more information and flexibility to the researcher.

7 Conclusions

Comparison between the initial and final coverings of a problem allow the evaluation of the behavior of the classifying algorithm independently from other circumstantial factors in the problem, such as the quality of the control sample in the case of supervised problems. Thanks to the definitions previously established, such comparison is a common element between supervised and non-supervised problems and unifies the evaluation methodology.

The specification of what is meant by structural properties allows us to include in the analysis of the coverings both, the basic elements considered by the quality functions (membership assigned to each pattern in each class), and those considered by most of the structural indexes with which non-supervised problems are evaluated. At the same time, the main disadvantages of classic methodologies are avoided. Notoriously, the discussed methodology neither requires a previously known solution to the problem, nor evaluates the algorithm by considering such solution as a reference point.

The flexibility of the discussed methodology may be seen in two main aspects: first, the possibility of changeing the set of structural properties to be used during the analysis of the coverings, and second, the possibility of accounting for the abstentions of the classifying algorithm by using the complementing class technique.

References

1. Fukunaga, K., Hayes, R.R. Estimation of classifier performance, IEEE Transactions on Pattern Analysis and Machine Intelligence, 11(10), 1087 – 1101, 1989.
2. Berikov V., Litvinenko A. The influence of prior knowledge on the expected performance of a classifier. Pattern Recognition Letters, 24, 15, 2537 – 2548, 2003.

3. Fawcett, T. An introduction to ROC analysis. Pattern Recognition Letters, 27, 8, 861-874, 2006.
4. Arbel, R., Rokach, L. Classifier evaluation under limited resources. Pattern Recognition Letters. 2006 Available online.
5. Martínez-Trinidad, J.F., Guzman-Arenas A. The logical combinatorial approach to Pattern Recognition an overview through selected works. Pattern Recognition, 34, 4, 1-11, 2001.
6. Xie, X.L., Beni, G. A validity measure for fuzzy clustering. IEEE Transactions on Pattern Analysis and Machine Intelligence, 13(8), 841-847 ,1991.
7. Lee-Kwang, H., Song, Y.S., Lee, K.M. Similarity measure between fuzzy sets and between elements. Fuzzy Sets and Systems 62, 291-293, 1994.
8. Dae-Won, K., Kwang, H.L., Doheon, L. On cluster validity index for estimation of the optimal number of fuzzy clusters. Pattern Recognition 37, 2009-2025, 2004.
9. Bezdek, J.C. Cluster validity with fuzzy sets. Journal of Cybernetics, 3, 58-73, 1974.
10. Godoy-Calderón, S., Lazo-Cortés, M., Martínez-Trinidad, J.F. A non-classical view of Coverings and its implications in the formalization of Pattern Recognition problems. WSEAS Transactions on Mathematics, 2, 1-2, 60-66, 2003.
11. Bezdek J. C., Keller M. J., Krishnapuram R. *Will the Real Iris Data Please Stand Up?.* IEEE Transactions on Fuzzy Systems, 7, 3, 368-369, 1999.

Monte Carlo Evaluation of the Hausdorff Distance for Shape Matching

Arturo Perez-Garcia, Victor Ayala-Ramirez,
Raul E. Sanchez-Yanez, and Juan-Gabriel Avina-Cervantes

Universidad de Guanajuato FIMEE
Tampico 912, 36730, Salamanca, Mexico
{ayalav, sanchezy, avina}@salamanca.ugto.mx

Abstract. In this work, we present a Monte Carlo approach to compute Hausdorff distance for locating objects in real images. Objects are considered to be only under translation motion. We use edge points as the features of the model. Using a different interpretation of the Hausdorff distance, we show how image similarity can be measured by using a randomly sub-sampled set of feature points. As a result of computing the Hausdorff distance on smaller sets of features, our approach is faster than the classical one. We have found that our method converges toward the actual Hausdorff distance by using less than 20 % of the feature points. We show the behavior of our method for several fractions of feature points used to compute Hausdorff distance. These tests let us conclude that performance is only critically degraded when the subsampled set has a cardinality under 15 % of the total feature points in real images.

1 Introduction

Shape matching is necessary for several robotic vision tasks such as visual object tracking and visual servoing [1]. Locating a model in an image consists in, given a template composed by a set of features that characterize an object, determining its position and pose in a target image. A pose is the set of parameters, e.g., size and orientation, that defines the object appearance in the image under test. Many methods have been developed for model based recognition (for example, Zitova [2] and Zhang [3] present recent surveys). A non exhaustive list includes correlation methods, template matching, frequential methods and scale-space methods. Each approach has its advantages and drawbacks in view of the specific application.

Hausdorff distance [4] is a similarity measure between two sets of points issued from a feature extraction step. Features like line segments [5], curves and skeletons[6], edge points and salient points [7] have been used for image matching. In our work, we use the edge points as features of the model obtained by applying a Canny-like edge operator. We can compare how similar is our model to a region in the image under test. If we use an exhaustive search approach, we need to look at all the possible positions and at each location, all the possible

J.F. Martínez-Trinidad et al. (Eds.): CIARP 2006, LNCS 4225, pp. 686–695, 2006.

poses of our model in the zone where the model could be present in the image under test. Recent applications of Hausdorff distance for shape matching include face detection and tracking [8]. Medical image registration also uses Hausdorff distance techniques for kidney images acquired using CT devices [9]. A generic object tracking framework is presented by Polat [10]. Another application addressed recently using Hausdorff distance-based methods is image retrieval [11].

Main drawback of Hausdorff distance is the high computational complexity involved in its calculation. When the object model presents some transformation in the test image, some works report search times up to $6s$ [4]. We need then to implement some heuristics to reduce necessary time for locating the object in an image. Monte Carlo techniques [12] enable us to compute static properties of models by using only a fraction of the points (chosen in a random manner) where these properties apply. Computing the static properties with randomly sampled points reduces the computational load. The only question consist in how to determine if the value converges toward the value computed using all the points where the property holds. Monte Carlo techniques have been used previously in Hausdorff-based shape matching for the generation of outlier shapes by Boykov in the testing of a Bayesian recognition method [13] and for the reduction of an affine transformation parameter space search by Jian-qiu [14].

Our approach is to use Monte Carlo sampling to obtain a pattern with a lesser number of feature points and to apply Hausdorff-based shape matching on the sampled patterns. We have applied this approach and experimentally we have found that it converges by using only a small fraction $f = 0.12$ of the points composing the original model. Rest of this paper is organized as follows: In Section 2, we present the formal definition of Hausdorff distance and an alternative interpretation of it. This analysis leads in Section 3 to define the Monte Carlo version that we propose. Test and results for our experimental validation related to the convergence of the proposed approach are found in Section 4. Finally, our conclusions and perspectives are presented in Section 5.

2 Hausdorff Distance and an Alternative Interpretation

2.1 Hausdorff Distance Formulation

Hausdorff distance is computed as follows:

Given two set of points $A = \{a_1, \ldots, a_p\}$ and $B = \{b_1, \ldots, b_q\}$, Hausdorff distance $H(A, B)$ is:

$$H(A, B) = max(h(A, B), h(B, A)) \tag{1}$$

where $h(A, B) = \underset{a \epsilon A}{max}\, \underset{b \epsilon B}{min} \|a - b\|$ and $\|.\|$ is a two-dimensional Hilbert metric applied to points a and b.

The function $h(A, B)$ is named the forward Hausdorff distance from A to B and defines the point $a \,\epsilon\, A$ that is farther from any point in B according to the norm $\| \cdot \|$. Distance $h(B, A)$ is known as the reverse Hausdorff distance. Thus, Hausdorff distance $H(A, B)$ is the maximum between $h(A, B)$ and $h(B, A)$.

In computer vision tasks, sets A and B are usually named M and I, standing for the model set and the image set respectively. Rest of this paper will use this notation.

2.2 Alternative Interpretation of the Hausdorff Distance

Let us define distance d_m^f as follows:

$$d_m^f = \min_{i \in I} \|m - i\| \quad for\ all\ m \in M \tag{2}$$

Thus d_m^f is the minimal distance from the point $m \in M$ to any point $i \in I$. We have then for the computation of h(M,I) a decreasing ordered set of distances, called D^f, such that:

$$D^f = \{d_0^f, d_1^f, \ldots, d_p^f\} \tag{3}$$

where p is the cardinality of M; (i.e., $p = \sharp(M)$) and in a similar way, we define distance d^r from the point $i \in I$ to any point $m \in M$. We have then for the computation of h(I,M) a decreasing ordered set of distances, called D^r, such that:

$$D^r = \{d_0^r, d_1^r, \ldots, d_q^r\} \tag{4}$$

$q = \sharp(I)$. Evaluation of Hausdorff distance can be interpreted according to these two sets D^f and D^r where, The Hausdorff distance (Equation 1) can be redefined as:

$$H(M, I) = max(d_0^f, d_0^r) \tag{5}$$

3 Monte Carlo Hausdorff Distance (MCHD)

3.1 Random Sampling for the Hausdorff Distance Evaluation

Hausdorff distance is a very time demanding method. Even if some works have proposed optimizations for computing the current pose of the model [15,16], computational load remains heavy specially when considered for dynamical vision applications as visual servoing, where $4\,Hz$ operating frequencies are typical. The proposed method evaluates the Hausdorff distance by using a Monte Carlo approach. This method provide, in one hand, efficiency because we will compute the similarity property between a model M and an image I by using only a randomly sampled points subset for each model. In the other hand, our method is robust because we can overcome some of the problems associated with model based recognition methods as a result of random sampling.

Let us consider the sets $I_{MC} \subset I$ and $M_{MC} \subset M$. The sets I_{MC} and M_{MC} are random samples of cardinality n taken using an uniform probability sampling function from the sets I and M, respectively. Thus, we can also say:

$$\lim_{n \to p} I_{MC} = I \tag{6}$$

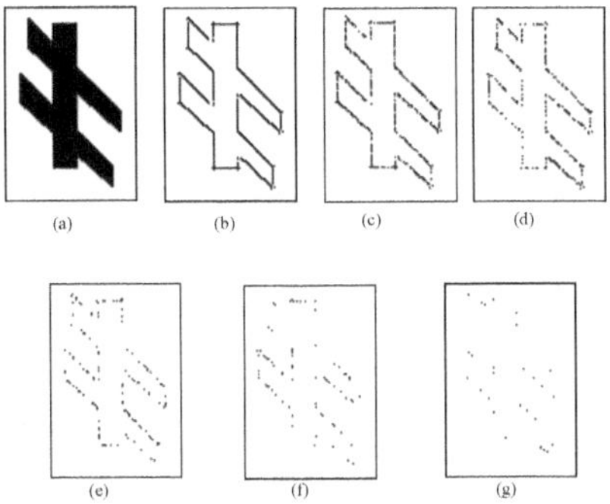

Fig. 1. (a) A synthetic target, (b) its edges, (c) the sampled edges using 75 %, (d) 50 %, (e) 25%, (f) 15 % and (g) 5 % of the feature points

$$\lim_{n \to q} M_{MC} = M \tag{7}$$

Probability of a point belonging to the random sample subset is defined by the ratio of points being kept to the total number of feature points in the I and M sets. For each feature point in both sets, we decide to include it in the sampled subset by using a random number ζ chosen from a uniform distribution in $[0, 1]$. The feature point will be included in the Monte Carlo sampled subset if $0 \leq \zeta < th$, th being a *a priori* chosen threshold.

Figure 1 shows the effect of random sampling for choosing feature points (in this case, edge points). In this example, we use a synthetic image (a) and the resulting edge points models when we use all the edge points (b). The subset M_{MC} is also shown when using (c) 75 %, (d) 50 %, (e) 25 %, (f) 15 % and (g) 5 % of the feature points.

3.2 MCHD Definition

We can define Monte Carlo variants for the forward and reverse Hausdorff distances by using the sub-sampled sets of I and M.

$$h_{MC}(M, I) = h(M_{MC}, I) = \max_{m \epsilon M_{MC}} \min_{i \epsilon I} \|m - i\| \tag{8}$$

$$h_{MC}(I, M) = h(I_{MC}, M) = \max_{i \epsilon I_{MC}} \min_{m \epsilon M} \|i - m\| \tag{9}$$

We define the Monte Carlo Hausdorff Distance (MCHD) as:

$$H_{MC}(M, I) = max(h_{MC}(M, I), h_{MC}(I, M)) \tag{10}$$

If M and I present a perfect matching (as only arises in ideal images) then

$$H_{MC}(M, I) = H(M, I) \tag{11}$$

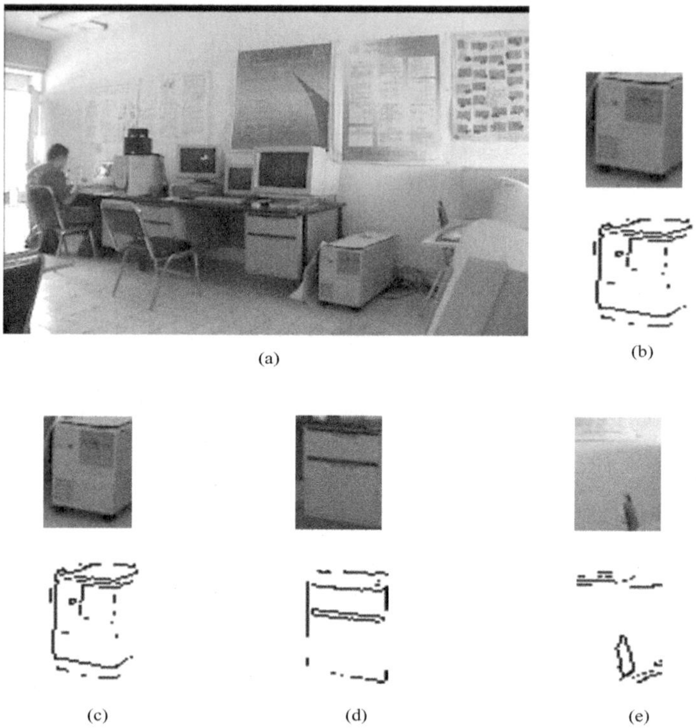

Fig. 2. (a) Image for model selection, (b) the selected model and its feature map, (c) near perfect matching zone, (d) partial matching zone and (e) non matching zone. Images (c), (d) and (e) were taken from a second image acquisition.

regardless of the cardinalities for I_{MC} and M_{MC}. The fraction of points considered for the computation will influence the MCHD estimation when we deal with real images (i.e., images that present different feature maps even in very similar environmental conditions).

For example, in Figure 2, we consider two images where the time interval between acquisitions was approximately 100 ms. Camera position was fixed and the environment had not any mobile objects. This setup let us know ground truth about the object of interest in the scene. We define the model M (shown in Figure 2b) from the first image and we try to locate it in the second one. If we compute $h(M, I)$ in the best matching point (the image zone shown in 2(c)), the value is typically not zero. This behavior is caused mainly by acquisition noise and varying illumination conditions.

We analyze the matching behavior for three cases: i) A near perfect matching, where the model is compared against the image subset located in the same position than the previous model location. These sets of points differ only in the outlier points caused by the imaging artifacts cited above. ii) A partial matching, where we compute the distance between the model zone and the image subset

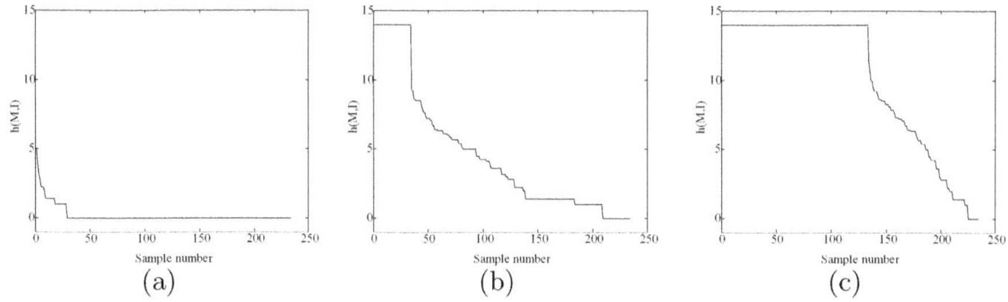

Fig. 3. Graph of the set $\|m - i\|$ for a (a) Correct, (b) Partial and (c) Null matching

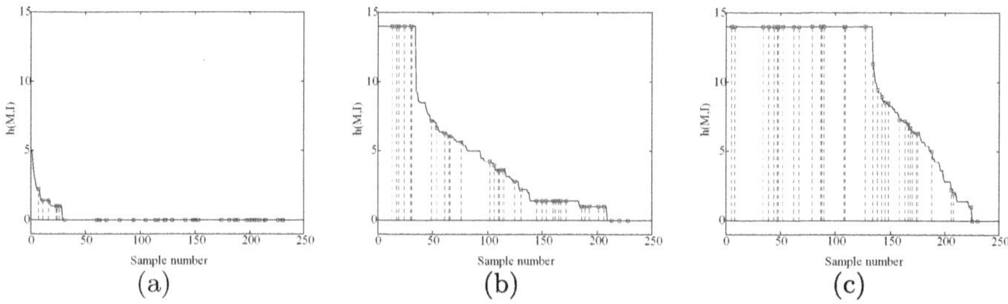

Fig. 4. Selected points belonging to M_{MC} for a (a) near perfect, (b) partial and (c) null matching of the model in the image under test

located on a zone that has a similar feature map than the model zone and iii) A null matching, where the distance between the image zone and the image subset located on a non matching nor similar zone in the image is computed. In each of these cases we have plotted the sorted values of $\|m - i\|$ in decreasing order. Figure 3 shows these plots for: (a) a near perfect matching, (b) a partial matching and (c) a null matching when the original Hausdorff distance definition is used.

Our proposed approach uses randomly sampled subsets of M and I. In Figure 4 we show the randomly selected points to evaluate the Hausdorff distance in a run where we have used only 20 % of the points. In this graph, randomly selected points are marked with a small square and with a vertical dotted line.

Let us consider how the random sampling influences the computation of the Hausdorff distance and the Monte Carlo variants proposed in this paper. Consider again the sets D^f and D^r (defined in Section 2.2).

For the computation of $h_{MC}(M, I)$, we have a set D^f_{MC} such that:

$$D^f_{MC} = \{d^f_{MC_0}, d^f_{MC_1}, \ldots, d^f_{MC_n}\} \tag{12}$$

and for the computation of $h_{MC}(I, M)$, we have a set D^r_{MC} such that:

$$D^r_{MC} = \{d^r_{MC_0}, d^r_{MC_1}, \ldots, d^r_{MC_n}\} \tag{13}$$

where n is the cardinality of the sets M_{MC} and I_{MC}.

We can then apply the alternative interpretation of the Hausdorff distance and obtain the following definition for the Monte Carlo variant of the Hausdorff distance:

Monte Carlo Hausdorff distance (MCHD) is defined as:

$$MCHD(M,I) = max(d^{f}_{MC_0}, d^{r}_{MC_0}) \tag{14}$$

Next section presents how the proposed approach converges toward a useful estimate of Hausdorff distance between a model and a target region in the image under test.

4 Experimental Work

4.1 Convergence Validation of the MCHD

The fraction of points f taken into account for the computation of $H_{MC}(M,I)$ impacts on the precision of the estimation. In this section, we use the cumulative histogram of the D_{MC} and D vectors to show the effect of random sampling in the performance of the computation of Hausdorff distance and the determination of what is a good choice for f.

Each point hic_i in the cumulative histogram $HISC$ is defined as

$$hic_i = \sum_{j=1}^{i} \frac{f_j}{n} \tag{15}$$

Let us consider the cumulative histogram $HISC$ of those points in the D set from $h(M,I)$ and $D_{MC}(M,I)$ from $h_{MC}(M,I)$, from the three cases of matching presented in the previous section.

The cumulative histogram for the set D for the near perfect matching is shown in Figure 5a. In Figure 5d, we have the D $HISC$ for the partial correspondence. The plots in Figure 5b and 5e show $HISC$ for the D_{MC} for the correct and partial matching cases, respectively, but using only 20% of the points. In the histogram in Figure 5a, we can see that the point distribution has a significant upward slope, indicating that the 100% of the points in D has a very small distance value. From this plot we can see that the distance for the 80% of the points is equal to 0. The same tendency is observed in Figure 5b. Plots in Figures 5d and 5e have similarities each other. Because of the cumulative histograms show the tendencies in function of the point percentage, we can over plot the graphs for D and D_{MC}. In Figure 5c, we can observe the histograms in 5a and 5b in the same axes. Plots in Figures 5d and 5e are compared in Figure 5f. From these graphs, we can say that D and D_{MC} follow the same trend in their cumulative histogram. A certain difference between the D_{MC} histogram with respect to the D one is observed in Figures 5c and 5f. Such a deviation depends on the amount of points taken into account.

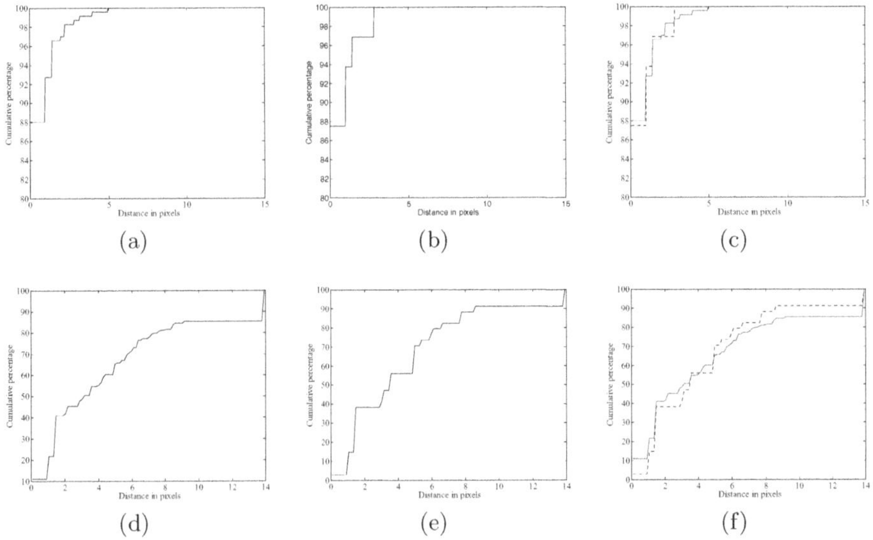

Fig. 5. Cumulative histograms for D and D_{MC}, respectively (a) and (b) for a near perfect matching (d) and (e) for a partial matching. (c) Comparison between histograms (a) and (b). (f) Comparison between histograms (d) and (e).

Figure 6 shows the $HISC$ results using (a) 75%, (b) 25%, (c) 15%, and (d) 5% of the points. We see that the number of points taken for M_{MC} determines the deviation of the D_{MC} $HISC$ from the one for D. Taking the 75% of points, vector D_{MC} has the same tendency than D, but with less points the variation increases. Using the 5% of the points produces a great variation. Such a variation implies a variation in the $H_{MC}(M, I)$ with respect to the $H(M, I)$ value. From Figure 6, we can see that the deviation between (a) and (b) is lower than that between graphs (c) and (d). All the results were estimated as the mean value for 100 experiments in each test. Main conclusion we can infer from these results is that variance of the cumulative histograms augments as we reduce the fraction of points we use to estimate MCHD. Nevertheless, accuracy is only degraded when we use a fraction of points lower than 15 % (Figure 6d). So if we use some $f = 0.15$ we will have an enough accurate estimate of Hausdorff distance but a reduced computation time (only about 15 % of the original computational time).

Applying an evaluation method for determining the Hausdorff distance to the D_{MC} vector, the result can be a lower or an equal distance than the obtained if we would apply such an evaluation to vector D.

$$|h(M, I) - h_{MC}(M, I)| \leq \varepsilon \qquad \varepsilon \geq 0 \tag{16}$$

where ε depends on the amount of points taken into account in the M_{MC} set. The higher the number of points is, the lower the maximum ε will become, but computation time will not be reduced significantly. A design choice has to be made to select f. For example, in an application developed for a robotic object

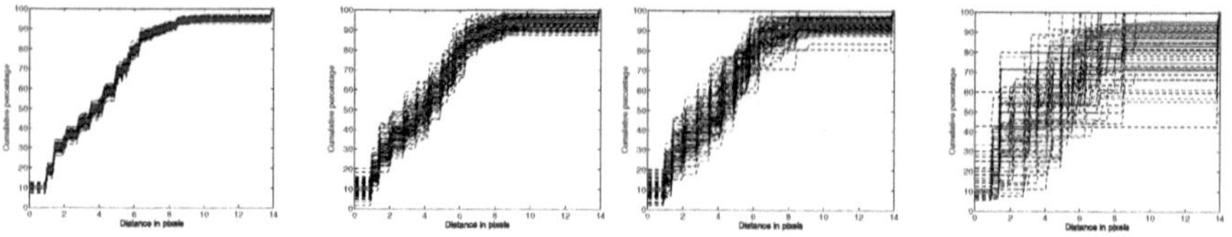

(a) (b) (c) (d)

Fig. 6. Variation of cumulative histograms of D_{MC} with respect to D using (a) 75%, (b) 25%, (c) 15%, and (d) 5% of the points. All data were computed for 100 runs of each case.

tracking and visual servoing system, $f = 0.15$ has shown to be a good choice for successful results.

5 Conclusions and Perspectives

We have presented a method for computing image similarity using a novel approach to compute Hausdorff distance. Our method computes Hausdorff distance on a random subsample of the feature point set and consequently it reduces the computational time needed to compute Hausdorff distance on real images that are linked by a translational transformation. We have shown the trend that follows the cumulative histograms for different fractions of randomly subsampled sets of feature points. We have found that our method's performance critically degrades when use under 15 % of the total of feature points of real images. Over this threshold, our method converges toward the classical Hausdorff distance value but as mentioned before, reducing the computational time needed to compute image similarity.

In the near future, we will also apply the alternative interpretations for the partial (PHD) and modified (MHD) Hausdorff distance in methods similar to the one presented here. That will result in even more substantial time reduction for complexity management in robotic vision tasks using shape matching. Specially, we aim to apply this approaches to dynamic vision problem as the visual tracking and visual servoing problems.

Acknowledgments

This work has been partially funded by the French-Mexican LAFMI Project "Concepción de funciones de percepción y planificación para la navegación topológica de un robot móvil en ambiente semi-estructurado interior o natural", the University of Guanajuato project "Funcionalidades visuales para la navegación topológica de robots móviles" and the Concyteg project "Herramientas Mecatrónicas para la Implementación de Entornos Virtuales".

References

1. Corke, P., Hutchinson, S.: Real time vision, tracking and control. In: Proc. of the Int. Conf. on Robotics and Automation (ICRA'2000). Volume 1., San Francisco, CA., IEEE (2000) 622–629
2. Zitova, B., Flusser, J.: Image registration methods: a survey. Image and Vision Computing **21** (2003) 977–1000
3. Zhang, D., Lu, G.: Review of shape representation and description techniques. Pattern Recognition **37** (2004) 1–19
4. Huttenlocher, D.P., Klanderman, G.A., Rucklidge, W.J.: Comparing images using the Hausdorff distance. IEEE Transactions On Pattern Analysis And Machine Intelligence **15** (1993) 850–863
5. Gao, Y., Leung, M.K.H.: Line segment Hausdorff distance on face matching. Pattern Recognition **35** (2002) 361–371
6. Sebastian, T.B., Kimia, B.B.: Curves vs. skeletons in object recognition. Signal processing **85** (2005) 247–263
7. Ayala-Ramirez, V., Parra, C., Devy, M.: Active tracking based on Hausdorff matching. Conference on Pattern Recognition Proceedings **4** (2000) 706–709
8. Odisio, M., Bailly, G., Elisei, F.: Tracking talking faces with shape and appearance models. Speech Communication **44** (2004) 63–82
9. Rao, M., Stough, J., Chi, Y.Y., Muller, K., Tracton, G., Pizer, S.M., Chaney, E.L.: Comparison of human and automatic segmentations of kidneys from CT images. International Journal of Radiation Oncology*Biology*Physics **61** (2005) 954–960
10. Polat, E., Yeasin, M., Sharma, R.: a 2D-3D model-based object tracking framework. Pattern Recognition **36** (2003) 2127–2141
11. Cinque, L., Giocca, G., Levialdi, S., Pellicano, A., Schettini, R.: Color-based image retrieval using spatial chromatic histograms. Image and Vision Computing **19** (2001) 979–986
12. Thijssen, J.M.: Computational Physics. 1st edn. Cambridge University Press (1999)
13. Boykov, Y., Huttenlocher, D.P.: A new bayesian framework for object recognition. In: Proc. Int. Conf. on Computer Vision and Pattern Recognition CVPR'99. Volume 2., IEEE Computer Society Press (1999) 517–524
14. Jian-qiu, J., Zhang-ye, W., Qun-sheng, P.: Constrained branch-and-bound algorithm for image registration. Journal of Zhejiang University Science **6A suppl. I** (2005) 94–99
15. Ni, M., Tao, Q., Reichenbach, S.E.: MCMC-based peak template matching for GCxGC. IEEE Workshop on Statistical Signal Processing (2003) 514–517
16. Olson, C.F.: A probabilistic formulation for Hausdorff matching. Proceedings Conference on Computer Vision and Pattern Recognition (1998) 150–156

A Fast Probabilistic Model for Hypothesis Rejection in SIFT-Based Object Recognition*

Patricio Loncomilla and Javier Ruiz-del-Solar

Department of Electrical Engineering, Universidad de Chile

Abstract. This paper proposes an improvement over the traditional SIFT-based object recognition methodology proposed by Lowe [3]. This improvement corresponds to a fast probabilistic model for hypothesis rejection (affine solution verification stage), which allows a large reduction in the number of false positives. The new probabilistic model is evaluated in an object recognition task using a database of 100 pairs of images.

1 Introduction

Object recognition approaches based on local invariant features have become increasingly popular and have experienced an impressive development in the last years ([1][3][5][8][11]). Typically, local invariant features are extracted from a test image, then characterized by invariant descriptors and finally matched against a reference database. Most employed local detectors are the Harris detector [2] and the Lowe's sDoG+Hessian detector [3], being the Lowe's detector multiscale and the Harris detector single scale. Best performing affine invariant detectors are the Harris-Affine and the Hessian-Affine [10], but they are too slow to be applied in general-purpose object recognition applications. The most popular and best performing invariant descriptors [9] are the SIFT (Scale Invariant Feature Transform) features [3].

When building real-world object recognition applications as for example robot self-localization systems based on invariant visual landmarks [12] or robot head pose detection systems [6], the algorithm recognition capabilities and processing speed are both important. Lowe's system [3] using the sDoG+Hessian detector, SIFT descriptors and a probabilistic hypothesis rejection stage has acceptable recognition capabilities and works in near real-time (1-3 images per second). However, Lowe's system main drawback is the large number of false positive detections. This is a serious problem when using it in vision tasks that need to process video sequences of images.

For that reason, the aim of this paper is to improve the traditional SIFT-based object recognition method from Lowe, by proposing a fast probabilistic model for hypothesis rejection (affine solution verification stage), which allows a large reduction in the number of false positives. The new probabilistic model is evaluated

* This research was partially supported by FONDECYT (Chile) under Project Number 1061158.

J.F. Martínez-Trinidad et al. (Eds.): CIARP 2006, LNCS 4225, pp. 696 – 705, 2006.

in an object recognition task using a database of 100 pairs of images (UCH100 database).

This article is structured as follows. In section 2 we describe the proposed fast probabilistic model for hypothesis rejection. Experimental results of applying this probabilistic model in the recognition of objects present in real work images (UCH100 database) are presented in section 3. Finally, in section 4 some preliminary conclusions of this work are given.

2 Fast Probabilistic Model for Hypothesis Rejection

As already mentioned Lowe's system use the sDoG+Hessian detector, SIFT descriptors and a probabilistic hypothesis rejection stage. The system is very complex, having several sub-stages (local extrema detection, accurate keypoint localization, orientation assignment, etc.). A detailed description can be found in [3].

One of the main weaknesses of Lowe's algorithm is the use of just a simple probabilistic hypothesis rejection stage, which cannot successful reduce the number of false positives. Lowe's method for calculating a probabilistic model for hypothesis rejection [4] requires that the explicit affine transformation must be known in advance, and that all matches that fall onto the projected region must be counted. Given that the probabilistic model is applied after the matching stage, all bins with more than 4 votes must be full-processed. This computation can slow down the process if the number of bins and matches is large.

In this section an additional fast probability rejection test is proposed. It consists on assigning a probability value to all bins with more than 4 votes, without knowing an explicit transformation. This probability values are calculated directly in the quantized Hough bins space. This allows the rejection of bins with very low probability without the requirement of additional processing.

A general similarity transformation from $\mathbb{R}^2$ to $\mathbb{R}^2$ has the following expression:

$$\begin{bmatrix} x' \\ y' \end{bmatrix} = \begin{bmatrix} e\cos\theta & e\sin\theta \\ -e\sin\theta & e\cos\theta \end{bmatrix} \begin{bmatrix} x \\ y \end{bmatrix} + \begin{bmatrix} t_X \\ t_Y \end{bmatrix} \Leftrightarrow \mathbf{x}' = \mathbf{A}\mathbf{x} + \mathbf{t} \quad (1)$$

A,**t** depend on the $(\Delta x, \Delta y, \Delta\theta, \Delta n)$ differences of the object pose between the two compared images, Δn being the differences in the scale dimension.

A similarity transformation that quantizes the pose difference $(\Delta x, \Delta y, \Delta\theta, \Delta n) = (x_1 - x_2, y_1 - y_2, \theta_1 - \theta_2, n_1 - n_2)$ in bins of size $\left(\frac{L_X}{4}, \frac{L_Y}{4}, 30^\circ, 1\right)$, as a function of integer variables (i, j, k, z), has the following expression [3]:

$$\begin{pmatrix} x' \\ y' \end{pmatrix} = 2^Z \begin{pmatrix} \cos(30^\circ k) & \sin(30^\circ k) \\ -\sin(30^\circ k) & \cos(30^\circ k) \end{pmatrix} \begin{pmatrix} x - 0.25L_X i \\ y - 0.25L_Y j \end{pmatrix} \quad (2)$$

From (1) and (2) we obtain fractional values for (i, j, k, z):

$$i_{FRAC} = \frac{2^{\frac{n_1-n_2}{2}} x_2 - x_1\cos(\theta_1-\theta_2) + y_1\sin(\theta_1-\theta_2)}{(1/4)L_X \times 2^{\frac{n1-n2}{2}}}$$

$$j_{FRAC} = \frac{2^{\frac{n1-n2}{2}} y_2 - y_1\cos(\theta_1-\theta_2) - x_1\sin(\theta_1-\theta_2)}{(1/4)L_Y \times 2^{\frac{n1-n2}{2}}} \tag{3}$$

$$k_{FRAC} = \frac{\theta_1-\theta_2}{30^\circ}$$

$$z_{FRAC} = \frac{n_1-n_2}{2}$$

Each match $(x_1, y_1, \theta_1, n_1) \leftrightarrow (x_2, y_2, \theta_2, n_2)$ has 16 nearest values (i, j, k, z) for which it must vote. It can be observed that (i, j) quantizes translation, k quantizes rotation and z quantizes scale difference in the similarity transformation.

The probability that a random incorrect match votes for a given bin $B = (i, j, k, z)$ in the bin-space is $p_B = p(i, j, k, z) = p(z)p(k)p(i, j \mid k, z)$. When a correct mapping m_B for the bin B does not exist, all the votes in bin B are of random origin. Each random match votes for the 16 different nearest bins. We can estimate the probability that k or more random incorrect matches of a total of n vote for a bin B (cumulative binomial distribution):

$$P(\#B \geq k \mid \neg m_B) = \sum_{\alpha=k}^{N} \binom{N}{\alpha} p_B{}^{\alpha}(1-p_B)^{N-\alpha} \tag{4}$$

with $\#B$ the number of votes in the bin B and $N = 16 \times n$ the total number of random votes generated by the n matches that exists in all the bin-space. This approximation is acceptable when k is much smaller than n, as each random match produces 16 random (distinct) votes.

The probability of a bin B representing a true mapping m_B of an object can be approximated as [4]:

$$P(m_B \mid \#B \geq k) = \frac{P(m_B)}{P(m_B) + P(\#B \geq k \mid \neg m_B)} \tag{5}$$

An exact value of $p_B = p(z)p(k)p(i, j \mid k, z)$ is essential for obtaining an exact computation of (4) and (5). Lowe approximates $p(z) = 0.5$. But, if it is assumed that the density of interest points along the sub-sampled scale space is constant, an analytical value for $p(z)$ exists and can be computed. Lowe also approximates $p(i, j \mid k, z)$ as a fixed value. But, $p(i, j \mid k, z)$ can be estimated as a ratio between the space covered by the matches compatibles with the bin (i,j,k,z) and the space covered by all the possible matches that can be generated between the pair of images. Finally, the probability $p(k)$ can be calculated as $w/360^\circ$, where w is the angular width of a bin.

2.1 Analytical Computation of $p(z)$

Suppose we have a pair of images I and I'. $\{D_0, D_1, ...\}$ and $\{D'_0, D'_1, ...\}$ will be their respective sub-sampled scale space representations, and two images per octave will be used. The area of a scale space image can be expressed as:

$$area(D_k) = \frac{area(D_0)}{4^{floor(k/2)}}, \; area(D'_k) = \frac{area(D'_0)}{4^{floor(k/2)}}$$

If the density of interest points is constant in each of the scale spaces, and the point-matches are of random origin, the probability that a random match will be associated to a (m, n) scale space level can be written as:

$$P(match : m \rightarrow n) = \frac{area(D_m)area(D'_n)}{\sum_{i=0}^{\infty}\sum_{j=0}^{\infty} area(D_i)area(D'_j)}$$

If we simplify the last expression, a simple analytical probability expression can be obtained:

$$P(match : m \rightarrow n) = \frac{9}{64}\left(\frac{1}{4}\right)^{floor(m/2)}\left(\frac{1}{4}\right)^{floor(n/2)}$$

It will be defined a Z function that depends on m, n: $Z(m,n) = FLOOR(m/2) - FLOOR(n/2)$. Now, the following set can be evaluated:

$$B(z) = \{(m,n) \mid Z(m,n) = z\}$$
$$= \begin{cases} \{(2k, 2k+2z), (2k+1, 2k+2z), (2k, 2k+1+2z), (2k+1, 2k+1+2z) \forall k > 0\}, z > 0 \\ \{(2k-2z, 2k), (2k+1-2z, 2k), (2k-2z, 2k+1), (2k+1-2z, 2k+1) \forall k > 0\}, z < 0 \end{cases}$$

Using this set, probabilities in the (m, n) space can be mapped to the z space.

$$\begin{aligned} p(z \mid z \geq 0) = {} & \sum_{k=0}^{\infty} P(match : 2k, 2k+2z) + \sum_{k=0}^{\infty} P(match : 2k+1, 2k+2z) + \\ & + \sum_{k=0}^{\infty} P(match : 2k, 2k+2z+1) + \sum_{k=0}^{\infty} P(match : 2k+1, 2k+2z+1) \end{aligned} \quad (6)$$

$$\begin{aligned} p(z \mid z < 0) = {} & \sum_{k=0}^{\infty} P(match : 2k-2z, 2k) + \sum_{k=0}^{\infty} P(match : 2k+1-2z, 2k) + \\ & + \sum_{k=0}^{\infty} P(match : 2k-2z, 2k+1) + \sum_{k=0}^{\infty} P(match : 2k+1-2z, 2k+1) \end{aligned} \quad (7)$$

Finally, (6) and (7) can be simplified to:

$$p(z) = \frac{3}{5}\left(\frac{1}{4}\right)^{|z|}$$

It can be easily demonstrated than $\sum_{z=-\infty}^{\infty} p(z) = 1$. The new $p(z)$ expression can be used to get a modified probability test to reject incorrect bins.

2.2 Analytical Computation of $p(i, j \mid k, z)$

The $p(i, j \mid k, z)$ calculation considers the space of all positions (x_1, y_1) in the test image and all the (x_2, y_2) positions in the reference image. Random matches between the images generate random (x_1, y_1, x_2, y_2) points in a 4D space. If the reference image size is $L_X \times L_Y$ and the test image size is $M_X \times M_Y$, the 4D random points belong to the following space:

$$\mathbf{c} = (x_1, y_1, x_2, y_2) \in S = [0, M_X] \times [0, M_Y] \times [0, L_X] \times [0, L_Y]$$

The S space has a 4D volume that can be expressed as $L_X L_Y M_X M_Y$. A bin B covers a subset of S that will be named $Q(B)$. If the 4D volume contained by $Q(B)$ is known, the probability $p(i, j \mid k, z)$ can be estimated as:

$$p(i, j \mid k, z) = \frac{Q(i, j, k, z)}{L_X L_Y M_X M_Y}$$

The last equation can be approximated and written in terms of the (i, j) space instead of the (x_1, y_1, x_2, y_2) space. We will analyze 3 cases:

Case 1: If we assume that $\Delta\theta = 0°$ in (3), the equations for i_{FRAC} and j_{FRAC} are reduced to:

$$i_{FRAC} = \frac{2^z x_2 - x_1}{(1/4) L_X \times 2^z}$$

$$j_{FRAC} = \frac{2^z y_2 - y_1}{(1/4) L_Y \times 2^z}$$

The minimum and maximum admissible values for i_{FRAC} and j_{FRAC} while (x_1, y_1, x_2, y_2) belongs to S are the following.

$$i_{FRAC} \in \left[-\frac{M_X}{(1/4) 2^z L_X}, \frac{2^z L_X}{(1/4) 2^z L_X} \right], j_{FRAC} \in \left[-\frac{M_Y}{(1/4) 2^z L_Y}, \frac{2^z L_Y}{(1/4) 2^z L_Y} \right] \quad (8)$$

We define the following variables.

$$R_{XX} = \frac{M_X}{2^z L_X}, R_{YY} = \frac{M_Y}{2^z L_Y}$$

Then, expression (8), which expresses the domain for (i, j), can be rewritten as:

$$(i_{FRAC}, j_{FRAC}) \in [-4R_{XX}, 4] \times [-4R_{YY}, 4]$$

All the (i, j) bins have size 1 in the (i_{FRAC}, j_{FRAC}) space. Them the probability that a random (x_1, y_1, x_2, y_2) match produces a random (i_{FRAC}, j_{FRAC}) which vote for a particular (i, j) bin can be expressed as:

$$p(i,j \mid k,z) \approx \frac{1}{4(R_{XX}+1)\cdot 4(R_{YY}+1)}$$

Case 2: If we assume that $\Delta\theta = 90°$ in (3), a calculation similar to case 1 gives the following results:

$$R_{YX} = \frac{M_Y}{2^z L_X}, R_{XY} = \frac{M_X}{2^z L_Y}$$

$$p(i,j \mid k,z) \approx \frac{1}{4(R_{XY}+1)\cdot 4(R_{YX}+1)}$$

Case 3: If we do not assume a particular $\Delta\theta$ it is difficult to get an analytical solution. But an approximation can be obtained by mixing the two results. As R_{XX} and R_{YX} stands for two different orthogonal cases, they can be mixed as $R_X^2 = R_{XX}^2 + R_{YX}^2$. In a similar way, $R_Y^2 = R_{XY}^2 + R_{YY}^2$ can be assumed. This leads to the following equations:

$$R_X(\theta_1-\theta_2) = \frac{\sqrt{M_X^2\cos^2(\theta_1-\theta_2)+M_Y^2\sin^2(\theta_1-\theta_2)}}{2^z L_X}$$

$$R_Y(\theta_1-\theta_2) = \frac{\sqrt{M_Y^2\cos^2(\theta_1-\theta_2)+M_X^2\sin^2(\theta_1-\theta_2)}}{2^z L_Y}$$

$$p(i,j \mid k,z) \approx \frac{1}{4(R_X+1)\cdot 4(R_Y+1)}$$

3 Experimental Results

In this section is presented an experimental evaluation of the proposed improvement over Lowe's work. The performance of the introduced verification and merging hypothesis stages are tested in the UCH100 object recognition database (available in [13]). This database is composed by 100 pairs of real-world images $\{(I_{2k-1}, I_{2k}), k=1,...,100\}$, being I_{2k-1} a reference image and I_{2k} the corresponding test image. Each reference image shows a different, single object. The same object appears in the corresponding test image, viewed under different conditions (position, view angle, partial occlusion, in-plane and out-of the-plane rotation). In the test images can also appear objects not included in the reference images. In figure 2 are shown some examples of reference-test images pairs.

Object recognition experiments were performed in all image's pairs $\{(I_j, I_k), k, j=1,...,100\}$. The experiments consist on finding the mapping that relates each pair of images. A pair of images has a common object only in 100 of the 10,000 cases to be analyzed. In these pairs of images (100) the recognition methods generate a variable number of transformations (0 to 10, or even more in some cases), although ideally just one transformation should be obtained. For the proposed experiment, a pair of images is *solved* when the transformation with the best priority, i.e. the highest probability value, is a good-mapping transformation, and almost all the associated point-matches are correct. The other obtained transformations are not analyzed. The algorithms are compared in terms of:

- DR (Detection Rate): DR is computed as the rate of correct best-priority transformations. Just one per image can be correct in the 100 pairs having a common object.
- FPR (False Positive Rate): FPR is computed as the rate of incorrect best-priority transformations. Just one incorrect transformation per image is added when incorrect objects are matched.
- DR/FPR Ratio: Ratio between correct and incorrect best-priority transformations.
- Mean PT: Mean Processing time for the matching and verification stages.

The algorithms under comparison are:

- *Lowe*: Lowe's recognition system without any improvement.
- *FastProb*: Lowe's recognition system using the fast probabilistic model for hypothesis rejection.
- *Lowe+OVS*: *Lowe* plus other verification and merging stages proposed in [7].
- *FastProb+OVS*: *FastProb* plus other verification and merging stages (see [7]).

Table 1. Comparative evaluation of the different algorithms. DR=Detection Rate. FPR=False Positive Rate. Mean PT: Mean Processing time for the matching and verification stages.

Algorithms	DR (%)	FPR (%)	DR/FPR Ratio	Mean PT [ms]
Lowe	41%	85.5%	0.48	21.56
FastProb	39%	78.3%	0.50	14.38
Lowe+OVS	44%	4.87	9.03	26.56
FastProb+OVS	49%	3.74	13.10	19.38

The comparative evaluation of these algorithms is displayed in table 1. As it can be observed, the new FastProb rejection test reduces the FPR from 85.5% to 78.3%, while keeping the DR in about 40%. More important, the time required for performing the matching and verification processes is reduced from 21.56ms to 14.38ms (about 33% reduction). However, the FPR is still too high and other verification stages are required (see detailed explanation in [7]). When using these additional stages together with FastProb (FastProb+OVS) the DR is increased to 49%, while the FPR is strongly decreased to just 3.74, achieving a DR/FPR ratio of 13.10. When using the Lowe's algorithm together with the additional verification stages (Lowe+OVS), DR increases to 44%, FPR decreases to 4.87, and the resulting

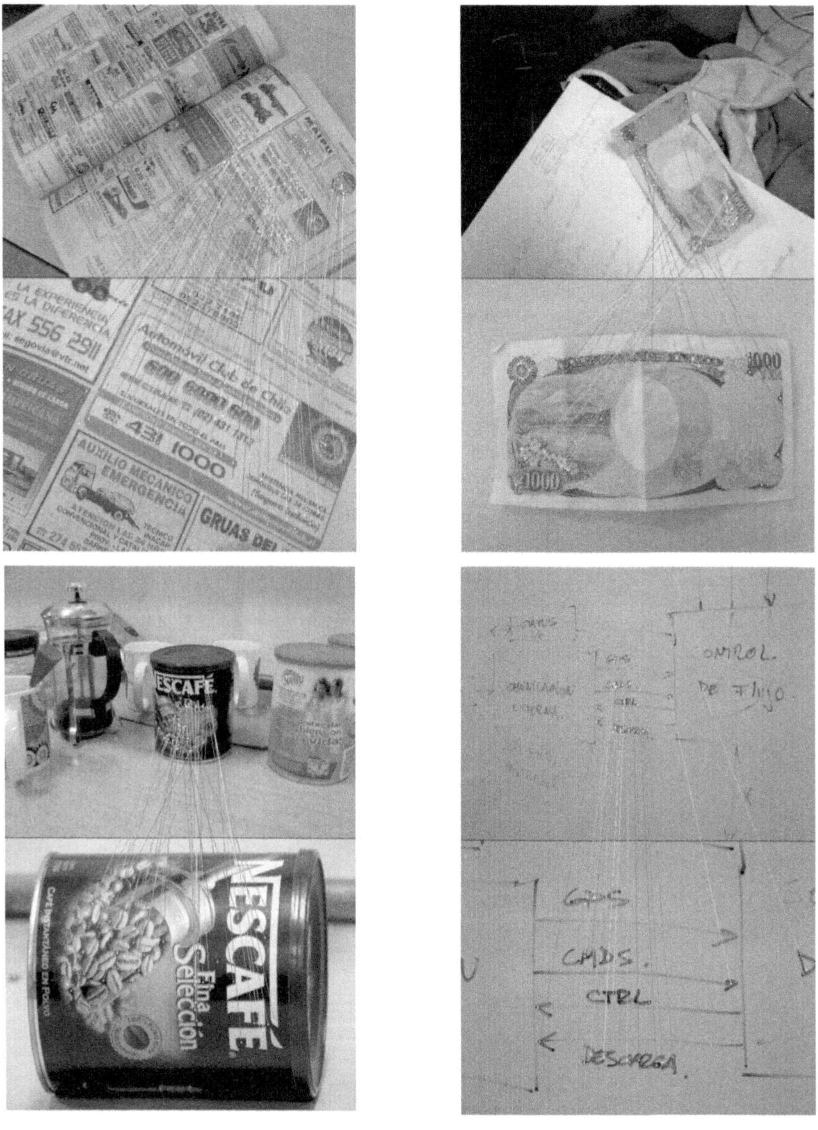

Fig. 1. Some examples of object recognition results that can be obtained with the new probabilistic model for hypothesis rejection

DR/FPR ratio is 9.03. Thus, FastProb+OVS achieves a DR/FPR ratio 45% higher than Lowe+OVS. That means that the proposed fast probability model for hypothesis rejection is essential for obtaining high recognition rates. Figure 1 shows some examples of the excellent object recognition results that can be obtained when using this new model.

Fig. 2. Selected images from the UCH100 database (see [13]). Left: reference images. Right: corresponding test images.

4 Conclusions

In this work was proposed an improvement over the traditional SIFT-based object recognition methodology proposed by Lowe. This improvement corresponds to a fast probabilistic model for hypothesis rejection (affine solution verification stage), which allows a large reduction in the number of false positives. The new probabilistic model was evaluated in an object recognition task using a real-world database of 100 pairs of images. Objects in these images are very hard to recognize. The obtained results show that with the probabilistic model for hypothesis rejection is obtained a reduction in the number of false positives of about 9%, and the time required for the matching and verification processes is reduced in about 33%. This reduction is very important for several real-world applications.

References

1. V. Ferrari, T. Tuytelaars, and L. Van Gool. Simultaneous Object Recognition and Segmentation by Image Exploration. *Lecture Notes in Computer Science* 3021, 40 - 54.
2. C. Harris and M. Stephens, A combined corner and edge detector, *Proc. 4th Alvey Vision Conf.*, 147-151, Manchester, UK, 1988.
3. D. G. Lowe. Distinctive Image Features from Scale-Invariant Keypoints. *Int. Journal of Computer Vision*, 60 (2): 91-110, Nov. 2004.
4. D.G. Lowe. Local Features View Clustering for 3D Object Recognition. *Proc. of the IEEE Conf. on Comp. Vision and Patt. Recog.*, 682 – 688, Hawai, Dic. 2001
5. P. Loncomilla and J. Ruiz del Solar. Improving SIFT-based Object Recognition for Robot Applications. *Lecture Notes in Computer science* 3617, Springer, 1084 - 1092.
6. P. Loncomilla and J. Ruiz-del-Solar. Gaze Direction Determination of Opponents and Teammates in Robot Soccer. *Lecture Notes in Computer Science* 4020, Springer, 230 – 242.
7. P. Loncomilla and J. Ruiz-del-Solar. An improved SIFT-based Object Recognition Methodology, *Tech. Report UCH-DIE-VISION-2006-03*, Dept. of E. Eng., U. de Chile, 2006.
8. K. Mikolajczyk and C. Schmid. Scale & Affine Invariant Interest Point Detectors. *Int. Journal of Computer Vision*, 60 (1): 63 - 96, Oct. 2004.
9. K. Mikolajczyk and C. Schmid. A performance evaluation of local descriptors. *IEEE Trans. on Pattern Analysis and Machine Intelligence*, Vol. 27, No. 10, 1615 – 1630.
10. K. Mikolajczyk, T. Tuytelaars, C. Schmid, A. Zisserman, J. Matas, F. Schaffalitzky, T. Kadir, L. Van Gool. A Comparison of Affine Region Detectors. *Int. Journal of Computer Vision* (accepted).
11. F. Schaffalitzky and A. Zisserman. Automated location matching in movies. *Computer Vision and Image Understanding* Vol. 92, Issue 2-3, 236 – 264, Nov./Dec. 2003.
12. S. Se, D. Lowe, and J. Little. Mobile robot localization and mapping with uncertainty using scale-invariant visual landmarks. *Int. J. of Robotics Research*, Vol. 21, No. 8, 2002, 735 – 758.
13. UCH100 database. Electronically available in: http://vision.die.uchile.cl/.

Diagnosis of Chronic Idiopathic Inflammatory Bowel Disease Using Bayesian Networks

Nicandro Cruz-Ramírez[1], Héctor-Gabriel Acosta-Mesa[1], Rocío-Erandi Barrientos-Martínez[1], and Luis-Alonso Nava-Fernández[2]

[1] Facultad de Física e Inteligencia Artificial, Universidad Veracruzana, Sebastián Camacho 5, Col. Centro, C.P. 91000, Xalapa, Veracruz, México
[2] Instituto de Investigaciones en Educación, Universidad Veracruzana, Diego Leño 8 esq. Morelos, Col. Centro, C.P. 91000, Xalapa, Veracruz, México
{ncruz, heacosta, lunava}@uv.mx, erandi_bm@yahoo.com.mx

Abstract. In this paper, we evaluate the effectiveness of four Bayesian network classifiers as potential tools for the histopathological diagnosis of chronic idiopathic inflammatory bowel disease (CIIBD) using a database containing endoscopic colorectal biopsies. CIIBD is the generic term for referring to two ailments known as Crohn's disease and ulcerative colitis. The results show that the defined histological attributes, considered relevant in the medical literature for the diagnosis of CIIBD, are very good for the distinction between normal samples and CIIBD samples (Crohn's disease and ulcerative colitis combined into a single category) but less good for the explicit distinction between Crohn's disease and ulcerative colitis. The findings suggest an intrinsic impossibility of selecting a set of features for achieving good balance for both sensitivity and specificity for Crohn's disease and ulcerative colitis.

1 Introduction

Chronic idiopathic inflammatory bowel disease (CIIBD) is the generic term for referring to two disorders of the digestive tract known as Crohn's disease and ulcerative colitis (UC) [5, 12, 15, 16, 19, 21]. Both of them are characterized by acute and chronic inflammation of the bowel. Crohn's disease involves the small intestine at its junction with the large intestine, or the small and the large intestines or the colon alone; the ulcerative colitis is restricted to the large intestine. Because the two diseases involve common symptoms, the distinction in the diagnosis of one or another is not an easy task. Needless to say, the correct diagnosis is imperative for a proper patient management, which, among other things, can help treat the disease properly and reduce the danger for the patient to develop cancer. Actually, there are two important distinctions in making the diagnosis: a) does the patient have CIIBD or not? b) If the patient has CIIBD, is it Crohn's disease or ulcerative colitis? In the first distinction, this implies that the patient receives/does not receive a long-term follow-up. Such a follow-up might include a colonoscopy every year; a procedure that unfortunately has a small associated mortality, high discomfort for the patient and high cost. However, if a patient who has CIIBD is not treated, it is possible that she/he could develop colorectal

J.F. Martínez-Trinidad et al. (Eds.): CIARP 2006, LNCS 4225, pp. 706–715, 2006.

carcinoma. In the second distinction, this implies that the patient, who has ulcerative colitis and is not responding to the medical therapy, can have her/his colon removed. If the patient has Crohn's disease, such a surgical removal is not recommended.

Histopathology is considered the gold-standard technique for the diagnosis of CIIBD [5]. However, it is important to mention that the accurate diagnosis of CIIBD, by means of histopathology, heavily relies on the histopathologist's expertise [5, 19]. This situation can be perceived when noticing the fact that the time it normally takes in some countries (such as United Kingdom) to a medical doctor to become an independent histopathologist is about 5 years as a minimum [5]. Such a fact gives certain indication of the very complex learning process through which medical doctors have to pass and the subjective nature of the histopathological diagnosis. In other words, a well-trained eye is needed for the correct and consistent diagnosis of CIIBD. Regarding this subjectivity, it is often the case that even expert histopathologists disagree on the interpretation of a sample; the so-called interobserver variability problem. This might suggest that there could be many factors responsible for impeding the reproducibility of the results, ranging from their expertise and the amount of stress and tiredness to the level of diligence when looking at the specimens. Due to the mentioned situations, a natural and sensible question arises: is it possible to construct computational support tools that help reduce this subjectivity? In this paper, we will explore the possibility of extracting some "objective" features, from a database, relevant for determining the presence/absence of CIIBD using a graphical-modeling approach called Bayesian networks [20]. Such an approach allows both the visual representation of the probabilistic interactions among variables of interest and the quantitative measure of the impact of those interactions. These two important properties permit to perform some inferential processes, such as prognosis and diagnosis. In order to do this, we assess the performance of four Bayesian network classifiers so as to determine their effectiveness for accurately diagnosing CIIBD using a real-world dataset.

Although some researchers have analyzed the same datasets using different techniques such as logistic regression and GCS (growing cell structure) [5], there are no studies, to the best of our knowledge, involving the analysis of CIIBD using Bayesian networks. The double nature of Bayesian-network classifiers (qualitative and quantitative) [9] can give some other insights of the phenomenon under study. For instance, an intrinsic limitation of logistic regression is the change in the classification accuracy if different orderings of the explanatory variables are considered [4]. Bayesian networks not only permit to visualize the interactions among variables but also provide local probability distributions which, despite their numerical nature, can be traced from beginning to end so that it is possible to know why and how a Bayesian network arrived at a specific conclusion. Furthermore, in contrast to logistic regression, the Bayesian network classifiers we use here are not sensitive to variable ordering.

The remainder of this paper is organized as follows. In section 2, we present the materials and methods used for the experiments reported here. In section 3 we present the experimental methodology and the results. In section 4, we provide a discussion of these results and finally, in section 5, we give some conclusions and mention future work.

2 Materials and Methods

2.1 The Datasets

The real-world database for this study comes from the field of histopathological diagnosis of endoscopic colorectal biopsies received at the Department of Histopathology, Royal Hallamshire Hospital in Sheffield, United Kingdom, between 1990 and 1995 inclusive. This database is partitioned in three subsets. The first one is the complete dataset (called "All IBD & Normal"), which contains 809 cases of which 165 are normal, 473 are ulcerative colitis (UC) and 171 are Crohn's disease. The second one ("All IBD") contains 644 cases of which 473 are UC and 171 Crohn's disease. The third one ("Active IBD") contains 370 cases of which 283 are active UC and 87 active Crohn's disease ("active" refers to the presence of active inflammation as indicated by polymorphs in the lamina propria). 23 independent variables and one dependent variable (the outcome) form part of these datasets. The diagnosis was confirmed by endoscopy, radiology and microbiological culture results. Continuous variables were

Table 1. The observed features of CIIBD

Variable	Type
1. Age	Real number
2. Sex	Binary
3. Active inflammation	Binary
4. Mucosal surface	Ordinal, categorical
5. Crypt architecture	Ordinal, categorical
6. Crypt profiles	Real number
7. Increased lamina propria cellularity	Binary
8. Superficially increased lamina propria cellularity	Binary
9. Increased lymphoid aggregates	Binary
10. Patchy increased lamina propria cellularity	Binary
11. Transmucosally lamina propria cellularity	Binary
12. Cryptitis: extent	Ordinal, categorical
13. Cryptitis: polymorphs	Ordinal, categorical
14. Crypt abscesses: extent	Ordinal, categorical
15. Crypt abscesses: polymorph	Ordinal, categorical
16. Increased lamina propria polymorphs	Binary
17. Epithelial changes	Ordinal, categorical
18. Mucin depletion	Ordinal, categorical
19. Intraepithelial lymphocytes	Binary
20. Subepithelial collagen	Binary
21. Lamina propria granulomas	Binary
22. Submucosal granulomas	Binary
23. Basal histiocytes	Binary
24. Outcome	Binary

discretized using the CAIM algorithm [18]. Table 1 briefly explains the meaning and types of each of the variables. Most of them have to do with the dimension, architecture and counts of the cells coming from endoscopic colorectal biopsies. For more details on these variables, the reader is referred to [15].

2.2 Bayesian Network Classifiers

Classification refers to the task of assigning class labels to unlabelled instances. In other words, given a set of cases having values for each variable or attribute (including a special kind called class), we have to build a model (in our case a Bayesian network) that best describes the class or concept using the rest of the attributes. Once this is done, the model is used for classifying new cases that do not have a label for the class. This kind of learning is known as supervised learning [8, 13, 17]. For the sake of brevity, we do not write here the code of the 4 procedures used in the tests carried out in this work. Instead, we only describe them briefly and refer the reader to their original sources. The procedures used in these tests are: a) the Naïve Bayes classifier, b) MP-Bayes, c) Greedy and d) algorithm B [1, 2, 6, 7].

1. The Naïve Bayes classifier (NB) is one of the most effective classifiers [7, 8, 13] and against which state of the art classifiers have to be compared. Its main appeals are its simplicity and accuracy: although its structure is always fixed (the class variable has an arc pointing to every attribute), it has been shown that this classifier has a high classification accuracy and optimal Bayes' error [7, 13]. In simple terms, the NB learns, from a training data sample, the conditional probability of each attribute given the class. Then, once a new case arrives, the NB uses Bayes' rule to compute the conditional probability of the class given the set of attributes selecting the value of the class with the highest posterior probability.
2. MP-Bayes [6] is a constraint-based algorithm that uses information measures for building a Bayesian network structure from data. Its parsimonious nature allows it to represent the joint probability distribution underlying the data with the least number of arcs.
3. Greedy [6] is a search and scoring algorithm, which uses greedy-hill climbing for the search part and the Bayesian Information Criterion (BIC) metric for the scoring part [10, 11, 14]. For the experiments reported here, procedure Greedy takes as input an empty graph and a database. Other alternatives for the initialization space are a complete graph, a random graph or a graph suggested by a constraint-based procedure. In every search step, it looks for a graph that minimizes the BIC score. Such an algorithm is a modification of that proposed by Friedman et al. [8]. In brief, procedure Greedy applies, whenever possible, 3 different operators: the addition of an arc (in either direction), the deletion of an arc and the reversal of an arc. In every step, the BIC score is calculated and procedure Greedy keeps the structure with the best (minimum) score. It finishes searching when no structure improves the BIC score of the previous network.
4. Power Constructor is a software package which contains two different algorithms (algorithms A and B) to build BN structures from data [1]. For the tests carried out here, we used algorithm B because it does not need a node ordering to work. Algorithm B uses mutual information and conditional mutual information tests to decide when to connect/disconnect a pair of nodes.

We have selected different types of Bayesian network classifiers: the Naïve Bayesian classifier, two constraint-based classifiers (b, and d) and one search and scoring classifier c). We have chosen them to check the behavior and performance of different statistical measures, heuristics and metrics in classification tasks.

3 Experimental Methodology and Results

In this section, we describe the experimental methodology and present the results for 3 different experiments. In section 4, we discuss such results. Because of the lack of space, the Bayesian network structures resultant from running these databases are not presented.

Experiment 1. We used the "All IBD and Normal" database split into 2 subsets: the training and the test sets. The size of the training set is 2/3 of the data (540 cases) and the remaining 1/3 of the data forms the test set. All the algorithms described in the previous section use these training data to learn a classification model. Then, they use such a classification model and the test set to compute two tests, commonly used in the medical domain, for comparing the performance of these four classifiers: sensitivity (the ability to correctly identify those patients who actually have the disease) and specificity (the ability to correctly identify those patients who do not have the disease). The central goal of Experiment 1 is to assess the discriminant power of the independent variables to tell normal samples from CIIBD samples (Crohn's disease and UC are combined into a single category). The results of experiment 1 are shown in table 2, which shows the sensitivity and specificity for Normal vs. CIIBD samples. For these tests, their respective 95% confidence intervals (CI) are shown in parentheses.

Table 2. IBD vs. Normal's sensitivity and specificity with their respective 95% confidence intervals in the "All IBD vs. Normal " dataset

	Naïve-Bayes	**MP-Bayes**	**Greedy**	**Algorithm B**
Sensitivity	96% (92-100)	0	0	0
Specificity	69% (63-75)	100% (100)	100% (100)	100% (100)

Experiment 2. We used the "All IBD" database split into 2 subsets: the training and the test sets. The size of the training set is 2/3 of the data (430 cases) and the remaining 1/3 of the data forms the test set. All the algorithms described in the previous section use these training data to learn a classification model. Then, they use such a classification model and the test set to compute sensitivity and specificity tests. The main objective of Experiment 2 is to assess the discriminant power of the independent variables to tell Crohn's disease samples from UC samples. The results of experiment 2 are shown in tables 3 and 4, which show the sensitivity and specificity for Crohn's disease and UC respectively. For these tests, their respective 95% confidence intervals (CI) are shown in parentheses.

Table 3. Crohn's disease's sensitivity and specificity with their respective 95% confidence intervals in the "All IBD" dataset

	Naïve-Bayes	MP-Bayes	Greedy	Algorithm B
Sensitivity	65% (53-78)	16% (7-26)	20% (9-31)	27% (16-39)
Specificity	68% (61-75)	93% (89-97)	96% (92-99)	94% (90-97)

Table 4. UC's sensitivity and specificity with their respective 95% confidence intervals in the "All IBD" dataset

	Naïve-Bayes	MP-Bayes	Greedy	Algorithm B
Sensitivity	68% (61-75)	93% (89-97)	96% (92-99)	94% (90-97)
Specificity	65% (53-78)	16% (7-26)	20% (9-31)	27% (16-39)

Experiment 3. We used the "Active IBD" database split into 2 subsets: the training and the test sets. The size of the training set is 2/3 of the data (247 cases) and the remaining 1/3 of the data forms the test set. All the algorithms described in the previous section use these training data to learn a classification model. Then, they use such a classification model and the test set to compute sensitivity and specificity tests. The main objective of Experiment 3 is to assess the discriminant power of the independent variables to tell active Crohn's disease samples from active UC samples. The results of experiment 3 are shown in tables 5 and 6, which show the sensitivity and specificity for active Crohn's disease and active UC respectively. For these tests, their respective 95% confidence intervals (CI) are shown in parentheses.

Table 5. Crohn's disease's sensitivity and specificity with their respective 95% confidence intervals in the "Active IBD" dataset

	Naïve-Bayes	MP-Bayes	Greedy	Algorithm B
Sensitivity	57% (39-75)	14% (1-27)	14% (1-27)	14% (1-27)
Specificity	72% (63-81)	99% (97-100)	99% (97-100)	99% (97-100)

Table 6. UC's sensitivity and specificity with their respective 95% confidence intervals in the "Active IBD" dataset

	Naïve-Bayes	MP-Bayes	Greedy	Algorithm B
Sensitivity	72% (63-81)	99% (97-100)	99% (97-100)	99% (97-100)
Specificity	57% (39-75)	14% (1-27)	14% (1-27)	14% (1-27)

4 Discussion of the Results

According to the medical literature, all 22 defined histological observations mentioned in table 1 are considered relevant for the histopathological diagnosis of CIIBD [4]. Age is also considered relevant as it provides useful information for making the final diagnosis. All variables are random variables and take on values as described in table 1. In the experiments we call such variables a1, a2, and so on. The 4 procedures presented here select the relevant attributes according to their own metrics, as described in section 2.2. Now, let us describe our findings for the described experiments.

Experiment 1. The central goal of Experiment 1 is to assess the discriminant power of the independent variables to tell normal samples from CIIBD samples. Table 2 shows a high sensitivity value for the NB classifier (96%) but 0% sensitivity for the remaining classifiers. This significant difference strongly suggests that it is important to consider all the attributes in order to achieve high sensitivity values. If only few attributes are considered relevant for explaining the outcome (a7 for MP-Bayes; a2, a3 and a4 for Greedy; and a5 and a16 for procedure B), 0% sensitivity is achieved. On the other hand, a regular specificity value is achieved by NB (69%) but a perfect specificity value (100%) is reached by the remaining classifiers. The attributes selected by MP-Bayes, Greedy and procedure B (a7; a2, a3 and a4; and a5 and a16 respectively) as the most discriminant attributes for the absence of CIIBD seem to work excellently. This supports the findings in Cross and Harrison [5]: histopathological examination of endoscopic colorectal biopsies is very good for the distinction between Normal samples and CIIBD samples. It is important to mention that the human expert achieves 82% for sensitivity and 99% for specificity [5] for this same database. This important finding suggests that the expert is taking into account more information than that portrayed by the variables in table 1 for making the final decision; otherwise, the NB classifier would perform as well as he does.

Experiment 2. The main objective of Experiment 2 is to assess the discriminant power of the independent variables to tell Crohn's disease samples from UC samples (see tables 3 and 4). Both tables 3 and 4 show a regular performance of the NB classifier in terms of sensitivity and specificity (65%-68% and 68%-65% respectively). These results seem to indicate that the consideration of all attributes for deciding whether a sample belongs to one or the other disease is insufficient. The human expert reaches a sensitivity value of 44% and a specificity value of 99% for the same experiment of table 3 and a sensitivity value of 58% and a specificity value of 99% for the same experiment of table 4 [3]. These results also support the findings in Cross and Harrison [5]: histopathological examination of endoscopic colorectal biopsies is less good for the distinction between Crohn's disease and UC than that between Normal samples and CIIBD samples. Furthermore, in the case of specificity, it also seems that the expert is taking into account more information than that portrayed by the attributes in table 1 for making the final decision. The remaining classifiers select the following attributes as the most discriminant ones: a1 and a2 for the case of MP-Bayes; a1, a2, a4 and a21 for Greedy; and a1, a5 and a21 for procedure B. This selection is very bad for detecting the presence of Crohn's disease (sensitivity values of 16%, 20% and 27%) but excellent for detecting its absence (specificity values of 93%, 96% and 94%; see table 3). This same selection shows the opposite result for detecting the presence of UC (sensitivity values of 93%, 96% and 94%) and for detecting its absence (specificity values of 16%, 20% and 27%; see table 4). Such mixed results reveal the difficulty in differentiating samples belonging to one or the other disease.

Experiment 3. The main objective of Experiment 3 is to assess the discriminant power of the independent variables to tell active Crohn's disease samples from active

UC samples (see tables 5 and 6). Both tables show a regular performance of the NB classifier in terms of sensitivity and specificity (57%-72% and 72%-57% respectively). Once again, these results seem to indicate that the consideration of all attributes for deciding whether a sample belongs to one or the other active disease is insufficient. The human expert reaches a sensitivity value of 30% and a specificity value of 93% for the same experiment of table 5 and a sensitivity value of 61% and a specificity value of 76% for the same experiment of table 6 [5]. These results also support the findings in Cross and Harrison [5]: histopathological examination of endoscopic colorectal biopsies is less good for the distinction between active Crohn's disease and active UC than that between Normal samples and CIIBD samples. Furthermore, in the case of specificity, it also seems that the expert is taking into account more information than that portrayed by the attributes in table 1 for making the final decision. The remaining classifiers select the following attributes as the most discriminant ones: a21 for the case of MP-Bayes; a10 and a21 for Greedy; and a10 and a21 for procedure B. This selection is very bad for detecting the presence of active Crohn's disease (sensitivity values of 14% for all the classifiers) but excellent for detecting its absence (specificity values of 99% for all the classifiers; see table 5). This same selection shows the opposite result for detecting the presence of active UC (sensitivity values of 99% for all the classifiers) and for detecting its absence (specificity values of 14% for all the classifiers; see table 6). Such mixed results reveal the difficulty in differentiating samples belonging to one or the other active disease.

5 Conclusions and Future Work

In this paper, we have explored the possibility of extracting some "objective" features, from a database, relevant for determining the presence/absence of CIIBD using the Bayesian network framework. The results show that, in sum, the attributes selected by procedures MP-Bayes, Greedy and B allow us to accurately detect the absence of CIIBD. On the other hand, the results also show that it is much more difficult to clearly differentiate samples belonging to Crohn's disease or to ulcerative colitis. Thus, such results suggest an intrinsic impossibility of selecting a set of features for achieving good balance for both sensitivity and specificity for Crohn's disease and UC, given that the only information we can use is that portrayed by the attributes. In other words, these results seem to indicate that the attributes in table 1 are not enough for making the final diagnosis and that the human experts are taking into account more information for arriving to their conclusions.

In the paper by Cross and Harrison [5], they run the same tests described in tables 2 and 6 using logistic regression and a technique known as GCS (growing cell structure); this last technique is described in [22]. The sensitivity and specificity results for logistic regression running the same tests as in table 2 are 78%% and 89% respectively. The results for these same tests for GCS are 76% and 86%. The sensitivity and specificity results for logistic regression running the same tests as in table 6 are 84% and 62% respectively. The results for these same tests for GCS are 66% and 66%. It is important to mention the root of such differences: while in a Bayesian network different value combinations of the same set of variables determine whether it is a normal sample or a CIIBD sample (or whether it is Crohn's disease or UC), in the logistic regression and in GCS different sets of variables determine the presence or absence of the disease being considered. As can be inferred, different combinations of such variables for both techniques, as well as the order of the explanatory variables for logistic regression, are a key ingredient for obtaining good/bad results. In the case of procedures MP-Bayes, Greedy and B, there is no prior knowledge that privileges specific variables in the analysis; i.e., not a single variable is treated with a special distinction. Moreover, the very nature of these three procedures is to follow Occam´s razor: they keep the least number of arcs among variables. The Bayesian network structures not only show the interactions between the attributes and the class but also the interactions among the attributes themselves. Such features may be helpful for both describing the phenomenon under study and classifying new samples with unknown class label. In contrast, logistic regression and GCS only allow the classification of new samples but do not provide a description of the phenomenon under investigation.

It is important to keep in mind that the process or processes that histopathologists follow to make their final diagnoses have not been yet fully understood and can only be partially explained in terms of pattern recognition with occasional use of heuristic logic. Hence, the information provided there is subjective rather than objective. To ameliorate this problem, alternative data collection methods such as image analysis techniques could be used so that objective measures from sample raw digitalized images can be extracted. In sum, our contribution has mainly to do with the discovery of an intrinsic impossibility of manually selecting a set of features for achieving a good balance for sensitivity and specificity in Crohn's disease and UC. We plan to investigate the possibility of building a pre-processing vision module capable of extracting "objective" features from raw images and, again, check the performance of the Bayesian network classifiers using the dataset produced by this module.

Acknowledgements

We are very grateful to Dr. Simon S. Cross, Clinical Senior Lecturer at the Academic Unit of Pathology of the University of Sheffield, United Kingdom, who provided the databases used in this study.

References

1. Cheng, J., Bell, D.A., Liu, W. Learning Belief Networks from Data: An Information Theory Based Approach. in Sixth ACM International Conference on Information and Knowledge Management. 1997: ACM.
2. Cheng, J. and R. Greiner. Comparing Bayesian Network Classifiers. in Fifteenth Conference on Uncertainty in Artificial Intelligence. 1999.
3. Cross, S.S., Dataset of Observed Features on Endoscopic Colorectal Biopsies from Normal Subjects and Patients with Chronic Inflammatory Bowel Disease (Crohn's disease and Ulcerative Colitis). 1999, Department of Pathology, University of Sheffield Medical School. p. 1-15.
4. Cross, S.S., et al., Which Decision Support Technologies Are Appropriate for the Cytodiagnosis of Breast Cancer?, in Artificial Intelligence Techniques in Breast Cancer Diagnosis and Prognosis, A. Jain, et al., Editors. 2000, World Scientific. p. 265-295.

5. Cross, S.S. and H. R.F., Discriminant histological features in the diagnosis of chronic idiopathic inflammatory bowel disease: analysis of a large dataset by a novel data visualisation technique. Journal of Clinical Pathology, 2002(55): p. 51-57.
6. Cruz-Ramirez Nicandro, N.-F.L., Acosta-Mesa Hector Gabriel, Barrientos-Martinez Erandi, Rojas-Marcial Juan Efrain, A Parsimonious Constraint-based Algorithm to Induce Bayesian Network Structures from Data, in IEEE Proceedings of the Mexican International Conference on Computer Science ENC 2005, IEEE, Editor. 2005, IEEE: Puebla. p. 306-313.
7. Duda, R.O., Hart, Peter E., Stork, David G., Pattern Classification. 2001: John Wiley & Sons, INC.
8. Friedman, N., D. Geiger, and M. Goldszmidt, Bayesian Network Classifiers. Machine Learning, 1997. **29**: p. 131-163.
9. Friedman, N. and M. Goldszmidt, Learning Bayesian Networks from Data. 1998, University of California, Berkeley and Stanford Research Institute. p. 117.
10. Grunwald, P., Introducing MDL, in Advances in Minimum Description Length: Theory and Applications, P. Grunwald, I.J. Myung, and M.A. Pitt, Editors. 2005, The MIT Press.
11. Grunwald, P., Tutorial on MDL, in Advances in Minimum Description Length: Theory and Applications, P. Grunwald, I.J. Myung, and M.A. Pitt, Editors. 2005, The MIT Press.
12. Guindi, M. and R.H. Riddell, Indeterminate colitis. Journal of Clinical Pathology, 2004(57): p. 1233-1244.
13. Han, J. and M. Kamber, Data Mining. Concepts and Techniques. First ed. Data Management Systems, ed. J. Gray. 2001: Morgan Kaufmann. 550.
14. Heckerman, D., A Tutorial on Learning with Bayesian Networks, in Learning in Graphical Models, M.I. Jordan, Editor. 1998, MIT Press. p. 301-354.
15. Jenkins, D., et al., Guidelines for the initial biopsy diagnosis of suspected chronic idiopathic inflammatory bowel disease. The British Society of Gastroenterology Initiative. Journal of Clinical Pathology, 1997(50): p. 93-105.
16. Jenkins, D., et al., What is colitis? Statistical approach to distinguishing clinically important inflammatory change in rectal biopsy specimens. Journal of Clinical Pathology, 1988(41): p. 72-79.
17. Kohavi, R. A Study of Cross-Validation and Bootstrap for Accuracy Estimation and Model Selection. in 14th International Joint Conference on Artificial Intelligence IJCAI'95. 1995a. Montreal, Canada: Morgan Kaufmann.
18. Kurgan, L.A., Cios, Krzysztof J., CAIM Discretization Algorithm. IEEE Transactions on Knowledge and Data Engineering, 2004. **16**(2): p. 145-153.
19. Lessells, A.M., et al., Observer variability in the histopathological reporting of abnormal rectal biopsy specimens. Journal of Clinical Pathology, 1994(47): p. 48-52.
20. Pearl, J., Probabilistic Reasoning in Intelligent Systems: Networks of Plausible Inference. First ed. Representation and Reasoning, ed. R.J.B.A.T.B. Laboratories). 1988, San Mateo, California: Morgan Kaufmann. 552.
21. Sheperd, N.A., Pathological mimics of chronic inflammatory bowel disease. Journal of Clinical Pathology, 1991(44): p. 726-733.
22. Walker, A.J., S.S. Cross, and R.F. Harrison, Visualisation of biomedical datasets by use of growing cell structure networks: a novel diagnostic classification technique. The Lancet, 1999. **354**: p. 1518-1521.

Learning Variability of Image Feature Appearance Using Statistical Methods

Rodrigo Munguía and Antoni Grau

Department of Automatic Control, UPC,
c/ Pau Gargallo, 5 E-08028 Barcelona, Spain
{rodrigo.munguia, antoni.grau}@upc.edu
http://webesaii.upc.es

Abstract. Motivated by the problems of vision-based mobile robot map building and localization, in this work, we show that using statistical learning methods the performance of the standard descriptor based methodology for matching image features in a wide base line can be improved. First, we propose two kinds of descriptors for image features and two statistical learning methods. Later, we present a study of the performance of descriptors with and without the statistical learning methods. This work does not pretend to present an exhaustive description of the mentioned methods but to give a good idea the effectiveness of using statistical learning methods together with descriptors for matching image features in a wide base line.

1 Introduction

Possibly the hardest problem in robotic mapping is the *correspondence problem*, also known as the *data association problem* [13]. The correspondence problem is the problem of determining if sensor measurements taken at different points in time correspond to the same physical object in the world. For example two instances of the correspondence problem in robot mapping are closing cycles in large cyclic environment and the kidnapped problem. When a mobile platform moves through its environment a single video camera can be used in order to build a map of its surroundings and to determine its position (absolute or relative). Because in computer vision a great amount of information is available, this information can be used for solve or at least to reduce the challenging correspondence problem. In computer vision, sparse image statistics called *features* are used in order to create a model that is rich enough to represent the environment and sparse yet to be stored efficiently. A *descriptor* can be viewed like a distinctive representation of the feature and its variations among the time in a compact way respect the original data without lose of its statistical meaning. In this scenario, the correspondence problem is represented for matching image features descriptors in a wide base line. We understand "wide base line" as a big difference in time and camera point of view, between learning and recognition phases. To address the whole problem descriptors can be very helpful because they can provide distinctive signatures of different locations in space. Furthermore, descriptors have to be as much invariant as possible to changes in scale, rotation, illumination or

J.F. Martínez-Trinidad et al. (Eds.): CIARP 2006, LNCS 4225, pp. 716–725, 2006.

projection (point of view) and algorithms must be efficient and robust to a number of environmental variations such as lighting, shades, and occlusions among others.

Some approaches [3, 4] have been presented to address the problem of image features representation for tracking, recognition or reconstruction, the affine invariant descriptors. Generally these methods search for extrema in image scale space for obtaining good candidates locations for detection. Lowe's scale invariant feature transform (SIFT) [5] has showed to match reliably across a wide range of scales and orientation changes; it uses a cascade filtering approach in an isotropic Gaussian scale space to identify points of interest, then it samples gradients to create an orientation histogram represented in a 128-element descriptor. In [6] an approximate version of Kernel Principal Component Analysis (KPCA) was used to estimate features descriptors for wide base line matching.

Invariance to some changes like point of view or illumination are difficult to represent in descriptors created from a single frame since there does not exist a single-view statistic that is invariant with respect to viewpoint or lighting conditions. In applications like structure from motion or robot localization a video stream is available making possible to detect and then track the features across the images with small base line (frame to frame); several trackers [1, 2] can be used for this. The correspondence problem is easy in a small base line. While a robot move through their environment and detect image features with its camera, the appearance of the features changes due to natural changes in illumination and changes in the point of view. We can take advantage of matching in a small base line for capture the variations in the appearance of each feature along the time to make the feature descriptors more robust to changes like illumination and point of view.

In our previous work [14] we design a image feature descriptor called ICAD based in ICA (independent component analysis) for matching image features with a wide base line from the incoming video at real time with the feature descriptors previously stored in a data base. Now, in this work we propose to use statistical learning methods for capture variability of image feature appearance. In the learning phase we use small base line tracking methods for capturing the appearance of the image feature along the time, then we build their descriptors, assigning a specific label; these labeled descriptors will be the input to the statistical learning method. In the recognition phase we use the statistical methods to identify the labels of the image features from the incoming video, in real time.

In section 2, we explain the general methodology followed by the implementation of the methods. In section 3 we briefly explain the image feature descriptors and the statistical learning methods used in this work. In section 4 we show the experiments and discuss their results, and finally in section 5 the conclusions and future work are presented.

2 General Methodology

We consider the feature matching wide baseline problem under the context of map building and localization of mobile robots. The viewing conditions change drastically between the phases of map building (learning) and localization (recognition). Such changes affect both the domain of the image (deformations of the scene and geometric distortion due to changes of the viewpoint) as well as its range (changes in illumination). Such changes are due to both intrinsic properties of the scene (shape, reflectance) and to nuisance factors (illumination, viewpoint).

A feature is a statistic of the image that is intended to make easier the matching process; ideally one would want a statistic feature invariant to all kind of changes. Invariant descriptors to changes like scale or rotation can be created from one single view and they are suitable for many applications, nevertheless in the context of mobile robot, changes like viewpoint or illumination can be appreciably significant between learning and recognition stages. Unfortunately there exist no single view statistic that is invariant respect to the point of view or lighting conditions. On the other hand in the context of mobile robots a high frame-rate video is available during both building and localization. So multiple adjacent views of the same scene are available, as for instance in a video from a moving camera and, at least in theory, the point of view could be explicitly accounted for. Additionally, changes in viewpoint cause irradiance changes that are due to the interplay of reflectance and illumination.

In this work we want to find if the performance of a scheme for matching image features in a wide base line based in a single feature descriptor is increased, if we use multiple descriptors from the same feature taken at different time, for training a statistical learning method, and then use this learning method for the matching process.

So in this work we are interested in the results of a general scheme for matching images features in a wide base line, instead of a specific method performance. Next, a general and modular scheme is presented to address the problem, the idea is to attempt different kind of descriptors and statistical methods of learning and classification, the modularity makes possible to interchange different methods and descriptors. Therefore, the scheme is divided into two stages: learning (map building) and recognition (localization).

Learning phase:

1. **Small base-line tracking:** Features are detected and tracked using a conventional small base-line tracker, specifically in this work the Lucas-Kanade Tracker (KLT) was used, but any efficient tracker could be used.
2. **Window extraction:** For each feature detected a *p*-by-*p* pixels window around the feature center is extracted, in our work we used a *12-by-12* pixel window. Other window sizes have been tested but the results were worse.
3. **Descriptor creation:** A descriptor x_i is obtained for each window area. A good descriptor has to be as invariant as possible to changes like rotation or scale and insensitive to changes like illumination. We used two statistical techniques: principal component analysis (PCA) and independent component analysis (ICA), but others descriptors like SIFT can be used.
4. **Storage in database:** For each frame, descriptors have to be scaled and stored in a data base. Descriptors created from the same feature tracked along the time with small base-line are stored with the same label y_i.
5. **Feature class creation:** A statistical method is used in order to create and represent the descriptors stored in the database with the same label y_i like a unique class V that represent the feature. This feature class V is created with the purpose of capturing the variations in the appearance of the feature along the time.

The capacity of V to represent these variations depends on the number of descriptors and the changes of scene conditions in which it was created. For this study we used Support Vector Machine (SVM) and variations of K-Nearest Neighbor (KNN).

Recognition phase:

1. **Feature Detection:** In order to improve the computational performance in the recognition phase, the same small base-line tracker in the learning phase is used to detect features, but it is not used to track feature candidates to match.
2. **Descriptors candidates:** For each candidate feature a descriptor x_j is created in the same way that it was created in the learning phase.
3. **Recognition:** The same statistical method used in the learning phase is used now to classify the candidate descriptor x_j in the more adequate feature class V. Depending on the kind of selected statistical method a quality scheme of correspondence between the candidate descriptor and its associated class can be implemented.

3 Statistical Methods for Matching Features in a Wide Base-Line

In this work we employ two image features descriptors: The ICAD [14] and the PCAD, based in [14] too, but using PCA (principal component analysis) instead of ICA (independent component analysis). We used two statistical learning methods: KNN (k-nearest neighbor) and SVM (support vector machine). The idea is comparing the performance of ICAD and PCAD alone, with their performance using them together with KNN and SVM. Consequently in the experiments we are comparing six methods: ICAD, PCAD, SVM-ICA, SVM-PCA, KNN-ICA, and KNN-PCA. In this section first we explain the theoretical bases for ICA, PCA, SVM and KNN, and later, we briefly explain our methods used in this work.

3.1 PCA and ICA

Principal Component Analysis (PCA) [7] is a standard statistical tool used to find the orthogonal directions corresponding to the highest variance. It is equivalent to a decorrelation of the data using second-order information. The basic idea in PCA is to find the components $p_1, p_2, \ldots, p_n$ that explain the maximum amount of variance, by n linearly transformed components. Then, the principal components are given by $p_i = w_i^T X$, where $X = [x_1, \ldots, x_m]^T$, x_i is an observed data vector, and w_i is a basis vector (an eigenvector of the sample covariance matrix $E\{XX^T\}$). It can be written, in matrix form, as:

$$P = WX \qquad (1)$$

where $P = [p_1, \ldots, p_n]^T$ and p_i is a principal component vector.

The Independent Component Analysis (ICA) [8] attempts to go one step further than PCA, by finding the orthogonal matrix H which transforms the data P into Z having $Z_1, Z_2, \ldots Z_m$ statistically independent. The ICA is thus more general than PCA in trying not only to decorrelate the data, but also to find decomposition, transforming the input into independent components. The simplest ICA model, the noise-free linear ICA model, seems to be sufficient for most applications. This model is as follows: ICA of observed random data X consists of estimating the generative model:

$$X = AS \tag{2}$$

where $X = [x_1, \ldots, x_n]^T$ x_i is an observed random vector, $S = [s_1, \ldots, s_n]^T$, s_i is a latent component, and A is the constant *mixing* matrix. The transform we seek is $B = VW$, then

$$Z = BX = BAS = CS \tag{3}$$

If an orthogonal matrix D that transforms the mixed signals X into Z with independent components could be found, and assuming that at least one independent source s_k is normally distributed, then Z=CS with C being a non-mixing matrix. The ICA algorithms attempt to find the matrix B which ensures that Z is independent.

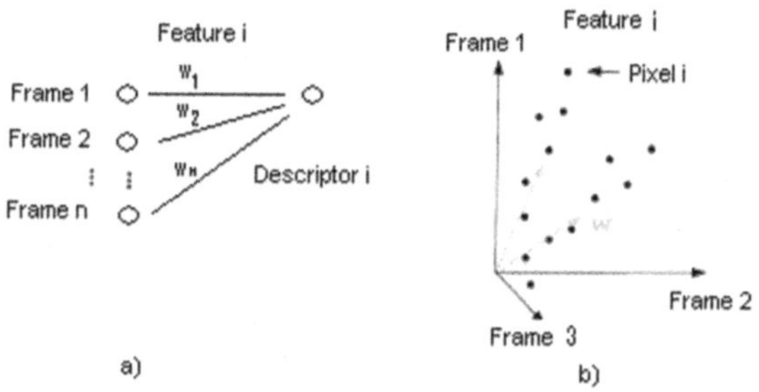

Fig. 1. a) Applying ICA or PCA a matrix is formed where each row is a feature i tracked in frame n. b) ICA or PCA finds a weight vector w in the directions of statistical dependencies among the pixel locations. In the case of ICA, data are decorrelated and decompositions found, transforming the input into independent components.

3.2 ICA and PCA Applied to Window Based Images Features

If we consider a feature as a window of p x p pixels in a frame, we can organize each feature as a long vector with as many dimensions as number of pixels in the feature. ICA or PCA can be applied to this data organizing each vector into a matrix X where each row is the same image feature for different frames (Fig.1 left). In this approach, images features are random variables and pixels are samples (Fig.1 right).

3.3 SVM and KNN

Support Vector Machine (SVM) is a technique used in data classification. The goal of SVM is to produce a model which predicts target value of data instances in the testing set which are given only the attributes.

Given a training set of instance-label pairs $(x_i, y_i), i = 1,\ldots,l$ where $x_i \in R^n$ and $y \in \{1,-1\}^l$, the SVM [9] require the solution of the following optimization problem:

$$\min_{w,b,\xi}\left(\frac{1}{2}w^t w + C\sum_{i=1}^{l}\xi_i\right),\ \text{with } C>0$$

subject to $y_i(w^t\varphi(x_i)+b)\geq 1-\xi_i$, where $\xi_i\geq 0$.

Here training vectors, x_i, are mapped into a higher (maybe infinite) dimensional space by the function φ. Then SVM finds a linear separating hyper-plane with the maximal margin in this higher dimensional space. C is the penalty parameter of the error term. Furthermore, $K(x_i,x_j)=\varphi(x_i)^T\varphi(x_j)$ is called the kernel function. In this work a radial basis function (RBF) was used like kernel function:

$$K(x_i x_j)\equiv\exp(-\gamma\|x_i-x_j\|^2),\gamma>0 \tag{4}$$

The K-nearest neighbor (KNN) is a statistical method of classification well known and very simple, nevertheless has come to demonstrate to be very effective in a wide variety of applications. It works based on minimum distance from the query instance x_j to the training samples (x_i,y_i), to determine the K-nearest neighbors. After we gather K nearest neighbors, we take simple majority of these K-nearest neighbors to be the prediction of the query instance.

In this work we use a 5-nearest neighbor; we use a parameter α like a threshold for considering a good match between an x_j candidate descriptor and the selected more voted feature class V:

$$\alpha=\frac{K\sum_{j=1}^{l}d(x_j,x)}{l^2} \tag{5}$$

where $x_j\in V$, $d(x_j,x)$ is the Euclidean distance and l is the number of votes for the more voted class V. In this way the average Euclidean distance is used like threshold but is penalized according to the number of votes received for V respect to K.

3.4 ICAD and PCAD Methods

Many ICA and PCA algorithms are available. A computationally efficient ICA algorithm, called the FastICA [10] algorithm and the PCA Snapshot Method [11] have been chosen for this work.

When the KLT (small base-line tracker) locates a feature (feature i at frame f), a p-by-p pixels window around the feature center is stored as a vector u_{fi} of length p-by-p, with a distinctive label; in the following frames the feature is tracked and repeating the above process, storing the window with the same label. Immediately vectors with the same label (same feature i) are regrouped in a matrix $U_i=[u_{1i},\ldots,u_{ni}]^T$ where n is the number of frames where the feature has been tracked.

Then for each matrix U the ICA or PCA is applied as it has been shown in the section 3.2 along with dimensional reduction selecting the largest eigenvalue to be retained. At the output of the ICA or PCA we obtain a descriptor q_i with a dimension that equals to the feature window size. The descriptors are stored in a database with a unique label for each feature.

In the recognition phase features are detected but not tracked by the KLT for each incoming frame. Then for each feature detected a window is obtained in the same way than the learning stage and sorted in a vector v_i, the ICA or PCA is directly applied to this vector without dimensional reduction producing a descriptor x_j. A fast k-nearest neighbor algorithm is applied to the database in order to look for the 2-nearest neighbor descriptors q_{i1} and q_{i2}. Be $k_1 = d(x_j, q_{i1})$ and $k_2 = \mathrm{d}(x_j, q_{i2})$ (d is the Euclidean distance), $k_1 \leq k_2$, and $\eta = k_1 / k_2$, this factor will be used by our algorithm as a threshold for considering a good match between the candidate descriptor r_i and its corresponding nearest descriptors q_{i1} *and* q_{i2} in the database. When η tends to 0 means a great distance between candidates and, empirically, the results are better.

3.5 SVM-ICA and SVM-PCA Methods

We used the LIBSVM [12] for the implementation of the SVM. The method follows exactly the same steps than the feature-class method (section 2): In step 3 (descriptor creation) unlike the ICAD and PCAD methods, the ICA or PCA is applied directly to the vector u_{fi} obtained from de p-by-p pixels window (step 2) and stored in the database (step 4). In the output of the ICA or PCA we obtain a descriptor with the same dimension than the pixel window.

For step 5 (feature-class creation) we employ the descriptors-database for training a SVM classifier with a radial basis function (RBF) as a kernel function, equation 4. The parameters $C = 8$ and $\gamma = 1$ used in RBF were selected by cross-validation and grid search. For the recognition phase the SVM output model is used to predict the feature class V of the candidate descriptor x_j, as it has been explained in section 2 (recognition phase).

3.6 KNN-ICA and KNN-PCA Methods

For the implementation of KNN we employ a computationally efficient algorithm called approximate nearest neighbor (ANN). The method follows the same steps than SVM-ICA and SVM-PCA except that a training model is not generated from the descriptor-database. Prior to the recognition phase the whole database is loaded in memory by the ANN algorithm. In experiments we used 5-NN. For recognition phase ANN is applied as it has been explained in section 3.3. The threshold α is used to consider a good match between a candidate descriptor x_j and the more voted selected feature class V (equation 5).

4 Experiments

We have implemented a C++ version of the methods that runs on a PC 2GHz Pentium IV processor, 512MB RAM. A non-expensive USB Webcam with a maximum resolution of 640-by-480 pixels and 30 fps has been used.

We performed a variety of experiments in order to show the performance of the aforementioned methods. For each method in the learning phase, a video sequence of a rigid environment desktop scene was recorded moving the camera slowly and continuously in order to obtain a change of some degrees in the 3D point of view and rotation of the camera. Later, twenty descriptors were created from this video sequence as it was described in section 3. In Fig. 2 (center image) the scene used in the learning phase is showed.

Together with these 20 descriptors, the database contains another 1000 descriptors corresponding to other video sequences. The objective of these experiments consists of observing the response of the methods when a set of descriptors coming from an online video sequence (close to the learning sequence, as it is explained below) will be matched with the descriptors database. The response was observed in four different situations:

- case a) change in 3D viewpoint with respect to the position in the learning phase and little change in illumination,
- case b) change in 3D point of view plus change in rotation and little change in illumination,
- case c) change in 3D point of view plus change in scale (camera zoom) and little change in illumination,
- case d) change in 3D point of view plus great change in illumination.

Fig. 2(left and right) show some frames used in the recognition phase.

Fig. 2. Descriptors created in the learning phase (central image). Examples of descriptors matched in the recognition phase: (left and right image) we can observe changes in the point of view and illumination.

We define the response of the methods in terms of two measurements:

1) ***Error of classification*:** It is the ratio between the *percentage of false positive* and *percentage of classification*. We define *percentage of false positive* as the ratio between the number of features wrong classified and the total of features classified in the scene (correctly or incorrectly). We define *percentage of classification* as the ratio between the total of features classified in the scene (correctly or incorrectly) and the total that potentially could be matched (we consider only a finite number of possible locations in each frame to be matched, step 1 of recognition phase). For example in the methods based in KNN the *percentage of false positive* for a threshold $\alpha = 0.6$ could be 16 percent but the *percentage of classification* is 50 percent, consequently we define the *error of classification* as 0.32. On the other hand in SVM is difficult to establish a threshold for classification, because SVM is a method of the kind "choose the best candidate". Therefore we consider the *percentage of classification* for SVM

as 100 percent. For example a 38 percent of false positive in SVM means 38 percent of classification error.

2) ***Computational cost*:** We have calculated the time for each frame (or the frequency, it is the same) that the different methods take to classify 30 possible features with the 1000 descriptors that are in the database.

The results for the experiments and the measurements are shown in Table 1.

Table 1. Error of classification for each condition case (a, b, c and d) in the recognition phase and their computational cost. CPU* does not include the time to detect features by KLT tracker.

Case	PCAD	ICAD	SVM-PCA	SVM-ICA	KNN-PCA	KNN-ICA
a	.40	.35	.33	.21	.26	.21
b	.47	.45	.44	.38	.31	.32
c	.47	.33	.41	.28	.50	.35
d	.48	.47	.43	.42	.37	.32
CPU	5.34 Hz	5.05 Hz	2.32 Hz	2.20 Hz	5.34 Hz	3.84 Hz
CPU*	16.30 Hz	10.70 Hz	3.22 Hz	2.94 Hz	21.72 HZ	7.09 Hz

5 Conclusions

In this work we propose the use of statistical methods for learning variability of image feature appearance, for matching image feature in a wide base line.

In the results of the experiments (Table 1), we can observe a lower error of classification in the methods based in statistical learning (SVM-PCA, SVM-ICA, KNN-PCA and KNN-ICA) comparing with ICAD and PCAD methods. Therefore the performance of the ICAD and PCAD methods was increased using statistical learning approaches.

On the other hand, as we expected, ICA-based descriptors show lower error of classification than PCA-based descriptors but computationally the cost for ICA is greater than PCA. We observe a similar computational cost in the case PCAD and ICAD with KNN-PCA and KNN-ICA. Finally we also observe that KNN shows better performance than SVM in error of classification as well as in computational cost.

A feature of our approach is the modularity, so in a future work we pretend to use a more robust descriptor like SIFT. Looking the results of this work, we can expect that using SIFT together with a scheme of statistical learning we can improve the performance of SIFT alone, for applications like a mobile robot where an incoming stream video is available.

References

1. Shi, J., Tomasi, C.: Good features to track, Proc. IEEE CVPR, 1994.
2. Harris, C., Stephens, M.: A combined corner and edge detector, Alvey Vision Conf., 1988.
3. Mikolajczyk, K., Schmid, C.: An affine invariant interest point detector, Proc. ECCV, 2002.

4. Lowe, D.: Object recognition from local scale-invariant features, Proc. ICCV, Corfu, Greece, September 1999.
5. Lowe, D.: Distinctive image features from scale-invariant keypoints, International Journal of Computer Vision, 60 (2): 91-110, 2004.
6. Meltzer, J., Yang, M H., Gupta, R., Soatto, S.: Multiple view feature descriptors from image sequences via kernel principal component analysis, Proc. ECCV, 2004.
7. Jolliffe, I.T.: Principal Component Analysis. Springer Verlag, 1986.
8. Comon, P.: Independent component analysis, a new concept?, Signal Processing, Elsevier, 36(3): 287-314, April 1994.
9. Boser, B. E., Guyon, I., Vapnik, V.: A training algorithm for optimal margin classifiers, Proc. of the Fifth Annual Workshop on Computational Learning Theory 5, pp. 144-152, 1992.
10. Hyvarinen, A., Oja, E.: A fast fixed-point algorithm for independent component analysis, Neural Computation, 9 (7): 1483-1492, 1997.
11. Sirovich, L.: Turbulence and the dynamics of coherent structures, Part 1: Coherent Structure, Quarterly of Applied Mathematics, 45 (3): 561-571, October 1987.
12. Chih-Chung Chang, Chih-Jen Lin: LIBSVM : a library for support vector machines, 2001. Software available at http://www.csie.ntu.edu.tw/~cjlin/libsvm.
13. Sebastian Thrun: Robotic Mapping *CMU-CS-02-111*.2000.
14. R. Munguía, A. Grau, A. Sanfeliu: Matching Images Features in a Wide Base Line with ICA Descriptors. IAPR 18th International Conference for Pattern Recognition, ICPR 2006, Honk Kong, to be appeared.

Probabilistic Shot Boundary Detection Using Interframe Histogram Differences*

Alvaro Pardo[1,2]

[1] DIE, Facultad de Ingeniería y Tecnologías, Universidad Católica del Uruguay
[2] IIE, Facultad de Ingeniería, Universidad de la República
apardo@ucu.edu.uy

Abstract. In this paper we study a method for the detection of shot boundaries using interframe histogram differences. Instead of using traditional distance between histograms, we use a probabilistic distance that indicates the chance of a given distance to be a shot boundary. We declare a shot change when the interframe histogram difference is a large deviation from the expected histogram interframe differences given past evidence. Like other histogram based methods the proposed one is very simple while being very robust and effective. The proposed method outperforms similar methods proposed in the literature for the detection of hard cuts and achieves good recall and precision performances for gradual transitions.

1 Introduction

Shot boundary (SB) detection algorithms are one of the most important methods for video analysis. They allow the segmentation of the original video sequence into basic units called shots that facilitate high level processing and abstraction of the video signal. Although it may seem a simple task, the automatic and reliable extraction of SB it has some difficulties, mainly due to the different types of video sequences. Since a video sequence contains a great amount of data, we should avoid unnecessarily complicated methods. For this reason we will explore possible improvements of classical and simple methods. In this work we will present a simple online method based on color histograms with only a few parameters that performs well for a representative set of tested video sequences.

Existing methods for SB detection can be divided into the following basic categories: pixel, histogram, block matching, object segmentation and tracking, and feature tracking based methods. Pixel based methods usually compute interframe differences between frames (adjacent or not). The main drawback of pixel-based methods is their sensitivity to camera and object motion and noise. For this reason filtering is usually applied before computing interframe differences [1]. Regarding the measure of difference, we can make a distinction between distance based methods and thresholding ones. Usually these methods are not

* Supported by Proyecto PDT-S/C/OP/17/07.

J.F. Martínez-Trinidad et al. (Eds.): CIARP 2006, LNCS 4225, pp. 726–732, 2006.

very reliable and therefore are mostly used as indicators of probable SB that are the confirmed by more sophisticated methods [2].

Histogram based methods compare the histograms of a pair of frames using a suitable histogram distance [3]. In contrast to pixel based methods, histogram based methods are robust against camera and object motions since histograms do not contain any spatial information. Unfortunately, the main limitation is that frames of different shots can have similar histograms and in this way these methods will fail. In addition, like pixel-based methods, these methods are not robust against lighting changes. Strong color changes in part of the image may produce false detections.

Block-matching methods divide each frame into blocks and then match a given set of block features (pixel colors, histograms, and so on) between frames. That is, the best match for each block in the source frame is found in the destination frame and the similarity of these block is used as an indicator for SB existence [3,1].

Segmentation and object tracking are typically computational demanding. The main idea behind these methods is that frames within a shot contain the same objects, therefore, they use algorithms for object tracking and segmentation to achieve SB detection.

Feature tracking methods detect shot transitions when there is an abrupt change in the number of features tracked. For example, if the frame edges have strong variations [1]. In [4] the authors propose feature tracking as a measure of frame dissimilarity. Instead of tracking edges, they propose to track fine grained features as corners and textures. SB are then detected as points with high inter-frame feature loss.

Nearly all of the previous methods rely on a set of thresholds in order to decide whether there is a SB in a given frame. The problem of selection of the right threshold is a key point that has big influence in the overall system performance. Unfortunately, it has received little attention in the literature [1] and most of the authors propose heuristics for their selection. Furthermore, it has been demonstrated that global thresholds led to sub optimal methods, with too many false positives or false negatives [1]. To solve this problem adaptive thresholds have been proposed. However, when using adaptive thresholds we must design an updating rule based on, for example, the statistics of non-boundary frames. This introduces additional problems concerning the correct estimation of this statistical information. Traditionally the problem is solved introducing a learning stage where several video sequences are processed to obtain the desired statistics.

In this paper we introduce a simple method for the detection of SB using only interframe histogram differences. The method is inspired in the works of Computational Gestalt [5,6]. The key idea in this framework is to define a meaningful event as large deviation from a known background process. Here we will extend those ideas to label a SB when its interframe histogram differences have little probability to be produced given past interframe histogram differences of non-SB frames. The use of past information of non-SB differs from other existing methods which usually evaluate distances between adyacent histograms. This is a difference between our proposal and other existing probabilistic histogram (or probability distribution) distance. Also, the use on non-SB allows using a non-supervised technique; we do not use any training step considering known SB information. Even though the mentioned limitations of histogram based methods will show that they achieve reasonable results. Furthermore, they are less sensitive to compression artifacts as some of the other discussed methods (feature and pixel based for example). In our case all sequences are compressed in mpeg format; some of them with strong compression artifacts.

In the first step of the algorithm we compute a measure of SB probability or meaningfulness. Then in a second stage we apply an adaptive thresholding technique that only uses the information of the video sequence being processed to find the SB. This makes our method very simple and fast.

2 Proposed Method

As we said in the previous section our method is based on interframe histogram differences. In what follows we will consider histograms of image pixels computed over a predefined set of bins. Let $H_i(t)$ be the histogram of the i color component of the frame t[1], and H_d the histogram of (color) histogram differences computed also over a predefined set of bins. That is, if we define $d = |H_i(t+1) - H_i(t)|$, H_d will contain the histogram of d for previous frames. That is, in each bin it counts the number of points (bins from H_i) where the difference falls within it.

Now let $P_\mu = \text{Probability}(d(b) > \mu)$ be the probability of the interframe histogram difference at bin b to be above μ. If there is no shot change we expect the histogram differences to be small, and in agreement with previous histogram differences. On the other hand, when a shot change occurs the histogram differences do not follow previous evidence.

Given a fixed threshold μ we can compute the number of bins in d exceeding the threshold μ, N_μ. To obtain a probabilistic measure of shot change meaningfulness we follow [5,6] and compute its probability of occurrence given previous interframe histogram differences. This can be done computing the probability of at least N_μ bins out of the total number of bins N_b exceeding the threshold μ by using the Binomial distribution:

$$B(N_b, N_\mu, P_\mu) = \sum_{k=N_\mu}^{N_b} C_k^{N_b} P_\mu^k (1 - P_\mu)^{N_b - k}$$

Using this probability, we say that the actual histogram difference is meaningful if its probability is very low given previous histogram differences [2]. This means that we say that the event is meaningful if it is a large deviation of what is expected given past information.

[1] In this work we use the YUV color space.

[2] In the computational gestalt theory instead of working only with the probabilities the authors propose to estimate the expectation via multiplying the probability by the number of test performed [6].

Finally, the meaningfulness of a histogram difference is obtained as the minimal probability over a set of fixed thresholds:

$$M = \min_{\mu_i} B(N_b, N_{\mu_i}, P_{\mu_i}) \tag{1}$$

where each term corresponds to a threshold $\mu_i \in \{\mu_1, ..., \mu_n\}$. The smallest threshold μ_1 is estimated from the past values of histogram differences using an $\alpha - \beta$ filter. The upper threshold is set to a reasonable value. In this work we set $\mu_n = 512$. According to our experiments this parameter does not influence the results.

The probabilities P_μ are obtained from past histogram differences. To deal with non-stationary statistics we use an $\alpha - \beta$ filter. The histogram H_d is updated with the following rule:

$$H_d(t+1) = \alpha \text{Histogram}(d(t)) + (1-\alpha) H_d(t) \tag{2}$$

with $\alpha = 0.2$.

For the computation of the binomial distributions we use the Hoeffding approximations [7] to obtain an upper bound for the logarithm of M when $k/n \geq p$ using[3]:

$$\log(B(k,n,p)) \leq k \log\left(\frac{pn}{k}\right) + n\left(1 - \frac{k}{n}\right) \log\left(\frac{1-p}{1-\frac{k}{n}}\right)$$

Since we propose an online method we must decide the occurrence of a shot change using only past values. In fact we introduce a delay in the response in order to consider a window, $W = [t-4, ..t+4]$, centered in t. We will say that there is a SB at frame t if the following conditions are fulfilled: $M(t) = \min_{s \in W} M(s)$, $M(t) < \delta \min_{s \in \{t-4,..,t-1\}} \hat{M}(s)$ or $M(t) < \delta \min_{s \in \{t+1,..,t+4\}} \hat{M}(s)$, $M(t) < \gamma \text{Threshold}(t)$ where $\hat{M}$ are the local maxima of M and $\text{Threshold}(t)$ adaptively computed using only the accumulated values for non-SB X [1]:

$$\text{Threshold}(t) = \alpha \text{Threshold}(t-1) + (1-\alpha) \text{Mean}(X)$$

For the all the results presented in next section we set: $\delta = 4$, $\gamma = 10$ and $\alpha = 0.01$.

3 Results and Evaluation

To validate the results of the proposed method we are going to test our algorithm against a set of sequences used in [4] where a method for hard cut detection was presented. In figure 1 we show the first frame and the outcome of the proposed method for three sequences. As we can see there are a set of well defined peaks that correspond to SB. In table 1 we present the our results restricted to hard

[3] Since the probabilities are very small is more combinient to work with logarithms.

Table 1. Comparison for the detection of hard cuts for sequences in figure 1

	Proposed Method			Feature tracking [4]			Pixel based [4]			Histogram based [8]		
Seq	Prec	Rec	F1	Prec	Rec	F1	Prec	Rec	F1	Prec	Rec	F1
A	1	1	1	1	1	1	1	1	1	1	1	1
B	1	1	1	1	1	1	.825	.825	.825	1	.375	.545
C	.946	.898	.922	.595	.870	.707	.764	.778	.771	.936	.536	.682
D	1	1	1	1	1	1	1	1	1	1	.941	.969
E	1	.957	.978	.938	1	.968	.867	.867	.867	.955	.700	.808
F	1	1	1	1	1	1	0	0	0	1	1	1
G	1	1	1	.810	.944	.872	.708	.994	.809	1	.666	.800
H	.769	.976	.860	.895	.895	.895	.927	1	.962	.971	.895	.932
I	1	1	1	1	1	1	1	1	1	1	.500	.667
Average	.968	.981	.973	.915	.968	.938	.788	.829	.804	.985	.735	.823
Variance	.006	.001	.002	.019	.003	.010	.099	.104	.099	.001	.055	.027
Std dev	.077	.035	.050	.137	.052	.100	.314	.323	.315	.025	.234	.165

cuts for comparison purposes with [4]. As in [4] we measure the performance of our method using precision (Prec), recall (Rec) and F1 defined as:

$$\text{Prec} = \frac{\text{T+}}{\text{T+} + \text{F+}}, \ \text{Rec} = \frac{\text{T+}}{\text{T+} + \text{F-}}, \ \text{F1} = \frac{2 \times \text{Prec} \times \text{Rec}}{\text{Prec} + \text{Rec}}$$

where $T+$, $F+$ and $F-$ means true positives, false positives and false negatives respectively.

The precision of the proposed method (PM) outperforms, on average, the feature tracking (FT) and pixel based (PB) methods while performs close to the histogram based (HB) one. On the other hand, considering the recall capabilities, PM outperforms, on average and for each sequence, the precision of the other three methods. Finally, the F1 measure of PM outperforms on average and for each sequence but the H, the results of the other methods. Looking at the individual sequences, the only sequence where PM is defeated is sequence H. For this sequence, the precision is worse than other three methods while its recall outperforms FT and HB methods and is close to the PB one.

We conclude that PM outperforms (specially looking at the F1 figures) the other three methods reported for the same sequences. The sequence H is a problematic case with too many false positives. These false positives are located around frame 3000 where strong lightning change occur, and may be eliminated using a better detection strategy. Particularly, a strategy adapted for this sequence. In our case we used the same strategy (with the same parameters) for all sequences.

When considering the detection of gradual transitions, PM detected all of them in the tested sequences achieving 100% of precision and recall. Although the obtained results seem very promising the total number of gradual transition considered is not big enough to expect this kind of performance in every case. The numbers of gradual transitions for each sequence are: A 1, C 2, E 4, F 2 and G 2. However, it is important to note that the detected gradual transitions are of different type. For example, even though the transitions in sequence F expand along several frames the output of the proposed method has two clear peaks at boundary positions, see figure 1.

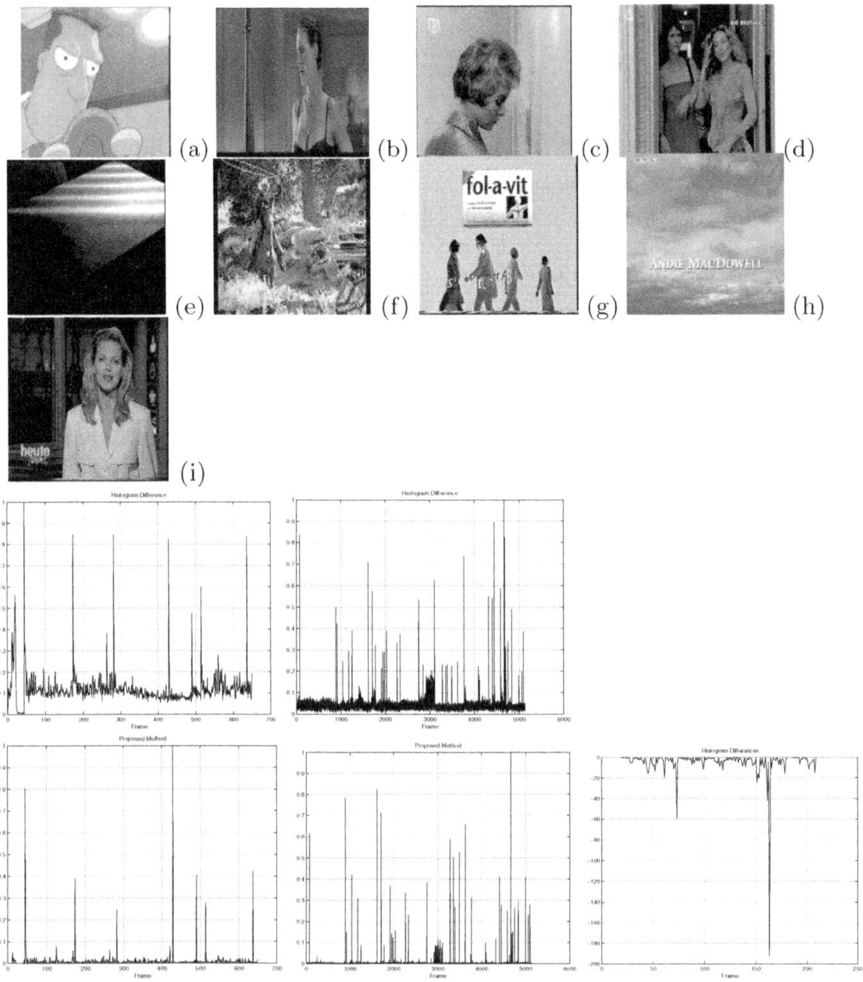

Fig. 1. Top: Sequences. A (Lisa): Cartoon video with substantial object motion. B(Jamie): Strong motions. C(Psycho): Black and white movie with substantial action and motions and many close hard cuts. D(Sex in the city): High quality digitalization TV show. E(Highlander): Low quality digitalization of TV show. F(TV Commercial): TV Commercial with only a dissolve. G(TV Commercial): TV commercial with hard cuts and gradual transitions. H(Video): Movie with strong lightning changes. I(News): TV news program. Bottom: Comparison of proposed method (meaningfulness M) and standard bin-wise histogram difference for sequences A and H. Results for sequence F.

To exemplify the advantages of PM against traditional histogram based methods we compare the outputs of PM and standard histogram difference. We normalized both results dividing each one by its maximum. The results are presented in figure 1 for videos A and H. As we can see the results of PM are less noisy and the peaks at SB positions are clearly separated from non-SB ones.

4 Conclusions and Future Work

We have presented a simple method that uses histogram differences and improves the results of previously reported methods. The method obtains a measure for shot change meaningfulness with clear peaks at SB. This allows for simpler adaptive threshold and offline detection methods. We formulated the problem inspired in the computational gestalt theory and presented a novel method to compute shot changes based on histogram differences. In future work we will address the limitations of the method with respect to strong color and lightning changes together with better detection strategies.

References

1. Hanjalic, A.: Shot-boundary detection: Unraveled and resolved. IEEE Transactions on Circuits and Systems for Video Technology (2002)
2. Huang, C.L., Liao, B.Y.: A robust scene-change detection method for video segmentation. IEEE Transactions on Circuits and Systems for Video Technology (2001)
3. Gargi, U., Kasturi, R., Strayer, S.H.: Performance characterization of video-shot-change detection methods. IEEE Transactions on Circuits and Systems for Video Technology (2000)
4. Whitehead, A., Bose, P., Laganiere., R.: Feature based cut detection with automatic threshold selection. In: Proceedings of the International Conference on Image and Video Retrieval. (2004) 410–418
5. Desolneux, A., Moisan, L., J.-M-Morel: A grouping principle and four applications. IEEE Transactions on Pattern Analysis and Machine Intelligence **25** (2003) 508–512
6. Desolneux, A., Moisan, L., J.-M-Morel: Maximal meaningful events and applications to image analysis. The Annals of Statistics **31** (2003) 1822–1851
7. Desolneux, A.: Evnements significatifs et applications l'analyse d'images. PhD thesis, ENS-Cachan, France (2000)
8. Pfeiffer, S., Leinhart, R., Kuhne, G., Effelserberg, W.: The MoCa Project - Movie Content Analysis REsearch at the University of Mannheim. In: Informatik 1998. (1998) 329–338

A Probabilistic Approach to Build 2D Line Based Maps from Laser Scans in Indoor Environments

Leonardo Romero and Carlos Lara

Michoacana University
Morelia, Mich., Mexico
lromero@umich.mx, calara@lsc.fie.umich.mx

Abstract. In this work we consider a mobile robot with a laser range finder. Our goal is to find the best set of lines from the sequence of points given by a laser scan. We propose a probabilistic method to deal with noisy laser scans, in which the noise is not properly modeled using a Gaussian Distribution. An experimental comparison with a very well known method (SMSM), using a mobile robot simulator and a real mobile robot, shows the robustness of the new method. The new method is also fast enough to be used in real time.

1 Introduction

This paper focuses on methods to resolve the problem of fitting a set of lines to a sequence of points. Specifically, the sequence of points are acquired by using a laser range finder mounted on a mobile robot. The set of lines can be used in complex activities such as Localization and Mapping in indoor environments.

Localization is a key activity for mobile robots which consists of determining the robot's position in its environment. Localization can be done by matching the newest sensed data against information in a priori map. There are two common matching techniques that have been used in mobile robotics: point–based matching and feature–based matching.

In the feature–based matching approach it is necessary to learn features from the environment. Features are recognizable structures of elements in the environment [12]. The simplest feature is a line or a line segment. A Line Based Map (LM) is a set of lines which represent the robot's environment. Owing to indoor environments are usually rich in planar surfaces, LMs are the natural way to represent them. In addition, LMs are more compact and more accurate than point–based maps.

For extracting a LM from a laser scan, many algorithms have been proposed, but all of them have their shortcomings. Forsyth [6] identifies three principal difficulties in this process: 1) find the best number of lines, 2) determine which points belong to which line, and 3) estimate the line parameters given the points that belong to a line. Furthermore, if the robot navigates within a high cluttered

J.F. Martínez-Trinidad et al. (Eds.): CIARP 2006, LNCS 4225, pp. 733–742, 2006.

environment, a lot of points do not belong to any line, and the process becomes more difficult.

This paper introduces a new approach called WSAC–GE, Window SAmpling Consensus with Global Evaluation. The algorithm begins with an empty map, and successively proposes a new map by adding or removing lines from the previous map. The current map is selected from two maps: the proposed new map or the previous map, according to which map is best evaluated by a global function. Problems associated with outliers (atypical data) are handled by a probabilistic search and different segments of the same line are identified easily. Other methods have difficulties with outliers or report many disconnected segments when in fact they belong to the same line.

This paper is organized as follows: Section 2 describes how a laser acquires information from the environment. Section 3 describes related works, and it focuses on the most used algorithms to extract lines. Section 4 describes the proposed method. Section 5 compares the performance of WSAC–GE against a good and well known method called SMSM (Split–Merge–Split–Merge). Finally, section 6 explains the advantages of the proposed method.

2 Data Acquisition

In a single measurement, a laser range finder calculates the distance to the object in a given orientation. Usually, each measurement is expressed in the form (r_i, α_i); where r_i is the distance from the sensor to the detected object at direction α_i. A laser scan performs n consecutive measurements from the environment changing the orientation in $\Delta\alpha$. Also, the laser scan can be expressed in its equivalent cartesian form $\mathcal{P} = \{(x_i, y_i) \,|i = 1 \ldots n\}$.

3 Related Works

To obtain a LM from a 2D laser scan many algorithms have been proposed. Two approaches, *Line Tracking* (LT) [4] and *Iterative End-Point Fit* (IEPF) [4] represent the classical way to solve the problem. These two algorithms take advantage of the sequentiality of the laser scan. The principal drawback of LT and IEPF is their poor performance when the laser scan is noisy. On other hand they are extremely fast. The Hough Transform Algorithm (HT) [8] is another common alternative used to generate line Maps . This technique has a good performance even when there are outliers. However, the principal drawbacks are associated with the discretization, its slow speed and that it ignores the uncertainty for estimating the line parameters. Finally, the well known Expectation-Maximization algorithm (EM) [3] is a technique used in several kind of problems with missed data. But it requires to know in advance how many line models exist in the environment. In [7] this difficult is solved by incrementally adding and removing models. Due to the SMSM algorithm has been widely used with good results [11], we compare the proposed method against SMSM. The next section describes the SMSM algorithm and section 3.2 focuses in methods commonly used to manage atypical data.

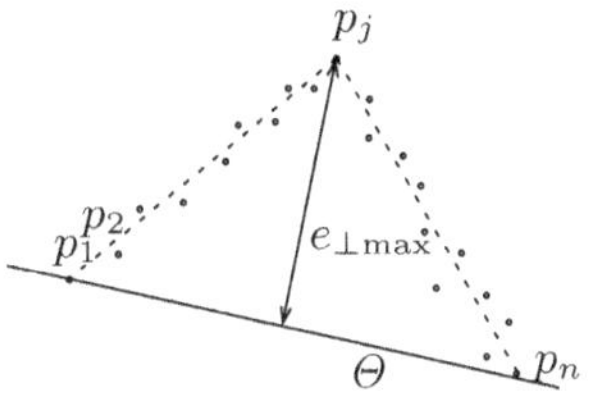

Fig. 1. Iterative End Point Fit

Algorithm 1. IEPF Algorithm

Input: The laser scan $\mathcal{P} = (p_1, p_2, \ldots, p_n)$ and a threshold t
Output: The map of lines $\mathcal{M}$

1. Initialize the set of sequences $\mathcal{L} \leftarrow \{\mathcal{P}\}$ and $\mathcal{M} \leftarrow \{\}$.
2. While $\mathcal{L} \neq \{\}$ do
   (a) Move an element of $\mathcal{L}$ to S
   (b) Calculate the line Θ joining the first and last point of S.
   (c) Detect the point p_j with maximum distance $e_{\perp max}$ to the line Θ
   (d) *If* $e_{\perp max} > t$ *then* Put $S_0 = (p_k | k = 1 \ldots j-1)$ and $S_1 = (p_k | k = j \ldots n_j)$ into $\mathcal{L}$
   (e) *If* $e_{\perp max} \leq t$ *then* Fit a line Θ^* to all the points in S and put Θ^* into $\mathcal{M}$.
3. Merge collinear segments in $\mathcal{M}$.

3.1 The SMSM Algorithm

The *Split–Merge Split–Merge* algorithm (SMSM)[17] is based in the IEPF algorithm. The IEPF algorithm [4] is described by the algorithm 1. and it is illustrated graphically in the figure 1.The SMSM algorithm is an extended and more robust version of the IEPF algorithm. At the beginning it finds clusters applying a breakpoint detector [1]. The idea behind this step is to detect and eliminate outliers, because they are not going to be included into any cluster. Then it merges two consecutive clusters if their distance (the distance between the final point of the first cluster and the first point of the second cluster) is less than a predefined threshold. In the second phase, SMSM applies the IEPF algorithm to all clusters. Finally it combines collinear segments.

3.2 Robust Regression

The goal of regression is to describe data using a model. Unfortunately, in the data set often exists a kind of data called outliers that makes the regression a hard problem. An outlier is a single observation far away from the rest of the data. Two techniques are frequently used to obtain a model from data contamined with outliers: The Random Sample Consensus Algorithm (RANSAC) [5] and the M–Estimators [9].

Algorithm 2. RANSAC Algorithm

Input: The laser scan $\mathcal{P} = (p_1, p_2, \ldots, p_n)$, a threshold t and a maximum number of iterations m

Output: Θ^* (the best line given $\mathcal{P}$)

1. $j \leftarrow 0$, $n^* \leftarrow 0$.
2. While $j < m$ do
   (a) $j \leftarrow j + 1$
   (b) Select randomly two points from $\mathcal{P}$ and compute the line Θ, that joins them
   (c) Count the number of inliers, n, from $\mathcal{P}$ given Θ and t
   (d) if $n > n^*$ then $n^* \leftarrow n$, $\Theta^* \leftarrow \Theta$
3. Reestimate Θ^* using all the inliers.

The Random Sample Consensus algorithm consists in to iteratively propose new random models, and to evaluate each model proposed. After a number of tries, RANSAC selects the best evaluated model to represent the data. The version of RANSAC applied to the problem of fitting a line is described in the Algorithm 2.. The RANSAC algorithm has the advantage of estimating parameters of a model with accuracy even when outliers are present in the data set. Frequently RANSAC is a better choice than other algorithms due it can be better adapted to complex data analysis situations [10]. One of the problems of RANSAC is deciding the threshold t for considering a point as an inlier. If t is set too high then the model estimation can be very poor.

Algorithm 3. A generalized RANSAC Algorithm which uses a M–Estimator

Input: Tha laser scan $\mathcal{P} = (p_1, p_2, \ldots, p_n)$ a weight function g and a maximum number of iterations m

Output: Θ^* (the best fit line given $\mathcal{P}$)

1. $j \leftarrow 0$, $n^* \leftarrow 0$.
2. While $j < m$ do
   (a) $j \leftarrow j + 1$
   (b) Select randomly two points from $\mathcal{P}$ and compute the line Θ, that joins them
   (c) Calculate $n = \sum_{i=1}^{n} g(e_i)$. Where e_i is the distance from the point p_i to the line Θ
   (d) if $n > n^*$ then $n^* \leftarrow n_j$, $\Theta^* \leftarrow \Theta$
3. Reestimate Θ^*.

In the other hand, M–Estimators reject outliers by weighting each point using a so called weight function. Under certain circumstances, M-estimators can be vulnerable to high-leverage observations [2]. Many authors [13,16,15] proposed the combination of the RANSAC and M–Estimator methods to improve the performance. As an example, the algorithm 3. shows a RANSAC algorithm where the count of inliers in the algorithm 2. is replaced using a weighting function g.

4 Proposed Method: WSAC-GE

Suppose that there is an evaluation function $\mathcal{H}(\mathcal{M}, \mathcal{P})$ which returns a real value related with the correspondence of the map $\mathcal{M}$ (a set of lines) given the laser scan $\mathcal{P}$ (a sequence of points). Using $\mathcal{H}$ it is possible to decide if the map $\mathcal{M}'$ is better than $\mathcal{M}$, for a given laser scan $\mathcal{P}$, if $\mathcal{H}(\mathcal{M}', \mathcal{P}) > \mathcal{H}(\mathcal{M}, \mathcal{P})$. It is the basic idea under the WSAC-GE algorithm. The algorithm 4. proposes a new map $\mathcal{M}'$ from the previous one $\mathcal{M}$ and then it decides which one is better. The line addition and line deletion mechanisms provide ways to obtain $\mathcal{M}'$ from $\mathcal{M}$.

Algorithm 4. WSAC–GE

Input: The laser scan $\mathcal{P} = (p_1, p_2, \ldots, p_n)$ and a maximum number of iterations m
Output: A line based map $\mathcal{M}$

1. Let $\mathcal{M} \leftarrow \{\}$ and $i \leftarrow 0$
2. While $i < m$ do
   (a) $i \leftarrow i + 1$
   (b) Line addition
      i. Select randomly a window w of consecutive points in $\mathcal{P}$
      ii. From the point in w, fit a line Θ
      iii. Propose a new map $\mathcal{M}' \leftarrow \mathcal{M} \cup \{\Theta\}$,
      iv. If $\mathcal{H}(\mathcal{M}', P) > \mathcal{H}(\mathcal{M}, P)$ then $\mathcal{M} \leftarrow \mathcal{M}'$ and $i \leftarrow 0$.
   (c) Line Deletion
      i. Select randomly a line $\Theta_j \in \mathcal{M}$,
      ii. Propose a new map $\mathcal{M}' \leftarrow \mathcal{M} - \{\Theta_j\}$,
      iii. If $\mathcal{H}(\mathcal{M}', P) > \mathcal{H}(\mathcal{M}, P)$ then $\mathcal{M} \leftarrow \mathcal{M}'$ and $i \leftarrow 0$.
3. Associate points with lines and refine the final lines.

4.1 Line Addition Mechanism

The first mechanism, line addition, generates a new map $\mathcal{M}'$ by adding a new line Θ_j to $\mathcal{M}$, where $j = |\mathcal{M}| + 1$. The line's parameters Θ are obtained by fitting a line into a small quantity of points w called a window.

Given the line Θ_j the algorithm calculates the weighted–error c_{ij}, from each point p_i to line Θ_j, using:

$$c_{ij} = g(e_{\perp ij})$$

Where e_{ij} is the orthogonal distance of the point p_i to the line Θ_j and the function $g(x)$ is the Beaton-Tukey function [14] (an M-Estimator):

$$g(e) = \begin{cases} [1 - (e/k)^2]^2 & \text{if } |e| < k \quad \text{inliers} \\ 0 & \text{elsewhere outliers} \end{cases}$$

To improve the results we propose to penalize points which belong to small segments. Recalling that the weighted function $g(\cdot)$ is evaluated with 0 for $|e_{\perp ij}| > k$ and then it is possible to get a set of inliers S. With the ordered set S and using a breakpoint detector [1] it is possible to find the segments of Θ. A Breakpoint finds the segments of a line by finding the discontinuities of a ordered set of points. Finally, the algorithm penalizes every point p_i which belong to small–length segments by doing: $c_{ij} \leftarrow k\,(c_{ij})$,.where $0 \leq k < 1$ is a penalization constant.

4.2 Line Remotion Mechanism

The objective of the line–remotion mechanism is to remove small-length segments supported by points which belongs to larger segments. This mechanism randomly selects a line Θ from the map $\mathcal{M}$ and generates a new maps by removing Θ, as showed in the algorithm 4..

4.3 The Global–Evaluation

Let $\mathcal{M} = \{\Theta_1, \ldots, \Theta_l\}$ be a map with l lines. Table 1 shows a matrix representation of $\mathcal{M}$, each cell has the weighted error c_{ij}. The i–th column represents the point $p_i \in \mathcal{P}$ and the j–th row represents the line $\Theta_j \in \mathcal{M}$.

Table 1. Weighted–Errors c_{ij}

	p_1	p_2	$\cdots$	p_n
Θ_1	c_{11}	c_{21}	$\cdots$	c_{n1}
	$\vdots$	$\vdots$	$\ddots$	$\vdots$
Θ_l	c_{1l}	c_{2l}	$\cdots$	c_{nl}
	s_1	s_2	$\cdots$	s_n

Where s_i in Table 1 is computed by

$$s_i = \begin{cases} s'_i & \text{if } s'_i > u \\ 1 & elsewhere \end{cases}$$

and s'_i is the maximum value of the i-th column $(c_{ij}, j = 1, \cdots, l)$ and u is a threshold. Using s_i, a normalized weight h_j of the j–th line is given by

$$h_j = \sum_{i=1}^{n} \frac{c_{ij}}{s_i} \tag{1}$$

A high value for h_j denotes a line with a high support given the set of points. Finally the function $\mathcal{H}$ is given by

$$\mathcal{H}(\mathcal{M}, \mathcal{P}) = \sum_{j=1}^{l} h_j^2 \tag{2}$$

4.4 Associating Points with Lines

If After m tries the algorithm can not find a better map, then it finishes. The result is the best map $\dot{\mathcal{M}}$. WSAC–GE associates the point p_i to its the closest line by selecting the maximum value of the i–th column in the table 1.

5 Experimental Tests

We perform two tests: the first one is based on simulated data of a laser range finder mounted on a mobile robot in a structured environment and in the second one we use our mobile robot equipped with a LMS209-S02 laser.

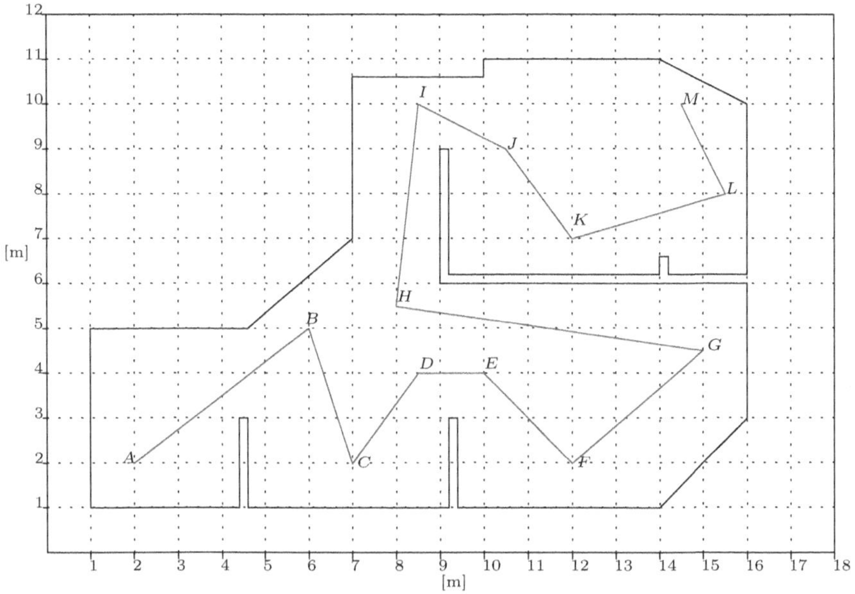

Fig. 2. Synthetic Environment

5.1 Test Using Synthetic Data

The computer–simulated environment has 12 walls, as shown in figure 2. The aim of this experiment is to evaluate the robustness of the proposed method against the popular SMSM method. In the experiment the robot follows the path ABCDEFGHIJKLM getting a total of 300 synthetic laser scans.

The parameters of the laser are $\Delta\alpha = 0.5°$, maximum distance $32m$ and the number of lectures $n = 361$. Also, 20 percent of the measures distances were contaminated by spurious noise simulated by adding a uniform random value between 0 and the maximum distance. The remaining measures were only contaminated with a Gaussian random noise with $\sigma_r = 0.03m$.

For this test we use a laptop HP Pavilion with Celeron processor, 1.1 GHz with 256 Mb and we use the C language to program the algorithms. The table 2 summarizes the results in the simulated environment. As it is shown, WSAC–GE is getting favorable results both in the parameters of the line ($|\Delta r|$ and $|\Delta\alpha|$) and in the assertivity. The assertivity a is given by $\text{a} = (100) \cdot \frac{n_s}{n_n}$ where n_s is the number of lines that match with lines in the simulated environment, and n_n is the total of lines extracted.

Table 2. Test Results for 300 simulated cases

Algorithm	Maximum time [ms]	$\|\Delta\sigma_r\|$ [mm]	$\|\Delta\alpha\|$ [°]	lines n_n	Assertivity %
SMSM	29.5	6.37	0.2670	1557	87.4
WSAC–GE	94.5	4.12	0.1323	1620	94.8

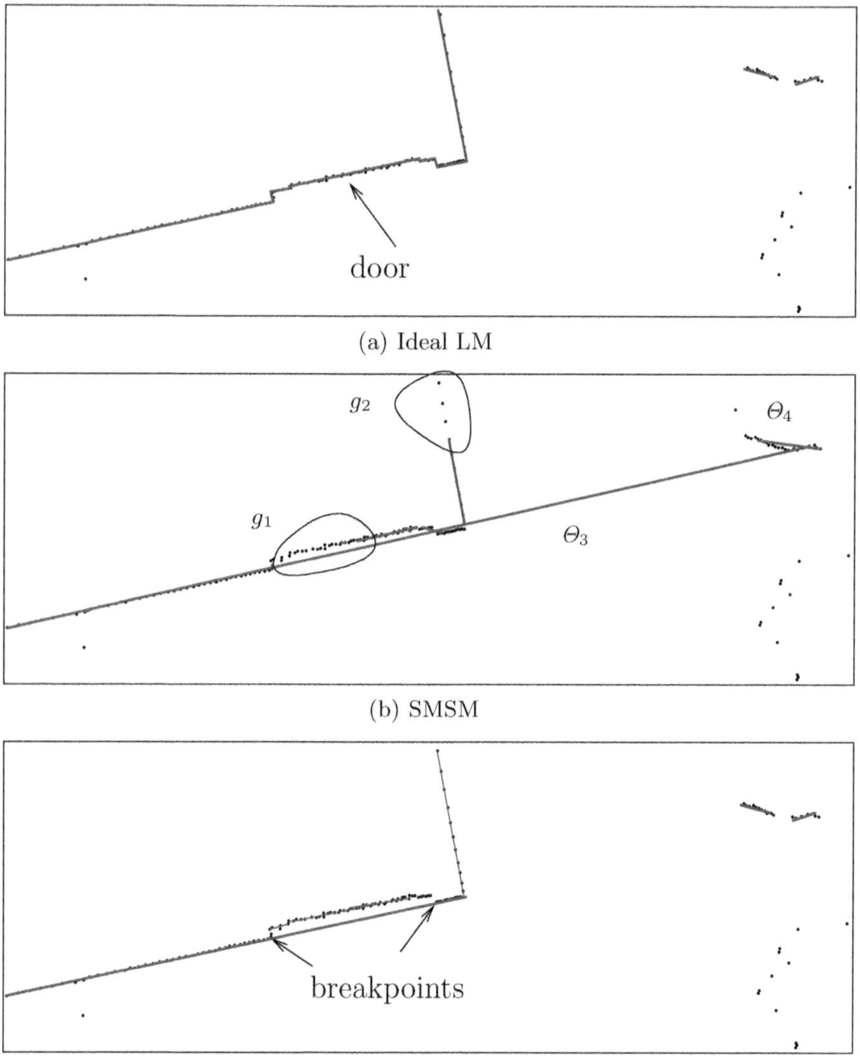

(a) Ideal LM

(b) SMSM

(c) WSAC–GE

Fig. 3. Results on real environment

5.2 Test Using Real Data

Figure 3 shows the results of SMSM and WSAC-GE methods in a real environment. The figure 3(a) shows the ideal map for this sample. As shown in the figure 3(b) the SMSM algorithm does not associate some points with lines (groups g_1 and g_2). In other cases, SMSM merges segments which do not represent the same object, lines Θ_3 and Θ_4 obtained does not represent precisely the environment. As shown in the figure 3(c) WSAC–GE finds lines more precise than SMSM and the asociation between points and lines is better.

6 Conclusions

We propose a robust method to find multiple lines in a laser scan, avoiding problems due to noisy data (outliers). Outliers typically does not follow a Gaussian Probability Distribution and in most cases do not have known probability distributions. While simple and fast algorithms work fine with Gaussian noise, the presence of outliers increase the complexity of the problem. The new method merges local and global strategies to solve the problem of outliers. We use a M-Estimator within a RANSAC method to find a line from a short sequence of points of the laser scan (the local strategy), then the line is evaluated and refined using the whole set of points (the global strategy), discarding those points belonging to very small segments. Once a line segment is found, the process continues looking for more lines. The key idea of this approach is to use a global evaluation function to add or remove lines from the map. The global evaluation function have higher values when more points are assigned to lines, when points belongs to single lines and when lines have more points. The proposed method is fast enough to be used in real time and it is able to find better results than the SMSM method, a very well known method reported in the literature as a very good and fast algorithm. Given its probabilistic nature WSAC–GE is able to deal with noise (outliers) with unknown probability distributions.

References

1. Geovany Araujo Borges and Marie-José Aldon. Line extraction in 2d range images for mobile robotics. *J. Intell. Robotics Syst.*, 40(3):267–297, 2004.
2. H. Chen and P. Meer. Robust regression with projection based m–estimators. In *In Proceedings of the 1991 IEEE International Conference on Computer Vision and Patern Recognition*, 2003.
3. A. P. Dempster, N. M. Laird, and D. B. Rubin. Maximum likelihood from incomplete data via the em algorithm (with discussion). *Journal of the Royal Statistical Society*, 1977.
4. Richard O. Duda and Peter E. Hart. *Pattern Classification and Scene Analysis*. Wiley-Interscience, 1976.
5. Martin A. Fischler and Robert C. Bolles. Random Sample Consensus: a paradigm for model fitting with applications to image analysis and automated cartography. *Commun. ACM*, 24(6):381–395, 1981.

6. David A. Forsyth and Jean Ponce. *Computer Vision: A Modern Approach.* Prentice Hall, 2003.
7. D. Hähnel, W. Burgard, and S. Thrun. Learning compact 3D models of indoor and outdoor environments with a mobile robot. In *Robotics and Autonomous Systems 44 (2003).* ELSEVIER, 2003.
8. P.V.C. Hough. Machine analysis of bubble chamber pictures. In *International Conference on High Energy Accelerators and Instrumentation*, 1959.
9. P. Huber. Robust location of a location parameter. *Annals of Mathematical Statistical*, 35, 1964.
10. P. Meer, C. V. Stewart, and D. E. Tyler. Introduction, robust computer vision: An interdisciplinary challenge. *Computer Vision and Image Understanding*, 2000.
11. Viet Nguyen, Agostino Martinelli, Nicola Tomatis, and Roland Siegwart. A comparison of line extraction algorithms using 2d. laser rangefinder for indoor mobile robotics. In *International Conference on Intelligent Robots and Systems (IROS 2005)*, 2005.
12. Roland Siegwart. *Introduction to Autonomus Mobile Robots.* The MIT Press, 2004.
13. Charles V. Stewart. Minpran: A new robust operator for computer vision. *IEEE Transactions on Pattern Analysis and Machine Intelligence*, 1995.
14. Charles V. Stewart. Robust parameter estimation in computer vision. *SIAM Review*, 41(3):513–537, 1999.
15. P. Torr and A. Zisserman. MLESAC: A new robust estimator with application to estimating image geometry. *Computer Vision and Image Understanding*, 78:138–156, 2000.
16. P H S Torr and A Zisserman. Robust computation and parameterization of multiple view relations. In *ICCV6*, pages 727 – 732, 1998.
17. Xu Zezhong, Liu Jilin, and Xiang Zhiyu. Map building and localization using 2d range scanner. In *Proceedings 2003 IEEE International Symposium on Computational Intelligence in Mobile Robotics and Automation*, pages 848–853, 2003.

Egomotion Estimation as an Appearance-Based Classification Problem

Pedro Sánchez[1], Cornelio Yáñez[2], Jonathan Pecero[3], and Apolinar Ramírez[1]

[1] Instituto Tecnológico de Ciudad Madero, Tamaulipas, México
[2] Instituto Politécnico Nacional, Centro de Investigación en Computación, D.F. México
[3] Instituto Nacional Politécnico de Grenoble, France
sanchezorellana_pedro@yahoo.com.mx

Abstract. In this paper a probabilistic approach is considered to develop a methodology to solve the problem of estimation of the position of the observer. The base of this methodology is the appearance vision with which an environment map is constructed using Kernel PCA. For the experiments an image set is acquired in unknown locations in the same environment. The performance of Kernel PCA technique was tested according to the optimum dimension of the environment model and the quantity of images correctly classified using a Bayesian algorithm. To validate the results obtained with Kernel PCA the same experiments were performed with PCA and APEX techniques, then the results were compared showing that Kernel PCA has better performance than PCA and APEX.

Keywords: Egomotion estimation, probabilistic approach, Kernel PCA.

1 Introduction

One of the key tasks inside the systems of visual navigation is the estimation of the position of the observer, which allows an autonomous mobile robot to have constant feedback of its position regarding to a reference point in the environment. By means of this information a mobile robot can make more complex tasks like target pursuit or optimum route planning.

The estimate of the position has been approached using geometric focuses that allow to estimate the observer position calculating the rotation and translation speeds [1], [2], [3], [4], [5], [6], [7], nevertheless this approach requires the consideration of restrictions in the environment conditions, for example, illumination conditions must be uniform. In this work we use a probabilistic focus; the base of this focus is the use of appearance based models, where the appearances of the environment depends on the positions – the location T:(x, y) and the orientation Ω –, from which the observer captures images. This finite set of images is used to create an environment model, against which the current appearance of the environment (a new captured image) is compared in order to estimate the current position of the observer.

This approach has been applied to solve different problems, for example, object recognition [8], tracking of human figures [9] and face recognition [10]. However, the main complexity in this focus resides in the quantity of images (and the dimension of

J.F. Martínez-Trinidad et al. (Eds.): CIARP 2006, LNCS 4225, pp. 743 – 752, 2006.

these) employed to create the environment model. This problem has been overcome by means of the use of techniques of compression of images like PCA (Principal Components Analysis) [11].

The contribution of this paper is the use of a variant of classic PCA known as Kernel PCA (Section 3 no. 2), which recently has been used to solve classification tasks, for example, face recognition [12], showing a better performance than classical compression techniques (PCA). In addition this technique is combined with a Bayesian algorithm and an Active Vision strategy (Section 3 no. 4), which allowed us to improve the obtained results.

2 Formal Definition of the Egomotion Estimation from a Probabilistic Approach

A sequence of images of an environment is obtained from $T = \{T_1, ..., T_N\}$ different locations. In each one of them a set of images is captured $\Omega = \{\Omega_1, ..., \Omega_p\}$, where Ω is a set of the possible orientations from a T-esim location, each orientation is separated X degrees of the subsequent orientation, see Section 5.1, creating a database indexed by the N locations. This database is used to create an environment model by means of the technique of principal components analysis "Kernel PCA". The probability that a new image I_A is obtained in the same environment (environment model) in a location T_i and with certain orientation Ω_j is given by eq. 1 [13].

$$p(\Omega_j : T_i | I_A) \tag{1}$$

Where Ω_j is the observer orientation in the environment T_i is the location of the observer (x, y) in the environment and I is an image captured by the observer in the current position in the environment.

Using the equation (1) the problem of estimating the position of the observer can be solved as an image classification problem; this means, now the objective is to classify a new image (obtained by the observer in an unknown position) into a set of known images.

Considering the a priori information (environment model) the current observer position $(\Omega_j : T_i)$ can be recovered, rewriting the equation (1) by means the Bayes theorem $p(I_A | \Omega_j : T_i)$ as it is shown in the (Section 3 no. 4).

3 Solution Methodology

The solution methodology consists of four steps (Fig. 1).

1. - Capture of images: The locations (T) and the orientations (Ω) are defined for the capture of the gray tone images. These images are indexed for location so a location contains all the possible appearances of the environment from that specific point; that means, the appearance of the environment from a location T_i is captured

rotating the camera *X* degrees and captures an image in each turn until completing the 360º. The obtained images are of dimension 60 x 60, each of those are vectorized, the resulting images are m-dimensional (m = 60 x 60), $x_1,\ldots,x_n \in \mathbb{R}^m$.

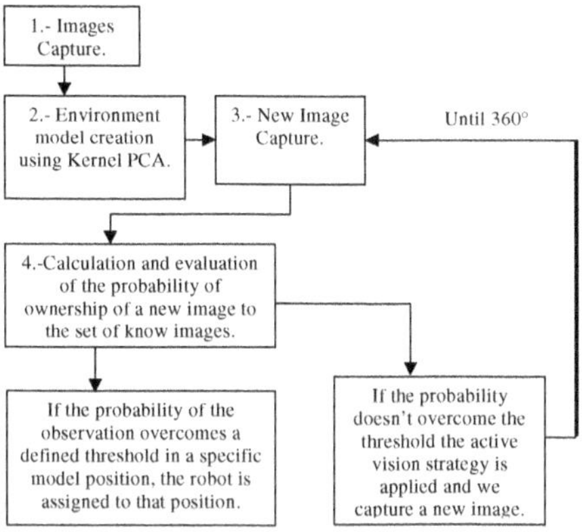

Fig. 1. Solution methodology

2. – The model of the environment: In order to deal with the amount of images and the dimensionality to them, the Kernel PCA technique was used. The basic idea of this technique is to find a map function to a space of characteristics (generally of greater number of dimensions), which allows to simplify the classification. The disadvantage is that the problem gets complicated when increasing the number of dimensions in that the original data are represented. However, by means of the use of the functions Kernel we can obtain the advantages in the classification without the need of having to use or knowing the map function [14], this means, the work is directly done in the characteristics space by means of the map function as follows:

Applying the Kernel PCA technique the information is taken from the input space $x_1,\ldots,x_n \in \mathbb{R}^m$ to a space of characteristics F by means of a function of non-linear mapping and later the linear PCA is applied in F. The covariance matrix is calculated $C = 1/n\sum_{j=1}^{n}\Phi(x_j)\Phi(x_j)^T$, and the principal components are calculated solving the Eigenvalue problem, calculating the eigenvalues $\lambda \geq 0$ and the eigenvectors $V\setminus\{0\}$ and solving $\lambda V = CV = 1/n\sum_{j=1}^{n}(\Phi(x_j)V)\Phi(x_j)$.

Every solutions of V with $\lambda \neq 0$ are inside of the mapped data set, for example, $V \in span\{\Phi(x_1),\ldots,\Phi(x_n)\}$ this is expressed by means of $V = \sum_{i=1}^{n}\alpha_i\Phi(x_i)$. By multiplying both sides of $\lambda V = CV$ by $\Phi(x_k)$ (to $k = 1,\ldots,n$) the eq. 5 is obtained.

$$\lambda(\Phi(x_k)\cdot CV) = (\Phi(x_k)\cdot CV) \tag{2}$$

Substituting the values of C and V in eq. 2 and considering a $n \times n$ matrix $K_{ij} = k(x_i, x_j) = (\Phi(x_i) \cdot \Phi(x_j))$, the resulting equation can be reduced to $n\lambda K\alpha = K^2\alpha$, where α represents the column eigenvectors. In order to obtain the solutions of the equation 2 the eigenvalue problem $n\lambda\alpha = K\alpha$ is solved for nonnegative eigenvalues.

Once obtained the new space F it is necessary to centre the projected data (by means the kernel function K) using the following equation $\overline{K} = K - 1_n K - K 1_n + 1_n K 1_n$ [15], where $(1_n)_{ij} = 1/n$ that is a measure of proportion necessary for the normalization of K, and n is the number of elements of the main K.

Now that we already have centred the data in F we calculate the λ's eigenvalues of the matrix K, with their corresponding α's eigenvectors. It is defined the optimal number of principal components to carry out the projection by means of this equation $\sum_{i=1}^{p} \lambda_i \Big/ \sum_{i=1}^{n} \lambda_i = 60\%$, which represents a variation percentage used in this work for the reconstruction of the original space, in this case 60%, and p the number of necessary main components to obtain variation percentage.

To obtain a reduction of the images (matrix K), in terms of the edges (eigenvectors) that represent 60% of the space original, a projection function is applied multiplying the eigenvectors by the matrix K. $Y_i = \lambda_i^{\mathrm{T}}(\mathrm{K})$, where $i = 1, \ldots, p$ are the vectors and Y_i represent the images projected to the principal axes in the space of characteristic F.

3. Captures of a new image: To test the classification a new image is captured in a different position to those of the obtained model, but in the same environment. With the purpose of being able to compare this image with those of the model the new image is projected to the eigenspace calculated by means of eq. 3.

$$(kPC)_n(x) = (V^n \cdot \Phi(x)) = \sum_{i=1}^{p} \alpha_i^n k(x_i, x) \tag{3}$$

4. Bayesian Algorithm with an Active vision strategy for searching in F: The probability of generating a vector image Y (random variable Y) in the eigenspace starting from a localization T_i and an orientation Ω_j of the robot in a continuous environment (because the number of positions in the environment is infinite) is given for $P(Y \mid T_i, \Omega_j)$. By means of the rule of Bayes we can calculate the probability that the robot is in a position (localization and orientation) starting from an image Y_A in the eigenspace:

$$P(T_i, \Omega_j \mid Y_A) = P(Y_A \mid T_i, \Omega_j) P(T_i, \Omega_j) \Big/ \sum_{ij} P(Y_A \mid T_i, \Omega_j) P(T_i, \Omega_j) \tag{4}$$

Where $P(T_i, \Omega_j)$ is the a priori probability of the location T_i and orientation Ω_j.

Because the projected data to the eigenspace are samples taken from a population where it was considered the same mean (environment mean) and the same covariance matrix, by means of the central limit theorem is considered that their probability distribution approaches to a multivariate normal distribution. This allows us to calculate the probability $P(Y_A \mid T_i, \Omega_j)$ by means of the eq. 5, considering as centre an image of the database (image projected to the eigenspace) $Y_{T_i \Omega_j}$.

$$P(Y_A \mid T_i, \Omega_j) = \exp[-1/2(Y_A - Y_{T_i,\Omega_j})^T \Sigma^{-1}(Y_A - Y_{T_i,\Omega_j})]/2\Pi^{k/2} \mid \Sigma^{-1/2} \mid \quad (5)$$

This formula allows us to know the distance between the vector Y_A and a known vector in the database Y_{T_i,Ω_j}. The probability that the robot is in a position T_i, starting from an image Y observed from a localization T_i and an orientation Ω_j can be calculated by means of $P(Y_A \mid T_i) = \sum_{ij} P(Y_A \mid T_i, \Omega_j) P(T_i, \Omega_j)$.

Applying the Bayes rule we can obtain the probability distribution of the independent location of the orientations $P(T_i \mid Y_A) = P(Y_A \mid T_i) P(T_i) / \sum_i P(Y_A \mid T_i) P(T_i)$.

If the probability of the observation overcomes a defined limit (50% of probability) the robot is assigned to that position, otherwise an active vision strategy is used, active vision basically says that in accordance with the necessities are the actions taken, if the new image does not obtain a bigger probability than 50% (that which indicates that the current information is insufficient) a rotation movement of (X°) is performed in order to obtain a new probability of a new image besides considering the current information:

$$P(T_i \mid Y_A, Y_B) = P(Y_A, Y_B \mid T_i) P(T_i) / \sum_i P(Y_A, Y_B \mid T_i) P(T_i) \quad (6)$$

Considering that Y_A and Y_B are conditionally independent events the equation 6 is rewritten as follow:

$$P(T_i \mid Y_A, Y_B) = P(Y_A \mid T_i) P(Y_B \mid T_i) P(T_i) / \sum_i P(Y_A \mid T_i) P(Y_B \mid T_i) P(T_i) \quad (7)$$

The success condition is that the obtained probability overcomes the defined limit, or the number of images settled down by location are captured until reaching the 360°, if these conditions are not completed it is determined that the current position of the robot is unknown.

4 Experiments and Results

4.1 Algorithms for the Validation of the Proposed Method

To measure the efficiency of the results obtained of the proposed techniques for the performance in the compression of the data we will use the results obtained by two techniques: Linear PCA which has been employed in the solution of the problem of the estimate of the position [16] considering a covariance matrix between the pixels, and APEX which although it has not been proven in this problem, possesses an important characteristic, according to its authors that it is the adaptation, that allows us to optimise the process of the extraction of the main components [17] [18], the results of the experiments are shown next.

Basically two types of experiments were carried out. The variations among the experiments consist in: the quantity of positions, initial orientation in the positions as well as the distance between each one of these. The quality of the solutions was measured according to the precision in the classification, that means, the number of test positions were classified in the positions of the environment model.

4.2 Experiment 1

Conditions for the creation of the environment model. In order to not capture the information repeatedly, pixels variations from 50 to 70% were searched in the consecutive images, for this, 12 locations were defined with "1 distance meter" among each one of them. In each one of the locations the robot rotates 360° with the objective of capturing with the camera all the possible appearances of the environment from the current location. It was defined that the rotation intervals to capture an image are of 20°, this way, when we refer of orientations we refer to the 20° that the robot should rotate before stopping, once detained a new image is captured, this image belongs to the location T_i and orientation Ω_j (see Fig. 4-a).

Table 1. Results of the realized tests in experiment 1. N.C. means that the test position was not classified in a position of the environment model.

Precision of the Algorithms in the Classification							
		PCA		APEX		Kernel PCA	
Test Images	Real Positions	Estimation	Classification	Estimation	Classification	Estimation	Classification
1	1 or 2	2	Correct	1	X	2	Correct
2	3 or 4	NC	X	12	X	5	X
3	5 or 6	NC	X	3	X	NC	X
4	7 or 8	NC	X	NC	X	4	X
5	9 or 10	11	X	NC	X	NC	X
6	10	6	X	NC	X	10	Correct
7	11 or 12	NC	X	NC	X	NC	X
8	8 or 9	8	Correct	12	X	8	X
9	7 or 6	NC	X	NC	X	7	Correct
Learning Peercentage		22,22%		0,00%		33,33%	

Eficiency: Principal Components (PC).			
	PCA	APEX	Kernel PCA
Number of PC	11	26	9
Time to calculate the PC	10minutes	15minutes	4minutes
Time to classify a test image	1,36secs.	1,42secs.	1,3secs.

To prove the compression techniques as well as the classification algorithm the robot was positioned in 9 unknown random locations and initial orientation, but within the same environment, and the same process of compression of images was applied. The random positions allowed us to simulate the real conditions in which the position estimation would be done. The results in the experimentation are shown in the Table 1.

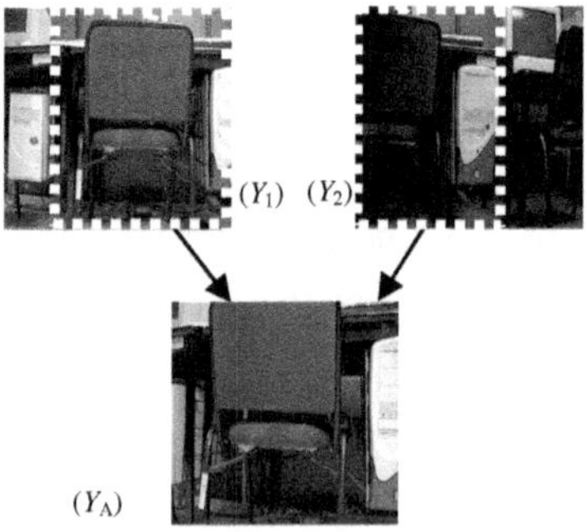

Fig. 2. Inconsistency in the classification. Y_1 Image belongs to the position 5 with 300° orientation, Y_2 Image belongs to position 7 with 320° of orientation. Test Image acquired between the position 5 and 7 with 310° of orientation.

In the percentages of correctly classified images the superiority of the Kernel PCA technique is appreciated with 33.33% in comparison with 0% (APEX) and 22.22% (PCA). Also the number of components required for the 60% reconstruction, and the time to calculate them was smaller using the Kernel PCA technique, because as is shown in the methodology, the matrix dimension employed to calculate PCA are of a smaller dimension (n x n in the Kernel PCA (by means of a covariance among images) instead of m x m (covariance among pixels of the images) in the PCA and APEX, where n is the quantity of images and m is the pixel number in each image) using the technique Kernel PCA.

The reason for which the classification percentages were very low is: the variation that existed in the pixels of the images was such that in occasions only 30% of the image coincided with the next one, this produced ambiguity in calculating the ownership from an image to a well-known position. For this reason when varying the initial orientation in the test images the possibility that the test images did not coincide with some of the database increased; since the pixels of the test image could belong in a part to the beginning of an image and the rest to the final-center of another different image (see Fig. 2).

4.3 Experiment 2

The solution proposed for the problem in the experiment 1 is by means of the reduction of the pixels variation between an image and another, reducing the turn angle in each position (orientation angle in the positions), this way instead of having variations of between 50 and 70%, variations of between 25 and 35% were obtained. To achieve this new positions (27 in total) and orientations (24 in total) were defined, the positions now would take half a meter with 15° turns in each one of them, this allowed us to reduce the variations among the images. The distribution of the positions is shown in the Fig. 4-b. The results obtained in the experiment 2 are shown in the Table 2.

Table 2. Results of the realized tests in experiment 2. N.C. means that the test position was not classified in a position of the environment model.

Precision of the Algorithms in the Classification							
		PCA		APEX		Kernel PCA	
Test Images	Real Positions	Estimation	Clasification	Estimation	Clasification	Estimation	Clasification
1	5 or 6	2	Correct	5	Correct	5	Correct
2	5 or 8	N.C.	X	8	Correct	5	Correct
3	8 or 11	11	Correct	3	X	11	Correct
4	12	12	Correct	N.C.	X	12	Correct
5	14 or 17	11	X	N.C.	Correct	N.C.	X
6	17 or 18 or 19	10	Correct	N.C.	X	10	Correct
7	20 or 23	N.C.	X	N.C.	X	23	Correct
8	23 or 22 or 27	8	Correct	1	X	22	Correct
9	25 or 26	N.C.	X	12	X	19	X
10	20 or 21	20	Correct	23	X	20	Correct
11	17 or 16	2	X	16	Correct	N.C.	X
12	14 or 15	11	X	N.C.	X	15	Correct
13	10 or 11	15	X	10	Correct	10	Correct
Learning Percentage		46,15%		38,47%		76,98%	

Eficiency: Princial Components (PC).			
	PCA	APEX	Kernel PCA
Number of PC	15	33	7
Time to calculate the PC	13 minutes	19 minutes	8.4 minutes
Time to classify a test image	2,26 secs.	2,43 secs.	2,21 secs.

With a time average of classification of 2.64 seconds in each image, this time increased (according to the time classification average in the experiment 1) because the number of images was increased from 216 to 648. Although the quantity of images in the model increased, the precision of the three algorithms was also increased.

To show the operation of the classification Bayesian algorithm in the Fig. 1 the behaviour of the probabilities of ownership of the position of test 8 is shown as mentioned in Table 2 in experiment 2. In this position an image was captured with random initial orientation (8°), the initial orientation is different to the initial orientation of the positions in the model, the calculated probability did not overcome the established threshold (50%), for this reason strategy of active vision was applied to register more information of the environment by means of capturing a new image in the same position but now in the orientation 1, rotating the robot 360/24°. Combining the information of the first one with the second image it is possible to overcome 50% of ownership in the position 22 although the biggest probability of ownership in the first image was obtained in the position 8 of the model (see Fig. 3).

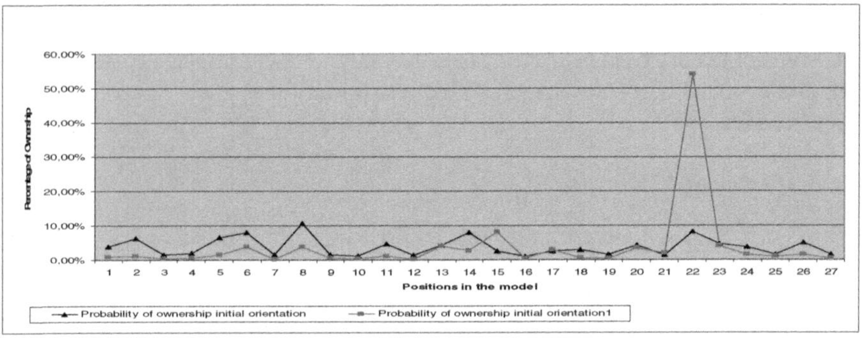

Fig. 3. Probabilities of Ownership for the classification of the position of test 8. The graphic shows the behaviour of the Bayesian algorithm, in the first stage (initial orientation) the success condition wasn't reach; the active vision strategy was performed and a second image was taken. Considering all the available information (the two images), the ownership probability was computed. The result is the classification of the current position of the robot into the twenty-two position in the environment model.

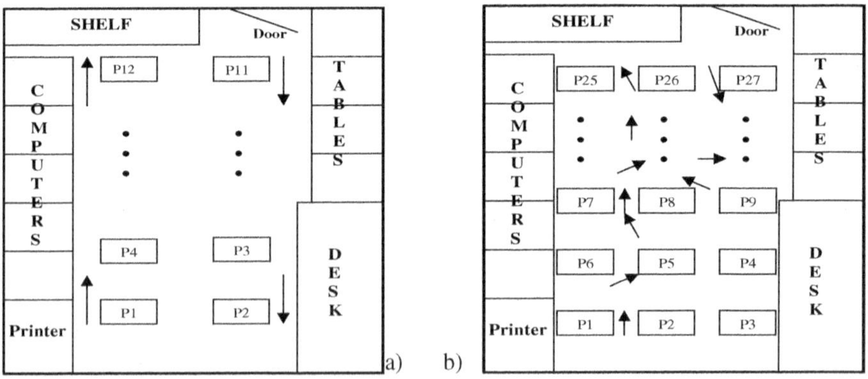

Fig. 4. Situation of the environment for the experiment 1 (a) and experiment 2 (b), the arrows indicate the orientation of the test positions. The numbers in the stalls indicate the position in the environment. The arrows indicate the initial orientation in each test position.

5 Conclusions

The results obtained in the experimentation show that the Kernel PCA technique allowed us to improve the acting (bigger percentage of correct classifications, smaller time of calculation and number of required principal components) of the algorithms PCA and APEX. It can bee easily seen that the algorithm APEX requires more time to calculate the eigenvalues and the eigenvectors and the resulting components are not completely orthogonal, this explains the biggest quantity of necessary components to achieve the percentage.

References

1. Longuet-Higgins, H.C., Prazdny K.: The Interpretation of a Moving Retinal Image. In Proc. of the Royal Society B, London, 1980
2. Lourakis M.I.A.: Using Constraint Lines for Estimating Egomotion. Proc. of ACCV'2000, vol. 2, Taipei, Taiwan, Jan 2000, pp. 971 – 976.
3. Convertino G., Branca A., Distante A.: Focus of Expansion Estimation with a Neural Network. IEEE International Conference on Neural Networks, June 1996, pp. 1693 – 1697
4. Tomasi C., Kanade T.: Factoring images sequences into shape and motion. Proc. IEEE Workshop o Visual Motion, 1991, pp. 21 – 28.
5. Negadharipour S.: Direct Passive Navigation. PhD thesis, Department of Mechanical Engineering, MIT, 1986.
6. Daniilidis K., Spetsakis M.: Understanding noise sensitivity in structure from motion. Y. Aloimonos, editor, Visual Navigation, 1996, pp. 61 – 88.
7. Burger W., Bhanu B.: Estimating 3D egomotion from perspective image sequence. Pattern Analysis and Machine Intelligence, IEEE, Honeywell Syst. & Res. Center, Minneapolis, MN, nov 1990, pp. 1040-1058.
8. Murase H., Nayar S. K.: Visual learning and recognition of 3D objects from appearance. International Journal of Computer Vision, 14(1):5--24, Jan. 1995.
9. Cai Q., and Aggarwal J.K.: Tracking Human Motion in Structured Environments Using Distributed-Camera System. IEEE Transactions on Pattern Analysis, 1999, pp. 1241–1247.
10. Turk M., Pentland A.: Eigenfaces for recognition. J. Cog. Neurosci., 3(1), 1991, pp. 71-86.
11. Krose B. J., Bunschoten A. R.: Probabilistic Location by Appearance Models and Active Vision. Proceedings of the IEEE International Conference on Robotics and Automation,1999, pp. 2255-2260.
12. Yang M. H.: Kernel eigenfaces vs. kernel fisherfaces: Face recognition using kernel methods. in Proc. IEEE International Conference on Automatic Face and Gesture Recognition, pp. 215--220 (2002).
13. Pourraz F., Crowley J.: Continuity properties of the appearance manifold for mobile robot position estimation. In Proceedings of the 2nd IEEE Workshop on Perception for Mobile Agents, Ft. Collins, CO, IEEE Press, 2001, pp. 741-752.
14. Muller K., Mika S., Ratsch G., Tsuda K., Scholkopf B.: An introduction to kernel-based learning algorithms. IEEE Transactions on Neural Networks, March 2001, pp. 181-201.
15. Schölkopf B., Smola A. J., Müller K. R.: Nonlinear component analysis as a kernel eigenvalue problem. Neural Comput., vol. 10, 1998, pp.1299 – 1319.

16. Krose B. J. A., Bunschoten R.: Probabilistic Location by Appearance Models and Active Vision. Proceedings of the IEEE International Conference on Robotics and Automation,1999, pp. 2255-2260.
17. Diamantaras K.I., Kung Y.: A Neural Network Learning Algorithm for Adaptive Principal Components Extraction. Prinsceton University, pp 860-864.
18. Oja E.: A simplified Neuron Model as a Principal Componet Analyser. J.Math. Biology, vol. 15, pp 267-273.

Decoding of Ternary Error Correcting Output Codes

Sergio Escalera[1], Oriol Pujol[2], and Petia Radeva[1]

[1] Computer Vision Center, Dept. Computer Science, UAB, 08193 Bellaterra, Spain
[2] Dept. Matemàtica Aplicada i Anàlisi, UB, Gran Via 585, 08007, Barcelona, Spain

Abstract. Error correcting output codes (ECOC) represent a successful extension of binary classifiers to address the multiclass problem. Lately, the ECOC framework was extended from the binary to the ternary case to allow classes to be ignored by a certain classifier, allowing in this way to increase the number of possible dichotomies to be selected. Nevertheless, the effect of the zero symbol by which dichotomies exclude certain classes from consideration has not been previously enough considered in the definition of the decoding strategies. In this paper, we show that by a special treatment procedure of zeros, and adjusting the weights at the rest of coded positions, the accuracy of the system can be increased. Besides, we extend the main state-of-art decoding strategies from the binary to the ternary case, and we propose two novel approaches: Laplacian and Pessimistic Beta Density Probability approaches. Tests on UCI database repository (with different sparse matrices containing different percentages of zero symbol) show that the ternary decoding techniques proposed outperform the standard decoding strategies.

1 Introduction

Machine learning studies automatic techniques for learning to make accurate predictions based on past observations. There are plenty of classification techniques reported in literature: Support Vector Machines [1][2], decision trees [3], nearest neighbors rules, etc. It is known that for some classification problems, the lowest error rate is not always reliably achieved by trying to design a single classifier. An alternative approach is to use a set of relatively simple sub-optimal classifiers and to determine a combination strategy that pools together the results. Different types of systems of multiple classifiers have been proposed in the literature, most of them use similar constituent classifiers, which are often called base classifiers (dichotomies from now on). Adaboost [4], for example, uses weak classifiers as predictions that showed to be slightly better than random guessing and combines them in an ensemble classifier.

Although binary classification is a well-studied problem, building a highly accurate multiclass prediction rule is certainly a difficult task. In those situations, the usual way to proceed is to reduce the complexity of the problem by dividing it into a set of multiple simpler binary classification subproblems. One-versus-one pairwise [5] or one-versus-all techniques are some of the most frequently used

J.F. Martínez-Trinidad et al. (Eds.): CIARP 2006, LNCS 4225, pp. 753–763, 2006.

schemes. In the line of the aforementioned techniques Error Correcting Output Codes [6] were born. ECOC is a general framework based on coding and decoding (ensemble strategy) techniques to handle multiclass problems. One of the most well-known properties of the ECOC is that it improves the generalization performance of the base classifiers [7][5].

In this technique the multiclass to binary division is handled by a coding matrix. Each row of the coding matrix represents a codeword assigned to each class. On the other hand, each column of the matrix (each bit of the codeword) defines a partition of the classes in two sets. The ECOC strategy is divided in two parts: the coding part, where the binary problems to be solved have to be designed, and the decoding technique, that given a test sample, looks for the most similar codewords. For the coding strategies, the three most well-known strategies are one-versus-all, all-pairs (one-versus-one) and random coding.

The decoding step was originally based on error-correcting principles under the assumption that the learning task can be modelled as a communication problem, in which class information is transmitted over a channel [8]. The decoding strategy corresponds to the problem of distance estimation between the test codeword and the codewords of the classes. Concerning the decoding strategies, two of the most standard techniques are the Euclidean distance and the Hamming decoding distance. If the minimum Hamming distance between any pair of class codewords is d, then any $[(d-1)/2]$ errors in the individual dichotomies result can be corrected, since the nearest codeword will be the correct one. The original two-symbol coding matrix M was extended to the ternary case $M \in \{-1,0,1\}^{N_c \times n}$ by Allwein et. al [5]. The new zero symbol indicates that a particular class is not considered by a given dichotomy. This fact allows to obtain a higher number of possible dichotomies that create different decision boundaries, allowing more accurate results for multiclass classification problems. Nevertheless, the effect of increasing the sparseness of the coding matrix has not been previously analyzed enough.

The goal of this article is twofold: firstly, we extend the standard state-of-art decoding strategies to the ternary case. We analyze the effect of the zero symbol in the ECOC matrix M. We show how this symbol affects to the decoding strategy, and we take into account the two main properties than define the problem: the zero symbol may not introduce decoding errors, and the coded positions have different relevance depending on the number of zeros contained on each coding matrix M row. We compare the evolution results for standard decoding strategies as Hamming (HD), inverse Hamming (IHD) or Euclidean distance (ED) when the number of zeros is increased. Secondly, we extend the state-of-art coding strategies to the ternary case: Attenuated Euclidean distance (AED), and Loss-based decoding (LB). In this context, we propose two new decoding techniques to solve the exposed problem: Laplacian decoding (LAP), and Beta Density Distribution Pessimistic score (β-DEN).

The paper is organized as follows: section 2 explains the ECOC framework, section 3 reviews the state-of-art decoding strategies, shows the ternary adapta-

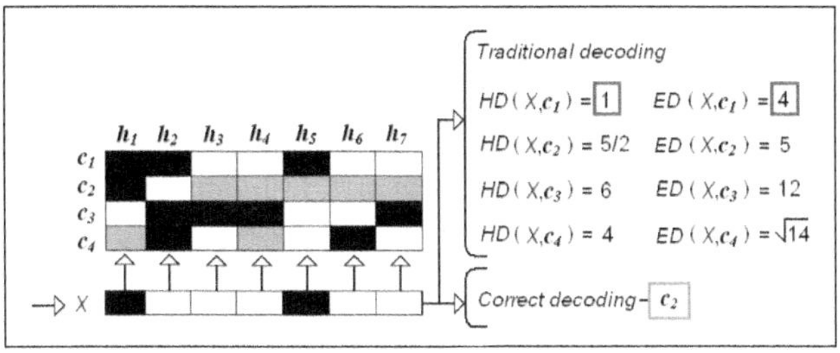

Fig. 1. Example of ternary matrix M for a 4-class problem. A new test codeword is missclassified due to the confussion of using the traditional decoding strategies.

tion and the new decoding approaches. Section 4 contains the experiments and results, and section 5 concludes the paper.

2 ECOC

The basis of the ECOC framework is to create a codeword for each of the N_c classes. Arranging the codewords as rows of a matrix, we define a "coding matrix" M, where $M \in \{-1,0,1\}^{N_c \times n}$ in the ternary case, being n the code length. From point of view of learning, M is constructed by considering n binary problems (dichotomies), each corresponding to a matrix column. Joining classes in sets, each dichotomy defines a partition of classes (coded by +1, 0 or -1, according to their class set membership). In fig. 1 we show an example of a ternary matrix M. The matrix is coded using 7 dichotomies $h_1, ..., h_7$ for a four multiclass problem (c_1, c_2, c_3, and c_4). The white regions are coded by 1 (considered as positive for its respective dichotomy, h_i), the dark regions by -1 (considered as negative), and the grey regions correspond to the zero symbol (not considered classes for the current dichotomy). For example, the first classifier is trained to discriminate c_3 versus c_1 and c_2, the second one classifies c_2 versus c_1, c_3 and c_4, and so on. Applying the n trained binary classifiers, a code is obtained for each data point in the test set. This code is compared to the base codewords of each class defined in the matrix M, and the data point is assigned to the class with the "closest" codeword.

To design an ECOC system, we apply a coding and a decoding strategy. The most well-known decoding strategies are Hamming and Euclidean distance. The Hamming distance is estimated by $d(x,y^i) = \sum_{j=1}^{n} \mid (x_j - y_j^i) \mid /2$, where $d(x,y^i)$ is the distance of the codeword x to the class i, n is the number of dichotomies (and thus, the components of the codeword), and x and y are the values of the input vector codeword and the base class codeword, respectively. For the Euclidean distance, the measure is based on minimizing the distance $d(x,y^i) = \sqrt{\sum_{j=1}^{n}(x_j - y_j^i)^2}$. To classify a new input $x = [-1,1,1,1,-1,1,1]$ in fig. 1, the traditional Hamming or Euclidean distances are applied, obtaining in both cases the minimum distance corresponding to class one. Note that the correct decoding corresponds to c_2 since both first dichotomies trained on c_2 classify the new example correctly.

Most of the discrete coding strategies up to now are based on predesigned problem-independent codewords. When the ECOC technique was first developed it was designed to have certain properties to enable them to generalize well. A good error-correcting output code for a k-class problem should satisfy that rows, columns (and their complementaries) are well-separated from the rest in terms of Hamming distance. These strategies are one-versus-all, dense and sparse random techniques [5], and one- versus-one [9]. Crammer et. al [10] were the first authors reporting improvement in the design of the ECOC problem-dependent codes. However, the results were rather pessimistic since they proved that the problem of finding the optimal discrete codes is computationally unfeasible since it is NP-complete [10]. Specifically, they proposed a method to heuristically find the optimal coding matrix by changing its representation from discrete to continuous values. Recently, new improvements in the problem-dependent coding techniques have been presented by Pujol et. al. [11]. They propose embedding of discriminant tree structures in the ECOC framework showing high accuracy with a very small number of binary classifiers. Escalera et. al [12][13] propose a multiple tree structures embedding to form a Forest-ECOC and design of a problem-dependent ECOC-ONE coding strategy. The procedure is based on generating a code matrix by searching for the dichotomies that best split the difficult classes in the training procedure guided by a validation subset.

Many decoding strategies have been proposed in the ECOC framework. Nevertheless, very few attention has been given to the ternary case. Often techniques add errors due to the zeros, while other approaches do not consider the effect of this symbol for the decoding strategy. In the next chapter, we address the ternary case of the decoding strategies in depth.

3 Ternary ECOC Decoding

The zero symbol allows to ignore some classes for a certain dichotomy. Although the binary matrix M is extended with the zero symbol, the decoding strategies are not adapted to the influence of that symbol. The use of standard decoding techniques that do not consider the effect of this symbol frequently fail (as shown in fig. 1). To understand the extension to the ternary case, first we define the reasons why the zero symbol needs special attention. As shown in fig. 1, the error accumulated by the zero symbol has to be non-significative in comparison with the failures at coded positions. Another important aspect is that if a codeword of length n has k zeros, the rest of the positions $(n - k)$ not containing zeros must have more importance either in case of coincidence or failure. For example, if we consider two codewords y_1 and y_2, we can not consider the same error for the codeword y_1 if it has one fail and two coded positions than if there are ten coded positions in y_2. Therefore, the large difference in the number of coded positions between codewords is an important issue that must be taken into account. Allwein et. al [5] studied numerically the effect of the symbol zero and they proposed the Loss-based decoding technique in order to take this symbol into account.

3.1 Traditional Decoding Strategies

Analyzing the Hamming distance in the ternary case, we can observe that it introduces a high error for the zero values (ignored classes by certain dichotomies) and all positions obtain the same importance at the decoding step. Euclidean distance accumulate half of the error estimated by Hamming distance. Equally, it still assigns a considerable error to the symbol zero and does not increase the relevance of the rest of the coded codeword positions. Another traditional strategy for decoding is the Inverse Hamming distance.

Inverse Hamming Distance. Let $D(x) = [d(x, y^1), d(x, y^2), ..., d(x, y^{N_c})]$ be define as the set of estimated distances from a test codeword to the N_c classes codewords. Let us define Δ as the matrix composed by the Hamming distances between the codewords of M. Each position of Δ is defined by $\Delta(i, j) = d(y^i, y^j)$, where $d(y^i, y^j)$ defines the Hamming distance between codeword i and j. If the set D is evaluated using the Hamming distance, Δ can be inverted to find the vector $Q = [q_1, q_2, ..., q_{N_c}]$ containing the N_c individual class probabilities by means of $Q = \Delta^{-1}D^T$. This approach is based on the Hamming minimization theory, hence its properties are the same for the ternary case.

3.2 Extended Decoding Strategies

The following techniques are adaptations of some traditional decoding strategies to the ternary case.

Attenuated Euclidean Decoding. This technique is an adaptation of the Euclidean distance to take into account the symbol zero. To solve the previously commented problem of the Euclidean distance, we redefine the decoding as $d(x, y^i) = \sqrt{\sum_{j=1}^{n} \mid y_j^i \mid (x_j - y_j^i)^2}$, where the factor $\mid y_j^i \mid$ rejects the errors accumulated by the zero symbol at codeword of class i. Using this technique, we consider that the relevant information is only represented by the coded positions, though the rest of coded positions still obtains the same relevance in the decoding process. Extending this discrete idea of the importance of zeros to the probabilistic case, we find the Loss-based decoding strategy.

Loss-based Decoding. The loss-based decoding method [5] requires that the output of the binary classifier is a margin score satisfying two requirements. First, the score should be positive if the example is classified as positive, and negative if the example is classified as negative. Second, the magnitude of the score should be a measure of confidence in the prediction.

Let $f(\ell, j)$ be the margin score for example ℓ predicted by the classifier corresponding to column j of the code matrix M. For each row i of M and for each example ℓ, we compute the distance between $f(\ell, j)$ and $y^i = M(i,j)$ $\forall j \in \{1, ..., n\}$,

$$d^i(\ell, i) = \sum_{j=1}^{n} L(M(i,j) \cdot f(\ell, j)) \tag{1}$$

where L is a loss function that depends on the nature of the binary classifier. The two most common loss functions are $L(\hbar) = -\hbar$ and $L(\hbar) = e^{-\hbar}$, where $\hbar = M(i,j) \cdot f(\ell, j)$. We label each example x with the label that minimizes d_L. Note that this technique attenuates the error for the zero symbol while maintaining the weight for all the coded positions independently of the number of zeros from each codeword. This technique attenuates the errors introduced by zeros in the same way that the discrete Attenuated Euclidean distance strategy extending the measure estimation to an additive probabilistic model.

3.3 Novel Decoding Strategies

The previous methods attenuate the errors from the zero symbol in a discrete and probabilistic way. The following novel approaches are based on considering the distance and probability conditions to decode the coding matrices depending on their structure, adding new conditions on coded positions to adjust the analysis of the ternary case.

Laplacian Strategy. We propose a Laplacian decoding strategy to give to each class a score according to the number of coincidences between the input codeword and the class codeword, normalized by the errors without considering the zero symbol. In this way, the coded positions of the codewords with more zero symbols attain more importance. The decoding score is estimated by:

$$d(x, y^i) = \frac{C_i + 1}{C_i + E_i + K} \tag{2}$$

where C_i is the number of coincidences from the test codeword and the codeword for class i, E_i is the number of failures from the test codeword and the codeword for class i, and K is an integer value that codifies the number of classes considered by the classifier, in this case 2, due to the binary partitions of the base classiers. The offset $1/K$ is the default value (bias) in case that the coincidences and failures tend to zero. Note that when the number of C and E are sufficiently high, the factor $1/K$ does not contribute:

$$\lim_{C \to 0, E \to 0} d(x, y^i) = \frac{1}{K} \qquad \lim_{C \to \infty, E \to \infty} d(x, y^i) = \frac{C}{C + E} \tag{3}$$

Beta Density Distribution Pessimistic Strategy. The method is based on estimating the probability density functions between two codewords, extending the Laplacian ternary properties from the discrete to the probabilistic case. The main issue of this strategy is to model at the same time the accuracy and uncertainty based on a pessimistic score to obtain more reliable predictions. We use an extension of the continuous binomial distribution, the Beta distribution defined as:

$$\psi(z, \alpha, \beta) = \frac{1}{K} z^{\alpha}(1 - z)^{\beta} \tag{4}$$

where ψ_i is the Beta Density Distribution between a codeword x and a class codeword y^i for class i, α and β are the number of coincidences and failures respectively, and $z \in [0, 1]$. The expectation $E(\psi_i)$ and the variance $var(\psi_i)$of the distribution are:

$$E(\psi_i) = \frac{\alpha}{\alpha + \beta} \qquad var(\psi_i) = \frac{\alpha\beta}{(\alpha + \beta)^2(\alpha + \beta + 1)} \tag{5}$$

where the expectation tends to the Laplacian estimation when $C \to \infty, E \to \infty$ in (2).

Let Z_i be the value defined as $Z_i = argmax_z(\psi_i(z))$. To classify an input codeword x given the set of functions $\psi(z) = [\psi_1(z), \psi_2(z), ..., \psi_{N_c}(z)]$, we select the class i with the highest score $(Z_i - a_i)$, where a_i is defined as the pessimistic score satisfying the following equivalency:

$$a_i : \int_{Z_i - a_i}^{Z_i} \psi_i(z) = \frac{1}{3} \tag{6}$$

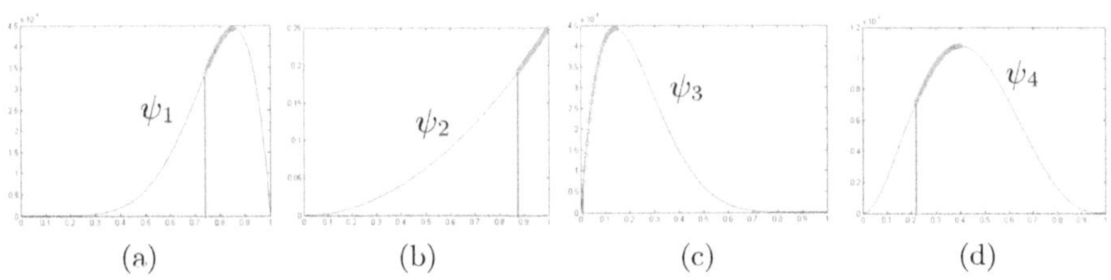

Fig. 2. Pessimistic Density Probability estimations for the test codeword x and the matrix M for the four classes of fig. 1. The probability for the second class allows a successful classification in this case.

In fig. 2 the density functions $[\psi_1, \psi_2, \psi_3, \psi_4]$ of fig. 1 for the input test codeword x are shown. Fig. 2(b) corresponds to the correct class c_2, well-classified by the method with the highest pessimistic score. One can observe that the Beta Density Probability decreases faster in c_1 compared to c_2 due to the failure of one code position for the codeword of class 1 compared to the pessimistic score of the second codeword with five zeros and two code coincidences.

It can be shown that when a function ψ_i is estimated by a combination of sets α and β of z and (1-z) respectively, the sharpness is higher than when it is generated by a majority of one of the two types. Besides, this sharpness depends on the number of code positions different to zero and the balance between the number of coincidences and failures.

4 Results

To test the different decoding strategies, we used the UCI repository databases. The characteristics of the 5 used databases are shown in table 1. As our main goal is to analyze the effect of the ternary matrix M, we have generated a set of matrices with different percentages of zeros. Once generated the coding matrices, the dichotomies are trained. The generated set of experiments is composed by 6 sets of matrices for each database, each one containing 10 different random sparse matrices of different percentage of zeros. We increase the number of zeros by 10% starting from the previously generated matrices to obtain more realistic analysis. Besides, each matrix from this set is evaluated with a ten-fold cross-validation. The decoding strategies used in the comparative are: Hamming distance (HD), Euclidean distance (ED), Inverse Hamming distance (IHD), Attenuated Euclidean Distance (AED), Loss-based decoding with exponential loss-function (ELB), Loss-based decoding with linear loss-function (LLB), Laplacian decoding (LAP), and Beta Pessimistic Density Probability (β-DEN).

Table 1. UCI repository databases characteristics

Problem	#Train	#Test	#Attributes	#Classes
Dermathology	366	-	34	6
Ecoli	336	-	8	8
Glass	214	-	9	7
Vowel	990	-	10	11
Yeast	1484	-	8	10

Table 2. Mean ranking evolution for the methods on the UCI databases tests when the number of zeros is increased

Strategy	0% zeros	10% zeros	20% zeros	30% zeros	40% zeros	50% zeros	Global rank
HD	3.2	3.2	4.4	4.2	4.6	4.0	3.9
ED	3.2	3.2	2.4	2.2	2.6	3.2	2.8
AED	3.2	3.6	4.6	3.8	2.4	4.0	3.6
IHD	3.4	4.0	5.8	4.0	6.0	5.2	4.7
LLB	**1.6**	6.8	7.0	6.8	6.6	7.2	6.0
ELB	**1.6**	4.2	6.8	5.2	5.8	5.6	4.9
LAP	2.4	**2.2**	2.2	2.0	**1.8**	1.6	**2.0**
β-DEN	2.4	2.4	**1.8**	**1.0**	2.4	**1.2**	**1.9**

The tests for the five databases are shown graphically in fig. 3(a)-(e). The graphics show the error evolution for all the decoding strategies at each database. In table 2 and fig. 3(f) the ranking of each method at each percentage step of zeros is shown. The ranking values of the table correspond to the average performance position for each method for all runs on all databases. One can observe that some methods obtain reasonable well-positions at the ranking in all percentages of sparseness, as our proposed Laplacian and Beta Pessimistic Density Probability decoding. Euclidean distance also can contribute to reduce the error of zeros better than techniques as loss-based function, although the last one shows the best accuracy with dense matrices (0% of zeros). However, its

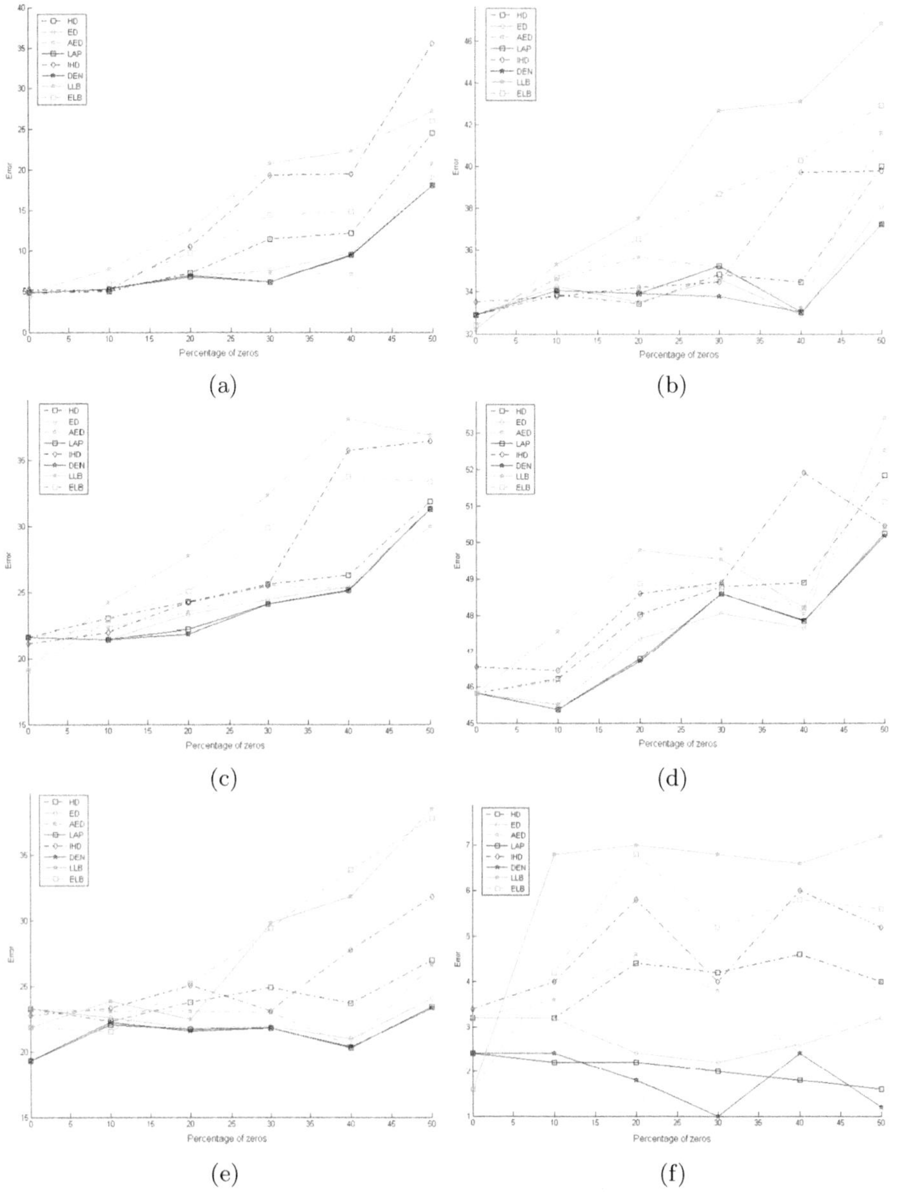

Fig. 3. Error evolution for decoding strategies on Dermathology (a), Glass (b), Ecoli (c), Yeast (d), and Vowel (e) UCI databases. (f) Mean ranking evolution for the methods on the UCI databases tests. The x-axis correspond to the percentage of ceros (increased 10% by step) of 10 sparse matrices M.

performance is reduced as the number of zeros increases. Observing the global rank of table 2, the first position is for Beta Pessimistic Density Probability followed by Laplacian decoding.

Table 2 shows that Loss based decoding is the best option for the dense matrix case, and Beta Pessimistic Density Probability and Laplacian decoding are the best choices when we have an increase of the sparseness degree. If we do not have information about the composition of the code matrix M, we can use the general rank of table 2, being the Beta Pessimistic Density Probability and Laplacian strategies the more suitable for each case.

5 Conclusions

The ternary ECOC when applying a decoding strategy has not been previously enough analyzed. In this paper, we show the effect on reliability reduction when the number of zeros (non considered class by a given dichotomy) is increased. We analyzed the state-of-art ECOC decoding strategies, adapting them to the ternary case, taking into account the effect of the ternary symbol and the weights of the code positions depending on the number of containing zeros. We propose two new decoding strategies that outperform the traditional decoding strategies when the percentage of zeros is increased. The validation of the decoding strategies at UCI repository databases gives an idea about the techniques that are more useful depending of the sparseness of the ECOC matrix M, where our proposed Pessimistic Density Probability and Laplacian strategies obtain the best ranking in the general case. We are planning to extend the proposed decoding strategies to the continuous case.

Acknowledgements

This work was supported in part by the projects TIC2003-00654, FIS-G03/1085, FIS-PI031488, and MI-1509/2005.

References

1. V. Vapnik, Estimation of dependences based on empirical data, Springer, 1982.
2. V. Vapnik, The nature of statistical learning theory, Springer, 1995.
3. L. Breiman, J. Friedman, Classification and Regression Trees, Wadsworth, 1984.
4. J. Friedman, T. Hastie, R. Tibshirani, Additive logistic regression: a statistical view of boosting, (38), 1998, pp. 337-374.
5. E. Allwein, R. Schapire, Y. Singer, Reducing multiclass to binary: A unifying approach for margin classifiers, (1), 2002, pp. 113-141.
6. T. Dietterich, G. Bakiri, Solving multiclass learning problems via error-correcting output codes, (2), 1995, pp. 263-286.
7. T. Windeatt, R. Ghaderi, Coding and decoding for multi-class learning problems,(4), 2003, pp. 11-21.
8. T. Dietterich, G. Bakiri, Error-correcting output codes: A general method for improving multiclass inductive learning programs, in: A. Press (Ed.), Ninth National Conference on Artificial Intelligence, 1991, pp. 572-577.
9. T.Hastie, R.Tibshirani, Classification by pairwise grouping, (26), 1998, pp. 451-471.

10. K. Crammer, Y. Singer, On the learnability and design of output codes for multi-class problems, (47), 2002, pp. 201-233.
11. O. Pujol, P. Radeva, J. Vitrià, Discriminant ECOC: A heuristic method for application dependent design of error correcting output codes, (28), 2006, pp. 1001-1007.
12. S. Escalera, O. Pujol, P. Radeva, ECOC-ONE: A novel coding and decoding strategy, ICPR, Hong Kong, China, 2006, (in press).
13. S. Escalera, O. Pujol, P. Radeva, Forest extension of error correcting output codes and boosted landmarks, ICPR, Hong Kong, China, 2006, (in press).

Context-Based Gesture Recognition

José Antonio Montero[1,3] and L. Enrique Sucar[2]

[1] Instituto Tecnológico de Acapulco
Av. Instituto Tecnológico S/N
Acapulco, Guerrero, México
[2] Inst. Nacional de Astrofísca, Óptica y Electrónica
Luis Enrique Erro #1
Tonantzintla, Puebla, México
[3] ITESM Campus Cuernavaca
Av. Reforma 182-A, Lomas Cuernavaca, Morelos, México

Abstract. Most gesture recognition systems are based only on hand motion information, and are designed mainly for communicative gestures. However, many activities of everyday life involve interaction with surrounding objects. We propose a new approach for the recognition of manipulative gestures that interact with objects in the environment. The method uses non-intrusive vision-based techniques. The hands of a person are detected and tracked using an adaptive skin color segmentation process, so the system can operate in a wide range of lighting conditions. Gesture recognition is based on hidden Markov models, combining motion and contextual information, where the context refers to the relation of the position of the hand with other objects. The approach was implemented and evaluated on two different domains: video conference and assistance, obtaining gesture recognition rates from 94 % to 99.47 %. The system is very efficient so it is adequate for use in real-time applications.

1 Introduction

In everyday life, humans make intensive use of their hands to communicate with other humans, or to manipulate their environment. We denote such hand motions as *gestures*. The automatic recognition of human gestures is useful for many applications, such as human computer interaction (HCI), surveillance, collaborative environments, training and entertainment systems, and medical support. In many domains, gestures are characterized by the spatio-temporal structure of their motion patterns. These structures are intrinsically probabilistic and often ambiguous. In general, they can be treated as temporal trajectories in a high dimensional feature space representing closely correlated measurements on visual observations. For example, the spatio-temporal structure of a simple behavior such as moving the hand towards a key, could be represented by the trajectory of an observation vector given by the position and displacement of the hand centroid (Fig. 1). However, there are many gestures, in particular *manipulative* gestures [6], where the motion trajectory information is not sufficient to discriminate the gestures; for example, gestures realized with the same object (*erasing/writing* on a notebook). In these cases it is necessary to use addi-

J.F. Martínez-Trinidad et al. (Eds.): CIARP 2006, LNCS 4225, pp. 764–773, 2006.

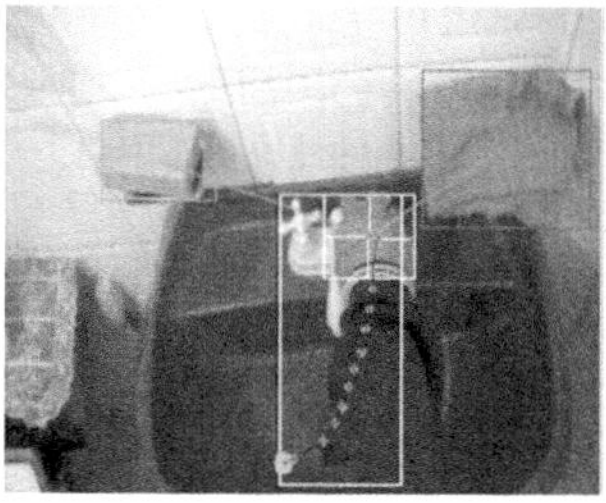

Fig. 1. Trajectory described by the hand centroid while realizing the gesture *opening the key*

tional information relative to the interacting objects (context) so the recognition process is more reliable.

An adequate selection of the visual features is very important for the success of gestures recognition systems. Current non intrusive approaches use a single camera (or a stereo system) to extract relevant features while detecting and tracking the hands, or other parts of the body of a person; which are used as input to a recognition system. The most commonly used methods for feature representation are: trajectory-based features [6], optical flow, and region-based features [11]. The choice is closely related to application and environmental conditions, and as mentioned before, this type of features are not enough for manipulative gestures.

The task of gesture recognition is a very challenging problem in computer vision. In most previous approaches, the gestures are confined to a predefined set, which requires that the subjects are well trained and the motions are uniform. The features and recognition algorithms are totally data-driven without any high level context information. For example, in [3], functions of different coordinates (cartesian, polar, angular) are used as feature vectors and applied in the recognition of six Tái Chi movements. Joint arm angles have been used by Quan, as a feature vector for human activities recognition [8]. However, the gestures realized in many real environments (office, washstand) where the person interacts with surrounding objects, are much more difficult than the above. In these cases, the motion is more natural, complex and dependent on the scenario. Then, it is necessary to use context information.

Hidden Markov Models (HMMs) are widely used for modeling temporal structures. They have been applied to speech recognition [9], learning and more recently to gesture recognition [6]. In this work we propose a novel approach that integrates motion and context features using HMMs to recognize manipulative gestures. These features are obtained using a single ceiling mounted camera observing the user hand interacting with surrounding objects. The motion or trajectory-based features selected are based on a previous study performed by the authors [12], and consist of the orientation and the magnitude in polar coordinates. The context features consider the relative position of the objects that interact with the user hand. We use these features to train HMMs and perform recognition. We evaluated experimentally the gesture recognition system in two different domains: a video conference environment and a scenario in which a someone is washing his hands (for assisting senior or disabled persons). We focus our attention on human gestures performed by the hand that include interaction with surrounding objects and do not have a characteristic trajectory.

Given that the features are continuous, we discretized them into a set of symbols using vector quantization [4]. We then tested the recognition rate using HMMs with different number of hidden states and different number of training data. The results show a variation on the recognition rate depending on these parameters, ranging from 94 % to 99.47 %. We contrasted our models to those based only on motion information.

This paper is organized as follows. In Section 2 we describe hand localization and tracking using color-based, adaptive histograms techniques. Section 3 describes the feature extraction process. In Section 4 we present the learning and recognition system using HMMs. Section 5 includes the experimental results. We conclude with a summary and directions for future work.

2 Hand Detection and Tracking

For this work we consider hand gestures performed in two environments (office and washstand). Hand gestures are made on a planar space. The view of the scene is provided by a downward pointing, ceiling-mounted camera which offers several advantages for hand and object tracking, such as a less unobstructed perspective of the gestures. Our hand detection and tracking approach is divided in two phases. The first phase is the hand localization process that obtains the hand region using an adaptive color histogram. The second phase consists of the tracking algorithm, that generates the gesture trajectory by connecting the hand centroid along the continuous time sequence.

2.1 Hand Detection

For detection of the hand region in an image we use a color-based approach [10]. The human skin color is usually more distinctive and less sensitive to illumination changes if we use the *rgy* normalized color space proposed by [5]. Table 1 compares the *rgy* color space with others models for skin detection. Color histograms is the technique used to model the skin color space. To determine if a blob in the image contains skin pixels we apply the technique proposed by Ballard and Swain known as *histogram intersection* [10]. However, to improve the constraint of a fixed threshold value used by Swain, we are using Otsu's algorithm [7]. Based on Otsu's algorithm, our method incorporates adaptive thresholding, so it is able to tolerate changes in lighting conditions. Initial detection of the hand combines the color-based approach with motion information (Fig. 2), to make it more robust with respect to occlusions and illumination changes in real environments.

2.2 Hand Tracking

Once we have detected skin regions in an image sequence, the next step consists on tracking the hand using only color information. (Currently we assume that

Table 1. Average recognition obtained with the Bayesian classifier used to determine the skin class on different colors spaces

Color Space	Average Recognition
RGB	94.42
HSV	93.50
Yc_rc_b	91.46
RGY	97.20

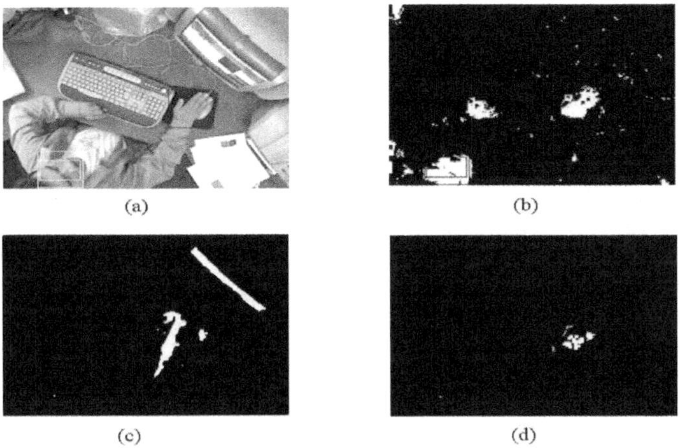

Fig. 2. Detection of human body parts using integration of color and motion information. (a) image original, (b) image segmented using color information, (c) image segmented using motion information, (d) integration of regions using color and motion segmentation.

the person performs all the gestures with the right hand.) For hand tracking, we first have to decide if the skin regions in the image are the face or the hand of a person. Hand/face detection is based on three rules. The first rule considers that only the hands and face of the person cause a significant movement in the images sequence. The second rule establishes a minimum threshold (number of skin labeled pixels) than a region must have to be considered a hand or face of a person. Experimentally we found that the region with the biggest skin area corresponds to the face of the person. The third rule indicates that the person is near the objects of interest, and his hand is the only skin region that establishes contact with the objects.

Based on these rules we detected the user hand in an image sequence, so the system starts tracking it. During tracking, we obtain the center points of the hand region. The center point of an object is defined using the centroid (X_c, Y_c):

$$X_c = \frac{\sum_x \sum_y B(x,y)x}{A}, \quad Y_c = \frac{\sum_x \sum_y B(x,y)y}{A} \; . \tag{1}$$

where A is the number of pixels in the object and B is the binarized input object which takes two values, 1 for the hand and 0 for the background. Then we adjust a search window over the region defined by X_c, Y_c.

Hand tracking is realized by applying the hand detection process over the search window based on motion heuristics (maximum motion between frames), in the images sequence. The sequences of centroid points are detected by the hand localization algorithm, and thus, the gesture trajectory, G, is produced by connecting centroid points (see Fig. 1):

$$G = (x_1, y_1), ..., (x_n, y_n) \ . \tag{2}$$

Our system detects the gestures realized by a person in real environments when his hand interacts with relevant objects.

3 Object Detection and Tracking

Context information for supporting gesture recognition has been used in others works [1,11,6], but their methods impose many restrictions or are computationally complex, so it difficult apply them to real environments. We propose a simple approach based on the color and position of relevant objects in a domain. We use this information to support the gesture recognition process. The object detection and tracking process is a color-based approach. The objects existing in a scenario represent the contextual information that supports the gesture recognition process. The detection and localization of relevant objects is done using an adaptation of the work of Swain [10] and Bradsky [2]. Objects are modeled using color histograms for *hue-saturation* in the *hsv* color space. Training images are used to generate color histograms for each object using 30x32 bins. Initially each object is searched over the full image, and then only in a search window (Bradsky applies the search over the entire image). Objects are detected using histogram intersection [10], so we obtain an image in gray scale where pixels close to 255 are from the object detected. Once an object is detected, we use a tracking algorithm proposed by Bradsky [2] over an appropriate search window

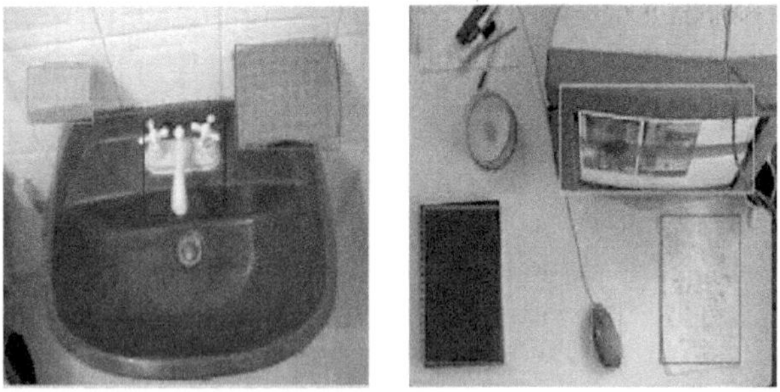

Fig. 3. Objects detected in two domains. Left image: towel, soap and key in a washstand. Right image: screen, book, mouse and note pad in an office environment.

for each object. The system maintains the position of each object in the scene. Figure 3 illustrates the object detection process in two domains: washstand and office environment. Objects detected in the washstand domain are: (1) a towel (pink rectangle), (2) a soap (green rectangle), and (3) a key (blue rectangle). Objects detected in the office environment are: (1) a notepad (blue rectangle), (2) a book (red rectangle), (3) a mouse (green rectangle), (4) a screen (aquamarine rectangle).

Objects interacting with the hand of a person represent contextual information. The gesture recognition system integrates this information with the motion attributes from the hand trajectory.

4 Recognition System

Gesture recognition is based on hidden Markov models (HMMs), integrating motion and contextual features.

4.1 Feature Selection

Motion features are obtained from the trajectory described by the right hand centroid when interacting with surrounding objects. In a previous analysis, we found that magnitude and orientation in polar coordinates are the best motion features for describing this type of gestures [12]. Context features include the distance from the hand centroid to each of the relevant objects that are detected in the scene. An example is shown in Fig. 4. Thus, we use the following set of features: (i) orientation, ρ, (normalized value) in polar coordinates, ii) magnitude, ϕ, (normalized value) in polar coordinates, and iii) context information (relative position of the objects in the scene). To obtain those features the following procedure is applied.

The center point, (C_x, C_y), of the gesture trajectory is obtained:

$$(C_x, C_y) = (\frac{1}{n}\sum_{t=1}^{n} X_t, \frac{1}{n}\sum_{t=1}^{n} Y_t) \ . \tag{3}$$

Based on this center point, the angle, θ_t, and distance, r_t, of each sample in the trajectory is obtained, relative to the center point:

$$\theta_t = tan^{-1}(\frac{Y_t - C_x}{X_t - C_y}) \ . \tag{4}$$

$$r_t = \sqrt{(X_t - C_x)^2 + (Y_t - C_y)^2} \ . \tag{5}$$

By calculating the longest distance from the center point to any point in one gesture, r_{max}:

$$r_{max} = max_{t=1}^{n}(r_t) \ . \tag{6}$$

the normalized $(0 - 1)$ distance, ρ_t; and normalized angle, ϕ_t, are:

$$\rho_t \frac{r_t}{r_{max}}, \phi_t = \frac{\theta_t}{2\pi} \ . \tag{7}$$

By integrating the motion and context parameters, we obtain the following feature vector:

$$F = (\rho, \phi, Context) \ . \tag{8}$$

Given that these are continuous variables and we are using discrete models, these features are codified in 64 discrete observation symbols using the k-means algorithm [4].

Fig. 4. The distance between the user hand and objects determine the context. In this case, the red line shows the closest object.

4.2 Hidden Markov Models

HMMs have the ability to accurately characterize data exhibiting sequential structure in the presence of noise, such as human gestures, finding the most likely sequence of states that may have produced a given sequence of observations. The HMM topology used in this paper is the classical left–right structure, which is typical for motion ordered paths. As usual, one model was trained for each gesture class, and for recognition we selected the model with the highest probability. The complete parameter set of the HMM can be expressed compactly as $\lambda = (A, B, \Pi)$, where A is the probability transition matrix, B is the observation probability matrix, and Π is the initial probability vector. Three basic problems must be solved for the application of HMMs: evaluation (classification), decoding, and training. We approach the above problems with the standard techniques [9]: forward algorithm, Viterbi algorithm, and the Baum-Welch algorithm.

5 Experimental Results

In this study, we focus our attention on human gestures performed by the hand that include interaction with known objects. The type of gestures considered in the experiments are the realized in two domains: office environment and washstand room. The gestures that recognition system will try to identify are the following: *erasing, writing, using the mouse and turning the leaves of a book*, in the office environment (see Fig. 5); and *using soap, opening the key, closing the key, drying the hands, taking the towel, and washing hands*, in the washstand domain (see Fig. 5).

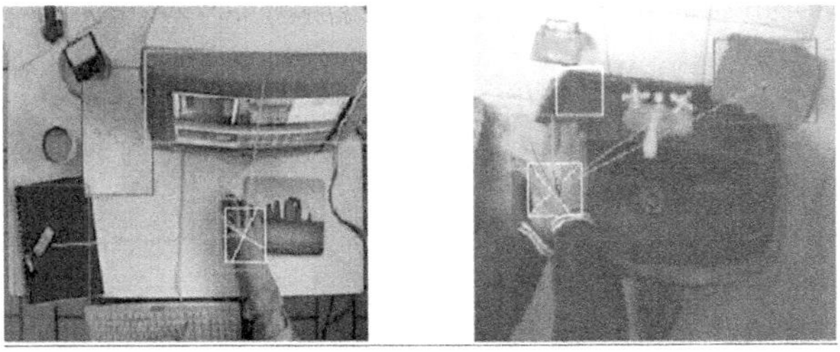

Fig. 5. Example of gestures recognized in the two domains: left image office environment, right image washstand

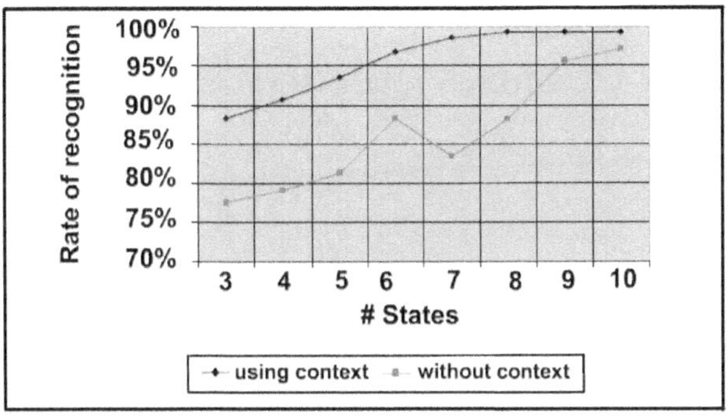

Fig. 6. Gesture recognition rates with and without context information vs. number of hidden states for the office domain

5.1 Training

We use two different training data set: one set for the office domain and another for the washstand domain. In the office domain a data base with 4200 data points was generated for training and testing. Data stored in the DB was obtained from 100 gestures sequences with 5 different gestures realized by a person in a sitting position and interacting with objects in the office environment. We used 2100 data points for training and 2100 for testing. In the washstand domain, we use a data base with 3600 data points generated for training and testing. These data were obtained from 50 gestures sequences with 6 different gestures realized by a person in a standing position and interacting with surrounding objects. In this case, we used 2560 data points for training and 1040 data points for testing. In both cases, gesture data was captured by a ceiling mounted camera pointed downward, under normal illumination conditions in an office and in a bathroom.

5.2 Results

We tested the gesture recognition system for the 11 different types of gestures, related to the manipulation of each object in the two scenarios.

For the office environment, we compared the recognition rate with only motion information vs. motion and context, for different number of hidden states in the HMM. Figure 6 shows graphically the difference between both schemes. With only motion, the recognition rate varies from 75% for 3 hidden states to 97% for 10 hidden states. In the other case, when we integrate motion and context, the recognition rate varies from 88% using 3 hidden states to 99.47% using 10 hidden states. There is a significant improvement by incorporating context.

For the washstand domain, we only show the results with motion and context features. The confusion matrix is depicted in Table 2. The recognition rate varies from 80% to 100%. The average recognition in this domain is 94%.

Table 2. Confusion matrix for the washstand domain

	Open/close Key	Washing hands	Take soap	Soaping	Take towel	Dry hands	Av %
Open/close Key	15	0	0	0	0	0	**100.00**
Washing hands	0	14	0	0	1	0	**99.33**
Take soap	0	1	12	0	1	1	**80.00**
Soaping	0	0	0	14	1	0	**93.33**
Take towel	0	0	0	0	14	1	**93.33**
Dry hands	0	0	0	0	0	15	**100.00**

5.3 Implementation

The system was implemented in a personal computer, Intel Pentium 4, with a 1.3 Ghz processor; and a Sony TRV19 CCD color video camera. The video card (PixelView) captures 30 frames of 320x240 pixels per second. The processing rate of the recognition system is between 12 and 15 fps. The system is codified in Visual C++ 6.0 over Windows XP.

6 Conclusions

In this work we propose a novel approach that integrates motion and context features using HMMs to recognize manipulative gestures. These features are obtained using a single ceiling mounted camera observing the user hand interacting with the surrounding objects. The motion features consist of the orientation and the magnitude in polar coordinates. The context features consider the relative position of the objects that interact with the user hand. We evaluated experimentally the gesture recognition system in two different domains: a video conference environment and a scenario in which a someone is washing his hands. The results in both domains are very good, showing a significant improvement in relation to using only motion features. We believe that using additional context information, such as the relation between hands, or hands and face, could provide another important set of features to improve gesture recognition for more complex scenarios.

References

1. D. Ayers and Mubarack Shah. Monitoring human behavior in an office environment. *PAMI*, 7:780–794, July 1997.
2. G.R. Bradski. Computer vision face tracking as a component of a perceptual user interface. *Workshop on Applications of Computer Vision*, 1:214–219, 1998.
3. Lee W. Campbell, David A. Becker, Ali Azarbayejani, Aaron F. Bobick, and Alex Pentland. Invariant features for 3-d gesture recognition. *In Proc. of the Intl. Workshop on Automatic Face and Gesture Recognition, Zurich*, 5:157–162, 1996.
4. Robert M. Gray. Vector quantization. *IEEE ASSP Magazine*, 7:407–467, Apr 1984.
5. Miriam Martnez and Luis E. Sucar. Learning and optimal naive bayes classifier. *36vo Congreso de Investigacion y Desarrollo del Tecnolgico de Monterrey: Impulsando la Economa Basada en Conocimiento*, 2006.
6. Darnell J. Moore, Irfan A. Essa, and Monson H. Hayes. Exploiting human actions and object context for recognition tasks. *Proc. IEEE of the 7th International Conference on Computer Vision*, 1, Sep 2000.
7. N. Otsu. A threshold selection method from gray-evel histograms. *IEEE, Trans. Sys, Man, and Cybernetics*, 1:62–66, Jan 1979.
8. D. L. Quan. Gesture recognition with a data glove. *IEEE Proc. National Aerospace and Electronics Conf.*, 2, 1990.
9. L. R. Rabiner. A tutorial on hidden markov models and selected applications in speech recognition. *Proc. of the IEEE*, 77(2):267–293, 1989.
10. M. J. Swain and D. H. Ballard. Color indexing. *International Journal of Computer Vision*, pages 11–32, 1991.
11. M. Thonnat and N. rota. Video sequence interpretation for visual surveillance. *Third International Workshop on Cooperative Distributed Vision*, pages 1–9, November 2000.
12. Jose Antonio Montero V. and Luis Enrique Sucar S. Feature selection for visual gesture recognition using hidden markov models. *Fifth Mexican International Conference on Computer Science*, 1:196–203, 2004.

Spectral Median Graphs Applied to Graphical Symbol Recognition

Miquel Ferrer[1], Ernest Valveny[1], and Francesc Serratosa[2]

[1] Computer Vision Center, Dep. Ciències de la Computació
Universitat Autònoma de Barcelona, Bellaterra, Spain
{mferrer, ernest}@cvc.uab.es
[2] Departament d'Enginyeria Informàtica i Matemàtiques
Universitat Rovira i Virgili, Tarragona, Spain
francesc.serratosa@urv.cat

Abstract. Generalized median graph is a general concept useful to capture the essential information of a set of graphs. In addition, spectral techniques can be used to obtain approximate solutions of graph matching problems in a reasonable time. In this work we use the novel concept of spectral median graph which takes advantage of both the median concept and the spectral techniques, to synthesize the representative of a set of graphical symbols. The results show that this concept represents appropriately the most important intra-class features, while rejecting small distortions and, for extension, it can be used to infer a prototype of a set of symbols.

1 Introduction

Graphs, specially labelled or attributed relational graphs, are general and powerful data structures for object representation in structural pattern recognition and computer vision applications. When objects are represented by graphs, *graph matching* is used to compare such objects. Algorithms for graph matching include graph and subgraph isomorphism [1]. However, due to errors and noise in the input data, many times it is not possible to find a perfect match between two elements and then, algorithms for approximate or error-tolerant matching must be considered. These algorithms compute a similarity measure between two given graphs. Numerous applications for exact and error-tolerant graph matching such as character recognition, schematic drawing analysis, 2D shape analysis, 3D object interpretation and machine learning have been reported in the literature [2].

In some of these applications it may be necessary to obtain the prototype of a set of objects. Given a set of noisy samples of a certain object, error-tolerant graph matching can be useful to infer a representative model that captures the essential information of the class while rejecting small distortions due to noise. In this context the concept of median graph [3] can be very useful and it has already been applied to the synthesis of a prototype of a set of graphical symbols[4].

[1] This work was sponsored research Fellowship number 401-027 (UAB) / Cicyt TIC2003-09291 (Ministerio Ciencia y Tecnología).

J.F. Martínez-Trinidad et al. (Eds.): CIARP 2006, LNCS 4225, pp. 774–783, 2006.

It is well-known that one of the drawbacks of graph matching is its computational complexity. However, in the last years, spectral graph theory have been applied to graph matching as an alternative way to obtain approximate solutions in a reasonable time [5]. We have used spectral graph theory to develop an efficient algorithm to compute the generalized median graph [6]. In this paper, we propose an application of the spectral median graph to compute the representative prototype of a set of graphical symbols. Graph matching has been widely used for recognition of graphical symbols and the definition of symbol prototypes is one of the open issues [7]. Thus, we will define a graph representation of symbols that is suitable for applying spectral techniques and we will show how the spectral median graph yields a good prototype of the set of symbols, in terms of recognition rates and theoretic definition. Results are compared with those obtained using the Graduated Assignment Algorithm [8].

The rest of the paper is organized as follows. In section 2, we present some theoretical concepts required to understand the rest of this work. Section 3 presents the concept of spectral median graph. In section 4 we introduce the representation of graphical symbols used to perform the experiments. Section 5 presents the experiments and the results obtained. We terminate with some conclusions and possible future research lines.

2 Definitions and Notation

In this work, we consider undirected labeled graphs. Given L_V and L_E, the sets of vertex and edge labels respectively, formally speaking a labeled *graph* G is a 4-tuple $G = (V, E, \mu, \beta)$ where V is the set of nodes, $E \subseteq (V \times V)$ is the finite set of edges, $\mu : V \longrightarrow L_V$ is a function which labels each vertex $v \in V$ and $\beta : E \longrightarrow L_E$ is a function which labels each edge $e \in E$.

2.1 Median Graph

Median graph [3] is an useful concept in object prototyping. Given a set of graphs, the median is defined as the graph that has the smallest sum of distances to all graphs in the set. We can distinguish between set and generalized median graph. Formally speaking, median graph can be defined as follows:

Definition 1. *Let Z be the set of graphs that can be constructed using labels from L_V and L_E. Given $S = \{G_1, G_2, ..., G_n\} \in Z$, the generalized median graph $\bar{g}$ and set median graph $\hat{g}$ of S are defined as follows:*

$$\bar{g} = arg\left(\min_{G \in Z} \sum_{G_i \in S} d(G, G_i)\right) \tag{1}$$

$$\hat{g} = arg\left(\min_{G \in S} \sum_{G_i \in S} d(G, G_i)\right) \tag{2}$$

For the median graph computation of a similarity or distance measure between two given graphs, $d(G_1, G_2)$ is needed. Error-tolerant graph matching [9] can be used to find the best correspondence between two graphs, providing such a measure of similarity.

The only difference between both definitions is the space where the median is computed. The generalized median graph is computed among the set of all possible graphs. Thus, it is a more general concept and usually gives a better representation than set median graph, which is computed among the set of sample graphs. Notice that $\bar{g}$ is usually not a member of S, and in general more than one generalized and set median graph can be found for a given set.

Conceptually, while the computation of set median graph is exponential in the size of input graphs and polynomially bounded in the number of those graphs (we must compute $\frac{1}{2}n(n-1)$ pairwise graph distances), the computation of generalized median graph is exponential in both the size of input graphs and the number of those graphs. As a consequence, we are committed to use suboptimal methods to compute approximate solutions in a reasonable time.

An application of median graph used in the synthesis of graphical symbols has been presented in [4]. In this work a genetic algorithm has been employed to compute the generalized median graph. The results obtained by such algorithm have been compared with those obtained by an A^*-search optimal algorithm.

3 Spectral Median Graph

Spectral graph theory is concerned with understanding how the structural properties of graphs can be characterized using the eigenvalues and eigenvectors of the adjacency matrix of a graph. A pioneering work concerning inexact graph matching using spectral techniques is [5]. Using this work, we have extended the median graph concepts to the spectral graph theory to define set and generalized median eigenmode [6] using the modal matrices (matrices containing the eigenvectors obtained from an adjacency matrix):

Definition 2. *Let K be the set of all modal matrices of order n. Given a set of modal matrices $L = \{\boldsymbol{U}_1, \boldsymbol{U}_2, \ldots, \boldsymbol{U}_m\}$, the generalized median eigenmode $\overline{U}$ and the set median eigenmode $\widehat{U}$ of L are defined by:*

$$\bar{U} = arg\left(\max_{U \in K} \sum_{U_i \in L} \Gamma(U, U_i)\right) \tag{3}$$

$$\hat{U} = arg\left(\max_{U \in L} \sum_{U_i \in L} \Gamma(U, U_i)\right) \tag{4}$$

where $\Gamma(A, B)$ is the correlation between two matrices A and B and is computed with the method described in [5].

The generalized median eigenmode and the set median eigenmode maximize the sum of the correlations to all modal-matrices in K or L. Nevertheless, the computation of both medians is drastically different. While $\hat{U}$ is obtained in polynomial time with respect to the number of elements, $\bar{U}$ is obtained in exponential time (see [6] for more details).

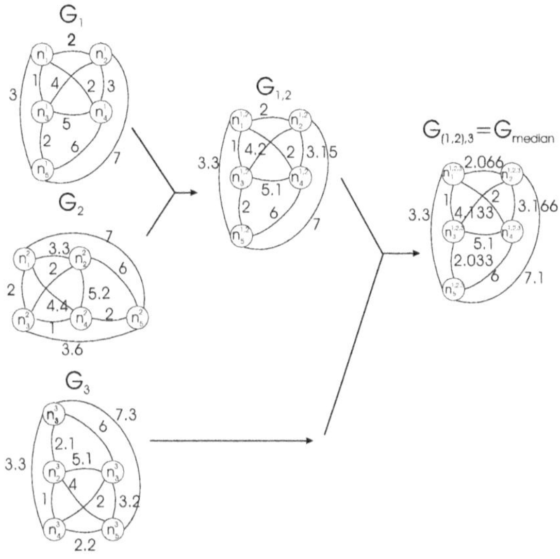

Fig. 1. Synthesis of median spectral graph

Synthesis of the Generalized Median Eigenmode: An incremental algorithm has been used in [6] to compute the generalized median eigenmode. First, we maximize the correlation between the modal matrices of two graphs in the set using the procedure explained in [5], giving an intermediate median graph. Then, the modal matrix of this intermediate median graph is used to maximize the correlation to the next graph in the set, and the process is repeated iteratively until the last graph in the set is processed, giving the final median graph. Figure 1 shows an example of such algorithm.

4 Synthesis of Graphical Symbols

In order to test the spectral median graph we have applied this method to compute the prototype of a given set of graphical symbols. We have chosen a subset of the symbols used in the *Sixth IAPR International Workshop on Graphics Recognition - GREC 2005* [10]. This subset contains 80 different symbols (classes), extracted from architectural, electric and other technical fields. Some representative symbols of such subset are shown in figure 2. Notice that all of them are composed of a set of straight lines. Each segment terminates either with a terminal point or a junction point (confluence point between two or more segments). For convenience, from now to the end of this work, we will refer to these kinds of points as TP and JP respectively.

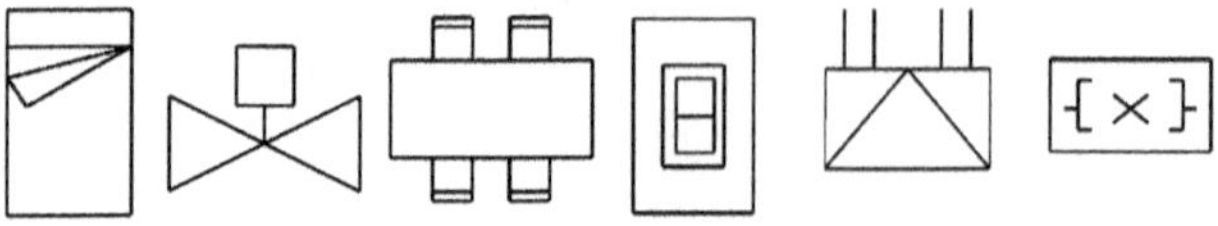

Fig. 2. Six symbols corresponding to *GREC 2005* database

In order to prove the robustness of the prototypes against noise, 7 different levels of distortion have been introduced. Distortion is generated moving each TP or JP randomly within a circle of radius r, given as a parameter for each level, centered at original coordinates of the point. If a JP is randomly moved, all the segments connected to it are also moved. With such distortion, gaps in line segments, missing line segments and wrong line segments are not allowed. But the number of nodes of each symbol is not changed. Figure 3 shows an example of such distortions. For each class and for each distortion, we have created 100 images. Thus for each class we have 700 elements (100 for each distortion). Therefore, we have 5600 (80*700) images to perform the experiments.

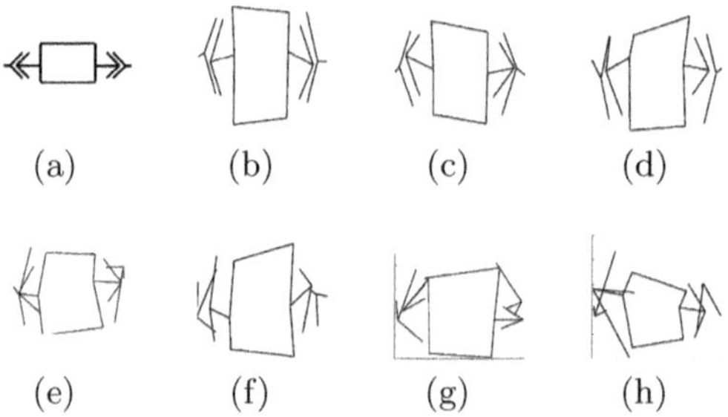

Fig. 3. Original model (a) and distorted models from level 1, (b) to level 7, (h)

In order to compute the prototypes a graph-based representation of the symbols must be defined. This representation must take into account some restrictions imposed by the two approximate methods that have been used to compute the prototypes, namely the spectral median graph and the Graduated Assignment algorithm. Spectral techniques can only work with graphs with the same number of nodes. On the other hand, the adjacency matrices used in the graduated assignment algorithm must have 0-element in the main diagonal. In addition, in both cases the attributes of nodes or edges must be real positive numbers.

We have defined two different representations, namely *node-based* representation and *edge-based* representation. In both of them a symbol is represented as an undirected labeled graph, where the TPs and JPs are represented as nodes. Edges correspond to the segments connecting those points. The information associated to nodes or edges are their coordinates (x, y). As labels can only be real numbers we have created two adjacency matrices for each symbol, one of them containing x-coordinates and the other containing y-coordinates. In the *edge-based* representation, information associated to nodes is always 0 while edge labels are the coordinates (x, y) of the mid point of the segment. In the *node-based* representation, labels of nodes are the coordinates (x, y) of the point while labels of edges are always 1. In both cases we store a 0 when no edge exists between two nodes. The distance between two symbols will be the mean between the x and y distances. Figure 4 shows the two representations of a symbol.

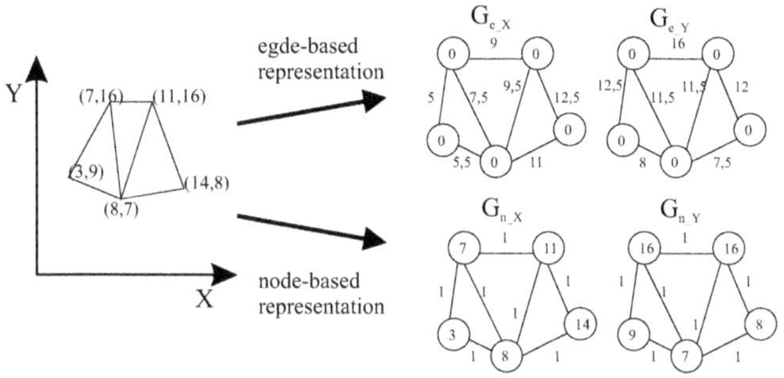

Fig. 4. Two graph-based representations of a graphical symbol

5 Experiments and Results

In this paper, two methods are compared, namely spectral median graph and the graduated assignment algorithm for graph matching. While the spectral graph method has been tested using the two graph-based representations cited above, the graduated assignment has only been tested using the edge-based representation. We will refer to such combinations as S-edge, S-node (for spectral applied to both edge and node-based representations) and GA-edge (for graduated assignment). In addition, we propose three measures in order to test the accuracy and the robustness of such methods to compute the prototype of a set of a given models. We call these measures *Intra-class Median Accuracy*, *Recognition Rate* and *Median Evolution*. The two first measures are quantitative measures while the third one is more qualitative and is useful to perform a visual evaluation of the methods. In order to make the results more general, we have calculated for each class and for each level of distortion, the corresponding median using 1,5,10,30,50,70 and 100 images in the class. In the next lines, these three experiments will be explained and the results obtained for each one will be presented.

Intra-class Median Accuracy: This measure computes the similarity between the computed median graph and the true median graph. The sum of distances (SOD) of the median to all the other elements in the class is computed and compared to the SOD of all the elements in the class. According to its definition, the median graph would always have the minimum SOD. So, if we rank the median and all the other elements according to SOD, the lower is the position of the median, the better is the representation for the median. The results obtained

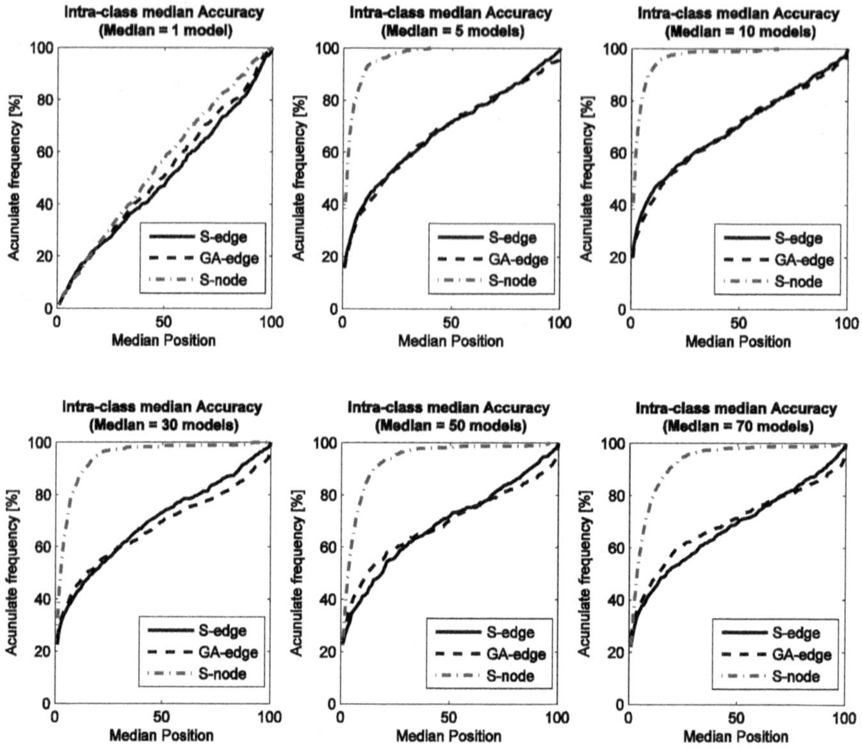

Fig. 5. *Experiment 1:* Intra-Class Accuracy

for all the classes are shown in figure 5. Curves show the mean accumulate position of the median over all distortion levels for a certain number of images used to compute the median.

When the median is computed with only one model, the position of the SOD of the median with respect to the rest of the elements in the class is distributed randomly. As a consequence, the accumulative frequency tends to be linear from 0 to 100. For the other cases, we can see that S-edge and GA-edge methods have a very similar behavior. In both cases, the SOD of the median is the minimum around the 20-25% of times and around 40-45% is among the fifth best positions. Results are much better for the S-node method. The accumulative frequency at the fifth position is between 80-90% depending on the number of images. Moreover, the evolution is much more abrupt than for S-edge and GA-edge. From these results we can draw three main conclusions: firstly, the *node-based* representation is more appropriate to compute the median; secondly, there is no significant differences between spectral methods and graduated assignment with respect to the correctness of the computed median; and thirdly, there is no significant improvement in the median accuracy when using more than 5 images per class. It seems that using between 5 and 10 images per class is enough to compute the median.

Recognition Rate: In this case, one median was computed for each class. Then, all the models in the database were matched against the computed medians and classified according to the median with minimum distance. It must be noticed, that, as spectral graph matching requires the two graphs to have the same number of nodes, only 20 classes, those with the same number of nodes in their elements, have been used. Table 1 shows the mean recognition rates. On the left, recognition rates are the mean for each level of distortion while on the right, recognition rates are the mean (over all classes and distortion levels) for the median computed with 1,5,10,30,50,70 and 100 images/class.

Results show that S-edge and GA-edge methods have similar recognition rates, being S-edge slightly better than GA-edge while S-node has the best results in all cases. As expected, recognition rate decreases as distortion level increases, being this tendency more clear in the S-node results. No significant improvement of recognition rates can be seen as a function of the #images, beginning with 5 images. Thus, the behavior pattern of the methods is very similar to that detected with the *intra-class median accuracy* measure.

Median Evolution: This experiment shows the evolution of the median as a function of the distortion level and the #images used to compute the median. Since experiments 1 and 2 show that the best combination is the S-node method, this third experiment has only been performed with such method. Figure 6 shows the results obtained for a particular class (the ideal model for this class is shown in figure 2). In this figure, rows correspond to the distortion level while columns correspond to the number of images used to compute the median. We can see that the largest is the number of symbols used to compute the median graph, the bigger is the similarity between it and the ideal model. Obviously, the number of images to obtain a close representation of ideal symbol by means of median graph depends on the distortion level. For instance, we obtained a similar results in median computation using 5 symbols for a distortion level of 10 and 100 symbols for a distortion level of 7. It must be noticed that even with high degrees of distortion, using enough number of images, the median always tends to the ideal shape.

Table 1. *Experiment 2:* Recognition Rate

Recognition Rate vs. Distortion			
Distortion	**S-edge**	**GA-edge**	**S-node**
1	96.10	93.54	99.78
2	93.19	92.43	98.28
3	93.46	90.75	97.24
4	92.94	92.81	96.27
5	92.55	92.19	96.10
6	93.54	93.97	94.84
7	92.05	93.12	93.78

Recognition Rate vs. #symbols			
# symbols	**S-edge**	**GA-edge**	**S-node**
1	92.02	93.22	94.50
5	93.35	92.62	96.62
10	93.17	91.87	96.45
30	93.35	92.71	97.03
50	94.68	93.52	97.12
70	94.27	92.14	97.23
100	93.01	92.72	97.35

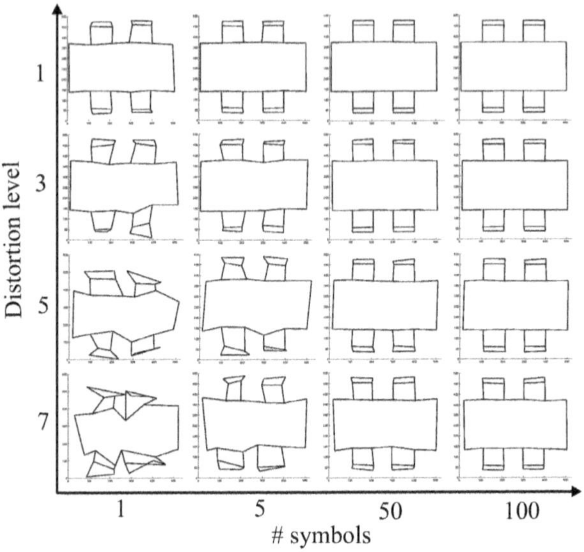

Fig. 6. *Experiment 3:* Median Evolution

Table 2. Computation time (minutes): S-edge, GA-edge and S-node algorithms

Algorithm	# Symbols/median						
	1	5	10	30	50	70	100
S-edge	15.6	16.2	16.5	18.1	20	20.9	23
GA-edge	14.7	27.7	45.1	109.6	174.3	241.23	337.05
S-node	9.87	10.15	10.25	11.56	13.37	14.71	16.26

Computation Time: Table 2 shows the computation time required for S-edge, GA-edge and S-node to perform experiment 3 on a Intel Centrino 1.73 GHz with 512 MB of RAM. In the case where the median is computed with one symbol all the methods have similar computation times. In the other cases, GA-edge computation time is always greater than those obtained by S-edge and S-node, being this difference bigger as the number of symbols used increases. The difference in computation times in S-edge and S-node is due to the representation, but in both cases is practically constant with respect to the number of symbols.

6 Conclusions

Median graph is a useful concept to compute the prototype of a given set of symbols. In this work we adopted a spectral approach to compute the generalized median graph of a set of graphical symbols. We compared the results obtained by our method with those obtained using the graduated assignment algorithm.

We have shown the practical usefulness of the proposed approximate method to represent the concept of median graph. In particular, the experimental results have demonstrated the ability of the solutions to represent the prototype of graphical symbols keeping the most important information in the class and rejecting small distortions due to some form of noise. Although S-edge and GA-edge have similar intra-class accuracy and recognition rate results, computation times are drastically different being significantly lower in the S-egde. We have defined two graph representations of graphical symbols, obtaining better results with the node-based representation. These results suggest that a deep study of the influence of the representation and the structure of the adjacency matrix should be done in order to characterize as well as possible the behavior of spectral techniques. In this sense it would be useful to extend this study to other matrices such as the Laplacian matrix, and compare the results with those obtained with the adjacency matrix.

References

1. Ullman, J.R.: An algorithm for subgraph isomorphism. Journal of ACM **23**(1) (1976) 31–42
2. Bunke, H., Messmer, B.T.: Recent advances in graph matching. IJPRAI **11**(1) (1997) 169–203
3. Jiang, X., Münger, A., Bunke, H.: On median graphs: Properties, algorithms, and applications. IEEE Trans. Pattern Anal. Mach. Intell. **23**(10) (2001) 1144–1151
4. Jiang, X., Münger, A., Bunke, H.: Synthesis of representative graphical symbols by computing generalized median graph. In Chhabra, A.K., Dori, D., eds.: GREC. Volume 1941 of Lecture Notes in Computer Science., Springer (1999) 183–192
5. Umeyama, S.: An eigendecomposition approach to weighted graph matching problems. IEEE Transactions on Pattern Recognition and Image Analysis **10**(5) (1988) 695–703
6. Ferrer, M., Serratosa, F., Sanfeliu, A.: Synthesis of median spectral graph. In Marques, J.S., de la Blanca, N.P., Pina, P., eds.: IbPRIA (2). Volume 3523 of Lecture Notes in Computer Science., Springer (2005) 139–146
7. Lladós, J., Valveny, E., Sánchez, G., Martí, E.: Symbol Recognition: Current Advances and Perspectives. In Blostein, D., Kwon, Y.B., eds.: Graphics Recognition – Algorithms and Applications. Volume 2390. (2002) 104–127
8. Gold, S., Rangarajan, A.: A graduated assignment algorithm for graph matching. IEEE Trans. Pattern Anal. Mach. Intell. **18**(4) (1996) 377–388
9. Sanfeliu, A., Fu, K.: A distance measure between attributed relational graphs for pattern recognition. IEEE Transactions on Systems, Man and Cybernetics **13**(3) (1983) 353–362
10. Dosch, P., Valveny, E.: Report on the second symbol recognition contest (to appear in lncs series). (2006)

Deterministic Tourist Walks as an Image Analysis Methodology Based

André R. Backes[1], Odemir M. Bruno[1], Mônica G. Campiteli[2], and Alexandre S. Martinez[2]

[1] Instituto de Ciências Matemáticas e de Computação (ICMC)
Universidade de São Paulo (USP)
Avenida do Trabalhador São-carlense, 400
13560-970 São Carlos SP Brazil
backes@icmc.usp.br, bruno@icmc.usp.br
[2] Faculdade de Filosofia, Ciências e Letras de Ribeirão Preto (FFCLRP)
Universidade de São Paulo (USP)
Avenida Bandeirantes, 3900
14040-901 Ribeirão Preto SP Brazil
monicacampiteli@pg.ffclrp.usp.br, asmartinez@ffclrp.usp.br

Abstract. Textures are important visual attribute used in image analysis. This paper presents a novel methodology, based on a deterministic walk, to texture analysis and texture characterization. Most of the methods adopted to classify textures deal with a defined fixed scale of texture. The method proposed here explores the set in all scales and is able to characterize efficiently different texture classes. The paper presents the deterministic walk technique and its results for two experiments using Brodatz images.

1 Introduction

Image Analysis is a field of computer vision and artificial intelligence responsible for the extraction of meaningful information from images. Among several attributes, texture is an important visual attribute used in image analysis. Texture analysis has a broad range of applications, such as: aid of diagnoses in medical images [1], remote sensing [2], analysis of geological images [3] and microscope images [4].

Although there is not a formal specification of the texture analysis, this attribute is directly related to the distribution of pixels in a certain region of the image. It represents an important source of information. Generally, textures can be classified as micro and macro textures according to the size of the set of pixels analyzed. By micro textures we mean the analysis of a small parts of the image, while for macro texture the analysis of the whole image. Most of the techniques used in image retrieval are devoted to the micro textures analysis [5,6]. The number of methods applied to macro textures is still restricted, due to the inherent difficulty in the analysis [7].

Recently we have proposed a new method for texture characterization based on a deterministic dynamics. Consider walkers leaving each pixel of an image.

J.F. Martínez-Trinidad et al. (Eds.): CIARP 2006, LNCS 4225, pp. 784–793, 2006.

Each walker does not interact with the others. For a given time step, each walker has information about the eight next nearest neighbor pixels and moves towards the direction of minimum intensity difference among the ones that have not been visited in the previous μ time steps. For $\mu = 0$, no dynamics is allowed. For $\mu = 1$, the walker always goes to the mininum intensity difference direction, so that after a time transient, the trajectories end on cycles of period two. This cycle consists of two pixels having mutually the minimum intensity differences between themselves. More interesting cycle distributions occur for $\mu \geq 2$. In this case each trajectory, after a transient time, ends in a cycle with period $p \geq \mu = 1$. In particular, cycles with period p much greater that the memory μ are allowed. It is the range of cycle periods which allows the image analysis from the local scale of μ pixel up to a large scale of size of the number of pixels N.

Our main interest is to obtain an image signature from the time transient and cycle period joint distribution. A naive approach to this analysis has been described in Ref. [8], where we have shown the potential use of these joint distributions for texture analysis in images. A more sofisticated analysis, using the non-parametric Flexible Discriminant Analysis (FDA) on the joint distribution furnished a more reliable classification [9].

Our presentation is divided as follows. A brief review of the considered deterministic walk in Section 2. In Section 3, we modify these walks t apply them to image analysis. In Section 4, from the transient time and cycle period obtained from the walker trajectory we build texture signatures vectors. Also we set up experiment sets to compare the performance of two of the proposed texture signature vectors to 400 images of 40 different Brodatz's texture classes. In Section 5, we show the superior performance when multiple μ values are used. Finally in Section 6, the conclusions and improvement of the methods are discussed.

2 Deterministic Tourist Walk

Although not as thoroughly studied as random walks [10,11], the study of deterministic walks has attained the interest of researchers [12,13,14,15]. Here, we are interested in exploring a partially self-avoiding deterministic walk algorithm, known as the tourist walk (TW) [16,17,18,19,20,21] for image analysis purposes.

The tourist walk algorithm can be pictorially viewed as a tourist wishing to visit N cities randomly distributed in a map of d dimensions. The tourist starts his route in a given city of this map and moves according to the following deterministic rule: *go to the nearest city, which has not been visited in the last μ time steps.* For $\mu \geq 1$, self-avoidance is limited to the memory window $\tau = \mu - 1$, which represents a characteristic time to the city to become attractive to the tourist again (refractory time). The trajectories can intersect outside this memory range. Each tourist trajectory consists of a transient part of length t (new cities are visited) and a final cycle of period p (no new cities are visited any longer). The trajectory is complex and depends strictly on the starting point and on the configuration of the data set. The only known relation that holds is $p \geq \mu + 1$. The tourist movements are entirely performed based on the neighborhood rank. These ranks are conveniently represented by a neighborhood table, which neglects the distances among the cities. This feature leads to invariance in scale transformations [21].

We call the attention to several aspects of these deterministic walks:

1. At each time interval the tourist moves from one city to another, regardless the distance between them.
2. Starting from different cities in the map, the tourist performs different trajectories with variable transient times (which can even be null $t = 0$) and end in cycles with period $p \geq \mu + 1$.
3. The trajectories are different for different initial conditions, but several trajectories can end in the same cycle with a given period p.

Although easy to formulate and not too complicated to implement numerically, this algorithm may present a complex behavior according to the chosen memory window μ. This intriguing behavior can be captured with the transient time and period joint distribution $S_{d,\mu}^{(N)}(t,p)$. Here we show that the joint distributions $S_{d,\mu}^{(N)}(t,p)$ can be efficiently used as features for image analysis. In the following we show some examples of known analytical joint distributions for Poissonic landscape.

The deterministic tourist walk with memory $\mu = 0$ is trivial since the walker does not move at each time step. The joint distribution is simply given by: $S_{d,0}^{(N)}(t,p) = \delta_{t,0}\delta_{p,1}$, where $\delta_{i,j}$ is the Kronecker's delta.

With memory $\mu = 1$, the walker must leave the visited city at each time step. The transient and period joint distribution is obtained for $N \gg 1$ [22]: $S_{d,1}^{(\infty)}(t,p) = \Gamma(1 + I_d^{-1})(t + I_d^{-1})\,\delta_{p,2}/\Gamma(t + p + I_d^{-1})$, where $t = 0, 1, 2, \ldots$, $\Gamma(z)$ is the gamma function and $I_d = I_{1/4}[1/2, (d+1)/2]$ is the normalized incomplete beta function. We stress that this transient time distribution has been calculated for Poissonic process. It does not lead to exploration of the random medium since after a short transient time, the tourist gets trapped in pairs of cities that are mutually nearest neighbors.

Interesting phenomena occur when greater memory values are considered. In this case, the cycle distribution is no longer peaked at $p_{min} = \mu + 1$, but presents a whole spectrum of cycles with period $p \geq p_{min}$, with possible power-law decay [16,17,18]. Determinism imposes serious restrictions as it can be seen in $\mu = 2$ one-dimensional systems, where all odd periods above $p_{min} = 3$ are forbidden, as well as the even period $p = 6$.

3 Modified Tourist Walk

In the context of images ($d = 2$), one can consider each pixel as a point (or city). In the original algorithm the neighborhood table has size of the order N^2, where each point is ranked with respect to the remaining $N - 1$ other points. Notice that μ ranges from zero to $N - 1$, where all cities are visited (full self-avoiding circuit).

For images, the algorithm has been modified since each pixel interacts only with its first and second neighbors and the walker goes always to the direction of minimum intensity difference (gradient). Thus the neighborhood table has a maximum size of $N \times 8$. For open boundary condition, the surface and corner pixels have five and three next and second next nearest neighbors, respectively.

Starting from each pixel, the walker moves according to the deterministic rule of going to the pixel with nearest intensity compared to the present pixel intensity, so that the given intensity difference has not been attained in the preceeding μ steps. From these walks, the transient time and cycle period of the trajectories are calculated and the joint distribution is constructed.

The occurrence of ties is resolved by choosing the first pixel in the counter clockwise direction, preserving the deterministic nature of the algorithm. This approach is not invariant to image rotation. For a given image and the same image with 90°-tilt feeded to the algorithm, different joint distributions are produced. This suitable difference for texture characterization is due the deterministic way of resolving intensity difference ties.

Differently from the original problem, the tourist walk is not performed in a non-correlated random media but in a correlated medium, the image. Similarly to the previous studies [8,9], the image analysis consists exploring the joint distribution properties over the image and compose a texture signature curve.

4 Experiments

The tourist walk transient time and cycle period joint distributions have been obtained for different memory values using open boundary conditions to the images from the book of Brodatz [23]. These images form a set largely used in computer vision and image processing literature as benchmark for texture analysis. In the computer experiment, each image has 200×200 pixels with 256 gray levels and 40 classes, with 10 samples each, have been employed. One example of each these 40 classes are dipicted in Figure 1. Experiments have been idealized to show the high potential of the method to analyze and characterize texture images.

4.1 Transient Time and Cycle Period Joint Distribution

It is important to stress that the transient time has the role of counting different intensity gradients while the cycle detects a kind of pattern that eventually an image may display. The memory μ has the role of setting the minimum pattern scale.

In Figure 2 three different classes of Brodatz's textures are dipicted and for each class, the transient time and cycle period joint distribution of the modified tourist walk is display for three different memory values. Observe the existence of a pattern for the joint distribution for each considered texture class. This stresses the potentiability to discriminate different texture classes from these distributions. Also, it is clear that the large the memory values are, the broader the distribution is. This means that different μ values sample different image characteristics indicating the possibility to have an optimum μ value for better

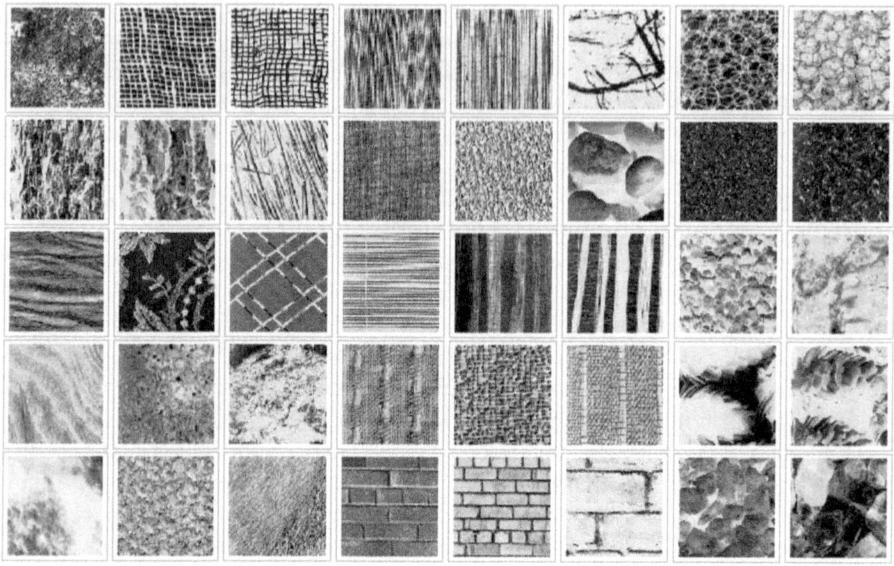

Fig. 1. One example of each of the 40 Brodatz's classes considered. Each image has 200×200 pixels and 256 grey levels.

image classification. The signature curves obtained from the joint distributions have been used to characterize and classify the images used in the experiment.

Operationally one has a three-dimensional array where one of the axis represents the transient time. The other axis represents the cycle period. When these two axes are combined, they represent the joint distribution $S_{\mu}^{(N)}(t,p)$. The third axis represents the memory, so that slices along the μ axis give $S_{\mu}^{(N)}(t,p)$.

A large amount of information is contained in this three-dimensional array. This implies to difficulties when dealing with pattern recognition. Our main objective is to extract texture information, in a simple form, using signatures.

4.2 Texture Signature Vector

Signatures concentrate the desired texture information to few elements of a vector. For instance, for images of 200×200 pixels, signatures are vectors is a typical size of 25 elements.

The signature curves are feature vectors extracted from the joint distributions and they are used to characterize and classify the images by the texture pattern. In the first approach the feature vector ψ is constructed from the joint distribution of a specific μ value. The parameters t and a indicate the maximum number of transient time and the maximum number of attractors to be considered, respectively:

$$\psi_{\mu}(t,a) = [S_{2,\mu}^{(N)}(0:t,\mu+1) S_{2,\mu}^{(N)}(0:t,\mu+2) \ldots S_{2,\mu}^{(N)}(0:t,\mu+a)] \,. \quad (1)$$

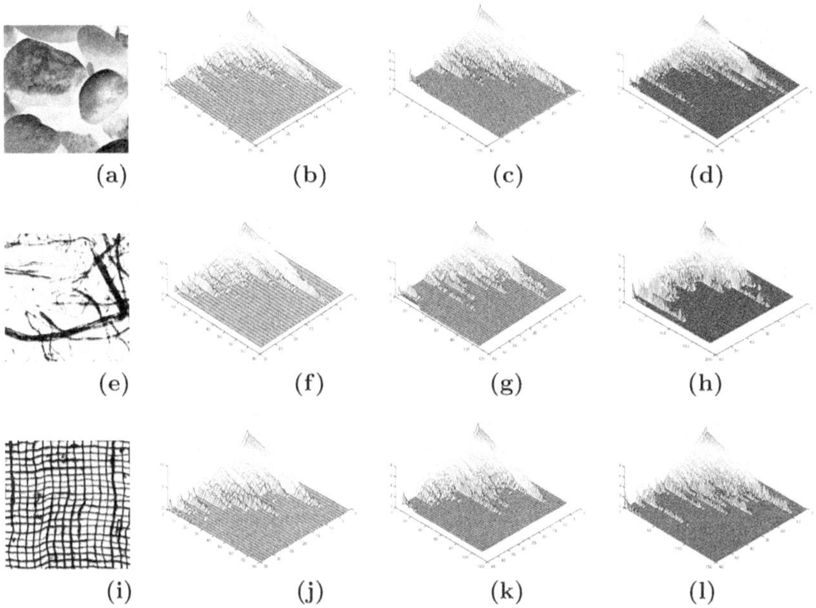

Fig. 2. Three different classes of Brodatz's textures are dipicted in panels from **(a)**, **(e)** and **(c)**. For each class, the transient time and cycle period joint distribution of the modified tourist walk is display for three different memory values: $\mu = 2$ (pannels: **(b)**, **(f)** and **(j)**), $\mu = 3$ (pannels: **(c)**, **(g)** and **(k)**) and $\mu = 5$ (pannels: **(d)**, **(h)** and **(l)**).

To study the influence of the memory on the time transient and cycle period distribution and consequently its influence in the sample classification, the experiments have been performed with $t = 4$ and $a = 5$ so that each signature vector has 25 elements. Experiments have been carried out for $\mu = 2, 3, 5, 7$ and 11.

In the second experiment only the first two time transients ($t = 0$ and $t = 1$) and two cycle periods $a = 2$ are considered for $\mu = 2, 3, 5, 7$ and 11 and the signature vector in this case is the concatenation of the simpler fixed signature vectors

$$\varphi(\mu_i, \mu_f) = [\boldsymbol{\psi}_{\mu_i}(2,2) \ldots \boldsymbol{\psi}_{\mu_f}(2,2)] . \quad (2)$$

4.3 Flexible Discriminant Analysis

In both experiments, the Brodatz's images have been characterized by modified tourist walk texture signature. A discriminant data analysis technique has been performed, based on these features. The statistical analysis has been carried out with the R 2.1.1 system [24] and the employed technique has been the *flexible discriminant analysis* (FDA) [25]. This is a generalization of *linear discriminant analysis* (LDA). It is more sofisticate analysis than LDA, once it uses non-parametric fits to achieve a more flexible classifier than LDA. The experimental results and the discussion about the performance of the modified tourist deterministic walks are presented in the following.

5 Results

Table 2 shows the confusion matrix obtained for the first experiment, i.e., when the μ values are not combined. The signature vector has the most 24 representative elements of the transient time and cycle period joint distribution of the modified tourist walk. This signature vector has been submitted to a flexible determinant analysis. Table 1 shows that as the memory μ increases, the error tends to increase.

The second set of experiments have been performed concatenating part of the μ image signature vector from the first set of experiments into a single image

Table 1. The error as a function of the memory μ for the fixed memory experiment

μ	2	3	5	7	11	multiple μ
error	0.1225	0.1775	0.2025	0.1725	0.2625	0.0525

Table 2. Confusion matrix showing the classification results for 40 classes of texture images, for signature extracts for $\mu = 5$. Classification error = 0.2025.

true obj	01	02	03	04	05	06	07	08	09	10	11	12	13	14	15	16	17	18	19	20	21	22	23	24	25	26	27	28	29	30	31	32	33	34	35	36	37	38	39	40
01	5			1			1										1	1									1															1	
02		5						1																		1					1											
03	1		7													1																									
04	1			8																																			1	
05					8											1																							
06						10																																		
07			1				9												1							1									1						
08		1						4											1								1						1								
09									8																						1								
10									1	9																													
11		1			1						8	1																											
12												9																											
13													7										1																	1	
14														10																									
15	1														8																		1						
16																7									1														1	
17																	6	2															1								1
18								1			1							8																1							
19																			7																						1
20																				10																			
21																					10	1																	
22																						9																	
23		1										1										8	1					1										1	
24		1			1			3																8																
25			1								1														7						1								1
26	1																		1							7							1							1
27																											10												
28																												10											
29																													8										
30													2										1							9								1		
31			1	1					1									1														8									
32		1						1								1	1									1						6									
33																			1							1							7							
34																																		10					
35																																			10				
36																																				10	1			
37																																					9		
38																														1								7		
39										1																													7	
40	1														1																1								6

Table 3. Confusion matrix showing the classification results for 40 classes of texture images, for the combining μ method. Classification error = 0.0525.

true obj	01	02	03	04	05	06	07	08	09	10	11	12	13	14	15	16	17	18	19	20	21	22	23	24	25	26	27	28	29	30	31	32	33	34	35	36	37	38	39	40
01	8																																						
02		9																														2							
03			9	1								1																											
04				9				1																								1							
05					10																																			
06						10																																		
07							10																																	
08		1						8										1																					
09									10																														
10										10																													
11											10																												
12												9																											
13													10																										
14														10																									
15															10																								
16																10																							
17																	10																						
18																		9																					
19																			10																				
20																				10																			
21																					10																		
22																						10																	
23																							10	2															
24																								8	1														
25																									8														
26																										10						1							
27																											10												
28																												10											
29																													10										
30																														10									
31								1																						9									1
32																									1							7							
33																																	9						
34																																		10	1					
35																																			9					
36																																				9				
37																																				1	10			
38																																						10		
39			1																																				10	
40		2																													1									9

signature vector. This approach leads to a significant increase of the method classification capacity. The composed signature vector has been generated colecting the five more significant elements from each single μ signature vector leading to 25 elements. The confusion table of this set of experiments is presented in Table 3 and the error is of 0.0525.

Collecting six elements from the single signature vector leading to 30 elements in the composed signature, the error is of 0.0500.

The results of these preliminary experiments with the modified tourist walk transient time and cycle period joint distribution with several memory values combined with a signature vector and a powerfull statistical multivariate analysis show the potential use of them as an efficient image classification method.

The new treatment proposed here diminishes the individual importance for each μ value, but stresses the role of small values either for μ or the transient time and cycle period. This conclusion is corroboreted with the small error taxes for the second experiment

6 Conclusion

We have presented a new method of feature extraction of image textures based on the deterministic tourist walk. The methods most commonly used deals with defined scales of pixel distributions. The distribution of transient times and periods of a set of data (image) present a wide range, capturing details on the organization of pixels from the micro to the macro scales and the resulting curve is strictly related to the configuration of the data set. We have showed that the joint distribution of the modified TW is an efficient tool for texture classification. We have realized two experiments using the modified TW and discriminant analysis to classify Brodatz textures. The results presented in this paper, show the great potential of the modified TW to be used as a texture analysis methodology.

Acknowledgements

O.M.B. acknowledges support from CNPq (303746/2004-1). M.G.C. acknowledges support from CAPES. A.S.M. acknowledges support from CNPq (305527/2004-5) and FAPESP (2005/02408-0).

References

1. Wu, C.M., Chen, Y.C., Hsieh, K.S.: Texture features for classification of ultrasonic liver images. IEEE Transactions on Medical Imaging **11** (1992) 141–152
2. Yang, C.Z.X.: Study of remote sensing image texture analysis and classification using wavelet. International Journal of Remote Sensing **19**(16) (1998) 3197–3203
3. Heidelbach, F., Kunze, K., Wenk, H.R.: Texture analysis of a recrystallized quartzite using electron diffraction in the scanning electron microscope. Journal of Structural Geology (2000) 91–104
4. Anguiano, E., Oliva, A.I., Aguilar, M.: Surface texture parameters as a tool to measure image quality in scanning probe microscope. Ultramicroscopy **77**(3) (1999) 195–205
5. Li, S.: On discontinuity-adaptive smoothness priors in computer vision. IEEE Transactions on Pattern Analysis and Machine Intelligence **17**(6) (1995) 576–586
6. Howarth, P., Ruger, S.: Evaluation of texture features for content-based image retrieval. Lecture Notes in Computer Science **3115** (2004) 326–334
7. Jain, A.K., Farrokhnia, F.: Unsupervised texture segmentation using gabor filters. Pattern Recognition **24**(12) (1991) 1167–1186
8. Campiteli, M.G., Martinez, A., Bruno, O.M.: A statisitcal texture classification framework using deterministic tourist walks - submited. INFOCOMP Journal of Computer Science (2006)
9. Campiteli, M.G., Martinez, A.S., Bruno, O.M.: An image analysis methodology based on deterministic walks - to appear in lecture notes in computer science. Ibero-American Conference on Artificial Intelligence (2006)
10. Scholl, J., Schol-Paschinger, E.: Classification by restricted random walks. Pattern Recognition **36** (2003) 1279–1290
11. Derrida, B.: From random walks to spin glasses. Phys. D **107**(2–4) (1997) 186–198
12. Freund, H., Grassberger, P.: The Red Queens walk. Physica A **190**(3-4) (1992) 218–237
13. Bunimovich, L.A., Troubetzkoy, S.E.: Recurrence properties of Lorentz lattice gas cellular automata. J. Stat. Phys. **67**(1-2) (1992) 289–302

14. Bunimovich, L.A.: Deterministic walks in random environments. Physica D **187** (2004) 20–29
15. Gale, D., Propp, J., Sutherland, S., Troubetzkoy, S.: Further travels with my ant. Math. Inteligencer **17**(3) (1995) 48–56
16. Lima, G.F., Martinez, A.S., Kinouchi, O.: Deterministic walks in random media. Phys. Rev. Lett. **87**(1) (2001) 010603
17. Stanley, H.E., Buldyrev, S.V.: Statistical physics - the salesman and the tourist. Nature (London) **413**(6854) (2001) 373–374
18. Kinouchi, O., Martinez, A.S., Lima, G.F., Loureno, G.M., Risau-Gusman, S.: Deterministic walks in random networks: an application to thesaurus graphs. Physica A **315**(3/4) (2002) 665–676
19. Boyer, D., Miramontes, O., Ramos-Fernandez, G., Mateos, J.L., Cocho, G.: Modeling the searching behavior of social monkeys. Physica A **342**(1-2) (2004) 329–335
20. Boyer, D., Larralde, H.: Looking for the right thing at the right place: Phase transition in an agent model with heterogeneous spatial resources. Complexity **10**(3) (2005) 52–55
21. aes Campiteli, M.G., Batista, P.D., Kinouchi, O., Martinez, A.S.: Deterministic walks as an algorithm of pattern recognition. submitted. (2006)
22. Terçariol, C.A.S., Martinez, A.S.: Analytical results for the statistical distribution related to memoryless deterministic tourist walk: Dimensionality effect and mean field models. Phys. Rev. E **72** (2005) 021103
23. Brodatz, P.: A Photographic Album for Arts and Design. Volume 1. Dover Publishing Co., Toronto (1966)
24. R Development Core Team: R: A Language and Environment for Statistical Computing. R Foundation for Statistical Computing, Vienna, Austria. (2005)
25. Webb, A.: Statistical Pattern Recognition. Volume 1. Newnes (1999)

Approaches to Classification of Multichannel Images

Vladimir Lukin[1], Nikolay Ponomarenko[1], Andrey Kurekin[2], Kenneth Lever[2], Oleksiy Pogrebnyak[3], and Luis Pastor Sanchez Fernandez[3]

[1] National Aerospace University, Dept of Transmitters, Receivers and Signal Processing, 17 Chkalova St, 61070 Kharkov, Ukraine
lukin@xai.kharkov.ua, uagames@mail.ru

[2] Department of Computer Science, School of Engeneering, Cardiff University, 5 The Parade, Roath, Cardiff CF24 3AA, UK
A.Kurekin@cs.cardiff.ac.uk

[3] Instituto Politecnico Nacional, Centro de Investigacion en Computacion, Ave. Juan de Dios Batiz S/N, C.P. 07738, Mexico, D.F., Mexico
olek@pollux.cic.ipn.mx

Abstract. The comparison of different approaches to classification of multichannel remote sensing images obtained by spaceborne imaging systems is presented. It is demonstrated that it is reasonable to compress original noisy images with appropriate compression ratio and then to classify the decompressed images rather than original data. Two classifiers are considered: based on radial basis function neural network and support vector machine. The latter one produces slightly better classification results.

Keywords: Multichannel image classification, image compression, remote sensing.

1 Introduction

Nowadays airborne and spaceborne remote sensing (RS) systems produce a lot of data that are valuable for such applications like ecological monitoring, forestry, agriculture, catastrophe prediction, etc [1]. Most of such systems operate in the so called multichannel mode [2]. Term "multichannel" means that for some terrain lot several component images are formed in different bands or using different polarizations of transmitted and/or received signals. Multichannel RS systems are potentially able to provide more reliable retrieval of useful information from RS data and/or more accurate estimation of sensed terrain parameters.

Multichannel data can be transferred from airborne or spaceborne carrier to an on-ground processing center without any compression, coded in a lossless manner, or lossy compressed. In case of lossless coding the provided compression ratio (CR) is commonly within the limits from 2 to 3 [3, 4] that often is inappropriate. Recently, several papers that report on possibilities of applying lossy compression to multi- and hyperspectral images have appeared (see, e.g., [5-7]). It has been demonstrated that quite good classification of multichannel RS data can be provided even if the used CR is from 20 to 50. It can be explained by the fact that the original multichannel RS

J.F. Martínez-Trinidad et al. (Eds.): CIARP 2006, LNCS 4225, pp. 794 – 803, 2006.

images often are noisy [8] and noise suppression using image compression techniques leads to increasing the reliability of correct classification simultaneously decreasing the data size [8-10]. The only important item is that CR should be adjusted in correspondence with noise variance for providing a proper trade-off between noise suppression and distortions introduced due to lossy compression [9,10]. This allows expecting that the probability of correct classification of multichannel RS data can be of the same order for two cases: a) applying classification procedure to original (noisy) data; b) applying classification to data compressed in a lossy manner with proper selection of a compression ratio.

The aim of this paper is twofold. The first goal is to compare both aforementioned approaches and to make up the corresponding practical recommendations. The second goal is to consider two modern classifier types based on using support vector machines (SVM) and radial basis function (RBF) neural networks (NN), both trained in a supervised manner.

2 Lossy Compression of Noisy Images

First, it is worth noting that in case of lossy compression of noisy images it is reasonable to use not typical criteria of compressed image quality [9, 10]. Recall that if one deals with traditional lossy compression of still images, the compression is basically characterized by the rate-distortion curve (PSNR vs CR) [11]. $PSNR_{or}$ for decompressed image is calculated with respect to the corresponding original image. On the contrary, if a noisy image is subject to compression, it is also expedient to control similarity of decompressed and noise-free images that can be characterized by $PSNR_{nf}$ calculated with the use of MSE between decompressed and noise free images. Certainly, $PSNR_{nf}$ can be obtained by simulations with test images to which noise has been artificially added.

Fig. 1 presents the corresponding curves for the test gray-scale image Lena corrupted by additive, zero mean Gaussian noise with variance σ^2=50. Two compression methods have been considered, the standard JPEG 2000 [12] and the recently introduced AGU coder [13].

For both considered coders the dependencies of $PSNR_{or}$ behave in conventional manner, i.e., $PSNR_{or}$ becomes smaller when the compression rate increases. The behavior of the $PSNR_{nf}$ curve is more specific. As seen, for both considered coders $PSNR_{nf}$ increases when CR reduces from 2 to approximately 0.35 bpp. At CR≈0.35bpp the maximums for both curves are observed, and further reduction of CR leads to rapid $PSNR_{nf}$ decreasing. Such a compression rate for which the maximum of $PSNR_{nf}$ is observed called optimal operation point (OOP). Intuitively, this can be favorable for image classification.

As shown in [9], for OOP determination one should know in advance or to pre-estimate the noise characteristics, and it can be done in a blind manner [15, 16]. Approaches to provide OOP in an automatic manner have been proposed in [9, 17]. Since AGU coder provides for OOP better $PSNR_{nf}$ than JPEG2000 (see [9] and particular data in Fig. 1), below we will consider the application of AGU coder for compressing multichannel images.

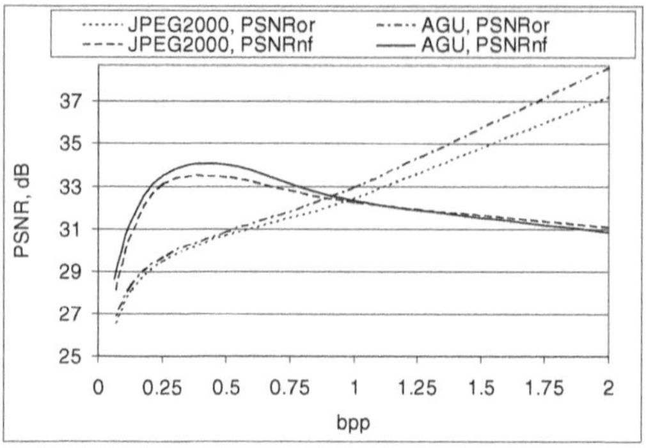

Fig. 1. Dependencies $PSNR_{nf}$ and $PSNR_{or}$ vs CR for JPEG2000 and AGU techniques for test image Lena corrupted by additive noise with σ^2=50

3 Considered Approaches to Classification of Original Noisy and Compressed Images

Classification has been applied to the three-channel test image presented in Fig. 2,a. This image has been obtained by using Landsat TM images of three bands (ftp://ftp.glcf.umiacs.umd.edu/glcf/Mosaic_Landsat), for which the corresponding ground truth map is available.

There are five basic classes in the observed scene, namely, soil, grass, water surface, roads and urban areas, bushes. The percentage of pixels (more exactly, voxels) belonging to each class is rather different and it varies from 7.4% for roads and urban areas to 43.6% for grass. Two classifiers have been employed. The first one is based on Support Vector Machines (SVM) that has superior performance comparing to many standard classification techniques in various applications [18].

The SVM classifier uses a "kernel trick" method for mapping the original feature space of classified data into a higher-dimensional non-linear feature space. For

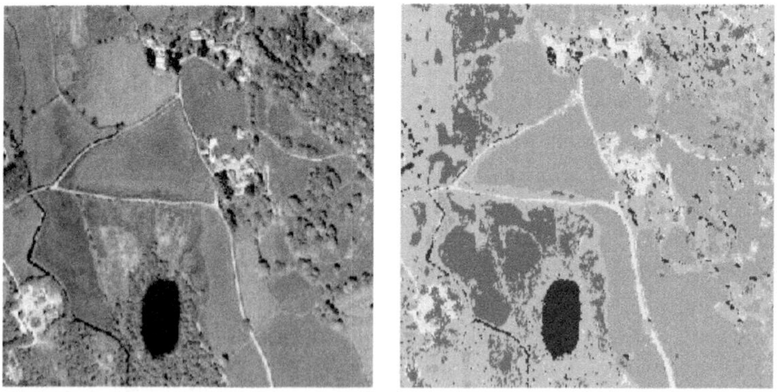

a b

Fig. 2. The test three-channel image in RGB representation (a) and the corresponding classification map for noise-free multichannel data (b) two-class (binary) classification problem the SVM classifier uses a hyperplane to subdivide the feature space into two regions and attributes the input feature vector to one of two classes. There are different ways for choosing a hyperplane in a feature space. One of them is a maximum margin approach that maximizes the distance from the hyperplane to the nearest training samples in a feature vector space. This approach is not applicable for training data with classification errors and data corrupted by noise, such as multichannel RS images considered in this paper. Obviously, classification errors are natural for some part of noisy data used for SVM training, and maximum margin condition can not be satisfied for all vectors of the training data set.

For training the SVM classifier we used a more practical approach. It is based on choosing a soft margin hyperplane that allows a small amount of errors in training data by introducing slack variables in the objective function. For binary classification the soft margin hyperplane is found by solving the primary optimization problem [18]

$$\min_{\mathbf{w},b,\xi_n} \{\frac{1}{2}\mathbf{w}^T\mathbf{w} + \sum_{n=1}^{N} C\xi_n\} \tag{1}$$

subject to

$$\begin{aligned} y_n(\mathbf{w}^T\varphi(\mathbf{x}_n)+b) &\geq 1-\xi_n, \\ \xi_n &\geq 0 \qquad \text{for} \quad i=1,\dots,N \end{aligned} \tag{2}$$

where N is a number of training samples, $\{(\mathbf{x}_n, y_n)\}_{n=1}^{N}$ is the training dataset and y_n=1 for the first class and y_n=-1 for the second class of training data. ξ_n are slack variables. If $\xi_n > 0$, the slack variables indicate training data with classification errors. C>0 is an error penalty parameter that determines the trade-off between the hyperplane margin and classification errors; **w** and b are the parameters of hyperplane $(\mathbf{w}\cdot\mathbf{x}_n)+b=0$. By introducing Lagrange multipliers $\alpha_n \geq 0$, the constrained optimization problem (1) can be expressed as dual optimization problem [20]

$$\max_{\alpha_n} \{\sum_{n=1}^{N}\alpha_n - \frac{1}{2}\sum_{m,n=1}^{N}\alpha_m\alpha_n y_m y_n \varphi(\mathbf{x}_m)^T\varphi(\mathbf{x}_n)\} \tag{3}$$

subject to the constraints

$$\sum_{n=1}^{N}\alpha_n y_n = 0, \text{ and } C \geq \alpha_i \geq 0 \text{ for } n=1,\dots,N \tag{4}$$

where $\alpha_n \geq 0$. For Lagrange multipliers α_n not equal to zero the corresponding training vectors are named "support vectors".

The dot product of two feature vectors in (3) is calculated indirectly by application of "kernel trick" method. A kernel function $K(\mathbf{x},\mathbf{y})$ is expressed as

$$K(\mathbf{x},\mathbf{y}) = \varphi(\mathbf{x})^T\varphi(\mathbf{y}) \tag{5}$$

where function $K(\mathbf{x},\mathbf{y})$ is subject to Mercer's condition [18, 20]. One of the frequently used kernel functions is a radial basis function (RBF)

$$K(\mathbf{x},\mathbf{y}) = \exp(-\gamma\|\mathbf{x}-\mathbf{y}\|^2),\ \gamma > 0 \tag{6}$$

where γ is the function control parameter. The RBF kernel has only one parameter, it provides the same performance as linear kernel, for certain parameters it behaves like some other kernel types and is a reasonable choice for the considered classification task. Application of (5) for a hyperplane equation gives the output of SVM classifier

$$f(\mathbf{x}) = \mathrm{sgn}\left(\sum_{n=1}^{N} y_n \alpha_n K(\mathbf{x}, \mathbf{x}_n) + b \right) \tag{7}$$

where $\mathbf{x}$ is the input feature vector. For the considered scenario of classifying three-channel test images, the feature vector is composed of three pixel values for RGB image components $\mathbf{x} = (x^R, x^G, x^B) \in R^3$.

The SVM classifier given by equations (1)-(7) is designed for solving binary classification tasks. Several approaches have been proposed for solving multi-class problems based on direct classification of all data in one optimization formulation and combining several binary SVM classifiers [21]. The first one has to deal with all SVM parameters for the objective function optimization and it is usually more computationally expensive than the second approach that we applied for classification of the test image in Fig.2,a. It is based on one-against-one classification strategy that divides multi-class problem into $K(K-1)/2$ separate binary classification problems for all pair combinations of K classes. The binary classification problems are solved by SVM classifiers and a majority voting rule is applied to find the output class [21].

While the number of class training samples is not equal, we used different error penalty parameters C_i in the objective function (1) to provide equal contributions from every image class and achieve similar probability of correct classification. For i-th class the parameter C_i is given by

$$C_i = C^* \frac{N}{KN_i} \tag{8}$$

where C^* is a constant. N_i is a number of training samples for class i and N is a total number of samples. The error parameter C^* and the RBF control parameters are evaluated by cross-validation [19].

Another approach presumes the use of radial basis function (RBF) neural network (NN) classifier [22]. The RBF NN demonstrates high efficiency, low computational demands and simplicity of software and hardware implementation at training and classification stages [23, 24]. The RBF NN classifier we used had an input layer, single hidden layer with nonlinear neurons and an output layer with linear neurons. The number of neurons in the input layer was the same as the number of input features, and the number of output layer neurons was equal to the number of data classes. The number of neurons in the hidden layer depends on such factors, as classification complexity and feature space dimensionality. The activation function of the hidden layer neurons had the same form as the RBF kernel function (6) we considered for SVM classifier. The training of RBF NN was performed by minimizing the mean square error E of the NN output

$$E = \frac{1}{KN} \sum_{k=1}^{K} w_k \sum_{n=1}^{N} \left(z_{n,k} - y_{n,k} \right)^2 \tag{9}$$

where $Z_{n,k}$ is the output of the NN output layer representing the accumulated membership of the n-th data sample to the object class k. $y_{n,k}$ is the desired output of neural network, N is the number of training samples and K is the number of classes. The error function (9) was weighted by w_k values to provide equal contributions from every image class for the different numbers of class training samples. The weight for every class is equal to the reciprocal of the number of class training samples.

A cascade-correlation algorithm that provides nearly optimal training results with the extended number of neurons in the RBF NN hidden layer was used to minimize the objective function (9). Training starts with one hidden layer neuron and the new ones are added iteratively to reduce the total residual error. The weighting coefficients of new hidden neuron are selected to provide the condition of maximum correlation between the new unit output and the trained NN output error [25]. The optimal number of hidden layer neurons is selected automatically by cross validation [19].

Classifiers have been trained in a supervised manner using small portions of images from 181 to 1610 pixels depending upon the class. In Fig. 3 the lots from which the training sets were taken are shown. After learning, the classifiers have been applied to the entire image. The pixels to which classification has been applied are depicted by black color in Fig. 3.

Learning of classifiers has been performed for each particular case of the test image. First, it was done for the original noisy image and, second, for the image compressed with optimal CR. Note that different sets of classifier parameters have been obtained for these cases. Two values of additive Gaussian noise variance have been used in simulations: 49 and 100 for byte component images. In the first case the optimal CR was about 8, and for σ^2=100 the optimal CR≈10.7.

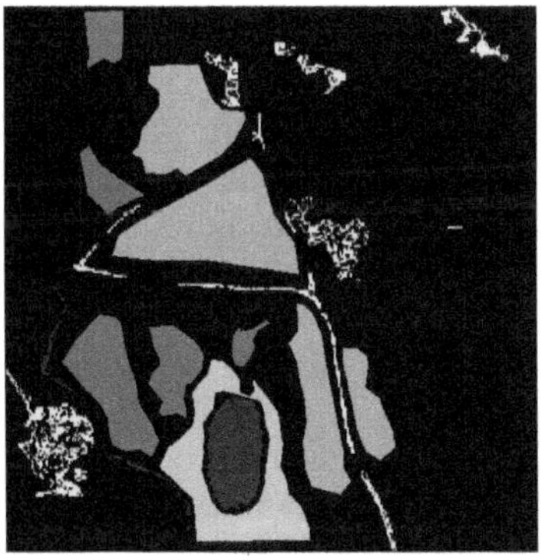

Fig. 3. The lots (image fragments) used for training the SVM and RBF NN classifiers

4 Experimental Result Analysis

The results obtained for SVM classifier for both variance values (σ^2=49 and σ^2=100) are presented in Table 1. For the class bare soil we have obtained 87.25% of correctly classified pixels, for grass 99.71%, for water surface – 98.38%, for roads and urban areas – 67.34%, and for bushes – 87.13% with overall accuracy $P_{cor\ ov} = 91.48\%$. As seen, the lowest probability of correct classification is observed for classes for which RS data are either rather heterogeneous of appear themselves as prolonged or small size objects.

Some tendencies observed from data in Table 1 are trivial and expectable. In particular, the probabilities $P_{cor\ k}$ for particular classes as well as $P_{cor\ ov}$ for noisy images are smaller than for noise-free data irrespectively is classification applied to original images or to compressed ones. Practically for all classes increasing of σ^2 leads to decreasing of $P_{cor\ k}$ and, respectively, these results in reduction of $P_{cor\ ov}$.

Table 1. Precentage of correctly classified pixels for the trained SVM

Noise variance	Classified image	Bare soil	Grass	Water	Roads	Bushes	Overall
49	Original	82.00	94.37	96.17	67.62	71.27	85.46
49	Compressed	83.39	91.57	95.59	65.60	81.43	85.80
100	Original	74.90	91.68	94.24	59.81	67.30	81.13
100	Compressed	83.43	93.43	92.76	62.07	76.23	85.21

The most interesting fact is that for both considered values of σ^2 the probabilities $P_{cor\ ov}$ are larger if classification is applied to compressed RS data. For the case σ^2=100 the benefit attained due to classifying compressed data in comparison to classifying original multichannel images is considerable. This means that a positive effect due to the noise suppression taking place in case of image compression is larger than a negative effect due to the introduced distortions. Concerning particular classes, sometimes better values of $P_{cor\ k}$ are provided if classification is applied to the original data.

The classification maps for applying the SVM based approach to original and compressed data in the case of σ^2=100 are presented in Fig 4,a, and Fig. 4,b, respectively. Comparison of these classification maps between each other and to the more accurate classification map (Fig. 2,b) shows the following. Being applied pixel-wise to original noisy image, the classification results in quite many misclassifications represented as separate pixels surrounded by the pixels referred to another class (see Fig. 4,a). This effect appears in less degree if trained SVM classifier is applied to the compressed data.

The classification results for RBF NN are presented in Table 2. For all cases of NN training the number of hidden units was 17. The percentages of correctly classified pixels are equal to 82.42, 99.67, 97.76, 71.72, 85.14% for the classes bare soil, grass, water, roads and urban areas, and bushes, respectively; $P_{cor\ ov}$=0.9062. As seen, these probabilities are, in general, slightly worse than for SVM classifier.

The obtained results are quite similar to those ones presented in Table 1. The values $P_{cor\ ov}$ for the corresponding classifiers and noise variances differ by less than 0.01. SVM recognizes better the class "soil" while RBF NN provides better classification of water surface. Again, the overall percentage of correctly classified pixels is larger if the classifier is applied to the compressed RS data. And the difference becomes more evident if the noise variance increases (see data for σ^2=100).

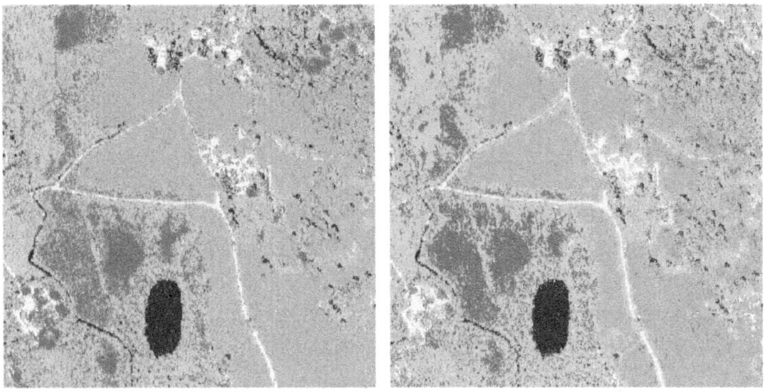

a b

Fig. 4. Classification maps for SVM applied to original (a) and compressed (b) RS data

Table 2. Precentage of correctly classified pixels for the trained RBF NN

Noise variance	Classified image	Bare soil	Grass	Water	Roads	Bushes	Overa ll
49	Original	75.22	95.81	99.48	66.50	75.51	85.41
49	Compressed	76.41	94.95	99.56	65.41	80.80	85.98
100	Original	73.62	91.58	99.66	67.14	65.50	81.79
100	Compressed	74.59	93.21	99.52	64.24	78.29	84.32

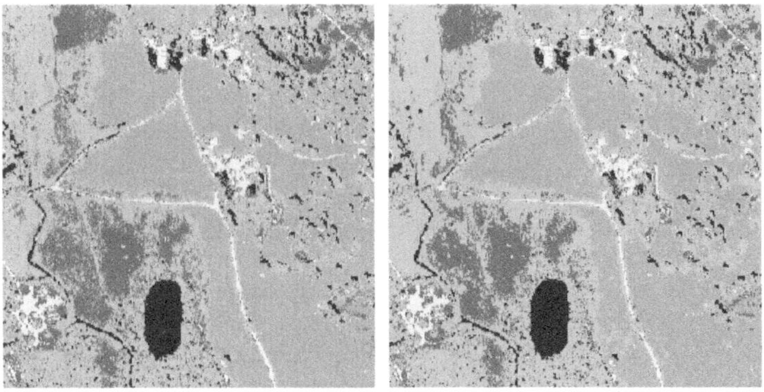

a b

Fig. 5. Classification maps for RBF NN applying to original (a) and compressed (b) RS data

Examples of multichannel image classification using RBF NN for σ^2=49 are given in Fig. 5. There are some noticeable differences in the spatial structure of the classified data. In particular, there are more separate pixel misclassifications if RBF NN classifier is applied to the original noisy data (see Fig. 5,a). The most problematic class is "roads and urban areas". Both classifiers recognize the corresponding regions with the smallest probability of correct classification. One possible reason is that we have considered pixel-by-pixel classification without taking into account any spatial features. Besides, no post-processing of the obtained primary classification maps has been utilized. These opportunities for further classification improving can be subject of the future work.

5 Conclusions

Two approaches to classification of multichannel RS data are considered. It is shown that in case of presence of rather intensive noise in obtained images it is reasonable to perform on-board lossy compression and then to apply on-land classification of decompressed images instead of data lossless compression and using the classification of original noisy images. The CR provided for such lossy compression can be about 10 and this is considerably better than in case of lossless coding. Moreover, we considered component-wise compression of multichannel images. And if the noise level is approximately the same in all component images, the same quantization step can be used in compressing multichannel images as multidimensional data. This can lead to further improvement of CR for given performance of the coder.

The obtained results and observed tendencies are in good coincidence for two different approaches to classification, one based on SVM and the other exploiting trained RBF NN. No obvious superiority between these two classifiers has been observed.

Acknowledgements. This study was partially supported by the CONACyT as a part of research project SEMAR No.11055.

References

1. Xiuping Jia, Richards, J.A., Gessner, W., Ricken, D.E.: Remote Sensing Digital Image Analysis. An Introduction. 3-rd edn. Springer-Verlag, Berlin Heidelberg New York (1999)
2. Kulemin, G.P., Zelensky, A.A., Astola, J.T., Lukin, V.V., Egiazarian, K.O., Kurekin, A.A., Ponomarenko, N.N., Abramov, S.K., Tsymbal, O.V., Goroshko, Y.A., Tarnavsky, Y.V.: Methods and Algorithms for Pre-processing and Classification of Multichannel Radar Remote Sensing Images, TICSP Series #28, Tampere, Finland, TTY Monistamo (2004)
3. Aiazzi, B., Alparone, L., Baronti, S.: Near-Lossless Comprerssion of 3-D Optical Data. IEEE Trans. On Geoscience and Remote Sensing, V. 39, 11 (2001) 2547-2557
4. Kaarna, A., Zemcik, A., Kalviainen, H., Parkkinen, J.: Compression of multispectral remote sensing images using clustering and spectral reduction. IEEE Transactions on Geoscience and Remote Sensing, V. GRS-38, 2 (2000) 1073-1082
5. Du, Q., Chang, C.-I.: Linear Mixture Analysis-Based Compression for Hyperspectral Image Analysis. IEEE Transactions on Geoscience and Remote Sensing, V. GRS-42, 4, (2004) 875-891
6. Faulconbridge, R.I., Pickering, M.R., Ryan, M.R., Jia, X.: A New Approach to Controlling Compression-Induced Distortion of Hyperspectral Images. Proceedings of IGARSS, (2003) 1830-1832
7. Pal, M.D., Brislawn, C.M., Brumby, S.P.: Feature extraction from Hyperspectral Images Compressed Using the JPEG-2000 Standard. CD-ROM Proceedings of the Fifth IEEE Southwest Symp. On Image Analysis and Interpretation, (2002) 5 p.

8. Kurekin, A., Dolia, A., Marshall, D., Lukin, V., Lever, K.: Mitigation of image impairments for multichannel remote sensing data fusion. Visual Information Processing XIV; Proc. of SPIE, V. 5817 (2005) 145-156
9. Ponomarenko, N., Lukin, V., Zriakhov, V., Egiazarian, K., Astola, J.: Lossy compression of images with additive noise. Proceedings of International Conference on Advanced Concepts for Intelligent Vision Systems, Antwerpen, Belgium (2005) 381-386
10. O.K. Al-Shaykh, R.M. Merserau: Lossy Compression of Noisy Images. IEEE Trans. On Image Processing, V. 7 12 (1998) 1641-1652
11. Salomon, D.: Data Compression. The Complete Reference. 3-rd edn. Springer-Verlag, Berlin Heidelberg New York (2004)
12. Taubman, D., Marcellin, M.: JPEG 2000: Image Compression Fundamentals. Standards and Practice. Kluwer, Boston (2002)
13. N.N. Ponomarenko, V.V. Lukin, K.O. Egiazarian, J.T. Astola: DCT Based High Quality Image Compression. Lecture notes in computer science, Vol. 3540, Springer-Verlag, Berlin Heidelberg New York (2005) 1177-1185
14. Ponomarenko N., Lukin V., Zriakhov M., Pogrebnyak O.: Methods for Lossy Compression of Images Corrupted by Multiplicative Noise. Proceedings of the International Conference "Modern Problems of Radioengineering, Telecommunications and Computer Science" (TCSET), (2006) 278-281
15. Carton-Vandecandelaere, M.-P., Vozel, B., Klaine, L., Chehdi, K.: Application to Multispectral Images of a Blind Identification System for Blur, Additive, Multiplicative and Impulse Noises. Proceedings of EUSIPCO, V. III (2002) 283-286
16. Lukin, V.V., Abramov, S.K., Vozel, B., Chehdi, K.: A method for blind automatic evaluation of noise variance in images based on bootstrap and myriad operations. Proceedings of SPIE/EUROPTO Symp. On Satellite Remote Sensing, SPIE V. 5982 (2005) 299-310
17. Ponomarenko, N., Lukin, V., Zriakhov, M., Egiazarian, K., Astola, J.: Estimation of accesible quality in noisy image compression. *accepted to EUSIPCO*, (2006) 4 p.
18. Christianini, N., Shave-Tailor, J.: An Introduction to Support Vector Machines and Other Kernel-based Learning Methods. Cambridge University Press (2000)
19. Duda, R.O., Harrt, P.E., Stork, D.G.: Pattern Classification. 2nd Edition. John Wiley and Sons (2001)
20. Schölkopf, B., Burges, J.C., Smola, A.J.: Advances in Kernel Methods: Support Vector Learning. MIT Press, Cambridge, MA (1999)
21. Hsu, C.-W., Lin, C.-J.: A comparison of methods for multi-class support vector machines. IEEE Transactions on Neural Networks, 13(2) (2002) 415–425
22. Bose, N.K., Liang, P.: Neural Network Fundamentals with Graphs, Algorithms and Applications. McGraw-Hill (1996)
23. Roli, F., Serpico, S.B., Bruzzone, L., Vernazza, G.: Classification of multispectral remote-sensing images by neural networks. Proc. of the VIII European Signal Processing Conference, V. I (1996) 172-175
24. Foody, G.M.: Supervised image classification by MLP and RBF neural networks with and without an exhaustively defined set of classes. International Journal of Remote Sensing, 25, (15) (2004) 3091-1304
25. Zelenskyj, O., Kurekin, A., Lukin, V.: Techniques of Multichannel Radar Images Processing and Interpretation by Multilayer Neural Network. Proceedings of the Third All-Ukrainian International Conference on Signal/ Image Processing and Pattern Recognition, (1996) 231-233

Fast Fingerprint Matching Based on the Novel Structure Combining the Singular Point with Its Neighborhood Minutiae*

Peng Shi[1,2,3], Jie Tian[1,2,3,**], Weihua Xie[1,2,3], and Xin Yang[1,2]

[1] Center for Biometrics and Security Research
[2] Key Laboratory of Complex Systems and Intelligence Science, Institute of Automation, Chinese Academy of Sciences
[3] Graduate School of Chinese Academy of Sciences, P.O. Box2728, Beijing 100080, China
tian@doctor.com, jie.tian@ia.ac.cn
http://www.fingerpass.net

Abstract. It is a very demanding task to design a reliable fingerprint matching approach with high accuracy and speed. An algorithm based on the novel structure combining the singular point with its neighborhood minutiae proposed in this paper can solve this problem efficiently. The structure introduced in this paper has two novel ideas as follows: First, we give an efficient singular points detection method by the inter-relationship between the singular points and the minutiae around them. It can reject the spurious singular points detected by the Poincare index. Second, an improvement of minutiae pairing strategy is introduced, which can sharply decrease the number of candidate minutiae pairs. Experiment results show that these improvements can highly speed up the matching with a preferable accuracy. This algorithm can be used in the one-to-many matching of the on-line fingerprint identification system.

Keywords: Fingerprint; Matching; Singular Point; Minutiae Pairing.

1 Introduction

Fingerprint is one of the most widely used features in biometric identification. The most crucial technology in the Automated Fingerprint Identification System (AFIS) is the matching method. A big challenge to the matching method is to reduce the matching error and to improve the matching speed. The features used in the matching process can be basically divided into two types: the global features and the local features. The most widely used global features in fingerprint recognition are the

* This paper is supported by the Project of National Science Fund for Distinguished Young Scholars of China under Grant No. 60225008, the Key Project of National Natural Science Foundation of China under Grant No. 60332010 and 60575007, the Project for Young Scientists' Fund of National Natural Science Foundation of China under Grant No.60303022, and the Project of Natural Science Foundation of Beijing under Grant No.4052026.
** Corresponding author. Tel.: 8610-82618465; Fax: 8610-62527995.

J.F. Martínez-Trinidad et al. (Eds.): CIARP 2006, LNCS 4225, pp. 804 – 813, 2006.

orientation field and the singular points, including cores and deltas, while the local features are mostly minutiae, such as the ridge endings and bifurcations.

For seeking a high accuracy, many matching algorithms use minutiae as the main features because that the local structure is more stable. Nandakumar and Jain used local correlation of minutiae to ascertain the quality of fingerprint image [1]. Jiang and Yau used the minutiae matching based on the local structure and global structure respectively [2]. And a fingerprint matching using the minutiae triangulation is provided by Parziale and Niel in [3]. The stability of triangle structure is efficient in avoiding the non-linear deformations of the fingerprint image. But at the same time, the traditional minutiae-based method encounters some difficulties in the matching process.

1. The minutiae extraction process could be difficult if the input image has a very low quality. The lost of true minutiae and the extraction of spurious minutiae caused by the low quality image would heavily affect on the following matching process. It will directly cause the matching failure.

2. The arrangement of all minutiae in a fingerprint is a time consuming process. Usually there are 30-60 minutiae in a fingerprint, if we construct local structures for all minutiae, the template size will be very large, and the large template will decrease the system's efficiency.

As a result, the matching method only using the minutiae cannot perform the one-to-many matching efficiently. Though many state-of-art AFIS have good performance on small databases, it is not satisfactory for large-scale applications. A fast and reliable matching strategy is necessary for the fingerprint identification system.

As global features, singular points are used as important features in fingerprint recognition, mostly in the classification. By the relative position of the singular points, a fingerprint database can be primarily classified under the Henry classification scheme as NIST4 fingerprint database [4]. Jain et al. used a multi-channel approach to fingerprint classification including the singular points [5]. The correlation between singular points was also used in indexing the fingerprint in Liu et al.'s paper [6]. But the singular points were seldom used in the matching process. The main reason is that is difficult to detect all the genuine singular points and reject the spurious ones. In order to do matching efficiently, one of the singular points can be chosen as the reference point to accelerate the matching speed as part of the matching structure.

In this paper, we provide a matching algorithm based on the novel structure combining the singular point with its neighborhood minutiae, which gives attention to both efficiency and accuracy. The paper is organized as follows: In Section 2, a new method based on the relationship between singular points and their neighborhood minutiae is used in the singular point detection. The matching process using the novel structure is illuminated in Section 3. Experimental results are presented in Section 4. Finally, we finish with conclusions and future directions in Section 5.

2 Singular Point Detection

After pre-processing of the input image, the orientation field is calculated by the method described in [7]. There have been several approaches for the detection of singular points on the orientation field map. The most popular method is the one proposed by Kawagoe and Tojo [8] and is based on the Poincare index. For these algorithms, a point in the orientation field is classified as a singular point if along a closed curve around that point the orientation changes $\pm 180^{\circ}$, but it heavily depends on the quality of the input image. The noise of the input image always causes spurious singular points detection by Poincare index. And the impact of singular points detection on matching is discussed by Chikkerur and Ratha in [9]. It is proved that the singular point detection will be not reliable if only based on the traditional Poincare index. In this paper, we define the novel structure including the singular points and their neighborhood minutiae. By computing the inter-relationship of them, we can detect the spurious singular points efficiently and give a reliable reference point to the following matching process.

2.1 Defining the Singular Point Area

In a fingerprint image, the singular points detection algorithm is described below.

1. Estimate and smooth the directional fields of the input fingerprint image;
2. In each block (8×8), we compute the Poincare index. The Poincare index is defined and computed as follows:

$$Poincare(i,j) = \frac{1}{2\pi}\sum_{k=0}^{N-1}\Delta(k) \tag{1}$$

$$\Delta(k) = \begin{cases} \delta(k), if\ |\delta(k)| < \pi/2 \\ \pi + \delta(k), if\ \delta(k) < -\pi/2 \\ \pi - \delta(k), otherwise \end{cases} \tag{2}$$

$$\begin{aligned} &\delta(k) = \theta(X(k'),Y(k')) - \theta(X(k),Y(k)) \\ &k' = (k+1) \bmod N \end{aligned} \tag{3}$$

where θ is the orientation field, $X(k')$ and $Y(k')$ denote coordinates of the kth point on the arc length parameterized closed cure. We consider as singular point candidates those pixels whose Poincare index calculated from Eq. (1) exactly equals to $\pm 1/2$.

2.2 Spurious Singular Points Detection and Reference Point Selection

After computing the Poincare index of the orientation field of the input image, several singular points may be detected as candidate points, including the genuine and some spurious singular points. Certainly, if the input fingerprint belongs to the arch class, or its singular point was missed in the fingerprint collection, there is no singular point can be detected. So we will still use all minutiae to form local structures for matching. In fact, the arch class contains a very small portion of 3.7% in nature [10], it will affect very little on the matching performance of the whole database. With little affect of no singular point in the image, we continue matching with our novel algorithm.

Fig. 1. The spurious singular points detection using their neighborhood minutiae. (a) illustrates the singular points detected by Poincare Index. The minutiae are marked in (b), and (c) is the sketch map of structure in the detection of spurious singular point, which takes the singular point S_i as the centre. The red points P are minutiae around the singular point.

Wu and Zhou presented a model-based spurious singular points detection method in [11]. But these model-based approaches need much orientation field calculation and are time consuming. As illustrated in Fig. 1, we can see that the spurious singular points always occurs in the borders of the foreground region, where there are little other local features can be detected. We use the inter-relationship of singular points and there neighborhood minutiae to detect the spurious singular points as follows:

1. As shown in Fig. 2, at the same time of singular point detection, we get all the minutiae of the fingerprint image by the minutiae extraction process.

2. Defining each of the singular point S_i ($i \geq 1$) as the centre, several circles can be drawn with the equal radius of r pixels, which is shown in Fig. 1. In this process, r is defined by an experimental value as 14.

$$|P_i - S_i| \leq r \tag{4}$$

3. Computing the number of minutiae M_i and the average distance d_i between each minutia with the centered singular point of each circle. As the Eq. (6), the singular point which has the smallest d_i and a reasonable number M_i ($M_i \geq 2$) can be defined as the reference point.

$$d_i = \frac{1}{M_i} \sum_{j=1}^{M_i} d_j \tag{5}$$

$$R = \min(d_i) \tag{6}$$

After these processes, we acquire the most reliable singular point of the fingerprint. According to the experiment results, this reference point is often the core point and the centre area of the image, where most minutiae occur. Therefore, it is a perfect feature for the fast matching.

3 Fingerprint Matching

Matching is the key step of fingerprint recognition. Many approaches were taken to improve the speed and accuracy of matching process. In Wang and Rong's algorithm, they mainly abandoned the global features and controlled the number of evolutionary species [12]. Ratha et al. employed an elastic matching algorithm to keep the matching accuracy [13]. In this paper, we get the reference point after the singular points detection. In order to keep the matching accuracy with a smaller template and a higher speed, the novel structure combining the global feature and the local features is constructed for the matching step. The algorithm's process using the combined template of singular point with minutiae is illustrated in Fig. 2.

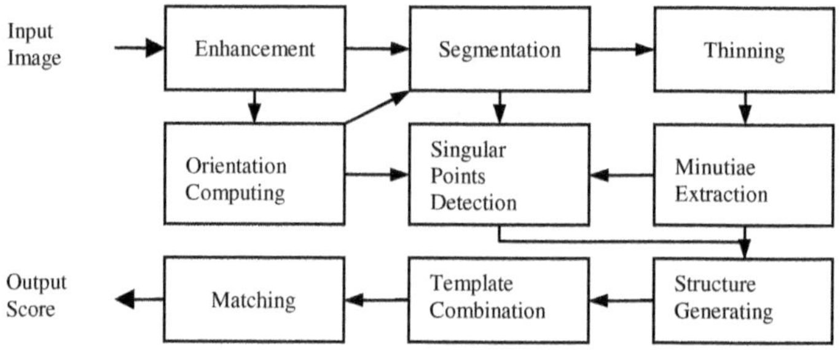

Fig. 2. The algorithm's process based on the novel structure combining the singular point with its neighborhood minutiae

In the matching process, we firstly give the definition of the novel structure, which contains the reference point and the minutiae around it. Then, many minutiae pairs are generated under defined rules in the structure. Finally, we complete the matching process by comparing the matching pair vectors and calculating the matching score.

3.1 Definition of Novel Structure

In the traditional core-based matching algorithms, the information of the singular points doesn't participate in the matching process for two reasons as follows: First, the singular points detected often vary in position and type. It is difficult to choose the most suitable singular point as the reference point. Second, the uncertainty of singular points can decrease the performance of the algorithm. In Section 2, the reference point choosing problem has been solved. Further, to improve the performance of matching, a novel structure is defined combining the reference point and the minutiae around it.

$$\overline{P_i} = [(x, y), \theta, ZOD] \tag{7}$$

The equation above is the traditional definition of minutiae, where (x, y) is the position, θ is the orientation and *ZOD* is the orientation field information of the minutiae. In our algorithm, the new definition of minutiae also contains the information of the reference point as follows, which can be seen in Eq. (8) as $\overline{P_i'}$.

$$\overline{P_i'} = [(x, y), \theta, \ell, ZOD] \tag{8}$$

$$\ell = \frac{|P_i - R|}{r} \tag{9}$$

where ℓ is the level which P_i belongs to. As illustrated in Fig. 3, defining the reference point R as the centre, we draw several circles around R with the radii kr ($1 \le k \le 15$), where r is the pre-defined radius 14 pixels, the same as r in the singular points detection process. Then, we can divide the neighborhood area around R into k levels. Minutiae belonging to the kth level have the parameter ℓ equals to k. If there is no singular point in the input image, ℓ is defined as 0.

Each ℓ is wide enough to avoid excursion of the reference point in fingerprint image. On the other hand, since ℓ classifies different minutiae, it will speed up the searching process of the matching minutiae.

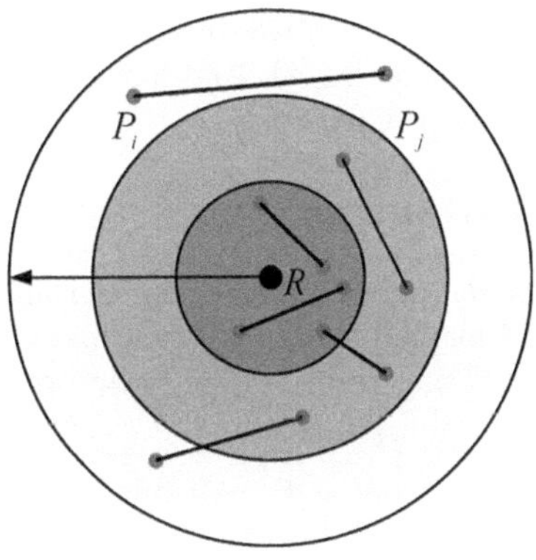

Fig. 3. Sample of the novel structure for matching. Every circle takes the reference point as the centre, and the radius is kr. Different color denotes different level ℓ around the reference points. The red points such as P_i and P_j are minutiae and the thin lines denote minutiae pairs defined in our algorithm.

3.2 Minutiae Pairing

The traditional minutia-to-minutia matching algorithm is heavily affected by the low quality and the distortion of fingerprint image, so it is necessary to use a kind of minutiae combination to perform matching. It can both reduce the affect of noise and distortion to matching and increase the matching speed. But many minutiae pairing strategy such as [14] encounter a problem that too many minutiae pairs will cause a large template and a low speed. In this paper, we use the minutiae pair to do matching. It can cut down the size of the template and increase matching speed with little accuracy losing, and it is suitable to the one-to-many matching system.

In the fingerprint matching algorithm based on the minutiae pairs, the number of minutiae pairs will affect the performance heavily. The theoretical number of the matching pairs is calculated as:

$$Num = M(M-1) \times N(N-1)/4 \tag{10}$$

where M is the number of input minutiae and N is the number of matching minutiae. In this case, many false matching pairs waste a lot of searching time. In our fast matching algorithm, the level of minutiae is used in matching as the a rule of matching minutiae pairs' selection.

If P_i and P_j are the minutiae of input minutiae set, Q_i and Q_j are the minutiae of template minutiae set. The minutiae pair $\overline{p_i p_j}$ and $\overline{q_i q_j}$ will be selected as the possible matching pairs as:

$$\begin{cases} \overline{p_i p_j} \mid \ell^i_p - \ell^j_p \le 1 \\ \overline{q_i q_j} \mid \ell^i_q - \ell^j_q \le 1 \end{cases} \tag{11}$$

where ℓ^i_p, ℓ^j_p, ℓ^i_q and ℓ^j_q are the levels which the minutiae P_i, P_j, Q_i and Q_j belong to. Because the minutiae are pre-classified by the level ℓ, the number of possible minutiae pairs will be rapidly decreased. And the searching process for the matching minutiae pairs will be highly speeded up.

3.3 Matching by the Novel Structure

Since the candidate minutiae pairs are selected, the matching process can be done favourably. An improved method using alignment-based matching [2] is provided in our algorithm, where the fingerprint minutiae information is like the following structure. The fingerprint minutiae matching process includes 4 steps as follows:

1. Getting the minutiae vectors as $\overline{P_i}$. All minutiae vectors represent the unique fingerprint. Since these vector structures only contain the local information, so the set of these fingerprint minutiae possesses excellent differentiability.

2. In the first match, we use the fingerprint minutiae vector to get the matching pairs like the following structure.

$$Fl_k = (d_{ki}, d_{kj}, \theta_{ki}, \theta_{kj}, Z_{ki}, Z_{kj}, n_{ki}, n_{kj}, t_k, t_i, t_j)^T \tag{12}$$

The structure was generated as a kind of multi-dimensional vector, where d_{ki}, d_{kj} is the distance between the minutia k and minutia i, j; z_{ki}, z_{kj} is the minutiae orientation difference between k and i, j; θ_{ki}, θ_{kj} is the angle between $\overrightarrow{k_i}$, $\overrightarrow{k_j}$; and φ_k, n_{ki}, n_{kj} is the number of crossed ridge line respectively.

3. Using Fl_k' as the template to match the structure Fl_k with Fl_k'. Through the process, two matching arrays can be obtained, one records the power of the position shift, another posts the power of angle deviation. The shifting parameter and rotation parameter are calculated by the two arrays.

4. After getting the shifting and rotation parameters, we translate the template minutiae set into the aligned minutiae set through the global shifting and rotation translation. Since the aligned minutiae set is very close to the inputting minutiae set, the second match only compares the position of corresponding minutiae and gets the matching score.

4 Experimental Results

The experiments reported in this paper have been conducted on the public domain collection of fingerprint images. Both DB1 in FVC2002 and FVC2004 [15] are selected to be computed the matching performance of our algorithm. Each database is 100 fingers wide and 8 impressions per finger deep (800 fingerprint in all). The image size of DB1 in FVC2002 is 388×374 pixels, and that of DB1 in FVC2004 is 640×480 pixels with much lower quality. They both have the resolution of 500 dpi.

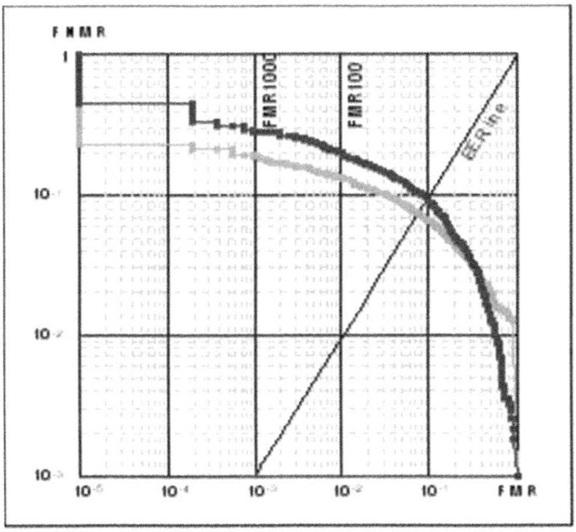

Fig. 4. ROC-curves of experiments on DB1 in FVC2004. The red line denotes the performance of our algorithm based on the novel structure, the green line denote that of the algorithm based on the traditional matching strategy of minutiae pairing.

We employed a set of experiments in order to validate our algorithm. Both the accuracy and speed were considered in the matching experiments. Firstly, we employed an experiment of our algorithm with novel structure on DB1 in FVC2002. There were 2800 genuine matches and 4950 imposter matches executed in the experiment under the test protocol of FVC. The Equal Error Rate (EER) was 1.64%. This proves that our algorithm can have a good performance on the public database. Secondly, under the same protocol on DB1 in FVC2004, we employed two experiments of algorithm with novel structure and without the novel structure to validate our algorithm. The Receiver Operating Characteristic (ROC) curves obtained by the two algorithms are illustrated in Fig. 4.

The average template size is 0.8 KB in experiment with the novel structure, and we employed the experiments on CPU of 2.8GHz, 512MB RAM. The average match time was 0.001 second in the experiments, and it was far less than the time consuming of most of the algorithms. Because the tests of FVC2004 were performed on CPU of 1.4GHz, the time consuming of P068 was divided by 2 as shown in Table 1. P068 is the algorithm in FVC2004 on DB1 which obtain the 10th place ranked by EER.

Table 1. Comparison of our algorithm with P068 in light category on DB1 in FVC2004. Each time consuming is supposed on CPU of 2.8GHz.

Algorithm	EER	Average enroll time	Average match time	Average model size
Our algorithm with novel structure	9.25%	0.031s	0.001s	0.8KB
Our algorithm without novel structure	7.31%	0.221s	0.034s	1.0KB
P068	9.92%	0.080s	0.090s	2.0KB

From Table 1. we can see that our algorithm has a considerable improvement on the time consuming of matching, and the rank of EER is also in the first 10 place in FVC2004. The least average match time of DB1 in FVC2004 is 0.035 second (supposed on CPU of 2.8GHz), far more than that of our algorithm. The template size is also reduced by using the novel structure as shown in Table 1. Because of the high speed, the preferable accuracy and the small template, our algorithm has a better performance in the large scale application.

5 Conclusions and Future Directions

With the increasing demand of on-line verification for large scale fingerprints database [16], the time and memory consuming of the matching algorithm is becoming more and more important in AFIS designing. In this paper we define a novel structure by choosing the most reliable singular point and reducing the number of candidate minutiae pairs in our algorithm. The experiment results show that these improvements can highly speed up the matching with only a little accuracy loss. Because the novel structure performed in this paper centralizes much useful information for the following matching process, the template size will be decreased and the time consuming in matching can be cut down remarkably. It can have a good performance in the real-time matching system for large scale fingerprint database.

Furthermore, if different thresholds can be defined in the detection of spurious singular points, all the genuine singular points can be correctly detected by the novel structure rather than only one reference point. By the relative positions of core(s) and delta(s), we may get useful classification information of the input fingerprints, and write it into the templates. This classification work can give a further considerable acceleration to the following matching process, which can reduce the size of scanning database. And the matching error can be further reduced by improvements in generating minutiae vectors in the novel structure. Future works on the integration of classification with fast matching can make the AFIS more efficient in performing the one-to-many matching task in public use.

References

1. Nandakumar, K., Jain, A.K.: Local Correlation-based Fingerprint Matching. The Indian Conference on Computer Vision, Graphics and Image Processing (ICVGIP), Kolkata (2004)
2. Jiang, X., Yau, W.Y.: Fingerprint Minutiae Matching Based on the Local and Global Structures, Proc. of the 15th Int'l Conf. on Pattern Recognition (ICPR), Barcelona: IEEE Computer Society (2000) 1038-1041
3. Parziale, G., Niel, A.: A Fingerprint Matching Using Minutiae Triangulation, Biometric Authentication: First International Conference (ICBA), Hong Kong (2004) 241-248
4. NIST Special Database 4. http://www.nist.gov/srd/nistsd4.htm
5. Jain, A.K., Prabhakar, S., Hong, L.: A Multichannel Approach to Fingerprint Classification, IEEE Transactions on Pattern Analysis and Machine Intelligence, IEEE Computer Society (1999), vol. 21, no. 1, 348-359
6. Liu, T., Zhu, G., Zhang, C., Hao, P.W.: Fingerprint Indexing Based on Singular Point Correlation, Int'l Conf. on Image Processing (ICIP), Genova (2005), vol. 3, 293-296
7. Hong, L., Wan, Y., Jain, A.K.: Fingerprint Image Enhancement: Algorithm and Performance Evaluation, IEEE Transactions on Pattern Analysis and Machine Intelligence, IEEE Computer Society (1998), vol. 20, no. 8, 777-789
8. Kawagoe, M., Tojo, A.: Fingerprint Pattern Classification, Pattern Recognition, Pergamon Press, Oxford, (1984) vol. 17, no. 3, 295-303
9. Chikkerur, S., Ratha, N.: Impact of Singular Point Detection on Fingerprint Matching Performance, Fourth IEEE Workshop on Automatic Identification Advanced Technologies (AutoID), (2005) 207-212
10. Maltoni, D., Maio, D., Jain, A.K., Prabhakar, S.: Handbook of Fingerprint Recognition, Springer Verlag, Berlin Heidelberg New York (2003) 176
11. Wu, N., Zhou, J.: Model Based Algorithm for Singular Point Detection from Fingerprint Images, Int'l Conf. on Image Processing (ICIP), Singapore (2004), vol. 2, 885-888
12. Wang, Q., Rong, L.: A Fast Fingerprint Matching Approach in Medicare Identity Verification Based on Gas, Advances in Natural Computation: First International Coference, (ICNC), Changsha, (2005) 151-160
13. Ratha, N.K., Karu, K., Chen, S., Jain, A.K.: A Real-time Matching System for Large Fingerprint Database, IEEE Transactions on Pattern Analysis and Machine Intelligence, IEEE Computer Society (1996), vol. 18, no. 8, 799-813
14. Lee, D., Choi, K., Kim, J.: A Robust Fingerprint Matching Algorithm Using Local Alignment, Proc. of the 16th Int'l Conf. on Pattern Recognition (ICPR), Quebec: IEEE Computer Society (2002), vol 3, 803-806
15. Fingerprint Verification Competition. http://bias.csr.unibo.it/fvc2002/, http://bias.csr.unibo.it/fvc2004/
16. Jain, A.K., Hong, L., Bolle, R.: On-line Fingerprint Verification, IEEE Transactions on Pattern Analysis and Machine Intelligence, IEEE Computer Society (1997), vol. 19, no. 4, 302-314

A New Nearest Neighbor Rule for Text Categorization

Reynaldo Gil-García and Aurora Pons-Porrata

Center of Pattern Recognition and Data Mining
Universidad de Oriente, Santiago de Cuba, Cuba
{gil, aurora}@app.uo.edu.cu

Abstract. The nearest neighbor (NN) rule is usually chosen in a large number of pattern recognition systems due to its simplicity and good properties. In particular, this rule has been successfully applied to text categorization. A vast number of NN algorithms have been developed during the last years. They differ in how they find the nearest neighbors, how they obtain the votes of categories, and which decision rule they use. A new NN classification rule which comes from the use of a different definition of neighborhood is introduced in this paper. The experimental results on Reuters-21578 standard benchmark collection show that our algorithm achieves better classification rates than the *k*-NN rule while decreasing classification time.

1 Introduction

Text Categorization (TC - also known as text classification) is the task of assigning documents to one or more predefined categories (or classes, or topics). This task relies on the availability of an initial corpus of classified documents under these categories (known as training data). Depending on the application, TC may be either single-label (i.e., exactly one category must be assigned to each document) or multi-label (i.e., any number of categories may be assigned to each document). This task, that falls at the crossroads of Information Retrieval and Machine Learning, has witnessed a booming interest in the last ten years from researchers and developers alike [1].

Text Categorization is an important component in many information management tasks such as spam filtering, real time sorting of email or files into folders, document routing, document dissemination, topic identification, classification of Web pages and automatic building of Yahoo!-style catalogs. Different learners have been applied in the TC literature, including probabilistic methods, decision tree and decision rule learners, example-based methods, support vector machines and classifier committees.

Nearest neighbor (NN) rule [2] is a very popular nonparametric and example-based method. This approach classifies an unknown sample into the categories of its nearest neighbors, according to some similarity measure. A particular case of NN classifiers is the *k*-nearest neighbor rule (*k*-NN), which assigns the category most frequently represented among the *k* nearest training samples. The NN classifiers include the following features: 1) conceptual simplicity, 2) easy implementation, 3) they can be designed even if training samples are few, 4) known error rate bounds, 5) they can be implemented when categories are overlapped with each other, 6) good performance, 7) they have no design phase and simply store the training set, and 8) they can be performed in time linear in the cardinality of the training set.

J.F. Martínez-Trinidad et al. (Eds.): CIARP 2006, LNCS 4225, pp. 814–823, 2006.

During the last years, a large number of NN algorithms have aroused from various scientific communities. Many of them focus on reducing classification time [3,4]. Other algorithms focus on increasing classification rates, either changing the method to find nearest neighbors [5], varying the voting schema [6] or improving the training data [7].

NN classification rule has shown to be very effective in Text Categorization tasks. WAKNN [8] is a k-NN classification algorithm that learns importance of attributes and utilizes them in the similarity measure. Galavotti [6] proposed a variant of the basic k-NN approach based on the exploitation of the negative evidence. Yang [9] presents an examination of thresholding strategies on the performance of the k-NN classifiers under various conditions.

In this paper we introduce a new NN classification rule that obtains classification rates better than k-NN algorithm while decreasing classification time. This approach is based on a new definition of neighborhood. The effectiveness of the proposed algorithm is evaluated on different subsets of Reuters-21578 test collection, which is the standard benchmark for the Text Categorization tasks.

2 A New Classification Rule

As mentioned above, the nearest neighbor algorithms classify an unknown document d into the categories of its nearest neighbors. These classifiers usually involve three phases: (i) the *nearest neighbor finding* from the training documents, (ii) a *voting phase*, in which each category assigns a vote to d, and (iii) a *decision rule*, in which a decision is made from these votes.

The first phase assumes a neighborhood definition. Intuitively, the concept of neighborhood should be such that the neighbors are as close to an unknown document d as possible. The traditional k-nearest neighbor rule starts at d and grows a spherical region until it encloses k training documents. This kind of neighborhood suffers from some drawbacks: 1) the k nearest neighbors may be too far from the document to classify d (see Figure 1(a)), and 2) it may be not spatially homogeneous, that is, there are few neighbors very similar whereas others are not sufficiently close to d (see Figure 1(b)), and hence the far documents can be decisive in the classification. The second one could occur, for example, when the training set is imbalanced (some categories are represented by a very small number of examples compared to the other categories).

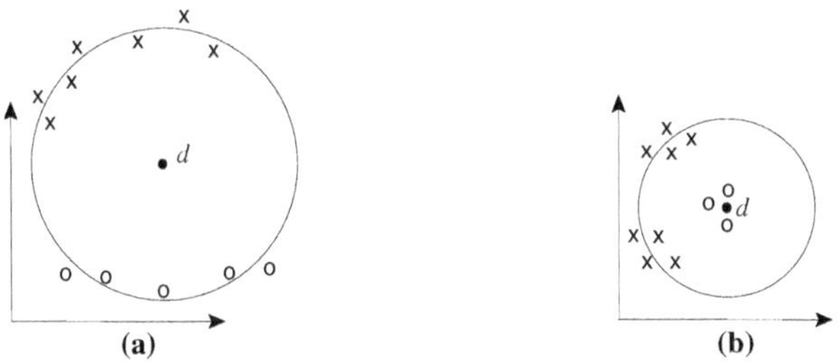

Fig. 1. Drawbacks of k-NN neighborhood. The big circles denote the "influence area" of the classifier. Here, we consider k=7. Note that, for ease of illustration, document similarities are here viewed in terms of Euclidean distance rather than in terms of cosine measure.

In order to tackle these problems just described, we propose an alternative of neighborhood definition. The lower the neighborhood density of d, the greater the radius of spherical region defined by the k nearest neighbors is. A natural way of avoiding that far documents influence in the classification is to fix a radius β and take into account the training documents only whose similarities with d are greater than or equal to β. Thus, documents which are not close to d are excluded from the neighborhood.

However, this solution is not enough. A large value of β may be very restrictive because many documents can not be classified. On the contrary, a small value of β could cause many documents in the neighborhood, which may produce an important deterioration of the classification accuracy, in particular with documents belonging to the less represented categories. In order to focus on a sufficiently small neighborhood of training examples homogeneously distributed, we propose to automatically adjust the neighborhood radius from the nearest neighbor of d. With this aim, we define a spherical region, whose radius is the difference between the similarity of nearest neighbor of d and a certain threshold α. Thus, the neighborhood of the document to classify is defined by the intersection between this region and the spherical region of radius β. Notice that the conventional neighborhood takes into account the k neighbors from the nearest neighbor. The neighborhood we propose takes into account instead all neighbors enclosed within a spherical region defined from the nearest neighbor. The parameters α and β provide a convenient way of obtaining such a neighborhood.

The neighborhood definition proposed is graphically depicted in Figure 2. In the first case, the similarity (*max*) between the document to classify d and its nearest neighbor is less than β; hence, the neighborhood is empty and the document can not be classified. The figures 2(b) and (c) show the cases where $\beta < max - \alpha$ and $\beta > max - \alpha$, respectively. In both cases, the shady region represents the neighborhood of d.

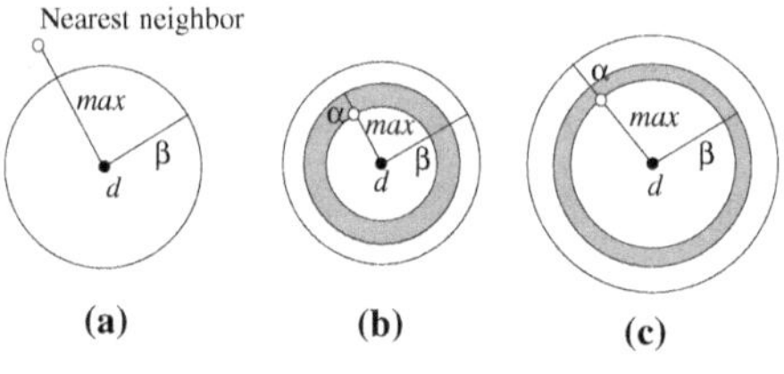

Fig. 2. Our neighborhood definition

Different methods have been used to calculate the votes of each category (second phase). In the basic k-NN classifier, the vote of the category c_i is the number of nearest neighbors labeled with it. Another well-known method considers the similarity of the nearest neighbors and their category association to calculate the votes [10], i.e.,

$$V(c_i, d) = \frac{\sum_{d_j \in N(c_i)} cos(d, d_j)}{\sum_{d_j \in N} cos(d, d_j)} \tag{1}$$

where N is the set of all nearest neighbors of the document d, $N(c_i)$ is the set of the nearest neighbors labeled with the category c_i, and $cos(d, d_j)$ is the cosine between the two document vectors, which is the similarity measure commonly used in TC tasks. In this paper, we used the second method.

From these category votes, several rules can be applied for deciding whether d should be classified under c_i (third phase). A simple decision rule classifies the document into the category that has the greatest vote. Instead, we used the thresholding decision rule. According with this rule, the document is assigned to categories with the score greater than a certain threshold value γ. Notice that this decision rule allows a multi-label categorization. There are various policies for determining the thresholds [9]. We adopt the policy *CSV thresholding*, which consists in testing different values on a validation set and choosing the value which maximizes effectiveness (we use $\gamma = 0.3$).

To sum up, the steps of our NN classifier is shown in Algorithm 1.

Algorithm 1. Our NN classifier.

1. Let d be the document to classify.
2. Build the set $N_\beta = \{d_j / cos(d, d_j) \geq \beta\}$.
3. Let max be the similarity between d and its nearest neighbor.
4. Let $N_{\alpha\beta}$ be the neighborhood of d, $N_{\alpha\beta} = \emptyset$.
5. For each $d_j \in N_\beta$:
   (a) If $cos(d, d_j) \geq max - \alpha$:
      i. Add d_j to $N_{\alpha\beta}$.
6. Compute the votes $V(c_i, d)$ for each category c_i using formula 1 and $N_{\alpha\beta}$.
7. For each c_i:
   (a) If $V(c_i, d) \geq \gamma$:
      i. Assign d to c_i.

Like k-NN, in our algorithm the classification of a document is performed in linear time with respect to the cardinality of the training set.

3 Experiments

We have conducted some experiments to test the validity of our NN rule for Text Categorization tasks.

3.1 Document Indexing

Because of texts cannot be directly interpreted by a classifier, an *indexing* procedure that maps a document into a compact representation of its content needs to be applied. In this paper, we adopt the traditional vector space model, in which a document d_j is represented as a vector of term weights $d_j = (w_1^j, ..., w_{|\tau|}^j)$, where τ is the set of terms that occur in the document collection and quantifies the importance of term t_l in characterizing the semantics of d_j. The selection of terms includes removing tags and stop words, lemmatization and proper name recognition. Weights are computed by using the standard *ltc* variant of *tf-idf* function [11], i.e., $w_l^j = (1 + \log TF(t_l, d_j)) \cdot$

$\log \frac{|Tr|}{df_{Tr}(t_l)}$, where $TF(t_l, d_j)$ denotes the number of times t_l occurs in d_j, Tr is the set of training documents and $df_{Tr}(t_l)$ is the number of documents in Tr in which t_l occurs at least once.

In TC, unlike in Information Retrieval, a dimensionality reduction phase is often applied so as to reduce the size of the document representations from $|\tau|$ to a much smaller, predefined number $|\tau'|$; the value $\varepsilon = \frac{|\tau|-|\tau'|}{|\tau|}$ is called the *reduction factor* [12]. Dimensionality reduction techniques reduce overfitting (i.e., the tendency of the classifier to better classify the data it has been trained on than new unseen data), and makes the problem more manageable for the classifier. Also, standard classification techniques cannot deal with a large feature set, since processing is extremely costly in computational terms, and the results become unreliable due to the lack of sufficient training data.

Usually, these techniques consist in scoring each term in τ by means of a category-based term evaluation function f and then selecting a set τ' of the highest scoring terms. The *information gain* [13] is a standard function of the trade in the dimensionality reduction literature, i.e.,

$$f(t_l, c_i) = \sum_{c \in \{c_i, \overline{c_i}\}} \sum_{t \in \{t_l, \overline{t_l}\}} P(t,c) \cdot \log_2 \frac{P(t,c)}{P(t) \cdot P(c)}$$

In this formula, probabilities are interpreted on an event space of documents (e.g. $P(\overline{t_l}, c_i)$ indicates the probability that, for a random document d, term t_l does not occur in d and d belongs to category c_i), and are estimated by maximum likelihood. We use this function to select terms according to the maximum global policy, i.e.,

$$f_{max} = \max_{i=1}^{|C|} f(t_l, c_i)$$

3.2 Experimental Settings

In our experiments we have used the Reuters-21578, Distribution 1.0 corpus[1], currently the most widely used benchmark in TC research. Reuters-21578 consists of a set of 12902 news stories classified under 135 categories related to economics. This collection is partitioned (according to the "ModApté" split we have adopted) into a training set of 9603 documents and a test set of 3299 documents.

Several researchers have preferred to carry out their experiments on different subsets of categories. The three subsets that have been most popular [12] are: 1) the set of the 10 categories with the highest number of positive training examples, hereafter, *reu10*, 2) the set of 90 categories with at least one positive training example and one test example, hereafter, *reu90*, and 3) the set of 115 categories with at least one positive training example, hereafter, *reu115*. The characteristics of these subsets are summarized in Table 1. The last four columns contain the average number of categories per document, and the maximum, minimum and average number of training examples per category, respectively.

[1] The Reuters-21578 collection may be freely download from http://kdd.ics.uci.edu.

Table 1. Characteristics of Reuters-21578 subsets

Collection	# Train Docs.	# Test Docs.	Multi-label	Category size		
				Max	Min	Average
reu10	5920	2313	1.11	2709	160	657
reu90	7058	2740	1.24	2709	1	98
reu115	7063	2740	1.25	2709	1	76

TC effectiveness is usually measured in terms of the classic Information Retrieval notions of *precision* (π_i), the proportion of documents classified into c_i that indeed belong to c_i, and *recall* (ρ_i), the proportion of documents belonging to c_i that are indeed classified into c_i. Since a classifier can be tuned to emphasize precision at the expense of recall, or vice versa, only combinations of the two are significant. The most popular combination nowadays is: $F1(c_i) = \frac{2\pi_i \rho_i}{\pi_i + \rho_i} = \frac{2TP_i}{2TP_i + FP_i + FN_i}$, where TP_i, FP_i and FN_i refer to the sets of true positives wrt c_i (documents correctly deemed to belong to c_i), false positives wrt c_i (documents incorrectly deemed to belong to c_i), and false negatives wrt c_i (documents incorrectly deemed not to belong to c_i), respectively.

When effectiveness is computed for several categories, the results for individual categories must be averaged in some way. Two methods may be adopted: micro-averaging (categories count proportionally to the number of their positive test examples) and macro-averaging (all categories count the same). Micro-averaging gives equal weight to every document, while macro-averaging gives equal weight to each category. The former rewards classifiers that behave well on heavily populated ("frequent") categories, while classifiers that perform well also on infrequent categories are emphasized by the latter.

3.3 Results

The first experiments we have conducted compare the categorization performance of our NN rule against *k*-NN classifier on the three above-mentioned Reuters-21578 subsets. Both approaches use the same method to calculate the votes of each category and the thresholding decision rule.

Different values of parameters have been tried on each algorithm to ensure that the experimental results can reflect the best performance. The values of *k* tried for the *k*-NN algorithm include 1, 3, 5, 7, 10, 20, 30, 40 and 50. There are two parameters of importance in our NN algorithm: α and β. The values of α tried are 0.1, 0.15, 0.20, 0.25 and 0.3. However, the value of β is fixed to 0.1, since its role is only to guarantee that far documents do not influence in the classification. Then, we chose the parameters with the best performance according to micro-averaged $F1$ to represent each algorithm.

The results of our experiments are reported in Figure 3. This figure includes 6 plots: the leftmost plots show micro-averaged $F1$ scores while the rightmost show macro-averaged $F1$ scores. Each individual plot, which corresponds to a dimensionality reduction factor, includes the results for both NN approaches in each document collection.

Several observations can be made by analyzing the results in Figure 3. First, the best performance is obtained in Reu10 subset for both algorithms. This was largely to be expected, given that its categories are the ones with the highest number of training

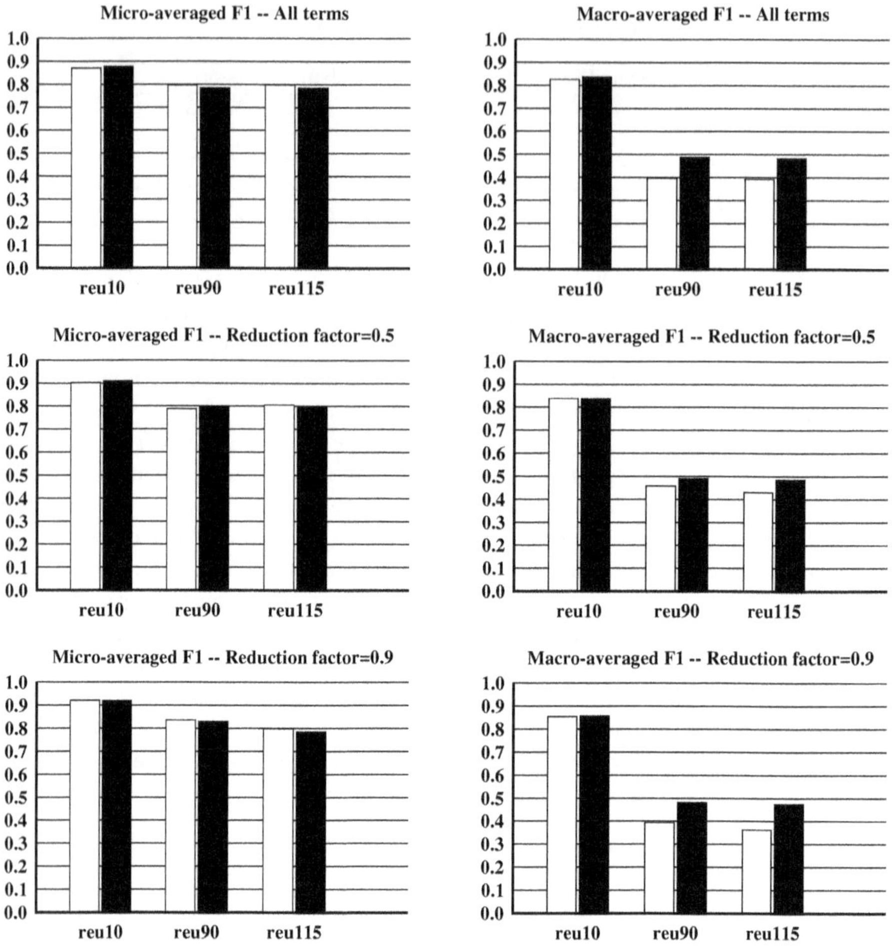

Fig. 3. $F1$ scores obtained with k-NN (white bars) and our NN rule (black bars)

examples, and as such allow taming the "curse of dimensionality" more effectively. The decrease of performance in going from Reu10 to Reu90 is much larger for macro-averaged $F1$ than micro-averaged $F1$. However, the performances of Reu90 and Reu115 have a similar behavior. This can be explained by the fact that micro-averaged effectiveness is dominated by the performance of the classifiers on the most frequent categories. Note that the 10 categories in Reu10 have altogether 2313 test examples, while the other 80 categories in Reu90 have altogether just 427 them. Also, the differences between Reu90 and Reu115 are limited to 5 documents and 25 very small categories. These conclusions are in agreement with the results presented earlier in [12].

A second fact that also emerges clearly from the figure 3 is that the best micro-averaged $F1$ scores are achieved with the most aggressive reduction in all collections. Macro-averaged effectiveness maintains this behavior in Reu10 subset. Instead, in the other subsets the behavior of the algorithms is different. Our NN rule obtains the same

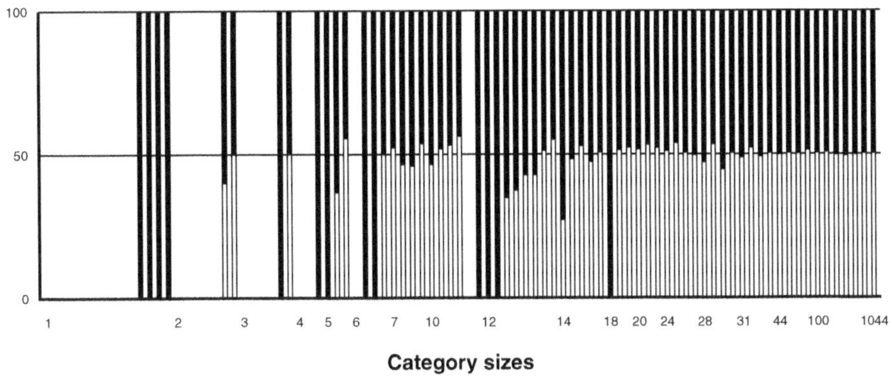

Fig. 4. $F1$ scores per category with k-NN (white bars) and our NN rule (black bars)

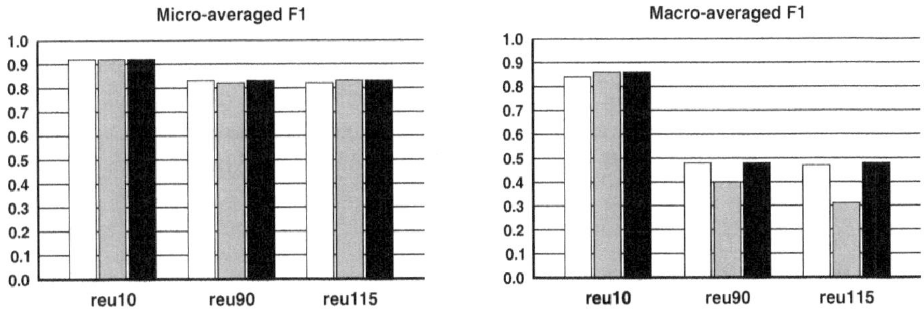

Fig. 5. Impact of the parameters in our NN rule

macro-averaged $F1$ score disregarding the reduction factor whereas k-NN improves effectiveness when term reduction is 50%, but decreases it with 90% of reduction.

Finally, the micro-averaged $F1$ scores obtained by both algorithms are similar in all collections. However, with regard to the macro-averaged $F1$ our NN rule clearly overcomes k-NN in Reu90 and Reu115 subsets. This observation seems to suggest that our algorithm yields better results when categories have few training examples. In order to know what really happens, Figure 4 shows a percentage diagram of $F1$ scores per category in Reu90 collection with 90% of reduction factor.

As it can be noticed, both algorithms obtain similar results for the most frequent categories. Nevertheless, our approach achieves better results than k-NN when categories have few training examples. This can be explained because the best results in k-NN algorithm are obtained with k=30, and hence it is difficult that small categories achieve the required votes. Since the number of neighbors in our algorithm is not fixed, this problem is reduced. It must be pointed out that there are still some less represented categories whose documents are not well-classified.

Our second experiment was focused on evaluating the impact of the parameters α and β in the classification rates. Figure 5 shows the $F1$ scores obtained when disregarding the β parameter (white bars), disregarding the α parameter (gray bars) and considering

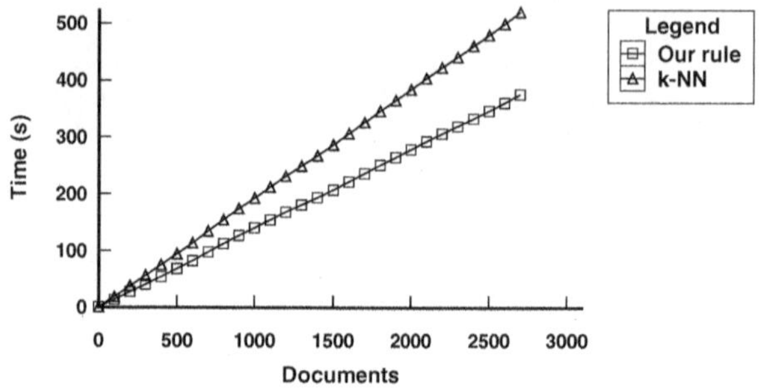

Fig. 6. Time performance

both parameters (black bars). As it can be noticed, the $F1$ scores are similar when we only consider the α parameter and both parameters together. Despite these results, we believe that β parameter is useful to avoid that far documents influence in the classification, although it seems that this problem is not presented in the Reuter collection.

Finally, Figure 6 shows the time spent by k-NN and our algorithm. As can be seen, despite both algorithms have a linear behavior, our algorithm clearly overcomes k-NN. This can be explained because we do not need to create a sorted list of k nearest neighbors.

4 Conclusions

A new NN classification rule has been proposed in this paper. It is an attempt to minimize the drawbacks pointed out for the k-NN rule. This approach is based on the general idea of estimating the category of an unknown document d from its neighbors, but considering a kind of neighborhood which allows one to inspect a sufficiently small and near area to d. In our rule the number of neighbors is not fixed, but rather the neighborhood radius is automatically adjusted from the nearest neighbor of d.

The experiments carried out on Reuters-21578 standard benchmark collection show that our rule not only obtains similar micro-averaged $F1$ scores, but it also achieves better macro-averaged $F1$ scores than k-NN. It is very important since producing classifiers that perform well also on infrequent categories is the most challenging problem of Text Categorization [1]. Furthermore, our algorithm reduces the classification time.

In the future, one key issue we face is the automatic choice of the threshold value α. Future work also includes exploring the use of our NN rule in adaptive document filtering tasks, where the category distribution is not given a priori and it must be learned incrementally over time.

References

1. Sebastiani, F.: Text categorization. In: Text Mining and its Applications to Intelligence, CRM and Knowledge Management. WIT Press, Southampton, UK (2005)
2. Duda, R., Hart, P., Stark, D.G.: Pattern Classification. Wiley-Interscience (2000)

3. Ramasubramanian, V., Paliwal, K.K.: Fast nearest-neighbor search algorithms based on approximation-elimination search. Pattern Recognition **33** (2000) 1497–1510
4. Moreno-Seco, F., Micó, L., Oncina, J.: A new classification rule based on nearest neighbour search. In: 17th International Conference on Pattern Recognition. Volume 4., IEEE Computer Society (2004) 408–411
5. Sánchez, J., Pla, F., Ferri, F.: On the use of neighbourhood-based non-parametric classifiers,. Pattern Recognition Letters **18** (1997) 1179–1186
6. Galavotti, L., Sebastiani, F., Simi, M.: Experiments on the use of feature selection and negative evidence in automated text categorization. In: ECDL-00, 4th European Conference on Research and Advanced Technology for Digital Libraries, Lisboa, PT (2000) 59–68
7. Shin, K., Abraham, A., Han, S.: Improving knn text categorization by removing outliers from training set. In: 7th International Conference of Computational Linguistics and Intelligent Text Processing,CICLing 2006. (2006) 563–566
8. Han, E.H., Karypis, G., Kumar, V.: Text categorization using weight adjusted k-nearest neighbor classification. In: 5th Pacific-Asia Conference on Knowledge Discovery and Data Mining (PAKDD). (2001) 53–65
9. Yang, Y.: A study on thresholding strategies for text categorization. In: SIGIR-01, 24th ACM International Conference on Research and Development in Information Retrieval, New York, ACM Press (2001) 137–145
10. Yang, Y.: Expert network: Effective and efficient learning from human decisions in text categorization and retrieval. In: SIGIR'94,17th ACM International Conference on Research and Development in Information Retrieval, Ireland (1994) 13–22
11. Salton, G., Buckley, C.: Term-weighting approaches in automatic text retrieval. Information Processing and Management **24** (1988) 513–523
12. Debole, F., Sebastiani, F.: An analysis of the relative hardness of Reuters-21578 subsets. Journal of the American Society for Information Science and Technology **56** (2005) 584–596
13. Lewis, D.D.: An evaluation of phrasal and clustered representations on a text categorization task. In: SIGIR-92, 15th ACM International Conference on Research and Development in Information Retrieval, Denmark (1992) 37–50

Alignment of Paragraphs in Bilingual Texts Using Bilingual Dictionaries and Dynamic Programming*

Alexander Gelbukh and Grigori Sidorov

Natural Language and Text Processing Laboratory,
Center for Research in Computer Science, National Polytechnic Institute,
Av. Juan Dios Batiz, s/n, Zacatenco, 07738, Mexico City, Mexico
sidorov@cic.ipn.mx
www.Gelbukh.com

Abstract. Parallel text alignment is a special type of pattern recognition task aimed to discover the similarity between two sequences of symbols. Given the same text in two different languages, the task is to decide which elements—paragraphs in case of paragraph alignment—in one text are translations of which elements of the other text. One of the applications is training training statistical machine translation algorithms. The task is not trivial unless detailed text understanding can be afforded. In our previous work we have presented a simple technique that relied on bilingual dictionaries but does not perform any syntactic analysis of the texts. In this paper we give a formal definition of the task and present an exact optimization algorithm for finding the best alignment.

1 Introduction

Given the same text in two different languages, the parallel text alignment task consists in deciding which elements of one text are translations of which one of the other text 9. The task is useful in learning bilingual dictionaries and in training statistical machine translation algorithms. Viewed more generally as a pattern recognition task, the problem consists in identifying correspondences in two sequences of objects, which could be, say, text and speech or video recordings from different cameras 1314. While both the task and our suggested method are quite general, in this paper we concentrate on alignment of paragraphs in bilingual texts.

Various researchers have tried different approaches to text alignment, usually at sentence level 3517, and a number of alignment tools are available.[1] Some methods rely on similarity between certain words in the two text—for example, words that are graphically similar can be considered pivots for rough alignment 18. In a previous

* Work done under partial support of Mexican Government (CONACyT, SNI) and National Polytechnic Institute, Mexico (CGPI, COFAA). We thank an anonymous reviewer for attracting our attention to valuable resources and publications.

[1] *Bilingual Sentence Aligner* by Robert C. Moore, research.microsoft.com/research/downloads/default.aspx; *Geometric Mapping and Alignment* (GMA) by Dan Melamed, nlp.cs.nyu.edu/GMA/; *Champollion Toolkit* by LDC, champollion.sourceforge.net/; an on-line sentence aligner, 143.107.183.175/site2001/projetos/pesa.htm.

J.F. Martínez-Trinidad et al. (Eds.): CIARP 2006, LNCS 4225, pp. 824 – 833, 2006.

paper 8 we have suggested an alignment method based on measuring similarity using bilingual dictionaries and presented an approximate heuristic greedy alignment algorithm. In this paper our goals are:

- To formalize the paragraph alignment task, casting it as an optimization problem;
- To introduce an algorithm that finds the exact optimum of this problem, instead of the approximate heuristic-based algorithm;
- To suggest a distance measure for paragraphs that guarantees unbiased solution;
- To propose a baseline distance measure and to compare the results obtained with our suggested measure against such a baseline.

The optimization problem resulting from our formalization of the task strongly resembles string alignment problems, such as optimal string alignment or calculating the Levenshtein distance between strings. Inspired in standard methods for solving problems of this class, we developed a dynamic programming algorithm. However, our formalization differs from the optimal string alignment. That latter task requires aligning some symbols in a string with at most one symbol in the other string; in our case, we align every symbol with at least one symbol in the other string. This leads to a modification of the algorithm.

The paper is organized as follows. In Section 0, we explain the task in detail and formalize it as an optimization problem. In Section 0, we introduce a baseline and a suggested distance measures between paragraphs, which are used for calculation of the cost function to be optimized. In Section 0, we present a dynamic programming algorithm that finds the exact optimum of the problem. In Section 0, we discuss its complexity. Finally, in Section 0 we present the experimental results and in Section 0 give conclusions and discuss the possible future work.

2 Paragraph-Level Text Alignment

Given a text and its translation into another language, the text alignment task consists in determining which text elements (such as words) are translations of each other, as shown in Fig. 1, where words that are translations of each other are connected by lines. In such simple cases the text alignment task can be formalized as building a bipartite graph whose vertices are the text elements and an arc connects two vertices if the corresponding elements are translations of each other.

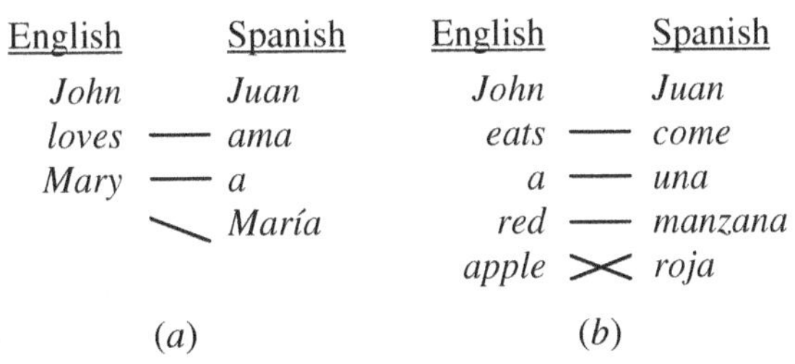

Fig. 1. Word-level alignment for the sentences *John loves Mary* and *John eats a red apple*

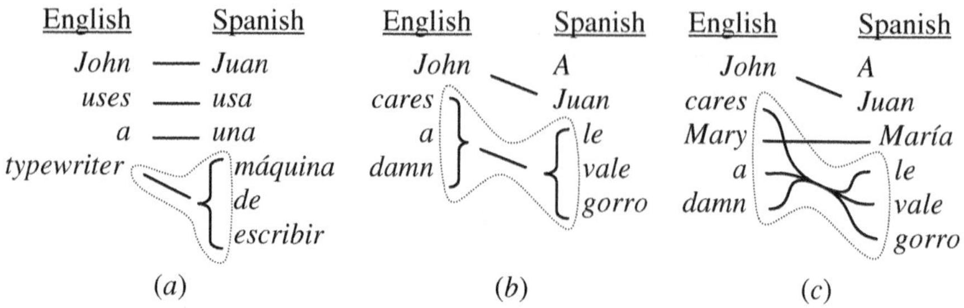

Fig. 2. Set-to-set alignment (literally: (*a*) 'device of writing', (*b*, *c*) 'is worth a cap to him'). The dotted lines mark single hyperarcs.

However, in more complex cases a whole set of text elements are translated by another set of elements, while this correspondence cannot be broken down into pair-wise correspondences of individual elements, as shown in Fig. 2. In Fig. 2 (*a*), one word is translated by a whole run of words. In Fig. 2 (*b*), a whole run is translated by another run, while there is no pair-wise translation correspondences between the individual words in these two runs. Finally, Fig. 2 (*c*) shows the most general case: the correspondence holds between (non-contiguous) sets of elements.

While the structure shown in Fig. 1 can be formalized by a graph, the structure shown in Fig. 2 (*c*) is formalized by a generalization of the notion of a graph called *hypergraph*. Given a set of vertices $\mathbf{V}$, a hypergraph $\mathbf{G}$ on $\mathbf{V}$ is defined as a graph whose vertices are non-empty subsets of $\mathbf{V}$, a *hyperarc a* being a pair of subsets of $\mathbf{V}$: $a = \{\mathbf{X}, \mathbf{Y}\}$, $\mathbf{X}, \mathbf{Y} \subseteq \mathbf{V}$, $\mathbf{X}, \mathbf{Y} \neq \varnothing$. A hyperarc can be graphically represented by a link with several "ends", as in Fig. 2 (*c*), or in a simplified form as a connection between grouped vertices, as in Fig. 2 (*a*, *b*). The bilingual text alignment task deals with *bipartite* hypergraphs. A (hyper)graph is called bipartite if its vertices are of two kinds: $\mathbf{V} = \mathbf{A} \cup \mathbf{B}$, $\mathbf{A} \cap \mathbf{B} = \varnothing$, and arcs connect elements of different kinds: $\mathbf{X} \subseteq \mathbf{A}$, $\mathbf{Y} \subseteq \mathbf{B}$.

The peculiarities of the task depend on the text units considered: words (as in our examples) 12, clauses 10, sentences 146, paragraphs, sections, etc.; see Fig. 3.

If the units are too large, such as whole sections, the task is usually trivial: the text and its translation consist of the same number of sections, which correspond to each other in the natural order. On the other hand, if the text units are too small—such as morphemes or words—the very definition of the task becomes complicated, as Fig. 2 shows. In particular, in this case there are elements without translations, as in Fig. 1 (*a*), the order of the elements is not preserved, as in Fig. 1 (*b*), or even the indivisible groups of elements may be not contiguous, as in Fig. 2 (*c*).

The medium-size units such as sentences and paragraphs are an intermediate case: while the alignment task is not trivial, it does not usually present most of the

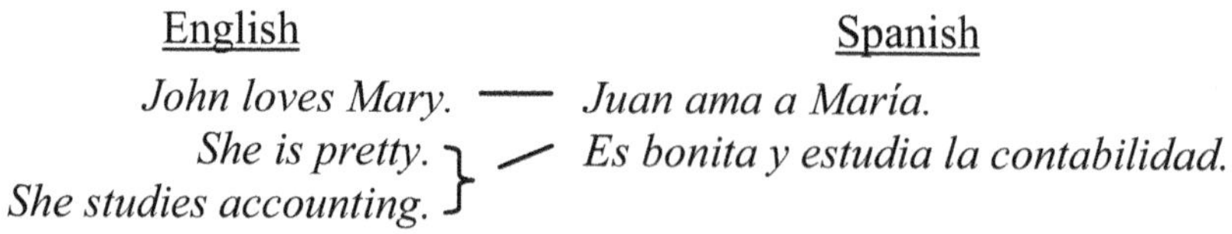

Fig. 3. Sentence-level alignment (literally: 'She is pretty and studies accounting')

English		Spanish
When she saw my baffled look, she corrected herself: "My grandmother."	—	*Luego, al percatarse de mi gesto estupefacto, corrigió:* *— No. Es mi abuela.*

Fig. 4. One-to-many paragraph alignment (here the direct speech is translated as a separate paragraph)

English		Spanish
John loves Mary. She is pretty. She studies economy. *Her father is a professor. They live in Boston.*	—	*Juan ama a María. Es bonita.* *Estudia economía. Su padre es profesor.* *Viven en Boston.*

Fig. 5. An artificial example of many-to-many paragraph alignment (here the third and fourth sentences are translated as a separate paragraph)

complications discussed above. Particularly in the case of paragraphs, the order of the elements is preserved and every element has a translation, cf. Fig. 1. What is more, we assume that the translator can join two or more source paragraphs into one translated paragraph or split one source paragraph into several translated paragraphs, as in Fig. 4, cf. Fig. 2 (*a*) and Fig. 3, but cannot re-arrange the sentences in the paragraphs in such a way that, say, a final part of a paragraph be translated as a beginning of another paragraph, as in Fig. 5, which would lead to patterns such as those shown in Fig. 2 (*b*, *c*). Though these assumptions are not completely true to life, they significantly simplify formalization of the task and the algorithm.

Thus, we define the paragraph-level bilingual text alignment task as the problem of constructing a bipartite hypergraph (cf. Fig. 2 (*c*)) whose vertices are the paragraphs of the texts in the two languages, respectively, and whose hyperarcs—standing for the sets of vertices to be mutual translations—satisfy the following conditions:

- Every vertex is incident to an arc, i.e., no paragraph disappears or appears from nothing in the translation process;
- At least one side of each arc has only one end, i.e., an arc can connect element to element, element to group, group to element, but not group to group;
- The ends of each arc are contiguous, i.e., a group of paragraphs that is the translation of a paragraph in the other language occupy a contiguous run of the text;
- The arcs are not crossing, i.e., the order of paragraphs is preserved in translation.

The (sets of) paragraphs that are translations of each other are *similar* in the sense of Section 0 below. This similarity measure can be assigned to the hyperarc connecting the paragraphs; we call this value the *weight* of the hyperarc. Our hypothesis is that the total weight of all hyperarcs gives the quality of a particular alignment. With this, the task is reduced to finding, among all possible hypergraphs satisfying the above conditions, the one with the maximum total weight of its hyperarcs.

3 Distance Measure

To assign the weight to a hyperarc as described in Section 0 above, we need to calculate the similarity between two sets of paragraphs (in our algorithm at least one of the two sets consists of only one paragraph). We define it as the similarity between the two texts that are obtained by concatenation of the corresponding paragraphs.

3.1 Baseline Distance Measure

Common sense suggests that the corresponding pieces of texts are located at approximately the relative same distance from the beginning of the whole text. We define the baseline distance between two pieces of text, T_A in the language *A* and T_B in the language *B*, as follows:

$$\text{Distance}(T_A, T_B) = |\text{start}(T_A) - \text{start}(T_B)| + |\text{end}(T_A) - \text{end}(T_B)|, \quad (1)$$

where start(T_X) is the relative position of the first word of the text T_X measured in percentage of the total number of words in the text in the corresponding language, and similarly for end(T_X). We could also use the position of the paragraph instead of word as percentage of the total number of paragraphs, but the measure based on word counts has been reported as better than the one based on paragraph counts, which agrees with our own observations.

3.2 Proposed Distance Measure

We define the similarity between two texts in different languages as the number of words in both texts that are not mutual translations of each other 12. For this, we first define which words are such translations.

1. Set T_X, := the shortest one of T_A and T_B; T_Y := the longest
2. Set translations := 0
3. for each word token *w* in T_X
4.   if any of its translations $D_{XY}(w)$ is found in T_Y
5.   increase translations by 1

where $D_{XY}(w)$ is a function returning a set of the dictionary translations of the word *w*. Then the number of word tokens without translation in both paragraphs, under the hypothesis that these two paragraphs correspond to each other, is:

$$\text{Distance}(T_A, T_B) = |T_A| + |T_B| - 2 \times \text{translations}. \quad (2)$$

The cost of an alignment hypothesis is the total number of words in both texts that are left without translation under this hypothesis. Note that under different hypotheses this number is different: here we consider two word tokens to be translations of each other if both of the following conditions hold: (a) they are dictionary translations (as word types) and (b) the paragraphs where they occur are supposed to be aligned.

Note that we represent the texts as vectors of word frequencies, ignoring the order of the words. In particular, concatenation of the paragraphs into text pieces is performed simply as summation of the corresponding vectors.

The above algorithm for calculating the number of translations has a drawback: in line 828, the same word in T_Y can potentially be counted twice, as in the English sentence T_A = "*The bank is at the French border*" and Spanish sentence T_B = "*Juan vive a la orilla de la ciudad*" 'John lives at the border of the city.' However, addressing this problem would lead to a more complicated and computationally more expensive algorithm, which we may consider in our future work.

Recall that in our formalization of the task we select the optimal hypergraph out of hypergraphs with different number of arcs. This leads to that the algorithm would usually prefer a smaller number of hyperarcs: in an extreme case it might tend to align the firs paragraph of A with all but one paragraphs of B, and the rest of A with the last paragraph of B, which gives only two hyperarcs. However, the specific measure we suggest here is linear in the sense that it does not depend on the number of arcs: the cost is proportionally greater for the hyperarcs that align more paragraphs with one. Thus with this particular measure the algorithm is not biased towards a smaller number of larger pieces being aligned. Note that our experiments show (see Table 2) that our baseline measure suffers from such a bias.

4 Algorithm

To find the exact optimal alignment, we apply a dynamic programming algorithm. It uses a $(N_A + 1) \times (N_B + 1)$ chart shown in Fig. 6, where N_X is the number of paragraphs in the text in the language X.

The algorithm works as follows. First, the chart is filled in:

1. $a_{00} := 0$, $a_{i0} := -\infty$, $a_{0j} := -\infty$ for all $i, j > 0$.
2. for i from 1 to N_A do
3. for j from 1 to N_B do
4. $a_{ij} := \min (a_{xy} + \text{Distance}(T_A[x + 1 .. i], T_B[y + 1 .. j]))$

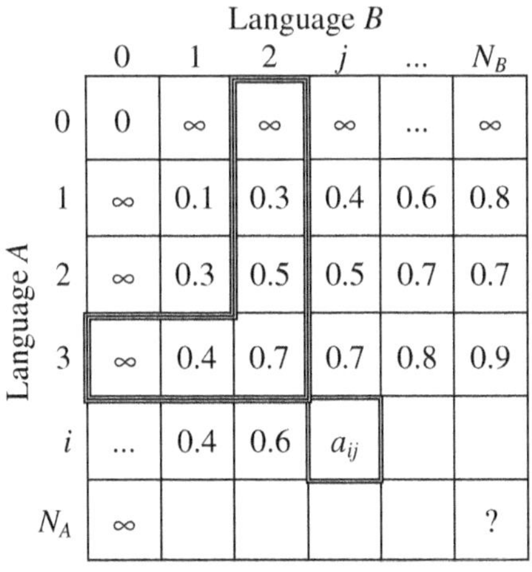

Fig. 6. The chart of the dynamic programming algorithm

Here, a_{ij} is the value in the (i,j)-th cell of the chart, $T_X[a .. b]$ is the set of the paragraphs from a-th to b-th inclusive of the text in the language X, and the minimum is calculated over all cells (x,y) in the ┘-shaped area to the left and above the (i,j)-th cell, as marked with a triple-line border in Fig. 6. In our implementation we star from the corner of this area, thus preferring of equal variants the ones with fewer paragraphs being aligned with one paragraph. Note that at least one of the two $T_X[a .. b]$ consists of only one paragraph, according to the conditions from Section 0. In Fig. 6, arbitrary values such as 0.3 are shown only to indicate that the corresponding cells have been already filled by the step of calculating a_{ij}.

As in any dynamic programming algorithm, the value a_{ij} is the total weight of the optimal alignment of the initial i paragraphs of the text in the language A with the initial j paragraphs of the text in the language B. Specifically, upon termination of the algorithm, the bottom-right cell (marked by "?" in Fig. 6) contains the total weight of the optimal alignment of the whole texts. The alignment itself is printed out by restoring the sequence of the assignments that led to this cell:

```
(i,j) := (N_A, N_B).
while (i,j) ≠ (0, 0) do
    (x,y) := argmin (a_xy + Similarity (T_A [x + 1 .. i], T_B [y + 1 .. j]))
    print "paragraphs in A from x + 1 to i are aligned with
            paragraphs in B from y + 1 to j."
    (i,j) := (x,y)
```

Here, again, the minimum is sought over the same ┘-shaped area to the left and above the current cell (i,j). Upon termination, this algorithm will print (in the reverse order) all pairs of the sets of paragraphs in the optimal alignment. Note again that in each pair at least one of the two sets consists of only one paragraph. We omit here the proof of optimality, which is quite standard for dynamic programming algorithms.

5 Complexity Analysis

In this paper our goal was to prove that the task of finding the exact optimal alignment is tractable, and present the general idea of the algorithm. We did not have the goal of discussing its fast implementation.

The algorithm as presented here has the complexity $O(N^4)$, where $N = N_A \approx N_B$ is the size of the text to be aligned. Indeed, the chart contains $O(N^2)$ cells, calculating of each cell requires $O(N)$ calculations of similarity between one paragraph and a set of paragraphs, which in turn can require $O(N)$ comparisons of individual words. We assume that the size of a paragraph and the number of translations for a word in the dictionary are $O(1)$.

The algorithm can be trivially modified to have the complexity $O(N^{3.5})$. Indeed, the Heaps law 2 states that the number of different word types in a text of length N is $O(N^{0.5})$. Assuming a faster implementation of the algorithm from Section 0 dealing with word vectors and not with individual tokens, we get the complexity of the function Similarity (T_A, T_B) to be $O(N^{0.5})$ instead of $O(N)$. In case of our suggested distance measure, the complexity can be even lowered to $O(N^3)$ by incremental calculation of the distance in the inner loop of the algorithm, due to linearity of our measure.

In practice, the complexity can be lowered to $O(N^2)$ by limiting the size of the ┘-shaped area in the chart calculation (which will also reduce to $O(1)$ the calculation of the similarity function). Indeed, as reported in 8, the correspondences longer that 1 to 3 paragraphs are low-probable.

We even believe that a linear on average (though not in the worst case) algorithm can be constructed, but this should be a topic of a future research.

6 Experimental Results

We experimented with a science fiction novel *Advances in genetics* by Abdón Ubídia and its original Spanish text *De la genética y sus logros*, downloaded from Internet. The English text consisted of 114 paragraphs and Spanish 107, including the title.[2] The texts were manually aligned at paragraph level to obtain the gold standard, see Table 1. In this table, only non-one-to-one pairs are shown: e.g., 2–3=2 stands for the fact that English paragraphs 2 and 3 constitute the translation of Spanish paragraph 2. The one-to-one pairs are trivially inferred from the data shown in the table: for example, 48–50=47 continues as 51=48, 52=49, etc.

Table 1. Comparison of the methods

Method	Alignment
Gold	2–3=2; 4–5=3–4 (4–5=3, 5=3–4); 6=5–6; 9–10=9; ∅=21; 46–47=46; 48–50=47; 51–53=48; 58–59=53; 87–88=81
Proposed	2–3=2; 4–5=3; 6=4–6; 9–10=9; 22=21–22; 46–47=46; 48–50=47; 51–53=48; 58–59=53; 67=61–62; 68=63–64; 69–71=65; 85=79–80; 86–88=81
Baseline	2–3=2; 4–6=3; 7=4–7; 9–10=9; 11–12=10; 13=11–13; 15–16=15; 22=21–23; 23–24=24; 25–32=25; 33=26–27; 35=29–32; 36–37=33; 38=34–35; 39=36–38; 41=40–41; 42–43=42; 44=43–44; 46–47=46; 48–50=47; 51–53=48; 54=49–50; 55–56=51; 57–58=52; 59–60=53; 61=54–55; 63–64=57; 65=58–60; 66–68=61; 69=62–63; 72–73=66; 76–77=69; 78=70–71; 79=72–73; 82=76–77; 83–84=78; 85=79–80; 86–87=81; 88–89=82; 91–92=84; 94–96=86; 97=87–89; 98=90–91; 99–100=92; 101–102=93; 103–104=94; 105=95–99; 106–108=100; 109=101–102; 111–112=104; 113=105–106

As often happens with literary texts 15, the selected text proved to be a difficult case because of violation of two of our assumptions; see the underlined pairs in Table 1. In one case, two paragraphs were aligned with two: the translator broke down a long Spanish paragraph 3 into two English paragraphs 4 and 5, but joined the translation of a short Spanish paragraph 4 with the English paragraph 5; in Table 1 we illustrate this situation in parentheses. In another case, the translator completely omitted the Spanish paragraph 21. This illustrates that our assumptions from Section 0 above are not always correct. Obviously, our algorithm (with both distance measures) did not align correctly these cases.

[2] We did not experiment with a larger corpus because we are not aware of a gold-standard manually aligned Spanish-English parallel corpus.

Both texts were preprocessed by lemmatizing 7, 19 and POS-tagging, which allowed for correct dictionary lookup. Stop-words were removed to reduce noise in comparison; leaving the stop-words in place renders our method of comparison of paragraphs completely unusable. Then our algorithm was applied, with both baseline and suggested distance measures. The resulting alignments are shown in Table 1.

We evaluate the results in terms of precision and recall of retrieving the hyperarcs 10; see Table 2: precision stands for the share of the pairs in the corresponding row of Table 1 (including one-to-one pairs not shown explicitly in the table) that are also found in its first row; recall stands for the stare of the pairs in its first row that are also found in the row corresponding to the method. Alternatively, we broke down each hyperarc into pair-wise correspondences: 48–50=47 was broken down into 48 ~ 47, 49 ~ 47, 50 ~ 47, and calculated the precision and recall of our algorithm on retrieving such pairs; see the last two columns of the table.

Table 2. Comparison of the distance measures

Measure	Hyperarcs		Single arcs	
	Precision, %	Recall, %	Precision, %	Recall, %
Proposed	89	85	88	90
Baseline	65	28	43	54

One can see that the proposed distance measure based on the bilingual dictionaries greatly outperforms the pure statistically-based baseline.

7 Conclusions and Future Work

We have suggested a formalization of the paragraph alignment task as finding a least-cost hypergraph with certain properties. We also described a dynamic programming algorithm that finds the exact optimum of the corresponding problem. The assumptions that allowed for our formalization and thus the algorithm hold most of the time though not always, as our test corpus showed.

The following directions of future work can be mentioned:

- Error analysis: to analyze the causes of the errors made by the algorithm on our corpus. Actually only such analysis will define the ways of future improvements.
- Algorithm improved as to its complexity, preferably linear.
- More accurate similarity measures, for example, to avoid possibly counting some translations more than once. However, this is complicated and would lead to much higher complexity: in fact it implies word-level alignment.
- A similarity measure taking into account the order of words in the paragraphs.
- Weighting schemes such as TF-IDF instead of removing keywords.
- Formalization of the task considering many-to-many correspondences.
- Application of the method to sentence-level alignment.
- Using the results of alignment to enrich existing bilingual dictionaries.

References

1. Brown, P. F., Lai, J. C. & Mercer, R. L. 1991. Aligning Sentences in Parallel Corpora. In: *Proceedings of the 29th Annual Meeting of the Association for Computational Linguistics*, Berkeley, California, pp. 169–176.
2. Baeza-Yates, R., B. Ribeiro-Neto. Modern Information Retrieval. Addison-Wesley, 1999.
3. Caseli, H. M., and M. G. Volpe Nunes. 2003. Evaluation of Sentence Alignment Methods on Portuguese-English Parallel Texts. *Scientia* 14(2):1–14.
4. Chen, S. 1993. Aligning sentences in bilingual corpora using lexical information. In: *Proceeding of ACL-93*, pp. 9–16.
5. Bing Zhao *et al.* 2003. Efficient Optimization for Bilingual Sentence Alignment based on Linear Regression. In: *HLT-NAACL 2003 Workshop: Building and Using Parallel Texts: Data Driven Machine Translation and Beyond*. p. 81–87.
6. Gale, W. A. & Church, K. W. 1991. A program for Aligning Sentences in Bilingual Corpora. In: *Proceedings of the 29th Annual Meeting of the Association for Computational Linguistics*, Berkeley, California.
7. Gelbukh, Alexander, and Grigori Sidorov. 2003. *Approach to construction of automatic morphological analysis systems for inflective languages with little effort*. Lecture Notes in Computer Science, N 2588, Springer-Verlag, pp. 215–220.
8. Gelbukh, Alexander, and Grigori Sidorov. 2006. Paragraph-Level Alignment of an English-Spanish Parallel Corpus of Fiction Texts using Bilingual Dictionaries. Proc. of TSD-2006. Lecture Notes in Artificial Intelligence, Springer-Verlag, in press.
9. Kay, Martin and Martin Roscheisen. 1993. Text-translation alignment. *Computational Linguistics*, 19(1):121–142.
10. Kit, Chunyu, Jonathan J. Webster, King Kui Sin, Haihua Pan, Heng Li. 2004. Clause alignment for Hong Kong legal texts: A lexical-based approach. *International Journal of Corpus Linguistics* 9:1. pp. 29–51.
11. Langlais, Ph., M. Simard, J. Veronis. 1998. Methods and practical issues in evaluation alignment techniques. In: *Proceeding of Coling-ACL-98*.
12. McEnery, A. M. & Oakes, M. P. 1996. Sentence and word alignment in the CRATER project. In: *Using Corpora for Language Research*, London, pp. 211–231.
13. Melamed, I. Dan. 1996. A Geometric Approach to Mapping Bitext Correspondence. *Proc. EMNLP-1996*, ACL, p. 1–12.
14. Melamed, I. Dan. 2000. Pattern Recognition for Mapping Bitext Correspondence. In *Parallel Text Processing: Alignment and Use of Translation Corpora*. Kluwer, p. 25–47.
15. Meyers, Adam, Michiko Kosaka, and Ralph Grishman. 1998. A Multilingual Procedure for Dictionary-Based Sentence Alignment. In: *Proceedings of AMTA'98: Machine Translation and the Information Soup*, pages 187–198.
16. Mikhailov, M. 2001. Two Approaches to Automated Text Aligning of Parallel Fiction Texts. *Across Languages and Cultures, 2:1*, pp. 87–96.
17. Robert C. Moore. 2002, Fast and Accurate Sentence Alignment of Bilingual Corpora. *AMTA-2002*. p. 135–144.
18. Simard, M., George Foster, Pierre Isabelle. 1992. Using Cognates to Align Sentences in Bilingual Corpora. TMI-1992, p. 67–81.
19. Velásquez, F., Gelbukh, A. & Sidorov, G. 2002. AGME: un sistema de análisis y generación de la morfología del español. In: *Proc. of Workshop on Multilingual information access & natural language processing of IBERAMIA 2002*, pp 1–6.

Document Mining Based on Semantic Understanding of Text

Khaled Shaban, Otman Basir, and Mohamed Kamel

Electrical and Computer Engineering, University of Waterloo, Waterloo, Canada
{kshaban, obasir, mkamel}@uwaterloo.ca

Abstract. This paper presents a new paradigm for mining documents by exploiting the semantic information of their texts. A formal semantic representation of linguistic inputs is introduced and utilized to build a semantic representation for documents. The representation is constructed through accumulation of syntactic and semantic analysis outputs. A new distance measure is developed to determine the similarities between contents of documents. The measure is based on inexact matching of attributed trees. It involves the computation of all distinct similarity common sub-trees, and can be computed efficiently. It is believed that the proposed representation along with the proposed similarity measure will enable more effective document mining processes. The proposed techniques to mine documents were implemented as components in a mining system. A case study of semantic document clustering is presented to demonstrate the working and the efficacy of the framework. Experimental work is reported, and its results are presented and analyzed.

Keywords: Document mining, semantic understanding, text representation, similarity measure, document clustering.

1 Introduction

As the sheer number of documents that are available online grows exponentially, the need to manage these documents also grows. The result of this exponential growth is what has become known as the *information overload* problem. Taking into consideration only the volume of information available via the Internet and the World Wide Web (WWW) presents a non-trivial real problem. The extent of this problem is immediately apparent to anyone who has tapped into the WWW, and attempted to locate specific desired information. Solving this problem involves processes such as *information gathering*, *information filtering* (IF), *information retrieval* (IR), *information extraction* (IE), *document classification*, and *document clustering*. The goal of these processes is to help users to have better access to documents that satisfy their information needs. The needs can be to discover or derive new information from documents, to find patterns across documents, and to separate the desired information from the noise. These computational processes constitute cornerstone tasks in the ever-developing study field of *document mining*.

The goal of this work is to introduce, build, and demonstrate a novel document mining system that is based on semantic understanding of the document contents. The

J.F. Martínez-Trinidad et al. (Eds.): CIARP 2006, LNCS 4225, pp. 834 – 843, 2006.

system is composed of components that facilitate semantic analysis of text, measuring similarity between documents, and applying the different mining processes. The aim is to show the working of the method and how this system can provide better performance than it is possible otherwise.

There are three aspects pertain to document mining approaches: a) Representation models. b) Similarity measures. c) Mining processes.

Representation Models: Conventional text representation models focus on whether a document contains specific keywords, and their appearance frequencies. For example, in the vector space model (VSM) [5, 21, 22], documents are represented by vectors containing the frequency of all possible words (*features*) in a document set. Since many words rarely occur in a particular document, many of these features will have zero or low frequencies. Therefore, features are selected according to their importance as dictated by criteria such as *Document Frequency-Inverse Document Frequency*, *Information Gain*, *Mutual Information*, a *Chi-Square–test*, and *Term Strength* [1, 29]. Moreover, before applying feature selection, a common practice is to reprocess text by removing stop-words and applying word-stemming algorithms. Stop-words, such as *the*, *and*, and *a*, are believed to have no significance in capturing meaningful information. Word-stemming algorithms convert different word forms into a similar canonical form. Two popular stemming algorithms are used; the Porter stemmer [20], and using a lexicon dictionary lookup, such as WordNet [18].

Despite the widespread use of these word-based approaches to represent documents, it is believed that these approaches contribute to the lack of reliable performance of document mining systems. These approaches consider the document as a bag of words, and ignore meanings and ideas the document wanted to convey. It is this deficiency that causes the similarity measures to either fail to perceive contextual similarity of text passages due to the variation of words the passages contain, or perceive contextually dissimilar text passages as being similar because of the resemblance of words the passages happen to have. An illustration of this deficiency that causes the failure is the two sentences '*John eats the apple standing beside the tree*' and '*The apple tree stands beside John's house*', where despite using the same words, their meanings are different. Moreover, the following two sentences have more or less the same meaning but have been constructed from different sets of words, '*John is an intelligent boy*', and '*John is a brilliant lad*'.

Similarity Measures: Similarity measures are used to determine distances between documents, after transforming the textual data into a useable and intelligible format. There are various techniques to measure similarities and they all rely on the chosen model to represent the text. In VSM, for instance, the feature space constitutes a geometric space where documents are represented as points in a multidimensional space. Thus, measuring the similarity can be easily calculated. Two measures are often used; they are the *cosine measure*, and the *Jaccard measure* [12, 25]. The cosine measure is defined as: $cos(x,y)=(x.y)/(|x||y|)$, where $(x.y)$ denotes the vector dot product of x and y, and $|x|$ and $|y|$ are the lengths of vectors x, y, respectively. The cosine measure gives high similarity values to documents that share the same set of words with high term frequencies, and lower values to those that do not. The Jaccard measure is defined as: $sim(x,y)=|x\cap y|/|x\cup y|$. It finds the overlap between two documents by calculating the number of terms that are common between them. The Jaccard measure can work for both continuous and binary feature vectors.

Although these techniques could be appropriate to measure distances between vectors of numerical features, the inherent inadequacy of word-focused approaches still exist. There is no perfect correlation between comparing words and comparing meanings. As the example sentences in the previous section show, the correlation can be very low indeed. Better mining results can be attained by measuring meanings instead of counting words found in documents. Thus it is imperative to develop semantic representations of text, and distance measures that can determine whether one statement is an instance of, or quite different from, another statement.

Mining Processes: Document mining processes may vary in their requirements and specifications, yet their goals are to discover and extract knowledge from documents. IR is concerned with finding relevant documents in response to a user request and ranking them accordingly [2, 17]. This is normally done by measuring the distances between documents and queries in their transformed form in an index. When relevancy and similarity measuring is performed with the intent of transmitting a document to a user(s), it is usually referred to as IF [3, 19]. It is also used to either accept or reject an incoming document, as in e-mail filters that attempt to screen for junk mail. The goal of IE is to locate specific information and produce structured format from unstructured or semi-structured documents [24]. The output of an extraction system is usually tabular or fixed-format forms that are filled out with unambiguous data. This is done through analyzing those portions of each document that contain relevant information. Relevance here is determined by predefined domain guidelines which specify what types of information the system is expected to find. The aim of the document classification task is to assign a new document to one of a pre-existing set of document classes. In this setting, the task of creating a classifier consists of discovering useful characterization of the documents that belong to each class. Although this can be done by hand, the standard approach is to use supervised machine learning. In particular, classifiers can be trained on a set of documents that have been labeled with the correct class. The classification task assumes existing categories, or clusters, of documents. By contrast, the task of document clustering is to create, or discover, a reasonable set of clusters for a given set of documents. A reasonable cluster is defined as one that maximizes the within-cluster document similarity, and minimizes between cluster similarities [4].

2 The Semantic-Based Document Mining System

The proposed approach is based on analyzing text in documents before proceeding with the different mining processes requirements. The text analysis step comprises syntactic analysis to extract syntax structural descriptions (e.g. part of speech tags, phrasal chunks, and parse trees), and semantic analysis that produces formal knowledge representations of the documents contents. Thus, a generic semantic-based document mining system consists of three major components: (1) Text parser, (2) Similarity estimator, and (3) Mining processes. These components are interconnected, which makes the system highly integrated, but yet modular.

2.1 Semantic-Based Text Representation

We introduce a representation, called the *Semantic Graph Model* (SGM), where the focus is on the ability to express distinct readings of sentences as distinct formulas that capture their intuitive structures and meanings. We start by creating predicate structures of sentences, augmenting the structures elements with valuable attributes, and taking all parsed sentences as the document representation (Figure 1). The representation is a graph-based data structure where entities, such as *agents*, *objects*, *states*, *actions*, *events*, and *locations* are represented as vertices, and relations between them are represented as arcs. Each node holds information that could include its original text, syntactic information, semantic meaning, and relations with other nodes.

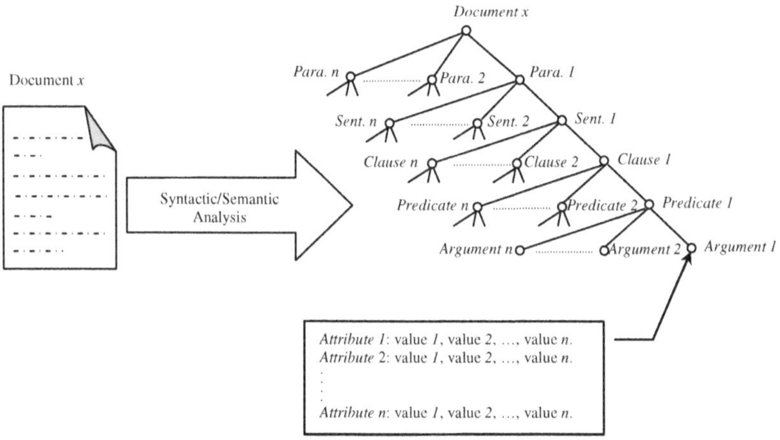

Fig. 1. SGM Skeleton for a Document

2.2 Semantic-Based Similarity Measure

The similarity estimator component is responsible for searching the abstract representations of two documents, finding elements that are sufficiently similar, and yielding an overall similarity index. An inexact graph matching technique to approximately match graphs is utilized to calculate semantic distances between documents. Since SGMs are in essence trees with multiple symbolic node attributes, the semantic distance measure is defined over attributed-trees. The measure involves the computation of all similarity common sub-trees that do not overlap.

Figures 2 (a) and (b) demonstrate the proposed distance estimator. The figures depict the finding of the common similarity sub-trees in the SGMs of two sentences. The symbol (**x**) denotes the nodes that are not matched, while (⇔) represents the similarity matching of nodes that are included in the common similarity sub-trees. Note that in order to match only distinct sub-trees the overlapping resulting from considering one node in Figure 2 (a) (status: '*stands beside John's house*') should be eliminated. Thus, only one matching node (Action 2 or Object 2) would be considered as a match.

Clearly, the summing up of similarities for the first pair of sentences is lower than the second pair, which reflects the closeness of their meaning distances. An index number indicating the similarity between a pair of sentences (or documents) can be determined by normalizing the similarity of all found similarity sub-trees. Applying this on the sample sentences in figure 2 (a) and (b), assuming the similarity values between the sub-trees are estimated through matching of nodes attributes will produce a low similarity for the first sentence pair an a high similarity for the second pair.

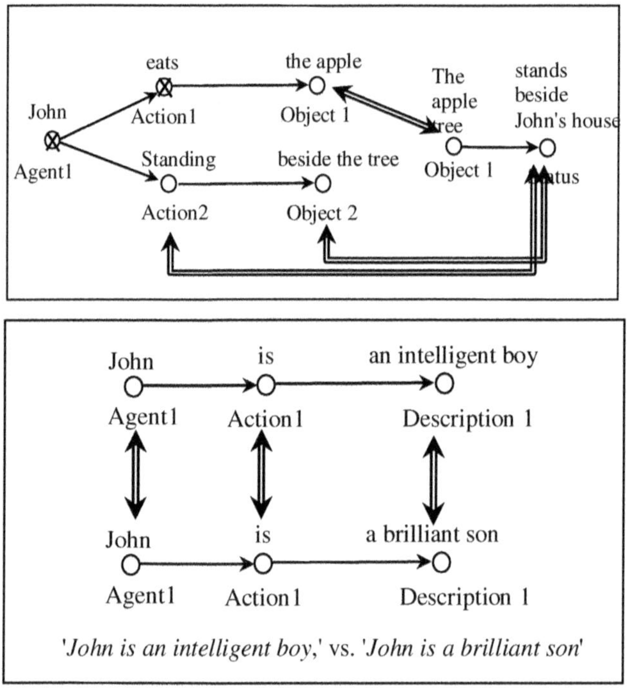

Fig. 2. (a) Similarity Estimation for Sample Texts. (b) Similarity Estimation for Sample Texts.

2.3 Semantic-Based Mining Processes

At a certain level of abstraction we can look at the different mining processes as being relatively similar. We maintain that they can all benefit from the semantic-based representation, i.e., the SGM, produced by a text parser, and can make use of the similarity measure estimator as needed. And then proceed with their specific tasks. The text analysis and the similarity estimation should be as much independent as possible of the specific mining process to allow for modularity and scalability. In Section 3, a case study of the proposed approach on one of these document mining processes (semantic-based document clustering) is presented. Implementations and experimental work have been carried out and results are also presented and analyzed.

3 Semantic Document Clustering: A Case Study

While a large number of statistical document clustering approaches have become available, relatively, a little attention has been paid to the clustering of documents represented using symbolic structures. In principle, however, given suitable documents similarity (or dissimilarity) measurements, many of the clustering algorithms originally developed in the context of statistical pattern recognition, can be applied in the symbolic domain. This is the course we have adapted to cluster documents represented semantically. Text documents were syntactically and semantically parsed and represented by their SGMs. Pair-wise similarities were computed using our developed inexact tree similarity measure. The similarity matrix was fed to different clustering algorithms to produce clusters for the data sets. The clustering results were then evaluated using standard evaluation techniques in document mining. In what follows we detail the steps taken and give an analytical discourse on findings.

Text Parser: A parsing system, which performs the syntactic analysis, and builds the semantic structures of SGM is implemented. We are utilizing the open source GATE (General Architecture for Text Engineering) project from University of Sheffield in the UK (http://gate.ac.uk) [11], and a commercial integrated development environment (IDE), Visual Text [26], from Text Analysis International, Inc. GATE provides an extensible framework for information extraction and text analysis, and Visual Text integrates NLP++ programming language for rapid parsers building. We have based the design of our text analysis system on a multi-pass, and a multi-strategy architecture that could be implemented within Visual Text IDE. The syntactic and semantic parser developments are built upon the TAIParse general analyzer [27] that is provided as an open source from Text Analysis. The analyzer contains 123 passes that build syntactic (parse trees), and semantic (the SGM) structures. Many other external processing components and language resources are wrapped and made usable interchangeably within the system. Specifically, every document in the processed data set goes through tokenization, part of speech tagging, syntactic parsing, semantics and discourse analysis.

Data Set: A Web documents collection is used. The document set is a collection of 2340 Reuters news articles posted on Yahoo! News. This corpus is especially interesting for evaluation, as it comes along with a *hand-crafted* classification. All documents have been classified manually by Yahoo experts to one or more of six main categories of Reuter's news feed, namely, business, entertainment, health, politics, sports, and technology. The data set has been collected and used by Boley et al [6, 7, 8] for clustering.

Text Representations: All text documents are represented using the proposed semantic graph model (SGM). The SGM representation model constitutes trees that have attributes for their nodes. Each document is represented as a tree rooted in a node describing its file name, and branches to sub-trees represent paragraphs, sentences, clauses, and predicate-argument nodes with attributes describing the arguments. As applicable, the node attributes include *Name*: a unique identification for the node, *Type*: the semantic role of concept, *Text*: the original text, *Syntax*: the part of speech tag, *Synonyms*: dictionary senses of the concept, *Semantic*: the disambiguated meaning of the concept, and *Relation*: other nodes IDs that are connected to the node. Different algorithms are employed and integrated in the parser to produce the SGM representations. The documents are also represented by the VSM. Some pre-processing procedures are performed such as normalizing words, analyzing words globally, and words weighting. To normalize words, numeric, and stop words are removed. All words are converted to lowercase, and words of length 2 or less are also removed. Note that no stemming is done. Analyzing words globally is done by building a list of unique words from all documents, and calculating the document frequency of each word. Then, for each document, the word frequency is calculated and weighted using the following formula: $w_{i,j} = f_{i,j} \log(\frac{N}{df_j})$, where $f_{i,j}$ is the term frequency of word j in document i, N is the number of documents, df_j is the document frequency of word j. Finally, an output of the term-by-document matrix is produced.

Similarity Measures: Our distance measure technique is used to measure distances between documents. It follows the similarity calculation approach that is based on finding all distinct common similarity sub-trees. The algorithm is applied to the semantic trees of the SGMs produced by the semantic parser. Various attributes are considered in the testing. Attribute consideration starts from taking into account only the original text to represent a node and extends to consider other attributes the parser accumulates. Specifically, we carried out the experiments with mainly five options of sets of attributes to include in measuring the similarities. These options are (1) original text only, (2) original text, and syntax tag, (3) original text, syntax tag, and semantic role, (4) original text, syntax tag, semantic role, and semantic disambiguated sense, and (5) original text, syntax tag, semantic role, semantic disambiguated sense, and semantic variation. To measure similarities of documents represented in the vector space, the commonly used cosine correlation measure is utilized.

Clustering Algorithms: The semantic approach to represent text and determine similarity between them is evaluated by allowing clustering algorithms to use the produced similarity matrix of the document set. We run the test with standard clustering algorithms that accept the pair-wise (dis)similarity between documents, rather than the internal vector-space or SGM representations of the documents. The employed algorithms included: Single-Pass Clustering [10, 15], k-nearest neighbour (*k*-NN) Clustering [10, 13], and Hierarchical Agglomerative Clustering (HAC) [16]. The different parameters of these algorithms (i.e., the clustering threshold parameters) are tuned so the best results of clustering are obtained.

Evaluation: To evaluate results, we used a benchmark of manually classified document set; Routers news feeds. The main aspect of the evaluation is the quality of the clustering task output, which is measured in terms of clusters quality. The widely used evaluation indices, F-measure that combines precession (*P*) and recall (*R*) [9, 14, 28], Entropy, and Overall-Similarity are used for this purpose as clustering quality evaluation measures. *R* for cluster *c* is the ratio of processed documents manually classified as *c* with regard to the whole document set, and *P* is the ratio of these documents clustered as *c* by the process that were also manually classified as *c* regarding the produced set of results. The *F-measure* is calculated as: $F=[(\beta^2+1)PR]/[\beta^2 P+R]$, the parameter β influences how much to favor recall over precision. The *F1* score where $\beta=1$, weighs precision and recall equally. The entropy E_i of a cluster i is calculated using Shanon [23] standard formula: $E_i = -\sum_j p_{ij} \log(p_{ij})$, where P_{ij} is the probability of documents of cluster i belong to class j. An overall entropy E for all clusters can also be calculated as the sum of entropies for each cluster weighted by the size of each cluster as follows: $E = \sum_i^n (\frac{N_i}{N} \times E_i)$, where N_i is the size of cluster i, and N is the total number of documents. Overall similarity uses the weighted similarity of the internal cluster similarity as: OverallSimilarity(S) = $\frac{1}{|S|^2} \sum_{x,y \in S} sim(x, y)$, where S is the cluster under consideration, and $sim(x, y)$ is the similarity between the two objects x and y.

3.1 Analysis of Results

The clustering algorithms were utilized to cluster the data set using document-to-document similarities produced by the semantic-based approach, and the vector space model. Results show the effectiveness of the semantic-based approach for clustering. In addition, the experiments illustrate improvements when more semantic clues are included in the process of measuring similarity between SGMs of documents. The improvements were achieved at a factor up to 72% from the base case of considering only the original text of nodes (option 1) to considering all five semantic analysis results (option 5). The threshold parameters for the different clustering algorithms were manually tuned and the ones that produced the best results were reported. The *F-measure* index showed noticeable improvement. The same can be noticed about the entropy and the overall similarity indexes.

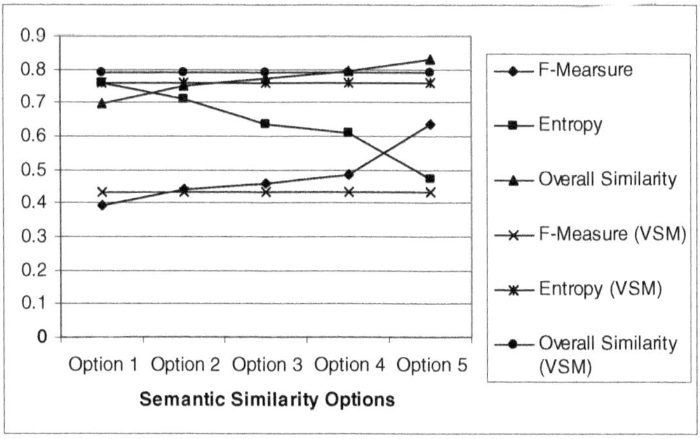

Fig. 3. Clustering Results

To better understand the effect of the inclusion of semantic information when calculating similarity on the clustering quality, we plot the clustering quality profile indices against the similarity options in Figure 3. The plotted values are the averages of *F*-measure, entropy, and overall similarity of the different clustering algorithms. We also plot the value of these measures with regard to the VSM. It is easy to notice the enhancement of the clustering as we consider more semantic information. The enhancement is, however, non-linear. Options 2 and 3 seem not to have as much effect on the clustering quality, but they never bring it down. Option 5 had the most effect to bring up the quality of clustering. As anticipated; keywords alone cannot capture all the similarity information between documents, thus the quality of semantic clustering with option 1 was as low as the VSM.

4 Conclusions

We demonstrated a system composed of semantic components in an attempt to improve the accuracy of measuring the similarity between documents and using the similarity in applying document mining. We considered semantic document clustering as a case study. By exploiting the semantic analysis findings we could achieve better clustering results. We implemented document analysis components that are capable of identifying the meaning structures of text in documents. The second part is to measure similarity between parsed documents. The measure has the most impact on the performance as how much of semantic information it considers. Using the maximum amount of the semantic information enables us to perform similarity calculations between documents in a very robust and accurate way. The quality of clustering achieved using this model significantly surpasses the traditional vector space model based approach.

References

1. Aas, K., and Eikvil, L., "Text categorisation: A survey," Tech. Report 941, Norwegian Computing Center, 1999.
2. Baeza-Yates, R., and Ribeiro-Neto, B., *Modern Information Retrieval*, ACM, 1999.
3. Belkin, N. J., and Croft, W. B., "Information filtering and information retrieval: Two sides of the same coin?" Comm. of the ACM, vol. 35, no. 12, pp. 29-38, 1992.
4. Berkhin, P., "Survey of Clustering Data Mining Techniques," Tech, Report, Accrue Software, 2002.
5. Berry, M. W., Dunais, S. T., and O'Brien, G. W., "Using Linear Algebra for Intelligent Information Retrieval," SIAM Review 37(4), pp. 573-595, 1995.
6. Boley, D., "Principal direction divisive partitioning", Data Mining and Knowledge Discovery, 2(4):325-344, 1998.
7. Boley, D., Gini, M., Gross, R., Han, S., Hastings, K., Karypis, G., Kumar, V., Mobasher, B., and Moore, J., "Partitioning-based clustering for web document categorization", Decision Support Systems, 27:329-341, 1999.
8. Boley, D., Gini, M., Gross, R., Han, S., Hastings, K., Karypis, G., Kumar, V., Mobasher, B., and Moore, J., "Document categorization and query generation on the World Wide Web using WebACE", AI Review, 13(5-6):365-391, 1999.

9. Chakrabarti, S., *Mining the Web: Discovering Knowledge from Hypertext Data.* Morgan Kaufmann Publishers, 2003.
10. Cios, K., Pedrycs, W., and Swiniarski, R., Data Mining Methods for Knowledge Discovery. Kluwer Academic Publishers, 1998.
11. Cunningham, H., Maynard, D., Bontcheva, K., Tablan, V., "GATE: A Framework and Graphical Development Environment for Robust NLP Tools and Applications" Proce. of 40th Anniversary Meeting of the ACL (ACL'02). Philadelphia, July 2002.
12. Cutting, D.; Karger, D.; Pedersen, J.; and Tukey, J.: "Scatter/gather: A cluster-based approach to browsing large document collections." In 16th International ACM SIGIR Conference on Research and Development in IR, pp 126-135, 1993.
13. Dasarathy, B.V. "Nearest Neighbor (NN) Norms: NN Pattern Classification Techniques." McGraw-Hill Comp. Scie. Series. IEEE Comp. Soci. Press, 1991.
14. Eikvil, L., "Information Extraction from World Wide Web – A Survey," Technical Report 945, Norwegian Computing Center, July, 1999.
15. Hill, D.R."A vector clustering technique" In Samuelson, ed. Mechanized Information Storage, Retrieval and Dissemination. North-Holland, (1968).
16. Jain, A. K., and Dubes, R. C., "Algorithms for Clustering Data", Prentice Hall, Englewood Cliffs NJ, U.S.A, 1988.
17. Lee, D. L., Chuang, H., and Seamons, K., "Document Ranking and the Vector-Space Model" IEEE Comp., Issues on Assessing Measurement, 14(2):67-75, 1997.
18. Miller, G. A., Beckwith, R., Fellbaum, C., Gross, D., and Miller, K., "Introduction to WordNet: An On-line Lexical Database" Cognitive Science Lab, Princeton University, 1993.
19. Mostafa, J., Mukhopadhyay, S., Lam, W., Palakal, M., "A Multi-level Approach to Intelligent Information Filtering: Model, System & Evaluation," ACM Transactions on Information Systems, 15(4): pp. 368-399, 1997.
20. Porter, M. F."An algorithm for suffix stripping" Program,14(3),pp.130-137, 1980.
21. Salton, G., and Mcgill, M. J., *Introduction to Modern Information Retrieval*, McGraw-Hill, 1984.
22. Salton, G., Wong, A., and Yang, C., "A vector space model for automatic indexing," Communications of the ACM, 18(11), pp.613-620, 1975.
23. Shannon, C.E.: "A Mathematical Theory of Communication", Bell Syst. Tech. J., 27, 379-423, 623-656, 1948.
24. Soderland, S., *Learning Information Extraction Rules for Semistructured and Free Text.* Machine Learning, 1999.
25. Steinbach, M.; Karypis, G.; and Kumar, V. "A comparison of document clustering techniques" KDD-2000 Workshop on TextMining, August 2000.
26. Text Analysis International, Inc. "Integrated Development Environments for Natural Language Processing", White Paper, www.textanalysis.com, October 2001.
27. Text Analysis International, Inc. "Multi-Pass Multi-Strategy NLP", White Paper, http://www.textanalysis.com/, October 2003.
28. van Rijsbergen, C. J.: *Information Retrieval*, Woburn Massachusetts. Butterworths, 1979.
29. Yang, Y., and Pedersen, J., "A Comparative Study on Feature Selection in Text Categorization" In Proceeding of the 14th International Conference on Machine Learning, ICML, pp. 412-420, Nashville, TN, 1997.

Authorship Attribution Using Word Sequences

Rosa María Coyotl-Morales[1], Luis Villaseñor-Pineda[1],
Manuel Montes-y-Gómez[1], and Paolo Rosso[2]

[1] Laboratorio de Tecnologías del Lenguaje,
Instituto Nacional de Astrofísica, Óptica y Electrónica, México
{mcoyotl, villasen, mmontesg}@inaoep.mx
[2] Departamento de Sistemas Informáticos y Computación,
Universidad Politécnica de Valencia, España
prosso@dsic.upv.es

Abstract. Authorship attribution is the task of identifying the author of a given text. The main concern of this task is to define an appropriate characterization of documents that captures the writing style of authors. This paper proposes a new method for authorship attribution supported on the idea that a proper identification of authors must consider both stylistic and topic features of texts. This method characterizes documents by a set of word sequences that combine functional and content words. The experimental results on poem classification demonstrated that this method outperforms most current state-of-the-art approaches, and that it is appropriate to handle the attribution of short documents.

1 Introduction

Authorship attribution is the task of identifying the author of a given text. It can be considered as a typical classification problem, where a set of documents with known authorship are used for training and the aim is to automatically determine the corresponding author of an anonymous text. In contrast to other classification tasks, it is not clear which features of a text should be used to classify an author. Consequently, the main concern of computer-assisted authorship attribution is to define an appropriate characterization of documents that captures the writing style of authors.

There are several methods for authorship attribution, ranging from those using stylistic non-topic features such as the vocabulary richness of the author and the frequency of occurrence of some functional words[1] [12], to those based on the traditional bag-of-words representation that consider all content words of documents [5, 8]. In this paper, we propose a new method for authorship attribution. This method relies on the hypothesis that a proper identification of authors must consider both stylistic and topic features of texts. Therefore, an adequate characterization of documents must effectively combine functional and content words. Our proposal is to construct this characterization by means of word sequences.

It is important to mention that word sequences (specially, fixed-length word *n*-grams) have been applied without much success in topic-based text classification [3].

[1] Words having little semantic content of their own, such as prepositions, conjunctions, and articles. In information retrieval, they are also known as stopwords.

J.F. Martínez-Trinidad et al. (Eds.): CIARP 2006, LNCS 4225, pp. 844 – 853, 2006.

Nevertheless, there are not enough studies on their application to non-topic-based classification, and in particular to the task of authorship attribution [10].

On the other hand, another less studied difficulty is the impact of the document size on the classification accuracy. It is known that some approaches for authorship attribution are very sensible to the length of documents. Specially, the methods based on stylistic features tend to fail when confront short documents [11]. This behavior motivates us to apply our method on the classification of poems by authors. Given that poems are very short documents, our experiments not only contribute to evaluate the usefulness of word sequence features for authorship attribution, but also allow analyzing their appropriateness to handle difficult classification scenarios.

The rest of the paper is organized as follows. Section 2 discusses some previous works related to the task of authorship attribution. Section 3 introduces the proposed method. Section 4 describes the experimental setup. Section 5 presents some experimental results on the use of word sequences features. Finally, section 6 depicts our conclusions and future work.

2 Related Work

The analysis of style for authorship attribution is mainly based on the assumption that each author has habits in wording (i.e., in the use of words) that make their writing unique. However, this assumption is not completely true, since the style of an author may be variable depending on the target audience, or may change because of differences in topics or genre. For this reason, it is difficult to determine a set of features stable to these variations but adequate to distinguish between writings of different authors.

There are several methods for authorship attribution. These methods may be clustered in the following three main approaches:

Stylistic measures as document features. This approach considers features such as the length of words and sentences as well as the richness of the vocabulary [7, 9]. Its results are not conclusive, but have demonstrated that these features are not sufficient for the task. It seems that they vary depending on the genre of the text, and that they lost most of their meaning when dealing with short texts.

Syntactic cues as document features. This approach uses a set of style markers. These markers go beyond the stylistic measures by integrating information related to structure of the language, which is obtained by an in depth syntactic analysis of documents [4, 5, 11]. Basically, texts are characterized by the presence and frequency of certain syntactic structures. This characterization is very detailed and relevant; unfortunately, it is computationally expensive and even impossible to build for languages lacking of text-processing resources (e.g. POS tagger, syntactic parser, etc.). Besides, it is also clearly influenced by the length of documents.

Word-based document features. This approach includes at least three different kinds of methods. The first one characterizes documents using a set of functional words, ignoring the content words since they tend to be highly correlated with the document topics [2, 12]. This method works properly, but it is also affected by the size of documents. In this case, the document length not only influences the frequency of occurrence of the functional words but also their sole presence. The second method applies the traditional bag-of-words representation and uses single content-words as document features [5, 8]. It is very robust and produces excellent results when there is a noticeable relation between authors and topics. Finally, a third method considers word n-gram features, i.e., features consisting of sequences of n consecutive words. This method attempts to capture the language structure of texts by simple word sequences instead of by complex syntactic structures [10]. Somehow, it purpose is to obtain a rich characterization of texts without performing an expensive syntactic analysis. Nevertheless, due to the feature explosion, it tends to use only n-grams up to three words.

In general, our method is very similar to the n-gram based approach. In both cases, documents are characterized by a combination of function and content words. However, ours considers a special kind of word sequences (namely, maximal frequent word sequences), which are determined by their frequency of occurrence instead of by their length. Using this strategy, it selects the most relevant word sequences, and indirectly tackles the problem of feature explosion. The following section describes in detailed the proposed method.

3 Our Method

As we previously mentioned, this paper presents a new method for authorship attribution. This method characterizes documents by a set of relevant sequences that combine functional and content words. The idea is to use these sequences to classify the documents in view that they express the most significant lexical collocations[2] used by an author. Traditionally, these sequences are extracted by applying a general n-gram computation. In contrast, we propose to discover them by means of a process for mining maximal frequent word sequences.

The following subsections define the maximal frequent word sequences, the process for their extraction, as well as a classification algorithm using them as document features.

3.1 Mining Maximal Frequent Word Sequences

Assume that D is a set of texts (a text may represent a complete document or even just a single sentence), and each text consists of a sequence of words. Then, we have the following definitions [1].

Definition 1. A sequence $p = a_1 \ldots a_k$ is a *subsequence* of a sequence q if all the items a_i, $1 \leq i \leq k$, occur in q and they occur in the same order as in p. If a sequence p is a subsequence of a sequence q, we also say that p occurs in q.

Definition 2. A sequence p is *frequent* in D if p is a subsequence of at least σ texts of D, where σ is a given frequency threshold.

Definition 3. A sequence p is a *maximal frequent sequence* in D if there does not exist any sequence p' in D such that p is a subsequence of p' and p' is frequent in D.

---

2 A collocation is defined as a sequence of words or terms that co-occur more often than would be expected by chance.

Once introduced the maximal frequent word sequences, the problem of mining them can formally state as follows: given a text collection D and an arbitrary integer value σ such that $1 \leq \sigma \leq |D|$, enumerate all maximal frequent word sequences in D.[3]

It is important to mention that the implementation of a method for sequence mining is not a trivial task because of its computational complexity. The algorithm used in our experiments is described in [6].

3.2 Classification Algorithms

Authorship attribution is a classification problem, where a set of documents with known authorship are used for training and the aim is to automatically determine the corresponding author of an anonymous text. Table 1 shows the direct classification algorithm based on the use of maximal frequent word sequences as document features.

Table 1. Direct Algorithm

Let D_T be the set of labeled documents that will be used for training
Let d be an anonymous document

TRAINING

1. Set the value of the frequency threshold σ
2. Enumerate all maximal frequent word sequences in D_T corresponding to the given frequency threshold
3. Build the training instances using the discovered word sequences as Boolean features
4. Give the learning algorithm the training instances and perform training

CLASSIFICATION

1. Build the representation of d in accordance to the training feature space
2. Let the trained classifier label the new instance

The proposed direct algorithm is conceptually simple and appropriate. However, it greatly depends on the adequate definition of the frequency threshold σ. It is expected that different values of σ generate different sets of word sequences, and consequently produce different performance rates. For instance, low σ-values allow for extracting large sequences and favor the precision rate, while high σ-values tend to generate many short sequences that support the recall percentage. Unfortunately, the most adequate σ-value is influenced by the size of the given document collection, and therefore, it need to be empirically determined for each particular situation.

In order to reduce the dependency of the classification performance to the used frequency threshold, we propose to construct the feature set by combining the maximal frequent sequences extracted by different σ-values. The idea is to construct the feature set by an iterative process, incrementing the σ-value at each step. This process starts with the inclusion of sequences corresponding to the frequency threshold $\sigma = 2$, and ends when there are no more lexical collocations (sequences of at least two words) to aggregate to the feature set. Table 2 describes the enhanced algorithm.

---

3 It is important to notice that a maximal frequent sequence may consist of only one single word.

Table 2. Enhanced Algorithm

Let D_T be the set of labeled documents that will be used for training
Let d be an anonymous document

TRAINING

1. Set the value of the frequency threshold $\sigma = 2$
2. Set the feature set $F_1 = \{\emptyset\}$
3. DO
   a. Enumerate all maximal frequent word sequences in D_T corresponding to the frequency threshold σ. Name the set of sequences S_σ
   b. Integrate new sequences to the feature set, i.e., $F_\sigma = F_{\sigma\text{-}1} \cup S_\sigma$
   c. Increment the frequency threshold; i.e., $\sigma = \sigma + 1$

   WHILE ($S_{\sigma\text{-}1}$ contains at least one sequence of two or more words not included in $F_{\sigma\text{-}2}$)
4. Build the training instances using the discovered Boolean features
5. Give the learning algorithm the training instances and perform training

CLASSIFICATION

1. Build the representation of d in accordance to the training feature space
2. Let the trained classifier label the new instance

4 Experimental Setup

4.1 Corpus

Unfortunately, there is not a standard data set for evaluating authorship attribution methods. Therefore, we had to assemble our own corpus. This corpus was gathered from the Web. It consists of 353 poems written by five different authors. Table 3 sums up some statistics about this corpus. It is important to notice that, on the one hand, the collected poems are very short documents (176 words on average), and on the other hand, that all of them correspond to contemporary Mexican poets. In particular, we were very careful on selecting modern writers in order to avoid the identification of authors by the use of anachronisms.

Table 3. Corpus Statistics

Poets	Number of documents	Size of Vocabulary	Number of Phrases	Average Words by Documents	Average Phrases by Documents
Efraín Huerta	48	3831	510	236.5	22.3
Jaime Sabines	80	3955	717	155.8	17.4
Octavio Paz	75	3335	448	162.6	27.2
Rosario Castellanos	80	4355	727	149.3	16.4
Rubén Bonifaz	70	4769	720	178.3	17.3

4.2 Classifier

The Naïve Bayes classifier has proved to be quite competitive for most text processing tasks including text classification. This fact supported our decision to use it as main classifier for our experiments. It basically computes the probability of a document d to belong to a category c_i given the set of features $F = \{f_1, f_2,\ldots, f_{|F|}\}$.[4] This probability can be expressed using Bayes' rule as follows:

$$P(c_i \mid d) = \frac{P(d \mid c_i)P(c_i)}{P(d)}$$

Simplifying and assuming statistical independence of the features:

$$P(c_i \mid d) = P(c_i)\prod_{j=1}^{|F|} P(f_j \mid c_i)$$

These probabilities can be estimated directly from the training set as follows:

$$P(c_i) = \frac{N_i}{N}, \quad P(f_j \mid c_i) = \frac{1 + N_{ji}}{|F| + \sum_{k=1}^{|F|} N_{ki}}$$

where N is the number of documents in the whole collection, N_i the number of documents of category c_i, and N_{ji} the number of documents from category c_i having the feature f_j. Finally, $|F|$ indicates the number of features.

4.3 Baseline Configurations

Because of the difficulty of comparing our approach with other previous works – mainly caused by the absence of a standard evaluation corpus–, we performed several experiments in order to establish a baseline. These experiments consider the use of four different kinds of word-based features: (i) functional words, (ii) content words, (iii) the combination of functional and content words, and (iv) word n-grams. Table 4 shows the results corresponding to each one of these approaches.

Table 4. Baseline Configurations

Features	Accuracy	Average Precision	Average Recall
Functional words	41.0%	0.42	0.39
Content words	73.0%	0.78	0.73
All kind of words	73.0%	0.78	0.74
n-grams (unigrams plus bigrams)	78.8%	0.84	0.79
n-grams (from unigrams to trigrams)	76.8%	0.84	0.77

It is important to mention that because our main interest was to determine an appropriate document characterization for authorship attribution, we used in all cases the same classification algorithm, namely, the naïve Bayes classifier. As well, we applied the same technique for dimensionality reduction (information gain) and the same evaluation schema (a 10-cross-fold validation).

The results shown in Table 4 are very interesting since they confirm some of our major assumptions. First, functional words by themselves do not help to capture the writing style from short documents. Second, content words contain some relevant information to distinguish between authors, even when all documents correspond to

4 Text classification is the problem of assigning a document d to one of a set of $|C|$ predefined categories $C = \{c_1, c_2,\ldots, c_{|C|}\}$.

the same genre and discuss similar topics. Third, the lexical collocations, captured by word n-gram sequences, are useful for the task of authorship attribution. Fourth, due to the feature explosion and the small size of the corpus, the use of higher n-gram sequences does not necessarily improve the classification performance.

5 Experimental Results

In this paper, we have proposed the use of *maximal frequent word sequences* as document features for authorship attribution. This section presents the results of two basic experiments. The first one evaluates the classification performance of the direct algorithm using different frequency thresholds (σ). The second experiment applies the enhanced algorithm. Its goal is to evaluate the impact of using a feature set that combines maximal sequences extracted by different σ-values.

In these experiments, as in the baseline generation, we used sequences considering not only content words, but also function words as well as punctuation marks. In the same way, we used the naïve Bayes classifier, the information gain technique for dimensionality reduction[5], and a 10-cross-fold validation schema.

5.1 Experiments with the Direct Algorithm

Table 5 shows the results obtained using different frequency threshold values. It can be noticed that for all σ-values our results were worst than those obtained using the n-gram features (combining unigrams and bigrams). However, it is interesting to point out that the number of sequences –for the best case– was much less than the number of n-grams, 4276 and 45245 respectively. Moreover, after the dimensionality reduction, the number of sequences was less than the number of n-grams, 203 and 455 respectively. This condition indicates that even when our method did not outperform the n-gram based approach, it could obtain a reduced set of features with a better discrimination capacity.

Table 5. Results of the Direct Algorithm

σ	Number of Sequences	Average Words per Sequence	Accuracy	Average Precision	Average Recall
2	141	2.59	68.60%	0.76	0.69
3	203	2.32	77.30%	0.82	0.77
4	225	2.26	77.30%	0.82	0.77
5	195	1.67	77.10%	0.81	0.77
6	156	1.59	75.40%	0.79	0.75
7	129	1.57	74.80%	0.78	0.74
8	124	1.50	74.20%	0.76	0.74
9	105	1.46	71.40%	0.73	0.71
10	94	1.45	70.50%	0.72	0.70

In addition, the results of Table 5 demonstrate the great influence of the frequency threshold on the classification process. It is clear that the σ-value determines the

[5] In particular, we selected all attributes with information gain greater than 1.

number and kind of discovered sequences and, therefore, it has a direct effect on the overall classification performance. In particular, it is noticeable that the accuracy decreases while increasing the frequency threshold. This is because high σ-values tend to fragment sequences, losing several relevant lexical collocations.

5.2 Experiment Using the Enhanced Algorithm

The Enhanced Algorithm (refer to section 3.2) constructs the feature set by combining maximal frequent sequences corresponding to different σ-values. In this way, it attempts diminishing the dependency of the classification performance on the used frequency threshold. Table 6 shows some data on the construction of the feature set. This process started with the inclusion of large sequences (those having more discriminatory capacity) and ended with the insertion of short sequences (those having more coverage). In total, we assembled a set of 425 features.

Tabla 6. Construction of the Enhanced Feature Set

σ	Extracted Sequences	Added Sequences	Average Length of Added Sequences	Number of Features
2	141	141	2.58	141
3	203	100	1.71	241
4	225	80	1.76	321
5	195	53	1.74	374
6	156	23	1.35	397
7	129	13	1.46	410
8	124	12	1.25	422
9	105	3	1	425

Table 7 shows the results related to the enhanced algorithm. From these results, it is clear that the enhanced algorithm not only does better than the direct algorithm, but also that it outperforms all baseline configurations. Furthermore, given that the resultant feature set is comparable in size to the n-gram set, the obtained results validate our hypothesis that determining the word sequences by their frequency of occurrence instead of by their length is a good strategy, which allows to select the most relevant word sequences and to tackle the problem of feature explosion.

Table 7. Results of the Enhanced Algorithm

Poets	Precision	Recall
Efraín Huerta	1.00	0.75
Jaime Sabines	0.83	0.83
Octavio Paz	0.95	0.75
Rosario Castellanos	0.65	0.91
Ruben Bonifaz	0.94	0.87
Average Rates	0.87	0.82
Overall Accuracy	83%	

6 Conclusions

In this paper, we proposed a new method for authorship attribution. This method is supported by the idea that a proper identification of author must consider both stylistic and topic features of documents. In particular, it characterizes the documents by a set of word sequences that combine functional and content words.

Other previous approaches for authorship attribution also characterized documents by word sequences. Specifically, they used word *n*-gram features, that is, word sequences of a fixed predefined size. In contrast to these approaches, our method considers a special kind of word sequences (namely, maximal frequent word sequences), which are determined by their frequency of occurrence instead of by their length. The experimental results demonstrated that this kind of sequences are superior to the *n*-grams, since they allow capturing the more significant lexical collocations used by an author.

It is also important to mention that our method, without using any sophisticated linguistic analysis of texts, could outperform most of the state-of-the-art approaches for authorship attribution. Furthermore, our method, on the contrary to other current approaches, is not very sensitive to the size of documents and the document collection.

As future work, we plan to apply the proposed method (document characterization) to other problems of text classification. In particular, we want to investigate the contribution of function words to topic-based text classification.

Acknowledgements

This work was done under partial support of CONACYT (project grants 43990 and U39957-Y, SEPSEBYN-C01-40), R2D2 CICYT (TIC2003-07158-C04-03) and ICT EU-India (ALA/95/23/2003/077-054).

References

1. Ahonen-Myka H. (2002). *Discovery of Frequent Word Sequences in Text Source*. Proceedings of the ESF Exploratory Workshop on Pattern Detection and Discovery. London, UK, 2002.
2. Argamon, S. & Levitan, S. (2005). *Measuring the Usefulness of Function Words for Authorship Attribution.* Association for Literary and Linguistic Computing/ Association Computer Humanities, University Of Victoria, Canada.
3. Bekkerman, R. & Allan, J. Using (2004). *Bigrams in Text Categorization*. CIIR Technical Report IR-408 Center for Intelligent Information Retrieval, University of Massachusetts Amherst.
4. Chaski, C. (2005). Who's at the Keyword? Authorship Attribution in Digital Evidence Investigations. *International Journal of Digital Evidence*. Volume 4, Issue 1.
5. Diederich, J., Kindermann, J., Leopold, E. & Paas, G. (2003). *Authorship Attribution* with Support Vector Machines. Applied Intelligence, 19(1):109-123, 2003.
6. García-Hernández, R., Martínez-Trinidad F., and Carrasco-Ochoa A. (2006). *A New Algorithm for Fast Discovery of Maximal Sequential Patterns in a Document Collection*. International Conference on Computational Linguistics and text Processing, CICLing-2006. Mexico City, Mexico, 2006.

7. Holmes, D. (1995). Authorship Attribution. *Computers and the Humanities*, 28:87-106. Kluwer Academic Publishers. 1995.
8. Kaster, A., Siersdorfer, S., & Weikum, G. (2005). *Combining Text and Linguistic Document Representations for Authorship Attribution*. Workshop Stylistic Analysis of Text for Information Access, 28th Int. SIGIR 1. MPI, Saarbrücken 2005, 27-35.
9. Malyutov, M.B. (2004). Authorship Attribution of Texts: a Review. *Proceedings of the program "Information transfer" held in ZIF*. University of Bielefeld, Germany. 2004. 17 pages.
10. Peng, F., Schuurmans, D., Keselj, V. & Wang, S. (2004). Augmenting Naïve Bayes Classifiers with Statistical Languages Models. *Information Retrieval*, vol. 7, 317-345. Kluwer Academic Publishers. 2004.
11. Stamatatos, E., Fakotakis, N. & Kokkinakis,G. Computer-Based Authorship Attribution Without Lexical Measures. *Computers and the Humanities* 35: 193-214, 2001. Kluwer Academic Publishers. 2001
12. Zhao, Y. & Zobel, J. (2005). Effective and Scalable Authorship Attribution Using Function Words. *Lecture Notes in Computer Science*, vol. 3689, 174-189. Springer Verlag. 2005.

Document Representation Based on Maximal Frequent Sequence Sets

Edith Hernández-Reyes, J. Fco. Martínez-Trinidad, J.A. Carrasco-Ochoa, and René A. García-Hernández

National Institute for Astrophysics, Optics and Electronics
Luis Enrique Erro No.1 Sta. Ma. Tonantzintla, Puebla, México C. P. 72840
{ereyes, fmartine, ariel, renearnulfo}@inaoep.mx

Abstract. In document clustering, documents are commonly represented through the vector space model as a word vector where the features correspond to the words of the documents. However, there are a lot of words in a document set; therefore the vector size could be enormous. Also, the vector space model does not take into account the word order that could be useful to group similar documents. In order to reduce these disadvantages, we propose a new document representation in which each document is represented as a set of its maximal frequent sequences. The proposed document representation is applied for document clustering and the quality of the clustering is evaluated through internal and external measures, the results are compared with those obtained with the vector space model.

1 Introduction

Currently there is a lot of digital information in the World Wide Web and the amount of digital text documents is growing every day. In consequence, we need automatic methods for organizing these text documents, because if we have organized the text documents it is easier to look for the information that we want.

Document clustering consists in dividing, automatically, a set of documents into different groups [1]. Therefore, the document clustering methods can be seen as tools which allow us to organize documents. Document clustering has been used for tasks such as information retrieval and generating hierarchies of documents [2].

In order to cluster documents, we need to represent them in a suitable way to be compared. Commonly, text documents are represented with the vector space model proposed by Salton in 1975 [3]. This model represents the documents as a word vector in which the features correspond to the words of the documents. However, the vector space model presents some disadvantages such as very high dimensionality, because a document collection can have a huge amount of different words. Another drawback, of the vector space model, is that it does not preserve the word sequential order.

The words are not the only features that can be used in order to represent documents; there is another kind of information that can be extracted from the documents, for example word sequences which appear frequently in the document. But the amount of frequent word sequences could be large; however, the amount of frequent word sequence can be reduced if only the maximal frequent sequences are used.

J.F. Martínez-Trinidad et al. (Eds.): CIARP 2006, LNCS 4225, pp. 854–863, 2006.

In this work, we propose a new document representation using the maximal frequent sequences, with this proposed representation each documents is represented as a set of its maximal frequent sequences which reduce the number of features used and preserve part of the word sequential order of the document. In order to test the proposed document representation, some document clustering experiments were done with two document collections: the English document collection Reuters-21578 [4] and the Spanish document collection Disasters. The quality obtained in the document clustering experiments, with the proposed representation, was compared against the one obtained with the vector space model, through internal and external clustering quality measures.

This paper is organized as follows. Section 2 describes the maximal frequent sequences. Section 3 introduces the new document representation. Section 4 gives the methodology used in this works and the experimental results. Finally, in section 5 we present our conclusions and some directions for future work.

2 Maximal Frequent Sequences

The text of a document is expressed by words in a sequential order. Therefore, it could be useful determining the consecutive word sequences that appear frequently in a document. Also, it is possible to determine which of the frequent sequences are not contained in any other frequent sequence *i.e.* which of them are maximal. In this work we will focus in the MFS's because they are a compact representation of the frequent sequences.

Ahonen [5] developed the first algorithm to find sequential patterns in a document collection. Recently, the MFS's have been used by Doucet [6] in the document retrieval task, his algorithm finds the MFS's from a document collection too. In [7] an algorithm to find efficiently the maximal consecutive frequent sequences of words but unlike Ahonen and Doucet algorithms from a single document was proposed.

The maximal frequent sequences are formally defined as follows [7]:

Definition 1. A sequence $P=p_1p_2...p_n$ is a subsequence of a sequence $S=s_1s_2...s_m$, denoted $P\subseteq S$, if there exists an integer $1\leq i$ such that $p_1=s_i, p_2=s_{i+1}, p_3=s_{i+2},...,p_n=s_{i+(n-1)}$.

Definition 2. Let $X\subseteq S$ and $Y\subseteq S$ then X and Y are exclusive if X and Y do not share items *i.e.*, if ($x_n=s_i$ and $y_1=s_j$) or ($y_n=s_i$ and $x_1=s_j$) then $i<j$.

Definition 3. Let T be a text expressed as a sequence, a sequence S is *frequent* in T if it is contained at least β times in T in an exclusive way, where β is the user-specified threshold.

Definition 4. A frequent sequence is *maximal* if it is not a subsequence of any other frequent sequence.

Table 1 presents, as example, two documents and their MFS's with β=2

The MFS's present some important characteristics. First, they keep the sequential order of the words; it means the MFS's do not lose the sequential order of the text. Second, the length of the MFS's is not previously determined; it is determined by the document content. And third, the MFS's can be obtained independently of the language of the documents.

In this work, the algorithm proposed in [7] was used to obtain the MFS's of each document.

Table 1. MFS's for two documents

d_1= *bank said had provided money market further billion assistance bank afternoon session brings billion bank total help compares revised shortage forecast money market.*   **MFS's** = bank, money market, billion
d_2= *bank billion provided money market late assistance system brings bank total help compares money market latest forecast shortage system today.*   **MFS's** = bank, money market, system

3 Representation Based on MFS Sets

The document representations such as vector of words have some disadvantages like high dimensionality and loss of important information from the sequential order of the original text. In order to reduce these drawbacks we propose a new document representation using MFS's. This representation consists on obtaining the MFS's from each document and use them to represent the document as a set of MFS's. For example, in Table 1 two documents, D_1 and D_2, are given and they are represented with the set of their MFS's. The first document is represented with the MFS's "bank", "billion" and "money market" and the document D_2 is represented with "bank", "money market" and "system".

In the example from table 1, with the proposed document representation, each document is represented with 3 MFS's while using the vector space model, each document would be represented with a vector of 22 words. Therefore, the number of features which are used in the proposed document representation is less than the number of features used to represent each document with the vector space model. In this sense, the problem of high dimensionality presented in the vector space model could be reduced with the proposed document representation.

It is important highlight that with the MFS's, the sequential order of the words is preserved which could help to distinguish among documents with almost the same words but in different order.

The similarity between two documents represented as MFS sets is based on the intersection of their MFS's and it is obtained with the next expression.

$$sim(d_1, d_2) = \frac{2|MFS(d_1) \cap MFS(d_2)|}{|MFS(d_1)| + |MFS(d_2)|} \quad (1)$$

Where: *MFS(dj)* is the set of MFS's of the document *j*

j=1, 2

Following the idea of the vector space model, the TF-IDF weighting can be used in order to assign a weight to each MFS in the set. Thus the weight *w* of each MFS S_i for a document d_j can be computed as the product of its frequency f in d_j and the log of its inverse frequency in the collection C.

$$w_{dj}(S_i) = fS_i(d_j)\log\left(\frac{1}{fS_i(C)}\right) \tag{2}$$

The expression (3) is another way to evaluate the similarity between two documents represented as MFS sets and taking into account the TF-IDF weighting.

$$sim(d_1,d_2) = \frac{2\left[\sum_{i=S_i\in\{MFS(d_1)\cap SFM(d_2)\}}\left[w_{d_1}(S_i) * w_{d_2}(S_i)\right]\right]}{\sum_{i=1}^{|MFS(d_1)|} w_{d_1}(S_i) + \sum_{i=1}^{|MFS(d_2)|} w_{d_2}(S_i)} \tag{3}$$

Where: $w_{dj}(S_i)$= weight in document d_j of the MFS S_i. j=1,2

If the Boolean weight is used, instead of the TF-IDF weighting, in expression (3), this expression will be the same one that the expression (1).

4 Experimentation

In order to test the proposed representation we used the Reuters-21578 and Natural Disasters collection which are written in English and Spanish, respectively. Table 2 and 3 present a description of the data used for the experiments done with Reuters-21578 and Natural Disasters collection. For each experiment, the name of the used

Table 2. Data used for the experiments with the Reuters-21578 collection

	Exp. 1	Exp. 2	Exp. 3	Exp. 4
Classes	Acq earn	Money, acq, earn	Acq, earn, crude	Gold,acq,trade, reserve,earn
Documents	100	120	120	253
Required clusters	2	3	3	5
Total words	1546	2354	2541	4294
Average of MFS's per document	5	6	7	7

Table 3. Data used for the experiments with the Natural Disasters collection

	Exp. 1	Exp. 2	Exp. 3	Exp. 4	Exp. 5	Exp. 6
Classes	Forest, hurri-cane	Forest, inundation	Drought, Inundation	Forest, earth-quake, inundation	Forest, drought, inundation	Forest, drought, hurricane
Documents	80	80	80	120	120	120
Required clusters	2	2	2	3	3	3
Total Words	4611	4583	4825	5963	6059	4593
Average of MFS's per document	8	11	12	11	22	10

classes, number of documents and the number of required clusters are shown. Also, the number of words and MFS's, from each experiment, are provided. A β=2 was used in order to extract the MFS's.

4.1 Methodology

In all the experiments, the methodology showed in figure 1 was used. We pre-processed the documents removing punctuation, numbers, special characters and stop words. Then the MFS's from each document were obtained in order to represent each document as a set of its MFS's. For extracting the MFS's, we have used the algorithm described in [7] taking the threshold β equal to 2 since it is the lowest threshold which produced longer MFS's. On the other hand, in order to represent the documents with the vector space model, the bag of words was obtained. Then, with this word set, the documents were represented as word vectors using the Boolean and TF-IDF weighting. After documents were represented with the vector space model and as MFS sets, a clustering algorithm was applied in both document representations.

For documents represented with the vector space model the cosine similarity was used. It is calculated with the next expression:

$$\cos(d_1, d_2) = \frac{(d_1 \cdot d_2)}{\|d_1\|\|d_2\|} \quad (4)$$

For our proposal document representation, the expressions 1 and 3 were used to evaluate the similarity among documents. The used clustering algorithm was the k-means algorithm.

Finally, the clustering was evaluated with internal and external quality measures [8]. Internal measures evaluate the internal cohesion and external separation of the resulting groups without using previous knowledge about the original classes of the collection. In this work, the global similarity and the global silhouette were used as internal measures. For both internal measures, higher values represent better quality of the clusters.

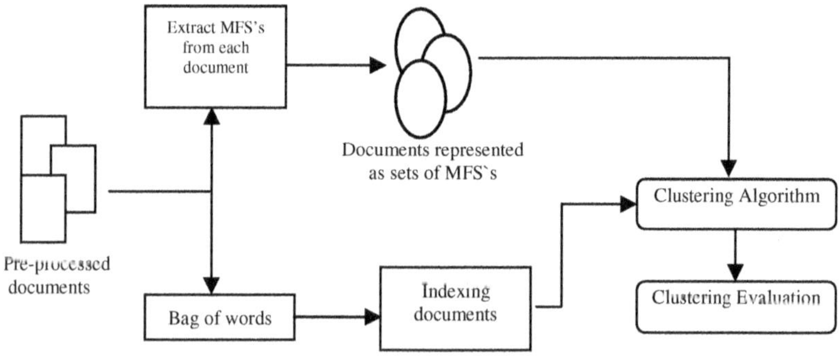

Fig. 1. Methodology of the experiments

It is appropriate to underline that in real clustering problems the original classes are unknown and for this reason the internal measures have been widely used for evaluating clustering. In spite of this, the external measures [8] are employed to evaluate the clustering quality by comparing the obtained groups against the previously defined classes, which have been determined by a human criterion. In this paper, we evaluated the clustering quality with the external measures total entropy and general F-measure. For general F-measure higher values represent better quality of the clusters and for the total entropy, smaller values represent better quality.

The internal and external measures used in this work are described in table 4.

Table 4. Internal and external measures for evaluating clustering quality

INTERNAL MEASURES

Silhouette value of the *i*th document $s(i) = \frac{MIN(AVGD\_BETWEEN(i,k) - AVGD\_WITHIN(i))}{MAX(AVGD\_WITHIN(i), AVGD\_BETWEEN(i,k))}$

AVGD_BETWEEN(i,k): average distance from the *i*-th document to all documents in other clusters.
AVGD_WHITHIN(i): average distance from the *i*-th0 document to the others documents in its own cluster.

Cluster Silhoutte $S_j = \sum_{i=1}^{|C_j|} s(i)$ $|C_j|$ = number of documents in cluster C_j

$$GlobalSilhoutte = \frac{1}{K}\sum_{j=1}^{K} S_j$$ K = number of clusters

$$GloabalSimilarity = \frac{\sum_{i=1}^{K} similarity(C_i)}{K}$$

where:
K = number of clusters
C_i = cluster i

$$Similarity(C_i) = \frac{1}{|C_i|^2}\sum_{\substack{d \in C_i \\ d' \in C_i}} \cos(d, d')$$

EXTERNAL MEASURES

$$GeneralFmeasure = \sum_{i=1}^{K}\left[\frac{|class_i|}{N}\max_{j=1..k}\{Fmeasure(i,j)\}\right]$$

where:
K = number of classes = number of clusters
$|class_i|$ = number of documents in the class i
N = total number of documents

$$Fmeasure(i,j) = \frac{2P_{ij}R_{ij}}{P_{ij}+R_{ij}}$$

P_{ij} = precision of class i with cluster j
R_{ij} = recall of class i with cluster j

$$TotalEntropy = \sum_{j=1}^{K}\frac{n_j * Entropy_j}{N}$$

where:
K = number of clusters
n_j = number of documents in cluster *i*
N = total number of documents

$$Entropy_j = -\sum_i p_{ij}\log_2(p_{ij})$$

p_{ij}= probability that a documents from the cluster *j* belongs to class *i*.

4.2 Results

The results of the experiments for the Spanish and English collections are show in tables 5 and 6, respectively. In these tables, the first column specifies the used document representation while second column shows the term weighting used for each representation, the next columns provide the results of each experiment. For each experiment the best results are highlighted.

For the experiments whit the Natural Disasters collection, table 5 shows the quality clustering, obtained by the two document representation, evaluated with the internal measures. We can observe that the document representation using MFS's obtained clusters with higher internal cohesion and external separation than the groups obtained with the word vector. This shows that using MFS's as a document representation is a good option. Also, we can observe that the best clustering quality was obtained by document representation using MFS's with Boolean weights, and the smallest quality was obtained by the word vector with TF-IDF term weighting.

Table 5. Clustering quality for the Spanish collection evaluated with the internal measures

GLOBAL SILHOUETTE							
DOCUMENT REPRESEN TATION	WEIGHT	Exp. 1	Exp. 2	Exp. 3	Exp. 4	Exp. 5	Exp. 6
Words	Boolean	0,0460	0,0421	0,0651	0,04218	0,05084	0,1623
Words	TF-IDF	0,0186	0,0213	0,0351	0,02487	0,04895	0,0612
MFS's	**Boolean**	**0,4417**	**0,3144**	**0,7192**	**0,2889**	**0,3976**	**0,5230**
MFS's	TF-IDF	0,1402	0,0848	0,2425	0,1032	0,1354	0,3240
GLOBAL SIMILARITY							
DOCUMENT REPRESEN-TATION	WEIGHT	Exp. 1	Exp. 2	Exp. 3	Exp. 4	Exp. 5	Exp. 6
Words	Boolean	0,0334	0,0331	0,0167	0,0159	0,0158	0,0618
Words	TF-IDF	0,0156	0,0164	0,0086	0,0077	0,0268	0,0169
MFS's	**Boolean**	**0,1959**	**0,1863**	**0,4372**	**0,1892**	**0,0853**	**0,0999**
MFS's	TF-IDF	0,0668	0,0596	0,1725	0,0660	0,0268	0,0599

Table 6. Clustering quality for the Spanish collection evaluated with the internal measures

GLOBAL SILHOUETTE					
DOCUMENT REPRESENTATION	WEIGHT	Exp. 1	Exp. 2	Exp. 3	Exp. 4
Words	Boolean	0,1211	0,1039	0,10314	0,1315
Words	TF-IDF	0,0722	0,0607	0,07701	0,0948
MFS's	**Boolean**	**0,4295**	**0,3654**	**0,34480**	**0,1564**
MFS's	TF-IDF	0,1825	0,1595	0,13696	0,0827
GLOBAL SIMILARITY					
DOCUMENT REPRESENTATION	WEIGHT	Exp. 1	Exp. 2	Exp. 3	Exp. 4
Words	Boolean	0,0484	0,0456	0,0194	0,0251
Words	TF-IDF	0,0228	0,0228	0,0108	0,0136
MFS's	**Boolean**	**0,1619**	**0,0689**	**0,1512**	**0,2173**
MFS's	TF-IDF	0,0543	0,0213	0,0482	0,0335

Table 6 presents the results of the clustering quality trough internal measures, obtained with the documents in English. The results show that using MFS's for representing documents, the formed groups have high internal cohesion and external separation. The biggest clustering quality was obtained by the document representation using MFS's with Boolean weights, and the smallest quality was obtained by the word vector with TF-IDF term weighting. In both tables, 5 and 6, we can see a great difference of the quality clustering obtained by the MFS's and the word vector is very huge.

In all the experiments, the number of features which were used in the proposed document representation was less than the number of features used to represent each document with the vector space model. For example, in table 2 for the English experiment 3, using the vector space model the documents were represented with 4294 features, words; and using the proposed document representation the average number of MFS's used to represent each document was 7.

In real clustering problems the original classes are unknown and for this reason the internal measures are widely used for evaluating clustering. However, in this paper, the quality clustering was evaluated with external measures too. These measures could be used because we knew the categories of the documents collections that were used.

Table 7 presents the result of the experiments with the Spanish document collection, evaluating the clustering quality with the external measures. Although the document representation using MFS's was not the best in all the experiments it was the best in most of the cases. As we mentioned before, these external measures are based on evaluating the clusters according to a previously defined classification. However we do not always have this information in real problems of document clustering.

Table 7. Quality clustering for the English collection evaluated with the external measures

GENERAL F-MEASURE							
DOCUMENT REPRESEN-TATION	WEIGHT	Exp. 1	Exp. 2	Exp. 3	Exp. 4	Exp. 5	Exp. 6
Words	Boolean	0,9875	1	0,9624	0,9492	0,9412	0,9499
Words	TF-IDF	1	1	0,9498	0,9492	0,9497	0,9499
MFS's	Boolean	0,9875	1	0,6521	0,9749	0,9751	0,9834
MFS's	TF-IDF	0,9875	1	0,9750	0,9624	0,9916	0,9833
TOTAL ENTROPY							
DOCUMENT REPRESEN-TATION	WEIGHT	Exp. 1	Exp. 2	Exp. 3	Exp. 4	Exp. 5	Exp. 6
Words	Boolean	0	0	0,1450	0,0565	0,2141	0,1921
Words	TF-IDF	0	0	0,1962	0,0565	0,2141	0,1526
MFS's	Boolean	0	0	0,9344	0,1450	0,1537	0,1133
MFS's	TF-IDF	0	0	0,1686	0,1962	0,0565	0,1127

Table 8 presents the results of the experiment with the English document collection, evaluating the clustering quality with the external measures. The word vector and document representation using MFS's, both obtained very similar results, and in some cases they were tied.

Table 8. Quality clustering for the English collection evaluated with the external measures

		GENERAL F-MEASURE			
DOCUMENT REPRESENTATION	WEIGHT	Exp. 1	Exp. 2	Exp. 3	Exp. 4
Words	Boolean	0,8886	1	0,90756	0,9123
Words	TF-IDF	0,8886	1	0,90756	0,9123
MFS's	Boolean	0,8782	0,9007	1	1
MFS's	TF-IDF	0,8782	0,8946	1	0,8547
		TOTAL ENTROPY			
DOCUMENT REPRESENTATION	WEIGHT	Exp. 1	Exp. 2	Exp. 3	Exp. 4
Words	Boolean	0,4152	0	0,39332	0,4229
Words	TF-IDF	0,4152	0	0,39332	0,4229
MFS's	Boolean	0,4394	0,4099	0	0
MFS's	TF-IDF	0,4394	0,4381	0	0,4678

5 Conclusion

In this paper, we have introduced a new document representation based on MFS's where each document is represented as a set of MFS's. The number of features which are used in the proposed document representation is less than the number of features used to represent each document with the vector space model. In this sense, the problem of high dimensionality presented in the vector space model could be reduced with the proposed document representation. The experiments established that using the maximal frequent as document representation is a good option for document clustering.

Some experiments were made using two documents collections, the results showed that the documents represented as sets of MFS's always obtained clusters with best internal cohesion and external separation. Also, the quality clustering was evaluated with external measures and the document representation using MFS's obtained better quality in most of the experiments.

The objective of the work was to analyze the MFS's performance as document representation for document clustering. However the MFS's have some useful characteristics that could improve even more the document clustering, therefore as future work we propose defining a new way to evaluate the similarity among documents represented by MFS's.

References

1. Zhong Su, Li Zhang, Yue Pan. Document Clustering Based on Vector Quatization and Growing-Cell Structure. Lecture Notes in Computer Science vol. 2718, pp. 326-336, Springer-Verlag 2003.
2. Yoelle S., Fagin, Ronald, Ben-Shaul, Israel Z. y Pelleg, Dan. Ephemeral Document Clustering for Web Applications. IBM Research. Report RJ 10186, 2000.
3. G. Salton, A. Wang, C.S. Yang. A Vector Space Model for Information Retrieval. Journal of the American Society for information Science, pp. 613-620, 1975.
4. [http://www.ics.uci.edu/~kdd/databases/reuters21578/reuters21578.html]
5. Helena Ahonen-Myka. Finding All Maximal Frequent Sequences in Text. Proc. of the ICML99 Workshop on Machine Learning in Text Data Analysis, pp. 11-17, 1999.

6. Antoine Daucet. Advanced Document Description, a Sequential Approach. Thesis PhD. University of Helsinki Finland. 2005.
7. René A. García-Hernández, José Fco. Martínez-Trinidad and Jesús Ariel Carrasco-Ochoa, A Fast Algorithm to Find All the Maximal Frequent Sequences in a Text, 9th Iberoamerican Congress on Pattern Recognition (CIARP'2004), Lecture Notes in Computer Science vol. 3287, pp. 478-486, Springer-Verlag 2004.
8. M. Steinbach, G. Karypis, V. Kumar. A Comparison of Document Clustering Techniques. Proc. Text mining workshop, KDD, 2000.

Building an Optimal WSD Ensemble Using Per-Word Selection of Best System

Harri M.T. Saarikoski[1] and Steve Legrand[2]

[1] KIT Language Technology Doctorate School, Helsinki University, Finland
Harri.Saarikoski@helsinki.fi
[2] Department of Computer Science, University of Jyväskylä, Finland
stelegra@cc.jyu.fi

Abstract. In Senseval workshops for evaluating WSD systems [1,4,9], no one system or system type (classifier algorithm, type of system ensemble, extracted feature set, lexical knowledge source etc.) has been discovered that resolves all ambiguous words into their senses in a superior way. This paper presents a novel method for selecting the best system for target word based on readily available word features (number of senses, average amount of training per sense, dominant sense ratio). Applied to Senseval-3 and Senseval-2 English lexical sample state-of-art systems, a net gain of approximately 2.5 - 5.0% (respectively) in average precision per word over the best base system is achieved. The method can be applied to any base system or target word in any language.

1 Introduction

Based on recent evaluation of WSD systems, progress in disambiguation methods have reached a standstill. The 15 best systems in Senseval-3 English sample task ended up within 2% of each other [10] while in Senseval-2 the number of systems within that range was only five [1]. Numerous methods of disambiguation have been tried out in Senseval evaluations. For instance, most classifiers found effective in data mining experiments have been tried out: in Senseval-3 for example there were experiments with support vector machines (IRST-kernel, nusels), Naive Bayes (CLaC1, all htsa systems), Neural Networks (MC-WSD, UJAEN) and Maximum Entropy algorithms (HKUST-me, CLaC2) [10]. Multi-classifier experiments have also been very popular [3,19,12,17]: in Senseval-3 evaluation, classifier ensembles were as popular as single-classifier systems (e.g. SyntaLex, NRC, HKUST-all and BCU systems, and Duluth-ELSS) [10].

The first conclusion from these experiments has been that different disambiguation methods result in different performance results. A second conclusion is that there is a 'word bias', i.e. each word poses a different set of learning problems. To solve these biases, all we need is an exact definition of the type of system that is best equipped to handle a particular target word. [18] showed that word grain, amount of training and most frequent (dominant) sense bias in training data are factors that have a profound influence on system performance. For instance, disambiguating a hard word (40

J.F. Martínez-Trinidad et al. (Eds.): CIARP 2006, LNCS 4225, pp. 864 – 872, 2006.

senses, average of 4 training examples per sense out of which dominant sense gets 25%) is a different type of learning task than disambiguating an easy word (2-sense word with 40 examples at 80% dominant share). Since classifiers have different solutions to deal with the different learning tasks, it is reasonable to assume that system strengths tend to follow changes (drops and rises) in these three word factors. We further propose that system strength is focused on a particular region of this 'word space' (see Figures 1 and 2), which allows effective predictors of best system per word to be built.

This paper presents a novel method using the three word features that fairly accurately predicts the strong regions of given base systems. To our knowledge, only one such per-word ensemble using word features as system selection criterion has been implemented [11] where they selected the system according to target word part-of speech. Despite the fact that the two-system ensemble ended up at the bottom of the Senseval-2 evaluation (20% off the state of the art), it still achieved three wordwins, which indicates the viability of the per-word selection method in general.

In section 2, we present the machine-learning tools we used for predictions. In section 3, we define the three word-based factors and the predictors built on them. In section 4, we present the disambiguation method based on those predictors, and in section 5, we test the method in practice on two different datasets. Sections 6 and 7 discuss and conclude on the findings.

2 MOA-SOM Toolkit

Study of disambiguation systems lacks a diagnostic tool that could be used to meta-learn the effects of these factors. As a result, the following types of questions are largely unanswered: Which are the words where a system is at its strongest? What type of ensembles of systems achieve optimum performance for give target word?

We are developing a meta-classifier (MOA-SOM, 'mother-of-all-self-organizing-maps') to handle such learning tasks. The tool clusters publicly available WSD system scores [10,1,4] stored in database [13] based on features defining the systems (e.g. classifier algorithm, feature sets) and target words (e.g. PoS, training, word grain) by calculating the amount of correlation between systems and words. The output from MOA-SOM is the optimal classifier, feature and configuration for that target word. The feature matrix can be fed to SOM using either system names as labels and words as data points or vice versa. The SOM used is based on hierarchically clustering DGSOT [7] which was found useful in earlier WSD experiments [6]. For these tests we additionally employed the machine-learning algorithms implemented in Weka toolkit [16] for predictors.

In the next section, we present the three factors in more detail and how we combined them to build machine-learning predictors of system differences.

3 Predictor Building

In this section we present the factors predicting system performance and the predictors using those factors for prediction of system differences.

3.1 Factors

We introduce here the three word-based factors in explaining variations in system performance (Train, Grain, and DomSub). *Train* is average number of training instances per sense, *Grain* is the number of senses (as recorded in WordNet / WordSmyth sense repositories used in Senseval evaluations). DomSub is aimed to differentiate between systems that differ in their inherent bias to deal with big vs small dominant (most frequent) sense shares. The formula we used for DomSub is `DomSub = dom² + sub²` where *dom* and *sub* are the shares of dominant and subdominant sense out of all training instances for the current target word[1]. For example, for a word with 80% / 20% shares for dominant / subdominant senses, DomSub is $0.8^2 + 0.2^2 = 0.68$.

Next we present the types of predictors we used in our experiments.

3.2 Predictors

A few factor formulas emerged as best predictors of system difference predictors. To train the predictors, we used both manual rules and machine-learning algorithms:

(1) Bisections (baseline). To achieve a bisection baseline, we first sort the data according to a selected factor (e.g. T, G, D, T+G+D), then split the data in two and calculate the net gain by each system for each half and average that by dividing it by two. The best weighting scheme we found was the square root of the unweighted sum of normalized values of the three factors: `sqrt (a*T + b*G + c*D)` where *G* stands for Grain, *T* for Train, *D* for DomSub values of target words and integers *a*, *b* and *c* normalize the weights of the three factors. Note that since this set of predictors is limited to one factor at a time, it cannot express decision rules containing multiple factors which tends to make them less reliable.

(2) Machine-learned models. To predict the best system for words, we trained some of the most efficient learning algorithms implemented in Weka toolkit [16] (Support Vector Machine, Maximum Entropy, Naive Bayes, Decision Trees, Random Forests as well as voting committee, training data bagging and algorithm boosting methods). For training we used the abovementioned word factors both individually and in various permutations (e.g. T-G).

Next we outline the method of using these predictors for system-word pairing.

4 Method

In this section, we outline a method for defining and selecting maximally complementary base systems integrated inside a disambiguation algorithm:

1. **Base system selection.** Run candidate base systems on training words. Investigate their performance at different types of words. Based on their performance at training words, select systems whose strong regions are as large and as distinct as possible using the following criteria:

---

[1] We consider the increment from the rest of the senses (typically < 0.05) as largely negligible.

- biggest gross gain (see Evaluation) from candidate base systems
- largest number of training words won by the system

2. **Training the predictor.** Using the training run data, train the predictors to recognize the best base system using readily available factors (e.g. word grain). Predictor can be constructed by setting decision rules manually, e.g. "use system#1 (Decision Tree -based) when number of senses (grain) < 5, system#2 (Naive Bayes -based) when grain is > 5 but not when 20 < train < 25". Alternatively, use a machine-learning algorithm to induce the rules from the training data.
3. **Testing.** Run selected base systems and the ensemble (according to the best predictor for that ensemble) on test words.
4. **Evaluation.** Evaluate the ensemble by comparing it to the better of the base systems. Also evaluate the predictor using *net gain* measure calculated from the following formula:

```
((PredictionAccuracy - (1.0 / NumberOfSystems))
                  *2)
             * GrossGain
```

PredictionAccuracy is the number of correct system-for-word predictions out of all test words and *NumberOfSystems* is the number of classes/systems to predict. *GrossGain* is a measure of the potential of the base systems when they form an ensemble, resulting from a perfect system-for-word prediction for all test words. It is calculated from all-words average net gain by either base system (e.g. in a test set of two words, if system#1 wins over system#2 by 2% at word#1 and system#2 wins over system#1 by 4% at word#2, then gross gain for all test words is (2+4) / 2 = 3%). Net gain is then calculated as follows: in a two-system ensemble with 0.80 prediction accuracy and 8.0% gross gain, net gain is ((0.80-0.50)*2)) * 8.0% = 4.8%. It should be noted that in a two-system prediction task, prediction accuracy of 0.50 results in zero net gain, same as random selection of system.

Next we apply this method to two separate Senseval datasets (four prediction tasks each), using state of the art systems and predictors that proved best in our tests.

5 Testing

In this section, we apply the method to two Senseval evaluations.

5.1 Senseval-2 English Lexical Sample

System Selection. We trained the predictors with 39 words [2] and considered all supervised systems as candidates for base systems [3]. We selected the systems based on criteria in Step 1 of the method: looking at wins by best systems in training words, SMU [9] got 10 wins, JHU [17] nine, KUN(LP) [14] got four and CS(224N) [8] three.

---

[2] We discarded words where the wordwinner system's margin over next best system was < 2%.

[3] We ignored low-recall (<99%) and low-precision (> 4% behind best) systems.

Strong region of the latter was almost identical the same as that of JHU, yet smaller, and even though the abovementioned Alicante system [8] scored 3 wordwins, it cannot be used because of its poor overall performance (20% behind top) (criteria 3). In Figure 1, we see the Train-Grain regions (most important criteria 1) of the two top 'wordwinners' (SMU and JHU).

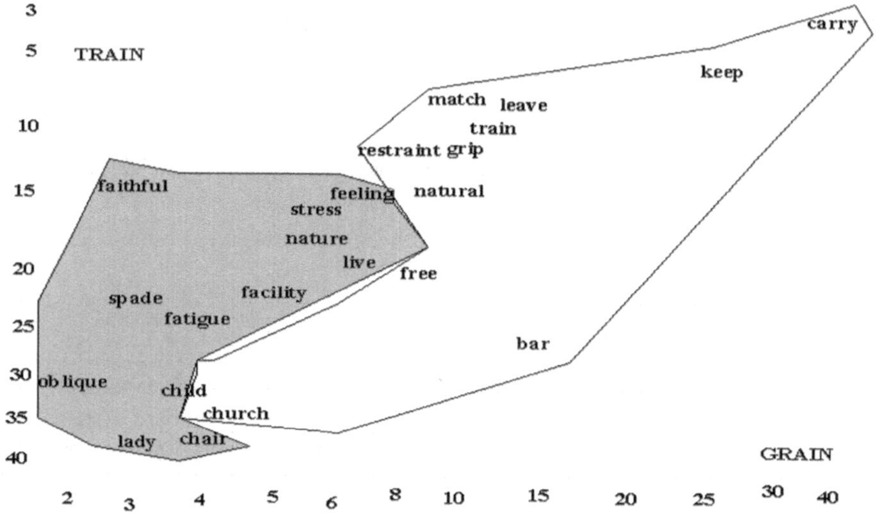

Fig. 1. Strong regions of two Senseval-2 systems in Train-Grain space (sample of training words shown). JHU region can be found on right (mid/high-grain), SMU region on left (low-grain, mid/high-train).

Table 1. Results from applying the method on selected base systems from Senseval-2

system pair (gross gain)	best predictor (factor/classifier)	prediction accuracy	net gain of ensemble
JHU+SMU (8.0%)	(1) (T-G) / (T+G)	0.63	2.6%
	(2) SVM *	0.80	4.8%
SMU+KUN (**8.4%**)	(1) T+G+D	0.70	3.4%
	(2) SVM	**0.82**	**5.0%**
JHU+KUN (5.5%)	(1) T+G+D	0.56	1.7%
	(2) SVM	0.75	2.8%
JHU+SMU+KUN (9.5%)	(3) SVM	0.55 [4]	4.2%

We see from Figure 1 that SMU and JHU populate distinct and large learning regions in Grain-Train space. KUN (not showing) also occupies a large region, focused on high-grain, low-train words such as *call* and *dress* and would be located approximately between JHU's strong words *keep* and *leave*.

[4] Note that having three systems to predict yields a naturally lower prediction accuracy.

Strength of KUN is, however, in the steady quality of its performance with all words, not manifesting any huge drops with any word.

Testing. We tested the model(s) on 19 words and three possible two-system combinations of the three top wordwinning systems (SMU, JHU and KUN) as well as an ensemble of all three systems.

SMU+KUN appears to have the highest gross gain, prediction accuracy and net gain, making it the maximally complementary system pair for this dataset. Furthermore, it seems that 3-system prediction (JHU+SMU+KUN) with more gross gain loses to 2-system predictions in prediction accuracy ending up with a slightly lower net gain.

5.2 Senseval-3 English Lexical Sample

System Selection. We trained the predictors again with 39 words and considered 15 top systems and selected the three top wordwinners for candidate base systems: IRST-kernel [15] with 8, htsa3 [2] 4 and nusels [5] with 3 training words won. Let us investigate the strong Train-Grain regions of the two top wordwinners.

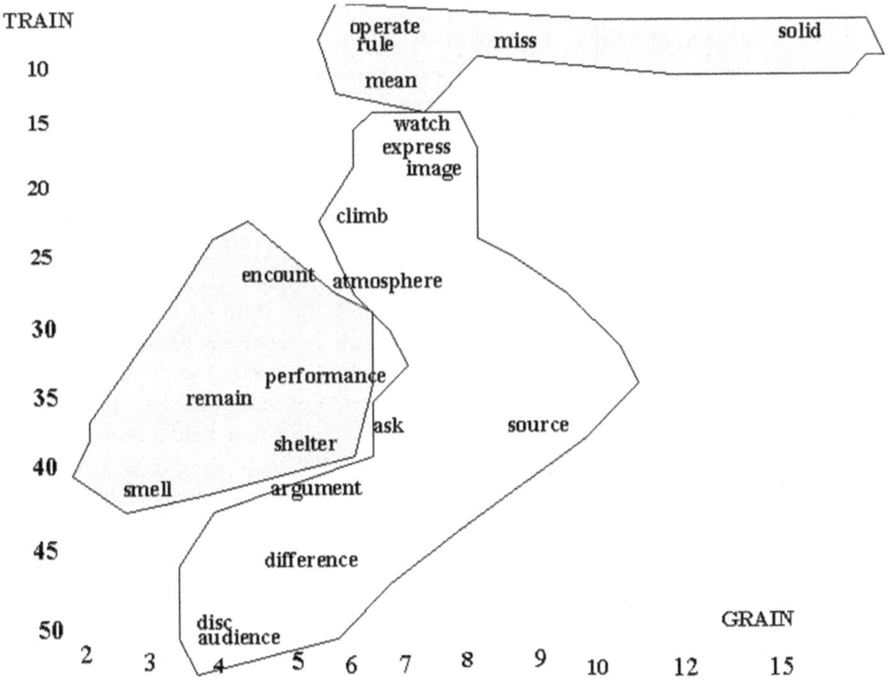

Fig. 2. Strong regions of two Senseval-3 systems in Train-Grain space (sample of training words shown). htsa3 is the lighter shade intact region in the middle, IRST-kernel holds the other two regions, one on left, one on top.

These two systems (htsa3 and IRST-kernel) complement each other very well. IRST-kernel occupies two regions but since training data contains no words from this area the regions cannot be merged.

Testing. We tested the model on 19 words and three two-system combinations of the three wordwinning systems (htsa3, IRST-kernel and nusels) as well as an ensemble of all three systems.

Table 2. Results from applying the method on selected base systems from Senseval-3

system pair (gross gain)	best predictor (factor/classifier)	prediction accuracy	net gain of ensemble
htsa3+IRST-kernel (4.1%)	(1) T+G+D	0.80	2.5%
	(2) NaiveBayes	**0.82**	**2.7%**
htsa3+nusels (3.6%)	(1) T+G+D	0.65	1.2%
	(2) DecisionTree	0.70	1.4%
nusels+ IRST-kernel (**4.4%**)	(1) (T-G) / (T+G)	0.80	2.6%
	(2) SVM	0.80	2.6%
htsa3+IRSTk+nusels (6.1%)	(2) MaxEnt	0.55	**2.7%**

Table 2 shows nusels+IK is the maximally complementary system pair in terms of net gain but another system pair (nusels+IRST-kernel) has the higher potential (gross gain). It should also be noted that the more challenging three-system prediction task (htsa3+IRSTk+nusels) produces equally high net gain as htsa3+IRST-kernel pair.

6 Discussion

Best predictors turned out to vary according to base system pair, both in terms of learning algorithm and input features. The most reliable learning algorithms turned out to be Support Vector Machines and slightly less consistently Maximum Entropy and Naive Bayes classifiers. Machine-learning models (2) tend to work better than the corresponding bisection baseline (1). The contribution of individual factors to system differentiation seems to depend heavily on the base system pair: combination of factors tended to work better than individual factors but there were (e.g. T+G+D for SMU/JHU pair) but sometimes one factor differentiated better (e.g. DomSub for IRST-kernel/htsa3). These findings lead us to conclude that this system prediction task - just like word sense disambiguation task itself - is in fact a set of tasks dependent on details and the difficulty of the task, and therfore, a customized predictor may need to be developed for given system pair.

7 Conclusion

We have presented a novel method for constructing effective WSD system ensembles. Predictors built on word-based factors (Grain, Train, DomSub) seem to yield very good predictions of optimal systems for words. The method was tested with two evaluations: in Senseval-2 the best net gain was 5.0% (out of maximal 8.4%) for

SMU/JHU pair, while in the more contested Senseval-3 it was 2.7% (out of 4.1%) for three-system ensemble (htsa3/IRST-kernel/nusels). The method is scalable to any ambiguous word and any assortment of base systems and the factors used to build predictors are readily available for all words.

Although most predictors exceed random selection baseline (zero net gain), further work is needed to make the prediction method more accurate and thereby maximize net gain. It should be kept in mind that base systems and their optimal predictors form a pair. Based on a more covering set of factors, we can then learn more reliable predictors, including for more than two or three systems. Particularly we need to account for other factors found influential to system performance: choice of feature sets [6,18] as well as choice of the classifier algorithm as well as the specifics of its sense decision procedure [2,18,19]. We also believe it is possible to fabricate two strong, 'opposite' systems that together optimally cover the word space, which probably makes predictions more reliable too. Furthermore, as with any supervised prediction system, providing more training words to a machine learner is likely to improve prediction accuracy (e.g. all the 165 English words and around 100 systems that have participated in the three English Senseval evaluations). Evaluation data from other languages can also be used since our preliminary comparisons with Spanish Senseval-2 data indicate that the same systems (JHU, CS, Duluths, UMCP) that excelled in a particular region in the English evaluation did so in Spanish as well. This phenomenon can be explained by the language-independence of both word factors and WSD systems and suggests that it is possible to build one 'optimal ensemble' that would be as effective for all languages.

Acknowledgments

Authors would like to express their gratitude to professor Alexander Gelbukh of Instituto Politecnico Nacional, Mexico, for his review of our paper. Work of first author is supported by Department of Translation Studies (Language Technology Doctorate School) of Helsinki University, Finland, and second author by COMAS Doctorate School of Jyväskylä University and Instituto Politecnico Nacional, Mexico.

References

1. Edmonds, P., and Kilgarriff, A. Introduction to the Special Issue on evaluating word sense disambiguation programs. Journal of Natural Language Engineering 8(4) (2002).
2. Grozea, C. Finding optimal parameter settings for high performance word sense disambiguation. In SENSEVAL-3: Third International Workshop on the Evaluation of Systems for the Semantic Analysis of Text, Barcelona, Spain (2004).
3. Hoste, V., Hendrickx, I., Daelemans, W. and A. van den Bosch. Parameter optimization for machine-learning of word sense disambiguation. Journal of Natural Language Engineering, 8(4) (2002) 311-327.
4. Kilgarriff, A. SENSEVAL: An Exercise in Evaluating Word Sense Disambiguation Programs. In Proceedings of LREC, Granada (1998) 581--588.
5. Lee, Y-K., Ng, H-T., and Chia, T-K. Supervised Word Sense Disambiguation with Support Vector Machines and Multiple Knowledge Sources. In Proceedings of SENSEVAL-3 workshop (2004).

6. Legrand, S., Pulido JGR. A Hybrid Approach to Word Sense Disambiguation: Neural Clustering with Class Labeling. Knowledge Discovery and Ontologies workshop at 15th European Conference on Machine Learning (ECML) (2004).
7. Luo, F., Khan, L., Bastani F., Yen I-L and Zhou, J. A dynamically growing self-organizing tree (DGSOT) for hierarchical clustering gene expression profiles, Bioinformatics 2004 20(16):2605-2617, Oxford University Press.
8. Manning, C., Tolga Ilhan, H., Kamvar, S., Klein, D. and Toutanova, K. Combining Heterogeneous Classifiers for Word-Sense Disambiguation. Proceedings of SENSEVAL-2, Second International Workshop on Evaluating WSD Systems (2001) 87-90.
9. Mihalcea, R. Word sense disambiguation with pattern learning and automatic feature selection. Journal of Natural Language Engineering, 8(4) (2002) 343-359.
10. Mihalcea, R., Kilgarriff, A. and Chklovski, T. The SENSEVAL-3 English lexical sample task. Proceedings of SENSEVAL-3 Workshop at ACL (2004).
11. Montoyo, A. and Suárez, A. The University of Alicante word sense disambiguation system. Proceedings of SENSEVAL-2 Workshop (2001) 131-134.
12. Mooney, R. Comparative experiments on disambiguating word senses: An illustration of the role of bias in machine learning. Proceedings of the Conference on Empirical Methods in Natural Language Processing (1996).
13. Saarikoski, H. mySENSEVAL: Explaining WSD System Performance Using Target Word Features. In NLDB-05, Natural Language for Databases: Proceedings of 10th International Conference on Applications of Natural Language Processing to Information Systems. Lecture Notes in Computer Science, N 3513, Springer (2005) 369–371.
14. Seo, H-C., Rim, H-C. and Kim, S-H. KUNLP system in Senseval-3. Proceedings of SENSEVAL-2 Workshop (2001) 222-225.
15. Strapparava, C., Gliozzo, A., and Giuliano, C. Pattern abstraction and term similarity for Word Sense Disambiguation: IRST at Senseval-3. In Proceedings of SENSEVAL-3 workshop (2004).
16. Witten, I., Frank, E. Data Mining: Practical Machine Learning Tools and Techniques (Second Edition). Morgan Kaufmann (2005).
17. Yarowsky, D., S. Cucerzan, R. Florian, C. Schafer and R. Wicentowski. The Johns Hopkins SENSEVAL2 System Descriptions. Proceedings of SENSEVAL-2 workshop (2002).
18. Yarowsky, D. and Florian, R. Evaluating sense disambiguation across diverse parameter spaces. Journal of Natural Language Engineering, 8(4) (2002) 293-311.
19. Zavrel, J., S. Degroeve, A. Kool, W. Daelemans, K. Jokinen. Diverse Classifiers for NLP Disambiguation Tasks. Comparisons, Optimization, Combination, and Evolution. TWLT 18. Learning to Behave. CEvoLE 2 (2000) 201–221

Pixel-Wise Histograms for Visual Segment Description and Applications*

Alvaro Pardo[1,2]

[1] DIE, Facultad de Ingeniería y Tecnologías, Universidad Católica del Uruguay
[2] IIE, Facultad de Ingeniería, Universidad de la República
apardo@ucu.edu.uy

Abstract. In this work we present an overview of several methods that extract information from a video segment using pixel-wise histograms or pixel-wise probability distributions. We will show that most of these algorithms that have been presented in the literature are specific implementations of a more general approach. Finally, we will present some applications based on these ideas to video segment retrieval and target detection in surveillance applications with static and dynamic backgrounds. We present a visual segment descriptor based on pixel-wise histograms that outperforms similar reviewed methods. In this way we show the advantages on this approach for this kind of problems.

1 Introduction

The idea of pixel-wise information for video segment processing has been extensively studied in the literature. Probably, one of the most known algorithms in this area is the one of static background learning for object detection. In this case each pixel from the background is represented by its mean value. The mean value can be calculated online or offline taking a set of frames and estimating the mean or median for each pixel in the background. When the background is static these procedures estimate the true value of the background removing undesired variations. In other cases, although the background is physically static, for instance a street crossing, it changes along time due to illumination changes. Although, the same ideas can be applied taking a long set of frames to estimate the background, the most effective systems remove lightning and shadows computing an intrinsic image of the scene [1].

Another possible improvement is to assign to each pixel a Gaussian distribution that is represented with its mean and variance [2]. That is, in each pixel we have a probability distribution of background pixels along time. With this probability distribution we can evaluate each pixel in a new frame to judge if it belongs to the background or moving object. Once again, the estimation of the mean and variance can be done online or offline. The advantage of Gaussian distributions is that all the information is encoded in only two values per pixel. On the other hand, the disadvantage of this approach is that not always the

* Supported by Proyecto PDT-S/C/OP/17/07.

J.F. Martínez-Trinidad et al. (Eds.): CIARP 2006, LNCS 4225, pp. 873–882, 2006.

background obeys a Gaussian distribution. This can be considered true when the background is static and background variations can be taken as Gaussian. However, when the background is slowly changing due to waving trees, water, etc, its variations do not follow a Gaussian distribution and other methods must be considered.

To capture more general background distributions we can consider a mixture of Gaussians (MoG) or any other parametric distribution [3]. Parametric distributions are interesting since they can be encoded with a set of parameters. For now on, we will consider MoG. The most difficult problem in the use of MoG is the selection of the number of Gaussians to be used. Although there are methods that automatically estimate the number of Gaussians [4] they tend to overestimate it leading to overfitting to the training data.

This led us to non-parametric probability estimators like histograms or kernel methods, for instance see [5,6,7]. In this case no assumptions need to be made on advance; only the kernel must be selected. The drawback is the great amount of data that is obtained as we end up with a vector of probabilities with a length equal to the number of colors bins used. Nevertheless, we must consider the following facts. First, data storage is no longer a limitation nowadays. Second, the process done in each pixel is exactly the same so it can be successfully implemented in hardware or in parallel.

The problem of static background estimation has received a lot of attention in the literature. Although, there is always room for improvement we believe one of the most challenging problems is dynamic backgrounds. This is an important and practical case. In outdoor surveillance the cameras are exposed to wind and other factors that affect the captured background resulting in backgrounds which are rarely completely static. Weaving trees, water, weather conditions, etc, causes that background to slowly change along time. Abrupt and big changes are difficult to model with low level features because they cannot be distinguished from other truly moving objects. Recently several approaches have been proposed to deal with non-static backgrounds [6].

Now we are going to discuss other applications where information from a set of frames must be extracted either online or offline. In video analysis, the entire video is partitioned into basic units which we define as video segments (VS). Each VS is composed by a set of consecutive frames. For video indexing and retrieval the visual content of the VS must be extracted. In the literature there are several approaches to this problem. The most basic solutions is to summarize the VS in one or more key frames. These key frames can be any of the frames within the video segment, or other criteria such as color or motion can be used to select the best set of key frames [8]. Although this is a straight forward solution its performance is relatively poor. To obtain a more stable and global visual description color histograms computed using all frames in the video segment must be used [9]. For example, mean histogram, median histogram or alpha-trimmed histograms. As is well known, global histograms do not provide any spatial information and different VS with similar color content may produce erroneous retrievals.

As a solution to this problem in [10] the authors propose to compute pixel-wise based histograms. In this way this description provides the probability of occurrence of a given pixel in a given spatial position. They propose two VS descriptors. The first one constructs a frame where each pixel corresponds to the value with maximum probability. To improve the retrieval power, the second descriptor considers more values for each pixel. That is, in the proposal, after the computation of the histogram the descriptors retain only a small set of values representing the most likely ones defined as peaks in the histogram.

As we can see in both problems overviewed above, we need to extract the visual content of VS. In the first case of background modeling, we need to learn the visual content of the background to detect moving objects in the scene. For VS indexing and retrieval we need visual content descriptions to unambiguously describe them. As we saw in the literature there are several algorithms that propose online or offline pixel-wise estimators for the VS visual content. Here we are going to show that most of them fall in the same category and can be seen as specific implementations of a more general method of pixel-wise histogram or probability estimation. Contrary to existing methods we are going to exploit all the information in the pixel-wise histograms to show its potential. We do not want to address the study of the different techniques for effective and efficient estimators. Our goal is to formulate the problem in a general setting while showing the possible improvements that can be achieved when using all the information from the pixel-wise probability distributions estimators.

2 Proposed Method

Lets suppose that we have a video segment with a set of frames $\{f_1, ..., f_n\}$. Then we define the pixel-wise video segment histogram at pixel x as $H(x;q)$ and the probability of occurrence $p(x;q)$ of each color bin q.

Once we have $H(x;q)$ we can compute several statistical descriptions used for background modeling such as: mean or median background, fit a Gaussian to each pixel distribution, fit a MoG or any parametric distribution to this data [2,3], compute minimal and maximal values per pixel as used in [11]. So, $H(x;q)$ contains all the information needed to implement these methods. Furthermore, some of them summarize the information contained in $H(x,q)$ in a small set of parameters: mean, median, variance, maximal and minimal values, etc.

For video indexing and retrieval applications with $H(x;q)$ we can compute the classical per-frame histograms [9] or the recently proposed keyframe in [10].

As we can see several methods can be seen as simplifications of pixel-wise $H(x;q)$ and $p(x;q)$. In order to support the benefits of increasing the amount of data retained, in next section, we evaluate the performance of the proposed method with two applications: VS description and background modeling. In the case of VS description we are going to apply an offline method while in the later one we are going to test an online one.

3 Applications

3.1 VS Description

Here we present a VS descriptor that considers all the information in $H(x;q)$ or $p(x;q)$, i.e., we are going to compute and store them for each VS.

For VS retrieval we consider $g(x)$ as the query frame. The distance between this frame and the VS is computed in a probabilistic sense. For each pixel we have the probability of $g(x)$ to occur at x within the VS as: $p(x, B(g(x)))$ where $B(g(x))$ maps colors to bin histograms. Assuming independence and taking the logarithm the probabilistic distance between $g(x)$ and the visual segment is defined as:

$$PD(g, VS) = \sum_{k=1}^{n} \log p(x_k, B(g(x_k))),$$

where n is the number of pixels in the frame.

Now we are going to show that this method improves the results of the method proposed in [10] since it considers the entire histogram and not a representative set of values. In this way we capture a more precise description of the VS. As we can see in Figures 1 and 2 it has two main advantages. First, if we concentrate on the distances of frames within the VS our method produces more stable results. Second, if we compare the distance for frames outside the VS the PD is always greater than the one proposed in [10] (TMOF). In [10] the authors propose another descriptor that uses the k pixels with maximum frequencies to improve the results. According to our experiments, several histograms within VS have a unique maximum.

In Figure 1 we show the distance of each frame to a given VS (shot) in the sequence using PD and TMOF. The results are normalized in each case with respect to the closest frame to the descriptor. This sequence is a challenging one due to its almost constant blueish color. In Figure 1(b) we show the distance to the first VS (frames 1 to 154), in Figure 1(c) the distances to the second VS (frames 155 to 215), and in Figure 1(d) the last VS (frames 791 to 959). In all cases the proposed PD outperforms the method TMOF. The last VS (frames 791 to 959) contains strong variations in scene content, however, the results are still very stable. In this case is clear how the PD outperforms TMOF. When considering TMOF there are frames outside the VS that are closer than other frames within the VS. This is not a problem in the case of PD. Furthermore, the variations inside the VS are almost constant and its variations are insignificant with respect to the ones of TMOF.

For the second example in Figure 2 we consider a sequence with a gradual transition at frame 128. Therefore, the descriptors of adjacent VS contain some mixing of information. Even though this, the results of PD outperforms the ones of TMOF.

To further test the performance of PD against TMOF we segmented three sequences in shots, computed the VS description for each shot in the sequences, and retrieved the shot using each frame in the sequence as a query. The first sequence used was Jamie (Figure 1(a)). In this case PD gave a 0% of errors.

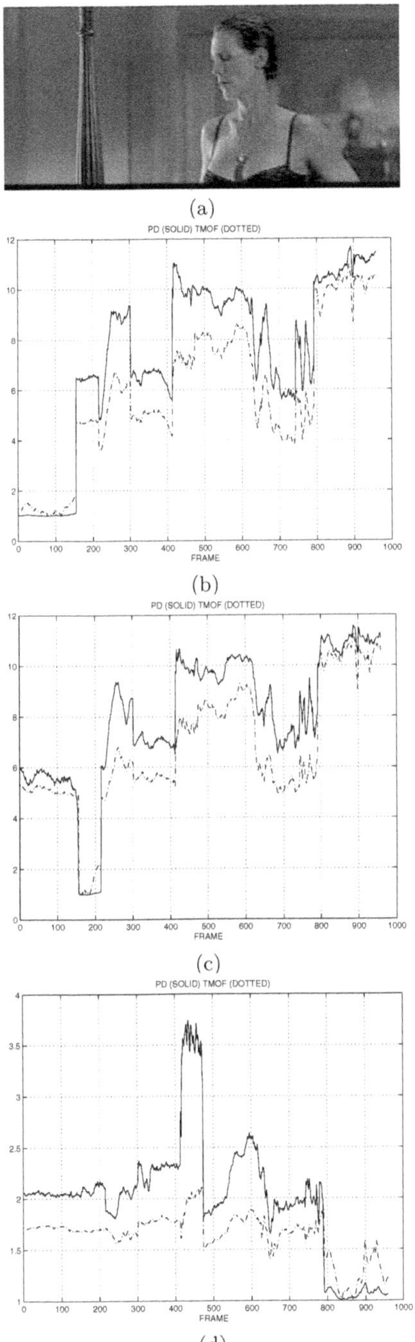

Fig. 1. Jamie sequence. (a) First frame. Comparison of PD(solid) against TMOF(dotted) for three VS. In (b) first VS (frames 1 to 154), (c) second VS (frames 155 to 215), in (d) last VS (frames 791 to 959).

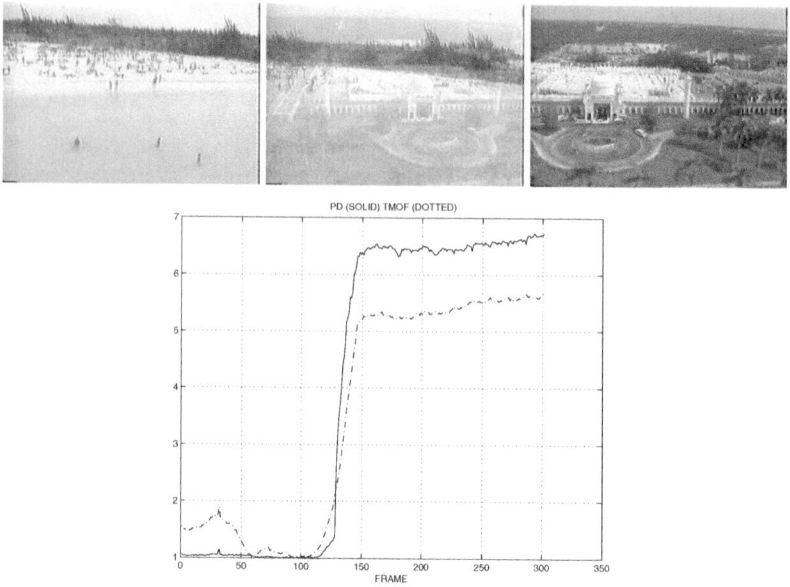

Fig. 2. Dissolve sequence. (a) First frame. (b) Comparison between PD and TMOF for first VS (frames 1 to 128).

Fig. 3. Comercial sequence. First frames of some of the VS.

TMOF, on the other hand, failed in 41 frames out of 959 giving a 4.3% of errors. The second sequence contains a series of TV commercials (see Figure 3) with several shots. We proceeded in the same way and found that PD produced no errors while TMOF failed in 20 out of 500 frames giving 4% of errors. Finally we considered a TV commercial with only smooth transitions (see Figure 4). We identified three shots with boundaries at frames 56 and 159. While PD gave 0% of errors TMOF gave 16.3% (34 errors over 209 frames).

Fig. 4. Comercial sequence. First frames of the VS.

Fig. 5. Original frames of sequence crossing ladies

To test the method when the sequence used for computing the VS descriptor and the one used for the query have different dimensions, we downsampled the sequences with factors two and four. For the sequence Jamie PD produce 0% of errors in both cases and TMOF produced erorrs around 4.2% in both cases. In the case of the commercial sequence PD produced no errors in both downsampled versions while TMOF gave 16.2% of error.

Although more extensive testing must be carried out to assess the quality of this descriptor for indexing and retrieval, the results presented here clearly show its potential. In [10] the authors show how their methods outperform other global histogram methods, for this reason we concentrated our efforts in comparing against their work.

3.2 Background Modeling

In this section we apply the pixel-wise histograms to the problem of background learning. First we consider the offline scenario where a set of frames from the background are used for learning $p(x, q)$. Once we have learned the background, each for each pixel x in a new frame g we compute the probability of $g(x)$ given the background: $p(x, B(g(x)))$. If this value is below a given threshold, it has a small probability to correspond to the background the pixel is classified as foreground.

Fig. 6. First and second columns likelihood of each pixel and final detection using online histogram estimation. Second and third columns results without online learning.

For static background this approach has no big differences with respect to other solutions proposed in the literature. When considering dynamic backgrounds, the advantage of pixel-wise histograms is that we only may need to specify the kernel parameters but we do not need to set other critical parameters such as the number of Gaussians in MoG. Other parameters may be used in the detection step when based on the background we must decide if a pixel in a new frame corresponds to background or moving object.

In Figure 6 we show the results of offline and online pixel-wise background learning for the sequence in Figure 5. In the online version the histogram of background pixels are adapted with a $\alpha - \beta$ filter. As we can see the proposed method can be successfully adapted to work in an online fashion and improves the results of the offline versions in the case of dynamic backgrounds.

4 Conclusion

In this work we reviewed different algorithms that exploit pixel-wise estimators. The algorithms came from two different areas, background estimation and visual segment indexing and retrieval. First, we showed that several of these algorithms have a lot of elements in common that can be summarized in the pixel-wise histograms. Also, we showed that the information used in these algorithms can be extracted from pixel-wise histograms. In this way we connected two different areas and showed that a more general algorithm can be used.

Based on the discussion of pixel-wise histograms we presented a novel method for VS description that considers all the information in the histograms and not a small set of values as in [10]. The presented VS descriptor outperforms, in the experiments conducted, the VS descriptor proposed in [10]. Also we presented an example of online pixel-wise histogram estimation applied to dynamic background learning. Based on the results here presented, we presented importante evidence on the advatages of pixel-wise statistics.

We believe that this work can give some light to these problems. We expect to improve the performances of other algorithms considering pixel-wise statistics. Here we considered temporal pixel-wise statistics but spatio-temporal ones may improve even more the performances of the algorithms. In future work we will address the complete evaluation of the proposed VS descriptor for video indexing and retrieval and the application of these ideas to sureveillance.

References

1. Matsushita, Y., Nishino, K., Ikeuchi, K., Sakauchi, M.: Illumination normalization with time-dependent intrinsic images for video surveillance. IEEE Transactions on Pattern Analysis and Machine Intelligence **26** (2004) 1336–1347
2. Wren, C., Azarbayejani, A., Darrell, T., Pentland, A.: Pfinder: real-time tracking of the human body. IEEE Transactions on Pattern Analysis and Machine Intelligence **19** (1997) 780–785
3. Stauffer, C., Grimson, W.: Learning patterns of activity using real-time tracking. IEEE Transactions on Pattern Analysis and Machine Intelligence **22** (2000) 747–757

4. Figueiredo, M., Jain, A.: Unsupervised Learning of Finite Mixture Models. IEEE Transactions on Pattern Analysis and Machine Intelligence **24** (2002) 381–396
5. Elgammal, A., Duraiswami, R., Harwood, D., S.Davis, L.: Background and foreground modeling using nonparametric kernel density estimation for visual surveillance. Proceedings of the IEEE **90** (2002) 1151–1163
6. Monnet, A., Mittal, A., Paragios, N., Ramesh, V.: Background modeling and subtraction of dynamic scenes. In: Proc. Int. Conf. Computer Vision. (2003) 1305–1312
7. Mittal, A., Paragios, N.: Motion based background subtraction using kernel density estimation. In: Proc. Computer Vision and Pattern Recognition. (2004)
8. Zhang, H., Zhong, J., Somaliar, S.: An integrated system for content-based video retrieval and browsing. Pattern Recognition **30** (1997) 643–658
9. Ferman, A., Tekalp, A., Mehrotra, R.: Robust color histogram descriptors for video segment retrieval and identification. IEEE Transactions on Image Processing **11** (2002) 497–508
10. Sze, K., Lam, K., Qiu, G.: A new key frame representation for video segment retrieval. IEEE Transactions on Circuits and Systems for Video Technology **15** (2005) 1148–1155
11. Haritaoglu, I., Harwood, D., Davis, L.S.: W4: Real-time surveillance of people and their activities. IEEE Transactions on Pattern Analysis and Machine Intelligence **22** (2000) 809–830

eVLBI Development in TIGO*

Sergio K. Sobarzo[1,2], Sergio N. Torres[1], and Hayo Hase[2]

[1] Department of Electrical Engineering, University of Concepción.
Casilla 160-C, Concepción, Chile
[2] Transportable Integrated Geodetic Observatory (TIGO)
Casilla 4036, Correo 3, Concepción, Chile
ssobarzo@udec.cl, sertorre@udec.cl, hayo.hase@tigo.cl

Abstract. Very Long Baseline Interferometry (VLBI) is a geometric technique which measures the time difference between the arrivals of a radio wavefront emitted by a distant quasar to at least two Earth based radio telescopes. Because the time difference measurements are precise to a few picoseconds, VLBI determines the relative positions of the cooperating radio telescopes to a few millimeter and the positions of the quasars to a few milliarcseconds. The transfer of the collected data from the radiotelescopes to the correlation centers is made through physical shipment of data discs which implies a delay of weeks in the turnaround. eVLBI is a technique which allows the direct transmission of the data to the correlators through Internet with multiples advantages. TIGO is a VLBI station located in Concepción, Chile with a limited bandwidth of few Mbps which must be increased in order to achieve an usable speed to work as an eVLBI station. The challenge and approaches to dodge the difficulties of achieving eVLBI in TIGO are explained in the present paper.

Keywords: Astronomy, Geodesy, VLBI, Network, Internet, Multipath Routing.

1 Introduction

Global reference systems are realized by measuring platforms, which represent reference points in the universe or on the Earth. Measurements between reference markers contain information about the relationship between them. This relationship can be expressed as directions or distances at a given epoch.

The existing reference frames are used in a hierarchical manner. The geodetic principle *from the big to the small* is applied here. Therefore quasars at the edge of the known universe form a quasi-inertial celestial reference frame (CRF) in which the position of the Earth is determined. On the next hierarchy level

* S. Sobarzo acknowledges support from CONICYT Doctoral Fellowship program. S. Torres acknowledges support to grant Milenio ICM P02-049. The authors also acknowledge the support for the eVLBI tests of Florencio Utreras (Red Clara), Paola Arellano and Sandra Jaque (Reuna), Eduardo Riveras (UdeC-DTI), Alessandra Bertarini (MPIFR), Sergei Pogrebenko (JIVE) and Ed Himwich (MIT).

J.F. Martínez-Trinidad et al. (Eds.): CIARP 2006, LNCS 4225, pp. 883–891, 2006.

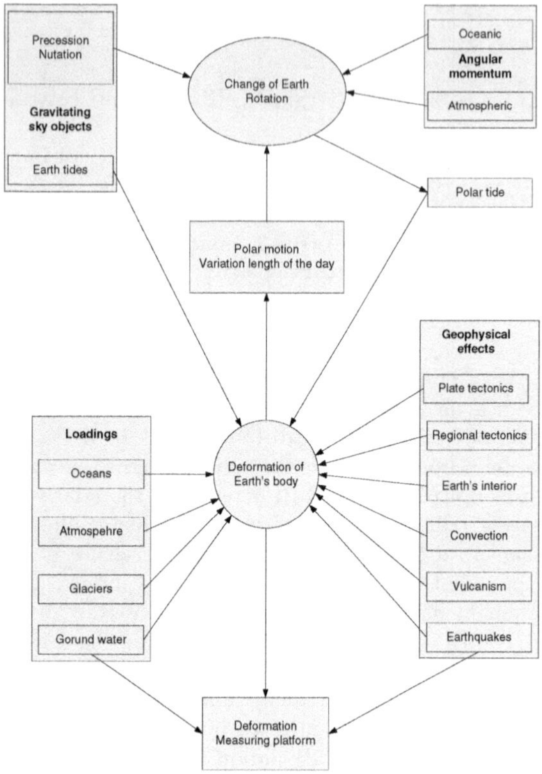

Fig. 1. Geodynamic phenomena with significant signals in measurements with geodetic space techniques. A proper modelling of the phenomena allows the determination of precise global reference frames [10].

comes the terrestrial reference frame (TRF). Any other continental, national, regional or local geodetic network appears in subsequent steps in the hierarchy of reference frames and makes use of reference points of the preceding level as an outer large scale frame. It is therefore mandatory that the most precise measuring techniques are applied at geodetic observatories, which have to supply data for the generation of the celestial and terrestrial reference frames. The reference points at different continents require measurements with techniques, which provide the relation between them. These techniques are summarized as geodetic space techniques.

The measurements of geodetic space techniques are biased due to geodynamic phenomena which vary the observation conditions at individual network stations. These local effects must be monitored in local surveys in order to complement the geodetic space techniques. The correct modeling of the geodynamic phenomena (Figure 1) allows finally the determination of precise reference frames.

The most remote objects in the universe are quasars in a distance of about 3-15 billion light years. Those objects can be detected with very sensitive radiotelescopes. With the Very Long Baseline Interferometry (VLBI) technique it is possible to relate the position, orientation and rotation of the Earth to the quasi-inertial reference frame realized by quasars. Due to the large distance of the quasars the gravity field of Earth is not predominant in the VLBI measurements.

eVLBI is a technique which allows to analyze the data for the correlators as long as they are captured. TIGO (http://www.tigo.cl) is a VLBI station located in Concepción, Chile, with a limited bandwidth of few Mbps. This paper deals with the challenge and approaches for achieving eVLBI in TIGO.

2 VLBI

Very Long Baseline Interferometry (VLBI) is a geometric technique which measures the time difference between the arrivals of at least two Earth based radio telescopes of a radio wavefront emitted by a distant quasar as is shown in Figure 2. Because the time difference measurements are precise to a few picoseconds, VLBI determines the relative positions of the cooperating radio telescopes to a few millimeter and the positions of the quasars to a few milliarcseconds [1]. The very distant quasars provide an inertial reference frame which is two orders of magnitude more accurate than the well-known fundamental catalog of fix stars FK5. Since the radio telescopes are fixed on the rotating Earth, VLBI tracks instantaneously the orientation of the Earth in an inertial reference frame, indispensable information for any kind of satellite orbit determinations and space navigation.

VLBI observations, as a microwave technique, can be performed under all meteorological conditions. The elements of a geodetic VLBI station consists in general of:

- A radio telescope with a cryogenic dual band S/X-band receiver.
- A data acquisition terminal for bandwidth frequency synthesis
- A hydrogen maser as very precise frequency standard to which all local oscillators in a VLBI-system must be phase-locked.
- A data formatting and a recording device for the temporary storage of digitized quasar noise.

Usually the VLBI-data are acquired during 24h on about 30 quasars in about 300 different directions. The VLBI-data consists of digitized noise from the quasar and is recorded with a time stamp on magnetic tapes or hard disks arrays at the stations. After the completion of the observations within an experiment, the magnetic tapes or disc arrays must be shipped from all co-observing stations to a VLBI correlator. After the arrival of these tapes the interferometer is setup at the correlator. The correlation process plays back the recorded data from all the station simultaneously and the processor searches for the maximum of the cross-correlation function. The correlator output are the fringe phase and the fringe amplitude from which the delay and delay rate of the wavefront can be derived. The delay is the primary observable in geodetic VLBI. Radioastronomers

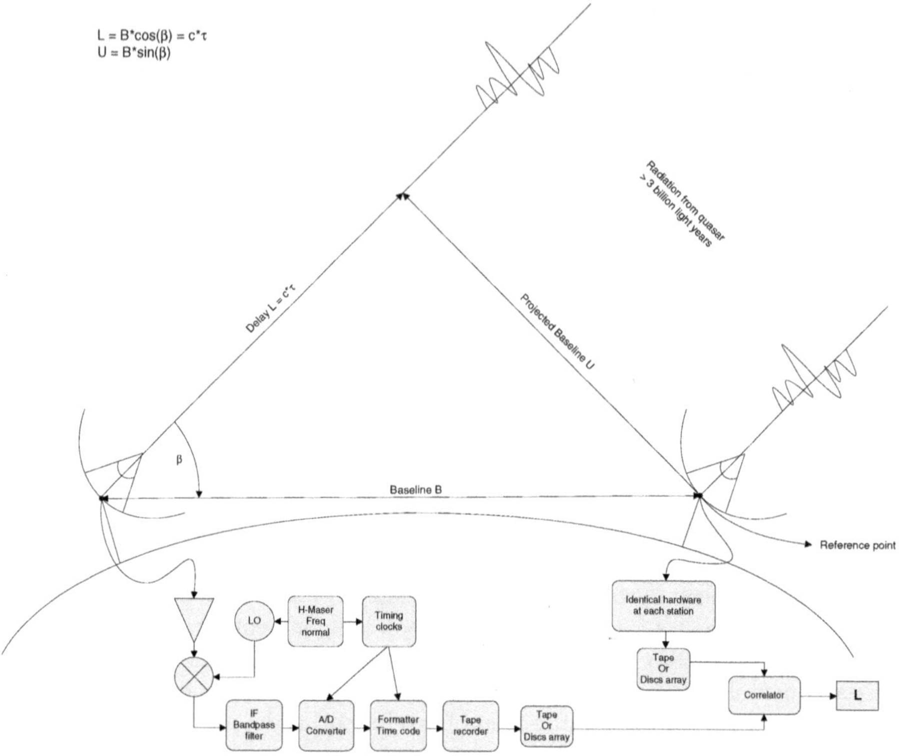

Fig. 2. Principle of Very Long Baseline Interferometry shown in a tape recorder correlation interferometer [10]

are using from the VLBI data the fringe phase and amplitude of the correlation process to derive images of the radio objects.

Usually the VLBI operation is scheduled within the International VLBI Service (IVS). The main program is the continuous observation of the rotation of Earth (CORE) in which a VLBI station observes in different global VLBI networks one to three times a week for 24 hours. Each 24 hours experiment consists of about 300 quasar observations about 3-5 minutes each.

3 eVLBI

Every year near 3 Petabytes of VLBI data are recorded on magnetic tapes or hard disks and physically transported to one of the few VLBI correlator sites (3 in The U.S., 2 in Europe, 2 in Japan and 1 in China). It's expected that this data volume will increase rapidly in the coming years. Disks and/or tapes are erased and re-cycled to between the telescopes and the correlation centers after correlation processing. This means that the data is ready to be used by the correlator near one week after the data is captured. This fact and other technical reasons had pushed to develop research about e-VLBI implementations.

e-VLBI has been developing rapidly in past 2-3 years, with increasing amounts of data transferred electronically, around 50 TB transferred in 2004 and 300 TB were transferred in 2005.

e-VLBI technique offers many advantages over the current operation:

- Bandwidth growth potential for higher sensitivity. VLBI sensitivity (SNR) is proportional to square root of bandwidth resulting in a large increase in number of observable objects. The only alternative is the use of bigger antennas but this is a more expensive alternative.

$$\Delta S \approx \frac{1}{\sqrt{B \times T}} \frac{T_{sys}}{A} \tag{1}$$

  where ΔS is the noise in flux density, T_{sys} is the noise expressed as system temperature, B is the bandwidth, T is the integration time and A is the radiotelescope area.
- Rapid processing turnaround. In astronomy it gives the ability to study transient phenomena with feedback to steer observations. In geodesy higher precision measurements for geophysical investigations can be achieved and better earth-orientation predictions can be obtained, particularly UT1, important fact for military and civilian navigation. The growth of the bandwidth will produce a need of growth of storage capacity therefore a near real-time processing will be necessary at the correlator side.
- Lower costs. The media pool represents a great cost that can be removed. Big bandwidths make possible to lead the VLBI stations to an automated operation eliminating manual handling and shipping of storage media.
- Increased reliability. Removal of recording equipment and tapes or disks shipping will increase the robustness of the process. The use of high speed networks will allow at the same time remote performance monitoring and control capability in near real-time which can lead the station to a full automation.

4 Current Status

The international Internet connection of TIGO can be divided in 3 sections as is shown in Figure 3:

- The path from the TIGO facility to the University backbone.
- The link between the University and the REUNA (Red Universitaria Nacional) academic Chilean network.
- The REUNA International link.

The current configuration has a total speed of 5Mbps. In the last mile connection from TIGO to the University there is an optical path with a monomode optical fiber with a speed of 100Mbps. The connection between the University and REUNA has a speed limited to 15 Mbps for national traffic with a capacity

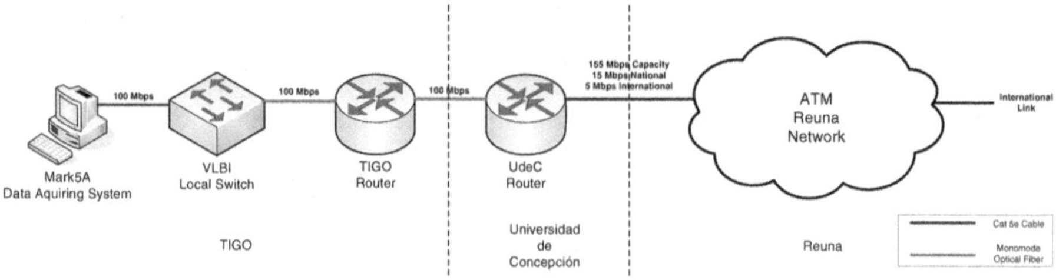

Fig. 3. Current status of TIGO connection

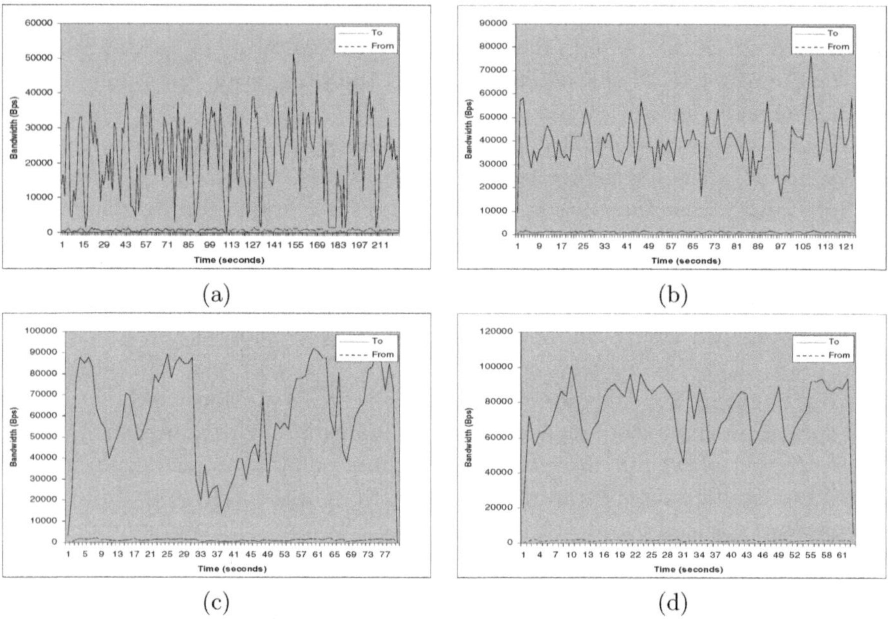

Fig. 4. a) Speed results of transferring from Concepción to Boston during working hours. b) Speed results of transferring from Concepción to Boston during non-working hours. c) Speed results of transferring from Concepción to Bonn during working hours. d) Speed results of transferring from Concepción to Bonn during non-working hours.

of 155 Mbps. The international link of REUNA has a capacity of 96 Mbps, but the University has a contract for 5 Mbps only.

A test of the real speed connection from Concepción to United States and Germany is shown in Figure 4. This test was conducted during working and non-working hours sending a 4 MB file to show the influence of the Universidad de Concepción traffics. The results show a clear influence of the difference between working and non-working hours and the destiny. The transmission to United States is slower due to high demand of commercial sites over there. The average speed obtained for a transfer to Boston during working and non-working hours was 21.8 and 38.8 KBps respectively. For a transmission to Bonn the speed was 58.9 and 73.5 Kbps for working and non-working hours, respectively.

5 Approaches

There are two possible solutions to increase the final speed of the connection. It's possible to use Multipath Routing or increase the bandwidth identifying the bottlenecks and upgrading the links and/or equipments.

In 2004 the first world wide eVLBI test was made among Britain, Sweden, Holland, Poland and Puerto Rico with a total speed of 32 Mbps. At the end of 2005 United States, Japan, Sweden and Holland were connected at 512 Mbps in other eVLBI experiment. Therefore a minimal speed of 32 Mbps can convert TIGO into an eVLBI station, however higher speeds will benefit the sensitivity of the station.

5.1 Multipath Routing

eVLBI has special requirements since it needs a fix point to point path between the VLBI station and the correlation facilities. It has been proved that the use of multiple streams can increase the final speed of a connection since it's possible to bypass bottlenecks using alternative routes [5].

A closer look of the Reuna network shows that while the infrastructure can support higher speeds, the final speed of every connected university is limited due the inherent sharing feature of Reuna. Besides the speed achieved for international connections is limited by contract for each university. This scenario gives the opportunity to apply the Multipath Routing as a plausible solution for eVLBI transmissions at high speeds.

In Figure 5 a Multipath Routing scheme is presented. The main route path is what is obtained when a connection is done using default routing algorithms, like OSPF [12] or BGP [13] limited by the constraints described before. The alternative routes can be used to send data as parallel streams to the destination. In the Reuna particular case, Universidad de Concepción has a bandwidth of 15 Mbps for national traffic but the international traffic is limited to 5 Mbps, with the installation of custom eVLBI data routers in other universities it is possible to bypass the international speed restriction of Universidad de Concepción *masquerading* the data to the correlators as national traffic increasing the total speed.

The expected result is a theoretically raise of the transmission speed from 5 Mbps to 15 Mbps. However, the imminent upgrade of Reuna network to 1 Gbps will allow higher speeds.

5.2 Expres Project

The Expres project [14] aims to identify the bottlenecks of the route from the TIGO VLBI station to a correlator in Europe and expand the bandwidth in order to join the European VLBI network as an eVLBI station. The lowest speed of the path from TIGO to Europe is limited by a contract bandwidth of 5 Mbps

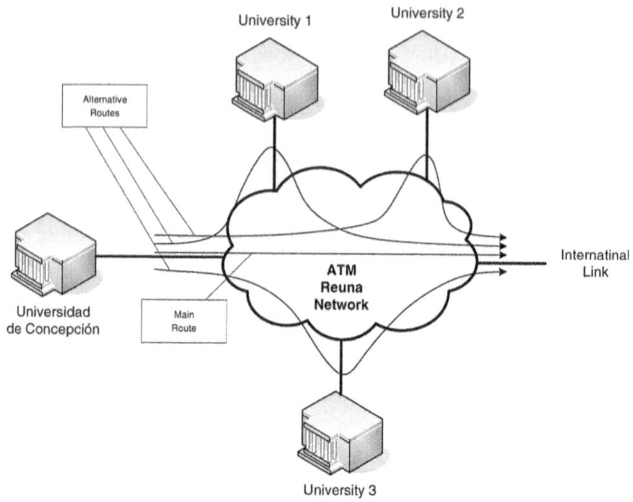

Fig. 5. Multipath Routing in Reuna Network

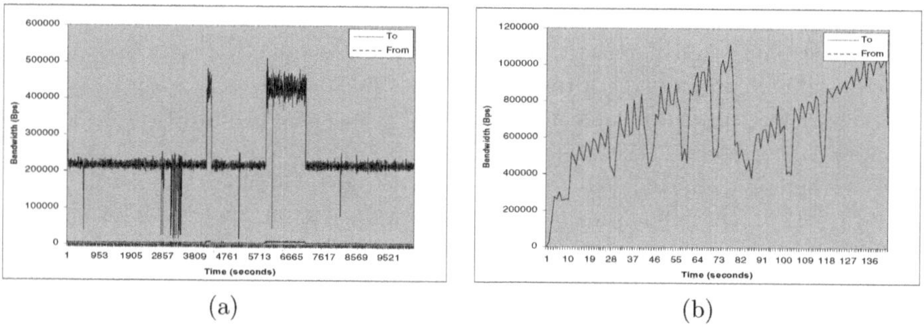

Fig. 6. a) Speed results of transferring from Concepción to Netherlands when Reuna restrictions applied. b) Speed results of transferring from Concepción to Netherlands without any kind of restriction.

provided by Reuna. This speed can be increased buying more bandwidth up to 64 Mbps (96 Mbps are available but $\sim$ 32 Mbps are in use as normal traffic). Besides, in order to achieve this maximum speed it's necessary to release the 15 Mbps constraint of Universidad de Concepción, which can be selectively made by Reuna for the TIGO traffic only. The path from TIGO to Universidad de Concepción has a total speed of 100 Mbps which is not a problem but there are plans to upgrade this path to 1 Gbps. Therefore, 64 Mbps is the expected total speed for the Expres project if no change is made in the Reuna network.

The first step is to find the bottlenecks along the path in order to identify a needed upgrade of the equipments/links involved. According to this, Reuna opened their restrictions with interesting results. Two test were conducted to JIVE VLBI correlator in Netherlands which are shown in Figure 6. The first test was made using two parallel streams with a per flow restriction applied in the Reuna border router linked to Concepción. The first streams was started with an upload speed of ~ 200 KBps, at 68 and 98 minutes of transmission a second stream was started with a resulting total upload speed of ~ 400 KBps. The second test was made without any restriction in TIGO, Universidad de Concepción, Reuna or JIVE VLBI correlator networks showing that a restriction of 10 Mbps exists.

6 Conclusions

The VLBI technique and its contribution to the earth geometry measurements and rotation parameters has been shown. At the present time, the speed achieved by TIGO is not enough to be an eVLBI competent station for the VLBI network. However two approaches were discussed. The use of cooperative nodes from other universities connected to Reuna is a plausible solution. Also, the Expres project in execution can remove the bottlenecks buying bandwidth or upgrading equipments where it's possible. Further, in the near future a creation of custom VLBI data routers software for Linux is planned.

References

1. F. Takahashi, T. Kondo, Y. Takahashi, Y. Koyama, "Very Long Baseline Interferometer", Ohmsha and IOS Press, 1997.
2. M. Felli, R. Spencer, "Very Long Baseline Interferometry, Techniques and Applications", Kluwer Academic Publishers, 1989.
3. R. Thompson, J. M. Moran, G. W. Swenson, Jr., "Interferometry and Synthesis in Radio Astronomy", Krieger Publishing, 1991.
4. R. Wohlleben, H. Mattes, Th. Krichbaum, "Interferometry in Radioastronomy and Radar Techniques", Kluwer Academic Publishers, 1991.
5. N. F. Maxemchuck, "Dispersity Routing", Proceedings of ICC'75, San Francisco, June 1975.
6. S. Savage, A. Collins, E. Hoffman, J. Snell, T. Anderson, "The end-to-end effects of Internet path selection", Proc. of ACM SIGCOMM, 1999.
7. David G. Andersen, Alex C. Snoeren, Hari Balakrishnan, "Best-Path vs. Multi-Path Overlay Routing", In the proceedings of the ACM SIGCOMM Internet Measurement Conference '03, October 2003.
8. L. Qiu, Y. Zhang, S. Keshav, "On Individual and Aggregate TCP Performance," Proc. of 7th Intl. Conference on Network Protocols (ICNP'99), Toronto, Canada, 1999.
9. E. Gustafsson, G. Karlsson, "A literature survey on traffic dispersion", IEEE Network, vol. 11, no. 2, pp. 28-36, March/April 1997.
10. Hase, H.: Theorie und Praxis globaler Bezugssysteme, Mitteilungen des BKG, Band 13, 1999.
11. Haejung Lim, Kaixin Xu, Mario Gerla, "TCP Performance over Multipath Routing in Mobile Ad Hoc Networks", In Proceedings of ICC 2003.
12. J. Moy, "The OSPF Specification", RFC 1131, October 1989.
13. Y. Rehkter and T. Li, "A Border Gateway Protocol 4 (BGP-4)", RFC 1771, T. J. Watson Research Center, IBM Corp., Cisco Systems, March 1995.
14. "A Production Astronomy e-VLBI Infrastructure", Proposal/Contract No.: 026642 EXPReS. Annex I - Description of Work.

Satellite Tracks Removal in Astronomical Images

Haider Ali, Christoph H. Lampert, and Thomas M. Breuel

Image Understanding and Pattern Recognition (IUPR) Research Group
German Research Center for Artificial Intelligence (DFKI)
and Technical University of Kaiserslautern
D-67663 Kaiserslautern, Germany
{ali, chl, tmb}@iupr.net

Abstract. This paper describes a new system for "Finding Satellite Tracks" in astronomical images based on the modern geometric approach. There is an increasing need of using methods with solid mathematical and statistical foundation in astronomical image processing. Where the computational methods are serving in all disciplines of science, they are becoming popular in the field of astronomy as well. Currently different computational systems are required to be numerically optimized before to get applied on astronomical images. So at present there is no single system which solves the problems of astronomers using computational methods based on modern approaches. The system "Finding Satellite Tracks" is based on geometric matching method *"Recognition by Adaptive Subdivision of Transformation Space (RAST)"*.

Keywords: Satellite Tracks, Geometric Matching, Astronomical Images, RAST.

1 Introduction

1.1 Motivation

Astronomical images play an important role in man's effort to understand the universe. These images are taken by space observatories spread across the globe. Acute weather conditions are required for image capturing. It takes several minutes to take a single astronomical image. Therefore it is important to extract maximum information from the astronomical images. These images contain important information about stars and galaxies and irrelevant information (like satellite tracks) which appear quite often. The target of our application is "weak lensing", which is a statistical method to estimate mass distributions in the universe by measuring galaxy ellipticities. Therefore, astronomers want to measure the ellipticity of very many small objects in an image which has to be done automatically. The presence of satellite tracks would disturb those measurement. Since data collection is time consuming, the images containing additional objects can not be simply discarded. Instead, irrelevant objects have to be removed from these images [5].

Currently astronomers remove these satellite tracks manually from images according to [4]. We replace this traditional approach by using a computational

J.F. Martínez-Trinidad et al. (Eds.): CIARP 2006, LNCS 4225, pp. 892–901, 2006.

system. This system is based on a *Geometric Matching* technique called *"Recognition by Adaptive Subdivision of Transformation Space (RAST)"*. A working system will help in saving a lot of human effort to remove these tracks manually.

1.2 Problem Formulation

The objective of this research work is to find satellite tracks in the images taken by astronomers. The images taken from the sky are contaminated by a lot of noise (Cosmic rays, CCD defects, ghost images and satellite tracks) which disturbs the detection or identification of important objects in the images like stars and galaxies. These tracks can be characterized as straight lines in the images. The major aim of this part of work is to develop a system to find and remove satellite tracks in astronomical images. In this system a well known algorithm RAST is applied based on Geometric Matching techniques.

1.3 Related Work

There is no computational method to reliably identify and remove satellite tracks at present. Currently astronomers do this job by hand after selecting and masking the images having satellite track. After masking satellite tracks they ignore the masked area while doing further processing of the objects. A general adaptive method *Cleaning Sky Survey databases using Hough Transform and Renewal String Approaches* was introduced by A.J. Storkey et al. (2004) to remove unusual objects in the astronomical images. This method was developed to remove four types of objects - satellite or aeroplane tracks, scratches, fibres and other linear phenomena introduced to the plate, circular halos around bright stars due to internal reflections within the telescope and diffraction spikes near to the bright stars in the sky survey data using catalogue of objects as described in [8]. The system we present is different from the adaptive method. As our system uses pixel based representation of images instead of using catalogue of objects. This system is based on geometric matching techniques a modern approach. This paper is organized as follows: Section 2 gives a brief overview of image pre-processing and related work including data preparation for satellite tracks system. Then the use of RAST algorithm in the system is described for finding straight lines in the image in Section 3 and Section 4. Section 5 presents the evaluation of the tasks and Section 6 leads to the conclusion, discussion of unsolved problems and future work.

2 Finding Satellite Tracks

2.1 Image Pre-processing

The available astronomical images are generally in Flexible Image Transport System (FITS) format. This format is widely used in astronomy for convenient exchange of astronomical data. FITS images are composed of a sequence of header data units (HDUs). A header data unit contains keywords (value statements) that describe the organization of the data in HDUs and the format of

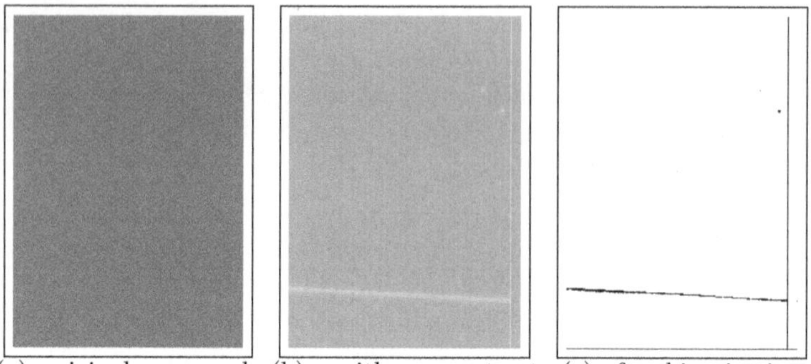

(a) original grayscale image (b) with contrast stretching (c) after binarization

Fig. 1. Example of binarized image (foreground objects become visible), the binarized image is inverted to white background and black foreground

the data contents. Based on the special structure of these header data units, FITS images may provide additional information like used instrument, status and history of the data etc. [6]. The given images were binarized and converted from FITS grayscale images to Portable BitMap (PBM) images. In this work the binarization is done by using global thresholding. Global thresholding sets all pixels above a defined value to white and the rest of the pixels to black in the image. It is very important to decide the appropriate threshold value to binarize the image, though it is difficult to decide a global value which is suitable for all images [7]. In this case the intensity range does not vary much from image to image. After looking at grayscale values in different images on the available data set, 102 were founded as a suitable value (40 %) threshold of total intensity range $0-255$. `Convert`, a utility in the ImageMagick software package was used to binarize the grayscale images. An example image before and after binarization is shown in Figure 1.

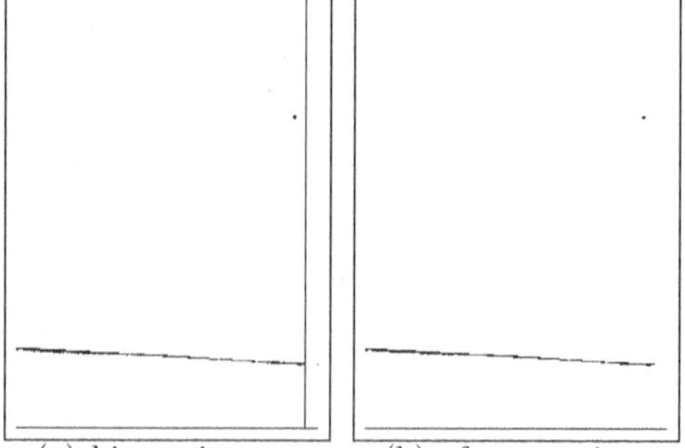

(a) binary image (b) after opening

Fig. 2. Example of opening effect (CCD defect and bad pixels are removed), Both the images are inverted to white background and black foreground

After binarization the morphological operation *Opening* was applied to remove noise and CCD defects in the images. Opening is based on the morphological operations Erosion and Dilation. Opening smoothes the inside of the object contour, breaks narrow strips and eliminates thin portions of the image. It is done by first applying erosion and then dilation operations on the image. Erosion shrinks the foreground objects in the image by certain amount. The amount of growing and shrinking the size of objects depends on the structuring element. CCD defects and noise have to be eliminated. These defects have a typical size of one to three pixels. So the opening is performed by using 3×3 structuring element. `Pgmmorphconv` is used for the opening operation. It is a utility in the Netpbm software package, a graphics programming library. The opening effect is demonstrated in Figure 2.

3 Geometric Matching

3.1 General Description

There are different algorithms to perform geometric matching. Many geometric matching problems in computer vision are based on image models. A model of an image can have geometric features like points, lines, arcs etc. Different algorithms are developed to match these geometric features in the model image [3]. As satellite tracks have geometric resemblance to straight lines, we look for line features in the image. In this work the RAST algorithm is applied for finding satellite tracks in the image.

3.2 Data Preparation

RAST takes sample points as input features. The computation of these sample points is described in this section. In binarized images these input features consist of the pixel positions of the foreground objects. The binarized images contains white foreground objects on a black background. A routine is written in C++, which computes the (x, y) positions of all the white pixels in the image. These pixels constitute the sample points.

3.3 Recognition by Adaptive Subdivision of Transformation Space (RAST) Algorithm

The RAST algorithm was developed by Breuel [1]. RAST consists of a family of geometric matching algorithms, one of these are for finding lines.

3.4 Geometric Transformation

The RAST algorithm is applied on prepared sample data points. RAST is based on forward transformation (model to image) and an error model [2]. In this case, the algorithm takes a collection of sample data points and tries to fit an optimal line on these sample points in the image.

The algorithm is implemented using hierarchical and adaptive subdivision of the space of line parameters. RAST implements a "best first" search by a binary tree based on recursive subdivision of the parameter space [2].

The RAST algorithm considers a set of all possible parameters as region of interest before execution. Then it recursively divides the parameter space into sub regions. For each region in the parameter space there is a set of consistent image features under bounded error. During the execution RAST eliminates the regions of disinterest. These are the regions which do not contain a solution [2]. An illustration of sample points and RAST line fitting is presented in Figure 3.

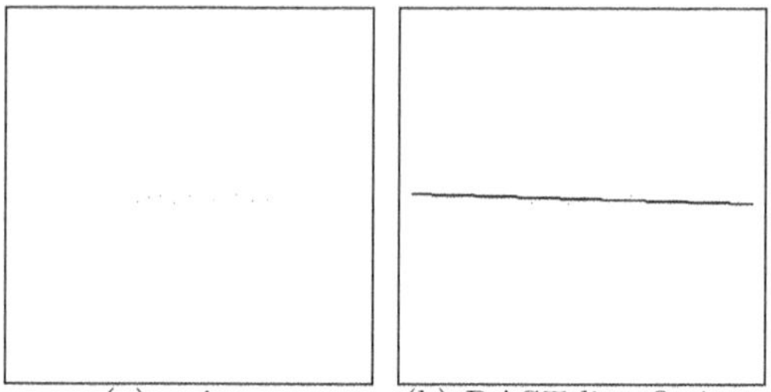

(a) points (b) RAST line fitting

Fig. 3. A hand made image with sample data points and reconstructed copy of the hand made image with RAST line fitting

3.5 Parametrization

The RAST algorithm for finding lines based on the parametric model, described by line parameters (r, θ). In the xy-plane, r is the distance of the line from the origin and θ is the angle between the perpendicular and the x-axis. The angle θ is always measured anticlockwise from the positive side of the x-axis. As shown in 1.

$$x\text{cos}\theta + y\text{sin}\theta = r \tag{1}$$

An illustration of line parameters in xy-plane is presented in Figure 4. There are different parameters to the algorithm like the *epsilon*, *quality*, *tolerance* and *angle tolerance*.

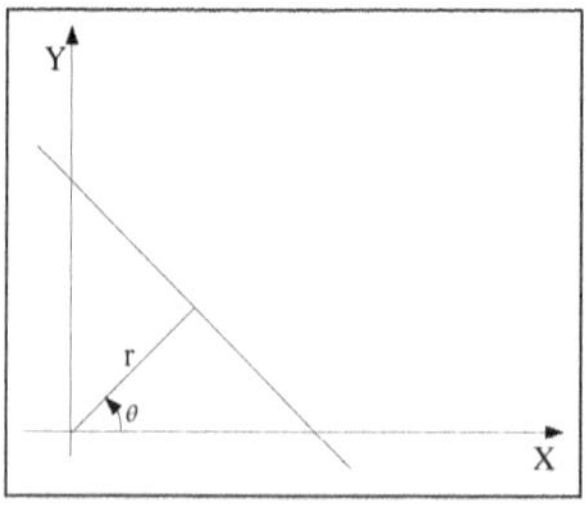

Fig. 4. Representation of r and θ in xy-plane

- The epsilon (eps) parameter defines the distance up to which a point can contribute to the line.
- The quality (minquality) parameter specifies the minimum acceptable quality of a line as given by:

$$q(\vartheta, P) = \sum_{k=1}^{N} max(0, 1 - \frac{d_k^2}{\varepsilon^2}) \tag{2}$$

  where ϑ is the set of parameters (r,θ), P is set of points, N is total number of points and d_k is the distance of kth point from the line.
- The tolerance (tol) and angle tolerance (atol) parameters specifies the allowed deviation of the parameters r and θ respectively from their optimal values.

The RAST algorithm is used with default values of these parameters. The default values of tolerance is set to 0.1 and the value of angle-tolerance is set to 0.001 in the implementation by Breuel [2]. To find lines in the astronomical images the the epsilon (eps) parameter value is set to 2 and the weight (minweight) of the line is set to 1000.

3.6 The Algorithm

The algorithm is used with the interest of finding the best match of all possible lines in the image. The execution steps of RAST algorithm are explained to calculate the quality function and error tolerance function. [2]. Following are the steps involved in the execution of RAST for finding lines.

- Step 1. Choose an initial region T in parameter space containing all specified parameter values.
- Step 2. Define a priority queue Q, where the priority of the queue Q is based on the upper bound on the quality of possible best match in that region as defined by the equation 2. The initial region is inserted into the priority queue Q.
- Step 3. Extract the element of the highest priority from the queue Q.
- Step 4. If the upper bound on the quality of the match in the extracted region T is less than the minimum quality threshold, go to step 7.
- Step 5. If the size of the region T is less than the tolerance size of the region dimensions r and θ then the region T is reported as a solution and continue to step 3.
- Step 6. If the specified size of the region T is greater than the minimum size of the interval for a solution then it is subdivided into two sub regions $T1$ and $T2$ and these sub regions are pushed into the priority queue Q and the algorithm continues to step 3.
- Step 7. Terminate

3.7 Output

The algorithm returns a list of parameter values r and θ. The RAST algorithm provides an output parameter *maximum result* to find more than one lines in the images.

4 Image Reconstruction

4.1 General Description

To remove lines from the image the position of the lines are computed by the RAST algorithm. To visualize the removal of the satellite tracks having geometric resemblance to lines, a new image is reconstructed from the binarized copy of the image. It is important to make a decision whether a line founded by RAST algorithm is a satellite tracks or not. This decision is based on the size of the line, that is how many pixels contribute to this line. An assumption is made that if the weight of the line is 1000 or greater, then the line found by the algorithm is considered as satellite track.

4.2 Painting Image

This algorithm reads the original image (PGM file) and data (line file) of pixel positions computed by the RAST algorithm. The number of lines returned by the RAST algorithm depends on the value of maxresult parameter. By setting the value of the maxresult parameter to more than one, the algorithm returns the optimal quality lines in decreasing order. The line found by the algorithm is painted black in the reconstructed image with a width of 20 pixels. The painted width of the line is decided on the basis of observed thickness of the satellite track. Examples of binarized image before and after the removal of a satellite track are shown in the following 5.

5 Evaluation

The evaluation of the satellite tracks removal system is done using a large database of astronomical images. This database consists of 1000 images. A total of 102 random images are chosen to evaluate this method. To generate ground truth information, the images are visually examined and annotated whether they contain satellite tracks or not. The system described in Section 2 is applied to find satellite tracks in the given dataset of images.

5.1 Results

The results of the system are presented in table 1. The table gives *true positive* (T_p), *true negative* (T_n), *false positive* (F_p) and *false negative* (F_n) number of satellite tracks detection.

(a) binarized (b) reconstructed (c) binarized (d) reconstructed

Fig. 5. Example: Binarized image containing satellite track : Reconstructed image after removal of satellite track, in these images few objects are removed because they were very close to the satellite track

Table 1. Different types of errors made by satellite tracks detection application. Each column represents the different type of error. The column labels are: total true positive (T_p), total true negative (T_n), total false positive (F_p), total false negative (F_n).

	Total Images	T_p	T_n	F_p	F_n
Satellite Track Detection	102	2	87	5	8

True positive (T_p) are the satellite tracks which actually exists and are reported as tracks as well. True negative (T_n) are the images without satellite tracks, which are correctly separated as free of tracks. False positive (F_p) are the images which do not contain satellite tracks but are detected as images containing satellite tracks. False negative (F_n) are the images containing satellite tracks but are not reported as images containing satellite tracks. The system has detected 2 true positive (T_p) images containing satellite tracks which are processed by the system as well. There are 87 true negative (T_n) images identified by the system where there is no satellite track exists. Therefore the accuracy of system for finding satellite tracks is 87.3%, which is the total number of correct detections. The system has detected 5 false positive (F_p) images. The false positive (F_p) images are analyzed and it turned out to some expanded stars and galaxies in the image due to the brightness and make a *Light Spike* in the available database of images. These light spikes look like vertical satellite tracks. While considering these light spikes as satellite tracks the algorithm detects and removes them as well. These light spikes are removed completely except the circular shaped bright stars or galaxies due to their thickness. An illustration of the images having stars and galaxies affected with the telescope light spikes before and after removal of these light spikes are presented in the Figure 6.

The system has detected 8 False negative (F_n) images. These False negative (F_n) images are analyzed and the images were found to contain satellite tracks but in very low brightness. The system was not able to detect satellite tracks

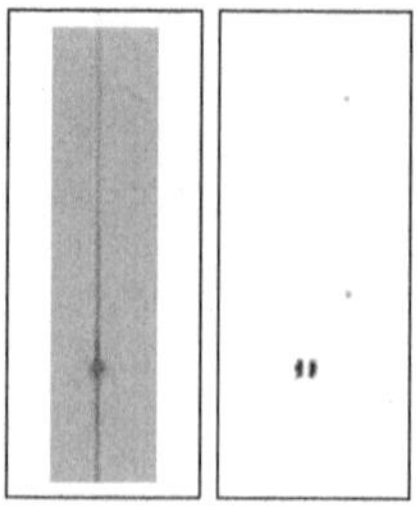

Fig. 6. The original image containing light spikes, there after the removal of these light spikes a few points of the galaxies still remains visible in the output image

Table 2. Different types of results made by RAST algorithm while finding satellite tracks in the images. Each column represents different type of error. The column labels are: true positive (T_p), true negative (T_n), false positive (F_p), false negative (F_n).

Algorithm	Total Images	T_p	T_n	F_p	F_n
RAST	94	2	87	5	0

in them. After analyzing False negative (F_n) images deeply, it is found that the original FITS images do not contain *DATAMIN* and *DATAMAX* fields. As the header data units (HDUs) of FITS images have DATAMIN and DATAMAX containing the range of grayscale values in the images. DATAMIN describes the minimum and DATAMAX describes the maximum gray value in the image. The foreground objects are lost already in the conversion step, so there is no chance of detection by RAST algorithm. This failure was not because of the RAST algorithm but was due to the missing information about DATAMIN and DATAMAX in FITS header data units (HDUs) which are the essential information required for the conversion process. Therefore a new evaluation scheme was decided where these black images were removed from the test set. The results of this new evaluation scheme is presented in a separate table 2. As the table shows that the RAST algorithm did not find any false negative (F_n) results. The accuracy of our algorithm is increased to 94.7% with this evaluation scheme.

6 Conclusion and Future Work

In this paper a computation method for identification and removal of satellite tracks in astronomical images is presented as an alternative of manual approach. This computation method is based on geometric matching techniques for finding lines in the images. There are different methods available for finding geometric shapes in images. As satellite tracks has geometric resemblance to lines, so the focus of this part of thesis was to find lines in the astronomical images. The RAST algorithm is applied to find these satellite tracks. The problem in this method was to find the right size of a satellite track. The problem of measurement of the size of satellite track is solved by visualizing satellite tracks of different sizes.

While identifying the satellite tracks in astronomical images, it is important to know the actual size of the satellite tracks. Currently, the system is implemented based on the assumption that if 1000 or more pixels contribute to make a line then this line is considered as a satellite track. This assumption could be refined after knowing the minimum size of the satellite track. Results of this method are visualized by reconstructing the image after removal of satellite tracks. The provided solution is quite fast. It can find and remove satellite tracks from an image of size $2000X4000$ pixels on a pentium 4 processor running at 2 GHz with a typical computational time less than 30 seconds. This computation time could be decreased with high performance hardware. The system did not have any false negatives, which means that all satellite tracks were removed, which is the main priority of the system when it should be applied for weak lensing. This solution will provide ease to astronomers for their further processing of objects in the images.

References

1. T.M. Breuel. *Geometric Aspects of Visual Object Recognition.* PhD thesis, Massachusetts Institute of Technology, 1992.
2. T.M. Breuel. Finding lines under bounded error. *Pattern Recognition Letters*, 29(1):167–78, 1996.
3. T.M. Breuel. A practical, globally optimal algorithm for geometric matching under uncertainty. In *International Workshop on Combinatorial Image Analysis (IWCIA August 2001), Philadelphia, CA*, 2001.
4. T. Erben. Personal communication, 2005.
5. T. Erben and M. Schirmer et. al. Gabods: The garching-bonn deep survey; iv. methods for the image reduction of multi-chip cameras. `arXiv.org:astro-ph/0501144`, 2005.
6. William D. Pence. Fits overview. http://fits.gsfc.nasa.gov, 2004.
7. R. E. Woods R. C. Gonzalez. *Digital Image Processing, 2nd Edition.* Prentice-Hall, Inc., 2002.
8. A.J Storkey, Hambly N.C., C.K.I. Williams, and R.G. Mann. Cleaning sky survey databases using Hough Transform and renewal string approaches. *Monthly Notices of the Royal Astronomical Society*, 347(1):36–51, 2004.

Detection of Coding Regions in Large DNA Sequences Using the Short Time Fourier Transform with Reduced Computational Load

Aníbal Rodríguez Fuentes[1], Juan V. Lorenzo Ginori[1], and Ricardo Grau Ábalo[2]

[1] Center for Studies on Electronics and Information Technologies
[2] Center for Studies on Informatics, Universidad Central "Marta Abreu" de Las Villas, Carretera a Camajuaní, km 5 ½, Santa Clara, VC, CP 54830, Cuba
anibalr@uclv.edu.cu, juanl@uclv.edu.cu, rgrau@uclv.edu.cu
http://www.fie.uclv.edu.cu

Abstract. Due to the non-uniform distribution of codons in coding regions, a three-periodicity is present in most of genome coding regions which, after a previous numeric conversion, show a notable peak at frequency component N/3 when calculating the Fourier Transform. Taking into account the veracity of this result, the Short Time Fourier Transform has been applied to large DNA sequences to predict coding regions. This paper presents a new approach to reduce the computational burden associated with STFT computation, for coding regions detection purposes. Experimental results show significant savings in computation time when the proposed algorithm is employed.

1 Introduction

Bioinformatics has become one of the most exciting areas of research in science today. The whole description of the human genome is about three billion characters in length. In the last years, scientists have completed the sequencing of a few other organisms, which are very useful in the study of general features and the architecture of entire genomes. The speed at which data is currently being acquired is growing at very high rates. Interpreting the meaning of these genome sequences is a big challenge for scientists today.

The standard approach used to represent genome sequences consists in representing the genomic information by sequences of nucleotide symbols in the strands of DNA and RNA molecules, by symbolic codons (triplets of nucleotides), or by symbolic sequences of amino acids in the corresponding polypeptide chains (for the genes). This approach limits the methodology for handling the genomic information to mere pattern matching or statistical procedures. However, numerical assignments can also be made as an alternative for analysis purposes. Many approaches [1-6] have been used in order to transform a DNA sequence into a numerical signal. For example, one of the most used approaches is the computation of four binary sequences (one per each base A, T, C and G), called binary indicator sequences, where 1 at position k indicates the presence of the base at that position, and 0 its absence. Another approach consists in assigning numerical values to each one of the nucleotide bases, as is used in this work and explained in detail below.

J.F. Martínez-Trinidad et al. (Eds.): CIARP 2006, LNCS 4225, pp. 902 – 909, 2006.

It is known that due to the non-uniform distribution of codons in coding regions, a three-periodicity is present in most of genome coding regions, which show a peak at frequency N/3 when calculating their Discrete Fourier Transform (DFT). Many authors have used this result to propose approaches to detect coding regions in large DNA sequences. In [1], the Short Time Fourier Transform (STFT) is used to detect five coding regions in an 8000 base pairs DNA stretch of *C. elegans*, and in [7] a new measure, based on the DFT phase at a frequency *N*/3, is presented. It is important to notice that when applying the STFT in these cases, usually the frequency component that corresponds to the periodicity three is the only one to be calculated.

In this paper a new approach to reduce the computational load when calculating the STFT for coding regions detection purposes is presented. It is based on a computational simplification obtained when calculating the Fourier Transform (FT) for a data window centered in a certain point, knowing the FT of a data window of the same size, but shifted one point backwards in the sequence. To complement this result, the Goertzel algorithm was used to calculate the frequency content in the first window of the entire sequence.

2 Materials and Methods

In the following paragraphs there is a presentation of the method introduced in this work to perform the computations associated to the spectral analysis of a genomic sequence. For this purpose, the nucleotide bases are previously mapped into a sequence of complex numbers according to

$$A=1+j;\quad T=1-j;\quad C=-1-j;\quad G=-1+j\,.$$

As a result a discrete sequence of complex numbers is obtained, that can be analyzed through standard techniques like the Discrete Fourier Transform [1].

2.1 Reducing the Computational Load When Calculating the Discrete Fourier Transform for Sliding Windows

The STFT uses a sliding window along the sequence and calculates the Fourier Transform of each subsequence. We consider here the case where a rectangular window is used, so that we do not have to multiply the data samples by any coefficient, as occurs when using a weighting window.

The k-th coefficient of the Discrete Fourier Transform of a signal x[n] of length N can be computed as:

$$X[k]=\sum_{n=0}^{N-1}x[n]e^{-j2\pi kn/N}\quad . \tag{1}$$

Assume now that $X_p[k]$ is the k-th coefficient of the DFT for the subsequence starting at position p within the sequence, and with a window of length N:

$$X_p[k]=\sum_{n=0}^{N-1}x[p+n]e^{-j2\pi nk/N} \tag{2}$$

So $X_{p+1}[k]$ can be computed as:

$$X_{p+1}[k] = \sum_{n=0}^{N-1} x[p+n+1] e^{-j2\pi nk/N} \tag{3}$$

Making the change of variables m = n + 1 (n = m − 1) we can show that

$$X_{p+1}[k] = e^{j2\pi k/N} \sum_{m=1}^{N} x[p+m] e^{-j2\pi mk/N} \tag{4}$$

Now it is possible to compute $X_{p+1}[k]$ using the previous result (2) for $X_p[k]$:

$$X_{p+1}[k] = e^{j2\pi k/N}(X_p[k] - x[p] + x[p+N])$$

In the particular case of interest in this study, for the periodicity three when k = N/3 we have:

$$X_{p+1}[N/3] = e^{j2\pi/3}(X_p[N/3] - x[p] + x[p+N]) \tag{5}$$

Using the previous equation, we can just calculate the DFT for the first subsequence (window) instead of calculating a Fourier Transform for each window, and then use its N/3 frequency component to calculate the same component in the next subsequence. This procedure can be continued for all the window displacements until the whole DNA sequence is analyzed. Notice that with this approach, only one DFT, corresponding to the first subsequence, is to be fully calculated. This is the basis for the significant reduction in the computational cost that was obtained. The same savings in computational load can be obtained for every frequency component of the STFT, which makes the proposed method very suitable to detect any periodicity that could appear in the DNA sequence [8].

2.2 The Goertzel Algorithm

To calculate the DFT frequency component at N/3 for the first subsequence, we can use the Goertzel algorithm [9] instead of using the DFT in order to increase the computational efficiency. The Goertzel algorithm computes the DFT for specific indexes in a vector or matrix by using the periodicity of the sequence $e^{-j2\pi kn/N}$ to reduce the computational load. It computes the k-th DFT coefficient of the input signal $x[n]$ using a second-order filter. The algorithm can be implemented as:

$$v_k[n] = x_e[n] + 2\cos(2\pi k/N)v_k[n-1] - v_k[n-2] \tag{6}$$

where

$$v_k[-2] = v_k[-1] = 0$$

$$x_e[n] = \begin{cases} x[n], & 0 \le n \le N-1 \\ 0, & n < 0, n \ge N \end{cases} \tag{7}$$

and

$$X[k] = v_k[N] - W_N^k v_k[N-1] \tag{8}$$

It can be seen that this method uses recursion to compute $\cos(2\pi k / N)$ and $W_N^k = e^{-j2\pi k/N}$, which are evaluated only at $n = N$. The direct DFT does not use recursion and must compute each complex term separately.

The real cost of this algorithm is $2N$+4 real multiplications, and $4N$ real sums, for the general case of a complex signal.

Notice that although there is a computational saving by using the Goertzel algorithm when it is desired to compute only one DFT coefficient, the main savings result from the application of equation (5). This makes useful the proposed method even for the case in which more than one frequency component is to be evaluated and DFT calculations could be more efficient than the Goertzel algorithm.

3 Results

Using the Goertzel algorithm to compute the N/3 frequency component of the first subsequence and then the algorithm developed previously to compute the same frequency component for the next subsequences, we reduced considerably the computation complexity of the application of the STFT to detect coding regions in large DNA sequences.

In Table 1 it is shown a detailed comparison between the direct method and the algorithm we propose, when a complex signal is used to describe the DNA sequence, assuming that the length of the DNA sequences is L and the sliding rectangular window has length N.

Table 1. Comparison between the direct method and the proposed algorithm when calculating the STFT for a complex signal

	Direct method		Proposed algorithm		
	Per point	Total	Goertzel	Per point	Total
Real multiplications	$4N$	$4L*N$	$2N$+4	4	$4L+2N$
Real sums	$4N$-2	$L*(4N$-2)	$4N$	6	$6L+4N$-6
Computational load	Order $L*N$		Order $L+N$		

As Table 1 shows, the proposed algorithm can reduce significantly the computational burden for the calculation of the Short Time Fourier Transform to detect coding regions in DNA sequences. If we use binary indicator sequences to obtain the power spectrum of the signal like in [1] the reduction is more significant because we need to compute 4 times the DFT per point, although in this case the signals are real. The use of the STFT involves completing the sequence with 2N/3 ceros at the beginning and with N/3 ceros at the end, and this reduces the amount of operations when computing the N/3 frequency component in the first 2N/3 windows and last N/3 windows of the cero-padded sequence. However, this reduction is not shown in Table 1 because it is not significant for large sequences.

It is also important to compare the computation load between the Fast Fourier Transform and the proposed algorithm when it is necessary to compute all frequency components per window, which is the case when calculating complete spectrograms. The FFT computation load is $N*\log_2 N$ for a window, which is totalized as $L*N*\log_2 N$, for L windows, while the computation load for the proposed algorithm when computing all frequency components is $L*N*(1+(\log_2 N)/L))$. Here an FFT is used instead the Goertzel algorithm to compute all frequency components of the first window. Comparing $\log_2 N$ and $1+(\log_2 N)/L$ it is possible to realize that a noticeable saving in computational load is obtained when using the proposed algorithm.

In Table 2 it is shown the average execution time, in seconds, of the expression: $|aA + tT + cC + gG|^2$, where A, T, C and G are respectively the DFT values at N/3 for each subsequence of length N corresponding to binary indicator sequences Xa, Xt, Xc and Xg, and a, t, c and g are complex constants obtained in [1] as the solution of an optimization problem to maximize the discriminatory capability between protein coding regions and random DNA regions. The values of these complex constants are:

$$a = 0.10 + 0.12j \qquad t = -0.30 - 0.20j$$
$$c = 0 \qquad g = 0.45 - 0.19j \tag{9}$$

In the computer experiments, different DNA strings contained in Chromosome III of *C. elegans* were analyzed, and both approaches, the direct method and the algorithm we propose, were used for this purpose. The 8000 base pairs DNA stretch was the same used by Anastassiou in [1] for a sliding window of length 351.

Table 2. Computation time comparison, in seconds, between the direct method and the algorithm we propose for different DNA strings contained in Chromosome III of *C. elegans*

DNA stretch	8000 bp DNA stretch		15100 bp DNA stretch		42799 bp DNA stretch	
Window Length	351	702	351	702	351	702
Direct Method (DM)	4.9370	8.6130	8.8630	15.6730	26.1270	46.4470
Proposed Algorithm	0.0550	0.0551	0.0800	0.0800	0.2300	0.2310
% of DM time	1.11%	0.64%	0.90%	0.51%	0.88%	0.50%

Practical results confirm the computational orders shown in Table 1. Notice that when we increase the length of the window, the execution time using direct method is increased at about the same rate, whereas the time spent by the proposed algorithm is almost invariable. In general sense, our algorithm employs less that 1% of the time required when the direct method is used.

The graph shown in Figure 1, obtained using our algorithm, coincides with the one obtained by Anastassiou in [1]. Figure 2 shows the graph for the first 42799 bp of the same Chromosome. Most of the notable peaks correspond to coding regions.

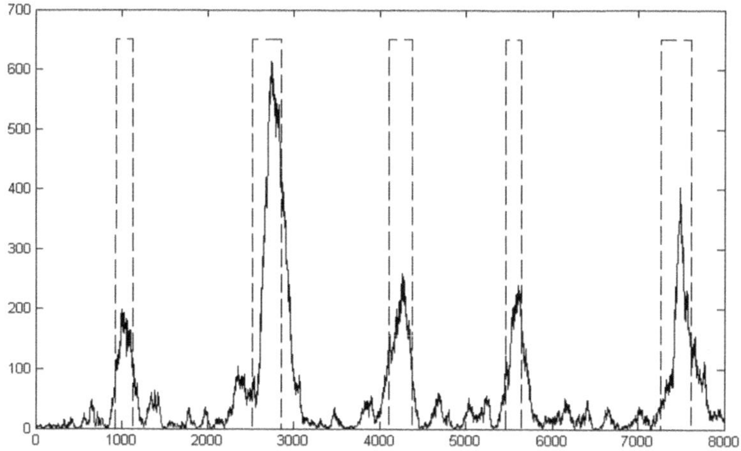

Fig. 1. Plot of $|aA + tT + cC + gG|^2$ for the 8000 bp stretch starting at position 7020 inside Chromosome III of *C. elegans.* using a sliding window of length 351. Noticeable peaks correspond to coding regions, which are represented using dashed lines.

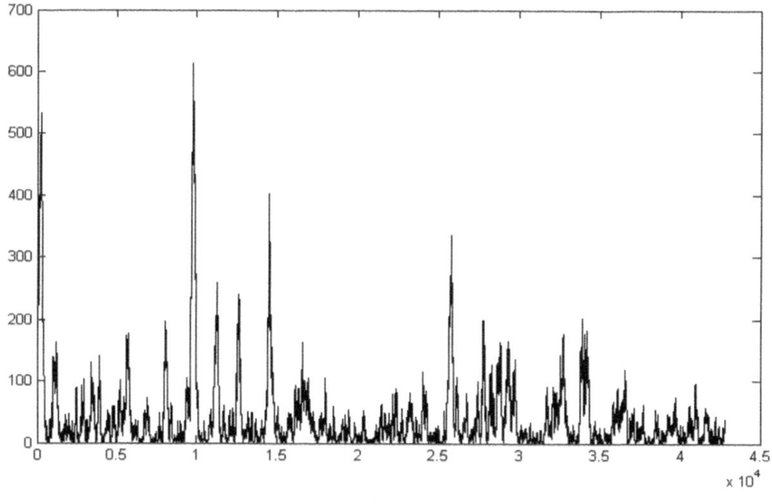

Fig. 2. Plot of $|aA + tT + cC + gG|^2$ for the first 42799 bp inside Chromosome III of *C. elegans*

4 Discussion and Conclusions

Various Digital Signal Processing based methods are being used currently to detect coding regions in large DNA strings. Among them, there are several frequency-domain techniques that make extensive use of the Discrete Fourier Transform. Some of these techniques use the amplitudes of the DFT coefficients and others their phase angles. When using these methods, a typical situation arises in which it is necessary to calculate only the frequency component at $N/3$ in a repetitive process, which involves the calculation of the DFT for many subsequences obtained from a sliding window applied to the whole sequence. This could mean a high computational load when dealing with large DNA databases.

In this work, an algorithm was introduced to reduce the computational burden associated to the calculation of the *N/3* frequency component of the STFT for a sliding window with a one-sample step. The proposed algorithm was derived from the properties of the DFT, and combined with the well-known Goertzel algorithm, which allowed further improvements when calculating only one DFT coefficient for a particular frequency, that is precisely the situation in this application.

The computational experiments performed consisted in the calculation of the STFT for long sequences using both the proposed algorithm and the conventional method, and using the computation time as the basis to evaluate the computational efficiency. The results showed that the application of the algorithm introduced in this work, reduced at great extent (typically less than 1% for the computed cases) the computational load associated to this task. It is worth to mention that the precision of the results is not affected significantly, given that this is only influenced by the different way in which roundoff errors propagate. These errors are usually negligible when using floating point as is usual in modern computers.

A very significant reduction in computation time can be also expected when calculating more frequency components, or even the complete STFT (with all the frequency components). The results obtained suggest that the proposed algorithm can be used efficiently in analyzing long DNA strings, even in large studies involving many sequences. Practical comparison results demonstrated the good performance of the proposed algorithm.

Acknowledgements

This work was supported partially by the Canadian International Development Agency Project Tier II-394-TT02-00 and by the Flemish VLIR-UOS Programme for Institutional University Co-operation (IUC). The authors wish to thank Dr. Julián L. Cárdenas-Barrera for the revision of the manuscript.

References

1. D. Anastassiou, "Genomic signal processing," *IEEE Signal Processing Magazine*, vol. 18, pp. 8-20, 2001.
2. P. D. Cristea, "Conversion of nucleotides sequences into genomic signals," *J. Cell. Mol. Med.*, vol. 6, pp. 279-303, 2002.
3. J. A. Berger, S. K. Mitra, and J. Astola, "Power spectrum analysis for DNA sequences," *University of California*, 2002.
4. G. Dodin, P. Vanderghenynst, P. Levoir, C. Cordier, and L. Marcourt, "Fourier and Wavelet Transform Analysis, a Tool for Visualizing Regular Patterns in DNA Sequences," *J. Theor. Biol*, vol. 206, pp. 323-326, 2000.
5. J. A. Berger, S. K. Mitra, M. Carli, and A. Neri, "New approaches to genome sequence analysis based on digital signal processing," *University of California*, 2002.

6. S.-C. Su, C. H. Yeh, and C. J. Kuo, "Structural Analysis of Genomic Sequences with Matched Filtering," *IEEE Signal Proccessing Magazine*, vol. 3, pp. 2893-2896, 2003.
7. D. Kotlar and Y. Lavner, "Gene Prediction by Spectral Rotation Measure: A New Method for Identifying Protein-Coding Regions," *Genome Research*, vol. 13, pp. 1930-1937, 2003.
8. J. A. Berger, S. K. Mitra, and J. Astola, "Power spectrum analysis for DNA sequences," *Proceedings of the International Symposium on Signal Processing and its Applications (ISSPA 2003), Paris, France*, pp. 29-32, 2003.
9. A. V. Oppenheim and R. W. Schafer, *Discrete-Time Signal Processing*: Prentice-Hall, 1989.

Time Series Pattern Recognition Based on MAP Transform and Local Trend Associations

Ildar Batyrshin and Leonid Sheremetov

Mexican Petroleum Institute, Av. Lázaro Cárdenas, 152,
Col. San Bartolo Atepehuacan, Mexico D.F., CP 07730, Mexico
{batyr, sher}@imp.mx

Abstract. The methods of pattern recognition in time series based on moving approximation (MAP) transform and MAP image of patterns are proposed. We discuss main properties of MAP transform, introduce a concept of a MAP image of time series and distance between time series patterns based on this concept which were used for recognition of small patterns in noisy time series. To illustrate the application of this technique to recognition of perception based patterns given by sequence of slopes, an example of recognition of water production patterns in petroleum wells used in expert system for diagnosis of water production problems is considered.

Keywords: Moving approximation transform, local trend association, time series, pattern recognition.

1 Introduction

Time series contain important information about measured parameters of systems changing in time. Such systems can be found in meteorology, economics, finance, geophysics, industry, and telecommunications. Time-series analysis is an important research area in these domains and more accurate analysis tools are consistently sought. Conventional techniques of time series analysis are based on statistical modeling, Fourier and wavelet transforms [4-6], [8], [12-14], [16], [17]. Techniques developed for noise suppression, data filtering and pattern recognition often suppose that time series describe some signal propagation or oscillating processes, contain large patterns, small noise, or noise with known statistical parameters. Many of these conditions are not fulfilled for time series describing economic or industrial systems [7], [9], [10]. In these application domains (i) time series are already obtained as a result of averaging of some parameter during given time intervals; (ii) they do not represent some oscillating processes; (iii) recognition of small patterns is important for decision making; and (iv) small patterns in time series can exist in presence of a noise. Moreover, in decision making procedures related with time series analysis in these domains, a trend or a tendency in a change of a parameter during some time interval usually becomes an important characteristic and the powerful signal processing techniques can not be applied.

J.F. Martínez-Trinidad et al. (Eds.): CIARP 2006, LNCS 4225, pp. 910–919, 2006.

The formal technique for analysis of such "local trends" was introduced in [1], [2]. The basis of this technique is an analysis of slopes of linear approximations of time series in a sliding window. This technique consists of two parts: i) moving approximation (MAP) transform calculates slopes in sliding window of a given size; and ii) a "local trend" association measure calculates a similarity between time series or time series patterns. This technique was applied in [1], [2] for analysis of associations between time series and representation of these associations as an association network of time series. The paper [3] considered the method of application of this technique to time series forecasting. In this paper we discuss the methods of application of MAP transform and local trend association measures to the recognition of time series patterns.

The rest of the paper is organized as follows. In the next section, we consider the basic notions of MAP transform and local trend associations. In section 3, we propose novel methods of coding of time series patterns by local trends and a pattern recognition procedure for extraction of given patterns from time series. Several measures of local trend association between time series patterns (E-distance, J-distance and EJ-distance) are introduced and compared on examples of time series pattern recognition in the presence of noise. Finally we discuss an application of this approach to the recognition of water production patterns in petroleum wells which are important for diagnosis of water production problems in petroleum industry. In Conclusions we discuss the main results presented in the paper and possible application and extension of the proposed technique.

2 Basic Notions of MAP Transform and Local Trend Associations

A time series (y,t) is a sequence $\{(y_i,t_i)\}$, $i\in I = (1,\dots, n)$, such that $t_i < t_{i+1}$ for all $i = 1,\dots, n-1$, where y_i and t_i are real numbers called time series values and time points, respectively. A time series (y,t) will be denoted also as y. A window W_i of a length $k > 1$ is a sequence of indexes $W_i = (i, i+1,\dots, i+k-1)$, $i\in\{1,\dots, n-k+1\}$. The sequence $y_{W_i} = (y_i, y_{i+1},\dots, y_{i+k-1})$ of the corresponding values of time series y is called a partial time series induced by window W_i. A sequence $J = (W_1, W_2,\dots, W_{n-k+1})$ of all windows of size k, $(1 < k \le n)$, is called a moving (or sliding) window. Such mowing window is used, for example, in statistics in moving average procedure for smoothing time series when the value in the middle of the window is replaced by the mean of values from this window.

Suppose J is a moving window of size k and $y_{W_i} = (y_i, y_{i+1},\dots, y_{i+k-1})$, $i\in (1,2,\dots, n-k+1)$, are corresponding partial time series in time points $(t_i, t_{i+1},\dots, t_{i+k-1})$. A linear function $f_i = a_i t+b_i$ with parameters $\{a_i,b_i\}$ minimizing the criterion

$$Q(f_i, y_{W_i}) = \sum_{j=i}^{i+k-1}\left(f_i(t_j) - y_j\right)^2 = \sum_{j=i}^{i+k-1}\left(a_i t_j + b_i - y_j\right)^2, \qquad (1)$$

is called a moving (least squares) approximation of y_{W_i}. The solution of (1) is well known and optimal values of parameters a_i, b_i can de calculated as follows:

$$a_i = \frac{\sum_{j=i}^{i+k-1} (t_j - \overline{t_i})(y_j - \overline{y_i})}{\sum_{j=i}^{i+k-1} (t_j - \overline{t_i})^2}, \quad b_i = \overline{y_i} - a_i \overline{t_i}, \tag{2}$$

where $\overline{t_i} = \frac{1}{k} \sum_{j=i}^{i+k-1} t_j$, $\overline{y_i} = \frac{1}{k} \sum_{j=i}^{i+k-1} y_j$.

Definition 1. A transformation $MAP_k(y,t) = a$, where $a = (a_1, \ldots, a_{n-k+1})$ is a sequence of slope values obtained as a result of moving approximations of time series (y,t) in moving window of size k is called a moving approximation (MAP) transform of time series y. The slope values $a_1, \ldots, a_{n-k+1}$ are called local trends.

Elements a_i, $(i = 1,\ldots, n-k+1)$ from $MAP_k(y,t)$ will be denoted as $MAP_{ki}(y,t)$.

In many applications time points $t_1, \ldots, t_n$ are increasing with a constant step h such that $t_{i+1} - t_i = h$ for all $i = 1,\ldots, n-1$. In such cases, in MAP transform the set of time points $t = (t_1, \ldots, t_n)$ can be replaced by the set of indexes $I = (1,\ldots, n)$ as follows: $MAP_k(y,t) = (1/h)MAP_k(y,I)$ and the formula (2) for local trends can be simplified as follows [2].

Theorem 1. Suppose time points $t_1, \ldots, t_n$ are increasing with a constant step h then the values of *MAP* transform $MAP_k(y,t)$ can be calculated as follows:

$$a_i = \frac{6\sum_{j=0}^{k-1} (2j - k + 1) y_{i+j}}{hk(k^2 - 1)}, \quad i \in (1,2,\ldots, n-k+1). \tag{3}$$

Formula (3) gives a simple method to calculate MAP transform for time series with a fixed step. Further, for such time series we will replace time points by indexes $I = (1,\ldots, n)$ and in (3) the value $h = 1$ will be used. We will denote time series also as $y = (y_1,\ldots,y_n)$ and will use a notation $MAP_k(y)$ for $k \in \{2,\ldots,n-1\}$.

As a measure of similarity between time series one can use measures of similarity between their MAP transforms.

Definition 2. Suppose $y = (y_1,\ldots,y_n)$, $x = (x_1,\ldots, x_n)$ are two time series and $MAP_k(y) = (a_{y1}, \ldots, a_{ym})$, $MAP_k(x) = (a_{x1}, \ldots, a_{xm})$, $(k \in \{2,\ldots,n-1\}$, $m = n - k+1)$, are their MAP transforms. The following function is called a measure of local trend associations:

$$coss_k(y,x) = \frac{\sum_{i=1}^{m} a_{yi} \cdot a_{xi}}{\sqrt{\sum_{i=1}^{m} a_{yi}^2 \cdot \sum_{j=1}^{m} a_{xj}^2}} \tag{4}$$

Suppose p,q,r,s, $(p,r \neq 0)$ are real values and (y,t) is a time series. Denote $py+q = (py_1+q, \ldots, py_n+q)$ and $rt+s = (rt_1+s, \ldots, rt_n+s)$. A transformation $L(y,t) = (py+q, rt+s)$ is called a linear transformation of time series (y,t).

Theorem 2. Suppose L_1 and L_2 are two linear transformations of time series *(y,t)* and *(x,t)* given by the sets of parameters (p_1,q_1,r_1,s_1) and (p_2,q_2,r_2,s_2), respectively, where p_1, p_2, r_1, $r_2 \neq 0$, then

$$coss_k(L_1(y,t), L_2(x,t)) = sign(p_1)\cdot sign(r_1)\cdot sign(p_2)\cdot sign(r_2)\cdot coss_k((y,t), (x,t)). \quad (5)$$

From this Theorem it follows a very nice invariance property of local trend association measure under various types of normalization of time series. For the lack of space, we leave the proving of the Theorems 1 and 2 out of the scope of this paper.

Analysis of associations between time series is based on the analysis of associations between them for different window size. The sequence of association values $AV(y,x)= (coss_2(y,x),\ldots, coss_n(y,x))$ for all sizes of window is called an association function [2]. A specific measure of association between time series is defined by the subset of window sizes $J \subset \{2,\ldots,n\}$ as a maximum or average of all associations $coss_k(y,x)$, $k\in J$. Examples of application of this association measure to the classification of time series are considered in [2]. In Section 3 it will be introduced a *J*-MAP image of time series pattern defined by a subset of window sizes *J*.

3 MAP Image and *J*-MAP Distance in Time Series Pattern Recognition

Suppose $y = (y_1, \ldots, y_n)$ is a time series with a constant time step. Our goal is to propose a method to find a pattern $p = (p_1,\ldots, p_m)$ in time series *y*. This problem is trivial if the pattern *p* coincides with some subsequence $x = (y_i, y_{i+1},\ldots,y_{i+m-1})$ of *y* such that $y_i= p_1$, $y_{i+1} = p_2,\ldots, y_{i+m-1} = p_m$. In real applications, such trivial cases usually do not take place and the problem is to find a subsequence in *y* which is most similar to the goal pattern. A simple algorithm to find such pattern is following: to move a window W_i of size *m* along time series and calculate a distance between goal pattern and partial time series $y_{W_i} = (y_i, y_{i+1},\ldots, y_{i+m-1})$ induced by this window. The partial time series minimizing this distance can be chosen as a found pattern. As a commonly used distance one can use Euclidean distance between time series patterns:

$$d_E(x,p) = \sqrt{\sum_{k=1}^{m}(y_{i+k-1} - p_k)^2}\,. \quad (6)$$

Before searching patterns in time series one can apply some methods of data smoothing, data filtering or noise suppression, but in the presence of large errors such procedures developed mainly for signal processing can essentially deform time series which do not describe some wave propagation or oscillating process but, instead, describe a change of some time dependent economical, financial or industrial parameter. Fig. 1 gives an example of such time series distorted by different types of errors.

Here we propose a novel method of pattern recognition in time series based on MAP transformation of patterns. MAP transform smoothes data in a sliding window. For this reason we can suppose that it is less sensitive to errors in data than original data.

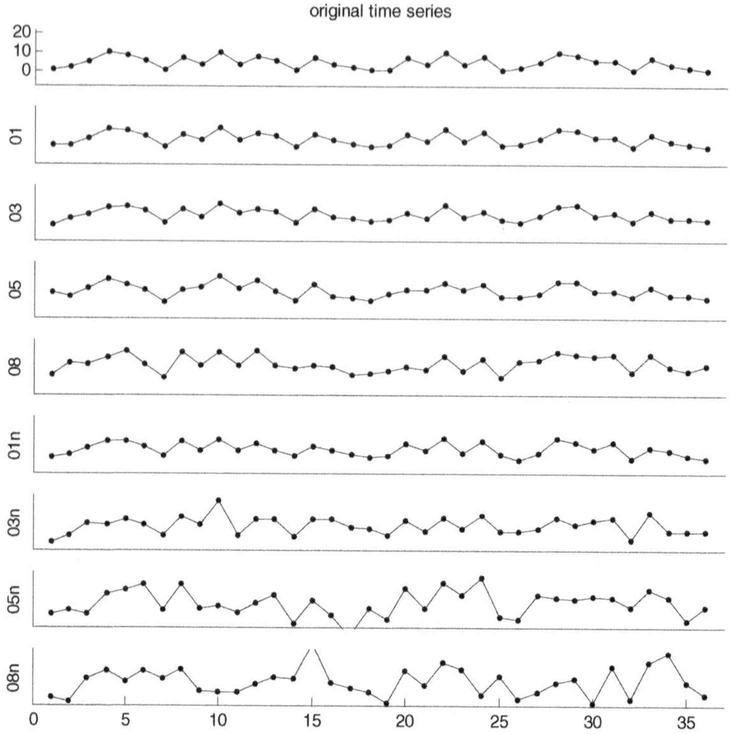

Fig. 1. Example of a synthetic time series (on the top of figure) taking values between 1 and 10 and noisy time series obtained from it by adding the following errors: 01, 03, 05, 08 denote time series with errors uniformly distributed in the intervals [0,1], [0,3], [0,5], [0,8], respectively; 01n, 03n, 05n, 08n denote time series with standard normal distribution errors multiplied by 1, 3, 5, 8, respectively.

Definition 3. A MAP image of pattern $p = (p_1,\ldots, p_m)$ is a sequence $MAPI(p)= (MAP_2(p),\ldots, MAP_m(p))$ of MAP-transforms of p for all possible window sizes. Suppose J is a subset of indexes $\{2,\ldots, m\}$. A J-MAP image of p is a sequence of MAP-transforms of p for all possible window sizes from J.

Fig. 2 shows an example of moving approximations of a pattern for different window sizes. The MAP transforms corresponding to these moving approximations contain the following sets of slope values of approximating lines: $MAP_2(p) = (1, 3, 5, -1, -3)$, $MAP_3(p) = (2, 4, 2, -2)$, $MAP_4(p) = (3, 2.6, 0.2)$, $MAP_5(p) = (2.4, 1.2)$, $MAP_6(p) = 1.4571$. The corresponding MAP image of p will be represented by a sequence: ((1, 3, 5, -1, -3), (2, 4, 2, -2), (3, 2.6, 0.2), (2.4, 1.2), (1.4571)). For $J = \{3, 4\}$ a J-MAP image of p will be equal to: ((2, 4, 2, -2), (3, 2.6, 0.2)).

Instead of a distance (6) between goal pattern p and partial time series $x = y_{Wi}$ in sliding window we propose to calculate a distance between J-MAP images of goal pattern p and partial time series $x = y_{Wi}$. This distance, called J-MAP distance, will be defined as follows:

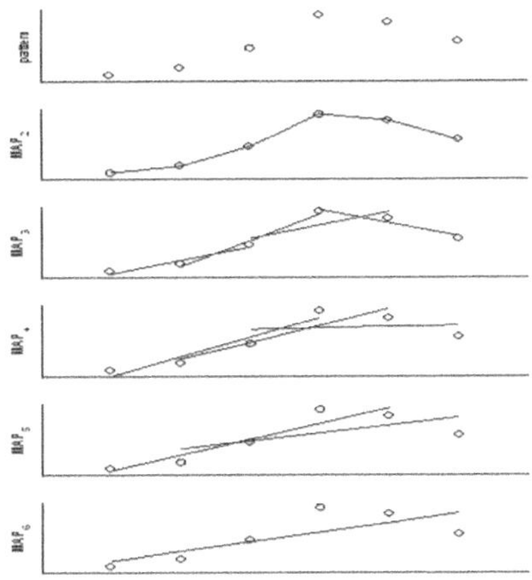

Fig. 2. Moving approximations of a pattern (given on the top of the figure) for all possible window sizes

$$d_J(x,p) = \sum_{k\in J} \sqrt{\frac{1}{m-k+1} \sum_{i=1}^{m-k+1} (MAP_{ki}(x) - MAP_{ki}(p))^2} \,. \tag{7}$$

As a distance measure combining both Euclidean distance and *J*-MAP distance we propose the following distance, which will be called *EJ*-MAP distance:

$$d_{EJ}(x,p) = d_J(x,p) + \frac{1}{\sqrt{m}} d_E(x,p)\,. \tag{8}$$

It is clear that instead of Euclidean distance one can use a normalized distance:

$$d_{NE}(x,p) = \sqrt{\frac{1}{m} \sum_{k=1}^{m} (y_{i+k-1} - p_k)^2} \,. \tag{9}$$

In this case (8) will be presented as follows:

$$d_{EJ}(x,p) = d_J(x,p) + d_{NE}(x,p)\,. \tag{10}$$

Experiments show that results of pattern recognition based on these distances can be different. Fig. 3 depicts an example of recognition of time series patterns in time series with noise. Fig. 3a shows search patterns in original time series and Fig. 3b depicts results of recognition of these patterns in time series distorted by noise.

Table 1 contains the results of comparison of considered three distance measures in their ability to recognize time series patterns in time series distorted by random errors. From time series shown on top of Fig. 1 were generated 300 random time series for each type of error described in the caption of Fig. 1. The distances for two sets of indexes J = {3,4,5,6} and J= {4,5,6} were applied. The results obtained for J = {3,4,5,6} are slightly better than for J = {4,5,6}. As one can see from Table 1, the *J*-MAP distance is more suitable for recognition of patterns in the presence of large

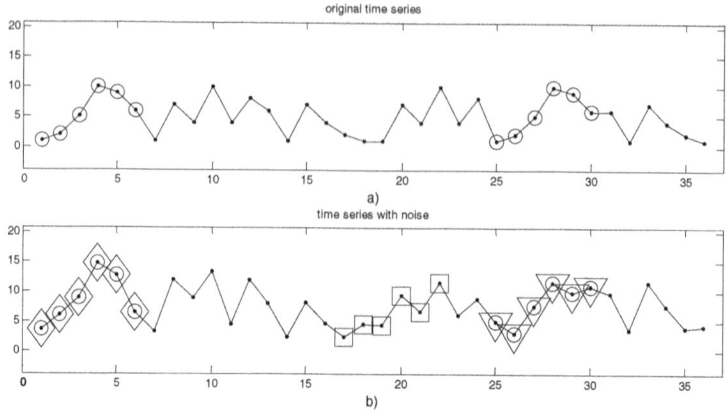

Fig. 3. a) Goal patterns (shown by circles "o") in original time series depicted also on top of Fig. 1; b) Two goal patterns in time series distorted by random errors are shown by circles (o). Patterns found by *J*-distance, *E*-distance and *EJ*-distance are shown by diamonds (◊), squares ( ) and triangles (∇) respectively

uniformly distributed errors and Euclidean distance has some advantage in recognition of patterns with normally distributed errors. *EJ*-MAP distance can be used as a compromise between these two distances when the type of error is unknown.

4 Recognition of Water Production Patterns in Petroleum Wells

The proposed methods of time series pattern representation and recognition were realized as modules of the Percept-Miner toolbox [15]. They were also used in SMART-Agua, an expert system for diagnosis of water production problems in petroleum wells.

In petroleum industry it is convenient to describe a water production patterns in petroleum wells by slopes. MAP transform and local trend associations based on MAP give a natural method for analysis of such patterns. As an example of the application of the proposed technique we consider the case of the recognition of the four water entrance patterns important for diagnosis of water production problems. The real data are analyzed against four typical patterns describing "quick increase" and "slow increase" of water production related to the certain problems of excessive water production (Fig. 4). A methodology for interpreting the behavior of waterflooding is applied in order to analyze the behavior of the water oil ratio vs. time curve in various time domains (for example, following the breakthrough).

Since expert patterns were given by sequences of slopes, *J-MAP* distance was applied for search patterns in time series closest to the goal patterns. A screenshot (Fig. 4) shows found patterns most similar to given ones. The first column shows goal patterns defined by expert. The second column shows found patterns in time series most similar to the goal patterns. The columns 3 and 4 give numerical values of slopes in goal patterns and in found patterns. Depending on the importance of the particular time interval for the expert, he can select the most appropriate pattern based on the similarity measure. This tool was developed as a support for knowledge engineer in describing his perceptions about water production patterns important both for diagnosis and for testing the expert rules considering such patterns.

Table 1. Percentage of correct recognition of patterns for different types of errors

Type of error	*E*-distance	*EJ*-distance	*J*-distance	*J* =
08	36	58	67	4,5,6
08	32	61	70	3,4,5,6
05	83	92	90	4,5,6
05	75	91	95	3,4,5,6
03	100	100	99	4,5,6
03	100	100	100	3,4,5,6
08n	17	16	16	4,5,6
08n	19	14	13	3,4,5,6
05n	28	24	21	4,5,6
05n	27	23	22	3,4,5,6
03n	64	62	55	4,5,6
03n	74	71	62	3,4,5,6
01n	100	100	96	4,5,6
01n	100	100	100	3,4,5,6

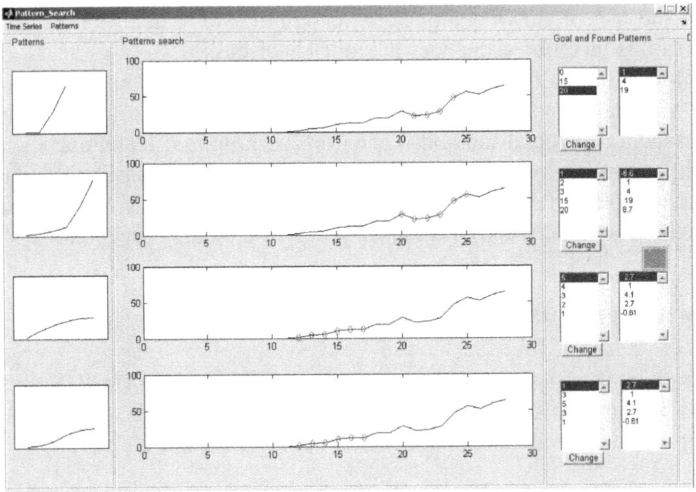

Fig. 4. Moving approximations of four patterns for all possible window sizes

5 Discussion and Conclusions

Human decision making in different application domains like economics, finance, or industry is often based on analysis of time series data bases. The main reasons for exploring a pattern recognition tools for time-series analysis are [17]: i) pattern recognition methods are more flexible than other available tools in signal processing, statistics and neural networks and offer the user the ability to optimize their design for the best results; ii) results using such tools are easy to explain to the users as opposed to neural networks whose behavior is often difficult to rationalize; and iii) pattern recognition methodologies already offer a range of existing techniques that are well suited for time-series analysis. Pattern recognition methods offer different services for time-series analysis including its recognition, classification and prediction, e.g. speech classification, source separation or forecasting.

Such analysis usually contains description of time series patterns important for decision making. Two tasks arise from searching for such patterns in time series. First, time series data can be noisy and can contain large errors. Many of conditions supposed by techniques developed in time series data mining, signal processing and time series analysis for noise suppression, data filtering and pattern recognition are not satisfied in time series describing economic or industrial time series. Moreover, the goal patterns can be small and known methods of smoothing of time series can delete them. New methods of recognition of such patterns in noisy time series are proposed in this paper. Section 3 introduces the new concepts of MAP-image and *J*-MAP distance which give possibility to recognize small patterns in time series in the presence of large evenly distributed errors. For noisy time series *J*-MAP image acts as a filter. This novel technique is based on analysis of slopes of moving approximations of time series in a sliding window. It can be used also for recognition of patterns in time series given by sequences of slopes. It is a natural way to describe time series patterns important for decision making in several application areas. As an example, in Section 4 the use of this technique for recognition of water production patterns in petroleum wells given by sequences of slopes is discussed.

Several directions of future research can considered: 1) combination of proposed methods with traditional time series analysis technique like smoothing and filtering; 2) development of special methods based on the proposed technique for recognition of specific complex patterns in real time series; 3) extension of the proposed technique to solution of perception based time series data mining tasks where linguistically described patterns are used in decision making procedures.

Acknowledgements

The research work was supported by projects D.00006 and D.00322. Special thanks to R. Herrera for his invaluable support in the development of the software. Authors also highly appreciate the valuable comments of the reviewers of the paper.

References

1. Batyrshin I., Herrera-Avelar R., Sheremetov L., Suarez R.: Moving Approximations in Time Series Data Mining. In: Proc. of the Int. Conf. Fuzzy Sets and Soft Computing in Economics and Finance, June 17-20, St. Petersburg, Russia, Vol. I (2004) 62-72
2. Batyrshin I., Herrera-Avelar R., Sheremetov L., Panova A.: Association Networks in Time Series Data Mining. In: Soft Computing for Real World Applications, Proc. of the Int. Conf. NAFIPS, June 22-25, Ann Arbor, Michigan, USA. IEEE Comp. Soc. (2005) 754-759

3. Batyrshin I., Sheremetov L.: Perception Based Time Series Data Mining with MAP Transform. In: Advances in Artificial Intelligence, Lecture Notes in Computer Science, Vol. 3789, Springer-Verlag, Berlin Heidelberg New York (2005) 514 – 523
4. Bowerman, B.L., O'Connell, R.T.: Time Series and Forecasting; An Applied Approach. Duxbury Press, Massachusetts (1979)
5. Brockwell, P.J., Davis, R.A., Fienberg, S.E.: Time Series: Theory and Methods, Springer Series in Statistics, Springer-Verlag, Berlin Heidelberg New York (1991)
6. Chatfield, C.: The Analysis of Time Series, an Introduction, Sixth Edition. London: Chapman and Hall/CRC (2004)
7. Cheung, J.T.: Representation and Extraction of Trends from Process Data. D.Sci. Th., Massachusetts Institute of Technology, Cambridge/MA, USA (1992)
8. Hand, D.J.: Intelligent Data Analysis: Issues and Opportunities. In: Proc. of the Int. Conf. IDA97. Lecture Notes in Computer Science, Vol. 1280. Springer-Verlag, Berlin Heidelberg New York (1997) 1-14
9. Kivikunnas, S.: Overview of Process Trend Analysis Methods and Applications. In: Proc. of Workshop on Applications in Chemical and Biochemical Industry. Aachen, Germany. (1999)
10. Konstantinov, K.B., Yoshida, T.: Real-time Qualitative Analysis of the Temporal Shapes of (Bio) Process Variables. J. of Am. Inst. of Chem. Eng., Vol. 38 No. 11 (1992) 1703-1715
11. Least Squares Fitting. Wolfram Research. Mathworld. URL: http://mathworld.wolfram.com/LeastSquaresFitting.html
12. Mörchen, F.: Time Series Feature Extraction for Data Mining Using DWT and DFT. Data Bionics, Philipps-University Marburg, Germany, October 9 (2003)
13. Ponomaryov, V., Gallegos-Funes, F., Sansores-Pech, R., Sadovnychiy, S.: Real-time noise suppression in 3D ultrasound imaging based on order statistics. Electronics Letters, Vol. 42, No. 2 (2006) 80-82
14. Ponomaryov, V., Pogrebnyak, O.: Novel Robust RM Filters for Radar Image Filtering. J. of Electronic Imaging, Vol. 5 No 3, (1996) 410-421
15. Sheremetov, L.B., Batyrshin, I.Z, Filatov, D.M.: Perception Based Hybrid Intelligent Systems in Petroleum Applications. In: Proc. of the NAFIPS'06 Int. Conf., June 3-6, Montréal, Canada. IEEE Comp. Soc. (2006)
16. Shumway, R.H., Stoffer, D.S.: Time Series Analysis and its Applications, Springer-Verlag, Berlin Heidelberg New York (2000)
17. Singh, S.: Noise Impact on Time-Series Forecasting Using an Intelligent Pattern Matching Technique, Pattern Recognition, Vol. 32, Issue 8 (1999) 1389-1398

System Classification by Using Discriminant Functions of Time-Frequency Features

Miguel Mendoza Reyes[1], Juan V. Lorenzo-Ginori[1], A. Taboada-Crispí[1], and Yakelin Luna Carvajal[2]

[1] Center for Studies on Electronics and Information Technologies, Universidad Central "Marta Abreu" de Las Villas, Carretera a Camajuaní, km 5 ½, Santa Clara, VC, Cuba, CP 54830
{mmendoza, juanl, ataboada}@uclv.edu.cu
[2] Ministry of Public Health, Santa Clara, VC, Cuba
yakelin@uclv.edu.cu

Abstract. Time-frequency representations (TFR) convey relevant information about systems that can not be obtained under stationary conditions. In this paper, a methodology to classify systems using the information obtained from time-frequency representations during transient phenomena is described and tested experimentally. The study includes an assessment of the features to be extracted from the TFR, which are relevant for the desired classification, as well as the construction of the appropriate discriminant functions using them. The methodology is tested by means of a biomedical example related to patient's classification.

Keywords: time-frequency distributions, feature extraction.

1 Introduction

System classification can be done through the analysis of the signals they produce. When the analysis is to be done in the frequency domain, there are considerations that should be addressed. In the case of a signal whose spectral characteristics vary with time, if there is a need of knowing the spectral content of that signal for every time instant, in order to perform a dynamic spectral analysis, the use of a time-frequency representation (TFR) of that signal is commonly required. This dynamic representation of the spectral behavior can be obtained by processing signals through the time-frequency distributions (TFD).

From the TFR of signals, a set of features can be extracted to characterize them. The selection of the most appropriated features depends mainly on the type of TFD used to process the signal, and the application where they will be employed. For those TFR that allow energetic interpretations, features values serve to estimate the form in which signal energy is locally distributed in the time-frequency (t-f) plane. For TFR computation, TFD from the Cohen group have been commonly assessed. The TFDs from this group of bilinear distribution have the general form

$$C_x(t,f;\varphi) = \int_{-\infty}^{\infty}\int_{-\infty}^{\infty}\int_{-\infty}^{\infty} e^{j2\pi\theta(u-t)} z(u+\tau/2) z^*(u-\tau/2)\varphi(\theta,\tau) e^{-j2\pi f\tau} d\theta du d\tau \;, \qquad (1)$$

J.F. Martínez-Trinidad et al. (Eds.): CIARP 2006, LNCS 4225, pp. 920–928, 2006.

where z(t) is the analytic signal and $\varphi(\theta,\tau)$ the kernel function, whose behavior in the (θ,τ) plane, or ambiguity domain, defines the general properties of the TFD 1.

A typical TFR contains a large amount of information. To reduce this, features are extracted from particular zones in the t-f plane. The size and location of these zones are mainly defined according to the specific application. After computing the features, the selection of the suitable ones is a mandatory task in the classification procedures.

To determine the feasibility of features for classification purposes, they must be evaluated in order to find their discriminatory possibilities. The combination of these selected features in discriminant functions allows system classification.

All the process should be repeated in order to find the configuration with the greater amount of features with discriminatory possibilities. This process includes the selection of the appropriate TFD used to obtain the TFR, and the sizes and location of the proper zones in TFR from which the features will be extracted.

This paper presents a methodology for system classification by using discriminant functions of statistical parameters of time-frequency features. Section two depicts the methodology proposed and describes the systems under classification. The methods used for the computation of TFR and its features, and the selection of statistical parameters and its combination, are also presented in this section. Section three shows the results of the system classification by following the proposed methodology. Finally, section four encloses the discussion of obtained results and resulting conclusions.

2 Materials and Methods

The global procedure followed to find the discriminant functions could be summarized in the following steps:

1. Set initial configuration for TFR computation: TFD type and parameters, window type and parameters.
2. Select zones of TFR to compute features: (depending on application)
3. Extract features from TFR zones.
4. Compute statistical parameters of features in selected zones.
5. Select parameters for analysis of variance (ANOVA): normality and homogeneity test.
6. Select parameters with discriminatory abilities: ANOVA and multiple comparisons.
7. Select the setup for TFR computation according to the number of parameters with discriminatory abilities.
8. Find combinations of parameters to form discriminant functions: LDA
9. Test discriminant functions: Wilk's lambda, Cross-validation.

In the present work, the systems to be classified were patients with different blood pressure (BP) behavior and therefore different influence on their autonomic nervous system (ANS). ANS controls heart rate through its sympathetic and parasympathetic branches. High blood pressure (HBP) can affects the performance of the ANS and, as a result, also influences the behavior of the heart rate variability (HRV) signal 2 3 4.

Spectro-temporal features of HRV, derived from an appropriate TFR, were used in this example for the classification of patients with different BP behavior. Features selection was done according to the proposed methodology.

2.1 Patients

Patients under study belonged to one of three categories: hyperreactive (HR) that comprised individuals whose levels of cardiovascular response to the left-arm isometric exercise (LAIE) were greater than the limits set to the normotensive (NT) group, but lower than those set for the hypertensive (HT). HR group has been considered prone to develop HBP 5.

The LAIE consists of three stages. During the first one, lasting two minutes, the rest stage, the patient sits relaxed with his hands on his legs. Then the effort stage begins, the patient extends his left arm horizontally with respect to the floor, while holding a 500 gram weight during two minutes. Finally, the patient releases the weight and put his left arm back to the rest position, keeping it that way for the two minutes that last this final recovery stage. The whole procedure lasts for six minutes.

The group of patients comprised 27 individuals, all male. Subjects with health conditions that are known, or suspected, to cause autonomic disorders, such as diabetes, epilepsy and asthma, were excluded.

Patients were selected according to confirmed diagnosis reached by a team of physicians after various studies and laboratory tests. The characteristics of the groups evaluated are shown in table 1.

Table 1. Groups of patients

Group		Number of patients	Age (m ± std), years
Normotensive	(NT)	11	31.18 ± 5
Hypertensive	(HT)	10	41.20 ± 7
Hyperreactive	(HR)	6	36.85 ± 12

m: mean value, std: standard deviation

2.2 TFD Configuration

Spectral analysis of HRV is the recommended method when the study of the effect of one of the systems that modulates this signal through the ANS is needed 3. To highlight the influence of a particular system on the ANS, HRV is commonly obtained from electrocardiographic (ECG) records acquired during the execution of exercises 2 6, as in this case. Due to the non-stationary characteristics of such records, the use of time-frequency analysis (TFA) is the most suitable approach for HRV dynamic spectral analysis 1.

In HRV studies, Wigner-Ville Distribution (WVD) and its smoothed versions have been commonly used 7–10. Choi-Williams distribution (CWD), a representative case of the reduced-interference distributions (RID) group, have also been addressed 11. In this study TFR were obtained by using the Choi-Williams distribution,

$$CWD_x(t,f)=\sqrt{\frac{2}{\pi}}\int_{-\infty}^{\infty}\int_{-\infty}^{\infty}\frac{\sigma}{|\tau|}e^{-2\tau^2(u-t)^2/\tau^2}z(u+\tau/2)z^*(u-\tau/2)\varphi(v,\tau)e^{-j2\pi f\tau}dud\tau\ , \tag{2}$$

and the smoothed-pseudo-Wigner-Ville distribution,

$$SPWVD_x(t,f)=\int_{-\infty}^{\infty}h(\tau)\int_{-\infty}^{\infty}g(u-t)z(u+\tau/2)z^*(u-\tau/2)e^{-j2\pi f\tau}dud\tau\ , \tag{3}$$

where $h(\tau)$ is the frequency smoothing window or data window, $g(u)$ is the time smoothing window and $z(t)$ is the analytic version of time signal $x(t)$ 7.

In (2), the parametrization function, or distribution kernel, $\varphi(v,\tau)$, has the form

$$\varphi_{(v,\tau)}=e^{-\frac{(\pi v\tau)^2}{2\sigma^2}}\ . \tag{4}$$

In this study, the value $\sigma = 0.1$ was used to favor interference reduction 12.

2.3 Feature Extraction

After computing the TFR of HRV, there were extracted instantaneous estimates of frequency, power and bandwidth from the LF band, 0.04 Hz to 0.15 Hz, and from HF band, 0.15 Hz to 0.4 Hz, as defined in 3 These features have been linked to the ANS in previous studies 2 3 6. Their values were computed from the moments and marginals of TFRs 1 7. A list of the TFR features evaluated in this study is presented in table 2.

Table 2. TFR features evaluated in this study

Feature	Meaning
IF	Instantaneous frequency
IB	Instantaneous bandwidth
IP	Instantaneous power
PS	Power spectral density
E	Local energy

The feature vectors, containing the values computed for the whole record, were divided according to the three exercise stages. Stages 2, effort, and 3, recovery, were subsequently divided in sections where statistical parameters were computed.

An appropriate configuration was elected after considering several alternatives. These involved different analysis windows, TFDs, and number of sections in which the stages of effort and recovery were divided. A preliminary selection of the configuration was made heuristically.

The statistical parameters evaluated were: mean value, M, trimmed mean, TM, and standard deviation, SD. The values corresponding to the effort and recovery stages were normalized with respect to those corresponding to the rest stage, to reduce inter-individual variations.

The names of the parameters were formed by appending the numbers of the corresponding stage and section, in that order, to the name of the feature. For example, L_H31SD represents the standard deviation of the values of the instantaneous LF to HF bands power ratio, computed for the first section of the recovery stage. MATLAB toolboxes were used for TFR computation and feature extraction 13.

2.4 Parameter Selection

For each evaluated configuration the parameters with higher probability to discriminate patients, according to the group to which they belonged, were searched. One-way ANOVA was used to determine if the parameter under test was significantly different in the groups evaluated, $p<0.05$. Previously to ANOVA analysis, these parameters were analyzed to ensure distribution normality and homogeneity of variances. Anderson-Darling test and Levene's test were used, respectively, for these purposes 14.

Parameters selected, according to ANOVA results, were further evaluated by using the Tukey-Kramer's multiple comparisons test, to investigate their possibilities for the discrimination of at least one group from the others. Statistical processing was performed with SPSS 15.

2.5 Discriminant Analysis

Linear discriminant analysis (LDA) was performed in order to find functions $f_i(p_k)$ of the N previously selected parameters p_k, suitable for the classification of patients. These functions have the form,

$$f_i(p_k) = \sum_{k=0}^{N-1} a_{ik}\, p_k \ , \qquad (5)$$

where

i =1..G-1, is the function number,
G = 3, is the number of groups,
a_{ik}: are the function coefficients.

The Mahalanobis distance in a stepwise analysis was used to obtain the functions. A significance level $p<0.05$ was selected for the inclusion of parameters. Functions were tested using leave-one-out cross-validation, a process in which every case is classified by using discriminant functions obtained from the rest of them.

3 Results

3.1 TFD Configuration Selection

Among the different configurations assessed to obtain the TFR, the one that used the CWD with Gaussian windows and six sections per stage had the greater amount of parameters with discriminatory possibilities, $p < 0.05$. The list of parameters and the corresponding p vales are shown in table 3.

According to multiple comparisons tests, none of the listed parameters was able to differentiate every group from the rest. For example, parameter L_H31SD, the standard deviation of the power ratio in the first section of recovery stage, was significant different for the group HT, but it could not discriminate the groups NT and HR. Figure 1 shows the time progression of this parameter during the effort ant recovery stage.

Table 3. Parameters selected according to established criteria

Parameter	p
L_H31SD	0.002
IPL31M	0.006
IPL31MT	0.009
IFH31DSD	0.012
L_H32DSD	0.015
IPL31SD	0.017
IFL34DMT	0.034
IFH22DMT	0.036
IFL26SD	0.038
IFL34DM	0.039
IFH22DM	0.040
IFL35DM	0.047

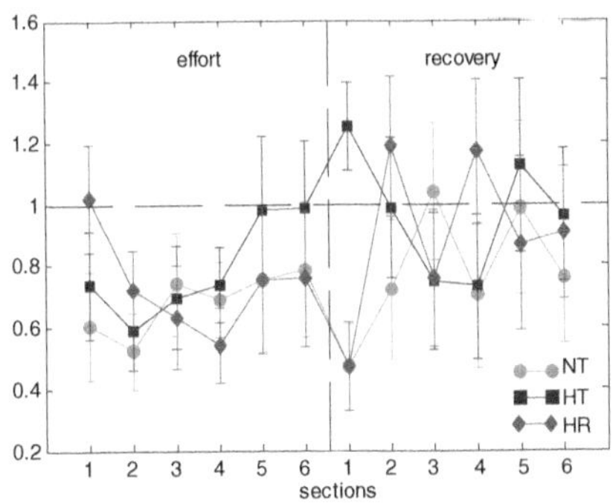

Fig. 1. Time progression of the parameter L_HSD

3.2 Discriminant Functions

Two discriminant functions were obtained from the set of selected parameters. The coefficients are shown in table 4.

Table 4. Coefficients of discriminant functions

k	p_k	Coefficients	
		a_{1k}	a_{2k}
0	(constant)	2,075	-0,996
1	L_H31SD	0,114	0,270
2	IFH31DSD	162,845	37,339
3	IFL34DMT	157,605	-23,029
4	IFH22DMT	-917,906	756,490
5	IFL26SD	-290,709	14,561
6	IFH22DM	832,625	-763,422
7	IFL35DM	75,769	-64,371

The feasibility of the use of discriminant functions for the classification of different cases was tested by determining Wilks' Lambda and significance value, Sig, table 5.

Table 5. Discriminant functions evaluation

Function	Wilks' Lambda	Chi-square	df	Sig.
1 through 2	0.051	62.351	14	0.000
2	0.407	18.861	6	0.004

The low value of Wilks' lambda, below 0.1, and the null value of significance, confirmed that the mean values of the functions were different for the groups, and proved the sufficiency of their application as discriminant functions. Figure 2 shows the scatter plot of the cases, classified by using the discriminant functions.

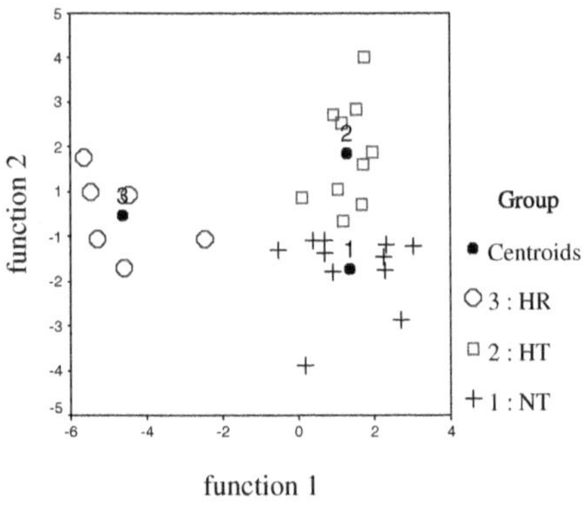

Fig. 2. Scatter plot for all groups

To get a more realistic evaluation of discriminant functions, leave-one-out cross-validation was performed; table 6 shows the results of this evaluation.

Table 6. Classification results with original cases and cross-validated evaluation

			Predicted Group Membership			
		group	NT	HT	HR	Total
Original Data	cases	NT	11	0	0	11
		HT	1	9	0	10
		HR	0	0	6	6
	%	NT	100.0	0.0	0.0	100.0
		HT	10.0	90.0	0.0	100.0
		HR	0.0	0.0	100.0	100.0
Cross-Validated	cases	NT	10	1	0	11
		HT	3	7	0	10
		HR	0	0	6	6
	%	NT	90.9	9.1	0.0	100.0
		HT	30.0	70.0	0.0	100.0
		HR	0.0	0.0	100.0	100.0

The difference between classification results obtained with original data from those of cross-validation is satisfactory according to the sample size. This suggests that the number of predictors accounted in the discriminant functions is acceptable.

4 Discussion and Conclusions

Due to the great amount of parameters that can be extracted from a TFR, the search of the appropriate features for classification purposes should be done through a combination of techniques.

The proposed methodology contributed to control the amount and quality of parameters with discriminatory abilities. The appropriate selection of feature parameters benefits dimensionality reduction, which is an almost obligatory process in the case of TFR analysis, due to the high dimensionality of the data to be processed.

The discriminant functions, obtained by following the proposed approach, gathered the most appropriate statistical parameters of spectro-temporal features of the signal used to represent the systems under study.

Cross-validation should be used to confirm classification results obtained with the discriminant functions. This procedure generates more realistic results, and is particularly useful if the number of available cases is small.

Acknowledgments

The authors wish to acknowledge M. D. Alina Pérez-de-Armas for her invaluable help in the completion of this work. We also thank Dr. Ricardo Grau-Abalo and Dr. Gladys Casas-Cardoso for their thorough review of the statistical issues. This research was partially supported by the Canadian International Development Agency Project Tier II-394-TT02-00 and by the Flemish VLIR-UOS Programme for Institutional University Co-operation (IUC).

References

1. L. Cohen, "Time Frequency Distribution – A Review", in *Proceedings of IEEE*, vol. 77, July, 1989, pp 941-981.
2. D. Luccini et al, "Impairment in Cardiac Autonomic Regulation Preceding Arterial Hypertension in Humans. Insights from Spectral Analysis of Beat-by-Beat Cardiovascular Variability," *Circulation*, November, 2002, pp. 2673-2679.
3. Task Force of European Society of Cardiology and the North American Society of Pacing and Electrophysiology, "Heart Rate Variability. Standards of Measurement, Physiological Interpretation and Clinical Use", *European Heart Journal*, Vol. 17, pp. 354-381, 1996.
4. L. R. Davrath, Y. Goren, I. Pinhas, E. Toledo and S. Akselrod, "Early autonomic malfunction in normotensive individuals with a genetic predisposition to essential hypertension," *Am J Physiol Heart Circ Physiol*, vol. 285, pp. H1697–H1704, 2003. Available: http://ajpheart.physiology.org/cgi/content/short/285/4/H1697.
5. M. Benet, J. Apollinaire, J. Torres and S. Peraza, "Reactividad cardiovascular y factores de riesgos cardiovasculares en individuos normotensos menores de 40 años," *Revista Española de Salud Pública*, vol. 77, no. 1, pp. 143-150, 2003.
6. H. G. Steenis, W. L. J. Martens and J. H. M. Tulen, "Time–Frequency Parameters of Heart rate Variability," *IEEE Engineering in Medicine and Biology*, vol. 21, no. 4, July / August 2002, pp. 46-58.
7. M. Houle and G. Billman, "Low-frequency component of the heart rate variability spectrum: a poor marker of sympathetic activity," *Am J Physiol Heart Circ Physiol*, vol. 276, no. 1, pp. H215-H223, January 1999.
8. M. Ebden, L. Tarassenko, S. Payne, A. Darowski A. and J. Price, "Time-frequency analysis of the ECG in the diagnosis of vasovagal syndrome in older people," in *Proceedings of the 26th Annual International Conference of the IEEE EMBS*, San Francisco, CA, USA, September 1-5, 2004, pp. 290-293.
9. K. Yoshiuchi et al, "Use of time-frequency analysis to investigate temporal patterns of cardiac autonomic response during head-up tilt in chronic fatigue syndrome," *Autonomic Neuroscience: Basic and Clinical*, vol. 113, pp. 55-62, 2004.
10. S. Jasson et al, "Instant Power Spectrum Analysis of Heart Rate Variability During Orthostatic Tilt Using a Time-/Frequency-Domain Method," *Circulation*, vol. 96, pp. 3521-3526, July, 1997.
11. F. Clariá, M. Vallverdú, R. Baranowski , L. Chonowska , P. Martínez and P. Caminal , "Time-Frequency Representation of the HRV: A Tool to Characterize Sudden Cardiac Death in Hypertrophy Cardiomyopatthy Patients," in *Proceedings of the 22nd Annual EMBS International Conference*, Chicago, IL, July 23-28, 2000, pp. 71-73.
12. W. Williams and J. Jeong, "Reduced Interference Time-Frequency Distributions," in *Time-Frequency Signal Analysis*, B. Boashash, Ed. Longman Cheshire, 1992, pp. 74-97.
13. F. Auger, P. Flandrin, P. Goncalves and O. Lemoine, *Time Frequency Toolbox for use with MATLAB*, Available: http://www-isis.enst.fr/Applications/tftb/iutsn.univ-nantes.fr/auger/tftbftp.html.
14. J. L. Romeu, "Anderson-Darling: A Goodness of Fit Test for Small Simples Assumptions," *RAC START*, vol. 10, no. 5. Available: http://rac.alionscience.com/pdf/A_DTest.pdf.
15. *SPSS for Windows, Release 9.01*, 1999.

Gabor Kernels for Textured Image Representation and Classification

Hugo Hidalgo-Silva

CICESE-Ciencias de la Computación,
Km. 107 Carr. Tijuana-Eda,
Ensenada 22800 México
hugo@cicese.mx

Abstract. A Gabor based representation for textured images is proposed. Instead of the ordinary filter bank, a reproducing kernel representation is constructed consisting of a sum of several local reproducing kernels. The image representation coefficients are computed by a basis pursuit procedure, and are then considered as the feature vectors. The feature vectors are used to construct a kernel for a support vector classifier. Results are presented for a set of oriented texture images.

1 Introduction

Classification and segmentation of digital images based on the texture content is a fundamental problem in computer vision. A lot of different techniques have been considered in literature, from signal processing [1,2,3], to statistical modeling based [4,5]. In the signal processing approach, the Gabor filter is the preferred building block. The textured image is submitted to a linear transform system named filter bank, consisting of a set of Gabor filters. The output of each filter is another image, applied then to a feature extractor. Several feature extractors are considered in literature [6], some use only the magnitude response, others the real component and some authors apply a full-wave rectifier, or a sigmoidal function to each filter's output. For every image, a large set of features are usually considered, those features are then applied to a classifier to identify the corresponding texture in the image.

In this work a Gabor based representation for the image is proposed. Instead of a filter bank, the image is considered as an element of a reproducing kernel Hilbert space. A kernel is constructed consisting of a sum of several local reproducing kernels. The image representation is assembled by a basis pursuit procedure, and the coefficients of the representation are taken as the feature vectors. The feature vectors are then used to construct a kernel for a support vector classifier. Results are presented for a set of test images from the Brodatz album.

J.F. Martínez-Trinidad et al. (Eds.): CIARP 2006, LNCS 4225, pp. 929–935, 2006.

2 Signal Representation

The Gabor transform is a fundamental tool for signal representation and decomposition. When a function f in $L^2(\mathbb{R})$ is used to represent an analog signal with finite energy, its Fourier transform

$$F(\omega) = \int_{-\infty}^{\infty} e^{-i\omega t} f(t)dt \tag{1}$$

reveals the spectral information of the signal. But the Fourier transform is not very useful for extracting information of the spectrum from a local observation of the signal f. The Gabor approach consider a window for time localization. The optimal window for time localization is obtained using a Gaussian function:

$$g_\sigma(t) = \frac{1}{2\sqrt{\pi\sigma}} e^{-\frac{t^2}{4\sigma}} \tag{2}$$

where $\sigma > 0$ is fixed. Optimality is characterized in terms of the uncertainty principle [7].

If $f(t) \in L^2(\mathbb{R})$, the Gabor transform $F_{\mu,\sigma}(\omega)$ is the Fourier transform of the product $f(t)g_\sigma(t-\mu)$:

$$F_{\mu,\sigma}(\omega) = \int_{-\infty}^{\infty} e^{-j\omega t} f(t) g_\sigma(t-\mu)dt. \tag{3}$$

The Gabor transform is also represented as $F_{\mu,\sigma}(\omega) = (\mathcal{G}_\mu^\sigma f)(\omega)$, and can be interpreted as a dot product relation that measures the similarity of $f(t)$ to the Gabor elementary function (GEF) $G_{\mu,\omega}^\sigma(t) = g_\sigma(t-\mu)e^{j\omega t}$ [7]:

$$(\mathcal{G}_\mu^\sigma f)(\omega) = \langle f, G_{\mu,\omega}^\sigma \rangle. \tag{4}$$

Gabor elementary functions, also named as Gabor atoms or windowed Fourier atoms, have great applicability to spectral analysis of textures. Some authors consider only the real part of the GEF to construct filter banks employed in the classification task [1,6]. Texture analysis with Gabor filters is usually performed by obtaining a bank of Gabor filters tuned at different μ, ω parameters. Then, a non linearity is applied to every Gabor function in order to select the proper feature of every filter. In this work, we are interested in the construction of a reproducing kernel Hilbert space (RKHS) for images with a kernel derived of the Gabor elementary functions. RKHS have acquired great importance in the learning community because they form the basis of the Kernel learning methodology [8,9]. By definition, a Hilbert space $\mathcal{H}$ es called a reproducing kernel Hilbert space if the following conditions are satisfied[10]:

1. the elements of $\mathcal{H}$ are (complex or real valued) functions defined on any set $\mathcal{D}$;
2. for every $t \in \mathcal{D}$ there exists $K_t > 0$ such that

$$\|f(t)\| \leq K_t|f| \quad f \in \mathcal{H}.$$

In an RKHS $\mathcal{H}$, for every $t \in \mathcal{D}$ there is a function $R(\cdot, t) \in \mathcal{H}$ such that

$$f(t) = \langle f, R(\cdot, t)\rangle \quad f \in \mathcal{H}$$

by the Riesz representation theorem and the evaluation functionals are determined by the function $R(s,t)$ on $\mathcal{D} \times \mathcal{D}$, called the kernel of the RKHS $\mathcal{H}$. The kernel $R(s,t)$ of an RKHS is a symmetric and positive definite function, i.e. $R(t,s) = \overline{R(s,t)}$ and for any finite set $\{s_i \in \mathcal{D}; i = 1, 2, \ldots\}$ and complex numbers λ_i $(i = 1, 2, \ldots, n)$,

$$\sum_{i,j=1}^{n} \lambda_i \overline{\lambda_j} R(s_i, s_j) \geq 0.$$

Besides, the RKHS $\mathcal{H}$ with kernel R is generated by $\{R(\cdot, t); t \in \mathcal{D}\}$. Another approach to construct a RKHS consist in considering the Loéve Transform [10]. For $x \in \mathcal{H}_1$, a closed subspace of $\mathcal{H}$ generated by $\{h(t); t \in \mathcal{D}\}$, the function $\hat{x}(t) := \langle x, h(t)\rangle$ is called the Loéve transform of x. The Loéve Transform form an RKHS with kernel

$$R(s,t) = \langle h(t), h(s)\rangle \quad s, t \in \mathcal{D}.$$

For example, considering a finite interval $[-A, A]$ and the subspace of $L^2[-A, A]$ generated by $h(t) = e^{-i\omega t}$ for $-\infty < t < +\infty$. In this case the kernel is

$$\langle h(t), h(s)\rangle = \frac{1}{2A} \int_{-A}^{A} e^{i\omega t} e^{-i\omega s} d\omega = \frac{\sin A(t-s)}{A(t-s)},$$

and the Loéve transform of $F \in L^2[-A, +A]$ is the Fourier transform

$$f(t) = \frac{1}{2A} \int_{-A}^{A} e^{i\omega t} F(\omega) d\omega.$$

Then, the finite Fourier transforms with fixed band limit A form an RKHS, the Hilbert space L_A of band-limited signals. Here, we are interested in an RKHS for band-limited signals but considering the Gabor representation. Consider the kernel obtained with the dot product of the GEF's:

$$\begin{aligned} Q(s,t) = \langle G^{\sigma}_{\mu,\omega}(s), G^{\sigma}_{\mu,\omega}(t)\rangle = \\ \frac{1}{2A} \int_{-A}^{A} e^{i\omega t} e^{-i\omega s} g_\sigma(t-\mu) g_\sigma(s-\mu) d\omega = \\ g_\sigma(t-\mu) g_\sigma(s-\mu) \frac{\sin A(s-t)}{A(s-t)}, \end{aligned} \tag{5}$$

by this formulation, we can represent an element of the Hilbert space of band-limited signals in terms of the kernel (5).

3 Image Representation

In the usual Gabor expansion texture recognition approach, a bank of Gabor filters is applied to a portion of the image [2]. The basic even-symmetric Gabor filter oriented at 0° is the real part of G with a variance parameter for each axis σ_x, σ_y:

$$h(k,l) = e^{-\frac{1}{4}(\frac{k^2}{\sigma_x}+\frac{l^2}{\sigma_y})}\cos(2\pi f_0 k),$$

where f_0 is the radial center frequency. Other orientations are obtained by rotating the reference coordinate system (k,l) some angle θ. We consider the image representation in terms of a kernel:

$$f(t) = \sum_{i=0}^{i=N} \beta_i \tilde{Q}(s_i, t), \tag{6}$$

where $\tilde{Q} = \sum_{j=1}^{M} R_j(s,t)$.

Each $R_j(s,t)$ with different parameters $\mu_x, \mu_y, \sigma_x, \sigma_y, \theta$. N is the number of pixels, M the number of kernels and the space coordinates are two-dimensional $t = (t_x, t_y), s = (s_x, s_y)$. For the kernel construction we have used the property that a sum of kernels is a kernel [9]. Observe that the number of coefficients is the same as the number of image pixels, contrary to the filter bank approach, where we have a much more large feature set.

The selection of the β coefficients is considered by a basis pursuit (BP) procedure [11]. In the BP approach, the basis dictionary is assumed overcomplete, and there may exist many representations as (6). In our implementation, the kernel is constructed by a sum of several local kernels, and we assume that the representation may not be unique. The BP technique consist on finding a representation whose coefficients have a minimal l^1 norm. For that purpose, the minimization problem is:

$$\min \quad \|\beta\|_1 \quad \text{subject to} \quad \mathbf{\Phi}\beta = \mathbf{d} \tag{7}$$

with $\mathbf{\Phi}$ the Gram matrix of kernel evaluations $\mathbf{\Phi}_{i,j} = \tilde{Q}(s_i, t_j)$, $\mathbf{d}$ is the image representation in a lexicographically ordered vector. The minimization problem is implemented by solving the equivalent linear program

$$\min \quad \mathbf{c}^t\mathbf{x} \quad \text{subject to} \quad \mathbf{A}\mathbf{x} = \mathbf{b}, \quad \mathbf{x} \geq 0, \tag{8}$$

making the translations $\mathbf{A} = (\mathbf{\Phi}, -\mathbf{\Phi})$, $\mathbf{b} = \mathbf{d}$, $\mathbf{x} = (\mathbf{u}, \mathbf{v})$, $\beta = (\mathbf{u} - \mathbf{v})$, and considering $\mathbf{c}$ a vector of ones. The solution of (7) is obtained by solving the linear program (8). The linear program can be efficiently solved with public available software like PCx [12].

4 Image Classification

For the image classification process, the kernel representation (6) is obtained for every element of a set of sub-images extracted from the training and testing images. The corresponding coefficients of the kernel representation are employed to construct a kernel machine; a support vector classifier (SVC). The SVC is constructed assuming a kernel function $k(x, z)$ implementing a dot product among elements of a feature space: $\langle \Phi(x), \Phi(z) \rangle$. The usual kernel construction for image classification has been to perform dot products of sub-elements of the image, then raise the resulting dot product to a power d_1 to form a local kernel. The final kernel is the sum over the whole image of the local kernels [8]. In this work, the kernel is constructed as a function of the dot product of the image coefficients, $\langle \beta_i, \beta_j \rangle$. The SVC is aimed to construct the classifier function $c(x) = sign(\sum_i^l y_i \alpha_i k(x, x_i) + b)$ in terms of a Gram matrix

$$\mathbf{K}_{i,j} = k(x_i, x_j), \tag{9}$$

by solving the system:

$$\max \quad W(\alpha) = \sum_{i=1}^{l} \alpha_i - \frac{1}{2} \sum_{i,j=1}^{l} \alpha_i \alpha_j y_i y_j k(x_i, x_j),$$

$$\text{subject to} \quad 0 \leq \alpha_i \leq \frac{C}{l} \quad \text{for all} \quad i = 1, \ldots, l.$$

$$\text{and} \quad \sum_{i=1}^{l} \alpha_i y_i = 0.$$

Where l is the number of patterns, y the corresponding output (± 1) and b is the threshold [8]. We construct our SVC kernel matrix $\mathbf{K}$ by performing the dot product among coefficients. Several other kernels can also be obtained using kernel properties [8,9].

5 Application Results

A set of 560 non-overlapping images of 40×40 pixels were extracted of the images observed in Fig. 1. The images correspond to textures D1,D11,D17,D20,D21,D22,

Table 1. Classification accuracy results for SVC's with different kernel functions

kernel	Classification Accuracy (%)
$< x, y >$	41.7
$< x, y >^2$	67.85
$< \beta_i, \beta_j >$	36.26
$< \beta_i, \beta_j >^2$	94.78
$< \beta_i, \beta_j >^3$	52.47
RBF	86.26

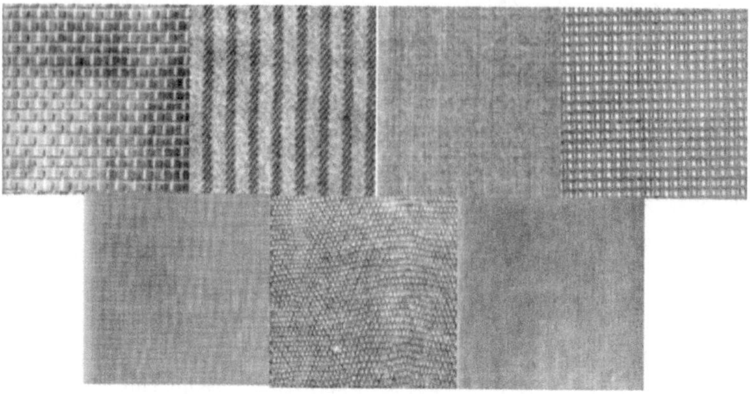

Fig. 1. Brodatz images (upper left to lower right) D1,D11,D17,D20,D21,D22 and D77

Table 2. Parameters of the kernel functions $R_j(s,t)$

kernel	μ_x	μ_y	σ_x	σ_y	θ	kernel	μ_x	μ_y	σ_x	σ_y	θ
1	20	20	40	40	0	21	20	20	20	20	0
2	20	20	40	10	45	22	20	20	20	5	45
3	20	20	40	10	90	23	20	20	20	5	90
4	20	20	40	10	135	24	20	20	20	5	135
5	10	10	20	20	0	25	20	30	20	20	0
6	10	10	20	5	45	26	20	30	20	5	45
7	10	10	20	5	90	27	20	30	20	5	90
8	10	10	20	5	135	28	20	30	20	5	135
9	10	20	20	20	0	29	30	10	20	20	0
10	10	20	20	5	45	30	30	10	20	5	45
11	10	20	20	5	90	31	30	10	20	5	90
12	10	20	20	5	135	32	30	10	20	5	135
13	10	30	20	20	0	33	30	20	20	20	0
14	10	30	20	5	45	34	30	20	20	5	45
15	10	30	20	5	90	35	30	20	20	5	90
16	10	30	20	5	135	36	30	20	20	5	135
17	20	10	20	20	0	37	30	30	20	20	0
18	20	10	20	5	45	38	30	30	20	5	45
19	20	10	20	5	90	39	30	30	20	5	90
20	20	10	20	5	135	40	30	30	20	5	135

and D77 of Brodatz's album [13]. For each class, 28 images were used as training, and 52 as testing data. The coefficients of (6) were obtained considering the kernel parameters shown on Table 1. Results for different kernel functions are presented in Table 2, observe that the first two kernels are constructed with dot products of the raw images.

From Table 2 observe also that using the dot products of the images or the dot product of coefficients alone produce similarly wrong results. The main improvement is obtained when the second order polynomial kernel is constructed. For the second order of the bare images an improvement to 67.85 % is obtained. But when the second order polynomial kernel for the coefficients is constructed, an increase of accuracy to 94.78% is observed. The result for the radial basis function (RBF) kernel $k_{i,j} = e^{\|\beta_i - \beta_j\|^2}$ was obtained with parameter $\gamma = 0.004$. All the results are presented for a νSVC with parameter $\nu = .5$.

6 Conclusions

An image representation is proposed to detect texture. The representation is based on an RKHS constructed using the Gabor elementary functions. The representation is assembled using a basis pursuit approach, and the coefficients are employed to implement kernels of support vector classifiers. Results are presented for a set extracted of Brodatz texture images, achieving 94% of classification accuracy.

References

1. Randen, T., Håkon Husøy, J.: Filtering for Texture Classification: A Comparative Study. IEEE Tran. on Pattern Analysis and Machine Intelligence, 21 (1989) 291–310.
2. Jain, A. K., Farrokhnia, F.: Unsupervised texture segmentation using Gabor Filters, Pattern Recognition,24 (1990) 1167–1186.
3. Teuner, A., Pichler O., Hosticka, B.J.: Unsupervised texture segmentation of images using tuned matched Gabor filters, IEEE Trans. Image Process. 4 (1995) 863–870.
4. Haralick, R.: Statistical and Structural Approaches to Texture, Proceedings of the IEEE, 67 (1979) 786–804
5. Varma, M., Zisserman, A.: A statistical Approach to Texture Classification from Single Images, International Journal of Computer Vision, 62 (2005) 61–81.
6. Clausi, D., Jernigan, M.: Designing Gabor filters for optimal texture separability. Pattern Recognition, 33 (2000) 1835–1849.
7. Chui, C.K.: An Introduction to Wavelets, San Diego, USA, Academic Press, (1992).
8. Schölkopf, B.,Smola, A.: Learning with Kernels, Cambridge, USA, MIT Press, (2002).
9. Shawe-Taylor, J., Cristianini, N. : Kernel Methods for Pattern Analysis, Cambridge, UK, Cambridge University Press, (2004).
10. Máté, L.: Hilbert Space Methods in Science and Engineering. Bristol, England: Adam Hilger (1989).
11. Chen, S.S., Donoho, D.L., Saunders, M.A.: Atomic Decomposition by Basis Pursuit, SIAM Review, 43 (2001) 129-159.
12. Czyzyk, J., Mehrotra, S., Wagner, M., Wright, S.: PCx User Guide, Optimization Technology Center, Technical Report OTC 96/01 (1997).
13. Brodatz, P. : Textures: A Photographic Album for Artists and Designers, Dover Publications, New York (1966).

Local Linear Approximation for Kernel Methods: The Railway Kernel

Alberto Muñoz[1], Javier González[1], and Isaac Martín de Diego[2]

[1] University Carlos III de Madrid, c/ Madrid 126, 28903 Getafe, Spain
{alberto.munoz, javier.gonzalez}@uc3m.es
[2] University Rey Juan Carlos, c/ Tulipán s/n, 28933 Móstoles, Spain
isaac.martin@urjc.es

Abstract. In this paper we present a new kernel, the Railway Kernel, that works properly for general (nonlinear) classification problems, with the interesting property that acts locally as a linear kernel. In this way, we avoid potential problems due to the use of a general purpose kernel, like the RBF kernel, as the high dimension of the induced feature space. As a consequence, following our methodology the number of support vectors is much lower and, therefore, the generalizacion capability of the proposed kernel is higher than the obtained using RBF kernels. Experimental work is shown to support the theoretical issues.

1 Introduction

Support Vector Machines (SVM) have proven to be a successful method for the solution of a wide range of classification problems [1], [6]. In particular, linear SVMs are optimal in the classical setting in which two normally distributed populations have to be separated. This assertion is supported by the fact that SVM classifier approaches the optimal Bayes rule and its generalization error converges to the optimal Bayes risk [4]. Our aim in this paper is to build a global kernel for general nonlinear classification problems that locally behaves as a linear (optimal) kernel. Within this approach we expect to avoid the problems due to the use of a general purpose kernel like the RBF kernel: in this latter case, the data are embedded in a high dimensional feature space and problems of overfitting and poor generalization may appear. Since the proposed kernel behaves locally as a linear kernel, the good properties of the SVM classifier will be inherited by our method. In particular, the number of support vectors will be much lower and, therefore, the generalizacion capability will be higher than the obtained using RBF kernels.

To motivate our approximation, consider the situation presented in Figure 1. The decision function is clearly nonlinear. However, this function can be approximated locally by linear functions. For instance, a linear SVM (with kernel K_3) solves the classification problem in the oval area. We build a global kernel that will behave locally as the linear kernels whose decision functions are shown in the figure. We denote this kernel by '**Railway Kernel**'. The name for this

J.F. Martínez-Trinidad et al. (Eds.): CIARP 2006, LNCS 4225, pp. 936–944, 2006.

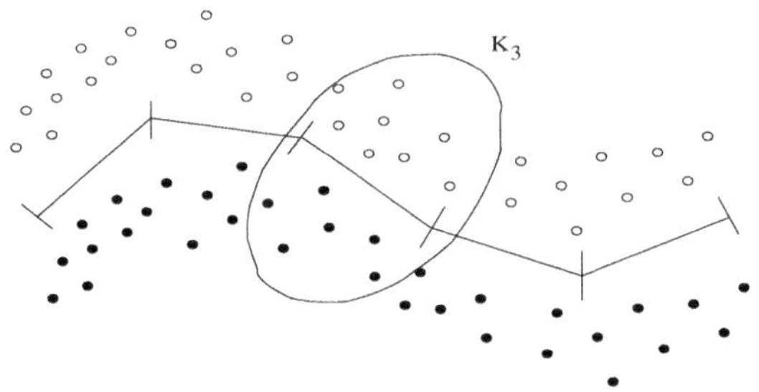

Fig. 1. Illustration of the Railway Kernel performance

kernel has been choosen because it is build like a railway where their wagons are the local decision functions.

The paper is organized as follows. The general framework for the proposed kernel is presented in Sections 2 and 3. The experimental setup and results on various artificial and real data sets are described in Section 4. Section 5 concludes.

2 Railway Kernel

In this section we will study our new type of locally linear kernel, the Railway Kernel. We proceed as follows: First, the kernel is defined on 'simple' areas where the linear SVM works. Then the kernel is extended to the intersection of such 'pure' areas.

Next we introduce a special kernel that acts as an indicator function on the proccess.

2.1 Indicator Kernel Functions

Given a data set, let assume that we are able to identify specific space areas where the problem can be solved using a linear SVM. In this section we define a special indicator function to identify such areas. For the sake of simplicity only spherical areas are considered in this paper. The generalization to more elaborated shapes is straightforward. The indicator kernel function takes value 1 if the point under consideration is in the circular area defined by a given center and a radius, and decreases to zero quite fast as the distance to the center grows. Assumming smoothness in the boundary of the areas, we can define the following indicator kernel function $\lambda(x)$:

$$\lambda(x) = \begin{cases} 1 & \text{if} \|x - c\|^{1/2} \leq r \\ e^{-\gamma(\|x-c\|^2 - r^2)} & \text{if} \|x - c\|^{1/2} > r \end{cases} . \tag{1}$$

where $\|\cdot\|$ denotes the Euclidean distance, $x \in R^d$ is a sample point, $c \in R^d$ is the center of the sphere and $r > 0$ is the radius. Parameter $\gamma > 0$ is fixed in order to obtain a fast transition from 0 to 1 and, in this case, $\lambda(x)$ will aproximate

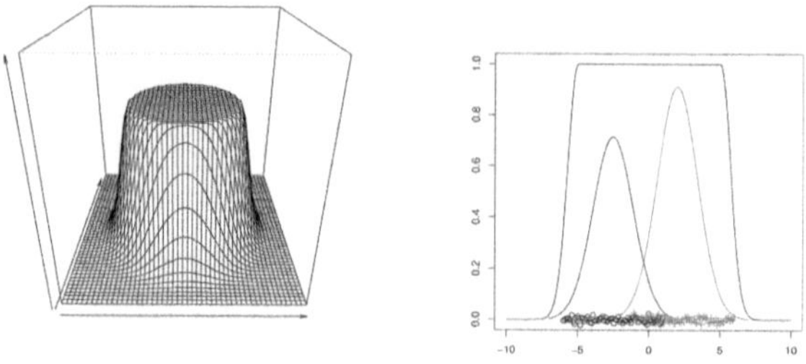

(a) (b)

Fig. 2. Indicator kernel funcions. (a) 2D case. (b) 1D case for a two-class classification problem. Class density functions are shown.

an indicator function. It is immediate to check that $\lambda(x)$ is a kernel. The two dimensional case is shown in Figure 2a. Figure 2b represents a two-class classification problem in one dimension and the corresponding indicator function. If a SVM kernel built from this indicator function is used to solve the classification problem, points outside the indicator influence will not be considered.

2.2 Railway Kernel for a Two Areas Problem

First consider the case of two areas without intersection. Kernel K_1 solves the classification problem in area A_1 and so does K_2 in area A_2. Let x and y be two sample data points. We define two functions: $H_1(x, y) = \lambda_1(x)\lambda_1(y)$ and $H_2(x, y) = \lambda_2(x)\lambda_2(y)$, where λ_1 and λ_2 are indicator kernel functions (with appropriate c and r parameters). The functions H_1 and H_2 take the value 1 when x and y belong to the same area, and 0 otherwise. In this particular case, we define the global Railway Kernel K_R as follows:

$$K_R(x, y) = H_1(x, y)K_1(x, y) + H_2(x, y)K_2(x, y) . \qquad (2)$$

Notice that the new kernel is obtained as a functional combination of linear kernels.

The Railway Kernel will approximate piecewise a global non-linear function by local linear functions. Notice that $K_R(x, y)$ is a block-diagonal matrix. This fact can be used to improve the optimization method used to solve the SVM problem (see [10] for details about the SVM optimization problem).

By the Representer Theorem (see [9] for details), the SVM solution takes the form: $f(x) = \sum_i \alpha_i K(x, x_i) + b$. In this case, due to the particular Railway Kernel structure the solution is given by:

$$f(x) = \sum_{x_i \in A_1} \alpha_i K_1(x, x_i) + \sum_{x_j \in A_2} \alpha_j K_2(x, x_j) + b \qquad (3)$$

Notice that K_R behaves like K_1 in the domain of indicator function H_1 and like K_2 in the domain of indicator function H_2.

We have not yet studied neither a multiarea problem, nor intersection between areas. These issues will be considered in Section 2.4.

2.3 A First Example

We generate four groups of observations (50 observations per group) corresponding to four bivariate normal distributions: $N(\mu_i, \Sigma_i)$ for group i, with $\mu_1 = (3,5)$, $\mu_2 = (7,5)$, $\mu_3 = (15,17)$, $\mu_4 = (15,13)$ respectively, and $\Sigma_1 = \Sigma_2 = diag(0.5, 1.5)$ and $\Sigma_3 = \Sigma_4 = diag(1.5, 0.5)$. Points in groups 1 and 3 belong to class $+1$ and points in groups 2 and 4 belong to class -1. Consider two areas defined by indicator kernel funcions with centers $c_1 = (5,5)$, $c_2 = (15,15)$ and radii $r_1 = r_2 = 5$ respectively. The point in this example is that the classes are linearly separable in each of these areas; however there is no a global proper linear kernel. In this case, the problem could be solved with a RBF kernel ($\sigma = 1$). Nevertheless when the Railway Kernel is used several advantages appear. The number of support vector is significatively lower than in the RBF case (13.5% vs. 73.5%). Figure 3a and 3b show the decision functions for the Railway and RBF kernels respectively. In addition, the number of positive eigenvalues of the kernel

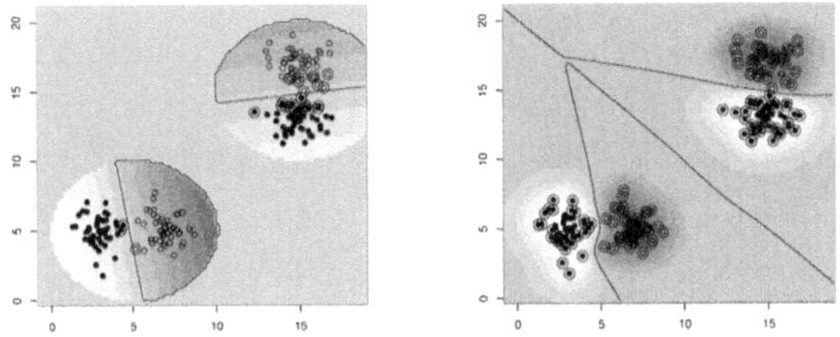

(a) Local linear kernels solution. (b) Global RBF solution.

Fig. 3. Two solutions for a modified XOR problem (support vectors are highlighted)

matrix is clearly lower using the Railway Kernel (2.0% vs. 25%). Therefore, the manifold induced by the Railway Kernel is of lower dimension than the obtained using the RBF kernel. Figures 4a and 4b show the eigenvalues for the Railway and RBF kernels respectively.

2.4 Building the Railway Kernel in the Intersections

Next we deal with the problem of intersection between areas. Let A_1 and A_2 the areas under consideration. In this case, the Railway Kernel is built as follows:

$$K_R(x,y) = \begin{cases} K_1(x,y) & \text{if} \quad x,y \in A_1 \cap A_2^c\,, \\ K_2(x,y) & \text{if} \quad x,y \in A_1^c \cap A_2\,, \\ \frac{1}{2}(K_1(x,y) + K_2(x,y)) & \text{if} \quad x,y \in A_1 \cap A_2\,, \\ 0 & \text{otherwise}\,, \end{cases} \tag{4}$$

where A_i^c represents the complementary set of A_i.

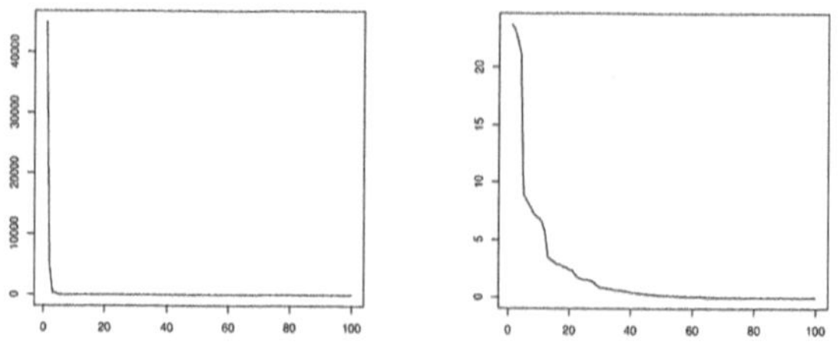

(a) Local linear kernel. (b) RBF kernel matrix.

Fig. 4. Eigenvalues of the kernel matrices for the modified XOR problem

Intersections between areas can be seen as areas where both kernels achieve the same performance, and should be equally weighted. Thus, the average of the kernels (which is a kernel [2]) is computed for points in the intersection. Figure 5a shows graphically the idea of intersection, and Figure 5b shows the Railway Kernel perfomance in a simple example.

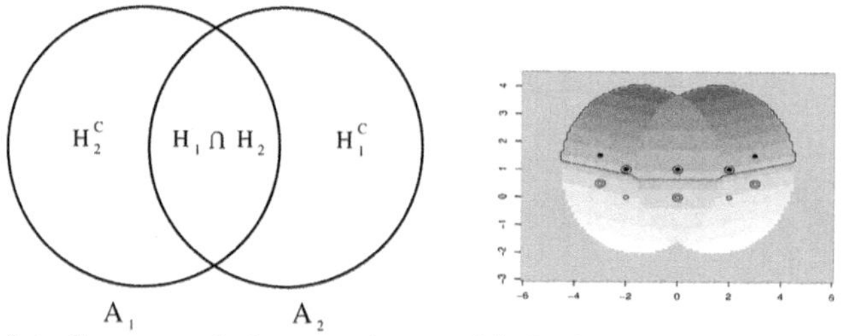

(a) Conceptual intersections in the Railway Kernel

(b) Railway Kernel performance in a simple example with curvature.

Fig. 5. The Railway Kernel performance in an simple example with intersection

The matrix computed in (4) is a semidefinite positive and block diagonal matrix. Thus, it comes from a Mercer kernel. It is possible to find an analytical expression for (4). Consider the example given in Figure 5a). Without loss of generality suppose that our sample is distributed in 3 zones: H_1^c, H_2^c and $H_1 \cdot H_2$, where $H_1^c(x, y)$ is the region of the space where the funcion H_1 vanishes and it is given by $H_1^c = (1 - \lambda_1(x))(1 - \lambda_1(y))$. Thus, it represents those points in A_2 and not in A_1. H_2^c represents those points in A_1 and not in A_2. The final kernel (K_R) will be the sum of three matrices. $K_R(x, y) = 0$ when x and y belong to different zones. In other case, $K_R(x, y)$ is exactly the kernel that works on the zone x and y belong to. The expression for the kernel is as follows:

$$K_R(x, y) = H_1^c(x, y) K_2(x, y) + H_2^c(x, y) K_1(x, y) +$$

$$(H_1(x,y)H_2(x,y))\frac{1}{2}(K_1(x,y)+K_2(x,y))\,. \qquad (5)$$

As before, K_R is a block-diagonal matrix where each block is a kernel matrix. Then, K_R is a positive semidefinite matrix and thus a kernel. The generalization of (5) to the case of more than 2 areas is straightforward.

Notice that, to compute the Railway Kernel it is enough to use the areas information and the local linear kernels on that areas. We have built a method to compute an aproximation to a nonlinear decision function with a sum of local linear hiperplanes.

3 Areas Location

In Section 2 we have assumed that each point in the sample belongs to one or more previously defined areas. Now we present a local algorithm to detect such areas in a classification problem. The algorithm works in two main steps. First, single labelled areas are created. A sample point is assigned to its nearest area if the label of the point is the same that the label in the area. In other case, a new area is defined. A new area is built when the distance between the new point under consideration and its nearest area is higher than the maximun of the average distances into the areas. We repeat the process until each sample point belong to an area. Once the areas $A_1, \ldots, A_M$ have been built, the final areas are obtained joining the nearest areas with different labels. In order to obtain the indicator function kernels needed to build the Railway Kernels, centers and radii are needed. Centers are computed as the $A_1, ..., A_M$ centroids, and radii in each area are computed as the maximun distance between the center and the farthest point in this area.

An example to illustrate of the performance of the algorithm is presented in Figure 6. Figure 6a presents a two class problem in two dimensions. In Figure 6b the result of applying the areas location algorithm is shown. The procedure is as follows. First, area 1 is created and completed. Next, we look for the next

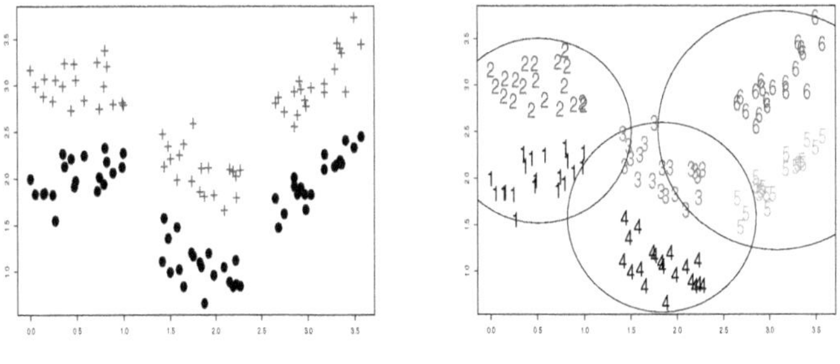

(a) Initial problem. (b) Areas Location Solution.

Fig. 6. An example of the Areas Location algorithm performance nearest point. Since a data point belongs to another class a new area is defined (area 2). This new area is completed and a new point is evaluated. Since the distance between the previous area (2) and the nearest point (the new point) is large enough, a new area is created (area 3), and so on. Figure 6b shows the six final spherical areas detected.

4 Experiments

To test the performance of the proposed method, a SVM (with the upper bound on the dual variables fixed to 1) has been trained on artificial and real data sets using the Railway Kernel matrix previously constructed. We have compared the proposed methods with two SVM classifiers built using RBF kernels. For the first classifier (SVM_1) the parameter σ is choosen as a function of the data dimension (see [8] and [7] for details). For the second (SVM_2), σ and the upper bound on the dual variables of the optimization problem are choosen following the ideas in [3].

4.1 Two Areas with Different Scattering Matrices

The first data set under consideration is presented in Figure 7 and corresponds to 400 points in $\mathbb{R}^2$. There are two areas of points (80% of the sample is in area A_1 and 20% is in area A_2). Each area A_i corresponds to a normal cloud. The first area center is $(0, 1)$ and the second group center is $(1, 1)$, while the diagonal covariance matrices are $\sigma_i^2 I$ where $\sigma_1 = 10^{-2}\sigma_2$, and $\sigma_2 = 1$. The point on this example is that the areas do not coincide with the classes $\{-1, +1\}$ that are to be learned. Half of the points in each class belongs to area A_1, and the other half to area A_2. Within each area, the classes are linearly separable. Therefore, the only way to build a proper classifier for this data set is to take into account the area each point belongs to. We use 50% of the data for training and 50% for testing.

To compare the performance of the Railway Kernel, consider a set of three RBF kernels with parameters σ =0.5, 5 and 10 respectively.

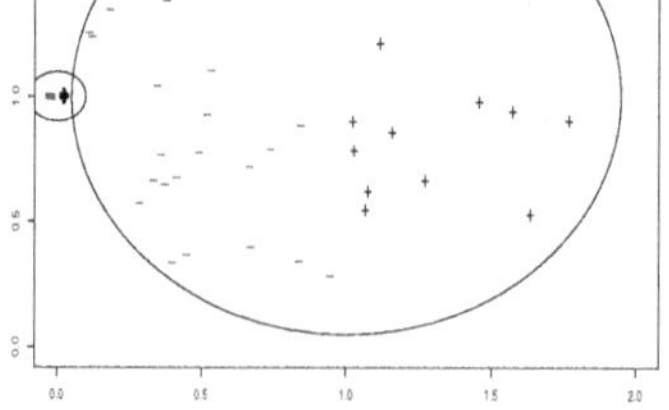

Fig. 7. Two areas with different scattering matrices. The first area center is $(0, 1)$ and the second area center is $(1, 1)$. The areas do not coincide with the classes $\{-1, +1\}$.

Table 1 shows the performance of our proposal for this data set. The results have been averaged over 10 runs. Given the geometry of the data, it is clear that is not possible to choose a unique best σ for the whole data set. As σ grows, the test error increases for the data contained in area A_1, and decreases within area A_2. The Railway Kernel clearly improves the best RBF kernel.

Table 1. Percentage of missclassified data and percentage of support vectors for the two different scattering data set: A_1 stands for the less scaterring group, A_2 stands for the most dispersive one

	Train Error			**Test Error**			**Support Vectors**
Method	Total	A_1	A_2	Total	A_1	A_2	Total
RBF$_{\sigma=0.5}$	2.4	3.0	0.0	13.4	4.1	51.0	39.2
RBF$_{\sigma=5}$	4.6	5.8	0.0	13.6	8.6	35.0	82.6
RBF$_{\sigma=10}$	29.1	36.2	0.5	36.0	44.1	10.0	94.4
Railway Kernel	3.7	3.6	15.6	4.2	0.1	20.6	14.1
SVM$_1$	2.1	2.6	0.0	13.5	4.1	51.0	39.6
SVM$_2$	2.1	2.6	0.0	11.0	3.3	41.5	37.6

4.2 The Breast Cancer Data Set

In this section we have dealt with a database from the UCI Machine Learning Repository: the Breast Cancer data set [5]. The data set consists of 683 observations with 9 features each. We use 80% of the data for training and 20% for testing.

Table 2 shows the performance of the Railway Kernel on this data set. Again, the results have been averaged over 10 runs. Our method clearly improve the RBF kernel with σ parameter choosen as a function of the data dimension. Our method does not take into account the penalization parameter of the SVM. However, our results are similar to the classification results obtained when both parameters, σ and the upper bound on the dual variables of the optimization problem, are choosen, but using significantly less support vectors.

Table 2. Percentage of missclassified data, sensitivity (Sens.), specificity (Spec.) and percentage of support vectors for the cancer data set. Standard deviations in brackets.

	Train			**Test**			**Support**
Method	Error	Sens.	Spec.	Error	Sens.	Spec.	**Vectors**
Railway Kernel	2.5 (0.3)	0.979	0.974	2.9 (0.4)	0.975	0.876	18.6 (3.6)
SVM$_1$	0.1 (0.1)	1.000	0.999	4.2 (1.4)	0.989	0.942	49.2 (1.0)
SVM$_2$	0.0 (0.0)	1.000	0.999	2.9 (1.6)	0.963	0.975	49.2 (1.0)

5 Comments and Conclusions

In this paper we have presented a new kernel, the Railway Kernel. This global kernel takes advantage of the good generalization properties of the local linear kernels for classification tasks. We have shown that the potential problems due to the use of a general purpose kernel like the RBF kernel have been avoid. The generalization capability of the proposed kernel is higher than the obtained using RBF kernels. The method could be generalized by using alternative non-linear local kernel. Further research will focus on the theoretical properties of the Railway Kernel and extensions.

References

1. C. Cortes and V. Vapnik. *Support Vector Networks.* Machine Learning, 20:273-297, 1995.
2. N. Cristianini and J. Shawe-Taylor. *An introduction to Support Vector Machine. Cambridge University Press, 2000.*
3. S.S. Keerthi and C. Lin. *Asymptotic Behaviors of Support Vector Machines with Gaussian Kernel.* Neural Computation, 15:1667-1689, 2003.
4. Y. Lin., G. Wahba, H. Zhang and Y. Lee. *Statistical Properties and Adaptive Tuning of Support Vector Machines.* Machine Learning, 48:115-136, 2002.
5. O.L. Mangasarian and W.H. Wolberg. *Cancer diagnosis via linear programming.* SIAM News, 23 (5):1-18, 1990.
6. J. Moguerza and A. Muñoz. *SVM with aplications.* Statistical Science, In press, 2006.
7. A. Muñoz and J. M. Moguerza. *Estimation of High-Density Regions Using One Class Neighbor Machines* IEEE Transactions on Pattern Analysis and Machine Intelligence, 28 (3):476-480, 2006.
8. B. Schölkopf, J.C. Platt, J. Shawe-Taylor, A.J. Smola and R.C. Williamson. *Estimating the Support of a High Dimensional Distribution.* Neural Computation, 13(7):1443-1471 , 2001.
9. B. Schölkopf, R. Herbrich, A. Smola and R. Williamson. *A Generalized Representer Theorem.* NeuroCOLT2 TR Series, NC2-TR2000-81, 2000.
10. B. Schölkopf and A. Smola. *Learning with Kernels.* MIT Press, 2002.

Fusion of Gaussian Kernels Within Support Vector Classification

Javier M. Moguerza[1], Alberto Muñoz[2], and Isaac Martín de Diego[1]

[1] University Rey Juan Carlos, c/ Tulipán s/n, 28933 Móstoles, Spain
{javier.moguerza, isaac.martin}@urjc.es
[2] University Carlos III de Madrid, c/ Madrid 126, 28903 Getafe, Spain
alberto.munoz@uc3m.es

Abstract. In this paper we propose some methods to build a kernel matrix for classification purposes using Support Vector Machines (SVMs) by fusing Gaussian kernels. The proposed techniques have been successfully evaluated on artificial and real data sets. The new methods outperform the best individual kernel under consideration and they can be used as an alternative to the parameter selection problem in Gaussian kernel methods.

1 Introduction

It is well known that the choice of kernel parameters is often critical for the good performance of Support Vector Machines (SVMs). Nevertheless, to find optimal values in terms of generalization performance for the kernel parameters is an open and hard to solve question. An a priori kernel selection for SVM is a difficult task [1]. The Gaussian kernel (or radial basis function (RBF) kernel) function is one of the most popular classical SVM kernels. The effect of RBF kernels parameter within a SVM framework has been studied from a theoretical point of view [5]. Several practical proposals to choose the RBF kernel parameter have been made [14,7,3,13]. However, there is not a simple and unique technique to select the best set of parameters to build a kernel matrix. Our proposal is based on the fusion of the different RBF kernel matrices that arise with the use of a range of values for the unkown parameters. Fusing kernels provides a solution that minimizes the effect of a bad parameter choice. An intuitive and usual approach to build this fusion is to consider linear combinations of the matrices. This is the proposal in [6], which is based on the solution of a semi-definite programming problem to calculate the coefficients of the linear combination. Nevertheless, the solution of this kind of optimization problem is computationally very expensive [16].

In this paper we propose several methods to build a kernel matrix from a collection of RBF kernels generated from different values of the unkown parameters in the RBF kernel function. The functions involved in the proposed methods take advantage of class conditional probabilities and nearest neighbour techniques.

The paper is organized as follows. The general framework for the methods is presented in Section 2. The proposed methods are described in Section 3. The

J.F. Martínez-Trinidad et al. (Eds.): CIARP 2006, LNCS 4225, pp. 945–953, 2006.

experimental setup and results on artificial and real data sets are described in Section 4. Section 5 concludes.

2 General Framework

Consider the general expression of the RBF kernel function:

$$K(x_i, x_j) = exp\left(-\frac{\|x_i - x_j\|^2}{2\sigma^2}\right), \tag{1}$$

where $\sigma > 0$ is the kernel parameter, and x_i and x_j are data points in the sample. The kernel parameter controls the flexibility of the kernel. Small values of σ gradually reduce the kernel to the identity matrix. On the other hand, large values of σ imply that the kernel matrix become close to a constant function. Notice that the RBF kernel matrix defines a similarity measure. As already mentioned, our proposal is based on the generation of a collection of kernel matrices using a wide range of values for the unkown RBF kernel parameter. Once the collection has been built, we will fuse the matrices in order to build a unique kernel.

In order to fuse the kernel matrices we make use of the concept of functional fusion of matrices. This concept is based on the one introduced originally in [10]. Let $K_1, K_2, ...K_M$ be a set of M normalized input RBF kernel matrices defined from (1) on a data set X, and denote by K^* the desired output combination. Let y denote the label vector, where for simplicity $y_i \in \{-1, +1\}$ (the extension to the multiclass case is straightforward).

Consider the following (functional) weighted sum:

$$K^* = \sum_{m=1}^{M} W_m \otimes K_m\,, \tag{2}$$

where $W_m = [w_m(x_i, x_j)]$ is a matrix whose elements are nonlinear functions $w_m(x_i, x_j)$, and '$\otimes$' denotes the element by element product between matrices (Hadamard product). Notice that if $w_m(x_i, x_j) = \mu_m$, where $\mu_m\,, m = 1, \ldots M$ are constants, then the method reduces to calculate a simple linear combination of matrices:

$$K^* = \sum_{m=1}^{M} \mu_m K_m\,. \tag{3}$$

Several methods have been suggested to learn the coefficients μ_m of the linear combination [2,6]. Thus, the formulation used in these papers is a particular case of the formula we propose. For instance, if we take $\mu_m = \frac{1}{M}$, the average of the input matrices is obtained.

Regarding our proposals, consider the (i, j) element of the matrix K^* in (2):

$$K^*(x_i, x_j) = \sum_{m=1}^{M} w_m(x_i, x_j) K_m(x_i, x_j)\,. \tag{4}$$

This is the general formula of our approximation. In this way, we will generate a particular weight for each pair of elements under consideration.

An aspect that has to be treated before describing the methods is the fact that the kernel matrix arising from the combination has to be a positive semi-definite matrix. Since this can not be guaranteed in advance, we make use of some of the several solutions that have been proposed to solve this difficulty [12]. For instance, consider the spectral decomposition $K^* = Q\Lambda Q^T$, where Λ is a diagonal matrix containing (in decreasing order) the eigenvalues of K^*, and Q is the matrix of the corresponding eigenvectors. Assume that Λ has at least p positive eigenvalues. We can consider a p-dimensional representation by taking the first p columns of Q: $Q_p\Lambda_p Q_p^T$. We will refer to this technique as 'Positive Eigenvalue Transformation'. A computationally cheaper solution is to consider the definition of a new kernel matrix as K^{*2}. Notice that, in this case, the new kernel matrix is: $Q\Lambda^2 Q^T$. We call this method 'Square Eigenvalue Transformation'. In practice, there seems not to be a universally best method to solve this problem [11].

3 Some Specific Proposals

The next section describes a common feature to the methods we will propose: The use of conditional class probabilities in order to build the weights $w_m(x_i, x_j)$ introduced in the previous section.

3.1 Conditional Class Probabilities

Consider the pair (x_i, y_i) and an unlabelled observation x_j. Given the observed value x_j, define $P(y_i|x_j)$ as the probability of x_j being in class y_i. If x_i and x_j belong to the same class this probability should be high. Unfortunately, this probability is unknown and has to be estimated. In our proposals, we will estimate it by:

$$P(y_i|x_j) = \frac{n_{ij}}{n}, \tag{5}$$

where n_{ij} is the number of the n-nearest neighbours of x_j belonging to class y_i. Notice that each kernel matrix induces a different type of neighborhood. In fact, there is an explicit relation between a kernel matrix and a distance matrix. For instance, consider a matrix K of inner products in an Euclidean space $\mathcal{F}$ (a kernel). Then $D^2 = ve^T + ev^T - 2K$ is a matrix of square Euclidean distances in $\mathcal{F}$ [4], where v is a vector made up of the diagonal elements of K. Hence, it is advisable to estimate this probability for each representation, that is, for the matrix K_m we will estimate the conditional probabilities $P_m(y_i|x_j)$ using the induced distances matrix D_m^2. We will need the average of this conditional probabilities over the kernel matrices:

$$\bar{\rho}(x_i, x_j) = \frac{\bar{P}(y_i|x_j) + \bar{P}(y_j|x_i)}{2}, \tag{6}$$

where $\bar{P}(y_i|x_j) = \frac{1}{M}\sum_{m=1}^{M} P_m(y_i|x_j)$.

To estimate the conditional class probabilities, the appropriate size of the neighbourhood has to be determined. We propose a dynamic and automatic method: given two points x_i and x_j, we look for the first common neighbour. For each data point (x_i and x_j), the size k of the neighbourhood will be determined by the number of neighbours nearer than the common neighbour. To be more specific, let $R(x_i, n) = \{n\text{-}nearest\ neighbours\ of\ x_i\}$, then $k = \operatorname{argmin}_n\{R(x_i, n) \cap R(x_j, n) \neq \emptyset\}$. Obviously, the size k of the neighbourhood depends on the particular pair of points under consideration.

At this point, we have the tools to implement some particular proposals of combination methods.

3.2 The 'MaxMin' Method

The 'MaxMin' method (first used in [10]) produces a functional fusion of two kernel matrices, namely, the maximum and the minimum of the ordered sequence of similarities, being zero the weight assigned to the rest of the similarities. Consider the ordered sequence:

$$\min_{1\leq m\leq M} K_m(x_i, x_j) = K_{[1]}(x_i, x_j) \leq \ldots \leq K_{[M]}(x_i, x_j) = \max_{1\leq m\leq M} K_m(x_i, x_j)\,,$$

where the subscript $[\cdot]$ denotes the position induced by the order. This method builds each element of K^* using the formula:

$$K^*(x_i, x_j) = \bar{\rho}(x_i, x_j)K_{[M]}(x_i, x_j) + (1 - \bar{\rho}(x_i, x_j))K_{[1]}(x_i, x_j)\,. \tag{7}$$

If x_i and x_j belong to the same class then the conditional class probabilities $\bar{\rho}(x_i, x_j)$ will be high and the method guarantees that $K^*(x_i, x_j)$ will be large. On the other hand, if x_i and x_j belong to different classes the conditional class probabilities $\bar{\rho}(x_i, x_j)$ will be low and the method will produce a value close to the minimum of the similarities. In the following, this method will be refered as **MaxMin**.

3.3 The Percentile-In Method

Next we propose a method whose assignment of positive weights $w_m(x_i, x_j)$ is based on the order induced by the similarities. The method builds each element of K^* using the following formulae:

$$K^*(x_i, x_j) = K_{\lceil \bar{\rho}(x_i, x_j)M \rceil}\,, \tag{8}$$

where the subscript $\lceil \cdot \rceil$ denotes the upper rounding of the argument.

We denote this method by **'Percentile-in'** method [10] . If the class probability $\bar{\rho}(x_i, x_j)$ is high, we can expect a high kernel between x_i and x_j and the method will guarantee a high $K^*(x_i, x_j)$. If the class probability $\bar{\rho}(x_i, x_j)$ is low, $K^*(x_i, x_j)$ will be also low.

3.4 The Percentile-Out Method

As in the previous method, the last proposed technique is based on the order induced by the similarities. However, in this case two similarities are considered. Each element of the K^* matrix is built as follows:

$$K^*(x_i, x_j) = \frac{1}{2}\left(K_{\lceil \bar{P}(y_i|x_j)M \rceil} + K_{\lceil \bar{P}(y_j|x_i)M \rceil}\right), \tag{9}$$

where the subscript $\lceil \cdot \rceil$ denotes the upper rounding of the argument. We denote this method by **'Percentile-out'** method [10] .

If the conditional class probabilities $\bar{P}(y_i|x_j)$ and $\bar{P}(y_j|x_i)$ are high, we can expect a high kernel between x_i and x_j and both methods will guarantee a high $K^*(x_i, x_j)$. If the conditional class probabilities $\bar{P}(y_i|x_j)$ and $\bar{P}(y_j|x_i)$ are both low, $K^*(x_i, x_j)$ will be also low.

4 Experiments

To test the performance of the proposed methods, a SVM (with the upper bound on the dual variables fixed to 1) has been trained on several real data sets using the output matrix K^* constructed.

In order to classify a non-labelled data point x, $K^*(x, i)$ has to be evaluated. We calculate two different values for $K^*(x, i)$, the first one assumming x belongs to class $+1$ and the second assumming x belongs to class -1. For each assumption, we compute the distance between x and the SVM hyperplane and assign x to the class corresponding to the largest distance from the hyperplane.

Since our technique is based on the calculation of the nearest neighbours, we have compared the proposed methods with the k-Nearest Neighbour classification (k-NN, using the optimal value $k = l^{\frac{4}{p+4}}$, where l is the sample size and p is the data dimension [15]). In order to evaluate the improvement provided by our proposals, we have carried out a Wilcoxon signed-rank test (see for instance [8]). This nonparametric test is used to compare the median of the results for different runs of each method. So, the null hypothesis of the test is that our methods do not improve the individual kernels.

4.1 Two Areas with Different Scattering Matrices

This data set, shown in Figure 1, is made up of 400 points in $\mathbb{R}^2$. Visually there are two areas of points (80% of the sample is in area A_1 and 20% is in area A_2). Each area A_i corresponds to a circle with radio σ_i. Here $\sigma_1 = 10^{-2}\sigma_2$, with $\sigma_2 = 1$. The first group center is $(0, 1)$ and the second group center is $(1, 1)$. Nevertheless, the areas do not coincide with the classes $\{-1, +1\}$ that are to be learned. Half of the points in each class belongs to aread A_1, and the other half to area A_2. Within each area, the classes are linearly separable. Therefore the only way to built a classifier for this data set is to take into account the area each point belongs to. We use 50% of the data for training and 50% for testing.

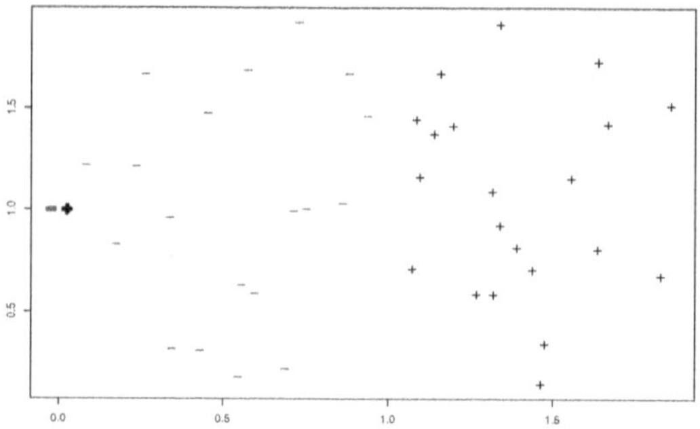

Fig. 1. Two areas with different scattering matrices. The first area center is $(0, 1)$ and the second area center is $(1, 1)$. The areas do not coincide with the classes $\{-1, +1\}$.

Let $\{K_1, \ldots, K_5\}$ be a set of five RBF kernels with parameters σ =0.5, 2.5, 5, 7.5 and 10 respectively. We normalize the kernel matrices: $K(x, z) = \frac{K(x,z)}{\sqrt{K(x,x)}\sqrt{K(y,y)}}$. In order to get a positive semi-definite kernel matrix K^*, we use the Square Eigenvalue Transformation technique described in Section 2.

Table 1 shows the performance of our proposals for this data set. The results have been averaged over 10 runs. Given the geometry of the data, it is clear that is not possible to choose a unique best σ for the whole data set. As σ grows, the test error increases for the data contained in area A_1, and decreases within area A_2. The LC method seems to work fairly. Nevertheless, the MaxMin method achieves the best results on classification. Regarding the Wilcoxon signed-rank test for the comparison of our methods with the LC technique, the p-value is smaller than 0.001 for the MaxMin method.

4.2 Cancer Data Set

In this section we have dealt with a database from the UCI Machine Learning Repository: the Breast Cancer data set [9]. The data set consists of 683 observations with 9 features each. Let $\{K_1, \ldots, K_{12}\}$ be a set of RBF kernels with parameters σ =0.1, 1, 10, 20, 30, 40, 50, 60, 70, 80, 90, 100 respectively. We use the Positive Eigenvalue Transformation to solve the problem of building a positive semi-definite matrix.

Table 2 shows the performance of the proposed methods when combining all these kernel matrices. Again, the results have been averaged over 10 runs. The MaxMin method, the Percentile-in method, and the Percentile-out method improve the best RBF kernel under consideration (test errors of 2.8% for the three methods vs. 3.1%). The results provided by all the combination methods are not degraded by the inclusion of kernels with a bad generalization performance. Our methods clearly outperform the SVM classifier using an RBF kernel with $\sigma = \sqrt{d}/2$, where d is the data dimension (see [14] for details). Regarding the Wilcoxon signed-rank test for the comparison of our methods with the SVM technique, the p-values are smaller than 0.05 for the MaxMin and the Percentile-out

Table 1. Percentage of missclassified data and percentage of support vectors for the two different scattering data set: A_1 stands for the less scaterring group, A_2 stands for the most dispersive one

	Train Error			Test Error			Support Vectors		
Method	Total	A_1	A_2	Total	A_1	A_2	Total	A_1	A_2
RBF$_{\sigma=0.5}$	2.1	2.6	0.0	13.5	4.1	51.0	39.6	25.1	97.5
RBF$_{\sigma=2.5}$	4.8	6.0	0.0	13.5	6.5	41.5	62.2	53.4	97.5
RBF$_{\sigma=5}$	6.6	8.2	0.0	14.0	10.1	29.5	82.8	79.2	97.0
RBF$_{\sigma=7.5}$	16.0	19.9	0.5	22.2	22.6	20.5	94.6	94.2	96.0
RBF$_{\sigma=10}$	30.7	38.2	0.5	37.3	44.1	10.0	94.2	95.4	89.5
MaxMin	0.3	0.4	0.0	4.9	0.9	21.0	27.7	9.6	100.0
Percentile-in	4.2	5.1	0.5	9.0	3.1	32.5	35.9	20.1	99.0
Percentile-out	0.7	0.9	0.0	7.7	1.1	34.0	29.0	11.4	99.5
***k*-NN**	14.5	3.5	58.5	15.5	3.5	63.5	—	—	—
LC	1.6	2.0	0.0	8.1	2.5	29.5	46.6	33.2	100.0

Table 2. Percentage of missclassified data, sensitivity (Sens.), specificity (Spec.) and percentage of support vectors for the cancer data using a battery of RBF kernels. Standard deviations in brackets.

	Train			Test			**Support**
Method	Error	Sens.	Spec.	Error	Sens.	Spec.	**Vectors**
Best RBF	2.3 (0.3)	0.979	0.976	3.1 (1.6)	0.976	0.966	13.6 (1.3)
Worst RBF	0.0 (0.0)	1.000	1.000	24.7 (2.3)	1.000	0.627	74.0 (2.4)
MaxMin	0.1 (0.1)	0.999	0.998	2.8 (1.6)	0.963	0.975	14.2 (1.5)
Percentile-in	2.0 (0.4)	0.982	0.979	2.8 (2.8)	0.975	0.969	7.8 (0.7)
Percentile-out	0.2 (0.1)	0.999	0.997	2.8 (1.7)	0.964	0.975	19.2 (4.5)
***k*-NN**	2.7 (0.5)	0.961	0.980	3.4 (1.5)	0.949	0.974	— (—)
LC	0.0 (0.0)	1.000	1.000	3.2 (1.6)	0.976	0.964	41.5 (4.4)
SVM	0.1 (0.1)	1.000	0.999	4.2 (1.4)	0.989	0.942	49.2 (1.0)

methods, and smaller than 0.1 for the Percentile-in method. Again, the improvement obtained by the use of our proposals is statistically significant.

5 Conclusions

In this paper, we have proposed some methods for the fusion of RBF kernels in order to improve their classification ability. The proposed techniques are specially usefull when does not exist an overall and unique best RBF kernel. The suggested kernel fusion methods compare favorably to the single use of one of the RBF kernels involved in the combination. Further research will focus on the theoretical properties of the methods. In particular, the methods shown in this paper do not take full advantage of the concept of the functional weighted sum described in (2): we think that there is room for improvement and more sophisticated ways for the calculus of the weights for the particular case of RBF kernel matrices may be designed. There are two natural extensions of this work. Firstly, the application of this methodology to kernels not defining a similarity (for instance, polynomial kernels). In this case, care has to be taken when transforming the kernel into a similarity. A second extension would be the generalization for the fusion of different types of kernels. In this case, the normalization of the kernels has to be carefully studied.

Acknowledgments. This work was partially supported by Spanish grants TIC2003-05982-C05-05, MTM2006-14961-C05-05, and SEJ 2004-03303.

References

1. S. Amari and S. Wu. Improving support vector machine classifiers by modifying kernel functions. *Neural Networks*, 12:783–789, 1999.
2. O. Bousquet and D.J.L. Herrmann. On the complexity of learning the kernel matrix. In S. Becker, S. Thurn, and K. Obermayer, editors, *Advances in Neural Information Processing Systems, 15*, pages 415–422. Cambridge, MA: The MIT Press, 2003.
3. O. Chapelle, V. Vapnik, O. Bousquet, and S. Mukherjee. Choosing multiple parameters for support vector machines. *Machine Learning*, 46(1/3):131–159, 2002.
4. J. C. Gower and P. Legendre. Metric and euclidean properties of dissimilarity coefficients. *Journal of Classification*, 3:5–48, 1986.
5. S.S. Keerthi and C. Lin. Asymptotic behaviors of support vector machines with gaussian kernel. *Neural Computation*, 15:1667–1689, 2003.
6. G. R. G. Lanckriet, N. Cristianini, P. Barlett, L. El Ghaoui, and M. I. Jordan. Learning the kernel matrix with semi-definite programming. *Journal of Machine Learning Research*, 5(Jan):27–72, 2004.
7. J.-H. Lee and C.-J. Lin. Automatic model selection for support vector machines. Technical report, National Taiwan University, 2000.
8. E. L. Lehmann. *Nonparametrics: Statistical Methods Based on Ranks.* McGraw-Hill, 1975.
9. O. L. Mangasarian and W. H. Wolberg. Cancer diagnosis via linear programming. *SIAM News*, 23(5):1–18, 1990.
10. J. M. Moguerza, I. Martín de Diego, and A. Muñoz. Improving support vector classificacion via the combination of multiple sources of information. In *Proc. of the IAPR International Workshops SSPR 2004 and SPR 2004, Vol. 3138 of LNCS*, pages 592–600. Berlin: Springer, 2004.
11. E. Pękalska, R. P. W. Duin, S. Günter, and H. Bunke. On not making dissimilarities euclidean. In *Proc. of the IAPR International Workshops SSPR 2004 and SPR 2004, Vol. 3138 of LNCS*, pages 1145–1154. Berlin: Springer, 2004.
12. E. Pękalska, P. Paclík, and R. P. W. Duin. A generalized kernel approach to dissimilarity-based classification. *Journal of Machine Learning Research, Special Issue on Kernel Methods*, 2(12):175–211, 2001.

13. K. Schittkowski. Optimal parameter selection in support vector machines. *Journal of Industrial and Management Optimization*, 1(4):465–476, 2005.
14. B. Schölkopf, S. Mika, C. J.C. Burges, K.-R. Müller P. Knirsch, G. Rätsch, and A. J. Smola. Input space vs. feature space in kernel-based methods. *IEEE Transactions on Neural Networks*, 1999.
15. B. Silverman. *Density Estimation for Statistics and Data Analysis.* Chapman and Hall, London, 1986.
16. L. Vandenberghe and S. Boyd. Semidefinite programming. *SIAM Review*, 38(1):49–95, 1996.

Support Vector Machine with External Recurrences for Modeling Dynamic Cerebral Autoregulation*

Max Chacón[1], Darwin Diaz[1], Luis Ríos[1], David Evans[2], and Ronney Panerai[2]

[1] Universidad de Santiago de Chile; Departamento de Ingeniería Informática, Av. Ecuador No 3659 - Casilla 10233; Santiago-Chile
mchacon@diinf.usach.cl, darwindiazh@gmail.com, lrios@diinf.usach.cl

[2] Medical Physics Group, Department of Cardiovascular Sciences, University of Leicester, Leicester Royal Infirmary, Leicester LE1 5WW, UK
dhe@le.ac.uk, rp9@le.ac.uk

Abstract. Support Vector Machines (SVM) have been applied extensively to classification and regression problems, but there are few solutions proposed for problems involving time-series. To evaluate their potential, a problem of difficult solution in the field of biological signal modeling has been chosen, namely the characterization of the cerebral blood flow autoregulation system, by means of dynamic models of the pressure-flow relationship. The results show a superiority of the SVMs, with *5%* better correlation than the neural network models and *18%* better than linear systems. In addition, SVMs produce an index for measuring the quality of the autoregulation system which is more stable than indices obtained with other methods. This has a clear clinical advantage.

Keywords: Support Vector Machine, biological signals, cerebral autoregulation.

1 Introduction

Support Vector Machines (SVMs) have shown their usefulness by improving over the performance of different supervised learning methods, either as classification models or as regression models. But the small number of papers involving the prediction of temporal series or signal modeling [1-2] shows a lack of assessment in this respect. When these applications are restricted to the field of biomedical signals, SVMs are used as classical classifiers following a process of extraction of signal characteristics [3-4]. At this time we are not aware of any applications that use SVMs as recurrent structures for modeling biomedical signals.

To evaluate SVMs in the field of biomedical signal modeling and prediction we have chosen to model the Autoregulation Blood Flow System (ABFS). Describing this system adequately is a complex problem for which currently there is no model that represents the phenomenon properly. This means that we can not have reliable methods that allow detecting, diagnosing and monitoring different cerebrovascular

* This works was supported by FONDECYT, Chile, under project 1050082.

J.F. Martínez-Trinidad et al. (Eds.): CIARP 2006, LNCS 4225, pp. 954 – 963, 2006.

conditions such as stroke, carotid artery disease, severe head injury, Alzheimer's disease, vascular dementia, arterial hypertension and others.

The ABFS performs the function of maintaining Cerebral Blood Flow (CBF) approximately constant within a given range, even if there are changes in Arterial Blood Pressure (ABP). The study of this system has been possible due to the development of Transcranial Doppler as a tool for measuring Cerebral Blood Flow Velocity (CBFV), which can be assumed to be equivalent to CBF from the studies of Newell et al [5].

The classical way of representing this system is to attempt the dynamic characterization of the ABP-CBFV relationship. Different techniques have been used to provoke changes in ABP and then observe the corresponding CBFV. Chiefly amongst them is the sudden release of thigh cuffs inflated above systolic pressure for 3 min. [5-9]. Different system identification methods have been used to evaluate the dynamic ABP-CBFV relationship. Those carried out in the time domain should be noted; they model the ABP-CBFV relation by means of a differential equation proposed by Aaslid-Tiecks (A-T) [9] which has the advantage of measuring the autorregulation of each subject with a unidimensional index. These methods assume that there is a linear relation between ABP and CBFV, but it is well known that there are a number of nonlinearities in the system [6,10-12].

As far as we know, the only papers that modelled the thigh cuff maneuver responses in a nonlinear way are those of Panerai [10-11]. The first of them uses Winer-Laguerre filters (with second order polynomials) and the second uses artificial neural networks (Time Lagged FeedForward, with Laguerre memory), but neither of them improved the predictive capacity of linear models such as those of A-T [9].

To carry out this work we have used *84* thigh cuff maneuvers performed to *15* healthy subjects. We propose to use the SVMs as static regression machines, adding to them external recurrences, allowing the temporal ABP-CBFV relation to be treated. To compare the results we used the same data to build models with neural networks and we also applied the equations of Aaslid-Tiecks [9].

2 Methods

2.1 Data Collection and Pre-processing

The study considers *16* voluntary subjects who did not have a history of cardiovascular problems, hypertension or nervous system disease. The average age ± SD of the subjects was *30* ± *7* years, with a range of *23* to *47* years. The measurements were made in a room at a temperature of approximately *30 ºC* at the University of Leicester, in England. The study was approved by the Leicestershire Ethics Committee.

Each of the 16 subjects underwent six thigh cuff maneuvers (a total of *96*). Seven maneuvers (in four subjects) had excessive noise at their origin, and three of them were concentrated in one subject. In order to have maneuvers that would allow a symmetric performance of training and tests (*2* or *3* maneuvers for training and the same number for testing), the subject who had the fewest maneuvers was discarded and three subjects remained with only four maneuvers. As a result, *15* subjects underwent a total of *84* maneuvers.

CBFV was monitored in the middle cerebral artery using a Scimed QVL-120 Transcranial Doppler system with a 2-MHz transducer. ABP was measured with a noninvasive Finapres 2300 Ohmeda pressure monitor.

Pressure and flow data were collected and stored on a digital audio tape on an eight channel recorder (Sony PC108M) for later processing. The data from the tape were transferred to a microcomputer in real time. Fast Fourier transform was used to extract the maximum frequency (i.e.velocity) envelope with a *5*-ms time window. The ABP signal was sampled at 200 [samples/sec]. Both signals were filtered with an eighth order lowpass Butterworth filter with a *20*-Hz frequency cut-off. The beginning of each cardiac cycle was detected from the diastolic value of the ABP wave, and mean values for ABP (MABP) and CBFV were calculated for each cardiac cycle, interpolated with a spline and resampled at 0.2 s interval to produce signals with a uniform sampling rate (5 samples/s).

2.2 Modeling Techniques

Support Vector Machine

The SVM algorithm that we used corresponds to the one called ν-SVM, which was introduced by Schölkopf et al. [13] in the late 1990s. This algorithm is based on the results of the statistical theory of learning given by Vapnik [14], which introduces regression as the fitting of a tube of radius ε to the data. The decision boundary for determining the radius of the tube is given by a small subset of training examples called Support Vectors (SV).

Vapnik's SVM Regression estimates the values of $\vec{w}$ to obtain the function

$$f(\vec{x}) = (\vec{w} \cdot \vec{x}) + b, \qquad \vec{w}, \vec{x} \in \mathbf{R}^N, b \in \mathbf{R}, \tag{1}$$

by introducing the so called ε-insensitive loss function shown in equation 2:

$$|y - f(\vec{x})|_\varepsilon = \max\{0, |y - f(\vec{x})| - \varepsilon\}, \tag{2}$$

which does not penalize errors smaller than $\varepsilon > 0$ (where ε corresponds to a value chosen a priori).

The algorithm is implemented by minimizing the functional risk $\|\vec{w}\|^2$ to which is added a penalty for leaving points outside the tube (identified by slack variables ξ). In this way the risk function to be minimized is given by equation 3, where C is a constant that determines the trade-off between the complexity of the model and the points that remain outside the tube. Figure 1 shows a geometric interpretation for the case of a linear regression.

$$\text{minimize} \quad \theta(\vec{w}, \xi) = \frac{1}{2}\|\vec{w}\|^2 + \frac{C}{l}\sum_{i=1}^{l} \xi_i, \tag{3}$$

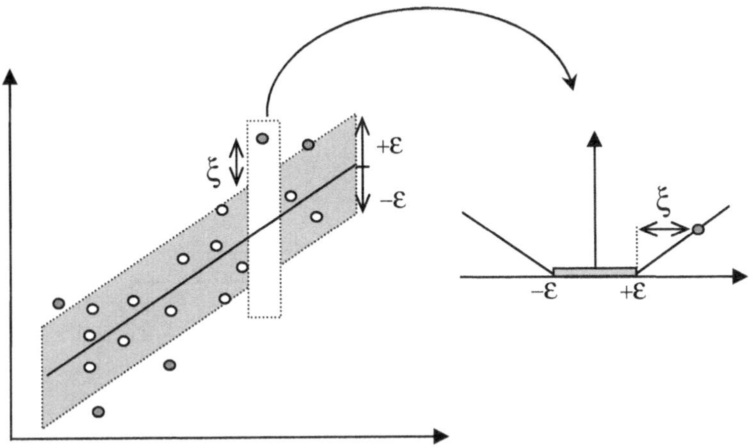

Fig. 1. Geometric interpretation of the SV regression in which the regression equation is estimated by means of a tube of radius ε. The trade-off between the complexity of the model and the points left outside the regression tube is controlled by the slack variables ξ. The dark points correspond to the *SVs*.

The variation of the ν-SVM introduced by Schölkopf et al. [13], consists in adding a variable ν≥0 that weights the size of ε making a trade-off between the complexity of the model and the slack variables (equation 4).

$$minimize\ \theta(\vec{w},\xi) = \frac{1}{2}\|\vec{w}\|^2 + C\left(\nu\varepsilon + \frac{1}{l}\sum_{i=1}^{l}\xi_i\right) \tag{4}$$

The solution of this minimization problem for obtaining the weight vectors $\vec{w}$ is found by the standard optimization procedure for a problem with inequality restrictions when applying the conditions of Kuhn-Tuker to the dual problem. The main advantage of introducing parameter ν ∈ [0-1] is that it makes it possible to control the error fraction and the number (or fraction) of *SVs* with only one normalized parameter.

To solve a nonlinear regression problem it is sufficient to substitute the dot product between two independent original variables $\vec{x}_i \bullet \vec{x}_j$ by a kernel function $k(\Phi(\vec{x}_i)\bullet\Phi(\vec{x}_j))$. This function carries out the dot product in a space of higher dimension such that it ensures the linearity of the regression function in the new space via a nonlinear map Φ. Several functions may be used as kernel, such as the Gaussian $k(\vec{x}_i,\vec{x}_j) = \exp(-\|\vec{x}_i - \vec{x}_j\|^2/(2\sigma^2))$ or the polynomial function $k(\vec{x}_i,\vec{x}_j) = (\vec{x}_i \bullet \vec{x}_j)^p$. In this way the nonlinear regression equation is given by equation 5.

$$f(\vec{x}) = k(\vec{w},\vec{x}) + b \tag{5}$$

To implement the recurrence in the SVM we used external feedback from the delayed outputs (*v(t-i)*=CBFV), and the present input (*p(t)*=MABP) and past time instants (*p(t-j)*) are considered, as shown in figure 2.

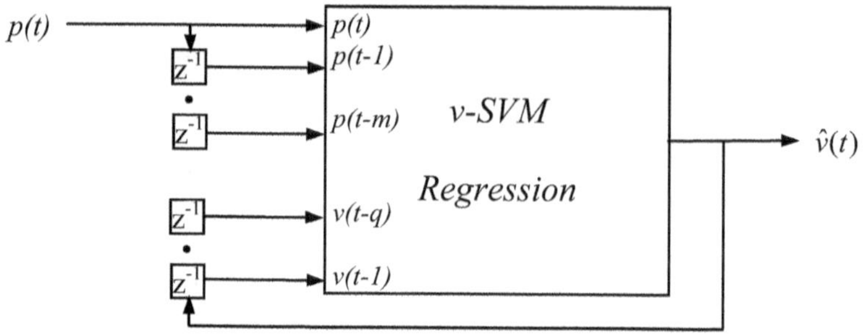

Fig. 2. Regression SVM with external recurrences for modeling the ABP-CBFV relation

Neural Networks

To implement the neural models we used the ideas that are introduced in the work of Nerrand et al. [15], where it is shown that a static neural network with external recurrences is equivalent to the neural networks with internal recurrences. The resultant model is similar to that shown in fig. 2 when the SVM is replaced by a static neural network.

The training algorithms for the static network correspond to variations of the backpropagation method, which is carried out by approximations of second order gradient descent methods.

The two methods used correspond to algorithms of the quasi-Newton type which avoid the direct calculation of the Hessian matrix. The One Step Secant method was used first; it uses an approximation for calculating the search direction of the best descending slope as the combination of the slopes calculated in previous steps. The second method corresponds to the algorithm of Levenbert-Marquardt, which uses a multiplication of Jacobian matrices to estimate the Hessian matrix.

Linear Model

As reference model, use implemented the most widely used linear method in the autoregulation literature, which is that of A-T [9]. This method estimates the CBFV from a second order linear differential equation that uses two state variables, x_1 and x_2, as shown in equations 6.

$$NP(t) = \frac{p(t)}{1-CCP}\ ;\ \ x_1(t) = x_1(t-1) + \frac{NP(t-1) - x_2(t-1)}{f \times T}$$

$$x_2(t) = x_2(t-1) + \frac{x_1(t-1) - 2\times D \times x_2(t-1)}{f \times T}\ ;\ \ \hat{v}(t) = 1 + dP(t) - K \times x_2(t) \tag{6}$$

where f is the sampling frequency and CCP refers to the Critical Closing Pressure. *NP(t)* is the change in the mean MABP normalized from a reference value. The model's parameters are given by *K*, *D* and *T*, where *K* is a parameter that represents the system's autoregulatory gain, *D* is the damping factor, and *T* is a time constant.

For every maneuver produced in the *p(t)*, a corresponding model velocity $\hat{v}(t)$ is predicted, which can be compared with the actual velocity *v(t)*. To choose the velocity given by the model, *10* different responses by the differential equation are generated, corresponding to *10* different values of parameters *K*, *T* and *D*. The combination of parameters to generate the $\hat{v}(t)$ outputs has been tabulated previously [9]. The model's response signal is chosen as the curve that shows the largest correlation (or smallest error) with the actual velocity signal $v(t)$.

This method has the advantage that the *10* tabulated responses for the combination of parameters correspond to an index that measures the quality of the autoregulation (ARI index) of the subjects who undergo the thigh cuff techniques. The ARI index classifies the subjects on a *0* to *9* scale in which *0* represents the complete absence of autoregulation and *9* refers to perfect autoregulation.

2.3 Selection of Parameters and Statistical Analysis

The main objective is to compare the different methods in terms of their predictive capacity, with the purpose of obtaining a method that generates models that represent adequately the ABFS. To evaluate the methods' predictions, the data were divided into two disjoint groups of similar size. One group consisted of odd-numbered maneuvers (1 3 5 for subjects with 6 maneuvers) and the other group contained the even-numbered maneuvers (2 4 6 for subjects with 6 maneuvers), in this way trying to avoid any bias due to physiological accomodation between one maneuver and another [11]. Therefore, a "balanced" cross-validation process takes place that consists in training with even-numbered maneuvers and performing the test with odd-numbered maneuvers, and vice versa. The model chosen corresponds to the training that produced the best correlation (or the smallest error) with the test set.

For the nonlinear models we have not made any a priori assumptions with respect to a general structure for autoregulation. Consequently, every parameter of the model must be fitted for each of the subjects; thereby obtaining what we call models "parametrized by subject".

In the case of the SVM one must seek the best combination of MABP and CBFV delays and of parameters ν, C and σ for each subject, and similarly for the case of the neural networks, where in addition to fitting the delays, the optimum number of neurons in the hidden layer must be established.

To measure the performance of the models, the correlation coefficient r as well as the mean square error (MSE) were used. The latter is defined according to equation 7.

$$MSE = \frac{\sum_{i=1}^{N} (v(i) - \hat{v}(i))^2}{N} \tag{7}$$

In order to compare different model results in terms of error and correlation, Wilcoxon's non-parametric sign test was used, and two results were considered significantly different when $p<0.05$.

In addition to evaluating the predictive capacity of each method, it is important to analyze the variability of the autoregulatory indices generated by each method. To calculate the autoregulatory indices in the nonlinear cases, it is possible to enter a step signal into the trained models and to fit the A-T equations [9] to obtain the corresponding autoregulatory index (ARI). To analyze the variability of this index, we simply calculated the coefficient of variation ($CV = \sigma / \bar{x}$).

It is also important to find out if the nonlinear models succeed in determining whether the model is able to capture the physiological dynamics of the ABFS, or if the model has only managed a numerical fit for the data. One way of determining whether this is or is not the case is to input an ABP step signal that simulates a thigh cuff technique to an already trained model, and examine the CBFV response signal.

3 Results

The three methods were applied to each of the *15* subjects, generating a parametrized model by subject in the case of the nonlinear models.

To build a model by subject using the SVM, from *1* to *10* delays were tested in the CBFV (which corresponds to the order of the model) and from *1* to *14* delays in the MABP. Parameter ν was evaluated from *0.1* through *1* in intervals of *0.1*. Parameter σ was tested from the units to the hundreds in an incremental way. Parameter C was increased by powers of two [16], and the best results were obtained when C reached higher values, deciding to leave it at infinity. This means that the solution is concentrated on minimizing the empirical risk, without considering the complexity of the model.

For the SVM, parameter ν varied form *0.1* to *0.9*, with a predominance of *0.9* values. Parameter σ varied between 5 and 60, with a predominance of a value of *15*.

In the case of the neural networks, the same delayed ranges used for the SVMs were applied to MABP and CBFV, and for the neurons of the hidden layer a range of *2* to *20* was used. When this parameter combination was applied to the subject population, the following results were obtained: the most frequent numbers of neurons in the hidden layer were *4* and *6*; the delays in CBFV varied between *1* and *3*, with *1* being the most frequent; the delays in MABP varied between *4* and *10*, with *7* as the most frequent. The best results in the neural networks were obtained when the training method of Levenbert-Marquardt was used. Table 1 shows the correlation and MSE results for both the training and the test.

Table 1. Training and test correlations for the different methods that model the ABP-CBFV relation

Method	Training Correlation	Training MSE	Testing Correlation	Testing MSE
SVM	*0.97*	*0.004*	*0.83*	*0.028*
NN	*0.85*	*0.043*	*0.79*	*0.066*
A-T	*0.77*	*0.074*	*0.70*	*0.094*

To evaluate if there is a significant difference between the models, Wilcoxon's test was applied to the correlations between the SVMs and the neural networks, showing that there is no significant difference, with $p=0.233$. When this test was applied to the SVMs and the linear model of A-T, the differences were significant, ($p=0.0001$).

Finally, the differences between the neural networks and the linear model were also significant (*p=0.0006*).

Figure 3 shows the average signals of the step response for the SVM and the neural network methods.

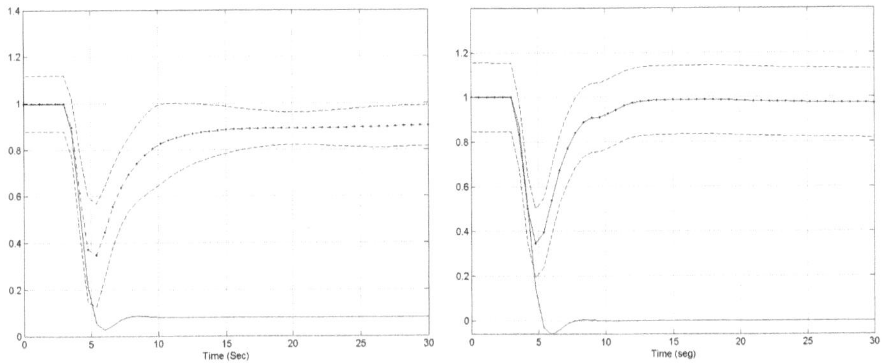

Fig. 3. CBFV response to the step signal for SVM (left) and Neural Networks (right). Solid line: step signal; dotted line: average CBFV response; dashed line: ± 1 standard deviation.

After applying a step signal to each nonlinear model, the method of A-T was used to obtain the ARI index of each subject represented by the model. In the case of the linear model of A-T, the ARI indices are obtained directly.

The mean ARI indices, standard deviations and coefficients of variation for all the subjects are shown in table 2.

Table 2. Mean values, standard deviations and coefficients of variation for the autoregulatory indices of the different methods

Method	Mean ARI	Standard Deviation	CV (%)
SVM	*5.38*	*1.44*	*26.7*
NN	*6.30*	*2.52*	*40.0*
A-T	*4.39*	*1.47*	*33.5*

4 Discussion and Conclusions

The correlation and error values in the test show that the method that best predicts, on the average, the CBFV responses for unknown cases is that of the SVMs, followed closely by neural networks. The same order, but with greater differences, is kept in the training sets.

The largest differences are found between the nonlinear and the linear methods, and they are significantly different when Wilcoxons test is applied. When the nonlinear methods are compared, even though there are differences between the average correlation values, they are not significant ($p>0.05$).

Evaluating the predictive capacity by means of the errors made in the test set is not sufficient to infer that the model represents the ABFS adequately. It is also necessary to know if the model captures the physiological dynamics of the ABFS. When examining the responses of the CBFV to the step signal (figure 3), it can be seen that the responses of the nonlinear models correspond to normal responses, recovering the CBFV level in less than 6 s. It is also seen that the ranges of the standard deviations are different, with the neural networks showing the greatest deviations, which means less precision of the neural networks compared to the SVMs.

Table 2 shows that the highest mean ARI indices correspond to the neural networks, but they also have great variance, in agreement with the results of the step responses. ARI values greater than 6 are those closest to the actual values, because they correspond to normal autoregulation values, in agreement with the set of subjects in the study. But the variance that exists between these indices must also be analyzed, and in this case the smallest corresponds to the SVMs. A way of combining in a single measure the mean ARI values and their variance is by through the coefficient of variation, which in this case shows that SVMs are the best method. Reducing the variability of the ARI index is of great clinical importance, because this variability is the main limitation to use this index in measuring the autoregulation system [17].

The results of this work show that the nonlinear models are significantly better than the linear models for representing the ABFS. Similar approaches had only been tested with other types of ABFS signals, such as spontaneous pressure changes [12-16, 18], but so far, the available work with thigh cuff maneuvers had not succeeded in improving on the linear models [10-11].

The idea of using external recurrences in the SVMs for the treatment of biological signals has proved to be adequate. Although the SVM predictive correlation and error were not significantly different from the corresponding figures for the neural network (Table 1), the trend showed by the slightly higher numerical values of correlation and smaller error, together with the much smaller coefficient of variation (Table 2) for estimating the autoregulatory index of individual subjects, suggest that this approach should take precedence as the best technique for modelling cerebral autoregulation by non-linear methods, as assessed by the thigh cuff technique. Future work should be performed to compare the performance of SVMs with alternative approaches in other conditions, such as spontaneous fluctuations in ABP or changes induced by the Valsalva maneuver or CO_2 reactivity tests.

References

1. Raicharoen T, Lursinsap C, Sanguanbhokai P, Application of critical support vector machine to time series prediction. Circuits and Systems, 2003. Proceedings of ISCAS '03. **5** (2003) 741-4.
2. Wan-Zhao C, Chang-Chun Z, Wen-Xing B and Jun-Hua L. Chaotic time series prediction using mean-field theory for support vector machine. Chinese Phys. **14** (2005) 922-9.
3. Jankowski S and Oreziak A, Learning system for computer-aided ECG analysis based on support vector machines. International Journal of Bioelectromagnetism **5** (2003) 175-6.

4. Acir N and Guzelis C. Automatic spike detection in EEG by a two-stage procedure based on support vector machines. Comput Biol Med. **7** (2004) 561-75.
5. Newell D, Aaslid R, Lam A, Mayberg T, Winn R. Comparison of flow and velocity during autoregulation testing in humans. Stroke **25** (1994) 793-7.
6. Panerai R. Assessment of cerebral pressure autoregulation in humans - a review of measurement methods. Physiological Measurement **19** (1998) 305-38.
7. Panerai R, Evans D, Mahony P, Deverson S, Hayes P. Assessment of thigh cuff technique for measurement of dynamic cerebral autoregulation. Stroke **31** (2000)476-80.
8. Panerai RB, Dawson SL, Eames PJ and Potter JF. Cerebral blood flow velocity response to induced and spontaneous sudden changes in arterial blood pressure. Am J Physiol **280** (2001) H2162-H2174.
9. Tiecks F, Lam A, Aalid R, Newell D. Comparison of static and dynamic cerebral Autoregulation measurements. *Stroke.* **26** (1995) 1014-19.
10. Panerai R, Dawson S and Potter J. Linear and nonlinear analysis of human dynamic cerebral autoregulation. Am J Physiol. **227** (1999) H1089-H1099.
11. Panerai R, Chacón M, Pereira R and Evans D. Neural network modeling of dynamic Cerebral Autoregulation: assessment and comparison with established methods. Med Eng & Phys **26** (2004) 43-52.
12. Mitsis G, Zhang G, Levine BD, Marmarelis VZ. Modeling of Nonlinear Physiological Systems with fast and Slow Dynamics. II. Application to cerebral Autoregulation. Ann. Biomedical Engineering **30** (2002) 555-65.
13. Schölkopf B, Smola A,Williamson RC, and Bartlett PL. New support vector algorithms. Neural Computation, **12** (2000) 1207-45.
14. Vapnik V. The Nature of Statistical Learning Theory, Springer Verlag. New York, (1995).
15. Nerrand O, Roussel-Ragot P, Personnaz L. and Dreyfus G. Neural networks and non-linear adaptive filtering: unifying concepts and new algorithms. Neural Comput. **5** (1993) 165-99.
16. Frohlich H. and Zell A. Efficient parameter selection for support vector machines in classification and regression via model-based global optimization, Neural Networks. IJCNN '05. Proceedings. 2005 IEEE International Joint Conference **3** (2005) 1431-6.
17. Panerai RB, Eames PJ and Potter JF, Variability of time-domain indices of dynamic cerebral Autoregulation. Physiol. Meas. **24** (2003) 367–81.
18. Chacón M, Blanco C, Panerai R and Evans D. Nonlinear Modeling of Dynamic Cerebral Autoregulation Using Recurrent Neural Networks. LNCS, CIARP 2005 **3773** (2005) 205-13.

An Approach to Automatic Target Recognition in Radar Images Using SVM

Noslen Hernández[1], José Luis Gil Rodríguez[1], Jorge A. Martin[2], Francisco Silva Mata[1], Ricardo González[1], and Raúl Álvarez[2]

[1] Advanced Technologies Application Center, MIMBAS
7a #21812 e/ 218 y 222, Rpto. Siboney, Playa. C.P. 12200
Ciudad de la Habana, Cuba
Office Phone number: (+) 537.271.4787; Fax number: (+) 537.273.0045
{nhernandez, jlgil, fjsilva, rgazapo}@cenatav.co.cu
http://www.cenatav.co.cu
[2] "Granma" Navy Academy, Micro X, Alamar, Habana del Este,
Ciudad de La Habana
Fax: 93 9676

Abstract. This paper introduces an Automatic Target Recognition (ATR) method based on X Band Radar image processing. A software which implements this method was developed following four principal stages: digital image formation, image preprocessing, feature selection through a combination of C4.5 Decision Tree and PCA and classification using SVM. The automatic process was validated using two images sets, one of them containing real images with natural noise levels and the other with different degrees of impulsive noise contamination. The method achieves a very nice computation behavior and effectiveness, high accuracy and robustness in noise environments with a low storage memory and high decision speed.

Keywords: target recognition, X Band radar, SVM, image processing, feature selection.

1 Introduction

X-band radar systems have been of great interest in the last few decades. The relative short wavelength at X-band frequencies (8-12 GHz) makes possible the obtaining of high-resolution radars (HRR) images for target identification and discrimination [1]. Some civil, military and government institutions often use X-band radar systems for: maritime and air traffic control, defense tracking, weather monitoring, and others applications. Target recognition is a challenging problem intensified on the extraction of target features from the available raw data as the recognition performance is strongly determined by the informative power of the features [2]. Furthermore, the objects feature extraction is an especially difficult problem highly dependent on three aspects: Radar Cross Section (RCS[1]) of targets; image formation process and particularly on the image preprocessing sequence applied. Target detection on the sea, under some abnormal conditions, is possible with an image of the sea surface. This

[1] RCS is "a measure of the reflective strength of a radar target" [3].

J.F. Martínez-Trinidad et al. (Eds.): CIARP 2006, LNCS 4225, pp. 964 – 973, 2006.

image is created with information given by the standard marine X-band radar. In these images we can visualize the changes in the wave behavior produced by the presence of objects as sea clutter, clouds or ships in sailing. The automatic recognition of ships navigating is the main purpose of this work.

This paper introduces an automatic target recognition (ATR) method based on X Band Radar image processing and it is organized as follows: digital image formation, image preprocessing, feature extraction and feature selection through a combination of C4.5 Decision Tree and PCA and classification using SVM. The automatic process was validated using two images sets, one of them containing real images with natural noise levels and the other with different levels of impulsive noise contamination. The method achieves a high accuracy in the classification process, permitting a good identification of the target of concern.

2 Radar Image Formation and Preprocessing

The formation of a radar image takes place starting from the digitization of the captured echoes when the electromagnetic signal emitted by the radar is reflected by the objects. The reception of the echoes depends on the maritime object characteristics, in particular on its RCS. The reception of the echoes also depends on the radar technical characteristics as: the power of transmitted signal, impulse time duration, width of the signal band and the antenna gain.

Received echoes digitization is obtained through a specialized acquisition hardware. It has an analog/digital converter used as the communication interface between radar and computer. The echoes are one-dimensional electromagnetic signals synchronized in time and also in exploration angles. At each angle, a one-dimensional signal is captured by the sensor during its rotation. Its digitized values are converted into a two-dimensional representation [4] from where an image is formed and whose intensity levels are normalized in the interval [0 ...255].

The RCS of maritime targets is expressed in square meters (m^2). Generalized values of RCS for a variety of ships are given in [5]. Taking averages values of RCS a division in small targets (<500 m^2), medium targets (500 to 2000 m^2) and big targets (>2000 m^2) was made. Present research attention focus was put on big targets in 15 miles scale.

The main objective of image preprocessing stage is to prepare the image for the automatic analysis, which includes the reduction of the impulsive noise, and some objects that are not of interest (sea clutter) applying a 3x3 pixels median filter and a 3x3 pixels high pass filter [6]. The next step is the image binarization in order to achieve the objects (target/no target) segmentation applying an automatic threshold algorithm following the iterative procedure proposed by González and Woods in [7].

3 Feature Extraction and Selection

The next step is to represent and describe these objects in a form suitable for further computer processing. A representation with 11 boundary and region descriptors was

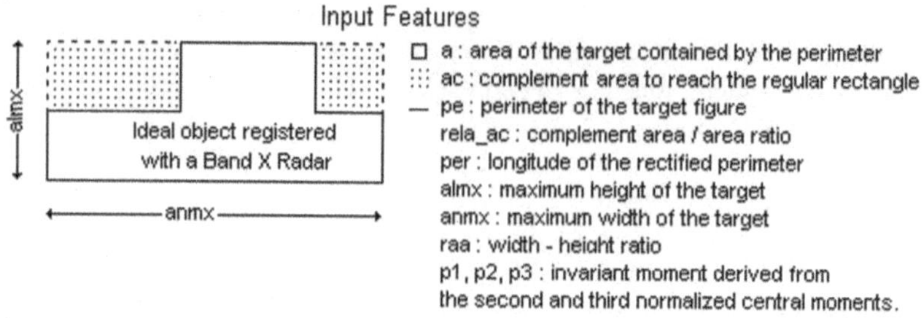

Fig. 1. Graphical representation of the 11 features in an ideal object present in a preprocessed X Band Radar image

chosen using a Geometric and Topologic Model [8] [9]. Fig. 1 shows the full feature set designed for the textural characterization of objects.

To known the most significant features to describe the Targets (object of interest), C4.5 Decision Tree and Principal Component Analysis (PCA) were used. Both techniques were applied separately on a set of samples, described by original features, composed by objects from different images in order to guarantee a high representativeness. We will refer to this set as "S", which contains 470 objects, 178 in the Target class and 292 in the No Target class.

3.1 C4.5 Decision Tree Used for Feature Selection

In general, decision trees represent a disjunction of conjunctions of constraints on the attribute-values of examples. The selection is based on a statistical property called *information gain* that measures how well a given attribute separates the training examples according to their classification. In this sense the tree' nodes will contain the more relevant features, being the more important feature located at the high levels of tree [10].

An instance is classified by starting at the root node of the decision tree, testing the attribute specified by this node and moving down by the tree branch corresponding to the value of the attribute. This process is then repeated at the node on this branch and so on, until a leaf node is reached which provides the classification of the instance.

Three different experiments were designed and applied to the set "S" (Fig. 2). In the Experiment 1, "S" was randomly divided in four disjoint training sets which have the same number of samples and also a good balance among target and no target ones. Four decision trees were built; each of them validated using 10 folds Cross Validation. In the Experiment 2, four different sets were prepared using resampling on "S"; each of them was divided in 75% of the samples for training and the other 25% for testing. This means that each classifier was built with training sets that could be contain common samples. In the Experiment 3, only one decision tree was built using the set "S" as training set and it was validated with 10 folds Cross Validation.

Results show that some of the initial features do not appear in any of the trees. This mean that they are not relevant for targets characterization and recognizing and it is possible to eliminate them. Finally were selected **a**, **ac**, **pe**, **p1**, **p2**, **per** as a result of the union of the partial results of each decision tree.

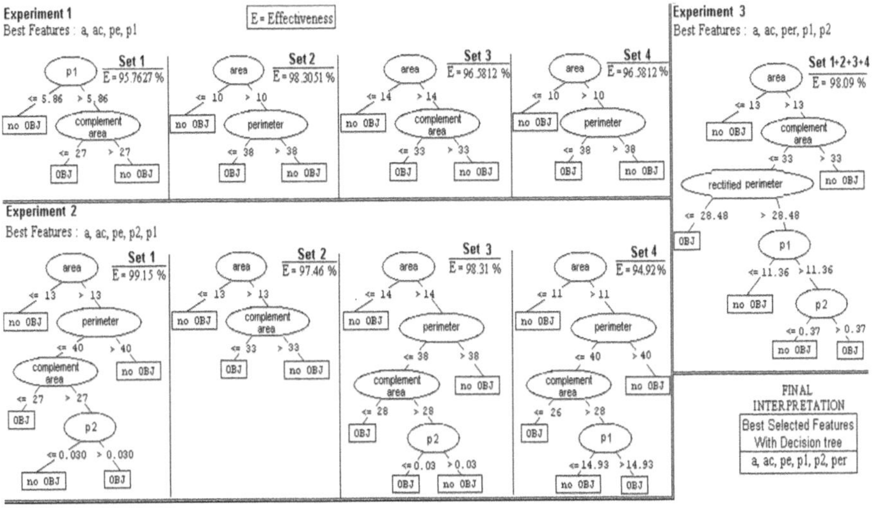

Fig. 2. Features selected with C4.5 Decision Tree

3.2 PCA Used for Feature Selection

PCA is a powerful tool used in exploratory data analysis. It provides a way to reduce the dimensionality of the data finding linear combinations of the original features which account for maximal amounts of variation, known as principal components or eigenvectors. PCA eigenvectors have several desirable properties. First, they are mutually orthogonal, which is the same as saying they are uncorrelated. Second, eigenvectors can be computed in order of decreasing variance. Thus, the first eigenvector accounts for the maximum amount of variance and each successive eigenvector accounts for less of the remaining variance in the data [11].

PCA is based on the idea of expressing a matrix **X** as the product of two other matrices, the scores matrix **T** and the transpose of the loadings matrix **L**: $X = TL^T$. If only the first k columns of the scores and loadings matrices are retained, then $X \approx \hat{X} = T_k L_k^T$. The concentration of variance in the first several PCs permits the omission of later factors without significant loss of information, so the transformed and preprocessed data matrix is imperfectly reconstructed from the trimmed scores and loadings, that is, within some residual error $E_k = X - T_k L_k^T$.

PCA has been done in a set of samples "S". With the aim to give the same importance to all features we scale our data before doing PCA to zero mean and unit variance. From the analysis of the correlation matrix obtained with PCA and some plots of features against features we conclude that the features **pe** and **per** are highly correlated.

To reduce the dimensionality of the data implies that it contain irrelevant or random variation, some of which can be removed by retaining only the principal components that capture relevant information. Only the first three principal components which explain 94.14 % of world variance were retained, as we can see in Fig. 3.

Cumulative variance
(first 3 principal components)

#PC	Variance	Percent	Cumulative
1	3970.0559	76.9539	76.95
2	522.8480	10.1346	87.08
3	363.5855	7.0475	94.14
4	181.0152	3.5087	97.64
5	69.4025	1.3452	98.99

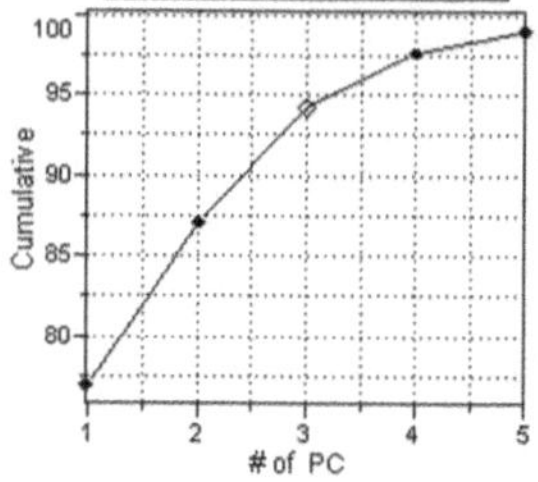

Contribution of the original features

	PC1	PC2	PC3
a	0.337577	-0.026405	0.040514
ac	0.337030	-0.022973	-0.049633
rela_ac	0.232434	0.153986	-0.673983
pe	0.336590	0.051287	-0.081255
per	0.336449	0.057543	-0.081227
anmx	0.308327	-0.190876	-0.255153
almx	0.319414	0.281617	-0.114021
p1	0.331767	-0.102732	0.220360
p2	0.305833	-0.180671	0.374666
p3	0.287611	-0.267265	0.384976
raa	0.092318	0.859508	0.336451

Fig. 3. Cumulative variance versus principal components and contribution of the original features to the first three components

The contribution of the original features to the first three principal components is shown in the same figure. All the original variables contribute in a significant manner to any one of the PC_S. For this reason none of them can be removed in this step. In order to look for the relevant features is necessary to obtain the modeling power of them.

Modeling Power

Modeling Power varies with the number k of principal component selected (k = 3 in our case) but is variable-oriented. Typically, it is not helpful in determining the optimal number of factors to retain, but *does point out important variables.*
Modeling Power of a variable is defined as:

$$MP_j = 1 - \frac{\hat{S}_j}{S_{0j}} \tag{1}$$

where $\hat{S}_j$ is the root square of variable residual variance $\hat{S}_j^2$, which is calculated using the jth column of the residual matrix E_k defined above:

$$\hat{S}_j^2 = \frac{\hat{e}_j \hat{e}_j^T}{n-k-1} \tag{2}$$

and S_{0j} is the root square of the total variance of that variable calculated as:

$$S_{0j}^2 = \frac{1}{n-1}\sum_i^n (x_{ij} - \bar{x}_j)^2 \tag{3}$$

When the power of a variable to model information in the data increases, MP approaches 1; contrary when it decreases, MP approaches 0. Even with random data, some features will exhibit high modeling power, so *an absolute threshold cannot be specified*. Instead, the different variables should be compared based on their relative modeling power.

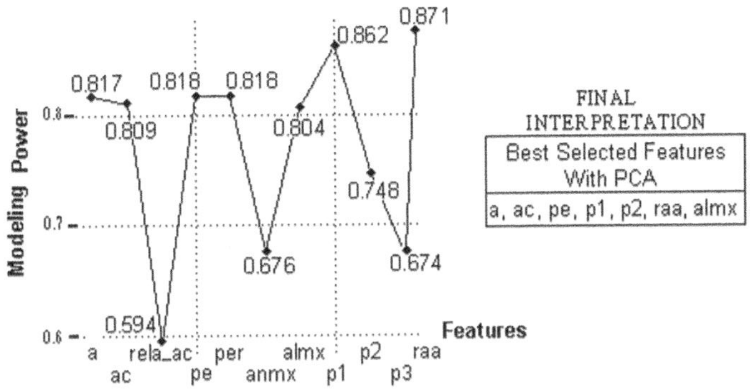

Fig. 4. Modeling power versus features

Comparing the 11 original features by their modeling power value (Fig. 4) is possible to conclude that features **a**, **ac**, **pe**, **per**, **p1**, **p2**, **raa**, **almx** have the highest values of discriminator power.

As we can notice there are interceptions between features selected as relevant by both techniques. For final feature selection, a combined interpretation of the results was made and the union of the features selected as relevant by both methods was used as final criterion. Taking into account the high correlation that exist between **pe** and **per** it is necessary to reject one of them. The selection of **pe** instead of **per** was based in the fact that **pe** appears more times in the experiments realized with Decision Trees.

The features selected (**a**, **ac**, **pe**, **p1**, **p2**, **raa**, **almx**) were used to build an automatic classifier.

4 Classification

In our case a binary classification problem (Target and No Target objects) is necessary to solve. One of the relatively new and promising methods for learning separating functions in pattern recognition (classification) tasks are the Support Vector Machines (SVM) developed by Vapnik and Chervonenkis [12] [13] [14] [15].

In a SVM learning for two linearly separable classes, one aims at finding a separating "maximal margin" hyperplane which gives the smallest generalization error among the infinite number of possible hyperplanes [12]. The data on margin and/or the closest ones are called support vectors. They are found by solving a quadratic programming (QP) problem. Very often the separation function between the classes is nonlinear. In this case, the data will be mapped from an input space into a high dimensional feature space by a nonlinear transformation $\phi(x)$. Because the QP problem in a feature space depends only on a dot product $\phi(x_i)^T \phi(x_j)$ the every learning can be performed by using Mercer theorem [13] for positive definite functions that allows replacement of $\phi(x_i)^T \phi(x_j)$ by a positive definite symmetric kernel function $K(x_i, x_j) = \phi(x_i)^T \phi(x_j)$. In our case a non-linear SVM with a Gaussian radial basis function (RBF) kernel [13] was used.

The QP optimization problem also have the convex properties and hence not local minima, given us a unique and optimal solution.

There are two basic design parameters that determine the goodness of an SVM Classifier. Here, they are, C which determines a tradeoff between maximizing the margin and minimizing the numbers of errors and γ that define the width of 7-dimensional Gaussian functions contained on the diagonal of the covariance matrix. Both parameters can be selected performing a "grid-search" using k folds cross-validation. Basically, pairs of (C,γ) values are tested and the one with the best cross-validation accuracy is picked.

The used of grid search is recommended when we may not feel safe to use methods which avoid doing an exhaustive parameter search by approximations or heuristics.

5 Results and Discussion

SVM were training with data given as vectors (x, y), where x is a seven-dimensional input vector of values of selected features, i.e., vector $x \in \Re^7$, the desired value y is a binary value variable, i.e., $y \in \{+1, -1\}$ for Target and No Target objects respectively. The set "S" defined in section 3 was used to train.

In order to obtain the best parameters value to train the SVM a grid search using 10 folds Cross Validation was done. The ranges assigned to each hyperparameter were $\log_2 C = (-5,-4,\ldots, 14,15)$ and $\log_2 \gamma = (-15,-14,\ldots,4)$. Then, with the values obtained by

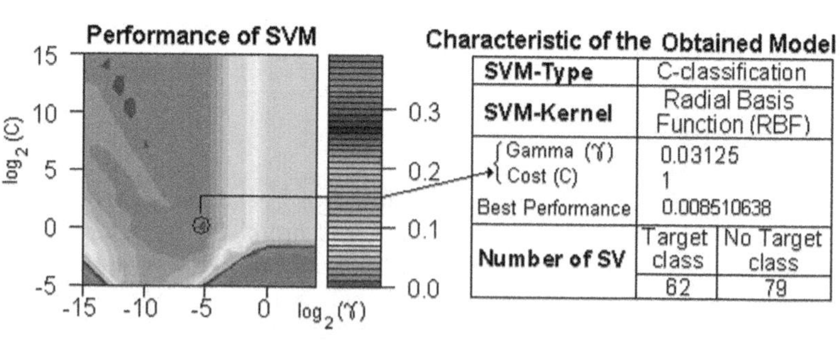

Fig. 5. Left: The best pair of parameter (C, γ) values was extracted from the area within the circle marked. Right: The general characteristic of the obtained model are presented.

grid search, the SVM Classifier was trained again and the model was validated using 10 folds Cross Validation, giving us an accuracy of 99.15 %.

The accuracy of SVM trained using different training parameters combination and the characteristic of the obtained model are shown in Fig. 5.

In order to SVM training and classification process was used the LIBSVM library [16].

In processed X Band radar images there are much more No Target objects than Target objects. In learning extremely imbalanced data, the overall classification accuracy is often not an appropriate measure of performance. A trivial classifier that predicts every case as the majority class can still achieve very high accuracy. We use metrics such as *true negative rate, true positive rate, G-mean and Precision* [17] to evaluate the performance of our learning algorithms on imbalanced data. These metrics are functions of the confusion matrix [17]. Different test sets were prepared in order to obtain statistics about the performance of the automatic method proposed. The process was applied repeatedly on each image belonging to these sets.

5.1 Performance with Real Images

In this experiment, a set of 27 X Band radar real images never employees during the training process were used as validation set. These images were collected during six months. They were processed using our method and the confusion matrix and metrics are shown in Fig. 6.

		Predicted Class	
		Targets	**No Targets**
Actual Class	**Targets**	**TP** = 74 (True Positives)	**FN** = 4 (False Negatives)
	No Targets	**FP** = 12 (False Positives)	**TN** = 9228 (True Negatives)

$$\text{True Positive Rate } (Acc^{+}) = \frac{TP}{TP + FN} = 94.87\ \%$$

$$\text{True Negative Rate } (Acc^{-}) = \frac{TN}{TN + FP} = 99.87\ \%$$

$$\text{G-mean} = (Acc^{+} \times Acc^{-})^{1/2} = 97.33\ \%$$

$$\text{Precision} = \frac{TP}{TP + FP} = 86.05\ \%$$

Fig. 6. Confusion Matrix and metrics calculated

The good results obtained in the classification task demonstrated the advantages attributed in the literature to the SVM as a two class classifier. The complete automatic process of an image was very fast, 3 sec by image approximately, doing this method very good and robust for a real time detection of maritime targets.

5.2 Performance with Artificial Noisy Images

In this experiment, the principal objective was investigated the performance of our method at different levels of signal-to-ratio (SNR) noise. An arbitrary X Band Radar image containing all kind of targets and not targets was chosen. A set of noisy images were synthesized adding Salt and Pepper noise with levels of 0.01, 0.02, 0.03, 0.04 and 0.05 noise density (dB). Table 1 presents the accuracy of the automatic method in noisy test conditions.

Table 1. Results of our method in a set of noisy image at different levels of noise

	Original Image	Original Image + Salt & Pepper Noise Density				
		0.01	**0.02**	**0.03**	**0.04**	**0.05**
True positive (%)	100	99.08	96.33	93.58	84.40	85.32
True negative (%)	98.55	98.27	98.19	98.11	98.01	97.93
G-mean	99.27	98.67	97.25	95.81	90.95	91.40
Noise Level Tolerance		**OK**	**OK**	**OK**	**No OK**	**No OK**

We can notice that our method has robustness in noisy images, staying above 90% for all tested levels of noise. However, only up to 0.03 noisy density levels were accepted as a consequence of the risk that implies a failure in the detection of Target objects. It is important to point out that these levels of not accepted noise are hardly found in real images after preprocessing stage.

Fig.7 shows a set of images representatives of all the process. After the final results are obtained, the user has the possibility of change any wrong response given by the automatic process.

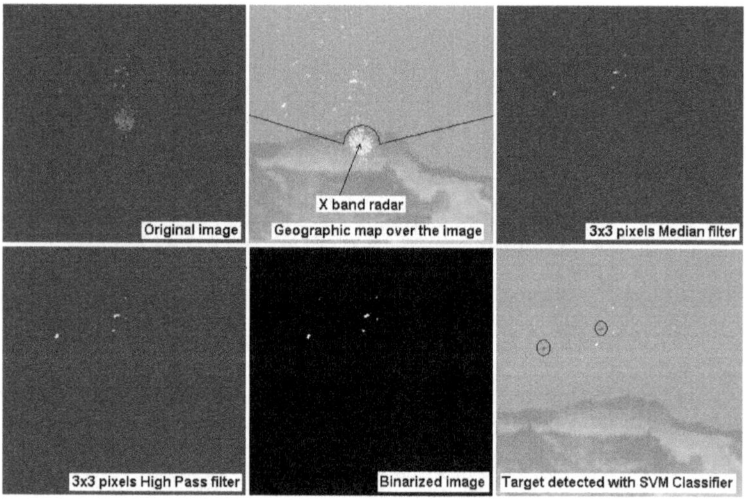

Fig. 7. Process for marine targets automatic recognition using X band radar sensor

6 Conclusions and Future Work

In this paper, the main concern was to obtain a novel and efficient approach for automatic target recognition in X band radar images. Its usefulness in two image sets, one of them with real image containing natural level of noise, and the other with noisy images at different levels of impulsive noise contamination was verified. We also applied successfully a combination of PCA and C4.5 Decision Tree to find out the relevant features among all features calculated by us.

The experimental results show that this method has a very good computational behavior and provide a very useful tool for real time ATR systems due to its simplicity and high decision speed.

We consider necessary to experiment with new king of features specially obtained from the frequency domain of the image.

References

1. Gallego, J., Pérez, F.: Detección de Blancos Extensos en Entornos Marinos y Terrestres Basada en Descriptores. Available in Internet at http://w3.iec.csic.es/URSI/ articulos _gandia_2005/articulos/RA/334.pdf. Date: May 14, 2006.
2. Turhan-Sayan, G.: Real Time Electromagnetic Target Classification Using a Novel Feature Extraction Technique with PCA-Based Fusion. IEEE Trans. on Antennas and Propagation, Vol. 53, No. 2, February 2005.
3. Bairachefski A. M., Sistemas de radiolocalización naval, Editora Transporte, Moscú, 1982.
4. Shinozawa, et al.: A weather radar image prediction method in local parallel computation. International Conference on Neural Networks, 1994.
5. Skolnik, M. I. (1980). *Introduction to Radar Systems*. McGraw-Hill Book Company, New York, 2. Ausgabe, 1563 pp.
6. Martin, J.A. y J.L. Gil: Cálculo de la navegación de altura empleando señales de posicionamiento global e imágenes meteorológicas. IPEN Journal, No. 29, Published by Pan American Institute of Naval Engineering, ISSN – 1011 – 5951. (2005).
7. Rafael C. González, and Richard E. Woods, "Digital Image Proccesing", 2nd ed. Addison-Wesley Publishing Company, 2002.
8. Gil, J.L.: Estado actual de la representación y análisis de textura en imágenes (inédito). (2005).
9. Silva, F.J.: Estado actual de la representación y análisis de formas. (inédito). (2005).
10. Quinlan, R. J.: C4.5: Programs for Machine Learnig (Morgan Kaufmann Series in Machine Learning). Paperback- January 15. (1993).
11. Jackson, J.E.; A User's Guide to Principal Components, (John Wiley & Sons: New York, 1991).
12. Vapnik, V.: The Nature of Statistical Learning Theory. New York: Springer Verlag. (1995).
13. Scholkopf, C., Burges, J., Smola, A.: Advances in Kernel methods: Support Vector Learning.MIT. Press. (1999).
14. Cristianini, Shawe-Taylor, J.: An introduction to Support Vector Machine. Cambridge University Press. (2000).
15. Burges, C. J. C.: A Tutorial on Support Vector Machines for Pattern Recognition. Data Mining and Knowledge Discovery 2(2): 121-167. (1999).
16. Chih-Chung Chang and Chih-Jen Lin: LIBSVM: A Library for Support Vector Machines, Dpt. Computer Science and Information Engineering, National Taiwan University. (2003). Available in Internet at http://www.csie.ntu.edu.tw/~cjlin/libsvm/. Date: May 14, 2006.
17. Computer Science 831: Knowledge Discovery in Databases. Dept. of Computer Science. University of Regina. Canada. Available in Internet at http://www2.cs.uregina.ca/~dbd/ cs831 /index.html. Date: May 15, 2006.

Analysis of Algebraic Expressions Derived from Genetic Multivariate Polynomials and Support Vector Machines: A Case Study

Ángel Kuri-Morales[1] and Iván Mejía-Guevara[2]

[1] Departamento de Computación, Instituto Tecnológico Autónomo de México, Río Hondo No. 1, 01000 D. F., México
akuri@itam.mx

[2] Posgrado en Ciencia e Ingeniería de la Computación, Universidad Nacional Autónoma de México, IIMAS, Ciudad Universitaria, 04510 D. F., México
imejia@uxmcc2.iimas.unam.mx

Abstract. We discuss how algebraic explicit expressions modeling a complex phenomenon via an adequate set of data can be derived from the application of Genetic Multivariate Polynomials (GMPs), on the one hand, and Support Vector Machines (SVMs) on the other. A polynomial expression is derived in GMPs in a natural way, whereas in SVMs a polynomial kernel is employed to derive a similar one. In any particular problem an evolutionary determined sample of monomials is required in GMP expressions while, on the other hand, there is a large number of monomials implicit in the SVM approach. We make some experiments to compare the modeling characterization and accuracy obtained from the application of both methods.

1 Introduction

Function approximation from experimental data is an issue that many researchers have tackled in the past. The specification of certain functions given a dataset is commonly used to model interesting phenomena. Genetic Multivariate Polynomials (GMPs) modeling [2] relies on specific polynomial functions given a dataset. A simple and explicit algebraic expression is derived form the application of GMPs. The relationship and specification of the explanatory variables arises in a natural way. In classical methodologies a full polynomial model is attained from an exhaustive exploration of the linear combinations of the set of monomials corresponding to the independent variables. In this case the number of possible combinations can increase unmanageably. In the latter case, it turns out to be not only impractical but impossible to tackle the modeling problem for even a modest number of independent variables. This drawback is eliminated in GMPs by a) Changing the commonly used approximation least square error norm by a minimax norm and b) Employing Genetic Algorithms (GAs) to reduce the number of monomials in the final model. This is achieved

J.F. Martínez-Trinidad et al. (Eds.): CIARP 2006, LNCS 4225, pp. 974 – 984, 2006.

without losing the capability of this model ("learning machine") to represent the phenomenon under analysis.

Another approach that has been proved to be successful relies on Support Vector Machines (SVMs). This methodology relies on finding a functional that is nonlinear in the input space, but linear in a higher dimensional feature space and is capable of making classification, regression or function approximation [10]. Acting, in effect, as a Neural Network with one hidden nonlinear layer, SVMs, as all other connectionist schemes, have been labeled "black boxes" [1], since the complex relationships between explanatory variables are not explicit in its structure. However, one of the main goals of this paper is to show that we are able to build algebraic explicit expressions (which depend on the appropriate selection of the kernel function) from such SVMs. In particular, we use a polynomial kernel that allows us to find an expression comparable to the ones arising from GMPs.

In section 2, we point out the main theoretical characteristics of GMPs and the advantage of using genetic algorithms (GAs). In section 3, the general foundations of SVMs are presented. Particularly, we discuss the way in which, via SVMs, one may find a solution to the nonlinear regression problem. We also show how a polynomial kernel can be used in SVMs in order to derive an explicit algebraic expression from the support vector solution. In section 4, some experiments and results are shown applying both methodologies to a set of representative regression problems. Finally, in section 5 we advance some conclusions and discuss the results of the previous section.

2 Genetic Multivariate Polynomials

Given a training sample $\varsigma = \{(\mathbf{x}_i, y_i)\}_{i=1}^{N}$, where $\boldsymbol{x}_i$ denotes the i-th input vector pattern and y_i its corresponding target output, the goal of GMPs is to find an explicit algebraic expression of the form:

$$F(v_1,\ldots,v_n) = \sum_{i_1=0}^{d_1} \cdots \sum_{i_n=0}^{dn} c_{i_1 \cdots i_n} v_1^{i_1} \ldots . v_n^{i_n} \tag{1}$$

The sets of coefficients in (1) (denoted as **C'**) yield an explicit mathematical relationship between the independent variables ($\boldsymbol{x}_i$) and dependent variables (y_i). This approximation problem has been the subject of many studies in the past and it has been pretty much solved except for certain practical issues. First of all, we have to contend with the fact that the cardinality of **C'** (which we denote as γ') is large enough to make it unwieldy for all except the simplest cases. Second, considering a certain floating point number representation (8 bytes for example), the storage of a hypothetical solution will normally require a huge number of bytes. Third, and most important, the usual numerical methods with which these approximations are normally tackled imply the solution of systems of linear equations of large order with the consequent inevitable numerical instability. Finally, fitting a relatively large set of data under least squares error measure leads to Hilbert matrices which are known to be particularly sensitive to rounding error [13]. Hence, even though it is theoretically possible to solve the approximation problem even for large samples, in practice it is both impossible and impractical to do so with the usual methods [2]. The approximation given by GMPs replaces the equation (1) by another one in which we retain the algebraic polynomial of the solution while removing the need for large γ' by introducing the constant $\boldsymbol{\mu}$ as shown by:

$$F(v_1,\ldots,v_n)=\sum_{i_1=0}^{d_1}\cdots\sum_{i_n=0}^{d_n}\mu_{i_1\ldots i_n}c_{i_1\ldots i_n}v_1^{i_1}\ldots.v_n^{i_n} \tag{2}$$

The coefficients are represented as $c_{i_1\ldots i_n}$ where d_i represents the maximum allowed exponent of the *i*-th independent variable. The elements of $\boldsymbol{\mu}$ determine whether a given monomial in (2) is to be included in the purported polynomial solution. For this reason we must establish a priori the cardinality of $\boldsymbol{\mu}$. Obviously, we want to have a manageable number of coefficients so that we do not longer need to contend with the problems derived from large storage needs. Therefore, we will replace the least squares (or L_2) norm with less common minimax (or L_∞) norm. In so doing we will avoid the need to solve large systems of equations and get around the inherent precision problems. The minimax norm is not as popular as least squares because the approximation algorithms are normally slower. In what follows we give a brief account of the principles behind the minimax multivariate approximation algorithm. Once this is done we will discuss the genetic algorithm that allows us to determine **C'** for a given γ.

2.1 The Ascent Algorithm

The algorithm to approximate the sample under the minimax norm is based on three observations: a) The minimax approximation coefficients of a set *M* of size *m* are uniquely determined by finding the adequate signs of the errors for the elements of the set, b) if a larger set *N* of size *n* has elements outside the minimax solution it is always possible to exchange one of elements in *M* by an element in *N* such that the minimax condition is still met for the new *M* and c) Continuing exchanges will eventually lead to a target set *M* which satisfies the minimax norm for all elements in *N*.

In what follows we denote with *F(x)* the function which is able to minimize the error $\ell_\varphi = \max|F_i(x_i)-d_i|$. In order to find the approximator of (2) we map the vectors $\boldsymbol{x}$ to a higher dimensional space yielding matrix **V** of dimension $p\times N$ where $p=\prod_{i=1}^{n}(1+d_i)$. Let us arbitrarily select a sub-matrix of **V** of size m×m (call it **V'**). Then we solve the following system:

$$\begin{bmatrix} \eta_1 & (v_1^0\ldots v_n^0)_1 & \cdots & (v_1^{d_1}\ldots v_n^{d_n})_1 \\ \eta_2 & (v_1^0\ldots v_n^0)_2 & & (v_1^{d_1}\ldots v_n^{d_n})_2 \\ \cdots & \cdots & \cdots & \cdots \\ \eta_m & (v_1^0\ldots v_n^0)_m & & (v_1^{d_1}\ldots v_n^{d_n})_m \end{bmatrix}\begin{bmatrix}\ell_\theta \\ c_1 \\ \cdots \\ c_{m-1}\end{bmatrix}=\begin{bmatrix}y_1\\y_2\\ \cdots \\ y_m\end{bmatrix} \tag{3}$$

Denoting the approximation error for the *i*-th vector as ℓ_i and the largest absolute such error as ℓ_θ we may define $\ell_i = \eta_i \ell_\theta$; clearly, $\ell_i \eta_i \le \ell_\theta$. We also denote the elements of row *i* column *j* of (3) as $\boldsymbol{\delta}_{ij}$ and the *i*-th cofactor of the first column as $\boldsymbol{\kappa}_i$. From Cramer's rule we immediately have:

$$\ell_\theta = \frac{\begin{vmatrix} y_1 & \cdots & \delta_{1m} \\ \cdots & \cdots & \cdots \\ y_m & \cdots & \delta_{mm} \end{vmatrix}}{\eta_1 \kappa_1 + \ldots + \eta_m \kappa_m} \tag{4}$$

To minimize ℓ_θ we have to maximize the denominator of (4). This is easily achieved by a) selecting the maximum value of the $\boldsymbol{\eta}_i$'s and b) making the signs of the $\boldsymbol{\eta}_i$'s all equal to the signs of $\boldsymbol{\kappa}_i$'s. Obviously the $\boldsymbol{\eta}_i$'s are maximized iff $abs(\boldsymbol{\eta}_i)=1$ for $i=1,\ldots,m$ which translates into the well known fact that the minimax fit corresponds to approximation errors of the same absolute size. On the other hand, to achieve (b) we must simply set the signs of the $\boldsymbol{\eta}_i$'s to those of the cofactors. Making $\sigma_i = sign(\kappa_i)$, system (3) is simply re-written as:

$$\begin{bmatrix} \sigma_1 & \cdots & \delta_{1m} \\ \cdots & \cdots & \cdots \\ \sigma_m & \cdots & \delta_{mm} \end{bmatrix} \begin{bmatrix} \ell_\theta \\ \cdots \\ c_{m-1} \end{bmatrix} = \begin{bmatrix} y_1 \\ \cdots \\ y_m \end{bmatrix} \tag{5}$$

Once having all the elements in (5) it suffices to solve this system to obtain, both, the value of ℓ_θ and the coefficients **C'** which best fit the elements of $\boldsymbol{x}$ in the minimax sense. To obtain the coefficients for the whole sample we apply the Exchange Algorithm (EA) (for details see [2]).

2.2 Genetic Algorithm

Another reason to choose the minimax norm is that the EA is not dependent on the origin of the elements in **V**. We decided them to be monomials of a full polynomial but it makes no difference to the EA whether the v_i are gotten from a set of monomials or they are elements of arbitrary data vectors. This is important because the number of monomials in (3) grows geometrically. One way to avoid the problem of such coefficient explosion is to define γ a priori and then properly select which of the γ' possible ones these will be. There are $\binom{\gamma'}{\gamma}$ possible combinations of monomials and even for modest values of γ an exhaustive search is out of the question. This optimization problem may be tackled using genetic algorithms as follows.

The genome of the GA is a binary string of size γ'. Every bit in it represents a monomial. If the bit is '1' it means that the corresponding monomial remains while, if it is '0', such monomial is not to be considered. This simple strategy corresponds to determining the values of μ in equation (2). All one has to ensure is that the number of 1's is equal to γ.

It is well known that an elitist GA will converge to a global optimum [3]. It has also been shown that a variation called Vasconcelos' GA (VGA) displays superior behavior on a wide range of functions [4]. VGA uses: a) Deterministic selection, b) annular crossover, c) uniform mutation. All results reported here are based on VGA's application.

3 Support Vector Machines

SVMs were developed by Vapnik et al [5] based on statistical learning theory. Particularly, a SVM is an approach to the problem of structural risk minimization, based on the fact that the generalization error rate is bounded by the sum of the training-error rate and a term that depends on the Vapnik-Chervonenkis (VC) dimension [6].

SVMs have been successfully used in practical applications [7]. In the case of classification tasks, the objective is to build a linear surface that separates points belonging to different classes. The objective in regression problems is similar, but in this case the data is enclosed in a ε-tube of the function approximation.

Given the training sample ς, the goal of SVMs for non-linear regression problems is to find a function *f(x)* that has at most ε deviation from the actually obtained targets $\hat{y}_i$ for each element of ς and, at the same time, is as flat as possible. In other words, errors are disregarded as long as they are less than ε. This functional has the form $f(\mathbf{x}) = \boldsymbol{\omega}\mathbf{x} + b$ with $\mathbf{w} \in \Re^k, b \in \Re$. As in the case of classification problems, *f(x)* can be obtained by solving a quadratic optimization problem (QOP) of the form [8]:

$$\begin{aligned} &\underset{w,b,\xi}{Min} \frac{1}{2} \|w\|^2 + C\sum_{i=1}^{N}\left(\xi_i + \xi_i^*\right) \\ &\textit{subject to:} \\ &\quad y_i - wx - b \le \varepsilon + \xi_i \\ &\quad wx + b - y_i \le \varepsilon + \xi_i^* \\ &\quad \xi_i, \xi_i^* \qquad \ge 0 \\ &\quad \text{for } i = 1, 2, \ldots, N \end{aligned} \tag{6}$$

According to this formulation, the objective is to minimize the empirical risk $R_{emp} = \frac{1}{N}\sum_{i=1}^{N} L_\varepsilon(y_i - \hat{y}_i)$, where $L_\varepsilon(y_i - \hat{y}_i)$ is called the ε-insensitive loss function[1].

The formulation (6) is known as the primal problem for nonlinearly separable patterns, where the constant *C*>0 determines a trade off between the flatness of *f(x)* and the tolerated amount of points which deviations larger than ε. The appropriate selection of *C* is a very important issue not only in regression, but in classification problems [9] for an appropriate approximation. The value of ε is inversely proportional to

[1] Other loss functions may be used, but we use the most common $L_\varepsilon(y_i - \hat{y}_i) = |\xi| - \varepsilon$ if $|\xi| > \varepsilon$ and 0, otherwise.

the number of support vectors (sv) [10], which are a subset of ς, resulting from the solution of (7) and which defines completely *f(x)*; i. e., increasing ε-insensitivity decreases the number of sv. In this paper we use the approach of [11] for the selection of C and ε, where $C = 3\sigma_d$ and $\varepsilon = \psi\sigma\sqrt{\ln(N)/N}$; σ_d, σ and ψ are the standard deviation of output values of ς, the noise standard deviation and a constant, respectively. The determination of σ and ψ is explained in section 4.

For the solution of this problem it is more appropriate to solve the so-called dual problem [8], which is derived applying the Karush-Kuhn-Tuker (KKT) [8] conditions to (6). The dual formulation is as follows:

$$\max_{\alpha} \; -\frac{1}{2}\sum_{i=1}^{N}\sum_{j=1}^{N}\left(\alpha_i - \alpha_i^*\right)\left(\alpha_j - \alpha_j^*\right)K\left(x_i, x_j\right) - \varepsilon\sum_{i=1}^{N}\left(\alpha_i + \alpha_i^*\right) + \sum_{i=1}^{N} y_i\left(\alpha_i - \alpha_i^*\right)$$

$$\text{subject to:} \qquad (7)$$

$$\sum_{i=1}^{N}\left(\alpha_i - \alpha_i^*\right) = 0$$

$$\alpha_i, \alpha_i^* \in [0, C]$$

The solution of (7) is given by $\boldsymbol{\alpha}$, which is a vector of Lagrange Multipliers, where the values that satisfy $(\alpha_i - \alpha_i^*) \neq 0$ correspond to the sv of the problem. Once sv are determined, the regression function *f* is given by:

$$f(\mathbf{x}) = \sum_{i=1}^{N}\left(\alpha_i - \alpha_i^*\right) K(\mathbf{x}, \mathbf{x}_i) + b \qquad (8)$$

This function is non-linear in the input space, but linear in a high dimensional feature space. The translation of input data to a higher dimensional space is possible because the use of *K(.)* in (7). These functions must satisfy certain known conditions to be admissible as kernels in a SVM. Specifically they must satisfy Mercer´s condition [6]. Many functions may be used as kernels [10], but the most popular are: a) Polynomial learning machines (PLM), b) Radial-basis functions (RBF) and c) Two-layer perceptrons (LP) [6].

In this paper, the selection of Polynomial learning results very appropriate for the construction of an explicit algebraic expression, as we explain below.

3.1 Polynomial Kernel

As shown in (8), *f(x)* is determined by the kernel function and the values of $\boldsymbol{x}$ that appear in that expression as function of *K(.,.)*. The theory of SVM asserts the construction of Kernels of the form $K(\mathbf{x}, \mathbf{x}_i) = \varphi(\mathbf{x})^T \varphi(\mathbf{x}_i)$; $\varphi(.)$ is a mapping that allows the transformation of points from input space to higher dimensional spaces. The knowledge of $\varphi(.)$ is relevant because it allows *f(x)* to be expressed in an explicit way and shows the functional relation involved between independent variables of some specific problem.

However, for many kernels the functional $\varphi(.)$ is given implicitly and it is very difficult (even impossible) to derive it form the particular Kernel chosen. For example, if a Radial Basis Function Kernel is used, it is very difficult to propose a function $\varphi(.)$, such that $\varphi(\mathbf{x})^T.\varphi(\mathbf{x}_i) = \tanh(\beta_0\mathbf{x}^T\mathbf{x}_i + \beta_1)$.

In the case of polynomial kernel, $\varphi(.)$ can be known because it represents a polynomial expression. Its monomials are combinations of independent variables with distinct exponents. The polynomial kernel is given by $K(\mathbf{x},\mathbf{x}_i) = (\beta_0\mathbf{x}^T\mathbf{x}_i + \beta_1)^\rho$. In this paper, we consider $\beta_0=\beta_1=1$ and applying recursively the Newton's binomial theorem, this Kernel can be expanded as:

$$\begin{aligned}(1+\mathbf{x}^T\mathbf{x}_i)^\rho &= \left(1+\sum_{j=1}^{k} x_j x_{ij}\right)^\rho \\ &= \sum_{i=1}^{\rho}\binom{\rho}{i_1}\left[\sum_{j=1}^{k} x_j x_{ji}\right]^{\rho-i_1} \\ &= \sum_{i_1=1}^{\rho}\binom{\rho}{i_1}\sum_{i_2=1}^{\rho-i_1}\binom{\rho-i_1}{i_2}(x_1x_{i1})^{i_2}\left[\sum_{j=2}^{k} x_j x_{ij}\right]^{\rho-i_1-i_2} \\ &= \sum_{i_1=1}^{\rho}\binom{\rho}{i_1}\sum_{i_2=1}^{\rho-i_1}\binom{\rho-i_1}{i_2}(x_1x_{i1})^{i_2}\cdots\sum_{i_k=1}^{\rho-\sum_{j=1}^{k-1} i_j}\binom{\rho-\sum_{j=1}^{k-1} i_j}{i_2}(x_{k-1}x_{ik-1})^{i_k}(x_k x_{ik})^{\rho-\sum_{j=1}^{k} i_j}\end{aligned} \tag{9}$$

With (9) we conclude that the binomial coefficients for a polynomial with degree ρ and k independent variables can be obtained from the following expression:

$$\binom{\rho}{\mathrm{i}_1}\binom{\rho-\mathrm{i}_1}{\mathrm{i}_2}\binom{\rho-\mathrm{i}_1-\mathrm{i}_2}{\mathrm{i}_3}\cdots\binom{\rho-\sum_{j=1}^{k-1} i_j}{\mathrm{i}_k} \tag{10}$$

The number of elements in the vector $\varphi(.)$ is equal to the number n_m of monomials in (9), where $\varphi(\mathbf{x}_i)$ contains the section of the corresponding monomial where terms $\boldsymbol{x}_i$ appears ($x_{i1}, x_{i2}, \ldots, x_{ik}$) and $\varphi(\mathbf{x})$ contains the section of the monomial where elements of $\boldsymbol{x}$ appears ($x_1, x_2, \ldots, x_k$). In each case, both terms are multiplied by the square root of the coefficient monomial's given by (10). For instance, if $\rho=2$ and $k=2$, $\varphi(\mathbf{x}_i)$, $\varphi(\mathbf{x})$ and $K(x, x_i)$ we have:

$$\begin{aligned}\varphi(\mathbf{x})^T &= (x_1^2, \sqrt{2}x_1x_2, x_2^2, \sqrt{2}x_1, \sqrt{2}x_2, 1) \\ \varphi(\mathbf{x}_i)^T &= (x_{i1}^2, \sqrt{2}x_{i1}x_{i2}, x_{i2}^2, \sqrt{2}x_{i1}, \sqrt{2}x_{i2}, 1) \\ K(\mathbf{x},\mathbf{x}_i) = \varphi(\mathbf{x})^T.\varphi(\mathbf{x}_i) &= x_1^2x_{i1}^2 + 2x_1x_2x_{i1}x_{i2} + x_2^2x_{i2}^2 + 2x_1x_{i1} + 2x_2x_{i2} + 1\end{aligned} \tag{11}$$

Finally, $f(x)$ can be obtained from (8) and (9) once the sv are estimated. The coefficients of $f(x)$ are combinations of $(\alpha_i - \alpha_i^*) \neq 0$ and binomial coefficients (10). As in the case of GMPs, the $C_{i_1 i_2 \ldots i_m}$ are the coefficients of the final expression, where i_j is the power of the j-th independent variable for that particular monomial.

4 Experiments

A set of two nonlinear regression problems is presented here in order to illustrate the application of GMPs and SVMs methodologies. The set of problems are explained as follows:

mpg. This data is available in UCI Machine Learning Repository[2]. The data concerns city-cycle fuel consumption in miles per gallon, to be predicted in terms of 3 multi-valued discrete and 4 continuous attributes: 1) cylinders, 2) model year, 3) origin, 4) displacement, 5) horse power, 6) weight and 7) acceleration. Attributes 1 and 2 were eliminated from our analysis because they turned out to be highly correlated. We considered 392 instances in this dataset.

bodyfat. This dataset was obtained from the StatLib--Datasets Archive[3] and corresponds to some estimates of the percentage of body fat determined by underwater weighing and various body circumference measurements for 252 men. The dataset consists of 14 independent variables: 1) Percent body fat, 2) Age (years), 3) Weight (lbs), 4) Height (inches), 5) Neck circumference (cm), 6) Chest circumference (cm), 7) Abdomen 2 circumference (cm), 8) Hip circumference (cm), 9) Thigh circumference (cm), 10) Knee circumference (cm), 11) Ankle circumference (cm), 12) Biceps (extended) circumference (cm), 13) Forearm circumference (cm), 14) Wrist circumference (cm).

4.1 Results of GMPs and SVMs Applied in mpg

The experiments we performed for in this article (applying GMPs and SVMs to the **mpg** dataset) are:

GMPs. The VGA was run in this experiment with probability of crossover equal to 0.9 (Pc=0.9) and probability of mutation of 0.005 (Pm=0.005)[4]. The number of individuals was 50 (np) over 50 (ng) generations. The maximum value allowed for di was 2, for the 5 independent variables. The number of monomials was $\gamma = 20$. The RMS of this method was 14.5%. The coefficients are shown in Table 1.

SVMs. A Polynomial Kernel of degree $\rho=3$[5] was applied here. The value of $C=0.62$ was determined as explained in section 3. The noise variance σ^2 was calculated with the equation $\hat{\sigma}^2 = \frac{1}{n-d}\sum_{i=1}^{N}(y_i - \hat{y}_i)^2$ [11], where $\hat{y}_i$ is the output of a polynomial

---

[2] http://www.ics.uci.edu/~mlearn/MLSummary.html.

[3] http://lib.stat.cmu.edu/datasets/.

[4] The values for P_c and P_m were chosen after vast experimentation with several plausible values.

[5] A value of $\rho=3$ allows more coefficients of Polynomial SVM to match with different coefficients of GMPs (given $d_i=2$).

SVM with degree $d = 5$ (degrees of freedom). The value of ψ was set to 3, as is done in [11]. Once σ and ψ are determined, the value of ε used for training was 0.0228. With a polynomial Kernel of degree 3 and 5 independent variables, the total number of monomials that represent $f(x)$ is 56. All of them are shown in table 1. The RMS of this method was 6.6%. We use LIBSVM (ver 2.81) in our experiments [12].

Table 1. Results of GMPs and SVMs methods for mpg problem

COEF	SVM	GMP	COEF	SVM	GMP	COEF	SVM	GMP
C00003	0.02	-	C10101	-0.09	-	C10010	-0.16	-
C00012	-0.04	-	C10110	-0.17	-	C10100	0.02	-
C00021	0.15	-	C10200	0.07	-	C11000	0.02	-
C00030	-0.21	-	C11001	-0.14	-	C20000	-0.06	-
C00102	-0.09	-	C11010	0.14	-	C00001	-0.02	-
C00111	-0.05	-	C11100	-0.02	-	C00010	0.10	-
C00120	-0.03	-	C12000	0.05	-	C00100	0.00	-
C00201	0.11	-	C20001	-0.04	-	C01000	-0.33	-
C00210	0.24	0.57	C20010	0.09	-	C10000	-0.10	-0.70
C00300	-0.08	-	C20100	-0.14	-	C00000	0.57	0.72
C01002	-0.02	-	C21000	0.06	-	C02020	-	-2.35
C01011	0.26	-	C30000	0.03	-	C01112	-	3.84
C01020	0.00	1.81	C00002	0.01	-	C11222	-	0.88
C01101	-0.10	-	C00011	-0.11	-	C12002	-	2.35
C01110	-0.01	-	C00020	0.23	-	C12100	-	5.48
C01200	0.03	-	C00101	0.12	-	C10221	-	-0.92
C02001	-0.09	2.33	C00110	-0.02	-0.30	C11102	-	-13.94
C02010	0.17	-	C00200	-0.12	-	C11122	-	-14.40
C02100	0.15	-	C01001	0.04	-	C12201	-	15.99
C03000	0.02	-	C01010	-0.20	-	C21211	-	165.70
C10002	0.06	-	C01100	-0.07	-2.05	C22100	-	-3.00
C10011	-0.08	-	C02000	0.07	-0.04	C22211	-	-425.66
C10020	0.07	-	C10001	0.04	-			

4.2 Results of GMPs and SVMs Applied in Bodyfat

The experiments applied to bodyfat dataset with GMPs and SVMs are as follows:

GMPs. The parameters used for VGA in this experiment were: P_c =1.0, P_m =0.005[4], n_p=50 and n_p=50. The maximum value allow for d_i was 1, for the 14 independent variables. The number of monomials was γ=20. The RMS of this method was 8.0%. The coefficients are shown in Table 2.

SVMs. A Polynomial Kernel of degree ρ=2 was applied here. The value of C was 0.5 and the value of ε=0.024, where the noise variance was also estimated applying first a polynomial SVM with d=5 degrees of freedom. With a polynomial kernel of degree 2 and 14 independent variables, the total number of monomials that represent $f(x)$ is 120. Only those coefficients that also appear in the GMP approach are shown in Table 2, the rest (118) are not displayed because of lack of space. The RMS for this problem was 2.5%. Likewise, we used LIBSVM (ver 2.81) [12].

Table 2. Results of GMPs and SVMs methods for bodyfat problem

COEF	SVM	GMP	COEF	SVM	GMP
C01001000000000	0.005	-1.27	C10010100110000	-	8.740
C00000000000000	0.871	0.93	C11000111000100	-	7.475
C00010110111000	-	-15.81	C10011001100010	-	-2.069
C00011001010111	-	-22.50	C01010101100010	-	-20.024
C00100111111001	-	13.37	C10100000001110	-	1.657
C00001110111101	-	53.13	C11000110011011	-	-116.780
C00100000101111	-	-6.17	C10110110001011	-	43.529
C01100010110100	-	-16.57	C11001101011011	-	78.219
C01011011101101	-	26.18	C11100100100111	-	-34.857
C01011110100011	-	34.23	C01001000110010	-	6.291

5 Conclusions

From both of our methods we are able to achieve the explicit algebraic representation of the behavior of complex dynamic systems. This is a goal that has eluded many researchers in the past. We believe that this is a major contribution of our paper. In determining which approach is better we have to point out that SVMs are theoretically sounder than GMPs. However, as shown in the previous experiments, the number of monomials in SVM approach is substantially greater than those obtained with GMPs. Even though the accuracy of SVMs is superior in both experiments, this is so only at the expense of having to consider larger sets of monomials. The results also suggest that GMP can approximate very well, displaying an explicit algebraic expression with a relatively few number of terms (monomials). Many more experiments are necessary to establish a proper comparison between these methods. In this paper we focused on the fact that GMPs and SVMs with polynomial kernels can build similar expressions for some tasks, particularly nonlinear regression problems. A more detailed analysis with other kind of problems is a matter for future work.

References

1. Salcedo, S., Fernández, J., Segovia, M., Bousoño, C.: Genetic programming for the prediction of insolvency in non-life insurance companies, Computers & Operations Research 32 (2005) 749–765.
2. Kuri, A., Approximation and Classification with Genetic Multivariate Polynomials, WSEAS Transactions on Computers, Issue 3, (2006) 645-652.

3. Rudolph, G.: Convergence Analysis of Canonical Genetic Algorithms, IEEE Transactions on Neural Networks, Vol. 5, Issue 1, (1994) 96-101.
4. Kuri, A.: A Methodology for the Statistical Characterization of Genetic Algorithms. Proceedings of the Mexican International Congress on Artificial Intelligence, Springer-Verlag, (2002) 79-88.
5. Boser, E., Guyon, I., Vapnik, V.: A training algorithm for optimal margin classifiers. 5th Annual ACM Workshop on COLT, ACM Press, (1992) 144-152.
6. Haykin, S.: Neural Networks. A comprehensive foundation. 2nd ed., Prentice Hall, New Jersey (1999).
7. Chapelle, O., Haffner, P., Vapnik, V.: Support vector for histogram-based image classification. IEEE transactions on Neural Networks Vol. 10, 5, (1999) 1055-1065.
8. Smola, A., Schölkopf B.: A Tutorial on Support Vector Regression. NeuroCOLT Technical Report NC-TR-98-030, Royal Holloway College, University of London, UK, (1998).
9. Kuri, A., Mejía, I.: Evolutionary Training of SVM for Classification Problems with Self-Adaptive Parameters. Advances in Artificial Intelligence Theory, (Gelbukh, A., Monroy, R., Eds.), IPN, (2005) 207-216.
10. Vapnik, V.N.: The Nature of Statistical Learning Theory. Springer-Verlag, NY, (1995).
11. Cherkassky, V., Ma, Y.: Practical Selection of SVM Parameters and Noise Estimation for SVM Regression. Neural Networks, Vol. 17 No. 1, (2004) 113-126.
12. Chang, C., Lin, C.: LIBSVM: a library for support vector machines, (2001). Software available at http://www.csie.ntu.edu.tw/~cjlin/libsvm/.
13. Choi, M. D.: Tricks or Treats with the Hilbert Matrix. American Mathematical Monthly Vol. 90, (1983) 301-312.

Image Compression by a Time Enhanced Self Organizing Map

Pascual Campoy and Pedro Gutiérrez*

Departamento de Automática, Ingeniería Electrónica e Informática Industrial
Universidad Politécnica de Madrid, Spain
pascual.campoy@upm.es, pgutierrez@etsii.upm.es

Abstract. This paper presents the promising results of an innovative modification of the Kohonen's algorithm, the time enhanced self-organizing map (TESOM), when used for low bitrate image compression. The time enhanced map is used in this paper to learn codebooks of subimages, in a similar way as other classical algorithms based on LVQ or SOM do, but taking advantage of the fact that it learns the sequence order of the input data (i.e. subimages) during the training phase. The codebook learned by the new proposed algorithm TESOM presents the advantage that the vicinity of the codes in the output map is not only established by their visual similarity, as in SOM, but also by the sequential order of the subimages during the training phase. Since this sequential order of the subimages determines the vicinity of the codes, the increment of the representative code of two consecutive subimages has been proved to have a lover Entropy and can therefore be codified by a lower bit rate. The advantage of the proposed algorithm is thoroughly evaluated and quantified over a set of experiments, which include several images, used in different ways in the training phase for codebook design and in the compression phase, and a variety of parameters.

Keywords: Time enhanced, self-organizing map, image compression, vector quantization, low bitrate, entropy.

1 Introduction

Millions of digital images are generated each day: from the few daily shots of an amateur photographer to the countless files at a newspaper's multimedia archive, and there is a real and pressing need to store these images at the lowest possible cost. Furthermore, the advent of the Internet has set a new requirement: the transmission of digital content through bandwidth-limited channels. A very effective, although partial, solution to these problems is the use of lossless and lossy image compression algorithms. There are many lossy compression methods but when high compression ratios are sought codecs based on vector quantization (VQ) represent an attractive alternative because they easily attain 64:1 or higher compression ratios without a

* Supported by CONACYT and CONCYTEA, Mexico.

J.F. Martínez-Trinidad et al. (Eds.): CIARP 2006, LNCS 4225, pp. 985–992, 2006.

noticeable quality loss 1]. For the design process of the codebook Linde, Buzo and Gray's algorithm 2] is the classical method, but in the 1980s Kohonen 3] opened the way for a new generation of design processes with his well-known work on artificial neural networks (4] and 5] for example).

The original self organizing map has, however, an inherent limitation: it was designed for spatial representation and can not model the sequential aspects of the data. It is open to discussion whether modeling the *sequentiality* of the input stream yields better results for a particular problem, but several researchers have modified the original SOM to model *non spatial* relations 6] –[8]. Campoy et al.[9] developed a novel self organizing map that models the temporal redundancy of the input data: the time enhanced self organizing map (TESOM). By training both a classical map and a TESOM with ordered vectors of known probability density function in $\Re^2$, Campoy et al. showed that the time enhanced map had better performance, expressed as a lower entropy of the incremental position in the template index. Here this novel algorithm will be reviewed and compared to a standard SOM for image compression. The capacity of the time enhanced map for lower entropy and equivalent image quality will be showed, as will its ability to *learn* long and complex sequences.

2 Time Enhanced SOM Algorithm for VQ Image Compression

A k-dimensional memoryless vector quantizer (VQ) consists, in general, of a coder-decoder pair: the coder maps input vectors to channel symbols and the decoder maps these symbols to values of a reproduction alphabet. In this particular scenario a finite index set I of N consecutive integers, beginning with 0, represents the channel symbols. The alphabet is a set of carefully selected reproduction vectors, the codebook, which sets the partition of the $\Re^k$ space into Voronoi cells through a closest neighbor rule, using the Euclidean distance as the criterion. These conditions define a codec that is fully described by the indexed vectors of the codebook: the compressor matches $w \times h$ subimages to indexed templates and stores the increment of the index, then the decompressor constructs a mosaic with said templates. Therefore the codebook design is critical.

The self organizing map can be used to design VQ codebook, but instead of fully describing the standard algorithm and its modification we will present only the latter and state that for the SOM $RA_i(j)=0$. Campoy et al [9] introduced the concept of Residual Activity: each neuron holds energy, which decays with time and is reinforced by the Neighborhood Activity. The Residual Activity changes the criterion for selecting the best matching node: past "winners" are more likely to be selected. The Residual Activity decay is modeled with a Gaussian function and at the beginning of each iteration of the learning algorithm $RA_i(j)$ is updated to reflect the energy decay:

$$RA_i(j)=e^{\frac{\left(1+\sqrt{-2\sigma_i^2(j)*\log[RA_i'(j-1)]}\right)}{-2\sigma_i^2(k)}}$$

where RA_i' is the Residual Activity that was reinforced by the Neighborhood Activity *at the end* of the last iteration:

$$RA'_i(j) = 1-(1-NA_i(j))*(1-RA_i(j))$$

This novel modification is remarkable because it does not store several past states of the network; for a full description of the time enhanced map and its properties consult [9].

2.1 Algorithm

1. Create the network of N nodes and set the synaptic weights to random values.
2. Map the input vector $x(j)$ and the synaptic weights $w_i(j)$ to $\hat{x}(j)$ and $\hat{w}_i(j)$ in the $\Re^{k+1}$ space:

$$\hat{v} = [v, \hat{v}_{k+1}], \text{ where } \hat{v}_{k+1} = \sqrt{1-v_1^2-v_2^2-\cdots-v_k^2}$$

3. Calculate both the Instantaneous Activity IA_i and the Residual Activity RA_i for each neuron. Then compute the Total Activity TA_i and select the winning node i_j:

$$i_i(j) = \max(TA_i(j)), \text{ where } TA_i(j) = 1-(1-IA_i(j))*(1-RA_i(j)) \text{ and}$$
$$IA_i = \hat{w}_i(j) \bullet \hat{x}_i(j)$$

4. Compute the Neighborhood Activity and Learning Factor:

$$d_{im}(j) = \left\|P_{i(j)} - P_m\right\| \qquad \sigma_v(j) = \sigma_{v0} \cdot e^{-j/t_c} \qquad NA_i(j) = e^{-d_{im}^2(j)/2\sigma_v^2(j)}$$

$$\alpha(j) = \alpha_0(j) \cdot e^{-j/t_c}$$

where $P_{i(j)}$ is the of the i-th neuron and P_m is the index of the winning neuron, both expressed as the *position* in the output map.

5. Update the Residual Activity RA'_i (see previous section).
6. Update the synaptic weights:

$$w_i(j+1) = w_i(j) + \alpha(j) \cdot NA_i(j) \cdot [x(j) - w_i(j)]$$

7. Iterate from step 2 until $j = 5t_c$. No significant adaptation occurs beyond this value.

3 Benchmarking

3.1 Input Data

For image compression systems, where the probability density function of the data is unknown, it is common to use a large set of vectors from a reference image or group of images. The training vectors are used in no particular order because the SOM only models the similarity of the inputs, but the TESOM needs ordered training data so it can *learn* its patterns. Obviously the input sequence used for training must be used for image coding, and because there is no previous knowledge on this topic one of the simplest sequences is used, as shown in Fig. 1. As the order of the training vectors is not relevant for the SOM performance the same training data will be used for both design processes.

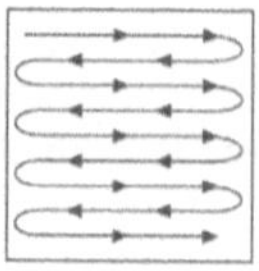

Fig. 1. Input sequence

3.2 Input Data Correlation

The VQ compressor transforms a digital image into a set of increments of indexes $A' = \{i'_0, i'_1, i'_2, \ldots\}$. As the input vectors are neighboring partitions of the digital image they are, presumably, correlated: they are similar and there exist sequence patterns. As the TESOM models both the spatial and temporal aspect of the input data vectors close in the input space map to indexes close in the output space, like the typical SOM, but it is also true that vectors close in the *input sequence* map to a sequence of indexes close in the output space. These rules, while not mutually exclusive, compete at the learning stage and produce a *better* codebook when the patterns are also present when compressing data.

3.3 Training parameters

To train a self organizing map five parameters must be set: the order of the input space, the number of neurons, the characteristic time, the initial neighborhood variance and the initial learning factor. For the TESOM an extra parameter exists: the initial temporal variance. For each parameter a fixed value or range is selected.

The order of the input space is set by the size of the partitions of the digital image: $k = w \times h$, and in this case only the results for 8×8 and 12×12 subimages will be reported. Previous experience with SOMs lead to fixed values of the initial neighborhood variance ($\sigma_0 = 0.25$) and the initial learning factor ($\alpha_0 = 1.5$), as they guarantee a good differentiation and specialization of neurons. The remaining parameters are discussed below.

- Number of neurons (N): small values boost compression ratio but maximize the quantization error. Since subimage size has a bigger impact in image quality than the value of N *standard* values may be used: 64, 128 and 256.
- Characteristic time (t_c): it sets the number of learning iterations ($5 * t_c$). It is assumed that the training data is a large collection of patterns that must be recycled several times so the map will be able to *learn* them, hence the training data will be recycled 25, 50 and 100 times, being the characteristic time a multiple of the quantity of vectors.
- Initial temporal variance (σ_{t0}): in the range $(0, \infty)$ this is the extra parameter of the time enhanced algorithm. For small values the TESOM is *less enhanced* as the effect of past inputs decays more rapidly, but large values distort the learning process with neurons that win all the time. To gather additional data on the properties of the TESOM 20 different values will be tested: 1-15, 20, 25, 30, 35 and 40. This means that for each SOM codebook there will be 20 TESOM codebooks with *equivalent* parameters.

3.4 Performance Evaluation

Two indexes are used to establish the comparison between the algorithms: entropy of the compressed data and the PSNR of the decoded image. The entropy $H(A')$ is calculated for each compressed image, and for the TESOM-compressed images is reported as a percentage gain or loss against a reference SOM-compressed image:

$$\Delta = 100 * \left(1 - \frac{H(A')_{tesom}}{H(A')_{som}}\right)\% \quad \text{,where } H(A') = \sum_j P(i'_j) * \log_2 P(i'_j)$$

A positive Δ represents a **higher compression ratio** of the TESOM algorithm. This is possible because the time enhanced algorithm has an extra training parameter (σ_{t0}) with 20 different values, so each one of those maps may be compared to one SOM with identical standard parameters.

4 Results

The full suite of tests comprises 4,326 codebooks: 7 images were used for training and 13 images for compression test over a wide range of training/coding parameters, that has yield to 60,564 different experiments for compression of 8bpp (grayscale) images. A subset of the compressed images is shown in Fig. 2. From left to right: Lena (512×512 pixels), Mandrill (512×512), self-portrait (400×500) of Dutch neoimpressionist Vincent van Gogh, "Woman with parasol" (288×360) and "Woman with parasol – Madame Monet and her son" (268×400) of French impressionist Claude Monet. They will be referred hereafter as *lena*, *mand*, *gogh*, *mon1* and *mon2*, respectively. It is important to note that the training data is a set of subimages (quarter of total area) of the test images.

The presented results are clustered into three possible scenarios: best-case, where the compressed image fully contains the training image; normal-case, where the compressed image is of the same *class* (i.e. visually similar) as the training image (i.e. *gogh* and *mon1*); and a worst-case, where the compressed image is not *related* to the training image.

Fig. 2. Subset of test images

The first battery of tests uses 12×12 subimages and reveals that the TESOM algorithm has an average of 10% performance advantage over the SOM in terms of the Entropy of the code increment, i.e. in actual terms of bitrate. The leftmost graph of

Fig. 3 shows the better compression of the TESOM for a range of σ_{t0} values when a *lena*-subimage is used to train the map and *lena* and *mand* are compressed. The image quality is equivalent for both cases, as shown as values of PSNR in Table 1 and visually in Fig. 4. The middle graph of Fig. 3 shows *a similar* situation when training with a *mand*-subimage, and the results are consistent with the previous test. These graphs demonstrate both the best and worst case scenarios with two unrelated images while the rightmost graph of Fig. 3 presents the results for a normal scenario where one image is representative of the group of images to be compressed and shows even better performance (see Table 1 for the image quality comparison).

Compression with smaller templates of 8×8 pixels leads to a smaller TESOM advantage, down to an average value of 6% in the bitrate. Image quality is still equivalent, and even if in some cases the TESOM performs equally than a SOM it can be said that in general the time enhanced algorithm keeps a small lead in performance.

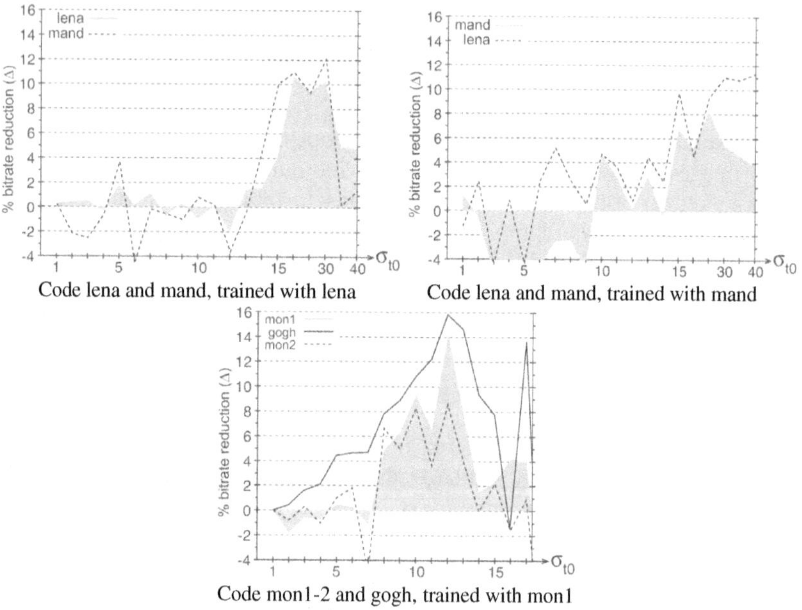

Fig. 3. Bitrate reduction for 12×12 subimages and $N=128$

Table 1. Image quality comparison in dB (PSNR)

Training subimage	Compressed image	SOM-coded PSNR	TESOM-coded average PSNR
lena 12x12	*Lena*	23.55	23.46
	mand	18.42	18.42
mand 12x12	*mand*	18.62	18.61
	lena	21.62	21.77
mon1 12x12	*mon1*	22.10	22.08
	gogh	21.14	21.05
	mon2	21.56	21.53

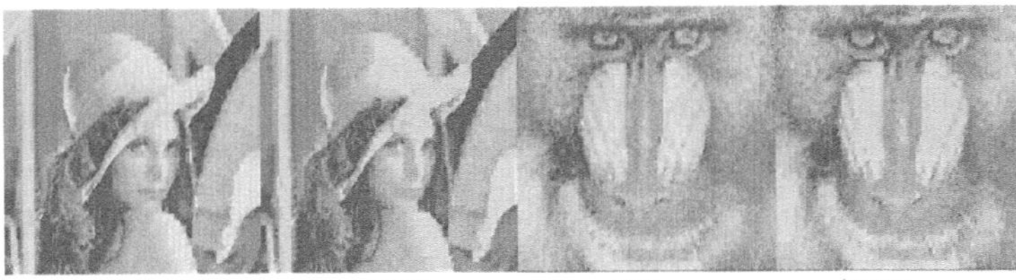

Fig. 4. Visual results: TESOM vs. SOM (trained with *lena*, 12×12 subimages, $\sigma_{t0}=30$)

5 Conclusions

A new and innovative modification to Kohonen's algorithm, the time enhanced self organizing map TESOM, has been reviewed and its application extended for the design of VQ codebooks for digital image compression. The performance of the time enhanced algorithm was compared to that of a standard SOM using two quality indexes: the compression ratio (measured as the entropy of the of the code increment) and the objective quality of the decoded images (PSNR).

Tests show that maps obtained by TESOM are able to learn the sequence order of th long and complex sequences that exist in the training data (i.e. subimages). This additional information is taken into account for a better ordering of the vectors in the codebook, which leads to a performance advantage when coding data with similar *patterns*. This bitrate improvement is most remarkable when compressing with *big* subimages (12×12 pixels), when the subimages are not very similar and the sequential order is therefore more relevant.

It is important to note that the TESOM algorithm introduces only one extra training parameter and that its value is **not** critical, since a good performance is possible for a wide range of temporal variances $10\le\sigma_{t0}\le30$. Furthermore, typically the worst performing TESOM is equivalent to the reference SOM in both compression ratio and image quality. Additionally better performance was demonstrated for the three scenarios tested: a best case where the compressed image fully contains the training data, a normal case where the compressed image is of the same class as the training data and a worst case where the compressed image is not related to the training data.

Future work will focus on different ordering sequences of the subimages, video compression and enhancements to the algorithm based on the knowledge and data acquired with the experiments and results.

References

1. N. M. Nasrabadi, R. A. King, Image coding using vector quantization: a review, IEEE Transactions on Communications 36 (8) (1988) 957–971
2. Y. Linde, A. Buzo, R. M. Gray, An algorithm for vector quantizer design, IEEE Transactions on Communications 28 (1) (1980) 84–95
3. T. Kohonen, The self-organizing map, Proceedings of the IEEE 78 (9) (1990) 1464–1480
4. H.-C. Wei, Y.-C. Chang, J.-S. Wang, A Kohonen-based structured codebook design for image compression, in: TENCON '93 IEEE Region 10 Conference on Computer Communication, Control and Power Engineering, Proceedings of, Vol. 3, 1993, pp. 426–429

5. C. Amerijckx, M. Verleysen, P. Thissen, J.-D. Legat, Image compression by selforganized kohonen map, IEEE Transactions on Neural Networks 9 (3) (2002) 503–507
6. Kangas, Phoneme recognition using time-dependent versions of selforganizing maps, in: IEEE International Conference on Acoustics, Speech and Signal Processing, Proceedings of, 1991, pp. 101–104
7. L. James, R. Miikkulainen, SARDNET: A self-organizing feature map for sequences, in: NIPS'94 Advances in Neural Information Processing Systems, Proceedings of, 1994, pp. 577–584
8. R. Euliano, J. C. Principe, Spatiotemporal self-organizing feature maps, in: International Joint Conference on Neural Networks, Proceedings of, Vol. 4, 1996, pp. 1900–1905
9. Campoy, C. J. Vicente, Residual Activity in neurons allows SOMs to learn temporal order, International Conference on Artificial Neural Networks, September 11-15, 2005, Warsaw, Poland.

Author Index

Lecture Notes in Computer Science

For information about Vols. 1–4153

please contact your bookseller or Springer

Vol. 4270: H. Zha, Z. Pan, H. Thwaites, A.C. Addison, M. Forte (Eds.), Interactive Technologies and Sociotechnical Systems. XVI, 547 pages. 2006.

Vol. 4264: J.L. Balcázar, P.M. Long, F. Stephan (Eds.), Algorithmic Learning Theory. XIII, 393 pages. 2006. (Sublibrary LNAI).

Vol. 4249: L. Goubin, M. Matsui (Eds.), Cryptographic Hardware and Embedded Systems - CHES 2006. XII, 462 pages. 2006.

Vol. 4248: S. Staab, V. Svátek (Eds.), Engineering Knowledge in the Age of the Semantic Web. XIV, 400 pages. 2006. (Sublibrary LNAI).

Vol. 4243: T. Yakhno, E. Neuhold (Eds.), Advances in Information Systems. XIII, 420 pages. 2006.

Vol. 4241: R.R. Beichel, M. Sonka (Eds.), Computer Vision Approaches to Medical Image Analysis. XI, 262 pages. 2006.

Vol. 4239: H.Y. Youn, M. Kim, H. Morikawa (Eds.), Ubiquitous Computing Systems. XVI, 548 pages. 2006.

Vol. 4238: Y.-T. Kim, M. Takano (Eds.), Management of Convergence Networks and Services. XVIII, 605 pages. 2006.

Vol. 4233: I. King, J. Wang, L. Chan, D. Wang (Eds.), Neural Information Processing, Part II. XXII, 1203 pages. 2006.

Vol. 4232: I. King, J. Wang, L. Chan, D. Wang (Eds.), Neural Information Processing, Part I. XLVI, 1153 pages. 2006.

Vol. 4229: E. Najm, J.F. Pradat-Peyre, V.V. Donzeau-Gouge (Eds.), Formal Techniques for Networked and Distributed Systems - FORTE 2006. X, 486 pages. 2006.

Vol. 4228: D.E. Lightfoot, C.A. Szyperski (Eds.), Modular Programming Languages. X, 415 pages. 2006.

Vol. 4227: W. Nejdl, K. Tochtermann (Eds.), Innovative Approaches for Learning and Knowledge Sharing. XVII, 721 pages. 2006.

Vol. 4225: J.F. Martínez-Trinidad, J.A. Carrasco Ochoa, J. Kittler (Eds.), Progress in Pattern Recognition, Image Analysis and Applications. XIX, 995 pages. 2006.

Vol. 4224: E. Corchado, H. Yin, V. Botti, C. Fyfe (Eds.), Intelligent Data Engineering and Automated Learning – IDEAL 2006. XXVII, 1447 pages. 2006.

Vol. 4223: L. Wang, L. Jiao, G. Shi, X. Li, J. Liu (Eds.), Fuzzy Systems and Knowledge Discovery. XXVIII, 1335 pages. 2006. (Sublibrary LNAI).

Vol. 4222: L. Jiao, L. Wang, X. Gao, J. Liu, F. Wu (Eds.), Advances in Natural Computation, Part II. XLII, 998 pages. 2006.

Vol. 4221: L. Jiao, L. Wang, X. Gao, J. Liu, F. Wu (Eds.), Advances in Natural Computation, Part I. XLI, 992 pages. 2006.

Vol. 4219: D. Zamboni, C. Kruegel (Eds.), Recent Advances in Intrusion Detection. XII, 331 pages. 2006.

Vol. 4217: P. Cuenca, L. Orozco-Barbosa (Eds.), Personal Wireless Communications. XV, 532 pages. 2006.

Vol. 4216: M.R. Berthold, R. Glen, I. Fischer (Eds.), Computational Life Sciences II. XIII, 269 pages. 2006. (Sublibrary LNBI).

Vol. 4213: J. Fürnkranz, T. Scheffer, M. Spiliopoulou (Eds.), Knowledge Discovery in Databases: PKDD 2006. XXII, 660 pages. 2006. (Sublibrary LNAI).

Vol. 4212: J. Fürnkranz, T. Scheffer, M. Spiliopoulou (Eds.), Machine Learning: ECML 2006. XXIII, 851 pages. 2006. (Sublibrary LNAI).

Vol. 4211: P. Vogt, Y. Sugita, E. Tuci, C. Nehaniv (Eds.), Symbol Grounding and Beyond. VIII, 237 pages. 2006. (Sublibrary LNAI).

Vol. 4210: C. Priami (Ed.), Computational Methods in Systems Biology. X, 323 pages. 2006. (Sublibrary LNBI).

Vol. 4209: F. Crestani, P. Ferragina, M. Sanderson (Eds.), String Processing and Information Retrieval. XIV, 367 pages. 2006.

Vol. 4208: M. Gerndt, D. Kranzlmüller (Eds.), High Performance Computing and Communications. XXII, 938 pages. 2006.

Vol. 4207: Z. Ésik (Ed.), Computer Science Logic. XII, 627 pages. 2006.

Vol. 4206: P. Dourish, A. Friday (Eds.), UbiComp 2006: Ubiquitous Computing. XIX, 526 pages. 2006.

Vol. 4205: G. Bourque, N. El-Mabrouk (Eds.), Comparative Genomics. X, 231 pages. 2006. (Sublibrary LNBI).

Vol. 4204: F. Benhamou (Ed.), Principles and Practice of Constraint Programming - CP 2006. XVIII, 774 pages. 2006.

Vol. 4203: F. Esposito, Z.W. Raś, D. Malerba, G. Semeraro (Eds.), Foundations of Intelligent Systems. XVIII, 767 pages. 2006. (Sublibrary LNAI).

Vol. 4202: E. Asarin, P. Bouyer (Eds.), Formal Modeling and Analysis of Timed Systems. XI, 369 pages. 2006.

Vol. 4201: Y. Sakakibara, S. Kobayashi, K. Sato, T. Nishino, E. Tomita (Eds.), Grammatical Inference: Algorithms and Applications. XII, 359 pages. 2006. (Sublibrary LNAI).

Vol. 4199: O. Nierstrasz, J. Whittle, D. Harel, G. Reggio (Eds.), Model Driven Engineering Languages and Systems. XVI, 798 pages. 2006.

Vol. 4198: O. Nasraoui, O. Zaiane, M. Spiliopoulou, B. Mobasher, B. Masand, P. Yu (Eds.), Web Minding and Web Usage Analysis. IX, 177 pages. 2006. (Sublibrary LNAI).

Vol. 4197: M. Raubal, H.J. Miller, A.U. Frank, M.F. Goodchild (Eds.), Geographic, Information Science. XIII, 419 pages. 2006.

Vol. 4196: K. Fischer, I.J. Timm, E. André, N. Zhong (Eds.), Multiagent System Technologies. X, 185 pages. 2006. (Sublibrary LNAI).

Vol. 4195: D. Gaiti, G. Pujolle, E. Al-Shaer, K. Calvert, S. Dobson, G. Leduc, O. Martikainen (Eds.), Autonomic Networking. IX, 316 pages. 2006.

Vol. 4194: V.G. Ganzha, E.W. Mayr, E.V. Vorozhtsov (Eds.), Computer Algebra in Scientific Computing. XI, 313 pages. 2006.

Vol. 4193: T.P. Runarsson, H.-G. Beyer, E. Burke, J.J. Merelo-Guervós, L. D. Whitley, X. Yao (Eds.), Parallel Problem Solving from Nature - PPSN IX. XIX, 1061 pages. 2006.

Vol. 4192: B. Mohr, J.L. Träff, J. Worringen, J. Dongarra (Eds.), Recent Advances in Parallel Virtual Machine and Message Passing Interface. XVI, 414 pages. 2006.

Vol. 4191: R. Larsen, M. Nielsen, J. Sporring (Eds.), Medical Image Computing and Computer-Assisted Intervention – MICCAI 2006, Part II. XXXVIII, 981 pages. 2006.

Vol. 4190: R. Larsen, M. Nielsen, J. Sporring (Eds.), Medical Image Computing and Computer-Assisted Intervention – MICCAI 2006, Part I. XXXVVIII, 949 pages. 2006.

Vol. 4189: D. Gollmann, J. Meier, A. Sabelfeld (Eds.), Computer Security – ESORICS 2006. XI, 548 pages. 2006.

Vol. 4188: P. Sojka, I. Kopeček, K. Pala (Eds.), Text, Speech and Dialogue. XIV, 721 pages. 2006. (Sublibrary LNAI).

Vol. 4187: J.J. Alferes, J. Bailey, W. May, U. Schwertel (Eds.), Principles and Practice of Semantic Web Reasoning. XI, 277 pages. 2006.

Vol. 4186: C. Jesshope, C. Egan (Eds.), Advances in Computer Systems Architecture. XIV, 605 pages. 2006.

Vol. 4185: R. Mizoguchi, Z. Shi, F. Giunchiglia (Eds.), The Semantic Web – ASWC 2006. XX, 778 pages. 2006.

Vol. 4184: M. Bravetti, M. Núñez, G. Zavattaro (Eds.), Web Services and Formal Methods. X, 289 pages. 2006.

Vol. 4183: J. Euzenat, J. Domingue (Eds.), Artificial Intelligence: Methodology, Systems, and Applications. XIII, 291 pages. 2006. (Sublibrary LNAI).

Vol. 4182: H.T. Ng, M.-K. Leong, M.-Y. Kan, D. Ji (Eds.), Information Retrieval Technology. XVI, 684 pages. 2006.

Vol. 4180: M. Kohlhase, OMDoc – An Open Markup Format for Mathematical Documents [version 1.2]. XIX, 428 pages. 2006. (Sublibrary LNAI).

Vol. 4179: J. Blanc-Talon, W. Philips, D. Popescu, P. Scheunders (Eds.), Advanced Concepts for Intelligent Vision Systems. XXIV, 1224 pages. 2006.

Vol. 4178: A. Corradini, H. Ehrig, U. Montanari, L. Ribeiro, G. Rozenberg (Eds.), Graph Transformations. XII, 473 pages. 2006.

Vol. 4177: R. Marín, E. Onaindía, A. Bugarín, J. Santos (Eds.), Current Topics in Artificial Intelligence. XV, 482 pages. 2006. (Sublibrary LNAI).

Vol. 4176: S.K. Katsikas, J. Lopez, M. Backes, S. Gritzalis, B. Preneel (Eds.), Information Security. XIV, 548 pages. 2006.

Vol. 4175: P. Bücher, B.M.E. Moret (Eds.), Algorithms in Bioinformatics. XII, 402 pages. 2006. (Sublibrary LNBI).

Vol. 4174: K. Franke, K.-R. Müller, B. Nickolay, R. Schäfer (Eds.), Pattern Recognition. XX, 773 pages. 2006.

Vol. 4173: S. El Yacoubi, B. Chopard, S. Bandini (Eds.), Cellular Automata. XV, 734 pages. 2006.

Vol. 4172: J. Gonzalo, C. Thanos, M. F. Verdejo, R.C. Carrasco (Eds.), Research and Advanced Technology for Digital Libraries. XVII, 569 pages. 2006.

Vol. 4169: H.L. Bodlaender, M.A. Langston (Eds.), Parameterized and Exact Computation. XI, 279 pages. 2006.

Vol. 4168: Y. Azar, T. Erlebach (Eds.), Algorithms – ESA 2006. XVIII, 843 pages. 2006.

Vol. 4167: S. Dolev (Ed.), Distributed Computing. XV, 576 pages. 2006.

Vol. 4166: J. Górski (Ed.), Computer Safety, Reliability, and Security. XIV, 440 pages. 2006.

Vol. 4165: W. Jonker, M. Petković (Eds.), Secure, Data Management. X, 185 pages. 2006.

Vol. 4163: H. Bersini, J. Carneiro (Eds.), Artificial Immune Systems. XII, 460 pages. 2006.

Vol. 4162: R. Královič, P. Urzyczyn (Eds.), Mathematical Foundations of Computer Science 2006. XV, 814 pages. 2006.

Vol. 4161: R. Harper, M. Rauterberg, M. Combetto (Eds.), Entertainment Computing - ICEC 2006. XXVII, 417 pages. 2006.

Vol. 4160: M. Fisher, W.v.d. Hoek, B. Konev, A. Lisitsa (Eds.), Logics in Artificial Intelligence. XII, 516 pages. 2006. (Sublibrary LNAI).

Vol. 4159: J. Ma, H. Jin, L.T. Yang, J.J.-P. Tsai (Eds.), Ubiquitous Intelligence and Computing. XXII, 1190 pages. 2006.

Vol. 4158: L.T. Yang, H. Jin, J. Ma, T. Ungerer (Eds.), Autonomic and Trusted Computing. XIV, 613 pages. 2006.

Vol. 4156: S. Amer-Yahia, Z. Bellahsène, E. Hunt, R. Unland, J.X. Yu (Eds.), Database and XML Technologies. IX, 123 pages. 2006.

Vol. 4155: O. Stock, M. Schaerf (Eds.), Reasoning, Action and Interaction in AI Theories and Systems. XVIII, 343 pages. 2006. (Sublibrary LNAI).

Vol. 4154: Y.A. Dimitriadis, I. Zigurs, E. Gómez-Sánchez (Eds.), Groupware: Design, Implementation, and Use. XIV, 438 pages. 2006.

GPSR Compliance

The European Union's (EU) General Product Safety Regulation (GPSR) is a set of rules that requires consumer products to be safe and our obligations to ensure this.

If you have any concerns about our products, you can contact us on ProductSafety@springernature.com

In case Publisher is established outside the EU, the EU authorized representative is:

Springer Nature Customer Service Center GmbH
Europaplatz 3
69115 Heidelberg, Germany

Batch number: 10761593

Printed by Printforce, the Netherlands